Historical Dictionary
of
European Imperialism

Historical Dictionary
of
European Imperialism

James S. Olson,
EDITOR

Robert Shadle,
SENIOR ASSOCIATE EDITOR

ASSOCIATE EDITORS:
Ross Marlay
William G. Ratliff
Joseph M. Rowe, Jr.

GREENWOOD PRESS
New York • Westport, Connecticut • London

Library of Congress Cataloging-in-Publication Data

Historical dictionary of European imperialism / James S. Olson, editor ;
   Robert Shadle, senior associate editor ; associate editors, Ross
Marlay, William G. Ratliff, Joseph M. Rowe, Jr.
     p.   cm.
   ISBN 0–313–26257–8 (alk. paper)
    1. Europe—Colonies—History—Encyclopedias. 2. History, Modern—
Encyclopedias. 3. Europe—History—1492– —Encyclopedias.
  I. Olson, James Stuart, 1946–   . II. Shadle, Robert.
  D217.H57   1991
  903—dc20   90–38413

British Library Cataloguing in Publication Data is available.

Library of Congress Catalog Card Number: 90–38413
ISBN: 0–313–26257–8

First published in 1991

Greenwood Press, 88 Post Road West, Westport, CT 06881
An imprint of Greenwood Publishing Group, Inc.

Printed in the United States of America

The paper used in this book complies with the
Permanent Paper Standard issued by the National
Information Standards Organization (Z39.48–1984).

10 9 8 7 6 5 4 3 2 1

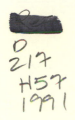
CONTENTS

CONTRIBUTORS

ERNEST ANDRADE, JR., is a member of the History Department at the University of Colorado, Denver.

GARY M. BELL is a member of the Department of History at Sam Houston State University, Huntsville, Texas.

CATHERINE A. BOEHM is currently a Fulbright Fellow conducting research in Great Britain.

JAY O. BOEHM is currently a Fulbright Fellow and graduate student at the University of Virginia.

PHILIP A. BUCKNER teaches history at the University of New Brunswick in Fredericton, New Brunswick, Canada.

MICHAEL DENNIS teaches history in the Cypress-Fairbanks Independent School District in Houston, Texas.

BRUCE R. DRURY is a professor of political science at Lamar University in Beaumont, Texas.

SAMUEL FREEMAN teaches political science at the University of Texas campus in Edinburgh, Texas.

RONALD FRITZE is a historian at Lamar University in Beaumont, Texas.

CATHERINE G. HARBOUR is a graduate student in history at Stephen F. Austin State University in Nacogdoches, Texas.

CHARLES W. HARTWIG teaches political science at Arkansas State University at State University, Arkansas.

BASCOM BARRY HAYES is a professor of history at Sam Houston State University in Huntsville, Texas.

WILLIAM T. HAYNES is an associate professor of history at Sam Houston State University in Huntsville, Texas.

CRAIG HENDRICKS teaches history at Long Beach City College in Long Beach, California.

ARNOLD P. KAMINSKY teaches in the Asian Studies Program at California State University, Long Beach, California.

ARTHUR J. KNOLL teaches at the University of the South in Sewanee, Tennessee.

ERIC C. LOEW is a graduate student in history at Sam Houston State University in Huntsville, Texas.

SAID EL MANSOUR CHERKAOUI is an adjunct professor of history at several colleges in the San Francisco area.

ROSS MARLAY is a political scientist at Arkansas State University, State University, Arkansas.

FRANK MAROTTI, JR., is a graduate student in the Department of History at the University of Hawaii.

ALAIN G. MARSOT is a political scientist at California State University, Long Beach.

JOSEPH L. MICHAUD is a graduate student in history at Sam Houston State University in Huntsville, Texas.

J. LARRY MURDOCK is head of government documents at Purdue University in West Lafayette, Indiana.

LEE E. OLM is a historian at Sam Houston State University in Huntsville, Texas.

JAMES S. OLSON is a professor of history at Sam Houston State University in Huntsville, Texas.

JUDITH E. OLSON is a graduate student in linguistics and ESL at Texas A & M University in College Station, Texas.

CARLOS PÉREZ is a graduate student in the history department of the University of California at Berkeley.

ANITA PILLING teaches history at Willis High School in Willis, Texas.

AMANDA POLLOCK is a graduate student in the Department of History at Sam Houston State University in Huntsville, Texas.

WILLIAM G. RATLIFF teaches history at California State University in Chico, California.

VEULA J. RHODES teaches in the Department of History and Political Science at Albany State College in Albany, Georgia.

RANDY ROBERTS is a historian at Purdue University in West Lafayette, Indiana.

WILLIAM B. ROBISON teaches in the History Department of Southeastern Louisiana University in Hammond, Louisiana.

JOSEPH M. ROWE, JR., teaches history at Sam Houston State University in Huntsville, Texas.

PHILIPPE-JOSEPH SALAZAR is Professor of French Language and Literature at the University of Cape Town in the Republic of South Africa.

JERRY PURVIS SANSON teaches history at Louisiana State University in Eunice, Louisiana.

WILLIAM H. SCHNEIDER teaches history at Indiana University-Purdue University at Indianapolis, Indiana.

ROBERT SHADLE is a historian at Sam Houston State University in Huntsville, Texas.

PETER T. SHERRILL teaches history at the University of Arkansas at Little Rock, Arkansas.

MARK R. SHULMAN teaches history at Yale University in New Haven, Connecticut.

KAREN SLEEZER is a graduate student in the Department of History at Sam Houston State University in Huntsville, Texas.

JOHN W. STOREY is a historian at Lamar University in Beaumont, Texas.

WALTER A. SUTTON teaches history at Lamar University in Beaumont, Texas.

ROY E. THOMAN is a political scientist at West Texas State University in Canyon, Texas.

JUSTUS M. van der KROEF is a member of the Department of Political Science at the University of Bridgeport in Bridgeport, Connecticut.

PREFACE

Five hundred years ago today, Christopher Columbus was shuttling back and forth among the courts of the major royal families of Western Europe trying to secure financing for his visions. He intended to reach the East by sailing west, and he promised to bring back the wealth of China and break the backs of the Italian and eastern Mediterranean middlemen who were profiteering in Asian goods. Columbus managed to get his financing, and although he never really understood the nature of his achievement in 1492, his landfall on San Salvador launched the peoples of the world on a process of economic and cultural integration that still continues today. In the wake of Columbus's voyage to the New World, the major powers of Western Europe established imperial systems that shaped global politics and economics for centuries.

The Historical Dictionary of European Imperialism is designed to provide a ready reference tool for students and scholars. Its major focus is the Spanish, Portuguese, British, Dutch, French, German, Belgian, and Italian empires during the past 500 years. This volume represents a general overview. Subsequent volumes on the individual European empires will provide substantially more detail. The *Dictionary* provides brief descriptive essays on a variety of topics—colonies, prominent individuals, legislation, treaties, conferences, wars, revolutions, and technologies.

Several guidelines were used in selecting topics. For an individual to be included in this introductory volume, he or she had to have a historical significance which transcended his or her own country. Essays on individual colonies usually end with the winning of independence or formal incorporation into the body politic of the mother country. References at the end of each entry provide sources of additional information for those wishing to pursue the subject further. Cross-references within the text, designated by an asterisk, will help the reader to find related items. Three appendixes provide a guide to contemporary languages in former colonial areas, a chronology of European imperialism, and a complete table of island systems in the world.

I wish to express my thanks to the scholars who wrote essays for the *Dictionary*, especially to those associate editors who contributed so much material. Their names appear at the end of the entries they wrote. All unsigned entries were written by me. I am especially grateful to Professor Robert Shadle, whose extensive understanding of European imperialism helped shape this book at every stage of its development. I would also like to thank the librarians who assisted me in locating hard-to-find material. Bill Bailey, Frank Marotti, and Ann Holder of the Newton Gresham Library at Sam Houston State University were particularly helpful.

James S. Olson

Historical Dictionary
of
European Imperialism

A

ABU DHABI. See UNITED ARAB EMIRATES.

ABYSSINIA. See ETHIOPIA.

ACADIA. In 1603 King Henry IV of France issued a land grant to Pierre du Guast, who promptly established a fur trading post, commanded by Samuel de Champlain,* on the Bay of Fundy. The colony of Acadia expanded around the main settlement of Port Royal. Acadians supported themselves by fishing, fur trading, and farming, but the severe winters and mosquito-infested summers made life difficult. Immigration was slow, and strong village kinship systems developed. The original families of the early seventeenth century became the Acadian clans of the eighteenth century. They were Roman Catholic in religion, Gallic in culture, and bound together in strong extended families.

Anglo-French rivalry eventually disrupted Acadian society. After Queen Anne's War ended in 1713, England acquired Acadia from France, and for the next forty years the Acadians preserved their culture, but it was an untenable position, living in an English colony while loyal to France. England perceived the Acadians as potential traitors ready to rise up in rebellion. When Acadians refused to take a loyalty oath to England at the outset of the French and Indian War,* English politicians expelled them.

The exile began in 1755, when there were probably 10,000 Acadians in Nova Scotia* and another 5,000 on Prince Edward Island*. In a matter of days, most of the Acadians were forced onto ships and deported. Eventually, thirty years after the exile, Spain recruited 1,600 Acadians living in France to colonize the Spanish possession in Louisiana. They became the nucleus of the large Acadian

(Cajun) settlement in southwestern Louisiana. (Naomi Griffiths, *The Acadians: Creation of a People*, 1973.)

ACCRA. Accra is a port on the Gulf of Guinea. It was once the capital of the British colony of Gold Coast*. The British, Dutch, and Danes all had trading stations there, but in 1851 the Danes ceded their interests to Great Britain, and in 1871 the Dutch did the same, making it British territory exclusively. (Peter Kemp, *The Oxford Companion to Ships and the Sea*, 1976.)

ACT OF ALGECIRAS OF 1906. The Act of Algeciras was signed on April 7, 1906, at the conclusion of the Algeciras Conference*. It confirmed Moroccan independence and assured freedom of trade for all nations. The act created a state bank with equal shares for the Great Powers but controlled by a French bank. It granted France and Spain joint control of the police forces in Moroccan ports. It marked the defeat of Germany's efforts to weaken the Anglo-French entente and to move into Morocco*. France became the dominant power in Morocco but did not succeed at that point in making that country its protectorate. (Eugene N. Anderson, *The First Moroccan Crisis, 1904–1906*, 1930; reprint, 1966; Edmund Burke III, *Prelude to Protectorate in Morocco*, 1976.)

Walter A. Sutton

ADEN. Strategically located at the southern entrance to the Red Sea near the strait of Bab el Mandeb, Aden attracted the British interest in the late 1830s because of the advent of oceanic steamships. It was not possible for such vessels to carry sufficient fuel for the voyage to India*; a coaling station in the vicinity of the mouth of the Red Sea was thus necessary. The town of Aden, built on a peninsula, was well situated for use as a defensible British base. British naval and army forces occupied the town on January 16, 1839. A treaty was signed the following June granting the Sultan of Lahej an annual stipend of 6,500 Maria Theresa dollars. This was the first of a series of agreements with some thirty local sheikhs. These treaties extended British authority throughout the region and accorded British protection to rulers who agreed not to have relations with foreign states. The strategic importance of Aden was enormously enhanced when the Suez Canal* was opened in 1869.

The territory acquired by Britain in 1839 consisted only of the peninsula of Aden itself. In 1868 Little Aden was purchased from the Sheikh of Aqrabi; in 1882 the connecting neck of land and the town of Sheikh Othman were bought from the Sultan of Lahej. Local government began with a settlement committee in 1876 and a port trust in 1889. By 1931 both institutions included representatives of the Arab community. On April 1, 1937, Aden became a Crown Colony directed by a governor assisted by an executive council. By that time England had launched a pacification program in the Protectorates to terminate the blood feuds and other forms of violence that were stifling trade, agriculture, and economic development in general.

A legislative council was inaugurated in Aden in 1947. Further constitutional developments went into effect in November 1958 with an Aden order in council providing for a reconstituted legislative council with an elected unofficial majority. Half the membership of the executive council was to be composed of unofficial members of the legislative council who would be designated "Members in Charge" of certain departments of the government of Aden. The first elections for the twelve contested seats on the legislative council in January 1959, however, were boycotted by certain political groups, supported by the Aden Trades Union Congress, which maintained that Britain should grant the area complete independence. The winning candidates were either independents or members of the Aden Association, whose goal was self-government within the British Commonwealth of Nations*. The governor announced in January 1961 that the Members in Charge would henceforth have the title of "Minister," and would be given greater responsibilities.

Prior to the 1934 Treaty of Sana, Britain played a limited role in the domestic affairs of the protected states. There were British troops and police in Aden proper, but none in the protectorates; the tribal sheikhs were encouraged to form their own locally recruited police forces, called Tribal Guards. They were later strengthened in the Western Protectorate by armed police known as the Government Guards, a force directed by the British agent, who represented the governor of Aden in the Western Protectorate. A similar force was initiated in the Eastern Aden Protectorate in 1940.

By the mid–1950s the British concluded that political and economic progress was being thwarted by the lack of an appropriate structure that would facilitiate cooperation among the many states of the area. On February 11, 1959, six sheikhdoms of the Western Protectorate established a Federation of Arab Emirates of the South. The objectives of the new organization were to ensure mutual defense and to promote social, political, and economic development. By late 1962 the Federation of South Arabia, as it had been renamed, consisted of eleven states. Aden joined the Federation in January 1963.

By September 25, 1965, terrorist attacks in Aden had become so troublesome that the British decided to dismiss the government of Abdul Qawee Mackawee and the legislative council. Sir Richard Turnbull, the British high commissioner, assumed direct rule. In 1966 the political situation became more complicated as the National Liberation Front (N.L.F.) merged with the Organization for the Liberation of the Occupied South to form a new anti-British and militant Front for the Liberation of Occupied South Yemen (F.L.O.S.Y.). Before long, however, the N.L.F. had second thoughts and decided that the merger had been a mistake; the N.L.F. announced its independence on December 12, 1966.

By February 1967 British security forces were preparing for one of the worst periods of civil disorders in the history of Aden. In April the split between the N.L.F. and F.L.O.S.Y. intensified into a form of gangster warfare. Sir Humphrey Trevelyan, the new British high commissioner, announced in May 1967 that Britain supported the federal government as the legal government of South

Arabia. He indicated that if the N.L.F. and F.L.O.S.Y. wanted to take part in discussions, they would be welcome, but they would not be allowed to resort to blackmail. Sir Humphrey was unable, however, to slow the rush toward disintegration.

On July 5, 1967, it seemed as though the South Arabian federal government had decided, in effect, to phase itself out of existence. It did this when the supreme federal council chose Hussain Bayoomi to be South Arabia's prime minister, giving him the task of forming a provisional administration. Nothing positive resulted, however, because the N.L.F. and its rival, the Egyptian-backed F.L.O.S.Y., decided not to cooperate with Bayoomi. Events then began to move quickly. While the special United Nations mission was in Geneva holding discussions on the future of South Arabia, the N.L.F. began to displace the Federal authorities. By the middle of August the N.L.F. had extended its control over the state of Lahej, the wealthiest state of the South Arabian Federation, after having taken over several other states. The N.L.F.'s sweep of the Eastern Protectorate was completed when it was announced on October 16 that its forces had captured the Mahra sultanate.

The extent of the collapse of federal authority was indicated by the fact that by the end of August twelve of the South Arabian Federation's seventeen states were in the hands of the nationalists. Aden state, where 12,000 British troops were still stationed, was completely encircled. It was obvious that the system of the past was being rapidly swept away. On September 5 Prime Minister Harold Wilson called a meeting of the defense and overseas policy committee of the cabinet at No. 10 Downing Street to discuss the new situation caused by the disintegration of the South Arabian federal government and seizure of power in many parts of the federation by the N.L.F. This meeting was followed shortly by Sir Humphrey's statement that sealed the fate of the Federation of South Arabia. He declared that he recognized the nationalist forces as representatives of the people, and that he was ready to have discussions with them.

On November 6 the South Arabian army openly sided with the N.L.F. In its statement, the army called for negotiations between Britain and the National Liberation Front concerning the transference of power. Great Britain granted sovereignty on November 30, 1967, to the new state, which adopted the name of the People's Republic of Southern Yemen. The N.L.F–run nation originally was composed of Aden and sixteen of the twenty states; the remaining four states later became part of the country. Salim Robea Ali was the first chairman of the presidential council. South Yemen united with North Yemen in May 1990 to create the Republic of Yemen. (R. J. Gavin, *Aden Under British Rule, 1839–1967*, 1975.)

Roy E. Thoman

ADMIRALTY ISLANDS. The Admiralty Islands are part of the Bismarck Archipelago.* There are forty of the islands scattered out over 800 square miles of territory, with the geographic center of the islands located about 250 miles north of the Huon Peninsula of New Guinea. The first European to discover the islands was Alvaro de Saavedra,* who landed there in 1528, and in 1767 the English explorer Philip Carteret named the islands. Germany annexed the Admiralty Islands in 1884 and maintained sovereignty there until 1914, when World War I started and the British Navy drove them out. The Treaty of Versailles of 1919* allowed Australia to establish a mandate over the islands. By that time the Admiralties formed Manus Province, part of Papua New Guinea*. (Paul Hasluck, *A Time for Building: Australian Administration in Papua and New Guinea 1951–1963*, 1976.)

AFGHANISTAN. Central to the history of Afghanistan in the nineteenth and early twentieth centuries was the "Great Game" of imperialism played by Czarist Russia, expanding southward toward Afghanistan, and Great Britain, driving northward from India*. Russian expansion was perceived by British officials to be a threat to India, while the Russians suspected that Great Britain intended to project her power north of the Hindu Kush.

By 1830 the internal situation in Afghanistan revealed enough division and weakness to attract foreign meddling. The empire was split into three independent states. Kabul was ruled by Dost Muhammad, while his brother, Kohendil Khan, reigned in Qandahar. Sadozai Kamran, last of the legitimate ruling house and an enemy of the two brothers, was sovereign in Herat. In 1837 the Shah of Persia, in pursuit of his policy of eastward expansion, led a military expedition that laid siege to Herat. Russian agents supported him. Ultimately, however, to avoid war with Great Britain, the Shah decided to end the nine-month siege and return to Tehran. As he had been in league with the Russians, the outcome amounted to a defeat for St. Petersburg in its maneuver to gain a strategic base in Afghanistan.

British intervention in the country's internal politics led to the First Afghan War, 1838–1842. For strategic reasons, British military forces helped Shah Shuja regain power in Afghanistan, a move strongly opposed by Dost Muhammad and his supporters. In April 1839 the invading force reached Quetta. By the end of the month Shah Shuja and his British allies took Qandahar; on August 6, 1839, he occupied Kabul after an exile of thirty years. What had seemed to be an easy victory, however, turned into a tragedy for the British. In a complicated turn of events involving a combination of isolation and logistical problems, a large number of Britons were massacred. As an act of retribution, British troops returned to Kabul in the fall of 1842 and burned the great bazaar. The British then left the country and permitted Dost Muhammad to return to power, Shah Shuja having been murdered earlier in the year. The first attempt of the British to gain control of the Hindu Kush thus ended unsuccessfully. Dost Muhammad died in 1863 and was succeeded by his third son, Sher Ali.

The Second Afghan War, 1878–1881, was precipitated by British formulation of a new "forward policy." Noting the relentless Russian push to the south, British statesmen were determined not to allow Russia to control or outflank the frontier barrier to India—the mountains of the Hindu Kush. This region in northern Afghanistan had throughout history been the key venue for invasion of the Indian subcontinent. The ultimate objective of the viceroy's forward policy would be to locate the Indian defensive line on the northern heights of the Hindu Kush. In the implementation of this grand scheme, little regard was expressed for the wishes of the Afghan leaders.

British forces began their conquest in November 1878. Victories came swiftly, and by mid-January one column had reached Jalalabad; in the south, another column captured Qandahar and occupied the surrounding region. Peace talks then opened with Yaqub Khan, Sher Ali's son and successor, and the Treaty of Gandamark was concluded by the end of May. The main provisions of the treaty were as follows: the amir would conduct relations with foreign states only in accordance with the advice of the British government; permanent British representatives would be stationed in Kabul and other places in Afghanistan; the British would retain control of the Khyber Pass and the districts of Kurram, Pishin, and Sibi; and the amir would receive an annual subsidy of £60,000.

The peace, however, was short-lived. After members of the British mission reached Kabul in July they were attacked by a mob of mutinous Afghan soldiers. The amir made little effort to intervene, and all of the Britons were massacred. British forces then attacked and defeated Afghan levies. Shortly thereafter the amir abdicated. The British took control of Kabul and the country's treasury and set up a court to try those accused of taking part in the killings.

In March 1880 Sardar Abdur Rahman, son of Sher Ali's elder half-brother, returned to Afghanistan. As he was a talented leader and friendly to England's interests, the British welcomed his assumption of power. They permitted him to take control of the country, except for Qandahar. There were limits placed on his external sovereignty, however. The amir was prohibited from having direct political relations with any other foreign powers. If he followed British advice in foreign relations, Britain promised to help him repel aggressors. (Forty years later Abdur Rahman's grandson went to war with Great Britain to end this provision, which by 1919 was viewed as degrading.) Afghanistan thus became the long sought-after buffer state between Russia and India.

In the summer of 1895 an agreement between Russia and Great Britain precisely defined, with one exception, the international boundary between Afghanistan and Russia. The exact location of the boundary along the Oxus was not defined, leading to numerous disputes. (The problem was solved in 1946 when a Soviet-Afghan agreement defined the boundary as the *thalweg*, or mid-channel of the river.) In an agreement signed in St. Petersburg in 1907, the Czarist regime declared that it regarded Afghanistan as outside the Russian sphere of influence and promised to send no agents into that nation. Russia also agreed to deal only through the British government concerning political matters involving Afghanistan. For its part, Great Britain pledged not to annex or occupy any part of Afghanistan or to interfere in its internal administration. Afghanistan became fully independent through the 1919 Treaty of Rawalpindi. (W. K. Fraser-Tytler,

Afghanistan: A Study of Political Developments in Central and Southern Asia, 1967.)

Roy E. Thoman

AGADIR CRISIS. Agadir is a seaport on the Atlantic coast of Morocco*. Its estimated population in 1984 was 623,000. In 1911 it was the focal point of the second Moroccan crisis between France and Germany, with France having British support. Because France landed troops in April 1911 to protect the native government from a rebellion at Fez, Germany assumed that France intended to take over all of Morocco. To protect its interests and to secure concessions from France, Germany sent the battleship *Panther*, which arrived at Agadir on July 1. Germany appeared to France and Britain to be seeking a naval base and territory in Morocco, and the two powers cooperated to block German penetration. During the course of the crisis David Lloyd George, British chancellor of the exchequer, in a famous speech at Mansion House on July 21, appeared to threaten the Germans with war if they persisted in Morocco. For a while war seemed possible, but Germany backed down in October, signed an agreement with France early in November, and withdrew the *Panther*. The agreement allowed France to make Morocco a protectorate and gave to Germany a part of the French Congo*. The crisis brought France and Britain closer, and the British cabinet began to discuss the possibility of military support of France in case of a future crisis. (Ima C. Barlow, *The Agadir Crisis*, 1940; Edmund Burke III, *Prelude to Protectorate in Morocco*, 1976.)

Walter A. Sutton

AJMAN. See UNITED ARAB EMIRATES.

AJMER-MERWARA. Ajmer-Merwara was a small principality in India* ceded to Great Britain in 1818 by the ruler of Gwalior. In 1832 Ajmer-Merwara was administratively incorporated into the North-West Frontier Provinces*, where it remained until 1871. Great Britain changed that arrangement in 1871, designating the agent for the viceroy of Rajputana as the chief commissioner of Ajmer-Merwara. In 1947 Ajmer-Merwara became part of India. (David P. Henige, *Colonial Governors from the Fifteenth Century to the Present*, 1970.)

ALAGÔAS. Throughout most of the colonial period, Alagôas was a district in the Portuguese colony of Pernambuco* in Brazil*. In 1817 it became a separate captaincy, but Alagôas did not receive its own governor until 1819. Two years later, in 1821, Alagôas became a province of the empire of Brazil. See BRAZIL.

ALASKA. In 1728 the Danish mariner Vitus Bering, on contract from the Russian tsar, explored the Bering Sea and realized that Alaska was not connected to Siberia. He made a second voyage in 1741, landed a group of men on the Alaska coast, and brought back sea otter furs to Russia, launching what became a lucrative trade. In 1784 a permanent Russian settlement was established on Kodiak Island. The Russian-American Company, formed in 1799, assumed political jurisdiction over Alaska in 1806. A bitter competition raged between Russian, English, and American trappers for control of the sea otter trade, but in 1824 Russia, limited by treaties to the territory north of 54° 40', resolved the dispute by opening the traffic on an equal basis to everyone. They all too soon trapped the sea otter to near extinction.

With the otter trade disappearing, the tsar lost interest in Alaska. The Crimean War (1853–1856) depleted the tsar's treasury, and in 1867 Russia sold Alaska to the United States for $7.2 million. The American interest there was primarily strategic—to eliminate the Russian presence in the Western Hemisphere and prevent British expansion. Although critics dubbed the purchase ''Seward's Folly'' after Secretary of State William Seward, the Senate ratified the treaty by 37 to 2. Alaska was under control of the War Department (to 1877) and the Treasury until 1884 when Congress upgraded it to a civil and judicial district. Gold discoveries at the Stikine River in 1861, Juneau in 1880, the Klondike in 1897–1900, Nome in 1898, and Fairbanks in 1903 boosted the Alaskan population. In 1903 the United States and Canada* settled a boundary dispute over Alaska, placing the border along the peaks of the Boundary Range Mountains. In 1906 Alaska sent a non-voting representative to Congress. Alaska became a formal territory of the United States in 1912. In the twentieth century oil discoveries at the Kenai Peninsula and Cook Inlet created a new industrial base, and between 1940 and 1959 Alaska's population increased from 70,000 to more than 250,000. In 1959 Alaska became the 49th state in the United States. (Ernest Gruening, *The State of Alaska*, 1954; C. C. Hulley, *Alaska: Past and Present*, 1970.)

AL-FUJAYRAH. See UNITED ARAB EMIRATES.

ALGECIRAS CONFERENCE OF 1906. The Algeciras Conference took place in Algeciras, Spain, from January 16 to April 7, 1906, to end the first Moroccan crisis, which began early in 1905. France tried to make Morocco* a protectorate, and Germany intervened to support the Moroccans, to gain influence over them, and to test the Anglo-French *entente*. Kaiser Wilhelm even visited Tangier on March 31, 1905. Faced with growing German hostility at a time when its ally Russia was worn out from the Russo-Japanese war, France agreed to an international conference. Thirteen nations attended: Britain, France, Russia, Germany, Italy, Austria-Hungary, Spain, Belgium, the Netherlands, Sweden, Portugal, the United States, and, of course, Morocco. It was the first conference that the United States attended concerning strictly European affairs.

The Powers believed that Morocco should remain independent but under European domination. They began by dealing with noncontroversial matters of freedom of trade, illegal arms, the customs service, public works, and taxes. The difficult questions of control of the Moroccan police force and a new Moroccan bank took longer to resolve. The Powers believed that whatever nation controlled the police and the bank would control Morocco. They did not pay much attention to what Morocco wanted. As the discussions progressed, Germany was more and more isolated, with only Austria-Hungary and Morocco's support. Even Italy, one third of the Triple Alliance, voted with France, as did Great Britain and the rest. Germany failed to get an international police force when France and Spain secured joint control of the police in Moroccan ports. A state bank was created under the control of a French bank but with each of the Great Powers having an equal share. The Powers signed the Act of Algeciras*, the formal agreement, on August 7. Germany was humiliated but did succeed in blocking French desire to make Morocco a protectorate.

British support for France was of great significance. Russia, France's ally, had been gravely weakened by its defeat by Japan. Consequently, Germany sought an advantage, and Britain rescued France. Germany throughout the crisis had been unduly belligerent (although it never contemplated war) and had alarmed other nations. Germany's diplomatic defeat meant that its attempts to move into Morocco and to weaken the Anglo-French agreement of 1904 helped produce the results that Germany had tried to prevent. Britain and France grew even closer, and the alignments of World War I were fixed. (Eugene N. Anderson, *The First Moroccan Crisis, 1904–1906*, 1930; reprint 1966; Edmund Burke III, *Prelude to Protectorate in Morocco*, 1976.)

Walter A. Sutton

ALGERIA. Largest of the three states of the Maghrib (North Africa), Algeria has a heritage characterized by Berber and Arab elements as the result of the spread of Islam to North Africa in the seventh century. The adoption of Islam and Arabic culture were the enduring results of that invasion, which followed successive invasions of Phoenicians, Romans, Vandals, and Byzantine Greeks. In the sixteenth century Algeria became the westernmost province of the Ottoman Empire. It was the Regency of Algiers which was used as a naval base, notably from the ports of Algiers and Oran, in the Ottoman wars against the West. It constituted a permanent threat to the Spanish navy. Later, when Ottoman control loosened and the Regency became semiautonomous, it continued to be for 300 years (until 1800) a base for attacks on European ships by the corsairs of the "Barbary Coast."

In 1830 a dispute between the French consul and the ruler of Algiers—the dey—about an alleged debt by Algiers going back to the time of Napoleon, led to insults. Refusal by the dey to apologize led to French intervention. The increasingly unpopular regime of Charles X of France, the last of the Bourbon kings, needed an external diversion to deflect French discontent at home and permit passage of authoritarian measures. It did not work, as the king and his regime were toppled by the July 1830 Revolution. Meanwhile a French fleet blockaded Algiers, and a French army landed, facing very little resistance at the onset. The dey went into exile.

The July Monarchy in France, under King Louis Philippe, inherited a new colony in North Africa. It expanded French control, facing much opposition soon led by a very able leader, the Amir Abd al-Qadir, who carried on guerrilla warfare against the French with such success that they had to sign a treaty recognizing him as amir of Masacara in the interior. Hostilities soon resumed and bitter campaigns demanded more and more French troops: 64,000 in 1840, and more than 100,000 by 1847. The French used total war methods, destroying crops, killing animals, even exterminating whole tribes. In 1847 Abd al-Qadir was finally captured, imprisoned, and sent into exile. He was the first Algerian nationalist.

The vicious character of the fighting, accompanied by the appalling ravages of disease, produced much political criticism in France, where the Algerian conquest was unpopular. But French expansion in Algeria continued under Napoleon III and the Second Empire, especially since French immigrants had been brought in to consolidate the French hold. There were 27,000 in 1841, 75,000 in 1845, and close to 300,000 by 1860. After 1871, when the whole country had been subjugated, it was divided into three French departments (Algiers, Oran, Constantine) with representatives in the chamber of deputies in Paris. But the franchise was granted only to European colonists and small numbers of Europeanized North Africans, who had to give up Islam to become French citizens. This small minority dominated political life. The other native Algerians, 90 percent of the population, had an inferior status and were isolated economically from the more developed European sector. As far as they were concerned, Algeria was really a colony. The European colonists (the "colons") had taken the best land, on which they grew wine and vegetables.

When Algerian nationalist leaders started to appear, the first ones were French educated, spoke better French than Arabic, and had received French citizenship. Later on, other Algerians became increasingly influenced by successful nationalist movements in other Arab countries. Until 1940 most Algerian leaders did not demand independence, only equal rights with the Europeans. French colons, mostly townspeople and businessmen, were determined to hold on to their privileges and oppose progress toward political and social equality. By the end of World War II, when Algeria had been for a time under Vichy control, Muslim leaders came to the conclusion that armed struggle was the only solution.

In May 1945 an outbreak of violence was repressed by the French army, accompanied by the burning of Algerian villages. In the following years, there were other eruptions of violence, some engineered by the Secret Organization (OS). Many Arab (or nationalist) leaders were jailed. In 1952 one of them, Ahmed ben Bella*, escaped to Cairo. A major insurrection, which marked the beginning of the Algerian war, was launched on November 1, 1954, All Saints Day, a French holiday. It was led by the National Liberation Front (FLN). Bombs exploded throughout the European residential areas, often smuggled out of the native quarter, the Casbah, by Algerian women, and settlers were murdered. Within a year, the rebellion had spread across Algeria.

The French government, under Premier Pierre Mendes-France and Interior Minister Francois Mitterrand, attempted to quell the rebellion through a police action. They would not call it war. France had just extricated itself from Indochina*, but Algeria was supposedly part of France, not a colony. Nevertheless, the conflict escalated in intensity, lasting eight years, as long as the Indochina war, and proving to be much more intractable than Tunisia* and Morocco*, most of all because of the presence of one million European settlers who opposed any concession to the indigenous Algerians. France sent up to 500,000 men, including draftees (unlike in Indochina), which made it a domestic political problem, to fight 6,000 guerrillas. Those guerrillas enjoyed widespread support within the Muslim population, and also in Morocco and Tunisia from where supplies and weapons were smuggled. The rebellion also received assistance and support throughout the Arab world, notably from Egypt*, which was an added reason for France joining the Suez expedition in 1956.

The French set up electric fences along the Tunisian and Moroccan borders, and they managed to control urban terrorism. But the widespread use of torture by the army, even though atrocities were committed on both sides, profoundly divided public opinion in France. Many intellectuals openly supported the rebellion. On the other hand, many French career officers, who had fought in Indochina, saw in Algeria another instance of the world communist conspiracy. They thought they had learned a lesson in Indochina and had mastered the techniques of psychological action and revolutionary warfare. They were also more willing to practice a genuine integration of the Muslim population, which put them at cross purpose with the French settlers.

The Algerian war ultimately caused the collapse of the Fourth Republic when a coalition of colons and army officers started an insurrection in Algiers against a new government in Paris deemed favorable to the rebels. This happened on May 13, 1958, leading to the return to power in France of General Charles de Gaulle and the advent of the Fifth Republic. By then the war had produced inflation and social and industrial unrest, and the number of casualties had mounted. By the end of the war, 300,000 Algerians and 21,000 Europeans had been killed. De Gaulle's position was ambiguous at first and interpreted by all sides as favorable to their cause. However, he attempted to settle the problem by allocating large sums to the economic development of Algeria, increasing the number of Muslims in positions of authority, and transferring unreliable officers. In 1959 he offered to the Algerians self-determination four years after the end of the fighting. But it was not enough for the FLN and too much for the infuriated colons and some army officers. Military revolts erupted, one in April 1961 led by four prominent French generals. Most of the army remained loyal to the government, and the revolt collapsed. An outbreak of right-wing French terrorism, with the formation of the OAS (Secret Army Organization) was likewise unsuccessful. Meanwhile, secret negotiations between the French government and FLN leaders led to a ceasefire in March 1962, a referendum in Algeria, and the proclamation of independence on July 3, 1962. A constitution was ratified in September 1963, and Ahmed ben Bella was elected president. (Raphael Danziger, *Abd al-Qadir and the Algerians. Resistance to the French and Internal Consolidation*, 1977; Alf A. Heggoy, *Insurgency and Counterinsurgency in Algeria*, 1972.)

Alain G. Marsot

AMERICAN COLONIZATION SOCIETY. In 1816 Robert Finley, a Presbyterian minister, founded the American Colonization Society. He believed it would be a solution to the problems of slavery and the place of black people in American society. Finley proposed sending freed slaves back to Africa. Because it seemed a peaceful way of addressing the problem of slavery, the American Colonization Society attracted considerable attention and, for a time, the support of such prominent Americans as Thomas Jefferson, Henry Clay, and James Monroe. Most of the financial support for the American Colonization Society came from slaveowners in Kentucky, Maryland, and Virginia. They felt that large numbers of emancipated slaves living in the United States would inevitably undermine the institution of slavery.

In 1821 the American Colonization Society bought a strip of land known as Cape Mesurado on the west coast of Africa. They named the region Monrovia. But the scheme was largely stillborn. Henry Clay failed to secure congressional support for a compensated emancipation scheme which would have purchased slaves and then sent them to Africa. Congress balked because the scheme was too expensive. Also, relatively few freed slaves were interested in relocating to Africa. By 1820 most of them had been born in the United States. Throughout the 1820s the American Colonization Society promoted the relocation idea, but by 1831 only 1,420 black people had moved to Monrovia. In 1847 the black settlers of Monrovia declared their independence from the United States and launched the Republic of Liberia*. The American Colonization Society finally dissolved in 1912. (Philip J. Staudenraus, *The African Colonization Movement, 1816–1865*, 1961.)

AMERICAN EMPIRE. For most of its early history, the United States was preoccupied with internal expansion—the Manifest Destiny* crusade to reach from the Atlantic to the Pacific. It was not until 1867 when the United States, concerned about the Russian presence along the northern Pacific coast, purchased Alaska* from the tsar for $7.2 million and acquired some non-contiguous territory. New acquisitions soon followed. Intent on developing the China trade and securing naval coaling stations in the Pacific, the United States established a naval station at Pago Pago in Samoa* in 1878. Ten years later, in 1888, the United States, Great Britain, and Germany almost went to war over Samoa, and the dispute was not settled until 1899 when Germany and the United States divided up the islands and Great Britain surrendered her claim.

By that time the American empire had expanded. The Spanish-American War of 1898* was a triumph for the United States. During the conflict the United

States annexed Hawaii*, and in the treaty concluding the war the United States acquired the Philippines*, Guam* in the Marianas*, and Puerto Rico* in the Caribbean. To those colonies the United states added the Panama Canal Zone* in 1903 and the Virgin Islands*, purchased from Denmark in 1917 to prevent a possible German expansion there. The United States also had naval bases at Wake Island* and Midway Island* in the Pacific.

After fighting a bitter guerrilla war against Filipino nationalists between 1898 and 1902, the United States governed the Philippine Islands with an even hand, and between 1936 and 1945 gradually extended independence to them. Puerto Rico became a commonwealth of the United States, while Alaska and Hawaii became states in 1959. That left the United States with colonial dependencies at Guam, Wake, and Midway islands in the Pacific, the Virgin Islands in the Caribbean, and the Panama Canal Zone in Central America. (Ernest R. May, *American Imperialism: A Speculative Essay*, 1968.)

AMERICAN REVOLUTION. The American Revolution and the War for American Independence ended what historians refer to as the First British Empire. Both had a fundamental impact on the formation and subsequent development of the Second British Empire. The American Revolution and the War for American Independence are different concepts. The War for American Independence involved only the limited military contest over the issue of American independence; whereas the American Revolution encompassed the longer festering ideological alienation of Americans from Britons. As such, the Revolution started long before the first shot was fired at Lexington and Concord.

Chief among these alienations were economic, political, and constitutional differences. Economic friction resulted from a growing competition between mother country and colonies, which in the 1760s led to new commercial regulations and restrictions on the colonial economy and a renewed determination by Britain to enforce the long-ignored and evaded Acts of Trade and Navigation. Political and constitutional differences evolved around the concept of self-government, which was an American colonial tradition of long standing. Americans identified with the constitutional history of the mother country, particularly with concessions won for the representative principle by the English Glorious Revolution of 1688.

The British empire was significantly altered in 1763. With the successful conclusion of the French and Indian War*, Britain acquired new territories and for the first time a large number of alien people to be absorbed, some 60,000 French Canadians. The shift from a basic commercial empire to a territorial empire required fresh imperial thinking and new responses for the 1760s. Aside from William Pitt the Elder (Earl of Chatham), there were no innovative thinkers on broad imperial themes able to adjust policies constructively, and some of the responses by tradition-bound ministers and unreformed parliaments alienated the older colonies. For example, it was determined early to raise a revenue in America to defend the enlarged empire and to keep a standing army in America for this

purpose. Pontiac's Indian Rebellion in the spring of 1763 and the Royal Proclamation of October 7, 1763, temporarily closed the American West to white
settlement. Settlement of the West had been a major objective of American
efforts during the French and Indian War. What was asserted to be temporary
appeared to become permanent by the Quebec Act of 1774. Although the act
did deal intelligently with the new problem of an alien group of French within
the British empire, the content convinced suspicious Americans that it was a
coercive measure. The Northwest was attached to the French-speaking province
of Quebec and reserved for Indians and the fur trade. No provisions were included
for a representative government in Quebec, and Roman Catholicism was granted
official recognition. It looked as if England wanted to thwart American agricultural expansion, undermine the principle of representative government, and
surround Protestant America with Papists.

Furthermore, much of the British legislation of the 1760s requiring Americans
to defray imperial expenses, such as the Sugar Act, the Stamp Act, the Quartering
Act, and the Townsend Duties Act, violated American concepts of the rights of
Englishmen. Despite frequent references to King George III* in the Declaration
of Independence, rebellion when it came was primarily aimed against Parliament,
not the King. Colonials believed that the empire was not a unitary empire with
all power vested in Parliament, but that it was a federal empire with sovereignty
divided among equal units. Indeed Americans were moving toward a common-
wealth-of-nations concept with the idea of coordinate legislatures under a common sovereign. For a time Americans acknowledged Parliament's right to
legislate on external imperial matters while asserting that the sole right over
internal taxation resided with the colonial representative assemblies. That time
had passed by July 1776.

Britons viewed the empire very differently. To them, the empire was unitary,
and since the Glorious Revolution, the British Parliament was considered supreme over all—King, empire, and everything. This was good Whig doctrine
in Britain. Even George III accepted the Whig view and expressed no desire to
restore monarchy to the powers it had enjoyed under the Stuart kings during the
previous century. Both King and Parliament clearly considered the various colonial assemblies subordinate and colonials inferior to Britons. Obduracy by
King, Parliament, and Britons led to military conflict with colonial Americans
and the collapse of the First British Empire. (John R. Alden, *A History of the
American Revolution*, 1969; Bernard Bailyn, *The Ideological Origins of the
American Revolution*, 1967).

Lee E. Olm

AMERICAN SAMOA. American Samoa is an archipelago stretching 290 miles
across the South Pacific. It consists of six islands: Tutuila, Ta'u, Olosega, Ofu,
Aunu'u, and Rose. Swain's Island, located about 210 miles northwest of Tutuila,
was added to American Samoa in 1925. Jacob Roggeveen, the Dutch explorer,
became the first European to visit Samoa in 1722. Later in the eighteenth century

a number of European expeditions came into contact with Samoans, particularly Tutuilan, and the results were often violent, giving the Samoans a reputation for ferocity. Although a handful of escaped convicts from New South Wales* and navy deserters reached Samoa in the early 1800s, regular contact was not established until the 1830s, when European missionaries began arriving.

United States interest in Samoa commenced when Americans became attracted to the Asian trade potential. The islands were a midway point between Australia* and Japan and China. The harbor of Pago Pago on Tutuila was especially attractive. In 1872 Richard W. Meade, commander of the U.S.S. *Narragansett*, arrived at Pago Pago and negotiated exclusive rights to build a naval base there. Although the United States Senate did not ratify the arrangement, it raised the interest of Great Britain and Germany in Samoa. Throughout the 1870s the three countries tried to win the loyalty of various Samoan factions, creating violence and political instability on the islands.

A tripartite convention in 1879 between Germany, Great Britain, and the United States temporarily reduced those tensions. But ten years later, in March 1889, the issue came to a head again when German, American, and British ships all reached Apia harbor in what is today Western Samoa*. War threatened until an enormous hurricane destroyed most of the ships. Later in the year the Berlin Act created a tripartite condominium of Germany, the United States, and Great Britain to govern the Samoan Islands. The arrangement was cumbersome at best and handicapped by squabbling between the European powers and constant internecine warfare among the Samoans. In 1900 Britain withdrew from the arrangement, and the United States and Germany divided up Samoa. In return Germany and the United States recognized the British right to establish a protectorate in Tonga. The Samoan islands east of longitude 171 degrees W. went to the United States and became American Samoa. Those west of the line went to Germany and eventually became Western Samoa.

On April 17, 1900, a number of Samoan chiefs in the eastern islands signed documents surrendering sovereignty to the United States. The United States Navy assumed jurisdiction over the islands, leaving governance to the feuding Samoan chiefs. The local economy boomed during World War II* when troops arrived to train there for the assault on Japan, but when the naval station closed in 1951, President Harry S Truman turned American Samoa over to the Department of the Interior and the islands went into an economic tailspin. Thousands of people left the islands. In 1956 Peter Tali Coleman became the first native Samoan appointed governor. Not until the 1960s, when the United States government began spending millions of dollars to improve the Samoan infrastructure, did the economy revive. Although American Samoa received its own bicameral legislature in 1948 and its own constitution in 1960, a Future Political Status Commission in 1969 rejected every alternative—unification with Western Samoa, unification with Hawaii*, independence, or statehood—in favor of maintaining the status quo in its relationship with the United States. In 1977 Peter Tali Coleman became the first elected governor of American Samoa. It remains a self-governing colony of the United States. (James Bishop, ''America Samoa: Which Road Ahead?,'' *Pacific Studies*, 1, 1977, 47–53; J. A. C. Gray, *American Samoa*, 1960.)

ANDAMAN AND NICOBAR ISLANDS. Great Britain began using the Andaman Islands, a chain of small islands in the Bay of Bengal as a penal colony in 1789, but evacuated the colony in 1796. The British re-established the penal colony in 1850, and in 1858 sent a superintendent—James Pattison Walker—to govern the area. The title of superintendent was changed to chief commissioner in 1872. That year Andaman was the sight of the assassination of Lord Mayo, the British viceroy, by a Muslim fanatic. In 1869, Great Britain acquired the neighboring Nicobar Islands from Denmark and brought them into the Andaman jurisdiction. Both island groups became part of India in 1947. (David P. Henige, *Colonial Governors from the Fifteenth Century to the Present*, 1970.)

ANGLO-DUTCH WAR OF 1780–1783. The Anglo-Dutch War began as an outgrowth of the American Revolution*. Spain joined France in June 1779 as an ally of the United States against England. In 1779–1780 Spain laid siege to Gibraltar* and sent its fleet to attack British shipping in the Atlantic and Mediterranean. In retaliation, the British navy expanded its practice of boarding neutral vessels in search of enemy goods. On several occasions the British searched Dutch vessels and found evidence of secret agreements between the city of Amsterdam and representatives of the United States. King George III* of England demanded the punishment of the Amsterdam officials. The Dutch government refused and, instead, joined with Russia, Denmark, and Sweden in a united ''Declaration of Armed Neutrality,'' which vowed to resist Great Britain's policy of boarding the vessels of neutral nations. Subsequently, Britain declared war against Holland in December 1780. During almost three years of war, the British captured nearly all Dutch shipping and crippled the Dutch economy. In the Treaty of Paris of 1783* ending the hostilities between Britain and the United States, the interests of Holland were forgotten. Holland was forced to surrender Negapatam in south India* to Britain. Britain was also given free navigation through the Moluccas* in the southwestern Pacific. (J. P. W. Ehrman, *The British Government and Commercial Negotiations with Europe, 1783–1793*, 1962; P. Mackesy, *The War for America, 1775–1783*, 1964; A. W. Ward and G. P. Gooch, eds., *The Cambridge History of British Foreign Policy*, Vol. I, 1922.)

William G. Ratliff

ANGLO-EGYPTIAN SUDAN. Sudan, located in the central Nile Valley of Africa, is that continent's largest country. It is bordered on the north by Egypt*, the east by the Red Sea and Ethiopia*, the south by Kenya*, Uganda*, and Zaire*, and on the west by the Central African Republic*, Chad*, and Libya*. Until the early 1820s the Sudan was comprised of small independent states ruled by sultans of the Funj Dynasty. The chief sultan of the Funj was known as the "mek." His wealth came from taxes imposed on the slave trade. Farming and herding were well established in the fertile area of Al Jazira. In 1821 Egypt (which at the time was under the Ottoman Empire and ruled by a khedive) invaded and unified the northern portion of Sudan. The population was primarily Arabic Muslims. Even though Egypt claimed sovereignty over all of Sudan, it was unable to establish complete control over the southern Sudanese area, whose people were primarily black and practiced tribal religions. Sudan remained loosely under Egypt's rule until the early 1880s, when the tribes of the western and central Sudan rose in an Islamic holy war against the Egyptians. The movement was led by Muhammad Ahmad bin Abdallah, a Muslim fundamentalist who called himself the Mahdi ("Rightly Guided One").

Egypt had established its administrative headquarters at Khartoum. For many years British influence had been present in Egypt, and the Egyptians employed British officers to head their military forces in the Sudan. Charles Gordon was made governor-general of the Sudan in 1877. One of Gordon's major tasks was the eradication of the slave trade. Having strong convictions about the evil of slavery, he zealously pursued its extinction. This policy alienated many Arab tribes who felt Gordon was destroying their economy. Gordon was replaced for a short time (1880–1883) as governor of the Sudan, but he was reappointed after the Mahdi had become a major problem in the Sudan. Gordon's principal task was to evacuate all Egyptian military and civilian personnel from Khartoum, as the English and Egyptians had decided to relinquish possession of the Sudan to the Mahdi. The Mahdist forces, known as Ansars, had enjoyed several impressive victories, including the annihilation of an 8,000 man Egyptian force commanded by British Colonel William Hicks.

Unfortunately, when Gordon reached Khartoum in February 1884, he realized time would not permit the evacuation of the Egyptians. He requested reinforcements from Egypt and set out to defend Khartoum. After a lengthy siege, the Ansars attacked Khartoum on January 26, 1885, overwhelmed the Egyptian garrison, and killed and beheaded Gordon. Two days later, when advance elements of a British relief column reached Khartoum, it was securely held by the forces of the Mahdi. Although the Mahdi died within six months from typhus, his successor, Khalifa Abdallahi, continued the quest to unite the Sudan under the Mahdist fundamentalism.

In 1895 the British, fearing encroachment by other nations in the Sudan, decided to reestablish their presence. General Herbert Kitchener was made commander of the Anglo-Egyptian forces with instructions to retake the Sudan. Starting from Wadi Halfa on the Egyptian-Sudan border in March 1896, Kitchener's expeditionary force moved up the Nile with 25,000 men. After a hard-fought advance up the Nile, the battle of Omdurman was fought on September 2, 1898. Kitchener's attacking force was supported by river boats mounting artillery. The Khalifa's army, 52,000 strong, met Kitchener's forces on a plain just outside Omdurman, across the river from Khartoum. Eleven thousand of the Khalifa's men were killed in the morning battle while Kitchener suffered the loss of only 48 men with 400 wounded. It was during this battle that the 21st Lancers made the last British cavalry charge with sabers, accounting for a large number of the 48 men Kitchener lost. Winston Churchill* was a young officer in the 21st Lancers and participated in this famous but foolish charge.

Even though the Khalifa escaped from Omdurman, he was later killed in the battle at Umm Diwaykarat in November 1899. It took several years to defeat all followers of the Mahdi, but the battle of Omdurman put an end to any effective resistance by the Mahdists. A French attempt to occupy an abandoned Egyptian fort at Fashoda with one hundred Senegalese troops was also dealt with by General Kitchener, who moved up the Nile with a vastly superior Anglo-Sudanese force. Captain Jean Baptiste Marchand was ordered by his government to evacuate the fort to the British without a fight. History refers to this as the Fashoda Incident* (September 1898), and it was the last attempt by France to colonize the Sudan. In 1899 an Anglo-Egyptian agreement, devised by Lord Cromer, created a joint Anglo-Egyptian Condominium for the Sudan, which was, in fact, British controlled. Sir Reginald Wingate, who succeeded Kitchener as governor-general (1889–1916), deserves mention as the soldier and statesman chiefly responsible for the establishment of peace, order, and a stable administrative structure in the Sudan under British rule.

The British handling of southern Sudan differed greatly from that of the north. Christian missionaries, both Catholic and Protestant, had established churches and schools in the southern area. The schools ultimately became government subsidized, with instruction in English. Graduates of these mission schools were given favored treatment in civil service jobs. Arab businessmen and traders were expelled from the south and replaced by the educated southerners, and tribal chieftains were allowed to do most of the local governing, under British administration. There was considerable disagreement and rivalry between the northern and southern British officials of the Sudan Political Service. Overall, however, British control of the Sudan was quite efficient, and the country generally enjoyed peace and economic growth. Telegraphs and railroads were built in the more populated areas, and improved agricultural techniques were introduced, with cotton being the primary product.

Soon after World War I*, Sudanese nationalist movements began to surface but were of little consequence until World War II*. During World War II, the nationalist movement was given impetus when a British-led Sudanese force turned back a much larger Italian army. After World War II two major Muslim parties emerged. The Khatmaya, led by Sayyid Ali al-Marghani, wanted the Sudan to become a part of the Egyptian empire, a move supported by Egypt's King Faruk. The other party, the Ansar, under the leadership of Sayyid Abd al-Rahman-al-Mahdi, son of the Mahdi, wanted complete independence for the Sudan. After King Farouk was deposed in Egypt* in 1952, Britain agreed to self-government for Sudan. The Anglo-Egyptian Agreement of 1953 set forth the steps which would bring the condominium arrangement to an end. A parliament was established in 1954, and on January 1, 1956, Sudan became an independent republic. Its first prime minister was Ismail el Azhari. (Robert Collins and Robert Tignor, *Egypt and the Sudan*, 1967; David L. Lewis, *The Race to Fashoda*, 1987.)

Amanda Pollock

ANGLO-FRENCH CONVENTION OF 1908. The Anglo-French military convention of 1908 was part of a series of British-French discussions between January 1906 and August 1914. The 1908 convention followed the French request during the First Moroccan Crisis of 1905 that the British government should agree to a common strategy in the event of armed conflict with Germany. Among the plans proposed between France and Britain in both 1906 and 1908 were the employment of some 100,000 British troops in France and the use of Royal Navy warships in attacks on German naval installations in the Baltic and North Sea.

The Anglo-French conventions from 1906 to 1914 were held in secret until 1911, when the talks were divulged to the British cabinet. The British government had, however, been fully involved in the planning—the British Foreign Secretary Sir Edward Grey and Prime Minister Sir Henry Campbell-Bannerman both endorsed the possibility of joint British-French military operations. The Anglo-French conventions greatly extended the scope of the Anglo-French Entente of 1904*. The conventions meant that, inevitably, the Entente had evolved into a European military alliance, a turn of events far removed from its original intent as a deterrent to German colonial expansion and as a medium for the settlement of outstanding colonial differences. (Paul M. Kennedy, ed., *The War Plans of the Great Powers, 1880–1914*, 1979. Z. S. Steiner, *Britain and the Origins of the First World War*, 1977; K. M. Wilson, *The Policy of the Entente: Essays on the Determinants of British Foreign Policy*, 1904–1914, 1985.)

William G. Ratliff

ANGLO-FRENCH CONVENTION OF 1919. A series of agreements reached during the Peace Conference of 1919, the Anglo–French Convention of 1919 centered on British-French rivalry over the remains of the Ottoman Empire. By late December 1919 France agreed, in accordance with British demands, to support the expulsion of Turkish influence from Constantinople and the neutralization of the Straits, to be guaranteed by creation of a neutral state under international control. In Syria*, the French government recognized King Faisal as head of an autonomous Arab state under a French mandate. France also agreed to abandon Palestine* and Mosul to the British on the condition that France share equally in the exploitation of Mesopotamian oil. In addition, France approved the construction by Britain of two railways and two oil pipelines across Syria to the Mediterranean.

The only major difficulty in the Anglo-French convention centered on the southern boundary between Syria and Palestine. Since the end of the war Zionists had been pressing for a "big Palestine" along the Litani River in the north. The

British also wanted to redraw the frontier determined by the Sykes–Picot Agreement of 1916*. France, however, refused to give up any more mandated territory and conceded only a guarantee of water rights to Jewish settlers in northern Palestine. A final boundary settlement, based largely on the original Sykes-Picot plan, was reached in 1920. (Christopher M. Andrew and A. S. Kanya-Forstner, *The Climax of French Imperial Expansion, 1914–1924*, 1981; Elie Kedourie, *England and the Middle East*, 1978.)

William G. Ratliff

ANGLO-FRENCH ENTENTE OF 1904. The Anglo-French Entente, or Entente Cordiale, was formed between 1904 and 1907 and during World War I served as the basis for the alliance of more than twenty states against the Central Powers. The creation of the Entente was preceded by the conclusion of a Franco-Russian alliance from 1891 to 1893, in response to the formation of the 1882 Triple Alliance among Germany, Austria-Hungary, and Italy. The Anglo-French Entente was sparked by the intensification of the Anglo-German rivalry beginning in 1900. Specifically, Britain was deeply concerned by Germany's Second Naval Law, which provided for the construction of thirty-eight battleships, thus giving Germany parity with the British navy. To meet the German threat, Britain took diplomatic and military countermeasures. In 1902, abandoning its traditional policy of nonalignment, the British government signed a defensive alliance with Japan. An Anglo-French agreement was signed in 1904, and an Anglo-Russian accord in 1907. In effect, these conventions formalized the creation of the Entente.

In the Entente system, Britain and France were allies, bound to each other by mutual military obligations fixed by the convention and the subsequent decisions of the general staffs of both states. Despite the contacts between the British and French general staffs and naval commands established in 1906 and 1912, Britain assumed no definite military obligations. When in May 1906 Germany passed the Third Naval Law, providing for battleships capable of matching the British dreadnoughts in displacement and firepower, the Anglo-German breach was irreparably widened.

British statesmen believed that nothing less than acknowledgment of German superiority on the Continent and the high seas would satisfy Berlin, and that it had become essential for Britain to safeguard its imperial interests by giving full support to France and Russia. In 1907 Britain settled its outstanding diplomatic differences with Russia over the Middle East and signed a treaty similar to the Entente Cordiale. The agreement did not call for automatic military assistance, but it left no doubt with whom Britain would side in a conflict with the Austro-German bloc.

After 1907 relations between the great powers soured due to a succession of dangerous crises, each capable of sparking a major war. In 1908 the Austrians annexed the Balkan regions of Bosnia-Herzegovina, bringing Russia to the brink of war with the empire. During the Moroccan crisis of 1911, Kaiser William II interfered in the French sphere of influence in North Africa, again pushing Europe to the brink of war. These and similar incidents galvanized the respective alliance systems and widened the gulf between the two European blocs. When war came in August 1914 the countries of the Entente made common cause against the Central Powers. In September 1914 an agreement was concluded by Britain, France, and Russia whereby none would conclude a separate peace—thus serving as the equivalent of an allied military treaty.

In imperial terms, the participants in the Entente—Britain, France, and Russia—engaged in secret negotiations beginning in 1914 on specific war aims, which included the seizure of enemy colonial possessions. The Anglo-French-Russian agreement of 1915 provided for the transfer of the Black Sea straits to Russia upon the defeat of the Ottoman Empire. The Treaty of London of 1915 between the Entente and Italy determined Italy's territorial gains, to be achieved at the expense of Austria, Turkey, and Albania. The Sykes-Picot Agreement of 1916* provided for the division of Turkey's Asian possessions among Britain, France, and Russia. (P. J. V. Rolo, *Entente Cordiale: The Origins and Negotiation of the Anglo-French Agreements of 8 April 1904*, 1969; Samuel R. Williamson, *The Politics of Grand Strategy: Britain and France Prepare for War, 1904–1914*, 1969.)

William G. Ratliff

ANGLO-FRENCH TREATY OF 1860. The first in a series of European bilateral commercial agreements, the Anglo-French Commercial Treaty, known popularly as the Cobden–Chevalier Treaty, was a symbol of the era of liberal free trade in the mid-nineteenth century. It provided a major restructuring downward of the European tariff system. The agreement was championed by Richard Cobden, president of the British Board of Trade and chief exponent of free trade as a guarantor of international peace, and Michel Chevalier, advisor to Napoleon III. France sought the treaty in order to improve relations with Britain following the 1859 Italian War and the subsequent French annexation of Nice and Savoy. Napoleon III also wanted to stimulate the moribund French economy through lower tariff rates on foreign imports. The treaty was signed on January 23, 1860. The treaty terms included a reduction of existing trade duties by as much as two-thirds. All French goods would be admitted free to Britain, except for distilled spirits and wine. The agreement was to be in force for ten years and included most-favored-nations clauses whereby both Britain and France would benefit from any trade treaty involving a third country. The treaty and subsequent agreements reduced French customs duties as a proportion of the value of imports from 17.2 percent in 1849 to only 4 percent by 1865.

Among the consequences of the Anglo-French agreement were benefits to the British overseas empire. When the American Civil War, 1861–1865, reduced supplies of southern cotton to French textile manufacturers, the low tariff rates allowed for easy and inexpensive importation of Indian cotton. Also in Britain's favor, the treaty personified the school of economic thought prevalent in Britain that insisted on maximum economic freedom as the only way to achieve for all the greatest and healthiest prosperity and to effect an economic integration of the world essential for the maintenance of the empire. (A. L. Dunham, *The Anglo-French Treaty of Commerce of 1860 and the Progress of the Industrial Revolution in France*, 1976.)

William G. Ratliff

ANGLO-GERMAN AGREEMENT OF 1886. By the late nineteenth century German and British rivalry over East Africa was assuming major proportions, primarily because of its strategic location on the Indian Ocean and its domination of the sea lanes to India and the Red Sea. Tensions in the area were increasing, and to stabilize them the two countries signed the Anglo-German Agreement of 1886, dividing East Africa into two separate spheres of influence. A boundary line from the Indian Ocean between the Pangani River and Mombasa went inland on a northwesterly direction to Mt. Kilimanjaro, north around the mountain, and then to Lake Victoria. German interests, including today's Rwanda*, Burundi*, and Tanzania,* were confined south of the line, and British interests, in what became British East Africa*, were north of the line and eventually became Uganda*, Kenya*, and Jubaland. A collateral treaty signed in 1890 extended the boundary line west from Lake Victoria to the Belgian Congo* and gave the British control over Zanzibar*. (R. A. Oliver, *History of East Africa*, 3 volumes, 1963–1973.)

ANGLO-GERMAN AGREEMENT OF 1899. Throughout the late nineteenth century, the major European powers engaged in a scramble for new colonies in Africa and the Pacific. In 1889 Germany, the United States, and Great Britain agreed to joint jurisdiction over Samoa*, but the arrangement was unstable. When King Malieta Laupepa, the local puppet, died in 1898, civil war erupted among various Samoan factions, with the Europeans backing the different rivals. War threatened to erupt. But war was the last thing Great Britain needed, particularly with the Boer War* raging in South Africa. So late in 1899 diplomats from Great Britain and Germany negotiated the dispute. Great Britain agreed to surrender her claims to Samoa in return for territorial concessions in Tonga* and the Solomon Islands*. The Anglo-German Agreement was signed on November 14, 1899. One month later all three powers agreed to German sovereignty over the western islands—Upolu and Savai'i—and American control over the eastern islands—Tutuila and Manu'a. (Paul M. Kennedy, *The Samoan Tangle: A Study in Anglo-German-American Relations, 1878–1900*, 1974).

ANGLO-JAPANESE ALLIANCE OF 1902. The Anglo-Japanese Alliance was signed on January 30, 1902. One ally was to afford the other benevolent neutrality in case it went to war with one nation and military support if it went to war with two. Its term was ten years. The agreement clearly showed that Britain could no longer alone protect its interests in the Far East. The pact also indicated that Europe had come to recognize Japan's emergence as an Asiatic power. The Alliance grew out of a mutual concern about Russia. Japan wanted to block Russian moves into Korea. It made initial proposals to Britain in April and July 1901. At the same time Japan pursued the possibility of an understanding with Russia, but Britain refused to sign an agreement if Japan continued those negotiations, and Japan broke them off. Britain wanted protection of its Chinese interests from Russian encroachment.

The existence of the Alliance encouraged Japan to begin the Russo-Japanese War in 1904. Britain supported Japan. There was a fear that Britain would go to war with Russia over the Dogger Bank incident. The Russian Baltic fleet, on route to the Orient, mistakenly attacked British trawlers in the Channel, believing them to be Japanese torpedo boats. Russia apologized and the crisis was resolved. War would have been disastrous to the Anglo-French entente since Russia had an alliance with France. Britain closed its overseas ports to the Russian fleet, which was slowly moving toward the straits of Tsushima and the Japanese ambush. Russia's defeat destroyed its power in the Far East.

On August 12, 1906, the two powers strengthened the Alliance by agreeing to reciprocal protection of Britain's interests in India* and Japan's interests in Korea. They also agreed to mutual defense if a signatory was attacked by only one nation. These new provisions were aimed at Russia. The Alliance was renewed on July 13, 1911. Japan declared war on Germany in August 1914, although against initial British wishes. Japan wanted to to take China's Shantung peninsula from Germany, and Britain was afraid of the consequences. Japan went on to seize German islands in the Southwest Pacific and to make the twenty-one demands of China. Britain was not happy but had no power to restrain its ally. World War I* made Japan dominant in the Far East.

After the war, as American-Japanese relations deteriorated, the United States became unhappy with the Alliance. Britain, initially, had no desire to abrogate the treaty because it seemed to provide protection for the British Pacific empire against potential Japanese attack. At the Washington Conference of 1921–1922*, the British and the Japanese agreed to cancel the Alliance when they, the Americans, and the French signed the Four Party Treaty* to uphold the status quo in the Pacific. In the naval disarmament treaty signed at the same time, Japan received in return assurance of its navy's supremacy in the Far East. The four also joined with five others to create the Nine Power Treaty* which internationalized the open door in China*. (Peter Lowe, *Great Britain and Japan, 1911–15*, 1969; Peter Lowe, *Britain in the Far East*, 1981; Ian H. Nish, *The Anglo-Japanese Alliance, 1894–1911*, 1985.)

Walter A. Sutton

ANGLO-PORTUGUESE TREATY OF 1891. The Anglo-Portuguese Treaty of 1891 involved a major exchange of territory between South Africa* and Portuguese East Africa.* From the early 1870s to mid–1880s British attempts at gaining increased territory at the expense of Portugal had succeeded, with Cecil Rhodes* in charge of British efforts. By 1890 Rhodes's agents had negotiated a treaty with the chief of Gazaland for concessions in his kingdom, which lay along the border between the British and Portuguese colonies. Confronted with the potential loss of more territory in Gazaland and apprehensive that an armed clash might erupt between British and Portuguese forces, Portugal resolved to settle any territorial disputes with Great Britain. In return for concessions in the Zumbo region, Portugal agreed to freedom of navigation on the Zambezi River, a long-sought British goal, and promised to build a railroad from the Rhodesian frontier to the Indian Ocean coast. The treaty was signed in June 1891 and final frontier settlements were made in subsequent agreements between 1891 and 1896. (James Duffy, *Portuguese Africa*, 1959; Norman Dwight Harris, *Europe and Africa*, 1914.)

William G. Ratliff

ANGLO-SIAMESE TREATY OF 1909. British-Siamese relations centered largely on British colonial interests in the Malay Peninsula. From the late eighteenth century British colonial expansion in Southeast Asia focused on the Malay states. From 1786 to 1824 the British seized Penang* Island, Wellesley Province, and the island of Singapore.* In 1824 the Anglo-Dutch Treaty of London declared Malaya* to be within the British sphere of influence. Great Britain's possessions in Malaya were united in 1826 to form the Straits Settlements* Presidency. From 1824 to 1867 British influence in Malaya was consolidated. The Straits Settlements became a crown colony in 1867. In the 1870s and 1880s Britain seized the Malay states of Perak*, Selangor*, Negri Sembilan*, and Pahang*.

Britain's final territorial acquisition in the peninsula came directly at Siamese expense. Britain and Siam signed the Anglo-Siamese Treaty in 1909. Under the terms of the agreement, including several secret annexes, Siam transferred to Britain its rights of suzerainty over the Malay states of Kelantin*, Trengganu*, Kedah*, and Perlis*. In return the British transferred their consular jurisdiction over all British subjects in Siam to the Siamese courts. Britain also received a number of tax concessions on plantation land. Furthermore, the British government received the exclusive right to finance and control the construction of a Singapore-Bangkok peninsula railway. Finally, Siam promised not to allow any third power to establish a military or naval presence in the areas of the Malay Peninsula still under its control.

While the treaty ensured Siamese independence, the Siamese government ultimately was required to cede to Britain (and to a lesser extent France in several separate agreements) nearly half the area of the peninsula held under Siamese hegemony since the seventeenth century. The treaty enabled Britain to add some 176,000 square miles of territory to its holdings in southern Asia. (M. R. D. Foot, *British Foreign Policy Since 1898*, 1956; David K. Wyatt, *Thailand: A Short History*, 1984.)

William G. Ratliff

ANGOLA. Formerly known as Portuguese West Africa*, Angola is the seventh largest nation in Africa. It is bordered by Zaire* to the north and northeast, by Zambia* to the east, and by Namibia* to the south. The Portuguese first arrived there in 1483, landing in the Kingdom of Kongo. Initially an attempt was made to modernize Kongo and bring its people into the Christian community, but as Portugal expanded into the richer colonies of Brazil*, Guinea, and the East Indies, these ambitions were abandoned. Instead, the Portuguese were lured by the huge profits that could be made in the slave trade. At first the slaves were sold to the sugar plantations on São Tomé*, but larger markets developed in the middle of the sixteenth century in Brazil. In 1556, envious of the growing slave trade to the south in Luanda*, the Portuguese persuaded Diogo, the Kongo king, to wage war against the king of Angola. The attempt ended in failure, however, and when Diogo died in 1561, the ensuing civil war closed the Kongo to ships from São Tomé, and thus the slave trade passed to Angola.

When the Portuguese arrived in Angola, a small Mbundu kingdom was emerging called Ndongo. Its king was known as the Ngola and it was from this title that the region got its name. Lisbon ignored Ndongo until 1557 when an ambassador from the Ngola arrived asking that a representative be sent to his kingdom. Portugal sent an expedition headed by Paolo Dias de Novais. When he returned after a five-year captivity, de Novais lobbied for a charter that would allow him to conquer Angola and form a proprietary colony. The charter was issued in 1571. The Donation Charter divided Angola into two parts: the section between the Kongo border and the Cuanzo River was to be governed by de Novais for the crown and an area south of the river was given to de Novais. He was not obligated to develop the already thriving slave trade, but was required to settle European colonists and maintain an army for their protection. By the time of his death in 1589, de Novais was able to establish only a few forts, and his attempt to colonize the region was a failure.

In 1592 Francisco d'Almeida was appointed governor-general and a colonial government was created in Angola. This action came as a result of recommendations made by Domingo de Abreu e Brito, who called for the methodical occupation of Angola by force, the establishment of forts, an overland connection between Angola and Mozambique*, and tighter control over the slave trade. However, until the twentieth century there was no systematic implementation of colonial policy. By the seventeenth century, after a brief period of Dutch occupation (1641–1648), the military and civil administration of Angola was in the hands of the governor-general, whose authority was substantial. He named his own staff and had a voice in choosing the captains of the interior forts. He also controlled the police and treasury. His powers were great if he chose to exercise them, but in most cases the governors left matters in Luanda alone. Any attempt to exercise real authority was complicated by the opposition from the locally entrenched power structure of slave traders and Jesuits*. In addition, Lisbon refused to adequately compensate local administrative officials and soldiers, who turned to the slave trade to supplement their incomes. The result was an increase in local wars to supply slaves who could then be taxed as property by the local government.

These incessant wars, which carried into the twentieth century, prevented any serious attempt to assert colonial rule or subdue and colonize the interior. The Jesuits, who might have been a force for reform, were also involved in the slave trade. The only serious attempt at reform prior to the twentieth century was made by Francisco de Sousa Coutinho, who arrived in the colony as governor in 1765. Although his efforts brought only temporary order, he was the first modern colonial administrator in Africa. His most lasting contribution was the development of local industry, especially the tapping of Angola's great mineral wealth. The slave trade, however, remained Portugal's most profitable venture in Angola, providing more than 80 percent of Angola's commerce before 1832. By the time the Portuguese slave trade was abolished in 1836, over three million Africans had been exported from Angola. The abolition of the slave trade and the eventual end to slavery in 1858 resulted from liberal legislation passed in Portugal in the 1830s. But the practice of forced labor still kept many Africans enslaved.

With the revival of colonial interest in Europe, Portugal attempted to better secure her sovereignty over Angola in the 1880s. At the Berlin West Africa Conference of 1884–85* the limits of Portugal's claims to Angola were established. It was not until 1915, after intense warfare, that Portugal secured the Angolan interior. During the republican era in Portugal (1910–1926) an attempt was made to establish colonial policies with respect to civil administration. The focus was on increased white colonization and the decentralization of local administration from Lisbon. With the overthrow of the republican regime in 1926, however, Angola's drift toward autonomy was ended. In the 1930s and 1940s Lisbon's policy was to integrate Angola into the Portuguese nation, making it self-supporting and a market for Portuguese goods. With the increased emigration of whites into Angola after World War II*, Portuguese abuse and black inequality became more focused. Blacks were excluded from certain government jobs because the education they needed was not available to them. Also, the practice of forced labor came under renewed attack. Those Africans who had been officially assimilated and, therefore, were eligible for higher education and exemption from forced labor, were only about 0.75 percent of the population. It was evident to many educated Africans that Portuguese rule offered them nothing.

The earliest anticolonial political group to emerge in Angola was the *Partido da Luita Unido dos Africanos de Angola* (PLUA). Founded in 1953, it later combined with other nationalist movements in 1956 to form the *Movimento Popular de Libertaçao de Angola* (MPLA). The MPLA was founded partly by members of the Angola and Portuguese Communist Party and attracted educated blacks and city dwellers. In 1954 another group, this one calling for an independent Kongo, was founded as the *Uniao das Populaçoes do Norte de Angola* (UPNA). In 1962 the UPNA formed an alliance with another ethnic group and became the *Frente Nacional de Libertaçao de Angola* (FNLA). Jonas Savimbi broke with Holden Roberto and the FNLA in 1964, accusing them of tribalism, and in 1966 he formed the *Uniao Nacional de Independencia Total de Angola* (UNITA). The main weakness of these liberation movements was their inability to set aside ethnic differences and pursue a truly nationalist agenda.

In 1961 Angola erupted into violence. Although the fighting was intense, the Portuguese were able to subdue the uprising. The rebels, for their part, were not able to sustain their initial cohesion, and hostility broke out between the FNLA and the MPLA in the mid–1960s over ideological and tribal issues. Events took an abrupt turn in 1974, however, when a coup led by young officers took control of the government in Lisbon and called for an end to colonialism. A tripartite government of transition, consisting of the MPLA, FNLA, and UNITA, was formed but broke down as the FNLA and UNITA forces moved into armed confrontation with the MPLA. Their main concern, other than ethnic, was the communist nature of the movement. By late 1975 the civil war in Angola had become international with the United States and South Africa* supporting the FNLA and UNITA, while the Marxist-leaning MPLA received Soviet and Cuban backing. By July MPLA units were able to oust FNLA and UNITA forces from the capital and by mid-September the MPLA controlled twelve of sixteen districts. When independence came on November 11, 1975, the MPLA declared the People's Republic of Angola and a Marxist government headed by Agostino Neto was installed. (Ronald H. Chilcote, *Portuguese Africa*, 1967; James Duffy, *Portugal in Africa*, 1962.)

Michael Dennis

ANGUILLA. Anguilla is a flat, dry island located 150 miles east of Puerto Rico* and 60 miles northwest of St. Kitts*. Though discovered by Christopher Columbus* in 1493, it generally was ignored by Spanish colonizers. In the early seventeenth century Anguilla attracted the attention of Dutch saltpanners, who erected a fort. In 1634, Spaniards scavenged this post for construction materials, which they transported to St. Martin.* Sixteen years later Abraham Howell and a band of planters from Antigua* founded a small English settlement. Buccaneers, Caribs, and Frenchmen threatened the fledgling community constantly in the 1600s and 1700s. During the Second Dutch War, Irish indentured servants from Montserrat* raided Anguilla. The island also received an influx of English refugees fleeing the French takeover of their St. Kitts holdings. In 1688, while Europe fought the War of the Grand Alliance, France seized Anguilla, but the English retook it in 1689 and evacuated its inhabitants to Antigua, which required reinforcements to stave off Carib warriors. Britain did not reoccupy the deserted island until 1696.

The eighteenth century brought more warfare. English forces launched a successful assault from Anguilla upon French St. Martin in the War of the Austrian Succession (1744–1748). France's efforts to retaliate in 1745 failed after 100 Anguillian militiamen checked 600 invaders. When Paris and London again opposed one another in 1796, the French torched the islanders' property but were driven away by a British naval vessel.

The low coral island contains pockets of fertile land, yet much of it is rocky and lacking in rainfall. Large sugar estates never predominated. Fishing, boat-building, salt-gathering, subsistence farming, and stock-raising constituted the major economic activities. Residents traded salt to British North America in the eighteenth century, but this relationship ended as a result of post–1783 commercial restrictions that applied to intercourse with the newly independent United States. The salt-rakers found themselves in a miserable state by the 1830s. After the emancipation of the slaves in 1838, many Anguillians moved to Trinidad* and British Guiana*. When the sugar cultivation ceased, sea-island cotton served as a cash crop.

Throughout Anguilla'a history, Britain administered the island in connection with St. Kitts and Nevis*. Frequently an an official based on one of these islands was responsible for its well-being. After 1882 St. Kitts–Nevis–Anguilla was a unified "presidency" of the Federation of the Leeward Islands*. Despite the implementation of various political arrangements to join territories for administrative convenience, inter-island rivalries flourished in the British West Indies. As the twentieth century progressed, friction between Anguilla and its Kittician overlords intensified. During the 1950s and 1960s Robert Bradshaw's Labor Party spearheaded the drive for self-government by appealing to sugar workers, a strategy which failed to capture the enthusiasm of most Anguillians. Anguilla remained tied to St. Kitts–Nevis when the United Kingdom dissolved the Leeward Islands Federation in 1956. From 1958–1962 Anguilla, still linked to St. Kitts–Nevis, belonged to the West Indies Federation*. Subsequently St. Kitts–Nevis–Anguilla was granted local autonomy when, in 1967, it became a state in association with the United Kingdom.

Plebiscites held in 1967 and 1969 demonstrated overwhelming Anguillian popular support for secession from the Associated State. On February 7, 1969 Anguilla declared its independence. A prominent leader in this movement was Ronald Webster, head of the People's Progressive Party. The United Kingdom sent paratroopers in March and placed in power a British commissioner. Anguilla nominally remained attached to St. Kitts–Nevis until 1980. In reality, the Anguilla Act passed by Parliament in July 1971 transferred the island to the direct control of London. Britain provided a new constitution in 1976. Formal separation from St. Kitts–Nevis occurred in December 1980 when Anguilla became a British Dependent Territory.

Anguilla's present political system dates from the Anguilla Constitutional Order of 1982. A governor appointed by the British monarch oversees internal and external security, as well as its foreign relations. A house of assembly, with seven of its eleven members elected by universal adult suffrage, functions as a legislature. Lobster-fishing, livestock-raising, boat-building, salt production, and the growing of food for local consumption remain the major occupations. Tourism, however, has become important recently. (William J. Brisk, *The Dilemma of a Ministate: Anguilla*, 1969; Donald E. Westlake, *Under an English Heaven*, 1972.)

Frank Marotti

ANNAM. The French called the central part of Vietnam* "Annam." They ruled it as a protectorate, and as part of their Federation of Indochina, from 1883 to 1954. Annam lay between the protectorate of Tonkin* to the north and the directly ruled colony of Cochin China* to the south. Although the colonial division of Vietnam was artificial, Annam possessed distinct geographic, cultural, and economic characteristics. Unlike Tonkin and Cochin China, Annam had no great river basins for growing rice. Instead, there were only small deltas where short rivers drained the Annamite mountains. Such topography inhibited communication and economic development. In fact, the mountains were occupied by tribes whom the lowland Vietnamese regarded as savages.

Annam had a number of good ports, though (Cam Ranh, Nha Trang, Qui Nhon, Da Nang), which attracted Arabs, Portuguese, and later Frenchmen seeking ports of call along the trade route to China*. French interest in Asia quickened in the mid-nineteenth century and Paris listened to Catholic missionaries appealing for protection against xenophobic Vietnamese emperors ruling from the capital of Hue. By 1883 France's appetite for control of all Vietnam led to bloody military intervention in Annam. The result was a treaty (ratified in 1886) that allowed the Vietnamese emperor to remain on the throne while real power was exercised by a French superior resident and a French-dominated bureaucracy. Naturally, the emperor and his bureaucrats, who sought to preserve their privileges by serving foreigners, completely lost legitimacy in the eyes of ordinary Vietnamese.

Control of Annam was never a paying proposition for the French. There was little tropical agriculture and few minerals for export, and since the region contained some of Vietnam's most rebellious provinces, maintaining control was always hard. But as the seat of traditional rule, and strategically linking Tonkin and Cochin China, Annam was too important for the French to abandon, at least until their defeat at the Battle of Dien Bien Phu* in 1954. Annam itself was divided by the Geneva Accords of 1954. A "demilitarized zone" separating the states of North Vietnam and South Vietnam ran through its middle at the 17th parallel. That line, and legal recognition of a region called Annam, were erased in 1975 when Vietnam was united under communist rule. (Bernard Fall, *The Two Vietnams*, 1967; Stanley Karnow, *Vietnam: A History*, 1983.)

Ross Marlay

ANTIGUA. Antigua, an island of 108 square miles in the Lesser Antilles, lies north of Guadeloupe* and east of St. Kitts* and Nevis* in the Caribbean Sea. Today it is an independent nation formally named Antigua and Barbuda, and includes the islands of Barbuda* and Redonda. Christopher Columbus* first discovered Antigua in 1493 during his second voyage to the New World, but because the Spanish were preoccupied with the conquest of Cuba*, Hispaniola*, Mexico*, and Peru*, they did not develop the Lesser Antilles, and Antigua remained inhabited by Arawak and Carib Indians. In 1627 King Charles I of England gave the Earl of Carlisle a land grant in the Caribbean which included Antigua. The English established a settlement there in 1632. The colony had a marginal existence at first, primarily because of chronic water shortages and the attacks of Carib Indians from neighboring Dominica*. The economy began to grow later in the seventeenth century when sugar became the dominant crop. The importation of slaves to work the plantations made the Antiguan population primarily African.

From the very beginning of the settlement Antigua had a body of elected representatives, which evolved into a legislative assembly. Periodically over the years, England tried to consolidate Antigua into island federations, but its insularity was quite strong. Political power on the island, however, was narrowly exercised by the English planters. Slavery was abolished in 1834, freeing nearly 30,000 slaves, but universal manhood suffrage was not introduced until 1951. Cabinet government was introduced in 1956. Antigua became an associated state of Great Britain in 1967, with full internal self-government, and Antigua and Barbuda became independent on November 1, 1981. (Cyril Hamshere, *The British in the Caribbean*, 1972.)

ANTILLES. The Antilles is a term referring to the islands of the Caribbean Sea. The Greater Antilles include Cuba*, the Cayman Islands, Jamaica*, Haiti*, the Dominican Republic*, and Puerto Rico*. The Lesser Antilles include the Virgin Islands*, St. Martin*, St. Barthelemy*, St. Christopher*, Antigua*, Guadeloupe*, Dominica*, Martinique*, St. Lucia*, St. Vincent*, Barbados*, Grenada*, Trinidad and Tobago*, Bonaire, Curacao, and Aruba. (Noel Grove, "The Caribbean: Sun, Sea, and Seething," *National Geographic*, 159, February 1981, 244–71.)

ANTIOQUIA. Antioquia is a region in northwestern Colombia near the isthmus of Panama*. Spaniards first began arriving in the region in 1537 as *conquistadores* looking for new tribes to conquer and new treasures to be found. Settlers began arriving a few years later. Antioquia was part of the province of Popayan* until 1579 when it received its own governor. In that year Antioquia became a separate province under the authority of the Audiencia of New Granada.* After the end of the wars of independence in Colombia, Antioquia became part of Gran Colombia. See COLOMBIA.

ARABIA. Arabia is a large desert peninsula of 1,100,000 square miles located south of Jordan* and Iraq*, west of the Persian Gulf, north of the Arabian Sea and the Gulf of Aden, and east of the Red Sea. From the seventeenth century to the end of World War I*, much of Arabia was controlled by the Ottoman Empire, although the local Wahhabi Kingdom fought with the Turks for control.

By the nineteenth century Great Britain had established several small colonies and dependencies in Arabia, primarily to protect the sea lanes to India. After World War I the Ottoman Empire disintegrated completely and the British Empire* began a long period of decline. Out of the imperial vacuum a number of new nations emerged in Arabia: Bahrain*, Kuwait*, Oman*, Qatar*, Saudi Arabia*, the United Arab Emirates*, the Yemen Arab Republic*, and the People's Democratic Republic of Yemen*. (Richard H. Sanger, *The Arabian Peninsula*, 1954.)

ARGENTINA. At the time of the initial Spanish conquest of Mexico* and Peru* in the early 1500s, the region of present-day Argentina was inhabited by a variety of native American tribes. Argentina's conquest by Spain came from two directions: expansion out of the original settlements in Peru and Bolivia* and exploration of the Atlantic coast and up the Río de la Plata. The rich silver mines in Bolivia needed supplies and pack animals, and the first settlements in northwestern Argentina were designed to fill those needs. Spaniards came to Argentina from Peru, Upper Peru, and Chile*. Francisco de Aguirre founded Santiago del Estero in 1553. Juan Perez de Zorita established Catamarca in 1559, and two years later Pedro del Castillo founded Mendoza. Other Argentinian settlements soon followed: Tucumán* (1565), Córdoba (1573), Salta (1582), La Rioja (1592), Jujuy (1593), and San Luis (1594).

Spanish exploration of the Atlantic coast was proceeding at the same time. Juan Díaz de Solís discovered the Río de la Plata in 1516, and Ferdinand Magellan* reached Patagonia and the southern straits in 1521. In 1527–1528 Sebastián Cabot explored the Río Uruguay and the Río Paraná and discovered the Río Paraguay and the Río Pilcomayo. He established Sancti Spiritus near present-day Rosario, but Indians destroyed the settlement in 1529. Pedro de Mendoza founded Buenos Aires* on the Río de la Plata in 1536, but the expedition then headed up the Río Parana and the Río Paraguay to establish Asunción in 1537, abandoning the Buenos Aires settlement. Asunción prospered, and from there explorers established Santa Fe in 1573, Buenos Aires in 1580, and Corrientes in 1588. By 1600 the cattle industry, feeding the American and European empire, was flourishing.

Portugal founded the Novo Colônia do Sacramento* across the Río de la Plata from Buenos Aires in 1680, and the settlement soon became a source of imperial rivalry. Spain thought Portugal had designs on Argentina. For nearly a century the two countries struggled, militarily and diplomatically, over the settlement, until the issue was resolved with the Treaty of San Ildefonso* in 1777: the Colônia do Sacramento and the missions east of the Río Uruguay went to Spain, while Portugal kept Santa Catarina*, Guaira, Mato Grosso*, and both banks of the Rio Jacuy and Rio Grande in Brazil.

During the seventeenth century a frontier society emerged in northwestern Argentina. The Indian tribes underwent a rapid population decline. The encomiendas* exploited Indian labor, but the Argentinian economy originally revolved

around cattle ranching, pack animals, and grains to supply Asunción and the
Bolivian mines. By the time those mines declined in the mid-eighteenth century,
northwestern Argentina was thriving economically. To institutionalize control
over the region, Spain created the Viceroyalty of the Río de la Plata in 1777.
Juan José Vértiz y Calcedo was the first viceroy. Within a year Spain defined
the viceroyalty boundaries to include Argentina, Uruguay*, Paraguay*, and
southern and eastern Bolivia. Spain also established a royal treasury there in
1778, an audiencia in 1785, and a consulado in 1794. With the demise of the
old fleet system, which had given Panamanian and Peruvian merchants monopolies on New World trade, the economy of Buenos Aires boomed, with northwestern Argentina becoming a breadbasket for much of Spain's New World
empire.

Argentina remained loyal to Spain until the Napoleonic Wars allowed Generals
Manuel Belgrano, J. M. de Pueyrredón, and José de San Martín* to deliver
Argentina to self-rule. The independence movement had several sources. By the
turn of the century Buenos Aires merchants were increasingly critical of Spanish
imperial regulations, which they viewed as stifling and expensive. At the same
time, the American Revolution* had deprived Great Britain of her North American colonies, and she turned to South America as a new trade source. Argentinian
merchants welcomed the attention. Spain allied herself with France in the Napoleonic Wars, and in 1805, at the Battle of Trafalgar, Great Britain destroyed
much of the Spanish fleet, leaving the Spanish colonies unprotected. Great Britain
invaded Buenos Aires in 1806 and 1807. Local forces managed to expel the
British, but the combination of nationalism and a new self-confidence born of
their successful military campaigns inspired the independence movement. When
Napoleon invaded Spain in 1808 and deposed King Ferdinand VII, *criollo* leaders
in Buenos Aires refused to recognize the puppet government of Joseph Bonaparte.
In 1810 they deposed Viceroy Baltasar Hidalgo de Cisneros, installing their own
government. The event is known as the May Revolution. They established a
provisional revolutionary junta to govern the area, but their hopes that a spontaneous independence movement would sweep through the country did not materialize. On the contrary, spontaneous uprisings against the junta developed in
Montevideo* and Asunción*, guaranteeing that Argentina would eventually not
include what is today Uruguay and Paraguay.

During 1812 and 1813 the revolutionaries successfully resisted several invading royalist armies. In the liberated area of northern Argentina, demands for
formal independence escalated. The region was divided into fourteen separate
provinces, and in 1816 representatives from each province convened in Tucumán.
On July 9, 1816, they declared their independence from Spain and established
the United Provinces of South America. The delegates were, however, unable
to agree on a government. Intense ideological differences emerged between
unitarists favoring a strong central government and federalists demanding local
autonomy. Civil war erupted between the factions in 1819–1820, and in 1825
the United Provinces went to war with Brazil over possession of Uruguay. Brazil

was defeated in the conflict and Uruguay emerged as an independent nation in 1828.

Argentinian politics stabilized somewhat in 1829 when General Juan Manuel de Rosas was elected governor of Buenos Aires. A strong believer in federalism, Rosas reached out to surrounding provinces, building political relationships while assuring them that the province of Buenos Aires was not interested in dominating them. Slowly during the 1830s and 1840s Rosas extended his authority over the United Provinces. In 1852, with the assistance of Brazil* and Uruguay, General Justo Urquiza deposed Rosas and the next year the United Provinces adopted a federal constitution, creating the Argentine Republic. The province of Buenos Aires refused to cooperate, however, and rebellions broke out there in 1859 and again in 1861. That problem was resolved in 1862 when General Bartolome Mitre, leader of the Buenos Aires' army, was elected president of Argentina and Buenos Aires was designated the country's new capital. (Jonathan C. Brown, *A Socio-Economic History of Argentina, 1776–1860*, 1979; Tulio Halperin-Donghi and Richard Southern, *Politics, Economics, and Society in Argentina in the Revolutionary Period*, 1975.)

Mark R. Shulman

ARUBA. See NETHERLANDS ANTILLES.

ASCENSION ISLAND. See ST. HELENA.

ASHANTI. In 1896 British forces took over the Kingdom of Ashanti, north of the Gold Coast* colony on the West African coast. The governor of Gold Coast had the authority to appoint the resident administrator of Ashanti. The resident was replaced by a chief commissioner in 1902. The political status of Ashanti remained unchanged until 1951, when Gold Coast received internal autonomy. At that point Ashanti became a political unit of Gold Coast with the former chief commissioner designated as a resident officer. When Gold Coast received its independence in 1957, Ashanti was fully integrated as one of its political subdivisions. See GOLD COAST.

ASSAM. The province of Assam emerged out of the Ahom Kingdom which existed in the Bengal* region of India*. It was under the direction of the province of Bengal until 1874 when it received its own chief commissioner. For seven years beginning in 1905 Assam was part of the province of East Bengal and Assam, but that political unit was dissolved in 1912. Assam then became a separate province with a chief commissioner as executive officer. Its status was again elevated in 1921 when it received its own governor. Assam remained a separate province until 1947 when most of it became part of independent India. (In the partition of India about one per cent of the area of Assam was assigned to East Pakistan.) In 1950 Assam became an Indian state. See INDIA.

ASSINIBOIA. Beginning in the early 1800s, the Hudson's Bay Company*
began settling Irish and Scotch immigrants along the Red River in western
Canada*. The area was known as Assiniboia, although the settlement was frequently referred to as the Red River Colony or the Red River Settlement. Miles
Macdonell became its first governor in 1811. The North West Company, a rival
to the Hudson's Bay Company, intensely opposed the colony and frequently
harassed its settlers, but the settlement survived. In 1870 the colony was absorbed
by the Province of Manitoba. (David P. Henige, *Colonial Governors from the
Fifteenth Century to the Present*, 1970.)

ASTROLABE. The astrolabe was a simple device used by seamen to measure
the altitude of the sun or a star. It consisted of a graduated brass ring fitted with
a sighting rule pivoted at the center of the ring. The astrolabe was suspended
vertically by a thread or from the thumb and altitude readings taken. Although
the astrolabe was in use in the late thirteenth century, it was not until Martin
Behaim's invention in 1484 that it was adapted to navigation. Although it was
of little use in heavy seas, the European explorers used the astrolabe to fix the
latitude of their new discoveries. (Peter Kemp, *The Oxford Companion to Ships
and the Sea*, 1976.)

AUDIENCIA. The *audiencia*, based on a judicial institution that existed in
Spain, had administrative and judicial functions in the Spanish imperial system.
The *audiencias* existed in the principal cities of important provinces in the New
World and the Philippines*. The first *audiencia* was established in 1511 in Santo
Domingo* and then in Mexico City after the conquest of the Aztec empire. They
soon appeared in the newly conquered territories of the Americas where they
shared power with the viceroy or captain-general and served to check his arbitrary
use of it.

The number of bureaucrats who staffed the *audiencia* depended on the importance of its location. The two principal *audiencias* in Mexico City, New
Spain*, and Lima, Peru* initially had a president and four judges (*oidores*), but
as the empire gained in complexity the number of judges grew. In the seventeenth-
century Mexico City *audiencia* there were twelve judges divided into two chambers: civil, composed of eight judges, and criminal, composed of four. There
were also a civil and a criminal attorney (*fiscales*) for the crown. The viceroy
or captain-general was the ex–officio president who had no vote in judicial matters
and was forbidden to meddle in judicial affairs. There were also many lesser
officials, such as reporters, notaries, a lawyer, and solicitor for the poor. At the
end of the eighteenth century there were ten civil judges, five criminal judges
(*alcaldes de crimen*), and three attorneys. The Lima *audiencia* operated in much
the same way. In the less important *audiencias* there were three to five judges
who tried both civil and criminal cases and one or two attorneys. Many times
these lesser *audiencias* did not have the requisite members because of death,

illness, and failure to fill the vacancies. In order to ensure governmental continuity at the highest level, the appointment of a judge was for life.

The *audiencias* had manifold judicial duties. It heard appeals from the lower courts, and their decision in criminal cases was final. Any appeal of decisions in important civil cases, on the other hand, went to the Council of the Indies. One of the most important functions of the *audiencia* was the protection of the Indians. Two days a week were set aside to hear suits between Indians or between Indians and Spaniards. Also, the Indians did not have to pay lawyer fees. This duty was later taken up by the *juzqado de indios*, a special court for Indians. The *audiencia* also had original jurisdiction over criminal cases that occurred in the city, or within a radius of five leagues, where it resided. It also sat in judgment of ecclesiastical cases of a secular nature.

Besides its judicial functions the *audiencia* also had administrative ones. As a council of state it conferred with the president on political administration. Through these sessions, known as *acuerdos*, and the decisions arrived at, known as *autos acordados*, the *audiencia* was able to exercise administrative and legislative power. It also made sure that all royal decrees and orders were carried out. If the viceroy or captain-general died, the *audiencia* would rule until his replacement arrived. Whether the viceroy or *audiencia* would dominate depended on the personality of the viceroy.

From the inception of the *audiencia* in 1511 in Santo Domingo, the Spanish crown tried to prevent *audiencia* members from becoming *radicados* (being rooted to the New World community where they resided) because *audiencia* members were much more permanent than the viceroy. During the period from 1687 to 1750, the age of impotence, the Spanish crown, forced to bow to its fiscal needs by selling *audiencia* posts to those who had the money, allowed many creoles, or New World Spaniards, to acquire an *audiencia* office and increase their influence in government. During this period there were also many *radicado* peninsulars, or Old World Spaniards, on the *audiencias*. This trend shifted during the age of authority from 1751 to 1808 under the later Bourbons, who fought against this tendency to local influence by appointing *peninsulares* who had few local ties. By the end of the Spanish colonial period there were far fewer creoles who sat on the *audiencia*. The Spanish American independence movement put an end to this institution. The newly independent Spanish American nations often defined their borders by the colonial *audiencia* jurisdictional limits. (Mark A. Burkholder and D. S. Chandler, *From Impotence to Authority: The Spanish Crown and the American Audiencias, 1687–1808*, 1977; C. H. Harin, *The Spanish Empire in America*, 1963.)

Carlos Pérez

AUSTRAL ISLANDS. The Austral Islands are a chain of five islands in French Polynesia*. The islands of Tubuai and Raivavae became Tahitian territory in 1824 but then reverted to France when France established its protectorate over Tahiti* in 1842. France established protectorates over Rapa in 1867 and Rurutu and Rimatara in 1889, and formal annexation took place for Tubuai and Raivavae in 1880; Rapa, Rurutu, and Rimatara in 1900; and Maria in 1901. The Austral Islands are part of Tahiti. (Colin Newbury, *Tahiti Nui: Change and Survival in French Polynesia, 1767–1945*, 1980.)

AUSTRALIA. Australia comprises an entire continent of 2,967,877 square miles of mostly flat and dry territory. The land was left to the aborigines who arrived some 20,000 years ago. The Dutch first reached Australia in 1606, when they sighted the northwest coast, but they did not realize they had come upon a new continent. The Dutch did not follow up on their discovery because the northwestern coast seemed so barren that there appeared little potential for economic development. When Captain James Cook* sailed into Botany Bay in 1770, he claimed the fertile east coast for Great Britain. No Europeans, however, emigrated there until the first fleet sailed into what is now Sydney Harbor in 1788. In 1779 Joseph Banks suggested Botany Bay as a penal settlement to relieve overcrowding in British jails. The British government accepted the suggestion in 1786, and the first fleet brought 1,500 people, almost half of them convicts, in January 1788. They settled somewhat further to the north in what is today Sydney. Captain Arthur Phillip was the first governor. Eventually more than 160,000 convicts were transported to Australia. New South Wales* ended convict transportation in 1840 and Tasmania* did so in 1852. Convicts never settled in South Australia*. Western Australia* was settled primarily by free immigrants, but between 1850 and 1868 it also accepted convicts. Convict labor was used to build roads, bridges, and the transportation network, although the law provided for emancipation in return for good behavior. Convicts who had served their terms, as well as soldier–guards who had left their service, started to farm in the outlying regions.

Free immigration to Australia began to increase rapidly in the 1820s after merino sheep* were introduced and became the foundation for the wool industry. By mid-century large numbers of free settlers were arriving for inexpensive land, founding Tasmania in 1825, Western Australia in 1829, South Australia in 1836, Victoria* in 1851, and Queensland* in 1859. Various notions of planned settlement, inspired primarily by E. B. Wakefield, did not succeed, leaving Australia to be settled sporadically around the major cities of each state. Great gold rushes in 1851 and 1892 further contributed to the unplanned growth.

By the 1880s more than two million of Australia's three million inhabitants were native born and identified themselves as Australians. The country had more than 106 million head of sheep; railroads reached the southeastern coast, opening up millions of new acres for farming; and irrigation and scientific agriculture brought a new level of sophistication to crop production. By 1900 the Australian population exceeded 4 million people and the country boasted 10,000 miles of railroads. Melbourne and Sydney each had populations of more than 500,000 people.

The growing population, economic expansion, and the deepening sense of

Australian identity fostered a movement for federation that was debated throughout the 1890s. Economic differences posed one obstacle. The people of New
South Wales believed strongly in free trade while those in Victoria were committed to protective tariffs. Localism was also a powerful force in the six Australian colonies: New South Wales, Western Australia, Victoria, Tasmania,
Queensland, and South Australia. But such differences were resolved. National
conventions drafted a constitution providing for a federal government and reserving most powers to the colonies, which were renamed states. It was approved
in colonial referendums in 1898–99. In 1900 the British parliament approved
the constitution and on January 1, 1901, the Commonwealth of Australia came
into existence. (Gordon Greenwood, ed., *Australia: A Social and Political History*, 1968; A. L. McLeod, *The Pattern of Australian Culture*, 1963.)

Mark R. Shulman

AZORES. The Azores are an archipelago of nine major islands located in the
North Atlantic Ocean. At the time of their discovery by Portuguese navigator
Diogo de Sevilla in 1427, the islands were uninhabited. Prince Henry the Navigator annexed the islands in 1432 and that same year began settling Santa Maria
under the direction of Gonçalo Velho Cabral. Portuguese settlers reached São
Miguel in 1444, Terceira in 1449, and Flores and Corvo in 1452. By 1500 all
of the islands had been settled. Like the rest of the Portuguese realm, the Azores
were under Spanish rule between 1580 and 1640. Because of their location as
a point of rendezvous and resupply along the sea lanes to the New World, the
islands were subject to frequent English and Dutch attacks in the sixteenth and
seventeenth centuries. In 1766 Portugal established local government institutions
in the Azores, centered on the island of Terceira, and in 1832 the islands were
divided into three administrative districts, on equal footing with Portugal's nineteen other political subdivisions. In 1976 the Azores were given partial autonomy
by the Portuguese government, and although they have elected to remain part
of Portugal, they are looking for economic benefits from special status in the
European Economic Community. (Francis M. Rogers, *Atlantic Islanders of the
Azores and Madeira*, 1979.)

AZTECS. See CORTES, HERNAN.

B

BAHAMAS. The Commonwealth of the Bahamas stretches almost 600 miles from southeastern Florida* to northwestern Haiti*. On October 12, 1492, Christopher Columbus* made his first New World landfall at Samana Cay, where the Lucayans, an Arawak people, warmly greeted him. Columbus spent fifteen days exploring the archipelago. In 1513 Juan Ponce de Leon* scoured the Bahamas for the fabled Fountain of Youth. The generally infertile territory lacked gold, but slave raiders frequently seized the gentle Lucayans, thus depopulating the entire island chain by 1520.

No permanent colony existed until 1648, when William Sayle led religious dissenters from Bermuda* to Eleuthera. Another party established themselves on New Providence around 1666. In 1670 the Bahamas received its first official government, after the English Crown granted them to five lords proprietors who also held patents to the Carolinas. Proprietary rule never was strong. Colonists lived by salvaging shipwrecks and exporting dyewoods, salt, and ambergris. Wrecking brought them into conflict with Spain, whose treasure fleets passed by the Bahamas en route to Europe. Two Spanish attacks in 1684 wiped out Charles Towne, present-day Nassau. New Providence remained deserted for two years.

A strategic location was both a blessing and a curse. Privateers utilized the Bahamas' numerous anchorages as bases for raids against Spanish and French shipping. English pirates filtered in when they were forced from Tortuga*. The two Catholic powers retaliated by destroying Nassau in 1703. For the next fifteen years, privateers and corsairs held sway over the colony, prompting the Crown to dispatch an able royal governor, Woodes Rogers, in 1718. The new governor suppressed piracy, restored trade, encouraged agriculture, and repelled a Spanish invasion. Moreover, in 1729, Rogers presided over an elective assembly that continued almost uninterrupted throughout the colonial period.

Between 1738 and 1768, under governors John Tinker and Thomas Shirley, the colony boomed as a privateering center and entrepot for illegal commerce with France. Warfare boosted the Bahamian economy. The American Revolution* occasioned two rebel attacks on Nassau, as well as Spanish occupation of the port. Subsequent to United States independence, an influx of southern Loyalist refugees tripled the islands' population, raising the proportion of slaves to 75 percent. Sea-island cotton flourished briefly, but insect pest infestation and soil exhaustion initiated its decline in 1788. Planters gradually abandoned their estates over the next half century. Slavery's abolition in 1838 encouraged further migration.

The American Civil War (1861–1865) transformed Nassau into a colorful haven for Confederate blockade runners who brought unprecedented wealth to the colony. From 1920 to 1933, during prohibition in the United States, the Bahamas were the headquarters for bootleggers engaged in smuggling liquor to the mainland. During the remainder of the hundred-year period between 1840 and 1940, wrecking and sponging were the economic mainstays, the former peaking in 1870 and the latter reaching its height in 1925. Attempts to export citrus, pineapples, sisal, and tomatoes never proved successful. Moreover, the Bahamas lost a sizable income in 1848 when London decided to detach the salt-rich and restive Turks and Caicos Islands* from Nassau's domain. Poverty caused 20 percent of its inhabitants to emigrate to America in the first half of the twentieth century.

During the 1950s the black majority moved to wrest power from the white minority. The islands' first political party, the Progressive Liberal Party (PLP), was born in 1953. It was opposed by the mostly white United Bahamian Party (UBP) formed five years later. An anti-discrimination resolution in 1956 and a taxi strike in 1957 signaled the dawn of another era. The United Kingdom bestowed internal self-government in 1964. As the result of the first elections under universal adult suffrage in 1967, the PLP was able to construct a majority government under the leadership of Lynden Pindling. On July 10, 1973, the Commonwealth of the Bahamas, guided by the PLP, won its independence. (Paul Albury, *The Story of the Bahamas*, 1975; Michael Craton, *A History of the Bahamas*, 1962.)

Frank Marotti

BAHIA. Early in the 1500s the Portuguese began their conquest of Brazil*, and they promoted development and settlement through the medium of "donatárias," or land grants to well-to-do individuals and groups. The donatária of Bahia (Bahia de Todos os Santos, or Bay of All Saints) was granted in 1534, and the first governor arrived in 1549. There were a series of loosely organized donatarias all along the east coast of Brazil, and the governor of Bahia tried to coordinate their activities and provide at least a minimum of political direction. Between 1574 and 1578, and again between 1608 and 1612, the southern captaincies of Brazil were governed out of Rio de Janeiro,* and by the early seventeenth century the east-west coastal axis of Brazil became known as the Estado do Maranhão, which was established in 1621. The rest of Brazil, called the Estado do Brasil, continued to be administered from a headquarters in Bahia. During the late seventeenth century and eighteenth century, the economic focus of Portuguese development in Brazil shifted toward the south, and Bahia gradually became less and less significant. In 1763 the Portuguese transferred the seat of colonial government from Bahia to Rio de Janeiro. Bahia remained a captaincy-general until 1822 when it was incorporated as a province in the empire of Brazil. See BRAZIL.

BAHRAIN. Bahrain is an island of 262 square miles located in the Persian Gulf. Middle Eastern traders have used the island as a commercial center for thousands of years. In 1507, as part of their expansion into the Indian Ocean, the Portuguese seized Bahrain and kept it until 1602, when they abandoned the island. In 1820 the Khalifa, the ruling family in Bahrain, signed a commercial treaty with Great Britain, and from that legal base the British tightened their control of Bahrain. The British stake in India* made the Persian Gulf strategically significant, and the construction of the Suez Canal* in the 1860s only exaggerated its importance. In 1861 Bahrain signed a treaty of protection with Great Britain, and the treaty was renewed in 1892 and 1951. By that time the discovery of vast oil reserves in the Persian Gulf region heightened British interest. Late in the 1960s Bahrain flirted with joining a federation of the smaller Persian Gulf kingdoms, but eventually she decided on complete independence. Great Britain signed a treaty of friendship with Bahrain in 1971 and on August 15 of that year Bahrain became an independent nation. (Alvin Cottrell, *The Persian Gulf States: A General Survey*, 1980; John B. Kelly, *Britain and the Persian Gulf, 1795–1880*, 1968.)

BAKER. Baker is a small coral island in the central Pacific Ocean, part of the Line Islands group. The United States claimed Baker in 1857, but in 1889 Great Britain sent colonists there. American and British companies harvested guano deposits on Baker for years, but when the threat of war with Japan grew in the 1930s, the United States decided to assert itself. In 1935 the United States sent colonists from Hawaii* to live there. Baker was under the jurisdiction of the United States Department of the Interior. Japan captured the island in 1942 but the United States recaptured it in 1944. There are no permanent inhabitants there. See EQUATORIAL ISLANDS and JARVIS.

BALBOA, VASCO NÚÑEZ DE. Vasco Núñez de Balboa was born in 1475 in Jerez de los Caballeros in Badajoz Province, Spain. As an adolescent, Balboa served as a page to a prominent member of the nobility, and in 1501 he sailed along the coast of South America searching for pearls. When that voyage was completed, Balboa stayed on in Santo Domingo* and tried his hand at sugar planting, but mounting debts forced him to flee. He tied on with an exploring expedition and emerged as its leader. In 1510 the group established the town of

Santa María de la Antigua del Darién along what is today the east shore of the isthmus of Panama.*

A local Indian leader, enraged by the Spaniards' lust for gold and wealth, told Balboa that on the west side of the isthmus the streams were full of gold. With a party of 1,000 Spaniards and Indians, Balboa cut his way through the jungle terrain, and on September 27, 1513, became the first European to view the Pacific Ocean from its eastern shore. Balboa plied the coast for three months, collecting pearls and gold from the Indians, and in January 1514 he returned to the Caribbean shore. During the next five years, however, political infighting doomed Balboa. Pedro Arias de Ávila, governor of Darién, schemed against Balboa, arrested and convicted him for treason, and executed him in January 1517. (Charles L. G. Anderson, *The Life and Letters of Vasco Núñez de Balboa*, 1941; Kathleen Romoli, *Balboa of Darién: Discoverer of the Pacific*, 1953.)

BALFOUR DECLARATION. Issued by Great Britain on November 2, 1917, the Balfour Declaration served as the basis for the British mandate on Palestine* until the mandate was liquidated by United Nations* resolution on November 29, 1947. The one sentence declaration stated that "His Majesty's Government views with favor the establishment in Palestine of a national home for the Jewish people, and will use their best endeavors to facilitate the achievement of this object, it being clearly understood that nothing shall be done which may prejudice the civil and religious rights of existing non-Jewish communities in Palestine, or the rights and political status enjoyed by Jews in any other country."

Britain had both concrete and abstract objectives in issuing the declaration. The immediate objectives included using Russian Jews to influence the revolutionary government to continue participation in World War I*, achieving propaganda victories in countries with Jewish populations, and forestalling an expected German declaration favoring Jews. In retrospect there is no reason to have assumed the declaration would produce these anticipated gains. Longer range political objectives included the belief by some that a large-scale Jewish settlement in Palestine might thwart French colonial designs on Palestine and bring the entire country under British domination. The abstract objectives were humanitarian rather than politically based and involved sympathy for Zionist aspirations, respect for the Zionist movement earned by Chaim Weizmann and Sir Herbert Samuel, and a paternalistic desire to assist the regeneration of the Jewish people.

International recognition for a Jewish National Home in Palestine produced considerably less immigration than expected after World War I, but Hitler generated a flood of immigration from 1934 until 1940. The flood resumed after World War II*. Throughout these years the British worked to narrow the mandate. To reduce Arab fears and subdue Jewish expectations, Britain issued the Churchill White Paper in 1922, which reinterpreted the mandate by excluding Transjordan* from the Jewish National Home area and clarifying the rights of Palestinians. Arab attacks against the Jewish community in 1929 prompted a reaffirmation of the White Paper's provisions on protecting Arab rights in Palestine and restricting Jewish immigration. In 1936 increased Jewish immigration prompted renewed Arab violence and a series of failed British attempts to ensure Arab numerical, or at least political, superiority in Palestine. In 1937 a royal commission recommended that the mandate be abandoned completely in favor of partitioning Palestine into Arab, Jewish, and British zones. While Jews accepted this proposal, Arabs rejected it. A subsequent British commission concluded that partition was impractical.

World War II bonded Jews in Palestine into a cohesive, determined community. As the world learned the full extent of the Holocaust and reacted with sympathy to world Jewry generally and Jews in Palestine particularly, Zionists moved quickly to defy British restrictions on Jewish immigration. When Britain, in frustration, took the Palestinian issue to the United Nations, Zionists lobbied effectively for a resolution that ultimately permitted creation of a Jewish state. Humanitarian motivations should be neither minimized nor ignored, but it also should be realized that superpower politics was deeply enmeshed in the debate over Palestine. Britain and France wanted to fill the post-World War I vacuum created by the Ottoman Empire's collapse. Britain saw Jewish aspirations as a means of gaining advantage over Russia, Germany, and France. It retreated from the Balfour Declaration when it no longer served Britain's Middle East interests. (Frank Gervasi, *The Case for Israel, 1967;* Nadav Safran, *Israel: The Embattled Ally,* 1978; Harold Wilson, *The Chariot of Israel*, 1981.)

Samuel Freeman

BALI. Bali is an island of 2,100 square miles near the east tip of Java*. Its lush environment is matched by its people's obsession with perfecting their intricate culture. Balinese find life's meaning in Sivaite Hinduism, blended with ancestor worship and cults of the sun, earth, mountains, and sea. Monsoon rains and fertile soil enable them to grow two crops of rice a year and still find time everyday for elaborate religious rituals. No other culture is so devoted to art, music, flower arrangement, temple-building, and woodcarving. Bali's high mountains divide the island into a wet southern portion, culturally and politically dominant, facing the open Indian ocean, and a drier northern region with no good harbors on the Java Sea. Herein lies the secret of Bali's survival as the only enclave of Hinduism outside India, an island of fewer than three million Hindus surrounded by 140 million Muslims. The Indian Ocean has high winds and huge waves. Arabs and Dutchmen sailed the safer Java Sea, bypassing Bali. Also, the Balinese are oriented toward their sacred mountain, Gunung Agung, the navel of the earth, and fear the sea.

Early Balinese history was interwoven with that of Java. When Islam spread through Java in the 1500s, Hindu priests, nobles, and court retainers fled to Bali. When the first Dutch fleet landed in 1597, sailors jumped ship and refused to leave, forcing the ships to limp home half-manned. Dutch commercial interest focused first on the Spice Islands* and later on Javanese coffee plantations, so

Bali was left alone for almost 250 years. The island's only commerce with the Dutch East India Company* was to sell them cattle and slaves and provide them with soldiers.

Nineteenth-century commercial and strategic developments ended Bali's isolation. The Dutch insisted that the Balinese stop plundering shipwrecks and end the slave trade. Bali was not, and never had been, a political unit. Many small kingdoms vied for power, which made it easy for the Dutch to play divide-and-rule. Four Balinese rajas signed treaties in 1841, but plundering continued, so the Dutch attacked in 1846, 1848, and 1849, and took direct control of Singaraja (north Bali) in 1855. Their rule was inconspicuous at first but soon became more intrusive. Unfamiliar with the language or local conditions, the Dutch resident delegated power to uncooperative nobles who often had to be replaced. Christian missionaries met with complete disinterest. Most gave up and went home; some abandoned mission work for anthropology.

Commerce changed Bali fundamentally in the nineteenth century. From 1839 to 1856 trade flourished at Kuta under the direction of Mads Lange, a Dane with more than a dozen ships. The great plantation crops of Java—coffee, indigo, rice, sugar, tobacco, coconuts—were also cultivated on Bali, but by smallholders. After Lange's death, trade fell off at Kuta and picked up at Singaraja, but the Balinese became addicted to opium. Customs duties on chests of opium grew so profitable that the Dutch repealed all other taxes and made Singaraja a free port. Enough money was left over to pay for administering the neighboring island of Lombok.

Bali's traditional royal politics persisted into the twentieth century. Rajas ruled over "theatre states" whose real function was not to govern—that was taken care of by village councils—but to sponsor spectacular religious ceremonies. The Dutch grew dissatisfied with indirect control and took Lombok in 1894. Ten years later they used an incident involving a looted Chinese shipwreck as a pretext for impossible demands on the raja of Badung. A Dutch war fleet anchored off Sanur in 1906 and bombarded Denpasar. The Balinese princes, knowing they were beaten, decided on ritual suicide. They purified themselves, put on their cleanest clothes and brightest jewels, burned their palaces, and marched straight into the Dutch lines. The horrified Dutch saw what was coming and tried to convince them to halt, but failing to, opened fire. Three thousand died—rajas, priests, relatives, men, women and children.

By the early 1900s, Dutch officials began to see Bali as a kind of museum of pre–Islamic Indonesian culture and sought to protect the island from disruptive change. A remarkable process of acculturation began in the 1920s when European artists "discovered" Bali and went there to live. A whole new style of art sprang from a union of French impressionism and Balinese design. Bali became part of Indonesia in 1949. (Willard A. Hanna, *Bali Profile: People, Events, Circumstances 1001–1976*, 1976.)

Ross Marlay

BANDA ISLANDS. The Banda Islands form part of the southern Moluccas*. Located in the Banda Sea, the ten islands are approximately 75 miles south of Ceram. The Portuguese first discovered the islands in 1512, but the Dutch East India Company* conquered them in 1621. England occupied the islands between 1796 and 1800 and throughout the Napoleonic Wars, but the Treaty of Paris in 1814 restored them to Dutch control. In 1949 the Banda Islands became part of the Republic of Indonesia, under the local jurisdiction of Maluku Province. (C. R. Boxer, *The Dutch Seaborne Empire: 1600–1800*, 1965.)

BANTAM. Bantam was one of the few British outposts in the East Indies. Located in West Java*, Bantam became the site of a British factory in 1603 under the direction of the British East India Company*. The company appointed a chief factor in 1613, but four years later the company raised Bantam to the status of a presidency and gave it control over the other British posts in the East Indies and over the Coromandel coast of India*. That status lasted until 1630 when the company reduced it to an agency again and placed it under the authority of Surat*. Between 1634 and 1652 Bantam was a presidency again, but it became an agency in 1652 when the presidency was transferred to Madras*. Bantam's status even as an agency, however, became more and more tenuous in the 1660s and 1670s when Dutch power in the East Indies steadily increased. The British East India Company, convinced that the Dutch were destined to dominate the East Indies, abandoned Bantam in 1682. (David P. Henige, *Colonial Governors from the Fifteenth Century to the Present*, 1970.)

BARBADOS. Barbados, the easternmost of the numerous islands in the Caribbean Sea, has a total area of 166 square miles. Originally Barbados was densely forested, but the rapid expansion of the sugar industry in the seventeenth century practically defoliated the entire island. Barbados' economy has historically centered on agriculture, especially sugar production. The Spanish were the first Europeans to discover the island (in 1519), but the prevailing winds and ocean currents made it a difficult place to reach in sailing vessels, and they did not attempt to plant any settlements. Instead, Spanish slavers carried off the bulk of the native Arawak Indians to work the mines of Hispaniola*, leaving Barbados virtually depopulated by 1541. Her attention focused on her more prosperous American colonies, Spain allowed her claims to Barbados to lapse.

An Englishman, Henry Powell, rediscovered Barbados in 1625 on his return to England from Brazil*. Finding the island uninhabited and densely forested, Powell claimed the fertile land of Barbados in the name of James I. Two years later settlers from England arrived, bringing with them African slaves they had captured during the journey. At first, the English colonists, assisted by their few slaves and indentured servants, raised tobacco, cotton, ginger, and indigo, but in 1637 Dutch trader Pieter Brower introduced sugarcane (a far more valuable crop) to the island. By the mid–1640s, sugar production had become the foremost economic activity on Barbados. The expansion of sugar production stimulated a massive importation of West African slaves. Slaves became the majority of the population.

In 1663, as a result of the turmoil of the English Civil War, the colonists of Barbados canceled the proprietary grant James I had given to the Earl of Carlisle in the 1620s, gaining more control of their internal affairs. The Barbados general assembly, which had been formed some time before 1641, continued to serve the colony's legislative needs, only with enhanced powers.

Economic conditions on the island were relatively stable throughout the eighteenth century, although the sugar industry suffered somewhat during the American Revolution*. Another economic setback was the emancipation of the slaves in 1834, but the subsequent transition to a wage-based labor system progressed fairly smoothly. In 1935, however, economic conditions had reached their nadir, leading in 1937 to widespread rioting. An investigation into the causes of disruption resulted in a variety of British-sponsored reforms throughout the 1940s culminating in 1954 with complete internal self-government. In November 1966 Barbados became an independent nation within the Commonwealth. (Jerome Handler and Frederick W. Lange, *Plantation Slavery in Barbados*, 1978; J. H. Parry, Philip Sherlock, and Anthony Maingot, *A Short History of the West Indies*, 1987.)

Jay O. Boehm

BARBUDA. Barbuda is one of the Leeward Islands* in the West Indies*. Totaling 62 square miles, the island is approximately 25 miles north of Antigua*. Columbus* discovered Barbuda during his second voyage in 1493, but its isolation and fierce native Carib Indians made it an inhospitable place for colonization. Not until the 1630s did Europeans look again at Barbuda as a permanent settlement. The English moved in under the proprietorship of the Codrington family, which named the island "Dulcina." Between 1680 and 1872 the Codringtons controlled Barbuda. Although Barbuda had modest hopes of separate status, its political existence became inextricably entwined with the interests of its southern neighbor Antigua*. Between 1958 and 1962 Antigua and Barbuda were part of the West Indies Federation*, and in 1967 they became a self-governing associated state with Great Britain. Some Barbudans began campaigning in the 1970s for separate, independent status, but the British refused, arguing that the Barbudan population of 1,400 people was insufficient for independence. On November 1, 1981, Antigua and Barbuda became a single independent state, part of the Commonwealth. (J. H. Parry, Philip Sherlock, and Anthony Maingot, *A Short History of the West Indies*, 1987.)

BARINAS. Spain created the province of Barinas in Venezuela in 1782. It was the last province established in Venezuela before the wars of independence. Fernando Miyares y González served as the first governor. Spanish control of the province deteriorated rapidly after 1810 because of the military situation, and in 1819 Barinas became part of Gran Colombia*. Later it was incorporated into the Republic of Venezuela*. See VENEZUELA.

BASUTOLAND. Once known as Basutoland or Basotholand, home of the Basotho people, and now known as Lesotho, the country is an isolated, mountainous area entirely surrounded by the Republic of South Africa. The land was inhabited only by Bushmen (San) hunters until the end of the sixteenth century when various Bantu-speaking peoples began to enter the region. Moshoeshoe I (c. 1786–1870), one of the outstanding figures in the history of southern Africa, welded the Basotho nation together from the remnants of tribes scattered by the destructive inter–African wars known as the "Lifaqane" (or hammering) in the early nineteenth century. These wars spread from present day Zululand* to most of southern and central Africa by the 1820s. Under the wise and skillful leadership of Moshoeshoe I, thousands of refugees from broken clans established themselves in the mountain fortress of Thaba-Bosiu, which was to become the heart of the Basotho nation, or Basotholand.

During the reign of Moshoeshoe I, Basotholand was caught up in the Anglo-Boer conflict. Between 1856 and 1868 the Boers repeatedly sent envoys to try to rouse the Basotho to join them. Though initially successful against the Boers, Moshoeshoe, seeing the balance of power swinging against the Basotho, sought the protection of the United Kingdom. Meanwhile, Boers from the Orange Free State* launched another attack in July 1867 and gained control over a rich fertile strip of Basotholand. Moshoeshoe appealed once more to Queen Victoria for assistance, and on March 12, 1868, Britain agreed to place Basotholand under Crown protection.

Reluctant to incur expense, the British handed over Basotholand to the white dominated Cape Colony* in 1871, a change emphatically opposed by the Basotho. In 1884, after a seven month conflict between the Basotho and the Cape Colony (the Gun War, 1880–1881), Britain resumed responsibility for Basotholand, which it retained until the territory achieved its independence. From 1884 Basotholand was governed under a system of indirect rule in which an appointed colonial official advised the traditional ruler. The British hoped to disturb local affairs as little as possible while still maintaining colonial rule. A resident commissioner at Maseru administered the government under the direction of the British high commissioner (i.e., the governor or governor-general) in Cape Town or Pretoria. The traditional leader (also known as the paramount chief or king) governed from the capital of Matsieng.

In 1903 an informal Basotholand council composed of 99 appointed Basotho members was informally established, and it was regularized in 1910 as an advisory body. In 1955 the Basotholand council asked for the authority to legislate on internal affairs; and in 1959 a new constitution ended the legislative authority of the high commissioner and gave Basotholand its first elected legislature. In 1960 the newly formed, indirectly elected, Basotho national council became effective; however, Basotholand remained under British executive authority.

Political organizations emerged in 1952 with Ntsu Mokhehle's formation of the Basotholand Congress Party (BCP). Other parties soon appeared. The first general elections for district councils took place in 1960 and gave a majority to the BCP, which proposed negotiating with Britain for independence. The British finally acceded to the demands for full independence and, in 1964, a constitutional conference held in London approved recommendations for a constitution. On April 30, 1965, another general election was held and the more conservative Basotholand National Party (BNP) won with 31 seats in the 60 seat legislature. In April 1966 a conflict in parliament between the King, who felt the constitution deprived him of powers that should have been his, and Prime Minister Leabua Jonathan, who wanted a limited monarchy, nearly jeopardized autonomous development. The final independence conference was held in June 1966, and on October 4, 1966, Great Britain granted full independence to the newly named Kingdom of Lesotho. Moshoeshoe II was proclaimed king. (Peter Sanders, *Moshoeshoe of Lesotho*, 1975; Colleen and Dirk Schwager, *Lesotho*, 1975.)

Eric C. Loew

BATAVIA. Batavia, a city on the northwest coastal plain of Java*, was the capital of the Dutch East Indies*. Batavia was the name given to a fortress built by Jan Pieterszoon Coen in 1619 on the ruins of a small port variously known as Sunda Kelapa, Jaya Karta, or Jacatra. The site was swampy and unhealthy due to malaria and other tropical diseases, but it possessed three strategic advantages: a good harbor, proximity to the strategic Sunda Strait, and enough distance from the native Mataram Empire to become the seat of government of the Dutch East Indies. Today it is the capital of modern Indonesia*. The name was changed to Djakarta in 1949 and to Jakarta in 1972. (O. W. Wolters, *Early Indonesian Commerce*, 1967.)

Ross Marlay

BAY ISLANDS. The Bay Islands are located in the Bay of Honduras off the coast of Honduras.* Ever since the seventeenth century the British had had an interest in the Caribbean coast of what is today Honduras and Nicaragua,* but settlement on the Bay Islands had been sparse and sporadic. But late in the 1830s a wave of British immigrants from the Cayman Islands* began to settle on the Bay Islands, and in 1841 Great Britain announced its claim to the region. Honduras bitterly protested the claim, but in 1852 Great Britain designated the area as a crown colony with the governor of Jamaica* serving as its governor-in-chief and the superintendent of British Honduras* serving as its lieutenant governor. But British interest in the region was limited. They were not willing to create a hemispheric conflict over the Bay Islands, and in 1860 Great Britain ceded them to Honduras. (David A. G. Waddell, "Great Britain and the Bay Islands, 1821–1861," *Historical Journal*, 2 (1959), 59–77.)

BECHUANALAND. Bechuanaland, now known as Botswana, was an area of southern Africa located north of the Molopo River between German Southwest Africa* to the west and the Transvaal* to the east, with the Chobe River at its northern border. The frontiers of Bechuanaland were very similar to the modern boundaries of Botswana. The area was named for the principle tribe of the region, the Tswana, or as the British later called them, Bechuana. The Tswana are believed to be of the Sotho group of Bantu-speaking peoples. The Tswana's first contact with the Europeans occurred when Scottish missionary Robert Moffat, a colleague of David Livingstone, arrived in Kuruman in 1821. Moffat in 1858 urged Sir George Grey to send British police from the Cape Colony* to portions of Bechuanaland in order to preserve his mission against the encroachment of the Boers as well as the Ndebele tribe. The British occupation of the Cape Colony had begun the "Great Trek" of Boer settlers northward in the 1830s. For decades the Tswana faced the danger of losing their lands to the Boer trekkers. From 1878 to 1884 the British missionary John Mackenzie appealed to Britain to declare the region a protectorate. When the Transvaal Boers declared their own protectorate over the area, British authorities at the Cape responded with military force in 1885, pushed out the Boers, and formally placed Bechuanaland under the protection of the Queen.

Until 1891 the protectorate was governed very loosely. The British policed the area to curb raids and "free-booters," and the Tswana chiefs were permitted to govern their areas in their own way. Very little land was ceded to the British in exchange for protection, since the British were mainly interested in Bechuanaland as a connection between the Cape Colony and the interior trade rather than as an area for settlement. A royal charter was granted to the British South African Company, a conglomeration of trapping, mining, and trading companies, headed by Cecil Rhodes*, in 1889. The company could acquire and exercise governing powers of any kind for the preservation of public order. However, the company met with resistance from Tswana chiefs, mainly over taxation. By the 1890s the position of the British government had changed. Bechuanaland had become vital to Britain as a secure line of communication from the Cape to her interior colonial holdings.

In 1891 the British government declared the Bechuanaland Protectorate under the jurisdiction of the high commissioner of South Africa Sir Henry Loch, giving him legislative powers, taxing powers, and the authority to appoint officials in Bechuanaland. Loch quickly extended British control over the inhabitants of the region. By 1895 Tswana chief Ngwato Khama III was appealing directly to London for a return to the autonomy of the individual tribes. These appeals prompted the establishment of native reserves, in which the five major tribes maintained their boundaries and governed themselves. However, they would still be subject to taxation to pay for British protection. The remaining lands outside of the reserves were granted to private charter companies. For almost twenty-five years the administration of the protectorate remained the same.

When the Union of South Africa* was created in 1909, the law called for

Bechuanaland to be annexed into South Africa at a later date, but South Africa left the Commonwealth* in 1961, before the annexation of Bechuanaland could be initiated. In 1950 a joint European and African advisory council was established in Bechuanaland. African executive and legislative councils in Bechuanaland were formed in 1961. It was at this time that political parties seeking independence for Bechuanaland were organized. In 1965 the first elections were held based on universal suffrage. The new 1965 constitution provided for a cabinet to be chosen from an elected legislative assembly. Seretse Khama, leader of the majority Bechuanaland Democratic Party, became prime minister in September 1965. In addition, a house of chiefs, an advisory body made up of the chiefs from the eight major tribes and representatives of four smaller tribes, was established. The Queen's commissioner (formerly the resident commissioner, or governor) remained in control of foreign affairs, defense, and public service until 1966 when the Republic of Botswana came into being. (Anthony Siller, *Botswana: A Short Political History*, 1974; Gideon S. Were, *A History of South Africa*, 1974.)

Karen Sleezer

BELGIAN CONGO. European penetration of west-central Africa began with the Portuguese explorer Diogo Cao's discovery of the estuary of the Congo River in 1483. European settlement, however, began largely with the development of the slave trade, which reached its peak during the early nineteenth century. After 1850 explorers such as David Livingstone and Richard Francis Burton reached the headwaters of the Congo. Henry Morton Stanley, however, first explored the entire length of the river from 1874 to 1877. Stanley offered his discoveries to Great Britain and was turned down, but subsequent dealings with King Leopold II* of the Belgians proved fruitful. The king established a private company that claimed ownership of the entire basin south of the Congo and Ubangi rivers. Within a decade Belgian emissaries signed hundreds of "treaties" with local chiefs placing the land and native peoples under the protection of Leopold. The Berlin West Africa Conference of 1884–1885* granted international recognition to what was called the Congo Free State, with Leopold II as King and head of state.

Following two decades of repressive rule, King Leopold had to relinquish personal rule. The Congo Free State, renamed the Belgian Congo, was placed under control of the Belgian parliament in 1908 as an official colony. From the 1920s to the 1950s the colony was governed centrally from the capital of Leopoldville (now Kinshasa). Belgian rule was efficient, the Congo's rich mineral resources were fully exploited by international corporations, and an educational system was established for the African population. But peasant uprisings broke out continually during the interwar period, largely because of the emerging African nationalism. The rebellion of the Kivu in 1919–1923 was brutally suppressed, but secret societies, such as the "leopard men," called for African unity against European colonialism both before and after World War II*.

Until 1955 Belgium isolated the Congo from growing African anti-colonialism. Although locally-elected municipal councils were permitted in several cities, no African nationalist political parties were allowed to exist. Only after violent riots broke out in Leopoldville in January 1959 did Belgium make concessions to the African Congolese. Finally, after increased political tensions, Belgium agreed to independence beginning June 30, 1960, and called for parliamentary elections. Provisions for the transfer of power and outlines of future political organizations were laid out by the Brussels Round Table Conference in January and February 1960. The leading political party, the *Mouvement National Congolais* (MNC), under the leadership of Patrice Lumumba*, formed a coalition government with Joseph Kasavubu of the *Alliance des Bakongo* (Abako) following elections in May 1960. The Belgian Congo became the independent Republic of the Congo* on June 30, 1960. In October 1971, the name of the country was changed to the Republic of Zaire. (Georges Brausch, *Belgian Administration in the Congo*, 1961; Basil Davidson, *Let Freedom Come*, 1978; Roland Oliver and Anthony Atmore, *Africa Since 1800*, 1967.)

William G. Ratliff
{: style="text-align: right"}

BELGIAN EAST AFRICA. See RWANDA-BURUNDI.

BELIZE. See BRITISH HONDURAS.

BEN BELLA, AHMED. Algerian nationalist leader Ahmed Ben Bella was born in 1916 in Marnia, Algeria*, to a traditional Muslim family. He attended school at Tlemcen, where racial relations were tense, but he was educated in French and was not completely fluent in Arabic. There in 1937 he encountered a political group, the PPA (Algerian People's Party), which favored ridding Algeria of the French. During World War II* Ben Bella fought in the French Army, but in 1945 he joined the PPA. He then ran for the office of municipal councillor but gave up because of French pressure tactics against his family. In 1947 Ben Bella helped found the Secret Organization (OS), which advocated armed insurrection, and he became its chief. In 1949 OS men robbed the Oran post office to get funds for the operation. Ben Bella was arrested in 1950 and sentenced to 8 years in jail for the robbery. He escaped in 1952 and went into hiding, first in Paris and then in Cairo. In 1954 Ben Bella was one of the nine original members of the Revolutionary Committee for Unity and Action (CRUA), the group that planned the November 1 uprising that marked the beginning of the Algerian war. He was in charge of organizing the "wilayas," regional military sections of the FLN (National Liberation Front), which carried the struggle for independence against the French. Ben Bella was also in charge of supplying weapons to the insurgents and getting financial support from friendly Arab countries.

In 1956 the insurgents held a congress at Soumman which marked the predominance of the interior group led by Abane Ramdane over Ben Bella's exterior group. Ben Bella was accused of not providing enough money and weapons for the cause. In October of that year on a flight to Morocco* with other Algerian leaders, Ben Bella's plane was diverted to Algiers by order of French authorities. They all spent the rest of the war in jail. Ben Bella was released in 1962 when Algeria became independent. After the September elections Ben Bella became prime minister, and a year later, president for a five-year term. He was overthrown by Defense Minister Houari Boumedienne and jailed for 14 years without trial until Boumedienne's death in 1979. Then he was placed under house arrest, but all restrictions on him were lifted in 1982 and he went to France, where he was somewhat associated with fundamentalist Islamic sentiments. (Jules Roy, *The War in Algeria*, 1961.)

Alain G. Marsot

BENCOOLEN. The British East India Company* established an agency at Bantam* on West Java* in 1603 to exploit the trade of the East Indies, but they were not able to displace Dutch hegemony in the region. Late in the 1600s the interest of the British East India Company shifted from West Java to Sumatra*, and in 1685 the company established York Fort in the Bencoolen region. Other posts were established at Fort Marlborough, Tapanuli, Natal, and Air Bangis. Bencoolen was administratively subject to Madras until 1760, when it was raised to the status of a presidency by the company. Profits there, however, were extremely limited, and in 1785 the company reduced its status and placed it under Bengal.* For the next forty years Bencoolen retained that status. By the early 1800s, Great Britain was willing to surrender its foothold in the East Indies in return for complete control over Malaya*. The British and Dutch agreed to that settlement in 1825 and Bencoolen became the property of the Netherlands. (John Bastin, ed., *The British in West Sumatra, 1685–1825*, 1965.)

BENGAL. Bengal is a historically significant region of the Indian sub-continent bounded by Sikkim and Bhutan* on the north, Assam* and Burma* on the east, the Bay of Bengal on the south, and Bihar* on the west. Bengal today includes the state of West Bengal in India and the nation of Bangladesh. Before the independence of India in 1947, the region of Bengal consisted of the British ruled province of Bengal and the princely states of Cooch Behar and Tripura on the Assam border. The major city of Bengal is Calcutta. The British first became interested in Bengal in 1633, and it became the springboard for their subsequent conquest of the entire subcontinent of India. The British established a factory in 1690 at the site of present-day Calcutta, and in 1700 raised its status to that of a presidency. At the time the post was known as Fort William*.

The presence of the British East India Company* in Bengal steadily expanded in the eighteenth century, and in 1774 the governor of Bengal was designated governor-general, with authority over Bengal, Bombay* and Madras*. In 1834 Agra, which became known as the North-West Provinces (United Provinces*), was detached from Bengal, and twenty years later a separate lieutenant-governor took charge of Bengali affairs to relieve the governor-general of the burden of dealing with local matters. Assam was separated from Bengal in 1874, Bihar in 1912, and Orissa* in 1912. Great Britain extended local autonomy to Bengal in 1937. After World War II, Britain briefly assumed power again in Bengal, but in 1947, when India became indepenent, Bengal was divided between India and Pakistan*. See INDIA.

BENIN. See DAHOMEY.

BERBICE. In the early seventeenth century, the Dutch began their expansion into the Caribbean, challenging British and Spanish interests there. Like the British, they used joint stock companies* as the vehicle for expansion. In 1627, the government gave the House of Van Pere, a Dutch commercial and financial enterprise, a concession to develop Berbice, one of four Dutch settlements on the coast of Guiana. Until 1803, Berbice was governed by the House of Van Pere and then by the Berbice Association. Great Britain occupied Berbice in 1803 during the Napoleonic Wars. They kept Berbice and eventually it became part of the colony of British Guiana. (David P. Henige, *Colonial Governors from the Fifteenth Century to the Present* 1970.)

BERLIN ACT OF 1889. The Berlin Act of 1889, signed on June 14, 1889, by Germany, Great Britain, and the United States, established three-power joint rule over Samoa*. In the scramble for new colonies in the late nineteenth century, the western powers looked greedily on Samoa, even though the islands were south of the main Pacific sea lanes. In the spring of 1889 the three powers sent naval vessels to Samoa to protect their claims, but just as tensions reached the point of war, a devastating typhoon swept through Samoa, destroying six of the seven warships in the harbor at Apia. After the disaster the three countries returned to the negotiating table and reached an agreement setting up a supreme court, presided over by a chief justice, to rule Samoa, with the advice of diplomatic consuls from Germany, Great Britain, and the United States. A land commission would determine ownership of contested property. The Berlin Act brought only a temporary peace to Samoa. In the 1890s civil war erupted again, precipitating the Anglo-German Agreement of 1899*. (R. P. Gilson, *Samoa 1830 to 1900: The Politics of a Multi-Cultural Community*, 1970.)

BERLIN WEST AFRICA CONFERENCE OF 1884–1885. The Berlin West Africa Conference met from November 15, 1884, to February 26, 1885. Although the conclave was hardly a decisive event in the scramble for Africa, it did succeed in moderating tensions that had worsened relations among the powers since the 1870s. In fact, the two most obvious antagonists of Europe, the victor and the vanquished in the Franco–Prussian War of 1870–1871, were responsible for the Berlin Conference after finding a basis for collaborating on various African issues.

Aside from the rivalry of the French, British, Italians, and Spanish in North

Africa and the conflict between the British and the Boers at the southern end of the continent, one development in particular required the attention of the European Concert. The penetration of the Congo Basin had become increasingly critical since King Leopold II* of Belgium convoked the conference of 1876 at Brussels to explore the possibility of "opening up" Africa. The meeting formed an International African Association to promote this process. King Leopold financed explorations by Henry Stanley in the Congo Basin which resulted in the negotiation of hundreds of treaties with native chieftans for the use of natural resources and establishment of numerous stations by the early 1880s.

Soon other powers were intruding. French premier Jules Ferry* was responsible for French successes in North and West Africa, which led to competition with Stanley for treaties with tribal leaders. The Portuguese were suddenly reminded of their ancient claims, which the British were wont to support. But the Anglo-Portuguese Treaty of 1884 recognized Lisbon's claims to both sides of the Lower Congo River from 5 degrees 12 minutes south latitude and as far as Noki in the interior. An Anglo-Portuguese commission was to control navigation on the river, with the British enjoying free navigation and most–favored–nation status. But the agreement would have denied the projected Belgian empire a commercial access to the sea, so King Leopold appealed to the French and German governments. Jules Ferry then engineered the Franco-Belgian Treaty of April 23, 1884, whereby France would respect the Association's territory and reserve an option to buy it if the Association ever decided to sell. Germany also protested the Anglo-Portuguese Treaty, which the British formally abandoned in June 1884.

The Egyptian problem was also involved. Late in June 1884 the British convened a conference in London with France and Germany. Faced with an enormous financial burden since the occupation of Egypt* in 1882, Britain wanted to abandon bondholders in the hope that with a major reduction in the Egyptian debt, political stabilizaiton would allow them to withdraw their troops. Although the British presence in Northeast Africa stood in the way of French expansion from Tunisia*, Gabon*, and Senegal* across Saharan Africa to Somalia, France worked with Germany to frustrate Britain at the conference by insisting on protecting the bondholders. The conference ended in failure.

The Germans then proposed to France the conclusion of a formal "colonial marriage" for mutual Franco-German cooperation against the British Empire* in Egypt, West Africa, and the Congo. Otto von Bismarck* challenged London and the Cape Colony* in Southwest Africa*, and in July 1884 Germany established protectorates over Togoland* and Cameroon*, challenging British claims in the vicinity of Benin and Biafra. In November 1884 Karl Peters, leader of the German Colonial Society, started a series of events which led to the formation of German East Africa* in February 1885.

Suspicious of German intentions, the French agreed to cooperate, but only on specific colonial issues. The Berlin West Africa Conference convened, therefore, with a narrow agenda. Representatives from Germany, France, the Habsburg monarchy, Belgium, Denmark, Spain, the United States, Italy, the Netherlands, Portugal, Russia, and the Ottoman Empire attended. The central issue was the status of King Leopold's International Association. With its sovereignty widely recognized, the main challenge was to give that sovereignty a foundation in international law. The conference defined the Congo Basin in a geographic sense, even though poor cartography required numerous bilateral and multilateral treaties before the turn of the century; allowed Leopold's colony to declare itself "neutral"; guaranteed freedom of trade and equal treatment for the commerce of all nations, not only on the river and its tributaries but on collateral roads, railways, and canals; extended the free trade zone from the Congo all the way across the continent to the Indian Ocean between latitude 5 degrees north and the mouth of the Zambezi River; created an international commission for the navigation of the Congo to supervise implementation of these provisions; and declared that henceforth no power was to declare a protectorate in coastal Africa without first giving due time to allow other interested nations to respond and without having already established "effective occupation." In typical rhetorical fashion, the conference also concluded that the European powers should protect the native tribes, suppress the slave trade, and promote Christianity and freedom of religion.

Such noble experiments in European cooperation were scarcely evident in the eventual partition of Africa. Leopold's International Association made itself the "Congo Free State" with Leopold as its sovereign in July 1885, but it was not subject in any way to Belgium, whose anti-colonialist parliament opposed the union. Ignoring the commitments at Berlin by imposing highly restrictive economic policies, Leopold made the enterprise enormously profitable for himself. Not until 1908 did the Belgian parliament annex the Congo.* Britain chartered the Royal Niger Company to circumvent the decisions of the Berlin conference by excluding foreign competitors from the Niger and Benue rivers. Between 1885 and 1900 an increasing number of entrepreneurs, mining interests, soldiers, and consuls became aware of the potential riches of Africa and influenced all of the powers to place greater value on formal empire than on the traditional "free trade" system, which the diplomats had tried to perpetuate in 1885. (Sybil E. Crowe, *The Berlin West African Conference, 1885–85*, 1942; A. J. P. Taylor, *Germany's First Bid for Colonies, 1884–1885*, 1938; Howard E. Yarnell, *The Great Powers and the Congo Conference*, 1934.)

Bascom Barry Hayes

BERMUDA. Bermuda is a series of 145 islands and rocks stretching across a twenty-two mile area, 570 miles off the coast of North Carolina* in the Atlantic Ocean. The islands are primarily coral in composition, and only twenty of them are inhabited. In 1503 the Spanish explorer Juan Bermudez discovered the islands, but it was not until 1609 that the islands were settled when the English navigator George Somers shipwrecked there. The Virgina Company brought 60 settlers to Bermuda in 1612, and in 1616 the first slaves arrived. Bermuda established its own legislature in 1619. Bermuda's early history closely paralleled that of Virginia*, which was founded in 1607, received its first slaves in 1619, and established its House of Burgesses in 1619.

Along with the general trend in her other North American colonies, England forced the Somers Island Company to cede control of Bermuda in 1684, making it a royal colony. Its population grew very slowly. In 1815 the colonial capital was established at its present location in Hamilton on Great Bermuda (main island). Bermuda never sought independence from the British Empire.* Not until 1968 did its population go past 50,000 people, and the populated area consists of only twenty square miles of land. In 1968 the people of Bermuda approved a constitution permitting England to appoint a governor responsible for foreign affairs and internal security, along with an appointed legislative council and an elected, forty member house of assembly. The population of Bermuda is approximately 60 percent black and 40 percent white, with most whites of British extraction. (Jean de Chantal Kennedy, *Biography of a Colonial Town*, 1961; Terry Tucker, *Islands of Bermuda*, 1970.)

BHUTAN. Bhutan is a landlocked country of 18,000 square miles located in the Himalaya Mountains between India* and China*. Its original inhabitants migrated there from Tibet* in the early middle ages. The Bhutanese first confronted the British Empire* in 1772 when British troops expelled a Bhutanese invasion of Cooch Behar. A treaty ended the conflict in 1774. Periodically Britain tried to establish peaceful contacts with the Bhutanese, but they were very suspicious of foreigners and frequently attacked British expeditions. In 1865 Britain made a concerted effort and took military control of the strategic entrances to Bhutan; later in the year Bhutan accepted a British protectorate.

In 1907 the British installed Ugyen Dorji Wangchuk as king of Bhutan, and in 1910 the two countries signed the Treaty of Punakha. Great Britain agreed not to interfere in the internal affairs of Bhutan, and the Bhutanese accepted British direction of their external affairs. After India achieved her independence in 1947, the British severed their relationship with Bhutan. The Indo-Bhutanese Agreement of 1949 gave India control of Bhutanese external affairs. During the 1960s Bhutan abolished slavery and embarked on a land-distribution program. In 1972 Jigme Singye Wangchuk became king and moved the country toward a constitutional monarchy. (Arabinda Deb, *India and Bhutan: A Study in Frontier Political Relations*, 1976; Leo Rose, *The Politics of Bhutan*, 1977.)

BIHAR. Bihar is a region of India bordered by Nepal* on the north, Pakistan* on the northwest, the Indian state of West Bengal on the southeast, Orissa* and Madhya Pradesh on the south and southwest, and Uttar Pradesh on the west. The British East India Company* acquired Bihar in 1765 and merged it administratively with Bengal*. In 1912 Bihar and Orissa were detached from Bengal and became known as the governor's province of Bihar-Orissa. Bihar was detached from Orissa in 1936 and became part of India in 1947. See INDIA.

BISMARCK, OTTO EDUARD LEOPOLD VON. Otto Eduard Leopold von Bismarck was born on April 1, 1815, in Mark Brandenburg, some 20 miles southwest of Berlin near the town of Magdeburg at Schönhausen, the ancestral estate of his father, Ferdinand von Bismarck. In addition to a large estate, Otto inherited from his father the characteristic Junker devotion to Fatherland and a love for the simplicity of rural life. Bismarck was a loyal subject of the Kingdom of Prussia. He venerated tradition, the authority of the crown and nobility, and the values of the rural, patriarchal world. Bismarck studied law at the University of Göttingen and then spent several years in Berlin and Aachen preparing for a civil service career, plans which he eventually abandoned before returning to the family estates, first at Kniephof in Pomerania and after 1845 at Schönhausen. During this time, in the company of some Pietistic neighbors, including Johanna von Puttkamer, who became his wife in 1847, Bismarck found a religious faith that helped curb his youthful exuberance. Left intact, however, was his zest for power, a will to dominate others, and a perception of a chaotic world of diverse, competing elements without much inner meaning or purpose. Bismarck became a member of the Conservative Party, which opposed the revolutionary institutions emerging from the political rebellions of 1848. He believed in the need for a greater concentration of political power. And he saw that a potentially catastrophic conflict could result from dissension between the two most powerful German states—Austria and Prussia. Both had to realize that the conservation of the values of the traditionally pluralistic social order of old feudal Germany might be possible only if the ancient federative system were mitigated somewhat by a strong executive authority, preferably an Austro-Prussian duumvirate. Conservative political leaders had to develop a new formula for a German federation, although Bismarck insisted that Prussia, not Austria, be the driving force behind that federation.

Bismarck's political career was dedicated to that quest. He was a member of the United Diet of Prussia in 1847, the second chamber of the Prussian Diet in 1849, and the Erfurt Parliament in 1850. Between 1851 and 1858 Bismarck served as the Prussian ambassador to the Germanic Diet at Frankfurt, where he opposed Austrian ascendancy and worked for German consolidation under Prussian leadership. Bismarck was ambassador to Russia from 1859 to 1862 and then briefly ambassador to France in 1862, when he became Prussian prime minister and foreign minister. From that post Bismarck began his lifelong work—the creation of a unified Germany as the most powerful nation in Europe. After Prussia defeated Austria in the Seven Weeks War, Bismarck excluded Austria from the new North German Confederation. The Franco-Prussian War the next year, in which several German states defeated France, led to the creation of the German Enpire*, with Wilhelm I of Prussia as emperor.

Bismarck became the first chancellor of the new German Empire, a position he retained until 1890. His tenure was marked by a broad range of economic and social reforms. Bismarck suppressed socialism but established the modern welfare state, including workmen's compensation, health insurance, and old-age pensions, as well as government ownership of certain industrial enterprises. He dominated the Congress of Berlin of 1878*, which focused on the future of the Balkans and the Middle East after the Russo-Turkish War, and he arranged the highly successful Berlin West Africa Conference of 1884–1885* which led to the partitioning of Africa. Bismarck established the Alliance with Austria-Hungary in 1879 and the Triple Alliance of Germany, Italy, and Austria-Hungary in 1882.

Bismarck's bid for a colonial empire was consistent with his continental ambitions. An integrated *Mitteleuropa* was the necessary foundation for *Weltpolitik*. Bismarck saw that relationship as early as 1878 when he took a step toward the later Franco-German "colonial marriage" that led to the Berlin West Africa Conference of 1884–1885 and toward the creation of an African colonial empire that was to emerge as a necessary component of the *Mittelafrika–Mitteleuropa* ideology—the doctrine that the Balkans and the Near East constituted the bridge between Central Europe and a Central African empire. With a view toward an eventual collaboration between France and the Dual Powers, he had the Austrian government assist him in securing Reich–German and Austrian capital invested in a bankrupt and politically troubled Egypt. This initiative of 1879 came just after the Congress of Berlin where he had encouraged the French to move into North Africa.

A second problem germane to the question of the interrelationship between continental policy and overseas colonial expansion stems from the obvious point that the "protectionist" impulse of neomercantilism presupposes a threat against which the Reich must intervene. There was a widespread perception in the Reich that Great Britain and the "sub-imperialists" of Australia* and New Zealand* were obstructing German enterprises from Africa to Oceania. Accordingly, Bismarck advertised the debut of the Reich in *Weltpolitik* with a highly Anglophobic propaganda. He was deliberately combative in his challenges to England on a number of occasions, including April 1884 when he initiated the first Reich colonial protectorate in South West Africa* on behalf of the Bremen firm of F. A. Luderitz; in July 1884 when he responded similarly on behalf of Gustav Nachtigal in Cameroon* and Togoland*; in February 1885 when the beneficiary was Karl Peters in German East Africa*; or in May 1885 when Bismarck so favored the Hamburg firm of Johann Ceasar Godeffroy and Son in New Guinea.

The anti-English offensive was also directly related to the "ideological warfare" which Bismarck waged not only against the Liberal cabinet of William Gladstone* but also the chancellor's excessively "English" antagonists in the Reich. Bismarck was most concerned that the old and infirm Kaiser might die any day and leave the throne to his son, the rather liberal and somewhat anti-Bismarckian Crown Prince Friedrich Wilhelm whose wife, Victoria, was the eldest daughter of the English queen. Bismarck suspected that certain leaders of his left-liberal coalition were already the probable choices of Friedrich Wilhelm to form his government. The colonial policy thus became the basis for a highly successful nationalistic appeal against both English and German Gladstonism during Bismarck's determined effort to defeat his political opposition.

Also, a German "protectionist" impulse had been evident for many decades in the desire to provide cultural and economic assistance to the "islands" of "endangered Germandom" in Eastern Europe and the advocacy of "state interventionism" on behalf of the Austrian and Bohemian Germans and the Siebenburgen "Saxons" of Hungary. Such had been the logic behind the formation of protective associations as early as the 1840s to defend and nurture German interests, especially in Bohemia—but also in Texas and the South Pacific. The connection between overseas and Middle–European protectionism was evident in the career of Karl Peters, as he was an architect of both the *Kolonialverein*, organized in 1882 to agitate for overseas expansion, and of the General German Educational Association for the Preservation of Germandom Abroad, which he hoped could defend the German cause in the Habsburg Monarchy against the Russian Pan-Slav and Austro-Slav threats. Out of the close association of these organizations, which were holding joint congresses by the mid–1880s, the Pan-German League ultimately emerged to combine their Middle-European and overseas programs under the guidance of a single organization.

Although Bismarck left office in 1890 in the midst of a political struggle with the followers of Friedrich Wilhelm, he remained active in German politics until his death on July 30, 1898. Known as the "Iron Chancellor," Bismarck was a towering figure of the nineteenth century, the greatest diplomat of his age and the individual most responsible for transforming Germany from a series of divided kingdoms and principalities into a unified country and a world power. (George O. Kent, *Bismarck and His Times*, 1978; Otto Pflanze, *Bismarck and the Development of Germany: The Period of Unification, 1815–1871*, 1963; Woodruff D. Smith, *The German Colonial Empire*, 1978; Fritz Stern, *Gold and Iron: Bismarck, Bleichroder, and the Building of the German Empire*, 1977.)

Bascom Barry Hayes

BISMARCK ARCHIPELAGO. While the bulk of the German colonial empire was centered in Africa, other colonial holdings were acquired in the Pacific. Germany took northeastern New Guinea* on November 16, 1884. The New Guinea protectorate also embraced the Bismarck Archipelago, and the Northern Solomons. By 1906 German colonial holdings had been expanded to include the Mariana*, Caroline*, Palau*, and Nauru* islands. Chancellor Otto von Bismarck* established formal protectorates only in northeastern New Guinea (also known as Kaiser Wilhelmsland), the Bismarck Archipelago, Palau, and the Marshall Islands*. The establishment of a protectorate in New Guinea and the Bismark Archipelago was influenced by Adolf Hansemann, a leading industrialist and an avid supporter of colonization in the Pacific basin. Hansemann's New Guinea Company (*Neu Guinea Kompaqnie*, or NGK) was established as concessionaire in New Guinea and the Bismarck Archipelago in May 1885. The NGK was intended by its owners to control all aspects of colonial economic development. The German government also put the company in full charge of administration. The NGK explored the interior of New Guinea and developed the copra industry.

German colonial efforts in both New Guinea and the Bismarck Archipelago, however, were dismal failures. Costs regularly exceeded income, both in administration and in commercial operations. Especially unprofitable were the islands of the Bismarck Archipelago. The protectorate was not valuable enough to show a measurable profit without expensive capital investment. The colonial effort was also hampered by the NGK's enormous bureaucracy. Consequently, by 1886 the German government was forced to provide the funding for such essential services as naval patrols and communications. By 1898 the NGK could not perform its mandated administrative functions and the German government assumed full colonial control on October 7, 1898. The Bismarck Archipelago, as part of the German New Guinea, became an official colony in 1899. The first imperial governor was Rudolf von Benningsen, an able administrator who effectively remedied most of the problems. But when World War I* began in 1914, the takeover of the area by Australia* and Great Britain was practically unopposed. In 1919 the region was given to Australia under a League of Nations* mandate. (John A. Moses and Paul M. Kennedy, *Germany in the Pacific and Far East, 1870–1914*, 1977.)

William G. Ratliff

BLACK HOLE OF CALCUTTA. The Black Hole of Calcutta* was a room eighteen by fourteen feet with two barred airholes for windows. It was used as a jail to house no more than three or four drunken soldiers for a night. On Sunday, June 20, 1756, at 8:00 P.M., 146 British prisoners were forced into this enclosure by the Nawab of Bengal,* Siraj-ud-Daula. When the prisoners were released the following morning, 22 men and one woman staggered out, leaving 123 people dead. In retaliation a British army of 800 Europeans and 2,000 sepoys under Robert Clive defeated a 50,000 man army led by Siraj-ud-Daula at the Battle of Plassey on June 23, 1757. As a result the British became the virtual rulers of Bengal.

At the root of the tragedy was a growing Muslim distrust of the British East India Company*. The relationship became more strained after the death of the Nawab of Bengal, Aliverdi Khan, in April 1756. His successor, Siraj-ud-Daula, hated the British, especially Roger Drake, then governor of Calcutta. Shortly before Aliverdi's death Drake had enraged Siraj-ud-Daula by allowing his cousin and rival, Kissindas, to take refuge in Calcutta. Ten days after Aliverdi's death, the new nawab, Siraj-ud-Daula, demanded that both the French and British delegations pull down their newly built fortifications. While the French treated the Nawab's emissary with courtesy, Drake wrote a letter which so enraged Siraj-ud-Daula that he became determined to expel the British from Bengal.

The British at Fort William were ill-prepared for a siege. The fort's walls were crumbling, the gunpowder in storage was damp, and the garrison commander did not have a plan to defend the fort. In the past, threats of attack had always been diverted by payoffs. On June 16, the day of the first attack upon the fort, the British mustered 515 men to defend against Siraj-ud-Daula's 50,000. The attack was repulsed and neither the Nawab nor his commander, Roy Dolub, seemed to have a coherent plan of battle. During the British evacuation of women and children on Friday night, June 18, Charles Manningham, the export warehouse keeper, and William Frankland, the import warehouse keeper, deserted, claiming they needed to remain aboard the ship *Dodaldy* to protect the women and children. On Saturday, June 19, Drake and the garrison commander, George Minchin, deserted. John Holwell, the senior magistrate, assumed command and vowed to fight to the end. By now he had only 170 men to defend against 50,000. The situation was not entirely hopeless. If the fort could not be held the garrison could still be evacuated aboard the *Prince George*. Unfortunately for the British, this avenue of escape became closed when the ship ran aground. Fort William had only two choices—honorable death or surrender. Holwell had no other option left but to surrender and hope for honorable treatment.

A few survivors escaped in the confusion by walking out the river gate and later being picked up by passing ships. After capturing the fort, the Nawab felt it would be too dangerous to allow the prisoners the relative freedom of the fort. He probably did not intend to massacre the British prisoners, but when he inquired about a suitable place in which to confine them, he was told the British used the Black Hole. The evidence suggests the Nawab did not know whether the prison was large or small. However, his senior officers had seen the prison and knew its size. Their motive for not informing the Nawab was probably revenge for their heavy losses.

The ten hours spent in the Black Hole was an indescribable horror. Holwell was among the lucky ones; he got near one of the two small windows, and this probably saved his life. Those who sought refuge under a long platform, however, died rapidly of suffocation. Some of the survivors were able to hold out because they drank their own urine. Holwell reported that he sucked perspiration from his shirt sleeve. Water was brought to the prisoners, but since they had no containers except hats in which to hold it, it only made matters worse as the desperate men fought and spilled the water. None of the guards risked the displeasure of the Nawab by waking him up to report what was happening to the prisoners, so it was not until 6:00 A.M., that he learned about the tragedy. When the door was finally open, 22 men and one woman tumbled out. Upon his release from prison, Holwell was placed in irons along with three others chosen at random. The Nawab released Holwell and his companions a few weeks later.

The irony of this episode was that it had been an attempt to drive the British out of Bengal, but with the victory of Robert Clive at Plassey, the East India Company was able to extend its control over all of Bengal, which became the source of almost two-thirds of all British imports from Asia. (Noel Barber, *The Black Hole of Calcutta*, 1965.)

Michael Dennis

BLACK LEGEND. Apparently coined by Julian Juderias y Loyot (1877–1918), who took exception to the anti-Spanish view of history, the term "black legend" refers to a body of literature as well as an attitude critical of Spain's alleged cruelty in the conquest of the New World and its presumed decadence, political corruption, hypocrisy, laziness, bigotry, and pride as a nation. Ironically, a Spaniard, Father Bartolomé de las Casas*, fueled the image. In 1552 las Casas documented the harshness of Spain's treatment of the Indians in a polemic entitled *Very Brief Recital of the Destruction of the Indies*. His motive was humanitarian; he hoped to reform Spanish policies toward the Indians. Driven by less noble impulses, however, Spain's enemies quickly saw in las Casas's pamphlet "proof" of Spanish rapacity. Replete with lurid illustrations, the bishop's work was soon translated into French, English, Dutch, and other languages. Since the early twentieth century many scholars have challenged the veracity of the black legend, suggesting that it was at least an exaggeration if not an outright distortion of Spanish history. The result has been a more balanced treatment of Spain in the New World, frequently at the expense of las Casas's reputation as an unbiased observer. (Charles Gibson, ed., *The Black Legend*, 1971.)

John W. Storey

BOER WAR. An important development that contributed to the Anglo-Boer War of 1899–1902 was the discovery of gold in the hills of Witwatersrand in the Transvaal* in 1886. The newly founded Johannesburg became a large mining camp as prospectors immigrated to the area. Before long the *Uitlanders*, or foreigners, felt victimized by the Boer regime. By 1895 foreigners outnumbered Boers by about two to one. Even though they paid almost all of the taxes and earned most of the foreign exchange, the *Uitlanders* lacked the right to vote and had virtually no voice in Transvaal policymaking. An 1890 law required immigrants to have fourteen years of residence before being allowed to vote. English-speaking immigrants chafed under the uncompromising Boer insistence on upholding Dutch as the official language. The president of the Transvaal, Paul Kruger, angered investors and miners by having the *Volksraad* (parliament) pass legislation providing for a government monopoly over the importation, manufacture, and distribution of dynamite, an essential factor in obtaining gold ore.

Tension mounted when the Nederlands Railway, which dominated rail traffic in the Transvaal, set prohibitive rates upon trains traveling back and forth from Natal*, the Cape Colony*, and the Free State. The British continued to supply the Rand by ox wagons, but in November 1895 Kruger closed the fords by which the wagons crossed the Vaal River. Cecil Rhodes*, the South African diamond and gold magnate, was a dedicated British imperialist who had dreams of a consolidated empire in southern and central Africa ruled from the Cape. He secretly informed the high commissioner in Capetown that an "economic federation" with the Transvaal could be accomplished. He was able to acquire a territorial cession near Mafeking, located in extreme eastern Bechuanaland*, for the British South Africa Company to use as a staging area. Dr. Leander Starr Jameson, who ruled for Cecil Rhodes in Rhodesia, headed south with company police; at the same time, guns were smuggled to the *Uitlanders* in the Transvaal. Rhodes' maneuver was supported by Joseph Chamberlain*, British secretary of state for the colonies, who was an enthusiastic imperialist. The plot called for an attack to be coordinated with a *Uitlander* uprising. Kruger, however, made certain conciliatory gestures; this development, among others, led Rhodes and the *Uitlanders* to cancel the plan. Dr. Jameson had meanwhile severed the telegraph lines and Rhodes' wire ordering the cancellation was never received. The famous Jameson Raid ended in failure. Transvaal's General Pieter Cronje defeated the invaders on January 1, 1896, and captured Jameson the following day.

One significant result of the Jameson Raid was that the Free State shifted from neutrality to an alliance with the Transvaal. Kruger consolidated his position and easily won reelection in 1898. In 1897 Sir Alfred Milner was appointed as the new high commissioner. Two years later the *Uitlanders* sent a petition with more than 21,000 signatures to the Queen listing their complaints. Milner followed this up by sending a message to London in early May reviewing the mistreatment of the *Uitlanders* at the hands of the Boers. *The Times* of London began championing the cause of the *Uitlanders*. Negotiations between the British and the Boers broke down in early September 1899; meanwhile, 10,000 imperial troops embarked for South Africa. On October 9 Kruger and Marthinus Steyn, president of the Free State, cabled a joint ultimatum which the British rejected. The Boer War began three days later.

In the earliest stage of the war Republican troops outnumbered British forces two to one. The Boers did not, however, press their advantage. Instead of defeating British forces in the Cape Colony, which would have compelled the British to invade from overseas, the Boers moved on the Kimberley mines, Mafeking, and Ladysmith, targets of secondary strategic importance. At first the British armies assumed a defensive posture, but before long, thanks to their secure position in the Cape, they took the offensive. The tide turned as almost all of the Indian Army, together with volunteers from Canada and Australia, flooded into Capetown.

In late February 1900 the Boers were driven back. The British entered the Rand in June; Johannesburg and Pretoria fell with little difficulty. The Boer government retreated along the Nederlands Railway and sought asylum with the Portuguese in August. Before long Kruger had exiled himself in the Netherlands. The British declared peace. In reality, however, only the first phase of the war had ended. The conflict took an ugly turn when Boer guerrillas struck near the end of the year in the Orange River Colony*. Soon other Boer commandos emerged, forcing the proclamation of martial law in all areas outside of Capetown. Lord Kitchener, now in command of the war effort, moved to protect the railways by stringing barbed wire and constructing blockhouses. Farmhouses used by guerrillas were burned.

To defeat the guerrillas, Kitchener resorted to the tactics of total war. Men not killed in the fighting were detained at the Cape or exiled to islands such as St. Helena* or Ceylon*. Women, together with their children and native servants, were placed in detention camps. Farms, together with crops, animals, and equipment were destroyed to break the back of the guerrilla movement. By mid–1902 almost 250,000 people were detained in prison camps.

On May 31, 1902, the Peace of Vereeniging was signed. The Republics became colonies of the Crown. The British agreed to provide funds for reconstruction. Milner was given the enormous task of rehabilitation and reconstruction. The Empire had mobilized approximately 450,000 soldiers for the war effort, while the Boers had raised an army of 87,000. Milner was now responsible for about 1,300,000 people in the conquered territories. There were 35,000 Boer prisoners of war; 210,000 Boer women, children, and native servants were in concentration camps. Within ten months almost all of the Boers had been released. Royal subsistence grants to Boer families continued for several years. (Theodore C. Caldwell, *The Anglo-Boer War*, 1965; Thomas Pakenham, *The Boer War*, 1979.)

Roy E. Thoman

BOLÍVAR, SIMÓN. Simón Bolívar was born on July 24, 1783, in Caracas, Venezuela*, to wealthy parents who died when he was very young. An uncle administered his inheritance. Bolívar's chief tutor was Simón Rodríguez, who introduced him to the rationalist thinkers. In 1799 Bolívar was sent to Europe to complete his education. In 1801 he met and married the daughter of a Spanish nobleman, María Teresa Rodríguez del Toro y Alaiza. Bolívar and his new bride returned to Caracas, where she died of yellow fever in less than a year. He returned to Europe in 1804, where his ideas about independence began to take shape. He believed that revolutions depended upon ideas; therefore, educated creoles would have to lead a Latin American revolution. At Monte Sacro in Rome, Bolívar vowed to liberate his country.

In 1807 Bolívar returned to Venezuela, and in 1808 the independence movement was launched, sparked by Napoleon's invasion of Spain, which weakened her authority over the colonies. On April 19, 1810, the Spanish governor Don Vincente Emparan was expelled, and a junta took charge in Caracas. Bolívar went to London in July to seek recognition and obtain arms, but England was more concerned with defeating Napoleon, and the mission failed. He did, however, induce the exiled revolutionary leader, Francisco de Miranda, to return and assume leadership of the independence movement. In March 1811 the national congress in Venezuela drafted a constitution, and on July 5, 1811, it declared independence. Bolívar entered the army and took command of Puerto Cabello, a vital port. As a result of betrayal by one of his officers, Puerto Cabello fell to the royalists after Bolívar was forced to retreat. Miranda then entered into negotiations with the Spanish commander-in-chief, Juan Domingo Monteverde, which led to the Treaty of San Mateo and capitulation by Miranda to the royalists.

On July 25, 1812, Bolívar, incensed at the "betrayal" by Miranda, had him delivered over to the Spanish. Miranda eventually died in a Spanish dungeon.

By the end of 1812 Venezuela had returned to the status of a Spanish colony. Determined to continue the revolution, Bolívar made his way to Cartagena in New Granada. There he published *El Manifesto de Cartagena*, in which he called for the destruction of Spanish power in Venezuela. To ensure the safety of New Granada, Venezuela had to be liberated. To this end Bolívar was named commander of an expeditionary force. In a lightning campaign of six battles Bolívar gained control of the Venezuelan capital on August 6, 1813. Upon his entry into Caracas he was proclaimed captain-general and given the title Liberator. The war was not over, however. In 1814 Bolívar was defeated by José Tomás Boves, a former pirate, at the Battle of La Puerta. Boves commanded an exceptionally effective cavalry which captured Caracas in July 1814 and ended the second Venezuelan republic.

Bolívar barely escaped to Jamaica*, where he wrote *La Carta de Jamaica*, in which he proposed the creation of constitutional republics throughout Latin America. He believed the legislative body should be created on the British model—hereditary upper house and an elective lower house. The executive should be a president chosen for life. Jamaica appeared unlikely to supply the resources needed to carry on the revolution, so the Liberator sailed to Haiti*. In Haiti Bolívar obtained the aid he needed from President Alexandre Sabes Petión. While Bolívar was in exile, General Pablo Morillo arrived in South America with the largest Spanish expeditionary force yet sent against the rebellious colonies. After three years of indecisive fighting, Bolívar moved his headquarters to the lower Orinoco River in 1817 where he recruited a patriot army which included many foreign soldiers and officers who had experience fighting Napoleon. He also gained the collaboration of José Antonio Páez, who was popular among the much feared llaneros, the horsemen of the plains. The llaneros were further won over with the promise of land and cattle. By establishing the Venezuelan congress at the revolutionary capital in Angostura in February 1819, Bolívar gave the patriot regime a legal basis. In his address to the congress, he outlined the system of government he would establish and again rejected political democracy.

In May 1819 Bolívar abandoned efforts to regain Caracas and instead turned westward to attack New Granada. He and his 2,500 men crossed the Andes, surprising the Spanish, who thought the mountain route was impassable. In the Battle of Boyacá on August 7, 1819, the royalist army surrendered and Bolívar marched into Bogotá on August 10. Leaving Francisco de Paula Santander to organize and administer the newly liberated territory, Bolívar went before the Angosturan congress to declare union of Venezuela, New Granada, and Quito* as the Republic of Colombia* (Gran Colombia). Two of its three provinces remained under the control of the royalists, however, and Bolívar returned to the struggle.

Recent events in Spain had confused the issues. A revolution had forced the king to recognize the ideas of liberalism and seek accommodation with the patriot movement. Bolívar concluded a six months armistice in November 1820, and when fighting resumed, he won a victory at the Battle of Carabobo in June 1821, which freed Venezuela and New Granada. That fall a constitution was drafted for Gran Colombia which proclaimed Bolívar president, but he had to continue his military campaign. With the assistance of Antonio José de Sucre, Bolívar trapped the Spanish in Ecuador*. On May 24, 1822, Sucre won a victory at Pinchincha, which freed Ecuador. With the incorporation of the Province of Quito into Gran Colombia, only Peru* remained in Spanish hands.

The problems of Peru brought Bolívar and José de San Martín* together on July 26, 1822, at Guayaquil. San Martín wanted military aid to defeat Spanish royalists entrenched in the highlands surrounding Lima. Because of differences over the nature of the future government, the meeting was a failure and San Martín returned to Lima, where he resigned and sailed for Europe. In September 1823 Bolívar arrived in Lima and in 1824 he moved against the royalist troops. At the Battle of Junin on August 24, Bolívar defeated the Spanish. The rest of the campaign was left to Sucre, who on December 9, 1824, defeated Spanish forces in the Battle of Ayacucho. By April 1825 he had ended the last royalist bastion in upper Peru, which was named Bolivia in honor of the Liberator.

Although Bolívar was at the height of his career, most South Americans did not share his continental views, but thought in terms of nation-states. In 1826 the Panama Congress convened with only Colombia, Peru, Central America, and Mexico sending delegates. They signed a treaty of alliance and created a biannual assembly to represent the federated states. In April 1826 civil war erupted between Páez in Venezuela and Santander in New Granada. Bolívar, determined to preserve Gran Colombia, appeased Páez by promising him a new constitution that would grant Venezuela a degree of independence. Thus reconciled, Páez recognized Bolívar as the supreme authority. After the failure of the 1828 convention in Ocaña to bind the many wounds of the union, Bolívar established a military dictatorship. After an attempt on his life in September 1828, Bolívar suspended liberal reforms. His dictatorship continued to provoke many minor revolts, including a civil war in Peru, and in 1829 a rebellion in Venezuela. Disheartened, Bolívar decided to sail for Europe, but remained when he learned that Sucre had been assassinated. The Liberator lived the remainder of his life on an estate near Santa Marta*, Colombia, where he died of tuberculosis on December 7, 1830. (Daniel F. O'Leary, *Bolivar and the War of Independence*, 1970; J. B. Trend, *Bolivar and the Independence of Spanish America*, 1951).

Michael Dennis

BOLIVIA. Bolivia's long and turbulent history has its roots in the colonial period with its clash of cultures, people, and social classes. What became known as Bolivia after independence was known as Upper Peru during this period. The territorial jurisdiction of this area was under the *audiencia* of Charcas with its seat in Chuquisaca (now Sucre). The *audiencia* was a part of the Viceroyalty of Peru until the late eighteenth century, when it became attached to the new Viceroyalty of the Río de la Plata.

Its discovery and conquest by Spain was made from two directions: north to south and from the east. The north to south conquest was begun after the Inca defeat in July 1535 by Diego de Almagro, an associate of Francisco Pizarro*. When this expedition returned from the *altiplano* to Lower Peru, Almagro rebelled, but was defeated and beheaded in 1538. That same year Pizarro sent an expedition to Charcas, or Upper Peru, which founded the towns of Chuquisaca and Porco near Potosí. The eastern expeditions came from the Rio de la Plata and had outposts in the Chiquitos and Mojos regions by the 1540s. They were forced to settle in the Santa Cruz region by the Lima and Cuzco groups. These regions, difficult to colonize because of the Indians there, provided agricultural products necessary for the mines.

In 1544 Francisco Pizarro revolted against the first Peruvian viceroy who tried to implement the New Laws. In 1545 the Potosí silver veins were discovered, and with Pizarro's defeat in 1548, its wealth attracted Spaniards who started the city as a mining camp. After the civil wars, La Paz, which became a commercial and agriculture center, was founded in the middle of the Aymara Indians. Other rebellions in the region occurred. On September 18, 1559, the *audiencia* of Charcas, installed in Chuquisaca, was established. The bishopric of La Plata, with its seat in Chuquisaca, was founded in 1552.

From 1569 to 1581, under Viceroy Francisco de Toledo, major changes occurred in the region. The declining Indian communities and the prevention of the development of a *criollo* nobility made Toledo pass laws to have existing *encomiendas* revert to the crown. The *mita* was reorganized to provide labor for the mines. Indian communities were put into *reducciones* and forced to pay tribute in specie, not in goods, forcing their participation in the Spanish market system. To increase silver production, Toledo introduced the mercury amalgam system, created a royal mint, and established a mining code. He founded new towns along the eastern frontier to control the Indians and provide agricultural products for the mines. Upper Peru became one of the richest jewels of the Spanish empire.

In the seventeenth century there were struggles between the *Vasconqados*, who came from Spain's Basque provinces and had political, social, and economic power in Potosí because of their control of mining, and the *cabildo* and the *Vicuñas*, composed of Castilians, Extremadurans, and *criollos*, who did not have any opportunities. The worst lasted from 1622–1625 and ended with the defeat of the *Vicuñas*, but animosity continued and was exacerbated by silver production declines in the middle of the century.

The seventeenth century was Chuquisaca's golden age, reflected by the establishment of a university in 1624, but silver production decline had profound effects. A growing population affected the relationship between the cities and supply networks as agricultural demand decreased. Cochabamba, a typical example, drifted into self-subsistence because its products were too costly to transport. Indian *mita* participation decreased, and a call for the system's abolishment was sounded. Revolts began near the end of the century. The Jesuits* explored and set up missions in the frontier regions. Potosí's position within the imperial system changed.

The eighteenth century began with regional decline. In 1730 a Cochabamba revolt, centered around the grievances of *mestizos* and *criollos* who resented their inclusion on tribute lists, failed but others followed. The Jesuit expulsion from the Spanish empire affected the frontier missions. On August 8, 1776, the Viceroyalty of Río de la Plata was created. It included the *audiencia* and had an impact on Upper Peru's trade patterns by shifting them from Lima to Buenos Aires. The powers of the *audiencia* were curtailed, and administrators arrived to stimulate silver production and economic growth.

The Tupac Amuru* rebellion of 1780–82 had a profound impact on everyone. The rebellion was fueled by the Indians' dissatisfaction with the tribute demands of the *corregidor* and *hacendado*. They were led by their *kurakas* (Indian nobility) who resented the decline of their privileges and attacks on their religious beliefs. Beginning in Lower Peru, it spread to Upper Peru, where it continued as people from all social and ethnic classes became involved against the Spanish. La Paz was put under siege by the rebels, and other regions were engulfed in violence. After defeat of the rebels, the *corregimientos* were abolished and the *kuraka* class destroyed, with Spaniards put in their places to rule directly over the Indians. Although destruction of lives and property was great, population and economic production had reached pre-rebellion levels by the late 1780s.

In 1784 intendancies replaced the *audiencias* in La Paz, Cochabamba, Potosí, and Chuquisaca. In the 1790s silver production was disrupted as mercury shipments from Spain failed to arrive. Besides a general crisis in mining, agricultural production suffered and epidemics occurred at the beginning of the nineteenth century. The economy went into severe depression. On May 25, 1809, a rebellion in Chuquisaca was the harbinger of independence. The initial revolt led to one in La Paz on July 16, 1809, under the leadership of Pedro Domingo Murillo. On July 27, independence was declared; Royalist forces from Peru and Buenos Aires invaded Upper Peru, crushed the rebellion, and executed its leaders on January 10, 1810. Events moved quickly when Buenos Aires declared independence on May 25. The *Audiencia*, in royalist hands, returned to the Viceroyalty of Peru. New rebellions occurred in the principal cities. Between 1810–1817, four Argentine expeditionary forces invaded Upper Peru to liberate it but were defeated. Internally, the struggle for independence was carried on by the *republiquitas*, irregular guerrilla units representing the popular forces, which harassed the royalists.

In 1823 absolutism was once more installed in Spain and, in early 1824, General Pedro Antonio Olaneta, a royalist and conservative was in control of Upper Peru. He had opposed Spain's previous liberal regime, breaking with Viceroy La Serna, a liberal, and declaring himself head of Upper Peru. La Serna had sent a force against him but signed the Treaty of Tarapaca on March 9 when he realized Olaneta's strength. In Peru, forces of Simón Bolívar won the Battle of Ayacucho on December 9 but Olaneta, not recognizing the royalist surrender, remained in control of Upper Peru. On April 1, 1825, his troops rebelled in Tumusula and he was shot by his own men. On August 6, 1825, Bolivia declared its independence. (Charles Arnade, *Bolivian History*, 1984; Herbert S. Klein, *Bolivia: The Evolution of a Multi-Ethnic Society*, 1982; Huberto Vásquez Machicado, José de Mesa, and Teresa Gilbert, *Manuel de Historia de Bolivia*, 1983.)

Carlos Pérez

BOMBAY. Bombay, with its unrivaled, sheltered harbor of 70 square miles, is India's largest seaport. After taking Goa* in 1510, the Portuguese moved closer and closer to Bombay, eventually taking control of the city in 1534. In 1661 Great Britain took control of Bombay as part of Portugal's dowry for the marriage of Princess Catherine of Braganza to Charles II. Britain passed title to Bombay to the British East India Company* in 1668. It reverted to Crown control in 1858, by which time it was a major depot for South Asian and Indian Ocean trade. (Peter Kemp, *The Oxford Companion to Ships and the Sea*, 1976.)

BONAIRE. See NETHERLANDS ANTILLES.

BONIN ISLANDS. See OGASAWARA ISLANDS.

BORNEO. Borneo, the third largest island in the world (287,000 square miles), located between the South China Sea, Java Sea, and Celebes Sea. It has never been politically unified. Three fourths of its area and population are contained in Indonesian Kalimantan, the former Dutch Borneo. The north and northwest coasts were colonized by Britain. Borneo is one of the world's last great tracts of unspoiled wilderness. Jungle covers 75 percent of the island; less than 2 percent is farmed. The interior has many mountain ranges. Rivers flowing from them have gradual gradients in their middle courses; they overflow in the rainy season, creating vast swamps. There are almost no roads, nor has anyone tried to build a railroad. Inland towns are small and only three coastal towns have grown to notable size: Pontianak in the west, Bandjarmasin in the south, and Balikpapan in the east. These are the only good ports in Kalimantan, for Borneo rises from a shallow sea, and much of the coast is lined with mangrove swamp.

The indigenous population is divided between coastal groups (Javanese, Malays, Bugis) and upland tribes. The latter live along riverbanks or else grow rice, corn, or cassava by the swidden method. Some tribes hunt with blowguns and fish with poison. It is not surprising that Europeans stayed near the coast. Jungle vines, wild animals, stinging insects, and headhunters were bad enough, but tropical diseases (elephantiasis, smallpox, malaria, dysentery, cholera, and intestinal worms) were worse. A Dutch explorer, A. W. Nieuwenhuis, is thought to have been the first white man to penetrate the interior in the 1890s. Large areas have not been surveyed yet.

Kalimantan's coastal towns have a colorful history. Islam had just been adopted by people along the north coast of the Java Sea when the Portuguese and Dutch came at the turn of the seventeenth century seeking spices. The Dutch experience was particularly discouraging. They established a trading post at Bandjarmasin in 1603, but a ship's entire crew was massacred in 1607. Other early contacts with Sambas and Sukadana were equally short-lived. The persistent Dutch convinced the Sultan of Bandjarmasin to sign another trade agreement in 1635, but rebels killed more than a hundred Dutchmen in 1638. The Dutch were interested in Bandjarmasin solely for its strategic value: it could be used as a base against Makassarese and Buginese pirates. After the Makassarese submitted in 1669, the Dutch abandoned Bandjarmasin, only to see it occupied by the British (1698). The Dutch tried again, constructing a factory in 1747 but abandoning it in 1809. While this fitful relationship sputtered along, Hakka Chinese had begun moving to the southwest coast of Borneo, at Sambas, where they worked gold and diamond deposits, alarming both the sultan and the Dutch. Dutch military expeditions against the Hakkas commenced in 1818, and continued for more than 30 years.

The Dutch had very limited aims in Kalimantan; they only wanted to deny the use of Bornean ports to native or European rivals. No one thought seriously about trying to open up the forbidding interior. Most of Borneo remained outside the control of any foreign power. The sultans of Pontianak, Mampawah, Sambas, Bandjarmasin, Tarakan, Balikpapan, and Kutai still ruled their domains. One last bitter war with Bandjarmasin was fought from 1859 to 1863. Dutch control was thereafter more or less uncontested. Dutch interest in Kalimantan was then quickened by two factors. The British were carving out colonies in Sarawak* and Sabah* on the north coast of Borneo. An 1891 Anglo-Dutch treaty defined their respective territories. Also, oil was discovered in eastern Borneo. A company that evolved into Royal Dutch Shell was formed in 1898. Drilling doubled output from 1901 to 1904, and a pipeline was built.

There was no nationalist sentiment on Borneo before World War II*. Japanese treatment of Europeans, Chinese, and Bornean natives was even more brutal than elsewhere in Indonesia*. The Dayaks rose against Japanese control but were efficiently slaughtered. After the war Kalimantan was briefly incorporated into Holland's last foothold in Southeast Asia, the Republic of Eastern Indonesia. In 1949 it became part of independent Indonesia. (J. J. Van Klavern, *The Dutch Colonial System in the East Indies*, 1953.)

Ross Marlay

BOTHA, LOUIS. Louis Botha was born on September 27, 1862, near Greytown, Natal*. In 1884 he joined an expedition led by Lukas Meyer to restore the Zulu king Dinizulu to the throne. In return Botha received a grant of land. In August 1884 he helped to create the New Republic. Although his formal education was limited, he displayed a unique ability to lead. In the New Republic Botha served as one of the land commissioners. In 1885 Botha married Annie

Emmet, built a farm in Vryheid, and began to raise a family. When the New Republic became part of the South African Republic* in July 1888, Botha held a number of political positions before becoming the member from Vryheid in the Transvaal* Volksraad. Politically, Botha was a moderate, siding with those who opposed President Paul Kruger's hostile policy toward *Uitlanders* (non-Boers). On October 9, 1899, when Kruger issued an ultimatum to the British government, which meant war, Botha and six others voted against the measure.

With the outbreak of war, Botha joined Lukas Meyer's commandos as a Field Cornet in the Transvaal army under the supreme command of Petrus Jacobus Joubert. On November 15, Botha captured a British armored train, and among his prisoners was the young Winston Churchill*. In late November Joubert was thrown from his horse and had to be sent to Pretoria for recovery. Botha was appointed acting assistant general. At the battle of Colenso in December, Botha demonstrated his genius for defensive strategy in his victory over a vastly superior enemy. On March 27, 1900, General Joubert died, and Botha took over complete command of the Transvaal forces. On June 5 Pretoria surrendered as the British began to gain the upper hand, and after the battle of Dalmanutha on June 11–13, Botha dispersed his forces to carry on guerrilla warfare. Botha met with Lord Kitchener at Middleberg in March 1901 for negotiations which eventually led to the signing of the Peace of Vereeniging on May 31, 1902. Among the provisions of the treaty was a promise to eventually grant South Africa self-government.

With the war over, Botha returned to politics, becoming chairman of a new party—the *Het Volk* (The People). When the Transvaal was granted self-government in 1907, Botha was chosen prime minister. In 1908 a national convention was held in Durban to unite the four territories of Transvaal, Orange Free State,* Natal, and Cape Colony.* Botha was instrumental in establishing a unitary form of government instead of a federation, in maintaining the political color bar, and in making Pretoria the executive capital of the Union of South Africa*.

In the first election, Botha's South Africa Party captured 67 out of 121 seats, and on May 31, 1910, Botha became the first prime minister of the Union of South Africa. His chief aim was to bring about a conciliatory policy between Boers and Britons. He wanted a merging of the two language groups into a single white South Africa within the British Empire*. Botha's policy of merging two cultures, and his ties to the British, caused a split in his party led by J. B. M. Hertzog, who favored a "two-stream" policy which would preserve Afrikaner culture and national identity. By 1912 the differences had become so great that an open split occurred. Botha resigned and formed a new government that excluded Hertzog. During the years 1913–1914 Botha was plagued with labor unrest in the railway and mining industries. Because the strikes crippled the country's trade and commerce, Botha was forced to take more drastic action. Using an old law that allowed the government to deport Boer rebels, he had the labor leaders arrested and deported to England. With their leaders gone, the strike ended. Botha also had to deal with Mohandas Gandhi*, who used his technique of passive civil disobedience to protest legislation restricting the movement of Indians and Indian immigration.

The differences between Botha and the Afrikaner nationalists were exacerbated during World War I when he acceded to a request by the British government to conquer German Southwest Africa*. Although the rebellion of 1914–1915 was frowned upon by Hertzog and his Nationalist Party, it was fueled by Afrikaners who saw the war as an opportunity to restore Boer independence. Not wanting to make race an issue, Botha declined to use British troops and relied upon Boer volunteers to put down the rebellion. Botha then personally led the campaign that defeated the Germans in South West Africa in July 1915. After the war Botha participated in the 1919 Versailles Peace Conference, where he advocated leniency for the former enemies. On August 27, 1919, Louis Botha died in Pretoria. (Harold Spencer, *General Botha: The Career and the Man*, 1916; Thomas Pakenham, *The Boer War*, 1979.)

Michael Dennis

BOTSWANA. See BECHUANALAND.

BOUGAINVILLE, LOUIS ANTOINE DE. The French navigator Louis Bougainville was born on November 11, 1729, in Paris. He was educated in the law but became a soldier and then secretary to the ambassador to London where he published his *Traite du calcul integral* in 1756 and was accepted as a member of the Royal Academy. He served with Montcalm in the French and Indian War*. After the war Bougainville was commissioned to conduct France's first around-the-world sea expedition. On December 5, 1766, he left Brest, France, stopped at Rio de Janeiro, and passed through the Strait of Magellan into the Pacific. He discovered several Tuamotuan islands and on April 2, 1768, anchored on the eastern side of the island of Tahiti*. Bougainville claimed the island for France, not knowing that the English navigator Samuel Wallis had just been there. After visiting several other Pacific islands, he returned home. He later took part in the American Revolution under the command of the Count de Grasse. Napoleon named him senator and then count. He died on August 31, 1811, in Paris. (Charles la Conciere, *A la gloire de Bougainville*, 1942).

BOUGAINVILLE. Bougainville, also known as North Solomons, is a large, copper-rich island in the Solomon Islands*. Bougainville came under German control in 1882, and German sovereignty was confirmed in 1899 when Bougainville was declared part of German New Guinea*. British and Australian forces seized the island in 1914 when World War I* erupted, and Bougainville remained Australian territory, part of Papua New Guinea*. When Australia* granted independence to Papua New Guinea in 1975, a secessionist movement in Bougainville, led by Leo Hannett and John Morris, demanded independence of their own. Ethnically, the dark-skinned Bougainvillians are part of the Solomon Islands, not New Guinea. They also felt that their rich copper mines were simply being exploited by outsiders. Although the secessionist movement did not succeed in the 1970s, the Bougainville nationalists remained a serious political problem for Papua New Guinea. (Ralph R. Premdas, "Ethno-nationalism, Copper, and Secession in Bougainville," *Canadian Review of Studies in Nationalism*, Spring 1977, 247–65.)

BOXER REBELLION. The Boxer Rebellion, which erupted in China* in 1900, was based on anti-foreign and anti-Christian sentiments. In an edict issued in November 1899, the Empress Dowager Tz'u Hsi ordered officials throughout the country to resist foreign aggression. The Boxers themselves were members of a secret society known in Chinese as *I-ho Ch'uan* meaning "Righteous and Harmonious Fists" or simply in English, "Boxers." They were called "Boxers" by Westerners because they included a boxing-like dance in their ceremonies. They held the fanatical belief that they had been endowed with powers that would protect them from physical harm in battle. It was a very old society that expanded rapidly in 1898, especially in the impoverished provinces of Chihli and Shantung.

When false rumors spread that foreigners had been expelled from Peking, anti-foreign emotions escalated. In the autumn of 1899 the Boxers began to persecute Christians in the Shantung Peninsula. Local government officials encouraged the Boxers. These activities aroused the British, who protested, but the persecutions continued and grew worse. Early in 1900 the imperial court began to encourage the Boxers to organize more units. Clearly the Boxers were anxious to cause trouble for the foreigners. Missionaries were attacked and missionary property was looted and vandalized. Following vigorous protests from the legations in the capital, the Chinese government issued orders to protect foreigners, missionaries, and Chinese Christians. At the same time, however, the throne issued secret instructions that encouraged the anti-foreign movement.

The xenophobic Tz'u Hsi, receiving advice from such anti-foreign members of the imperial court as Grand Eunuch Li Lien-ying, made the fateful decision to form an alliance between the Boxers and the Chinese army to expel foreigners. On June 11, 1900, a secretary of the Japanese legation was killed. Following the seizure of Peking by the Boxers on June 13, Baron von Kettler, the German minister, was murdered on the 20th. On June 21 the Chinese government declared war on the foreign powers. The legations were under siege and cut off from the outside world.

The Empress Dowager and her advisers seemed to perceive the extreme vulnerability of China's position as the court pursued the ambivalent policy of concurrently making war and hinting at a peaceful solution. The diplomatic compounds in Peking, although protected by only 533 defenders, were able to hold out despite repeated attacks by thousands of Boxers and regular Chinese troops. International military units moved out of Tientsin on August 4 to rescue the legations. Chinese forces were defeated on the 6th in a battle at Yangtsun; on August 12 Tungchow fell to the advancing forces. On August 14 the foreign armies captured Peking and lifted the eight-week siege of the legations. In the course of the rebellion a total of 242 missionaries and civilians had been murdered by the Boxers.

When the international forces occupied Peking, the Imperial Court immediately fled from the capital. Accompanied by the Emperor and a few members of the royal household, Tz'u Hsi made Sianfu, the capital of Shensi province, her temporary headquarters. The court returned to Peking on January 7, 1902, four months after the final terms of the peace settlement had been reached. Diplomats representing Austria, Belgium, France, Germany, Great Britain, Italy, Japan, Spain, Russia, the United States, and the Netherlands submitted the following demands as a basis for opening negotiations with the Chinese. First, the main culprits, as designated by the representatives of the powers, were to be punished; second, the ban against the importation of arms would be maintained; third, appropriate indemnities would be assessed; fourth, provision would be made for instituting a permanent legation guard in Peking; fifth, the forts at Taku were to be dismantled; sixth, foreign military occupation of two or three points on the road from the capital to the sea would be conceded to guarantee that the legations would never again be cut off from outside help. After a period of negotiations, the Chinese representatives agreed to terms essentially in accord with these demands, and on September 7, 1901, a protocol was signed ending the conflict.

The indemnity, supposedly based on what the powers had calculated China could afford to pay, was set at the ruinously high figure of 450,000,000 taels, or $330,900,000. If China elected to pay in installments, which of course she would have to do, there would be an interest charge of 4 percent per year on the unpaid balance. Payments were to be made in gold, although China was prohibited from collecting tariff duties in gold. Considering all aspects, the indemnity totaled almost one billion taels, or approximately $650,000,000. To insure that the indemnity, as well as previous debts, would be paid, it was further stipulated that the Chinese government would adopt financial reforms acceptable to the powers. In effect, these arrangements gave control of China's finances to the powers for the next thirty-nine years. The Manchu dynasty did not last long after the humiliating settlement. A decade after the signing of the protocol a revolution began that swept away the old imperial system. (O. Edmund Clubb, *Twentieth Century China*, 1964; John A. Harrison, *China Since 1800*, 1967; George Nye Steiger, *China and the Occident: The Origin and Development of the Boxer Movement*, 1966.)

Walter A. Sutton and Roy E. Thoman

BRAZIL. Colonial Brazil must be viewed in the wider context of European and Portuguese overseas expansion in the fifteenth and sixteenth centuries. European powers reached out to Africa, India, and Asia, eager to tap the rich commerce available there. Portugal first ventured seaward under the leadership of Prince Henry (1394–1460), christened "the Navigator" by an appreciative English writer. By 1488 Bartolomeu Dias had rounded the Cape of Good Hope and the

Portuguese were soon deeply involved in a commercial empire stretching the length of the Indian Ocean and beyond. Under the leadership of Affonso d'Albuquerque, governor of India* (1509–1515), the Portuguese extended their commercial control over the Indian Ocean sea routes. In these early decades of the sixteenth century, the Portuguese were mainly interested in establishing commercial footholds, with an emphasis on trade, not settlements. As a result of such enterprises, a small nation exerted an enormous influence over the developing world system of the sixteenth century through its factories, trading forts, and commercial agents.

The discoveries of Columbus* in the 1490s created a dispute between Portugal and Spain which was settled by the Treaty of Tordesillas of 1494*, granting Portugal a large part of the eastern coast of South America. In early 1500 Pedro Alvares Cabral* left Portugal with a large fleet bound for India to exploit the earlier discoveries of Vasco da Gama*. During the voyage Cabral sailed further west in the Atlantic than intended and made landfall on the Brazilian coast in April. However, the discovery was greeted with no great enthusiasm at home, as the commercial empire in the East commanded far keener attention. In the years after 1500, sporadic Portuguese voyages to Brazil uncovered no great Amerindian empires and no vast treasures to be plundered. In fact, the only item of commercial value discovered was the bark of a native tree—brazilwood—which was processed into a valuable commercial dye.

It was this dyewood that forced the Portuguese to guard their possession more closely. French corsairs regularly visited the coast of Brazil in the years 1502–1530, bartering trade goods with Tupi-Guarani people for the red bark found in abundance along the coast. After years of complaining in vain to the French monarch, Portugal sent Martim Afonso da Souza with five ships and 400 men to found permanent settlements in Brazil in 1532. Along the southern coast, they built the town of São Vicente*, near the modern port city of Santos.

Although São Vicente was a success, it soon became clear that other settlements must follow to effectively control the vast Brazilian coast. The Portuguese king began to offer large grants to those with the means to undertake colonization of the new land, and by 1536 fifteen huge grants, called captaincies, existed, extending from the northern Amazon coast to the border of present-day Uruguay*. Most of these captaincies failed due to lack of population, adverse conditions for agriculture, and constant attacks by hostile Indians and corsairs.

However, two of the hereditary grants did succeed. In Pernambuco,* on the northeastern coast, Duarte Coelho achieved great success through the cultivation of sugarcane, tobacco, and cotton. He avoided conflict with local Indians and soon had over fifty sugar mills processing cane. By the 1580s his heirs were sending hundreds of sugar ships annually to Europe and were among the wealthiest of all Portuguese. The captaincy at São Vicente also flourished with sugar and reported six mills by mid-century. The others languished, however, and the king soon instituted changes. In 1549 he sent Tome da Souza as the first governor-general of Brazil. Salvador da Bahia, a major disappointment as a captaincy, became the seat of a new central administration and the king committed one thousand soldiers and artisans to ensure the success of da Souza.

In the years that followed sugar quickly became the dominant agricultural enterprise and Brazilian producers supplied the insatiable European markets. A pattern of monoculture, heavily dependent upon fickle world markets, was set in place in Brazil. Sugar was followed by gold and diamonds in the early eighteenth century, coffee and cotton in the nineteenth century, and rubber in the early twentieth century. The prosperity of the colony and its development was tied to the fortunes of its export products. This is a trend that has bedeviled Brazil throughout its history.

One serious problem Tome da Souza and his successors faced was the need for a steady, reliable source of labor. Local Amerindians at first supplied these needs, but as plantations grew in size and complexity, they could no longer fill the demand. Harsh working conditions, susceptibility to European diseases, and a lack of Crown officials to supervise Indian-Portuguese relations led to a disastrous decline in Amerindian numbers. Despite attempts by Portuguese Jesuits* such as Manoel da Nobrega, and official policy that forbade exploitation, mortality rates as high as 80 percent were recorded in many areas in the sixteenth century. Survivors fled to the interior, although they were hunted by slave-catching expeditions for another century.

The continuing labor problem led to the importation of Africans in large numbers after 1550. More than 3.5 million Africans came to Brazil in the next three centuries. A racial heritage of African, Amerindian, and European mixtures grew out of the institution of plantation agriculture. Labor conditions remained harsh, and slaves imported to the sugar areas of northeastern Brazil or to the developing center-south region, with its mineral resources and cattle ranches, often survived less than a decade. The colony had its share of slave revolts, with runaway slaves at times forming refugee communities in the interior. The famous slave republic, or *quilombo*, known as Palmares, appeared in 1603 and eventually encompassed a dozen villages spread over a 100-square mile area. Palmares survived nearly a century.

As the eighteenth century began, local and international events altered the path of Brazilian development. Northeastern Brazil began a long and serious decline as its grip on the world sugar market loosened and then faded completely. In 1630 the Dutch West India Company invaded the northeast and held it for nearly a quarter century. Although ultimately expelled, the Dutch took the valuable knowledge of sugar production with them to the Caribbean. Within fifty years, rival European colonies were out-producing Brazil and had captured three-fourths of its sugar business.

This unfortunate turn was partially saved by the discovery of gold in the center-south region known as Minas Gerais* in 1693. Thirty-four years later, a major diamond strike occurred there, drawing population and commerce from the northeast and leading, along with increased Portuguese interest in the Plate River region (present-day Uruguay), to the establishment of Rio de Janeiro* as the colonial capital in 1763. Although the mineral cycle played out within a half-century, it did spark economic development in Brazil's southern regions. The cattle industry began producing large herds after the mineral discoveries and soon extended from the northeast interior to the extreme south.

The ironic situation of a small Atlantic kingdom governing a huge Latin American colony became more apparent as the nineteenth century began. By 1800 Brazil possessed a handful of small port cities and a few mining centers, with its remaining population dispersed over a two-thousand mile frontier. The masters of large plantations and cattle ranches governed themselves, and Portuguese royal authority was confined to the small urban centers. In the interests of tightening control, Portuguese ministers, such as the capable Marquis de Pombal, instituted new regulations in the 1760s and 1770s that strengthened the mother country's hold, but Brazil was too large and geographically diverse for the small number of Portuguese officials to govern it. Moreover, Brazilians were affected by the new fiscal policies and chafed under restrictions that favored Portuguese interests over their own. There were several abortive revolts in the 1780s and 1790s.

The decisive revolution began in 1807 when Napoleon invaded the Iberian peninsula. The result for Portugal was the improbable escape of the regent, Dom João (later João VI), and thousands of his royal retinue, courtesy of an English fleet, to Brazil. João remained in Brazil until 1821, long after Napoleon's defeat and the restoration of Portuguese independence. He and his family enjoyed life in the colony and their presence brought prosperity and a closer connection with Europe. The eager purveyors of European goods to the now suddenly elevated colony (João decreed Brazil a kingdom co-equal with Portugal in 1815) were the English. They flooded Brazil with all manner of formerly scarce merchandise and eagerly bought raw materials. When a political crisis in Portugal forced João's hand in 1821, he returned to claim his throne, but left his son Pedro behind as regent. When the Portuguese cortes formally attempted to abrogate Brazil's new status and demanded the return of the popular young prince, Pedro refused, and with the backing of the Brazilian elite, he declared the country independent on September 7, 1822. After several months of slight resistence, Pedro became Brazil's constitutional emperor. Brazil retained an emperor until 1889, when a mild revolution created a republic. (E. Bradford Burns, *A History of Brazil*, 1984; C. R. Boxer, *The Golden Age of Brazil*, 1967.)

Craig Hendricks

BRITISH COLUMBIA. British Columbia is the western-most province of the nation of Canada.* The first European ''discovery'' of British Columbia occurred in 1774 when Juan Pérez Hernández, sailing for Spain, explored that part of the Pacific coast of America as far north as the Queen Charlotte Islands. In 1778 Captain James Cook*, on a voyage in search of a Northwest Passage*, anchored and repaired his ships in Nootka Sound on the west side of Vancouver Island. As a consequence of knowledge gained from Cook's visit, British merchants soon arrived by sea and began to engage in a lucrative trade with coastal Indian tribes for sea-otter pelts to be exchanged for tea at Canton*. Spanish and Russian traders also became active in the area, competing with the British. In 1789 the Spanish, who claimed a monopoly of the entire Pacific coast and waters, seized three British merchant ships at Nootka Sound. The ensuing crisis, known as the Nootka Sound Controversy, almost led to war between Britain and Spain, but was resolved in the early 1790s by agreements that recognized the right of British subjects to trade and settle on any part of the northwest coast of North America not effectively occupied by Spain. The thorough exploration and charting of the coast of northwest America, including the circumnavigation of Vancouver Island by Lt. George Vancouver in 1792–1794, further strengthened British claims in the region.

At the same time, fur traders of the North West Company began to traverse the mainland interior of British Columbia. Alexander Mackenzie crossed the Rockies and reached the Pacific shore at Bella Coola inlet in 1793. Simon Fraser explored the central interior highlands, which he called New Caledonia, early in the nineteenth century and descended to the mouth of the Fraser River in 1808. David Thompson in 1811 followed the Columbia River to the ocean. The fur trade posts established by the North West Company in that period became the first permanent settlements in the future province.

Following the merger of the North West Company with the Hudson's Bay Company* in 1821, it fell upon the Bay Company to maintain British rule in the vast fur trade area west of the Rocky Mountains. But the arrival of American settlers in the Oregon country in the 1830s and the subsequent dispute over conflicting territorial claims between the United States and Great Britain undermined the authority of the company in the southern part of its domain. In anticipation of the diplomatic resolution of the Oregon question—that is, the loss of the Oregon Territory—the Hudson's Bay Company in 1843 established its headquarters at Fort Victoria on Vancouver Island. In 1849 Vancouver Island was declared a British crown colony, and in 1851 James Douglas, an official of the company, was named governor. Douglas—the "Father of British Columbia"—upon instructions from the British government established an elected assembly for Vancouver Island in 1856.

The discovery of gold along the Fraser River in 1857 resulted in a gold rush to the mainland, especially from the California goldfields. In order to control the influx of American miners and preserve British authority, Great Britain created the separate mainland colony of British Columbia in 1858, the name "New Caledonia" having been taken already by a French possession in the South Pacific. James Douglas carried on as governor of both Vancouver Island and the new colony.

In 1866, after the gold rush had come to an end, Vancouver Island was joined to the colony of British Columbia for the purpose of reducing government expenses. Confronted with grave financial difficulties, the enlarged province of British Columbia weighed the possibilities of union with the new Dominion of

Canada or union with the United States. Rejecting annexation to the United States, British Columbia entered the Canadian Confederation in 1871 on the promise that the Dominion would complete the construction of a transcontinental railway to the Pacific within two years. The Canadian Pacific Railroad was not open for through trains from Montreal to the village of Vancouver on the Pacific coast until 1886. (J. Lewis Robinson, *British Columbia*, 1973.)

Robert Shadle

BRITISH COMMONWEALTH OF NATIONS. The British Commonwealth of Nations, today known as the Commonwealth of Nations, is a group of 50 independent nations—Great Britain and most of her former colonies—tied together in a voluntary political association. Membership in the Commonwealth imposes no legal or constitutional obligations on participating countries, only the right to consult widely with other Commonwealth nations on matters of mutual concern. The Queen is the acknowledged head of the Commonwealth, and the Commonwealth Secretariat is the coordinating body for the political association.

The British Commonwealth of Nations traces its origins back to 1839 when John George Lampton, the Earl of Durham, issued a report to parliament explaining the nature of the political unrest in Canada. At the time there was a great deal of concern in Great Britain that Canada* and perhaps other colonies would follow the lead of the thirteen British North American colonies and launch revolutionary rebellions against the empire. Lord Durham recommended that the governor of Canada appoint only ministers who had the confidence of the Canadian assembly and that Great Britain extend self-government to Canada, except in foreign relations and a few other areas. This notion of "responsible government" was extended first to Canada (the British North American Provinces) and then to Australia*, South Africa*, New Zealand*, the Irish Free State, and Newfoundland*.

During World War I*, British officials first began using the term "commonwealth" to describe the relationship between Great Britain, Canada, Australia, South Africa, and New Zealand. At the Treaty of Versailles* negotiations in 1919, the "dominions" of Canada, Australia, New Zealand, and South Africa were permitted to sign the treaty separately and join the League of Nations* as independent entities. A Dominion Office was established in 1925 to direct Britain's relations with the self-governing nations of the Empire, and the Imperial Conference of 1926* further defined the status of the dominions when A. J. Balfour proclaimed that dominion governments could pass legislation that was inconsistent with British laws and that Britain had no power to enforce its laws in a dominion without its consent. Voluntary allegiance, not compulsion, was the operating feature of the Commonwealth. In 1931 parliament passed the Statute of Westminister, which gave the British Commonwealth of Nations its legal status.

Since World War II* most former British colonies have elected to become part of the Commonwealth upon gaining their independence. In addition to Canada, Australia, South Africa, New Zealand, the Irish Free State, and Newfoundland, the following countries joined the Commonwealth: India* (August 15, 1947); Sri Lanka* (February 4, 1948); Ghana* (March 6, 1957); Malaysia* (August 31, 1957); Cyprus* (March 13, 1961); Nigeria* (October 1, 1960); Sierra Leone (April 27, 1961); Tanganyika* (December 9, 1961), Zanzibar* (December 10, 1963), United Republic of Tanganyika and Zanzibar (April 26, 1964), which was renamed Tanzania* (October 29, 1964); Jamaica* (August 6, 1962); Trinidad* and Tobago* (August 31, 1962); Uganda* (October 9, 1962); Kenya* (December 12, 1963); Malawi* (July 6, 1964); Malta* (September 21, 1964); Zambia* (October 24, 1964); Gambia* (February 18, 1965); Singapore* (August 9, 1965); Guyana* (May 26, 1966); Botswana (September 30, 1966); Lesotho (October 4, 1966); Barbados* (November 30, 1966); Nauru* (January 31, 1968); Mauritius* (March 12, 1968); Swaziland* (September 6, 1968); Tonga* (June 4, 1970); Western Samoa* (August 28, 1970); Fiji* (October 10, 1970); Bangladesh (April 18, 1972); Bahamas* (July 10, 1973); Grenada* (February 7, 1974); Papua New Guinea* (September 16, 1975); Seychelles* (June 29, 1976); Solomon Islands* (July 7, 1978); Tuvalu (October 1, 1978); Dominica* (November 3, 1978); St. Lucia* (February 22, 1979); Kiribati* (July 12, 1979); St. Vincent and the Grenadines* (October 27, 1979); Zimbabwe* (April 18, 1980); Vanuatu (July 30, 1980); Belize* (September 21, 1981); Antigua* and Barbuda* (November 1, 1981); Maldives* (July 9, 1982); St. Kitts and Nevis* (September 18, 1983); Brunei* (January 1, 1984); and Namibia (March 21, 1990). There are also 15 remaining dependent territories of Great Britain: Anguilla*; Bermuda*; British Antarctic Territory; British Indian Ocean Territory*; British Virgin Islands*; Cayman Islands; Falkland Islands*; Gibraltar*; Hong Kong*; Montserrat*; Pitcairn Islands*; Ducie, Henderson, and Oeno; South Georgia and the South Sandwich Islands; St. Helena*; Dependencies (Ascension, Tristan da Cunha*); and the Turks and Caicos Islands*. When Newfoundland voluntarily surrendered her dominion status in 1933 to become directly administered by Great Britain, she ceased to be a member of the Commonwealth. Four nations over the years have left the Commonwealth: Ireland* (1949), South Africa* (1961), Pakistan* (1972), and Fiji (1987). (W. David McIntyre, *The Commonwealth of Nations. Origins and Impact, 1869–1971*, 1977.)

BRITISH EAST AFRICA. See KENYA.

BRITISH EAST INDIA COMPANY. For much of the sixteenth century, the Indian Ocean was, for all intents and purposes, a Portuguese lake. The lucrative spice trade in Southeast Asia was dominated by Portugal, which in fact provided a model for Great Britain's later imperial rule in India—particularly with respect to (1) control of strategic routes to India, (2) use of factories (warehouses) to secure goods on a year-round basis; and (3) the use of subsidiary alliances to gain cooperation of native princes. But Portuguese power declined as the century neared its end, and the coup de grace came when the Portuguese Kingdom was annexed to Spain in 1580. The defeat of the Spanish Armada in 1588 signaled Holland and England that the road lay open for a new Eastern adventure.

On December 31, 1600, Queen Elizabeth I extended monopoly rights for all trade with the "Indies" (between the Cape of Good Hope and Magellan), for fifteen years, and allowed the twenty four "Committees" (Directors) to export 30,000 specie for each voyage. This initial effort, however, was by comparison less than one-tenth of its soon to be rival, the Dutch East India Company (VOC) founded in 1602. Initially the Protestant powers, England and Holland, cooperated to break the Iberian presence and, in fact, the company turned an average profit of 170 percent on each of its first voyages. The East India Company also established its presence at the Mughal court through various embassies (Captain William Hawkins and Sir Thomas Roe), which led to Mughal recognition of an English factory at Surat in western India.

In 1623 the Dutch effectively expelled the English from Southeast Asia, and India became the company's chief theater of activity in Asia. By the end of the seventeenth century, the company set up a tripod of bases on the periphery of the Mughal empire in Calcutta, Madras and Bombay, destined to become the great colonial port cities of the Raj. The company traded in bulk, and had to operate within the constraints of Mughal demands for silver vis-a-vis Britain's prevailing mercantilist philosophy (requiring minimum export of specie). To solve this dilemma, the company engaged in a triangular trade involving limited amount of specie for Indian cotton goods and indigo, then traded for spices from Southeast Asia, and then sold for profit at home. The company also developed opium for export and it became the basis for the Anglo-Chinese tea trade.

The East India Company at home was not immune to the gyrations of English politics in the turbulent seventeenth century. King Charles I encouraged a rival company, and under the protectorate of Oliver Cromwell, virtual free trade operated until 1657. The Company, however, survived these events and the Restoration and Glorious Revolution too, until in 1708–1709 all rival entities were merged into the original company.

While the Mughal Empire declined in the first half of the eighteenth century, the Company limited its disputes with the Mughals to dialogue over trade. But the East India Company was aware of a growing French presence in India (first established in 1664), which had located itself proximate to the Company's key India bases. Contextually, Anglo-French rivalry worldwide for Empire was also played-out in India between 1740–63. Legendary figures such as Joseph Francios Dupliex, and Robert Clive* emerged at this time. Each company discovered that it could effectively intervene in local politics through subsidiary alliances, and by employing regularly drilled and armed Indian sepoys, could contest even vastly superior Indian armies. While most of the contests (eventually won by the English) occured in the south, a major "revolution" unfolded in Bengal,* by far the wealthiest Indian province.

Following the famous "Black Hole of Calcutta"* incident, Clive made a daring move on Bengal and, with careful planning, achieved a military victory at Plassey in 1756. Several year later, the Company bahadur ("Valiant" or "Exalted" Company) accepted the Diwani from the Mughals, attaining legitimization as the official tax collector of the Mughals. However, the period of unbridled Nabobism, during which individual company men made their fortunes while those of the company declined, finally prompted Parliament to intervene in the company's affairs. Lord Cornwallis was sent to India in 1784 to put the company on a proper footing, and progressively, through acts of Parliament (1773, 1784) and charter renewals (1793, 1813, 1833, 1853), the East India Company's political and financial independence was circumscribed. The fortunes of John Company seemed to flourish in the first half of the nineteenth century. Through a series of annexations, the company came to control roughly two-thirds of the subcontinent by mid-century. It also ministered to the modernization of certain sectors of the economy, building railways, the telegraph and public works. But such efforts were also accompanied by an infusion of western ideologies in India, particularly Utilitarianism, Evangelicalism and Free Trade. All these changes impacted certain groups of Indians (e.g., landlords, peasants, the military), and resulted in a series of unconnected upheavals in the so-called Mutiny of 1857. Finally, following the traumas of 1857, the company was formally wound-up and Indian governance was assumed by the Crown. (C. H. Philips, *The East India Company, 1784–1834*, 1961; Holden Furber, *John Company at Work*, 1948; B. B. Misra, *The Administration of the East India Company*, 1960.)

Arnold P. Kaminsky

BRITISH EMPIRE. Of all the European empires that developed in the wake of Christopher Columbus's voyage to the New World, the British Empire became the most extensive and the most long-lasting. In the 1490s John Cabot* explored the northern North American coastline for Britain, and a century later several prominent English promoters—Humphrey Gilbert*, Walter Raleigh, and Richard Hakluyt*—had made abortive colonization attempts in North America and were actively calling for more extensive English colonization activity there. By that time the English had already established plantations across the Irish Sea in Ireland*, especially in and around Dublin in what became known as the Pale. By the early 1600s joint stock companies from England had financed the first permanent settlements in Bermuda* and Jamestown*.

Within a generation English-speaking colonies had also been established at Plymouth*, Massachusetts* Bay, and Maryland* on the mainland, as well as on Antigua*, the Bahamas*, Barbados*, St. Vincent*, Montserrat*, St. Christopher*, and the Turks and Caicos Islands* in the Caribbean. Geographic expansion in New England* also led to new colonial settlements in Connecticut* and Rhode Island. These early colonial endeavors on the part of the English were due more to the efforts of private entrepreneurs and corporate concerns than formal imperial programs by the Crown. The early 1600s also marked the settlement of Ulster by Scots Presbyterians intent on taking land and power from the native Roman Catholic population in northern Ireland.

Expansion of the British Empire was stalled by the bloody English Civil War between 1640 and 1660, but when peace returned the government and the entrepreneurs renewed their colonization efforts. The Duke of York seized New Netherland* from the Dutch, creating the New York* colony, and other mainland colonies appeared in Pennsylvania* and the Carolinas. New Caribbean settlements developed in the Virgin Islands*, the Cayman Islands*, Jamaica*, and Guiana. On the African coast, the British placed small trading settlements in present-day Gambia* and St. Helena*.

By that time the government was taking a more direct interest in the colonial settlements. Mercantilism* was gaining more and more prominence as a theory of political economy, and the colonies increased in significance as sources of raw materials and markets for British goods. Parliament began passing a series of laws known as the Navigation Acts* to coordinate the imperial economy. Early in the 1700s a new English-speaking colony was established in Georgia*. The English had also captured Gibraltar* in 1704 to protect their access to the Mediterannean.

England's real rival in the contest for North America and the Caribbean was France, whose empire included Canada* and a number of sugar colonies in the Caribbean. Beginning in the 1690s England and France fought four wars for supremacy in North America, and England emerged the victor. Nova Scotia* and Newfoundland* became British territory in 1713, and when the Treaty of Paris of 1763* ended the French and Indian War*, France ceded the rest of Canada to Great Britain. The French Empire* in North America was dead.

By that time, however, the British Empire in North America was in trouble. The French and Indian War left the British with a huge debt, and beginning in the early 1760s parliament passed a series of laws designed to raise tax revenues in the thirteen mainland colonies. Such measures as the Stamp Act, the Townshend Acts, the Tea Act, the Quebec Act, and the Coercive Acts inspired the American Revolution* in 1776, and when the war for American independence* was over, so was the first British Empire. The thirteen colonies became the United States of America.

With the thirteen North American colonies gone, Britain began looking elsewhere to salvage its imperial interests. The most promising site was India, which the British East India Company* was already trying to subdue. British settlements appeared in Australia* at the end of the eighteenth century, and to protect the sea lanes to India, Great Britain established protectorates at Aden*, the Seychelles*, Mauritius*, and Ceylon*, and took the Cape Colony* from the Dutch early in the nineteenth century. British trading posts and protectorates were also established at Singapore* and Hong Kong* to exploit East Asian trade. The Australian settlements were thriving by mid-century, as was the English colony of New Zealand*, and British India had become the crown jewel of the Empire.

The British Empire managed its global expansion during the nineteenth century because of the power of the British navy and strength of the British economy as it led the Industrial Revolution in Europe. In the late nineteenth century Great Britain took part in the great scramble for colonies in Africa and the Pacific Ocean, which eventually brought into her sphere of control the areas of Basutoland*, Bechuanaland*, British Somaliland, Egypt*, Gambia*, Gold Coast, Kenya*, Nyasaland*, Nigeria*, the Solomon Islands*, the Gilbert Islands, the Ellice Islands*, Fiji*, South Africa*, Sudan, Tanganyika*, Northern Rhodesia, Southern Rhodesia, New Hebrides*, Tonga, and Uganda.* The British had also consolidated their control over Burma*, Malaya, and Brunei* in Asia. On the eve of World War I*, the British proudly claimed that "the sun never sets on the British Empire."

But World War I proved to be the undoing of the British Empire. In its immediate aftermath, the League of Nations* gave the British mandates over former German and Ottoman colonies, actually increasing the extent of the British Empire. Iraq*, Palestine*, Kaiser Wilhelmsland, Southwest Africa*, Tanganyika*, Transjordan*, and Western Samoa* all became British mandates or colonies. But even as it was adding colonies to British control, World War I was undermining the Empire. The war was an economic disaster for Europe, draining national resources and rendering the Empire increasingly indefensible, especially in face of concerted drives for independence. At the Imperial Conference of 1926* and then in the Statute of Westminister in 1931, Great Britain created the British Commonwealth of Nations*, a loose association of self-governing countries equal in status to one another but bound together by common loyalties. Canada, South Africa, the Irish Free State, Australia, New Zealand, and Newfoundland were the first members of the Commonwealth. The Commonwealth was a way for Great Britain to retain some imperial economic power without the burdens of political rule.

World War II* only accelerated the dissolution of the Empire. India and Pakistan led the way, securing independence from Great Britain in 1947, followed by Ceylon (Sri Lanka) in 1948 and scores of other colonies in the next generation: Bahamas (1973), Barbados (1966) Basutoland (1966), Belize (1981), Botswana (1966), Brunei (1984), Cyprus* (1960), Dominica (1978), Ellice Islands (1978), Fiji (1970), Gambia (1965), the Gilbert Islands (1979), Gold Coast (1957), Grenada* (1974), Guyana (1966), Jamaica (1962), Kenya (1963), Malaya (1957), Malta* (1964), Mauritius (1968), Nauru (1968), New Hebrides (1980), Nigeria (1960), Northern Rhodesia (1964), Nyasaland (1964), Papua New Guinea* (1975), St. Kitts and Nevis (1983), St. Lucia (1979), St. Vincent and the Grenadines* (1979), the Seychelles (1976), Singapore (1965), Solomon Islands (1978), Southern Rhodesia (1980), Swaziland* (1968), Tanganyika (1961), Tonga (1970), Trinidad and Tobago (1962), Uganda (1962), Western Samoa (1962), and Zanzibar (1963). (T. O. Lloyd, *The British Empire 1558– 1983*, 1984.)

BRITISH EMPIRE IN WORLD WAR II. During the interwar period (1919–1939), there emerged a bifocal perception about the British Empire* as a security issue. On the one hand, many people considered the Empire a liability—an expansive frontier which would inevitably drain Britain's limited resources. Additionally, reconciliation of a variety of diplomatic perspectives was surely problematical. On the other hand, British imports from the dominions and dependent territories increased from 24 to 37 percent of overseas trade, while exports to the Empire increased from 32 to 39 percent. The Empire was a formidable part of the British economy.

The situation was exacerbated by the fact that significant adjustments in relations between Great Britain and the self-governing dominions had emerged in the interwar period, not the least of which was the Statute of Westminster, which redefined imperial relationships and, in theory, established a Commonwealth of equals (as applied to Canada*, Australia*, New Zealand*, South Africa*, the Irish Free State, and Newfoundland*). The dependencies were not part of this consideration. The fact was, however, that there was no unity of purpose or even common perception of the Commonwealth's role in general, let alone in any future war. During the war, the dominions and colonies contributed nearly five million troops (over one half from India). Critics pointed out that most of these were involved in defending their own lines and that this required much American help. Also, many British troops were used in the Empire. Nevertheless, all of the dominions (except Ireland) came to Britain's aid, even though they were no longer formally obliged to do so. Even India*, consumed by nationalist and communal politics, contributed mightily to the war in both men and materials. Still, both Canada and Australia faced important domestic crises over the issue of conscription for the war effort, and resistance of some Afrikaaners to war contributions strained internal relations in South Africa. Only New Zealand had a relatively effortless entry into the war.

In the end, imperial troops were used in several important theaters. ANZAC troops were used in Crete, Indians in Southeast Asia, Canadians at the abortive raid on Dieppe, and South African troops in North Africa and Ethiopia. This fact also led to tensions between Britain and her allies over the use of Commonwealth troops by British commanders, and to considerable Anglo-American tensions related to questions of continuation of the Empire after the war.

During the war the question of an imperial war cabinet was raised, but it never materialized. When the Allies met in San Francisco after the war to set up the United Nations*, there were important differences on matters of substance among the members of the British Commonwealth of Nations*. Great Britain, of course, was one of the great powers with a veto in the proposed security council. There was, however, no British Empire* delegation as there had been at Versailles, but rather each of the dominions signed the U.N. Charter in alphabetical order as independent Allied nations which had fought in the war.

The election of a Labour government at the end of the war, committed to devolution of power and withdrawal from Empire, signaled further institution-alization of the notion of equality among Commonwealth members. The Following the war, the Dominions Office became the Commonwealth Relations Office, and with the admission of India and Pakistan* to its ranks, a multiracial Common-wealth of Nations finally emerged. This transformation had been greatly facil-itated by the experiences of World War II*. (Nicolas Manserge, *The Commonwealth Experience*, Vol. 2, rev. ed., 1982; Bernard Porter, *The Lion's Share*, 2nd ed., 1984.)

Arnold P. Kaminsky

BRITISH GUIANA. British Guiana (Guyana) lies on the north coast of South America between Venezuela* on the west, Surinam on the east, and Brazil* on the south. Christopher Columbus* first sailed along the coast in 1498 on his third voyage to the Americas. In 1594 the Englishman Sir Robert Dudley in-vestigated rumors of the empire of Guiana. Later, another Englishman, Sir Walter Raleigh, commanded expeditions looking for El Dorado, the legendary empire of gold. Other attempts by the English to establish colonies in 1604 and 1609 proved unsuccessful. The Dutch made their first appearance in 1598, and in 1621 the Dutch West India Company was formed to establish colonies. By the 1630s the Dutch were well entrenched on the Guiana coast. In 1662 the thriving Dutch colony was attacked by a British force under Lord Willoughby, and the Dutch planters moved east to what became Dutch Guiana* (Surinam). The Dutch returned in 1704 and by 1775 had established a profitable sugar trade.

In 1781, during the war between England and Holland, the English captured the Dutch colonies of Demerara,* Essequibo*, and Berbice*. A few months later the French, who were also at war with England, captured the colonies from the English. When the colonies were restored to the Dutch in 1783 they moved their capital to the newly built French town of Longchamp at the mouth of the Demerara River. The Dutch renamed the town Stabroek; it would eventually become Georgetown under the British. In 1815 Essequibo, Demerara, and Ber-bice were officially ceded to the British, and in 1831 they were united to form the crown colony of British Guiana.

The British abolished slavery in 1833, and to replace slaves, indentured ser-vants, most of whom came from India*, were brought into British Guiana. When India abolished the indenture system in 1917, the East Indian population of British Guiana was 126,577 and by 1970 that number had risen to 212,300, making East Indians the largest ethnic group. The Sugar Act of 1846, leveling sugar prices, badly crippled the sugar industry in British Guiana, which had to compete with sugar producers from other countries using slave labor. An alter-native crop, rice, began to be cultivated on land not being used for sugar pro-duction. By 1905 the colony had become self-sufficient in rice and began to export it to other countries. Sugar remained the most important crop, however.

Before 1928 the colonial constitution provided for a bicameral division of legislative powers. One council controlled non-financial legislation and included the governor, seven appointed officials, and eight unofficial (elected) members. The second council wielded authority over financial legislation and consisted of six elected members, called financial representatives. The constitution of 1928 created a more typical British crown colony arrangement. It established a legislative council consisting of fifteen members appointed by the governor and fourteen elected members. Two members of the elected group also served in the executive branch. In 1945 a new constitution created a legislative council composed of the governor, a colonial secretary, the attorney general, a financial secretary, and five elected members. The franchise was also extended to all literate persons over 21 who owned property or had an annual income of at least $120. In 1949 the People's Progressive Party (PPP) was formed calling for self-government, economic development, and social revolution. A new constitution in 1953 established universal suffrage and granted the colony a large measure of self-government. It also created a bicameral legislature consisting of a House of Assembly composed of twenty-four elected members and three ex-officio members appointed by the governor. The executive council was made up of the governor as president, three ex-officio members, and six elected members from the house of assembly. In the first elected government under the 1953 constitution, the PPP captured sixteen of the twenty-four seats in the house of assembly.

As a result of strikes and the fear that the leftist-leaning PPP would create a communist state, Britain suspended the constitution in 1953. In 1955 the PPP split along ethnic lines, and Forbes Burnham, an African, organized the People's National Congress (PNC), drawing black support away from the PPP. Cheddi Jagan, an East Indian, remained the leader of the PPP. In 1957, when the constitution was restored, both parties ran candidates, and the PPP secured a majority in the assembly. A new constitution was adopted in 1961 and the PPP dominated the new assembly. As the PPP began to press Britain for independence, the years 1962–1964 saw increased rioting and strikes, generally along racial lines. Under a new constitution providing for proportional representation, elections were held in December 1964. The PPP won twenty-four seats, the PNC twenty-two seats, and the United Force (UF) seven seats. The PNC and UF formed a coalition with Forbes Burnham as prime minister. On May 26, 1966, independence was granted, and the independent state of Guyana was created with a parliamentary form of government. On February 27, 1970, Guyana became the Cooperative Republic of Guyana. Unfortunately, the constitutional changes had the effect of politically dividing Guyana along ethnic and racial lines. (Raymond T. Smith, *British Guiana*, 1962.)

Michael Dennis

BRITISH-HEDJAZ AGREEMENT OF 1916. The British-Hedjaz Agreement of 1916 concerned alleged assurances made by Britain to promote the establishment of an independent Arab kingdom stretching from Damascus to Palestine* when World War I* ended. The British promises were part of a series of letters exchanged between the British high commissioner for Egypt*, Sir Arthur Henry

McMahon, and the Sharif of Mecca. In the exchange of letters, which occurred between October 1915 and the beginning of 1916, McMahon told the Sharif that Britain was prepared to recognize the independence of the Arabs across the whole of the Middle East. British reservations excluded from this independent Arab state the coastal areas lying to the west of the districts of Damascus, Homs, Hama, and Aleppo. The problem of interpreting this restriction involved the use of the ambiguous word for "district" (*vilayet*) which equally meant "province." In effect, the McMahon correspondence was unclear about the inclusion of Palestine in an Arab state—the ambiguous reference to areas west of the *vilayet* of Damascus might have included Palestine, or it might not. Moreover, the McMahon letters, which Arab leaders claimed were tantamount to a formal agreement, contradicted the Sykes-Picot Agreement of 1916*, which prevented any unilateral British action in the Middle East regarding the disposal of the former Turkish provinces. The result was a series of misunderstandings among the Arabs, Britain, and France over possession of most of the Turkish lands, including Palestine and the holy city of Jerusalem. In the end, Arab claims to the region were not honored. The peace settlement in 1919 provided for a British mandate over Palestine, while France was given mandates over Damascus and Syria*. The British-Hedjaz Agreement set the stage for seventy-five years of ethnic and religious tension in the Middle East. (Briton Cooper Busch, *Britain India and the Arabs, 1914–1921*, 1971; Elie Kedourie, *England and the Middle East*, 1978.)

William G. Ratliff

BRITISH HONDURAS. Christopher Colombus*, on his fourth voyage in 1502, sailed into the Bay of Honduras, southeast of present-day Belize. In 1507 Spanish navigators passed the coast of Belize during their exploratory voyages along the Central American coast, and Hernán Cortés* went through the southwestern corner of Belize on his march to the Golfo Dulce in 1525 to quell the Honduran revolt led by Cristóbal de Olid. Three years later the Yucatan governor, Francisco de Montejo, sailed down the coast of Belize and concluded that a settlement was feasible. He sent Alonso Dávila to Chetumal, a northern site, to carry out his plans. This proved to be a mistake, as the Mayas led successive attacks and drove Davila further south. The Spanish continued to meet opposition from the Mayas though they established and abandoned posts with regularity from 1540 onward. The brutality and diseases that accompanied these settlement attempts created social disorganization among the Indians.

The British first set foot on Belize as shipwrecked sailors in 1638. They established a settlement at the mouth of the Belize River, the purpose of which was to export logwood, a textile dyestuff. Previous to this settlement, British buccaneers used the coast of Belize to lie in wait for Spanish treasure ships. By 1705 the logwood trade was well established despite frequent skirmishes with Spaniards who continued to claim the area. The Treaty of Paris of 1763* gave the British the right to export logwood though they were not to build fortifications.

This encouraged the British settlement on St. George's Cay to codify logwood business regulations. However, the eventual lack of a logwood market created a need for a new product—mahogany, which remained the main export until the 1980s. In order to cut and ship mahogany, the British imported African slaves in the 1770s.

The fact of Spanish opposition and harassment until 1798 did not stop the British settlements from branching out. By 1804 they had reached the southern border of modern-day Belize. Belize maintained a self-governing rule until Britain, without claiming ownership, sent Edward M. Despard to govern the Bay Settlement, an area adjoining the Bay of Honduras. An executive council was established in 1840 and a legislative assembly in 1853. Nine years later the British formally acquired Belize, made it a colony, and named it British Honduras. Its colonial status, however, fell under the governorship of Jamaica*. In 1871 British Honduras abolished its legislative assembly and accepted the status of crown colony. Thirteen years later it gained its own governor after separating politically from Jamaica (1884). The early twentieth century saw Belize riddled with economic problems. The goal of independence was aided by constitutional reforms in the 1950s but hindered by frequent outbreaks of strife with Guatemala*. Guatemala laid claim to Belize as a portion of the Spanish Empire* in the New World. Independence came in 1981, led by Prime Minister George Price. However, due to Guatemala's threatening stance, Great Britain continues to maintain a vested military interest in the area. (O. Nigel Bolland, *Belize: A New Nation in Central America*, 1986; C. H. Grant, *The Making of Modern Belize*, 1976.)

Catherine G. Harbour

BRITISH INDIAN OCEAN TERRITORY. In November 1965 the British Indian Ocean Territory was formed to provide defense facilities for the United States and Great Britain. The colony included the Chagos Archipelago (consisting of Diego Garcia, Peros Banhos, Six Islands or Egmont Islands, Salomon Islands, and the Three Brothers group), the Farquhar Atoll of the Farquhar group, Des Roches, and the Aldabra Islands. The Chagos Archipelago had been detached from Mauritius* in return for a payment of three million pounds. The Farquhar Atoll, Des Roches, and the Aldabra Islands had been detached from the Seychelles in return for the international airport constructed on Mahe Island. Both territorial groups were administered by a commissioner in Seychelles*. Mauritius, itself independent since 1968, has never recognized the administrative separation of the Chagos Archipelago from its domain.

In 1814 Diego Garcia, the largest of the Chagos Archipelago, was ceded by France to the United Kingdom, which hoped to strengthen the British sea route to the east. Later, slave laborers from Mauritius worked the island's rich copra plantations. Following the Emancipation Act of 1833, these slaves became contract employees and subjects. Until the establishment of military facilities in 1966, Diego Garcia's principle enterprises were coconut plantations and fishing.

The island was used as a British air base and naval station during World War II*.

In 1966, following Diego Garcia's incorporation into the British Indian Ocean Territory, the United States and Great Britain reached preliminary agreements on the construction of a joint naval base. Great Britain bought out the privately owned copra plantations in 1967 and closed them. In 1968 the U.S. Joint Chiefs of Staff recommended setting up a joint British-American communications facility on Diego Garcia. Between 1967 and 1973 some 1,200 native copra workers (known as Ilois) were transferred from Diego Garcia, Ile du Coin, and Boddam to Mauritius. The naval airfield and communication center were built on Diego Garcia in 1973, and in July 1975, the U.S. Senate approved the expansion of its naval base and the construction of new airport and harbor facilities.

Until 1976 the British Indian Ocean Territory was administered by the governor of the Seychelles. However, following the return of the Aldabra, Farquhar, and Des Roches island groups to the independent Seychelles in 1976, the territory eventually came under the direct rule of the British government. Also, in 1980, the government of Mauritius, arguing that the construction of military facilities violated an assurance allegedly given by Britain in 1967, demanded the return of the island of Diego Garcia. The British government denied any such neutrality pledge in regard to Diego Garcia but nonetheless granted four million pounds to the Ilois on Mauritius and agreed to resettle them on the Agalega Islands, 600 miles to the north. (Ferenc Albert Vali, *Politics of the Indian Ocean Region*, 1976.)

Eric C. Loew

BRITISH KAFFRARIA. Great Britain took the Cape Colony* from the Dutch in 1806 and then steadily extended their control to the east. In 1847 the British established a separate crown colony west of the Kei River and called it British Kaffraria. For nineteen years they administered the colony, but it was too small to survive, especially when dwarfed by its much larger neighbor. In 1866 they reattached it to the Cape Colony. See SOUTH AFRICA.

BRITISH LEEWARD ISLANDS. During the seventeenth century, Great Britain expanded its presence in the Lesser Antilles of the Caribbean. Those islands consisted of Antigua*, Barbuda*, St. Kitts*, Nevis*, the British Virgin Islands,* Anguilla*, and Montserrat*. In 1671 Great Britain organized them into a single colonial government—the Leeward Islands. That political arrangement lasted until 1816 when Britain divided the islands into two separate administrations: Antigua-Montserrat-Barbuda and St. Kitts-Nevis-Anguilla-British Virgin Islands. Each of those two groups had its own appointed governor. It proved a cumbersome arrangement, however, and in 1833 they were recombined into a single unit. That same year the British added Dominica*, which they had acquired in 1761, to the Leeward Islands colony. Great Britain elevated the Leeward Islands in 1871 to the status of a federal colony. In 1960, however, Great Britain dissolved the Leeward Islands colony and the various islands became separate colonies. (Alan C. M. Burns, *A History of the British West Indies*, 1954.)

BRITISH MALAYA. See MALAYSIA.

BRITISH NEW GUINEA. Early in the 1880s, concerned about German expansion in the Pacific, Australia* requested a British protectorate over the south coast of eastern New Guinea, and Great Britain agreed in 1884, establishing the protectorate. Administrative headquarters was located at Port Moresby. In 1888 Britain annexed the territory, designating it the Crown Colony of British New Guinea. Authority over British New Guinea passed to Australia on September 1, 1906. It became known as the Australian Territory of Papua. After World War I Australia also received a League of Nations* mandate* over German New Guinea,* and the two territories were combined into one during World War II. Independence was achieved in 1975. (International Bank for Reconstruction and Development, *The Economic Development of the Territory of Papua and New Guinea*, 1965; David Stone, *Prelude to Self-Government*, 1976.)

BRITISH NORTH AMERICA ACT. See CANADA.

BRITISH NORTH BORNEO. British North Borneo is the name formerly applied to the large (29,000 sq. mi.), thickly forested but thinly populated East Malaysian state of Sabah. The capital of Sabah is Kota Kinabalu, (former Jesselton). Sabah occupies the northern end of Borneo*, with water on three sides: the South China Sea to the west, the Sulu Sea to the northeast, and the Celebes Sea to the southeast. There are land borders with Indonesian Kalimantan (former Dutch Borneo) and Sarawak*, another state of Malaysia*. The most porous and troublesome border is that with the Philippines*, for Manila and Kuala Lumpur disagree about where the boundary lies and about sovereignty over Sabah itself. Neither state effectively controls the Bajau sea-nomads, who smuggle goods across the Sulu Sea.

Sabah is mountainous and mostly inaccessible. There is but one short railway and very few miles of paved road. Travel to the interior is by airplane or river boat, but only one river, the Kinabatangan, is navigable for any distance upstream. The high Crocker Range, including 13,000-ft. Mt. Kinabalu, runs parallel to the northwest coast. North Borneo receives ample rain from October to March; its jungles are marvelously rich in many different species of plants and animals. Most of Sabah's cash income is from rubber plantations and timber concessions.

The total population of Sabah is about one million people, concentrated along the coast. Of this total, approximately 30 percent are Dusuns (also called Kadazans), 25 percent are Chinese (Hakka and Fukienese), 12 percent are Bajau, and 5 percent are Malay. The remainder consists of a scattering of Europeans,

Indians, and Javanese who immigrated during North Borneo's colonial period, and primitive inland tribes. Ethnic fragmentation is the essence of Sabah's communal politics today. The most densely populated part of Sabah lies on the narrow plain between the Crocker Range and the coast, but even here the largest towns contain less than 50,000 people.

North Borneo was not controlled by any outside power before the nineteenth century, although sultans from Brunei* and Sulu claimed loose suzerainty over coastal settlements. The sultan of Sulu allowed the British East India Company* to establish a station on Balembangan Island in 1773, but it was too vulnerable to pirate raids to be viable. The extraordinary Brooke family, the "white rajas" of Sarawak, might have gained control of all North Borneo, but they were checked by Claude Lee Moses, an American who in 1865 talked the Sultan of Brunei into giving him a ten-year cession of land along the northwest coast. Moses promptly went to Hong Kong and sold the rights to American merchants, including Joseph W. Torrey. The sultan obligingly appointed Torrey the "Maharajah of North Borneo," but that was not enough to prevent Torrey from selling his rights in 1875 to Baron von Overbeck, the Austro-Hungarian Consul in Hong Kong*. In 1877 Overbeck secured financial backing from the Dent brothers, a Hong Kong British trading firm. They formed a syndicate, paying rent to the sultans of Sulu and Brunei and applying to Queen Victoria for a royal charter, which was granted on November 1, 1881. The British North Borneo Company ran Sabah for the next sixty years.

The Company's charter provided that control should remain in British hands. This worried the Dutch, who controlled most of the rest of Borneo, and the Spanish, who feared that Britain might try to pry the Philippines from their grip. But international recognition of company control was granted by the Madrid Protocol of 1885, and the Anglo-Dutch Convention of 1891 defined the border more precisely. The company did not want to bother with foreign affairs, so in 1888 North Borneo became a protectorate. Great Britain would handle defense and diplomacy, while the Dent brothers could run Sabah as they pleased. The company suppressed what it called Bajau "piracy" and "slavery," ignoring nuances that made these activities less terrible in practice than they seemed to the Englishmen. A Bajau uprising led by Mat Saleh did not end when he was killed in 1900. Other rebellions among interior tribes continued until 1915. A company constabulary consisted of Sikhs, Pathans, and Malays, with British officers. Indian penal and civil codes were applied. Outside the market towns, civil control rested with traditional native leaders.

Financially the company was poorly managed and plunged deeply into debt. A railway, originally intended to run clear across Borneo, was left unfinished. A telegraph line proved a huge money-loser. Rubber plantations offered some promise, but the Great Depression of the 1930s undercut the export market. In the end, only by cutting magnificent hardwood trees could the company make money. Cacao, coffee, abaca, tobacco, and copra were also cultivated on a small scale. Company policies encouraged immigration, because the British reasoned that the Chinese would boost trade. That was correct, but it left an unfortunate legacy of racial suspicion in North Borneo, as elsewhere in the Malay world.

Japanese troops landed at Weston, on Brunei Bay, on January 3, 1942. The occupation years were terrible for Borneans. Some joined anti-Japanese partisan bands. Liberation entailed Allied bombing of the main towns. After the war, the North Borneo Company went bankrupt. Sabah became a direct colony of England until its incorporation into the Federation of Malaysia in 1963. That was controversial, as Indonesia and the Philippines protested. The Philippine government has asserted a claim to Sabah ever since, but receives no international support. (Robert Milne, *Malaysia: New States in a New Nation*, 1974; Nicholas Tarling, *Sulu and Sabah: A Study of British Policy Towards the Philippines and North Borneo From the Late 18th Century*, 1978.)

Ross Marlay

BRITISH PAPUA. See BRITISH NEW GUINEA.

BRITISH SOLOMON ISLANDS PROTECTORATE. See SOLOMON ISLANDS.

BRITISH SOMALILAND. See SOMALIA.

BRITISH SUDAN. See ANGLO-EGYPTIAN SUDAN.

BRITISH VIRGIN ISLANDS. See VIRGIN ISLANDS.

BRITISH WEST AFRICA. Although used during the nineteenth and twentieth centuries to describe the British sphere of influence in West Africa, the term ''British West Africa'' was merely descriptive, not the name of any formal federation or territorial administration. It generally included Gambia*, Gold Coast, Nigeria*, Sierra Leone*, British Togo*, and British Cameroons, but they were all governed under separate administrations.

BRITISH WEST INDIES. See WEST INDIES.

BRUNEI. Brunei is a small, rich, sultanate on the northwest coast of Borneo formally named Negara Brunei Darussalam, meaning ''Brunei, place of peace.'' It became independent in 1984. The current population of about 250,000 is 65 percent Malay, and 20 percent Chinese, the remainder consisting of inland tribal groups: Kedayans, Dusuns, Melanau, Ibans, and Dayaks. The total land area is only 2,226 square miles. The sultanate is actually divided into two separate sections by a small slice of Sarawak* (Malaysia). Physically, Brunei consists of a mangrove-fringed coastal plain, divided by rivers flowing from the hilly interior to the South China Sea. Three-fourths of the land is rain forest. There are few roads. To reach inland areas still requires a longboat. Brunei would have lapsed into obscurity but for the fact that it sits on a sea of oil.

Brunei's early history is not well known, but it was probably a vassal of the Javanese Majapahit empire, and definitely carried on trade with China. In the 1400s a Bruneian ruler converted to Islam, changed his name to Mohammed, and took the title sultan. An Arab from Taif married into the royal family, built a mosque, and enforced Islamic law. When the Portuguese took Malacca*, a rival sultanate, in 1511, Brunei achieved dominion over all the coastal areas of Borneo* and the southwest Philippines*. The sultanate repelled a Spanish attack in the late sixteenth century. A British East India Company* factory established in Brunei in the eighteenth century quickly closed, but the British North Borneo Company whittled away at Brunei's territory from the northeast (Sabah) while the so-called "white rajas" of Sarawak took over land to the southwest once claimed by Brunei. In 1841 the sultan of Brunei signed a treaty of commerce with the British recognizing their control over Sarawak. An 1888 treaty made Brunei a protectorate of Great Britain, and left the sultan in charge only of Muslim law within the territory. A third treaty in 1906 placed a British resident in Brunei Town. The sultan was put on a pension.

During the early British colonial period there was little trade between Brunei and the rest of the world. Some small rubber plantations were started, but they never amounted to much. Then oil was discovered at Seria in 1929. It attracted the Japanese, who occupied the territory from 1941 to 1945. Oil also led the sultan to keep Brunei out of Malaysia* when that federal nation was created in 1963. Today, revenue from petroleum and natural gas enables the sultan to maintain the only welfare state in Southeast Asia, with a per capita GNP in the 1980s of more than $20,000.

After World War II there was little sentiment for immediate independence in Brunei. The transition to self-government was gradual, emphasizing the introduction of democratic rights into the traditional hereditary sultanate. A Bruneian "People's Party" was formed in 1956 to press for independence, but was co-opted into a government formed after Brunei was given an internal sovereignty constitution in 1959. A brief revolt abetted by Indonesia flared in 1962 but was quickly suppressed by Gurkha troops. When the Malaysia Agreement (uniting Malaya, Singapore*, Sabah, and Sarawak) was signed in July 1963 Brunei stayed out, mostly because the sultan feared his oil fields might be nationalized. Under the terms of a 1979 treaty with Great Britain, Brunei gained full sovereignty on January 1, 1984. That year it joined the Commonwealth, the United Nations, and the Association of Southeast Asian Nations (ASEAN). (Donald Brown, *Brunei: The Structure and History of a Bornean Malay Sultanate,* 1970.)

Ross Marlay

BRUSSELS CONFERENCE OF 1889–1890. By the mid–1800s European competition for unclaimed territories in Africa had become so intense that the imperial powers concluded that it was necessary to regulate the process of annexation by international agreement. The Berlin West Africa Conference of 1884–1885* was the first meeting to address the problem, and the representatives of states assembled in Berlin agreed in 1885 to a legal document specifying rules for the colonization of the African coast. Five years later representatives of Germany, Belgium, France, Portugal, and Great Britain met in Brussels and drew up a second agreement relating to the colonization of the African interior.

The agreement reached at the Brussels Conference of 1889–1890 included a system by which the interior slave trade was to be eliminated within a specified number of years. It called for the institution of an active military administration with a series of fortified stations, and the establishment of effective means of communication and transport (i.e. railroads) between major colonial towns. The sale of firearms, with a few specified exceptions, was forbidden for twelve years between latitude 20 North and latitude 22 South, and reaching from the Atlantic to the Indian Ocean. The manufacture and sale of alcohol was also prohibited there. In other areas a heavy import duty was placed on distilled spirits. The conferees agreed to ban protective or differential duties and guaranteed freedom of access on equal terms in much of West Africa and in the Congo*, British East Africa and Northern Rhodesia*. In the English, French, and German protectorates, whose governments possessed a recognized and forceful organization, the agreement worked reasonably well. (L. H. Gann and Peter Duignan, eds., *Colonialism in Africa, 1870–1960*, 1969; Prosser Gifford and William Roger Louis, eds., *Britain and Germany in Africa*, 1967.)

William G. Ratliff

BRYAN-CHAMORRO CONVENTION. In 1913 Secretary of State William Jennings Bryan of the United States took over treaty negotiations initiated by the Taft administration to promote American interests in Nicaragua* by relieving the financial distress of that nation through "dollar diplomacy." At the same time, the agreement would eliminate the danger of a rival canal through Nicaragua by securing for the United States the exclusive right to build such a canal. Bryan also intended to include a provision modeled after the Platt Amendment giving to the United States the right to intervene in Nicaragua. When finally convinced that the Senate would not accept such a treaty, Bryan settled for a scaled-down version which did not include such a provision. The Bryan-Chamorro Convention, signed on August 5, 1914, consisted of three articles. Article I granted the United States, in perpetuity, exclusive right to build an inter-ocean canal through Nicaragua, if such a canal were ever to be built (a provision that was abrogated by mutual agreement in 1970). Article II granted the United States ninety-nine year leases to Great Corn Island, Little Corn Island, and the Gulf of Fonseca, together with the right to build naval bases there. In Article III, the United States agreed to pay Nicaragua $3 million for these concessions. The treaty was ratified on February 18, 1916. (Henry S. Commager, *Documents of American History*, 1949; Julius W. Pratt, *A History of United States Foreign Policy*, 1955.)

Joseph M. Rowe, Jr.

BUENOS AIRES. Sebastián Cabot explored the Río de la Plata in the 1520s, and in 1530, thinking that the river was a conduit to Peru, Pedro de Mendoza established a settlement at the site of present day Buenos Aires. When it became clear that the river would not reach all the way to Peru, the settlement was abandoned. Buenos Aires was permanently established in 1580 by Juan de Garay, who brought settlers from Asunción to build a livestock industry. At the time the entire region was under the political jurisdiction of the Viceroyalty of Peru. Spain established the province of Buenos Aires in 1618 by splitting the province of Río de la Plata into Buenos Aires and Paraguay. The Audiencia of Buenos Aires was created in 1661 to handle the population growth and economic development in the area, but it was discontinued in 1671 and the area continued to fall under the direction of the Audiencia of Charcas. By the end of the seventeenth century, Buenos Aires was a major exporter of hides, tallow, and beef jerky, the premier products of its burgeoning cattle industry. Wheat farming began in the late eighteenth century. In 1776 the Spanish crown created the Viceroyalty of the Río de la Plata, separating what is today Argentina, Uruguay, Paraguay, and Bolivia from the Viceroyalty of Peru. At the time the population of Buenos Aires totalled 24,000 people. By 1800 Buenos Aires totalled nearly 50,000 people and became a center of the independence movement. See ARGENTINA.

BUGANDA. See UGANDA.

BÜLOW, BERNHARD HEINRICH MARTIN VON. Bernhard von Bülow was born on May 3, 1849, at Klein-Flottbeck in the Duchy of Holstein. He was the son of Count Bernhard Ernst von Bülow. The elder Bülow served as the Reich state secretary of the foreign office and as Prussian state minister from 1873 until his death in 1879. The son entered the Reich diplomatic service with his father and for the next fifteen years held important posts at Rome, St. Petersburg, Athens, Vienna, and Paris. He was secretary for the Congress of Berlin* in 1878. He became the head of a mission for the first time in 1888 when he went to Bucharest as minister to Rumania. His transfer to Rome as ambassador to the Kingdom of Italy followed in 1893. Bülow returned to Berlin in 1897 to become Reich state secretary for foreign affairs.

Internal politics of the Reich were decisive in Bülow's career. Shortly after the fall of Otto von Bismarck*, Bülow became associated with the plotting of the camarilla to bring about the "personal rule" of Wilhelm II. They wanted to augment the authority of the king of Prussia as German Kaiser and replace key personnel in both the Prussian and Reich governments with loyal Wilhelmian servants. Bülow's promotion to the foreign secretaryship was one of those changes. Along with Johannes Miquel and Admiral Alfred von Tirpitz, Bülow worked to rally the nation behind the Kaiser by seeking new colonies, constructing a great battle fleet, and orchestrating a highly nationalistic campaign to win the support of Germany's agrarian and industrial producers for this new

Weltpolitik ("world policy"). Establishment of a German base at Kiaochow* was the springboard for the plan. Bülow was the key figure in the pursuit of *Weltpolitik*.

By aggravating the Reich government's persistent shortage of funds, *Weltpolitik* ultimately forced Bülow to rely increasingly on a parliamentary bloc of the National Liberal and Conservative parties. He thereby contributed to a process which one historian has recently characterized as "the silent parliamentarization" of German politics. Bülow also harmed the macroeconomic health of the Reich with his high tariffs to finance *Weltpolitik*. Bülow became perhaps the only "social imperialist" in Berlin's ruling circle; he wanted to use "colonial imperialism" as a deliberate means of eliminating internal social conflict and unifying the Reich. Bülow even allowed Wilhelm to become the object of ridicule in the Reichstag in November 1908 over an article in the *London Daily Telegraph* quoting some of the Kaiser's more tactless remarks. Wilhelm never forgave Bülow for failing to intercept the article, allowing criticism in parliament, and offering there at best a lame defense of the Kaiser. Bülow resigned as chancellor on July 14, 1909. He died in 1929. (Isabel V. Hull, *The Entourage of Kaiser Wilhelm II, 1888–1918*, 1982; Peter Winzen, *Bülow's Weltmachtkonzept Untersuchugen zur Fruhphase seiner Aussenpolitik, 1897–1901*, 1977.)

Bascom Barry Hayes

BURKINA-FASO. See UPPER VOLTA.

BURMA. Burma is a potentially rich Southeast Asian nation, whose people live in poverty. The country was severely traumatized by its collision with the imperial West. Its policies of isolation, neutrality, anti-capitalism, *and* anti-communism are a direct reaction to the humiliation and social disintegration of having been ruled by Great Britain as an appendage of British India.

The fertile, productive, densely populated parts of Burma are the long river valleys of the Sittang, the Salween, and the Irrawaddy, draining the eastern Himalayas. The Burmans (67 percent of the population) live in the lowlands. A plethora of unassimilated hill tribes (Karens, Chins, Kachins, Shans, Nagas, Lahus, and others) live in the hills and plateaus to the west, north, and east of the Irrawaddy heartland. Burma is cut off from Bangladesh, India*, China*, Laos*, and Thailand* by steep mountain ranges, yet it lacks natural borders. Burmese kings have always sought to control the mountains for strategic reasons. Burma is favored with extensive deposits of silver, tin, zinc, tungsten, copper, and lead as well as jade, rubies, and sapphires. The warm, wet climate favors rice, cotton, and rubber. Tremendous stands of teakwood are still being cut after a century of logging.

Powerful kingdoms and a rich culture arose in Burma more than a thousand years before the colonial period. The civilization was shaped by Hindu and Buddhist influences from India that melded with native Burmese animism. The Konbaung kings, the last Burmese dynasty, were militarily strong, but in 1819 they moved into Manipur and Assam, frontier zones deemed strategic by the British, who worried about defending their vast Indian empire. The English were not initially interested in annexing Burma, but a variety of irritants and misunderstandings inflamed Burmese-British relations. British merchants in Rangoon felt shabbily treated. British envoys arrogantly refused to remove their shoes when entering the royal palace, as protocol demanded. Above all, there were completely different concepts of world order and interstate relations. War broke out in 1823 and proved much tougher than the British had expected. They employed steam-powered gunboats on the Irrawaddy, driving the Burmese north. Then they annexed "Lower Burma" in 1824, and forced the Burmese to sign the humiliating Treaty of Yandabo (February 24, 1826), which included cession of Arakan and Tenasserim and an indemnity of one million pounds. The treaty also provided for future commercial and diplomatic intercourse, but it did not bring permanent peace.

Foreign merchants and missionaries, feeling ill-treated, urged Britain to intervene again. During the second Burmese War (1852–1853), the British took the area around Rangoon, turning "Upper Burma" into a landlocked kingdom whose only access to the sea was down the Irrawaddy through British territory. King Mindon (1853–1878) sought to appease the British and fostered limited westernization, including some factories, telegraph lines, and newspapers, and he tried to open relations with other European nations, a move that backfired. The English imagination became inflamed by a vision of Frenchmen moving west from Indochina to conquer Thailand and Upper Burma. Then the French would be on the very border of British India, and might even find a land route into China through the "back door" of Yunan. After King Mindon died in 1878, no strong ruler arose, and local rebellions sapped Burmese power. The British, racing against the French to divide up uncolonized parts of the world and obsessed with the security of India, extinguished Burmese sovereignty in a very short war at the end of 1885.

On January 1, 1886, Burma was made part of British India, an unbearable slight to the Burmese, who had little use for Indians. Indeed, the symbolic humiliations seemed worse than the economic exploitation. Villagers broke down crying when Thibaw, the last Burmese king, was deported to India. The British had to cart off his throne, too, because people believed that as long as it remained, a new dynasty would arise. The palace in Mandalay, the pivot of the universe to Burmese, was turned into a drinking club for British officers. Military pacification took five years.

British imperial rule in Burma wrought socioeconomic changes familiar elsewhere in Asia. Village autonomy yielded to administrative centralization. True cities arose, now with an economic, not a religious, focus. One great port city, Rangoon, dominated the commercial, political, and cultural life of the country. Railroads and river shipping linked inland Burma to Rangoon, and ocean steamers brought Burmese products to the world market. Far and away the greatest change was the clearing of extensive rice land in what had been the swampy Irrawaddy delta. Whole new social classes sprang up: landlords and paid field hands. Indian moneylenders provided the credit that made this system flourish—until the Great Depression. Then, impoverished peasants followed an ex-monk, Saya San, into blind, backward-looking rebellion. Saya San's amulets and charms did not protect his followers from bullets, as claimed, and the British put down the insurrection, though it required 12,000 troops.

Meanwhile, a more progressive nationalism had taken root among Burmese students, beginning with the innocuous Young Men's Buddhist Association, then the more inclusive General Council of Burmese Associations, the "We Burmans Association," and the Dobama Asiayone. In 1937 the British attempted to defuse the growing nationalism by granting Burma separation from India and a new constitution as a crown colony; but in fact many Burmese rejoiced when the Japanese invaded in 1942. At last fellow Asians would liberate Burma from Europeans. The honeymoon ended quickly as Burmese nationalists turned against the Japanese and gathered under the banner of the Anti-Fascist People's Freedom League.

Naturally, once the Japanese were beaten, the Burmese wanted to prevent the British from returning. Great Britain, too exhausted from World War II to fight again, agreed to independence for Burma. At 4:20 A.M. on January 7, 1948, an auspicious moment chosen by astrologers, Burma regained complete independence, declining to join the Commonwealth. The country has stagnated economically since then, as the government has chosen isolation from world capitalism over foreign investment and the entanglement it brings. (John F. Cady, *A History of Modern Burma*, 1958, and *The United States and Burma*, 1976; Oliver Pollak, *Empires in Collision: Anglo-Burmese Relations in the Mid-Nineteenth Century*, 1979.)

Ross Marlay

BURUNDI. See RWANDA-BURUNDI.

BUXTON, SIR THOMAS FOWELL, BARONET. Thomas Fowell Buxton served as a member of parliament from 1818–1837. After a series of brilliant scholastic achievements, he married and settled into a post with a brewing firm, from which he amassed considerable wealth. His Quaker heritage drew him to humanitarian causes. During his early days of public office, Buxton devoted himself to the reform of Britain's prisons and penal code. His *Inquiry into Prison Discipline* (1818), was distributed throughout Europe. In India*, it prompted an investigation of the horrifying conditions afflicting Madras jails. Buxton also campaigned against *suttee*, a Hindu custom whereby a widow would display her devotion by throwing herself upon her husband's funeral pyre.

These crusades earned the admiration of William Wilberforce, a venerable political warrior who had waged a twenty-year struggle culminating in parliament's abolition of the slave trade in 1807. Wilberforce chose Buxton to succeed him as head of the abolitionist party in the house of commons. On May 15,

1823, Buxton pressed for gradual emancipation by advocating the manumission of young slave children. His opponents, led by George Canning, countered with a proposal for "melioration"—humane treatment of slaves. Canning's arguments prevailed, but Caribbean planters and colonial assemblies refused to cooperate with what they believed was undue imperial interference.

For nearly a decade after the implementation of the melioration policy, Buxton toiled to rally the public to abolitionism. The British and Foreign Anti-Slavery Society, which he helped found in 1823, rendered great assistance. Furthermore, the Reform Act of 1832 brought the franchise to the middle class, thus ensuring that the house of commons would reflect a broader base than it had ten years earlier. When the first reformed parliament convened in 1833, Buxton immediately moved for abolition. This time, his motion carried. The Abolition of Slavery Bill, enacted on August 29, 1833, would take effect the following August 1. All slaves under six years of age were to be freed. Others, though technically emancipated, were required to serve their masters as apprentices until 1840, if they worked in agriculture. Domestic slaves would be free in 1838. Former owners also were to receive monetary compensation from the government. When apprenticeship proved unworkable, Buxton responded to a popular outcry by calling for its termination. Hence, on August 1, 1838, the program ceased.

While the emancipation process progressed, Buxton set his sights on another concern—the fate of the Hottentots of South Africa, who were coming into contact with English settlers. He played a major role in the 1835 creation of the Aborigines Protection Society. Buxton then chaired (1835–1837) the house of commons's select committee that investigated the treatment of native groups dwelling within the Empire. His *Report of the Aborigines Committee* was a stinging indictment of European imperialism.

Next Buxton strove to deal slavery its death by eliminating it from Africa. In 1839 he founded the Society for the Extinction of the Slave Trade and the Civilization of Africa. He also published the *African Slave Trade and its Remedy*. Buxton claimed that three times as many Africans were being shipped into slavery in 1837 as were in 1807. Only by signing treaties with local chiefs and providing alternate commercial opportunities could this evil be stemmed. Buxton proposed that former slaves be sent to Africa to introduce Christianity, as well as modern agriculture and industry. Europeans would fund these efforts.

Accordingly, the British dispatched an expedition to the Niger River in 1841, but many of its members perished from fever. The society collapsed in 1843 with Buxton on the public defensive. His health deteriorated and by early 1845, he was dead. The Niger expedition, it turned out, opened new areas of Africa to Christianity and to British mercantile and political influence. Also, it positively contributed to the long-term war against slavery. Thousands of ex-bondsmen donated funds to Buxton's memorial statue, which stands in Westminster Abbey. (Charles Buxton, ed., *Memoirs of Sir Thomas Fowell Buxton*, 1925; R. H. Mottram, *Buxton the Liberator*, 1946.)

Frank Marotti

C

CABILDO. The *cabildo* or municipal council, patterned after a similar institution which existed on the Iberian peninsula since Roman times and later evolving into the Castilian municipality of the Middle Ages, was brought to the New World and the Philippines by the Spanish conquistadores who founded new towns as they entered recently conquered territories. It not only ruled over these towns but also the surrounding rural areas which comprised the district. It would play an important role in the Spanish imperial system because it represented local interests in contradistinction to other institutions which represented the interests of the Spanish crown and Spain.

Alcaldes ordinarios (magistrates) and *regidores* (councilors), whose number would depend on the importance of the city and surrounding district which they administered, composed the *cabildo*. In the smaller towns there would be between four and six *regidores* and one *alcalde* whereas in the larger cities, such as Mexico City and Lima, there would be between eight or more *regidores* and two *alcaldes*. There were other municipal offices attached to the *cabildo* such as *alferez real* (herald or municipal standard bearer), *alguacil mayor* (chief constable), *receptor de penas* (collector of judicial fines). The *regidores* or *alcaldes* would many times exercise these extra functions.

During the initial period of conquest and colonization the *adelantado* or first governor of a conquered territory chose the *cabildo*'s first *alcaldes* and *regidores*. After this period the full *vecinos* ("citizens") or property owners elected the *cabildo* members. Under Philip II the fiscal necessities of the empire led to the sale of these offices to the highest bidder. Most of these offices, by the beginning of the seventeenth century, had become not only proprietary but also hereditary. In other towns these offices were part proprietary and part elective. In the less important towns many times the *cabildo* seats remained vacant because of lack of a buyer.

The *cabildo*'s functions were many and could be quite lucrative to the *cabildo* office holders. They distributed land to the citizens, imposed local taxes, raised a militia for self-defense, gave building permits, maintained jails and roads, and supervised market prices. They also had the added privilege of communicating directly with the king. The *cabildo* ceased to be a functional institution near the end of the colonial period because of the increasing centralization of the crown.

Besides the Spanish *cabildo*, there was a parallel Indian *cabildo*, which administered local government in the Indian towns and maintained order through its policing functions. The Indian *cabildo* contained the offices of *alcalde*, *regidores*, *escribano* (scribe), and *alquacil* (sheriff). The Indian *cabildo* had functions similar to the Spanish one, except that the Indian *alcalde* could only investigate, capture, and bring criminals to the jail located in the Spanish city of that district where major offenses were punished. He could, at times, punish minor offenses such as public drunkenness or failure to attend Mass. The Indian *cabildo* shared jurisdiction with the *cacique*, or dynastic ruler, the *corregidor* (Spanish lieutenant governors), Spanish priests, and *encomendero* (a holder of an inalienable grant of Indian labor). The *caciques* were responsible for the distribution of Indian labor while the Indian *alcaldes* and *regidores* were responsible for the rest of the duties regarding Indian government. The *cajas de comunidad*, or community treasuries, paid for municipal expenses.

The *cabildo abierto*, or open municipal council, revitalized the Spanish *cabildo* during the independence period. The *cabildo abierto* was a larger assembly which traditionally dealt with grave matters that affected the city or town. The most notable citizens, as well as the bishop and principal clergy, would attend the assembly. The Spanish American *cabildo* represented the local interests of the creoles against the *peninsulares*. During the independence period it was many times the *cabildo* which declared independence from Spain. (Constantino Bayle, *Los Cabildos Seculares en La America Espanola*, 1952; C. H. Haring, *The Spanish Empire in America*, 1963.)

Carlos Pérez

CABINDA. The enclave of Cabinda is a detached province of Angola* located north of the Congo River on the west coast of Africa. The area was dominated by the Loango kingdom until the fifteenth century. When the Portuguese arrived at the port of Tchiowa, now named Cabinda, in 1482, they established a trade relationship with the Mani-Kongo or monarch of the kingdom of the Kongo. In 1506 the Mani-Kongo, Nzinga Mbemba, accepted Christianity. The Portuguese competed with the British, French, and Dutch for trade in the area throughout the sixteenth century. The competition allowed the Cabinda kingdoms to expand their influence in the area and resist European control, but in 1665 the kingdom of the Kongo was defeated by a rebellious vassal state, the Ndongo, and the Portuguese. The French occupied Tchiowa (Cabinda) in 1783.

Portugal's influence around the Congo River declined in the early nineteenth century. The British established naval patrols along the coast to suppress the slave trade. However, near the end of the nineteenth century the Portuguese revived their interests in the Congo River by signing trade treaties with the African kingdoms in the region: Chinfuma in 1883, Chicamba in 1884, and Simulambuco in 1885. Cabinda became a Portuguese protectorate, and Angola was declared a Portuguese colony by the Berlin West Africa Conference of 1884–1885*. Cabinda's borders were finalized with French Congo* in 1886 and the Belgian Congo* in 1894.

A military coup in Portugal in 1926 installed a one-party regime in Portugal, the New State; and with the constitution of 1933 Angola and Cabinda were defined as separate overseas provinces. Africans in Cabinda were not legally Portuguese citizens, and they were required to carry identification cards labeling them as *indigenas* and forced to pay a head tax or work for the state for six months of each year. During the 1940s and 1950s anti-colonial movements were established in Angola and Cabinda. When Cabinda's status as a separate province was changed in 1956 to make Cabinda a district of the overseas province of Angola, nationalist movements in Cabinda organized. The war for Angola's independence (Cabinda attached) began in 1961 and lasted for thirteen years, with Cuba* assisting the Popular Movement for the Liberation of Angola (MPLA) in its efforts to liberate Angola and Cabinda as a united country.

Still under Portuguese control, the Cabinda oil fields were established in 1968 by the Gulf Oil Corporation. The spectacle of an American corporation financing the Portuguese war effort against a colony fighting for independence raised some controversy in the United Nations. In the 1970s the Front for the Liberation of the Enclave of Cabinda (FLEC) was organized and advocated secession of Cabinda from the new Republic of Angola, which was established in February 1976. FLEC proclaimed the independent Republic of Cabinda in 1977, but the guerrilla movement was suppressed by the presence of Cuban forces on behalf of Angola. Chevron Oil, having taken over the Gulf Oil Corporation, now operates the oil fields of Cabinda, the income from which is Angola's most substantial source of revenue. (Robin Cohen, ed., *African Islands and Enclaves*, 1983; Lawrence H. Henderson, *Angola: Five Centuries of Conflict*, 1979.)

Karen Sleezer

CABOT, JOHN. John Cabot was an Italian-born explorer who secured England's claim to the North American continent. His life is sparsely documented, but he was probably born in Genoa, later becoming a citizen of Venice where he was a merchant. Cabot told a contemporary that he had traveled as far as Mecca in the spice trade and conceived a plan to reach Asia by sailing westward across the North Atlantic Ocean. By the end of 1495 Cabot was in England where he secured royal sponsorship for his voyage. On March 5, 1496, Henry VII granted letters patent for the voyage to John Cabot and his three sons, authorizing them to "sayle to all partes, countreys, and seas, of the East, of the

West, and of the North" and to seek out and discover lands unknown to Christians. Cabot made an attempt to carry out his plan in 1496, but was forced to turn back.

Cabot set sail from Bristol about May 20, 1497, with eighteen to twenty men in a single small vessel, *Matthew*. He reached North American soil on June 24—either Cape Breton Island, Newfoundland*, Labrador, or Maine. Cabot claimed the land for Henry VII and England. After surveying some of the coast, Cabot sailed back to England. He had an interview with King Henry in London on August 10. Convinced that Cabot had reached Asia, the King financed a second voyage. Cabot left Bristol with a fleet of five ships in May 1498. Only one of the ships reached Ireland. Cabot's fate remains a mystery. (James A. Williamson, *The Cabot Voyages and Bristol Discovery under Henry VII*, 1962.)

CABRAL, PEDRO ÁLVARES. Pedro Cabral was born in 1467 or 1468 in Belmonte, Portugal, the second son of a nobleman. Little is known of his early life, other than that he was a *moce fidalgo* at the court of King John II, where he studied the humanities, and a *fidalgo* of the council of King Manuel I, a royal annuitant, and a knight of the Order of Christ. His fame owes entirely to a voyage begun in 1500, in which he logged two major achievements, the discovery of Brazil* and the beginning of profitable Portuguese trade with India*.

Cabral's feats were preceded by almost a century of Portuguese exploration along the coast of Africa, which culminated in Bartolomeu Dias* rounding the Cape of Good Hope in 1488 and Vasco da Gama* voyaging to India by that route beginning in 1497. Upon the latter's return in August 1499, the Portuguese were eager to mount a second expedition to open a commercial relationship with India* and wrest the eastern trade in silks, spices, and drugs from Moslem traders and the Venetians. Cabral was appointed a captain-general on February 15, 1500. The king wanted Cabral and other captains to impress native rulers in the East Indies with their ability to command. This was not meant to be a voyage of discovery, but of commerce and—where Muslims were concerned—of conquest.

Cabral's fleet of thirteen ships sailed on March 9, passing the Canary Islands* on March 14 and the Cape Verde* Islands on the 22nd. That night one of the ships was lost, and Cabral spent two days searching for it. Why he then steered or was deflected west of a southerly course has occasioned much debate. The best explanation seems to be that he did so, perhaps on da Gama's suggestion, to avoid the doldrums and make the best use of the trade winds and ocean currents, though he probably went further west than he intended. His landing on the Brazilian coast was an accident, not the result of a previous discovery known to the Portuguese.

The first sighting of land, a peak Cabral named Monte Pascoal, occurred on April 22. On the 24th the fleet moved to a safer harbor, which Cabral called Porto Sequro, where they remained eight days. Cabral did not take time to explore this new land, which he mistook for an island. He called it Vera Cruz, though Manuel subsequently renamed it Santa Cruz; the name Brazil, taken from a kind of dyewood found there, came later. To notify the king of his discovery, Cabral sent back to Portugal a ship commanded by Gaspar de Lemos.

On May 2 the remaining eleven ships set sail across the uncharted South Atlantic for the Cape of Good Hope. On the 12th the crew sighted a comet, traditionally a bad omen; and on the 24th off the Cape of Good Hope a severe storm struck, sinking four ships, damaging the others' sails, and separating them into three groups. Cabral's ship and two others landed briefly north of Sofala on the East African coast, where they encountered friendly Muslims, before being rejoined by three other ships on July 20 at Mozambique*, where they remained ten days for repairs. Meanwhile the seventh ship, under Diogo Dias, made the first European sighting of Madagascar*. The other six were greeted cordially in Mozambique and later, on August 2, were well received by the Arab king of Malindi, though they encountered suspicion from the king of Kilwa on July 26 and avoided altogether landing at Mombasa, which had been hostile to da Gama. They later stopped for supplies at the island of Andejiva, then departed for Calicut, India, arriving on September 13.

The zamorin (ruler) of Calicut was at first friendly, and the Portuguese gratified him by capturing an Indian ship with an elephant on it. They established a factory onshore, but because of opposition from Arab traders, they obtained only enough cargo for two ships. During the negotiations over trade, the Arabs attacked the factory, and about fifty Portuguese were slaughtered. Cabral captured and burned ten Arab ships, killed their crews, and bombarded Calicut for an entire day. He then moved on to Cochin, which he reached on Christmas eve. Here he was welcomed by the local king and was greeted by messengers from Cananore and Quilon, all of whom hated the zamorin as overlord of the Malabar Coast and were eager for trade with the Portuguese.

As the zamorin by early 1501 had amassed a fleet of about eighty ships to attack the Portuguese, Cabral quickly departed Cochin. One ship ran aground on the East African shore and was abandoned, the other five going to Mozambique for supplies and repairs. Cabral despatched Sancho de Tovar to reconnoiter Sofala, though he did not land there. Subsequently Pedro de Ataide's ship was separated from Cabral, leaving only his flagship and that of Simao de Miranda. Cabral and de Miranda reached Lisbon on July 21. It was a mixed reception. He had lost several ships with many men, and two more had returned empty, and he had failed to establish a factory in Calicut or good relations with the zamorin. However, he had won the friendship of the spice-producing kingdoms of Cochin and Cananore, planted a factory in the former, and demonstrated the viability of the all-water route to India, shifting the center of European trade with the East from Venice to Lisbon and greatly augmenting the power and prestige of Portugal. Ironically his discovery of Brazil, equally significant for the Portuguese empire and the more important of his accomplishments over the long run, received little notice. Cabral himself was soon eclipsed. Though he was originally given command of a proposed third voyage to India and worked for eight months to prepare for it, he was replaced before its departure on March

25, 1502 by da Gama, who now was or became his bitter enemy. Cabral left court for good, married about two years later, had six children, and spent the rest of his life on his small estate at Jardim, where he died in 1520. (Bailey W. Diffie and George D. Winius, *Foundations of the Portuguese Empire, 1415–1580*, 1977; William Brooks Greenlee, ed., *The Voyage of Pedro Alvares Cabral to Brazil and India*, 1938.)

William B. Robison

CALCUTTA. Calcutta is a major Indian seaport located on the Hooghly River and also close to the mouths of the Ganges and Brahmaputra rivers. It receives enormous volumes of commercial trade from those river valleys. Calcutta was founded in 1690 when Job Charnock of the British East India Company* established a settlement at the small village of Sutanati. Although the British contested Calcutta many times during the first half of the eighteenth century in struggles with the Indian nawabs, it was finally secured in the Battle of Plassey in 1757. By that time it had become a major commercial port in India. (Peter Kemp, *The Oxford Companion to Ships and the Sea*, 1976.)

CALIFORNIA. Spanish explorers reached the peninsula of Baja California in 1533, and within the next decade they explored the entire coast of Alta California and Baja California. There was no settlement of the area for the next century and a half. Late in the seventeenth century several missions were established along the coast, but Spain did not concentrate on establishing control of the region until the late 1760s. By that time they were worried about the possibilities of British or Russian expansion into the area. Baja California and Alta California were separate provinces but they were governed jointly until 1804 when each received its own governor. In 1822 they became part of Mexico.* See MEXICO.

CAMBODIA. Cambodia (Kampuchea) is a Southeast Asian country of about 66,000 square miles bounded by Thailand*, Laos*, and Vietnam*. Cambodia has a short coastline on the Gulf of Siam, but has been effectively landlocked, physically and psychologically, throughout its history. The country is unique in Asia, because it has much fertile land, but always has been thinly populated. For almost a thousand years Cambodia has been a tempting target for its more populous, expansionist neighbors, the Thais and Vietnamese. Cambodia's extraordinary fertility comes from the Mekong River. Tonle Sap, a great shallow lake and a catchment basin for Mekong floods, dominates the center of the country. In the rainy season Tonle Sap triples in size and when the water later recedes it leaves a rich layer of alluvial soil. Villagers harvest tons of fish as the lake shrinks. The Cambodian population is almost entirely Khmer—culturally and linguistically different from Thais or Vietnamese. Before all the recent turmoil, there were small urban minorities of Vietnamese and Chinese, but together these composed less than 10 percent of the population. There are also native tribes of people in the Cardamom and Elephant mountains.

Khmer culture was deeply influenced by that of India*. Hinduism, Indian classical music, and Sanskrit writing were adapted by the Khmers to their own traditions. The Khmers also absorbed Indian political ideas, according to which the king was divine, and his capital was a microcosm of the universe. The center of the temple, at the center of the capital, was the very axis of the universe. Cambodian architects, engineers, and stonemasons created over the course of four hundred years (ninth to thirteenth centuries, A.D.) the elaborate stone temple cities of Angkor, which are a perfection of the Hindu idea of the heavenly city. The temples now symbolize Cambodian nationalism, and are depicted on the national flag and currency, but had reverted to jungle and been almost forgotten during the centuries of Khmer decline after the Thais sacked Angkor in 1432.

Scholars debate the reasons why Khmer power faded. Some say the people were exhausted from massive building programs; others that the spread of Buddhism led to passivity in the face of aggression. But Cambodian history since the fifteenth century has revolved around a single strategic theme: How to preserve Khmer independence, Cambodian culture, and the Khmer race itself, when caught between two large, aggressive neighbors, Thailand and Annam* (Vietnam). When Frenchmen appeared on the scene in the mid-nineteenth century, Cambodia's plight meshed neatly with France's own imperial plans.

Cambodia had slipped into dual vassalage. Thailand annexed two northern provinces in 1814, and even manipulated Khmer royal succession. Thai troops swept through Cambodia in 1833, and the Vietnamese counterattacked the next year, sending 15,000 troops to occupy Cambodia and drive the Thais back. They also tried to "Vietnamize" Khmer society, driving priests from their temples and forcing officials to adopt Vietnamese names. Peasants revolted against foreign occupiers and their own ineffectual royal court. When the French offered Cambodia protectorate status in 1863, King Norodom leapt at the chance to enlist European power in the preservation of Cambodia. French rule, very indirect at first, seemed far preferable to the unpleasant alternatives.

France showed little economic interest in Cambodia, apart from some rubber plantations hacked out of the eastern forests. There was not much mining, and no industry. Rather, Cambodia's value to the French was strategic—it served as a buffer between Cochin China* and Thailand. The French were content to exercise control over Cambodian foreign policy, while allowing the royal family all the ceremonial perquisites of office. No one interfered much in the lives of the peasants. French popularity was cemented by their recovery of Cambodia's "lost provinces" from Thailand in 1907, and by their painstaking restoration of Angkor Wat, Angkor Thom, and other reminders of past glory.

No independence movement emerged to challenge French hegemony until World War II*. The rudimentary educational system and the absence of Cambodian-language newspapers retarded political development. But modern nationalism, when it came to Cambodia, did so with a fury, first in the guise of fascism, then neutralism, then the peculiar, intense, xenophobic communism of the Khmer Rouge. The Japanese interlude stimulated what had been until then only an embryonic Cambodian independence movement. The French governor-general placed a young, apparently compliant prince named Norodom Sihanouk on the throne in 1941. He, in turn, named Son Ngoc Thanh, a nationalist with pro-fascist leanings, prime minister. The French continued to administer Cambodian affairs until March 1945, but when the Vichy regime in France was replaced by De Gaulle's government, the Japanese jailed all French colonial administrators. King Sihanouk, acting on the advice of Son Ngoc Thanh, declared Cambodian independence. The date was March 12, 1945. But independence was not to be.

When Allied troops reached Phnom Penh in September 1945, they arrested Son Ngoc Thanh for collaboration. King Sihanouk, unable to defend Cambodia against the French, who were bent on returning, negotiated Cambodia's entry into the French Union. The promised autonomy was severely circumscribed until France, defeated by the Viet Minh, withdrew from Southeast Asia in 1954, giving independence to Cambodia, Laos, and Vietnam. Sihanouk abdicated his kingship in 1955, reclaimed the title of prince, and governed the new nation. (George Coedes, *The Making of Southeast Asia*, 1966; David Chandler, *A History of Cambodia*, 1983; Ben Kiernan, *How Pol Pot Came To Power*, 1985.)

Ross Marlay

CAMEROON. Cameroon is a country on the west coast of Africa. Its immediate neighbors are Nigeria*, Chad*, the Central African Republic*, Equatorial Guinea*, Gabon*, and the Republic of Congo*. Northern Cameroon is primarily Islamic in its religious background. It was not until late in the 1880s that the major European powers established trading posts in what is today Cameroon. The German African Society and the Woermann Company promoted German claims there, while the John Golt Company did the same for the British. On July 5, 1884, local tribal leaders gave the Woermann Company control of the Kamerun River, which became the basis for the German colony of Kamerun. France increased the size of the colony by 100,000 square miles in 1911 by ceding a large section of French Equatorial Africa to German Kamerun.

The area remained a German colony until World War I when a combined British-French force seized Kamerun in 1916. After World War I, France received a League of Nations mandate over most of what became known as Cameroon. It totalled approximately 167,000 square miles. Great Britain received a mandate over 17,500 square mile North Cameroon and 16,580 square mile Southern Cameroons. After World War II, a strong nationalist movement emerged in Cameroon, led by Reuben Nyobe of the *Union des Populations de Cameroun*. The French suppressed the rebels—Nyobe was killed in 1958—but the nationalist agitation could not be quelled, and in 1960 Cameroon became independent. Southern Cameroons voted to become part of Cameroon as well, while North Cameroon opted to become part of Nigeria. (Victor T. Levine, *The Cameroon Federal Republic*, 1971.)

Said El Mansour Cherkaoui

CANADA. The Dominion of Canada is the largest country in the area in the Western Hemisphere and the second largest in the world, but its population is only 25 million. The name Canada probably is derived from the Huron-Iroquois *kanata*, meaning a village or community. It was first used by Europeans in the early sixteenth century. The Dominion of Canada was formally created by the British North America Act of 1867 passed by the British parliament. This act, which the Canadian government has renamed the Constitution Act of 1867, joined together three British colonies—the Province of Canada, New Brunswick*, and Nova Scotia*. The Province of Canada was known as New France* until 1763, when the Treaty of Paris* ending the Seven Years War ceded the entire colony to Great Britain. Since then the region has been known as Quebec*, Upper Canada, Lower Canada, Canada East, and Canada West. The latter two made up the Province of Canada (1841–1867). The Dominion of Canada is a constitutional monarchy. The fathers of confederation believed that the United States of America would be offended by the creation of a kingdom on their northern border so they chose the word "dominion," which was vague and presumably less offensive.

Canada consists of ten provinces and two territories. The maritime provinces located on the Atlantic seaboard are Nova Scotia, New Brunswick, and Prince Edward Island*. Moving westward, the most populous provinces are Quebec and Ontario*. The prairie provinces are Manitoba, Saskatchewan, and Alberta. The westernmost province is British Columbia*. The newest province is the island of Newfoundland*, which joined Canada in 1949. Canada's two northern territories, the Northwest Territories and the Yukon Territory*, contain almost forty percent of Canada's total land area but less than one percent of the population, which, in part, explains their territorial status.

Upper Canada is the predecessor of the modern province of Ontario. It came into existence when the British parliament passed the Constitutional Act of 1791, dividing the colony of Quebec into Lower Canada in the east and Upper Canada in the west. Essentially, Upper Canada was the land enclosed by the Ottawa and the St. Lawrence rivers and the lower Great Lakes. Upper Canada was originally inhabited by Huron and Algonquian Indians. The first European to visit the area was the French explorer, Samuel de Champlain*, early in the seventeenth century. Champlain was followed by other French explorers and missionaries, particularly Jesuits*. By the eighteenth century the French were well established in the fur trade in the area. English fur traders began to move into the area early in the eighteenth century, and as a result of the Seven Years War (1756–1763) the French lost the area to the English.

In an effort to calm the Indians the Proclamation of 1763 closed the area to settlement, and by the beginning of the American Revolution* the population consisted of Indians and a few white soldiers, fur traders, and farmers. The situation changed rapidly in the 1780s as United Empire Loyalists began to establish the political and cultural tone of the colony. Rewarded with land and equipment by the British government, the Loyalists established farms along the upper St. Lawrence River, the north shore of Lake Ontario, and throughout the Niagara Peninsula. By 1790 the population exceeded 10,000. Most of the new population resented the restrictive government imposed on the area by the Quebec Act of 1774, and in 1791 in response to repeated appeals, the British government separated the newcomers from the French colonists to the north of them.

The Constitutional Act of 1791 created Upper Canada as a separate province with representative but not responsible government. The act also provided for the use of English common law and freehold tenure and reserved one-seventh of the province's land for the support and maintenance of a Protestant (i.e. Anglican) clergy, a provision that resulted in 50 years of political and social conflict. By the early nineteenth century political control of Upper Canada had fallen into the hands of an older and conservative oligarchy, the Family Compact. Conflict between the Family Compact and newer more progressive settlers dominated Upper Canada's politics. During the War of 1812 Upper Canada was invaded by the United States. Although the people of the area had mixed sympathies, the invasion was repulsed by British regulars and Canadian militia. The invasion strengthened the province's links to Great Britain, and fostered a growing and long lasting anti-American sentiment.

The increasingly bitter internal politics of Upper Canada turned violent in the 1830s. In 1837 William Lyon Mackenzie, who regarded himself as a spokesman for all the dissatisfied elements in Upper Canada and who favored a republican form of government, led an armed rebellion. Loyalty to Great Britain and the local government's strong stand quickly ended the rebellion, but the British government was sufficiently alarmed to investigate conditions in both Upper Canada and Lower Canada, where violence had also occurred. The investigation, led by John George Lampton, Earl of Durham, lasted only a few months in 1838, but the Durham Report brought significant change to both Upper and Lower Canada. Durham recommended a merger of the two colonies to assimilate the French population in Lower Canada, and the introduction of responsible government. Great Britain granted the former by the Union Act of 1840, but it viewed responsible government as being incompatible with imperial control. The Union Act also changed the name of Upper Canada to Canada West.

Between 1840 and 1849 the newly united Canada East and Canada West won responsible government by demonstrating that government without it was unmanageable, and one British governor general in Canada candidly admitted that responsible government virtually existed whether or not it was approved. The election of a Liberal government in Great Britain brought new instructions for Lord Elgin, the governor general in Canada, and the acceptance of the Rebellion Losses Bill by the imperial authorities in 1849 confirmed the existence of responsible government.

The union of Canada East and Canada West brought new political problems that responsible government did not resolve. Between the 1840s and the 1860s the Canadian government slowly ground to a halt. Increasingly, Canadian politicians looked to a union of all the British colonies in North America as a political solution. In 1864 the Canadian Liberal Party leader, George Brown, startled his Conservative counterpart, John A. Macdonald, by expressing his willingness to form a coalition government to consider a broader union. The Canadian politicians met with their maritime colleagues at Charlottetown, Prince Edward Island, and later in Quebec to discuss the scheme. Although there was formidable opposition in Nova Scotia and New Brunswick, and much doubt in Canada East, the British parliament passed the British North America Act in 1867, recently renamed the Constitution Act of 1867, which brought Ontario (Canada West), Quebec* (Canada East), New Brunswick, and Nova Scotia together in the Dominion of Canada.

In 1867 the newly created Canada faced a host of problems, including relations with the United States; the nature of its relationship with Great Britain; the strength of the provincial governments relative to the dominion government; and, above all, the presence of a large Francophone minority in the heart of the country determined to preserve its language and culture. The most immediate problem was the empty west. Canada had to acquire the territory between Ontario and the Pacific Ocean or the United States might settle the area and claim it. In 1869 Canada took a critical first step by acquiring the enormous Hudson's Bay Company* territory, which extended from Labrador to the Rocky Mountains. Almost immediately the Canadian government faced a rebellion by Metis settlers along the Red River in Manitoba. The Metis, a racial mixture primarily of French and Indians, feared the loss of their lands with the transfer of territory. The Manitoba Act of 1870 created Canada's first new province and ended the brief rebellion by conceding to the Metis land rights, denominational schools, and French language rights. For the most part the land rights did not materialize, and the Metis moved northwest to Saskatchewan and rebelled again in 1885 with no success. The lure of a transcontinental railroad brought British Columbia into the Dominion in 1871. Aided by huge land grants, government subsidies, special privileges, and Prime Minister John A. Macdonald's determination to make confederation work at all costs, the transcontinental Canadian Pacific Railroad was completed in 1885. By the early 1900s the railroads had fulfilled their mission. European immigrants filled in the Canadian west. Bankruptcy had brought Prince Edward Island into the Dominion in 1873, and in 1905 Saskatchewan and Alberta became provinces. Continental Canada was complete from the Atlantic to the Pacific.

As Canadians filled in the vast interior, relations with the United States improved. The Treaty of Washington of 1871 resolved several outstanding problems including fisheries, and the Boundary Waters Treaty of 1909 set a pattern for future relations by creating the International Joint Commission, the first permanent joint organization between the United States and Canada. Much of Canada's anger at the resolution of the Alaska Boundary Dispute in 1903 was directed at Great Britain rather than the United States. Canadians came to realize that as long as Great Britain represented Canada in international affairs British interests would be paramount, especially in cases involving relations with the United

States. Canada's major contribution to the imperial war effort in World War I assured it a separate and autonomous voice after the war. This status was confirmed in 1931 by the Statute of Westminster. Another tie to the mother country was severed in 1949 when the supreme court of Canada replaced the judicial committee of the privy council as the final court of appeal in Canada. However, the British North America Act of 1867, which could only be amended by the British parliament, remained Canada's constitution. Canada had to rely on this act because the provinces and the dominion government could not agree on an amendment process. Clearly the founding fathers had intended to give the dominion government dominance in confederation, but after 1882 a long series of court decisions had brought the provinces to a nearly equal position. In 1982, prompted by a threat of unilateral dominion action, nine of the ten provinces, Quebec dissenting, agreed on an amendment process. That process and a Charter of Rights made up the Constitution Act of 1982. This act and the British North America Act of 1867, renamed the Constitution Act of 1867, make up the constitution of Canada.

Quebec's dissent to the Constitutional Act of 1982 illustrates Canada's most persistent and critical political problem. The Francophone population of Quebec believes that the province deserves a special role in the Canadian confederation, a role that will ensure protection of their language, their culture, and their share of economic prosperity. The other provinces have been reluctant to grant such special status. The depth of Anglo-French antagonism has been revealed repeatedly since confederation in the Riel Rebellion, the Manitoba School Question, French resistance to conscription in both World Wars, and the separatist movement in Quebec. In 1980 a separatist proposal was defeated in a referendum in Quebec, but the nature of Quebec's future role in the confederation since the failure of the Meech Lake constitutional accord (1990) remains a major question. (J. Bartlet Brebner, *Canada*, 1970; J. L. Finley and D. N. Sprague, *The Structure of Canadian History*, 1984; E. W. McInnis, *Canada, A Political and Social History*, 1969.)

Peter T. Sherrill

CANARY ISLANDS. The Canary Islands are an archipelago in the North Atlantic Ocean, about 70 miles west of the Moroccan coast of Africa. There are seven major islands. In 1927 the Canary Islands became two formal provinces of Spain. Las Palmas Province consists of Gran Canaria, Fuerteventura, and Lanzarote, while Santa Cruz de Tenerife Province is composed of Tenerife, Gomera, La Palma, and Hierro. Although the islands were known to the Phoenicians, Romans, Carthaginians, Greeks, Arabs, and medieval Europeans, their modern history began in 1336 when Lanzarote Malocello first led a Portuguese expedition there. In 1402 French explorer Jean de Bethencourt claimed the Canaries for his sponsor, King Henry III of Castile. Between 1415 and 1466 Portugal tried but failed several times to conquer the Canary Islands. Spain emerged as the dominant power, crushing the native Guanches, who numbered approximately 80,000 people. By 1475 the Guanches controlled only three islands—La Palma, Tenerife, and Gran Canaria. Spain then conquered Gran Canaria between 1478 and 1483, La Palma between 1492 and 1493, and Tenerife between 1494 and 1496. The conquest brought diseases, cows, pigs, horses, sheep, and Mediterannean plants to the Canaries and annihilated the Gaunches by 1600. The conquest of the Gaunches was a model for the European conquests of other colonial people around the world in the next three centuries. (Alfred W. Crosby, *Ecological Imperialism: The Biological Expansion of Europe, 900–1900*, 1986.)

CANTON. Canton (Chinese Kwangchow, Guangzhou), a city of five million people, is the capital of Guangdong province and a bustling center for foreign trade. Canton has a distinctive cosmopolitan character that sets it apart from other Chinese cities. It has been south China's major trading port for two millennia and a window on the world for the sometimes xenophobic Chinese. The Cantonese speak their own dialect and are viewed by other Chinese as energetic and entrepreneurial. Most colonies of overseas Chinese originated in Guangdong. Canton is located on the left bank of the Pearl River, eighty miles upriver from Hong Kong* and the open sea. Ocean-going vessels can proceed only as far as Huangpu (Whampoa), a downstream suburb of Canton. The monsoon climate is subtropical, muggy most of the year, and rainy from April to September. Double-cropping of rice is possible, and the alluvial soil of Guangdong province is very fertile. Hence, the area around Canton is one of the most densely populated in all China.

Canton was first incorporated into an expanding China in the third century B.C. Merchants from Rome called there, but the city's real rise to prominence began with the arrival of Muslim Arab traders in the seventh century, when Canton's Great Mosque was built. The overland "Silk Route" was threatened by barbarian raiders, so long-range trade took to the sea. After the long journey from Arabia and India, through the straits of Southeast Asia and up the coast of Vietnam, Canton was the first Chinese port of call. With its quarters for Persians, Hindus, and Arabs, Canton had an international connection unique among Chinese cities. Suspicious T'ang emperors sent officials to oversee all foreign trade. The end of the T'ang Dynasty in 906 A.D. signaled the eclipse of Canton until European traders came six centuries later—first the Portugese, then the Spanish, Dutch, and British.

From the point of view of the emperor in Peking, a strictly regulated foreign presence in South China was useful but dangerous. The Europeans quickly subjugated most other Asian countries, and their religious and political ideas undermined the Confucian order, so in 1757 the Manchu emperor decreed that foreigners were to trade only with a few Chinese merchants incorporated into an official government monopoly (the *cohong* or Hong system). But Peking was very far away from Canton. Local officials and merchants found it easy to circumvent imperial restrictions on free trade. This was tolerable as long as the

Europeans bought more from China than they sold, paying for the surplus with Mexican silver, but became disastrous when the British reversed the balance of payments by selling opium grown in the hills of British India. Corruption, addiction, and the debasement of Chinese currency followed. When Peking sent an honest customs commissioner to destroy the narcotics, the British declared war. They humiliated the Chinese in the First and Second Opium Wars (1840–42 and 1856–60).

Canton became an open port with a European enclave on Shamian (Shameen) Island, a sandbar reclaimed from the Pearl River and connected to the city by a short bridge. Shamian had churches, villas, football fields, consulates, mansions, gardens, and an iron gate through which natives could be expelled at night. The arrangement pleased the Europeans but irritated Cantonese, who organized to overthrow the emperor, establish a republic, strengthen China, and expel the foreigners. Canton in the early 1900s was a hotbed of revolutionary activity. Sun Yat Sen's Nationalists staged an uprising in March 1911 that failed but produced 72 martyrs who are honored to this day. The Nationalists (Kuomintang, or KMT) held Canton during the tumultuous warlord period (1916–1926). They pulled down the old city walls, cleared slums, laid streets and sewers, and established a military academy. Meanwhile, the Chinese Communist Party (CCP), in temporary alliance with the KMT, established its own training school, the National Peasant Movement Institute, inside an old Confucian temple, with Mao Zedong himself as schoolmaster. The inevitable collision came in 1927, when the KMT turned on the communists, killing 5,000. The CCP reestablished its forces in the countryside. Twenty-two years later communist armies marched almost unopposed into Canton. The KMT had fled to Taiwan.

Since 1949 the communists have transformed Canton from a commercial city to one with a solid base of heavy industry. A semiannual trade fair highlights Chinese manufactured products for sale abroad. China opened dramatically to the West after 1978, and Canton has again become the city through which goods—and new ideas—enter China. Its proximity to Hong Kong and the Shenzhen Free Trade Zone ensures a leading role for Canton in China's modernization drive. (John K. Fairbank, *The United States and China*, 1979; Ezra F. Vogel, *Canton Under Communism: Programs and Politics in a Provincial Capital, 1949–68*, 1969.)

Ross Marlay

CAPE BRETON. Cape Breton Island, known by its initial French settlers as Ile Royale, was first occupied in 1710 after the British had seized Acadia*. It was strategically located in the Gulf of St. Lawrence. Its capital city was Louisburg.* Great Britain seized Cape Breton in 1745, returned it to the French in 1749, and permanently took it, along with much of the rest of New France*, in 1758. At the end of the Seven Years' War* in 1763, New France became permanent British territory. Settlement of Cape Breton was discouraged by the British until after the American Revolution, when Loyalists immigrated there from the American colonies. Great Britain designated Cape Breton a separate colony in 1784 and detached it from Nova Scotia. In 1820, however, Cape Breton was returned to Nova Scotia. (François Audet, *Canadian Historical Dates and Events, 1492–1915*, 1917.)

CAPE COLONY. Today known as the Province of the Cape of Good Hope, the Cape Colony was one of the original four provinces of the Union of South Africa*. In 1652 the Dutch East India Company* established a small colony at Table Bay, near what is today Cape Town, to service their fleet of ships going to and returning from the Dutch East Indies*. Located at the junction of the Atlantic and Indian Oceans at the southern tip of Africa, Cape Town became a port of major international importance. Late in the seventeenth and throughout the eighteenth century Dutch colonists, known as Boers, migrated to the Cape Colony. Great Britain seized the Cape Colony in 1795, returned it to the Dutch in 1803, and then seized permanent control after the close of the Napoleonic Wars in 1814.

The Boers chafed under British rule and in the 1830s they engaged in a mass migration—known as the Great Trek—out of the Cape Colony north into the Transvaal* and what became the Orange Free State*. Under British authority the Cape Colony annexed Kaffraria, now known as the Transkei region, in 1865, and then annexed Griqualand* West in 1871 after diamonds had been discovered there. The annexation of the Transvaal by the British (1877–81) led to the First Anglo-Boer War (1880–81) and the restoration of the Boer Republic (1881). The Second Anglo-Boer War* between 1899 and 1902 destroyed Boer resistance and gave Britain control over the Transvaal, and the Orange Free State, as well as Natal and the Cape. That control led to formation of the Union of South Africa in 1910. The Cape Colony then became known within the Union as the Province of the Cape of Good Hope. See UNION OF SOUTH AFRICA.

CAPE VERDE. The islands of Cape Verde are located off the coast of Senegal* in the eastern Atlantic Ocean. They were uninhabited when they were discovered around 1456 by Luigi da Cadamosto, a Venetian navigator in the service of Prince Henry of Portugal. The first permanent settlement was on the island of São Tiago in 1462. The Portuguese planted sugarcane, cotton, and fruit trees, and soon brought African slaves to work the crops. A small population of free Africans was also established on São Tiago. Slave trading became the most important economic activity during the sixteenth and seventeenth centuries. Slaves were trained to work the land on Cape Verde before being shipped elsewhere. The general decline of the slave trade along with the phaseout of slavery within the Portuguese empire (1858–78) contributed to steadily worsening economic conditions, which were aggravated by Portuguese restrictions on island exports and by periodic and devastating droughts. The economic situation improved slightly in the late nineteenth century when the island of Mindelo became an important refueling station for trans-Atlantic shipping.

Portugal ruled Cape Verde and the mainland enclave that is now known as Guinea-Bissau under one government until 1879, when each became a separate colony. Cape Verde's traditional role as a port of call was revived when the Portuguese used the islands as a staging area for troops in their African colonial wars of the mid-twentieth century. In 1951 Cape Verde became an overseas province of Portugal with representation in the Portuguese national assembly. This transition, however, did little to alter the restrictive and often brutally oppressive nature of Portuguese colonial rule. During the 1950s and 1960s, as the winds of change swept across Africa, a movement for independence emerged in the Cape Verde Islands.

In 1956, Amilcar Cabral, a Cape Verde-born, Portuguese-educated Marxist and African nationalist, founded the African Party for the Independence of Guinea and Cape Verde. PAIGC began as a peaceful, clandestine, political party, but in response to the violent repression of the Portuguese regime it developed into an armed guerrilla movement. The revolutionary struggle, which took place primarily in Portuguese Guinea* because the military strength of Portugal was sufficient to keep Cape Verde under tight control, continued until 1974 when a coup d'etat in Portugal led to a change in the African policy of the Portuguese government. The two sides negotiated an agreement that led to the establishment of the independent Republic of Cape Verde on July 5, 1975. Guinea-Bissau (Portuguese Guinea) had achieved independence separately in 1974. (James Duffy, *Portugal in Africa*, 1962; Richard Lobban, *The Cape Verde Islands*, 1974.)

Joseph L. Michaud

CARAVEL. The caravel was a small trading vessel common to the Mediterranean Sea from the fourteenth to the seventeenth centuries. The Spanish and the Portuguese both used caravels in their great voyages of exploration in the sixteenth century. Columbus*, Magellan*, Da Gama*, and Dias* all sailed in caravels. They were lateen-rigged on two masts originally, but the need to lower the long sail and bring the yard to the other side of the ship in order to tack into the wind made the caravel unworthy for long ocean voyages. That problem was overcome with the development of three-masted caravels with square rigging on the two forward masts and a lateen-rigged mizen. (Peter Kemp, *The Oxford Companion to Ships and the Sea*, 1976.)

CAROLINE ISLANDS. The Caroline Islands constitute a huge chain of nearly 1,000 islands in Micronesia,* stretching three thousand miles from Tobi Island in the west to Kosrae Island in the east. The population of the islands is primarily Micronesian in composition. Spanish explorers began reaching the Caroline Islands early in the 1500s: Gómez de Sequeira reached Yap in 1526; Alvaro Saavedra reached Ulithi in 1528 and Truk and Kosrae in 1530; and Pedro Fernández de Quiros explored Ponape in 1595. Despite the frequency of their contacts, the Spanish did not press their claims to the Caroline Islands until late in the nineteenth century when they began to fear German expansion there. But from the seventeenth century, maps of the Pacific showed the Caroline Islands as Spanish territory.

In the 1870s the German presence in the Pacific became more visible. German traders signed special trade agreements in 1878 securing preferred commercial rights in the neighboring Marshall Islands*, and in August 1885 a German naval flotilla captured Yap. Spain bitterly protested the invasion, and both countries submitted the dispute to Pope Leo XIII for arbitration. The settlement at the end of the year gave the Carolines to Spain, the Marshalls to Germany, and allowed Germany free trading privileges in the entire area. When Spain lost the Spanish-American War* to the United States in 1898, she also lost the Philippines* and Guam* in the Marianas*. Germany purchased the Caroline Islands and the other Marianas from Spain for $4.5 million.

German sovereignty in the Carolines was brief. When World War I* broke out, Japan occupied the islands and in 1919 received a League of Nations mandate* over them. Japanese control continued until the later stages of World War II*, when United States forces occupied them and used them for the military assault on Japan. In 1947 the United Nations granted the United States a trusteeship over the Caroline Islands. The administrative unit became known as the Trust Territory of the Pacific Islands*, and included the Mariana Islands, the Marshall Islands, and the Caroline Islands. Nationalist movements in the various areas of the Trust Territory of the Pacific led to political negotiations in the late 1960s and 1970s. Eventually those negotiations resulted in the establishment of the Federated States of Micronesia*, a new nation composed of the Caroline districts of Truk, Ponape, Kosrae, and Yap from the old Trust Territory of the Pacific. (F. W. Christian, *The Caroline Islands*, 1967; Donald M. Topping, "Micronesia: The Long, Long Haul to Ending the U. S. Trusteeship," *Pacific Islands Monthly*, January 1981, 13–18.)

CARTAGENA DE INDIAS. The city of Cartagena, Colombia, was established in 1533 by Pedro de Heredía and became an important port on the Caribbean Sea, especially for the shipment of mineral wealth out of the Viceroyalty of Peru. Because of its strategic location and economic significance, Cartagena was frequently the object of British and Dutch attack during the colonial period. In 1618 Cartagena was separated out as a discrete province with its own governor. It was subject to the Viceroyalty of Peru until the establishment of the Viceroyalty of New Granada in 1740. Cartagena proclaimed its independence from Spain in 1811 but fell under Spanish control again from 1816 to 1821. In 1821 Cartagena became part of Gran Colombia. See COLOMBIA.

CARTIER, JACQUES. Jacques Cartier was probably born in St. Malo in Brittany, France. Little is known about his early life, but when he married in 1520 he had already made voyages across the Atlantic. Financed by King Francis I, Cartier sailed in April 1534 to find a Northwest Passage* to China*. Cartier arrived in Newfoundland* twenty days later. He then continued northward along the coast, sailed through the Strait of Belle Isle, and eventually reached the Gulf of St. Lawrence. In June, he discovered Prince Edward Island*, explored Chaleur Bay, and proceeded northward to Gaspe Bay. Cartier took possession of his discoveries in the name of the king of France. He started home in early August.

Pleased with the first expedition, Francis I organized a second, which left St. Malo in May 1535. Cartier reached Funk Island off the coast of Newfoundland and reached the site of the present-day city of Quebec* on September 7, 1535. He continued sailing upriver as far as present-day Montreal. Cartier spent the winter at the St. Charles River and returned to France in May 1536. Five years later Cartier set sail for the New World and went up the St. Lawrence River again. He spent the winter in Canada and in June 1542 left for France. Cartier, the first European to survey the shores of the Gulf of St. Lawrence and the St. Lawrence River, died in St. Malo on September 1, 1557. (Samuel Eliot Morison, *The European Discovery of America: The Northern Voyages*, 1971.)

CATHAY. In the late fifteenth century, when the European voyages of discovery to the New World began, Cathay was the geographical term used to refer to China*. Marco Polo had traveled widely throughout Asia at the end of the thirteenth century, and in his published writings he had used the name Cathay in describing the land dominated by Kublai Khan. During the next two centuries Cathay was the reference word for China. In 1492, when Columbus* set out across the Atlantic, he was heading for Cathay where he hoped to find the riches and spices Polo had described. (David Quinn, ed., *New American World. Volume I. America from Concept to Discovery. Early Exploration of North America.* 1979.)

CATTLE. Cattle were one of Europe's most important biological transplants to the New World in the age of imperialism. Cattle are blessed with four important gifts, at least from a human perspective. First, they have an excellent thermo-regulating system, which allows them to survive very hot or cold climates. Second, they convert a variety of plants that humans cannot digest into meat, leather, milk, and fiber. Third, they can serve as draft animals. And fourth, cattle require relatively little care from humans. Columbus brought cattle to Hispaniola* in 1493, and they had spread throughout the West Indies* by 1510 and reached Mexico in the 1520s, Peru in the 1530s, Florida in the 1560s, New Mexico in the 1590s, and California in the 1760s. Northern Mexico was covered with millions of head of cattle by the end of the sixteenth century. On the Argentinan pampas, the region of Rio de la Plata, and the Rio Grande do Sul region of Brazil*, cattle multiplied rapidly, reaching as many as 50 million head by the eighteenth century, most of them wild. English and French colonists brought cattle to the eastern coast of North America in the seventeenth century and cattle then spread with them across the continent. A million head of cattle were in Australia* by the middle of the nineteenth century. Throughout the

European colonies in North America, South America, and Australia, cattle played a central role in the pre-industrial economies. (Alfred W. Crosby, Jr., *Ecological Imperialism. The Biological Expansion of Europe, 900–1900*, 1986.)

CAYMAN ISLANDS. The Cayman Islands are a British crown colony in the Caribbean Sea. All three of the islands—Grand Cayman, Cayman Brac, and Little Cayman—are coral formations located south of Cuba and northwest of Jamaica. The islands were first discovered by Christopher Columbus* in 1503, and he named them Las Tortugas. When Spain's fortunes declined in the seventeenth century, Great Britain filled the political vacuum in the Caribbean, and in 1670 Spain ceded the Cayman Islands to England. British settlers began moving there in 1734. The Cayman Islands were part of Jamaica until 1959, when they split off as a separate colony. In a 1959 plebiscite, the Cayman Islanders voted to remain a crown colony. By the mid–1980s, the population of the Cayman Islands—a mixture of Europeans and the descendents of African slaves—totaled just over 20,000 people. The colony is a center for tourism and finance in the Caribbean. (Peter Benchley, "Fair Skies for the Cayman Islands," *National Geographic*, 167 (June 1985), 798–824; H. H. Wrong, *The Government of the West Indies*, 1923.)

CEARÁ. The colony of Ceará, located in northeastern Brazil,* was given as a *donatária* in 1534 but actual settlement of the region by the Portuguese did not begin until 1603 when settlers from Pernambuco* came there. Ceará became a royal captaincy in 1619, but until 1656 its executive leaders were subject to Maranhão.* During seventeen of those years, between 1637 and 1654, Ceará was occupied by the Dutch as part of Netherlands Brazil*. The Portuguese were back in control of Ceará in 1656, when they moved it to the jurisdiction of Pernambuco. The colony remained there until 1799 when it was recognized as a separate captaincy. In 1822 Ceará became a province in the newly created empire of Brazil. See BRAZIL.

CELEBES. Celebes (Sulawesi) is a large island in eastern Indonesia* surrounded by the Flores, Celebes, Banda, and Molucca Seas and the Makassar Strait. It has four long peninsulas protruding from a central nucleus. Celebes' climate is equatorial, and wet enough for ebony, teak, and mahogany trees to flourish. The lightly populated eastern and southeastern peninsulas still have extensive tracts of virgin jungle. Celebes has a very long coastline and many bays, but only a few good ports, because of offshore coral reefs. No point on the island is far from the sea, but the terrain is so rugged that isolated mountain tribes have little contact with more cosmopolitan coastal people. Celebes' peculiar geography has allowed the island's seven major ethnic groups to develop apart. The Makassarese, Buginese, and Gorontalese are Muslim. The Minahasans, more westernized than the others, are Christian. The inland Mori and Toradja have a syncretic mixture of religions. The still primitive Toala are animists.

Celebes was influenced by Buddhist and Hindu ideas transmitted from powerful empires on Sumatra*, Java*, and Bali*. Islam reached southern Celebes only in the sixteenth century, just when Spaniards were converting Minahasans to Christianity. Portuguese, Spaniards, and Dutch struggled for control of Celebes' ports, strategically located on the sea lanes to the Spice Islands*. The Dutch expelled their European rivals more easily than they could subdue the stubborn sultans of Makassar* and Bone (Bugis) on the southwestern peninsula. Those two seafaring sultanates carried on a bitter rivalry for centuries, sometimes allying with Holland but rarely with each other.

Makassar's formal independence ended in 1667, but Makassarese continued to invade neighboring islands as late as the 1760s, and Buginese pirates were the terror of merchantmen until the nineteenth century. After the Dutch lost interest in Moluccan spices, Celebes was left to itself and was not "pacified" until 1860. The last revolts flared up in 1905 and 1911. The Japanese and Dutch fought bitterly over Celebes in World War II*, and Manado was heavily bombed. The Dutch used the island as a base for their "Republic of Eastern Indonesia" from 1946–1949. In December 1949, Celebes became part of the independent nation of Indonesia. In 1957, repeating an old pattern, Sulawesian nationalists revolted against the national government but were suppressed. The central authorities have encouraged transmigration from overcrowded Java and Bali to Celebes. The island is divided into four provinces, and for the time being, is politically integrated into Indonesia. (M. C. Ricklefs, *A History of Modern Indonesia*, 1981.)

Ross Marlay

CENTRAL AFRICAN FEDERATION. See FEDERATION OF RHODESIA AND NYASALAND.

CENTRAL AFRICAN REPUBLIC. The Central African Republic consists mainly of plateau surfaces, and is completely enclosed within the continent, sharing borders with Chad*, Sudan*, Cameroon*, Congo*, and Zaire*. Among various ethnic groups, the Banda and Baya represent half the population. Contact with Islam occurred through commercial relations with North Africa and close ties with the Hausa tribes. France became interested in the region in the late nineteenth century. Leading French imperialists, like explorer Savorgnan de Brazza, dreamed of creating a vast empire uniting French West Africa* with Algeria and land north of the Congo River. The French colonial penetration of Equatorial Africa was shaped by the acquisition of Congo-Gabon in 1886 and by a number of diplomatic conventions with other European powers. The convention of 1885 with Germany established the western border with German Cameroons, and the Convention of 1887 with King Leopold II* of Belgium established the southern border with the Congo Free State.* The eastern border with Sudan was established by an Anglo-French agreement of 1899. A French expeditionary force reached the Ubangi-Shari* region in 1889, signing treaties with tribal leaders in accordance with the rules laid down at the Berlin West Africa Conference of 1884–1885. When the agents of Leopold II established Zongo on the Ubangi River as an outpost of the Congo Free State, France countered and established Bangui (today the capital of the Central African Republic) on the other side of the river in 1889. In 1890, the *Comite de l'Afrique Francaise* sent a great expedition led by Paul Crampel to explore the region from the Ubangi to the Shari, but the expedition met with disaster when attacked by local tribes on the Shari River southeast of Lake Chad. Sustained resistance to French intrusion into the area—particularly from the Muslim Senussi sect— continued until 1912.

Nevertheless, the territory of Ubangi-Shari became a formal administrative entity under French rule in 1894. In 1905 administrative responsibility for Ubangi-Shari, Chad, Gabon, and Middle Congo* were all placed in a governor-general located at Brazzaville. Ubangi-Shari and Chad were fused into a single territory in 1906. Four years later Ubangi-Shari-Chad, Gabon, and Middle Congo were united to form the federation of French Equatorial Africa.* A 107,000 square mile area of French Equatorial Africa which included Bangi was ceded to Germany in 1911 as part of the agreement settling the Moroccon crisis. The Germans called it Neu-Kamerun. After World War I*, when Cameroon was divided up between France and Great Britain, Neu-Kamerun was returned to French control. By that time Ubangi-Shari and Chad had become separate political entities again.

The exploitation of raw materials and the sale of manufactured goods in Ubangi-Shari was left to private interest groups—concessionary companies— concerned with a rapid profit. The rapacious methods of collecting ivory and extracting wild rubber exhausted the labor force as well as the natural resources. By the 1920s and 1930s the French were emphasizing the production of coffee, cotton, gold, and diamonds in Ubangi-Shari. During the late 1920s and early 1930s the French were also preoccupied in another bloody guerrilla war in Ubangi Shari, known as the War of Kongo-Wara.

World War II* created new economic opportunities for Ubangi-Shari, which with the other territories of French Equatorial Africa, rallied to the "Free French" movement. External trade increased, as did the expansion of small scale local businesses. But the prosperity, as well as world politics, also gave birth to African nationalism in general and Ubangi-Shari nationalism in particular. In France, the constitution of the new Fourth Republic granted citizenship to Africans within their own overseas region of the French Union.* In the first elections held under the new constitution, Barthelemy Boganda was elected as the Ubangi delegate to the French National Assembly, confirming his rising political star. To protest discrimination and oppression at the hands of the French colons in Ubangi-Shari, Boganda helped found and lead the *Mouvement de l'Evolution Sociale de l'Afrique Noire* (M.E.S.A.N.). Boganda campaigned widely throughout Ubangi-Shari calling for civil rights; in the process he became an extraordinarily popular figure among native Africans. French colons, of course, considered him revolutionary and dangerous. In 1953, Boganda created the *Intergroupe Liberal Oubanguien* (I.L.O.). When the French arrested Boganda in 1951, he immediately became a national hero and MESAN became the dominant political group in the colony.

France's problems in maintaining her colonial empire were brutally exposed in the war in Indochina* in the early 1950s and by similar problems in Algeria*. She had neither the will nor the resources to fight similar guerrilla battles in all of her colonies, and in 1956 the French National Assembly passed the Enabling Act, or *Loi-Cadre* granting new power to all territorial assemblies in the French Union*. The next year MESAN won 347,000 of 356,000 votes cast in Ubangi-Shari elections, completely controlling the Ubangi-Shari Territorial Assembly. Boganda then formed the first Council of Government under the French governor of Ubangi-Shari. The constitution of the Fifth French Republic, implemented in 1958, provided for autonomous republics within the French Community*, and Ubangi-Shari was one of the first to avail itself of the option. On September 28, 1958, the people of Ubangi-Shari voted in a referendum to become an autonomous republic within the French Community. On December 1, 1958, Barthelemy Boganda became the first president of the new Central African Republic. Complete independence was attained on August 13, 1960. (Pierre Kalck, *Central African Republic, A Failure in Decolonisation*, 1971; Thomas O'Toole, *The Central African Republic, The Continent's Hidden Heart*, 1986.)

Said El Mansour Cherkaoui

CENTRAL PROVINCES AND BERAR. British India* annexed the Maratha kingdom of Nagpur in 1853 and attached it to Bengal* for administrative purposes. But it quickly became clear that the region was too far to be administered efficiently from Bengal, so in 1861 Great Britain created a new entity—the Central Provinces. The Central Provinces was also responsible for administering the Berar Province of Hyderabad. The Central Provinces and Berar became part of India in 1947. See INDIA.

CEUTA. Ceuta is a Spanish outpost of 7.5 square miles located on the north coast of Morocco*, at the Mediterranean entrance to the Straits of Gibraltar. In ancient times Ceuta was controlled by a succession of Phoenicians and Romans. The Visigoths overran Ceuta in 618 and Arabs seized it in 711 and used it as a springboard for their invasion of Iberia. Ceuta had great commercial significance as the Mediterranean outlet of the great trans-Sahara ivory, gold, and slave trade routes. But as the Reconquest took place over seven centuries, and as the Moors were gradually expelled from the Iberian peninsula, the Portuguese and the Spanish looked across the Mediterranean for conquests of their own.

Early in the fifteenth century the Portuguese began seeking commercial opportunities in North Africa; an army led by King John I captured Ceuta from the Moors on August 24, 1415. Although the Portuguese did not penetrate deeper into North Africa, Ceuta was the beginning of Portuguese expansion, first to

Madeira* and the Azores*, then down the west coast of Africa, and finally to the East Indies and New World. Ceuta remained under Portuguese control until 1580, when Philip II of Spain annexed Portugal. The Portuguese struggle against Spain lasted until 1668, when Spain finally recognized Portuguese independence in the Treaty of Lisbon. That treaty also ceded Ceuta to Spain. Except for the British occupation between 1810 and 1814, Ceuta has been under Spanish rule ever since. Over the years Moroccans have tried to regain control of Ceuta, periodically putting the region under siege. One siege lasted continually from 1694 to 1720. Until 1956, Ceuta was surrounded by Spanish Morocco*, but it was not part of the protectorate. When Morocco gained her independence in 1956, Ceuta remained under Spanish control. Today Ceuta is administered by the province of Cádiz. (Damiao Peres, *D. Joao I*, 1917; "Rabat: Loose Ends," *National Review*, 37, September 6, 1985, 45.)

CEYLON. Ceylon was the name the English gave to the island now called Sri Lanka*. The lush, tropical island off the southeast coast of India* was called Taprobane by the Greeks and Serendib by early travelers. The Sanskrit name Simhaladvipa, meaning "island of the Sinhalese," is thought to be the origin of "Ceylon." See SRI LANKA.

Ross Marlay

CHAD. The British explorers Dixon Denham and Hugh Clapperton (1822) and the German travelers Heinrich Barth (1853) and Gustav Nachtigal (1870–1871) were among the earliest Europeans to cross the Sahara from the north and reach the region of Lake Chad in north-central Africa. Pierre Savorgnan de Brazza established the French presence north of the Congo River (1880) and laid the groundwork for later French penetration of the Chad area from the south. After the Berlin West Africa Conference of 1884–1885* settled conflicting European claims in the Congo Basin, French expeditions moved north from the Congo into the Ubangi-Shari and Chad areas. British and German claims to the west (in Nigeria* and Cameroon*) by 1890 confined the French to the eastern shore of Lake Chad; but French expansion northward ultimately extended to the frontiers of the Niger district of French West Africa*, creating for France an African empire that stretched without interruption from the Congo to the Atlantic and the Mediterranean.

The French advance into the Chad region was opposed principally by Rabah Zubier, a Sudanese slave raider who had carved out for himself, through conquests and massacres, a formidable empire in Central Africa. In 1897 Emile Gentil, a French explorer and associate of Brazza, concluded a treaty of protection with the sultan of Baguirmi, whose kingdom was threatened by Rabah. In retaliation, Rabah attacked and pillaged Baguirmi. The French, after having secured British recognition of their rights in the area (1898), mounted a three-pronged campaign—with columns converging from Algeria, Niger, and the Congo—and defeated Rabah's forces in the battle of Kousseri on April 22, 1900.

In that engagement, both Rabah and the French commander, Francois Lamy, were killed. Some months later (September 1900) the French established the *Territoire Militaire des Pays et Protectorats du Tchad* with headquarters at Fort Lamy (now Ndjamena). Although the death of Rabah removed the chief obstacle to French control in central Africa, sporadic uprisings and clashes—particularly with the Senussi, a fanatical Moslem sect—prevented pacification of the northern Chadian areas until 1922.

In 1910 Chad, then part of the larger Ubangi-Shari-Chad colony, was joined with the French colonies of Gabon and Moyen Congo to form the federation of French Equatorial Africa* (FEA) under the administration of a governor-general in Brazzaville. Chad was separated from Ubangi-Shari in 1916 and was given a civilian administration and colonial status in 1920. In the 1920s cotton cultivation was forced upon the people of the southern areas to provide them with a means of paying their poll taxes and to help make the colony self-supporting. Cotton production notwithstanding, Chad remained one of the poorest and least developed colonies under French rule in Africa.

During World War II, the governor of Chad, Felix Eboue, a black man born in French Guiana, defied the Vichy government and rallied his colony and the rest of French Equatorial Africa to the Free French cause of General Charles de Gaulle. (Eboue was subsequently appointed governor-general of French Equatorial Africa by De Gaulle.) Chad became a vital supply base and air link for the Allies, as well as a launching point for desert campaigns against the Axis powers in North Africa.

After the war reforms involving the decentralization of colonial administration, representative institutions, economic development, and broadened educational and medical services—largely due to the influence of Eboue, who had died in 1944—began to be implemented. In 1946 the territories of FEA became part of the French Union*. Under the French Union, colonial Africans became French citizens and were permitted to participate in the election of representatives to their territorial assemblies, the French national assembly, and the assembly of the French Union.

In September 1958, despite severe inflation and religious clashes between northern Muslims (Arabic) and southern Christians and animists (blacks), the territory of Chad voted in a referendum to become an autonomous—but not independent—republic within the French Community*. In November 1958 the FEA was formally dissolved, though essential communications routes and customs and currency arrangements continued on an ad hoc basis. Efforts to reestablish a federation of the four FEA republics broke down when Gabon* withdrew and voted to become independent. Chad followed. On August 11, 1960, the independent Republic of Chad was established with Francois (Ngartha) Tombalbaye as head of state and prime minister. On April 4, 1962, the proclamation of a new constitution created a presidential system in Chad, with Tombalbaye as president. (Dougles Porch, *The Conquest of the Sahara*, 1984.)

Eric C. Loew

CHAMBERLAIN, JOSEPH. Joseph Chamberlain was a born on July 8, 1836, in London, to a middle class family. He spent his early years in the family screw-making business in Birmingham. Chamberlain entered politics in 1869 and was elected to the House of Commons in 1876 as a Liberal. William Gladstone* made him a member of the cabinet after the Liberal victory in the election of 1880. Chamberlain soon drafted a plan for Irish autonomy within the British Empire*, but the coercion-minded cabinet rejected it and Chamberlain resigned. After the Liberal victory of 1885 Gladstone again appointed Chamberlain to the cabinet, but when Gladstone proposed Irish Home Rule, Chamberlain resigned, believing that the prime minister's plan went too far and weakened the imperial connection. He emerged as a major leader of the Liberal Unionists who opposed Gladstone and who cooperated with the Conservatives to keep him out of power to block Home Rule. The Conservative-Unionist coalition succeeded in its goal.

In 1895 the Conservative P.M. Lord Salisbury made him colonial secretary, a post Chamberlain held until 1903. It was a fateful period for the British Empire. In late 1895 the English miners and other Uitlanders (outsiders) in the gold fields of the Transvaal* grew increasingly angry at their treatment by the Boer government. Chamberlain supported the plans of Cecil Rhodes*, the prime minister of Cape Colony*, to use the Uitlanders to overthrow the Transvaal government. The result was the botched Jameson raid*, which led to a growing crisis in South Africa*. Chamberlain's Liberal critics maintained that he and the colonial office had possessed prior knowledge of the Jameson raid, but the true extent of his involvement with Rhodes remains concealed. Nevertheless, Liberals continued to condemn him for what they called his unscrupulous handling of South African affairs.

Chamberlain pursued negotiations with the Transvaal, but its president, Paul Kruger, would not agree to the British demands, which included voting rights for Uitlanders, who had come to outnumber the Boers. The failure of compromise led to the Boer War* (1899–1902). During the conflict Chamberlain often spoke in support of the war and of the British Empire. Just after the British victory he traveled to South Africa and helped achieve a workable settlement.

Chamberlain promoted the creation of the Australian Commonwealth in 1900. He advocated imperial preference, a repudiation of the traditional liberal doctrine of free trade, but he made no immediate effort to secure cabinet support for such a radical change in British tariff policies. Chamberlain rejected the traditional foreign policy of "Splendid Isolation," which Britain had followed in the nineteenth century. Consequently he called for increased Anglo-American cooperation and helped to secure the Anglo-Japanese Alliance of 1902*. He also supported an Anglo-German alliance, and, when that proved impossible, helped arrange talks with France that later led to the Entente Cordiale.

After the elections of 1903 Chamberlain continued on in the cabinet of A. J. Balfour. Trying to get the cabinet to accept imperial preference, he made public his views in several speeches advocating tariffs to help increase trade within the Empire and to finance new social programs. The cabinet refused to accept his ideas, and Chamberlain resigned in September 1903. He continued to work for imperial preference for several years—without success. Chamberlain suffered a paralytic stroke in 1906 from which he never recovered. He died in Birmingham on July 2, 1914. (Richard Jay, *Joseph Chamberlain*, 1981; William L. Strauss, *Joseph Chamberlain and the Theory of Imperialism*, 1971.)

Walter A. Sutton

CHAMPLAIN, SAMUEL DE. Samuel de Champlain was born in 1570 at Brouage, France. He joined the French army and fought in Brittany in the 1590s. Between 1599 and 1601 Champlain sailed to the New World for Spain, visiting Cuba*, Mexico*, Puerto Rico*, Hispaniola*, and Central America. After returning to France, Champlain entered the service of Vice-Admiral Aymar de Chastes and sailed to what became New France* in 1603. He explored the St. Lawrence River and returned to France with a profitable cargo of dried fish and fur pelts.

Between 1604 and 1607 Champlain led exploring expeditions to Acadia* and down the North Atlantic coast. On a return voyage to North America in 1608, Chaplain established a trading post at Quebec*, which became the first permanent white settlement in New France. In 1609 he explored deep into what today is New York state. Between 1613 and 1616 Champlain led several other expeditions in an attempt to find the Northwest Passage*. He spent most of the rest of his life in Quebec, except for the years between 1629 and 1632 when England had captured Quebec. Champlain returned to New France in 1633 and died there on December 25, 1635. (Morris Bishop, *Champlain: The Life of Fortitude*, 1948.)

CHARLES V (CHARLES I OF SPAIN). Charles V was born in Ghent on February 24, 1500, and died September 21, 1558, at the monastery of Yuste in Spain. Of the Habsburg dynasty, he was king of Spain (as Charles I) from 1516 to 1556 and Holy Roman Emperor from 1519 to 1556. In 1516 Charles inherited the Spanish throne from his grandfather, Ferdinand II (Ferdinand of Aragon). He was elected emperor in 1519 and began a policy of expanding Habsburg influence in Europe and the New World. Charles V waged war against France, the Habsburg's main rival in Europe, and against the Ottoman Empire, which had expanded into southeastern Europe. In fighting the Reformation in Germany, he issued the Edict of Worms in 1521 against Martin Luther and defeated the German Protestant princes in the Schmalkaldic War of 1546–1547. As the result of military setbacks in the struggle against Protestantism in Central Europe, Charles was forced to sign the religious Peace of Augsburg in 1555.

During Charles V's reign, Spanish possessions in America expanded considerably. In 1515–1516 Juan Diaz de Solís explored and claimed for Spain the Río de la Plata. In 1519 Ferdinand Magellan*, a Portuguese who was employed by Charles, won the emperor's support for a voyage of discovery that resulted in the first passage around South America and the first circumnavigation of the globe. Between 1519 and 1521 Hernán Cortés*, seeking the gold of the Aztecs*, captured Mexico* for Spain. Charles V also commissioned Francisco Pizarro* with extensive powers in Peru*, and in 1535 Pizarro successfully completed the conquest of the Incas*. As Holy Roman Emperor, Charles authorized the exploration of the Caribbean coast of South America, which was carried out by the German adventurers Ambrosius Alfinger and Nikolaus Federmann in 1535 to 1538. By the end of his reign Charles V had witnessed the boundaries of his empire in the Americas expanded as far north as California and Texas. (Manuel Fernández Alvarez, *Charles V*, 1975.)

William G. Ratliff

CHARCAS. The Audiencia of Charcas, headquartered in what is today Sucre, Bolivia*, was established in 1559 when the population of Bolivia made it increasingly difficult for the Audiencia of Lima to deal with problems there. The region supervised by the Audiencia of Charcas had been officially under the authority of the Audiencia of Lima since 1542. The audiencia was under the jurisdiction of the Viceroyalty of Peru.* At first the Audiencia of Charcas had jurisdiction over most of what is today Bolivia, Paraguay*, southern Peru, and the Río de la Plata* region. As those areas gained in population and development, however, the geographical reach of the audiencia's authority was successively limited. In 1568 southern Peru was returned to the authority of Lima. Paraguay and Tucumán* were transferred to the Audiencia of Buenos Aires* when it was founded in 1661. With the establishment of the viceroyalty of Buenos Aires in 1776, the new viceroy also became the president of the Audiencia of Charcas, although cases continued to be heard in Charcas. That too stopped in 1783 when an audiencia was established in Buenos Aires. The region controlled by the audiencia was taken over by the troops of the United Provinces of Río de la Plata in 1810, reoccupied by Spanish forces from 1816 to 1824, but then liberated once again to become the nucleus of what is today Bolivia. See BOLIVIA.

CHILE. Located on the western coast of South America, Chile is a very long (over 2,600 miles) and narrow (nowhere over 250 miles) country. The harsh Atacama Desert in the north and the wet and stormy forest land of the south are inhospitable to settlement and are sparsely populated, while the fertile Central Valley, with its mild climate, is home to two-thirds of the population. Chile's southern hemisphere location, rugged Andes mountains to the east, vast expanse of the Pacific to the west, desert on the north, and Antarctic region to the south have isolated the country. Chile's population of over 12 million is predominantly mestizo, Catholic, and urban. By Latin American standards, the country is relatively industrialized and modern, with a 95 percent literacy rate and a per-capita GNP of over $1,700. The major contradiction to modernity is the poor distribution of wealth, a result of Spanish imperialism and the neo-imperialism of the post-colonial period.

The first permanent Spanish settlements were established in Chile by Pedro de Valdivia in 1541. An earlier effort in 1536 had been defeated by the Araucanian Indians, who contested European dominance for more than three centuries. The Spanish authorities issued *encomiendas** to soldiers, allowing them to exploit the land and extract tribute from the Indians. The Araucanians, who had a history of resisting Incan demands for tribute and dominance, fought Spain with great tenacity and restricted the Europeans to the Central Valley area. The resistance persuaded Spain to accept enslavement of the Indians by the *encomenderos* and to provide a royal subsidy for the maintenance of a standing army. Relations with the natives, in the form of settlement defense, pacification wars, and slave raids, were central to the economic life of the Chilean colony. Chile was not a profitable colony for the Spanish Empire*. The gold, grain, hides, and wine exported from Chile could not justify the tens of thousands of Spanish soldiers killed (and the hundreds of thousands of Araucanians) or the drain on the royal treasury. Colonial Chile was a highly stratified society where physical labor was to be avoided, laborers were to be exploited, and arbitrary use of political authority was accepted.

The occupation of Spain by Napoleon's army brought an end to Spanish control of Chile, but independence did not eliminate the imperial patterns of the society. A *cabildo abierto* (open council) abolished the royal government in 1810 but failed to agree on a successor government. In 1814 a royal army from Peru* reestablished control in the name of the Spanish crown but Argentine independence forces, led by José de San Martín* and joined by the Chilean *criollo* army of Bernardo O'Higgins, liberated Santiago in 1817 and formally declared the independence of Chile in 1818. O'Higgins was named the supreme director of Chile, but his government was marred by increasingly autocratic leadership and a conservative-liberal split between the *pelucones* (bigwigs) and the *pipiolos* (novices) within the *criollo* elite. O'Higgins was forced into exile in 1823 and the subsequent civil war brought the conservative *pelucones* to power in 1830. The Chilean constitution of 1833, written by the conservatives, embodied the patterns of Spanish colonialism without the conscience of the Crown. Primogeniture, a state church, limited male suffrage based on literacy and property, and a minimal government with a powerful president provided stability and little possibility of social change. Spanish imperialism was removed from Chile, but its local progeny, the landed elite, remained firmly entrenched in position to exploit the majority of Chileans through their control of the land and the government. (Robert J. Bauer, *Chilean Rural Society from the Spanish Conquest to 1930*, 1975; Brian Loveman, *Chile: The Legacy of Hispanic Capitalism*, 1979.)

Bruce R. Drury

CHINA. For centuries now, ever since Marco Polo's visit to Asia in the late thirteenth century, China has been a magnet attracting westerners interested in exploiting her enormous natural resources and huge market of consumers. During the age of imperialism, every major European power tried to stake out a sphere of influence in China, and although China never became a colony, she played a crucial role in European-Asian affairs in East Asia during the last five hundred years. The need to find a water route to Asia inspired Columbus's voyages in the 1490s and early 1500s, and the hope of discovering a Northwest Passage* to China was at the forefront in the minds of dozens of other European explorers in the sixteenth and seventeenth centuries. China was first opened to the European powers in 1555 when the Portuguese began constructing their factory and settlement at Macao* on the estuary of the Pearl River. The Dutch tried but failed to dislodge the Portuguese from Macao in the early 1600s, and although they kept trade avenues open to China, the Dutch concentrated their imperial efforts in the East Indies.

By the early nineteenth century it was the French and the English who were seeking to dominate the China trade. The English, because of their secure base in India* and Burma*, were in the best position to reap the benefits of commercial intrusion into China. France moved into Indochina* in the 1860s, hoping to use the Mekong River as an artery for entering China. Eventually they learned that the Mekong River would not provide a waterway into China, leaving the British in the premier position for exploiting China.

British merchants had been trading with China since the 1630s, but that trade did not assume significant proportions until 1760, when the Chinese government declared Canton* (Guangzhou) an open port, the only one in the whole country. The British purchased huge amounts of tea, as well as silk and other commodities, from the Chinese in Guangzhou, but not until the late eighteenth century did they find a product of their own which the Chinese wanted—opium from Bengal in India. By the 1820s China was purchasing enormous volumes of opium, turning her favorable balance of payments with the British into a massive deficit which was draining silver from the country. In 1839 Chinese soldiers destroyed 20,000 chests of British opium in Canton, and the next year the British attacked, starting the first Opium War. The Chinese were no match for British naval strength and firepower. China sued for peace in 1842, and the subsequent Treaty of Nanking* inflicted humiliating terms upon China. The treaty opened four new ports (Xiamen, Fuzhou, Ningbo, and Shanghai) to foreign trade, ceded Hong Kong* to Great Britain, established special zones in the trading cities where foreigners could buy property and build schools, gave foreigners the right of extraterritoriality* (exempting them from Chinese law and subjecting them only to the laws of their own governments), reduced the Chinese import tariff to 5 percent, and provided that any concessions given to one nation automatically applied to all other nations.

During the bloody Taiping Rebellion in China during the 1850s, France and Great Britain increased their penetration of China, launching the second Opium War. French and British troops sacked and looted Beijing before the Chinese government yielded in 1860. A series of treaties between 1858 and 1860 enlarged the European spheres of influence in China. Eleven new ports in north China, along the Yangtse River, on Hainan Island, and on Taiwan were opened to European merchants; the opium trade was legalized; western ships were exempted from transit taxes; and the western powers received diplomatic representation in

Beijing. Great Britain also acquired Kowloon on the mainland across from Hong Kong. More gains were made in the later years of the nineteenth century. By 1885 the number of open ports had increased to 29 and foreign police and troops were allowed to enforce the law and maintain order in them. China granted Portugal perpetual sovereignty over Macao in 1887.

But in the 1890s, instead of continuing their policy of cooperation in exploiting China, the imperial powers began carving out formal spheres of influence. Great Britain all but controlled the Yangtse Valley and received a 99-year lease on the New Territories in 1898, while the Russians took control of Darien and Port Arthur and increased their presence in Mongolia and Manchuria. Germany seized Kiaochow* and the Shantung Peninsula, while France gained a formal sphere of influence over the southern Chinese provinces bordering Vietnam*. The United States, afraid she would be frozen out of the Chinese markets, proposed the Open Door policy in 1899, demanding unrestricted access to all Chinese markets by any western power. Concerned about going to war over China, the European powers were ready to agree. The next year the Boxer Rebellion* resolved the issue. The Boxer Rebellion, which erupted in western Shantung in 1900, expressed powerful anti-foreign sentiments, especially toward Christian missionaries, merchants in the trade ports, and the diplomatic legations in Beijing. The Boxers seized the capital of Beijing and laid seige to the foreign legations. Only a combined European and Japanese army saved the legations from destruction.

By that time the Europeans were prepared to maintain the status quo in China, but the Japanese were not. Japan became the dominant imperial power in China until her defeat in World War II*. When the Chinese Communists triumphed in 1949, one of their central objectives was to expel the foreign imperialist powers from China. Their aims were not completely realized until the 1980s. In 1984 Great Britain agreed to turn Hong Kong over to the People's Republic of China in 1997, and in 1987 Portugal made the same promise concerning Macao. (Jean Chesneaux, Marianne Bastid, and Marie-Claire Bergere, *China from the Opium Wars to the 1911 Revolution*, 1976; Roger Pelissier, *The Awakening of China*, *1793–1949*, 1970; Hu Sheng, *Imperialism and Chinese Politics*, 1955.)

CHRISTMAS ISLAND. See KIRIBATI; LINE ISLANDS.

CHURCHILL, SIR WINSTON LEONARD SPENCER. Winston Churchill was born on November 30, 1874, at Blenheim Palace, Oxfordshire. Through his father, Lord Randolph Churchill, one of Britain's most notable Tory politicians, he was descended from John Churchill, the first Duke of Marlborough. His mother, Jennie Jerome, was an American, the daughter of a New York financier. Following an unhappy, neglected childhood and an indifferent scholastic career at Harrow, Churchill embarked on a military career, entering the Royal Military College at Sandhurst and graduating in 1894. From 1897 to 1899 Churchill served as a subaltern in India and Africa and, as a war correspondent, he followed the Spanish-American War in Cuba and the Boer War in South

Africa. In 1900 Churchill entered politics as a Conservative and won a seat in parliament in the same year. In 1904, however, he left the Conservative Party when he disagreed with that party's tariff policies. The same year he joined the Liberal Party and, in 1906, became undersecretary of state for the colonies, where he defended the policy of conciliation and self-government for South Africa. In 1908 Churchill joined the government of Prime Minister Herbert H. Asquith as president of the board of trade. He subsequently served briefly as home secretary and, in 1911, transferred to the Admiralty. As first lord, Churchill began a massive enlargement of the British Navy, largely in response to Germany's increasing naval expansion. The navy under Churchill received its largest naval expenditure in British history.

In the years before the outbreak of World War I he continued his interest in imperial affairs. Despite his conservative upbringing, Churchill enthusiastically supported the Liberal policy of home rule for Ireland*, moving the second reading of the Irish Home Rule Bill in 1912. The beginning of the war turned his interests back to naval affairs and, in 1915, Churchill became the chief advocate of the disastrous Dardanelles campaign, the failure of which caused him increasing political trouble. In November 1915 Churchill resigned his post at the Admiralty and served on the western front as an officer of the Royal Scots Fusiliers. After distinguished service in France and Belgium, Churchill returned to parliament in 1916 and was soon appointed minister of munitions in the government of Lloyd George. In 1921 Churchill went to the Colonial Office*, where his principal concern was the question of the mandated territories in the Middle East. Churchill pursued a policy of reduced British military force, relying instead on the establishment and support of rulers congenial to British interests. For Palestine* he produced in 1922 the white paper confirming Palestine as a Jewish national home while recognizing continued Arab rights. Churchill fell from political grace in 1922 following the Colonial Office's policy of urging a firm stand against Turkish attempts to reoccupy the Dardanelles neutral zone at Chanak (present-day Canakkale). British public opinion considered Churchill's stand provocative and a threat to peace, and the government collapsed.

Churchill remained outside the government for most of the years from 1922 to 1939, a time which he devoted largely to painting and writing. His work during this period includes his autobiographical history of the 1914–1918 war, *The World Crisis*, and a biography of his ancestor, *Marlborough: His Life and Times*. During the general strike of 1926, Churchill took the editorship of the reactionary *British Gazette*, an emergency official newspaper which he used effectively to attack the Labour Party. In the 1930s Churchill used his parliamentary seat to warn repeatedly of the menace of Hitler's Germany. After Germany invaded Poland in September 1939 Churchill was reappointed to the Admiralty. Following Germany's invasion of the Low Countries in 1940 and the collapse of Neville Chamberlain's government, he was installed as prime minister. Prime Minister Churchill served as a symbol of resistance to Hitlerism during the crucial period of 1940–1941 and, with the United States entry into

World War II, joined with President Franklin D. Roosevelt and Soviet leader Josef Stalin in the allied triumvirate which eventually defeated fascism. In the postwar era Churchill's Conservative Party was voted out of power in a Labour Party sweep in 1945. Churchill, however, remained a parliamentary gadfly, attacking Labour's policy of independence for India*, which he termed a "scuttle" of the Empire (although Churchill did not vote against the Indian independence legislation). Churchill returned as prime minister in 1951, but ill health forced him to resign in 1955. He received the Nobel Prize for literature in 1953 for his six volume *The Second World War*, and he was knighted in 1953. Sir Winston Churchill died in London on January 24, 1965.

With few exceptions (notably Ireland and South Africa) Churchill was an ardent supporter of the British Empire*. As early as 1897 Churchill spoke of his desire for the preservation of imperial rule. Addressing the critics of the Empire in the Jubilee Year 1897, he termed those who argued for the inevitable decline of the empire "croakers" and he fervently called for the continuation of "our mission of bearing peace, civilisation, and good government to the uttermost ends of the earth." In a City of London speech on November 4, 1920, Churchill excoriated the critics of the Empire as "a worldwide conspiracy against our country, designed to deprive us of our place in the world and rob us of victory." A self-described child of the Victorian era, Churchill always thought of the Empire as "an old lion, with her lion cubs by her side." Even with the end of the Second World War and loss of India, the "jewel in the Crown," he retained his imperialist views. (Martin Gilbert, *Winston S. Churchill*, 7 vols., 1966–1986.)

William G. Ratliff

CIPANGU. In the late fifteenth century, when the European voyages of discovery to the New World began, Cipangu was the geographical term they used to refer to Japan. Marco Polo traveled widely throughout Asia at the end of the thirteenth century, and in his published writings he described a land of riches lying 1,500 miles off the coast of Cathay, which he called "Chipangu." The term Cipangu soon became synonymous with Japan. Because Polo had placed Cipangu too far east of China, Columbus* mistakenly thought he had reached Cipangu when he reached Cuba. (David Quinn, ed., *New American World. Volume I. America from Concept to Discovery. Early Exploration of North America*, 1979.)

CLAYTON-BULWER TREATY. The acquisition of California by the United States in the Mexican War of 1846–1848, and the discovery of gold in California, renewed interest in an interocean canal across Central America. The most practical route seemed to be through Nicaragua.* For that reason, there was great concern in the United States over the expansionist moves of Great Britain in that region. Specifically, the United States objected to the assumption of a protectorate by Great Britain over the Mosquito Indians and their territory. And the British declined to relinquish their protectorate to allow construction of a canal under the auspices of the United States and Nicaragua. Both the United States and Great Britain feared that their conflicting interests in the area could lead to war, and agreed to negotiate their differences in 1850. The negotiations were held in Washington with Secretary of State John M. Clayton representing the United States and Sir Henry Bulwer representing Great Britain. Both countries agreed in the treaty never to obtain or maintain exclusive control over any ship canal through the region; never to fortify the same; and never to gain control over Nicaragua, Costa Rica*, the Mosquito coast, or any part of Central America. The United States Senate ratified the treaty by a vote of 42 to 10 on April 19, 1850. The Clayton-Bulwer Treaty remained in effect until abrogated by the Hay-Pauncefote Treaty of 1901*. (W. H. Callcott, *The Caribbean Policy of the United States, 1890–1920*, 1927.)

Joseph M. Rowe, Jr.

CLIVE, ROBERT. Robert Clive, widely considered to be the founder of the British Empire in India*, was born in 1725 in Shropshire, England. In 1744, while working as a writer for the British East India Company*, Clive was assigned to Madras. When French forces seized Madras soon after, Clive joined the military expeditions against the enemy and soon emerged as a courageous leader. He received the rank of captain in 1751 and further distinguished himself in battle with French troops. The French surrendered in 1752 and Clive returned to England in 1753. After an unsuccessful attempt to secure a seat in parliament, Clive returned to India in 1755. When the famous incident of the Black Hole of Calcutta* occurred in 1756, Clive was sent, now as a lieutenant colonel, to Bengal to punish the perpetrators. Through a series of threats, skillful negotiations, bribes, and military skirmishes, Clive defeated the nawab of Bengal in 1757. Two years later he defeated the Dutch at Biderra.

Clive returned to England in 1760 and was raised to the Irish peerage as Lord Clive of Plassey. He won his seat in parliament and was appointed governor of Bengal. Clive returned to India in 1765. During his tenure as governor of Bengal, Clive consolidated the power of the East India Company over the region and worked to eliminate graft and corruption among company officials. He also introduced the system of dual governments which characterized British administration thereafter. Clive returned to England in January 1767 to face charges of official corruption, and although he was eventually acquitted in 1773, by that time he had become severely depressed. Robert Clive committed suicide in 1774. (Mark Bence-Jones, *Clive of India*, 1974; T. G. P. Spear, *Master of Bengal: Clive and his India*, 1975.)

COCHIN-CHINA. Cochin-China is the southernmost part of Vietnam*, embracing the Mekong delta and surrounding regions, from the central highlands in the north to the Ca Mau peninsula in the south, and from the Cambodian border to the South China Sea. The name Cochin-China was bestowed by the

Portuguese, and later adopted by the French for their only directly ruled colony in Indochina*. (The other areas under French control were formally protectorates.) French control lasted from 1858 to 1954. Cochin-China was a frontier zone. Vietnamese history before the advent of French imperialism was a long march southward from the cradle of Vietnamese culture in Tonkin*. The Vietnamese had only recently wrested the northern part of Cochin-China from a people known as the Chams when the French arrived on the scene, and the Plain of Reeds west of Saigon was a region of mixed Vietnamese-Khmer settlement.

The changes wrought by French imperialism were more dramatic in Cochin-China than anywhere else in Indochina. Saigon arose where a fishing village had been; it grew into a colonial city of French expatriates and rootless Vietnamese who acquired a semi-Europeanized outlook. Saigon was more dynamic than traditional cities such as Hue, Haiphong, and Hanoi. With its French schools, its international orientation, and the constant coming and going of passenger and merchant vessels, Saigon became the center of modern Vietnamese nationalism. In the countryside, rice, sugar, and rubber plantations yielded handsome profits for French and Vietnamese landowners, but also bred a class of landless poor who were ripe for nationalist and communist organizers. When the French left in 1954, Cochin-China became the center of the ill-fated Republic of Vietnam which, being led largely by Vietnamese who had served the French, was unable to gain the allegiance of rural villagers. (John F. Cady, *The Roots of French Imperialism in Eastern Asia*, 1954; David G. Marr, *Vietnamese Anticolonialism*, 1971.)

Ross Marlay

COLOMBIA. Colombia is a country with great geographic diversity. Three ranges of the Andes mountains create an upland region with rugged terrain, but a mild and pleasant climate. East of the mountains are the hot grasslands of the Orinoco plains and the humid rain forest of the upper Amazon basin. West of the mountains are the Pacific coastal plain and the Caribbean coastal plain. Mountains and jungle have inhibited transportation and development and, as a result, the more comfortable Andean region is host to 75 percent of the population.

On his fourth voyage to the New World, Christopher Columbus* landed on the Caribbean coast of Colombia and took possession in the name of the Spanish crown, but the first permanent settlement was not established until the founding of Santa Marta* in 1525. Gonzalo Jiménez de Quesada, an Andalusian lawyer who led an expedition through difficult jungle in the quest for the legendary El Dorado, consolidated Spanish control when his forces defeated the Chibcha Indians and founded Santa Fe de Bogotá* in the Andean highlands in 1538. Colombia did not contain mineral wealth comparable to Mexico*, Peru*, and Bolivia*, nor were the natives as highly developed (and thus exploitable), as the Incas* and Aztecs*. Thus, the New Kingdom of Granada received far less attention than the more profitable colonies.

The first major challenge to Spanish imperial rule in Colombia was the Comunero revolt of 1781, an uprising of peasant Indians against new taxes imposed by the viceroy of New Granada. The *comuneros* received little support from the upper class *criollos* and were brutally repressed. The *criollos* had their own grievance with the Spanish officials concerning their subordinate social and political position, and some objected to continuation of Spanish absolutism. Antonio Nariño, a Bogotá aristocrat who translated and circulated Thomas Paine's *The Rights of Man*, became the inspiration for *criollo* resistance. Napoleon's invasion of Spain provided the opportunity for the Bogotá elite to rise up in 1810 to depose the viceroy and proclaim the Act of Independence. Simón Bolívar*, unable to defend independence in his home city of Caracas, recruited an army in Bogotá and proceeded to liberate other cities in Colombia and Venezuela*.

The Spanish, with Ferdinand VII back on the imperial throne, began a reconquest campaign in 1814. Bogotá was retaken in 1816 and a reign of terror was instituted to eliminate supporters of the independence movement. Bolívar, however, rebuilt his army and decisively defeated the Spanish in the battle of Boyacá in 1819. Having destroyed royal power in Colombia, Bolívar then went south to participate in the liberation of Ecuador*, Peru, and Bolivia. The Colombians formally declared the creation of the Republic of Gran Colómbia on December 17, 1819, with Bolívar as president and his top Colombian general, Francisco de Paula Santander, as vice president. Gran Colombia, by 1821, included Colombia, Venezuela, Panama, and Ecuador. Bolivar hoped to add Peru and Bolivia.

Gran Colombia was rent by a philosophical argument concerning the degree of government centralization and control. Bolívar, a centralist, wanted a single Spanish South American nation while Santander, a federalist, was only interested in Colombia. In 1828 Bolívar declared himself dictator of Gran Colombia and exiled Santander, but he was not able to prevent the withdrawal of Venezuela in 1829 and Ecuador a year later. Thus Gran Colombia became Colombia. (W. O. Galbraith, *Colombia: A General Survey*, 1966; Harvey F. Kline, *Colombia: Portrait of Unity and Diversity*, 1983.)

Bruce R. Drury

COLOMBO. Colombo is the main port city of Sri Lanka. Arabs controlled the city in 1517 when the Portuguese first took over, but they lost the city to the Dutch in 1656; they in turn surrendered it to the British in 1796. The British used Colombo as a naval base until the colony of Ceylon* gained its independence as Sri Lanka*. (Peter Kemp, *The Oxford Companion to Ships and the Sea*, 1976.)

COLONIAL CONFERENCE OF 1887. The Imperial Federation League, founded in 1884, encouraged closer constitutional union in the British Empire*. In 1886 the league, the membership of which included prominent politicians of both parties, adopted as its fundamental tenet the idea "that, in order to secure the permanent unity of the Empire, some form of federation is essential." In the same year, an Indian and Colonial Exhibition was held in London. The colonial exhibition, largely initiated by the league, also provided the opportunity to hold a conference that informally represented the entire Empire. In the wake of the exhibition, the league's monthly review, *Imperial Federation*, urged the government to call an official conference of accredited representatives of Great Britain and the self-governing colonies for the purpose of considering such matters as the defense of ports and the commerce of the Empire in time of war; the promotion of direct intercourse, commercial, postal, and telegraphic; and "other means" for securing the closer federation of the constituent parts of the Empire.

This first colonial conference, coinciding with Queen Victoria's Golden Jubilee, was held in London in the spring of 1887. More than one hundred delegates attended, most of them unofficial observers. All parts of the British Empire*— dependent colonies as well as self-governing—were represented, with the notable exception of India*. The opening address to the conference was given by the prime minister, Lord Salisbury, who focused attention upon mutual defense for the Empire, but ruled out any attempt at federation as being impractical for the foreseeable future. The prime minister also declined to support the idea of a customs union for the Empire. The conference as a body held only deliberative powers, and no binding resolutions were possible. The conference could agree only on the most general program for closer imperial cooperation. The conference did, however, establish a notable precedent by bringing together the governments of the Empire for a full exchange of views on matters of common interest.

In order to maintain the enthusiasm for imperial cooperation, the Imperial Federation League urged that the colonial conference be made a permanent imperial institution. The functions of the proposed permanent conference were not specified, but imperial defense was one immediate interest, with the adoption of preferential trading within the Empire being a long-term goal. When the league's proposal was broached to the government in 1893, William Gladstone* had replaced Salisbury as prime minister. Although Gladstone expressed sympathy with the idea of imperial federation, he was strongly opposed to the notion of abandoning free trade and he declared that the league's plan for a permanent colonial conference was impractical. Following Gladstone's denunciation, the conference idea lapsed, and the league disbanded in late 1893. (Max Beloff, *Imperial Sunset*, vol. I, 1970. C. A. Bodelson, *Studies in Mid-Victorian Imperialism*, 1924.)

William G. Ratliff

COLONIAL CONFERENCE OF 1897. The idea of a permanent colonial conference, first introduced by the Imperial Federation League in the early 1890s, was revived by Colonial Secretary Joseph Chamberlain* in 1897. Chamberlain's proposed conference was to meet on the occasion of Queen Victoria's Diamond

Jubilee celebration, an opportunity that the colonial secretary viewed as appropriate for drawing the self-governing colonies into a more active partnership with the United Kingdom. Unlike the Colonial Conference of 1887*, the 1897 Colonial Conference was restricted to only twelve delegates: the colonial secretary as presiding officer, and one delegate from each of the eleven self-governing colonies (Canada*, Newfoundland*, the six Australian colonies, New Zealand*, the Cape Colony*, and Natal*). As in 1887, India* was not represented.

Chamberlain proposed the creation of an imperial council (legislature) made up of representatives with power to commit their respective colonial parliaments on imperial matters. Most delegates, wary of anything that might undermine colonial autonomy, failed to endorse the proposal, resolving instead that the political relationship between Britain and the self-governing colonies was satisfactory as it stood. The delegates unanimously approved the idea of periodic colonial conferences. The colonial secretary had intended the Colonial Conference of 1897 to lead to imperial commercial union, but serious political disagreements within the British government made such an economic union impossible. The conference took a preliminary step away from free trade and toward economic cooperation by supporting the idea of preferential tariffs in imperial trade relations.

The conference also addressed imperial defense. The colonial delegates were reluctant to increase their contributions to the defense of the empire. The Canadians felt Canada had already contributed much to imperial defense by providing, in its transcontinental railway, a strategic line of communication and transportation of enormous benefit. The 1897 conference did adopt a resolution, however, agreeing in principle to the sharing of the defense burden. Moreover, both the Cape and Queensland delegates proposed an imperial tariff on foreign imports to provide a revenue for imperial defense. The conference failed to act on this idea, although the Australian colonies and several other colonies agreed voluntarily to increase their defense contributions, and the question of permanent colonial contributions to the defense of the British Empire was left for subsequent conferences. (J. L. Garvin, *Life of Joseph Chamberlain*, 1934; Donald C. Gordon, *The Dominion Partnership in Imperial Defense, 1870–1914*, 1965.)

William G. Ratliff

COLONIAL CONFERENCE OF 1902. The termination of the Boer War* sparked a renewed interest in imperial affairs and the coronation of Edward VII, the personification of the future of the British Empire*, inspired fresh demands for imperial unity. Colonial Secretary Joseph Chamberlain*, anxious to capitalize on the Empire's unselfish and voluntary contributions to the British war effort against the Boers, placed a priority on the issue of imperial defense at the first session of the Colonial Conference of 1902 in London. Conference delegates, however, were no more agreeable than they had been in 1897 to Chamberlain's proposal for the formation of an imperial council and the adoption of a general scheme of cooperative defense. In support of the Chamberlain plan, New Zealand proposed that each colony establish a special force for general imperial service in the event of war. Both Canada* and Australia*, however, derided the notion, insisting that the New Zealand* defense plan was inimical to self-government, and no further action was taken on the organization of a unified defense for the British Empire. Nevertheless, the 1902 conference agreed to increase the colonial annual contribution to the Royal Navy. But the delegates took only the smallest step toward institutionalizing imperial cooperation by passing a resolution for a colonial conference session every four years.

The second issue on the conference agenda, again introduced by the colonial secretary, was imperial economic union. On various occasions since 1897, Chamberlain had advanced the idea of a *Zollverein* (customs union) for the empire. At the 1902 conference, Chamberlain presented free trade within the Empire and a common tariff against the rest of the world as an ideal which was certain to be realized in the future. The colonial delegates, however, passed a resolution against imperial free trade. A vote in favor of imperial preference, a Canadian proposal put forward in 1897, was carried instead by the delegates, and the conference agreed to press the idea with the British government. (Peter Fraser, *Joseph Chamberlain: Radicalism and Empire, 1868–1914*, 1966; Donald C. Gordon, *The Dominion Partnership in Imperial Defense, 1870–1914*, 1965.)

William G. Ratliff

COLONIAL CONFERENCE OF 1907. See IMPERIAL CONFERENCE of 1907.

COLONIAL CONFERENCE OF 1911. See IMPERIAL CONFERENCE of 1911.

COLONIAL OFFICE. The department of the United Kingdom that administered to the colonies after 1801 was initially a division of the office of secretary of state (i.e. the Home Office)—itself directly descended from the thirteenth century office of king's secretary. The emergence of the modern Colonial Office dates from the early nineteenth century, and its role became increasingly complex as Britain's overseas territories increased. Only the Indian subcontinent and its related territories (including, for a time, parts of the Persian Gulf up to Aden* and select parts of Southeast Asia) remained outside the purview of the Colonial Office.

The Colonial Office came into being not as a carefully designed instrument of colonial government, but in response to long neglected needs of the colonies. But after 1812 the Colonial Office firmly established its place within the framework of British administration. The office underwent considerable restructuring after 1821, the most significant reorganization being the division of the Empire into four convenient geographical areas: Eastern colonies, North America, Mediterranean and Africa, and the West Indies.

The permanent undersecretaryship of Sir James Stephen was a seminal period for the Colonial Office. Between 1813–1846, Stephen was meticulous, methodical, and tireless in his management of the department. Stephen handled interdepartmental relations with great deftness, an increasingly difficult task as colonial assemblies evolved in the colonies of white settlement, setting the stage for selective granting of responsible government to Canada*, Australia*, New Zealand*, and the Cape Colony* in the ensuing decades.

The Colonial Office underwent its second major reorganization between 1868–1870 under 2nd Earl Granville. It was particularly affected by the arrival of better educated civil servants who successfully competed in new civil service examinations. Technological developments after 1870, particularly the steamship and telegraph, considerably altered the number and intensity of contacts between the Colonial Office and its outposts abroad. The office's telegraph bill jumped from £800 in 1870 to £2,800 ten years later, while it received over 4,000 telegrams in 1900—four times its total just eight years earlier (1892).

In the late nineteenth and early twentieth centuries the Colonial Office was dominated by the persona of Joseph Chamberlain*, conspicuously concerned with the material development of the Empire and the question of imperial tariffs. Following World War I*, another dominant colonial secretary, L. S. Amery, assumed the office (1924–29). Under Amery, the Colonial Office split off dominion affairs and the Dominions Office was created. Amery also was concerned with colonial development schemes around the Empire (for example, Kenya*, Cyprus*, Palestine*), and encouraged strategic emigration plans to the colonies. It was during the interwar years that the colonial service, in some eyes, surpassed its Indian counterpart (the ICS) in prestige, as many Eton and Oxford graduates went into colonial service.

After World War II*, the attention of Britain's newly elected Labour government turned inward. Committed to devolution of Empire, following divestiture of Empire in Asia (India*, Malaya*, Burma*), the Colonial Office tried to negotiate peaceful transitions to nationhood in Africa in the 1960s, plotting a careful tack amidst the wind of change sweeping that continent. In 1966 the Colonial Office was abolished. (John W. Call, *British Colonial Administration in the Mid-Nineteenth Century*, 1970; D. M. Young, *The Colonial Office in the Early Nineteenth Century*, 1961.)

Arnold P. Kaminsky

COLUMBUS, CHRISTOPHER. Christopher Columbus was born in Genoa, a major Italian seaport, between August 25 and October 21, 1451, to a weaver named Domenico and his wife Susanna Fontanarossa. He had two younger brothers, Bartholomew and Diego, who participated in some of his exploits. Between 1470 and 1476 Columbus sailed the Mediterranean on several Genoese ships, including one employed by René of Anjou in his war with Aragón and several involved in Genoa's trade with the island of Chios. When a Franco-Portuguese fleet attacked a Genoese convoy and sank his ship off Lagos, Portugal, on August 13, 1476, the wounded Columbus swam ashore and made his way to Lisbon. From 1477 to 1484 he sailed on various Portuguese vessels, principally to Madeira* and to Mina on the Gold Coast* in west Africa and possibly even to Iceland.

Columbus's "Enterprise of the Indies" proposed to reach Asia by sailing west, but vague biblical prophecies and the inaccurate theories of medieval authorities Pierre d'Ailly and Pope Pius II and the contemporary Paolo Toscanelli led him to underestimate the size of the earth. John II of Portugal rejected his proposal in 1484, so in 1485 Columbus left for Spain. His wife having died, he entrusted his son Diego to the Franciscans at La Rabida, who shared his interest in exploration and the spreading of Christianity. He then went to Córdoba, where he sought support from Ferdinand of Aragon* and Isabella of Castile*. The queen referred his proposal to a commission and in 1487 gave him a retainer. But the commission dallied, and in 1488 Columbus again approached John II, whose initial interest vanished when Bartholomew Dias* returned from his voyage to the Cape of Good Hope. Columbus's brother Bartholomew fared no better with Henry VII of England and Charles VIII of France in 1489–90, and late in 1490 the Spanish commission rejected the enterprise. Isabella urged Columbus to try again after the war with the Moors. In 1492 he did just that, audaciously asking not only to be made Admiral of the Ocean Sea if he succeeded, but also governor and viceroy of any lands discovered, with a tenth of all profits. Isabella accepted his terms, which were put into a contract signed in April.

At Palos—aided by the Pinzón, Niño, and Quintero families—Columbus assembled a small fleet, the *Santa María* as flagship, and the caravels *Niña* and *Pinta*. The latter's captain, Martín Alonso Pinzón, would be frequently at odds with Columbus. Departing on August 2, they stopped in the Canary Islands* then sailed westward on September 6, losing sight of land on the 9th. Columbus navigated by dead reckoning, plotting a course on the basis only of direction, time, and speed. The wind proved unreliable, and by October the crew was near mutiny. But after bearing southwest at the insistence of Pinzón, the fleet made landfall on October 12 at San Salvador, an island inhabited by friendly Tainos, whom Columbus inaccurately named Indians. With native guides the fleet explored the Greater Antilles*, also populated by natives who constantly, though never truthfully, promised gold was further on. The ships arrived on the 28th in Cuba*, where native references to gold raised false hopes of finding the "Great Khan." Instead they were introduced to tobacco.

On November 21 Pinzón and the *Pinta* stole away to seek gold elsewhere, but the other two ships explored Cuba until December 5 and then made a day's voyage to Haiti*—which Columbus named Hispaniola*—where they explored and feasted with hundreds of natives. At midnight on Christmas eve, the *Santa María* grounded on a reef, and taking this as a sign from God, Columbus left a small colony called Navidad there upon departing in the *Niña* on January 4. Rejoined by the *Pinta* on the 6th, and after making peace with Pinzón, he began a difficult voyage home on the 18th. Following a more northerly course, the ships were separated in bad weather in mid-February, part of the *Niña*'s crew was arrested by Portuguese authorities when it stopped in the Azores*, and they endured more fierce storms before arriving at Lisbon on March 4. Despite his jealous courtiers, John II welcomed Columbus on the 9th. The latter then departed in the *Niña* on March 13, reaching Palos two days later, just ahead of the *Pinta* and Pinzón.

The king and queen honored Columbus, confirmed his titles, and secured papal bulls dividing the newly discovered lands of the world between Spain and Portugal (prelude to the Treaty of Tordesillas of 1494*). On September 25, 1493, Columbus left Cádiz with seventeen ships and over 1,000 men to colonize and Christianize the "Indies." He arrived on November 3 in the Lesser Antilles*, discovering Puerto Rico* on the 19th. Reaching Hispaniola on the 22nd and learning that natives had destroyed Navidad, he moved east and founded Isabella on January 2, 1494. Sending Antonio de Torres back to Spain and leaving his own inexperienced brother Diego in charge at Isabella, Colombus searched for gold and built the fort Santo Tomás in Cibao between March 12–29, sailed to Cuba on April 29, discovered Jamaica* May 5, explored both islands, decided Cuba was the mainland, and returned to Isabella on September 29, after nearly dying of sickness and exhaustion. His brother Bartholomew arrived in the fall, and Torres returned soon after with confirmation of Columbus's authority. Columbus and Bartholomew captured a number of Indian slaves and in 1495 sent 500 to Spain with Torres and Diego. But Columbus and his brothers were on bad terms with Juan de Fonseca, royal administrator of the Indies, and complaints from colonists prompted the monarchs to dispatch Juan de Aguada to investigate. He and Columbus feuded for five months, then the latter appointed Bartholomew governor and Diego (now back) as assistant, and both Aguada and Columbus left on March 10, 1496.

Back in Spain, after spending several weeks with Franciscan friars, Columbus was summoned in July by the king and queen, overcame his opponents at court, and organized a third voyage, departing on May 10, 1498, with six ships and about 200 colonists. From the Canaries three ships sailed for Hispaniola, while Columbus and the other three headed south and then west. Sighting Trinidad* on July 28, he entered the Gulf of Paria, touched the South American mainland, observed natives wearing pearls, passed the mouths of the Orinoco River, and decided he had found the Garden of Eden. Arriving at Santo Domingo* on August 31, he found Francisco Roldan, mayor of Isabella, in revolt against his brothers in Xaragua in southwestern Hispaniola, and virtually capitulated to him to obtain peace. On September 5, 1499, a small fleet arrived led by Alonso de Ojeda, who was seeking pearls with Fonseca's approval, and stirred up more trouble. Meanwhile word of Columbus's handling of Roldan's revolt prompted Ferdinand and Isabella in spring 1499 to appoint Francisco de Bobadilla as royal commissioner with unlimited power to restore order. He arrived on August 23, 1500, as Columbus and his brothers were attempting to suppress rebellion with a rash of hangings. All three refused to accept Bobadilla's authority, and he had them put in chains and sent back to Spain. Columbus insisted on remaining in chains until he arrived in Cadiz at the end of November and was freed by the monarchs.

The sovereigns restored Columbus's lands but in February 1502 sent Nicolas de Ovando with thirty-two ships to replace Bobadilla as governor of Hispaniola. On May 11 Columbus left Cádiz with only four caravels*, seeking a strait leading to India. He reached Martinique* on June 15, violated orders by trying on June 29 to land at Santo Domingo (Ovando refused), sailed for Jamaica on July 14, then crossed the Caribbean July 27–30. Sailing down the coast of Honduras, Nicaragua, Costa Rica, and Panama—trading as he went—he arrived on January 6, 1503, at Belem on the Panama Coast and attempted to set up a trading post, but was foiled by hostile Indians. In May he sailed to Cuba, reached Jamaica on June 25, and remained stranded there until June 29, 1504, when Ovando reluctantly sent rescuers. He returned to Spain in October. Isabella died on November 26; Ferdinand received Columbus in May 1505, but did not restore his titles. Columbus died on May 21, 1506 in Valladolid. (Samuel Eliot Morison, *Admiral of the Ocean Sea: A Life of Christopher Columbus*, 1942.)

William B. Robison

COMMONWEALTH OF THE NORTHERN MARIANA ISLANDS. The Marianas are a group of volcanic, coral, and limestone geographic sites in the western central Pacific. The Spanish explorer Ferdinand Magellan* first reached the Marianas in 1521, and until the late 1800s the islands were widely considered Spanish territory, although Spain never really exerted her claims there. Spain lost Guam*, the southernmost of the Marianas, in the Spanish-American War of 1898*, and the next year she sold the rest of the Marianas to Germany. Germany held the islands until the outbreak of World War I*, when Japan seized them. They remained a Japanese mandated territory until the end World War II*, when United States soldiers captured them. In 1947 the United Nations awarded the United States a trusteeship over most of the Pacific Islands, and the Marianas, except for Guam, became part of the Trust Territory of the Pacific Islands*.

The United States hoped to grant independence to the entire trust territory as a single unit, but ethnic rivalries prevented it. In 1969 Guam rejected a proposal to unite with the other Mariana Islands. The United States began negotiating separately with the Northern Marianas Political Status Commission. In a 1975 plebiscite, the people of the northern Mariana islands voted overwhelmingly for independence as well as for a formal, permanent, free association with the United States. On April 1, 1976, they formally separated from the Trust Territory of the Pacific Islands, and in March 1977 the voters approved a new constitution for the Commonwealth of the Northern Mariana Islands. A governor and legislature took office in 1978, with the transition to complete independence finished in the mid–1980s. (Donald F. McHenry, *Micronesia: Trust Betrayed*, 1975; James H. Webb, *Micronesia and U.S. Pacific Strategy*, 1974).

COMOROS ISLANDS. The Comoros Islands are a volcanic archipelago located in the Indian Ocean between Mozambique and Madagascar. Centered at the crossroads of the Indian Ocean, the Comoros were originally settled by a mixed ethnic stock of African Bantu, Malayo-Indonesian, and Arab peoples, and in the 1400s and 1500s Arab missionaries converted most inhabitants to Islam. Independent sultans on each of the islands guaranteed constant strife between Grand Comore, Mayotte, Moheli, and Anjouan.

Portuguese sailors first landed at Grand Comore in 1505, and by 1527 the islands appeared on Portuguese maps. In the middle of the eighteenth century Madagascar slavers began raiding the Comoros Islands, delivering thousands of slaves to Madagascar, Mauritius*, and Reunion*. The raids on Mayotte were so serious that the island was nearly depopulated by 1810. The slavers were ethnic Sakalavans from Madagascar, and the Comoros sultans appealed to Europe in general and France in particular to intervene and stop the traffic. France refused. The slave raids did not stop until 1817 when the Hova people of Madagascar conquered the Sakalavans.

The French presence in the Indian Ocean began in 1634 when they established a settlement on southern Madagascar and seized the islands of Reunion* and Rodrigues. They claimed Mauritius* in 1715 and the Seychelles* in 1756. At the end of the Napoleonic Wars in 1814, France had to cede Mauritius, Rodrigues, and the Seychelles to England. Desperate for a new port in the Indian Ocean, France seized control of Mayotte in 1841. In 1886 France established protectorates over Grand Comore, Anjouan, and Moheli, and in 1908 France attached all four of them to Madagascar. French colonial administrators arrived in the Comoros in 1912. The Comoros Islands became an overseas department of France, with voting rights in the national assembly, in 1946, and in 1957 an internal governing council was appointed. A 1958 referendum indicated the willingness of Comorans to remain a part of France, and in 1961 France gave the governing council complete control over internal affairs.

The movement for independence got underway in the 1960s among Comorans living in Tanzania. The National Liberation Movement of the Comoros was established in 1962, and by 1967 it had branches on each of the islands. In 1969 the newly established Socialist Party of the Comoros began demanding independence, and in the early 1970s the conservative Comoros Democratic Union, led by Ahmed Abdallah, joined the independence movement. A coalition group called the Union for the Evolution of the Comoros began negotiating with France in 1973. A referendum in December indicated that 95 percent of the people of Grand Comore, Anjouan, and Moheli wanted independence, but 65 percent of those on Mayotte wanted to stay with France. When it became clear that France intended to treat independence on an island-by-island basis, Ahmed Abdallah unilaterally declared independence on July 6, 1975, claiming control of Mayotte as well. At the time the population of the Comoros was 374,000 people, with 45,000 of them on Mayotte. France sent military reinforcements to protect Mayotte. The new nation—the Federal Islamic Republic of the Comoros—included only Grand Comore, Anjouan, and Moheli. Mayotte remains a French colony. (Frederica M. Bunge, *Indian Ocean. Five Island Countries*, 1982.)

CONGO. The term "Congo" has been used in a variety of ways to describe European colonies near the Congo River in Africa. Today's Congo, or People's Republic of the Congo, was formerly known as Middle Congo (*Moyen Congo*), or French Congo, and was part of French Equatorial Africa. For a time it was also known as Congo-Brazzaville. The region was officially renamed Republic of Congo in 1958. Today's independent nation of Zaire was also known as Congo for a time, as well as Congo-Kinshasa and Belgian Congo. See BELGIAN CONGO and FRENCH CONGO.

CONGO FREE STATE. See BELGIAN CONGO.

CONGRESS OF BERLIN OF 1878. The Congress of Berlin met from June 13 to July 13, 1878, to settle the "Eastern Question"—the decline of the Ottoman Empire, the effects of the rise of nationalism in eastern Europe and the Balkans, the conflicting interests of the great powers with respect to the Balkans and the Straits, and a variety of North African and Near Eastern issues. The Eastern Question had become inextricably linked to the Middle European upheavals of 1859–1871 that resulted in the formation of the German Reich and the Kingdom of Italy and a major restructuring of the Austrian Empire. Following the Crimean War of 1854–1855 and the Paris Peace Conference of 1856, the Eastern Question continued to be a distraction for the powers, which were unable to act collectively. Only after Prussia defeated Austria in 1866 and France in 1870–1871 and formed the Reich of 1871 did Great Britain, France, Russia, and Austria become united in their concern over the potentially hegemonial power of Germany. A widely held view was that Berlin would attempt to "complete" the new Reich through the *Anschluss* with Austria and the Baltic provinces of Russia. This expansionist tendency struck fear among the major powers of Europe.

In 1874–1875 Germany relished the thought that the Eastern Question might replace the "German Question" as the major topic on the European agenda. The Reich foreign office had abundant evidence that revolutionary developments in Central Europe since the Crimean War had stimulated nationalism among Balkan Christians, making the Eastern Question more explosive than ever. The unification of Italy and the success of the Hungarians in gaining their equality in the Dual Monarchy under the *Ausgleich* of 1867 stimulated nationalist movements throughout southern and eastern Europe.

The major powers tried to exploit the unrest. With its traditional commitment to Pan-Slavism, Russia wanted to unite all Slavs under Russian influence as well as regain some of its influence after the defeat in the Crimean War. In 1870 the Tsar denounced the clauses in the Paris Peace of 1856 with respect to neutralization of the Black Sea. Austria wanted to pose as protector of the Balkan Slavs against the Turks, in the hope of staving off any Yugoslav nationalist movements as well as expanding Austrian influence in the Balkans to compensate for setbacks growing out of the Austro-Italian War of 1850 and the Austro-Prussian War of 1866. Serbia and Montenegro declared war on the Ottoman Empire in 1876, and Tsar Alexander II sent the Russian army into the fray on behalf of the Balkan Slavs in April 1877. The Russian victory over the Ottomans in the winter of 1877–1878 led to the Treaty of San Stefano* of March 3, 1878. With the peace settlement, previous Russian commitments to Austria and Britain concerning territorial modifications in the Balkans appeared to be broken. Austria and Britain reacted bitterly, and London sent a battle fleet to the Straits. In the midst of the talk of war, Germany appeared as a stabilizing force and Europe's leading statesmen assembled in Berlin to resolve the Eastern Question and revise the Treaty of San Stefano.

The participating powers at the Congress of Berlin were Great Britain, Austria-Hungary, France, Germany, Italy, Russia, and the Ottoman Empire. The chief of the German delegation and president of the congress was Prince Otto Eduard Leopold von Bismarck*, the chancellor of the recently formed Reich. He emerged as the central figure in the diplomatic maneuvering during the crisis, the dominant force in the deliberations, and the person primarily responsible for the peaceful outcome. Like Prince Klemens von Metternich, Bismarck understood the ethnic complexities of Central Europe, especially in the eastern borderlands, and its vulnerability to "foreign" domination. Since becoming Prussian minister-president in 1862 Bismarck had tried to gain the cooperation of the Austrians in building a new *Mitteleuropa*, the core of which would be a revised version of the German Confederation of 1815–1866, with dual Austro-Prussian leadership. But the Austro-Prussian War of 1866 had illustrated Austria's independent mood and the other powers supported it. As far as they were concerned, the Reich had already reached its penultimate form. Austria, they argued, must be treated as a completely separate and sovereign member of the European concert.

Bismarck was not prepared to accept such an arrangement. One way to subtly promote his vision of *Mitteleuropa* was to emphasize the Balkan problem. Bismarck's agents had close contacts with Hungarians, Romanians, and Serbs, hoping they would be useful in pressing Vienna to recognize the need for coming to terms with Berlin. Bismarck had also promoted extensive Prussian economic penetration of the Balkans since the early 1860s, including commissions, consuls, bankers, cartels, and interlocking directorates of Reich and Austro-German financial, manufacturing, and railway interests. He had also worked to shore up the financial soundness of the government in Constantinople as well as seen to the delivery of large numbers of weapons to the Turks during the mid–1870s. Bismarck was hardly an "honest broker" at the Congress of Berlin.

Bismarck also wanted to prevent a general war or even a localized eastern war in which both Austria and Russia would seek Reich-German support. He was especially careful about the eccentric Russophile, Kaiser Wilhelm I, who cherished his dynasty's familial ties with the House of Romanov and might try to force Germany to support St. Petersburg instead of Austria. So during the early stages of the Balkan crisis Bismarck was aloof, hoping to give Vienna and St. Petersburg enough time to disrupt their relationship. His occasional suggestions for partitioning the Balkans were not efforts to find a peace but to sow more discord. By the time the crisis became most dangerous in 1878, the eventual conclusion of an Austro-German alliance was virtually assured.

France played a minor role at the congress, consistent with her loss of diplomatic significance since the fall of Napoleon III and defeat by the Germans in 1870. Still, England and Germany suggested that France claim Tunis in North Africa. The French had no interest in the emerging "New Imperialism" at the time, but three years later Jules Ferry* took advantage of the congress mandate and established a French protectorate over Tunis in the Treaty of Bardo on May 12, 1881. The Ottomans counted for even less at the congress. The Turks were, after all, the most recent losers in European combat.

Russia's position at the congress was potentially as vulnerable as that of the Turks. Tsar Alexander's government was facing enormous economic problems and a seething discontent. One reason Tsar Alexander entered the Balkan War in 1877 was the hope that expansionism would strengthen his position against the forces of democracy and modernization, but Turkish successes at Plevna during the latter half of 1877 indicated a certain Russian vulnerability and the possibility of suffering a major defeat in a general conflict with the other great powers. But when Plevna fell and the Russian army advanced to the Straits, the Tsar dictated the Treaty of San Stefano. Shocked by Russian success, London, Vienna, and Berlin arranged the congress as a means of avoiding war.

Of the other interested powers, Italy could have posed some problems since her leaders had ambitions of their own in the Balkans. Fortunately, a conservative, Count Luigi Corti, had become foreign minister in March 1878 on the condition that Rome cooperate with the powers in opposing San Stefano.

But London and Vienna put up the strongest resistance to Russian policy in the Balkans. Great Britain wanted to prevent any Russian advance toward Constantinople and the Straits or anywhere in the Near East. London could not tolerate the endangering of the imperial life line to India through the Suez Canal*. Accordingly, preservation of the territorial integrity of the Ottoman Empire was the objective of the secret agreement of May 30, 1878, whereby London gained a pledge from St. Petersburg shortly after the mobilization of British forces that Russia would abandon the San Stefano plan to create a large Bulgarian state extending from the Danube to the Aegean Sea and into Macedonia. The two powers agreed to accept as the southern frontier of this new nation the Balkan Mountains. Great Britain also concluded with the Ottoman Empire the secret convention of June 14, 1878, whereby British forces were to occupy Cyprus.

The Eastern imbroglio produced a myriad of concerns for Austria-Hungary, and the German Reich shared most of them. The Austria-Hungary foreign minister, Count Julius Andrassy, was head of his country's delegation to the Congress of Berlin. By the time of the congress, Andrassy had already begun to angle for an Austro-German alliance that would serve the interests of Austria without making her a mere dependency of the Reich. His diplomatic exchanges with Bismarck during the crisis that preceded the congress showed that both men agreed that the Great Bulgarian project could thwart the economic penetration of both Central European empires into the Balkans and especially obstruct the construction of the railway network between *Mitteluropa* and Salonika on the Aegean. Bismarck was as concerned as Andrassy about Russian influence over the Slav subjects of both the Ottoman and Habsburg empires, especially the response of Austro-Slavs to Russian Pan-Slav propaganda which advertised these rebellions and the Russian military intervention as the beginning of a struggle for the liberation of all the little nations of the East. German and Austrian statesmen had no choice but to proceed in 1878 on the assumption that a Big Bulgaria under Russian protection could become a formidable Pan-Slav center for fomenting unrest among the Austro-Slavs and threatening the integrity of the Habsburg empire, as well as, indirectly, the German Reich.

Of more immediate concern was South Slav nationalism and the insurrection of July 1875 in Bosnia and Herzegovina, as well as the decision in neighboring Serbia to support the rebels. Bismarck wanted Austria to occupy Bosnia-Herzegovina. Andrassy and Bismarck eventually agreed on that point in order to prevent the creation of a Great Serbia which could benefit the Pan-Slav movement or promote the Yugoslav cause among the Austro-Hungarian Serbs, Croats, and Slovenes. Bismarck also suggested to Andrassy that London and Vienna settle their concerns. When the Anglo-Austrian accord was concluded on June 6, 1878, on such matters as the future organization of Bulgaria, length of the Russian military occupation in the eastern Balkans, and the Austrian occupation of Bosnia-Herzegovina, the main contours of the Berlin settlement were already determined.

The final treaty was signed on July 13, 1878. It included several main provisions. First, Russia's Great Bulgarian creation was divided into three parts. A new principality of Bulgaria, under Ottoman control but freed of all Ottoman troops and fortresses, was to encompass a narrow sliver of territory between the Danube and the Balkan Mountains, except for a small southwestern region, around and to the south of Sofia, that lay beyond this range (Articles I-XII). To the south of the principality of Bulgaria they created a second predominantly Bulgarian-speaking entity, dubbed Eastern Roumelia, which was to have a "Christian governor-general" while being subject to Ottoman control. Finally, the Macedonian and Thracian regions of the Great Bulgaria stipulated at San Stefano were to have their traditional status as lands under the direct authority of the regular Turkish administration. Second, the Russian army of occupation was restricted to Bulgaria and Eastern Roumelia and limited to a force not to exceed 50,000 people for a period of nine months from the date of the exchange of the ratifications of the treaty (Article XXII). Third, the Slav entities of the Northwest Balkans—those lying outside the Austro-Hungarian monarchy—were regulated by the Treaty of Berlin. The Ottoman provinces of Bosnia and Herzegovina were to be "occupied and administered" by Austria-Hungary, which could also exercise certain undefined garrison, communications, and economic rights in the Sanjak of Novi-Bazar, a narrow southern extension of Bosnia. This gave the Habsburg monarchy an opportunity to proceed with railroad construction through the Sanjak to Salonika, as well as a wedge for preventing the union of Montenegro and Serbia, which the treaty declared to be independent (Articles XXV-XLII). Fourth, from Romania, whose independence was affirmed and her territory increased through the acquisition of the Dobruja district from Bulgaria, Russia received Bessarabia, which she had lost at the end of the Crimean War. In Asia, Russia retained her recent conquests of Ardahan, Kars, and Batum. Restored to Turkey in contravention of the Treaty of San Stefano were the valley of Alaschkerd and the town of Bayazid (Articles XLIII-LI, LVII-LX).

Aside from these primary arrangements, the treaty also dealt with Turkish obligations on the island of Crete, recommendations for settlement of certain Greek claims to Turkish territory; freedom of navigation on the Danube; Turkish responsibilities in Armenia; and Ottoman obligations with regard to religious liberty and civil rights of all its subjects, especially the Christians (Articles XXIII, XXIV, LII-LVII, LXI, and LXII).

Although the Congress of Berlin was a success in international peacemaking, it left relations among the great powers badly shaken and the consequent diplomatic revolution would eventually leave the work of the congress in shambles. One effect of the Eastern Crisis was the eventual division of Europe into rival alliance systems. The Franco-Russian Alliance did not emerge for another sixteen years, but Bismarck turned within a year after the congress to building a Middle-European security system based on alliances: the Austro-German Alliance of 1879, the Italo-German-Austrian Triple Alliance of 1882; and the silent Reich partnership in the Austro-Serbian Treaty of 1882 and the Austro-Romanian Alliance of 1883. Europe was already taking steps on the road to World War I*. (M. S. Anderson, *The Eastern Question, 1774–1923: A Study in International Relations*, 1966; George C. Arnakas, *The Near East in Modern Times, Volume I, The Ottoman Empire and the Balkan States to 1900*, 1969; William L. Langer, *European Alliances and Alignments, 1871–1890*, 1950; William N. Medlicott, *The Congress of Berlin and After: A Diplomatic History of the Near Eastern Settlement, 1878–1880*, 1968.)

Bascom Barry Hayes

CONGRESS OF VIENNA OF 1815. Hardly a "congress" at all, the term is a misnomer for an incalculable series of formal diplomatic conferences and informal meetings in and around Vienna between September 1814 and June 1815. A lavish festival, it was symbolic of the widespread European hope for a revival of the monarchical order and aristocratic style of the eighteenth century following a long era of revolutionary turmoil. In residence as guests of Kaiser Francis of Austria were Tsar Alexander I of Russia, King Frederick William III of Prussia, King Frederick I of Wurttenberg, King Maximilian Joseph of Bavaria, and King Frederick VI of Denmark, as well as more than 200 lesser reigning princes, ministers of state, and counselors. The official host was Prince Klemens Lothar von Metternich-Winneburg, the Austrian chancellor. The other leading figures included Robert Stewart, the Viscount Castlereagh, who led the British delegation, and Prince Karl August von Hardenberg, the Prussian chancellor.

As a summary of the decisions reached during months of negotiations, the Final Act of the Congress of Vienna (June 9, 1815) dealt with some imperial issues. From the standpoint of continental politics, the collective effort of the powers was the antithesis of an "imperialist" imposition. Although some historians have criticized the Congress of Vienna for drastically altering European frontiers (such as the transfer of Belgians from Habsburg to Dutch rule, the shift of Norwegians from Danish to Swedish sovereignty, the redistribution of Polish soil among Russia, Prussia, and Austria, and the numerous transfers in Germany), far fewer Europeans lived under the rule of foreigners or were subject to an alien system of conscription after the Congress of Vienna than in 1810 when the Napoleonic empire was at its zenith.

As for the primary aim of the conferees at Vienna to reconstruct Europe territorially so that a fair balance of power and a new order of restraint and peace might be achieved, the congress was remarkably successful. It established certain barriers to future French expansionism, such as the enlarged Netherlands, Sardinia, and Prussia, as well as the strong Austrian presence in Italy. Furthermore, Prince Metternich led the way toward a German system capable of restraining both France and Russia, a concern which Castlereagh and the British shared. The Great Four (Britain, Austria, Prussia, and Russia) also established the Quadruple Alliance, pledging to prevent the return of Napoleon or his dynasty, to enforce by military action the provisions in the settlements of 1815, and to meet in the future "for the maintenance of the Peace of Europe." Historian C. W. Webster has said that "it marked definitely the ascendancy of the Great Powers and the principle of the European Concert."

But colonial imperialism was another matter, primarily because of Great Britain. Even as Lord Castlereagh worked for a military balance of power on the continent, he resisted attempts to have this principle applied on a global or naval scale. No conceivable alliance could rival either Britain's merchant marine or battle fleet. Moreover, none of the Allies could deny the importance to their cause of the British successes in the destruction of the combined Spanish and French fleets at Trafalgar in 1805 and the close blockade of the main French ports thereafter.

Great Britain was also in the midst of a transformation of colonial policy in the wake of the American Revolution*. In the shift from the "Old Colonial System" to the "Second Empire," naval power was to become even more important, since the new emphasis was on the strategic scattering of trading posts and naval stations instead of the consolidation of large territorial plantations. By no means abandoned was the mercantilist idea that colonies were the local branches of national trading companies and industrial corporations or farms for production not possible in England. But colonies were no longer going to be treated as the private property of the Crown or businesses; the colonial empire was to become a national institution under a highly centralized and regulatory administration whose policies were to be guided by political and strategic considerations as much as by economic interest.

Accordingly, Castlereagh played an important role at the congress in the emergence of the "Second Empire." Already vaguely discernible was the strategy of "free-trade" imperialism as a substitute for territorial expansion. Although the Congress of Vienna annulled a number of specific treaties from the Revolutionary and Napoleonic eras, Castlereagh managed to keep intact earlier agreements with Spain and Portugal which gave Great Britain most-favored-nation status in trade with South America. Castlereagh also pressed the congress on the question of putting an end to the slave trade, but he achieved only the Declaration of the Eight Powers (February 8, 1815), which morally condemned slavery.

At the Congress of Vienna Castlereagh also achieved several successes indicative of the British imperial "swing to the East" and away from the earlier concentration on the North Atlantic, a tendency evident since the expeditions of Captain James Cook* (1768–1779), the first settlement in Australia* (1788), the acquisition of Penang (1786) and Malacca* (1795), and the further emphasis on India* after the Seven Years War. During the peace process of 1814–1815 the "swing to the East" was most evident in Castlereagh's commitment to seizing control of the old Portugese sea lanes to the Orient. The acquisition of Malta* would eventually supplement Gibraltar* in helping to make secure a shorter route. The decision to keep the Cape of Good Hope, which was occupied provisionally in 1795, proved to be critical. One of Castlereagh's most impressive achievements was the treaty which he negotiated with Hendrik Fagel of the Netherlands, in which Great Britain paid two million pounds and bought the Cape from the Dutch. As a result of the congress, Great Britain retained Mauritius*, seized in 1810 from the French, as well as Rodrigues and the Seychelles*, and acquired Ceylon* from the Dutch (it had been captured in 1796, retained provisionally under the Treaty of Amiens of 1802* and permanently under the Anglo-Dutch Treaty of August 1814).

Finally, the Congress of Vienna provided a variety of evidence that the continental monarchies were continuing their decline as colonial powers. Portugal returned French Guiana* to French sovereignty. Castlereagh refused to support a Spanish military solution to the Latin American revolutions, not allowing the question on the Congress of Vienna agenda. Privately, Castlereagh was convinced that the revolutions would bring Great Britain substantial economic benefits. Although the Netherlands had lost all effective control of the Dutch East Indies* to the British during the recent wars, Britain returned the colony to Dutch sovereignty. Although France kept some of its enclaves in India, British ascendancy was so advanced that the French government had to dispense with regular garrisons and rely on police units for internal security. France regained Guadeloupe* from Sweden but had to restore certain parts of eastern Santo

Domingo (contemporary Haiti*) that Spain had ceded under the Treaty of Basel in 1795. Thus, the settlements at the Congress of Vienna signified not only the collapse of the French hegemonial designs in Europe but an inglorious end for Paris to the long Anglo-French global rivalry, sometimes referred to as the "Second Hundred Years War." (Geoffrey Bruun, *Europe and the French Imperium, 1799–1814*, 1938; Vincent T. Harlow, *The Founding of the Second British Empire, 1763–1793*, 1952; Enno E. Kraehe, *Metternich's German Policy. Vol. I: The Contest with Napoleon* and *Vol. II: The Congress of Vienna, 1814–1815*, 1963–1985; Sir Harold Nicolson, *The Congress of Vienna*, 1946.)

Bascom Barry Hayes

CONNECTICUT. Connecticut was a small colony in British North America that comprised 5,018 square miles on the shores of the Connecticut River and down to the coast of Long Island Sound. The name comes from the Mohican *quinnitukqut*, or "at the long tidal river." By the time of the American Revolution*, Connecticut had a population of 198,000, mostly of English descent, with a sprinkling of Huguenots, Acadians, and Dutch as well as some 5,101 blacks and 1,363 Indians. The land is generally poor and rocky except along the Connecticut, Thames, and Housatonic rivers.

Sailing for the Dutch West India Company, Adrian Block explored the lower Connecticut in 1614. Nineteen years later the Dutch founded a small trading house (House of Hope) where Hartford stands today. In November 1633, Puritans from Massachusetts Bay explored along the upper Connecticut. Finding the region to be fertile, they settled Wethersfield the next year and Windsor in 1635. In 1636 Reverend Thomas Hooker and Samuel Stone moved from Newtown, Massachusetts, to establish Hartford. By 1637 Windsor, Hartford, and Wethersfield had joined together in the so-called River Colony (Connecticut Colony).

The founding of the New Haven colonies began in 1638, first by Theophilus Eaton and John Davenport in New Haven, and later in the surrounding coastal areas. By 1639 the first constitution went into effect, uniting New Haven, Guilford, Milford, Stamford, and Southold on Long Island. These settlements represent some of the earliest examples of dissent against the Puritan rule in the Masschusetts* Bay Colony, but unlike others, the New Haven colonists had objected to religious laxity, rather than severity, in the parent colony.

Early neglect on the part of England gave way within a generation, as King Charles II granted a charter (1662) to John Winthrop II of the Connecticut Colony. This charter gave a great degree of self-government to the colony, but also placed the New Haven colonies under its control. New Haven resisted these imperial rearrangements until the fleet of the Duke of York (later James II) visited the region in 1664–1665. In a later effort to consolidate imperial control, James II revoked the charters of his northern royal colonies, consolidating them into the Dominion of New England* under Governor Edmund Andros. Patriotic Connecticut colonists resisted the change, first by hiding the charter itself in an oak, and then in 1689 by overthrowing Andros upon hearing of England's Glorious Revolution.

By the beginning of the new century Connecticut's imperial relations were comparatively stable. The charter had been restored and a period of salutary neglect allowed relative prosperity. Agricultural products and some manufactured goods were exported by the Yankee traders to the West Indies*, where they were traded for sugar, which was then brought to Connecticut to be made into rum. The rum was, in turn, sent to West Africa and traded for black slaves.

As the restrictions of Navigation Acts became more severe after the French and Indian War*, a crisis ensued, which eventually culminated in the American Revolution. In 1776, along with twelve other British North American colonies, Connecticut approved the Declaration of Independence, separating the United States from Great Britain. Despite being one of the colonial leaders of the revolution, Connecticut retained a strong conservative sentiment. In fact, Jonathan Trumbull was the only colonial governor to survive the revolution in office. For Connecticut, if not for the other colonies, the revolution was essentially fought to preserve traditional rights and privileges. (Jackson Turner Main, *Society and Economy in Colonial Connecticut*, 1985; Robert J. Taylor, *Colonial Connecticut: A History*, 1979.)

Mark R. Shulman

COOK, JAMES. James Cook was born on October 27, 1728, in Marton-in-Cleveland, England. Raised in a poor farming family, Cook apprenticed out to a storekeeper in 1744. Two years later he signed on as a sailor on a North Sea merchant ship and fell in love with the sea. Cook volunteered as a sailor in the Royal Navy in 1755. He was a quick learner, passing his master's examination in 1757 and becoming an expert ocean surveyer and navigator. During the Seven Years War, Cook surveyed the St. Lawrence River for General James Wolfe's army on its way to the English conquest of Quebec*. Between 1755 and 1765 Cook made a name for himself surveying the eastern coast of Canada*.

Cook received his first command in 1764—the *Grenville*. He spent a year on scientific and surveying expeditions, and by then his skill was well known among high-ranking Admiralty officials. In 1768 the Admiralty gave Cook command of the HMS *Endeavour* and sent him off to the "South Seas" to explore and to conduct astronomical observations. He reached Tahiti in June 1769 and sailed among the Society Islands. Between October 1769 and March 1770, Cook sailed to New Zealand* and circumnavigated both of its islands. During the rest of the year he charted the eastern coast of Australia*, naming the area New South Wales*. He returned to England in July 1771. The fact that not one of his sailors had died of scurvy earned Cook respect among both the Admiralty and his men.

In July 1772 Cook set out on his second major voyage, commanding the HMS *Resolution* and the HMS *Adventure*. His charge was to continue the search for the alleged "Unknown Southern Island." This time he sailed down the West African coast to Cape Town and from there south across the Antarctic Circle—

the first Europeans to complete such a journey. When ice blocked his path, Cook headed east to Polynesia and charted the New Hebrides*, New Caledonia*, and South Georgia*. Cook had also eliminated all beliefs in a great southern continent awaiting European exploitation. When he returned to England in July 1775, Cook was hailed as a great adventurer.

One year later Cook set out again, this time to find the fabled Northwest Passage*. Late in 1777 Cook discovered Christmas Island in the central Pacific, and in January 1778 reached the Sandwich Islands, today's Hawaii*. He moved on to the Pacific coast of North America and charted it from the Bering Strait down to Oregon in the spring and summer of 1778. Cook wintered in Hawaii, and on February 14, 1779, died in a clash with natives there. (J. C. Beaglehole, *The Life of Captain James Cook*, 1974; Alan Villiers, *Captain James Cook*, 1967.)

COOK ISLANDS. The Cook Islands consist of fifteen coral atolls and volcanic islands scattered over a 900-mile north-south axis in the South Pacific. The native people of the Cook Islands migrated there around 700 A.D. from what today is French Polynesia*. In 1595 the Spanish explorer Alvaro de Mendana de Neira discovered the Cook Islands, and in 1606 the Portuguese navigator Pedro Fernandez de Quiros came upon them. In the 1770s the British explored the Southern Cook Islands during the voyages of Captain James Cook*. Protestant missionaries arrived early in the 1800s, establishing a Christian and British sphere of influence there. Rarotonga is 2,800 miles from New Zealand*, and as the English colony there developed in the nineteenth century, the Cook Islands became even more closely associated with the British Empire*. Afraid that French designs in the Pacific would lead to annexation, the British established a protectorate over the Southern Cook Islands in 1888. In 1901 Britain saw to it that New Zealand annexed the Cook Islands, both the Northern and Southern groups.

After World War II*, a national independence movement emerged in the Cook Islands under the leadership of Albert R. Henry and his Cook Islands Progressive Association. New Zealand established an appointed legislative council for the islands in 1946, and in 1957 it was transformed into the legislative assembly with twenty-seven members, twenty-two of them elected and five appointed. The assembly focused exclusively on internal affairs, while New Zealand remained responsible for foreign affairs and defense. Late in 1964 the parliament of New Zealand passed legislation giving the legislative assembly of the Cook Islands complete self-government in domestic matters. The first elections were held in 1965, electing twenty-two people to the new parliament. Although the enabling act of 1965 allows the Cook Islanders to declare full independence from New Zealand at any time, they remain today citizens of New Zealand. The Cook Islands parliament and its cabinet system take care of all domestic matters, leaving defense and foreign policy to New Zealand. (J. C. Beaglehole, *The Life of Captain James Cook*, 1974; Richard Gilson, *The Cook Islands 1820–1950*, 1980; W. P. Morrell, *Britain in the Pacific Islands*, 1956.)

COORG. British India annexed the Kingdom of Coorg in 1834, and from then until 1869 the chief commisioner of Mysore* also handled Coorg. Great Britain raised Coorg's status to that of a chief commissioner's province in 1869. Coorg joined the new nation of India in 1947*. See INDIA.

CORAL SEA ISLANDS TERRITORY. The Coral Sea Islands are an uninhabited group located in the Coral Sea between the northern coast of Australia and the southern coast of New Guinea. Great Britain laid claim to the islands early in the nineteenth century, but after World War I Australia* assumed jurisdiction over them. In 1969 they were formally incorporated into Australia as the Coral Sea Islands Territory. (Robert D. Craig and Frank P. King, *Historical Dictionary of Oceania*, 1981.)

CORN LAW OF 1791. The Corn Laws were British laws that, from the fifteenth through the nineteenth centuries, regulated the import and export of grain (the term "corn" was used to denote basic food grains) and other agricultural products. The grain controls were enforced chiefly through the imposition of high import and low export duties. The net effect of the various corn laws was to limit the agricultural products available on the domestic market and to increase food prices. In general, the laws favored the interests of the big landowners, helped preserve the landlord-tenant system, restricted industrial development, and limited domestic dependency on grain imports from the colonial empire. In the long term, however, the effects of the corn laws were felt most keenly by the industrial working class in Britain, and imperial politics played little part in their imposition or, by 1869, their final abolition.

The Corn Law of 1791 was imposed by parliament when, for the first time in its history, Britain was unable to feed itself from the produce of its own soil. Until the second half of the eighteenth century, Britain was a net exporter of grain, but the trade balance tipped the other way at the time of the American Revolution*. By 1790 the rapidly increasing population of England, Scotland, and Wales was over ten million, and approximately one-fifth of the domestic requirements of food had to be imported, largely from Europe. To reduce this dependence on foreign supplies of grain, parliament determined to encourage domestic production by placing protective tariffs on imports. The 1791 corn law imposed prohibitive duties on foreign grain when the domestic price fell below fifty shillings per quarter (a "quarter" was equal to eight bushels, or one-quarter ton). The law allowed practically free importation only when the price exceeded fifty-four shillings, a price equivalent to about seven shillings per bushel, or two and one-half times the daily wage of a London workman.

The high food prices resulting from the passage of the Corn Law of 1791 and subsequent protective legislation helped spark demands for increased democracy in Britain by the 1830s. The stimulus of high prices also expanded the domestic production of food, so that Great Britain was relatively unscathed by the Napoleonic Wars. Following the demise of protectionism in 1869, when the last remaining tariffs were abolished, Britain maintained a policy of free trade into the twentieth century. In 1932, however, imperial economic conditions forced a re-imposition of limited protectionism under the policy of imperial preference. (Donald Grove Barnes, *A History of the English Corn Laws from 1660–1846*, 1930; Travis L. Crosby, *The English Farmers and the Politics of Protection*, 1977).

William G. Ratliff

CORN LAW OF 1815. The Corn Law of 1815 was one of the acts of the British parliament intended to provide economic protection for agricultural interests by restricting the import of cheap foreign grain. The imposition of corn laws began in England as early as the mid-fifteenth century. The laws became particularly important in the late eighteenth and early nineteenth centuries during the grain shortages created by Britain's growing population and the increasing trend toward industrialization. High prices during the Napoleonic Wars improved the economic position of the landlord and the farmer, but at the cost of recurrent urban disturbances, particularly in the new industrial cities. When, in 1813, a parliamentary committee, anticipating a post-Napoleonic grain surplus, demanded postwar agricultural protection, the working class in Britain countered with demands for cheap food. By 1814 an enormous grain harvest was followed by an unprecedented fall in wheat prices. In 1815, despite bitter protests from the industrial regions, parliament passed a new corn law.

The Corn Law of 1815 prohibited importation of foreign grain when the domestic price was less than eighty shillings per quarter (one "quarter" equals eight bushels, or one-quarter ton of grain). At this price, which was equivalent to ten shillings per bushel, or more than three times the average worker's daily wage, agricultural interests, especially large landowners, were guaranteed enormous profits. Although the act was intended to keep food prices, and thus farm profits, high, domestic prices fluctuated sharply, and neither landlords nor farmers were able to maintain their wartime prosperity between 1815 and 1822, when the corn law was amended.

On the whole, the corn laws were a grievous burden to industrial Britain. They increased the cost of production and, through European tariff retaliation, restricted markets. Moreover, because the Corn Laws kept food prices artificially high, British industrial workers had little money to spend on British manufactured goods. Parliamentary protectionism also restricted the development of British colonial possessions. The passage of the 1815 and other corn laws, intended to support the landed aristocracy, did, however, foster the growth of liberal democracy in Great Britain. During the nineteenth century middle-class opposition to protectionism sparked both economic and constitutional reform, most particularly the Anti-Corn-Law League (founded in Manchester in 1839) and the various reform bills enacted from 1832 to 1867. (Donald Grove Barnes, *A History of the English Corn Laws from 1660–1846,* 1930; L. W. Moffit, *England on the Eve of the Industrial Revolution,* 1963.)

William G. Ratliff

COROMANDEL COAST COLONY. See NETHERLANDS INDIA.

CORONADO, FRANCISCO VÁSQUEZ DE. Francisco Coronado was born in Salamanca, Spain, around 1510 and he came to New Spain* in 1535. After marrying the daughter of a prominent royal official, Coronado was appointed governor of New Galicia on the western coast of New Spain in 1538. In April 1540, Coronado led an expedition of several hundred Spaniards from Culiacan north into present-day Arizona, northern New Mexico, the Texas and Oklahoma panhandles, and central Kansas, searching for the fabled cities of "Cíbola." They located Cíbola, which turned out to be the Zuñi pueblo of Kawikuh. Some of Coronado's men explored further west into Arizona and discovered the Grand Canyon. After being thrown from a horse and injuring his head, Coronado returned to Mexico in 1542. He served as governor of New Galicia until 1544 and then moved to Mexico City to serve on the municipal council. His great expedition had not discovered the legendary wealth of the cities of Cíbola but had considerably expanded Spain's land claims in the New World. Francisco Coronado died in 1554. (Herbert E. Bolton, *Coronado on the Turquoise Trail: Knight of Pueblos and Plains,* 1949; George P. Hammond, *Coronado's Seven Cities,* 1940.)

CORTÉS, HERNÁN. Hernán Cortés was born 1485 in Medellín in the province of Extremadura, Castile. His father, Martín Cortés de Monroy, and mother, Doña Catalina Pizarro Altamarino, were poor but of the *hidalgo* class. Tradition has it that at fourteen he entered the university of Salamanca, where he studied law and became a Latin scholar, but the more mundane truth may be that he acquired his smattering of Latin while serving as a notary in Valladolid and Seville. Supposedly, by the turn of the century he was torn between fighting in the Italian wars and sailing to Hispaniola* with Nicolás de Ovando, royal governor of the Spanish Indies from 1501 to 1509, and having decided on the latter, was prevented from going by an injury suffered when a wall fell on him while he was escaping the house of a married woman. In any case he sailed in 1504 for Hispaniola, where he worked as a notary in the town of Azua for five or six years.

In 1511 Cortés served under Diego Velásquez in the conquest of Cuba* and, when the latter was appointed governor, became his secretary. Thereafter there was considerable friction between the two, perhaps because Cortés refused to marry Catalina Suárez Marcaida (his betrothed in 1513), who may have been related to Velásquez's wife; or possibly because he was involved in a conspiracy against the governor. Velásquez had him arrested, threatened to hang him, then pardoned him and put him on a ship for deportation to Hispaniola, whereupon

Cortés escaped, was recaptured, and evidently pardoned again. Eventually he married Catalina, made peace with the governor, and was twice elected *alcalde* of Baracoa (Santiago de Cuba), where he had settled in 1514. By 1517 he had acquired an *encomienda** and some gold mines, but was apparently not wealthy.

Meanwhile Velásquez had conceived the ambition to be *adelantado* (governor) of Yucatán and sent agents to the new king, Charles I (later Holy Roman Emperor Charles V*), to obtain the title for him, along with the right to conquer and settle new lands. Probably to bolster his claim, he sent to Yucatán the expeditions of Hernández de Córdoba in 1517 and Juan de Grijalva in 1518. Cortés seemingly showed no interest, possibly because the riches of the Aztecs* were as yet unknown. Why Velásquez chose to send a third expedition later in 1518 and selected Cortés to lead it is unclear. Supposedly the original purpose was to search for the overdue Grijalva. However, Velásquez's main motive, aside from the profitable trade, was surely to keep his claim alive while awaiting word from Spain. As for the choice of Cortés, perhaps he had wealthy partners. In any case Velásquez soon developed misgivings about entrusting so much power to Cortés, whose own influence was growing, and he tried to prevent Cortés from acquiring provisions.

Not to be denied, Cortés raided the Baracoa slaughterhouse and hastily departed on November 18, collecting additional supplies and men in Jamaica*, Macaca, Trinidad*, and back in Cuba, before departing on February 18, 1519, with eleven ships, about 600 soldiers and 100 sailors, and a few horses. He landed at San Juan de Ulua on April 22, already knowing that a powerful chieftain named Montezuma ruled the land, and that there would be no turning back from the goal of compelling Montezuma to acknowledge Charles' sovereignty, thus enabling Cortés to settle Mexico*, win new subjects for God and king, and acquire vast territory and great riches.

Cortés now scouted Montezuma's empire, won over most of Velasquez's adherents by promises of glory and gold, and established a "legal" justification for his actions by creating the town of Vera Cruz, which made him *alcalde* and captain-general. But Velásquez's court patron, Bishop Juan Rodríquez Fonseca, obtained for him the title *adelantado*, word of which reached Cortés on July 1. On July 26 Cortés sent his first letter to Charles, appealing over Velásquez's head. After foiling a plot against him and burning his ships, Cortés marched inland on August 16. By the end of the year he had a toehold in Tenochtitlán (Mexico City) and had "persuaded" Montezuma to submit to Charles, but Velásquez learned of his plans and on March 5, 1520, sent an army under Panfilo de Narvaez to stop him. Cortés defeated Narvaez near the coast on May 27, but by the time he returned to Tenochtitlán on June 25, the Aztecs were in revolt, and on June 30, 1520 (la *noche triste*) Montezuma was killed and the Spanish retreated from the city with heavy losses.

Cortés had not received a reply to his letter, but he had lost the empire he had offered to Charles. Meanwhile, the latter had gained another, the Holy Roman Empire, which had produced virtual revolt in Castile and delayed Charles' decision on the comparatively unimportant matter in Mexico. In this precarious position, Cortés sent a second letter, congratulating Charles on his election as emperor in Europe and offering the astonishing argument that he was already legal emperor in New Spain by virtue of Montezuma's submission—procured thanks to Cortés—even if his new subjects were temporarily in revolt. By the end of the summer of 1521 Cortés had retaken Tenochtitlán, but Fonseca had persuaded the regency government in Spain (Charles was in Germany) to send Cristóbal de Tapia to arrest Cortés and take over the government of New Spain. Undaunted, Cortés avoided Tapia, whom he probably bribed, arranged another demonstration of the "popular will" whereby Tapia was implored to ask the Spanish government to reconsider, and on May 22, 1522, sent a third letter with news of the capture of Tenochtitlán and attacks on his enemies. In July 1523 Juan de Garay, governor of Jamaica and Fonseca's ally, invaded New Spain, but in September there arrived Charles's decree of October 15, 1522, naming Cortés governor and captain-general, and Garay gave up.

Cortés sent Pedro de Alvarado and Cristóbal de Olid to conquer Guatemala* and Honduras* respectively, but the latter disavowed Cortés' authority at Velásquez's bidding. All this led to a fourth letter of October 14, 1524, in which Cortés denounced Fonseca by name and threatened to send a force to Cuba to arrest Velásquez (both were now dead). This alarmed Charles, who in November 1525 sent Luis Ponce de León to investigate. Earlier, in 1524, Cortés had set off to subdue Olid, and by the time he returned on May 24, 1526, New Spain was torn by civil war between Velazquez's partisans under Gonzalo de Salazar and Cortés' followers, whose leader—Rodrigo de Paz—had been captured and killed. Cortés' return led to triumph in June 1526, but in November de León arrived, and his death shortly thereafter aroused suspicians against Cortés, whose governorship he had suspended. Cortés left for Spain in March 1528 to seek redress. He was well-received by Charles, who made him Marqués del Valle de Oaxaca, but though the king confirmed his ownership of vast estates, he did not reappoint him governor. Though Cortés returned to Mexico in 1530, he had no official role, and in 1540 he returned, disillusioned, to Spain, where he lived until his death in 1547. (Hernán Cortés, *Letters from Mexico*, trans. and ed. by Anthony Pagden, 1986; Bernal Díaz, *The Conquest of New Spain*, ed. by J. M. Cohen, 1963; Francisco López de Gómara, *Cortés: The Life of the Conqueror by his Secretary*, trans. and ed. by Lesley Byrd Simpson, 1964.)

William B. Robison

COSTA RICA. During the colonial period, Costa Rica, a province of the captaincy-general of Guatemala*, was one of four *gobiernos* established to control the region and was one of the last Central American provinces to come under Spanish control. It was a peripheral area in a backwater region of the Spanish Empire* which had a small Indian population. The Spanish population soon outnumbered them although migration to the region was never large. Isolated and lacking mineral wealth, its inhabitants were condemned to poverty. Columbus* reconnoitered the coast on his fourth voyage and named the area Veragua. On June 9, 1508, the king named Diego de Nicuesa governor of Veragua, which was also named Castilla del Oro and included Nicaragua*.

In 1513 Pedrarias Dávila was named governor and captain-general of Castilla de Oro but Veragua province was not included. In 1522 and 1523 Gil González Dávila explored all Costa Rica on the Pacific side. When Pedrarias heard of the discoveries he sent Francisco de Hernández de Córdoba to conquer and settle the region. In 1524 he founded the first Spanish town, Bruselas, in Costa Rica, which was depopulated in 1525 by Córdoba who rebelled against Pedrarias. Pedrarias ordered the town repopulated in 1526 but it was destroyed by Honduras's governor in 1527.

Columbus's heirs continued a legal fight to get ownership of the region and in 1536 his nephew Luis won the title of duke of Veragua and part of the territory. In 1556 the territory reverted to the crown but the title was kept. The *conquistadores* of Panama and Nicaragua called the territory Costa Rica to distinguish it from the territory which comprised the Veragua dukedom. In 1539 the Audiencia of Panama named Hernán Sanchez de Badajoz *adelantado* and *mariscal* of Costa Rica with authorization to conquer and colonize the territory. A dispute with Nicaragua's governor led to his arrest and return to Spain. The king disavowed Sanchez's conquest because the Audiencia of Panama had no authority over the territory. In 1540 the king contracted Diego Gutiérrez to conquer it but his cruelty to the Indians led to his death.

Not much of the territory, only Nicoya, under Spanish control since 1524, was under Spanish rule after this but the *conquistadores* continued their attempts because they thought it contained great wealth. In 1560 the Audiencia of Guatemala gave Juan de Cavallón license to settle and conquer the territory. He brought the first livestock and founded towns. In 1562, when he returned to Guatemala, the territory was definitely under Spanish control. Juan Vásquez de Coronado continued the colonization but various Indian revolts plagued him. In 1565 Coronado went to Spain to petititon for the title of *adelantado* and governor of the province but drowned on his return. The Indians rebelled again in 1568 but were put down by governor Perafán de Ribera. After Ribera, the conquest phase was definitely over. It is through Cavallón, Coronado, and Ribera's efforts that Costa Rica became part of the Spanish empire.

The first settlers in the region were from Nicaragua. In 1573 there were about fifty families living in Cartago and Aranjuez. In 1601 a road was opened from Cartago to Chiriqui which allowed trade with Panama and mule breeding for export. The Talamanca Indians were one group which fought against the occupation of their territory. In 1608 Gonzalo Vázquez de Coronado gained permission to conquer the Talamanca territory. Various attempts were made to conquer the region, but finally a frontier fort was established in Chirripo.

Costa Rica's lack of minerals and population made it an extremely poor region besieged by many problems. In an attempt to bring back an Indian labor force, governor Alonso de Castillo y Guzmán reentered Talamanca in 1619, brought back 400 Indian prisoners to Cartago, and divided them among his soldiers. In 1622 the province requested incorporation into Panama but was rejected. Various attempts were made to open ports. Governor Rodrigo Arias Maldanado unsuccessfully attempted a reconquest of Talamanca in 1662.

Besides the Indians, the Spaniards had the added burden of protecting their borders from pirates who attacked the region frequently during the seventeenth century. The Matina valley was a prime target because of its cacao plantations. The Mosquito Indians, used by the English, raided cacao plantations and took African slaves working there. Cartago's citizens engaged in illegal trade with the English and the Dutch to get goods they needed. As Cartago's population grew, individuals moved to the valley to grow agricultural goods. The region's poverty was such that in 1709 the governor declared cacao as money. In the eighteenth century Costa Rica's situation had not improved much. The Talamancan Indians rebelled against the missionaries in 1709 because of their excessive zeal. The Audiencia of Guatemala sent an expedition to put down the rebellion in 1711. After the Talamanca rebellion of 1709–1711 new attempts at colonization were not attempted until 1742. The Mosquito Indians also kept up their attacks on Spanish settlements.

Taxes were raised by the crown through cacao and mule exports for the defense of the valley. In 1766 the tobacco *estanco* (monopoly) was created and the San José and Heredía tobacco growers, who previously had grown it freely, were required to bring it to a factory. In 1783 the *aquardiente* (liquor) *estanco* was also created. Militia were created to protect the province from Indian and pirate attacks. In 1787, because of the province's poverty, it received an exclusive monopoly to grow tobacco. The monopoly was abolished in 1792 because of the tobacco's bad quality. Tobacco growers were in a precarious situation. In 1804 new anil (indigo), cotton, cacao, coffee, and sugar plantations were exempt from paying taxes, but this did not help the province's situation. In 1808 an insurrection occurred in San José which demanded freedom for growing tobacco and making aguardiente.

When Napoleon invaded Spain in 1808, Cartago supported Carlos IV and his son, Ferdinand VII. The Costa Rican militia put down a revolt in Nicaragua in 1811, and as a reward in 1813, Cartago was given the title of *muy noble y muy leal*, San José the title of *ciudad*, and Heredia that of *villa*. In 1811 the Audiencia of Guatemala prohibited Costa Rican trade with Panama, forcing them to buy costlier goods from Guatemala. The Cartago, Heredía, and San José *ayuntamientos* (magistrates) protested before the Spanish Cortes in 1813. In 1815 the Casa de Enseñanza de Santo Tomás, a school, was founded in San José. Because the province did not have the 60,000 inhabitants necessary to elect a deputy to the 1820 Cortes, the district of Nicoya and towns of Santa Cruz and Guanacaste were attached to it. In October 1821 news of the independence declared in Guatemala City arrived in Cartago and on October 29 Costa Rica declared independence from Spain. (León Fernández Guardia, *Historia de Costa Rica durante la Dominación Española 1502–1821*, 1975; León Fernández Guardia,

Historia de Costa Rica, 1937; Ricardo Fernandez Guardia, *Cartilla Historica de Costa Rica*, 1909.)

Carlos Pérez

CUBA. Cuba is situated 90 miles south of the Florida Keys. When sighted by Colombus* on October 27, 1492, it was inhabited by 16,000 to 60,000 Amerindians representing three cultures: the Guanajatabey, Ciboney, and Taino. Raids by cannibalistic Caribs were threatening the dominant Taino, a peaceful, agricultural, Arawak people. In 1511, three years after Sebastián de Ocampo's circumnavigation of the 746 mile-long island, Diego Velásquez arrived from nearby Hispaniola*. By 1514 he had pacified the natives, though he encountered heroic resistance. To consolidate his power, Velasquez utilized the *encomienda** system, which gave settlers the right to exploit Indian labor as payment for Christianizing and "protecting" them. Bartolomé de las Casas*, a Dominican friar, embarked upon a lifetime mission of defending America's aborigines as a result of witnessing the ill-effects of the Cuban conquest. Velásquez founded Havana and Santiago, modern Cuba's two largest cities, and governed until his death in 1524.

Black slaves were introduced in 1523 to replace the dwindling Amerindian work force. Slavery would not be completely abolished until 1886. After Hernán Cortés* left the island to conquer Mexico* in 1518, other Spaniards used Cuba as a springboard for lucrative mainland enterprises. Havana, with its fine harbor and strategic location along the Gulf Stream, served as the key port of call for treasure fleets returning to Europe. It became Cuba's governmental seat in 1538. Cattle-raising developed into an important industry, providing salted meat and hides for export. Still, the island was primarily a "service colony" rather than a producer of goods.

Bullion-laden galleons attracted pirates. The French Huguenot, Jacques de Sores, sacked and burned Havana in 1555. Pedro Menéndez de Aviles, who governed Cuba in the 1560s, improved the convoy system that guarded Spanish shipping and transformed the capital into a military bastion. Santiago was torched by the infamous Henry Morgan in 1662. Nevertheless, despite a series of foreign attacks, Spain held the island until 1762. Ironically, the English capture of Havana in that year, during the Seven Years War, breathed new life into the colony. The port was opened to free trade for eleven months. Capital and slaves poured in. When Spain regained Cuba, it had to reconsider its monopolistic policies. The 1791 revolution in Haiti* led to a flood of refugees and the elimination of the world's top sugar producer. Commercial reforms, combined with growing trade with the United States, further stimulated cane planting. Coffee cultivation increased and peaked from 1820 to 1840. Consequently, by the late 1820s, Cuba had blossomed into the wealthiest colony on earth. Tobacco had boomed in the early 1700s, but now, sugar was "king."

Cuba and Puerto Rico* were Spain's last remaining American colonies after 1825. As the century progressed, however, Spanish rule was questioned. Cries for fiscal and political reform went unanswered. In October 1868 Carlos Manuel de Cespedes launched an unsuccessful rebellion ending in February 1878 with the Pact of Zanjón. After the Ten Years War, Madrid still refused to implement major colonial changes. Economic depression ignited another uprising in 1895 led by José Martí, Maximo Gómez, and Antonio Maceo. Rebel victories induced Spain to offer Cuba status as a self-governing province. The proposal was rejected.

In February 1898 the U.S.S. *Maine* mysteriously exploded in Havana harbor. Since the Ten Years War, United States businesses had increased their Cuban investments significantly. President William McKinley, pressured by a public outcry fueled by "yellow journalism," declared war on Spain on April 25, 1898. Although it had attempted to purchase the island earlier in the century, the United States promised in the Teller Amendment not to annex Cuba. In less than four months, Cuba was "liberated." The Cuban rebels, unfortunately, were not represented at the peace talks. From January 1899 until May 1902, the United States militarily occupied the former colony. Some improvements were made, especially in sanitation. Washington approved the Cuban constitution of 1901 only when the Platt Amendment was attached, which granted the United States the option to intervene for the purpose of protecting Cuba's "independence" or American "lives and property." On May 20, 1902, Tomas Estrada Palma assumed office as the first elected president of the Republic of Cuba. (Jaime Suchlicki, *Cuba: From Columbus to Castro*, 1985; Hugh Thomas, *Cuba: The Pursuit of Freedom*, 1971.)

Frank Marotti

CURACAO. See NETHERLANDS ANTILLES.

CYPRUS. Cyprus is an island of 3,572 square miles located about 40 miles south of the coast of central Turkey in the eastern Mediterranean Sea. Its population is primarily ethnic Greek, although Turks constitute a minority of approximately 19 percent. That difference between the Greeks, who are Greek Orthodox Christians, and the Turks, who are Sunni Muslims, has been a central theme in Cypriot history. Over the centuries Cyprus has been an international battleground, primarily because of its strategic location. Greeks, Persians, Byzantines, Lusignans of Jerusalem, and finally the Venetians successively dominated Cyprus over thousands of years until 1571, when the Ottoman Empire of the Turks conquered the island. Turkish rule was enlightened for more than two centuries, the government recognizing the Greek Orthodox Church and abolishing serfdom. But during the 1820s, when the Greeks successfully achieved their independence from the Ottoman Empire, the Turks grew suspicious of the Greek population in Cyprus and began to persecute them. Internal instability continued for years, with Greek Cypriots agitating for independence from Turkey.

In 1878, alarmed about the potential of Russian hegemony in the eastern Mediterranean, Great Britain formally leased Cyprus from the Turks, although

Cypriots continued to pay Turkish taxes. When Turkey entered World War I*
on the side of the Germans, Great Britain formally annexed Cyprus, making it
a crown colony in 1927. Greek Cypriots, however, still wanted independence,
from the British now, rather than from the Turks. Periodic riots had to be quelled
by British troops in the 1930s. The agitation subsided somewhat during World
War II*, but after the war it started up again, this time under the leadership of
George Grivas and his National Organization of Cypriot Fighters (EOKA). In
1954 Grivas launched an all-out revolt and guerrilla war against the British
administration.

That war continued throughout the 1950s. Greek Cypriots, supported by
Greece, wanted complete independence from Great Britain at least, and at best
unification with Greece, but Turkish Cypriots, supported by Turkey, resisted the
notion, realizing that in any independent nation or Greek-Cypriot unification
they would find themselves completely dominated by the Greek majority. Instead,
they wanted partition of the island and independence for both communities. For
the British colonial regime, it seemed an impossible dilemma.

The resolution of the dilemma came in February 1959, but it was only temporary. At meetings in Zurich and London, Great Britain, Greece, and Turkey
reached an agreement on Cypriot independence. All three countries agreed to
the island's independence, although the agreement also provided for small con-
tingents of Greek and Turkish troops to occupy the island and train a Cypriot
army. The agreement provided for a Greek president on Cyprus and a Turkish
vice president. The elected legislature would reserve 70 percent of its seats for
Greek Cypriots and 30 percent for the Turks, with all civil service appointments
allocated on the same basis. Independence came on August 16, 1960.

Political stability was very short-lived. Greek Cypriots resented the fact that
the new constitution had awarded Turks a number of legislative seats and government posts far in excess of their population. Civil war erupted between the
Greek and Turkish communities in 1963, with irregular troops on both sides
supplied by Greece and Turkey. A United Nations* peacekeeping force entered
Cyprus in February 1964. Thousands of regular soldiers from Greece landed
secretly on the island, while the Turkish irregulars retreated into defensive enclaves. A stalemate existed for ten years until 1974 when regular Turkish soldiers
invaded Cyprus in response to the seizure of the Cypriot government by Greek
officers. While negotiations took place in Geneva during 1974, Turkish forces
brought 40 percent of the island under their control. On February 13, 1975,
Turkish Cypriots declared the independence of all Turkish-controlled Cyprus,
and by June 1975 Turks had approved a new constitution there. On June 30,
1976, Rauf Denktash was elected president of the Turkish Federated State of
Cyprus. In November 1983, the Turks unilaterally proclaimed the existence of
the Turkish Republic of Northern Cyprus, a move which was not recognized by
the international community. (Doros Alastros, *Cypress in History: A Survey of
5,000 Years*, 1977; Halil I. Salih, *Cypress: The Impact of Diverse Nationalism
on a State*, 1978.)

CYRENAICA. Cyrenaica is the eastern region of Libya*. Its major city is Benghazi. Italy took much of Libya from the Ottoman Empire in 1911, and in 1919 Cyrenaica and Tripolitania* were separated as individual Italian colonies. They were rejoined in 1934 as the colony of Libya. See LIBYA.

D

DAHOMEY. Dahomey—today known as the People's Republic of Benin, is an elongated territory lying between Togo* to the west and Nigeria* to the east. To the north, Burkina-Faso and Niger are the bordering countries. The Gulf of Benin lies to the south. European slave traders reached the area in the 1580s, and their presence dramatically affected Dahomey's history. The Portuguese were first, establishing a trading post at Porto Novo. Early in the 1600s Portugal also established a slave trading base at Ouidah. By 1670 France and Britain did the same. The kingdom of Dahomey in the interior went to war with its neighbors in order to secure an outlet to the sea, which successful slave trading required. Until the early part of the nineteenth century, labor demand in the gold mines of Brazil and the plantations in Haiti kept the slave trade thriving in Dahomey.

France became active in the region in 1851 when she signed a treaty of friendship and trade with the king of Porto-Novo. New treaties in 1868 and 1878 with King Gelele of Dahomey and with King Toffa of Porto Novo in 1882 gave the French, in their own minds at least, sovereignty over the coastal areas of Cotonou and Porto Novo. The Berlin Act of 1885 precipitated the arrival of French occupation troops. When King Behanzin of the Kingdom of Dahomey succeeded King Gelele in 1889, a rebellion erupted against the French, one which was not crushed until Benhanzin was captured and exiled in 1894. Dahomey had become part of French West Africa*, although a formal constitution for the new colony was not complete until 1904.

During World War II, Dahomey supported the Free French forces against the Axis powers, and when the new French Fourth Republic of 1946 politically incorporated the colonies with metropolitan France, Dahomey became an overseas territory of the French Union. In 1946 the Progressive Dahomey Union became the first political party of Dahomey. Sorou Migan Apithy, protege of the French clergyman Father Aupiais, received 95 percent of the vote as Dahomey's first representative in the French National Assembly. But continuing discrimination against native Dahomeans by French colons as well as successful rebellions against French imperialism in Algeria* and Indochina* inspired a growing nationalism among the people of Dahomey. Hubert Maga, founder of the Democratic Movement of Dahomey in the early 1950s, emerged as the leading Dahomean nationalist.

The French Constitution of 1958 permitted a referendum regarding the status of Dahomey, and on February 14, 1959, Dahomey became an autonomous republic within the French Community*. In June 1960, during a meeting in Paris trying to create a federation of the former members of French West Africa, Prime Minister Hubert Maga requested independence. France agreed, announcing the independence of Dahomey on August 1, 1960. Elections in December designated Maga as president of independent Dahomey. In 1961 Dahomey annexed the Portuguese enclave of Sao Joao Baptista de Ajuda. Not until 1975 was the country's name changed to the People's Republic of Benin. (Patrick Manning, *Slavery, Colonialism and Economic Growth in Dahomey 1940–1960*, 1982; Dov Ronen, *Dahomey between Tradition and Modernity*, 1975.)

Said El Mansour Cherkaoui

DAMAN. Formerly known as Damao, Daman was once part of Portuguese India*, along with Diu* and Goa*. The city of Daman is located at the mouth of the Daman Ganga River on the Arabian Sea, approximately 105 miles north of Bombay. The Portuguese first attacked Daman in 1531 and permanently occupied it in 1559, although neither the British nor the native Indian government formally recognized that presence until 1780. Daman was a flourishing port city during the sixteenth and seventeenth centuries, but when the size of sailing ships began to increase, its harbor proved too small. By the eighteenth century Daman was declining in commercial importance, except for the coastal trade of western India. Daman remained under Portuguese control until December 18, 1961, when Indian troops occupied the city. Combat between Indian and Portuguese troops was intense but shortlived. Indian control was imposed quickly and Daman, along with Diu and Goa, was included in the new Union Territory. Portugal did not recognize Indian sovereignty over Daman until 1978. (Gervase Clarence-Smith, *The Third Portuguese Empire, 1825–1975. A Study in Economic Imperialism*, 1985.)

DANISH EMPIRE. If one considers Danish control of Iceland, Denmark had been an imperial power since 1380, but in 1611 the modern era of Danish imperialism began when enterprising merchants formed the Danish East India Company. They established a colonial outpost at Tranquebar* on the Indian coast in 1620. In the 1650s the company established outposts along the Guinea and Gold coasts of West Africa. Visits were made to the West Indies in the 1650s, and in 1671 the Danish West India Company was established. The Danish West

Indies eventually included St. Thomas, St. Croix, and St. John in what is today the Virgin Islands.* The Danish colonial empire was doomed, however, by Denmark's lack of resources. French, Dutch, and English interests eclipsed her. By the 1750s the government assumed administrative control of the two joint stock companies*, and a century later Denmark sold her colonies in India and West Africa to the British. Denmark's colonial empire finally dissolved in 1917 when she sold the Virgin Islands to the United States. (David P. Henige, *Colonial Governors from the Fifteenth Century to the Present*, 1970.)

DANISH GOLD COAST. In 1657 the Danish East India Company pushed Sweden out of its Fort Osu settlement near Accra on the coast of West Africa. The Danes renamed the post Christiansborg and then established other outposts at Keta, Teshi, Ningo, and Ada. The real profits from the forts came from the slave trade, but in 1792 Denmark became the first European country to outlaw the traffic. There was no money in the posts then, and Denmark began looking for a buyer. At the same time, Great Britain was searching for an opportunity to increase her presence in the area as a means of forestalling French expansion there. In 1850 Great Britain purchased the Danish colonies and incorporated them into her own Gold Coast* colony. (Georg Norregard, *Danish Settlements in West Africa, 1658–1850*, 1966.)

DANISH WEST INDIES. Danish merchants formed the Danish West India Company in 1671, and the next year the company established a settlement at St. Thomas*. The company staked a claim to neighboring St. John but did not send settlers there until 1716. France had claimed St. Croix since 1650 but had never settled it, so in 1733 the company purchased the island from France. Together the three islands constituted the Danish West Indies. In 1755 the Danish West India Company surrendered its control over the islands to the government, and the government began dealing with them as an administrative unit, with a governor-general on St. Croix, and St. Thomas and St. John administered as secondary units. During the Napoleonic Wars, Great Britain occupied the islands (1801–1802, 1807–1815) but returned them to Denmark in 1815. By that time the Danes knew that their hopes of a New World empire were doomed. Denmark simply did not have the resources to sustain it. In 1870 Denmark negotiated a treaty with the United States providing for American purchase of St. Croix, St. Thomas, and St. John, but the United States Senate refused to ratify the treaty. Not until 1917, when World War I threatened to bring German intervention into the Caribbean, did the United States conclude the purchase of the Danish West Indies (Virgin Islands*). (Waldemar Westergaard, *The Danish West Indies under Company Rule (1671–1754)*, 1917.)

DECLARATORY ACT OF 1766. In 1765 the English parliament had passed the Stamp Act in order to raise revenue in the American colonies and help pay the expenses of the recently concluded French and Indian War*. The American colonists resented the legislation, arguing that parliament did not have the right to tax them because they enjoyed no representation in that body. Insurgent groups, known as the "Sons of Liberty," emerged in several colonies offering violent resistance to the law. More significant, colonial representatives gathered in New York City in October 1765, forming the Stamp Act Congress and denying the right of parliament to levy direct taxes on the colonies. They also imposed a boycott of English products until the Stamp Act was repealed. American importers stopped bringing in English goods and American companies stopped payment on their debts to English merchants. Economic paralysis hit England, and in March 1766 parliament repealed the Stamp Act. But at the same time, parliament passed the Declaratory Act, which affirmed the right of parliament to tax the colonists in the future. The American colonists reacted to news of the repeal of the Stamp Act with unrestrained joy, all but ignoring the Declaratory Act, which they viewed as little more than a face-saving measure by the English. (Edmund S. Morgan, *The Stamp Act Crisis*, 1953).

DELAWARE. Delaware, the second smallest state in geographic area in the United States, lies on the Atlantic seaboard midway between Washington, D.C., and New York City. A small Dutch settlement at Lewes in 1631 was destroyed by local Indians, but seven years later a group of Swedes established Fort Christina, which eventually evolved into present-day Wilmington. In 1655 the Dutch, operating out of New Netherland*, conquered the Swedish settlement and retained control of it until 1664 when the English, under the Duke of York, invaded New Netherland and assumed sovereignty over all Dutch colonies on the North Atlantic coast.

The English referred to the area as "Delaware," a name honoring Thomas West, Lord De La Warr, an early governor of Virginia. By 1680 there were three counties formally organized in Delaware—New Castle, Kent, and Sussex. New York* governed Delaware until 1682, when the Duke of York ceded the three counties to William Penn so that Pennsylvania* would have access to the sea. In 1704 Pennsylvania granted Delaware its own legislature, even though the two colonies shared the same royal governor until the time of the American Revolution*. Delaware developed a diverse population composed of African, Swedish, Dutch, Welsh, English, and Scots-Irish settlers. By a close vote the Delaware delegation at Philadelphia voted for the Declaration of Independence in 1776 and at the same time severed their political relationship with Pennsylvania. On December 7, 1787, Delaware became the first state to ratify the United States Constitution. (John Munroe, *Colonial Delaware*, 1978.)

DELHI. Delhi was the capital city of the Mughal kingdom of India*. In terms of its place in British India, Delhi was part of the United Provinces of Agra and Oudh* from 1857 to 1859 and then of Punjab from 1859 to 1912. In 1912 the British changed the capital city of British India from Calcutta to Delhi, and in the process they created a separate chief commissioner's province for the city. In 1947 Delhi joined the new nation of India. See INDIA.

DEMERARA. In 1624 the Dutch West India Company established a settlement at the mouth of the Essequibo River in what is today Guyana, and from that base in 1750 settlers established the Demerara colony. It remained in Dutch hands until its seizure by the British in 1781. France occupied the colony from 1782 to 1784 and then returned it to the Dutch. During the Napoleonic Wars, the British occupied Demerara again, and although they gave it back to the Dutch in 1802, they seized it permanently in 1803. Eventually Demarara became part of British Guiana* and later Guyana. See BRITISH GUIANA.

DERNBURG, BERNHARD. Born July 17, 1865, Bernhard Dernburg was appointed director of the colonial department of the German foreign office in 1906 and became secretary of state of the newly created colonial office in 1907. He served as director of German colonial interests until 1910. Dernburg came to the colonial office after a successful career as an international banker. By the time he assumed office in 1906, he had already served on the directorial boards of 39 different banks and manufacturing concerns, including the Darmstädter Bank, one of Germany's most influential banking establishments. Dernburg was a member of the *Deutschfreisinnnige Partei*, a progressive-liberal party founded in 1884. He brought to the foreign office an interest in social and economic reform in the Germany empire*. Dernburg was most noted for the changes he introduced in the colonial section (*Kolonialabteilung*) of the foreign office. He dissolved the *Kolonialrat*, an advisory body that had represented the major colonial interest groups. Dernburg created four separate divisions within the colonial office, and appointed experts to head each of the divisions, among them Walther Rathenau, one of Germany's most brilliant intellectuals and industrialists. While Dernburg's most visible accomplishment was his push for the construction of railways, he was also responsible for the complete restructuring of the colonial bureaucracy. In general terms, Dernburg's policy involved the complete decentralization of colonial governance. He introduced financial self-sufficiency into the colonies by insisting that government subsidies be curtailed and revenue for colonial administration be raised from private investors, subject to financial guarantees given by Berlin. The German government, however, retained full responsibility for the cost of colonial defense.

Under Dernburg, the tone of Germany's colonial administration became more civilian and liberal in character. Dernburg took pains to turn his journeys to Africa into a political publicity campaign to strengthen the cause of reform. He worked to outlaw the corporal punishment of African workers. He also succeeded in making the colonial service more attractive to applicants and more professional in its administration. By 1910 Dernburg had regularized the positions of colonial officials, unified conditions of service, and laid down explicit conditions of tenure and benefits. He took considerable satisfaction in raising colonial service pay scales to a level equal to those of government service at home. In 1908 Dernburg helped found the Kolonialinstitut at Hamburg. The institute's purpose was to train colonial officials and to coordinate Germany's economic and scientific efforts in the colonies. The curriculum required students to gain expertise in the history of the indigenous peoples of the colonies, anthropology, and law. In addition, the students were expected to learn such practical matters as shipping and harbor construction, cartography, botany, and animal husbandry. Finally, Dernburg's links with German financial interests enabled him to facilitate the deployment of German capital in the African colonies, until 1910 an area largely neglected by German investors.

Dernburg resigned his cabinet post in 1910 following the political collapse of the government of Chancellor Bernhard von Bulow*. In 1914–1915 Dernburg directed anti-British propaganda in the United States. Following the war, he served as a Reichstag delegate from the politically moderate German Democratic Party. He died in Berlin on October 14, 1937. (Wilhelm Schiefel, *Bernhard Dernburg, 1865–1937: Kolonial Politiker und Bankier im wilhelminischen Deutschland*, 1975.)

William G. Ratliff

DE SOTO, HERNANDO. Hernando de Soto was born in Jerez de Badajos, Extremadura, Spain, in 1500. As a teenager he accompanied the expedition of Pedro Arias de Ávila to Panama, and in 1524 he was part of the Spanish army that conquered Nicaragua*. Between 1531 and 1536 de Soto served with Francisco Pizarro* in the conquest of Peru*. After a trip to Spain in 1536, he was named governor of Cuba* and received royal permission to explore the Gulf Coast of North America. He set out at the head of an expedition of 600 men in May 1539 and explored much of the Florida*, Georgia*, and Mississippi coastal regions. In search of gold, they headed inland and made their way all the way up to Tennessee. Late in 1540 and early in 1541 they traveled down through Alabama into Louisiana, discovering the Mississippi River in May. De Soto died on May 21, 1542, and his comrades buried him in the Mississippi River. (Edward Gaylord Bourne, ed., *Narratives of the Career of Hernando de Soto*, 1904; James Lockhart, *The Men of Cajamarca*, 1972.)

DIAS, BARTOLOMEU. Little is known about the early life of Bartolomeu Dias, and the few extant facts are obscured by the presence of several other individuals of that name in the court of King John II of Portugal. It is possible that Dias was importing ivory from Guinea* in 1478 and later commanded a ship in Azambuja's expedition of 1481 to found the fortress-factory of El Mina. Dias sailed from the Tagus River during August 1487 with two caravels and a larger storeship. Proceeding down the African coast, he anchored the storeship in an unidentified bay close to Cape Cross, the furthest southerly point reached by the previous expedition of Diogo Cao in 1486. Passing Cape Cross on December 4, 1487, the explorer reached Walvis Bay* on December 8 and entered

Elizabeth Bay on December 26. The Matsikama Mountains came into sight on January 6, 1488, but shortly after that a series of storms drove the Portuguese onto the high seas. As a result Dias actually bypassed the Cape of Good Hope and did not come upon land again until February 3 when he sighted Mossel Bay. From there the expedition proceeded eastward to Algoa Bay and Cape Receife, where the crew and officers demanded that they turn back. A disappointed Dias managed to persuade them to continue on for three more days so that the furthest point reached by the expedition was the Great Fish River. All of these discoveries definitely confirmed that Africa had been rounded; a sea route to India* was a reality.

On the way back to Portugal, Dias set up a stone cross at the Cape of Good Hope on June 6, 1488, which he incorrectly considered the southernmost point of Africa. Dias's ships entered the Tagus River in December 1488, having been gone sixteen months and seventeen days. Although King John II welcomed Dias enthusiastically, there is no record that the king rewarded him with the same generosity that had been accorded Diogo Cao. One Portuguese chronicler poetically commented that Dias like Moses was permitted to see the promised land but not allowed to enter. In 1494 John II placed him in charge of the construction of two heavy ships that were to be used in the voyage that would travel all the way to India. Since he was a commoner, the king passed over him for command of the expedition of 1497, naming instead the noble Vasco da Gama*. He did sail along with da Gama's fleet as far as the Cape Verde* Islands, where he turned aside to command a gold trading expedition to Guinea. When da Gama returned from India in 1499, he brought word of a thriving East African gold trade. This news prompted King Manuel to contemplate establishing a fortress-factory at the port of Sofala similar to El Mina. He placed Dias in charge of that enterprise, which was to be a subsidiary part of the expedition of Pedro Cabral* to India in 1500. Four caravels under the command of Dias were to proceed to Sofala after the Cape of Good Hope was rounded. As a result Dias participated in the discovery of Brazil*, but as the Portuguese fleet approached the Cape of Good Hope a great storm arose on May 24. Four ships were lost with all hands including Dias's flagship on May 29, 1500. (Eric Axelson, *Congo to Cape: Early Portuguese Explorers*, 1973; Bailey W. Diffie and George D. Winius, *Foundations of the Portuguese Empire 1415–1580*, 1977.)

Ronald Fritze

DIEGO-SUAREZ. Diego-Suarez was a short-lived French colony located on the northern tip of Madagascar*. When the French established their protectorate over southern Madagascar in 1886, they established a colonial outpost at Diego-Suarez on the northern coast of Madagascar to prepare for further imperial ventures in East Africa and the Indian Ocean. Only two colonial governors served there before France completed its conquest of Madagascar in 1896. At that point Diego-Suarez was dissolved and incorporated into the larger colony, becoming a political subdivision of Madagascar. (David P. Henige, *Colonial Governors from the Fifteenth Century to the Present*, 1970.)

DIEN BIEN PHU, BATTLE OF. The battle of Dien Bien Phu ended the First Indochinese War (1946–1954). It was a stunning defeat for the French and a decisive victory for the communist Viet Minh. Dien Bien Phu dramatically symbolized the French failure to reconstitute their colonial empire in Southeast Asia after World War II. The French were unable to pacify Vietnam* despite years of fighting and an ever-increasing volume of American aid. Ho Chi Minh's communist forces won the allegiance of most patriotic Vietnamese, and Viet Minh General Vo Nguyen Giap proved himself a master of the politico-military strategy the communists called "people's war." By 1953 France was ready to negotiate, but wanted to establish a strong military position from which to make political demands.

By the end of 1953 all of Tonkin* except the lower Red River delta was under Viet Minh control. General Henri Navarre decided to establish an impregnable bastion at Dien Bien Phu, a village in a rich agricultural valley nine miles long by five miles wide in the mountains of western Tonkin. Navarre believed that the site was strategic and that after fortifying it he could cut Viet Minh supply lines into Laos* and maintain a base from which his troops could sally forth to harass the Viet Minh. The whole idea was a classic military blunder, for the absence of roads meant that the French were immobilized while Giap's guerrilla forces could quietly ring the French position with artillery that had been disassembled, brought in on the backs of porters, and then reassembled for the final seige.

The French established their base at Dien Bien Phu in November 1953. Fifty thousand Viet Minh quickly and surreptitiously occupied the hills around the French base. They opened their seige on March 13, 1954, with an artillery barrage that completely surprised the 9,000 soldiers inside the French perimeter. The airfield was quickly knocked out. Henceforth, all resupply had to be by parachute. Although the French eventually increased the size of their garrison to 16,000 men, some of whom were Vietnamese, it was for nought. Well over half the garrison was killed, wounded, or taken prisoner.

France desperately sought direct American military intervention, even the use of atomic bombs, and there were some, but not many, in Washington who recommended that action to President Eisenhower. The United States advised the French to negotiate instead. Dien Bien Phu fell on May 7, 1954, when the Geneva Conference was already in session. The July 21 ceasefire ended French sovereignty in Indochina*. Ho Chi Minh, president of the communist Democratic Republic of Vietnam, proclaimed the Viet Minh porters, who had carried mortars and ammunition to the hills around Dien Bien Phu, the heroes of the day. General Giap went on to plan the successful Vietnamese war against the United States. (Bernard Fall, *Hell in a Very Small Place*, 1967; Ellen Hammer, *The Struggle for Indochina, 1940–1955*, 1966.)

Ross Marlay

DISEASE. In their expansion around the world in the age of imperialism, Europeans carried with them a host of Old World diseases that devastated native populations in North America, South America, Australia, and the islands of the Pacific. Because of the continental isolation for tens of thousands of years, aboriginal people did not have accumulated immunities to European diseases. In particular, the following diseases were unknown to them: smallpox*, measles, diptheria, trachoma, whooping cough, chicken pox, bubonic plague, malaria, typhoid fever, cholera, yellow fever, dengue fever, scarlet fever, amoebic dysentery, influenza, and a variety of helminthic afflictions. European diseases did not devastate the native populations of Africa and Asia because geographical contact and commerce over the millenia had made for bacterial exchanges, but in North America, South America, the Pacific, and Australia they brought epidemic death with them. Compared to the impact of disease on native population, European weapons and violence were relatively insignificant. Disease was imperialism's greatest weapon. (Alfred W. Crosby, Jr., *The Columbian Exchange. Biological and Cultural Consequences of 1492*, 1972.)

DISRAELI, BENJAMIN (EARL OF BEACONSFIELD). Born December 21, 1804, to a Jewish-Italian family in London, Benjamin Disraeli would serve twice as prime minister and be considered one of nineteenth-century Britain's most noted statesmen. In 1817 Disraeli's father converted his children to Christianity, thus removing any obstacle to young Disraeli's later political career. (Until 1858 Jews by religion were excluded from parliament). From 1821 to 1831, however, Disraeli exhibited little interest in either politics or the law, the profession chosen for him by his father. After his education at small, unfashionable private schools, he left the firm of solicitors to which he had been apprenticed and promptly lost a small fortune speculating in South American mining shares, incurring a debt that took him nearly thirty years to retire. After failing miserably to launch a daily newspaper, Disraeli turned to writing novels. Although he had limited literary talent, he produced a number of successful works throughout his life, including *The Young Duke* (1831), *Contarini Fleming* (1832), *Coningsby* (1844), and *Endymion* (1880). Most of his novels contained political themes that reflected Disraeli's interest in political reform. As early as 1831 he had decided to enter politics and he contested several elections from 1831 to 1836, but he failed to win a seat in parliament. Since his unsuccessful campaigns had been fought as an independent radical, Disraeli pragmatically changed to the more popular Conservative Party in 1837, whereupon he won a seat to the House of Commons.

Best known in London society and in the House of Commons as a literary fop who affected outlandish mannerisms and elaborate dress, Disraeli broke with the traditional conservative wing of his party in 1841. Disraeli became a leading spokesman for the Young England movement, a group of young Tories who opposed the middle class, stodgy conservatism represented by Sir Robert Peel. They opted for a romantic, aristocratic conservatism best exemplified by their opposition to the reduced-tariff, free-trade 1845 corn law proposals, a political stance that put Disraeli and the other Young Englanders in direct support of the country squires and landed interests. While Disraeli and his fellow protectionists could not prevent the corn law reforms from passing, his opposition to Peel catapulted him into a position of Conservative Party leadership in the Commons.

In 1852, 1858, and 1865 Disraeli served as chancellor of the exchequer in the shortlived Conservative governments of Lord Derby. Typical of Disraeli's political approach was his sponsorship of the 1867 Reform Bill, a measure intended to expand the British electorate, and a bill supported fully by Disraeli's archenemies in the Liberal Party. Disraeli justified the Reform Bill largely on the grounds of political expediency, that is, that the Conservatives could undercut the opposition by supporting a measure certain to pass eventually. In 1868 Disraeli became prime minister, a position which he likened to climbing a "greasy pole." In the following twelve-year period, Disraeli would find his Conservative Party in continuous confrontation with William E. Gladstone's Liberal Party, with Disraeli staunchly defending the monarchy, the House of Lords, and the church against what he took to be the threat of radicalism.

Disraeli's 1868 ministry was ended by Conservative defeat in parliament the same year. In 1874, however, Disraeli returned as prime minister, succeeding Gladstone, and devoted himself largely to matters of foreign policy and social reform. During his tenure as prime minister from 1874 to 1880, he presided over such reform measures as slum clearance, public health, and labor laws protecting the rights of trade unions. Disraeli's primary diplomatic interest centered on thwarting Russian expansion into the eastern Mediterranean and Afghanistan*. The prime minister left colonial affairs largely to the direction of the Colonial Secretary Lord Carnarvon. Nevertheless, Disraeli continued to defend the maintenance of the empire in general terms. In his Crystal Palace speech on June 24, 1872, for example, he enunciated his support for increased colonial self-government, but he also firmly advocated linking the empire closely together through an interlocking tariff structure and mutual defense agreements. Disraeli's most notable imperial enterprise, and an affair which he directed almost single-handedly, was the acquisition of the Suez Canal* shares in 1874–1875. In 1874 Disraeli discovered through the foreign office that the bankrupt Khedive Ismail of Egypt* was anxious to sell his share in the ownership of the Suez Canal. As British control of the canal would enable Great Britain to dominate both politically and economically all of Egypt and the Sudan*, plus ensure unhindered passage to India, Disraeli counseled an immediate buy-out of the unfortunate Khedive. After parliament balked at the expenditure and in the face of Liberal opposition, Disraeli, on his own initiative, overrode parliamentary objections and bought the Egyptian shares for Britain using funds provided by the Rothschild banking family. The deal eventually was hailed as a triumph for British prestige, and in 1876 Disraeli pushed through parliament a bill conferring the title Empress of India on Queen Victoria. Other imperial developments during Disraeli's second ministry included British acquisition of Fiji (1874), the establishment of the High

Commission for the Western Pacific Islands (1877), and the near disaster of the Zulu War and Second Afghan War (1879). In 1876 Britain completed the conquest of Indian Baluchistan. In 1878 Disraeli presided over the cession to Britain of Cyprus*—a key link in the chain of communication with India—by the Ottoman Empire.

Although Prime Minister Disraeli relegated colonial affairs to a secondary status, by the end of the 1870s the British Empire* comprised nearly a quarter of the land surface and included more than a quarter of the population of the world. Leaving office at the climax of his career in 1880, Disraeli was awarded the Order of the Garter from a grateful Queen Victoria. Following a short illness, Disraeli died April 19, 1881, in London. (Robert Blake, *Disraeli*, 1967.)

William G. Ratliff

DIU. Diu, once known as Dio when it was a Portuguese colony, is an island south of the Kathiawar Peninsula on the northwest coast of India*. Diu is in the Arabian Sea 170 miles northwest of Bombay. Early in the sixteenth century the Portuguese conquered and occupied the Kathiawar Peninsula, and in 1535 Portugal and Bahadar Shah of Gujerat signed a treaty ceding the island to the Portuguese. In the sixteenth and early seventeenth centuries, when sailing ships were small and resupplying stops more frequent, Diu was an important commercial entrepot, its population exceeding 50,000 people. But as the size and range of sailing ships increased in the late seventeenth and eighteenth centuries, Diu declined in importance. Her harbor was simply too small to accommodate the new ships. When India received her independence from Great Britain in 1947, the Portuguese presence became intolerable. In 1961 Indian troops occupied the island, in spite of Portuguese resistance. India then created the Union Territory out of Goa, Daman, and Diu. It was not until 1974 that Portugal recognized Indian sovereignty over Diu. (Gervase Clarence-Smith, *The Third Portuguese Empire, 1825–1975. A Study in Economic Imperialism*, 1985.)

DJIBOUTI. Formerly the colony of French Somaliland, Djibouti is located on the Horn of Africa, facing the Republic of Yemen across the strait of Bab el Mandeb. The British occupation of Aden in 1839 stimulated French interest in the region, and in 1856 France acquired trading rights in Ambabo and Obok from local Islamic sultans. French interest in the Gulf of Tadjoura was initiated by the traveler Dr. Albert Roche and promoted in 1859 by Henri Lambert, the French consul at Aden. In 1862 France bought Obok and what is now the Djibouti coast between Ras Bir and Ras Dumeira from another sultan. The European competition in the partition of East Africa, combined with the opening of the Suez Canal* and the French engagement in Tonkin* and Madagascar*, made the possession of a maritime base and coaling station for France at the intersection of the Asian and African continents particularly vital. Between 1883 and 1887 France negotiated treaties with Somali sultans giving her the entire Gulf of Tadjoura. The French holdings in the area were merged (1884–85) to form French

Somaliland.* The Anglo-French Treaty of 1888 then defined the French and British spheres of influence in Somalia*. Great Britain surrendered her claims to the Gulf of Tadjoura and the islands of Musha and Bab, and both Britain and France promised not to annex or establish a protectorate over Ogadan. The administrative capital of French Somaliland was transferred to the city of Djibouti in 1896, and in 1898 the French began constructing a railroad to Addis Ababa. A treaty of 1897 defined French Somaliland's boundary with Ethiopia*. Two protocols, in 1900 and 1901, between France and Italy, defined the boundary between Djibouti, or French Somaliland, and Eritrea.*

In 1912 the Salt Society of Djibouti opened salt mines and began extracting and exporting salt. Arms and ammunition traffic and native taxation also provided the French with revenues from the colony. The concentration of commercial activities in Djibouti created a no-man's-land in the rest of the territory. The European manipulation of intertribal disputes prevented local inhabitants from successfully opposing French domination and expropriation of the best land. In October 1935, when the Italians invaded Ethiopia, France remained neutral. Despite the Franco-Ethiopian agreement, the French administrator assisted the shipment of supplies from the Djibouti port to Italian soldiers in Addis Ababa.

Postwar politics was dominated by the struggle for power between the Afars and the Issas, two rival tribes, of which the Issas were the most numerous, as well as a struggle for power between those who wanted independence and those who wanted to remain part of France. Generally, the Afars wanted to retain ties with France; and citizenship laws discriminated in favor of them and against the more numerous Issas, who wanted independence. Ethiopia, which wanted French Somaliland to continue as a French colony, supported the Afars. In 1957 French Somaliland, sometimes called the French Somali Coast, received a territorial assembly and a local executive council to work with the French-appointed governor-general. In a 1958 referendum, which the Afars dominated, the voters of French Somaliland voted to become an overseas territory within the French Community. But the Issas continued to claim that they were being discriminated against. In 1967 France changed the name of the colony to the French Territory of the Afars and the Issas.

Not until 1975 did the French finally respond to Issa demands and change the colony's citizenship laws, giving the Issas more power. In the next referendum, held in May 1977, the Issa majority voted for complete independence. On June 27, 1977, France extended independence to French Somaliland, which became known as Djibouti. Hassan Gouled Aptidon became the country's first president. Because Djibouti did not have the economic resources to go it alone completely, France continues to supply it with economic and military assistance. (Virginia Thompson and Richard Adloff, *Djibouti and the Horn of Africa*, 1968.)

Said El Mansour Cherkaoui

DODECANESE ISLANDS. The more than fifty islands of the Dodecanese group sit off the coast of southwestern Turkey in the Aegean Sea. The most important islands in the group are Rhodes, Kos, and Karpathos. The Dodecanese islands were part of the Ottoman Empire until the outbreak of the Italo-Turkish War. Italy occupied them in 1912 and during World War I the Allied powers formally recognized Italian sovereignty there. In the Treaty of Sevre* of 1920, Turkey formally recognized Italian control as well. During World War II, Great Britain seized the islands from the Italians and kept them until 1947, when Greece was given formal possession of them. (David P. Henige, *Colonial Governors from the Fifteenth Century to the Present* 1970.)

DOMINICA. On November 3, 1493, Christopher Columbus* sighted and named this Caribbean island located 320 miles north of Venezuela. Winds and tides made Dominica the first landfall for numerous sailing ships arriving in the West Indies from the Azores, Canary Islands, and West Africa. Spanish ships called for water and provisions, but hostile Carib Indians discouraged colonization. From their rugged Dominican stronghold, the Caribs raided Puerto Rico* (1536), Antigua* (1640, 1674), Marie Galante (1653), and Barbuda* (1681). During the seventeenth, eighteenth, and early nineteenth centuries, the Caribs, British, and French fought for control of Dominica. The European settlers between 1632 and 1748 were predominantly French. Situated almost equidistant from France's colonies of Guadeloupe* and Martinique*, Dominica had more than 300 slaves by 1633. England, however, also claimed the island. In 1660 and 1731, Dominica was declared ''neutral'' in an effort to resolve the conflicting European assertions and to appease Carib raiders. Again, by the Treaty of Aix-la-Chapelle of 1748*, the British and French pledged to abandon the disputed territory. Even if both nations sincerely had desired to adhere to these pacts, enforcement would have proven difficult. War rather than diplomacy ultimately settled the question of possession.

French colonists arrived in increasing numbers. Their failure to evacuate helped precipitate the Seven Years' War (1755–1763) between England and France. In 1759, when the English seized Guadeloupe, the French presence on Dominica grew dramatically. The Caribs were driven to the remote areas where their descendants still survive. Britain reacted in 1761 by assaulting and capturing the island. The Treaty of Paris of 1763* confirmed the conquest. Between 1764 and 1774 both the white and black populations tripled. Approximately 19,000 slaves, some of whom were exported, entered Dominica during the same period. In 1763 blacks outnumbered whites three to one. By 1811 the ratio had climbed to sixteen to one. Even today, whites comprise a tiny minority of Dominica's population.

France regained control of the island during the American Revolution and ruled from 1778–1783. The Treaty of Versailles of 1783* restored it to England. The French unsuccessfully attempted to wrest it away between 1795 and 1805.

After the latter date Dominica remained British. French planters continued to dominate the coffee industry until blights in the 1830s ruined it. The influence of France has been strong, for 80 percent of Dominica's people speak French Creole and belong to the Roman Catholic Church. Even after Britain secured Dominica, internal threats plagued its landowners. The maroons, communities of runaway slaves, violently clashed with the authorities in 1808 and 1814. Coffee diseases, poor transportation, inefficient agricultural practices, and shifting British commercial policies spelled doom for the island's economy. Subsequent to the final emancipation of the slaves in 1838, peasant farming began to replace the plantation system. Sugar constituted three-quarters of Dominica's exports in 1880, but the industry received its death blow from 1881 to 1896 when prices fell by 50 percent. Limes, coconuts, and cocoa gained importance during the first three decades of the twentieth century. Starting in the 1930s, and receiving a strong boost in the mid–1950s, bananas became the primary cash crop. Overall, Dominica remained in an extreme state of poverty, hampered by rough terrain, difficult communications, and severe hurricanes.

Government on Dominica involving an elected legislative assembly dates back to 1763. Under this system, an extremely small planter class exercised power. At this time Dominica was part of the Windward Islands. In 1771 the British decided to administer it separately. To cut administrative costs, Britain joined Dominica to the Leeward Islands in 1833. The Leeward Islands became a federal crown colony in 1871. Dominica's electorate lost most of its influence in 1865.

Small concessions to responsible local government were granted in 1924 and 1936. Dominica gained more independence when the British transferred it back to the Windward Islands in 1940. A new constitution in 1951 provided for more elected representatives in the legislature and universal adult suffrage. Five years later the first steps toward ministerial government were taken. In 1960 the leader of the majority party in the legislative council became the island's chief minister. From 1958 to 1962 Dominica was a member of the West Indies Federation*. When the federation dissolved, the island chose to retain its ties to Britain. Dominica attained full internal autonomy as an associated state in 1967. Independence came on November 3, 1978, as the Commonwealth of Dominica was born. (Thomas Atwood, *The History of the Island of Dominica*, 1971; Basil E. Cracknell, *Dominica*, 1973.)

Frank Marotti

DOMINICAN REPUBLIC. This predominantly mulatto nation exercises sovereignty over eastern Hispaniola*, an island about 600 miles southeast of Florida. Prior to Christopher Columbus's sighting of the republic's northwestern coast on January 4, 1493, Alonzo Pinzón, the captain of the *Pinta*, had disembarked upon its shores. The Arawak name for the land was Quisqueya. On his second voyage in 1494, Columbus founded the town of Isabela near Pinzón's initial landfall. Two years later, Columbus moved his headquarters to Santo Domingo*, a settlement located at a superior site on Quisqueya's southern littoral. The socioeconomic, political, and religious patterns that emerged on the island strongly influenced Spain's subsequent colonization efforts.

Columbus proved to be a poor administrator, stirring the resentment of natives and Europeans alike. After defeating the Arawaks on March 27, 1495, in a full-scale battle, the discoverer began to exact tribute from them. Later, he was forced to grant Amerindian workers to individual Spaniards in order to regain the loyalty of a prominent rebel, Francisco Roldan. The cultural disruption resulting from this labor requirement, coupled with disease and warfare, precipitated a catastrophic decline in Hispaniola's Arawak population. By 1514, 90 percent of the island's 4,000,000 aborigines had perished. When reports of this chaos reached the Crown, an inspector, Francisco de Bobadilla, was sent to America. Bobadilla promptly clapped Columbus and his brothers in irons and shipped them to Castile.

Under Governor Nicolás de Ovando (1502–1509), Hispaniola thrived. Over 10,000 colonists flocked to the island, building towns, farms, plantations, and ranches which fueled the conquests of Puerto Rico*, Jamaica*, Cuba*, Panama, Mexico*, and Peru*. Ovando imported black slaves in 1503 to replace the rapidly disappearing Arawaks. Columbus's son Diego nominally ruled from 1509 to 1526. Although he constructed a fine palace in Santo Domingo and initiated the erection of the hemisphere's first cathedral, where his father's remains now lie, the distinguished scion saw his power curbed by the institution of a royal tribunal, the *audiencia*, in 1511.

Gold production quickly fell and more attractive mainland enterprises drew off Quisqueya's settlers so that by 1540 the colony's fortunes waned. In the next two decades a large number of inhabitants departed. Shifting trade routes caused Havana to replace Santo Domingo as Spain's premier West Indian port. Francis Drake* sacked the Quisqueyan capital in 1586. The cultivation of sugar, a crop first planted by Columbus, suffered from enemy depredations. Smuggling and foreign incursions occasioned the evacuation of western Hispaniola, thus creating a vacuum filled during the early 1600s by French adventurers from Tortuga*. After a seesaw struggle to expel the interlopers, the Spanish recognized France's ownership of Hispaniola's western third by the Treaty of Ryswick (1697).

While French Saint Domingue* developed into a valuable agricultural enterprise in which slaves outnumbered the free eight to one, Spain's colony languished. A relatively mild servitude prevailed and ranching dominated the economy. A sizable free-mulatto segment also existed. Subsequent to a minor expansion due to the Bourbon Reforms of 1778, Spanish Hispaniola became embroiled in a black uprising that shook Saint Domingue in 1791. The Spaniards invaded but were driven back in 1794, when Toussaint l'Ouverture*, a brilliant black commander, decided to support France's recently arrived revolutionary troops. Spain ceded its Hispaniolan holdings to the French in the Treaty of Basle (1795). Toussaint unified the island in January 1801, after eliminating his rivals by military skill and diplomacy. An expeditionary force dispatched by Napoleon captured eastern Hispaniola but was forced to abandon the west. On January 1, 1804, "Haiti*" proclaimed its independence.

The French held the former Spanish colony until local residents rebelled in 1809. Spain returned, misruling the territory for twelve years. The restive Quisqueyans expelled the Spaniards in 1821 and sought admission to Simón Bolívar's Republic of Gran Colombia. Jean-Pierre Boyer, Haiti's leader, then moved to reunify Hispaniola. His troops occupied the east from 1822 to 1844, a period which Dominicans regard as a time of barbaric repression. In the latter year patriots led by Juan Pablo Duarte, Francisco del Rosario Sánchez, and Ramón Mella overthrew the Haitians and announced the birth of the Dominican Republic. Fear of another Haitian takeover motivated the new nation's strong men to voluntarily submit to Spanish rule between 1861 and 1865. Following Spain's ouster, after narrowly rejecting an annexation treaty in 1866, the United States occupied the Dominican Republic in 1916–1924 and in 1965–1966. (Ian Bell, *The Dominican Republic*, 1981; Troy S. Floyd, *The Columbus Dynasty in the Caribbean, 1492–1526*, 1973.)

                                                                    Frank Marotti

DOMINION OF NEW ENGLAND. Five English American colonies were successfully established on the North American continent before 1650 with no help, and with minimum interference from the state. Seven more colonies were established before 1732 also with no help but with an increasing degree of interference from the state. The interference took political and economic forms during the Commonwealth and Restoration periods of English history. A new imperialism was then forged which resulted in the passage of mercantile legislation aimed at recovering for Britain shipping and trading benefits lost to the Dutch during the distractions of the English Civil War. Legislation was also intended to assure that certain colonial raw materials were reserved for the use of British industries and that British exports to America were encouraged over foreign exports. Mercantile legislation reflected a realization that the colonies had finally emerged as profit centers for British shippers, merchants, and industrialists. Early efforts to enforce the mercantile restrictions of the Navigation Acts* met with an almost solid wall of colonial resistance, especially with regard to imperial efforts to preclude Dutch shipping from English colonial waters. Although the lack of enforcement machinery allowed easy evasion in America, the new navigation system did improve Britain's economy, and the Dutch lost their lead in world commerce.

The new imperialism also intended the establishment of closer political controls and management over colonies. The New England* colonies and Massachusetts* in particular resisted administrative efforts by the Commonwealth and Restoration governments to accomplish this. Resistance cost Massachusetts its charter in 1684 and led Charles II to approve plans to consolidate all the New England colonies into a single colonial unit in order to bring them under closer imperial political and economic controls. The same might later be done for the southern American colonies. But before plans were completed, the King died (1685) and was replaced by his brother, James II. James, already proprietor of Maine and

New York*, was persuaded that combining his proprietary estates in America with the New England colonies into one great dominion would ensure even better administration and control. Consequently, in December 1686 Sir Edmund Andros arrived in Boston to assume the governor-generalship of the Dominion of New England, enlarged to include the vast territories and settlements between Nova Scotia* and the Delaware River and including over half of the settlers in America at the time. Francis Nicholson was dispatched to New York to function there as the governor-general's representative.

Andros's commission empowered him to govern with an appointive council and without a representative assembly. Charles II had intended to allow a representative assembly in his scheme; James reversed that decision. James believed that his was the only way to break the old regime and install the new commercial regime in America. Most of the measures subsequently taken by Andros as head of the dominion were opposed by colonials because of the lack of representation in the process rather than because the measures were deemed burdensome. For example, Andros actually reduced the tax burden during his two-year rule, but taxpayers objected because the taxes were levied without their consent.

By 1688 even colonial moderates had become alienated with arbitrary government. Improving the defense posture in the area was the only great success of the Andros regime; yet even this achievement proved transitory and disappeared with his fall. Religious changes which Andros initiated had a more lasting effect. The religious test for the franchise was abolished throughout the dominion, and religious toleration was imposed, although it too tended to disappear after the fall of the dominion. Andros also did well in the area of commercial regulation and control. This was the only time when a vigorous attempt was made to enforce the Navigation Acts in New England. Illicit, direct trade with Europe and the foreign West Indies* and piracy were reduced. However, arbitrary government was hated throughout the dominion—and when the arbitrary King James II was deposed in Britain by the Glorious Revolution, Massachusetts's leaders arrested Andros and sent him home. Colonies included in the dominion quietly resumed their former governments and waited to see what King William and Queen Mary would do. (David S. Lovejoy, *The Glorious Revolution in America*, 1972.)

Lee E. Olm

DRAKE, FRANCIS. Little is known of Francis Drake's early life. Probably born in 1542, Drake was, like his famous colleague Sir John Hawkins*, a seafaring Devon man. As his autobiographical comments suggest, he may well have been apprenticed at a very early age to a captain plying English coastal waters. He apparently bought the captain's boat, thus early in his career demonstrating the aggressive entrepreneurial drive that so marked his life. But staid trading responsibilities in domestic waters were not his destiny; he soon signed with his distant kinsman, Hawkins, for raiding and slave transporting activities down the Guinea coast and then on to the Spanish New World. He was with Hawkins at the disastrous confrontation at San Juan de Ulua in 1568. Perhaps this incident turned Drake toward a life of privateering on the Spanish Main. He certainly became the most notorious and the most successful of the English corsairs plundering American treasure. One infamous raid in 1573 was so fraught with excitement and danger that he lost two of his brothers (captains of ships in the expedition), looted numerous treasure sources, and returned with a £20,000 profit for his efforts. His reputation was established. The English made folk heroes of their more successful sea captains, the cowboys of their age; and the Spanish were terrified by "El Draque," or the Dragon, with whose name they frightened their misbehaving children.

His famous circumnavigation was a consequence of another privateering expedition, designed to plunder the hitherto secure west coast of South America, and to establish an English presence in the area. He sailed from England in 1577 aboard the *Pelican*, later renamed the *Golden Hind*, and with four additional ships. The lack of piratical activity in the Pacific Ocean had lulled the Spanish, with whom the English were unofficially at war, into laxness. The victims were taken by surprise, and Drake added extravagant amounts of treasure (reportedly £450,000) to the coffers of himself and his sponsors. Elizabeth*, a Queen always grateful for new sources of revenue, defied Spanish sensibilities and knighted Sir Francis on the deck of his ship upon his return in 1581.

It had been a return by the long route. At first Drake reportedly spent time exploring the coast of California, looking for the western terminus of the reputed Northwest Passage*. He claimed the area around San Francisco Bay for his queen. He then sailed west to get East, and further added to the success of his voyage with the acquisition of spices in the Indian Ocean area. Drake returned to England with just the *Golden Hind*, having become the first Englishman to circle the world. Subsequently, Drake was the point man in the increasingly hot war against Spain. In the mid–1580s he struck at the Caribbean and the North American coast and then in 1587 he was commissioned to "singe the King of Spain's beard." He raided what was now clearly understood to be a vast naval enterprise being outfitted for an invasion of England. As it turned out, the shipping he destroyed at Cadiz was less significant than the collateral damage he did. Assuming the task of burning parts of Cadiz during the raid, he managed to destroy the barrel staves that were curing for use to outfit the Spanish Armada*. In consequence, the Armada sailed with barrels of green wood, which in turn either leaked or permitted provisions to deteriorate. The great fleet was logistically crippled at the outset and the spoiled provisions contributed to sickness and staffing problems. Drake materially, even if inadvertently, was of paramount importance in the defeat of the Spanish Armada of 1588 due to his actions of 1587.

After the Armada, he returned to privateering and raiding, both in Spain and in the Caribbean. It was on one of these voyages, in 1596, that he became sick and died off Porto Bello. One of the greatest of English sea captains, Drake is perhaps most important as a role model in the English drive for naval supremacy. Moreover, his intrepidly adventurous spirit took him where no Englishmen had ever been, and gave England at least a tangential claim to land as disparate as areas around the Indian Ocean and off the California coast. He was the archetypal English "sea-dog." (Julian Corbett, *Drake and the Tudor Navy*, 1899; Julian Corbett, *Sir Francis Drake*, 1890; Derek Wilson, *The World Encompassed: Drake's Great Voyage, 1577–1580*, 1977.)

Gary M. Bell

DUBAI. See UNITED ARAB EMIRATES.

DUMONT D'URVILLE, JULES-SÉBASTIEN-CÉSAR. Dumont d'Urville, the great French Pacific explorer, was born in Conde-sur-Noireau, France on May 23, 1790. He sailed for the first time to the Pacific in 1822–1825. D'Urville led the next two voyages himself. From 1826 to 1829 he explored the western Pacific, visiting Australia*, New Zealand*, Fiji*, the Loyalty Islands*, and New Guinea, collecting scientific data, and charting new coastlines everywhere he went. His second voyage (1837–1840) was designed to explore the southern polar regions of the Pacific. Historians consider it the last of the great French voyages of discovery. He left France in September 1837, sailing south in the Pacific to the ice caps blocking the Antarctic continent. D'Urville then stopped in the Gambiers, Marquesa Islands*, Society Islands, Samoa*, Fiji, Solomon Islands*, Caroline Islands*, and Marianas*, returned to the Antarctic; sailed north to New Zealand, and finally returned to France. D'Urville was promoted to rear admiral in 1840 and died on May 8, 1842, in a railroad accident. (Camille Vergniol, *Dumont d'Urville*, 1920.)

DUTCH EAST INDIA COMPANY. The Dutch East India Company, along with the British East India Company*, was the most powerful of the European joint stock companies that laid much of the foundations of modern imperialism. Late in the 1500s Dutch private companies seeking to exploit trading opportunities in Asia multiplied rapidly, and in 1602, the states-general of The Netherlands consolidated them into the United Netherlands Chartered East India Company, or Dutch East India Company, a monopolistic corporation enjoying exclusive rights to all Dutch trade east of the Cape of Good Hope and west of the Straits of Magellan—all of Asia, the Indian Ocean, and the Pacific Ocean. The charter extended full sovereignty to the company over territories it penetrated, complete with the authority to levy taxes and make war. Until its demise in 1799, the Dutch East India Company was the moving force behind Dutch imperialism. See DUTCH EAST INDIES.

DUTCH EAST INDIES. The Dutch East Indies comprised the entire island world now called Indonesia*. The Dutch created a political unit from an archipelago in which people on different islands spoke different languages. Some islands already had long, complex histories. Java*, Sumatra*, and Bali* had known great empires (Srivijaya, the Sailendra dynasty, Majapahit, Kediri, Mataram) and a new politico-religious order, Islam, was on the horizon. The Dutch came to the islands of Southeast Asia at the end of the sixteenth century.

The Dutch aims were solely mercantile. They wanted a monopoly on the spice trade. To this end, the *Vereenigde Oost-Indische Compagnie* (United East Indies Company, or Dutch East India Company, or VOC) was created by royal charter in 1602. The VOC was delegated the powers of a sovereign state: it could (and did) use troops, conduct diplomatic relations, sign treaties, and claim islands for Holland. A seventeen-man board of directors in Amsterdam set overall policy but left day-to-day decisions to the company's captains and governors in the islands. Jan Pieterzoon Coen, VOC governor-general from 1618 to 1623, set up headquarters on the north coast of Java at a port he named Batavia*. VOC policy aimed at ruthless extermination of native and European competition in the marketing of Moluccan spices. To root out "piracy" the Dutch stormed through the Java and Banda seas conquering sultans who could not be persuaded to recognize Dutch suzerainty. The VOC monopoly was immensely profitable, for as sole purchaser in the Moluccas* they could buy cheap, and as sole vendor in Europe, they could sell dear.

It cost a lot to police the monopoly, however, and the Dutch quickly concluded that they could make more money by dominating the intra-Asian trade previously conducted by Arabs, Persians, Gujaratis, Sumatrans, Javanese, Malaccans, Portuguese, and Chinese. For example, the Moluccans wanted Gujarati cotton in payment for their spices, so the Dutch organized weavers at a factory in India. Spices could be sent to China, too, and Chinese silk taken to Japan, where it was sold for silver, which went to India for more cotton, and so on. Dominating the eastern seas required naval power. Once England showed herself nearly invincible, the Dutch settled down to exploit their islands, especially Java.

In Java, the Dutch nibbled away at the Bantam sultanate and the Mataram Kingdom by intervening in succession disputes. In the rest of the East Indies (the so-called outer islands), they would help one sultan against another, asking in return only for exclusive trade privileges. By the eighteenth century the East Indies belonged to the Dutch, except for Portuguese Timor and a single British factory at Benkulen on the south coast of Sumatra. The VOC yielded its highest profits in 1693, and then went into a slow, steady slide. The spice trade tailed off. Holland itself declined in power relative to Britain and France. Worst of all, corruption was sapping company revenues. Bookkeeping was lax. Employees neglected their duties for private deals. The VOC paid no dividends after 1782, its assets and debts were assumed by the Netherlands government, and its charter expired on December 31, 1799.

Henceforth, Dutch policy in the Indies depended on events in Europe. Holland became embroiled in the Napoleonic wars, and sent Willem Daendels to Batavia (1806–1810) to prepare for the expected British attack. Daendels centralized and rationalized Dutch administration, a process that Sir Stamford Raffles accelerated during the British interlude (1811–1816). Until then the Dutch had presided over a patchwork of principalities, sultanates, and fiefdoms. They had forced native princes to make their own villagers deliver coffee and sugar, at low prices fixed by the Dutch. The Javanese aristocracy became accomplices in exploiting their own people. They suffered a fatal loss of legitimacy.

Under the cultivation system (inaugurated 1830 under Governor van den Bosch) the exactions became intolerable. Indonesians were driven mercilessly to grow sugar and coffee, build roads and bridges, and pay other taxes in money and labor, and the only beneficiaries were the Dutch, the co-opted native royalty, and Chinese moneylenders. Douwes Dekker brilliantly satirized the immorality of this regime in his novel *Max Havelaar*, published in 1860. This book galvanized public opinion in Holland, and caused the adoption of a "Liberal Policy" (roughly 1870–1900). Free enterprise replaced mercantilism*. New products were encouraged. Most good land on Java was already being farmed, but sprawling new plantations were opened in the outer islands.

The Dutch feared that Britain or France, racing to divide the Southeast Asian mainland, might take the outer islands away from them. So, for the entire second half of the nineteenth century Batavia sent countless military expeditions to extinguish rebellions in Sumatra, Borneo*, Celebes*, Bali, and elsewhere. The last insurrections were suppressed in the first decade of the twentieth century, just when a reformist "Ethical Policy" was promulgated. The reforms were never fully implemented. On balance, the Dutch can be credited with laying the groundwork for Indonesian modernization and economic development. Their imperialism was also free of misplaced religious zeal. Many Dutchmen in the Indies grew to love their adopted land and fought to preserve Indonesian culture, but in pursuit of profit they undermined and discredited native leaders. They encouraged Chinese immigration, not knowing what terrible racial hatred would ensue. They improved public health with vaccination campaigns, only to see the population mushroom to the extravagant densities of modern Bali and Java. They set up some schools—too few and too late—and graduated discontented nationalists who eventually led a revolution. (M. C. Ricklefs, *A History of Modern Indonesia*, 1981.)

Ross Marlay

DUTCH EMPIRE. The Dutch colonial empire developed more than a century after the Portuguese and Spanish had launched their New World adventures, but the Dutch possessed the traditions and the inclination to look far beyond their own borders. The strategic location of The Netherlands on the North Sea, combined with the entrepreneurial spirit of her people, had given the Dutch a long history of commercial success and maritime experience. Continental and internal politics in the sixteenth century postponed Dutch expansionism. The Eighty Years War for independence from Spain and the political unification movement consumed Dutch resources in the late 1500s, preventing any attempt to exploit commercial opportunities in Asia or the New World.

But events in the 1570s and 1580s launched the Dutch on the road to empire. The Union of Utrecht in 1579 created the United Provinces of Holland joining

Zeeland, Utrecht, Duelderland, Overijssel, Groningen, and Friesland. Two years later Prince William I of Orange renounced Dutch allegiance to Philip II of Spain. A combined Anglo-Dutch fleet defeated the Spanish Armada* in 1588, and in the 1590s Dutch ships begin making their way around the world, hoping to capture a share of the mineral and spice profits monopolized by the Spanish and the Portuguese. There was a tremendous expansion of Dutch maritime activity in the West Indies*, the Mediterranean, and the East Indies, and in 1600 the first Dutch ship reached Japan.

Dozens of Dutch joint stock companies had appeared to profit in Asian commerce, and in 1602 the states-general of The Netherlands consolidated them into the Dutch East India Company*. The company was given sovereign power over the territories it conquered and it enjoyed a monopoly over all trade east of the Cape of Good Hope and west of the Straits of Magellan—the Indian Ocean, Asia, and the Pacific. The Dutch West India Company, formed in 1621, enjoyed similar powers, with a monopoly over the Atlantic and Caribbean trade. During the first half of the seventeenth century, the Dutch experienced a series of stunning successes and reverses in their attempt to establish a colonial empire. Their rise to power coincided with simultaneous declines in Portuguese and Spanish power.

In 1605 the Dutch captured Amboina and expelled the Portuguese from the Moluccas*. They established a factory at Hirado, Japan, in 1609, and inaugurated the settlements in Guiana and the Amazon region. The Portuguese, afraid of losing their control of Brazil*, drove the Dutch from northeast Brazil in the 1650s, but the Dutch had planted the roots of what eventually became Surinam. The English had settled that area in 1650 but the Peace of Breda of 1667 had ceded it to the Dutch. The Dutch established the settlement of New Amsterdam on Manhattan Island in what is today New York* in 1624, and in 1638 they took Elmina in Guinea* and invaded Ceylon*. The 1620s and 1630s also saw the Dutch penetration of what became known as the Netherlands Antilles*. The Dutch captured Malacca*, Maranhao, and Luanda from the Portuguese in 1641 and established the settlement at Cape Town between 1652 and 1654. Within the next decade the Dutch completed the conquest of the Amboina group of islands and took Malabar and Makassar* from Portugal.

By the mid-seventeenth century, England had become the chief imperial rival of the Dutch. The first Anglo-Dutch War was fought between 1652 and 1654. The English seized New Amsterdam in 1664, along with several Dutch forts on the Guinea coast. The Second Anglo-Dutch War was fought between 1665 and 1667, and they went to war a third time between 1672 and 1674. Gradually, almost piecemeal, the Dutch managed the conquest of what became the Dutch East Indies*. Matara recognized Dutch sovereignty in 1677, and between 1682 and 1684 the Dutch completed the conquest of Bantam. During the first half of the eighteenth century the Dutch fought a number of wars and crushed rebellions in Java*, finally taking control of the area.

But by the late 1700s the Dutch empire was feeling the pressure of its imperial responsibilities. The civil wars and rebellions in Java had been expensive, as

had the Fourth Anglo-Dutch War (1780–1783). In 1794 the English took the
Cape Colony*. The Dutch East India Company had long since suspended div-
idend payments to investors, and The Netherlands dissolved the company in
1799 and transferred its assets to what became known as the Batavian Republic.
Throughout the nineteenth century the Dutch consolidated and rationalized their
administrative control of the Dutch East Indies.

Like the British, French, and German empires, the Dutch empire fell victim
to the twentieth century. The Dutch East Indies were doomed by the spirit of
Asian nationalism which appeared in the early 1900s and was accelerated by
World War II. Sukarno, the leading Indonesia nationalist, began his campaign
for independence in the 1920s, but it was not until 1941, when Japanese troops
conquered the East Indies and humiliated the Dutch, that the incipient nationalism
became an obsession. World War II and the Nazi occupation left The Netherlands
with serious economic problems. She simply did not have the resources to fight
a war against Indonesian guerrilla nationalists, and in 1949 the Dutch East Indies
became Indonesia*, an independent nation. The Netherlands retained control of
Dutch New Guinea, but in 1962 they ceded that to Indonesia rather than risk a
war over it. Surinam* became independent in 1975. (C. R. Boxer, *The Dutch
Seaborne Empire: 1600–1800*, 1965.)

DUTCH GUIANA. Today known as the Republic of Surinam, Dutch Guiana
was a Dutch colony on the northeastern coast of South America, bordered on
the east by French Guiana*, on the south by Brazil*, and on the west by British
Guiana*. Throughout the sixteenth century a variety of Spanish expeditions, in
search of the fabled gold of "El Dorado," entered Surinam, but they established
no permanent settlements. The riches of Mexico and Peru were too distracting.
It was the English who first exploited opportunities there. Lord Willoughby, the
English governor of Barbados*, sent an expedition to Surinam in 1650 under
the leadership of Anthony Rowse. A decade later the English government officially recognized Willoughby's proprietary interests, and the colony soon
thrived with English settlers, African slaves, and Jewish immigrants from Europe. After the Second Anglo-Dutch War of 1665–1667, England ceded Surinam
to the Dutch in the Peace of Breda of 1667. That arrangement also recognized
English sovereignty over New Amsterdam, which the Duke of York had seized
in 1664. By that time, however, Dutch interests in the Caribbean were declining.
The growing power of the French and British navies, the economic collapse of
the Dutch West India Company in 1674, and the fact that the Dutch were more
interested in trade than in colonization condemned Dutch Guiana to backwater
status in the Dutch empire.

During the Napoleonic Wars, Great Britain controlled Dutch Guiana from
1799 to 1802 and from 1804 to 1816, but the Treaty of Paris in 1815 restored
Dutch sovereignty. The economy revolved around sugar for much of the nineteenth century, but when slavery was abolished in 1867 and sugar beet production
developed in the American West, the sugar industry declined. Large numbers

of immigrants from China, Java, and India came to Dutch Guiana. Not until the 1920s, when Dutch Guiana bauxite began to feed the aluminum plants of the United States and Royal Dutch Shell began to drill oil there, did the economy begin to recover. In 1922 a new Dutch constitution incorporated Dutch Guiana into The Netherlands, and during World War II the economy boomed with the enormous increases in demand for bauxite and oil. The Netherlands also promised to make necessary constitutional changes after the war to give Dutch Guiana internal autonomy. Negotiations continued between 1946 and 1954, when the Dutch government extended full autonomy to Dutch Guiana, now known again as Surinam. The Netherlands agreed to conduct foreign relations and military defense.

But the arrangement for internal autonomy and external dependence in Surinam did not survive the global wave of colonial nationalism in the 1950s and 1960s. The Surinam population—a mix of Africans, Europeans, Javanese, Chinese, and Indians—had acquired an identity of its own, one quite separate culturally from that of The Netherlands. Their economic resources gave them the means for independence, and bursts of nationalism in Africa and Asia inspired them. In 1972 the Dutch government established a special commission to study the question of Surinamese independence, and it recommended independence in 1974. On November 25, 1975, Surinam became an independent republic. (D. A. G. Waddell, *The West Indies and the Guianas*, 1967.)

E

EASTER ISLAND. Easter Island is an isolated, volcanic formation of 110 square miles located in the Pacific Ocean, 2,600 miles off the coast of Chile* and 1,200 miles east of the Pitcairn Islands*. Bleak and virtually treeless, without a natural harbor, Easter Island was first discovered by the Dutch mariner Jacob Roggeveen on Easter Day in 1722. Except for the huge statues erected by ancient inhabitants, Easter Island had little to interest Europeans. At the time there were approximately 3,000 people living there, but the diseases brought by European traders and missionaries soon reduced those numbers. In 1862–1863, more than 1,000 Easter Islanders were sold into slavery in Peru, and only a dozen returned, bringing back with them even more diseases. By the middle of the 1870s there were only 175 natives still alive on the island. Chile formally annexed Easter Island in 1888, but it was not until 1965 that Easter Islanders received Chilean citizenship and were transferred from naval to civilian administrative authority. The island is a province of Chile with an appointed military governor. (Michel Rougie, *Ile de Paques: Isla de Pascua*, 1979.)

EAST FLORIDA. Florida was the first part of the North American mainland to be colonized by Europeans. In 1513 Juan Ponce de León* discovered what he assumed to be an island, and since he landed on Easter Sunday (Sp. *Pascua florida*), he named the land Florida. Disaster overwhelmed every early Spanish attempt to explore and colonize the new land, however. The first permanent settlement was St. Augustine, founded in 1565 by Pedro Menéndez de Aviles. Although the Spanish had ambitious plans for the development of Florida, the dream was never realized and the colonial period was troubled by frequent conflicts with the French and British along the Atlantic and Gulf coasts. In the Treaty of Paris of 1763* ending the Seven Years War, Florida was transferred to British control. The next twenty years marked a period of prosperity, increased population, and development. During the American Revolution*, the people of Florida remained loyal to Great Britain. But in 1779 Spanish forces from New Orleans took the English post in West Florida* and captured Pensacola in 1781.

In the Treaty of Paris of 1783*, Florida went back to Spain. Disputes ensued, however, between the United States and Spain over the boundary. Treaty provisions between the United States and Britain had set the boundary at the 31st parallel. But Spain claimed considerable land north of that line. The matter was settled in the Treaty of San Lorenzo between the United States and Spain in 1795, and both nations accepted the 31st parallel.

Although West Florida was annexed by the United States in 1810 to the Pearl River and in 1813 to the Perdido River, East Florida remained under Spanish control. During the War of 1812, General Andrew Jackson invaded Florida and seized Pensacola (November 1814), but quickly withdrew to go to the defense of New Orleans. In 1818, during the First Seminole War, Jackson again invaded in pursuit of Seminole Indians and to punish the Spanish for assisting them. When Secretary of State John Quincy Adams supported Jackson and demanded that Spain either police the territory or give it up, Spain agreed to negotiate. The outcome was the Adams-Onis Treaty of 1819, part of which ceded East Florida to the United States in exchange for the United States government assumption of $5 million in claims of American citizens against Spain. Spain also relinquished claims to West Florida. The treaty was ratified by the United States Senate on February 24, 1819. Florida was formally organized as an American territory in March 1822. (Michael J. Curley, *Church and State in the Spanish Floridas (1783–1822)*, 1940; Gloria Jahoda, *Florida: A History*, 1984.)

Joseph M. Rowe, Jr.

EAST INDIA TEA ACT OF 1773. One of the items included in the Townshend Duties Act of 1767 intended to raise a revenue to defray expenses in British North America was a threepence per pound tax on East India tea to be collected upon import into America. The colonies resisted this and the other Townshend duties on paper, glass, lead, and painters' colors on grounds that they were not intended to regulate imperial trade but were intended to raise a revenue. Revenue measures could be levied only by their own representative assemblies, not by a distant parliament in which they were not nor could not be represented. A renewal of colonial non-importation agreements brought British merchant pressure on parliament to repeal the Townshend duties. The duties were repealed in 1770 except for the threepence tax on tea. Tea could not be produced in America; therefore, it was the tax best retained in order to uphold the principle of parliamentary supremacy. Rather than accept that principle, Americans continued to boycott British tea, preferring to smuggle it in duty free.

The loss of the American tea trade contributed to the problems of an already financially distressed British East India Company*. In 1773 parliament came to the assistance of the East India Company by granting it a monopoly of the

American market. Previously the company had been required to ship its tea to Britain, pay existing duties, and sell its tea at auction in London for transshipment to America where the threepence duty was to be collected. After May 10, 1773, the company was allowed to export tea to America without paying the English duties; and furthermore, instead of selling tea at auction to American merchants in London, the company decided to market the tea itself through pro-British agents in the colonies. The end result would be that Americans could buy East India Company tea cheaper than smuggled Dutch tea even if the threepence Townshend tea tax were paid. To Americans it appeared that Britain was attempting to use the lure of cheaper tea to have them pay the threepence tax and concede parliament's right to tax. Only somewhat less significantly, what was to prevent parliament from granting similar monopolies to other British companies and thereby gradually squeezing colonial merchants out of American commerce? The measure appeared to be a clever political and economic trap set by repressionist-minded ministers in London.

Colonial opposition to the East India Tea Act centered on the parliamentary supremacy and monopoly issues. East India Company tea ships destined for New York and Philadelphia were forced by popular demonstrations to return to England with their cargoes intact. Tea was unloaded in Charleston but locked up in government warehouses. In Boston, the three-ship consignment of tea worth about £15,000 was dumped into the harbor on December 16, 1773, by a band of men disguised as Indians.

The Boston Tea Party response to the Tea Act presented Great Britain with a crisis of staggering proportions. Britain's harsh reaction to the destruction of East India property and repeated American defiance of parliamentary authority led to the so-called Intolerable Acts in 1774 intended to bring Americans to their senses. Instead, colonial representatives at the First Continental Congress shattered the British Empire* asunder. (Benjamin W. Labaree, *The Boston Tea Party*, 1964.)

Lee E. Olm

EAST TIMOR. See PORTUGUESE TIMOR.

ECUADOR. During the colonial period, Ecuador was under the jurisdiction of the *audiencia** of Quito. Throughout the sixteenth and seventeenth centuries, the *audiencia* of Quito was subordinate to the viceroyalty of Peru*. It remained there until the creation of the viceroyalty of New Granada in 1717 and its reestablishment in 1739. The Real Audiencia de Quito, which had authority over most of present-day Ecuador, was established on August 29, 1563. There were *correqimientos* in Guayaquil, Cuenca, Loja, Guaranda, Riobamba, Otavalo, and Ibarra. On Francisco Pizarro's second expedition in 1526, Bartolomé Ruíz, a ship's pilot, first landed in Ecuador's Esmeraldas province. The province received its name from the emeralds which the Indians of the region wore. Pizarro undertook a third expedition in 1531, and he landed in Esmeraldas to begin a trek to Peru. An Inca dynastic feud between Atahuallpa of Quito and Huascar of Cuzco was taking place at the time and on November 16, 1532, Pizarro captured Atahuallpa at Cajamarca. The conquest of Quito soon followed.

Sebastián de Benalcazar organized the conquest of the kingdom of Quito. After Atahaullpa's capture, an Indian noble, Ruminahuí, retreated to Quito and began to organize its defense. In October 1533, Benalcazar left San Miguel for Quito and met stiff Indian resistance all along the way. Many Indian enemies of Ruminahuí joined the Spaniards. Before the Spaniards arrived in December 1533, Ruminahuí devastated and depopulated Quito. Diego de Almagro then arrived to ask why Benalcazar had abandoned San Miguel. On August 15, 1534, they founded Santiago de Quito. Pedro de Alvarado, the conquerer of Guatemala*, heard about the wealth of Peru*, landed on the coast, and marched to Quito. Almagro met him and convinced him to abandon the enterprise for 100,000 pesos. He left but many of his men stayed. Almagro, before he left for Peru, wanted a new foundation, and on August 28, 1534, the Villa de San Francisco de Quito was founded where the principal city of the Incas had been. He elected Benalcazar as *teniente gobernador* of Quito and gave him the chore of finishing the conquest. Benalcazar did not enter Quito again until December 1534. A cabildo was established and a new city laid out. Ruminahuí was captured and executed in January 1535, which ended the major Indian resistance. In 1535 Santiago de Guayaquil was founded but was twice destroyed by Indians. Francisco de Orellana founded it for the third time.

After pacification, the eastern territory, known as the Oriente, was penetrated by various expeditions. In September 1538 Gonzalo Díaz de Piñeda organized an expedition that did not find any of the riches they were looking for. In March 1541 Gonzalo Pizarro, the governor of Quito, organized a second expedition. Francisco de Orellana, one of his captains, discovered the Amazon River, but the expedition found no wealth. Other explorations of the territory followed during the colonial period, particularly when missionaries began arriving. In 1637 an expedition organized in Brazil went up the Amazon and then to Quito, but the *audiencia* of Quito had already laid claim to the area.

The Ecuadorean economy was based on pastoral farming, agricultural exports, mining, and textile production. The port of Guayaquil was used for shipbuilding and transporting exports to other parts of the empire along the Pacific coast. Mining, located around Zaruma and Zamora, was not a primary economic activity. A major agricultural export was cacao until its collapse in the 1620s by the ban on its exportation to Mexico.

Ecuadorean politics were tempestuous. Between July 1592 and April 1593 the Revolution of the *Alcabala* took place in Quito. It began as a revolt against the new *alcabala* (excise) tax imposed by the crown. Large numbers of Ecuadoreans resented the tax and refused to pay. They had already paid huge donations to the King and large ransoms to pirates who ravaged the coast. The revolt was not suppressed until Spanish troops from Peru arrived in the spring of 1593 and crushed the rebels. Pirates had taken Guayaquil in 1587 and their attacks continued into the eighteenth century. In 1705 and 1764 pirates razed the city.

The nineteenth century rebellion against Spain had its origins in the eighteenth century. Eugenio de Santa Cruz y Espejo was an influential political thinker with Enlightenment ideas. Spanish officials jailed him for his political liberalism in 1789 and again in 1795. During the last incarceration he died in jail. From December 1808 to October 1809, a group of Espejo's friends decided to form a *Junta de Gobierno* once Napoleon invaded Spain. Local officials quickly arrested them. Another *Junta*, established in August 1809, lasted for nearly three months before surrendering on October 28, 1809. Quito was caught up in the independence movement sweeping through South America, and on May 24, 1822, General José Antonio de Sucre, a subordinate of Simón Bolívar*, liberated Quito from royalist forces at the battle of Pichincha. Ecuador became the Department of the South, part of the confederation of Gran Colombia, which included Colombia* and Venezuela*. In 1830 Ecuador became independent from Gran Colombia. (Pedro Germín Cevallos, *Historia del Ecuador*, 3 volumes, 1985–1986; John Leddy Phelan, *The Kingdom of Quito in the Seventeenth Century*, 1967.)

Carlos Pérez

EGYPT. Located at the crossroads of the Mediterranean, Asia, and Africa, Egypt has occupied a strategic position throughout history. It is also the area where one of the three oldest civilizations appeared and developed on the banks of the Nile River. This geographical fact is of such significance that it has been said, by Herodotus, that Egypt is a gift of the Nile. Egypt has more than 5,000 years of recorded history. It was a united kingdom under many brilliant Pharaonic dynasties with considerable cultural achievements, from around 3200 B.C. until Alexander's conquest in 333 B.C. From that time until the middle of the twentieth century Egypt was under continuous foreign domination: Greeks, Romans, Persians, Arabs, Turks, and finally British. Hence the profound significance of Nasser's Revolution in 1952, when for the first time in close to 2,300 years Egypt was at last governed by true native sons.

However, among those successive invasions, the one which had the greatest impact was that of the Arabs in the seventh century. They gave Egypt and all of the Middle East the imprint of Arab civilization and the religion of Islam. After being ruled by several dynasties of Arab caliphs—Ummayyads, Abbassids, Fatimids, and then Mamluks—and a brief invasion by western crusaders in the thirteenth century, Egypt fell in 1517 under Ottoman rule. By the end of the eighteenth century, Egypt which was again under the effective control of the Mamluks, became exposed to the western world as a result of the French occupation led by Bonaparte between 1798 and 1801. At the beginning of the nineteenth century the Ottoman viceroy, Muhammad Ali (1805–1848), turned Egypt into an autonomous country, taking advantage of the increasing weakness of the Ottoman Empire. He also embarked on a drastic attempt at modernization of the economy and the army, and would have built an empire for Egypt in the Middle East had not his efforts been foiled by the interference of England. His successors, who were known as "khedives," fell prey to often unscrupulous European bankers and moneylenders all too willing to encourage their profligacy, thereby paving the way for western commercial and financial penetration. One of the most significant results of the increasing western presence—mostly French and British—was the building by the French of the Suez Canal*, joining the Mediterranean to the Red Sea, which was opened in 1869. If anything, the opening of the Suez Canal reasserted the strategic importance of Egypt, considerably shortening the sea route to the Far East.

The Western presence in Egypt benefited from the capitulation system, in which Europeans enjoyed privileges of extra territoriality and exemptions from taxation and tariffs which were economically detrimental to local business interests. But soon the disastrous level of Egyptian indebtedness and European financial interference led to nationalist stirrings and a revolt by an army officer, Ahmed Arabi (Arabi Pasha). This in turn brought about British intervention in 1882, ostensibly to reestablish the authority of the khedive. A British army occupied Cairo, and the British took control of the country. The occupation was supposed to have a short duration, but it lasted officially until 1922, and in reality it completely ceased only in 1954. During much of that time, relations between the khedive, his Ottoman suzerain, and the British occupants were never clearly defined. For all intents and purposes, Egypt was a protectorate, which was in fact officially declared by England in 1914 at the onset of World War I*.

From 1883 Sir Evelyn Baring, later Lord Cromer, as British agent and consul general, ruled Egypt autocratically until 1907. British advisers were placed in key ministries, notably a financial adviser in charge of fiscal matters. Civil and criminal codes were established by the British, and the police and the army were reorganized with a British commander in chief. Irrigation was developed with the building of the first Aswan dam. The financial situation remained chaotic as long as the French, who resented the British unilateral occupation, blocked British attempts at improvements through their participation in the liquidation of the Egyptian debt, as a consequence of the Treaty of London. The 1882 intervention had originally been a joint Franco-British endeavor, but the French had not continued beyond a naval show of force. Later, with the improvement in Franco-British relations, the French gave a free hand to England in Egypt in return for a green light in Morocco*. By 1889 the financial situation had improved, but the question of the British withdrawal was repeatedly postponed.

There was a progressive growth of Egyptian nationalism from the end of the nineteenth century, particularly under Abbas Hilmi Pasha (Khedive, 1892–1914). It was exacerbated by the brutal and insensitive actions of the British in 1906 in the Taba and Denshawai affairs. There were tentative attempts at liberalization under Sir Eldon Gorst, who replaced Cromer, but nationalist pressures were mounting by the time World War I started. During the war, Egypt became a military base for British troops in their Middle East operations against the Ottomans. Egypt was declared a British protectorate, and Abbas Hilmi was deposed and replaced by a relative, who was now called a sultan. Once the war was over, there was a great surge of nationalism with the foundation of a political movement, which later became a party, the Wafd, under the inspired leadership of Saad Zaghlul. When he was arrested and deported to Malta (1919), massive demonstrations and outbreaks of violence took place. Britain then ended the protectorate and granted formal independence to Egypt in February 1922. Sultan Fuad became king. But the reality of the political situation was a three way struggle between the king, the parliament of Egypt—dominated by the Wafd—and the British residency under a high commissioner. Two successive constitutions were promulgated—in 1923 and again in 1930. The Wafd, under the leadership of Nahas Pasha (from 1927), continued to play a dominant role in Egyptian politics, usually at odds with the king, who for a time imposed as prime minister Ismail Sidky Pasha—a virtual dictator. But there were still British troops in Egypt, and an Englishman was the commander in chief of the Egyptian army. The Anglo-Egyptian treaty of 1936, however, brought about the end of the capitulations.

At the beginning of World War II, Egypt severed diplomatic relations with Germany and Italy, and martial law was proclaimed. A large number of British and Commonwealth troops were stationed in Egypt, which was threatened by Rommel's Afrika Corps. Rommel advanced to within 70 miles of Alexandria when he was stopped by Montgomery at the battle of El Alamein. But Egyptian public opinion was chafing at the heavy British presence, especially after the British in 1942 forced King Farouk, whose attitude was deemed pro-fascist, to take Nahas Pasha as prime minister under threat of deposition.

After the war Egypt tried to renegotiate the 1936 treaty to no avail and even took its case to the United Nations with equal lack of success. The disastrous war with the new state of Israel in 1948 antagonized the last bastion of loyalty to the monarchy, the army. A bankrupt governing elite unilaterally abrogated the Anglo-Egyptian treaty, causing outbreaks of violence in Ismailia and culminating in the burning of Cairo by an angry mob in January 1952. On July 23, a military coup deposed King Farouk, and the following year Egypt was declared a republic with General Muhammad Naguib as president. In 1954 Gamal Abd al-Nasser*, the true brains behind the Free Officers' Movement, put Naguib under house arrest and took over the presidency. That same year he signed a treaty with Britain, which finally agreed to evacuate the Suez Canal Zone after 72 years of occupation. Egypt was at last independent. (John Marlowe, *A History* *of Modern Egypt and Anglo-Egyptian Relations, 1800–1953*, 1954; Robert Stephens, *Nasser: A Political Biography*, 1972.)

Alain G. Marsot

EIRE. See IRELAND.

ELIZABETH I. No monarch in English history experienced such a contrast between the prospects in the early stages of her life, and the retrospective on her reign, as Elizabeth Tudor (1533–1603). The daughter of the ill-fated Anne Boleyn, and a princess bastardized by the dynastic/personal imperatives of her father Henry VIII, she could only have been expected to be a minor player among the royals of sixteenth-century Europe. Although her mother had been executed by her father (on specious charges—Anne's real infraction was her failure to bear a royal son), Elizabeth's childhood was unremarkable and characterized more by neglect than anything else. Her stepmother, Katherine Parr, was instrumental, however, in securing an unusually substantial humanistic and Protestant education for her. When Henry VIII died, his will left the crown to his three children. Elizabeth's half-brother, Edward VI, inherited the throne in 1547, but the consumptive boy King died six years later. During his reign, Elizabeth lived in relatively pleasant if obscure circumstances, and was on good terms with the young monarch.

The next reign, however, was truly dangerous to Elizabeth. Her half-sister, Mary Tudor, was both Catholic and determined to have conformity in the land. Elizabeth's Protestant proclivities made her an irritant; and her royal blood, a threat. Worse, she inadvertently became a center of various conspiracies designed to resist Mary's Catholic renaissance and the Spanish marriage upon which Mary also insisted. Elizabeth's more aggressive supporters came close to costing the princess her life.

A second premature and heirless royal death in 1558 brought Elizabeth, the last of her father's line, to the throne. Besides the unexpectedness of her accession, no one could have predicted that her reign was to be the third longest in English history. Nor was the outlook in 1558 for a presumably weak, female ruler especially auspicious. Religious considerations were sure to bedevil the kingdom as they had ever since the Reformation. Royal finances were in a shambles after the war with France into which Mary had drawn England. She and her ministers dealt with each challenge in turn, and by the time of her death in 1603, men had come to characterize her reign as the "golden age of the English monarchy"—the standard by which subsequent reigns were measured.

The accomplishments of Elizabethan England were striking. First of all, the queen, with the assistance of the financial genius Sir Thomas Gresham, restored sound currency and the royal treasury. She next solved her religious dilemma by returning to her father's approach, a middle way between the old religion of Catholicism and the radicalism of Genevan-based Protestantism. She did, however, add to the theological mix the unusual ingredient of some of the first experiments with religious toleration ("I will not make windows into men's souls"). Prudently, for one of her sex, she chose to be the "governor," not the "head" of the established church. Anglicanism was thus born. Thirdly, she dealt with overseas threats by the twin expedients of not advertising her religious settlement and by flaunting her marital availability. These techniques kept foreign powers neutralized in their relations with the country for the first twenty years. Finally, Elizabeth surrounded herself with men who gave her sound statecraft (William Cecil, Lord Burghley; Robert Dudley, the Earl of Leicester; Sir Francis Walsingham; and others) but not suffocating domination. She played these capable and strong-willed males against each other, leaving her in undisputed ascendance.

As the reign matured, the nation enjoyed relative peace, prosperity, and a flourishing of culture. The kingdom survived a substantial threat from the Spanish Empire* in the Spanish Armada* incident of 1588. It saw the marked evolution of a robust representative parliament and its procedures; the economy was perhaps healthier than it had been or was to be in most other periods prior to the nineteenth century; and Shakespeare and a galaxy of other literary figures contributed in an unparalleled way to English letters. Most importantly, in the context of a study of imperialism, it was in the England of Elizabeth that the British began the long march toward controlling a fair portion of the earth's surface.

The expansion of Elizabethan England is especially noteworthy. American historians stress that it was during this era that the first English settlement (1587) was established in Virginia* (named of course for England's virgin queen— Elizabeth never married). Raleigh's Roanoke settlement failed, in part because the Spanish Armada made impossible a return to the area to succor the colonists in 1588, and the supply ships in 1591 found little evidence of what had happened to the lost colony. But through Roanoke and then the exploring voyages of Sir Humphrey Gilbert*, Sir Martin Frobisher*, and John Davis, Englishmen established a presence in what were subsequently to become the most important lands of their empire. The creation of what was ultimately to be the United States and Canada* was probably the single most important element in the Elizabethan expansion.

It was, however, far from the only element. During the great queen's era, merchants, explorers, and adventurers did much to focus English attention on other hitherto unknown or unexploited areas. Following the successful 1554 Willoughby and Chancellor expedition into Russia, and then Anthony Jenkinson's and Steven Burrough's voyages of exploration into the north in the 1560s, English trade under the auspices of the newly formed Muscovy Company began in all seriousness. New ambassadorial posts are usually a good indication of new trade patterns; the first English ambassador went to Moscow in 1566.

The same thing happened in the Mediterranean. Excluded from the Ottoman ports for decades by a French monopoly, the English forced their independent way into this lucrative trading area in 1553, and then consolidated their gains

y established in 1578 and the formation of the Levant
Company in 1581. North Africa fared similarly. Sporadic contact with the independent tribes and city states of the region became a fully functioning commercial relation in the Elizabethan era, as North Africans traded citrus and slaves
for the much sought English weaponry and cloth. The first English diplomat
went to Barbary in 1577, the Barbary Company was formed, and another component in a rapidly expanding commercial empire developed.

That empire certainly brushed the West African coast during Elizabeth's reign,
especially through the efforts of John Hawkins* and his slaving expeditions. But
perhaps the most remarkable of the commercial/exploration journeys took place
when John Newbery and Ralph Fitch made their way overland from the Ottoman
Porte into the Persian empire, and then subsequently into India*. Newbery
perished, but Fitch, after nine years, returned to England having opened communications and having brought Englishmen into contact with India, Burma*
and the Malay peninsula. Fitch and Newbery's exploits were the most remarkable. Those of Sir Francis Drake* were the most memorable. He further added
to the expansion of English horizons with his epic circumnavigation of the globe
1579–1581, the first by an Englishman.

Elizabethan England saw a remarkable spread of English interests throughout
the known world, and a substantial push into uncharted lands as well. Elizabeth,
the queen who presided over this expansionistic, aggressive, and inquisitive age,
deserves a share of the credit for its achievements. By nature cautious, she tried
to avoid direct confrontations with superior European powers, and preserved
both English independence and a relative peace that could be translated into
energies expended on exploration and commerce. She personally encouraged the
expansion of trade, for reasons of royal penury to be sure, but for whatever
reason, crown sponsorship was a substantial added stimulus. Her regime additionally assisted commercial expansion by stabilizing currency and ensuring that
crown finances did not provide a drag upon the economy. Finally, she trusted
clever and capable men—besides her politicians, we must add Drake, Hawkins,
Carew, Howard, and Frobisher—and this ability to recognize and exploit competence often is the best indication of leadership. Elizabeth Tudor contributed
markedly to England's "golden era." (J. B. Black, *The Reign of Elizabeth*,
1959; Paul Johnson, *Elizabeth, A Study in Power and Intellect*, 1974; J. E.
Neale, *Queen Elizabeth I*, 1938; A. L. Rowse, *The Expansion of Elizabethan
England*, 1955.)

Gary M. Bell

ELLICE ISLANDS. The Ellice Islands are nine coral islands and atolls, part
of Polynesia*, located in the South Pacific. The islands include Funafuti, the
most densely populated and the seat of government. Although they cover more
than 500,000 square miles of ocean, their land mass totals less than 20 square
miles. Spanish explorers first discovered the Ellice Islands in 1568, but their
isolation and sparce resources rendered them economically unattractive to the

early European empires, though whalers, copra traders, and slave labor contractors later visited the Ellice Islands regularly. The decline of the Spanish empire* in the eighteenth and nineteenth centuries left a political vacuum in the Pacific, and the rise of the prosperous English colonies in Australia* and New Zealand* brought the Ellice Islands into the British sphere of influence.

In 1877 parliament created a Western Pacific High Commission to supervise the Ellice and Gilbert Islands, and in 1892 England established a formal protectorate over both island groups. Political reorganization in 1916 established the Gilbert and Ellice Islands Colony. After World War II, Britain gradually prepared the Ellice Islands for self-government. In a popular referendum in 1975, Ellice Islanders voted to separate from the Gilbert and Ellice Islands Colony and became known as the Tuvalu Colony. Three years later, in 1978, Tuvalu received its independence and membership in the Commonwealth of Nations*. (C. J. Lynch, "Three Pacific Island Constitutions: Comparisons," *Parliamentarian*, 61, July 1980, 133–41; W. P. Morrell, *Britain in the Pacific*, 1953.)

EL SALVADOR. During the colonial period, El Salvador was a province of the captaincy-general of Guatemala. San Salvador was an *alcaldia mayor* until 1786 when it became an intendancy. Sonsonate was independent of San Salvador and Guatemala and did not become a part of El Salvador until after independence. Before the arrival of the Spaniards, the region of El Salvador was occupied by the Pipil Indians, who lived west of the Lempa River, and the Lenca, who were east of the Lempa River. In 1522 Andrea Niño and Gil González Dávila left Panama on an expedition to explore Central America. Niño became the first European to discover Salvadorean territory. His damaged ships went as far as the Bay of Fonseca, named after Bishop Fonseca, the president of the Council of the Indies.

Spaniards contested among one another for control of El Salvador. At the instigation of Hernán Cortés* in New Spain*, Pedro de Alvarado attacked Pipil Indians near Acajutla in June 1524, and in 1525 Gonzalo de Alvarado established San Salvador, although the settlement was destroyed by Indians in 1526. Pedro de Alvarado returned to El Salvador in 1526 and 1528, finally putting the region under Spanish control through brutal repression. In 1528 Diego de Alvarado refounded San Salvador and awarded *encomiendas** to his supporters. The last major Indian revolt was between 1537 and 1539.

But in Panama, Pedrarias Dávila resented the expansionism of Cortés's people, and in 1529 he sent an expedition led by Martín de Estete to claim the region as part of Nicaragua*. Pedro de Alvarado then founded San Miguel to protect the region from further incursions from Nicaragua and as a base against the Lenca Indians. When Pedro left for Peru* he took most of San Miguel's population with him. Some gold was found around San Miguel, which made a few dozen Spaniards rich, but El Salvador's wealth was in agricultural exports.

Cacao was the premier export crop. It was grown around the Los Izalcos region, which was settled after San Salvador and San Miguel. The Spanish settlement at Sonsonate, founded in 1552, became a center for cacao and balsam. The Indians kept control of cacao production. In 1558 Los Izalcos was granted local autonomy when the Sonsonate merchants petitioned the Council of the Indies that the *alcalde mayor* should be chosen directly by the king and the council instead of being under the jurisdiction of San Salvador or Guatemala City. This was a victory of the local merchants over the Guatemala *encomenderos* who controlled the Indian population. The third important export crop was indigo. The Indian population precipitously declined between 1550 and 1650 due to death and Indians escaping their villages to get away from paying tribute. This led to the gradual ladinoization of the population as they moved out of the villages and into the countryside where the haciendas were located. In 1549 El Salvador was placed under the jurisdiction of the Audiencia of Guatemala.

Land and labor patterns changed in the seventeenth and eighteenth centuries. Although the decline of the *encomienda* led to the appearance of the repartimiento in the early 1600s, labor shortages led to the introduction of African slaves by 1625. Because of economic competition from Ecuador and Venezuela, cacao declined in importance, but indigo and cattle production took its place. Gradually a hostility developed between the *hacendados*, who owned the large estates and controlled agricultural production, and the Guatemala City merchants, who controlled purchase and distribution. By the end of the colonial period, between 50 and 65 percent of the land was owned by subsistence cultivators, and the rest was in the hands of the *hacendados*.

The contradictions in the economic system began to find political expression in the early nineteenth century. On November 5, 1811, Father José Matias Delgado issued a formal call for independence from Spain. His proclamation was inspired by the outbreak of rebellion in Mexico. Manuel José Arce led rebellions against Spain in 1811 and 1814. But it was not until September 15, 1821, when Guatemala revolted from Spain, that San Salvador and Sonsonate and their environs won their independence. After a few short years as part of Agustín de Iturbide's Mexican empire, El Salvador became part of the United Provinces of Central America in 1824. The federation gradually disintegrated in the 1830s and El Salvador became an independent nation in 1839. (David Browning, *El Salvador: Landscape and Society*, 1971; Alastair White, *El Salvador*, 1973.)

Carlos Pérez

EMPIRE SETTLEMENT ACT OF 1922. The Empire Settlement Act was part of a threefold economic program formulated by Great Britain and the dominions for their mutual benefit. The program was designed to invigorate the economies of the dominions following the 1914–1918 war by supplying them with increased population, expanded capital investment, and trade benefits in the United Kingdom market. The economy of Britain was to be revitalized by solving the unemployment problem, bringing profitable returns on new investments, and rapidly expanding dominion markets for British products.

A special commonwealth conference held in February 1921 focused on the question of "assisted migration" to the dominions. The British government proposed to advance, through the dominion government or voluntary organizations, sums up to £300 sterling for each approved settler if the dominions would match these amounts, and to make £2 million per annum available to endow the emigration program. Dominion response to the British proposal was mixed. South Africa was not interested because of its "limited field for white labor," but Canada, Australia, and New Zealand supported the British offer. With the majority of the dominions behind assisted migration, parliament passed the Empire Settlement Act of 1922, which placed an upper limit of £3 million on the annual contribution of the British treasury.

Despite the abundance of funds, both from Britain and Australia, the project failed to stimulate much emigration. While emigration from Britain to the dominions in 1913 was 285,000, the total for all the years from 1922 to 1930 was only slightly over one million. Of this total, only about half migrated with government assistance. Moreover, the immediate absorptive capacity of the dominions was much less than the planners had anticipated. In addition, during the 1920s, the potential supply of settlers from the British Isles was declining, due largely to a declining birth rate which failed to compensate for the large numbers of young men either killed or incapacitated by World War I. Indeed, by 1930 the Empire Settlement Act was virtually abandoned due to the reverse flow of migration caused by the worldwide economic depression. Overall, the effects of the depression, especially unemployment, were felt more severely overseas. The Empire Settlement Act ultimately failed because its backers did not realize that the war had seriously impaired Britain's financial and demographic ability to assist commonwealth development. (C. L. Mowat, *Britain Between the Wars, 1918–1940*, 1955; G. F. Plant, *Overseas Settlement: Migration from the United Kingdom to the Dominions*, 1951.)

William G. Ratliff

ENCOMIENDA. Derived from the Spanish verb *encomendar*, to entrust, the *encomienda* was a manorial concept based upon reciprocal rights and obligations. More specifically, it was a relic of medieval feudalism used by the Spaniards to rationalize the virtual enslavement of New World Indians. Just as European peasants theoretically entrusted themselves to a manorial lord, for whom they performed special services in return for protection, Indians in Spanish America were to labor for *encomenderos* (favored conquistadores), who in turn were expected to protect and Christianize the natives. Contrary to common belief, the *encomienda* was not a landed estate, but rather a legalistic arrangement in which Spaniards justified the extraction of labor from the aborigines.

On paper, the *encomienda* was ideally suited to balance the dual and often conflicting religious and material aspirations of the Spanish crown and the conquistadores. With regard to the Indians, the crown was in a difficult position.

On the one hand, it sought to civilize the aborigines and defend them against exploitation, thereby placating the papacy and the religious orders; on the other, it was dependent upon Indian labor to operate the mines and harvest the fields. The *encomienda* offered a solution which, theoretically, was mutually beneficial to all. For their labor, the Indians would receive protection and religious instruction, while the crown and the conquistadores would reap the material rewards of colonization.

In 1503 Queen Isabella*, mindful of both the spiritual welfare of the aborigines and the material needs of the crown and the conquistadores, gave royal approval to the *encomienda*. From the outset, theory and practice diverged. Freed by distance from close royal scrutiny, the *encomenderos* either ignored their obligations to the Indians or performed them perfunctorily. In essence, it became little more than a ruthless system of forced labor, and in the sixteenth and seventeenth centuries it frequently prompted heated exchanges between the religious orders, the crown, and the conquistadores. Attempts to abolish the *encomienda*, such as the New Laws of 1542, not only aroused the anger of the conquistadores but also jeopardized the prosperity of the crown. Despite its sympathy for the Indians and its sensitivity to the protests of friars such as Bartolomé de las Casas*, the crown was unprepared to sacrifice its material interests to the spiritual and humanitarian claims of the Indians. So the *encomienda* with all its abuses survived throughout Spanish America until the early 1700s and lingered in the Yucatán and Chile until the late 1780s. (C. H. Haring, *The Spanish Empire in America*, 1947; John H. Parry, *The Spanish Theory of Empire in the Sixteenth Century*, 1940; Lesley B. Simpson, *The Encomienda in New Spain*, 1950.)

John W. Storey

ENTRECASTEAUX, ANTOINE DE BRUNI. Antoine d'Entrecasteaux (born 1737) was the French navigator who was appointed by the revolutionary French government to leave in September 1791 on a voyage to explore southwestern Oceania. He sailed around the Cape of Good Hope, investigated the western coast of New Caledonia*, explored the Solomon* and Admiralty* islands and New Guinea, circumnavigated Australia*, visited Tasmania*, and reached the Santa Cruz Islands. The expedition "discovered" the Kermadec group, Beautemps-Beaupre atoll, many small islands in the Louisade archipelago, and Entrecasteaux, Trobriand, and other islands near New Guinea. By the beginning of 1793 dysentery and scurvy had all but destroyed the exploration. Entrecasteaux died on July 20, 1793. The expedition disbanded at the Dutch East Indies* settlement of Surabaja in October 1793. (J. C. Beaglehole, *The Exploration of the Pacific*, 1966; John Dunmore, *French Explorers in the Pacific*, vol. 1, 1965; Andrew Sharp, *The Discovery of the Pacific Islands*, 1960.)

EQUATORIAL GUINEA. See SPANISH GUINEA.

EQUATORIAL ISLANDS. The Equatorial Islands—Howland*, Baker*, and Jarvis*—are located along the equator between the Gilbert Islands* and the Line Islands*. There was little interest in the islands until the mid–1930s when Pan American Airways and the Oceanic Nitrates Corporation expressed interest in establishing a guano mine there and an airport for trans-Pacific travelers. When Japanese expansion to the islands became a possibility, President Franklin D. Roosevelt had the United States Navy and the Department of Commerce send colonists there in March 1935. During World War II a radio station was established at Jarvis, an emergency airfield at Howland, and an operational airfield at Baker. After the war the islands retreated to uninhabited obscurity, though still territory of the United States. (Francis X. Holbrook, "Commercial Aviation and the Colonization of the Equatorial Islands, 1934–1936," *Aerospace Historian*, 17, 1970, 144–49.)

ERITREA. See ETHIOPIA.

ESPIRITU SANTO. Espiritu Santo was a Portuguese colony on the southeast coast of Brazil*. It was first created as a donatária in 1535 but in 1718 it went back to the Portuguese crown. At that point it was designated as a royal captaincy and placed under the jurisdiction of Bahia.* Espiritu Santo became a province of Brazil in 1822. See BRAZIL.

ESSEQUIBO. In 1624 the Dutch West India Company placed a settlement at the mouth of the Essequibo River in western Guiana. At the time the Dutch were interested in exploiting the commercial possibilities of the Caribbean as well as that of the South American interior. The colony remained intact until 1750 when settlers from Essequibo established the new colony of Demarara,* which eventually became the seat of the Dutch presence in western Guiana. Essequibo became subordinate to Demarara in 1784, and in 1803 the British took permanent control of Demarara and Essequibo. They became part of British Guiana.* See BRITISH GUIANA.

ETHIOPIA. Ethiopia (sometimes called Abyssinia) is located in eastern Africa. Its borders are with Somalia* on the east, Kenya* on the south, the Red Sea on the north, and Sudan* on the west. Tradition holds that the imperial families of Ethiopia were descended from the Queen of Sheba and King Solomon. Until the fourth century, Ethiopia was a pagan country with some Semitic influence. In about A.D. 326, two Syrian Christians, Frumentius and Aedisius, were shipwrecked and taken to King Aezana. They became his servants and converted him and the royal family to the Coptic Christian Church. Christianity was well established in Ethiopia, particularly in the central highlands, by the sixth century.

European influence was introduced in the fifteenth century by the Portuguese who were seeking the legendary Christian kingdom of Prester (Priest) John. Two of the earliest Portuguese travelers were Peros da Covilhão who arrived in Shewa in 1493 and Dom Rodrigo de Lima who arrived in Massawa in 1520. De Lima was accompanied by Father Francisco Alvarez, whose account of his visit contained more information than previously known of the area. Ethiopia relied on Portuguese military assistance in 1541 to stop a Muslim invasion led by Iman Ahmad. Ahmad was defeated and killed in 1543. However, when Portugal attempted to convert Ethiopia to Roman Catholicism, the Portuguese were expelled in the 1630s.

European contact was reestablished in the 1760s by James Bruce, a Scottish explorer who was seeking the source of the Blue Nile. He wrote about his journey in *Travels to Discover the Source of the Nile* (1790). By the 1850s the British had sent a consul to the Emperor Theodore. Theodore was friendly to the English at first but was disillusioned by what he perceived as their lack of assistance. He imprisoned the British consul and then members of the British mission sent to secure the consul's release. This led to the invasion of Ethiopia by an Anglo-Indian force under Sir Robert Napier. Following the Battle of Magdala (1868), the hostages were rescued and Theodore committed suicide. Having accomplished their mission, the British withdrew. They had no interest in Ethiopia as a colony.

In 1869 the first Italian influence was felt in Ethiopia with the purchase of the port of Aseb by an Italian company. On May 2, 1889, Menelik II, then emperor of Ethiopia, concluded the Treaty of Uccialli with Italy, permitting the Italians to occupy Asmara. This treaty became a source of trouble, as the Italian and Ethiopian copies differed. The Ethiopian copy stipulated that the Ethiopians might, at their option, employ Italy to conduct diplomacy for their country. The Italian copy stated that Ethiopia must employ Italy to conduct its diplomacy. The Italians used this document to declare a protectorate over Ethiopia. In May 1893 Ethiopia renounced the treaty, but not before Great Britain recognized the Italian protectorate and entered into the Anglo-Italian Agreement of 1891 which established each country's area of influence. The Italians pushed to extend their control over Ethiopia and met with early military success. However, Menelik II, with supplies from France and Russia, defeated a large Italian army at Adowa on March 1, 1896. (March 1st is still observed as a national holiday in Ethiopia.) On October 26, 1896, the Treaty of Uccialli was declared null and void and the Treaty of Addis Ababa was signed, the Italians recognizing Ethiopian independence.

Both Britain and France attempted to establish their presence in Ethiopia after the defeat of the Italians. By training and equipping the Ethiopian army, France gained important economic concessions. A secret Franco-Ethiopian treaty fixed Ethiopian boundaries on the Nile in 1897. Soon after this, Menelik signed a treaty with Great Britain settling the boundary with British Somaliland*. In 1906, France, Britain, and Italy signed the Tripartite Treaty ensuring Ethiopian independence, but agreed that if Ethiopia ever broke up, each would respect the others' interests.

Not long after Menelik died in 1913, Britain, France, and Italy became preoccupied with World War I. This enabled Ethiopia to address its own difficulties. In 1923, Ethiopia was admitted to the League of Nations*. Haile Selassie became emperor in 1930. He worked to create a unified and prosperous country. Italy, under Mussolini, magnified border incidents between Ethiopia and its neighbor, Italian Somaliland*, out of proportion to their true importance, and on October 3, 1935, invaded Ethiopia without a declaration of war. Mussolini, backed by Hitler's threats, prevented other nations from taking action against Italy. On May 5, 1935, Addis Ababa was occupied by the Italians and Emperor Haile Selassie fled the country to England. Italy formally annexed Ethiopia on May 9, 1936, establishing Italian East Africa* from Ethiopia, Eritrea, and Italian Somaliland. With the beginning of World War II, Italian power diminished. A combined British and Ethiopian army defeated the Italians in 1941 and Haile Selassie returned to power in Ethiopia. In 1952, by a United Nations decision, Eritrea, a northern province that had been under Italian rule, was returned to Ethiopia setting the stage for future ethnic conflict in the Horn of Africa. The Eritrean People's Liberation Front fought for independence from the Marxist regime of Ethiopia's Mengistu Haile Mariam, who fled in 1991. (Richard Greenfield, *Ethiopia*, 1965.)

Amanda Pollock

ETHIOPIAN WAR. Fascinated with dreams of empire and intent on making Italy a world power, Benito Mussolini looked enviously on Ethiopia as a future Italian colony. In 1932 Emilio De Bono, minister of colonies, hatched a scheme for gradually moving into Ethiopia from Eritrea*. De Bono expected the Ethiopians to try to expel the Italians militarily, which he thought would destabilize Emperor Haile Selassie's regime. But in 1934 Mussolini decided against the gradual penetration idea in favor of a full-scale military invasion. On October 3, 1935, Italian troops invaded from Eritrea in the north and Italian Somaliland* in the south. It was over in seven months. The Ethiopians did not have a chance against the Italian army. Mussolini sent 400,000 well-equipped troops to Ethiopia, and they enjoyed armored and air support. Selassie fled the country in May 1936. On May 9, 1936, Mussolini proclaimed the existence of Italian East Africa*. Although the League of Nations* condemned the invasion and imposed economic sanctions against Italy, the British and French decided not to attempt to intervene. Mussolini had his empire, but it would not survive him and would not survive World War II. (G. W. Baer, *Test Case: Italy, Ethiopia, and the League of Nations*, 1976.)

EXTRATERRITORIALITY. Extraterritoriality refers to the status of being, for legal purposes, outside the jurisdictional territory of a state. When a government grants extraterritorial privilege to the citizens of another state, the assumption is made that those individuals are not in the state where they are residing or visiting as aliens. The insistence on extraterritorial privilege arose to a large extent from the confrontation between European nations and non-Christian states. Faced with an exotic civil law rooted, for example, in Islamic or Buddhist precepts, the European alien felt that he could not obtain justice unless removed from local jurisdiction. The practice thus evolved of allowing foreigners to be subject to their own national laws. The system was normally established by treaties, with consuls functioning as judges. In the past a number of countries, including Turkey, Morocco, Egypt, Oman, Japan, and China conceded extraterritorial privileges.

The modern application of extraterritoriality is traced to the Muslim conquest of Constantinople. The sultan extended to his new Christian subjects virtually the same privileges they had previously enjoyed. In the ninth century the Chinese allowed a community of Arabs to construct a mosque in Canton* and to be governed by their own laws. In Macao*, the Portuguese were permitted local self-government. The most important manifestation of extraterritoriality in the nineteenth and twentieth centuries involved China. It began with provisions in treaties which followed the First Anglo-Chinese War. The Treaty of the Bogue, signed in 1843, stated that British subjects involved in criminal matters were to be tried by English officials according to British law. Shortly thereafter, in February 1844, an American diplomat, Caleb Cushing, arrived to open talks with the Chinese. The resulting Treaty of Wanghia extended to American citizens the same rights which the British had obtained, but also included a most-favored-nation clause. This provision guaranteed that American nationals would automatically receive all rights and privileges granted in the future by the Chinese to foreigners. Significantly, it called for extraterritorial jurisdiction in civil as well as criminal cases. The terms of the agreement became a model for treaties that were entered into later by other nations with China. The exercise of extraterritorial jurisdiction reached its zenith with the 1876 Chefoo Convention.

With a changing international environment, punctuated by the rise of Japan, attempts to end extraterritoriality were begun in the early 1930s. The United States submitted a draft treaty in July 1931 relinquishing jurisdiction over American citizens in China, subject to certain safeguards which would be in force for a period of five years. Provision was also made for a special zone in Shanghai in which American jurisdiction would be maintained for ten years. In the same year London also reached a tentative agreement with the Chinese to gradually end its extraterritorial privileges.

Negotiations were temporarily halted, however, when Japan invaded China in July 1937. It then seemed that it would be advantageous to continue extraterritoriality during the crisis. For example, it was speculated that foreign rights could act as a check on Japanese aggression, curbing violence toward foreign nationals and protecting the treaty ports from damage. The Chinese felt that the foreign concessions could be places of sanctuary. It soon became painfully obvious, however, that such a legalism was a frail shield. There were hundreds of incidents of bombings of foreign property, destruction of missions, and attacks on foreigners. London made strong but impotent protests to the Japanese concerning the stripping and searching of their nationals in Tientsin.

During World War II, because China had become a full partner in the struggle against Japan, and because it was deemed important to enhance the prestige of the Nationalist regime with its own people, the Powers moved to change the old policy of extraterritoriality. On January 11, 1943, the Treaty for the Relinquishment of Extraterritorial Rights and the Regulation of Related Matters was signed by China and the United States. On the same day the British entered into a similar agreement. The agreements began a new chapter in Chinese foreign relations and signaled the termination of extraterritoriality, concessions, and the stationing of foreign troops on Chinese soil. (Wesley R. Fishel, *The End of Extraterritoriality in China*, 1952; John W. Foster, *American Diplomacy in the Orient*, 1926; Graham H. Stuart, *American Diplomatic and Consular Practice*, 1952; Urban G. Whitaker, Jr., *Politics and Power: A Text in International Law*, 1964.)

Roy E. Thoman

F

FALKLAND ISLANDS. A British crown colony in the South Atlantic lying approximately 300 miles east of Argentina, the Falkland Islands are composed of East Falkland and West Falkland, separated by Falkland Sound, plus 100 smaller islands. The Falkland group was probably first discovered by the Englishman John Davis in 1592, but the first recorded landing was made by Captain Strong of the *Farewell* in 1690. The islands were visited regularly by most seafaring nations into the eighteenth century, and by the 1720s they were known as the Islas Malvinas to the Spanish and the Malouines to the French. The name Malvinas probably was derived as a result of exploration of the region by ships from St. Malo in the early eighteenth century. In 1765 a British naval squadron surveyed the islands and claimed formal possession of what became Port Egmont in West Falkland. The following year a small British garrison was established at Port Egmont. Also in 1766 Spain established a fortified settlement at Soledad in East Falkland. In 1770 a strong Spanish force sent from Buenos Aires succeeded in capturing the British garrison at Port Egmont. By an agreement between Great Britain and Spain concluded in 1771, the British force was allowed to return. The only stipulation included in the agreement was that Britain make no further claims to sovereignty over the islands. The British settlement subsequently was destroyed by Spain in 1777.

By 1800 Spain claimed full sovereignty over the Falklands based upon Article III of the Nootka Sound Convention of 1790. Spain, however, did not colonize West Falkland, but maintained a settlement and governor's residence at Soledad in East Falkland. In 1811 the Spanish government at Montevideo removed the island's inhabitants, who had been without a governor since 1806, and the Falklands remained uninhabited, visited only by whaling ships, until 1819. In 1820 the republican government of the United Provinces of La Plata claimed the islands as a former Spanish possession. In 1823 a new governor was appointed, but efforts to begin a new settlement were aborted. By 1829 the only successful colonization of the islands was accomplished by a private concern headed by Louis Vernet, a naturalized Argentine citizen. The same year Vernet was made governor.

The British government did not protest the Argentinian actions in 1820 and 1823, but the establishment of Vernet's thriving settlement in 1829 sparked retaliation. In December 1832 a British naval force took formal possession of Port Egmont and, in January 1833, the British squadron compelled the surrender of the Argentine defenders at Soledad. The formal protests made by the government of Argentina* received no support from the United States, even though the British action was a violation of the Monroe Doctrine*. From 1833 until 1945 the Argentine government took only limited diplomatic action to preserve its claim to the Falklands. The British government never recognized Argentina's claim of sovereignty over the islands and continued to maintain the islands for strategic naval purposes. On April 2, 1982, citing its own claim to the islands, Argentina invaded the Falklands and South Georgia* Island. War between Britain and Argentina followed, with the fighting taking place principally around Port Stanley, the largest British settlement on East Falkland Island. The war ended on June 15, 1982, with the surrender of the Argentine invasion force to British troops. Some 750 Argentine and 256 British soldiers were killed. The war did not, however, settle the dispute over the Falkland Islands sovereignty. (V. Boyson, *The Falkland Islands*, 1924; M. B. R. Cawkell, et al., *The Falkland Islands*, 1960; Max Hastings, *Battle for the Falklands*, 1983.)

William G. Ratliff

FASHODA INCIDENT. After the defeats of William Hicks and his 8,000-man force at El Obeid (1883) and Charles Gordon at Khartoum (1885) by the forces of the Mahdi, Britain decided to evacuate all British and Egyptian subjects from the Sudan*. This decision might have ended British colonialism in the Sudan had it not been for fear of subsequent French encroachment. Britain correctly believed that if they and the Egyptians did not reoccupy the Sudan, the void would soon be filled by the French. In 1895 General Horatio Herbert Kitchener received the blessing of the new British Conservative government to retake the Sudan. In March 1896 Kitchener launched his campaign with 25,000 troops from Wadi Halfa at the Egyptian-Sudan border. This campaign would last two and one half years, culminating with the battle of Omduran, September 2, 1898.

During this period France decided that the British and Egyptians had abandoned the Sudan to the Mahdi, and that it was their right to claim at least a part of the area. The French strategy was to enter the southern Sudan from French Congo* and move up the White Nile to Fashoda (now Kodok), an abandoned fort on the west bank of the White Nile some 469 miles south of Khartoum. From Fashoda, it would be possible to claim and control the Upper Nile Valley. Indeed, one French hydrologist and expert on the Nile, Victor Prompt, seriously suggested that the French might dam the White Nile at Fashoda and thus dictate the destiny of Egypt*.

Captain Jean-Baptiste Marchand, who was given command of the French venture, arrived at Loango on the coast of French Middle Congo in the summer of 1896. He found most of his supplies, which were to have been transported up-country in advance of the expedition, still on the beach. Pierre Savorgnan de Brazza, commissioner general of French Congo, had been unable to have them moved to Brazzaville, the official starting point for the Fashoda mission, because of the revolt of the Bashundi people against France. Before the supplies could be moved, the rebellion had to be crushed. After a delay of six months, some 17,000 loads were carried by African porters to Brazzaville on the Congo River. From there Marchand started up the river in March, seeking to reach the tributaries of the White Nile from the west, by way of the Ubangi country. Since much of the upper Ubangi River was not navigable, a large part of the journey was made on foot under incredibly difficult conditions. Dugout canoes were used when the water was deep enough, but usually this was only during the rainy season. Keeping porters, negotiating with local chiefs and sultans, and transporting supplies—including a disassembled steam launch—were continuing problems.

Marchand and his party finally reached Fashoda on July 10, 1898, almost two years after he had landed on the African coast, and having covered some 4,000 miles. They found the fort in disastrous condition. Under Marchand's direction, the place was put into shape. Not long after they were settled, Marchand's force of 120 Senegalese troops fought off an attempt of a Mahdist gunboat to travel up river past Fashoda. The French were ready to fight to the last man in the defense of Fashoda when a British flotilla arrived on September 19, 1898. General Kitchener had been dispatched to Fashoda immediately after the battle of Omdurman, with orders to remove the French. Fortunately for Marchand and his men, Kitchener, with two Sudanese battalions, a company of Cameron Highlanders, and five heavily armed gunboats, was not looking for a fight. When he arrived at Fashoda, he invited Marchand aboard his steamer to discuss the situation. Kitchener had the good sense to dress in an Egyptian uniform so as not at agitate Marchand. Over champagne, Kitchener informed Marchand he must leave Fashoda. Marchand refused until he communicated with his government. Kitchener agreed, and leaving a contingent of troops behind, he sailed back to Omdurman.

Marchand was soon called to Cairo and given the bad news from Paris: Fashoda was to be surrendered to the British. Negotiations at a later date between the two governments firmly settled the British presence in the Sudan and the France in the Congo*. Marchand, who was hailed by the French people as a national hero, never mentioned the name Fashoda again in his lifetime. The stand-off at Fashoda, a significant confrontation in the European imperialist rivalry for control of the Upper Nile Valley, almost brought the British and French to the brink of war. But the French government realized Fashoda could not be held by Marchand

and his men, and France was not in a position to go to war with Great Britain. (Robert Collins and Robert Tignor, *Egypt and the Sudan*, 1967; David L. Lewis, *The Race to Fashoda*, 1987.)

Amanda Pollock

FEDERAL COUNCIL OF AUSTRALASIA. In the late nineteenth century the European competition for colonies, especially the growing French and German presence in the Southwest Pacific, caused great concern among the people of New South Wales*, Queensland, Victoria*, Tasmania, and South Australia* in Australia, as well as New Zealand* and Fiji*, all of which were British colonies. Fear of the designs of Germany and France created a desire for some type of unification in the region, and in 1883 representatives from six of the colonies (South Australia, Tasmania, Victoria, Queensland, Western Australia, and Fiji) formed the Federal Council of Australia to discuss matters of common concern. New Zealand and New South Wales did not send representatives. Britain legalized the council in 1885, and representatives met yearly until 1899. Although a few delegates tried to implement a real political federation, their efforts were stillborn. Ethnic differences with Fiji were too great; New South Wales and New Zealand did not participate; and the vast distances between the colonies made federation difficult. Although the Federal Council of Australasia ceased to exist after the 1899 meeting, it did help stimulate the federation movement in Australia, which reached fruition in 1900. (H. E. Egerton, ed., *Federations and Unions within the British Empire*, 1924.)

FEDERAL ISLAMIC REPUBLIC OF THE COMOROS. See Comoros Islands.

FEDERATED MALAY STATES. Hoping to impose some political unity on the formerly independent sultanates of Perak*, Selangor*, Negri Sembilan*, and Pahang* on the Malay Peninsula, Great Britain established the Federated Malay States in 1895. They had a British resident-general and a form of central government. In 1945 the Federated Malay States became part of the Malayan Union. See MALAYSIA.

FEDERATED STATES OF MICRONESIA. On July 12, 1978, the United Nations sponsored a special election in several districts of the Trust Territory of the Pacific Islands*, a United States territory. The Trust Territory of the Pacific Islands had been created after World War II, and although both the United States and the United Nations preferred to see the trust territory evolve into a single nation state, the internal ethnic differences and vast distances between the various islands were simply too great. In 1975 representatives from most of the islands drew up a constitution under United Nations supervision, but the Northern Marianas Islands decided not to become part of the new nation, remaining instead in commonwealth status with the United States. The Marshall Islands* decided to separate from the rest of the Pacific Islands, becoming the Independent Republic of the Marshall Islands on May 10, 1979, as did the island of Palau*, becoming the Republic of Palau on January 1, 1981.

What remained of the Trust Territory of the Pacific Islands were the Caroline Islands*, except for Palau. The main islands were Yap, Truk, Ponape, and Kosrae. On May 10, 1979, they became known as the Federated States of Micronesia. The state of Yap consisted of four major islands, nine inhabited atolls, two inhabited smaller islands, and four uninhabited islands. The state of Truk had more than 300 individual islands, forty of which are inhabited. Ponape consisted of the volcanic island of Ponape and eight coral atolls. Finally, the state of Kosrae was made up of Kosrae, Ualang, and fourteen small islets. The population of the Federated States of Micronesia was just under 80,000 people in 1987. (John Wesley Coulter, *The Pacific Dependencies of the United States*, 1957; Barrie MacDonald, "Current Developments in the Pacific: Self-Determination and Self-Government," *Journal of Pacific History*, 17, January 1982, 51–61.)

FEDERATION OF RHODESIA AND NYASALAND. In the 1940s, as a means of maintaining white supremacy in the British colonies of central Africa, broadening the economic base of Southern Rhodesia by gaining access to the copper mines of Northern Rhodesia, and attracting investment money away fron South Africa*, a movement for the unification of Southern Rhodesia, Northern Rhodesia, and Nyasaland* emerged among European colonists. Initial discussions about the amalgamation of the two Rhodesias began during World War II.*. Godfrey Martin Huggins, prime minister of Southern Rhodesia from 1933–1953, led the unification movement, as did Roy Welensky, a trade union leader in Northern Rhodesia. Black Africans, especially the Nyasaland African Congress, bitterly opposed the federation because they were convinced it was designed to maintain white control over a broad area by extending the power of Southern Rhodesian whites.

A series of conferences between 1948 and 1952 hammered out details of the arrangement. In April 1952 a London conference, without the Nyasalanders, drafted a federal constitution for the region. Despite the opposition of the Nyasaland African Congress and some tribal chiefs, the imperial parliament approved the scheme in April 1953. Thus, the Federation of Rhodesia and Nyasaland was founded on the racial separation of eight million Africans from 200,000 Europeans living between the Limpopo River and Lake Tanganyika. The Federation of Rhodesia and Nyasaland was popularly known as the Central African Federation. Each of the three territories maintained its own administrative institutions and responsibility over internal matters. Godfrey Huggins served as prime minister from 1953 to 1956, and Roy Welensky succeeded him and served from 1956 to 1963.

The Central African Federation was inherently unstable politically. Africans north of the Zambezi River hated it and the English parliament became increasingly sympathetic with the idea of African political development in the late 1950s and early 1960s. The Monckton Commission, set up in 1959 to study the situation, recommended giving the individual territories the right to secede, and in 1962 parliament agreed. The Central African Federation was dissolved in 1963 when African nationalists in Northern Rhodesia (Zambia*) and Nyasaland (Malawi) voted for secession and independence. Great Britain awarded both of them independence in 1964. See NYASALAND; RHODESIA; ZAMBIA.

FERDINAND OF ARAGÓN. Ferdinand II of Aragón was born March 10, 1452, in Sos and died January 23, 1516. He was king of Aragon from 1479 to 1516, king of Sicily from 1468 to 1516, and king of Castile (as Ferdinand V, called the Catholic) from 1479 to 1504. As a result of his marriage to Isabella of Castile* in 1469, Ferdinand II was able to join the kingdoms of Aragón and Castile into what became modern Spain. Following Isabella's death in 1504, he was appointed regent of Castile for his daughter Juana. As king, Ferdinand II set upon a course to complete the *Reconquista*, the expulsion of the Muslim Moors from Europe, which he accomplished with the capture of Granada from the Moors in 1492. In 1493 he added Roussillon and Cerdagne to Spain under the Treaty of Barcelona with France. In 1504, during the Italian Wars of 1494–1559, he conquered the Kingdom of Naples, where he was proclaimed King Ferdinand III. Intending to strengthen Catholicism in Spain, Ferdinand and Isabella promulgated the Inquisition in Castile in 1480, and in 1492 they issued a decree banishing all Jews from Spain. They also increased the persecution of the Moors, forcing many of them to convert to Christianity.

Ferdinand's reign coincided with the discovery of the New World and the beginning of European colonization of the Americas. A sponsor, along with Isabella, of Christopher Columbus*, Ferdinand helped influence Spanish colonization to the extent that, by the middle of the sixteenth century, Spain controlled the Caribbean and the Gulf of Mexico, most of South and Central America, and a large portion of the southwestern North American continent. (Felipe Fernandez-Armesto, *Ferdinand and Isabella*, 1975; Denys Hay, *Europe in the Fourteenth and Fifteenth Centuries*, 1966.)

William G. Ratliff

FERRY, JULES FRANÇOIS CAMILLE. Jules Ferry, Republican prime minister of France on two occasions in the 1880s, was born in 1832. He descended from a long line of politically prominent middle class Lorrainers. An able student, he benefited when his family moved in 1850 from Strasbourg to Paris to facilitate their children's educations. Ferry studied law, economics, and history, and early in his career was numbered among the more prominent young attorneys in Paris. After a brief stint as a popular liberal Republican journalist, he was elected to parliament in 1869 (during the Second Empire) as a Radical Republican. Ferry's disinterest in colonial and imperial enterprise during the Second Empire presented a stark contrast to his active involvement while premier, especially during his second term, which lasted from February 1883 through March 1885.

During Jules Ferry's initial term (from September 1880 through November 1881) as Radical Republican premier, domestic interests superseded imperial matters. Although spending most of his energies on educational reform (the program upon which his reputation is primarily based), he found sufficient time to win legislative approval of the Republican program of civil and political liberties that conservative Monarchists had previously blocked. Only toward the end of Ferry's first premiership did the Tunisian imperial involvement assume significant proportions.

The surprising French military seizure of the Tunisian North African Regency (a European diplomatic creation designed to balance the interests of Britain, France and Italy in the region) by Jules Ferry's government in May 1881 initiated one of the more striking French colonial involvements during the Third Republic. He launched this preemptive "second step" to solidify French domination in face of a similar Italian threat to French Tunisian interests. Although domestic affairs had loomed larger than imperial matters, the Tunisian involvement became the political straw that drove Ferry's government from office. The first Ferry ministry fell in November 1881 when parliament failed to support his government's Tunisian policies.

The second Ferry ministry (from February 1883 through March 1885) witnessed a more active colonial involvement than the first. Initially, the successful acquisition of equatorial Africa, more precisely the Congo*, was an enterprise in which Ferry took great personal interest. He subsidized Pierre de Brazza's exploratory expeditions and supported France's subsequent claims by skillful diplomatic maneuvers against British, Belgian, and Portuguese objections. But in Madagascar*, Ferry lacked the personal interest he manifested in the Congo. Here a classical example of colonial momentum evolved, not by administrative policy from above but by local and regional bureaucratic, religious, and military pressures from below. Without clear ministerial planning and direction the "protectorate" forced on Madagascar in 1885 proved ineffective. In the case of French financial interests in the Suez Canal*, Ferry's personal concern in this matter, when given the added weight of Bismarck's support, succeeded against British imperial designs bent on removing French rights in Egypt*.

Together with his activities in Tunisia*, it was the creation of Indochina* that established Ferry's imperialistic reputation. The acquisition of Tonkin* and Annam* proved rich prizes despite their cost to France. Here the familiar imperial pattern repeated itself early in Ferry's second ministry. Once again old French claims were being reasserted by missionary groups, economic interests, an aggressive colonial administration, and a deeply involved military establishment. Such regional initiatives often predetermined Ferry's imperial alternatives. As was previously the case in Tunisia, the French Empire* in Southeast Asia expanded but the resulting military reverses finally brought Ferry's premiership to an end.

Premier Ferry's imperialistic reputation often rests on the legend that he followed a clearly defined program and that, furthermore, his primary imperialistic motivation came from pressures and inducements provided by special economic interests. According to such accounts his imperial scheme was a secret operation by which he built an empire without public support because he knew French voters considered imperialism a shameful, unpatriotic diversion from a policy of revanche which would force Germany to return the "lost provinces" of Alsace and Lorraine. More accurately, instead of consistently pursuing any clearly perceived imperial goals, Ferry stumbled along reacting to events and initiatives undertaken by others. Thus people on the spot, often autonomous missionaries and businessmen, and especially adventurous military officers, set in motion imperial activities that Ferry later approved. Furthermore, as to his motives, it should be noted that the New Imperialism of the 1870s and 1880s lacked fundamental economic goals. Indeed, French economic interests placed scarcely 10 percent of their overseas investments in French colonies and only enterprising bankers seemed to gain consistent profits from the colonies. A more positive motivating factor in this era and one that persisted in Ferry's case was his commitment to maintaining France's national and imperial prestige. Jules Ferry moved ahead of a disinterested French public opinion, for the parliaments which twice forced him from office eventually followed in his imperial footprints. Jules Ferry died in 1893. (E. Malcolm Carrol, *French Public Opinion and Foreign Affairs, 1870–1914*, 1931; Thomas F. Powers, *Jules Ferry and the Renaissance of French Imperialism*, 1966.)

                                                                          William T. Haynes

FEZZAN. Fezzan is the sparsely populated southern region of Libya*. Italy conquered much of Libya in 1911, driving the Ottoman Turks out of the area, and in 1919 separated Libya into three areas: the colonies of Tripolitania* and Cyrenaica* and the military district of Fezzan, which they called South Tripolitania. In 1934 they were rejoined again as the single colony of Libya. See LIBYA.

FIJI. In 1643 the Dutch navigator Abel Janszoon Tasman* was the first European to sail among the northeastern Fiji Islands. Captain James Cook* contacted the southernmost Fijis in 1774 and William Bligh, of "*Bounty*" notoriety, recorded other Fiji islands in 1789. British, French, and American sailors were soon landing there on whaling expeditions and to collect sandalwood. Missionaries followed, trying to win souls. With the passage of time Britain became dominant. The British Foreign Office considered Fiji a problem. Among native chiefs, such constant warfare raged that no "king" could permanently prevail, a condition that frustrated the British attempt to promote a secure local confederation. Problems with foreign white intruders loomed large too. Base characters and riffraff, adventurers anxious to exploit a world without law and order, arrived from New Zealand and Australia, bringing deadly diseases with them. Men who were debtors and without necessary capital were drawn to the Fijis by the lure of cheap land and labor to build plantations. To cope with these conditions, the British sought to "regularize" their position by appointing their first consul, W.T. Pritchard, in 1858.

The road to eventual British annexation proved to be a classic example of the undue impact of overzealous locals on colonial matters. Although the London foreign office emphasized a policy of native confederation, Pritchard pushed his own policy of native cession. For a year the foreign office sat on a native offer of cession which Pritchard had inspired and, after sending officials to Fiji to study his justifications, rejected them and finally dismissed him. But certain less manageable forces could not so easily be handled from London. The frontier mentality in Fiji persisted until, by 1870, the migration of Australian adventurers expanded into the "Fiji Rush." The intensification of earlier problems disturbed the foreign office because the intruders abused native land rights and increased the commercial marketing of native labor. Only annexation, London finally conceded, would give them the leverage necessary to bring such matters under control.

The official who expedited the annexation policy was the governor of New South Wales, Sir Hercules Robinson, whose powers were extended to Fiji. A strong advocate of annexation, Robinson insisted that cession be "unconditional." Most locals, incorrectly believing annexation would solve their serious social, political, and economic problems, acceded to Robinson's demands. Unconditional cession and annexation came in 1874 and, for a brief period, Robinson administered British imperial rule over its new crown colony through the offices of local senior officials.

In 1875 the foreign office selected the first locally based British governor of Fiji, the highly regarded Sir Arthur Gordon, known for his liberal outlook and his contributions to the techniques of colonial "indirect rule." Gordon designed the basic governing institutions for Fiji and all the British island possessions in the Western Pacific. He sought an efficient government to guarantee law, order, and commercial development. Specifically, Gordon's land policy attempted to preserve Fiji land for Fiji people; his tax policy allowed the natives to determine their own tax rules (though the governor's office collected all taxes); and his commercial policy focused on attracting Australian capital. One program of tragic consequence was the introduction of indentured Indian laborers into Fiji to work on European sugar plantations. Serious social and political results followed, and continue to the present day.

But liberalizing British imperial tendencies aimed at self-rule for colonial peoples have prevailed in Fiji. After World War II a legislative council comprised of 40 members was elected from communal and official rolls. Ethnically, council membership included 14 Fijians, 12 Indians, and 10 Europeans. Executive power rested in an executive Council presided over by the governor. The colonial office persisted in an attempt to reduce the longstanding practice of Fiji governmental ethnic separation which subsequently reduced Fijian initiative. By October 1970

the former Crown Colony of Fiji joined the British Commonwealth of Nations*
as an independent entity. That same year Fiji was accepted into the United
Nations. (Sir Alan Burns, *Fiji*, 1963; C. Hartley Grattan, *The Southwest Pacific
to 1900*, 1963.)

                                                                                                William T. Haynes

FIVE POWER PACT. Also known as the Naval Limitation Treaty, the Five
Power Pact was one of the major agreements negotiated at the Washington
Conference of 1921–1922*. In this treaty, the United States, Great Britain, Japan,
France, and Italy accepted the principal of naval arms limitations. In provisions
which applied to capital ships, then the backbone of all world fleets, the signatories agreed to a ratio of strength which had been worked out by the United
States based on the relative needs of each party. The ratio was 5:5:3:1.75:1.75,
which translated to 525,000 tons of battleships for the United States, 525,000
tons for Great Britain, 300,000 tons for Japan, 175,000 tons for France, and
175,000 tons for Italy. Battleship displacement was limited to 35,000 tons; gun
caliber to 16 inches. Although aircraft carriers were then in an early stage of
development, the signatories also agreed to accept the following limits: United
States and Great Britain, 135,000 tons each; Japan, 81,000 tons; France and
Italy, 60,000 tons each. On ships other than capital ships, on which no limitations
were accepted, gun caliber was not to exceed 8 inches. The only new capital
ship construction allowed was to replace ships then in service, and such new
ships had to be within the tonnage limitations specified in the treaty. And ships
then in service beyond the limitations had to be scrapped. In addition to the ship
limitations, as an assurance to Japan for accepting inferiority in relation to the
United States and Great Britain, the signatories pledged to maintain the status
quo in the Pacific in regard to fortifications and naval bases, with such exceptions
as specified in the treaty. Although the treaty was severely criticized during
World War II*, it was regarded as a major success at the time of its negotiations.
It was the first successful agreement of its kind and the only agreement to limit
armaments in the interwar period, despite the promise of the signatories of the
Treaty of Versailles of 1919* to limit land and sea armaments. It did stabilize
naval strength and avoided the danger and waste of a runaway naval arms race.
(Dexter Perkins, *Charles Evans Hughes and American Democratic Statesman-
ship*, 1953; J. Chalmers Vinson, *The Parchment Peace*, 1950.)

                                                                                                Joseph M. Rowe, Jr.

FLORIDA. See EAST FLORIDA.

FORMOSA. Ilha Formosa, meaning "beautiful isle," was the name given by
early Portuguese navigators to the island the Chinese and Japanese call Taiwan.
Steeply mountainous and lush, with jungle-clad cliffs dropping to the Pacific,
Formosa lies about ninety miles east of mainland China. The island is 240 miles
long, and about 80 miles wide, with a total area of approximately 13,000 square

miles. A high mountain range with peaks between 6,000 and 13,000 feet runs down the east side of the island, where there is no flat land at all. A fertile agricultural plain, about 20 miles wide, slopes down to the Straits of Formosa on the west. The capital, Taipei, is served by the port of Keelung (Chilung) 18 miles away on the north coast. The climate is damp and warm most of the year due to warm ocean currents, but winters in the northwest can bring freezing rain.

The original inhabitants were Malayo-Polynesians possibly related to the tribesmen of upland Luzon. They were driven to remote reaches of the island by Chinese invaders and are now called "aborigines." They number only 200,000, about one percent of the population, and face possible cultural extinction. The Chinese immigrants who displaced them beginning in the Ming Dynasty (Fukienese and Hakkas) are now called "Taiwanese." They number 16 million. In the late 1940s a new wave of two million people from all parts of China came across to Taiwan to escape the communists under Mao Zedong*. This group and their descendants, called "Mainlanders," dominate the political life of Taiwan.

Formosa was not mentioned by early Chinese historians and seemed an unexplored paradise to European traders and missionaries who made land in the sixteenth century, en route to Japan. Wild game abounded in deep forests. Spaniards established a small mission in the north but were driven out by the Dutch, who maintained a fort, Zelandia, on the east coast, until they, in turn, were expelled by a Chinese general and pirate known as Koxinga (Chinese name: Cheng Ch'eng-kung). The island then officially became part of China, a prefecture of Fukien province.

A perennial problem was that storms often drove ships onto the rocky coast of Formosa, where Western sailors were sometimes killed by aborigines or Chinese. For example, 43 hapless sailors of the wrecked British brig Ann were executed in 1842. Such abuses were ended by treaties imposed on China after her defeats in the Opium Wars. During the 1860s Formosa was opened to western traders and missionaries. The island might have been formally annexed by one of the European powers (the French bombarded Keelung in 1884 as part of their war for Tonkin) but a new, even more aggressive imperial power intervened: Japan attacked and defeated China and gained sovereignty over Formosa in the Treaty of Shimonoseki (1895). The island was ruled as part of the Japanese empire for the next fifty years.

The Japanese found it rough sledding at first. Taiwanese resistance was fierce. A "Republic of Taiwan" was proclaimed and the invaders had to subdue the people before they could occupy the island. Once the insurrectionists had been driven to the mountains, Japan developed Taiwan as a colonial appendage, after the European model. At first, the Japanese viewed the subtropical isle as a source of raw materials and agricultural products, but eventually they built roads and railroads, harbors and mines, factories and schools. The result was that Taiwan emerged from its imperial tutelage with the physical and demographic infrastructure for a modern economy. In contrast to the rest of Asia, where the Japanese are remembered chiefly for their brutality, Taiwanese of the older generation, many of whom speak some Japanese, think highly of the Japanese and now welcome them as tourists and investors.

During World War II* Taiwan was first a staging area for Japan's thrust into Southeast Asia; later a target of American bombers. Chinese rule was restored in 1945, but the Kuomintang was by then corrupt and in decline. Mistreatment of Taiwanese by Nationalist army officers led to an uprising in February 1947 that was bloodily suppressed. After Mao Zedong proclaimed the existence of the People's Republic of China in 1949, Chiang Kai-chek's Nationalist designated Taiwan "a province of the Republic of China." In the Shanghai Communique of 1972, the United States and China agreed that Taiwan was part of China, but that formula was so deliberately ambiguous that Taiwan's future is impossible to predict. Political power is passing from the older generals who came to the island in the 1940s to a younger generation of Taiwanese torn between their cultural ties to China and their desire to maintain their prosperity and relative freedom. (Ralph Clough, *Island China*, 1978.)

Ross Marlay

FORT-DAUPHIN. France established the outpost of Fort-Dauphin on the southern tip of Madagascar* in 1642 in hope of using the base as an entre into the Indian Ocean trade. Those hopes were never realized. Fort-Dauphin enjoyed trade only with the interior of southern Madagascar and served as a way station to India. Even the latter role was later eclipsed by the settlement at Reunion*. France abandoned the settlement in 1674 after repeated hostile attacks from indigenous Malagasy tribesmen. (David P. Henige, *Colonial Governors from the Fifteenth Century to the Present*, 1970.)

FORT WILLIAM. In 1690 the British East India Company* established a factory on the site of present-day Calcutta. In 1700 the company raised its status to that of a presidency and named the political entity Fort William. The company struggled with the Nawab of Bengal* for control of Fort William, but in 1757 company troops defeated him and took control of most of Bengal, of which Fort William was a part. See BENGAL; INDIA.

FOUR POWER TREATY. The Four Power Treaty was the first of the major agreements to emerge from the Washington Conference of 1921–1922*. In this treaty, the United States, Great Britain, Japan, and France promised to respect each other's rights and territorial possessions in the Pacific Ocean. If controversies did arise between the signatories relative to their Pacific possessions, they promised to negotiate such differences. And if aggression by other powers threatened the possessions of the signatories, they agreed to "communicate with one another fully and frankly in order to arrive at an understanding as to the most efficient measures to be taken, jointly or separately, to meet the exigencies of the particular situation.'' The treaty also provided that upon ratification, the alliance between Great Britain and Japan (renewed in 1911) would terminate. This provision was a major objective of the United States in order to preclude the danger that war with Japan would require Great Britain to support her Asian ally. (J. Chalmers Vinson, *The Parchment Peace*, 1950.)

Joseph M. Rowe, Jr.

FOUTA DJALLON. The Fouta Djallon is a mountainous highland area with elevations up to 4,500 feet in what is today the Republic of Guinea*, in West Africa. It is the source of three major rivers—the Niger, the Gambia, and the Senegal—as well as several smaller ones. It is historically significant as the area in which Fulani people established a major Muslim state, Fouta Djallon, in the early eighteenth century. The state survived until its conquest by the French in the late 1880s. The Fulani established control over a mostly non-Muslim population in Fouta Djallon by launching a holy war, or *jihad*. Their success inspired other *jihads* against existing states in western Africa, most notably the jihad of Usuman dan Fodio in Hausaland. (W. McGowan, ''Fula Resistance to French Expansion into Futa Jallon, 1889–1896,'' *Journal of African History*, 22, 1981, 245–61.)

Charles W. Hartwig

FRENCH AND INDIAN WAR. By the end of the seventeenth and beginning of the eighteenth centuries, the English and French empires in North America were on a collision course. The British colonies were poised for expansion west into the Ohio Valley, while French fur traders were ready to move south into the same area. The fighting began between the Virginians and the French in the Ohio Valley in 1754; and the French were generally successful in the early stages of the war. On May 18, 1756, England declared war on France. The conflict became known as the Seven Years' War in Europe and the French and Indian War in America. When William Pitt* assumed control of the British government in December 1756, he decided to eliminate France from the New World. Only then would England be able to achieve its mercantilist aims of securing a permanent source of raw materials and opening new markets for her goods.

The attack began in earnest in 1758, and in July the English conquered Louisbourg*, cutting Canada's supply line to France. Small in population and limited in resources, French Canada* could not resist the English onslaught without reinforcements and supplies. The French made alliances with most of the Indian tribes, the Iroquois being the notable exception, but even then the British drove them out of their forts in the Ohio Valley and the lake region of New York. By 1759 the English general James Wolfe had begun the siege of Quebec, which was defended by the Marquis de Montcalm. Using brilliant tactics, Wolfe attacked and defeated the French at Quebec in September 1759, breaking the back of the French empire in the New World. The French army in Canada surrendered to the British in September 1760. Because of the conflict in Europe and elsewhere in the world, formal peace did not arrive until 1763, but in that year the Treaty of Paris* gave England title to all of Canada and all territory east of the Mississippi River. The French also ceded Louisiana to Spain. Except for French Guiana*, the islands of Guadaloupe* and Martinique* in the Caribbean, and St. Pierre and Miquelon in the North Atlantic, the French empire in the New World no longer existed. (W. J. Eccles, *France in America*, 1976; Howard H. Peckham, *The Colonial Wars, 1689–1762*, 1964)

FRENCH ANTILLES. The French Antilles included the islands of Guadeloupe*, Martinique*, part of St. Christopher* until 1702, St. Croix* to 1733, Desirade*, Marie Galante*, Grenada*, and a number of smaller islands. Although the islands were governed in a number of individual and group arrangements over the years, France treated them as a single administrative unit beginning in 1667. The French Antilles had a single governor-general from 1667 until their capture by the British in 1759. When they were returned to France in 1762 the governor-generalcy was not re-established. It was reconstituted in 1768 but abolished in 1774. (David P. Henige, *Colonial Governors from the Fifteenth Century to the Present*, 1970.)

FRENCH COLONIAL EDUCATION. The educational system known as *école des chefs* (schools for chiefs' sons) in French Africa was first initiated in the territory of Upper-Senegal-Middle-Niger when General Faidherbe founded in Saint Louis (Senegal*) an *école des otages* to which recently pacified African chiefs were requested to send their elder sons. The experiment lasted only 18 years (1854–1872). The duties of the school were then taken over by ordinary primary schools until it resumed its activities under the name of *école des chefs* (1893). Following the three decrees of 1903, organizing education in French West Africa*, the St. Louis school was granted the same status as a metropolitan teachers' training college: students, hand-picked from leading Wolof families, were divided into two streams, educational and administrative. This plan fulfilled one of the aims set by French colonial ideologists to create a local and Frenchified elite for middle-rank positions in the various administrations fostered by the direct rule system. Since chiefs were often reluctant to send their sons to faraway boarding schools, they used to substitute them with slave boys, who later profited from this unexpected social promotion to the detriment of their ''benefactors.'' Post-colonial African ruling elites have usually sprung from such a stock.

In 1906, in recognition of the students' Muslim culture, the St. Louis school was renamed a *médersa* (Koranic school), along with ''Franco-Arabian'' schools in Timbukto*, Djenne, and Boutilmit (Mauritania*). Although their mission was to train interpreters, judges, and clerks for the Muslim judiciary, the experiment was brought to an end in 1922 under the pressure of the powerful Catholic missions. Until independence, the St. Louis school (relocated in Gorée and finally in Sibikitane) grew as an institution cast in the French Republican and non-confessional mold, to become the well-known École Normale William Ponty. Entrance took place after advanced primary education and studies lasted three years. From 1918 to 1923, following the creation of High Commission for Primary Education, similar schools were to be established throughout French West Africa and French Equatorial Africa*, as well as the former German colonies of Togo* and Cameroon*. Each school consisted of three sections, the first one reserved for the chiefs' sons. In addition William Ponty provided for the training of paramedical staff. Significantly, such an assimilatory and elite-making policy was more forcefully deployed in French West Africa than in French Equatorial Africa where, in spite of the 1903 law prohibiting religious congregations from managing public schools, education was left in the hands of mission stations (the 1925 decree organizing education in the French Equatorial Africa was never fully implemented: the capital city, Brazzaville, got her school only in 1935). It is ironic that the French Third Republic, so adamant on the democratic right to popular education, cultivated in its African colonies an elitist system. (Paul Désalmand, *Histoire de l'éducation en Côte d'Ivoire*, 1986.)

Philippe-Joseph Salazar

FRENCH COLONIAL IDEOLOGY. French writers occupy a specific position with regard to the development of the French colonial doctrine (1880–1930). As such their productions form a "literary field" (P. Bourdieu). Firstly, between Fromentin (1820–1876: *Un Eté dans le Sahara*, 1857; *Une Année dans le Sahel*, 1859) and A. Gide (1869–1951: *Voyage au Congo*, 1927; *Le Retour du Tchad*, 1929), French literature assimilated the colonial outer world by slowly transforming a specific literary code, the travelogue, into a literary genre which fusioned autobiography and exploration. The discovery of the inner regions of the self (sexual drives mostly) accompanied that of exotic and colonial lands, revealing in the process how the French mind apprehended its colonial experience. This was strikingly expressed by E. Psichari (1883–1914) in *Terres de soleil et de sommeil* (1908) which may be read as a psycho-analysis of the French colonial vision. Secondly, in the case of P. Loti (1850–1923: *Le Roman d'un Spahi*, 1881), A. de Gobineau (1816–1882: *Nouvelles Asiatiques*, 1876) and V. Segalen (1878–1919: *Les Immémoriaux*, 1907), the writer's projection onto the colonial African or Oriental map takes the form of a nostalgic meditation on the transience of culture, if not of an understated denunciation of European civilization: the imperialist enterprise is envisioned as an opportunity to reflect on the necessary decay of social, artistic, and religious beliefs. To a large extent it serves as a pretext for the writer to investigate the limits of his own endeavor. Thirdly, this "narcissistic" approach rapidly found its paradigm in a new literary language. R. Roussel (1877–1933) treats Africa as a metaphor of literary invention: his *Impressions d'Afrique* (1910) and *Nouvelles impressions d'Afrique* (1932) make use of Africa and the stock of narrative cliches bequeathed by colonialism to unveil most of the techniques of the "nouveau roman". In this case the hermeneutic function of the colonial experience is stretched to its limits. Fourthly, some writers transferred to the colonial reality methods and ideas elaborated by the realist and naturalist schools (G. Flaubert and E. Zola): either they applied their social critique to a new field, the colonial society, like A. Londres (1884–1932: *Terre d'ébène*, 1924), who denounced servile and forced labor, and the Belgian abolitionist L. Demer (*L'Esclave*, 1906), or they fell in line with the official Republican vision of colonization as the furthering of the French Revolution with other means, and produced a steady stream of novels celebrating this policy (L. Bertrand, *Le Sang des races*, 1899, *La Cina*, 1901; L. Noir, *Prisonnieres au Dahomey*, 1892; also the Belgian cartoonist L. Herge, *Tintin au Congo*, 1929). In these conditions it is significant that literature as a critical discourse of colonial imperialism (mainly in Africa) resulted in the development of the "new ethnology," which questioned the necessity of colonialism from a vantage point neither determined by a literary tradition nor an ideology. (M. Leiris, *L'Afrique fantôme*, 1934). (A. Buisine ed., *L'Exotisme*, 1988; W. B. Cohen, *Francais et Africains*, 1980; L. Fanoudh-Siefer, *Le mythe du negre et de l'Afrique noire*, 1980.)

Philippe-Joseph Salazar

FRENCH COMMUNITY. The *Loi-Cadre*, passed by the French parliament in 1956, dissolved French West Africa* and French Equatorial Africa* and constituted a giant step toward self-government for France's African colonies. Representatives from the African colonies attended the Bamako Conference in September 1957 in the French Sudan and expressed their desire for complete self-government along with a continuation of a special relationship with France, especially if economic assistance might be forthcoming. In 1958, the constitution of the Fifth Republic was submitted to the people of France and the overseas territories for rejection or ratification. It abandoned the old French Union in favor of a new French Community, which was a loose federation of self-governing nation states. Charles de Gaulle strongly supported the idea and traveled widely throughout the colonies prior to the referendum. All of the French colonies, except French Guinea, approved the new constitution of the Fifth French Republic. (Stewart Easton, *The Twilight of European Colonialism*, 1981.)

FRENCH CONGO. French Congo (today, the People's Republic of the Congo, also called Congo-Brazzaville) was a French colonial possession located in western equatorial Africa north of the Congo River. The mouth of the Congo River was discovered in 1484 by the Portuguese explorer, Diego Cao. The Portuguese, Dutch, English, and French—all interested in ivory and slaves—made frequent stops there in the seventeenth and eighteenth centuries. Later the coastal region near the Congo served as a base for French ships engaged in fighting the slave trade. No serious penetration of the interior was made by Europeans until the nineteenth century.

In 1875 Pierre Savorgnan de Brazza, starting out from Libreville on the Gabon* coast, began the first of three explorations of the hinterland for France. On his second expedition, Brazza reached the Congo River and signed a treaty (September 1880) with Makoko, chief of the Bateke tribe, placing the north shore of the river under the protection of the French and blocking the attempt by Henry M. Stanley to secure the area for King Leopold of Belgium. As a result of agreements made at the Berlin West Africa Conference of 1884–85*, boundary questions between the French Congo and Leopold's Congo Free State were settled and French claims to the region were formally recognized. Brazza was appointed commissioner of the French Congo in 1886, and in that position he was known as a friend of the African people. Brazza's dismissal in 1898 came about primarily because his ''negrophile'' policy was regarded by powerful interests as an obstacle to the exploitation of the area.

In 1899 the French government granted large monopoly concessions to companies that ruthlessly sought to extract ivory and rubber from the Congo basin. Lack of government supervision and control over the concessionary-companies regime led to widespread suffering and misery among the native Africans, who were forced to labor under conditions of extreme cruelty for little or no pay. After World War I*, France used African labor to build the Congo-Ocean Railroad at a cost of at least 14,000 African lives.

French Congo became known as Middle Congo (Moyen-Congo) in 1903, and in 1910 it was joined with several other colonies in the area to form the federal organization known as French Equatorial Africa. The Congo town of Brazzaville was made the capital of the federation. During the crisis of World War II*, the governor-general of the FEA federation, Felix Eboue, a Guyanese French Negro, rallied the people of the region to back the Free French movement. FEA loyalty was rewarded in 1944 at a Brazzaville conference which helped establish a new colonial policy in response to rising African nationalism. The end result of the conference was the achievement of greater freedom and self-government in the French colonies of sub-Sahara Africa.

In 1946 Middle Congo was designated an overseas territory of France with representation in the French parliament and with an elected territorial assembly of its own. France further accelerated the progress of Middle Congo toward autonomy with the enactment of the *Loi-Cadre** (Enabling Act) of June 1956, which expanded the electorate to include all adult Congolese and increased the powers and authority of the territorial assembly. In 1958 Middle Congo became the Republic of Congo and an autonomous member-state within the French Community. Full independence was achieved on August 15, 1960. (Maurice N. Hennessy, *The Congo: A Brief History and Appraisal*, 1961; Gordon C. McDonald, *Area Handbook for the People's Republic of the Congo*, 1971; Richard West, *Congo*, 1972.)

Joseph L. Michaud

FRENCH CREOLE. French creole is spoken on the islands of Reunion*, Mauritius*, Rodriques, and the Seychelles* in the Indian Ocean. It is the most noticeable linguistic outcome of a two-fold policy of settlement by French immigrants and African slaves deported from Senegal*, Guinea*, and Madagascar* (first in Reunion, then called Ile Bourbon, 1665; Mauritius, then known as Ile de France, 1721; the Seychelles, 1770; Rodriques, 1792). The process of creolization enfolded geographically, gaining greater momentum with two waves of emigration to the Seychelles during the French Revolution (overpopulation and political deportations). From a sociolinguistic viewpoint, the French settlers, already speakers of dialectal French (Norman in most cases), found themselves isolated from a French-speaking milieu, thus triggering the creolization process. Furthermore, in Reunion, European families withdrew to the Highlands, ("Hauts"), following an agricultural recession in the eighteenth century and the abolition of slavery in the nineteenth century. African, Malagasy, and Indian immigration (Mauritius, 1834) accelerated and completed the process, making French Creole a language no longer essentially used by original French speakers.

In fact, the French West Indies Company practiced the "seasoning" of slaves: Creole-speaking slaves were put in charge of newly arrived labor forces, teaching them the language. Although slaves from the Caribbean creolophone areas were imported by the company to perform the same task, there is little evidence that both groups of Creoles are historically related. This complex history explains why colonization, far from imposing French as a medium, fostered a highly original human community in the Indian Ocean: had settlements taken place during the heyday of French Republican imperialism, its aggressive linguistic policy would have impeded the formation of a Creole language. In many respects Creole is the remnant of "Ancien Regime" type of colonization. Creole falls at present in the following social categories: In Rodrigues it is the only spoken language (endogamous society, no immigration). In Mauritius, as a vehicular language it competes with Indian Creole among the working class, with Indian languages for cultural and religious reasons, while upper-middle class speakers consider it of a status inferior to French and English. In the Seychelles, perceptions distinguish between "créole fin," spoken by the bourgeoisie, "gros créole," spoken by peasants and poors in urban areas, and an artificial Creole used by the media. Finally, Reunion presents the classic case of linguistic diglossia, Creole and French cohabiting in a continuum from acrolect (upper class language) to basilect (lower class) through mediolects (intermediary ways of speaking).

The complexity of creolophone society came to the fore when colonization was questioned. Opposition parties accused the colonizers of ignoring Creole, seen as the language of the people, although linguistic evidence shows that diglossia does not recede once Creole is granted official status. In the Seychelles, Creole is perceived as a sign of ethnic authenticity. In Reunion, liberation movements prefer Creole to French, as the language of the oppressed to that of the oppressors, although creolophones belong to all social strata. In pluralistic Mauritius, the left-wing opposition promotes French (and Indian) Creole as a binding element to a plurilingual community. In Reunion nearly all political parties, including the local communist movement, agree on the "universality" of French as opposed to the parochiality of Creole: Creolophone intellectuals either emphasize that Creole, just as French, is part of the Francophone community or try to eradicate from Creole all French traces. (R. Chaudenson, *Les créoles francais*, 1979; J. C. Carpanin Marimotou, "Créolisation, créolité, littérature", *Cuisines/Identités*, 1988.)

Philippe-Joseph Salazar

FRENCH EMPIRE. The French empire had its beginnings in the voyages of Jacques Cartier* who, in search of the fabled Northwest Passage* to Asia, discovered the St. Lawrence River in North America. France followed up on the Cartier voyage in 1608 when Samuel de Champlain* established the settlement of Quebec* in what is today Canada*. Subsequent journeys by such other French explorers as Pere Marquette, Louis Joliet*, and Sieur de La Salle* established the French claim to the Mississippi River and the vast area that came to be known as the Louisiana* Territory in what is today the American Midwest. While the colonies in North America were developing, France also projected itself in the Caribbean in the 1630s and 1640s, establishing colonies on the islands of Martinique*, Guadeloupe*, St. Martin, and Santo Domingo, which developed into fabulously wealthy sugar plantations. Although France had not prevailed against the Portuguese in its struggle for Brazil*, the small colony of French Guiana* was retained. France also established itself in Asia with outposts in India*, like the one at Pondicherry, and naval posts in the Indian Ocean following the seizure of Mauritius* in 1715 and the Seychelles* in 1758. There was also the small Sakalava protectorate in Madagascar* and a few outposts on the Guinea* coast of West Africa.

But the first French empire reached its apogee in the 1750s, after which a steady decline set in. The Seven Years' War with Great Britain doomed much of the empire. In the Treaty of Paris of 1763*, France lost all of Canada to England and with that loss her presence in North America. The Napoleonic Wars of the 1790s and early 1800s were just as disastrous. England seized the Seychelles in 1794 and in 1814 France ceded Mauritius to the English. The slave revolt of Toussaint l'Ouverture* on Santo Domingo in 1798 resulted in the loss of the island to the independence movement, and in 1803, to raise cash to fight his war with Great Britain, Napoleon sold the Louisiana Territory to the United States. The first French empire was all but dead.

France soon began rebuilding its lost empire in the nineteenth century. To reestablish itself in the Indian Ocean, France seized the Comoros Islands* in 1843, and to gain a presence on the Red Sea and access to Suez, France established outposts in 1856 at Ambabo and Obock, in what became French Somaliland. Beginning in the 1830s, France established its presence in north Africa, occupying Algiers and other points on the Barbary Coast. Anxious to find an economical way of penetrating the China trade, France moved into Indochina* in the 1850s and 1860s, eventually establishing colonies in Tonkin*, Annam*, Cochin-China*, Laos*, and Cambodia*. In the latter part of the nineteenth century, France expanded her presence in Africa, the Indian Ocean, and the Pacific. French West Africa* and French Equatorial Africa* gave France much of West Africa, while the Sakalava protectorate evolved into a full-fledged colony on Madagascar. In the Pacific, France established colonies on New Caledonia*, the Marquesa Islands*, and Tahiti. The French empire reached its peak after World War I when the League of Nations* gave France mandates over the former Turkish protectorates in Syria* and Lebanon*.

By that time the winds of change were already blowing, and they would soon spell the demise of all the European empires, including that of France. World War II devastated France, politically and economically, and marked the beginning of the end of the empire. When France fell to Germany in 1940, Japanese troops marched unimpeded into Indochina. When the war was over, France was in no position to defend her global empire. The Fourth French Republic created the French Union* in 1946 and began extending autonomy to many colonies, declaring the Africans citizens of France and giving them representation in the French parliament. A number of the colonies became overseas territories of France. Although France returned to Indochina in 1945, she soon found herself embroiled in a bloody struggle against Ho Chi Minh* and his guerrilla troops, the Vietminh. In 1954, at the Battle of Dien Bien Phu*, the guerrillas defeated French troops and the Geneva convention that year gave independence to Vietnam*, Laos, and Cambodia.

In 1956 the French parliament passed the *Loi-Cadre*, or Enabling Act, which dissolved French West Africa and French Equatorial Africa in favor of the French Community*, a loose confederation of former colonies. By that time France was in another bloody colonial war in Algeria. That too ended in victory and independence for Algeria. Morocco and Tunisia* were also successful in breaking their ties to France. Independence soon came for Mauritania*, Mali*, Chad*, Guinea, Niger*, Togo*, Benin, Ivory Coast*, Upper Volta* (Burkina Faso) Cameroon*, Gabon*, the Central African Republic*, Madagascar*, and Senegal*. The Comoros Islands became independent in 1975. Except for small island outposts in the North Atlantic, the Caribbean, the Indian Ocean, and the Pacific, along with French Guiana, the French empire was dead. (Herbert Ingram Priestly, *France Overseas. A Study of Modern Imperialism*, 1966.)

FRENCH EQUATORIAL AFRICA. French Equatorial Africa (FEA) included Gabon*, Middle Congo, Ubangi-Shari, and Chad*. Today they are the independent countries of Gabon, the People's Republic of the Congo, the Central African Republic, and Chad. Its territory included 967,000 square miles of land and extended from the Atlantic coast of west Africa to the southern Sahara region of central Africa. Through centuries of contact with Berbers and Arabs, the region came under the influence of Islamic religious and cultural values. Portuguese sailors reached the area in the 1470s, and slave traders and Catholic missionaries were not far behind. Until the early 1800s, however, the only Europeans who remained on the coast were slave traders supplying colonies in North America, the Caribbean, and Brazil.

French interest in the region began when French priests established missions at Loango in 1645 and then at Bakongo in 1760. But in the early 1800s, when both France and Great Britain began working to abolish the slave trade, French interest in the region became more intense. France signed several treaties in 1839 with local chiefs for land on the estuary of the Gabon river. After annihilating Mpongwe tribal resistance, French navy officers founded Libreville in 1849. By 1862 France was in control of most of the coastal area.

The failure of several maritime and naturalist exploratory expeditions between 1862 and 1873 motivated the journeys of Pierre Savorgnan de Brazza on the Ogooue and the Congo rivers. On September 30, 1880, in exchange for French "protection," Makoko, chief of the Batiké tribe, ceded to France the northern bank of Congo*. On November 21, 1882, Brazza was appointed the commissioner for the Republic of French Congo*. Treaties with Portugal (1885) and Congo Free State (1887 and 1892) defined the French authority on the Niari and Oubangui rivers. The Berlin West Africa Conference of 1884–1885* established boundaries for French claims, German Kamerun, and the Congo Free State. By 1891 France had consolidated its control over Gabon and Ubangi-Shari. In the north, the Crampel (1890) and the Maistre missions (1893) led to the protectorate treaty between the Chadian sultan of Baguirmi and the Gentil mission in 1897. After the Fashoda crisis of 1898, France and Great Britain determined the eastern boundary of the French sphere of influence in Africa. The destruction of the Rabah empire in 1900 and the protectorate agreement with Kanem sealed French control from Gabon's coast to Ubangi-Shari and Chad. In return for German recognition of French rights and interests Morocco* in 1911, France ceded 100,000 square miles of its Congo territory to German Kamerun.

Despite Brazza's opposition, France created a corporate concession economy in the region, a monopolistic *cueillette entreprise* of 42 companies, in return for a modest rent and 15 percent of the profits realized. The companies were completely unregulated and notorious for exploiting native Africans. The concessionary exploitation of natural resources by the use of forced labor, combined with heavy taxation of the natives and the frequent recruitment of porters, caused enormous resentment and a local depression. The decline of rubber prices precipitated a crisis of the concessionary system. In 1910 France eliminated some of the worst abuses by imposing restrictions on the companies, at the same time consolidating the colonies into a new administrative unit—French Equatorial Africa. Gabon and Congo had been administratively united in 1888, and in 1891 France had begun calling the region French Congo. But in 1910 French Equatorial Africa came into being, composed of three colonies—Gabon, Middle Congo, and Ubangi-Shari. Chad did not gain separate colonial status until 1914.

During World War II French Equatorial Africa repudiated Nazi aggression and the Vichy government and pledged allegiance to Charles de Gaulle and the Free French forces. When the constitution of the Fourth French Republic extended new rights to the colonies, the four colonies of French Equatorial Africa became overseas departments of France with representation in the French national assembly. They were part of the French Union*. But the forces of nationalism rendered those arrangements only temporary. In 1946 Jean Felix Tchikaya founded the *Parti Progressiste Congolais* as the Middle Congo branch of the *Rassemblement Democratique Africain* (RDA). Another organization based on tribal origin was the twin party of the *Section Francaise de l'Internationale Ouvriere*, later named the *Mouvement Socialiste Africain* (MSA). The leader was Jacques Opangualt from northern Mboshi. In Chad, the French-dominated *Union Democratique Tchadienne* (UDT) appeared. Gabonese politics were dominated by two Fang politicians: Jean Aubame and Leon M'Ba. The Aubame-M'Ba antagonism was manifested in their respective creation of the *Union Democratique et Sociale Gabonaise* (UDSG) and the *Bloc Democratique Gabonais*. In Ubangi-Shari, Barthelemy Boganda founded the *Mouvement d'Evolution Sociale en Afrique Noire* (MESAN).

France was in no position to fight the budding nationalism. The debacle in Indochina* in 1954 and the bloody rebellion in Algeria* had doomed French imperialism, and in 1956 the *Loi-Cadre** expanded African political participation by providing for universal suffrage and autonomy for the African colonies "within the French Community." In 1958 the four colonies accepted the new French constitution and become self-governing entities in the new French Community*. French Equatorial Africa ceased to exist. Within a few years, all four of the former constituent members of French Equatorial Africa became independent republics. (Gwendolyn Carter Margaret, ed., *National Unity and Regionalism in Eight African States*, 1966; Virginia Thompson and Richard Adloff, *The Emerging States of French Equatorial Africa*, 1960.)

Said El Mansour Cherkaoui

FRENCH GUIANA. An overseas department of France, with a senator and deputy in the French parliament, French Guiana is located on the northeast coast of South America, between Surinam on the west and Brazil on the southeast. The Spanish explorer Vicente Pinzon first explored the coast of what became French Guiana in 1500. For over a century, European explorers went into the interior, searching for a fabled city of gold, but not until 1604 did a European colony appear. That year King Henry IV of France financed a settlement by La Touche de la Rivardiere, who founded the city of Cayenne. It was not until 1637 that French merchants sent permanent settlers there. The colony had a tenuous existence. Not only was the climate and geography inhospitable to European settlement, but Dutch and English privateers periodically attacked Cayenne.

Over the years France deported thousands of people and sent them to French Guiana, where most of them died of tropical diseases. The European population grew slowly, but plantation owners imported large numbers of West African slaves to fill labor needs. Until 1713 the Amazon River had been the boundary between French Guiana and Brazil, but the Treaty of Utrecht of 1713* moved the boundary nearly forty miles further north. Portugal seized the colony in 1809 but restored it to French control in 1817.

French Guiana became notorious after France established penal colonies there in 1852. The most infamous of them was the Ile du Diablo—Devil's Island. Incarceration at Devil's Island was tantamount to a death sentence since mortality rates among European convicts were so high. The prison, subject to world condemnation, was not abolished until 1945. A strong movement for independence never developed in French Guiana. The colony was always weak economically, dependent on France for money and supplies, and independence would have severed that economic lifeline. In 1848 France gave the Guianese citizenship and the right to vote. The colony gained representation in the French parliament in 1870, and in 1946 its political status was changed from a colony to a department, its status equal to that of an internal department of France. By 1980 the population of French Guiana was approximately 50,000 people. (John Hemming, *Red Gold. The Destruction of the Brazilian Indians, 1500–1760*, 1977; William Willis, *Damned and Damned Again*, 1959.)

FRENCH GUINEA. Beginning in the mid–1700s the Senegal Company, a French joint stock company*, began trading along the Guinea coast in West Africa. After more than a century of casual political relationships, France in 1850 began to negotiate treaties with local tribes and establish forts along the coast. In 1882 France formally established the colony of South Riviera, politically subordinate to Senegal*, with Jean-Marie Bayol serving as Lt. Governor. Throughout the 1880s French authority gradually extended deeper into the interior of what was known as Fouta Djallon,* expanding the size of South Riviera. In 1893 the name of South Riviera was changed to French Guinea, and the colony achieved separate status. French Guinea became a constituent part of French West Africa* in 1895. See FRENCH WEST AFRICA.

FRENCH INDIA. In 1642 French investors established the Oriental Indies Company to exploit trade with India*, and 26 years later a French factory was placed at Surat. The French colony at Pondicherry on the Coromandel coast south of Madras was founded in 1683. The French East India Company assumed the assets of the Oriental Indies Company in 1721 and soon established French outposts at Mahe on the Malabar coast, Yanam on the Orissa coast, and Karikal on the Coromandel coast. Other territorial acquisitions soon followed. By 1754 the French East India Company controlled an area of India larger than metropolitan France. But the Seven Years' War doomed the French presence in India. In the Treaty of Paris of 1763*, the victorious British stripped France of all her Indian possessions except the coastal enclaves of Pondicherry, Karikal, Yanam, Mahe, and Chandernagor. The French East India Company went bankrupt in 1769 and the five settlements were officially designated French India.

French India remained in existence for the next two centuries, but Indian independence from Great Britain in 1947 signaled the end of French colonial rule. France permitted a referendum election in Chandernagor in 1949, and the result was an overwhelming plurality for merger with India. France decided not to permit similar plebiscites in the other four territories, but in 1956 Pondicherry, Karikal, Yanam, and Mahe officials held their own elections with similar results. On May 28, 1956, they unilaterally merged with India, although France did not recognize the changed sovereignty until 1962. (Herbert Ingram Priestly, *France Overseas: A Study of Modern Imperialism*, 1938.)

FRENCH MEXICO. See MAXIMILIAN.

FRENCH POLYNESIA. French Polynesia consists of approximately 125 islands in the southeastern Pacific, scattered in the Society, Austral, Marquesa, Tuamotu, and Gambier Island groups of Polynesia*. More than fifty percent of the population of French Polynesia lives on Tahiti in the Society Islands. The Spanish explorer Ferdinand Magellan* reached the Tuamotu Islands in 1521, and 75 years later another Spanish captain—Alvarao de Mendana—discovered the Marquesa Islands. The English seafarer James Cook* came across the Austral Islands in 1768. In 1767 another English captain—Samuel Wallis—reached Tahiti and the Society Islands, and he was followed a year later by Louis-Antoine de Bougainville*, the French explorer. James Cook visited the Society Islands in 1769, 1773, and 1777.

In 1797 missionaries from the London Missionary Society landed at Tahiti, and by 1815 most of the islanders had accepted Christianity. The other islands in the southeast Pacific soon followed the lead of Tahiti in converting to Protestantism. In addition to religion and western trinkets, the Europeans also brought disease to the South Pacific. The Polynesians had no immunities to smallpox, scarlet fever, measles, dysentery, influenza, and venereal diseases, and the population declined dramatically, from 40,000 in 1600 to 8,000 in 1815 on Tahiti, and from 30,000 to 4,000 on the Marquesas.

France sent Roman Catholic missionaries to the islands in 1836, and when British Protestants had them expelled, a French naval expedition (1838) entered the harbor at Papeete, Tahiti. In 1842 France formally annexed the Marquesas and, in 1843, forced Tahitian rulers to sign an agreement establishing a French Protectorate of the Society Islands. Sporadic resistance from Tahitian natives was finally crushed in 1847. That protectorate lasted until 1880, when Tahiti was proclaimed a colony of France. France then formally annexed the Gambiers in 1881 and the Australs in 1900. Together they became known officially as *Etablissements Francais de l'Oceanie* (EFO) in 1903.

A strong nationalist movement did not come to French Polynesia until after World War II. In 1947 Marcel Pouvana'a a Oopa established the Tahitian People's Democratic Party and demanded more local autonomy and less French influence. By the 1950s Pouvana'a was demanding complete independence for

French Polynesia, but in a 1958 election, the majority decided to remain an overseas territory of France. Francis Sanford and John Teariki inherited Pouvana'a's political movement and carried it into the 1970s. In 1977 France granted autonomy to French Polynesia, allowing a Polynesian legislature to control all local affairs. The people of French Polynesia retained their French citizenship and the right to vote in national elections, as well as their right to send one senator to the French senate and two deputies to the national assembly. (David Howarth, *Tahiti: A Paradise Lost*, 1983; Colin Newbury, *Tahiti Nui: Change and Survival in French Polynesia, 1767–1945*, 1980; and Virginia Thompson and Richard Adloff, *The French Pacific Islands: French Polynesia and New Caledonia*, 1971.)

FRENCH-SIAMESE TREATY OF 1907. By a treaty signed on March 23, 1907, Siam* ceded to the French protectorate of Cambodia* the provinces of Battambang, Siem Reap, and Sisophon. In return, France restored to Thai control some much smaller territories it had seized shortly before. The real significance of this treaty was two-fold: for Cambodians, it restored the most important part of their once-great Khmer empire, especially the Siem Reap area with the supremely symbolic temples of Angkor Wat, which were—and remain—the focus of Cambodian nationalism. For Thais, the treaty represented an important milestone toward true international acceptance. The French agreed to a limited assertion of Thai jurisprudence over Indochinese subjects of France. Siam had barely escaped European colonization, and France, as a representative of European power, acknowledged in the 1907 treaty that Siamese reforms entitled that country to international legal protection. It was the beginning of the end for unequal treaties imposed on Siam.

Thai interest in the territories of northwest Cambodia did not cease, however; they pressed their Japanese allies in World War II* to give the territories once more to them, but this arrangement was quickly erased after 1945. In the 1980s the disputed frontier zone became a sanctuary where Thailand protected Khmer Rouge guerrillas fighting against a Vietnamese-supported government in Phnom Penh. (John F. Cady, *Southeast Asia: Its Historical Development*, 1964; D. G. E. Hall, *A History of Southeast Asia*, 1968.)

Ross Marlay

FRENCH SOMALILAND. See DJIBOUTI.

FRENCH SUDAN. See MALI.

FRENCH TOGO. See TOGO.

FRENCH UNION. The French Union grew out of realization that the post World War II era would produce significant changes in the relationship between France and its colonies. Its roots can be traced to declarations made at the

Brazzaville Conference in 1944 by De Gaulle's provisional government. These declarations were officially incorporated into the constitution of the Fourth Republic in Title Eight, Articles 60–104. While the general purpose of the French Union was to preserve French influence in Indochina*, its specific purpose was never clearly defined and agreed upon; not surprisingly, it ultimately failed to achieve anyone's objectives.

Postwar France simultaneously confronted problems of dealing with intense factional conflict between the communists, socialists, and Gaullists. Writing a new constitution to establish the Fourth Republic and devising a policy toward colonies pressing for independence was chaotic. Having had French domination broken by German and Japanese occupation, France's North African and Indochinese colonies were anxious to establish independence. Nationalists in Indochina, especially, hoped to establish independence before metropolitan France could resolve internal problems and again focus on its colonies.

Torn by internal dissent and denied the luxury of resolving domestic turmoil before addressing colonial questions, France adopted a series of stopgap measures aimed at patching over differences and buying time. French leftists wanted to restructure the French Empire* completely with independent former colonies affiliated with France in a manner similar to the British Commonwealth*. Gaullists, while recognizing the impossibility of "empire as usual," sought the minimum necessary appeasement of nationalist sentiment in the colonies and American opposition to European colonialism. Public officials were extremely reluctant to engage in anything more than temporizing incrementalism because there was no consensus of thought among metropolitian advocates of greater independence for French colonies.

In this environment, great latitude devolved upon colonial officials frequently representing the most conservative positions on colonial status. They wanted to permit limited increases in local autonomy and create the illusion of greater independence, while actually retaining for metropolitan France significant diplomatic, military, and economic authority. For example, High Commissioner Admiral d'Argenlieu successfully subverted the March 6, 1946, agreement between Ho Chi Minh* and Jean Sainteny, the delegate of the French provisional government, which recognized "the Republic of Viet Nam as a free state having its own government, parliament, army and treasury, and forming part of the Indochina Federation and the French Union."

Disorganization, diffusion of policymaking authority, and conflicting purposes produced confused and contradictory policies. For example, Article Eight of the new French constitution granted Indochina less autonomy than had already been granted under formal accords signed just after the war. While advocates of empire argued that too much had been given away, Indochinese nationalists correctly saw Article Eight as a step backward. Neither Vietnam's nominal Emperor Bao Dai nor Cambodia's Prince Norodom Sihanouk ratified membership in the French Union.

French officials underestimated the strength of nationalist sentiment and the determination of "natives" to achieve independence. They also systematically overestimated their ability to project French authority and penetrate their soon-to-be former colonies. The result was a series of failed political concessions and systematic military defeats culminating not at Dien Bien Phu*, France's most obvious military debacle, but with the ultimate loss of Algeria* and French colonies in North Africa. Ironically, France could have salvaged a semblence of the French Union had it been willing and able at the end of World War II to negotiate realistically and in good faith with nationalist leaders in Indochina and North Africa. However, confusion in France at the time and imperialist sentiment did not permit such rationality. Few imperialist nations realize that imperialism is self-defeating because it inevitably unleashes nationalist forces far greater than imperialist nations' containment capabilities. (Henri Grimal, *Decolonization: The British, French, Dutch and Belgian Empires, 1919–1963*, 1978; Ellen Hammer, *The Struggle for Indochina*, 1954; George Kelly, *Lost Soldiers: The French Army and Empire in Crisis, 1947–1962*, 1965.)

Samuel Freeman

FRENCH WEST AFRICA. French West Africa was the huge area in western Africa administered during the first half of the twentieth century by France as part of her colonial empire. Administrative headquarters for the territory, which officially existed from 1895 to 1958, was in Dakar, capital of present-day Senegal*. Stretching over 2,000 miles from the Atlantic Ocean to Lake Chad, the area comprised eight territories. These are now the independent African states of Benin, Burkina-Faso, Ivory Coast*, Guinea*, Mali*, Mauritania*, Niger*, and Senegal.

While a French company was granted a charter in 1624 by King Louis XIII to trade in Senegal, and trading posts such as St. Louis and Dakar were established on the coast of Senegal, the French did not seriously challenge the authority of the African states in the interior until the late 1800s. Numerous military campaigns were mounted by the French, who faced their toughest challenge when they engaged the forces of a remarkable Malinke leader named Samori Touré. Referred to by the French military as the "Napoleon of the Sudan," Samori was finally defeated in 1898.

Dakar became the headquarters of the governor-general for French West Africa in 1902, and a constitution for the "Federation of West Africa" was issued in 1904. In practice, the colony was directly ruled by French administrative officials, although in some areas, military authority was maintained until after 1945. In 1946 the eight territories became part of a federation within the French Union*. Citizenship was extended to the African inhabitants, although only limited numbers were allowed to vote. With the advent of the new French Fifth Republic in 1958, suffrage was extended to all Africans, in the French West African territories, which then voted with one exception to remain within a French Community*. French Guinea voted for immediate independence and became the Republic of Guinea in 1958. Senegal and the French Sudan united in a shortlived

Mali Federation in 1960, which split into independent Senegal and the Republic of Mali later in the same year. The five remaining former territories then asked for full independence, which was achieved by the end of 1960. (A. S. Kanya-Forstner, *The Conquest of the Western Sudan: A Study in French Imperialism*, 1969.)

Charles W. Hartwig

FROBISHER, MARTIN. Martin Frobisher was born about 1539 in Pontefract, Yorkshire, England, to a rural gentry family. His father died in 1545 and Frobisher went to live in London with his uncle, a merchant heavily invested in the African trade. In 1553 Frobisher sailed along the coast of West Africa, and after a number of other exploration voyages and military campaigns, he became a privateer. Frobisher met Sir Humphrey Gilbert* and decided to search for the Northwest Passage*. With financial backing from several investors, Frobisher sailed to Baffin Island in 1576. He thought that what was later termed Frobisher Strait was the Northwest Passage. He passed that news on to his backers when he returned to London, and they organized the Cathay Company, which financed two more Frobisher voyages in 1577 and 1578. He returned to London with nearly 1,400 tons of rock, which Frobisher thought could be processed to gold. The rocks were worthless and the voyages had failed to discover the Northwest Passage. Frobisher remained infatuated with the idea of the Northwest Passage for the rest of his life. Frobisher was knighted in 1588 for bravery in fighting against the Spanish Armada*. After being wounded in battle in France, Frobisher went back to England to recuperate but died on November 22, 1594. (William McFee, *The Life of Sir Martin Frobisher*, 1928; Vilhjalmur Stefansson, *The Three Voyages of Martin Frobisher*, 1938).

FUTUNA. See WALLIS AND FUTUNA.

G

GABON. The country of Gabon is a former French colony located on the west-central coast of Africa. The national government of Gabon is presently dominated by an ethnic group known as the Fang, a people whose warriors were once the most feared in the region. The Portuguese were the first Europeans to sight Gabon in 1470. They soon established permanent outposts near the mouth of the Ogooue River. Portuguese missionaries, followed by French Jesuits, came to Gabon to convert Africans to Christianity. In the seventeenth century French trading companies entered the region and built up the slave trade. The English also actively took slaves in the area. France established its first permanent base on the Gabon Estuary—near the present site of Libreville—in 1839, when naval officer Louis Edouard Bouet-Villaumez signed a treaty of trade, protection and territorial cession with the local tribe known as the Mpongwe. In 1843 the French navy, in an effort to discourage the slave trade (abolished by France in 1815) and encourage commercial development, established blockhouses at the mouth of the estuary. Libreville, the present capital, was founded by freed slaves in 1849.

Between 1855 and 1884 the region was explored extensively by Paul du Chaillu in the 1850s and Pierre Savorgnan de Brazza in the 1870s, and their reports cited the commercial potential of the Gabonese hinterland, sparking a new interest in the area. In 1886 France established the colony of Gabon. By the end of the nineteenth century the French government had turned Gabon over to commercial interests who exploited and abused the local people. From 1889–1910 Gabon was part of French Congo*, which in the latter year became French Equitorial Africa*—a federation of three colonies: Ubangi-Shari-Chad, Middle Congo, and Gabon. The removal of the regions' capital from Libreville to Brazzaville on the Congo River in 1907 opened up the Gabonese coast to terrible exploitation.

The commercial interests received huge tracts of land, on which they forced the local people to work for little or no pay.

The situation improved slightly after World War II because of the support of the Gabonese people for Charles de Gaulle and the Free French movement. At that time a liberalization of French colonial policy and the rise of an educated, articulate Gabonese elite also led to reforms and a certain measure of local autonomy. In 1946 Gabon became an overseas territory of France, with an elected legislature and representation in the parliament of France. A movement toward independence was started in 1946 by the *Union Democratique et Social Gabonese* (UDSG) and the *Bloc Democratique Gabonais* (BDG). The UDSG purportedly represented the Fang, but Leon Mba, himself a Fang, used the BDG to build a national coalition of both Fang and non-Fang people. In 1958 Gabon voted to become an autonomous republic within the French Community*. In 1959 a constitution was adopted, and a provisional government under the auspices of Mba was established. Independence was formally declared on August 17, 1960, and in 1961 Mba was elected president of the new Republic of Gabon. (Edward Mortimer, *France and the Africans, 1944–1966, A Political History*, 1969; K. David Patterson, *The Northern Gabon Coast to 1875*, 1975.)

Joseph L. Michaud

GADSDEN PURCHASE. With the acquisition of California and the Great Southwest in the Mexican War, the United States needed to develop railroad ties with the Far West. In 1853 President Franklin Pierce sent General James Gadsden to Mexico City as United States minister. Gadsden was a strong advocate of the southern route for the transcontinental railroad. In Mexico*, Antonio Lopez de Santa Anna was back in power and desperately in need of money. Convinced that Santa Anna would respond favorably, the United States authorized Gadsden to offer as much as $50 million for Lower California and a large portion of northern Mexico. Santa Anna rejected such a sweeping proposal, but did offer to sell just enough land to meet the administration's needs for the southern railroad route. From this came the Gadsden Treaty, signed December 30, 1853. Gadsden agreed for the United States to pay $15 million in cash for about 39,000 square miles of territory south of the Gila River. The terms also obligated the United States to assume the claims of American citizens against Mexico up to a limit of $5 million.

The treaty reached the United States Senate in 1854 during a heated debate over slavery in the territories. It was initially rejected on April 17, 1854, but rival factions settled their differences and forced reconsideration of the treaty. As finally approved, the treaty was scaled down to include only 29,640 square miles of territory in the Mesilla Valley south of the Gila River. Payment was reduced proportionally to $10 million, and the Senate refused to assume the cost of claims against Mexico. The Senate ratified that treaty on April 25, 1854. Santa Anna accepted it. (Nelson M. Blake and Oscar T. Barck, Jr., *The United States in its World Relations*, 1960.)

Joseph M. Rowe, Jr.

GALAPAGOS ISLANDS. The Galapagos Islands are located along the equator approximately 600 miles west of Ecuador* in the Pacific Ocean. The islands were first discovered by Tomas de Berlanga, a Spaniard stationed in Panama, in 1535, and for the next three hundred years the islands were used by pirates, fishermen, and whalers as places to rest and acquire fresh water supplies. In 1832 Ecuador annexed the Galapagos Islands, colonizing them temporarily in 1832 and permanently in 1869. (Irenaus Eibl-Eibesfield, *Survey on the Galapagos Islands*, 1959.)

GALLEON. In 1570, after noticing that the high-built forecastle on the typical ship of the time caught the wind and pushed the bow down to leeward so that it could not maintain its course to windward, Sir John Hawkins* eliminated the high forecastle. The new ship, known as a galleon, was far more weatherly and maneuverable. Spain began building them in 1588 and by the mid-sixteenth century the galleon was the principle type of Spanish trading ship. The new design reduced the time required for international voyages. (Peter Klemp, *The Oxford Companion to Ships and the Sea*, 1976.)

GAMA, VASCO DA. Vasco da Gama was born about 1460 at Sines in Portugal to Estevano da Gama and Isabel de Sodre, members of the lesser nobility. Originally King John II had wanted to appoint Estevano da Gama as commander of the expedition that would follow up the discovery by Bartolomeu Dias* of the Cape of Good Hope. But when he died, that post devolved on his son Vasco. Vasco da Gama's expedition consisted of four ships and departed from Portugal on July 8, 1497. Its objectives were to find a sea route to India*, engage in the Eastern spice trade, and make contact and treaties with local Christian rulers. The expedition was primarily one of exploration and not trade. After resting at the Cape Verde* Islands, the expedition took to the high seas on August 3, steering a southwesterly course and ignoring the coastal route used earlier by Diogo Cao and Dias. First sighting land again on November 4, da Gama's fleet rounded the Cape of Good Hope on November 22. Arriving at the hospitable port of Malindi on the east coast of Africa on March 29, 1498, they took on a skillful pilot, probably the famous Ahmed ibn Madgid. They proceeded north and caught the monsoon which quickly transported them to the Malabar coast of India on May 18. It was not until May 30 that Vasco da Gama managed to meet the Zamorin of Calicut, the most powerful local ruler and controller of the spice trade. By that time the Portuguese had discovered that their trade goods were better suited for the primitive Hottentots of southern Africa than the sophisticated Hindus who held the scruffy Portuguese and their goods in contempt. At the same time, da Gama remained hopeful because of his mistaken belief that the Hindus were Christians of some sort. Mutual suspicions built up, however, and the Portuguese only managed with the greatest difficulty to trade their shoddy cargo for some spices and precious stones. When the time came for them to depart, they literally had to fight their way out of Calicut harbor on August 30. Steering north, the expedition stopped at Angediva Island for a rest.

Vasco da Gama and his fleet left Angediva Island on October 5. Unfortunately on this passage they encountered unfavorable winds and little progress was made. Scurvy broke out with great intensity and eventually thirty men died. After the monsoons finally arrived, they sighted Africa on January 2, 1499. Losses among the crew forced them to abandon one vessel at Malindi before they went on to Portugal. Da Gama split the expedition at the Cape Verde Islands and rushed his ailing brother Paulo to the Azores* in the vain hope of saving his life. Meanwhile, Nicolau Coelho sailed for Portugal and arrived on July 10. It was not until late August or early September 1499 that da Gama reached Lisbon, where he received an enthusiastic reception.

King Manuel rewarded Vasco da Gama with the title of Admiral of the Sea of the Indies and made him proprietory owner of his birthplace, Sines. A second expedition under the command of Pedro Cabral* was readied for 1500 and da Gama prepared detailed sailing instructions for it. That expedition resulted in even greater hostilities between the Portuguese and the Muslim merchants of Calicut. Apparently dissatisfied with Cabral's performance, King Manuel named da Gama commander of the next expedition to India. This expedition's purpose was reprisal and conquest not trade and was the most powerful fleet yet sent to the Indian Ocean. It consisted of fifteen ships under the command of Vasco da Gama and another five ships under his brother Estevano. They sailed for India in February and March 1502, respectively. Arriving at Calicut on October 30, Vasco da Gama demanded the expulsion of the hostile Muslim merchant community. When the Zamorin refused, the Portuguese shelled the city and committed various other atrocities. Next they visited the friendly cities of Cochin and Cananore, picked up a cargo of spices, and returned to Portugal, arriving home on September 1, 1503. These expeditions of Cabral and da Gama forced the Portuguese into a policy of conquest as the Muslim merchants persuaded the Mamelukes of Egypt* and the Gujaratis of western India to form an alliance to drive the intruding Portuguese from the Indian Ocean.

After the expedition of 1502–1503, Vasco da Gama returned to a long period of private life. Meanwhile, the Portuguese empire in the East which had been established by his great successors Francisco de Almeida (1505–1509) and Affonso de Albuquerque (1509–1515) began to founder under a series of incompetent and corrupt governors. In 1524 King John III appointed da Gama as viceroy of India. He arrived at Goa* and immediately began restoring discipline and harassing Portugal's enemies. Traveling to Cochin, he arrested the departing governor Duarte de Menezes, but over-exertion and the tropical climate weakened the elderly da Gama, who died on December 24, 1524. (K. G. Jayne, *Vasco da Gama and his Successors 1460–1580*, 1910.)

Ronald Fritze

GAMBIA. The Republic of Gambia is a former British crown colony and protectorate located on the northwest coast of Africa. It consists of a narrow strip of land stretching about 200 miles upstream from the sea along both banks of the Gambia River, the major waterway and dominant physical feature of the country. Gambia is surrounded, except on the seaward side, by Senegal*. The first European contact with the people of Gambia occurred in 1455 when Portuguese explorers entered the mouth of the Gambia River. The Portuguese soon left when they realized that the riches they sought were not to be found there. The English chartered a number of companies to trade with the west coast of Africa in the sixteenth and seventeenth centuries—the Guinea Company, the Royal Adventurers, the Gambia Adventurers, and the Royal African Company— but these enterprises yielded negligible profits. In the same period, other Europeans, including Danes, Dutchmen, and even Latvians (from the Duchy of Courland) probed the commercial possibilities of the Gambia estuary, without notable success. The French also attempted to establish a colony on the Gambia River, but that effort failed and the French concentrated their settlements on the Senegal River to the north.

In 1661 the British took over from the Courlanders a fort on James Island in the Gambia River. Fort James served as the main British base in the Senegambia region until its destruction by the French in 1778. The French established a trading post in 1642 at Albreda across the river from the fort. This led to conflict in the 1600s and 1700s between Britain and France over domination of the slave trade there. From 1765 to 1783 the British controlled all of Senegambia, but the Treaty of Versailles of 1783* returned control of the northern territory to France.

With the outlawing of the slave trade in 1807, Britain dispatched naval patrols to the mouth of the Gambia River to suppress the traffic in slaves. In 1816 Britain established the town of Bathurst as a base on the island of Banjul, which they called St. Mary's Isle. Bathurst later became the capital of the colony. Peanuts first appeared in trade reports in 1829 and by 1851 formed 72 percent of the Gambian exports. British expansion into the interior was hindered by tribal warfare between the Marabouts, fanatically devout Muslims, and the Soninke "pagans," who would not abstain from the use of liquor. The wars destroyed the authority of the traditional Mandingo rulers and resulted in the conversion of most of the indigenous population to Islam. In order to make the area secure for commercial growth and safe from French influence, Britain purchased small pieces of land from local chiefs. The famous "Ceded Mile" on the north shore was acquired in 1826 and more land on the south shore of the river was obtained in 1840. The British also signed treaties with African tribal chiefs who agreed to place themselves under British protection. The French released Albreda to British control in 1857 as part of an exchange of colonial territories.

The British settlements in the Gambia had a checkered administrative history. From 1821 to 1843 they were governed at a distance by the British colony of Sierra Leone*. The Gambia was made a separate entity in 1843 and had its own colonial administration until 1866. In that year the area was placed once again under the jurisdiction of Sierra Leone. Finally, in 1888, the Gambia regained its status as a separate dependency with its own governor, executive council, and nominated legislative council.

In 1889 a convention was signed establishing a temporary border between French Senegal and the Gambia. Heavy French investment in Senegal and a growing feeling of responsibility toward the Gambians by the British ended any further exchange of territory in the area. Thus, the temporary boundaries became permanent. The crown colony of the Gambia consisted of a small area (about seventy square miles) around Bathurst at the mouth of the river. In 1894 a protectorate ordinance established the form of government for the upriver districts, providing a system of "indirect rule" using local chiefs supervised by British officials known as "traveling commissioners." British policy in regard to the Gambia stressed economic self-sufficiency, as opposed to the underwriting of development by the imperial government. As a result, Gambia could afford few economic or educational improvements in the early twentieth century.

After World War II, however, Britain advanced colonial development and welfare funds to Gambia, improving conditions dramatically. By 1950 Africanization of the civil service became the goal of the British authorities. The 1954 constitution provided for universal adult suffrage, an increase in the number of elected seats on the legislative council, and the appointment of Gambian members to work with British officials in the executive council of the colony. Under the 1960 constitution, universal suffrage was extended to the protectorate, and the legislature was enlarged and renamed the house of representatives. In the 1962 election, the Peoples Progressive Party gained a substantial victory. Its leader, Dauda Jawara, became the first prime minister. Internal self government was introduced in 1963, and Gambia became independent on February 18, 1965. (John M. Gray, *A History of the Gambia*, 1966.)

Joseph L. Michaud

GANDHI, MOHANDAS. Mohandas Karamchand Gandhi was born on October 2, 1869, at Porbandar in western India*. He belonged to the Vaisya caste, which stood third below the Brahmin caste. When he became a sophomore in high school at the age of thirteen, he married Kasturbai, who was the same age. Gandhi attended the University of Bombay and then decided to study law in England. His mother disapproved but consented when he promised not to touch wine, women, or meat. In London Gandhi joined the Inner Temple, considered the most aristocratic of the English legal societies by Indians. He had no difficulty passing his final examinations and was called to the bar on June 10, 1891. Gandhi had not enjoyed his stay in England but he did meet humanitarians and socialists such as George Bernard Shaw and Sir Edward Carpenter and found their ideas congenial with his own commitment to non-violence. Although a Hindu, Gandhi was not orthodox and did not feel bound to those aspects of his religion he felt were inhumane, especially the caste laws. A loose interpretation of Hinduism would characterize his entire life.

Gandhi returned to India in July 1891 but found the legal profession over-crowded and after two unsuccessful years sailed to Natal* to practice law. In South Africa* Gandhi first encountered the brutality of segregation when he was kicked off a train after refusing to give up his first class seat to a white passenger. Later he was beaten by a white stagecoach driver when he refused to give up his seat to a European passenger. The 24-year-old lawyer held meetings urging Indians to improve themselves by telling the truth, adopting more sanitary habits, forgetting caste and religious divisions, and learning English. At a farewell party held when his two-year contract expired, Gandhi learned that the Natal legislative assembly was going to deprive Indians of their right to vote. He decided to stay in South Africa and fight the discrimination.

Gandhi intended to establish the principle that Indians were subjects of the British Empire* entitled to equality under its laws. While in South Africa Gandhi also established ashrams, or religious retreats, at Phoenix Farm, outside Durban, and Tolstoy Farm, near Johannesburg. These hermitages would become the models for those he would later establish in India. Gandhi had become intrigued by the writings of Leo Tolstoy after reading *The Kingdom of God is Within You*, in which Tolstoy preached against serving or obeying evil governments and advocated peaceful resistance.

Because of his loyalty to the British Empire, Gandhi supported it during the Boer War* in 1899 and helped to raise an ambulance corps. However, after the war Indians found their condition little improved in South Africa. In August 1906 a new ordinance was introduced by the Transvaal* government requiring all Indians, including children over eight, to register with the government. The law also required Indians to be fingerprinted and obliged them to carry a certif-icate. When the Transvaal ceased to be a crown colony and established a re-sponsible government*, it passed this measure as the Asiatic Registration Act on July 31, 1907. During his seven-year struggle against the act, Gandhi em-ployed the new tactic of *satyagraha*, a technique to redress grievances through non-violent disobedience to the law and non-cooperation with the government. South Africa thus became the proving ground for the principle Gandhian tactic later employed to win Indian independence.

Gandhi led hundreds of Indians to South African jails for non-compliance before an agreement was finally reached between Gandhi and the South African statesman, General Jan Christian Smuts, on June 30, 1914. The Indian Relief Bill, passed by the Union of South Africa parliament in Cape Town, canceled the tax on indentured Indian laborers, declared valid Muslim and Hindu mar-riages, allowed Indians born in South Africa to enter the Cape Colony*, and allowed free Indians to enter the Cape Colony. Gandhi considered his victory as one more of principle than substance, but he felt the principle of racial equality had been upheld. The struggle completed, Gandhi sailed for England on July 18, 1914, and returned to India on January 9, 1915.

Upon his return to India Gandhi found rising agitation for self-rule. Gandhi did not become politically involved but kept his eyes and ears open. The focus of the struggle for self-rule became the Indian National Congress, founded in Bombay* on December 27, 1885. It was originally organized to moderate Indian protest against the British raj. With the emergence of a new Indian middle class, however, there arose increasing pressure for independence. A few extremists sought to make the Congress an active agent of this movement. Gandhi's emergence as India's leader and advocate of self-rule began in 1919 with his announcement of a satyagraha against the Rowlett Bills which allowed the government to imprison without trial those suspected of sedition. The subsequent protests resulted in the massacre of 379 Indians plus 1,200 wounded at a meeting in Amritsar on April 13, 1919, and the enactment of martial law. For Gandhi and India, Amritsar shattered any belief in Britain's ultimate goodwill or moral superiority. By the autumn of 1920 Gandhi had become the most important political leader in India opposing British rule, and he had been given the title of Mahatma, meaning Great Soul, by the common people. Gandhi, seeking to unite Hindus and Muslims, launched a general campaign of non-violent non-cooperation and civil disobedience in the early 1920s. It got out of hand and ended in tragedy, however, with outbreaks of violence such as the Moplah rising (1921) and the killing of 22 policemen at Chauri Chaura (1922). Gandhi concluded from this experience that the masses were not ready for this form of protest. In 1922 he was arrested for sedition and sentenced to six years but was soon released (1924) after an operation for appendicitis. During his absence the National Congress split into two factions. The Muslim minority resented Hindu economic domination of India. In an attempt to bring Hindus and Muslims into an accord, Gandhi began a 21-day fast, but this action failed as tensions between the two groups increased. Nevertheless, Gandhi continued to work for Hindu-Muslim unity and for removal of the stigma associated with the untouchable caste during the mid–1920s.

In 1927 the British parliament appointed a constitutional reform committee (the Simon Commission) which did not contain a single Indian, angering the politically aware among the Indian population. In response Gandhi began a new campaign of civil disobedience on February 12, 1928. Leading members of the National Congress disagreed with these tactics. Chandra Bose and Jawaharlal Nehru* desired a stronger response by declaring for immediate independence. Gandhi remained committed to a middle-of-the-road policy which precipitated protests from Nehru and his young followers. In December 1929 the National Congress passed a resolution committing it to the goal of complete independence and Gandhi acceded, having failed to arrive at a suitable plan with Britain to grant India dominion status. It was now left to Gandhi to choose the appropriate time and place to launch a new civil disobedience campaign. In March 1930 Gandhi launched a satyagraha against the tax on salt. Protesting the British salt monopoly, he led a march 200 miles to the sea, where he extracted salt from sea water against British regulations. This demonstration riveted the attention of the nation and was followed by the arrest of 60,000 people, including Gandhi, in 1930.

A year later Gandhi, now the leader of the Congress Party, ended the civil disobedience. The Mahatma had been released from prison and persuaded to attend a London round-table discussion in 1931. The conference was a failure, however, primarily because Hindus and Muslims could not agree on the future of India. The failure of the London Conference encouraged divisive tendencies within India. Muslims began calling for the partition of India, an eventuality which Gandhi emphatically rejected, believing the division of India to be a blasphemy.

Upon his return to India from England, Gandhi was arrested and imprisoned (1932) in an attempt to destroy his influence. While in prison he went on another fast to protest the British decision to politically segregate the untouchables from other Hindus by allotting them separate electorates. An alternative electoral arrangement was agreed upon in the historic 1932 Yervada Pact, which also directed that no one should be regarded as untouchable because of birth. Resigning his post as leader of the Congress Party in 1934, Gandhi continued his efforts to help untouchables and promoted programs providing social and economic uplift, including such cottage industries as handspinning and weaving.

When World War II erupted in September 1939, Britain brought India into the war without prior consultation. Although angered, the National Congress would have supported the British war effort if Indian self-rule had been assured. This assurance was not forthcoming from Britain and consequently, the National Congress took up Gandhi's position in 1942, demanding immediate British withdrawal from India. Gandhi had become convinced that India's problem of Hindu-Muslim division would not be settled until Britain left. The British attempted to achieve some form of compromise with the National Congress but failed because Indians were not willing to back away from their position on self-rule. Because of the war and Japan's immediate threat to India, Britain reacted sharply toward the opposition and imprisoned the entire leadership of the Congress Party, including Gandhi. This only led to a renewal of violence and the spread of self-rule movements throughout the country. While in prison at Poona, Gandhi began a 21-day fast in February 1943, in protest against his unjust imprisonment. A year later his wife died in prison, having become active in the free-India movement. In May 1944 Gandhi was released as his own health declined.

By 1944 the main struggle for Indian independence had passed to Nehru, Gandhi's chosen successor. Gandhi's most intractable problem was the Hindu-Muslim split. In September 1944 he met in Bombay with Mohammad Ali Jinnah*, leader of the Muslim League*. Jinnah's firm commitment to build a separate Muslim state sundered the two men irrevocably. In 1945 the Labour Party came to power in Britain determined to rid itself of the Indian problem. Britain negotiated with both the National Congress Party and the Muslim League. On June 3, 1947, the Mountbatten Plan was announced, calling for the creation of a separate Muslim state known as Pakistan. Although the partition of India was the greatest disappointment in his life, Gandhi continued to work toward healing the scars which had developed between the two religious communities. He toured areas where Hindu-Muslim riots had erupted and his mere presence calmed the turmoil. In August 1947 he succeeded in quelling the violence in Calcutta* by a fast. On January 13, 1948, he began his last fast, which brought a truce between Muslims and Hindus in New Delhi. On January 30, 1948, while walking to his evening prayer, he was shot down by Nathuram Godse, a young Hindu fanatic, who resented Gandhi's overtures to the Muslims. (Louis Fisher, *The Life of Mahatma Gandhi*, 1983; Mohandas K. Gandhi, *Gandhi: An Auto-biography*, 1957.)

Michael Dennis

GEORGE III (GEORGE WILLIAM FREDERICK). George III, King of Great Britain and Ireland from 1760–1820, was born June 4, 1738, to Frederick, the Prince of Wales, and Princess Augusta of Saxe-Gotha. George, at age twelve, became heir to the throne upon his father's death. He succeeded to the throne following the death of his grandfather George II in 1760, in the midst of the Seven Years' War (1756–1763). For most of his reign, George was dependent upon the counsel of his prime ministers, among them John Stuart (the Earl of Bute), George Grenville, Lord North, and William Pitt*. From the 1760s through the 1780s, the American colonial rebellion dominated British imperial politics. Under Grenville and subsequent Tory prime ministers, British policy lacked political consistency and overall direction. Only during the 1770s was any decisive colonial policy carried through, largely under the direction of Prime Minister Lord North. North, supported fully by King George, tried to force the American colonies to share the debts remaining from the Seven Years' War and to pay an increasing share of the costs of colonial security. With the outbreak of war between the colonies and Britain in 1775 (sparked in part by parliament's colonial revenue bills) the King argued that, though the war was economically ruinous, it had to be fought. Throughout the conflict, which ended with American victory in 1783, King George's belligerent view was based largely on his belief that if American disobedience were allowed to flourish, then the Empire was doomed to collapse, beginning first with the inevitable loss of Ireland.

The British Empire* flourished during his reign, the loss of the American colonies being assuaged by the expansion of British influence in Canada* and western North America. In 1788 settlement began in Australia* (New South Wales*) following the British claim to that continent made by Captain James Cook* in 1770. The Napoleonic Wars (1799–1815) brought new territory to the empire. By the early 1800s the Cape of Good Hope had been brought under British control. By the Treaty of Amiens of 1802* Britain gained Trinidad* and Ceylon*. By the Treaty of Paris in 1814 Britain gained Tobago*, Mauritius*, St. Lucia*, and Malta*. British imperial gains also included Malacca* (1795) and Singapore* (1819), the latter acquired by Sir Thomas Stamford Raffles on behalf of the British East India Company*. In India*, where British control had been solidified during the Seven Years' War by the military success of Robert Clive, the Napoleonic Wars resulted in the acquisition by the East India Company of the United Provinces of Agra and Oudh, followed shortly thereafter by British expansion into East Bengal and Assam.

The later period of King George III's reign was marked by the monarch's increasing ill health, which began as early as 1788, and which manifested itself in long bouts of delirium. By 1811 the king was hopelessly insane. George was remanded to the custody of his physicians, and parliament enacted the regency of the king's dissolute son George, the Prince of Wales. George III died January 29, 1820. (Stanley Edward Ayling, *George the Third*, 1972; John Brooke, *King George III*, 1972.)

William G. Ratliff

GEORGIA. Georgia was the thirteenth, and last founded, of the British North American colonies that became the United States. To protect the growing British colonies of North Carolina* and South Carolina* from the Spanish colony in Florida in the early 1700s, England wanted to establish a buffer colony, while private entrepreneurs hoped to develop an important source of furs and New World trade. Although Spain claimed the area under the Treaty of Madrid of 1670, England went ahead with the colonization effort anyway. In 1732 England granted a proprietary charter to James Oglethorpe and nineteen other trustees to establish a colony west of the Savannah River. In the beginning the trustees hoped to establish the colony along feudal lines and make a fortune by establishing silk culture. The trustees wanted to prohibit Catholics, liquor, slavery, and large plantations, but shortly after the arrival of the first settlers in 1733 their hopes were dashed.

The growth of the colony was slow and tempestuous. Settlers resented the restrictions on their ability to acquire land, slaves, and liquor. Silk culture proved to be an economic bust. James Oglethorpe served essentially as a military governor, but his frequent trips to England and forays against Spanish Florida kept him away from Savannah for extended periods. Discontent with his leadership led to repeal of the ordinances prohibiting alcohol and slavery and the formation of large landed estates was permitted. In 1751 the settlers organized their own assembly. The proprietary charter reverted to the crown in 1753 and Georgia became a royal colony. The assembly acquired real power, and the economy began to thrive on the production of rice and indigo. By 1760 Georgia had a population of nearly 10,000 people. Georgia joined with the other twelve rebellious North American colonies in declaring independence from Great Britain in 1776. (J. E. Callaway, *Early Settlement of Georgia*, 1948; A. A. Ettinger, *James Edward Oglethorpe*, 1933.)

GERMAN EAST AFRICA. Corresponding to present-day Rwanda and Burundi along with portions of Tanzania* and Mozambique*, German East Africa was one of the most important German colonies from the 1880s to the end of

World War I*. The early development of the colony was the work of Germany's leading explorer and colonial advocate, Karl Peters. Full of admiration for the British Empire following two visits to London, he founded the *Gesellschaft fur deutsche Kolonisation (Kolonialverein)* in 1884. In that same year Peters journeyed to the interior of eastern Africa and in six weeks concluded twelve treaties with native chiefs of the territories of Useguha, Nguru, Usagara, and Ukami. Peters then declared the native territories a German protectorate. In 1885 Peters returned to Berlin and the newly acquired East African lands were placed under the administration of the newly formed German East Africa Company. This arrangement, including German occupation of the port city of Dar es Salaam, was recognized by the British government in the Anglo-German Agreement of 1886*. Two years later Germany acquired the right of collecting customs duties on the coast, and in 1890 purchased an additional coastal strip from the sultan of Zanzibar*. The same year Germany added several coastal islands, not including Zanzibar and Pemba, to the protectorate. Also, by the Heligoland-Zanzibar Treaty of 1890*, Berlin recognized Zanzibar and Uganda* as British territories. In return Germany received the North Sea island of Heligoland.

The pacification of German East Africa fell largely to the German East Africa Company, which employed native troops to quell various uprisings. From 1891 to 1893 the German administration was engaged in a series of wars with the Wahehe people south of the Rufiji river. A period of comparative peace ensued, followed in 1905 by the largest native uprising in the German colonies. The Maji Maji rebellion took place in the southern districts of the colony between Lake Nyasa and the Kilwa coast. As many as 250 German missionaries, planters, traders, and government officials were killed. After almost two years of fighting the rebellion was subdued, at the cost of an estimated 120,000 African lives. The period following the conclusion of the rebellion witnessed even greater suffering for the natives due to the German punitive policy of food seizures and crop destruction.

In 1907, however, the German colonial office was given expanded authority in the colonies and the colonial secretary, Bernhard Dernberg*, initiated a number of reforms. Included in the Dernberg reforms were the abolition of forced labor and corporal punishment. From 1907 to 1914 Dernberg was also responsible for the establishment of a basic system of modern transportation and the creation of new forms of economic enterprise such as mining and improved horticulture. During World War I, the British occupied German East Africa. They received a mandate to administer the greater part of it by the Versailles Treaty. An additional portion of the former German colony (Ruanda-Urundi) was presented to Belgium. (Woodruff D. Smith, *The German Colonial Empire*, 1978; Mary E. Townsend, *The Rise and Fall of Germany's Colonial Empire, 1884–1918*, 1930.)

William G. Ratliff

GERMAN EMPIRE. Preoccupied with internal politics and the whole question of national unification in the nineteenth century, Germany was the last of the European powers to embark on imperialist ventures and, because of her defeat in World War I*, the first to lose her colonies. Once German unification was complete (1871), leading German political and intellectual figures grew more and more worried about the British and French scramble for overseas territories. During the 1880s and 1890s people like Otto von Bismarck* and Karl Peters pushed Germany toward colonial imperialism, and in a rush the country acquired a variety of territories overseas. German imperialists wanted to locate new sources of raw materials for German industry, acquire new markets for manufactured goods, establish naval stations to protect and promote German international commerce, and secure Germany's position in Central Europe against Russian and French designs.

The results were immediate. In less than two decades at the end of the nineteenth century, Germany established protectorates in Togo* and Cameroon* in West Africa; developed the full-fledged colonies of South West Africa*, German East Africa*, Kaiochow* on the Shantung Peninsula in China, German New Guinea and the Bismarck Archipelago*, and Western Samoa*; and placed naval bases in the Marianas* (except for Guam), the Marshall Islands*, the Caroline Islands*, and Palau*. German eagerness for colonial acquisitions brought them to the brink of war a number of times with France and Great Britain and helped inspire the alliance systems which eventually led to World War I. That war spelled the end of the German colonial empire. Soon after the outbreak of hostilities, British and French troops occupied most German overseas possessions, and when the conflict was over in 1918, the Allied powers decided to take the spoils of war themselves. German colonies were divided up between Great Britain, France, and Japan. (Woodruff D. Smith, *The German Colonial Empire*, 1978.)

GERMAN KAMERUN. See CAMEROON.

GERMAN NEW GUINEA. In 1884 a number of enterprising German investors formed the New Guinea Company and by 1885 they had established German control over northeastern New Guinea*, the Bismarck Archipelago*, and the Marshall Islands*. In 1888 they seized the island of Nauru*, which possessed rich phosphate deposits, and in 1899 Germany purchased the Marianas Islands* (except for Guam*), the Caroline Islands*, and the Palau Islands from Spain. The New Guinea Company named the New Guinea colony Kaiser Wilhelmsland and administered it. The Jaluit Company controlled the islands. Germany held those territories until World War I, when Allied forces and Japan seized them. In their disposition after the war, Japan received a mandate over the Mariana, Caroline, Marshall, and Palau islands, while Australia* received a mandate to

Kaiser Wilhelmsland, the Bismarck Archipelago, and Nauru. See NEW GUINEA.

GERMAN SAMOA. See WESTERN SAMOA.

GERMAN SOUTHWEST AFRICA. From its founding in the 1880s to its demise during World War I*, the colonial empire was of marginal value to Germany. German colonialism was begun as a small-time venture for a few private companies and, even at its peak, was designed to benefit only a few special-interest groups. While German colonialism provided many modern material benefits to Africa, the German impact was often double-edged in its effect—the act of conquest often involved prolonged violence and brutality to native populations. Nowhere was this more evident than in German Southwest Africa.

The colony, which was under German control officially from 1884 to 1915, was founded in 1883 by Adolf Luderitz, a merchant and adventurer from the North German city of Bremen. In 1883 Luderitz and several associates established a trading station at Angra Pequena, which was renamed Luderitzbucht, northwest of the Cape Colony.* Luderitz, who later drowned during an expedition on the Orange River, purchased the surrounding territory of the Nama and Herero people in 1884, naming the new acquisition Luderitzland. These areas formally became the first German colonial territory on April 24, 1884. When the German protectorate was declared in 1884, the majority of the native peoples in the region—the Bantu-speaking Herero, who lived inland from the coastal villages, the Nama, who occupied the colony's southern area, and the Ovambo, an agricultural people of the north—had already developed national state structures and had maintained for many years political relations with European merchants and settlers in South Africa. All resisted German colonial rule. By 1889 several native insurrections had been put down, but the increasing native African resentment of German colonial rule forced the German Colonial Company for Southwest Africa, a private company in charge of colonial administration, to turn over full authority to the Imperial German government. The German government increased the colony's territory and added to its economic viability as a result of the Heligoland-Zanzibar Treaty of 1890*. This agreement between Germany and Great Britain acquired for German Southwest Africa the Caprivi Strip (a narrow tract of land 280 miles in length in the northeast of the territory named for German Chancellor Count Leo von Caprivi), which provided access to the Zambezi River and Central Africa.

Further native troubles plagued the colony, however, and from 1894 to 1914 the colonial administration was occupied much of the time with suppressing them. Major Theodor Leutwein, governor of the colony in 1894–1904, faced serious insurrections by the Khoikhoi, a nomadic Hottentot people from the south, and the Herero. In 1904 the Herero mounted a large rebellion which included 8,000 men, many equipped with modern weapons. Reinforcements from Europe increased the size of the German colonial forces under the command of General Adolf von Trotha to nearly 20,000 troops, but for some time the rebels, led by Samuel Maherero, held out. Although the Herero were dealt a crushing defeat at the battle of Waterberg in August 1904, the war dragged on until 1908; and an estimated 70–80 percent of the Herero population perished as a result of the fighting and von Trotha's policy of extermination. In 1904 the Khoikhoi, led by Hendrik Witboi, also rose in a rebellion which the Germans did not put down until 1907. Full economic development of German Southwest Africa did not occur until the discovery of diamonds and copper in 1908. Almost immediately the number of European settlers increased (to a total of 15,000 by 1913) and, by 1912, some 766,000 carats total weight of diamonds had been exported. The overall colonial economy, however, declined by almost 25 percent from 1907–1914.

The outbreak of World War I in Europe brought a swift end to German colonial rule. As early as September 1914 the British government urged South African forces under General Louis Botha* to seize the two ports and destroy the three long-distance wireless stations in German Southwest Africa. The radio transmitters, in the British view, constituted a threat not only to the Union of South Africa, but also to the British line of communications around the Cape of Good Hope to the Far East. By late 1914 German Southwest Africa had been invaded by South African and British forces. Following a spirited defense, the outnumbered German troops (Schutztruppe) surrendered on July 9, 1915, and the colony was placed under Allied military control. In 1919 German Southwest Africa officially was mandated by the League of Nations* to South Africa. (L. H. Gann and Peter Duignan, *The Rulers of German Africa, 1884–1914*, 1977; Woodruff D. Smith, *The German Colonial Empire*, 1978.)

William G. Ratliff

GHANA. The Republic of Ghana is located on the southwestern coast of Africa, and was previously known as the Gold Coast. It was inhabited by the Fanti people in the coastal area, the Ashanti in the central and south central regions, the Guans along the Volta River plain, the Ga and Ewe in the south and southeast, and the Moshi-Dagomba in the north. Portuguese explorers discovered this area in 1471 and by 1482 had established a permanent trading post with the completion of Elmina Castle on a small peninsula next to the African settlement of Edina. The Portuguese soon established other forts at Axim, Shama, and Accra*. A British trading expedition under Thomas Windham landed on the coast in 1553, and over the next three centuries, forts were built by the British, Danish, and Dutch, often within sight of one another. By 1637 the Dutch had driven out the Portuguese.

The European countries set up trade in gold, ivory, and slaves. The slaves were supplied by the Ashanti who sold them to Fanti middlemen. With the end of the slave trade, the Danes and Dutch found it impossible to maintain a profitable economic posture in the area. They ceded their forts to the British and by 1872 had withdrawn.

The British consistently had problems with the Ashanti. During the seventeenth century, under outstanding leadership, the Ashanti had conquered neighboring tribes and formed a powerful confederation. The founder of the confederation was Osei Tutu, whose conquests greatly extended the Ashanti empire. Conquered tribes were accepted into the confederation and allowed a voice in the government. The Ashanti expansion ultimately took them to the Fanti territory where Europeans had established forts and trading posts. In 1807 the British outlawed the slave trade, directly affecting the Ashanti economy. This and other quarrels over the Fanti region led to open warfare between the British and the Ashanti in the 1820s. The Ashanti defeated a British force in 1824 and were themselves defeated by the British in 1826. A treaty was signed in 1831 which provided thirty years of peace. In 1863 the Ashanti under Kwaku Dua I invaded the Fanti coastal area, clashing with the British. In 1872, the British bought out the Dutch on the Gold Coast, acquiring Elmina, which the Ashanti claimed. A war soon followed, and in 1874 a British force under the command of Sir Garnet Wolseley invaded the Ashanti homeland. The 2,500 well-trained British soldiers and a large contingent of African troops occupied and burned the Ashanti capital of Kumasi. The last Ashanti uprising was put down in 1900, and the Ashanti had to accept British rule. In 1901 Ashanti became a British protectorate and was joined to the Gold Coast colony, which had been created in 1874. Part of the German colony of Togoland was put under British control by the League of Nations in 1922, after which the mandate was administered in conjunction with the Gold Coast dependencies.

Not until after World War II were Ashanti representatives given seats in the colony's legislative council. Africans gained a majority on the council in 1946 and were granted some control of local government. In 1947 the United Gold Coast Convention (UGCC) became the first nationalist movement. By 1949 the demand for self-government led to the appointment of an all African committee to look into constitutional reform. That same year Kwame Nkrumah* founded the Convention People's Party (CPP), which sponsored strikes and civil disorder, leading to outbreaks of violence. Nkrumah and some of his followers were arrested and jailed for sedition. But the CPP won the 1951 elections. Nkrumah was released from prison to become a member of the government and then prime minister in 1952. By 1954, through constitutional amendments, the Gold Coast became for all practical purposes self-governing. Nkrumah's party, the CPP, won the elections of 1954 and 1956.

On March 6, 1957, the Gold Coast, along with Ashanti, the Northern Territories Protectorate, and the Trust Territory of British Togoland gained independence and became a full member of the Commonwealth of Nations under the name of Ghana. On July 1, 1960, Ghana became a republic with Nkrumah as president. (J. D. Fage, *Ghana*, 1966; Irving Kaplan, *Area Handbook for Ghana*, 1971.)

Amanda Pollock

GIBRALTAR. A peninsula connected to Spain and extending into the eastern end of the Strait of Gibraltar, Gibraltar is a British crown colony. For centuries Gibraltar has enjoyed great strategic importance in European and African affairs because it guards the western entrance to the Mediterranean Sea. Although Gibraltar has been inhabited since ancient times, its modern history began in 711 when Berber tribesmen crossed the strait and occupied the area, maintaining it as a defensive outpost. The Moorish occupation of the Iberian peninsula led in 1160 to the establishment of an Arab city there, which Spain captured in 1309. The Moors regained Gibraltar in 1333 and held it until 1462, when Spain again took Gibraltar. By that time the Moorish presence in Iberia was confined to the outpost at Granada, and Gibraltar never again fell into their hands.

Spanish control of Gibraltar continued until 1704 when a British fleet commanded by Admiral George Rooke seized the city during the War of the Spanish Succession. As part of the Treaty of Utrecht* ending the war, Spain ceded permanent control over Gibraltar to England. Periodically over the years Spain has tried to regain Gibraltar. During the American Revolution, Spain placed Gibraltar under siege between 1779 and 1783, but the Treaty of Versailles of 1783* reconfirmed British sovereignty. Gibraltar became a crown colony in 1830. During the 1960s, in an attempt to squeeze the Gibraltar economy and bring about a repatriation of the region, Spain sealed off its border with Gibraltar and refused to permit any commerce and trade. But in 1966 the people of Gibraltar voted overwhelmingly to maintain their association with the British Empire* and remain independent of Spain. It remains a part of the British Empire today. (Howard S. Levie, *The Status of Gibraltar*, 1983; Maxwell Stamp, *Gibraltar: British or Spanish?*, 1976.)

GILBERT, HUMPHREY. Sir Humphrey Gilbert was born about 1539 in Compton, near Dartmouth, England. He pursued a military career, fighting for England in Ireland, France, and the Netherlands, and he was knighted for bravery. Obsessed with the idea of finding the fabled Northwest Passage* to Asia, Gilbert published his essay *Discourse* in 1576 explaining his ambition. Two years later Queen Elizabeth I* granted him a charter to begin his search and to establish a colony in the New World*. The expedition did not make it past the Cape Verde* Islands because of internal bickering and opposition from Spanish ships. With money from his half-brother, Sir Walter Raleigh, Gilbert tried again in 1583, sailing with five ships to Newfoundland, where he established a colony at St. Johns on August 5, 1583. Disaffected settlers began returning to England in a few weeks, and Gilbert died at sea in 1583 on his own return voyage. (Douglas Bell, *Elizabethan Seamen*, 1936.)

GILBERT ISLANDS. See KIRBATI.

GLADSTONE, WILLIAM EWART. Born December 29, 1809, to a wealthy Liverpool merchant family, William Ewart Gladstone was educated at Eton and graduated from Oxford University, where he studied theology and the classics.

In 1832 he decided on a political career and was elected to parliament as a Tory member for the tiny borough of Newark. His early career as a Tory MP focused largely on defense of the Church of England against the disestablishment movement. Gradually, however, his political views turned toward the left. By 1842 his primary interest had shifted from defense of the established church to economic reform. As president of the board of trade in the Robert Peel ministry, Gladstone worked toward the establishment of free trade through numerous tariff reductions. In 1846, however, the Corn Law repeal felled the Peel government and Gladstone's political career was temporarily derailed.

Gladstone was reelected to parliament from Oxford University in 1847. His outspoken attacks on protectionist trade policy brought him the office of chancellor of the exchequer in a coalition government headed by Lord Aberdeen in 1852. Gladstone, as a leader of the Tory liberals (Peelites), introduced a series of liberal, laissez-faire economic bills, most notably the 1853 budget bill. By the early 1850s Gladstone's religious views had become much more liberal, and he voted to support Nonconformist and Catholic civil rights. Gladstone also supported removing restrictions on Jews and he consistently opposed anti-Catholic legislation. According to Gladstone's own account, a visit to Naples in 1850–1851, where he witnessed appalling poverty and cruelty under the Kingdom of the Two Sicilies, removed the last vestiges of Toryism from his political conscience.

In 1867 Gladstone became leader of the Liberal Party. From 1868 to 1874 Gladstone served as prime minister. During this ministry, Gladstone was responsible for the passage of a number of liberal bills, including the Education Act of 1870, which established board schools at the elementary level; the removal of religious tests for admission to Oxford and Cambridge; the abolition of the purchase system for military commissions; the legalization of trade unions; and the introduction of the secret ballot. Following the defeat of the Liberal Party in the parliamentary elections of 1874, Gladstone led the opposition to Benjamin Disraeli's Conservative government.

In Gladstone's second ministry, from 1880 to 1885, his focus turned from domestic reform to imperial policy, most particularly the issue of Irish home rule. A bill intended to establish a system of fair land rents and land tenure for Irish tenants, the Second Land Act, was passed by parliament in 1881. Because of the bill's unpopularity in Ireland and the subsequent political violence, including the assassination of both the chief secretary and undersecretary for Ireland*, Gladstone was forced to suspend Irish land-reform legislation. At the same time, however, Gladstone opposed the idea of imperialism, which he considered to be a distraction from the pressing issues of domestic political and economic reform. Specifically, Gladstone was convinced that the economic exploitation of the native populations of India and Africa could serve no long-term useful purpose for Britain. Nevertheless, Gladstone supported Britain's intrusion into Egypt* and the Sudan* during the 1880s, although he was reluctant to send military aid to General Gordon at Khartoum during the Sudan uprising of 1885.

Gladstone headed the government as prime minister for a brief period in 1886, when he introduced a further Irish home rule bill, the defeat of which prompted his resignation. Gladstone introduced another home rule bill in 1893 during his fourth premiership (1892–1894), but opposition from the House of Lords defeated it. His opposition to imperialism and his support for home rule became increasingly unpopular with the British public, and Gladstone retired from politics in 1894. He died May 19, 1898. (Paul Adelman, *Gladstone, Disraeli and Later Victorian Politics*, 1970, Philip M. Magnus, *Gladstone: A Biography*, 1954.)

William G. Ratliff

GOA. The Goa settlement consisted of three cities on 1,426 square miles of territory on the western Indian coast, 250 miles south of Bombay. Goa originally comprised the four districts conquered by Portugal's Affonso du Albuquerque in 1510, the Velhas Conquistas. Over time, the 7 Novas Conquistas as well as the island of Angediva (Anjidiv) were added to Portugal's claims. Old Goa's first major Portuguese building was the cathedral, built in 1511 and rebuilt in 1623. The convent of St. Francis was added in 1517. These structures and Goa's archbishop marked Goa's establishment as a center for Catholicism in the East. In civil administration, however, the Portuguese outgrew Goa, establishing New Goa (Panjim) as the government's center and residence of the viceroy in 1759. But Goa's importance had already peaked in the last quarter of the sixteenth century.

Between 1603 and 1639 the city was blockaded by the Dutch, who in combination with an epidemic succeeded in damaging the trade-based colony's prospects. In 1683 and again in 1739 Goa was saved from being overrun by the warlike Marathas only by the last-minute appearance of a Mughal army and then the Portuguese fleet. The British occupied Goa during Napoleon's invasion of Portugal (1809), but returned it at the end of the wars.

Because of the relatively slight importance of the settlement, the minimal rule imposed, and the lack of any self-sustaining indigenous nationalism, the Portuguese managed to maintain a hold on the settlement longer than their British neighbors on the remainder of the subcontinent. In 1955 nonviolent activists attempted to penetrate Goa's territory, but were repelled. Soon the movement became too strong for the Portuguese. India invaded Goa in 1961, incorporating it into India in 1962. The Portuguese were the first Europeans to take territory on the subcontinent and the last to leave. The story in between makes a striking contrast to that of the British colonies. Although the mercantilist settlement was very similar to those of Britain in Bombay*, Calcutta*, and Madras, Portugal's vision of empire never grew to include formal rule of great populations and lands. These differences demonstrate the contrasts between the Portuguese Empire* which dragged on for over 450 years, and the British Empire* which burned so brightly for barely 150 years. (C. R. Boxer, *Four Centuries of Portuguese Expansion, 1415–1825, 1961; Gervase Clarence-Smith, The Third Portuguese Empire 1825–1975. A Study in Economic Imperialism*, 1985.)

Mark R. Shulman

GOD, GLORY, AND GOLD. The phrase "God, Glory, and Gold" was a catchword used by Spanish conquistadores in the sixteenth century to justify their drive for wealth and power in the New World. Those three words summarized the motivation behind early Spanish imperialism. They sincerely wanted to please God by exporting the Roman Catholic faith to the native inhabitants of Mexico*, Central America, South America, and the Philippines*; they wanted to bring adventure into their own lives, since so many of the conquistadores had been born to the extreme poverty of Extremadura, Spain; and they wanted to bring back bullion—gold and silver—to enrich themselves and the mother country. (Charles Gibson, *Spain in America*, 1958.)

GOIÁS. During the sixteenth century, the Portuguese imperial frontier in Brazil* was largely a coastal phenomenon, but by the late seventeenth and early eighteenth centuries, Portuguese settlers began pushing into the interior in the beginning of a vast "westward movement" which is still underway. They were searching for mineral wealth and grazing land for cattle. As that expansion into the interior highlands of Brazil took place, it became increasingly difficult to administer the region from Sao Paulo*. New political administrations were carved out of Sao Paulo, and Goiás was one of them, receiving its own governor in 1749. In 1822 Goiás became a province in the new empire of Brazil. See BRAZIL.

GOLD COAST. See GHANA.

GOLD COAST, NORTHERN TERRITORIES. The political unit known as Gold Coast, Northern Territories was the region of the Gold Coast, or contemporary Ghana*, north of Ashanti* in West Africa. British influence gradually extended into the area after the conquest of Ashanti. It received its own chief commissioner in 1899, and in 1953 the chief commissioner became known as a regional officer. The Gold Coast, Northern Territories was incorporated in Ghana when independence came in 1957. See GHANA.

GOLD COAST COLONY. The Gold Coast Colony was created as a separate region in the British empire* in 1945. It is that region of contemporary Ghana* which is south of Ashanti* along the coast of West Africa. The political unit was dissolved in 1953 and four years later incorporated into Ghana. See GHANA.

GOREE. Goree is an island off the coast of Senegal* in West Africa. The French first occupied Goree in 1677. It was a subordinate administrative district of Senegal until 1854, when it was governed in a new colonial arrangement with the French outposts in what is today Gabon* and the Republic of Guinea.* In 1859, however, Goree was reattached to Senegal. See SENEGAL.

GOVERNMENT OF INDIA ACT OF 1858. Following the traumatic upheavals in India* in 1857—during the so-called Indian Mutiny* or Sepoy Revolt—the Government of India Act of 1858 marked the formal transition from company to crown rule. It was the legal basis for Indian government from 1858 well into the twentieth century. The Act of 1858 was, in fact, the capstone on a series of charter renewals and parliamentary acts which had progressively stripped the British East India Company* of its authority and made the once powerful Company Bahadur (''Valiant'' or ''Exalted'' Company) a legal fiction even before its demise. The Act of 1858 abolished both the East India Company (and its court of directors) and the board of control (created to oversee Indian affairs in 1784). They were replaced with a full-blown department of state (the India Office*) headed by a principal secretary of state, and assisted by a council of fifteen members with India experience. (It also technically disposed of the Mogul empire once and for all.) Furthermore, the governor-general of India also received the title of ''viceroy'' to signify his enhanced status as the Queen's representative.

While in many ways little changed in 1858, the Act reconfigured Indian administration in some important new directions. First, unlike his colleagues in the cabinet, the secretary of state for India operated as a ''corporate entity''— the Secretary of State *in Council*. The council of India initially filled with former company directors or old ''India hands'' was envisioned as a way to provide Indian expertise to the secretary of state and to represent an ethos best described as ''India in England'' which would be salubrious to Indian administration from London. But the technical and legal relationship between the secretary of state and his council was unclear at times, and often made the work of the India Office cumbersome. The situation was exacerbated by the broader exposure of Indian affairs to parliament and the increasingly literate and interested British public.

The Government of India Act of 1858 ensured that all subsequent constitutional reform for India had to go through parliament and was, therefore, subject to the ebb and flow of British politics. This certainly created tension between Whitehall and Calcutta, where British officials on the spot often believed that they were better informed and regularly chaffed at the imposition of authority from London. Finally, the Act of 1858 required the government of India, through its revenues, to pay for the salaries and operation of the India Office and its top officials. While not being on the British Estimates gave the India Office some freedom of action, it also exposed it to the vagaries of international monetary crises in the nineteenth century and, ultimately, to the unpredictability of Indian revenues pegged, as they were, to the fortunes of the monsoons and agricultural produce. (T. R. Metcalf, *The Aftermath of Revolt*, 1964; Donovan Williams, *The India Office, 1858–1869*, 1983.)

Arnold P. Kaminsky

GOVERNMENT OF INDIA ACT OF 1919. The impact of World War I on India* was all pervasive—socially, economically, and politically—and relations between Britain and India were fundamentally and irrevocably altered. A wide range of problems emerged after the war which might collectively be labeled "dilemmas of dominion." These included, among other things, increasingly contentious internecine struggles among British interest groups and dilemmas related to the emergence of articulate groups of Indians making urgent and divergent demands on their strapped British rulers. With the Indian Councils Act of 1909, the British had taken an important step toward introducing representative government in India by increasing the number of non-official members elected to the central and provincial legislatures, allowing discussion on the Indian budget, and providing for admission of Indians to both the viceroy's executive council in Delhi and the council of India in London. Significantly, however, the 1909 Act did not introduce responsible government to India and, worse yet to the Hindu majority it introduced a "communal electorate" for Muslims which would remain an element of all subsequent constitutional legislation, gaining its final form as the partition of the subcontinent.

Despite the 1909 Act, Indian political aspirations and discontent continued unabated into the first years of World War I. To satisfy Indian demands for a larger share of government and to sustain Indian support during Britain's time of crisis, E. S. Montagu (secretary of state for India) announced on August 20, 1917, that the goal of British policy was "the progressive realization of Responsible government in India. . . . " He then traveled to India and issued a report in 1918 which was essentially given life as the Government of India Act of 1919. While it did not make any effective change in relations between Whitehall and Delhi, or in the central government (although the executive council was expanded to include three Indians), the Act of 1919 radically changed provincial administration by introducing into government the "dyarchy." While a number of subjects (such as public health, education, local self-government) became provincial subjects, some areas of responsibility were *transferred* to Indian ministers responsible to the provincial legislatures through the electorate. Transferred subjects included agriculture, public works, education, and local self-government. There were, however, a number of *reserved* subjects which remained in British hands—irrigation, land revenues, police, justice, press controls. Additionally, the Indian franchise was expanded so that roughly 10 percent of the adult male population could vote. The Act of 1919 expanded the principle of separate electorates for Muslims and other minorities, while certain privileged groups also had reserved seats in Indian government. In spite of its limitations, the introduction of direct election on a wider franchise, and the expanded opportunities for Indians not only in the consultative process but in administratively responsible positions, were landmarks in the constitutional development of India. (Edwin S. Montagu, *An Indian Diary*, 1930; Peter G. Robb, *The Government of India and Reform*, 1976.)

Arnold P. Kaminsky

GOVERNMENT OF INDIA ACT OF 1935. The Government of India Act of 1919 made important changes in the administrative set-up of India*. Most significantly, the 1919 Act provided for a good measure of Indian participation at the provincial level of government, although the principle of "dyarchy" sustained the British in their control of the raj. The 1919 Act, which became operational in 1921, failed to satisfy Indian aspirations and proved inadequate amidst the swirl of Indian politics following World War I. The 1920s and early 1930s were distinguished by an intensification of Indian nationalist politics, the most striking features of which were the appearance of Mohandas K. Gandhi* on the political scene, and the ominous upsurge of communal strife between Hindus and Muslims.

Faced with several widespread "non-cooperation" and "civil disobedience" movements, and concerned with the persistence of communal tension, the government of India equivocated between repression and reform as a solution to Indian agitation. The British strategy centered on convening a series of round table conferences with Indian parties and Indian princes (whose territory comprised roughly one-third of the subcontinent outside British rule, but within its sphere of influence). After three years of tedious work (1930–32) constructing a reform package, the Government of India Act was passed in 1935. The Act marked a major step toward "dominion status" for India, but fell short of it on several major counts. The Government of India Act of 1935 gave fiscal autonomy to the provinces, abolished dyarchy at the provincial level, and enabled elected Indian ministers to hold key portfolios hitherto reserved for the British. Still, provincial governments retained the technical ability to act independently of the provincial legislatures in certain cases. Moreover, the act retained the institution of dyarchy at the center, while allowing Indians increased participation in the inner sanctum of the Raj; and it still left a part of the executive "irremovable" by the people of India and responsible only to the British parliament. Finally, all acts of the central legislature were subject to approval or reservation by the governor-general, or disallowance of the crown. Such provisions approximated the conditions which the Colonial Laws Validity Act of 1867 had applied to British dominions. However, that restriction had been repealed with the Statute of Westminster in 1931, and yet it was here reasserted.

Another major feature of the 1935 Act was the proposal for a federation of British and Princely India with an elected council of state and federal assembly. But the princes were wary of such "democratic" features, and the scheme for federation remained a paper plan. Overall, the 1935 Act effectively shifted the locus of British rule in India to New Delhi. And in spite of its subtle provisions allowing for a British veto on important legislation, and from the standpoint of the Indian National Congress the odious retention of the Communal Award (Jawaharlal Nehru* called it a "new charter of slavery"), all Indian political parties contested elections when the Act went into operation in 1937. The election of 1937 began the penultimate phase of the Raj, under the provisions of the Act of 1935. But the chances for success were, of course, interrupted by the outbreak of World War II within two years. (Robin Moore, *The Crisis of Indian Unity, 1917–1940*, 1974; C. H. Philips and M. D. Wainwright, eds., *The Partition of India: Policy and Perspectives, 1935–1947*, 1966.)

Arnold P. Kaminsky

GRÃO-PARÁ. Early in the seventeenth century, the Portuguese colony of Grão-Pará developed inland on both sides of the mouth of the Amazon River. Francisco Caldeira Castelo Branco began serving as its first captain-general in 1615, but he was subject to the jurisdiction of Maranhão*. As the city of Belém, the capital of Grão-Pará, increased in size and political and economic significance, it eclipsed Maranhão in importance, and in 1754 the office of the governor-general was shifted from Maranhão to Grão-Pará, with Maranhão now under that jurisdiction. Maranhão and Grão-Pará received completely separate jurisdictions in 1775. By that time Grão-Pará's territorial extent had been circumscribed. Inland settlement up the Amazon made it impossible to govern the interior from Belém, and in 1757 Portugal created the new colonial province of São Jose do Rio Negro,* which still reported to Grão-Pará. In 1822, Grão-Pará became part of the new empire of Brazil as the Province of Pará. See BRAZIL.

GREATER ANTILLES. See ANTILLES.

GREAT LEBANON. See LEBANON.

GREENLAND. Greenland is an island of 840,000 square miles in the North Atlantic. More than 85 percent of the island is covered by a thick glacier. Inuits have lived on Greenland for thousands of years, but the first Europeans to arrive there were Viking explorers. Hans Egede, a Norwegian Lutheran missionary, established a mission on Greenland in 1721 to bring Christianity to the Inuits. That mission settlement at Godthaab eventually became the capital city of Greenland. In 1806 Denmark contracted Henrik Rink to survey the island, and during the rest of the nineteenth and early twentieth centuries, various American and British expeditions explored Greenland. The United States claimed title to Greenland, but in 1916, when Denmark sold the Virgin Islands* to the United States, the American government recognized Danish sovereignty over Greenland. In 1921 Denmark formally declared all of Greenland to be Danish territory, and although Norway protested, the World Court validated the claim in 1933. Denmark adopted a new constitution in 1953, which recognized Greenland as a Danish territory and gave Greenlanders representation in the national parliament. The population—Inuits, Danes, and a large mixed group—totaled 51,000 people in 1984. (Finn Gad, *The History of Greenland*, 2 volumes, 1971–1973).

GRENADA. Located 90 miles off Venezuela's coast in the southern Caribbean, Grenada has been a ping pong ball in the game of colonial imperialism. Although claimed by Spain in 1592, the first colonial settlement in 1608 was British. It was wiped out by Carib Indians. In 1650 M. De Parquet succeeded in building a French fort which became Grenada's first permanent colonial settlement. When the Indians realized that French intentions were to take over the island completely, they attempted to drive them out. In three years of war the French exterminated the Carib population. Grenada was safe for colonization. From 1654 to 1685

French entrepreneurs relied on the European underclass and religious and political dissidents for Grenada's labor force. The rise of European mercantilism* and industrial development reduced the availability of European labor just when the expansion of West Indies* tobacco and sugar plantations necessitated substantial increases in cheap labor. The African slave population grew from approximately 500 in 1700 to over 12,000 by 1753.

At the conclusion of the Seven Years' War in 1763, France ceded Grenada to Britain in the Treaty of Paris*. Grenada's Anglicization produced numerous cosmetic changes (for example, implementation of British law and changing the names of most settlements). For slaves, changing flags meant harsher conditions as British plantation owners tried to increase profit margins. Sugar exports more than doubled between 1763 and 1774. The American Revolution* prompted another war between Britain and France, with the French controlling Grenada from 1779 through 1783. However, Britain regained the colony in the Treaty of Versailles*. Inspired by the French Revolution, insurrection spread throughout the West Indies in the early 1790s. Grenada's revolt was led by Julien Fedon, a free black property owner. The revolt was crushed in 1796, but only after substantial loss of life on both sides and the destruction of Grenada's economy.

Access to "cheap" sugar from Cuba and South America coupled with British industrialization and economic development reduced the West Indies' economic importance and the profitability of slavery. Consequently, Britain abolished the slave trade in 1807 and slavery in 1833. The condition of "former" slaves did not improve. If anything, it worsened as a consequence of economic decline and efforts to maintain the plantation system. As sugar prices fell and Grenada's economy sank into depression, small landholders turned to cocoa and nutmeg to revitalize the economy.

Although economic conditions improved, the plight of the ex-slaves did not. By the late 1860s the former slaves, protesting their exclusion from political and economic power, posed a serious threat to the plantation aristocracy. To forestall powersharing with ex-slaves, Britain by the 1870s transformed most of the British West Indies into crown colonies, eliminating the old elected assemblies and vesting all political authority with the royal governor and a nominated legislative council. This did not quell black discontent. In the late nineteenth and early twentieth century, middle-class Grenadan leaders including William Donovan, founder of *The Federalist and Grenada People* newspaper, and T. A. Marryshow and C. F. P. Renwick, founders of the *West Indian* newspaper, worked to change the political, economic, and racial structure of colonial Grenada. Although they initially succeeded in achieving little more than cosmetic changes, they laid the foundation for Jamacia-born Marcus Garvey, a charismatic challenger to colonialism and racism. In the 1920s Garvey's movement was short-circuited, partially by the United States which felt threatened by the impact of Garvey's "subversive" message on American blacks; but not before motivating Marryshow and others to make vociferous demands for sweeping reforms. The British rejection was categorical.

With the Great Depression came truly wretched living conditions for an already generally impoverished population. The West India Royal (Moyne) Commission recommended welfare programs rather than socioeconomic restructuring. But the days of British colonial rule were numbered. In the aftermath of World War II, Britain realized it was better to grant independence from the top than to have it won from the bottom through rebellion. The process moved slowly with Jamaica* being the first West Indian colony to gain independence in 1962 and Grenada winning essential independence in the elections of 1967.

The story of imperialism in Grenada should end with independence in 1967, but the slow movement toward independence in Grenada contributed to the rise of Eric Gairy in the early 1950s. An opportunist more interested in self-advancement than independence and prosperity, Gairy was elected premier in 1967. Over the next twelve years he created the Mongoose Gang and turned Grenada into a dictatorship that exploited the general population for the benefit of Gairy and his cronies. Since he was strongly pro-capitalist and anti-communist, neither Britain nor the United States had serious problems with his regime. But on March 13, 1979, the New Jewel Movement, led by Maurice Bishop, overthrew Gairy's regime in "the Peaceful Revolution." The egalitarian, non-aligned, Marxist-influenced ideology of the New Jewel Movement and its close ties with Cuba won the intense displeasure of the Reagan administration, which made repeated accusations that large numbers of Cuban military forces were in Grenada and that construction of a new airport and improved port facilities were military installations intended to place a communist stranglehold on the Caribbean. When a power struggle within the New Jewel Movement resulted in the murder of Maurice Bishop, who was extremely popular with the Grenadan population, Reagan saw his chance.

On October 27, 1983, in the immediate wake of the slaughter of 240 U.S. marines in Lebanon, elements of the U.S. Marine Corps and 82nd Airborne Division invaded Grenada under the justifications that political turmoil in Grenada threatened the safety of United States citizens attending medical school there as well as the previous charges about the airport and Cuban soldiers. Virtually all of Reagan's allegations ultimately were proven false. (George Brizan, *Grenada: Island of Conflict*, 1984; Gordon Lewis, *Grenada: The Jewel Despoiled*, 1987.)

Samuel Freeman

GRENADINES. The Grenadines are an island chain in the Lesser Antilles. First discovered by Christopher Columbus* in 1498, the Grenadines are today divided between St. Vincent*, a British colony, and Grenada*, an independent nation. The Southern Grenadines associated with Grenada include Ronde, Les Tantes, Diamond, Large, Frigate, Saline, Carriacou, and Petite Martinique islands. The Northern Grenadines tied to St. Vincent include Petite St. Vincent, Palm, Union, Mayreau, the Tobago Cays, Canouan, Savan, Petite Mustique, Mustique, Baliceaux, Battowia, Isle a Quatre, Petit Nevis, and Bequia. (Ethel A. Starbird,

"Taking It as It Comes. St. Vincent, the Grenadines, and Grenada," *National Geographic*, 156, September 1979, 399–425.)

GRIQUALAND. Inhabited by and named after the Griqua people, Griqualand West and Griqualand East were two large areas of historical importance in southern Africa which are now located within the borders of the Cape Province of the Republic of South Africa*. The Griqua were light-skinned people of mixed descent: Hottentots, Sotho, Bushmen, and other tribal groups of southern Africa, intermixed with Europeans. It is believed that some of these light-skinned Africans migrated from the western part of the Dutch-ruled Cape Colony* to lands south of the Orange River in the late eighteenth century. They organized into a tribe calling themselves Basters, a name connoting white and black mix, and moved northward across the Orange River to escape European control in the Cape Colony. By 1813 the tribe called themselves the Griqua. Under the leadership of Adam Kok I, the small community of farmers and herders settled on the north bank of the Orange River in the area that came to be called Griqualand West.

When the British established permanent control of the Cape Colony in the early nineteenth century, Boer trekkers advanced into Griqualand West. With the discovery of diamond fields in 1867 at Kimberly, in the eastern region of Griqualand West, European settlement of the area increased, and the Griqua faced the danger of becoming subject to European rule. In 1871 a Griqua leader, Chief Nicholas Waterboer, encouraged Great Britain to declare Griqualand West a British territory in the hope of preserving Griqua claims to the land against the encroachment of the trekkers. For a short time (1873–1880) the territory was given the status of a crown colony, but on Oct. 15, 1880, Griqualand West was annexed into the Cape Colony. Most of the Griqua by that time had ceded their land claims to whites. By the end of the 1800s the few remaining Griqua in the area were impoverished and working for whites.

Griqualand East came about when a group of the Griqua in the early nineteenth century split away from the settlements on the Orange River, migrating under the leadership of Adam Kok II. By 1825 this branch of the Griqua tribe had settled east of the Vaal River in the area that later became the Orange Free State*. Adam Kok III assumed control of the tribe around 1837, and in 1843 he placed his people under British protection and negotiated the lease of Griqua lands to white settlers. When the Orange Free State was annexed into the Cape Colony in 1848–1854 the Griqua lost most of their claims to the lands they had leased to settlers.

From 1861 to 1862 Adam Kok III and about 2,000 Griqua began their own "great trek" south to the Transkei area where, due south of Basutoland*, they established Griqualand East. In 1868 this area too became a British protectorate. Shortly after the death of Adam Kok III, Griqualand East was formally annexed by the Cape Colony (1879). Today the Griqua are classified as a subgroup of the "Coloureds" in the South African Republic. (Gideon S. Were, *A Short History of South Africa*, 1974.)

Karen Sleezer

GRIQUALAND EAST. See GRIQUALAND.

GRIQUALAND WEST. See GRIQUALAND.

GUADELOUPE. Guadeloupe is an overseas department of France, complete with representation in the French national legislature. One of the Lesser Antilles* in the West Indies*, Guadeloupe is composed of Basse-Terre, a 35-mile long island also known as Guadeloupe, and Grand-Terre, an island just across a narrow channel from Basse-Terre. Together they total 583 square miles. Guadeloupe also includes another 105 square miles of territory: Marie Galante, a 60-square mile island 16 miles southeast of Basse-Terre; Desirade, an 11-square mile island just east of Grand-Terre; Les Saints, a small island group totaling 5 square miles of land south of Basse-Terre; St. Barthelemy*, a 9-square mile island north of Antigua; and St. Martin, a 37-square mile island, of which France controls the northern 20 square miles, located 43 miles northeast of St. Kitts.

Columbus* discovered Guadeloupe and most of its constituent islands during his second voyage to the New World in 1493, but because of the hostility of the native Carib Indians, the Spaniards did little to develop the island. Instead they invested their military and economic resources in conquering Cuba, Hispaniola, Mexico, and Peru. It was not until 1635 that Europe showed real interest in Guadeloupe, when France established a colony there. Twelve years later, in 1647, the French constructed their first sugar mill in Guadeloupe and began importing African slaves to work the plantations. By the middle of the eighteenth century Guadeloupe had become the crown jewel in the French overseas empire, the world's leading producer of sugar.

Administratively, Guadeloupe was ruled from Martinique. France lost control of the island when the British seized it in 1759 during the Seven Years' War, but in the Treaty of Paris of 1763*, Great Britain restored Guadeloupe to France. During the French Revolution slavery was abolished on Guadeloupe and in 1794, the same year Britain again invaded, the island was separated from Martinique and given its own colonial administration. Britain withdrew later in 1794. Life returned to normal in 1802 when Napoleon restored slavery and the sugar plantations began to thrive again.

During the Napoleonic Wars, Great Britain invaded Guadeloupe and maintained control until 1813, when the island was ceded to Sweden. Sweden supervised Guadeloupe until 1816 when it was once again returned to France. The island has remained French ever since. Guadeloupe came on hard times in 1848 when France abolished slavery, but her political connections to France were strong. In 1946 France changed Guadeloupe's status from colony to overseas department, with the same political status as France's internal departments. By

1988 the Guadeloupe population exceeded 335,000 people. (Nellis M. Crouse, *French Pioneers in the West Indies, 1624–1664*, 1972; Herbert Ingram Priestley, *France Overseas. A Study of Modern Imperialism*, 1966.)

GUAM. Located in the North Pacific approximately 5,043 miles west by south of San Francisco, Guam is 212 square miles in area, the largest of the Marianas* Islands. The first European discovery of Guam is attributed to Magellan*, who landed there in 1531. Spain made no attempt to bring the island under control until the seventeenth century, when it subdued the native population, the Chamorros, with considerable bloodshed. Spanish missionaries colonized the island in 1668 and converted the natives to Catholicism. Guam remained a Spanish possession until 1898, when the United States demanded it as part of the settlement ending the Spanish-American War*. In the Treaty of Paris of 1898*, Spain ceded Guam to the United States. Spain sold the remaining Mariana Islands to Germany in 1899. After World War I, Japan received these German possessions (together with the Caroline Islands* and Marshall Islands*) as a mandate from the League of Nations* (and in accordance with the secret treaties of London which promised to Japan all German colonies north of the equator).

Although Guam was demilitarized by the Washington Conference of 1921–1922*, the United States did little to change that status even after Japan withdrew from the agreement in 1936. Congress was not willing to provide the necessary funding, and many naval experts regarded the island as indefensible, given the fact that the Japanese island of Rota was only 30 miles away. Not until 1941 were funds provided to improve the harbor and airfield. The experts were correct. After the attack on Pearl Harbor in 1941, Japan invaded Guam and the small contingent of marines and sailors could not defend it. Guam fell to the Japanese on December 9, 1941, and remained under Japanese control until 1944, when United States troops recaptured it.

Until after World War II Guam was administered by the Department of the Navy. The commander of the naval station was also the governor, who ruled with almost unlimited powers. This archaic arrangement lasted until 1950, when the island was placed under the Department of the Interior. The Organic Act of 1950 also provided for a governor appointed by the President of the United States and a unicameral legislative body elected every two years. The residents of Guam were also given citizenship in the United States. Since 1970 the governor of Guam has been popularly elected, and since 1972 Guam has sent a non-voting delegate to the United States Congress. (*The World Almanac and Book of Facts, 1982*, 1982.)

Joseph M. Rowe, Jr.

GUATEMALA. Guatemala, once the seat of the captaincy-general of Guatemala, under the jurisdiction of the viceroyalty of New Spain*, not only included Guatemala but also the Central American nations of Costa Rica*, Nicaragua*, Honduras*, El Salvador*, the present-day Mexican state of Chiapas, and British

Honduras*. On December 6, 1523, Pedro de Alvarado left Mexico on an overland expedition to Central America to meet with a sea expedition sent by Hernán Cortés* to Honduras. The expedition consolidated Spanish control over Guatemala and made it a part of the Spanish Empire*. The Mayan population which Alvarado encountered on his journey was decimated by smallpox and factional struggles between the Cakchiquel and Quiché. Alvarado allied himself with the Cakchiquel against the Quiché and their allies, the Tzutzuhil. On July 25, 1524, after the Quiché's defeat, he established the first Guatemala City at Iximche, the Cakchiquel capital. The conquest continued as various Indian revolts sprang up. Spanish demands even caused their former allies to revolt. The pacification continued throughout the colonial period.

Guatemala City was moved various times throughout the colonial period. On November 22, 1527, Jorge de Alvarado, Pedro's brother, moved the city to Almolonga (now Ciudad Vieja, Guatemala). Pedro went to Spain in 1527 to petition the crown for the title of *adelantado*. Governor Alvarado, a restless administrator, used Guatemala as a base for further expeditions because of the area's paucity of precious metals. When Alvarado died, his wife, Doña Beatriz de la Cueva, became governor, but she died two days after taking command on September 10, 1541, when an earthquake destroyed Santiago de Guatemala. The city was moved to Panchoy (now Antigua, Guatemala) in November 1541.

During this early phase many struggles erupted between the various conquistadores, sent by different authorities, who converged on the region. The establishment of the Audiencia de los Confines on May 16, 1544, in Honduras, attempted to remedy the lack of unity and administrative confusion and give the isthmus political unity. The *audiencia's* removal to Santiago de Guatemala in 1549 showed the city's growing importance. The Audiencia de los Confines dissolved between 1564–1570, moved to Panama, and had jurisdiction over Panama, Costa Rica, and Nicaragua. Isthmian unity broke as the rest of Central America came under the jurisdiction of the Audiencia de Mexico. In March 1570 the Audiencia de Guatemala was reestablished in Santiago de Guatemala. The Audiencia, presided over by the president who also served as governor and captain-general, had political and administrative jurisdiction of Central America from Chiapas through Costa Rica. The viceroyalty of New Spain* had jurisdiction over the kingdom but its authorities were chosen directly from Spain. Guatemala remained unified until the end of the colonial period.

The region's lack of precious metals made Indian labor an important commodity, and the crown gave *encomiendas** to the region's conquistadores. The exploitation of Indian labor for the burgeoning economy of agricultural exports, initially cacao and indigo, led to many abuses. Indigo, a blue dye, survived throughout the colonial period as an important export commodity. To gain control over the *encomienda* and stop abuses, the crown promulgated the New Laws of 1541 which gave the *encomienda* grant for two generations and not in perpetuity. The New Laws legislated a system of forced labor, the *repartimiento*, where individuals could petition crown officials for procurement of an allotment of

Indian laborers to work in mines, agricultural lands, or public projects. The *encomienda* declined as a labor institution when Indian population dropped precipitously. But the *repartimiento* continued up to and through the eighteenth century.

Indian population decline, responsible for a long depression in the late 1500s and early 1600s, triggered the movement of Spaniards from towns to rural areas as land became available. They acquired title to empty village lands and drifted into self-subsistence. The kingdom's unity fragmented as internal trade diminished. English pirates ravaged the kingdom's coasts. Cultural and biological miscegenation produced the *latino*, a mixture of Spanish and Indian blood or an Hispanicized Indian. Throughout the colonial period the antagonism between *criollos*, New World–born Spaniards, and *peninsulares*, European Spaniards, increased. The *criollo*, condemned to minor government positions, could not expect a major colonial post. The *corregidor* represented the crown in the Indian villages and often subjected them to many abuses leading to resentment and open defiance of this official.

In the eighteenth century the replacement of the Habsburg rulers by the Bourbons in Spain heightened these antagonisms. This had a profound effect on the Spanish empire, in general, and the kingdom of Guatemala, in particular, as reforms for modernization encroached on the Indians' and *criollos'* traditional lives. The church, which played an important role in the region's colonization and administration, was also affected by this trend. The University of San Carlos's establishment in 1681 portended profound changes in the kingdom as its importance grew within the imperial system. In 1729 the first Guatemalan newspaper, the *Gazeta de Goathemala*, appeared, and a mint was established in 1733. In 1742 Guatemala was elevated to archdiocese status with jurisdiction over Chiapas, Honduras, and Nicaragua. The British effectively colonized parts of the kingdom along the Caribbean coast with the Mosquito Indians' help. In 1767 the Jesuits* were expelled from Guatemala. A major burden for the colony was the city's removal after an earthquake devastated Santiago de Guatemala on July 29, 1773. The new city was founded on January 1, 1776. The intendent system's introduction in 1786 infringed on the *audiencia's* central authority as intendents were set up in Honduras, El Salvador, Nicaragua, and Chiapas to maintain closer supervision and contributed to later fragmentation after independence. A merchants guild was established in 1794 to foment the economic development of the kingdom. An economic society was formed in 1795 to spread Enlightenment thought throughout the elite members of the society.

In the early nineteenth century indigo's decline and Spain's European wars led to Guatemala's economic decline and contributed to many *criollos'* desire for economic and political independence. Napoleon's invasion of Spain in 1808 intensified the *criollos'* desire. The appointment of a new captain-general, José Bustamante y Guerra, who perceived the *criollos* as responsible for the general agitation in the kingdom, led to harsh rule in the kingdom between 1811 and 1818. Guatemalan *criollos* participated in the Cortes de Cádiz' efforts to create a constitutional monarchy in 1812. The Spanish American independence movements influenced the *criollos*, and numerous revolts, such as the 1813 Belén conspiracy in Guatemala, occurred. The 1812 constitution was annulled with Ferdinand VII's return to the Spanish throne in 1814. The constitutional regime's reestablishment in 1820 did not prevent Guatemala's declaration of independence on September 15, 1821. (Jim Handy, *A Gift of the Devil*, 1984; J. A. Villacorta Calderon, *Historia de la Capitania General de Guatemala*, 1942; Ralph Lee Woodward Jr., *Central America; A Nation Divided*, 1976.)

Carlos Pérez

GUAYANA. Spain established the province of Guayana in eastern Venezuela* in 1591. It included the neighboring island of Trinidad*. The colony was subordinate administratively to New Granada*. In 1735 Spain separated Trinidad out as a colony in its own right and dissolved Guayana administratively, placing it under the authority of New Andalucia, its contiguous neighbor. In 1766 the Spanish crown transferred Guayana to the captaincy-general of Venezuela. Spanish authority survived there until 1817 when rebel forces occupied the region. After the wars of independence, Guayana was part of Gran Colombia and then Venezuela. See VENEZUELA.

GUAYAQUIL. Today Guayaquil is the largest city in Ecuador*. It was founded by Sebastian de Benalcazar in 1531, destroyed by Indians shortly thereafter, and then rebuilt by Francisco de Orellana in 1537 to serve as a port city for Quito. Because of its location at the Gulf of Guayaquil, the city prospered and grew as a center for the export of cacao and as the major site of the shipbuilding industry in Latin America. It was also known, however, for its abundance of yellow fever, malaria, and smallpox. Guayaquil and the surrounding region was a *corregimiento* under the Audiencia of Quito until 1763 when it became a separate province with its own governor. It fell to rebel forces in 1820 and was part of Gran Colombia until 1830 when it became part of Ecuador*. See ECUADOR.

GUINEA. Guinea, formerly known as French Guinea, is an independent country located on the western coast of Africa. In the middle ages, the vast Mali and Songhai empires extended into the area that became modern Guinea. The people who primarily make up the population (Fulani and Malinke) are descended from various tribes of the western Sudan region who emigrated to the plateaus of northern Guinea in the thirteenth to the seventeenth centuries.

The first recorded European contacts with the region were established by Portuguese traders in the fifteenth century. By the seventeenth century French, British, and Portuguese traders and slavers were competing for control of the region. French interests along the Guinea coast were recognized in the Treaty of Paris in 1814. In the late 1840s, the French began to make treaties of protection with tribes in the area, culminating with the establishment of a protectorate over

Fouta Djallon* in the early 1880s. Until 1890 the Guinea territories were ad-ministered as a part of Senegal, after which the area—then called Rivieres du Sud—was established as a separate colony and was renamed French Guinea (1893).

The French did not completely consolidate their control over Guinea until 1898 when the great Malinke leader Samori Toure was captured, bringing to an end the most effective resistance to the establishment of French colonial rule in West Africa. In 1895 French Guinea, while keeping its own colonial adminis-tration, was made part of the larger federation of French West Africa.

An independence movement began to emerge in Guinea shortly after World War II. France attempted to stall the move towards independence by liberalizing its administrative control of the colony. A territorial assembly was established and representation in the French legislature was offered to appease demands for independence. In September 1958, the people of Guinea were given an oppor-tunity to vote in a plebiscite conducted throughout France and the French Empire on a constitution for a Fifth French Republic. French overseas territories which accepted the new constitution could choose to remain as dependent colonies or could elect to become autonomous national republics within the French Com-munity. Of all the French African territories, Guinea alone rejected the new constitution, opting instead for complete independence. Guinea became inde-pendent on October 2, 1958. Sekou Toure, who had headed the independence movement, was elected as president of the new government. (American Uni-versity, *Area Handbook for Guinea*, 1975; Thomas E. O'Toole, *Historical Dictionary of Guinea*, 1978; Camare Laye, *The Dark Child*, 1969.)

Joseph L. Michaud

GUINEA-BISSAU. See PORTUGUESE GUINEA.

H

HAGUE CONFERENCE OF 1899. Several international peace conferences were held at The Hague, The Netherlands, beginning in the late nineteenth century. The first Hague Peace Conference was convened in 1899 at the request of the Russian minister of foreign affairs, Count Mikhail N. Muravyov. Acting on behalf of Tsar Nicholas II, Muravyov proposed to the foreign ambassadors in St. Petersburg that the assembled delegates of all the peace-loving nations discuss the general reduction of military armaments. Some of the governments, including the United States, immediately agreed to the tsar's proposal. By late December 1898 Muravyov proposed three specific topics for consideration: a limitation on the expansion of armed forces and a reduction in the deployment of new armaments; the application of the principles of the Geneva Convention of 1864 to naval warfare; and a revision of the unratified Brussels Declaration of 1874 regarding the laws and customs of land warfare. Following the exchange of additional correspondence between the interested governments, an invitation was sent out on April 7, 1899, for the conference to assemble on May 18 at The Hague.

The first Hague Conference of 1899 was attended by the representatives of twenty-seven nations, including Great Britain, the United States, Germany, France, Italy, the Scandinavian countries, and Japan, and over one hundred advisors and scientific experts. After prolonged discussions, the delegates ratified the three original conventions—peaceful resolution of international conflicts, the laws and customs of land warfare, and the application of the principles of the Geneva Convention of August 10, 1864, to naval warfare. The 1899 Conference also adopted three specific declarations: A five-year prohibition against throwing projectiles and explosives from balloons or ejecting them with the aid of any newly developed technique; the non-use of projectiles designed only for the diffusion of asphyxiating and harmful gases; and the prohibition of "dum-dum" projectiles, that is, bullets that easily turn or flatten in the human body. The most important and long-lasting proposal approved by the delegates, and the decision most directly affecting the issue of colonial relations, was the adoption of the Convention for the Pacific Settlement of International Disputes, which created the Permanent Court of Arbitration. (Joseph Hodges Choate, *The Two Hague Conferences*, 1913.)

                                                                        William G. Ratliff

HAITI. Haiti occupies the western third of Hispaniola*, an island that it shares with the Dominican Republic*. Only fifty miles east of Cuba, Haiti was discovered on December 5, 1492, by Christopher Columbus*. Twenty days later, after the *Santa Maria* was wrecked off its northern coast, Columbus constructed a small outpost, Navidad, near modern Cap Haitien. When the admiral returned almost a year later, he found that Navidad's 39 men had been killed by natives. In 1492 Hispaniola supported perhaps 4,000,000 Arawaks. Its western portion, the island's most densely-populated region, contained two chieftainships, one of which was centered at Xaragua, not far from Haiti's present capital, Port-au-Prince. Both were treacherously seized by the Spaniards in 1503. The Arawak population dwindled to 2,200 by 1518. Spain ordered the evacuation of the area in 1605 because of its flourishing contraband trade.

The abandoned territory's vast herds of feral cattle and hogs attracted roving bands of buccaneers who based themselves on Tortuga*, a small island hugging Hispaniola's northwestern shore. The Spaniards expelled English Puritans and Gallic adventurers in 1635 and 1654, but in 1664 Louis XIV granted western Hispaniola to the French West India Company. Its governor, Bertrand d'Ogeron, encouraged plantation agriculture in the main island's northern valleys. He also imported women and African slaves and induced buccaneers to plant or cut mahogany for export. Governor d'Ogeron died in 1675, after transforming a pirate's lair into the colony of Saint-Domingue.

Late seventeenth-century Saint-Domingue was involved in frequent international conflicts. Numerous raids on rival colonies were launched from its ports and it, in turn, suffered from both Spanish and English incursions. Finally, in 1697, Spain recognized France's sovereignty by the Treaty of Ryswick. Irrigation, modern machinery, efficient agricultural techniques, a highly developed infrastructure, and the massive importation of slaves spurred Saint-Domingue's phenomenal economic growth between 1697 and 1791. By the end of the 1760s, sugar exports equalled those of the entire British West Indies*. Coffee, cotton, and indigo were other significant cash crops. At the close of the eighteenth century, Saint-Domingue was the world's most valuable colonial possession.

Below the surface of this prosperity flowed an undercurrent of seething resentment. Slaves, mostly African-born, outnumbered free persons eight to one. Poor whites despised the mulattoes, many of whom owned slaves and were educated by their French fathers. French government officials looked down upon wealthy local planters. In 1758 Francois Macandal, an escaped slave and poison expert, was burned at the stake for conspiring to eliminate Saint-Domingue's whites. American and French Revolutionary ideals circulated widely in the latter 1700s. Vincent Oge headed a mulatto uprising and was promptly broken on the wheel in 1790. Social tensions strained Saint-Domingue's highly stratified caste system to its limits.

Voodoo priests secretly planned a revolt in the colony's North Province. Drummers coordinated the rebellion, which erupted in August 1791, with 100,000 slaves participating. French forces arrived the next year, but their Jacobin leaders sided with the Africans, causing 10,000 whites to flee overseas. England and Spain invaded with the support of the remaining planters. When the French National Convention abolished slavery in 1794, the commander of a 4,000-man mercenary army in the service of Spain, an idealistic, yet power-hungry Pierre-Dominique Toussaint L'Ouverture*, rallied to the side of France. Toussaint, an ex-slave educated by his master, expelled the Spaniards, who ceded eastern Hispaniola to the French in the 1795 Treaty of Basle. Combat and disease killed an estimated 100,000 British troops. Toussaint displayed his diplomatic acumen by negotiating an English withdrawal in 1798. He then defeated his remaining rivals so that by 1801 he ruled all of Hispaniola in France's name.

Napoleon Bonaparte could not stomach a Caribbean version of himself. General Charles le Clerc was dispatched to reconquer Saint-Domingue. Le Clerc's forces succeeded in eastern Hispaniola. Toussaint was captured and shipped to France. Soon afterward Saint-Domingue exploded when its people learned that slavery would be restored. Approximately 40,000 soldiers perished before France withdrew its troops. On January 1, 1804, Toussaint's former lieutenant, the vehemently anti-white, African-born Jean Jacques Dessalines proclaimed the independence of Saint-Domingue under an Arawak name, "Haiti." Thus, Haiti followed the United States as the second New World nation to cast off the yoke of colonialism. (C. L. R. James, *The Black Jacobins*, 1963; Thomas O. Ott, *The Haitian Revolution, 1789–1804*, 1973.)

Frank Marotti

HAKLUYT, RICHARD. Richard Hakluyt was born in Herefordshire, England, in 1552. From the time of elementary school he became fascinated with world geography and learned six languages to be able to read all the accounts of overseas exploration. He became a leading scholar at Oxford and in 1582 published *Divers Voyages Touching Upon the Discovery of America*. Seven years later, after leaving the priesthood and joining the clergy and serving as an aide to the English ambassador in Paris, Hakluyt wrote his most famous book, *The Principall Navigations, Voiages, Traffiques and Discoveries of the English Nation*. It was an extraordinarily popular book which legitimized the notion of English colonial expansion. Hakluyt rose through the Anglican ministry, eventually dying in 1616 at Gedney in Lincolnshire, where he was serving as rector. (G. B. Parks, *Richard Hakluyt and the English Voyages*, 1928.)

HAWAII. The Hawaiian Islands lie in an isolated position in the Central Pacific Ocean, 2,200 miles southwest of the United States mainland, 2,600 miles south of Alaska, and 3,800 miles east northeast of Japan. They lie along the main lines of communication both to the Far East and Australia and New Zealand and guard the approaches to North America from the western Pacific. The earliest value of the islands was as a stopover point in the trans-Pacific trade between Oregon and China and later as a trade connection with Australia and the United States. Hawaii also became the main way station and wintering ground for whaling ships. American domination appeared from the beginning. Late in the nineteenth century, the advent of the sugar industry with its West Coast market assured American control of that industry almost as soon as it began.

In addition to economic predominance, the Americans gained cultural ascendancy, mainly due to the efforts of New England missionaries who came to Hawaii in 1820. Within a short time they established Congregational Protestantism and an American-style cultural ethos among the Hawaiians. In the 1830s and 1840s missionary advisors to King Kamehameha III created a western government with a constitution, a cabinet, a legislature, and a legal system, although the monarch remained an absolute ruler. By 1850 the kingdom had survived bullying attempts by the British and the French, and President John Tyler made it clear that the United States would not tolerate a takeover of the islands by any other government.

In the years after the Civil War, Hawaiian prosperity grew as trade with the mainland increased. In 1876 a reciprocity treaty which allowed Hawaiian sugar to enter the United States duty-free tightened the economic bonds which joined the kingdom to the United States. Renewal of the treaty in 1887 was conditional upon the leasing of naval station rights to the basin of Pearl Harbor, but for the time being the United States was not interested in developing its option. By 1890 the relationship of Hawaii to the United States was that of a protectorate, but there is no evidence that the American government was interested in annexation.

Political events after 1880 brought increasing instability in Hawaii and the need for some kind of American action. King David Kalakaua and his chief advisor, Walter Murray Gibson, aroused the ire of white business leaders by creating a large debt, encouraging corruption in government, and above all increasing racial tension between the whites and the native Hawaiians. In 1887 the whites took up arms and forced Kalakaua to dismiss Gibson and accept a new constitution which reduced his powers to that of a constitutional monarch. Kalakaua accepted the situation, but his sister Liliuokalani did not. After his death in 1891, Queen Liliuokalani asserted the prerogatives remaining to her, and in January 1893 she tried to promulgate a new constitution.

Americans led a rebellion which overthrew her after American sailors and marines were landed from a warship in Honolulu harbor. The rebels, quickly recognized by the American minister, sent a delegation to Washington to draw up a treaty of annexation. The Harrison administration was willing, but the effort was forestalled by the inauguration of Grover Cleveland in March 1893. Cleveland withdrew the treaty and tried to restore Liliuokalani to her throne when he became convinced the American minister and military forces had acted in bad faith. As long as Cleveland was president Hawaii would have to wait for annexation.

The Hawaiian Republic was established in July 1894. Three years later William McKinley became president, and early in 1898 another attempt was made to bring about annexation. It languished in the Senate until the outbreak of the Spanish-American War*. With the impending American capture of the Philippines*, the vital importance of Hawaii to trans-Pacific communications suddenly became obvious, and on July 2 President McKinley signed a congressional joint resolution providing for Hawaii's annexation. After annexation the question of the organization of the new territorial government was addressed. On June 14, 1900, Congress passed an organic act establishing Hawaii as an incorporated territory with an elected legislature but an appointed governor. Representation in Congress was provided by an elected non-voting delegate. All residents at the time of annexation, except Asians, were made American citizens.

Hawaii's role as a territory within the American colonial system was to serve as a link and naval station between the West Coast and the Far East. Territorial status ruled out statehood for the time being but left the door open to longer term consideration. Over the years the second-class status of Hawaiians became a fact of life that they increasingly resented. Statehood seemed the best way to achieve equality. In 1940 a referendum showed a 2–1 majority favoring statehood. The campaign for statehood was halted abruptly by the Japanese attack on Pearl Harbor, but after the war serious efforts to bring Hawaii into the United States resumed. In 1950 a state constitution was drafted. But by that time the Cold War was underway, and the issue of communist infiltration of some of Hawaii's labor unions served as a pretext to defeat all efforts to push statehood resolutions through Congress. By the end of the decade the communist question was no longer important, and the petition of Alaska for statehood changed the situation. A mistaken decision to link the two territories together in the statehood fight delayed the entry of both, but when the two quests were separated, events moved rapidly. In 1958 Alaska was admitted to the Union, and a year later, on August 21, 1959, President Dwight Eisenhower proclaimed Hawaii the fiftieth state. (Gavan Daws, *Shoal of Time: A History of the Hawaiian Islands*, 1968; James A. Russ, Jr., *The Hawaiian Republic*, 1961.)

Ernest Andrade, Jr.

HAWKINS, JOHN. Next only to Sir Francis Drake*, John Hawkins is the most famous of the English sea-dogs who contributed so powerfully to the Elizabethan expansion and the advent of English naval supremacy. Born in 1532 in Devonshire to a maritime, commercial family, Hawkins quickly demonstrated the leadership that made him preeminent in English naval affairs. He established a reputation as a daring and ruthless merchant/sea captain/slaver with trips down the Guinea coast, and then a subsequent sale of Africans in Spanish America where such trade was officially prohibited. He made three such trips in the 1560s, which combined the capture of blacks in Africa with the plundering of Portuguese ships, followed by intimidation in the New World that forced Spanish settlements to deal with him. In the process, he established an English presence in Africa, the West Indies*, and southern North America. His first two trips, and perhaps even the ill-fated third expedition, were highly profitable. The third trip in 1567, however, went seriously awry. After his usual tactics of overawing local and scattered Spanish authority with a combination of attractive trade goods and a show of force, he found it prudent, owing to weather upon his return voyage, to put into San Juan de Ulua in Mexico for refitting. The heavily armed Spanish treasure fleet arrived the next day. Although peaceful accords were signed, and the two fleets temporarily shared the anchorage, the Spanish treacherously opened fire on the English fleet twenty-four hours later. Just two of the six original ships escaped. Hawkins and Drake, among the survivors, returned to England much worse for the affair but with most of their profits intact. The episode is often noted as the beginning of the English-Spanish hostility that would endure for forty years.

Hawkins turned to conventional trading activities, and acquired the additional responsibilities of serving as the treasurer of the Navy. In this latter capacity he made perhaps his greatest contribution to English supremacy. As overseer of the royal shipyards, and thus as both a royal shipbuilder and designer, he lowered the forecastles of newly constructed ships, lengthened them to increase seaworthiness, and made other modifications that greatly improved English naval capabilities. This was perhaps best proved with the battle of the Spanish Armada* in 1588. The sleeker and more maneuverable ships, abetted by weather and Spanish ill-preparedness, guaranteed that the Spanish objectives in this campaign were completely thwarted. Hawkins served as second in command during this greatest of threats to Elizabethan England.

Even prior to the Armada, Sir John Hawkins, knighted in 1565, had returned to his privateering ways against the Spanish, which further provoked Spanish retaliation in 1588. This time, of course, it was sanctioned piracy. And this time, he experienced none of the earlier successes. He died of an undefined illness upon precisely such a voyage in 1595 in a futile attempt to interdict the Spanish treasure fleet in Puerto Rico. Spanish defense preparations had increased substantively from the days of easy pickings in the 1560s.

Hawkins established a romanticized reputation as one of the more daring English captains on the Spanish Main; as one of the Englishmen most responsible for shifting domestic attention to the wealth and potential of the New World; and as an important naval defender of England. It was, however, in the more prosaic and bureaucratic function of modernizing the British Navy that he made his most important contribution. Due to his efforts, English naval supremacy had begun, a supremacy that was to prove to be the key component in both defense and then the aggressive overseas expansion of the next three centuries.

(Edward Arber, *The Third Voyage of Sir John Hawkins, 1567–8*, 1895; James Williamson, *Sir John Hawkins, The Time and the Man*, 1970.)

Gary M. Bell

HAY-BUNAU-VARILLA TREATY. After the Panamanian revolution of November 3, 1903, had declared the independence from Panama from Colombia*, the United States quickly recognized the new government of Panama on November 6. With great haste, Secretary of State John Hay initiated negotiations with Philippe Bunau-Varilla who, apart from representing the New French Panama Canal Company, had secured for himself appointment as Panamanian minister plenipotentiary to the United States. The two men signed an agreement on November 18, 1903, after negotiations facilitated by Bunau-Varilla's willingness to concede virtually everything Hay wanted.

The treaty was a close copy of the ill-fated Hay-Herran Treaty*, but even more favorable to the United States. The United States guaranteed and promised to maintain the independence of Panama. In return the United States received ''in perpetuity'' the ''use, occupation and control of a zone of land and land under water'' needed to build and maintain a canal across the Isthmus of Panama. The width of the zone was set at ten miles beginning in the Caribbean three marine miles from the low water mark and extending across Panama into the Pacific to a distance of three miles. However, the cities of Panama and Colon were excluded from the zone. The United States enjoyed sovereignty in the Panama Canal Zone*. To compensate Panama, the United States agreed to pay $10 million in gold and an annual payment of $250,000. Panama also agreed to sell or lease to the United States lands for naval bases and coaling stations on both the Caribbean and Pacific coasts of Panama. (Howard K. Beale, *Theodore Roosevelt and the Rise of America to World Power*, 1961.)

Joseph M. Rowe, Jr.

HAY-HERRAN TREATY OF 1903. After a fierce debate in the United States Congress over the prospective route for an Isthmian canal, the faction favoring the Panamanian route won out and secured passage of the Spooner Act in 1902. The measure stipulated that the Panamanian route would be used on condition that a satisfactory and timely treaty could be negotiated with Colombia*, to which the Isthmus then belonged. Secretary of State John Hay put unusual pressure on Colombia to sign the desired treaty. After the departure of the Colombian minister to the United States, who virtually fled the country in disgust, Hay secured a treaty from the Colombian charge d'affairs, Tomás Herran, on January 22, 1903. This agreement granted to the United States authority over an area six miles wide in which to build the canal. In return, Colombia was to receive the sum of $10 million in gold and an annual payment of $250,000. The concession was given for a period of 100 years, with renewal at the option of the United States.

Although the United States Senate quickly approved the treaty, Colombia delayed. The concession of the French Panama Canal Company would expire in 1904, at which time the French would have nothing to sell to the United States. Colombia, therefore, hoped for part or all of the $40 million the French were asking for their concession. But Secretary of State Hay, under the influence of the powerful lobby for the French interests, strenuously objected to any interference by Colombia with the money destined for the French company. In Colombia, Hay's actions increased concern about infringements upon Colombia's sovereign rights over Panama and led to the unanimous defeat of the treaty on August 12, 1903. This rejection prompted the United States to obtain the desired concessions by other means, which led to the Hay-Bunau-Varilla Treaty*. (Howard K. Beale, *Theodore Roosevelt and the Rise of America to World Power*, 1961.)

Joseph M. Rowe, Jr.

HAY-PAUNCEFOTE TREATY OF 1901. In the aftermath of the Spanish-American War*, there was renewed interest in the United States for the construction of an inter-ocean canal across Central America, both for naval and commercial reasons. But the obstacle was a legal one—the Clayton-Bulwer Treaty* of 1850. As early as 1898, Secretary of State John Hay began to impress upon Great Britain the desirability of revising that agreement to allow the United States to proceed with construction of a waterway. Britain delayed, hoping for a concession in United States-Canadian relations, but that tactic proved fruitless. Finally, the British foreign office agreed in 1900. On February 3, 1900, Secretary Hay and Sir Julian Pauncefote signed an agreement which provided for exclusive construction and management of a canal by the United States. But it was to be a neutralized waterway. Public revelation of that provision provoked an uproar in the United States. Leading the attack was Governor Theodore Roosevelt of New York. Under that pressure, the United States amended the treaty to the point that it was no longer acceptable to Great Britain. Faced with the prospect of a unilateral abrogation of the Clayton-Bulwer Treaty by an angry United States, the British government consented to renewed negotiations. The second Hay-Pauncefote Treaty, signed November 18, 1901, was much like the first except for the provisions allowing the United States to fortify and defend the canal. But the United States also had to pledge that the merchant vessels and warships of all nations would be treated with complete equity with no discrimination against any nation as far as access and charges for use of the waterway were concerned. The United States Senate ratified the treaty on December 16, 1901, allowing the United States to proceed with plans for an isthmian canal. (Howard K. Beale, *Theodore Roosevelt and the Rise of America to World Power*, 1961.)

Joseph M. Rowe, Jr.

HELIGOLAND-ZANZIBAR TREATY OF 1890. Also known as the Anglo-German Heligoland Treaty, the Heligoland-Zanzibar Treaty was an attempt by Great Britain and Germany to resolve several territorial disputes in Africa resulting from the late nineteenth-century European imperial rivalry. In the 1880s one of the pressing conflicts between Britain and Germany in Africa centered on the locations of interior trade routes affecting British and German interests in East Africa. The status of the independent sultanate of Zanzibar*, located just off the coast of the German protectorate of East Africa (a region encompassing Tanganyika* and Ruanda-Urundi), was also a topic of dispute. The importance of Zanzibar lay in its location as the ultimate terminus and transshipment point for the three major trade routes in East Africa. The most important of these was the central route which bisected the territory claimed as German East Africa*, running from Ujiji in the interior to Dar es Salaam on the coast. The principal German interest in East Africa lay in protecting that vital trade route.

The turning point in Anglo-German relations in Africa came in early 1890 when the leading German African explorer and colonial advocate, Karl Peters, secretly entered Uganda*, still a relatively independent African kingdom, and concluded a treaty with the king making the region a German protectorate. The British government reacted swiftly as Uganda was strategically located to the west and north of British East Africa. The government of Prime Minister Lord Salisbury proposed a treaty with Kaiser William II's government to settle all boundary disputes in East Africa. On July 1, 1890, the two governments signed the Heligoland-Zanzibar agreement. By the treaty terms Germany accepted that Zanzibar should become a British protectorate. In addition, Germany agreed to recognize Uganda and the whole territory northward to Egypt as a British sphere of influence. The boundary between German East Africa and British East Africa was settled when Germany was given access to the Pangani River basin, Usambara, and most of the region surrounding Mt. Kilimanjaro. The treaty provided for continued trade relations and for consultation on tariffs.

The key to the treaty was that the German government was willing to abandon its claim to Uganda and agreed to British domination of the strategic island of Zanzibar. The government of Chancellor Leo von Caprivi was willing to do so due to British acquiescence to a long-standing German goal, the acquisition of the strategic island of Heligoland in the North Sea. An important clause of the 1890 agreement ceded Heligoland to Germany; Britain had held it since the Napoleonic wars, and the German government wanted it as a guard for the entrance to the Kiel Canal (begun in 1887). The treaty thus served an important strategic purpose in Europe for Germany, allowed a virtually free hand for the expansion and consolidation of British interests in East Africa, and promoted an improvement of Anglo-German relations in colonial Africa. Nevertheless, German colonial enthusiasts attacked the Anglo-German agreement as an ''exchange of a whole suit of clothes for a trouser button.'' (Ralph A. Austen, *Northwest Tanzania under German and British Rule: Colonial Policy and Tribal*

Politics, 1889–1939, 1968; Woodruff D. Smith, *The German Colonial Empire*, 1978.)

William G. Ratliff

HERERO UPRISING OF 1904. Due largely to their inexperience in colonial affairs, the German authorities of South West Africa* were completely surprised by the rebellion of the Herero tribesmen in early 1904, yet three factors can be isolated as causes of the uprising. First, the German judicial system, which required the testimony of seven Africans to equal that of one European, had little regard for the legal status of native Africans; certainly, the inequality of punishment handed down to offenders did not encourage the Herero to bring their grievances before the courts. As long as judicial reform was delayed, the African resentment toward the German settlers and government grew. This lack of legal recourse led to the second cause of the rebellion, the German expropriation of the Hereroland. Soon after they began arriving in South West Africa in the 1890s, German settlers realized that the most profitable land for crops and grazing, the Hereroland, was occupied by the indigenous Herero tribe. Having already prevailed in several conflicts with the Nama tribe over the same fertile area, the Herero stubbornly resisted German pressure to vacate the region, but were powerless to stop the governmental expropriation of land for such public projects as railways and roads. The fact that much of this prime agricultural land was eventually sold to German farmers and ranchers contributed to the resentment of the Herero. Furthermore, the impending construction of the Otavi Railroad, slated to run north-south directly through the center of the Hereroland, was anticipated with trepidation by the Africans. A third cause for the rebellion of the Herero was their overwhelming indebtedness. An outbreak of rinderpest at the turn of the century had decimated Herero cattle herds. Not only were the Herero forced to work for Europeans in order to buy food, they had borrowed heavily to replace the lost herds. Governor Leutwein announced in 1902 a moratorium to begin in 1903 on debt payments. Rather than alleviating Herero suffering, as Leutwein had intended, the moratorium exacerbated the situation, for the European creditors attempted to collect their outstanding sums in the course of twelve short months, not the longer terms under which many of the loans originally had been made.

Fearing for their survival as a race and feeling as if they had no better options, the Herero under Supreme Chief Samuel Maharero rose in rebellion on January 12, 1904, killing over one hundred German settlers and soldiers. The Herero initially waged a successful campaign against the technologically superior (although outnumbered) German militia; all the Hereroland was recaptured and the military blunders of Governor Leutwein at Oviumbo resulted in abnormally high German casualties. A letter from Chief Samuel Maharero to the Nama tribe exhorting them to join the Herero in revolt was intercepted by the German authorities, who would be faced with a separate Nama rebellion later that same year. This was the high point of Herero fortunes. In mid-July 1904, Leutwein was relieved by General von Trotha, a veteran of both the Wahehe Rising in East Africa in 1896 and of the Boxer Rebellion in China. General von Trotha was determined to take no prisoners. His ruthless policy was supported by the Imperial high command, which believed that an extermination campaign would leave in its wake a native African laboring class who would never again question German authority. General von Trotha waited until fresh German troops and equipment arrived in August before opening a devastating offensive against the Herero designed to drive them into the Omaheke Desert. By September 1, 1904, most of the Herero had fled into the desert, yet scattered fighting persisted throughout the remainder of the year. Reports of German atrocities against the Herero and of von Trotha's no-prisoner policy led in December to an investigation of the conflict by the Kaiser and Chancellor Bernhard von Bulow*. Chief of the Army General Staff Alfred von Schlieffen flatly denied that the German troops had committed any atrocities, but the following month the no-prisoner order was rescinded and concentration camps for captured Herero were established. Over 8,000 Herero had surrendered by mid–1905. By the same time the following year, 14,769 Herero were incarcerated in concentration camps. Male prisoners of war were forced to work on a railroad in the city of Swakopmund under harsh conditions, which resulted in a high number of deaths, as did a typhoid epidemic which had broken out in early 1905. Military operations against the Herero ceased in January 1906, when General von Trotha was replaced by the more moderate Governor Friedrich von Lindequist. The costs of the rebellion were high: in 1911 only 15,130 of an original 80,000 Herero were still living in South West Africa. (Horst Drechsler, *Let Us Die Fighting: The Struggle of the Herero and Nama Against German Imperialism (1884–1915)*, 1980.)

Jay O. Boehm

HIGH COMMISSION TERRITORIES. The High Commission Territories was the term used by the British to describe their administrative supervision of Basutoland*, Bechuanaland*, and Swaziland*. Until 1964 the three territories were administered under the authority of a British High commissioner residing in the Union of South Africa*. After 1964 the High Commission Territories was dissolved when the three territories moved toward independence.

HISPANIOLA. See DOMINICAN REPUBLIC; HAITI.

HOBSON, JOHN ATKINSON. J. A. Hobson, the renowned English economist, was born in 1858. His greatest intellectual contribution was his theory of underconsumption. In a famous 1902 article entitled "The Economic Taproot of Imperialism," Hobson argued that the Industrial Revolution had concentrated enormous amounts of capital in the hands of a tiny elite. The increases of income they experienced far outpaced their own capacity to spend it, and in an industrial economy, especially like that of the United States, manufacturing capacity exceeds domestic demand. Imperialism is a necessity in order to acquire new

markets and stimulate demand. Otherwise, the result would be deflation, unemployment, and depression. Hobson expounded his ideas in a number of books,
most notably *Evolution of Modern Capitalism* (1894), *The Economics of Distribution* (1900), *Imperialism* (1902), and *Problems of a New World* (1921).
There he repeated his belief that modern imperialism was brought about by
investors seeking outlets for excess capital, and that they were the most powerful
advocates of aggressive foreign policies. Before his death in 1940, Hobson was
the leading exponent of the notion that imperialism was not inevitable, and that
the impetus for imperialism could be stunted by "removing the unearned incre-
ments of income from the possessing classes . . . " (Norman Etherington, *Theories of Imperialism. War, Conquest, and Capital*, 1984.)

HO CHI MINH. Ho Chi Minh was born on May 19, 1890, in Nghe An Province
in Vietnam*. He was a deeply revered Vietnamese revolutionary nationalist and
president of the Democratic Republic of Vietnam from its proclamation in 1945
until his death in 1969. He is more frequently thought of as an anti-colonial
patriot than as a communist dictator. In fact, he was both. Gaps in our knowledge
of Ho's life are partly due to the fact that for years he was a hunted agent of
the Comintern. During his life, he used more than a dozen aliases. His father
named him Nguyen That Thanh ("Nguyen Who Will Be Victorious"). He
changed that to Nguyen Ai Quoc (Nguyen the Patriot) while in Paris during
World War I, and finally adopted the name by which the world knows him, Ho
Chi Minh ("He Who Enlightens"), when leading anti-Japanese resistance forces
in Vietnam in 1942. A more fundamental reason for uncertainty about some
details of Ho's life is that he preferred to operate out of the limelight. Although
he became a national hero, he never sought one-man rule as did Mao and Stalin,
to whom he is sometimes compared.

Patriotism was in his blood. His father was a minor government official who
had joined a rebellion against the French that was crushed two years before Ho's
birth. As a schoolboy he carried messages for the anti-French underground. His
father was arrested and imprisoned, but nonetheless was able to get Ho admitted
to a prestigious Vietnamese *lycee* where nationalist thought flourished. It is
thought that Ho left school in 1910 and signed on as a cook aboard a French
ocean liner. He was in Paris by 1917, seeing French society in its most desperate
hour. In Vietnam he never would have seen French men at menial labor, nor
French prostitutes. The myth of white supremacy could not withstand scrutiny—
especially during wartime. Ho worked as a photographer's assistant, and in his
off-hours plunged into the exciting world of revolutionary politics. He put in an
especially poignant appearance at the Versailles Peace Conference in 1919, where
he read the delegates his call for Vietnamese independence from France. They
did not take him seriously.

Bolshevik success in Russia aroused great interest among Asian nationalists,
who saw in Marxism an explanation for imperialism and a blueprint for ending
it. Ho Chi Minh was strongly influenced by his reading of Lenin's *Imperialism:*

The Highest Stage of Capitalism, and in 1920 he became a founding member of the French Communist Party. In 1922 Ho attended the Fourth Comintern Congress in Moscow and the following year returned there to enter the University of the Toilers of the East, where he wrote a famous pamphlet entitled "French Colonization on Trial." The next decade of Ho's life is a confusing sequence of furtive missions to China, Thailand, Indochina, and Hong Kong, probably with some trips back to Moscow. In 1930 Ho founded the Indochinese Communist Party. Ho was arrested and jailed by British police in Hong Kong in 1931 but was soon released, whereupon he made his way to Shanghai and thence to Moscow. By 1938 Ho was back in China, where he was imprisoned again, this time by Kuomintang (KMT) authorities. When he was released as part of the KMT's "united front" policy, he made his way back to the jungles of northern Vietnam to organize the Viet Minh.

Japan had walked into Vietnam with no resistance from the French bureaucrats who now answered to the pro-Fascist Vichy regime in France. By fighting the Japanese, Ho was simultaneously fighting the French. Ho cooperated with the United States Office of Strategic Services (OSS) to evacuate downed American fliers from the Vietnam-China borderland. When Japan surrendered, Ho proclaimed the independence of Vietnam on September 2, 1945. The OSS parachuted him a copy of the American Declaration of Independence. Ironically, in view of later developments, Communist Vietnam's declaration reads, "All men are created equal. They are endowed by their Creator with certain unalienable rights. . . ."

Long and bitter fighting was the price of the independence so easily proclaimed. The French shelled Haiphong and fought hard to reconstruct their Indochinese empire, but by 1954 they surrendered. Vietnam became independent but was divided into communist and non-communist halves. For Ho this was only a temporary breathing spell before the final assault on South Vietnam, which he regarded as merely a creation of foreigners, completely lacking legitimacy. Ho did not live to see the victory he confidently expected, which eventually came after years of bloody warfare with the United States in the 1960s and 1970s. Ho Chi Minh embodied the Vietnamese mixture of communism and a fierce desire for independence. He presided over a collective leadership in North Vietnam that ruthlessly suppressed all civil liberties but remained popular during the long war for independence and national unification. Ho Chi Minh died on September 3, 1969. When communist forces overran Saigon in 1975, they immediately renamed it Ho Chi Minh City. (Frances Fitzgerald, *Fire in the Lake*, 1972; Robert Shaplen, *The Lost Revolution*, 1966.)

Ross Marlay

HONDURAS. During the colonial period, Honduras, a province of the captaincy-general of Guatemala, was divided into two administrative units: a *gobierno* in Comayagua and an *alcaldia mayor* in Tegucigalpa, which was reorganized in the eighteenth century when Comayagua became an intendancy. On

July 30, 1502, Columbus* discovered Honduras during his fourth voyage. This initial expedition led to others and the territory was disputed among various conquistadores. In 1524, Gil Gonzáles de Dávila arrived in Honduras followed by Francisco Hernández de Córdoba, sent by Pedrarias Dávila, governor and captain-general of Castilla de Oro (Panama), to challenge de Dávila's pretensions. On January 11, 1524, Hernán Cortés* sent an overseas expedition from Mexico under the command of Cristóbal de Olid. Olid betrayed Cortés who sent a second expedition under Francisco de las Casas. Olid captured Gonzáles de Dávila and Las Casas but, on January 15, 1525, they killed Olid in his headquarters. Cortés personally led a third expedition which left Mexico on October 12, 1524. With Cortés' arrival Las Casas and Gonzáles de Dávila left for Mexico*.

Cortés introduced livestock and founded the town of Navidad de Nuestra Señora, near the port of Caballos. On April 25, 1526, before he left, he named Hernando de Saavedra governor and captain-general of Honduras and left instructions to treat the Indians kindly. On October 26, 1526, Diego López de Salcedo, named by the emperor as Honduras' governor, replaced Saavedra. For the next decade the personal ambitions of the governors and conquistadores interfered with governmental organization. Spanish settlers rebelled against their leaders, and the Indians rebelled against the harsh treatment imposed on them. Salcedo, out to enrich himself, clashed with Pedrarias, the governor of Nicaragua*, who wanted Honduras as part of his domains. In 1528 he arrested Salcedo and forced him to cede territory, but the emperor rejected the agreement.

In 1527 Salcedo's Indian policy provoked an Indian revolt, and his punishment of the rebels contributed to the uprising. With Salcedo's death in 1530 the settlers became the arbiters of power as they put in and took out governors. The settlers petitioned Pedro de Alvarado, who had been in Honduras in 1526, to end the anarchy. In 1536, with Alvarado's arrival, the chaos subsided, and the region was brought under his authority. Francisco de Montejo arrived as governor in 1537. Alvarado's followers opposed Montejo when he annulled the *encomiendas** granted by Alvarado. Montejo's captain, Alonso de Cáceres, was responsible for putting down the Indian revolt of 1537–1538 led by the *cacique* Lempira and, in 1537, he founded Comayagua. In 1539 Alvarado's and Montejo's disagreements over the region got the attention of the council of the Indies. Montejo left for Chiapas, and Alvarado became governor of Honduras.

A new phase in Honduran history began when the New Laws of the Indies, signed on November 20, 1542, created the Audiencia de los Confines, whose jurisdiction included Central America. On May 16, 1544 the Audiencia was inaugurated with Alonso de Maldonado, the governor of Honduras, as its president. Maldonado's non-compliance with the laws, under pressure from the settlers, brought him into conflict with Bartolomé de las Casas*, bishop of Chiapas. Alonso López de Cerrato replaced Maldonado, who was found guilty of not executing the New Laws. Cerrato's arrival in 1548 signaled a consolidation of central power and the application of the laws which benefited the Indians.

The first religious orders arrived, convents were built, and the organized conversion of the Indians began. In 1552, on Cerrato's departure, the Audiencia lost direct control over the province. Thus ended the formative conquest phase as Honduras became a political entity.

Colonial Honduras had a dispersed, low density population. Although agricultural products were exported, mining was the province's most important economic activity. Silver production never competed against that of Mexico and Peru due to the instability suffered because of the veins' exhaustion and a lack of workers. Although a few *encomiendas* existed, the most important labor system was the *repartimiento* for work in the mines. The first important silver mines were discovered in Tegucigalpa in 1578. San Andrés de Nueva Zaragoza, also in a rich mining zone, was abolished as an *alcaldia mayor* in 1703 when the veins ran out. In 1649 African slaves arrived to work the mines. A mining boom occurred between 1730 and 1780, after which decline followed. Ranching, another important economic activity, replaced mining in significance near the end of the colonial period. The Bourbons stimulated tobacco production but transportation costs made it prohibitive. The end of the eighteenth century and beginning of the nineteenth saw the economy in decline.

The province was under continual assault by the unconquered Indians of the northeast and the English. Internally Honduras suffered from the non-incorporation of the northeast, known as Taguzgalpa. Colonization was left to the religious orders who underwent many hardships in their attempts to pacify and convert the Indians. The English occupied the area of Belize in 1667 and along the Río Tinto in 1699. They used these Indians in their struggles against the Spanish. The English also kept the area in constant agitation through pirate attacks. In 1556 and 1579 they attacked Trujillo. The Dutch attacked and burned Trujillo in 1643. When piracy was abolished the English and Spanish struggle continued. New Spanish settlements were established during the eighteenth century in the Mosquito region. In 1778 the new captain-general, Matias de Galvez, used Honduras as a base against the English. On October 16, 1779, the English occupied Omoa, and Galvez reoccupied it on November 29, 1779. Galvez reorganized trade by shifting military and commercial activity from the Guatemalan coast to the Honduran coast. Further struggles between the English and Spanish at the end of the eighteenth century engulfed the area. Contraband penetrated the captaincy-general through these English settlements.

During the eighteenth century the Bourbon reforms administratively restructured the province when Comayagua was made an intendancy, on July 24, 1791, and the *alcaldia mayor* of Tegucigalpa was formally put under its direct rule. Tegucigalpa's *vecinos* protested the move until the regency reestablished the *alcaldia mayor* in 1812. The province's political independence was relatively peaceful because the provincial offices were in the hands of the *criollos*. The last *alcalde mayor* of Tegucigalpa, Narciso Mallol, attempted to better the region through public works projects. In 1812 a disturbance in Tegucigalpa against the reelection of the *alcalde* and *regidores* was brought to an end when the captain-general sent a batallion to the city. In 1821 independence brought conflict between

Comayagua and Tegucigalpa as Comayagua sided with the independence proclaimed in Mexico and Tegucigalpa put itself under the authority of the independence proclaimed in Guatemala. War was avoided when Guatemala declared itself in favor of the Mexican empire in 1822. (Ralph Lee Woodward, Jr., *Central America: A Nation Divided*, 1976; Miles L. Wortman, *Government and Society in Central America, 1680–1840*, 1982.)

Carlos Pérez

HONG KONG. The colony of Hong Kong is located on the coast of Kwangtung in southern China* at the mouth of the Pearl River. It is only about 95 miles from Canton*. Sir Henry Pottinger arrived in the region in August 1841 with instructions to provide protection for British commercial activities. In the course of ensuing hostilities, he occupied Chinese ports and sailed up the Yangtze River, threatening Nanking. He forced the Chinese to sign the Treaty of Nanking* on August 29, 1842, which provided that Hong Kong, a small island with an area of only 29 square miles, would be a British possession in perpetuity. On June 26, 1843, Hong Kong was proclaimed a British colony and Sir Henry Pottinger, in addition to holding the titles of plenipotentiary and superintendent of trade, became the first governor. The Hong Kong Charter of April 5, 1843, provided for the establishment of advisory legislative and executive councils; Hong Kong thus became a crown colony, with control from London being accomplished by means of instructions to the governor.

The colony was expanded by three and one-half square miles with the acquisition of the small peninsula of Kowloon on the mainland, and Stonecutters Island, by the Convention of Peking in 1860. In 1898 the New Territories region, an area of 365.5 square miles, consisting of a section of the mainland north of the colony, along with 235 islands, was leased to Britain for 99 years. The Petition of 1894 called for political evolution beyond the stage of crown colony by requesting that certain members of the legislative council be elected. The problem with the proposal was that it focused only on the European facet of the colony's politics. It was not acted on favorably because it called for the kind of constitutional change more appropriate for colonies with a larger proportion of English settlers. Leaders of the two principal British political parties were in agreement that the devolution of increased political autonomy to the British residents was not compatible with the obligation to look after the welfare of the Chinese inhabitants, who composed the overwhelming majority of the colony's population. London felt that the interests of the Chinese could be better protected by the colonial office* than by the small local European community, regardless of how democratically the narrowly based elections might be conducted. Thus, the concepts of crown colony administration were clearly reaffirmed as an outcome of the 1894 petition. On July 9, 1926, Sir Chouson Chow became the first Chinese person to be appointed to the executive council. He was selected to promote loyalty among members of the Chinese community to the Hong Kong regime.

World War II caused a temporary eclipse of British authority in the colony. On December 7, 1941, the same day that Pearl Harbor was attacked, Japan began its conquest of Hong Kong. The colony surrendered on Christmas, following a short, heroic resistance. Japanese occupation continued for the rest of the war. Shortages, caused in part by the Allied blockade, plagued the colony. All British institutions were swept aside as General Rensuke Isogai established his harsh military government. There was some apprehension in London concerning the position the United States was taking regarding the postwar status of Hong Kong. President Franklin Roosevelt was urging the British to withdraw from the colony as a gesture of good will. At the 1945 Yalta Conference he stated in private talks with Stalin that Hong Kong should either be returned to China or internationalized as a free trading area. Nothing of substance, however, resulted from this pressure. Admiral Sir Cecil Harcourt, who was with the British Pacific Fleet, was dispatched to accept the Japanese surrender at the end of the war.

Colonial civil government was reestablished on May 1, 1946, when the governor, Sir Mark Young, returned to Hong Kong from his internment in Formosa. He immediately announced that he would propose constitutional reforms, under which the people of the colony would have greater responsibility in the management of their government. There were, however, no significant changes. Until the collapse of Chiang Kai-shek's regime in 1949, Hong Kong maintained close relations with the Nationalist Government. The Hong Kong authorities had, for example, helped the Nationalists to stabilize the gold yuan currency. Everything changed when the Chinese People's Republic came into being on October 1, 1949. Canton fell on October 15; the next day communist forces were in control of territory adjacent to the colony. In February 1950 Great Britain recognized the People's Republic of China.

From the time that Mao Zedong* had assumed power in China, the all-important issue for the residents of the colony involved Hong Kong's future. That question was answered in late 1984. A joint declaration concerning Hong Kong was signed by Chinese Prime Minister Zhao Ziyang and British Prime Minister Margaret Thatcher on December 19, 1984. According to the agreement, China will exercise sovereignty over all of Hong Kong beginning July 1, 1997. Hong Kong will be under the authority of the central government but will have a large measure of autonomy. It will be allowed to control its own taxes and revenues. As the sovereign authority, however, China will be responsible for Hong Kong's defense and foreign affairs. A legislative body will be elected locally, but China will appoint the chief executive. Perhaps the most important provision, assuming that it will be honored by the Communist regime, is the guarantee that the colony's current social and economic system—pure laissez-faire capitalism—will remain unchanged for 50 years after 1997. Various freedoms, such as those of speech, press, assembly, travel, movement, correspondence, choice of occupation, the right to strike, and religion, are to be guaranteed by law. The free movement of capital is assured, and the Hong Kong dollar will remain a convertible currency. The foreign exchange, securities, and futures markets will continue to operate. The agreement also called for a joint liaison committee to develop plans to facilitate the transfer of sovereignty.

In the wake of the bloody repression of the pro-democracy movement in China, Sir Geoffrey Howe, the British foreign secretary, visited Hong Kong in early July 1989. He was unable, however, to calm the fear and outrage expressed by the inhabitants. He had nothing specific to say concerning what measures Britain might be prepared to take to guarantee political and economic freedoms in the colony after the 1997 transfer. Some observers expressed the opinion that the joint declaration may turn out to be worthless. When martial law was imposed in Beijing, it was simply ordered by a few old leaders of the Communist Party; they ignored their own legal provision that requires martial law to be declared by the National People's Congress. (G. B. Endacott, *Government and People in Hong Kong, 1841–1962*, 1964).

Roy E. Thoman

HOOGHLY. Hooghly is a town in West Bengal on the Hooghly River in northeast India*, founded by the Portuguese in 1537 following the decline of Sataon. Hooghly (Hugli) was the commercial capital of lower Bengal. In 1632 the Shah Jehan drove out the Portuguese, but they returned the next year. The British also settled there in 1651, only to abandon it for Calcutta* in 1690. In 1742 the Marathas sacked the city. Robert Clive did the same in 1757, this time for the British East India Company*, establishing British rule. In 1865 Hooghly joined with nearby Chinsura to form a joint municipality, which was closely tied to Calcutta. Hooghly lies on a low, fertile alluvial tract, on which rice, jute, sugarcane, and mangoes are the major crops. (C. R. Boxer, *The Portuguese Seaborne Empire, 1415–1825*, 1969.)

Mark R. Shulman

HORMUZ. This ancient Persian trading center was strategically located on a waterless island at the mouth of the Persian Gulf. It was about 1300 A.D. that the original mainland city moved to the island. From that location it became a wealthy entrepôt controlling the Indian Ocean trade with Persia and the Aleppo caravan route. The general weakness of Persian rulers during the fourteenth and fifteenth centuries allowed the sultans of Hormuz to maintain virtual autonomy. At the beginning of the sixteenth century, the Safavid ruler of Persia, Shah Ismael (1502–1524), was on the verge of bringing Hormuz under his control when the Portuguese appeared.

During 1488–1489 Pedro da Covilha became the first Portuguese to visit Hormuz. He appreciated its wealth and strategic importance and sent back detailed reports to King John II. That appreciation was shared twenty years later by the great Portuguese conqueror Affonso de Albuquerque. After participating in the capture of Socotra, Albuquerque reached Hormuz in 1507 with seven ships and 500 men. He demanded that the twelve-year old sultan and his vizier

Khwaja Atar become vassals of King Manuel of Portugal. When they delayed answering, the ferocious Albuquerque attacked and destroyed their fleet. They quickly accepted the Portuguese king as their overlord. Unfortunately for Albuquerque, his captains became rebellious when he ordered them to begin building a great fortress next to Hormuz. Three of them deserted and fled to the Portuguese viceroy Francisco da Almeida to complain of Albuquerque's tyranny. The reduction in his forces compelled Albuquerque to abandon the island.

Affonso de Albuquerque never gave up his designs on Hormuz, and when he became governor of India* in 1509, he ultimately got a second chance. After capturing Malacca*, Albuquerque returned to India in the fall of 1513. There he found his existing desire to recapture Hormuz fueled by overtures of friendship from Shah Ismael. It was well-known that the Persians coveted Hormuz for themselves although they were willing to consider sharing it with the Portuguese. Such an arrangement was anathema to Albuquerque so he determined to capture Hormuz a second time before an alliance with Persia precluded further unilateral action. Meanwhile in Hormuz, the vizier Reis Hamed, a Persian, appeared to be in league with Shah Ismael.

Albuquerque arrived off Hormuz with 27 ships and 3,000 men in late March 1515 in response to the threat posed by Reis Hamed. A parley was called during which both sides behaved treacherously. Violence broke out and the Portuguese got the better of things, killing Reis Hamed. The frightened young Sultan Saifuddin agreed to become a vassal of King Manuel. Albuquerque then constructed a great stone fortress in Hormuz harbor. It was controlled by the Portuguese but paid for in tribute from the sultans of Hormuz. Furthermore, the Portuguese took over the customs house and decided who could or could not use the sea lanes around Hormuz. In return, the Portuguese allowed the merchants of Hormuz freedom of navigation in the Indian Ocean, provided they did not enter the Red Sea.

During their occupation of Hormuz, the Portuguese had little problem maintaining control. A native revolt in 1526 and a conspiracy in 1529 were easily suppressed. The Safavid Shahs of Persia also did not present a major threat since they did not possess a navy. In addition, the Persians were under serious attack by the Ottoman Turks, who captured Bagdad in 1534 and Basra in 1535. It was the Ottoman Turks who posed the greatest danger to the Portuguese control of Hormuz during the sixteenth century. The Portuguese actually began hostilities with the Turks in the Persian Gulf with an unsuccessful attempt to capture Basra in 1550. In retaliation, the Ottoman Turks in 1552 sent a fleet from the Red Sea under the command of Piri Reis to capture Hormuz. He failed and was beheaded on his return to Egypt. A further series of naval battles in 1554 ended the Ottoman naval presence in the Persian Gulf. After more inconclusive fighting, the two powers negotiated a peace settlement in 1564 that left the Portuguese in firm possession of Hormuz.

The Portuguese Asian empire was in decline by the early seventeenth century. In the Persian Gulf, the vigorous Shah Abbas I (1587–1629) ruled a resurgent

Safavid kingdom while the British East India Company sought to displace the Portuguese. Shah Abbas by 1617 was determined to capture Hormuz for himself. To accomplish this goal, he needed the ships of the East India Company. Securing their cooperation by threatening to withdraw trading privileges in Persia, Shah Abbas attacked and captured Hormuz in 1622. The victorious Persians practically destroyed the city. As a result, its trading activities shifted to Gombroom, a few miles away on the mainland, which was later renamed Bandar Abbas. (Peter Jackson and Laurence Lackhart, eds., *The Cambridge History of Iran*, Vol. 6, *The Timurid and Safavid Periods*, 1986; Salih Ozbaran, "The Ottoman Turks and the Portuguese in the Persian Gulf, 1534–1581," *Journal of Asian History*, 6, 1972, 45–87.)

Ronald Fritze

HORSE. The horse became extinct in the New World approximately 10,000 years ago, but in 1493 Columbus* brought several of them to Hispaniola*. The horse provided Europeans with mobility, a necessity in conquering native inhabitants, and horses thrived in North America, South America, and Australia. Horses multiplied rapidly and millions of them became wild. From northern Mexico the horse spread up and throughout the Great Plains of North America, giving those Amerindian tribes a new mobility and forever altering their way of life. The English settlers of the North American, Australian, and New Zealand colonies also brought horses with them. They also spread across the Argentinian Pampa by the hundreds of thousands. Throughout North America, South America, and Australia, the horse thrived and shaped the European way of life there, providing the mobility that allowed for subjugation of native populations and, in the absence of any formal infrastructure, the transportation mechanism for successful commerce in the interior. (Alfred W. Crosby, Jr., *Ecological Imperialism. The Biological Expansion of Europe, 900–1900*, 1986.)

HOWLAND. Howland Island is a small coral island in the Central Pacific Ocean, part of the Line Islands* group. United States sailors discovered Howland in 1842 and the United States formally claimed it in 1857. In 1936 the United States formally proclaimed it a territory. See EQUATORIAL ISLANDS and JARVIS.

HUDSON, HENRY. Henry Hudson was an English navigator and explorer who sailed twice for the English Muscovy Company trying to find a Northeast Passage* through the Arctic Ocean to China. In April 1609 he sailed for the Dutch East India Company* into the Barents Sea, but when he was stopped by ice flows, he headed south through the western Atlantic Ocean. Hudson's expedition reached the shore of Virginia* at the end of August and then coasted north and reached New York Bay. He sailed 150 miles up what is now called the Hudson River, demonstrating that the fabled Northwest Passage did not begin there. Hudson returned to England and in April 1610 set out again, this time on behalf of the English. They reached what is today Hudson Bay and spent three months exploring it before the crew mutinied and put Hudson adrift in a small boat. He was never heard of again. (G. M. Asher, *Henry Hudson the Navigator*, 1860; Leonard Powys, *Henry Hudson*, 1927.)

HUDSON'S BAY COMPANY. In the late 1650s Medard Chouart des Groseilliers and Pierre-Espirit Radisson collected furs out of Montreal, exploiting the region north of the Great Lakes in Canada. In 1659 they left on an unlicensed and highly successful fur expedition in the area of Lake Superior and present-day Michigan, but when they returned to Montreal their furs were confiscated by corrupt political officials who claimed they had broken the law by not getting the proper permission. For several years des Groseilliers and Radisson tried to get compensation from French officials, but finally they gave up and turned to the British, arguing that the fur potential of the Hudson Bay area was enormous. Anxious to gain a foothold in Canada, the British were interested. When an exploratory expedition to Hudson Bay proved its potential, Charles II of Great Britain granted to the new Hudson's Bay Company, on May 2, 1670, a huge portion of North America—all the land drained by Hudson Bay—which he called Rupert's Land after Prince Rupert, his cousin. The grant included much of northern Quebec* and northern Ontario*, all of Manitoba, most of Saskatchewan, southern Alberta, and part of the Northwest Territories. The Hudson's Bay Company enjoyed a monopoly of all trade there and virtual political sovereignty. In the Treaty of Utrecht of 1713*, France acknowledged Britain's claim to Hudson Bay. Nevertheless, sporadic warfare with the French for control of the region continued until 1763.

The most serious commercial threat to the Hudson's Bay Company came after the Treaty of Paris of 1763*. The French were expelled from Canada, but during the French and Indian War* large numbers of Scottish, English, and American entrepreneurs arrived in Montreal ready to replace the French in the fur trade. They formally established the North West Company in 1784 and began building forts along rivers normally used by Hudson's Bay Company traders. North West Company traders brought the furs by canoe from the interior to the lakes and then down to Montreal, cutting off the flow of furs to the Bay, where all of the Hudson's Bay Company posts were located. The competition between the two companies became increasingly intense and violent. In 1816 Lord Selkirk of the Hudson's Bay Company established a colony on the Red River where Winnipeg stands today. It posed a real threat to North West Company trade routes; and a band of Metis—an Indian-French ethnic group doing business with the North West Company—attacked the colony and slaughtered 21 people on June 19, 1816. The incident was known as the Seven Oaks Massacre. To bring the violence and ruinous competition to a halt, the North West Company and the Hudson's Bay Company merged in 1821. They retained the name Hudson's Bay Company. The company was soon under the energetic direction of Sir George Simpson, who remained governor until 1860.

With the merger, the Hudson's Bay Company gained control over even more territory, since people like David Thompson, Simon Fraser, and Alexander Mackenzie, working for the North West Company, had already explored territory west of the Rocky Mountains. Great Britain granted the Hudson's Bay Company sovereignty over Vancouver Island in 1849, and in 1851 James Douglas, the chief factor of the company, became governor of Vancouver. When gold was discovered on the mainland in 1857, Great Britain created the colony of British Columbia* with James Douglas as governor there too. By that time Hudson's Bay Company traders were trapping and collecting furs in what is today the Yukon Territory*.

The 1860s proved to be a momentous decade for the company. When the gold rush along the Fraser River declined, the colonies of Vancouver and British Columbia were merged in 1866. Because Hudson's Bay Company trading activity in the Pacific Northwest undercut the work of Russian trappers there and eliminated their profits, the Tsar sold Alaska to the United States in 1867 for $7 million. Because of the confederation movement in Canada in the 1860s, demands to annex Rupert's Land from the company increased. The British North America Act of 1867 contained a provision for the annexation of Rupert's Land, and after extensive negotiations, the Hudson's Bay Company agreed to sell the land to Great Britain for £300,000. The company retained 5 percent of the land to sell to settlers itself and kept all of its trading posts. Great Britain in turn allowed the Dominion of Canada to annex Rupert's Land and the North-Western territory, bringing the Hudson's Bay Company land under the jurisdiction of the new nation (1870). (Peter C. Newman, *The Story of the Hudson's Bay Company. Volume I. Company of Adventurers*, 1988.)

I

IFNI. Ifni is a 579 square-mile province of Morocco*, located on the Atlantic coast approximately two hundred miles southeast of Marrakech. The native people of Ifni were nomadic Berber tribesmen, and in 1860 Morocco ceded the region to Spain. The population was sparse and natural resources very limited, and Spanish control over the area was minimal at best. In 1934 Spain formalized its colonial supervision of Ifni. Between 1946 and 1958 Ifni was administered as part of Spanish West Africa. In 1958 the colony came under the administrative control of the Canary Islands as a Spanish Overseas Protectorate. That relationship persisted until 1969 when Spain returned Ifni to Morocco. (Richard M. Brace, *Morocco. Algeria. Tunisia*, 1964.)

ILE DE FRANCE. See MAURITIUS.

ILE ROYALE. See CAPE BRETON.

ILE SAINT-JEAN. See PRINCE EDWARD ISLAND.

IMPERIAL CONFERENCE OF 1907. Imperial Conference was the name adopted by the colonial conference in 1907 to describe the meetings of the prime ministers of the self-governing dominions and the prime minister and secretary of state for the colonies of Great Britain. The imperial conference grew out of the previous colonial conferences which were first held in 1887. At the meeting in 1907 the descriptions "colony" and "colonial" were dropped for the self-governing political entities and the term "dominion" was adopted. The general purpose of the 1907 conference (and the subsequent conference in 1911) was to bring the dominions into common defense arrangements and to give their leaders a greater awareness of the dangers facing the empire. The question of some advance toward representative institutions in India* was also to be raised, as well as possible devolution for Ireland*, provided Irish loyalty in case of war was assured. With the growing possibility of war in Europe, the imperial conference was to determine the imperial position regarding the United States, Japan, and Latin America.

The prime minister of Great Britain, Sir Henry Campbell-Bannerman (Liberal), served as president of the London conference with the prime ministers of the dominions serving as ex-officio members of the conference. Canada, Australia, New Zealand, South Africa, and, for the first time India, were represented. The most important delegates called for reciprocal imperial preference by Britain, but the topic was shelved due to the British prime minister's fervent support for free trade. Campbell-Bannerman, however, studiously refrained from dictating defense policy, and progress was made on strengthening imperial army and naval forces. It was agreed that an imperial general staff should be drawn from the forces of the Empire as a whole but without interfering with dominion autonomy in military matters. No uniform policy on naval defense, however, was concluded. Australia was in favor of an autonomous navy, but was dissuaded by New Zealand and South Africa. The delegates agreed, that for the time being, the dominions would continue to contribute men and money to the Royal Navy. Subsequently, when the naval scare of 1909 arose (based on German intentions to construct dreadnoughts), the dominions supported a drastic increase in the British building program. Both New Zealand and Australia contributed funds for dreadnoughts. A subsidiary imperial conference met in London to coordinate defense plans and it was agreed that Australia should create and control a naval squadron. In addition, Canada was allowed to build cruisers and destroyers to guard her Atlantic and Pacific coasts. The 1907 conference laid the groundwork for future political revision of the British Empire*. The conference also established the basic defense posture of the empire which was put to the test in World War I*. (Max Beloff, *Imperial Sunset*, Vol. I., 1970; G. E. H. Palmer, *Constitution and Cooperation in the British Commonwealth*, 1934.)

William G. Ratliff

IMPERIAL CONFERENCE OF 1911. The Imperial Conference of 1911 placed its emphasis on the constitutional basis for cooperation between Great Britain and her dominions. Before the 1911 meeting, again attended by the prime ministers of Australia, Canada, New Zealand, and South Africa, Sir Joseph Ward, the premier of New Zealand, submitted a proposal for a representative imperial council to advise the British government on imperial matters. At the first meeting of the delegations, Ward expanded his idea to include the setting up of an imperial parliament charged with the conduct of foreign policy, including the powers to declare war and make peace. The proposed council would be composed of members chosen from the dominions and Britain, and it would be presided over by an imperial executive. The council would hold no powers of taxation, leaving the issue of funding entirely up to the existing parliaments of the empire. As Ward's plan would infringe upon the foreign policy autonomy of Great Britain, the imperial conference's presiding officer, British Prime Minister Herbert H. Asquith, registered an immediate objection which was seconded by the other dominion delegates. Asquith, however, did concede the necessity for consultations with the dominion prime ministers on matters of pressing importance to the Empire. Later during the conference, British Foreign Secretary Sir Edward Grey gave the delegates in secret session an overview of the international situation. The result of Grey's briefing was the firm reluctance by the dominions to claim a voice in the management of imperial foreign policy. Several delegates requested frequent consultation with the foreign secretary on foreign policy, and Asquith offered to convene a standing committee on foreign affairs, but dominion premiers could not reach an agreement.

The 1911 conference did, however, see an agreement concluded on the negotiation of treaties affecting the constituent members of the Empire. The imperial conference resolved that the dominions were to be consulted in the preparation of instructions to British delegates to the Hague Peace Conferences, and conventions drafted by these conferences were to be circulated among the dominions before signatures. The same procedure was to be followed, within limits, in the negotiation of other international agreements. Indeed, as Japanese naval power grew from 1911 to 1914, the possibility of a challenge to Australia's interests became more likely. Thus Australia was consulted during the negotiations for the renewal of the Anglo-Japanese treaty. In the same vein, South Africa was consulted directly about negotiations with Germany on colonial matters in 1912. The result of this imperial cooperation was that the South African dominion government proved adamant against any extension of German territory in Africa. (Donald C. Gordon, *The Dominion Partnership in Imperial Defense 1870–1914*, 1965.)

William G. Ratliff

IMPERIAL CONFERENCE OF 1921. The Imperial Conference of 1921 was the first postwar effort of the British Commonwealth* to function as a partnership. The conference was called to create a central organ of imperial government which, according to a resolution of the Imperial War Conference of 1917, was intended to enable the dominions and the United Kingdom to act as one body, promptly and efficiently, in their common interest. The only solid support for this idea, however, came from New Zealand, and when the conference was convened in London in June 1921 the foreign policy question was again paramount.

The principal area of debate centered on the proposed renewal of the Anglo-Japanese alliance*, which was in apparent conflict with the League of Nations* Covenant. To the conference delegates (the prime ministers of Australia, New Zealand, Canada, South Africa, and Great Britain) the alliance had served its purpose as a protection against Russia and Germany in the Far East. By 1921, however, Japan appeared to be the primary threat to imperial interests, especially following her aggressive moves toward China. The United States attitude toward the Anglo-Japanese alliance had become increasingly hostile since its last renewal in 1911. American opposition to a renewed treaty would obviously strain Anglo-American relations. The United States failure to join the League of Nations, however, made Britain reluctant to abandon her only check upon Japan. Canadian Prime Minister Arthur Meighen argued that the Empire's foreign policy should be governed by its effect on the interests of the constituent members. In specific terms, Meighen proposed that in all questions affecting Canada and the United States, the dominion should have full and final authority.

The argument ultimately returned to the Anglo-Japanese alliance, with Canada favoring rejection and Australia and New Zealand championing renewal. The conference reached no decision since the dominions were deadlocked over the issue of Australian and New Zealand security versus Canadian interests. The threat to imperial cooperation was defused, however, by an agreement concluded at the Washington Conference of 1921–1922*. To the satisfaction of all concerned, the Anglo-Japanese alliance was buried by the Four Power Treaty* of December 1921, which bound the United States, Japan, France, and the British Empire* to respect one another's rights and possessions in the Pacific Ocean basin. The Four Power Treaty postponed the imperial debate on the interests of the dominions superceding those of the Empire as a whole. The question of dominion nationalism would continue to surface at subsequent imperial conferences, ultimately resulting in complete freedom of action for the dominions by the Statute of Westminster in 1931. (Max Beloff, *Imperial Sunset*, Vol. 1, 1970; Robert Borden, *Canada in the Commonwealth*, 1929.)

William G. Ratliff

IMPERIAL CONFERENCE OF 1923. The inherent weakness in one foreign policy for the whole British Empire*, controlled jointly by London and the dominions, was exposed by the Turkish crisis of 1922. In September 1922 the government of Mustafa Kemal abrogated the peace treaty imposed upon Turkey following World War I*. The Turks demanded the return of most of the territories stripped from the Ottoman Empire by the Allies and threatened British forces still occupying the Dardanelles. Britain called upon the dominions for military support. New Zealand and Australia complied, albeit reluctantly, but Canada and South Africa refused to send troops. The former automatic solidarity of the dominions on the issue of military support for Britain was shattered. The collapse of imperial cooperation in matters of foreign policy was indicated further by the negotiation of a new peace settlement with Turkey. The dominion governments neither shared in the talks leading to the Treaty of Lausanne of 1923*, nor did they ratify the agreement. Canada led the other dominions in declaring the treaty the sole obligation of Great Britain.

Moreover, in March 1923, Canada signed the Halibut Fisheries Treaty with the United States, thus effectively negating Britain's constitutional right to control the foreign relations of a dominion government. The result of both the Fisheries Treaty and the Lausanne Treaty was that new rules for the concluding of treaties were adopted by the Imperial Conference of 1923. The dominions, including for the first time the Irish Free State, set a further precedent for dominion autonomy by substituting separate for joint control and responsibility in foreign policy. While each dominion was to be responsible for its own international relations, a spirit of imperial cooperation was retained by the conference delegates. The dominions recognized the moral obligation of each member to avoid any action that would injure another member of the commonwealth. No government was to commit another to action without its consent. Consultation with other members of the empire was encouraged, but not required, during treaty negotiations. The new treaty guidelines were tantamount to a complete revision of the former practice of subjecting dominion interests to those of Great Britain. The imperial conference thus broke new ground in the continuing trend of dominion nationalism, culminating in the Imperial Conference of 1926*. (Max Beloff, *Imperial Sunset, Vol. 1*, 1970; A. B. Keith, *The Government of the British Empire*, 1935.)

William G. Ratliff

IMPERIAL CONFERENCE OF 1926. The Imperial Conference of 1926 was forced to address the growing question of dominion nationalism which had dominated imperial politics since the end of World War 1. The Irish Free State, having taken its place in the 1923 conference with full dominion status, led the demand for autonomy. The general Irish attitude on the question of status in the commonwealth was expressed in June 1926 when the Irish minister of external affairs insisted publicly that the Free State was a sovereign independent state and should be so recognized by Great Britain. South Africa, too, was inclined to be more importunate, led by the increasingly more popular Afrikanner nationalists. While the governments of both Australia and New Zealand were relatively content with the imperial status quo, by 1926 Canada, the senior member of the commonwealth, had joined the call for independence. The principal issue in Canada's demand for self-government was the so-called "constitutional crisis," an affair in which the dominion governor general, Lord Byng, ignored the request of Prime Minister Mackenzie King to dissolve the Canadian parliament and call new elections. When the Canadian electorate subsequently supported King, the prime minister determined to press the issue of Empire relations at the imperial conference.

Under the guidance of British Prime Minister Lord Balfour, Britain was prepared to make concessions to the dominions. At the 1926 Imperial Conference, the term "commonwealth" was adopted officially to designate the "autonomous communities within the British Empire*, equal in status, in no way subordinate one to another in any aspect of their domestic or external affairs, though united by a common allegiance to the crown. . . . " The conference also addressed the constitutional question of the commonwealth by initiating the Statute of Westminster, ultimately ratified in 1931. The Statute of Westminster contained two elements central to the issue of self-government in the commonwealth nations: that it would be inimical to the British constitution for the British government to take any action concerning the affairs of a dominion against the advice tendered by the government of that dominion; and that legislation by the British parliament applying to a dominion would only be passed with the consent of the dominion concerned.

While the 1931 Statute of Westminster erased most of the limitations on dominion independence, the 1926 Imperial Conference retained several basic elements of the old Empire. While recognizing the essentially autonomous character of the commonwealth, the conference was careful to observe that equality of status within the Empire did not necessarily imply equality of responsibility. In that vein, the Imperial Conference of 1926 continued to place the overall burden of defense and foreign policy of the Empire on Great Britain. (A. B. Keith, *The Government of the British Empire*, 1935; K. S. Wheare, *The Statute of Westminster and Dominion Status*, 1953.)

William G. Ratliff

IMPERIAL ECONOMIC CONFERENCE OF 1932. The onset of the depression intensified economic nationalism in the dominions and converted Great Britain to the policy of protection. London extended the process of imperial preference and, in February 1932, enacted a 10 percent ad valorem duty on all foreign goods, with certain specified exemptions. The complete exemption of Empire merchandise from the levy was intended to be tentative. The exemption could be curtailed or enlarged according to the response of the dominion governments. Negotiations between Britain and the commonwealth nations were scheduled for the summer of 1932 at Ottawa, Canada.

The Imperial Economic Conference of 1932 was the scene of complex economic bargaining. During the conference the governments of the commonwealth concluded fifteen bilateral trade agreements, known collectively as the Ottawa Agreements. The overall aim of these trade treaties was to expand the policy of trade reciprocity between the dominions. In addition, the commonwealth nations concluded a number of bargains with Britain, the gist of them being Britain's promise to continue the preferences already established and to extend them to other commodities—including minerals, wheat, and meat products—in return for an enlargement of dominion preferences, some by lowering tariffs on British goods, and some by raising levies on foreign products.

In general terms, the Ottawa Agreements embodied a mutual compromise among the Empire nations on economic nationalism. In more specific terms, the agreements reflected the combined response of the dominions and Great Britain to demands for increased imperial protection and retaliation for the United States's Smoot-Hawley tariff and the prohibitive tariffs, quotas, and commercial controls of the European states. (N. Mansergh, *Survey of British Commonwealth Affairs: Problems of External Policy, 1931–1939*, 1952.)

William G. Ratliff

INCAS. According to one legend, the sun created a son and daughter, placed them on an island in Lake Titicaca, gave them a golden rod, and instructed them to settle where the staff sank into the earth. At the site where the bar disappeared into the ground, the royal couple, Manco Capac and his sister-queen Mama Ocllo, obediently built the city of Cuzco and founded an empire. Such was the legend of Inca origins. About 1000 A.D. a tribe known as the Incas migrated north in the Peruvian Andes from Lake Titicaca to the Cuzco Valley. They promptly embarked upon a policy of conquest, and by the early 1500s their empire extended from Quito in Ecuador* to Tucumán in Argentina*, an area of about 380,000 square miles, or approximately one and one-half times the size of Texas. The Spaniards incorrectly referred to all the Indians of this vast realm as Incas. In fact, that term applied only to the ruling tribe, to the nobility.

With regard to scientific learning, the Incas lagged behind the Mayas and the Aztecs. They had only the crudest understanding of the relationship of the earth to other heavenly bodies; they had no system of writing, not even pictographs; and their numbering system was cumbersome. They used knotted strings of various colors called *quipus* for record keeping. A practical people, the Incas seemed more interested in the application of knowledge than in abstract learning. And when it came to pottery, textiles, metal working—gold, silver, platinum, and copper—road building, and the construction of an integrated empire, they had few equals.

Politically and socially, the Incan empire was a highly structured despotism, benevolent or cruel depending upon the nature of the Saca Inca, who was an absolute temporal and spiritual leader. Beneath the Saca Inca came the other Incas, nobles who held the most important political, military, and religious positions, followed by a second-class nobility composed of former rulers of conquered territories. At the base of the social pyramid was the mass of commoners, who were set apart by dress and a regimentation which left little or no room for individual choice. The people were divided into groups according to ability and assigned to work on the basis of skill and strength, and the daily life of farm workers was tightly governed by the *mita*, a system of forced, rotating labor supervised by Incan officials. Though life for commoners was obviously rigorous, the end result, if one accepts the chroniclers at face value, was the virtual elimination of hunger and destitution. From a material standpoint, the people of the empire appear to have been reasonably comfortable. Superb agriculturists, the Incas transformed Andean deserts and mountain slopes into arable land. Their system of terraces, aqueducts, irrigation canals, and dams is still a marvel. And by storing surpluses in royal granaries and warehouses, they were able to sustain themselves during difficult times.

As empire builders, the Incas surpassed all other pre-Columbian Indians. Whereas the Aztecs ruled by force and made little effort to win the allegiance of subjugated tribes, the Incas governed more subtly and without much brute force and shrewdly transferred the loyalty of the conquered peoples. The Incas always attempted to win new territory through persuasion. An area designated for conquest would be visited by diplomats who sought to convince the people of the advantages of being a part of the empire. Only if this failed was force used, but even then the Incas were restrained. The invading army took no captives for sacrifice, exacted no harsh taxes, and did no looting.

Once the military conquest was completed, the Incas moved quickly to establish bonds between themselves and their new subjects. First, a host of public officials, road builders, and artisans rushed into the area. Fortresses and government offices were built, and a careful census, which detailed the crafts of the people and the various products produced, was taken. Second, the defeated political leaders were taken to Cuzco for a period of training, then sent back to govern for the Incas. To ensure loyalty, however, their children remained in Cuzco as well-cared-for hostages and were educated in Incan ways. Third, the local gods of a conquered tribe were taken to Cuzco, where they were treated with respect. Meanwhile, the Incas built a temple in a privileged place to the Sun God, and Incan priests set about to convert the local populace. The Incas were not hostile to local deities, so long as the temple to their own god enjoyed a special location. Fourth, the Incas, while banning neither the native tongue nor ancient customs, insisted upon the acceptance of Quechua as the official language. And, finally, the Incas wisely made allowance for local customs, granted privileges to those who performed unusual tasks, and conducted feasts and festivals on holidays. Having established their authority in a new region, the Incas did not tolerate opposition. The slightest sign of rebellion led to mass deportations to distant parts of the empire, where among strangers the rebels' influence would be diminished.

That Francisco Pizarro* with about 180 men and twenty-seven horses toppled such a mighty empire so quickly in the early 1530s is astonishing. Several factors contributed to the Spaniard's accomplishment. First, the empire had recently been torn by civil war before the Spanish arrived. Second, Atahuallpa, the victor in the civil conflict, underestimated the Spanish, whom he held in contempt. And, finally, the political absolutism of the Incas ultimately was to their disadvantage. Once Pizarro captured and later executed the Saca Inca Atahuallpa and defeated the other nobles, the masses of corn farmers and craftsmen had little will to resist. For the masses, Pizarro's conquest meant that one set of rulers was replacing another, that Spanish feudalism was replacing Incan feudalism. (P. A Means, *Ancient Civilization of the Andes*, 1931; Alfred Metraux, *History of the Incas*, translated by George Ordish, 1970.)

John W. Storey

INDIA. A kaleidescope of distinct ethnic cultures and languages, India became the crown jewel in the British Empire*. When the expansion of the Ottoman Empire in the fifteenth century led to the conquest of the Middle Eastern caravan trade routes, Europe's access to Asian spices became more costly and difficult. Desperate to find a new route to Asia, the Portuguese led the way. Under the leadership of Prince Henry, Portuguese navigators began sailing down the west coast of Africa in the middle of the fifteenth century. In 1487–1488 Bartolomeu Dias* went around the Cape of Good Hope at the southern tip of Africa; and a decade later Vasco da Gama* rounded the same point, sailed up the coast of East Africa and then across the Indian Ocean to land at Calicut on the southwest Indian coast, launching the age of European imperialism in Asia. In 1510 Portugal conquered Goa*, and during the next half-century established factories and settlements at Diu*, Bombay*, Daman*, Calicut, Cochin, and Bijapur in India, and Jaffna and Colombo* on Ceylon*.

Portugal's decline in the seventeenth century was matched by the rise of the Dutch, French, and English as imperial powers. Between 1605 and 1663 the Dutch squeezed the Portuguese out of the spice trade of the East Indies and in 1663 captured most of the Portuguese settlements along India's Malabar Coast. But Dutch imperialism in Asia was centered on the East Indies, and they never followed up on their victories in India. There was too much money to be made by the Dutch on the cloves, mace, and nutmeg of the Moluccas*. The French Oriental Indies Company placed a trading post at Surat in 1668, and the French colony at Pondicherry on the Coromandel coast* south of Madras was founded in 1683. In the 1720s new French outposts were established at Mahe on the Malabar coast, Yanam on the Orissa coast, and Karikal on the Coromandel coast. Other territorial acquisitions soon followed. By 1754 the French East India Company, which had assumed the assets of the Oriental Indies Company, controlled an area of India larger than metropolitan France.

But it was British imperialism which eventually came to dominate the Indian subcontinent. In 1613 the British East India Company* established a factory at Surat, and by the end of the seventeenth century similar establishments had been placed at Bombay, Madras, and Calcutta. During the early years the company was interested in trade and profits only, and was quite willing to leave internal politics and Indian culture alone. But in 1757 Lt. Col. Robert Clive defeated the Nawab of Bengal* at the Battle of Plassey and established the company's political ascendancy. At the end of the Seven Years' War, Great Britain stripped France of all her Indian possessions except the coastal enclaves of Pondicherry, Karikal, Yanam, Mahe, and Chandernagor. During the next sixty years the British East India Company extended its influence and control over much of the subcontinent, usually through negotiations and subsidies, sometimes through conquest and annexation.

Gradually in the late eighteenth century, however, the British government began to assume greater control over the British East India Company. Political infighting at home and corruption abroad cost the company its financial stability and its reputation. In 1773 parliament increased its supervision of company affairs, and in 1784 the government took over company foreign policy and administrative oversight, leaving it independent to handle trade. The company lost its monopoly over the India trade in 1813, and in 1833 the British East India Company ceased to be a trading concern at all, becoming instead the political institution through which Great Britain ruled India. After the great Indian Mutiny of 1857*, the British East India Company was abolished and the government of India was placed under the crown.

During the nineteenth century Great Britain moved beyond trade to actual government in India, establishing political controls and regulations to replace the simple economic rules of the previous two centuries. During the viceroyalty of Lord William Bentinck (1828–1835), Great Britain abolished suttee (the burning of Hindu widows), suppressed the Thugs (a murder cult), declared English the language of instruction in the schools, and established the Indian penal code. During the viceroyalty of Lord Dalhousie (1848–1856), Great Britain ruled that if a prince died without natural heirs, all sovereign rights over his estate reverted to British control; constructed railroads, highways, and the telegraph; annexed the province of Oudh; built a public elementary school system; and established an excellent postal service.

The Indian Mutiny had a dramatic impact on British India. It marked not only the death of the British East India Company but the birth of Indian nationalism, although this was in gestation for twenty years. British education had produced a western-educated Hindu elite that came to accept Anglo political principles of individual civil rights and national self-determination. Improved global transportation and communication had allowed British officials in the late nineteenth century to bring their families with them to India, but they lived in segregated compounds and disdained Indian culture, creating a new animosity among native people proud of their Hindu, Muslim, or Sikh heritages. The Empire also led to economic problems for Indians. India became a market for mass-produced, cheap British factory goods, and in the process India's thriving handicraft industry declined, bringing unemployment to millions of Indian workers.

In 1885 Indian nationalists formed the Indian National Congress and demanded some degree of representative government and a program of social reform. They were led by Bal Gangadhar Tilak, a radical Hindu who demanded complete independence, and Gopal Krishna Gokhale, a moderate who wanted to work closely with the British in bringing about independence. Some of their demands bore immediate fruit. Lord Dufferin's Act of 1888 created native councils to cooperate with British civil servants, and the Lansdowne Act of 1892 established advisory councils of native Indians to consult with the British government. But the British didn't take the advice seriously, and the Indian National Congress gradually grew more militant in its policy positions. The demand for independence started gathering momentum.

In 1905 Indian politics grew more complex when the Viceroy Lord Curzon decided to divide up the huge province of Bengal for more efficient administration. The problem, of course, was that in the original province of Bengal, the Hindus had a majority, but in the divided province the Muslims controlled East Bengal. Anti-British sentiment erupted among Hindus throughout India, but particularly in Bengal. The British responded to the unrest by passing the Government of India Act of 1909, which took an important step toward introducing representative government by increasing the number of non-official members elected to the provincial and central legislatures, allowing discussion on the Indian budget, and providing for admission of Indians to the Viceroy's Executive Council and the Council of India in London.

But the Government of India Act also sowed the seeds of disaster, at least for the future of a united India. Before World War I unrest in India was almost exclusively confined to Hindus; the more than 70 million Muslims, who constituted perhaps 15 percent of the population and were scattered around the country, did not want a British withdrawal because it would then subject them to the Hindu majority. Recognizing the position of the Muslim minority, the Government of India Act provided for a "communal electorate," actually separate electorates for Muslim voters, a move the Hindus despised. It was the beginning of the notion of separate Hindu and Muslim spheres of influence in India, a position the Indian National Congress detested. The death of Gopal Gokhale in 1916 also gave Tilak and the radicals control of the Indian National Congress.

During World War I the Indians rallied around the British flag, but with the peace their demands for independence were heard once again, this time from a new leader—Mohandas K. Gandhi*, who advocated a campaign of widespread, non-violent civil disobedience to break the will of the British Empire. In 1919 Great Britain responded with the Rowlatt Act, which suspended civil rights and provided for martial law in areas disturbed by nationalist insurgency. Gandhi called for more passive resistance, and on April 13, 1919, a national day of mourning led to demonstrations and mass meetings everywhere. In the city of Amritsar in the Punjab, British troops dispersed a crowd by shooting 1,600 people, an act of violence which only inspired more resistance. Gandhi called for total noncooperation with British authorities. The British arrested and imprisoned Gandhi in 1922.

But Indian independence was not to be denied. By the end of the 1920s Gandhi was again out of prison and demanding dominion status for India, which the British denied in 1930. Gandhi then staged a massive violation of the British monopoly on salt production, dramatically marching to the Gulf of Cambay and boiling water to produce salt. Rioting broke out across the country, as did terrorist bombings, political assassinations, and acts of sabotage against railroads and telegraph lines. The British reacted by imprisoning 27,000 Indian nationalists. Rioting also erupted between Hindus and Muslims, primarily because the Muslim League was asking for separate political status for the Muslim minority. Great Britain arranged a truce with Gandhi and his associate, Jawaharlal Nehru*, and in 1935 passed a new Government of India Act*. It provided for autonomous legislative bodies in the provinces of British India and in more than 500 princely states, the creation of a bicameral national legislature representing those bodies, an executive branch under British control, and political protection of the Muslim minority. Gandhi reluctantly supported the measure, but in 1937 Mohammad Ali Jinnah*, head of the Muslim League, called for the creation of a separate Muslim state.

When World War II broke out, Lord Linlithgow, the viceroy of India, declared war on Germany without consulting the new national legislature, an act which enraged the Indian National Congress and led to new demands by Gandhi and Nehru for complete independence. Another campaign of civil disobedience led to the arrest and imprisonment of both men. The protests were so widespread and so large that the British realized they could no longer control the country and promised full independence after the war. But when the war ended, Gandhi and the Hindus found themselves in an irreparable political struggle with Jinnah and the Muslims, who wanted a separate Muslim state. Gandhi insisted on one India. The new viceroy, Viscount Mountbatten, steered the contending parties through negotiations to an agreement; and, in the end parliament passed the Indian Independence Act of 1947* which partitioned the sub-continent, creating two new nations—the Hindu-based India and the Muslim-based Pakistan. Between 1949 and 1956 all of French India* held referendum elections and merged with India, and in 1961 India drove the Portuguese out of their last outposts at Goa, Diu, and Daman. (T. O. Lloyd, *The British Empire 1558–1983*, 1984; B. N. Pandey, *The Break-up of British India*, 1969.)

INDIA ACT OF 1784. The British East India Company* was launched as a joint-stock enterprise in 1600 with monopoly privileges on all trade with the "Indies." For nearly a century and a half the company lay perched on the periphery of the great Mughal Empire (1526–1858), until the mid-eighteenth century when the dynamic convergence of the decline of Mughal power and Great Britain's victories in the so-called "Wars for Empire" over its European rivals allowed for a dramatic rise in the Company's fortunes in south India and in wealthy Bengal. However, the persistent mismanagement of the company's financial affairs, and frequent fighting among the company's servants in India and their allies at home, finally roused parliamentary concern over the state of the company's behavior in India. The first limitations on the East India Company were effected by the Regulating Act of 1773, which was designed to assert parliamentary control over the company's affairs in London and at the same time stabilize the company's administrative structure in India itself.

But the Regulating Act of 1773 proved inadequate in redressing the company's financial and administrative woes, and William Pitt* the Younger sought more rigorous control over the Company Bahadur ("Valient" or "Exalted" company) in 1784. Although the company's commercial independence was progressively reduced through a series of obligatory charter renewals (1793, 1813, 1833, 1853), the India Act of 1784 set the legal parameters for the company's relations with parliament until its formal dissolution in 1858.

In essence, the India Act of 1784 provided for a "double-government" and circumscribed the general court's ability to intervene in Indian administration. The court of directors was balanced by a board of control (BOC) which included six privy councillors, including a secretary of state and the chancellor of the exchequer. The East India Company could still handle trade, but matters related to Indian revenue, administration, war, and diplomacy fell to the new BOC. The operational aspects of the act, however, were somewhat anomolous, as the BOC could not communicate directly with the company's servants in India, but could send "secret orders" to India through a Secret Committee of the Court on select issues. Additionally, while the court of directors retained substantial patronage powers in company appointments, the Crown, on the advice of the president of the BOC, could recall the governor-general or any company servant from India. The Act of 1784, a compromise between Pitt, Charles Fox, and Edmund Burke (who wanted to take direct control of the East India Company), was put into effect with three of the ablest men of the day—William Pitt, the prime minister; Henry Dundas, president of the BOC; and Lord Cornwallis, governor-general of India, 1786–1793. (P. J. Marshall, *Problems of Empire: Britain and India, 1757–1813*, 1968; C. T. Philips, *The East Indian Company, 1784–1834*, 1961.)

Arnold P. Kaminsky

INDIAN COUNCILS ACT OF 1892. The transition from Company to Crown in 1858 did not substantially alter the de facto organization of government in India*, since the British East India Company's independence had eroded progressively in the first half of the nineteenth century through a series of charter renewals and government acts dating back to 1773. However, in part because they realized the profundity of their ignorance of the Indian scene, which had contributed to the so-called "Mutiny of 1857," British rulers instituted a measured policy of including Indians in the consultative process. The first step was enactment of the Indian Councils Act of 1861, which reconstructed the viceroy's executive council (creating a "mini-cabinet" of sorts), expanded the imperial legislative council, and provided for provincial legislatures. Non-official members, selected by the Government of India (GOI), were given a minority of places in the legislative council, but could only discuss legislation which was exclusively domestic in nature.

In large measure a response to the "politics of associations," growing Indian press criticism, and institutionalization of Indian nationalist politics (the Indian National Congress was founded in 1885), the Indian Councils Act of 1892 introduced *indirect* election of Indians by providing for "recommending bodies" (e.g., municipalities and district boards) to nominate additional members to provincial councils—but only for consultative purposes. Significantly, however, the provincial legislative councils could now discuss government finance and direct questions to government officials. With the Act of 1892, provincial councils became an increasingly important arena for political activity, providing the first generation of Indian nationalists with valuable training and experience which would bear fruit in the impending independence movement. Although a step forward in Indian constitutional development, British officials still formed an official majority in the provincial legislative councils and in the central government, thus providing the Raj with an effective safety valve as nationalist activity increased as the nineteenth century drew to a close. (S. Gopal, *British Policy in India, 1858–1905*, 1965; Anil Seal, *The Emergence of Indian Nationalism*, 1968.)

Arnold P. Kaminsky

INDIAN INDEPENDENCE ACT OF 1947. Although a few diehards retained the "illusion of permanence" about Britain's future in India*, the intensification of nationalist and communal politics in India after World War II, combined with the financial realities and reordered priorities of postwar Britain, made it clear to most that the British could no longer continue their sovereignty over India without the consent of the majority of the Indian people. On the one hand, for India, the 1940s formed a "great divide," the end of the Raj and the partition of the subcontinent. On the other hand, the 1940s can be seen as a "middle passage" of sorts which show far more continuity than change.

The British responded to increased nationalist activity by clamping down harshly on the Indian National Congress. At the same time, the Government of India tried to ameliorate the situation by sending Sir Stafford Cripps to India in 1942 with an offer of dominion status after the war—which Mohandas Gandhi called a "blank cheque on a failing bank." The failure of the Cripps Mission, followed by the collapse of the Gandhi-Muhammad Ali Jinnah talks, and the near-miss of the June 1945 Simla Conference* to resolve the constitutional impasse, was a striking set of reversals for the Raj. After the war, as tension increased with the Indian national army trials and a naval mutiny, a high level cabinet mission tried again to break the deadlock and failed. With the sudden victory of a Labour government in Britain, the increased imperatives for resolution of the "Indian problem" were matched by the determination of Clement Atlee and his colleagues to devolve power as quickly as possible and get on with the business of restoring Britain itself. Lord Louis Mountbatten*, Queen Victoria's grandson and head of Southeast Asia Command in World War II, assumed the viceroyalty and negotiated the turbulent waters of the Indian political scene. Sir Cyril Radcliffe set about his map-making to chart the partition of India and transfer of border populations, while parliament addressed questions on the final form of the transfer of power in India.

The central questions revolving about the Indian Independence Act of 1947 included concerns over the future dominion status of the two projected successor states; and the question of the accession of the Princely states to either India or Pakistan—but without provision for separate dominionhood for other units, especially Hyderabad. (This issue alone generated considerable debate in parliament.) It was a gruelling task to formulate the bill in just six weeks to end a 350-year-long connection. Cognizant of the historic importance of the act, Winston Churchill* and the Conservatives resisted the use of the term "Independence" in the title of the bill, preferring the "India Bill of 1947" or the "India Self-Government Act"—but to no avail. On August 15, 1947, the British left India, leaving behind two successor states (India and Pakistan*) to chart markedly different political paths. (R. J. Moore, *Escape from Empire: The Atlee Government and the Indian Problem*, 1983; R. J. Moore, *Making the New Commonwealth*, 1987.)

Arnold P. Kaminsky

INDIAN MUTINY OF 1857. See SEPOY MUTINY OF 1857.

INDIA OFFICE. For eighty-nine years the India Office ran the Home Government of Britain's largest and most complex overseas possession. Its multifarious responsibilities were carried out in a concerted fashion by a secretary of state of India*, key permanent officials, India office departments, and the Council of India—that unique imperial institution designed to represent the Indian ethos in the policymaking process in London. While the India Office was formally established by the Act for the Better Government of India in 1858, its character in its first decades was not markedly different than that of the "dual government" which operated under the court of directors of the British East India Company* and the board of control. Indeed, progressively from 1773, the home government of the East India Company had evolved into an institution exercising a system of dual control to accommodate both the commercial element and the government.

For all intents and purposes, the new India Office was a change in form but not substance. The personnel of the East India Company was by and large carried over to the fledgling department of state, while the committee system of the young office was directly descended from that of the Venerable John Company. However, the Act of 1858 defined new objectives—not the least of which was the new alignment of India Office responsibility to parliament, and increased controls over Indian affairs from London. The secretary of state for India's power exceeded that of the old president of the board of control since he could overrule the Council of India on "urgent" and "secret" matters. Such prerogatives were used only sparingly in the history of the office, and in the main the Home Government of India functioned as a corporate entity—the secretary of state for India *in Council*. This was especially important since all matters requiring expenditure of funds required council approval.

For much of its history, parliament was apathetic over Indian affairs. Later in the nineteenth century, when parliament woke up to India, the India Office worked meticulously to keep parliament at a distance, thus insulating itself from the ebb and flow of British domestic politics. Secretaries of state rotated the seals with each shift of administration. Throughout its history the India Office also had to work with other British departments of state. In this vein, special significance attached to the fact that from 1858 to 1919, the India Office establishment, and the salaries of the secretary of state and permanent undersecretaries were paid with Indian, not British, revenues. The India Office, then, was not subject to the usual pressures of the treasury until well into the twentieth century.

The structure and organization of the India Office received their first substantial revision in 1859 under Sir Charles Wood. Increasingly disillusioned with the cumbersome dispatch of office business, Wood designed reforms to streamline division of business between the permanent and parliamentary undersecretaries of state, and to effect closer cooperation with departments. In its first decades the initiative in writing dispatches gradually fell to department heads and, in fact, to the undersecretaries. Meanwhile, the character of the Council of India slowly edged away from the "tyranny of the past" and the spectre of the East India Company. Eventually, the departments and the committees of the Council of India were brought into alignment. The correspondence departments of the office were its heart and soul: financial, judicial and public, military, political and secret, public works, revenue, statistics and commerce.

Because of its wide-ranging responsibilities, the India Office processed nearly 100,000 documents annually. The volume increased when the telegraph reached India in 1870, and when technological innovations such as the typewriter were introduced into Whitehall at the turn of the century. The office handled not only correspondence from Indian officials but throughout its history was the focal point of much lobbying by Indian parties and their allies in Britain—in spite of the fact that they often castigated the office as that "great manufactory of lies." The major responsibility for guiding the India Office in its efforts fell to Sir Arthur Godley (later Lord Kilbracken), who served as permanent undersecretary of state for India under ten chiefs, from 1883–1909.

As a result of the Indian Council Act of 1909, two Indians joined the Council of India. In 1914 Lord Crewe introduced a Council of India Bill to strengthen the hand of the secretary of state vis-à-vis his council, but it was rejected. Lord Curzon, former viceroy of India, led the opposition, reminding parliament that the council was a bulwark against the India Office browbeating the Government of India. Indeed, the "Simla versus Whitehall" contest was hardly ever absent from Indian governance from 1858.

World War I proved to be the catalyst for the next major round of internal reforms for India, especially when the India Office went on the British estimates following the Government of India Act of 1919*. Significant reordering of the Office structure occured between 1920 and 1924, when its inefficient handling of the Mesopotamia campaign in World War I became public knowledge. In the interwar period, the number of Indians on the Council of India increased from two to three, and many of the departments were submerged into three units: services and general, public and judicial, and economic and overseas. An establishment officer took over personnel matters from the accountant-general and was the de facto liaison to the treasury department. The Council of India's weekly meetings were also cut back to once a month, and new requirements were effected to ensure that Indian experience was available to the consultative body. The Government of India Act of 1935*, operationalized in 1937, proved to be the coup de grace for the Council of India, which was transformed into advisors to the secretary of state who were consulted at the secretary's discretion. Additionally, Burmese affairs were slotted into a separate Burma Office in 1937, although it was housed within the India Office and there was much overlap in its personnel.

During World War II the India Office worked with a vast array of British, Indian, and Allied bureaucracies to prosecute the war and effectively monitor the intense Indian nationalism of the 1940s. With the British withdrawal from India in 1947, and the partition of the subcontinent, the India Office ceased to exist and was merged into the newly formed Commonwealth Relations Office. (Donovan Williams, *The India Office, 1858–1869*, 1983; Arnold P. Kaminsky, *The India Office, 1880–1910*, 1986.)

Arnold P. Kaminsky

INDOCHINA. French Indochina was a federation of states on the east side of mainland Southeast Asia, comprising all of what is now Vietnam*, Laos*, and Cambodia*. The federation made sense geographically, but not culturally. For France the coast of Vietnam was strategic because it had some ports along the shipping lanes to China. The Mekong River, in its middle course, formed a natural border between French Laos and the independent Kingdom of Siam*, while Cambodia produced an agricultural surplus and further buffered French territory from the Thais. Legally, French Indochina comprised one directly ruled colony, Cochin-China*, and four protectorates: Annam*, Tonkin*, Laos, and Cambodia. The Cambodians had nothing at all in common with Vietnamese and hated them. For this reason, the Cambodian king readily agreed to French protectorate status for his country.

France had long been interested in Catholic missionary work in Southeast Asia but did not actually seize any land until 1860 when they took an insignificant fishing village in the Mekong delta that later grew into Saigon. They occupied Cambodia by 1863, the Ca Mau Peninsula by 1867, the rest of Vietnam by 1883, and Laos by 1893. French control of Indochina was never secure, however. Vietnamese revolutionaries arose again and again to challenge the foreigners. French pacification campaigns were waged in the 1880s, the 1910s, and 1930s, and from 1946 until 1954, when the Geneva Accords rang down the curtain on France's Asian empire.

In colonial Indochina, the French governor-general enjoyed almost undiluted power over all parts of the federation, though a Vietnamese emperor continued to sit on the throne in Hue, and a Cambodian king enjoyed some measure of autonomy in Phnom Penh. There was a common budget for all Indochina, and the foundation for future economic development was laid: roads, canals, and railroads were built, mines were dug, and plantations were carved from jungle. Most importantly, the Mekong delta swamps were cleared for rice and sugar cultivation. *Lycees* were established in Hanoi and Saigon. Most development was intended to benefit the French, but their schools bred revolutionaries as well as functionaries; their plantations produced rural proletarians as well as export crops. While little nationalist agitation disturbed the peace in remote Laos and Cambodia, the opposite was true in Vietnam. Ho Chi Minh* founded the Indochinese Communist Party in 1930. He fought the French, the Japanese, the French again, and the Americans until his death in 1969. Ironically, after the

communists won in 1975, the Vietnamese immediately imposed extensive po-
litical and military control over Cambodia and Laos. (Joseph Buttinger, *Vietnam:
A Political History*, 1968; John F. Cady, *The Roots of French Imperialism in
Eastern Asia*, 1954.)

Ross Marlay

INDOCHINA UNION. Anxious to establish its own imperial presence in Asia,
France moved into Indochina* in 1858, landing a fleet at Tourane (Da Nang).
Two years later a French army seized Saigon and the three surrounding provinces:
Dinh Tuong, Gia Dinh, and Bien Hoa. A peace treaty in 1862 between Emperor
Tu Duc of Vietnam* and France ceded southern Vietnam to the French. In 1867
the French expanded west and seized three more provinces: Vinh Long, Cham
Doc, and Ha Tien. The French colony of Cochin-China* was born. Almost
immediately after their arrival in Saigon, the French began looking enviously
up the Mekong River delta into Cambodia*, but their ambitions collided with
those of Siam*. In 1863 France forced King Norodom of Cambodia to sign a
treaty giving France a protectorate over Cambodia. Sporadic fighting erupted
between French and Siamese forces, which did not end until 1867, when a
French-Siamese treaty recognized the French protectorate over Cambodia. In
return, France gave the three western Cambodian provinces to Siam.

Between 1879 and 1883, with British authority expanding out of India into
Burma*, France began looking north toward the Chinese border, fearful that the
British Empire* would fill a vacuum there. French forces moved north out of
Saigon and extended their imperial control over Annam and then Tonkin. The
protectorate over Tonkin was formalized in 1883. Hopeful of using Laos as a
buffer between British Burma and French Tonkin, France moved into Laos in
the 1890s. In 1893 Siam recognized the French protectorate in Laos. To provide
uniform government over their colonies, France established the Indochina Union
in 1887. After the addition of Laos in 1887, there were five colonies in the
union: Cochin-China, Annam, Tonkin, Cambodia, and Laos. Hanoi served as
the capital of the Indochina union. (John F. Cady, *The Roots of French Imperialism in East Asia*, 1954; Milton E. Osborne, *The French Presence in Cochin
China and Cambodia: Rule and Response (1859–1905)*, 1969.)

INDONESIA. Indonesia is a large, diverse nation composed of a great many
large and small islands stretching thousands of miles between the Indian and
Pacific Oceans. Its population, fifth largest in the world, speaks 250 different
dialects, but unifying factors include the prevalence of Islam (90 percent) and
a national language called Bahasa Indonesia, based on market Malay. Indonesia
inherited what was formerly the Dutch East Indies*. There might never have
been an Indonesia had the Dutch not conquered all the islands from Sumatra*
to New Guinea*. Patriotic Indonesian historians profess to see early expressions
of nationalism in Gadja Mada's fourteenth-century Javanese imperialism and
Diponegoro's war against the Dutch (1825–30), but this is unconvincing. In fact

the Dutch skillfully exploited disunity, playing on local suspicions to consolidate their power. Eventually however, rational colonialism demanded administrative uniformity, which was achieved when the last traditionalist revolts and separatist insurrections were snuffed out in the first decade of the twentieth century. The Dutch then implemented an "Ethical Policy" to rectify past abuses.

An elite, proto-nationalist group called Budi Utomo (Noble Endeavor) was organized in 1908. It eschewed political demands, seeking merely to reconcile traditional Javanese culture with the modern world. The Sarekat Islam (Islamic Association), founded in 1912, had far greater impact, but its ideology was vague. Sarekat Islam was discredited by its failure to expel radicals who had very different aims. The Indonesian Communist Party, founded in 1920 by the Dutchman Hendrik Sneevliet, launched a premature uprising on Java and Sumatra in 1927 that was easily suppressed by the Netherlands Indies government. The Dutch made few concessions to nationalism other than to permit a toothless consultative legislature called the Volksraad.

Pro-independence sentiment spread in the 1920s through the small class of educated Indonesians, but it lacked a clear focus. Three doctrines competed for followers: Marxism, Islamic revivalism, and simple anti-Dutch nationalism. Nationalism triumphed but then foundered on its inability to assimilate the first two. A young, spellbinding orator named Sukarno caught the attention of marginal men too educated to go back to their villages but unable to convince the Dutch to treat them as equals. Their tentative insubordination so unnerved the Dutch that it was forbidden even to use the word "Indonesia." Sukarno and other nationalists were repeatedly jailed, but their *Partai Nasional Indonesia* (PNI) emerged to lead the nation to independence. The economy rode an export boom to prosperity in the 1920s but crashed in the Great Depression. The population of Java multiplied at a frightening pace and peasants faced destitution. Dutch policy became so repressive that Indonesian nationalists made little headway—until World War II.

The Japanese arrived in March 1942, posing as Asian saviors. Indonesians gaped in amazement as Dutchmen were made to sweep the streets. But Japanese arrogance quickly dispelled the enthusiasm. Furthermore, all Muslims were repelled by the cult of emperor-worship. The Japanese set up youth groups and an Indonesian puppet army. Sukarno, Mohammed Hatta, and other nationalist leaders used these organizations for their own purposes. Sukarno proclaimed Indonesian independence on August 17, 1945. British troops sent to Java to accept the Japanese surrender found that Indonesians were determined to keep all foreigners out. The Indonesian Revolution began in November 1945 with a bitter three-week battle at Surabaya. Truce negotiations broke down and fighting continued for four years, ending with a nearly complete Dutch capitulation on December 27, 1949. They clung only to the western half of New Guinea and lost even that by United Nations decision in 1962. (George McT. Kahin, *Nationalism and Revolution in Indonesia*, 1952.)

Ross Marlay

INTERNAL PROVINCES. In 1777, to deal with expanding settlement patterns in northern Mexico as well as continuing problems with hostile Indian tribes, Spain created a new administrative unit known as the Internal Provinces. At first it included all of the northern provinces of New Spain with the exception of California. It was headed by a commandant-general and was independent of the viceroy. The exact authority of the Internal Provinces administration was poorly defined, since each of the constituent provinces had a civil governor who was dependent on the commandant-general in some provinces and independent of him in others. Between 1788 and 1793 and 1813 and 1821 the Internal Provinces was divided into a western and an eastern unit. It was dissolved in 1821 when Spanish authority ended in Mexico. See NEW SPAIN.

INTOLERABLE ACTS OF 1774. The Intolerable (or Coercive) Acts passed by the British parliament in 1774 were designed to force a colonial recognition of parliamentary sovereignty while punishing Massachusetts* and Boston in particular for destroying British East India Company* tea in Boston Harbor during December 1773. Effective June 1, 1774, the Boston Port Act closed Boston Harbor to all shipping until the East India Company was compensated for the destroyed tea. The harshness of the measure was supposed to isolate Massachusetts from sister colony support, but the colonies dispatched supplies to Boston and followed Virginia's lead in observing June 1 as "a day of fasting, humiliation, and prayer." The other Intolerable Acts passed in May and June included constitutionally alarming features which represented a sweeping attempt to reorganize the Empire along more tractable lines. A new Quartering Act required local officials to quarter and supply troops regardless of whether barracks were nearby and unoccupied. Most British Regulars initially stationed in the West had been relocated eastward after 1768 to reduce expenses and to provide control over mounting colonial resistance to parliamentary authority. The new Quartering Act was widely regarded as endorsing the use of military force to uphold arbitrary government. The dual appointment of General Thomas Gage as military commander of royal forces in America and civil governor for Massachusetts reinforced colonial suspicions of Britain's intent.

An Act for the Better Government of Massachusetts allowed the royal governor to appoint his council, which had formerly been chosen by the general court. The council could no longer veto executive decisions. The governor could forbid town meetings, except for annual meetings for the election of officers. Furthermore, governors were authorized to appoint and remove sheriffs, judges, and the attorney general and marshal of the colony. Juries were to be selected by the appointed sheriffs. The act was clearly regarded as an effort to enhance royal executive powers at the expense of colonial self-government. In like manner, the Administration of Justice Act was designed to strengthen imperial controls over the colonial judicial process. The Justice Act provided that British officials charged with offenses in America while enforcing British laws might be tried in another colony or in Britain if, in the opinion of the governor, a fair trial could not be had in the province in which the offense occurred.

In late June parliament passed the Quebec Act which colonials considered part of the punitive package. The Quebec Act extended the boundaries of Quebec to include the Ohio and Mississippi, withdrew the promise of representative government for Quebec included in the royal Proclamation of 1763, and granted religious freedom to French Catholics in Quebec. By legislative fiat, the act negated several colonial charter rights to the Northwest and seemed to substantiate the colonial view that the principle of representative government was under general imperial attack.

In one way or another the Intolerable Acts rejected most of the rights and privileges so strongly claimed by Americans since 1763. Britain's coercive policies adopted in 1774 presented Englishmen abroad in America with the alternative of abject submission or a more spirited self-defense. A more spirited self-defense was to be fashioned by the First Continental Congress in September and October 1774. (David Ammerman, *In the Common Cause*, 1974.)

Lee E. Olm

IONIAN ISLANDS. The Ionian Islands are off the west coast of Greece in the Mediterranean and consist of the islands of Cephalonia, Cerigo, Corfu, Ithaca, Leucas, Paxo, and Zante. Venice claimed them until 1797, when she ceded the islands to France. Two years later Russia occupied the islands and proclaimed the Septinsular Republic there. Shortly thereafter, during the Napoleonic Wars, Russia ceded the Ionian Islands to France. Great Britain occupied them in 1809 and then established its own protectorate. That arrangement lasted until 1864 when the British, at the request of Ionian Islanders, handed them over to Greece. (David P. Henige, *Colonial Governors from the Fifteenth Century to the Present* 1970.)

IRAN. Known anciently as Persia, Iran is a Shiite Muslim country located in the Middle East, south of the Caspian Sea and the Soviet Union, east of Iraq*, north of the Persian Gulf and Arabian Sea, and west of Pakistan* and Afghanistan*. Although Iran was never a formal colony of one of the European empires, her modern history has been inextricably linked with imperial politics. In the early sixteenth century, to protect her access to her Indian ports, Portugal established naval stations in Iranian territory, on Bahrain* and Hormuz* in the Persian Gulf. But in 1581, when Spain annexed Portugal, the Portuguese lost much of their capacity to defend those Persian Gulf installations. By 1600 the British were extending their reach into the Persian Gulf in order to protect their growing presence on the Indian subcontinent. Iran expelled Portugal from Bahrain in 1602, and in 1622, with British assistance, they captured Hormuz as well. The British established their headquarters at Bandar Abbas, and until the dawn of the nineteenth century it was the center of Persian Gulf commercial and economic activity.

By the early nineteenth century, Iran was growing more and more insecure about the southern expansion of Czarist Russia. Fath Ali Shah, the Iranian leader, signed an agreement with Napoleon in 1807. Napoleon supplied Iran with weapons to fight the Russians, and in return Iran granted Napoleon access to India through Iran. But the decline and ultimate defeat of France in the Napoleonic Wars compromised Iran's position vis-à-vis the Russians. In 1813 Iran signed the Treaty of Gulistan, ceding Georgia to Russia. The Treaty of Turkmanchai in 1828 resulted in the loss of Erivan and Nakhichevan to Russia.

The expanding Russian presence in Iran was unsettling to the British, who were anxious to keep open their access to India*. When Afghanistan rebelled against Iranian control in the 1850s, the British sided with the Afghans. The British governor-general of India declared war against Iran, and when Russia refused to come to Iran's assistance, Iran signed the Treaty of Paris in 1857, recognizing Afghanistan's independence and extending a variety of commercial privileges to Great Britain. Throughout the rest of the century, Iran's other boundaries were permanently fixed. In 1881 Iran ceded half of Sistan Province to Afghanistan. In 1884 Iran lost Merv to Russia, and in 1893 the British set the boundaries between Iran and British India at British Baluchistan, which is today part of Pakistan.

But political inroads from other European nations were not Iran's only problems. Because of her pre-modern economy and religious fundamentalism, Iran was vulnerable to foreign economic pressures. In 1889 the British established and controlled the Imperial Bank of Persia, and in 1901 British investors secured exclusive oil rights for most of Iran. Russia made huge loans to Iran in 1900 and in return received low tariff rates, road and railroad concessions, and the right to keep an army, the Persian Cossacks, inside Iran to protect her interests. On August 31, 1907, Great Britain and Russia signed an agreement dividing Iran into three commercial and protective zones. Both countries were concerned about German intentions to build a railroad across the Middle East to the Persian Gulf. Russia's zone included northern Iran, particularly Tabriz, Rasht, Tehran, Meshed, and Isafan. The British zone was much smaller and located in the southeast near Baluchistan. The rest of Iran was declared neutral territory.

When World War I* broke out, Iran declared her neutrality, but British, Turkish, and Russian troops entered the country shortly after the outbreak of hostilities. Russian troops defeated the Turks, but when the Russian Revolution broke out in 1917, Russian troops withdrew back to the border near the Caspian Sea, and Great Britain became the dominant power in Iran. When the war ended, the British presented a treaty which would have effectively given them complete control of Iran. The Iranians rejected it and in 1920 signed a treaty of friendship with the Soviet Union, in which the Soviets canceled all Iranian debts, withdrew all Soviet troops from Iranian soil, and ceded all Soviet assets on Iranian soil. In return Iran agreed to keep anti-Soviet groups from using Iran as a base of operations against the Soviet regime.

During the 1920s a new dynasty assumed power in Iran, and both Great Britain and the Soviet Union decided not to contest it. Iranian journalist Sayyid Zia al Din Tabatabai led a nationalist uprising against the Qajar dynasty in 1921, and he received military support from Reza Khan, a colonel in the Persian Cossack army. Tabatabai remained in office only three months before leaving the country. Reza assumed control of the government. Opposed to honorific titles, Reza chose to be identified by the Pahlavi family name, and on December 12, 1925, he was recognized as Reza Pahlavi, the shah of a new dynasty, with rights of succession granted to his heirs. His son, Mohammad Reza Pahlavi, was designated crown prince. During the next fifty years the Pahlavis worked to modernize and industrialize Iran, eliminating use of the Arabic language in favor of Farsi and requiring western-style dress. The revolution of 1979 was in part a rebellion against Pahlavi-imposed western values. (Amin Banani, *The Modernization of Iran, 1921–1941*, 1961; Richard N. Frye, *Iran*, 1954.)

IRAQ. Great Britain became involved in Iraq during World War I*. When Turkey, the sovereign authority over Iraq, entered the war on the side of the Central Powers, British troops landed at the mouth of the Shatt-al-Arab with the objective of protecting British oil interests in south Persia. They then advanced north and captured Baghdad in March 1917. By the time the Armistice was signed, the Turks had been virtually expelled from the country. In accordance with the terms of the Armistice with Turkey, the British Command received orders on November 2, 1918, to occupy Mosul. From then on the name ''Iraq'' began to be used to designate the territory comprising the Basrah, Baghdad, and Mosul vilayets; the old term ''Mesapotamia'' referred to the Basrah and Baghdad areas only. Under the aegis of the League of Nations*, Iraq became a British mandate. Nationalist extremists, however, resisted the British presence and a rebellion erupted on July 3, 1920, at Rumaitha. Trouble spread as the imams began calling for a jihad. Railway lines were cut, and isolated British garrisons were besieged; more than 65,000 British troops were required to defeat the rebels. The first high commissioner was Sir Percy Cox, who arrived in Iraq in October 1920. His task was to try to implement the British policy of establishing the beginnings of an independent Iraqi government.

The mandate concept was opposed by the Iraqis, and it soon became apparent that the relationship between Iraq and Britain would be structured by several bilateral treaties. Using this approach, Iraq became the first mandated territory to receive a parliament and a constitution. After 1920 Britain was involved in difficult treaty negotiations to generate a new agreement. Instead of the mandate, a new ''basis of alliance'' was developed. Britain recognized Faisal as Iraq's king, but there was no outright recognition of Iraq as a sovereign state. The main Iraqi objections involved the subsidiary agreements to the treaty. The British Officials Agreement, for example, provided that in the case of eighteen listed positions, including advisers in the ministry of finance and the ministry of defense, the Iraqi government would be required to appoint British officials when asked to do so.

The constituent assembly convened in 1924, and immediately major conflicts surfaced between the British and the nationalists. The latter objected to the proposed control of the military by British officers. They also condemned the proposal that would lead to the control of the governmental administration by British officials, and they also felt that the high commissioner's powers were too broad. The high commissioner issued an ultimatum to break the deadlock, threatening to ask the League of Nations to confirm the mandate in its original terms if the treaty were not swiftly ratified. The ploy worked; on June 11, 1924, the assembly voted to approve the treaty and subsidiary agreements. In September the League Council approved the agreements as being acceptable substitutes for the mandate.

King Faisal's formal accession to the throne had taken place in Baghdad on August 23, 1921. Before Faisal was selected as king and head of state, the British negotiated with him to receive assurances that he would support their policies. And, indeed, during his reign of approximately twelve years, the British could usually rely on his support. There was, however, some sentiment that he had become a British puppet and this weakened his position among his subjects. During the time he was king, Faisal had the difficult task of trying to balance the demands of the nationalists against those of the British.

Dissatisfaction with the treaty arrangements persisted, and in 1927 further efforts were made concerning revision. Negotiations were completed and a new treaty was signed in December. There was an understanding, however, that it would not be ratified until the financial and military provisions had been revised and then approved by the League. This initiated another tense period in British-Iraqi relations. In 1928 the two sides attempted to solve outstanding financial issues but failed to reach agreement. Britain demanded that debts owed her would have to be settled before Iraq could assume full control over the railways of the Basrah Port; the Iraqis rejected this demand.

Finally, there was a breakthrough with the ratification of a new treaty in 1930 by a specially elected parliament. The treaty provided for a military alliance. Britain was permitted to have right-of-way through Iraq for her armed forces, and British air bases would be allowed to continue west of the Euphrates. In exchange for these concessions, Britain agreed to work for the achievement of Iraq's sovereignty. The treaty lasted for 25 years. British assurances of Iraq's capacity to assume the status of a sovereign state were accepted, with some reluctance, by the Permanent Mandates Commission. The British argued quite logically that Iraq was at least as advanced as a number of other independent states. In any event, early resolution of the question of Iraq's sovereignty seemed guaranteed when the British Socialist government decided in 1929 to speed up the process of ending the mandate.

The Permanent Mandates Commission discussed the compatibility of the 1930 treaty with Iraq's independence and concluded that it was in the category of a treaty of alliance and, therefore, did not explicitly infringe the nation's independence. With respect to the railway system, which had been constructed by the British largely in connection with World War I, the commission accepted the settlement as fair. The railways were valued at £3,400,000 in 1930, but the British agreed to accept only about £2,000,000 in payment. To allay the fears of minorities, certain guaranteed rights were made part of Iraq's legal system. There was to be no discrimination involving elections, appointments, religion, language, or the expression of public opinion. These guarantees were accepted by Iraq in May 1932. On October 3, 1932, Iraq became a full, sovereign member of the League of Nations. The mandate was ended, and the high commissioner became an ambassador to an independent country. (Stephen H. Longrigg, *Iraq, 1900 to 1950*, 1953; Ernest Main, *Iraq From Mandate to Independence*, 1935.)

Roy E. Thoman

IRELAND. The Irish struggle for independence was an ancient one, beginning in 1169 when the Norman supporters of King Henry II of England invaded the island. Although culturally united by Celtic customs, the Gaelic language, and Roman Catholicism, Ireland before the Anglo-Norman invasions was politically decentralized into clan societies ruled by regional, tribal chiefs. English influence proved to be especially strong in eastern Ireland, an area known as the "Pale," but "beyond the Pale," to the west and southwest, native Irish control was progressively stronger. After the English Reformation in the sixteenth century, English officials insisted that the native Irish repudiate Catholicism as a test of loyalty. What had once been a political struggle now became a religious civil war between Anglo-Protestants and Irish Catholics.

Under the pressure of English persecution, Gaelic culture became indelibly stamped with the imprint of Roman Catholicism, and the more Catholic Ireland became, the more England worried about it. Faced with a rival in Catholic Spain in the sixteenth century, and worried about Catholic Ireland on its western flank, England decided to Anglicize all of Ireland. Queen Elizabeth* and later King James I awarded large plantations in Ireland to English landlords, who in turn invited Scots Presbyterians to settle there. The Scots fought ferociously against Catholic guerrillas, and between 1580 and 1690 Catholic ownership of the land declined from 95 to less than 15 percent. In the process the Catholic upper and middle classes were all but destroyed. In the region of northern Ireland known as Ulster, so many Catholics died that English and Scots Protestants became the majority group in the population.

In England the fear of Catholicism as well as the new concern for natural rights led to the Glorious Revolution; Catholic King James II was exiled to France, and Protestant William of Orange assumed the throne. Immediately after his flight from England, James II turned to Ireland, collected an army of French sympathizers and Irish Catholics, and summoned an anti-Protestant Irish parliament. But in July 1690 William of Orange invaded Ireland and defeated the Catholic army at the Battle of the Boyne. He then dissolved the Irish parliament and chased James II back to France. England then magnified the crisis by abolishing civil rights for Catholics. Bishops were exiled, monastic orders prohibited, and foreign priests no longer permitted in Ireland. Catholics could not vote, hold public office or government jobs, teach school, own property, or carry weapons. England even prohibited use of the Gaelic language throughout Ireland. English landlords controlled Ireland and Catholics became a helpless lower caste.

In the nineteenth century English policies only fanned the flames of Irish nationalism. The Irish Act of 1800* created the United Kingdom of Great Britain and Ireland in an attempt to fuse the two countries. Although some English officials called for "Catholic emancipation," the law excluded Catholics from serving in parliament, enraging Catholic nationalists. The Irish famine* of the 1840s, in which more than one million peasants perished from famine and starvation, inspired more hatred, particularly when England, in the name of laissez-faire classical economics, failed to provide adequate assistance to the Irish. Hating all things Protestant and all things English, the Irish became united, and a strong Irish-Catholic identity emerged.

Ever since the seventeenth century Irish political and terrorist organizations had fought for separation and independence from Great Britain, but it was not until the nineteenth century that their movement gained momentum. Robert Emmett led a rebellion in 1803, which the English easily suppressed, but in the 1820s the movement for Catholic emancipation gained strength on both sides of the Irish Sea. The Catholic Association, established in 1823 by Daniel O'Connell, called for an end to all anti-Catholic discrimination, and in 1828 Catholics were finally permitted to hold public office. The next year they gained the right to sit in parliament. The hated tithes to the Anglican Church ended in 1838. But concession to Irish Catholics only whetted their appetites for equality and independence.

The Home Rule movement, led by Charles Stewart Parnell, emerged in the 1860s, along with more violent insurgent and terrorist groups. In response to terrorist acts by a number of secret Catholic societies, England passed the Coercion Act of 1881 permitting authorities to arrest anyone even suspected of revolutionary activity. Catholic resentment increased. In 1900 Arthur Griffith founded the Sinn Fein, a political organization committed to complete independence. At the same time, Protestants in Ulster feared Irish independence because they would then become a tiny minority in Catholic Ireland. They began to campaign for a continuation of colonial status at best or at worst separation of northern and southern Ireland into two political entities, with the Protestant north remaining part of Great Britain. During World War I Irish nationalists stepped up their agitation for independence, and Irish Republican Brotherhood radicals staged the Easter Rebellion in 1916, which British troops had to crush. In the election of 1918, Griffith's Sinn Fein won 73 of the 106 seats allotted to Ireland in the English parliament.

In January 1919 those 73 members of parliament gathered in Dublin and organized the Dail Eireann, a national assembly, which proclaimed Irish independence and elected Eamon de Valera as president. War broke out between the Irish Republican Army, an irregular force of radical nationalists, and British troops in 1919. To quell the revolt, parliament passed the Government of Ireland Act of 1920, which provided Home Rule but at the same time separated Northern Ireland and southern Ireland. Northern Ireland remained united with Great Britain under this plan, but the "South" rejected the proposed arrangements. The fighting continued until the summer of 1921. A truce and negotiations then led to an Anglo-Irish treaty (December 6, 1921), which created the Irish Free State, with Dominion status, out of the 26 "Southern" counties of Ireland. During the 1920s and 1930s Eamon de Valera continued his drive for complete separation from Great Britain, and in 1937 the Dail Eireann deleted all references to the king in the Irish Free State constitution, renaming the country Eire. Thirteen years later, on April 18, 1949, the thirty-third anniversary of the Easter Rebellion, Eire became the Republic of Ireland, withdrawing from the British Commonwealth. (E. R. Norman, *A History of Modern Ireland*, 1971; John O'Beirne Ranelagh, *A Short History of Ireland*, 1983.)

IRELAND ACT OF 1949. See IRELAND.

IRISH ACT OF 1800. The Irish Act of 1800, also known as the Act of Union, was an attempt by the British parliament to merge the nominally independent kingdom of Ireland into Great Britain. The plan followed a period of discontent in Ireland from the end of the American Revolution to 1782, during which an independent Irish parliament was proposed, the Roman Catholic majority demanded emancipation, and the Irish peasantry verged on revolt against their English landlords. In 1782 the Irish parliament won limited legislative independence, although the British parliament retained the right to appoint the executive. In 1793 fewer than 40,000 Catholics were enfranchised, but even those allowed to vote were still excluded from parliament and public offices. During the 1790s Ireland remained little more than a British colony, with all political and social power held by a minority of Anglicans of English heritage.

Irish discontent reached a peak during the late 1790s. A rebellion led by the Irish revolutionary Wolfe Tone, who had anticipated French military support, was crushed in 1798. With the British government facing a desperate war against France and a hostile Irish population, Prime Minister William Pitt* the Younger proposed legislation to smother Irish independence by a union of the two kingdoms. Only after massive political corruption was the bill passed by the Irish parliament in 1800. The major British concession was Pitt's promise of Catholic emancipation, although a union would place the Catholic population in a minority position in Great Britain, still at the mercy of the Anglican majority. The Act of Union which created the United Kingdom of Great Britain and Ireland provided for the creation of 28 Irish peers in the House of Lords and 100 Irish seats in the House of Commons (bringing the total to 658). Roman Catholics were excluded from serving in parliament. The Anglican Church of Ireland was united with the Church of England. The policy of free trade was established between Ireland and the British Empire*. Pitt's promise of Catholic emancipation was vetoed by King George III on the grounds that such a policy would violate the king's oath to protect the Church of England. The "Irish Act" did little to prevent the growth of Irish nationalism and, instead, promoted even greater Irish resentment against Great Britain. (Donald Grove Barnes, *George III and William Pitt, 1783–1806*, 1965; Edmund Curtis, *A History of Ireland*, 1950.)

William G. Ratliff

IRISH FAMINE. Ever since the twelfth century, the English had set their sights on conquering Ireland, and the Protestant Reformation in the sixteenth century only added a new religious dimension to the Irish-English struggle. Anglo-Saxon England, now imbued with a powerful Protestantism, was intent on conquering a Celtic, Roman Catholic Ireland. In the late sixteenth century Ireland became the first English overseas colony.

In the early nineteenth century perhaps half of the Irish population lived on the edge of existence, in hovels and lean-tos, subsisting on milk and potatoes. Then came the Great Famine. Potatoes had become the staple because they flourished in poor soil, required little attention, and yielded enough per acre to feed a family. But they were also a risky crop because yield fluctuations could mean life or death for millions. Crop failures occurred in 1817, 1822, and the 1830s, but a fungus destroyed the entire crop in 1845. The blight continued in 1846 and 1847, bringing starvation to nearly a million people. Between 1847 and 1860, two million Irish emigrated to the United States.

The Great Famine occurred at the peak of the free trade movement in England, a time when the English upper classes were convinced that government intervention in economic problems was contrary to natural law. Since they viewed the Irish famine as an economic problem, England did little to relieve the suffering. While a million Irish peasants starved to death, the governing classes of England talked self-righteously about trade laws, the weaknesses of the poor, and the self-destructiveness of the Irish. In the process, the Irish acquired a hatred for the English which knew no bounds and a yearning for independence which had no rival anywhere else in the world. The Great Famine fueled the flames of Irish nationalism. (Cecil Woodham-Smith, *The Great Hunger*, 1962.)

IRISH FREE STATE. See IRELAND.

ISABELLA OF CASTILE. Isabella I, patroness of Christopher Columbus, was born April 22, 1451, in Madrigal. She was queen of Castile from 1474 until her death on November 26, 1504. In 1469 Isabella married Ferdinand of Aragón*, uniting the two kingdoms of Aragón and Castile, and providing the impetus for a unified modern Spain. With her husband, Isabella was responsible for completing the reconquest of Iberia from the Moors. By 1492, with the capture of the Moorish stronghold of Granada, Isabella became convinced of the necessity for Spain to expand its trade with Asia. Along with her chief advisor, royal treasurer Louis de Santangel, Isabella saw merit in the plan of Christopher

Columbus* to find a safe and profitable trade route to the Far East by sailing west across the Atlantic.

Spain's interest in a western trade route, however, brought it into conflict with the other great nation of explorers. Portugal had been interested in overseas expansion since the days of Prince Henry the Navigator in the early fifteenth century, but had been focusing its efforts toward finding an eastern route to the East Indies. In 1494 Isabella attempted to claim all the land mass discovered by Columbus for Spain, but the Treaty of Tordesillas* placed the demarcation line between Spanish and Portuguese interests in the New World east of the mouth of the Amazon. Isabella's failure thus allowed Portugal to colonize the entire eastern two-thirds of South America. (Irene A. Plunket, *Isabel of Castile*, 1919.)

William G. Ratliff

ITALIAN EAST AFRICA. Between 1935 and 1941, Italian East Africa was an administrative unit employed by Italy to govern its colonies in East Africa, which included Italian Somaliland, Ethiopia*, and Eritrea. Italian East Africa had its formal beginnings with the Italian invasion of Ethiopia in 1935 and ended in 1941 when British troops occupied the area. See SOMALIA and ETHIOPIA.

ITALIAN SOMALILAND. See SOMALIA.

IVORY COAST. Ivory Coast, or Cote D'Ivoire, is located on the west coast of Africa, and is bordered by Ghana* to the east, Liberia* and Guinea* to the west, and Mali* and Burkina-Faso to the north. Manding-speaking tribes inhabited the area when Portuguese explorer Soerio da Costa landed at the mouth of the Sassandra River in 1469. Europeans began trading in gold, ivory, ostrich feathers, pepper, and slaves with tribes on the coast, which were part of the kingdom of Bouna in the sixteenth and seventeenth centuries. In 1637 French missionaries landed at Assinie, but the mission was unsuccessful due to inhospitable terrain and climate. Fifty years later a second attempt also failed. However, by the end of the seventeenth century the French traders were successful at Grand Bassam.

In 1838 the French returned to Assinie as well as numerous other points along the coast, and by 1842 the French were making formal claims to the ports of Assinie and Grand Bassam. After 25 years of negotiating the French had made treaties to promote commerce and to regulate the slave trade with the tribes at Akapless, Dabou, Grand Lahou, Bereby, Fresco, Korohou, Trepoint, Sassandra, Drewin, Victory, and Calvary. These treaties gave the French full sovereignty and the right to build forts in exchange for payment of a "custom" to the tribal chiefs. After taking control of the post at Grand Bassam in 1858, the French entrepreneur Arthur Verdier formed the *Compagnie de Kong* and initiated efforts to occupy the interior of Ivory Coast. Calling his conquest *Campeign de Kong*, Verdier established the northern town of Kong as well as numerous other French strongholds within the interior. Verdier later set up the first coffee and cocoa plantations, began the mahogany timbering industry, and founded a "school of agriculture."

With the defeat of Louis Napoleon* in France, the French presence in Ivory Coast diminished during the 1870s. As a consequence of the Franco-Prussian War, the French withdrew garrisons at Assinie and Grand Bassam, but Verdier stayed on and in 1878 was named the *Resident de France* in Ivory Coast, representing and reporting to colonial officials in the French colony of Senegal*. The French renewed their interest in Ivory Coast in 1890 and established official claims to posts in the north. Yet, most of the remote forests remained unexplored and unexploited by the French. Ivory Coast was declared a colony in 1893, and Louis Gustave Binger was appointed governor. The colony's capital was in Grand Bassam.

In 1897 resistance to French rule, led by the Malinke warrior Samory Toure from Guinea, destroyed the city of Kong. Samory was captured in the Ivory Coast and exiled to Gabon in 1898, but the resistance continued. In 1900 the capital was moved to Bingerville. Shortly after, a program of "pacification" of the indigenous people was initiated. "Pacification" entailed economic reprisals in the form of a head tax (1901) and France's refusal to pay the promised "customs" to the tribal chiefs, along with a military campaign aimed at subduing the resistance between the upper Calvary and upper Sassandra Rivers. By 1918 the French proclaimed the "pacification" complete, but local tribes still resisted by retreating into the remote forest areas and refusing to deal officially with the French. Nevertheless, the French drafted approximately 20,000 Africans from Ivory Coast to fight for France during World War I and managed to disarm tribes, regroup villages, and impose a uniform and centralized administration.

After World War I cocoa, coffee, and mahogany became the mainstays of the Ivory Coast economy. During World War I portions of Upper Volta* were incorporated into Ivory Coast for administrative purposes, and a railroad from the coast to Upper Volta was begun. In 1919 Upper Volta was detached as a separate colony but was reincorporated during the Great Depression. Upper Volta did not separate permanently from Ivory Coast until 1948. The railroad was completed in 1935 and the port city of Abidjan was founded. In 1936 the Popular Front government in France initiated reforms in the French colonies such as extended suffrage and laws limiting forced labor. However, when the Vichy government of German-occupied France took over during World War II*, many of the reforms were suspended. In 1944 a unified organization of affluent Africans—planters, small farmers, and urban "evolues"—called the *Syndicate Agricole Africain* (SAA) headed up the movement for independence. The *Bloc Africain* was a conglomeration of special-interest groups and political parties pushing political and economic reforms during the 1940s. In 1945 Felix Houphouet-Boigny, a candidate of the SAA, was elected to the French constituent assembly in Paris where he proved his worth as a political leader and spokesman from Ivory Coast and Francophone Africa. Ivory Coast was declared a territory of the French Union* (1946) with representation in the French parliament. Due to the efforts of Houphouet-Boigny in the French chamber of deputies, compulsary labor was abolished in overseas France. A Regional Democratic African party (RDA) was organized in 1946. The party made significant political gains toward uniting French colonies in Western Africa and in pushing for reforms. However, the party affiliated with the French Communist Party, and when the communists lost political power in 1950, the RDA declined. Houphouet pragmatically broke RDA ties with the Communists and consolidated his position as the leading political figure in the Ivory Coast. In 1956 the Loi-Cadre*, passed in the French national assembly, provided for universal suffrage and free elections throughout the French Community*. With the new constitution of the Fifth Republic in France, Ivory Coast became autonomous and in 1960 achieved independence, with Felix Houphouet-Boigny as its first president. (Michael Crowder, *West African Resistance*, 1917; Robert J. Mudt, *Historical Dictionary of Ivory Coast*, 1987.)

Karen Sleezer

J

JAKARTA. Jakarta is a large city on the northwest coast of Java*, formerly the capital of the Dutch East Indies* and now the capital of independent Indonesia*. Jakarta was a muddy fishing village when the Dutch established the fort of Batavia* there in the early seventeenth century, but it survived Portuguese, British, and native Javanese assaults to grow into a great trading entrepot rivaling Malacca*, Singapore*, and Manila*. The site was inauspicious. Jakarta lies on a swampy plain, and its harbor is shallow near shore, though a number of small islands offer protection for ships anchored offshore. Most trade passes through the port of Tanjung Priok, six miles east of the heart of city but now swallowed up by a sprawling metropolitan area.

As Jakarta grew into the military and commercial center of Dutch power in Southeast Asia, it acquired a cosmopolitan character typical of Asian ports. The city center was built in Dutch style, complete with three-story houses and canals. There was an Arab section where navigators and gold traders lived, and a Malay quarter. There were also Eurasians, Javanese, and Chinese. The latter population expanded as Chinese shopkeepers and craftsmen stepped into the middleman role disdained by Dutch rulers and Javanese peasants. By 1740 the Chinese population had grown so large that the Dutch became afraid of a possible uprising; in that year many thousands of Chinese were slaughtered in a pogrom.

The lifeblood of Jakarta was trade, not manufacturing. Products of the hundreds of islands that comprised the Dutch East Indies flowed into Jakarta, and then were transshipped to Europe, India, and China. Chief among these were gold dust, pepper, other spices, fine cloths, tropical hardwoods, and such exotica as beeswax and edible bird's nests. Imports flowing through Jakarta for distribution to all parts of the colony included all manner of manufactured goods from Europe and luxury items from China.

At the end of the eighteenth century the Dutch East India Company* failed, and the territory it had controlled was henceforth ruled directly by the Dutch government. Jakarta steadily grew into the huge, sprawling metropolis it is today. In the early 1900s Indonesian nationalists in Jakarta began agitating for independence. Their cause was stimulated by the Japanese occupation of 1942–1945, when Dutchmen were interned and subjected to ridicule. Postwar Dutch attempts to reassert control were defeated by a bloody nationalist revolution which triumphed in 1949. (D. G. E. Hall, *A History of Southeast Asia*, 1968.)

Ross Marlay

JAMAICA. Jamaica is a large island of 4,470 square miles located in the Caribbean Sea about 80 miles south of eastern Cuba. The island is 144 miles long and 49 miles wide at its widest point. Christopher Columbus* discovered Jamaica on May 1, 1494, during his second voyage to the New World. During his fourth voyage, Columbus was stranded on the northern coast of Jamaica for more than a year in 1503 and 1504. Spanish rule lasted until 1655. The Spaniards completely exterminated the native Arawak Indians who were on the island when Columbus arrived, and eight Spanish families took control of Jamaica. Population growth was very slow. The Spanish families imported African slaves to replace the Arawak Indians, and by the middle of the seventeenth century, the Jamaican population was about 3,000 people, most of them Africans.

As Spanish fortunes declined and those of the British and Dutch rose in the seventeenth century, Spain's ability to maintain her Caribbean colonies declined. British admirals and pirates periodically attacked Jamaican ports beginning in the 1590s, but it was not until 1655 that the British attacked and held Jamaica. The last Spanish resistance there was wiped out by 1658. Spanish-owned slaves fled into the mountains and interior jungles and continued to carry out guerrilla warfare against the British for more than a century. Military governors ruled Jamaica until 1662, when a legislative assembly was established to make law. In the Treaty of Madrid of 1670, Spain formally ceded Jamaica to Great Britain. Jamaica was a headquarters for British pirates plundering Spanish treasure ships, and in 1672, when the Royal African Company achieved a monopoly of the African slave trade, Jamaica developed into one of the large commercial slave markets in the world. The Jamaican economy revolved around sugar production, but islanders also produced profitable crops of coffee, cocoa, pimento, indigo, and ginger.

The Jamaican economy peaked in the early nineteenth century and then began a long decline. In 1807 Great Britain outlawed the slave trade; there were approximately 320,000 African slaves in Jamaica at the time. When the anti-slavery forces in parliament succeeded in abolishing slavery in 1833, the Jamaican economy went into a tailspin. A huge slave revolt in 1831 in Jamaica had given the anti-slavery forces ammunition, but the revolt and emancipation further damaged the economy. When the political and social dust settled, the British planters were short on financial resources and labor to work their plantations. Most of the former slaves became small farmers and laborers. The free trade movement in Great Britain in the 1840s, by eliminating the subsidies for colonial produce, further damaged the Jamaican economy. Finally, new competition from beet sugar farms in the American West undermined prices. By 1880 sugar was selling for only one-half of what it had been at the beginning of the century.

The severe economic problems created tremendous hostility between the small elite of white planters and the large mass of black workers and farmers. In 1865 violence erupted in the Morant Bay Rebellion, but the British crushed it by declaring martial law. The next year Jamaica became a crown colony with a new governor, Sir John Peter Grant, who started a social and economic development program which restored internal stability. During the Great Depression of the 1930s, however, Jamaicans suffered terribly from low prices and unemployment. A royal investigation led to the constitutional reforms of 1944, which extended internal self-government to Jamaica. Two political parties appeared—the People's National Party, led by Norman Manley and the Jamaica Labour Party, led by Sir Alexander Bustamante. Although bauxite mining provided some new jobs, the economy was permanently depressed in the 1950s and 1960s. In 1958 Jamaica joined the West Indies Federation*, but in a 1961 referendum, Jamaicans voted to withdraw from the Federation, dooming it to failure. On August 6, 1962, Great Britain aknowledged Jamaican independence, and the Jamaican Labour Party formed a government with Alexander Bustamante as prime minister. (Aggrey Brown, *Color, Class, and Politics in Jamaica*, 1980; Douglas Hall, *Free Jamaica, 1838–1865: A Study in Economic Growth*, 1961; Katrin Norris, *Jamaica: The Search for an Identity*, 1972.)

Frank Marotti

JAMESON RAID. Dr. Leander Starr Jameson, a friend and comrade of Cecil Rhodes*, led an attack on the Boer republic of the Transvaal* in 1895 in order to overthrow its leader Paul Kruger. Under Kruger's leadership, and with the wealth of the Witwatersrand gold, the Transvaal was establishing a power base independent of Rhodes's South African empire. Jameson intended to spark off a revolution by the Uitlanders, the non-Boers, who were discontented with the Kruger administration. The government gave the Uitlanders no political voice and subjected them to the economic distresses of taxation, state monopolies of dynamite, and poor social services.

In 1895 Jameson, the British South Africa Company's administrator in Rhodesia*, along with 510 Europeans, 150 native drivers, maxims, cannons, and assorted horses and mules, planned to attack the Transvaal from the Bechuanaland* border. Although planning was disjointed, Jameson grew tired of delays. On December 29, 1895, he rashly attacked the forewarned and waiting Boers at Doornkop, near Krugerdorp, where he was soundly defeated. The Uitlanders had failed to join the revolution. Although Rhodes and British Colonial Secretary Joseph Chamberlain* denied any complicity with the fiasco, they did not completely abandon Jameson. Jameson was returned by Kruger to British custody to face trial in London, where he received a sentence of fifteen months in prison. His fellow raiders, who were also tried in London, received sentences from three to ten months. Several prominent Uitlanders were tried in Pretoria for their roles, and four of them received death sentences which were soon commuted to £25,000 fines and banishment. Because of Jameson's political connections, the Boers understandably feared that the British Empire was attempting to take over the Transvaal. Naturally, tensions between the Boers and the Cape South Africans increased, leading to the Second Anglo-Boer War of 1899–1902. (Alex Hepple, *South Africa*, 1966.)

Mark R. Shulman

JAMESTOWN. The first permanent English colony in America, Jamestown was founded by about 100 emigrants under the command of Christopher Newport in May 1607. Envisioned by the London Company, which controlled the settlement, as a profit-making venture, the enterprise almost floundered. A poor location some 32 miles up the James River on a low-lying peninsula near a malaria-breeding, mosquito-infested swamp almost destroyed the settlement, as did fear of the Indians, strife on the governing council between John Smith and Edward Wingfield, and "gold feaver." Only 32 of the original settlers survived the first seven months, and in the winter, 1609–1610, known as the "starving time," the number of colonials was reduced from 500 to 60. With the arrival of Lord Delaware in the spring, Jamestown survived. Conditions slowly improved. In 1612 John Rolfe, who two years later married Pocahontas, successfully raised and cured a crop of tobacco, a money-making product which improved the colonial economy. The year 1619 saw the arrival of more women, the introduction of slavery, and the establishment of representative government. The first colonial legislature in the New World consisted of the governor, his council, and the burgesses, composed of two representatives from each of the eleven plantations. In June 1924 the Virginia Company's charter was annulled, and Jamestown now became the royal colony of Virginia*. The colony was now more than an economic enterprise controlled by men motivated solely by profits.

Precipitated by the failure of Sir William Berkeley, the royal governor, to protect the frontier against Indian attacks, Nathaniel Bacon attacked Jamestown, drove out Berkeley's forces, and burned the city to the ground in September 1676. Although Jamestown was rebuilt, it accidentally burned again. This, along with the unhealthy location of the town, prompted Francis Nicholson in 1699 to move the seat of government seven miles farther up the river to Middle Plantation, which was renamed Williamsburg. Since the relocation of the capital, there has never been a town on the original Jamestown site. Indeed, except for an island in the James River with a few ruins, nothing remains of the original location. (Oliver Perry Chitwood, *A History of Colonial America*, 1961; T. J. Wertenbaker, *The Founding of American Civilization: The Old South*, 1942.)

John W. Storey

JARNAC CONVENTION OF 1847. On June 19, 1847, France and Great Britain signed the Jarnac Convention about the status of French Polynesia*. For years Great Britain had wanted to establish control over the Society Islands, but civil strife there prevented them from assuming control from the French. In the Jarnac Convention, both countries agreed to the independence of Bora Bora, Huahine, and Raiatea, which constitute the main units of the Leeward Islands, and that no ruler of either the Leeward or Windward Islands could assume control over the entire archipelago. France broke the Jarnac Convention in 1880 by annexing the Leeward Islands, and Great Britain protested until France agreed to surrender her aspirations over the New Hebrides*. French sovereignty over French Polynesia was secure. (Colin Newbury, *Tahiti Nui: Change and Survival in French Polynesia, 1767–1945*, 1980.)

JARVIS. Jarvis is a dry, equatorial, low-coral island located 1,360 miles south of Hawaii*. The uninhabited, two-square mile islet is part of the Northern Line Islands. At various times it has been called Brock, Brook, Bunker, Jervis, and Volunteer. A British expedition discovered Jarvis on April 21, 1821. The first American to visit Jarvis was Michael Baker, who arrived in 1835. In 1840 the United States Exploring Expedition surveyed the barren dot of land. Because of the strong American presence between Hawaii and Samoa, nineteenth-century geographers designated the area "American Polynesia."

Around 1840, farmers in the upper South began to read articles praising guano, a rich fertilizer derived from the droppings of sea birds. Their agricultural lands were wearing out at a time when the populations of east coast urban centers were burgeoning. Guano could help to restore their exhausted soils. Unfortunately, Peru* owned the islands containing top-quality guano deposits. Its control of the fertilizer meant high prices and a limited supply. Entrepreneurs realized that they could reap tremendous profits by finding alternative sources of guano. Alfred G. Benson, a New York merchant, decided to look for guano in American Polynesia. He and his associates formed the American Guano Company in 1855. The company acquired the rights to dig guano on two Pacific islands, Baker* and Jarvis, from Michael Baker. Moreover, with the support of Senator William H. Seward, Benson enlisted the backing of the United States. By the Guano Act of 1856, U.S. citizens were empowered to take possession of unclaimed, unoccupied islands for the purpose of extracting guano. Their island would be "appertaining to" the United States as long as guano was being mined.

In January 1856 a ship sent by the American Guano Company reached Jarvis. Its crew built a house as evidence of occupation. Another company vessel arrived in 1857, followed by the U.S.S. *St. Mary's* under the command of Charles Henry Davis, who formalized the firm's claim. Jarvis thus became one of the first overseas territories of the United States. C. H. Judd, acting as an agent for Benson's enterprise, supervised 23 native-Hawaiian laborers. The extraction of guano commenced in February 1858 and it reached the American market a year later. Working conditions were difficult. Water had to be shipped from Honolulu every three months. Nevertheless, guano extraction continued until 1879.

A decade after the American Guano Company abandoned Jarvis, Great Britain seized the desolate island. London feared the Pacific expansion of Germany and it required facilities for a planned trans-oceanic cable. In 1906 Britain leased the bowl-shaped atoll to the Pacific Phosphate Company, which exported little if any guano. Jarvis's ownership remained nebulous for almost a century. In the 1930s Jarvis once again attained strategic importance to the United States. The age of aviation was dawning and Jarvis might serve as a potential steppingstone to New Zealand* for airplanes flying from Hawaii. Furthermore, the island was a possible site for a military base or weather station. Consequently, in March 1935, William T. Miller, the Bureau of Commerce's superintendent of airways, landed on Jarvis with a small band of colonists. They constructed a settlement, Millersville, that consisted of several stone and wood structures.

The British ended up acquiescing in the matter. Franklin D. Roosevelt, by Executive Order No. 7368, placed Jarvis under the jurisdiction of the Department of the Interior on May 13, 1936. Richard Blackburn Black administered it, along with Baker and Howland* islands from a field office of the Division of Territories and Island Possessions that was established in Honolulu. Four boys from the Kamehameha School performed three-month tours of duty, gathering and transmitting daily meteorological data. In 1937 Black's Washington superior, Ernest Gruening, decided, after an on-site inspection, that Jarvis was ill-suited for a landing strip. After the Japanese attacked Pearl Harbor in December 1941, the Navy evacuated Jarvis's inhabitants and destroyed its facilities to prevent them from falling into enemy hands. Today, Jarvis continues to be administered as an unincorporated territory by the Department of the Interior. The U.S. Coast Guard makes an annual visit to the bleak islet. (Edwin H. Bryan, Jr., *American Polynesia and the Hawaiian Chain*, 1942; Roy F. Nichols, *Advance Agents of American Destiny*, 1956.)

Frank Marotti

JAVA. Java, an island 600 miles long and 80 to 100 miles wide, is the heartland of Indonesia*. It supports one of the most dense concentrations of people in Asia. Java lies east of Sumatra* and west of Bali*, with the Indian Ocean to its south and the Java Sea to its north. Lying just south of the equator, Java has a warm, humid climate. The island once was covered by jungle, but due to long habitation and intensive agriculture, little virgin forest remains. The north coast has a wide alluvial plain. South of the mountains the land drops off steeply to the sea. Jakarta* and Surabaya are the main ports. Because of its strong native traditions, its location on the Java Sea, and its topography, which is suitable for roads and railroads, Java may be considered the core of Indonesia—the cultural, political, educational, and economic center of gravity. Java's rich culture evolved in reaction to stimuli from India (Hinduism and Buddhism), Arabia (Islam), and Europe (commerce, industry, and nationalism). The Javanese language is rich in nuance. *Wayang* shadow plays convey moral lessons in the guise of popular entertainment. Gamelan orchestras make unique, complex music. The Javanese built magnificent stone monuments, including the famous Buddhist temple, Borobodur.

The eighth-century Mataram empire maintained cultural and diplomatic ties with Sumatra and mainland Southeast Asia. Under the Sailendra kings, Mataram abandoned Buddhism for Hinduism. Eventually Mataram was overshadowed by the Majapahit empire (thirteenth to sixteenth centuries), which tried to expand Javanese control to include much of what is now called Indonesia. Insofar as Majapahit power was based on elaborate Hindu ritual, it was sapped by the conversion of Javanese to Islam. Arab, Indian, and Malay traders brought the new faith to Java's north coast ports. From there it spread inland.

Batavia* was founded as a commercial port in 1619. During the seventeenth century, the Dutch steadily extended their control over Java. Their technique was to choose sides in royal succession disputes, and place the winner under their obligation. By 1705 they indirectly ruled all Java, using co-opted Javanese royalty. Their sole aim was commercial profit. Java's soil and climate were right for growing sugar, but the European market was taken by cheaper sugar produced by slaves in the West Indies*. Chinese were encouraged to come to Java and organize plantations, and the Dutch sold Javanese sugar all across Asia.

The Dutch East India Company* grew corrupt, fell into debt, and was nationalized in 1799. Following a five-year interlude of British rule (1811–1816) the Dutch returned more determined than ever to make a profit. They abandoned mercantilism for free trade, but for Javanese it meant only more exploitation. The Dutch suppressed one last gasp of Javanese independence, a five-year guerrilla war (1825–30) led by a prince named Diponegoro, then embarked on the notorious *kultuurstelsel*, or "cultivation system." This policy was the brainchild of Governer Johannes van den Bosch, who reasoned that instead of trying to collect taxes in money, the Netherlands Indies government should simply require each village to grow export crops. Village headmen then delivered the coffee, sugar, or indigo to the Dutch for free, in lieu of other taxes. Results included the extension of a commercial economy into the interior of Java, the progressive impoverishment of peasants, and a fatal erosion of the prestige of traditional village leaders. But tremendous profits were generated for the Dutch. Amsterdam became a world marketplace for coffee and other tropical products. The Netherlands Indies' debts were all paid off, and the surplus was used to build railways in Holland.

This system could not continue once starvation became common in Java. Cultivation programs for pepper, indigo, and tobacco were canceled in 1866, for sugar in 1890, and for coffee in 1917. By then new exports had been developed, and the focus of economic development shifted to Sumatra, where there were still vast tracts of "idle" land. After 1901 a new "Ethical Policy" protected Javanese from gross exploitation. Paradoxically, while Javanese peasants sank into poverty, their numbers multiplied. Colonial censuses estimate that the population of Java was about 6 million in 1813, 30 million in 1905, and 42 million in 1930. It is 90 million today. The Dutch initiated, and the government of independent Indonesia continues, a transmigration policy to relieve over-crowding on Java by sending people to live on other islands. (Clifford Geertz, *Agricultural Involution*, 1963.)

Ross Marlay

JAY'S TREATY. Also known as the Treaty of London of 1794, Jay's Treaty dealt with a variety of issues troubling United States–British relations in the 1790s. Some of the difficulties went back to the American Revolution*; others were by-products of the British–French War which had begun in 1793. Among the former were complaints about continued British occupation of portions of the American Northwest; accusations of British intrigue with the Indians in the West; restrictions and discrimination in British–United States trade; and argu-ments over prewar debts and postwar boundaries. Among the latter problems was United States outrage over British violation of maritime rights, that is, the seizure of United States merchant ships and cargoes, and the impressment of United States merchant seamen. Concerned that such continued disputes might well lead to war, President George Washington* determined to resolve the prob-lems through diplomacy.

Chosen to represent the United States was Chief Justice of the Supreme Court John Jay. He arrived in London in June 1794. Jay's bargaining position was not strong. Apart from his own Anglophilia, he was further undermined by Secretary of the Treasury Alexander Hamilton's secret assurances of benevolence conveyed to the British government. On November 19, 1794, Jay and the British repre-sentatives signed the treaty. It has been considered a failure for United States diplomacy. On the major issues of maritime rights, the British were uncompro-mising; little was said about them in the treaty and no real concessions were made. On the question of trade, the British made some minor concessions as far as United States-Canadian trade and the East Indies trade was concerned. But the concession in the area of the West Indies trade was inconsequential to the point of humiliation. It was later rejected by the United States Senate.

Among the few positive articles, the British promised to evacuate their gar-risons and troops from the Northwest by June 1, 1796, and to terminate their close association with the Indian tribes in the West. On such troublesome issues as debts and boundaries, a constructive solution was accepted—submit such differences to arbitration commissions. Most of the remaining articles dealt with minor issues. In the United States, Jay's Treaty set off a major dispute between the fledgling parties then emerging in American politics. After fierce debate, the Senate ratified the treaty in June 1795 by a slim margin. Because of opposition in the House of Representatives, the funds necessary to carry the treaty into effect were not appropriated until May 8, 1796, and the treaty was finally proclaimed. (Samuel F. Bemis, *Jay's Treaty*, 1926.)

Joseph M. Rowe, Jr.

JESUITS. Jesuits are members of a religious order of the Roman Catholic Church, the Society of Jesus. The Society was founded by Saint Ignatius of Loyola and several followers, including Saint Francis Xavier, in 1534 and confirmed as a religious order by Pope Paul III in 1540. The idea for the creation of the Society came to Ignatius, a Spanish nobleman, while he was recovering from a war wound in 1521. The avowed purposes of the Society were the spiritual growth of its own members and the salvation of all men and women. The fundamental philosophy of the Society is found in the *Spiritual Exercises*, written and revised by Ignatius over a period of years. The Jesuit organization was almost military in its highly centralized authority. Saint Ignatius was the first superior general, and he retained that title until his death.

Although not created for that purpose, the Society of Jesus rapidly became the most effective instrument of the Roman Catholic Reformation. The weapons of the Jesuits were education, missionary work, the confessional, and stringent obedience and loyalty to the pope. By the early seventeenth century, the Society had more than 15,000 members. Jesuit schools were synonymous with excellence in education and Jesuits were confessors to the Roman Catholic rulers of Europe. Moreover, the Jesuits had established missions in Japan, China, India, the Philippines, Africa, Latin America, and North America. In all of these locales the Jesuits suffered intermittent persecution, and often martyrdom, but with the exception of Japan where they were expelled in the early seventeenth century, the Jesuits retained lasting influence. In China they were the nucleus of the large Roman Catholic community that developed in that country. In India, after a slow beginning, Robert de Nobili attracted many converts by adapting Christianity to the customs of the people. De Nobili's practices drew criticism from his colleagues and from other sectors of the Roman Catholic Church, but they proved effective in the East. In Paraguay the Jesuits attempted to save the Indians by establishing the "reductions," self-supporting Indian communities from which most whites were barred. In New France* the Jesuits' successes and failures among the Huron and the Iroquois are recounted in detail in the *Jesuit Relations*. Jesuits were instrumental in the exploration of North America, and a Jesuit priest, Jacques Marquette, accompanied Louis Joliet* down the Mississippi River to the mouth of the Arkansas River where it became clear that there was a waterway from Canada to the Gulf of Mexico.

In the eighteenth century the Jesuits were opposed by the absolute monarchs, who resented their involvement in nationalist politics, and the Enlightenment liberals, who resented their conservative philosophy. The Jesuits were banned from the New World in 1767, and from several other countries, including France and Spain. Pope Clement XIV suppressed the Society in 1773. The post-Napoleonic period proved more hospitable, and Pope Pius VII reestablished the Society of Jesus in 1814. In the twentieth century the Society of Jesus has more than 30,000 members and there are more Jesuits in the United States than in any other country. (W. V. Bangert, *A History of the Society of Jesus*, 1972; Christopher Hollis, *The Jesuits—A History*, 1968.)

Peter T. Sherrill

JINNAH, MOHAMMAD ALI. Mohammad Ali Jinnah was born at Karachi on October 20, 1875. His father made a living as a hide merchant. Jinnah's family spoke Gujerati and he received his education at schools in Karachi and Bombay*. He read law in England between 1892 and 1896 and returned to India* where he built a thriving legal practice. Jinnah became active in the politics of the Indian National Congress and in 1909 was elected as the Muslim representative on the imperial legislative council. In 1913 he joined the All India Muslim League, although he retained his membership in the Congress. In both organizations Jinnah called for increased self-government as well as special safeguards for the Muslim minority in India. He resigned from the legislative council in 1919 in protest against the Rowlatt Acts, which denied basic civil liberties to militant Indian nationalists.

By 1920 Jinnah found himself in a rift with Mohandas K. Gandhi* which was never resolved. Jinnah, who was blessed with a fine legal mind and excellent parliamentary skills, found himself unable to support Gandhi's program of civil disobedience. Jinnah insisted that Indian nationalists use constitutional means to achieve independence. He also tired of what he considered Gandhi's "religious metaphysical politics." In it Jinnah saw a potential Hindu revivalism which would threaten the Muslim minority in India. He resigned his position in the Indian National Congress and never returned. In 1929 Jinnah formulated his Fourteen Points which outlined the evolving Muslim position on independence. By that time his own position was becoming more rigid. Throughout the 1920s Jinnah hoped to achieve a Hindu-Muslim compromise on Indian independence and protection of the Muslim minority, but by the 1930s he was growing increasingly alienated and inflexible. He spent the years between 1930 and 1935 dealing with the Government in London, but in 1935 Jinnah returned to India as the undisputed leader of the Muslim League.

During the late 1930s Jinnah complained about Hindu persecution of Muslims in India, and in October 1937 he publicly announced that Muslims would never enjoy justice, equality, or security in Hindu India. The break between the Indian National Congress and the Muslim League, and between Gandhi and Jinnah, was complete in 1940 when he supported the Lahore Resolution calling for creation of Pakistan* as a Muslim state. During World War II Jinnah enjoyed complete support from the British, who saw in him a counterweight to Gandhi's increasing influence. Gandhi and Jinnah met in Bombay in September 1944 to resolve their differences. Jinnah wanted two nations to emerge from the independence movement—a Hindu-dominated India and a Muslim-dominated Pakistan. The talks broke down quickly and Jinnah never retreated from his commitment to the two-nation theory. Eventually the British accepted the two-nation proposal of Jinnah and the Muslim League. When Pakistan became independent in 1947 Jinnah became its first governor-general. He died in 1948. (Hector Bolitho, *Jinnah, Creator of Pakistan*, 1954; M. H. Saiyid, *The Sound and the Fury: A Political Study of Mohammad Ali Jinnah*, 1981.)

JOHNSTON. Johnston atoll is located in the North Pacific Ocean approximately 715 miles southwest of Hawaii*. English sailors first discovered the island in 1807 and the United States seized control of it in 1858. Since then it has been used as a bird reservation, a small naval station, and a nuclear weapons test site. (*Webster's Geographical Dictionary*, 1986.)

JOHOR. Johor was an independent sultanate located on the southern tip of the Malayan Peninsula. Because of its strategic location just north of Singapore*, the British were intent on gaining political control of the region. In 1885 the sultan of Johor placed the state under British military protection, and that relationship became a formal protectorate in 1914. Administratively Johor became part of the Unfederated Malay States*. See MALAYSIA.

JOINT STOCK COMPANY. The joint stock company was among the most common techniques Europeans used in establishing overseas colonies. Used most frequently by the Dutch and the British, the corporate enterprise provided investment capital to finance the colonial ventures when central governments were unwilling or unable to do so. Many of the companies even exercised sovereign power over colonies, raising armies, levying taxes, and shaping political institutions. The typical pattern, however, was for private, corporate control to give way to the political sovereignty of the state. In some cases, that transition occurred rather quickly. The London Company financed the settlement of Jamestown*, Virginia, in British North America in 1607, but the colony of Virginia became a royal colony in 1624. For other joint stock companies, the transition took much longer. The British East India Company, founded in 1600, was not dissolved until 1858. During its more than 250 years of existence, the company exercised enormous power in East Asia and South Asia. For examples of joint stock company histories, see BRITISH EAST INDIA COMPANY, DUTCH EAST INDIA COMPANY, or HUDSON'S BAY COMPANY.

JOLIET, LOUIS. Louis Joliet was born in Quebec in 1645, the third son of a wagonmaker. At seventeen he entered the Jesuit order, where he received some formal education, but left after three years. Following a trip to France, he became a fur trader in 1668. Meanwhile, since 1643 the Iroquois nation had devastated much of New France*, but in 1666 they were crushed by an army sent by Louis XIV and his minister, Jean Baptiste Colbert, making it safe once again for the French to push west of Quebec*. The king sent a new administrator, intendent Jean Talon, who quickly saw that the key to making New France a profitable part of the mother country's mercantilist economy was the fur trade. He also heard rumors from fur traders and Jesuit missionaries of a great river called the Mississippi, which might become an important avenue of trade in the interior. Talon believed it was in the best interest of France to find out before the English or Spanish, and in 1672 he sent a team of explorers led by Joliet, who was to pay his own expenses in return for permission to trade with any Indians he encountered.

Joliet and eight others departed Montreal and on December 2 reached Michilimackinac (St. Ignace, Michigan), where they spent the winter trading with the Mackinac Indians and preparing the spring voyage. There they met Father Jacques Marquette, a Jesuit zealously committed to Christianizing the Indians, who spoke several tribal languages and whose superior had ordered him to join the expedition. Leaving three men to continue trading for furs, Joliet, Marquette, and five others set out on May 15 in two birchbark canoes carrying muskets, supplies, and trade goods. After a week of coasting along Lake Michigan, they reached Green Bay, where they found the Menominee tribe, who were friendly, but warned them that hostile Indians lived beside the Mississippi. After staying briefly at the St. Francis Xavier mission, they headed up the Fox River, arriving on June 7 at a village of Mascouten Indians, which was the limit of previous French exploration and where Marquette was delighted to find a wooden cross standing. Joliet obtained two guides here, and on June 10 made the portage to a tributary of the Wisconsin River, which led them on June 17 to the Mississippi. About 200 miles downriver they discovered a tribe of Illinois—enemies of the Iroquois—who after initial timidity, feasted the Frenchmen, smoked the calumet, or peace pipe, and presented them with a slave boy. Another 230 miles further down the team discovered that there were large petroglyphs painted on a cliff and that the roar associated with them was the Missouri River, feeding into the Mississippi. Several days later they reached the mouth of the Ohio, by which time it was clear that the Mississippi's course lay to the south. Near the mouth of the St. Francis River, they were attacked and then befriended by Quapaw Indians, who told them that the Spanish controlled the river below. On July 17 they turned back, to avoid capture and ensure that Talon received their report.

Near the mouth of the Ohio, they again met the Illinois, who told them about a shortcut up the Illinois River to Lake Michigan, which they reached at the end of September, after a short portage near present-day Chicago. They proceeded to Green Bay, where they wintered with the Jesuits*. Early in the spring Joliet departed for Montreal, leaving behind Marquette, who was ill and died soon after. By the end of June Joliet was headed down the St. Lawrence River for Montreal, but in the Lachine rapids his canoe was destroyed, the Indian slave boy killed, and his map and report lost—fortunately Marquette's journal survived. However, Joliet's feats were soon surpassed by those of La Salle, and with Talon back in France, he was not even able to get a license to trade for furs until 1679. In the interval he led another expedition to Hudson Bay to observe British actions. Eventually Joliet obtained a grant of the island of Anticosti in the Gulf of St. Lawrence, but the British destroyed his estate sometime later. Joliet died in 1700. (Jean DeLanglez, *Life and Voyages of Louis Joliet (1645–1700)*, 1948.)

William B. Robison

JORDAN. See TRANSJORDAN.

K

KAISER WILHELMSLAND. See NEW GUINEA.

KAMERUN. Worried that the British would expand their sphere of influence in Africa east from the Niger, German merchants in 1884 established a small settlement on the coast of Cameroon* near Duala. From that point the Germans gradually expanded into the interior, bringing more territory under their control. In 1912, as part of the settlement of the Agadir crisis, Germany acquired another 107,000 square miles of French Equatorial Africa. With that additional territory, German Kamerun extended to the Congo River. During World War I, England and France conquered German Kamerun, and when the war was over, England received a mandate over a small portion of territory bordering what is today Nigeria, while France received a much larger portion which became Cameroon. See CAMEROON.

KEDAH. Kedah was a sultanate in southern Siam* on the Malay Peninsula. In 1786 the sultan of Kedah gave the British East India Company* control over the island of Pinang*, which was the beginning of British Malaya. In the Treaty of Bangkok of 1909, Siam awarded Great Britain sovereignty over Kedah, and Kedah became one of the Unfederated Malay States*. See MALAYSIA.

KELANTIN. Kelantin was a sultanate in southern Siam* along the South China Sea on the Malay Peninsula. In the Treaty of Bangkok of 1909, Siam ceded Kelantin to Great Britain, and Kelantin became one of the Unfederated Malay States*. See MALAYSIA.

KENYA. The Republic of Kenya is located in East Africa and is bordered on the north by Ethiopia*, on the east by Somalia* and the Indian Ocean, on the south by Tanzania*, and on the west by Uganda* and Sudan. Little is known of the history of this land prior to 1500, except that it is mentioned in writings of the early Christian era as a place of trade. Arab writings indicated that by the eighth century trade was conducted on a regular basis along the Kenya coast for tortoiseshell, spices, and ivory. The earliest known inhabitants of Kenya were Cushitic, Bantu, and Nilotic-speaking people. Arab and Persian traders settled along the coast. Intermarriage between the Bantu and the Arabs created the Swahili language and culture.

In 1498 Vasco da Gama* landed at Malindi in East Africa. As a result, Portugal exercised a degree of control over the coastal area of Kenya for the next 200 years. This control was not without its problems. Friendly relations had been established early on with the sultan of Malandi, but further to the south, the people of Mombasa resisted the Portuguese. In order to extend their influence along the coast, the Portuguese constructed Fort Jesus at the entrance to Mombasa harbor in 1593, enabling them to dominate the area until 1631 when the fort was taken by an Arab sultan. It was recaptured by the Portuguese a year later, only to face repeated attacks by the imam of Oman*. Omani Arabs finally captured the great citadel of Fort Jesus in 1698 after a two-year siege. Although the Portuguese briefly reoccupied Mombasa in 1728–29, they failed to hold it, and Portuguese power on that part of the coast came to an end. During their two centuries of overlordship in Kenya, the Portuguese had concerned themselves primarily with trading and raiding. However, they made at least one major contribution to the area with the introduction of maize, potatoes, and cassava— foodstuffs from America which became important staples of the East African diet.

In the nineteenth century the British attempted to suppress the slave trade through the Moresby Treaty of 1822 and the Hamerton Treaty of 1845, both negotiated with the ruler of Oman and Zanzibar, Seyyid Said bin Sultan, who controlled much of the East Africa coast. Despite British efforts, slave trading continued along the Kenya coast until 1907. Additional British influence in Kenya was exerted by the Anglican Church Missionary Society (CMS), which backed the opening of a Christian mission station near Mombasa in 1846 by Johann Ludwig Krapf, a German pastor, and Johann Rebmann, a Swiss. At a later date Krapf established a second mission for the British Methodist Society. The religious missions also started the first European-type schools in Kenya.

In the mid–1880s German interest in East Africa became apparent. The German East African Company, headed by Dr. Karl Peters, signed numerous treaties of protection with tribal chiefs and advanced the German sphere. Since the opening of the Suez Canal* in 1869, British trade with the Kenya area had been on the increase. Concerned by the German expansion, the British concluded agreements with Germany in 1886 and 1890 defining boundaries and dividing their respective spheres of influence at approximately the present Kenya-Tanzania border. Meanwhile, William Mackinnon, who played much the same role in Kenya that Cecil Rhodes* did in Rhodesia, secured a coastal concession from the sultan of Zanzibar in 1887 and received a royal charter from the British government for the Imperial British East Africa Company, commonly called IBEA, in 1888. The IBEA, which had its own flag, army, money, and even postage stamps, maintained the British presence in East Africa, opposed the Germans, and sought to open up the hinterland for commerce and Christian civilization. When the chartered company encountered financial difficulties, the British government bought it out and on July 1, 1895, established the East Africa Protectorate, which included the area of present day Kenya between the coast and the Great Rift Valley.

Britain also controlled Uganda under a protectorate and needed easy access to that inland area to assure British ascendancy over the headwaters of the Nile. Construction of a railroad from Mombassa to Kisumu on Lake Victoria was started in 1895 using laborers imported from India, and was completed in December 1901. The railroad also opened up the highlands region of what is now central Kenya to European settlement. It became known as the White Highlands because its colonization was restricted mainly to settlers of British extraction.

The Crown Lands Ordinance of 1902 provided for the leasing of land for 99 years to Europeans, with one- to five-year leases for those Africans and Indians deemed qualified to work and manage the land. Europeans strongly objected to the short length of their leases; and this supposed problem was corrected by the Crown Lands Ordinance of 1915. Lease tenure for Europeans was increased to 999 years. However, lease terms for Africans and Indians were unchanged. The Indian community in particular strongly protested this discrimination but without results. Some areas were set aside as reserves for African occupation (not ownership), but the best land on one of these was taken over in 1919 for the resettlement of British soldiers. Legislation in 1938 and 1939 fixed the boundaries of the White Highlands, and African-held land in those areas was confiscated, often without compensation, fueling the fire of discontent among the displaced Africans.

Coffee, sisal, and corn were developed as profitable export crops, and by 1914 domestic revenues met government expenses. One problem that confronted the white settlers in British East Africa, even as they prospered on their farms and ranches, was the shortage of African labor. The native Africans often preferred to stay in their reserves rather than toil as field hands on the large European estates. The Protectorate Administration attempted to secure an adequate labor supply for the settlers by levying hut and poll taxes which, in effect, compelled native Africans to work for white planters, usually for three or four months a year, in order to earn enough money to pay the taxes. This, too, angered the Africans, who considered it forced labor.

In 1906 the Colonists Association, a settlers' political interest group under the leadership of Lord Delamere, the foremost spokesman of the white immigrants, requested the creation of a lawmaking body which would include settler representation. The Colonial Office* endorsed the idea, and in August 1907 the East Africa Protectorate's first legislative council, consisting of six government officials and two colonists—all appointed by the governor—met in Nairobi. No Indians or Africans were nominated to the council. In July 1920, the interior of the East Africa Protectorate, embracing the White Highlands, was declared a British crown colony and was renamed Kenya Colony (after Mount Kenya, the most imposing geographical landmark in the country). The narrow coastal strip which, legally, was still part of the domain of the sultan of Zanzibar, officially became the Kenya Protectorate, although it was administered as part of Kenya Colony. At that time, a representative element was introduced into the government of Kenya Colony, with eleven members of an enlarged legislative council being elected by the white settlers. A further constitutional change in 1927 allowed the election of five Indians and one Arab to seats on the legislative council, while one European was appointed to represent the interests of the African population. (The colonial government retained control through the appointment of a majority of the members.) Needless to say, these arrangements were less than satisfactory to the Indians, who outnumbered the white settlers by more than two to one, or to the African majority, who saw their land and the government controlled by Europeans.

The first African attempts at political organization took place in the 1920s and sprang mainly from the grievances of the Kikuyu people, the original occupants of the White Highlands. The most important African political organization before World War II was the Kikuyu Central Association (KCA), which demanded political rights, economic reform, and the return of lands that had been taken from the native African. The KCA was banned in 1940 along with other African groups considered subversive or detrimental to the war effort. At the end of World War II, the newly formed (1944) Kenya African Union (KAU) became the foremost political outlet for African opposition to settler and colonial domination. Jomo Kenyatta*, a Kikuyu scholar and radical nationalist who had recently returned to Kenya after a long stay in England, was elected president of KAU in 1947.

Members of the outlawed KCA formed the Mau Mau movement in the late 1940s. Those involved in Mau Mau, which was largely a Kikuyu phenomenon headed by younger militants from Nairobi and the rural areas, referred to themselves as the Land Freedom Army when the fighting began. The movement was secret, coercive, and insurrectionary, recruiting and holding members by means of powerful oaths which could not be broken without the most deadly consequences. Due to increasingly violent acts, such as arson, the maiming of cattle, and the assassination of Senior Chief Waruhiu, the leading supporter of government policies in Kikuyu country, the British declared a state of emergency and took military action against the Mau Mau in 1952. They confined tens of thousands of suspected rebels in detention camps and conducted intensive "cleansing" ceremonies to break the secret oaths and separate the detainees from their allegiance to Mau Mau. Kenyatta was also jailed in 1952 for his alleged leadership of the movement. The Mau Mau rebellion was brought under control by 1956, although the state of emergency was not ended until 1960. Some 11,500 Mau Mau adherents (mostly Kikuya) died in the fighting. On the other side, counting civilian and military casualties, 95 Europeans, 49 Indians, and over 2,000 pro-government Africans were killed before peace was firmly established.

Even though the Mau Mau movement was crushed militarily, it led to a major change in the direction of British policy in Kenya. Britain realized that the Mau Mau troubles had grown out of deeply rooted grievances and that African demands for political freedom could no longer be ignored. In 1954 the Colonial Office introduced the Lyttleton Constitution which provided seats in the legislative council for eight elected African representatives and granted Africans the right to vote on a separate roll. Elections for those representatives were held in March 1957. However, six of the new African members refused to accept their positions as they felt that Africans still were not properly represented. This impasse resulted in the Lennox-Boyd Constitution of 1958, which increased the African membership on the legislative council to 14, Asian to 8, and European to 14. For the first time, Europeans were not a majority of the elected representatives on the legislative council. In February 1961 Britain agreed to elections designed to permit the Africans to dominate a wholly elected colonial parliament. Kenyatta's new party, the Kenya African National Union (KANU), won the elections but refused to take office without the release of Kenyatta from custody, which the British authorities would not allow. Consequently, a rival party, the Kenya African Democratic Union (KADU), formed the government. Kenyatta was freed by the British in August 1961. Kenya was granted internal self-government on June 1, 1963. The KANU party won the elections, and Kenyatta became the country's first prime minister. The constitution was finalized in September 1963, and on December 12, 1963, Kenya became independent. (Jeremy Murray Brown, *Kenyatta*, 1973; Harold Nelson, ed., *Kenya, A Country Study*, 1983.)

Amanda Pollock

KENYATTA, JOMO. Jomo Kenyatta, a Kikuyu tribesman, was born in 1891 in Ngenda, some 25 miles northeast of Fort Smith, in what was then British East Africa (now Kenya*). He enrolled in the Scottish mission station at Thogoto in 1909 under his tribal name of Kamau wa Ngengi. Both of his parents had died so there were no family members to object to his participation in a system that would frequently be in conflict with Kikuyu traditions. He created the Christian name of Johnstone at baptism, wishing to be called after Jesus's two leading apostles, John and Peter. He knew his tribal background could never be rediscovered according to the simple legends he had learned from his mother, so he viewed his baptism as an initiation into the white man's world.

During World War I, Kenyatta worked as an administrative clerk and ranch hand responsible for getting cattle and sheep through to Nairobi. He also formed close ties with Masai relatives (an aunt had married a Masai chief) and began to affect some of their customs. Masai women wore thin strips of leather with brightly colored beads around the neck or arm, tied around the waist as a belt, or fastened in a band around a hat. The Kikuyu word for these beaded ornaments was *kinyata*. During the 1920s he entered the mercantile business with an establishment at Dagoretti called the Kinyata Stores. As he dispensed Nubian gin and danced with his patrons from all over the colony, church elders were disturbed. The church delayed blessing his marriage to Grace Watu and baptizing his son until he had served six months suspension of true contrition. Kenyatta agreed.

Following World War I the British East Africa Protectorate officially became the crown colony of Kenya. A system of registration for all natives leaving the reserves, *kipande*, as it was called, was also begun. By 1922 nearly half a million natives had been registered, Kenyatta among them. As a "detribalized" urban Kikuyu, he acquired a job as water meter reader for the Nairobi municipal council. He earned a high wage for an African at that time and he chose not to risk anything by getting mixed up in political agitation. The Kikuyu Central Association, a regional group protesting the abuses of the European settler system, approached Kenyatta for assistance in translating and drafting letters. In February 1928 he went as interpreter with a KCA delegation to Government House. The KCA delegates made no impression on the British commissioners who insisted that there were no natives of sufficient education to serve as representatives in government or any single native who could command the confidence of more than a section of the people. Kenyatta left the meeting determined to answer this challenge by assuming leadership of the KCA.

In 1929 the KCA put in a request to the colonial administration to send its secretary, Johnstone Kenyatta, to London. He went to England to discuss three questions: Kikuyu land rights, female circumcision, and the need for independent Kikuyu schools since the Presbyterian mission schools refused to admit circumcised girls. He returned to Kenya with permission for the Kikuyu to operate their own schools, but in 1931 he returned to England to testify concerning land rights and did not return to Kenya until 1946. During the intervening years Kenyatta traveled extensively in Europe, studied in several academic centers, including Moscow University and the London School of Economics, and in 1938 he published, under the name of Jomo Kenyatta, his book *Facing Mount Kenya*, a study of the tribal organization of the Kikuyu. Kenyatta's purpose in writing the book was to challenge the white man's view of history which assumed European superiority. He used the language of anthropology to insist the African was not a savage groping toward European enlightenment, but a man who inherited his social and cultural ideals from a different and equally worthy past. African tribal custom, Kenyatta argued, had cohesion and integrity better than anything the colonial system could offer.

When he returned to Kenya in 1946, Kenyatta helped to found over 300 schools and became principal of the independent Teachers' Training College established to promote an educational philosophy in harmony with Kikuyu values and traditions. He was instrumental in forming the Kenya African Union (KAU), since the Kikuyu Central Association had been proscribed during the war. As a nationalist movement, the KAU aimed at producing a synthesis, a way of life which would take the best from Europe, Asia, and America, while rejecting what was less suitable to Africans. It became the main force in Kenyan politics. Audiences at Kenyatta's speeches were from 30,000 to 50,000 strong. British Kenyans were so disturbed by the growth of the KAU that in 1948 they demanded that Kenyatta be deported.

Mau Mau terrorism began in 1950. Accusations that KAU was behind the Mau Mau increased and Kenyatta found several public occasions for disclaiming any connection. The growth of the Mau Mau movement occurred against a background of unusually rapid KAU successes. The colonial government proclaimed a state of emergency and arrested top KAU, trade union, and African religious leaders. In a short time, more than 50,000 Kikuyu were in concentration camps. If KAU could be identified with Mau Mau, the colonial government thought it would effectively discredit Kenyatta as a political leader of African nationalism. In September 1952 Kenyatta was charged with managing Mau Mau. During the trial, the prosecution shifted its argument from Kenyatta's alleged criminal activities as manager of Mau Mau to the politics of African nationalism. In an atmosphere of intrigue, intimidation, and fear, Kenyatta was found guilty and sentenced to seven years hard labor, to be followed by indefinite restriction.

By the late 1950s, when Kenyatta was released from prison but still under restriction (until 1961), it was clear to all but the most reactionary white men that history was moving toward Kenyan independence. Under a new constitution which promised decolonization and eventual independence, the Kenya African National Union or KANU was formed. After winning a majority in the elections of 1961, KANU refused to take part in any government until Kenyatta was freed. The British government accepted the inevitable. As head of KANU, Kenyatta became the first prime minister of a self-governing Kenya on June 1, 1963. In December 1963 Kenya became the thirty-fourth state in Africa to achieve independence. A year later, Kenya became a republic within the British Commonwealth*, with Kenyatta as president. Perhaps the greatest contribution Kenyatta gave to his country was his message of reconciliation: ''I have stood always for the purposes of human dignity in freedom and for the values of tolerance and peace.'' At the time of his death in Mombasa on August 22, 1978, he was revered as *Mzee*, wise father of Kenya and as a giant of African history. (Jeremy Murray-Brown, *Kenyatta*, 1973; Montagu Salter, *The Trial of Jomo Kenyatta*, 1955.)

Anita Pilling

KIAOCHOW. Some North German industries and trading companies had sought access to raw materials and new markets before the Reich of 1871 came into being, and the regime of Otto von Bismarck* prepared the way for the German penetration of Asia when he intervened between 1879 and 1885 to secure the port of Apia in Samoa*, as well as Papua New Guinea*, the Bismarck Archipelago*, the Solomon Islands*, and the Caroline*, Palau*, and Marshall* groups. After the Sino-Japanese War* of 1894–1895, in which the naval forces of China were destroyed, Japan intended to assume control of northern China. For a variety of reasons, Germany wanted its own foothold there.

Paul Kayser, the head of the colonial section of the foreign office in 1894, contended that the Reich government could gain prestige at home and abroad by constantly asserting itself overseas, mediating or taking sides in disputes among the colonial powers. Kaiser Wilhelm supported Kayser's ideas. The Second German Reich decided to establish itself at Kiaochow. Admiral Count Alfred von Tirpitz, Reich state secretary of the naval office, opposed those in the government who wanted Germany to seize the Chusan Islands, Wusung, Amoy, Weihaiwei, Samsah Bay, Mirs Bay, or the Montebello Islands off the coast of Korea. Tirpitz was impressed with Tsingtao at Kiaochow Bay, the location finally chosen after experts on harbor construction examined it. Tirpitz also concluded that Germany needed a much stronger navy to counter the British naval threat.

The Bay of Kiaochow is located on the southern coast of the Shantung Peninsula, the easternmost extension of the old Shantung Province in northeastern China. The town of Kiaochow, now called Kiaohsien, is located about ten miles northwest of the Bay of Kiaochow on the railway to the port city of Tsingtao. Tsingtao was a mere fishing village until the Chinese government established a naval station and fort there in 1891. The city was the primary objective when an armed force of the Second German Reich landed on November 14, 1897, under the command of Admiral Otto von Diedrichs. To gain support for naval expansion, the kaiser used as his pretext for the landing at Kaiochow Bay the killing of two German Catholic missionaries by a group of Chinese during a robbery in southern Shangtung in November 1891. Hoping that Russia would support Peking under the Sino-Russian Alliance of 1896, China protested the action, but Germany responded by sending additional ships and troops under the command of Admiral Prince Heinrich Albrecht Wilhelm, the brother of Kaiser Wilhelm II. When the Chinese government finally acceded to the *fait accompli* and agreed to "lease" the two capes guarding the entrance to Kiaochow Bay, a treaty of March 6, 1898, created the Kiaochow administrative district, a "neutral zone" of some 200 square miles. The treaty also allowed a Sino-German combine to construct two railroads into the heart of the Shantung Peninsula, and in a zone approximately ten miles on each side of the railroad, only German nationals could exploit mineral resources, of which iron and coal deposits were especially rich. The incursion in China made such an impression on the public and the political parties that the first naval bill could pass the Reichstag on March 28, 1898. Until the landing at Kaiochow the idea of naval expansion had not been popular at all.

The German government made Tsingtao a first-rate naval base and commercial port. As such it came under the control of the navy rather than the colonial administration. The governor was always a marine officer: Karl Rosendahl (1898–1899), Paul Jäschke (1899–1901), Oskar von Truppel (1901–1911), and Alfred Meyer-Waldeck (1911–1914). But Japan resented the German presence in Kiaochow from the very beginning, and with the outbreak of World War I* in 1914, Japanese naval forces seized control of Kiaochow after a month-long siege. (Arthur Julius Irmer, *Die Erwerbung von Kiaotchou, 1894–1989*, 1930; Paul M. Kennedy, *Germany in the Pacific and the Far East, 1870–1914*, 1977; John E. Schrecker, *Imperialism and Nationalism: Germany in Shantung*, 1971.)

Bascom Barry Hayes

KING PHILIP'S WAR. King Philip's war was one of the most savage racial conflicts in American history. Born in 1616 near what is today Warren, Rhode Island, King Philip became chief of the Wampanoag tribe in 1662. By the 1660s the British North American colonies in New England* were growing rapidly in population and pressing directly on Indian land. Resentful of white settlements, violations of land titles, and assaults on individual Indians, King Philip attacked a number of white settlements on July 4, 1675. Joined by such other tribes as the Narragansetts, Nipmucs, and Penobscots, the Wampanoags destroyed twenty New England towns and killed more than 3,000 people. It was only a temporary victory, however, for in the battle of Great Swamp in December 1675, Philip saw more than 1,000 of his warriors die. He too was killed in 1676. By 1678 colonial forces had cleared southern New England of Indians, opening the area to white settlers. King Philip's family was sold into slavery. The back of Indian resistance in New England was permanently broken. (Francis Jennings, *The Invasion of America: Indians, Colonialism, and the Cant of Conquest*, 1975.)

KINO, EUSEBIO FRANCISCO. Eusebio Kino was born in Segno, Trent, and baptized on August 10, 1645. He attended the Jesuit college in Trent before leaving for Hall, near Innsbruck, Austria, in 1663 to study rhetoric. In 1665 he joined the Jesuits* and devoted himself to a theological and scientific education. Kino initially petitioned Rome for missionary work in China but was turned down. On March 17, 1678, he received permission to work in New Spain*. He left Europe on January 29, 1681, and arrived in Mexico City on June 1. In the autumn of 1681 he published a book, *Exposición Astronómica de el Cometa*, on the 1680 comet which stirred controversy among scholars in Mexico City. He stayed in the capital until chosen to participate as Royal cosmographer, chaplain of the Spaniards, and superior of a scientific and exploring expedition to lower California.

The expedition hoped to create military bases to protect the Manila galleons coming and going from New Spain to the Philippines*, Christianize the Indian population, and lay the basis for future exploration. The fleet landed at La Paz, Lower California an April 1, 1683. Missionary work and exploration began immediately. On July 14 La Paz was abandoned after the slaughter of 13 Indians in retaliation for the supposed murder of the ship crier.

A second California expedition was attempted, and on October 6 construction began on a fort settlement named San Bruno. Kino explored the interior of California. Attempts were made to close down the mission because no source of wealth or fertile lands existed. The spring and summer of 1684 were spent at San Bruno in pearl fishing but not enough were found to justify the expedition. On December 22, 1685, the Spanish king ordered the suspension of the California mission. Kino found himself on the mainland when he learned of the suspension in April 1686.

Kino returned to Mexico City and remained until assigned as a missionary to the Indians in Nueva Vizcaya. He hoped to link the missions of Sonora with those established in California. On November 20, 1686, he went to Guadalajara, received instructions for his missionary work, and left for Sonora on December 16. On his arrival at Oposura he was instructed to go to the Pimeria Alta, which includes present day Sonora in the south and Arizona in the north, to work with the Pima Indians. On March 13, 1687, Kino arrived at his permanent residence in Cosari, renamed Nuestra Senora de los Dolores. He visited the villages, built chapels, and explored the surrounding territory. He entered what is today Arizona in 1690.

In 1694 Kino began more extensive explorations of the territory. A Pima rebellion broke out on March 29, 1695, and lasted until August 8. Although many missions and settlements were destroyed, Kino's mission was spared. Kino left for Mexico City in November, arrived January 8, 1696, and stayed for six months to recruit and get support. Criticism by the new rector of the Pimeria Alta did not stop Kino from further explorations and missionary activities on his return. In October 1699 an Indian tribe presented Kino with a gift of blue shells which led him to conclude that a land route to California existed because of the similarity of these shells with some he had seen in California. He began to search for this route to fulfill his wish of linking his mission with that of Lower California.

On April 23, 1700, he began another expedition but was recalled before he was able to investigate the hypothesis of the blue shells. On October 7, on another expedition, he climbed a mountain and saw contiguous land between California and the Pimeria Alta. In March 1701 a trip to the Colorado River definitely proved that California was not an island but a peninsula. On his return to Dolores he created the map "Paso por Tierra" (Land Passage to California and its neighboring New Nations and New Missions of the Company of Jesus in North America) designed to show that California was a peninsula. It was printed in Europe and became a standard. Troubles continued with the authorities because of his relationship with the Pima Indians. In the autumn of 1702 and spring of 1703 he began plans for another expedition but was prevented from taking it.

On September 16, 1710, he made one of his last requests, which was for new bells for Dolores Church. The response from Mexico City was that he would not need them since New Spain's Jesuit missions were suppressed. He continued his explorations until his death on March 15, 1711, in the village of Santa Magdalena. Kino's explorations established that California was not an island but a peninsula. He introduced many domestic animals and agricultural products into the region and built settlements for future colonization. His work as a cartographer, geographer, and explorer would gain him renown in the Old and New World. (Herbert E. Bolton. *Rim of Christendom: A Biography of Eusebio Francisco Kino*, 1936.)

Carlos Pérez

KIPLING, RUDYARD. Rudyard Kipling was born in Bombay*, India, on December 30, 1865, the son of an English museum curator. After education in England, he returned to India in 1882 to take a position on a newspaper. He began to publish verse and fiction immediately, soon gaining local fame. By 1890 he was known around the world. Among his early works are *Soldiers Three* (1888), *The Light that Failed* (1891), *Barrack Room Ballads* (1892), *Many Inventions* (1893), *The Jungle Book* (1894), and *The Second Jungle Book* (1895). For a while he traveled the world, then briefly settled in England (1890–1891). He lived in the United States from 1891 to 1896, when he returned permanently to England. In 1898 Kipling journeyed to South Africa and emerged as the chief apologist for British imperialism and the kind of nationalism called chauvinism.

Among his later works are *Captains Courageous* (1897), *Kim* (1901), and *The Irish Guards and the Great War* (1925). He wrote a number of works for children, including *Just So Stories* (1902), *Puck of Pooks Hall* (1906) and *Rewards and Fairies* (1910). His autobiography, *Something of Myself* appeared in 1937. Several of his poems are especially famous: "The Ballad of East and West," "Danny Deever," "Tommy," "Gunga Din," "Mandalay," "Recessional," and "The White Man's Burden." The last poem, published in 1899, celebrates the white virtues and the men and women who taught them to the "fluttered folk and wild" and calls by implication for the United States to do its duty by entering the race for empire. Thus it reflects the common belief of Englishmen (and Americans) in their own superiority and in the natural subordination of nonwhites. Kipling sent the first public copy to Theodore Roosevelt, who liked the ideas but not the poetry.

Kipling received the Nobel Prize for literature in 1907, a recognition that he was a master of the English language, a point admitted even by the critics who objected to his blunt imperialism. He died in London on January 18, 1936. (C. E. Carrington, *The Life of Rudyard Kipling*, 1955; Philip Mason, *Kipling*, 1975.)

Walter A. Sutton

KIRIBATI. Kiribati is an independent nation of Micronesia* and consists of the limestone-based island of Banaba and the coral groups of the Gilbert Islands, the Line Islands*, and the Phoenix Islands. They are scattered across more than two million square miles of the Pacific Ocean. At the far western perimeter of

Kiribati is the island of Banaba. In the center are the Gilbert Islands, with the capital at Tarawa. The Gilberts are at the equator just west of the international dateline. At the far east of the country are the Line Islands, of which the main atoll is Christmas Island* or Kiritimati. Kiritimati is approximately 1,300 miles southeast of Hawaii. The Phoenix Islands are uninhabited because of severe water shortages.

Spanish mariners first reached the Gilbert Islands in 1568, but because of the dearth of resources and strategic isolation, they made no political commitment there. English trading ships had mapped all of the Gilbert, Phoenix, and Line Islands by 1825. Christian missionaries, slave traders, and commercial traders overran the islands in the mid-nineteenth century. To forestall French and German interest in the area, Great Britain established the Western Pacific High Commission, located on Fiji*, in 1877 to administer the Gilbert and Ellice Islands*. Parliament formally made the area a British protectorate in 1892, and in 1900 Britain annexed Banaba because of its phosphate mines. In 1915 parliament upgraded the political status of the region by creating the Gilbert and Ellice Islands Colony. Banaba and the Line Islands were included in the colony in 1917, Kiritimati in 1919, and the Phoenix Islands in 1939.

Japan seized the Gilbert and Ellice Islands Colony in 1941, and Tarawa was the scene of a terrible battle between Japanese and American soldiers in November 1943. After World War II*, Great Britain began preparing the islands for self-government. Between 1963 and 1977, the establishment of appointed executive councils gave way to an elected legislature and internal control. The Ellice Islands voted out of the colony in 1976 and in 1978 became the independent nation of Tuvalu. On July 12, 1972, England granted independence to the Gilbert Islands, Line Islands, Phoenix Islands, and Banaba, and they took the name of the Republic of Kiribati. Kingman Reef and Palmyra Atoll in the Line Islands remained United States territory, as did Jarvis, Baker, and Howland islands, which lay between the Gilbert and Line Islands. (John Wesley Coulter, *The Pacific Dependencies of the United States*, 1957; Taomati Iuta, *Politics in Kiribati*, 1980.)

KOLONIALVEREIN. A propaganda organization founded by colonial enthusiasts in 1882 to promote German colonial policy, the *Kolonialverein* owed its origin to a meeting of the Frankfurt and Offenbach chambers of commerce and the members of the *Verein für Geographie und Statistik* (Institute for Geography and Statistics) during which the members pledged to support colonial commerce, exploration, and expansion. The primary political objective of the *Kolonialverein* was to block any efforts at reducing German colonial holdings and to push for colonial expansion, particularly in Africa. In the first year of its existence the organization numbered 3,000 individual and corporate members. By 1914 the *Kolonialverein* counted 42,000 members. From 1882–1887 the political influence of the league suffered due to a lack of support from the large industrial centers. Northern and eastern Germany were poorly represented in the *Kolonialverein* and the large numbers of businessmen and industrialists from Hamburg, Berlin, and the Ruhr expressed little interest in supporting the organization. The bulk of the league's influence stemmed from its connections with the upper level of German bureaucracy, municipal government officials, and German universities. The organization's executive committee included the respected Hanoverian politician Rudolph von Bennigsen; Dr. Johannes Miquel, the mayor of Frankfurt; Professor Friedrich Ratzel, Germany's leading geographer; and the historian Gustav Freytag.

In 1887 the *Kolonialverein* increased its political clout by merging with the *Gesellschaft für Deutsche Kolonisation* (Society for German Colonization), which had been founded in 1884 by Karl Peters, Germany's most renowned African explorer and colonial advocate. The new organization, the *Deutsche Kolonialgesellschaft* (DKG), was able to put considerable pressure on the Reichstag in favor of colonial expansion. The DKG was well organized; it influenced public opinion through its publications, by commissioning scholarly studies of German Africa, library exhibitions, and school lectures. The society sent scientific expeditions to the colonies, provided assistance to German colonial settlers, and attempted to promote the creation of German schools overseas. The DKG had considerable influence on the German colonial office since that bureaucracy looked for support not only in the Reichstag but also among pressure groups with a colonial interest. In World War I*, the DKG, in spite of severe military setbacks in Africa, demanded the expulsion of Britain and France from Africa to enable the creation of a German *Mittelafrika* (a German Central African empire). After 1919 the society fought for the return of the German colonies. After 1933 the DKG was merged into the *National Socialist Reichskolonialbund*, which promoted Nazi ideology in the former colonies. (Roger Chickering, *We Men Who Feel Most German*, 1984; L. H. Gann and Peter Duignan, *The Rulers of German Africa, 1884–1914*, 1977.)

William G. Ratliff

KOSRAE. See FEDERATED STATES OF MICRONESIA.

KOUANG-TCHEOU-WAN. Like Germany and Great Britain, France was interested late in the nineteenth century in penetrating the Chinese markets and carving out a sphere of influence. Such an endeavor, however, required a permanent naval station in East Asia. In the scramble for China*, Great Britain established such an outpost at Weihaiwei,* while Germany gained its foothold at Kiaochow*. The French found their spot in the northeastern part of the Liuchow peninsula, where they established their settlement—really a naval and coaling station—in 1898. In 1900 they formalized the arrangement by leasing the territory from China. That same year, Kouang-Tcheou-Wan became an administrative part of Indochina*. When France fell to Germany in 1940, the French could no longer defend the settlement, and it fell to Japan in 1943. When World War II was over, Kouang-Tcheou-Wan reverted to Chinese sovereignty. (David P. Henige, *Colonial Governors from the Fifteenth Century to the Present*, 1970.)

KRAMER, AUGUSTIN FRIEDRICH. Augustin Kramer was born in 1865, and studied medicine in Tubingen and Berlin and natural science in Kiel. In 1889 he joined the imperial navy and participated in several expeditions to German colonies in the South Pacific, where he collected a great deal of ethnological data. Eventually he visited Samoa*, the Bismarck Archipelago*, Truk, Yap, and Palau* in the Carolines*. Kramer headed up the Hamburg South Sea Expedition to the Caroline and Marshall islands in 1909–1910. Kramer later became the scientific director of the Linden-Museum in Stuttgart, and also published many scholarly works, including, *Die Samoa-Inseln* (1902–1903). (Hans Meyer, ed., *Das Deutsche Kolonialreich*, 1909–1910; Heinrich Schnee, *Deutsches Kolonial-Lexikon*, vol. 2, 1920.)

KUWAIT. Kuwait is an oil-rich nation of approximately 18,000 square miles located on the northwest edge of the Persian Gulf. In 1716 several clans of the Aniza people migrated to Kuwait from central Arabia, and in 1756 they selected the Al-Sabah family as the ruling dynasty. They remained in power until the Iraqi invasion of 1990, and were restored in 1991. Late in the nineteenth century the Ottoman Empire attempted to seize control of the Persian Gulf coast south of Kuwait, and to forestall that effort Sheikh Mubarak al-Sabah requested British assistance, something the British were only too willing to do. They wanted to protect the sea lanes to India from Turkish interference. In 1899 the Kuwaitis agreed not to give any of their territory to a foreign power without British consent. The British then began providing an annual subsidy to sustain the Kuwaiti ruling family. With the outbreak of World War I, the British, fearing new Turkish designs on the region, recognized the independence of Kuwait and extended them military protection. After World War II Kuwait became a major oil producer. She declared unilateral independence in June 1961, which led to the replacement of British troops by Arab League soldiers. In 1965 and 1969 Kuwait signed treaties with Saudi Arabia defining their mutual border. (J. S. Ismael, *Kuwait: Social Change in Historical Perspective*, 1982; David Sapsted, *Modern Kuwait*, 1980.)

L

LABUAN. Labuan is a Malaysian island of 35 square miles in the South China Sea near the coast of Borneo*. Labuan occupies a strategic location: it guards the entrance to Brunei Bay, the only good port along the entire northwest coast of Borneo. Labuan's colonizers hoped it would grow into a city to rival Singapore* and Hong Kong*, but that was not to be. The total population today is about 20,000: Malays, Chinese, Kadayans, Tamils, and some Europeans.

The sultan of Brunei* ceded Labuan to Great Britain in 1846 for use as a base for British anti-piracy campaigns along the coast of Borneo. Labuan was a crown colony until 1946 except for sixteen years (1890–1906) when it was administered by the British North Borneo Chartered Company. Schemes to develop Labuan's economy never amounted to much. A coal mine was dug, and a narrow-gauge railway laid between the mine and the wharf, but the mineshaft collapsed. Rubber, sago, and coconuts constituted the mainstays of Labuan's economy. The port remained merely a transshipment point for exotic Bornean products— beeswax and edible birds' nests—bound for Singapore.

Labuan's strategic location made it a focus of Japanese-Australian battles in World War II*. Victoria was leveled by Allied bombs, but was rebuilt after the war, when Labuan was again administratively joined to British North Borneo*. Labuan has been part of Sabah (as former British North Borneo was renamed) since 1963. (Nicholas Tarling, *Sulu and Sabah: British Policy Toward British North Borneo Since the 18th Century*, 1978.)

Ross Marlay

LANGUAGE IN FRENCH AFRICA. The French Republic pursued in its African colonies the same monolingual policy as in metropolitan France: the suppression of regional languages was paralleled by the complete disregard in which African vernaculars were held by colonization ideologists. First, J. Carde, governor general of French West Africa*, imposed the French language as the sole teaching subject in village schools (in 1938, 310 schools, 26,195 students, including 2,625 girls) arguing that "it is unacceptable that after 40 years of occupation chiefs are unable to converse with us in French" (1924 decree). French Equatorial Africa* followed suit in 1917 and 1922. All textbooks were written in French, although, in the recently acquired territories of Togo* and Cameroon*, mission schools were allowed to teach in the local languages for one hour a week. Throughout French Africa, French was the sole medium of instruction in rural, regional, municipal, and central primary schools as well as in secondary and technical college (in 1945, 110,951 pupils in French West Africa). Second, in 1927 some urban schools in Senegal*, the colony with the longest educational tradition (organized by Faidherbe, 1854) were granted the right to adopt the same syllabi as in France, doing away with the concept of "native programs" taught in French. Third, also in 1927, a short-lived decree, lobbied for by the principal of French West Africa's teachers' college, William Ponty, aligned its diplomas on the metropolitan degrees and placed the educational system under the jurisdiction of the Academy of Bordeaux. The assimilatory project met with such resistance from the metropolitan-trained teachers (225 in 1932, against 436 Africans, who were paid lower salaries) that it was never implemented. Contrary to British and Belgian administrators, who often allowed syllabi to be taught in the local languages, depriving Africans of an early access to the colonizers' printed world and largely preventing the emergence of these vernaculars out of "primary orality," French teachers in Africa gave a fraction at least of the colonial population such a possibility. Yet, at the same time, programs were strictly "Gallacentric," especially in history and geography. Finally, at a sociolinguistic level, the colloquial and substandard forms of French rapidly developed in the wake of colonization. Yet the fact that these variations have not triggered any true creolization process bears witness to the dominant nature of French in Francophone ex-colonies and to the impact of a colonial language once assimilated and officialized by the former colonies. (Jean Suret-Canale, *Afrique Noire. L'Ere coloniale. 1900–1945*, 1964; P. Desálmand, *Histoire de l'éducation en Côte d'Ivoire*, 1986; R. Stumpf, *La politique linguistique au Cameroun de 1884 à 1960*, 1979.)

Philippe-Joseph Salazar

LAOS. Laos is a remote, landlocked Southeast Asian country bordered by China*, Vietnam*, Thailand*, and Burma*. The long eastern border between Laos and Vietnam follows the crest of the Annamite mountains; most rivers run westward down to the valley of the Mekong, which, for its middle course, forms the border between Laos and Thailand. The terrain is steeply mountainous, and jungle covers most of Laos. There are no railroads and few roads. Movement is especially difficult during the rainy season, factors which have hindered national unity and retarded political development. The Lao language is a dialect of Thai, and most Lao-speakers actually live in northeastern Thailand. Within Laos, they live in the Mekong valley. Upland there are hill tribes such as the Ho, Yao, and Meo, closely related to tribes in Chinese Yunnan. The Lao-Theung in the south are regarded as savages by other Lao. Laos is hardly a nation-state in the modern sense. There is little sense of national unity among the people, who, representing a variety of races and speaking different languages, are oriented toward local rather than national action.

The dichotomy between lowlanders and hill tribes is a fundamental one in Southeast Asia. The former live in permanent villages with an elaborate social structure, practicing wet-rice agriculture. The latter farm by the slash-and-burn method, and are nomadic. Their social structure is simpler. A further distinction is that lowland Lao are Buddhist, while hill tribes are generally animist.

During the twelfth and thirteenth centuries the Lao moved from southwest China into territory that had been controlled by the great Khmer empire, then in decline. They fell into a pattern of internal squabbling and the kingdom was divided in three, with capitals at Luang Prabang in the north, Vientiane in the center, and Champassak in the south. Disunity invited Siamese intervention. The Thais asserted suzerainty over all Laos in 1828.

There was little European contact with Laos until the French began to carve out their Indochinese empire. After establishing a foothold in Cochin-China* and then, in the 1880s reducing Annam*, Tonkin*, and Cambodia* to protectorate status, France sought to buffer her new holdings against the ever-assertive Siamese and the rival British, who had already moved into Burma. French motives for incorporating Laos into Indochina* also included a desire to keep the British from what they vainly hoped would be a navigable route into China up the Mekong or Red river valleys. French conquest was accomplished nearly singlehandedly by the extraordinary Auguste Pavie, who promised to protect Laos from Siam and claimed that a dubious Annamese right of suzerainty over Laos had passed to France. Siam protested, but a French naval blockade of Bangkok settled the matter. In 1893 Siam renounced all rights to land east of the Mekong. France reunited Laos and added some more territory to it by another treaty with Siam in 1907.

French imperialism was hardly onerous for Laos. The Laotian king remained on his throne in Luang Prabang, while the rest of the country was divided into eight provinces, each governed by a French *resident*. A *resident superieur* exercised nearly unlimited power from Vientiane, but the French seemed to think of Laos as a quaint colonial backwater whose innocent people needed protection from modern ways. It is unlikely that most Laotians even knew they lived under French jurisdiction. Life went on as always in the self-sufficient villages. The French set up only a few schools, and no industry. They romantically called their protectorate "the land of a million elephants" or the "kingdom of the white parasol." A small number of towns grew up, with Chinese middlemen and Vietnamese clerks, but none was large enough to be called a city. The main exports of colonial Laos were rice, opium, tea, coffee, and some sugarcane.

There was some tin and iron mining, but it never amounted to much. Laos was spared deforestation, although there were magnificent stands of tropical hardwoods, because of an insuperable transportation problem.

This colonial idyll came to an end after World War II*. In 1945 the *Lao Issara* (Free Lao), a proto-nationalist movement, declared Laos independent. What began as jockeying for influence between rival branches of the royal family gradually became transmuted into a Cold War struggle between left-wing nationalists and a right-wing military. The left was ably led by the "Red Prince" Souphanouvong, who had been impressed by Viet Minh revolutionaries he had met in Paris. King Sisavang Vong welcomed the French back but they were eventually expelled from all Indochina by the Vietnamese communists, and when the Geneva Accords were signed in 1954, Laos was internationally recognized as an independent country. (Nina Adams and Alfred McCoy, eds., *Laos: War and Revolution*, 1970; Arthur Dommen, *Laos: Keystone of Indochina*, 1985; Milton Osborne, *River Road to China*, 1975.)

Ross Marlay

LAPÉROUSE, JEAN-FRANÇOIS DE GALAUP, COMTE DE. Lapérouse, a French navigator who explored the Pacific Ocean, was born on August 23, 1741, in southern France. He entered naval service in 1756. Lapérouse was wounded and captured by the British during the Seven Years' War. In 1779 he fought against the British during the American Revolution*. Under commission from the French government, Lapérouse launched an extensive, scientific expedition to the Pacific in 1785. For three years Lapérouse traveled widely throughout the Pacific gathering geographic and anthropological information. He visited Hawaii, Alaska, California, China, Japan, Easter Island, and Samoa, and he reached Botany Bay in Australia in January 1788, the last time any Europeans ever saw him or his crew again. (Maurice de Brossard, *Lapérouse: des combats a la decouverte*, 1978.)

LA SALLE, RENÉ ROBERT CAVALIER, SIEUR DE. La Salle was born in France in 1643 and emigrated to Montreal* in 1666. He obtained a land grant nine miles from Montreal, but he was interested in making money to use in exploring unknown regions of New France* and adding to its dominions. La Salle's original goal was to find the elusive Northwest Passage*. During the winter of 1668, however, he diverted his attention to charting the course of interior rivers after hearing descriptions of the Ohio River and of another greater river called the Missi-sepe from the Seneca Indians. La Salle sold his land to finance an expedition to explore these rivers.

He obtained authorization for his explorations from the Count de Frontenac, governor of New France, and his expedition set out in July 1669. He led a small group through the wilderness to the Ohio and followed it to the Mississippi River before returning to Montreal in the summer of 1671. Meanwhile, Jesuit priest Jacques Marquette and fur-trader Louis Joliet* reached the Mississippi by way of the Wisconsin River during the summer of 1673 and followed the river as far south as its juncture with the Arkansas. They turned back because they were convinced that it continued flowing south to the Gulf of Mexico, where they might be captured by the Spaniards they knew to be in the area.

La Salle, however, was dissatisfied because the French still did not know for sure where the Mississippi led. He returned to France to ask royal permission to follow the river to its mouth, which King Louis XIV granted in 1678. La Salle would have seigneurial rights over whatever lands he discovered. La Salle also encountered on this trip Henri de Tonti, who came to New France with him and became his most trusted lieutenant. In 1679 La Salle began building a chain of forts to serve as trading posts generating the resources to finance his explorations and symbolize French power on the frontier. Beginning along the Saint Joseph and Niagra rivers, he pushed slowly westward around the southern rim of the Great Lakes and down the Illinois River, but failed to reach the Mississippi because of delays caused by Indian attacks, loss of fur shipments, and bankruptcy threatened by his creditors.

Undaunted, La Salle gathered a group of twenty-two experienced frontiersmen and Tonti at the mouth of the Saint Joseph River in December 1681. They followed the southern shore of Lake Michigan to the Chicago River, the Chicago to the Illinois, and entered the Mississippi on February 6, 1682. After a quick descent, La Salle's party arrived at the Gulf of Mexico on April 9, where he claimed for Louis XIV all land drained by the river. La Salle returned to Canada* and from there to France. The French government granted him permission to return to the Mississippi and establish a French colony to threaten Spanish possessions in northern Mexico* and to guard against attacks on New France from Spain or England, either of which could use the river as a water route to the western edge of the French Empire*. He sailed from La Rochelle in late July 1684, but his expedition was destined to fail. Command was divided, for example, with La Salle having authority to determine the course to be followed and command of ground troops, while Sieur de Beaujeu commanded the four ships and the sailors.

One ship was captured by the Spanish, but the remaining three entered the Gulf of Mexico in mid-December 1684. La Salle failed to find the Mississippi approaching from the Gulf. Logs and silt deposited at the mouth of the river effectively disguised the entrance. La Salle's instruments had not allowed him to take accurate longitude readings in 1682, and bad advice about Gulf currents caused him to sail approximately 500 miles too far west. He established a temporary settlement at present-day Matagorda Bay, Texas, and from there searched for the Mississippi. The loss of his last ship convinced La Salle that he had to send to Canada and France for help. On the first leg of the journey, however, one of his own men ambushed and killed him in the early spring of 1687. La Salle had pushed the frontiers of New France far to the southwest and added considerably to French knowledge of North American geography. Also, he had planted the idea that the French must establish a colony along the Mississippi to guard the southern approach to Canada. (W. J. Eccles, *France in America*, 1972; Alcee Fortier, *A History of Louisiana: Volume I Early Explorers and the Domination of the French 1512–1768*, 1966; Sabra Holbrook, *The French Founders of North America and Their Heritage*, 1976.)

Jerry Purvis Sanson

LAS CASAS, BARTOLOMÉ DE. Born in Seville in 1474 of Spanish nobility and educated at Salamanca, Bartolomé de las Casas came to Hispaniola* as a gentleman soldier of fortune in 1502. Enormously successful, he became one of the richer men in the islands, possessing vast estates, gold mines, and Indian laborers. In short, the tall Spaniard was just another rapacious conquistador, and the angry sermon of Father Antonio de Montesinos was directed at him as much as anyone. In 1511 Father Montesinos, a Dominican, put the city of Santa Domingo in an uproar with a stinging denunciation of the enslavement of the aborigines. Las Casas, who heard the friar's barbed words, was irritated, as was almost everyone else in the colony, but apparently unmoved by the priestly condemnation. In any event, he shortly thereafter obtained more land and Indians in Cuba*.

Suddenly, in 1514 a dramatic change came over Las Casas. Acknowledging the injustice of the Spaniards to the Indians, the conquistador immediately freed his slaves, sold his properties, divested himself of all possessions, and became a priest. For the next 52 years he labored in behalf of the aborigines. In 1516 he returned to Spain and presented his case to Cardinal Jiménez de Cisneros, who then named him "Protector of the Indians." In 1517 Las Casas appealed directly to Charles V*. The young monarch and his aides were sympathetic but demanded a practical alternative to the *encomienda**. Las Casas offered two proposals, both unsatisfactory. First he suggested the substitution of black slaves for Indians but soon regretted and withdrew this advice. Second, he recommended the sending of Spanish peasants to the New World to work alongside the Indians, an arrangement which would be supervised by the friars. The king had no objections to the latter proposal, but Spanish landlords did—they were unwilling to allow peasants needed at home to migrate to the Caribbean.

Unable to alleviate the plight of the aborigines, a discouraged Las Casas retired to a monastery in Santa Domingo in 1520 and became a member of the Dominican Order. The ten-year period of seclusion afforded him the time to write his reputable *History of the Indies*, which was not published until 1875. Then, in the early 1530s, Las Casas abandoned monastic life and resumed his crusade. He wrote a pamphlet entitled *The Only Method of Attracting Men to the True Faith*, urging a new method of conversion through gentleness and persuasion rather than force and violence.

An opportunity to test his proposal came in 1537. In the mountainous area of Guatemala*, known as the Land of War, Mayan tribes had tenaciously resisted conquest. Las Casas issued a challenge. He would pacify the tribes without arms, provided Spanish officials would refrain from seizing Mayan lands and allow no Spaniards except Dominican friars into the area for five years. The challenge was accepted, and for a while Las Casas and the Dominicans enjoyed some success. But with the appearance of rival priests and land-hungry settlers, violence again flared, and Las Casas, who by then had become the bishop of Chiapas, was unable to overcome Indian suspicions. Still, his efforts were not altogether in vain, for Charles V, in part because of Las Casas, issued the New Laws in 1542 prohibiting enslavement of the Indians and abolishing the *encomienda*. Angry protests in the colonies prompted the king to revoke these laws three years later.

In 1547 Las Casas returned to Spain, where he spent his last nineteen years. He engaged Juan Gines de Sepulveda in a famous debate at Valladolid in 1550–1551 over the nature of the New World conquest and the treatment of Indians. While Sepulveda, drawing upon Aristotle's theory of natural inferiority, defended the *encomienda*, accepted the innate inferiority of the Indians, and justified force, Las Casas offered a vigorous dissent on all points. Not long afterward Las Casas wrote the most controversial polemic of his career, *Very Brief Recital of the Destruction of the Indies* (1552). A withering condemnation of Spanish practices toward the aborigines, the pamphlet was translated into several European languages, providing grist for anti-Spanish propaganda throughout Europe and a basis for the "black legend," the idea that Spain in the New World did very little more than rob, plunder, and kill. Las Casas was not a proponent of the black legend, but many of his writings, particularly *Very Brief Recital*, served that purpose for Spain's enemies in Europe and later America. (Manuel Jimenez Fernández, *Sobre Bartolomé de las Casas*, 1964; Hanke Lewis, *Aristotle and the Indians*, 1959.)

John W. Storey

LEAGUE OF NATIONS. The League of Nations was an organization whose purpose was to promote international cooperation, peace, and security. The Covenant of the League of Nations was created by a special commission formed at the Paris Peace Conference of 1919–1920 and was included in the Treaty of Versailles of 1919* and the other accords ending World War I*. The Covenant was signed by forty-four nations, including thirty-one states that had participated on the side of the Western Allies during the war. Thirteen other states that had remained neutral during the war ultimately joined the League. The United States was the only major world power not to ratify the Covenant or join the League.

The principal deliberative bodies of the League of Nations included the Assembly, in which all members participated and which met annually in September. The League of Nations Council was composed initially of four permanent members—Great Britain, France, Italy, and Japan, along with four rotating members chosen from the League signatories. The Council's primary duty was to mediate international disputes. The League also included a permanent Secretariat headed by a secretary-general. All decisions of the Assembly and Council, with the exception of decisions on procedural matters, had to be ratified by a majority of the League members. The League Covenant also created the Permanent Court of International Justice at The Hague. The Permanent Court was an autonomous body intended to serve as the final arbiter of international disputes.

One of the League's most significant undertakings was the disposal of the former German colonies and certain Turkish possessions which the League, following the defeat of the Central Powers in World War I, placed under the governments of the victorious powers on the basis of special commissions, or mandates. This mandate system* was formally established by Article 22 of the Covenant of the League of Nations. Subject to inclusion in the mandate system were colonies and territories which, as a consequence of the 1914–1918 war, had ceased to be under the sovereignty of the former colonial governments and which were inhabited by "peoples not yet able to stand by themselves under the strenuous conditions of the modern world." Ultimately the League mandate system simply ratified, with slight modification, the previously agreed upon system of territorial readjustment proposed by the Allied Powers before the end of the war.

Under the official League system, the mandated territories were subdivided into groups A, B, and C. Group A mandates were formally organized as states with their own citizenship and administrations. In reality, however, ultimate authority in legislation, domestic policy, and foreign relations was held by the mandate power, which was also given the authority to determine when the particular territory would be capable of fully governing itself. Included in Group A were Iraq*, Palestine*, and Transjordan* (all British mandates), as well as Syria* and Lebanon* (French mandates). Mandated territories in Group B were to be governed directly by the mandate power, with only the most limited local autonomy. These territories included part of the Cameroons* and part of Togo* and Tanganyika* (British mandates), and additional portions of the Cameroons and Togo (given to France as the mandate power). Belgium received a Group B mandate for the former German colonies in Ruanda-Urundi (German East Africa*). Group C territories were governed by the mandate powers as integral portions of its own territory which, in effect, gave the power of annexation to the mandatory government. Included in this group were South West Africa* (a Union of South Africa mandate), German New Guinea* (Australia), Western Samoa* (New Zealand), Nauru* (combined mandate of Australia, Great Britain, and New Zealand), and the Caroline Islands*, Marianas*, and the Marshall Islands* (to Japan).

Under the Covenant of the League of Nations, the slave trade and trade in weapons and alcohol were formally prohibited in the mandate territories. Furthermore, the state granted a mandate was obliged to guarantee freedom of conscience and religion, subject only to the "maintenance of public order and morals," and was prohibited from building fortifications and military and naval bases, and from providing the native inhabitants with military training. (James A. Joyce, *Broken Star: The Story of the League of Nations, 1919–1939*, 1978; F. P. Waters, *A History of the League of Nations*, 1952.)

William G. Ratliff

LEBANON. Lebanon is a creation of western imperialism, carved out of Syria*
along the lines of the "divide and rule" principle. Lebanon was the home of
the Phoenicians, a people of hardy navigators who sailed around Africa and
Western Europe and may even have reached North America. Their maritime
culture flourished from around 2700 to 450 B.C. But no central government was
ever established in Phoenicia. Tripoli, Byblos, Tyre, and Sidon were independent, rival city-states. Along with Syria, the area of Lebanon was occupied by
successive invaders: Assyrians, Babylonians, Persians, Greeks, Romans, and
Byzantines. In the seventh century Christian Maronites sought shelter in Mount
Lebanon, after theological disputes with the Byzantines. After the Arab conquest
the Maronites were joined on Mount Lebanon by other minority groups, Shiites
first and then Druzes, looking for a sanctuary from Sunni Muslim persecution.
During the Crusades the Maronites established close contacts with the French
and affiliated with the Roman Church.

The Ottomans, in turn, conquered the area but allowed the area of Mount
Lebanon a large amount of autonomy, in return for tribute. Powerful families,
both Sunni and Druze, governed the area in quasi-feudal fashion. In the nineteenth
century Maronites joined the ranks of feudal families. In the seventeenth century
French missionaries arrived, facilitating later European interventions. In the
1830s, occupation by the armies of Mohammed Ali of Egypt* resulted in the
development of Beirut and other coastal ports, for trade purposes, which was
detrimental to Mount Lebanon. This, plus heavy taxation, produced peasant
uprisings in 1840 and 1857. Those revolts were quelled by the Ottomans, with
European help. In 1860 the strife between the Maronites and the Druzes turned
into a civil war, and the Druzes, who were better organized, massacred thousands
from the larger Maronite community. French troops intervened on behalf of the
Christians, occupying Beirut and Damascus. The Ottoman government established the autonomous territory of Mount Lebanon, with an Ottoman Christian
governor, but the autonomy ended at the beginning of World War I* and was
replaced by direct Ottoman rule.

The secret Sykes-Picot Treaty of 1916* between the Allies had promised
Lebanon to France. After the Ottoman defeat, there came a brief interlude when
Amir Faysal attempted to form an Arab kingdom over the territories of Syria,
Lebanon, Palestine*, and Jordan, with its capital in Damascus. French forces
moved in and ousted Faysal. Over the protests of the local inhabitants, the League
of Nations established two mandates, one over a diminished Syria, and the other
over an expanded "Greater Lebanon." Twice the size of Ottoman Lebanon, the
new mandate reduced the Maronites to a small majority by adding the Sunni
Muslim regions of the coastal area thus permitting the French to play the "divide
and rule" game between the various sects.

Under the mandate, the French used martial law to put down disturbances,
controlled the press, and opened the country to French investors and French
banks. This was accompanied by cultural imperialism, part of the French "civ-
ilizing mission," notably the use of the French language, which was willingly

accepted by the elites of the Christian community. There was also economic progress, improved public health, and a general rise in the standard of living. A population census was conducted in 1932, the last one to be held because of the delicate ethnic balance and the political consequences of any change in the ratios between the Christian and Muslim communities. In the formal political domain, the French proclaimed a Republic of Lebanon in 1926, with a constitution and a Lebanese government allowed self-governance under the French high commissioner, who had a right of veto. The French also controlled Lebanon's international relations. The French military presence checked any overt resistance. In 1936 a treaty of friendship and alliance between the two countries, proposed by the Popular Front Government in Paris, would have granted more autonomy to Lebanon but was turned down by French conservatives. Up to the beginning of World War II, there were occasional outbursts of anti-colonial violence, as Muslims wanted to be part of an independent Syria, while most Christians wanted continued French protection.

With World War II, Lebanon came under the Vichy government until June 1941 when it was occupied by British and Free French forces. In November of that year the Free French proclaimed the independence of both Syria and Lebanon. In 1943, after general elections, there was the formation of a Lebanese cabinet, the signing of a national pact providing for the distribution of positions on a communal basis, and amendments to the constitution eliminating all references to the Mandatory power. But the French, reluctant to relinquish their prerogatives, arrested the president and the cabinet for supposed anti-French activities. Riots and strikes followed, until under pressure from the Allies the French had to release the arrested politicians and agree to a timetable for the evacuation of their troops. This took place on December 31, 1946, which marked the full independence of Lebanon. (A. J. Abraham, *Lebanon: A State of Seige*, 1985; Helen Cobban, *The Making of Modern Lebanon*, 1985.)

Alain G. Marsot

LEEWARD ISLANDS. The Leeward Islands are the part of the West Indies* located at the northern end of the Lesser Antilles. The islands include Antigua*, Dominica*, and St. Kitts*-Nevis, part of the West Indies Associated States; the British Virgin Islands*, Anguilla*, and Montserrat*, which are colonies of Great Britain; Guadeloupe*, a colony of France; the southern part of St. Martin*, St. Eustatius, and Saba, part of the Netherlands Antilles*; and St. Thomas*, St. John*, and St. Croix*, part of the United States Virgin Islands. (J. O. Cutteridge, *Geography of the West Indies*, 1956.)

LEGAZPI, MIGUEL LÓPEZ DE. Miguel López de Legazpi was born in Zubarraja, Guipuzcoa, Spain. Little is known of his early life. He studied law before coming to New Spain* in 1531. Legazpi became a member of the Mexico City *cabildo* on April 4, 1531, and he was *cabildo* secretary when he was appointed to head the expedition to the Philippines*. The Philippines, contested by both Portugal and Spain, were effectively colonized by Spain through Legazpi's efforts. Four previous Spanish expeditions to the island—Ferdinand Magellan* (1519–22), García Jofre de Loaysa (1525–27), Sebastián Cabot (1526), and Alvaro de Saavedra Cerón (1527–29)—preceded Legazpi's, which was the culmination of the previous efforts.

In 1559 New Spain's Viceroy Luis de Velasco advocated another Philippines expedition to the Spanish King Philip II. The king followed this suggestion and appointed Andrés de Urdaneta, an Augustinian friar and Legazpi's relative and close friend, to head the expedition. He was with Loaysa's expedition and had prior knowledge of the islands. On his recommendation Legazpi was appointed commander of the fleet. After the viceroy's death in July 1564, the New Spain *audiencia** took command of preparations for the journey. The expedition had three objectives: find a return route to New Spain, bring back spices and riches for trade, and convert the natives to Christianity. The fleet departed from Puerto de la Navidad on November 21, 1564, and after many delays arrived on February 13, 1565, near the island of Cebu, from where further exploration of the archipelago took place.

On June 1 Legazpi sent one ship, with Urdaneta aboard, back to New Spain to get provisions and inform the *audiencia* on the progress of the expedition. Urdaneta proceeded on to Spain to inform the king. That voyage established the route which the Manila Galleons* followed during the length of the colonial period. Through this action Legazpi fulfilled one of the main purposes of the expedition. But in July 1567 Legazpi sent another ship to New Spain when no news arrived from Urdaneta. A year later, in July 1568, he sent a third ship back loaded with spices but it wrecked off the Marianas*. Between November 1566 and October 1568 the hardships which the Spanish forces endured increased through Portuguese attacks and a two month blockade. In January 1569, after the blockade, Legazpi's forces moved from Cebu to the island of Panay, which served as an important stepping stone to the later colonization of the island of Luzon*.

From Panay, Legazpi sent out an expedition under the command of Martin de Goiti, an artillery officer. They encountered Raja Soliman's Moros who put up a fierce fight, but the town of Manila* fell and Goiti took formal possession of the island of Luzon on June 6, 1570. When this force returned to Panay three ships finally arrived from New Spain with provisions and instructions confirming Legazpi as governor and captain-general of the Philippines. These instructions formally set aside Portuguese claims to the archipelago. Permanent settlement began on Cebu when forty to fifty Spaniards took up residence and established a town council. Legazpi spent the winter of 1570–1571 on the island of Panay and moved to Manila* in May 1571. After military campaigns against the natives around Manila, the Spaniards gained effective control of the islands of Cebu, Panay, Mindoro, several smaller islands, and the central area of Luzon. These military campaigns were Legazpi's last because on August 20, 1572, he died suddenly. Guido de Lavesaris, treasurer of the colony, replaced him as governor and captain-general.

The accomplishments of Legazpi's expedition are important because he succeeded where four previous expeditions had failed. Legazpi's expedition gave
Spain effective possession of the Philippines as part of the Spanish Empire*. It
defeated Portuguese claims to the islands by undertaking permanent colonization
and settlement. This gave Spain an effective base in the Far East for trade with
China. It also established the trade route between New Spain and the Philippines
which the Manilla Galleons took during the colonial period. (Edward J. Mc-
Carthy, *Spanish Beginnings in the Philippines, 1564–1572*, 1943; Jose Sanz y
Diaz, *López de Legazpi (Primero Adelantado y Conquistador de Filipinas)*,
1950.)

Carlos Pérez

LENIN, NIKOLAI (VLADIMIR ULYANOV). Nikolai Lenin was born in
1870 to a middle-class Russian family. As a student he became a passionate convert to the ideas of Karl Marx, and during his years practicing law in Samara he
was an ardent socialist. Lenin moved to St. Petersburg in 1893 where he worked
actively against the czarist government. He was exiled to Siberia in 1897 and there
he wrote his first book, *The Development of Capitalism in Russia* (1899). Lenin
left Russia for the West in 1900, and for the next seventeen years he worked to
build what he considered the inevitable communist revolution in Russia. During
those years Lenin emerged as the leader of the Bolshevik faction of the Communist Party. In 1917 he wrote his most famous and enduring book, *Imperialism:
The Highest Stage of Capitalism*. There Lenin argued that imperialism was but an
extension of capitalism, that industrial monopolies and international financial
concerns used imperialism to extend their grip on the rest of the world. He also
argued that World War I* was essentially a struggle between imperial capitalists.
Germany appeared on the imperial scene after the other imperial powers had divided up the world into spheres of influence, and Lenin believed that the disparity
between economic strength and territorial control led to war. The only answer to
imperialism, according to Lenin, was socialist revolution at home and wars of national liberation abroad. In 1917 Lenin returned to Russia as leader of the Bolshevik
Revolution. He took Russia out of World War I and eventually became chief of state
in the new Soviet Union. Lenin died in 1924. (Norman Etherington, *Theories of Imperialism. War, Conquest and Capital*, 1984.)

LEOPOLD II. Born into the Saxe-Coburg dynasty on April 9, 1835, Leopold
was the second child of the reigning Belgian monarch Leopold I, and his wife
Louise, the daughter of King Louis Philippe of France. Leopold became a
member of the Belgian senate in 1855, thus beginning his official career as an
advocate of colonial expansion. Upon the death of his father in December 1865,
Leopold was crowned king of the Belgians. In domestic affairs, Leopold II's
reign was noted for liberal reform, including the creation of free, secular, compulsory education and the withdrawal of state support from Catholic schools.
By the 1890s radical left and social democratic pressure created the Labor party.

Increasing demands for social reform led Leopold in 1893 to accede to the adoption of universal male suffrage.

King Leopold II was best know, however, for his role in the development of a Belgian colonial empire in Africa. In 1876 Leopold organized the International Association for the Exploration and Civilization of the Congo. Under its organization, Leopold's emissaries (including travelers, army officers, and missionaries) imposed unilateral agreements on local tribal chiefs. By the early 1880s Leopold's personal control extended over a vast territory encompassing much of west-central Africa. The Berlin West Africa Conference of 1884–1885* recognized Leopold as sovereign of the accumulated territory, which was given the name of Congo Free State. The subjugation of native peoples was completed in ten years, but the brutal means by which Belgian control was established earned for Leopold the scorn of much of Europe. Leopold's personal control of the region was never accepted by the local population and frequent rebellions broke out during the 1890s and early 1900s. The rebellion of the Tetela, which erupted in 1901, threatened to engulf the entire region and was suppressed only after seven years of bloody fighting. Wary of other uprisings, Leopold authorized punitive expeditions against the Azande, Baluba, Basongo, and Lunda peoples. Belgian and colonial troops annihilated the local inhabitants, burned villages, and lay waste to thousands of acres. Other massacres of the African population ensued, due largely to their alleged failure to deliver ivory, rubber, and produce, and their refusal to fulfill labor conscription quotas.

In 1908 Leopold relinquished personal rule over the Congo Free State because of repeated condemnation of his administration by the Belgian Labor Party and foreign governments, especially Great Britain. The Congo Free State was "ceded" by Leopold to the Belgian government and the administration of the colony was placed under parliamentary control. On December 17, 1909, Leopold died. (Neal Ascherson, *The King Incorporated*, 1964; Robert O. Collins, *King Leopold, England, and the Upper Nile, 1899–1909*, 1968; Ruth Slade, *King Leopold's Congo*, 1962.)

William G. Ratliff

LESOTHO. See BASUTOLAND.

LESSER ANTILLES. See ANTILLES.

LEYTE. Leyte is the eighth largest island of the Philippines*, with 2,785 square miles. It lies in the eastern Visayas (central islands) forming a barrier between the huge waves of the open Pacific, to the east, and the inland Camotes Sea to the west. Leyte is separated from the large island of Samar only by the narrow San Juanico Strait. The two islands were joined in 1973 when the 7,000-foot long Marcos bridge was inaugurated. Leyte is only a short boat ride away from other southern Philippine islands such as Bohol, Mindanao*, and Cebu. The Waray and Cebuano-speaking people number about two million. Leyte is not densely populated compared to other Philippine islands, but most of the arable land is already cultivated, so as the population grows, people move to Mindanao. There are copper deposits, but no large mines.

Magellan* landed on Leyte in 1521. The island was governed as an integral part of the Philippines under Spanish, American, and Japanese colonizers, but its remote location excluded Leyte from the mainstream of the nation's economic and cultural life. Economic growth was retarded by Moro raids on Leyte's west coast and by devastating typhoons that annually wiped out villages along the island's east coast. Only two villages grew into sizable port towns: Ormoc and Tacloban. Tacloban was opened to international trade in 1874, after which coconuts, sugar, tobacco, bananas, and hemp were cultivated for export, but Leyte lacked sufficient level land for true plantations. Most farmers and fishermen were self-sufficient. Leyte endured ferocious battles in World War II*; it was the site of Douglas MacArthur's famous return. Tacloban later gained some notoriety as the birthplace of Imelda Marcos, who showered her hometown with ostentatious development projects of little practical use. (Frederick Wernstedt and J. E. Spencer, *The Philippine Island World*, 1967.)

Ross Marlay

LIBERIA. Liberia is a republic of 43,000 square miles on the west coast of Africa, just north of the equator. Through a series of treaty negotiations, land purchases, and forced takeovers Liberia's boundries now reach inland to the Nimba Mountains. The country is crisscrossed by seven rivers flowing to the Atlantic Ocean, with several rivers helping form boundaries with Guinea* to the north, the Ivory Coast* to the east, and Sierra Leone* on the northwest. A diverse region, Liberia has a rocky and indented coast, a series of hills and swamps, and heavily forested hinterlands which remain relatively unexplored. The present-day tribesmen, who speak a variety of languages and represent 20 tribes, supposedly came from ancestors who entered Liberia as refugees to escape the late sixteenth century onslaught of Muslim tribes during the military destruction of the kingdom of Songhai on the Niger River in the region of the western Sahara.

The Portugese were the first European explorers along the Liberian coastline. Arriving in 1461, these adventurers traveled along the coast from Cape Mount to Cape Palmas establishing trade in ivory, malagueta pepper, and human slaves. In 1816 the American Colonization Society was founded in the United States to assist emancipated slaves in their return to Africa. In 1818 the society sent representatives to West Africa to identify land suitable for settlement. By an act of Congress in 1819 the United States assumed responsibility for disposing of Africans who were rescued from the slave trade and allocated $100,000 to the American Colonization Society to work toward this end. United States naval squadrons patrolled the West African coast. A group of settlers, 88 blacks and three American whites serving as leaders, set sail for Sierra Leone in 1820. The land was infertile and fever-ridden. One third of the settlers died of malaria.

The settlers were left without a designated leader and turned to Elijah Johnson, an ex-slave, for guidance. A second group of United States settlers arrived in 1821 and were also plagued with disease and attacks from the local tribes. By 1822 the first permanent settlement was established at Cape Mesurado, later named Monrovia in honor of President James Monroe. The colony was named Liberia in 1824, meaning "free." Under the management of the Society, Liberia was directed by Jehudi Ashmun, who served as agent from 1822 to 1828. Aid from the United States helped the settlers resist both European powers and threats from local tribes. A constitution for Monrovia was drawn up in 1825 and approved by the American Colonization Society. By 1838, Maryland, New York, Pennsylvania, and Mississippi had each established settlements along the coast of Liberia. In 1839 these settlements, with the exception of Cape Palmos established by Maryland in 1827, found it economically and militarily advantageous to join together to form a commonwealth under a new constitution, with Thomas Buchanan as governor.

In 1841 Joseph Jenkins Roberts, an African-American from Virginia, became governor of Liberia. With an increased number of Europeans entering the colony to exploit her natural resources, trade increased, but England and France refused to recognize the colony because it was the enterprise of a private society. The society decided in 1847 to help the descendants of the settlers establish themselves as a sovereign power. A declaration of independence was issued and the Americo-Liberians convened and brought forth a constitution modeled after that of the United States. Roberts became the first president of this newly established centralized government, the Republic of Liberia, on July 26, 1847. Liberia, the land of liberty, thus became Africa's first independent republic and was joined by Maryland's Cape Palmas settlement in 1857. The United States did not recognize Liberia's sovereignty until 1862. (Raymond L. Buell, *Liberia: A Century of Survival* 1947; Hilton A. Phillips, *Liberia's Place in Africa's Sun* 1946.)

Veula J. Rhodes

LIBYA. Today known as the Libyan Arab Republic, Libya is a large desert nation on the Mediterranean Sea in North Africa. The Phoenicians first conquered Libya in the seventh century before Christ, and in succeeding generations it was conquered by Carthage, Greece, Arabs, and finally, in 1551, by the Ottoman Turks. Libya declared its independence in 1711, but Constantinople reasserted its authority in 1835. Italy began looking greedily on Libya in 1881 after it had lost Tunisia* to the French. At the time there was a powerful political movement in Italy arguing that the country needed room for its excess population. In 1902 France and Italy signed an agreement reserving Morocco* for French control and Libya for Italian development. Early in the 1900s Italy began making a number of banking, transportation, and commercial investments in the Libyan economy.

In 1911 Italy declared war on the Ottomans, attacking Tripolitania* and Cyrenaica*. During the next several years Italian troops conquered much of northwestern Libya, naming it the colony of Tripolitania, which totaled approximately 136,000 square miles. The Treaty of Ouchy ended the war with the Turks on October 12, 1912. By that time Libya was under Italian control. In 1919 Italy split the colony into two separate units, with the eastern region, totaling 330,000 square miles, known as Cyrenaica. Its capital was the city of Benghazi.

During the 1920s and 1930s Italy settled more than 100,000 Italians in Libya, giving them the best land and virtually all the civil service posts. Italian was declared the national language. Discrimination against native Libyans was overt and intense. Libyan guerrillas fought against the Italians, but by the mid–1930s most of the resistance had been crushed. In 1934 Italy joined Tripolitania and Cyrenaica into the single colony of Libya, with the southern territory of Fezzan* known as South Tripolitania. On January 9, 1939, Italy incorporated Libya into metropolitan Italy.

During World War II* allied troops invaded Libya and fought against the Italians. Great Britain seized control of Tripolitania and Cyrenaica, while France took over Fezzan. When the war was over, the allied powers were reluctant about making Libya an independent nation. Libya's illiteracy rate was the highest in the world and its per capita income the lowest. Many doubted whether it could survive as a sovereign country. In 1949 the British and Italians proposed a tripartite division of Libya, with England getting Cyrenaica, Italy getting Tripolitania, and France getting Fezzan. But the plan smacked of imperialism and failed to gain United Nations approval. Instead, the United Nations came out in favor of independence for Libya. The United Kingdom of Libya became an independent nation on December 24, 1951, with Idris I as King. (Claudio G. Segre, *Fourth Shore. The Italian Colonization of Libya*, 1974.)

LINE ISLANDS. The Line Islands are coral atolls located in the central Pacific. The largest of the Line Islands is Christmas Island, approximately 1,150 miles south of Hawaii*. Throughout much of the nineteenth and twentieth centuries, the Line Islands were known for their phosphate and copra production. The United States seized Palmyra* in 1898 during the Spanish-American War*, Kingman Reef in 1922, and Jarvis* in 1930. The other islands became British territory between 1866 and 1889. Fanning and Washington Islands became part of the Gilbert and Ellice Island Colony in 1916, as did Christmas Island in 1919. Washington, Fanning, Christmas, Malden, Starbuck, Vostok, Caroline, and Flint became part of the Republic of Kiribati* in 1979. (John W. Coulter, *The Pacific Dependencies of the United States*, 1957; Stuart Inder, *Pacific Islands Yearbook*, 1978.)

LOI-CADRE. In the spring of 1957, during the waning days of the Fourth Republic, a "framework" (*loi-cadre*) was created within which reforms were instituted in the French colonies by the Socialist Minister of Overseas France, Gaston Deferre. This illegal tactic of bypassing the legislature was adopted both in the interest of speed (given the recent independence of the Gold Coast* and the threat of Algerian-style resistance spreading elsewhere) and expediency to avoid an impasse in the Chamber over the specific details of the reforms.

The most important changes were the introduction of universal suffrage and the elimination of separate voting by European minorities in the colonies. Institutionally, the *loi-cadre* gave important legislative powers to territorial assemblies which, in turn, were empowered to elect government councils. Initially the council member with the highest number of votes became vice president and the governor served as president, but the following year the governors were removed from the councils. Although the division of power between the governors and indigenous councils was vague, an immediate effect was unmistakeably to limit the power of colonial governors.

The more important overall effect of the reforms was to grant indigenous populations a greatly increased role in political and administrative affairs. Politicians and political parties turned to problems of governance, while new civil servants were recruited into the administration from the local population.

At the time, Deferre declared that the *loi-cadre* was not intended to be the first step toward independence but rather, "to maintain and reinforce for many years to come the necessary union between metropolitan France and the peoples of the overseas territories." DeGaulle's policies in the new Fifth Republic soon rendered that prophecy false. (William B. Cohen, *Rulers of Empire*, 1971.)

William H. Schneider

LONDON CONVENTION OF 1884. Signed by Great Britain and the Transvaal* Republic on February 27, 1884, the purpose of the London Convention of 1884 was the abolition of the suzerainty Britain had held over the Transvaal Republic since the Pretoria Convention of 1881. In effect, the London Convention dropped the preamble of the Pretoria Convention, which had promised self-government for the Transvaal, but only under British supervision. All that Britain retained under the new agreement was a clause in Article IV that the British government's approval had to be obtained before the Transvaal Republic could sign a treaty or enter into any agreement with any state or nation (the Orange Free State* was excepted) or with any native tribe to the east or west of its borders. If the British government did not respond to any such request for a period of six months, the Transvaal government was allowed to act freely. The other major clauses of the 1884 Convention concerned colonial boundaries, freedom of religion, free trade, criminal procedures, and the treatment of the native African population. (Donald Denoon, *Southern Africa Since 1800*, 1972; D. M. Schreuder, *The Scramble for Southern Africa, 1877–1895*, 1980.)

William G. Ratliff

LOUISBOURG. Louisbourg became an important part of the French Empire* after the Treaty of Utrecht*, which ended the War of the Spanish Succession and transferred Acadia* and Newfoundland* from France to England in 1713.

After the cession, the French needed a port with facilities to repair and resupply their Atlantic fleet in the western part of that ocean. The location of Louisbourg on the southeastern coast of Cape Breton Island also provided a convenient headquarters for a fleet which could guard New France* against further encroachment by the English, protect the French fishing fleet, and threaten New England*. The French began construction of Louisbourg in 1713 as a combined military garrison and governmental and economic capital of the region which included Cape Breton and Prince Edward Island.* In 1715 the new settlement had only 720 inhabitants, but by the early 1750s approximately 4,000 people lived there, and it was the fourth busiest North American port, following New York, Boston, and Philadelphia.

Unfortunately for the French, however, success in Louisbourg caused concern in New England. The threat to their security posed by a strong French naval base and port to their north led many New Englanders to begin considering attacks to neutralize it. Raids conducted by French privateers headquartered there further strengthened their concern. The War of the Austrian Succession gave the New Englanders the excuse they needed to attack Louisbourg. Soldiers from the Louisbourg garrison captured the British settlement of Canso, Nova Scotia*, in 1744. Militia Colonel William Pepperell, a Kittery, Massachusetts* merchant, led a group of volunteers in a retaliatory attack on Louisbourg supported by the British fleet in 1745. Louisbourg was unable to withstand Pepperell's attack. Fortifications were in poor repair, and only a few months before the soldiers stationed there had rioted to protest their lack of weapons, ammunition, adequate clothing, and food. Louisbourg surrendered after a two-month seige. A French counterattack failed in 1746.

The strategic importance of Louisbourg in the minds of French officials was demonstrated by French Minister of the Marine Maurepas's agreement to yield territory captured by the French in Madras and the Netherlands in exchange for it. The Treaty of Aix-la-Chapelle* transferred Louisbourg back to the French in 1748. Permanent French loss of Louisbourg occurred in 1758 as part of the Seven Years' War. British Prime Minister William Pitt* ordered an attack on the fortress. British commander Jeffrey Amherst beseiged the town with 8,000 troops, but it still required sixty days and heavy bombardment to reduce its defenses. The Louisbourg campaign had lasted long enough to delay the British attack on Quebec* for a year. After the fall of Louisbourg, Quebec (in 1759), and Montreal (in 1760), the French New World empire in the north fell completely to the British, a transfer made official in the Treaty of Paris of 1763*. In 1760 Pitt ordered the complete destruction of Louisbourg. British military miners subsequently buried explosive charges within the fortress walls, and as they tore those walls apart, Louisbourg's usefulness as a French military outpost symbolically disappeared. (J. Bartlet Brebner, *Canada*, 1960; W. J. Eccles, *France in America*, 1972; George M. Wrong, *The Rise and Fall of New France*, reprint edition, 1970.)

LOUISIANA PURCHASE. By virtue of her extensive exploration of the region, France claimed the land west of the Mississippi River, known as Louisiana, until 1762. In the secret Treaty of Fontainebleau, France then transferred title to Spain. Thus, during the 1790s, the United States negotiated Pinckney's Treaty with Spain, securing the right of access and deposit at New Orleans, a matter crucial to the United States for the development of the west. In the secret Treaty of San Ildefonso of 1800, France secured the retrocession of the territory from Spain, although France did not take possession of it. When President Thomas Jefferson first learned of the retrocession, he wrote the United States minister to France, Robert R. Livingston, expressing his grave concern for the future of access to the Mississippi if France took control. Congress appropriated $2 million to be offered to France for purchase of New Orleans. If the purchase of New Orleans was refused by the French, then at least a treaty guaranteeing access was to be attempted. If that too failed, Jefferson clearly implied that the United States would have little choice but "to marry ourselves to the British fleet and nation," to secure Louisiana for the "common purposes of the united British and American nations."

Hoping to drive a wedge between the United States and Great Britain, Napoleon Bonaparte offered the entire territory to the United States for the sum of 60 million francs. Convinced that the opportunity should not be neglected for lack of authority, the American negotiators agreed to the terms. A treaty and two conventions, dated April 30, 1803, were signed early in May. The treaty ceded the Louisiana Territory to the United States, provided for the citizenship and guaranteed the rights of the people in the territory, upheld Spanish and Indian treaty rights in the area, guaranteed most-favored-nation status to Spain and France in New Orleans, and provided for United States assumption of French debts owed citizens of the United States. Although Jefferson had some constitutional doubts about the treaty, since the Constitution did not specifically delegate to the federal government the power to purchase territory, he decided to support the purchase, which the Senate approved on October 20, 1803. For the modest sum of $15 million, the United States acquired about 828,000 square miles of land between the Mississippi River and the Rocky Mountains, although the exact boundaries were not determined. The Louisiana Purchase doubled the size of the nation and solved forever the problems of access to and control of the Mississippi River. (William Macdonald, *Select Documents Illustrative of the History of the United States*, 1920; Thomas G. Paterson et al., *American Foreign Policy*, Volume I, 1983.)

Joseph M. Rowe, Jr.

LOWER CANADA. See QUEBEC.

LOYALTY ISLANDS. The Loyalty Islands are coral islands tied politically to New Caledonia*, a French Overseas Territory. They are located approximately 65 miles northwest of New Caledonia. Ouvea, Lifou, and Mare are the principal islands in the group. Antoine de Bruni d'Entrecasteaux*, the French explorer, visited the Loyalty Islands in 1793, as did Jules Dumont d'Urville* in 1827 and 1840. Protestant and Catholic missionaries from England and France began arriving in the islands in the 1840s, creating bitter cultural rivalries among the native population. In 1866 France took control of the Loyalty Islands and in 1946 attached them to New Caledonia. (Cyril S. Belshaw, *Island Administration in the South West Pacific: Government and Reconstruction in New Caledonia, the New Hebrides, and the British Solomon Islands, 1950*; K. R. Howe, *The Loyalty Islands: A History of Culture Contacts 1840–1900*, 1977.)

LUANDA. Luanda is a coastal town in Angola*. In 1641, the Dutch captured Luanda, driving the Portuguese into the interior of the colony. For the next several years, the Dutch used Luanda and other Angolan port cities to export slaves to their Brazilian plantations. But in 1648 the Portuguese regained the upper hand in Angola and expelled the Dutch. See ANGOLA.

LUMUMBA, PATRICE. The first prime minister of the Republic of the Congo*, Patrice Lumumba was educated in Protestant and Catholic missionary schools and worked as a postal clerk in Stanleyville before moving to Leopoldville and becoming active in the *Mouvement National Congolais* (MNC). Lumumba was charismatic, an eloquent speaker, fluent in each of the Congo's major languages as well as French. Consequently, he rapidly rose to prominence in the MNC. He was one of a few Congolese politicians who believed and worked for a unified, independent Congo and by 1959 was the nation's only truly national political figure. Lumumba quickly won the animosity of Europeans living in the Congo, Belgium, and the United States, and envious political rivals. In the 1960 general elections, Lumumba's MNC party won 41 of 137 seats in the national assembly, two and a half times the number of its nearest rival and more than five times the number of secessionist leader Moise Tshomsbe*. Lumumba was elected prime minister and Joseph Kasavubu, a low-keyed and consistently under-estimated moderate nationalist, became president with Lumumba's tacit support.

The Lumumba-Kasavubu government had a short, stormy life. Belgium and Congolese Europeans continuously maneuvered against the government, encouraging mutiny within the Congolese army and secessionist movements in Katanga Province under Tshombe and southern Kasai Province. Lumumba attempted to end Tshombe's secession efforts, but the presence of Belgian "advisors" and white mercenaries prevented a successful Congolese army offensive. Western nations and the United Nations turned a deaf ear to his entreaties for assistance for two reasons. First, Lumumba was seen as too "radical," too independent minded, too much the nationalist, and too much the leader for the tastes of Western Europe and the United States. Second, while Western nations favored a unified Congo, many were sympathetic to the "strongly pro-Western" Tshombe. They wanted Katanga to remain a part of the Congo, but were unwilling to destroy Tshombe's political standing in the process.

When Lumumba turned to the Soviet Union, which offered trucks and other military equipment to his army, President Kasavubu dismissed Lumumba from office. Colonel Joseph Mobutu led a coup when the national assembly reinstated Lumumba as prime minister. Lumumba was placed under house arrest under the protection of United Nations* forces from Ghana as his supporters began organizing a new government in Stanleyville. After escaping house arrest, Lumumba was arrested by Mobutu's soldiers and taken to Thysville. While imprisoned, Lumumba's political authority grew, moving his adversaries, including the United States, to conclude that their designs for the Congo would not be safe as long as Lumumba was alive. Consequently, the Central Intelligence Agency authorized his assassination—neither the first, nor the last time the CIA would order the death of chief of state. Under Mobutu's orders, Lumumba was flown from Thysville to Elisabethville, the Katanga capital, and turned over to a detachment of Kantangan troops which included white mercenaries. He was then placed in a vehicle, driven into the jungle and killed. A CIA agent loaded his body into the trunk of his car and drove through Lubumbashi trying to find a place to dump it. (Madeleine Kalb, *The Congo Cables*, 1982; Rene Lermachand, ''Patrice Lumumba'' in W. A. E. Skurnik, ed., *African Political Thought: Lumumba, Nkrumah, and Toure*, 1968; John Stockwell, *In Search of Enemies*, 1978.)

Samuel Freeman

LUZON. Luzon, with an area of more than 40,000 square miles, is the largest island in the Philippines*. It is so dominant that its history is nearly coincident with that of the nation as a whole. Luzon may be divided into the following regions: (1) Manila* and environs, the densely populated capital where nearly all important events in Philippine history have taken place; (2) Central Luzon, the only extensive plain in the islands, where land tenancy disputes have erupted into open rebellion; (3) Southern Tagalog, the fertile coconut-growing region south of Manila, home to many writers and political leaders; (4) Ilocos, the narrow northwestern coastal plain of infertile soil and hard-driving emigrants; (5) The northern cordillera, where non-Christian tribes who do not consider themselves Filipinos eke out a precarious existence while their mountains are rapidly denuded; (6) the Cagayan Valley, whose central river flows northward to the sea at the Babuyan Channel; and (7) Bicol, physically and culturally separated on the extreme southeast peninsula of Luzon.

The Philippines were ruled by three imperial powers between 1571 and 1946: Spain, the United States, and Japan. Each controlled the archipelago from Luzon, and Luzon from Manila. That city, with the finest harbor in the Far East, a fertile agricultural hinterland, and a strategic location at the center of all communication and transportation in the islands, dominates the political, cultural, educational, commercial, and industrial life of the nation. The imperialists came by ship, of course, so had no use for an inland capital. Manila was where Filipinos met the world, and where global commerce entered the islands.

Luzon developed various regional export economies in the nineteenth century in response to the new global market created by development of steamships and the opening of the Suez Canal* (1869). Bicol specialized in abaca. Ilocos grew marvelous tobacco. The Southern Tagalog area was planted to coconuts. Sugar estates were established where the swamps of central Luzon were drained to create big fields. Rice and fish remained the staple diet of Filipinos. Under Spanish rule, most large estates were owned by friars. When America took over, these lands fell into private hands. The Philippines has never known effective land reform.

Today Luzon exhibits all the pathologies that can thrive on a tropical island transformed by a colonial economy. It has little industry. Its export crops never bring in enough money to pay for imports, so the balance of payments registers a steady outflow. Luzon's population is much too heavily concentrated in the former colonial capital, placing an impossible burden on services. The land itself is scarred. Protective rain forests that once covered Luzon's mountains, soaking up monsoon rain then releasing it gradually during the dry season, have been cut down almost everywhere. The soil has laterized (turned to brick), so rain runs off immediately. There are floods from May to September, and drought the rest of the year. (Alfred W. McCoy and Edilberto de Jesus, *Philippine Social History*, 1982; Frederick Wernstedt and J. E. Spencer, *The Philippine Island World*, 1967.)

Ross Marlay

LYAUTEY, MARSHALL. Marshall L. H. Lyautey (1854–1934) was probably the most original ideologist of French imperialism. As "résident général" (high commissioner) of the Moroccan Protectorate (1912–1916, 1917–1925), he implemented a specific model for colonialism in the Cherifian empire. A theorist, he laid down his "principles of action" in a Grand Rapport (1916, addressed to the war minister): an intensive program of public works (roads, harbors, hospitals, schools, restoration of Almoravid monuments), the development of local industries in correlation with the training of skilled indigenous labor, and trade fairs to promote Moroccan industry and agriculture. He initiated the redistribution of land to Moroccans and set up cooperatives and land banks to combat usury. On a political level Lyautey strove to maintain the religious prestige of the sultan, seeing the Western Caliphate as an element of cohesion for the whole Maghreb and a future counterweight to the collapse of the Ottoman Caliphate, in which he was perceptive enough to foresee the rise of Islamic integrism: enlightened Morocco* would have to play a major role in a shattered Islamic world. He stressed the necessity of granting Arabs a "personal status" (based on Muslim principles, as opposed to French Civil Code status) and empowering the Moroccan government ("Maghzen") to deal with all religious, educational, judiciary, and welfare institutions related to the Moroccans themselves.

Lyautey moved cautiously in the direction of European colonization, first selecting a limited number of officers, entrepreneurs, and agriculturalists to modernize the economy. Colonization fell into four categories: small holdings in the vicinity of the major towns, settlements near railway stations, large holdings reserved to French settlers and locals, with the backing of private capital, and "great colonization" reserved to chartered companies. He employed his best officers, carefully chosen in France, to run *bureaux indigènes*, and established a schooling system for the offsprings of leading families, thus paving the way to the promotion of a new class of administrators. The "Moroccan economic miracle" attracted so many settlers (40,000) that his prudent policy could no longer be acceptable to France, since it ran contrary to the French Radical-Socialist conception of assimilation and to the Protectorate rule which relied heavily on French settlers, an imported bureaucracy, and the limited development of natural and human local resources. Lyautey, supported by Sultan Moulay Yussef (1912–1927), simply aimed at making Morocco a model for developing countries: he drew his conception of social development from nineteenth-century social catholicism (Albert de Mun) that emphasized a belief in natural hierarchy, social solidarity, and corporatism: "Colonial action is social action." After resigning from his post, he published *Paroles d'Action* (1927) in which he proposed Morocco as a model to the moral and economic reconstruction of France, since it "offers the spectacle of a human group where men of various origins, moeurs, professions and races, pursue an identical ideal of living together, without renouncing their individual beliefs." Lyautey's unique colonial doctrine was in fact deeply rooted in the French royalist tradition, which, from 1900 to 1930, shaped, along with Marxism, French intellectual elites. (L. H. Lyautey, *Du Rôle social de l'Officier*, 1927; P. Lyautey, éd., *Lyautey l'Africain*, 1956.)

Philippe-Joseph Salazar

M

MACAO. The Provincia da Macau currently has the legal status of an overseas province of Portugal. But after 450 years of ambiguous identity, the small territory of 6 square miles is scheduled to revert to full Chinese sovereignty on December 20, 1999. Macao consists of a peninsula and two tiny offshore islands, Taipa and Coloane (also spelled Colowan and Kuoloane). Macao's significance derives from its location near Hong Kong* and the rich south Chinese province of Guangdong. Guangzhou (Canton*), the capital of Guangdong, is forty miles up the Pearl River from Macao. Macao stands now as the last vestige of Portugal's once-extensive colonial empire, but in the 1500s it held promise of greater things. The Portuguese saw in Asia a vast field for trade and missionary work, and developed Macao as a base for both. By 1557 the Chinese allowed them to settle and erect factories, but they also isolated foreigners behind a barrier gate, which still stands. The Portuguese accepted this restriction in the hope of using Macao as a stepping-stone to Japan as well as to China.

The local Portuguese administration was virtually sovereign until the nineteenth century, governing the local Portuguese while Chinese residents of Macao remained subjects of the Chinese emperor. Portuguese power faded, while Britain and France expanded their empires. For a short time in the early 1800s the British occupied Macao, but they viewed with horror the "mixed element" of Macao's population—a natural result of the Portuguese lack of racial prejudice. The British were more interested in nearby Hong Kong, which possessed a superb harbor free of the silting affecting Macao.

When Britain and France forced the declining Manchu dynasty to open numerous "treaty ports" to world commerce, Macao's significance further declined. The Portuguese declared Macao a free port in 1845, to compete with Hong Kong, but Macao's economy depended on illicit activities such as smuggling gold and opium. Its sea breezes attracted vacationing British civil servants from Hong Kong, who also enjoyed gambling, banned in the more staid British crown colony. Macao's reputation slipped even further when the "coolie" trade flourished, until notorious abuses caused the Chinese and British jointly to force the Portuguese to put a stop to it in 1874. In 1887 China confirmed Portuguese occupation of Macao in perpetuity in return for a Portuguese promise never to "alienate" the territory.

Macao's condition as an isolated, tranquil colonial backwater continued until the 1960s, when the city became caught up in the storms of the mainland's Great Proletarian Cultural Revolution. The city initially sheltered many refugees, but in 1966 the Communist Chinese applied pressure in the form of riots among the Chinese population of Macao. The Portuguese then started repatriating refugees and also outlawed political activity by Kuomintang elements.

Portugal itself experienced a revolution in 1974 that brought socialist army officers to power. They sought to return Macao to China, but were surprised to find that China did not want it—for the time being. The Chinese calculus seemed to be that the status of Macao was strictly secondary to that of Hong Kong. Agreement was reached on March 26, 1987, that Macao is to become a "special administrative region" of the People's Republic of China at the end of this century, and its inhabitants (98 percent of whom are Chinese) will become citizens of China, but that Macao will be guaranteed a fifty-year period in which it may retain its capitalist economy. (C. R. Boxer, *Fidalgoes in the Far East, 1570–1750: Fact and Fancy in the History of Macao*, 1948; and *The Portugese Seaborne Empire*, 1969.)

Ross Marlay

MACASSAR. See MAKASSAR.

MACHINE GUN. The first machine gun appeared during the American Civil War. It was a hand-cranked, multi-barreled firearm known as the "Gatling gun." European versions were known as the Mitrailleuse, Nordenfelt, Gardner, and Hotchkiss. But the first reliable machine gun was invented in 1884 by Hiram S. Maxim, a one-barrel, smokeless weapon with gas pressure loading which could fire eleven rounds per second. The British used Gatling guns against the Zulus in 1879 and the Ashanti in 1874. Colonial troops in the French, British, Dutch, Portuguese, and German colonies all had machine guns in their possession by 1900. The gun proved decisive in the defeat of native armies. (Daniel R. Headrick, *The Tools of Empire. Technology and European Imperialism in the Nineteenth Century*, 1981.)

MADAGASCAR. The island of Madagascar is located 180 miles east of the Mozambique* coast. Its population reflects the waves of immigration from the Malayo-Indonesian archipelago, Africa, and Arabia. The first European landing was made by Dom Franciso de Alameda on February 1, 1508. Late in the sixteenth century, the development of Dutch trade from the Cape of Good Hope to the East Indies, with their exploitation of Mauritius* ebony, made Madagascar important as a source of food and as a slave labor reservoir. Until 1644 several short-lived British expeditions searched vainly for gold. Between 1643 and 1674 Fort Dauphin* and a settlement on the island of St. Marie* represented the first organized French attempts to colonize Madagascar, but native resistance dislodged the colonies. During the eighteenth century, European and American pirates used the Madagascar shore. The need of slaves brought more European intervention in Madagascar in the eighteenth century. In 1750 France permanently colonized St. Marie. They also established several other trading posts along the east coast of Madagascar.

The French were unable to penetrate the interior because of the powerful Hova kingdom. King Radama I (1793–1828) was hostile toward the French and instead invited the British into his homeland. Missionaries from the London Missionary Society arrived in 1820 and worked among the Hova, and British military officials helped train the Hova army. But when Radama died in 1828, an anti-European reaction swept through Madagascar, which resulted in persecution of Protestant missionaries and boycotts of British trade goods. Not until 1861 when Radama II came to the throne did political conditions for Europeans, especially the French whom he favored, improve. But traditionalists at the Hova court assassinated Radama II in 1863, precipitating a dynastic struggle and more anti-European rioting. The French intervened directly in the 1880s and in 1896 declared Madagascar to be a French colony.

After World War I, Madagascar nationalists like Jean Ralaimongo began demanding independence from France, and the Great Depression of the 1930s, which brought extraordinary suffering to Madagascar's towns and cities, further alienated the native population from the French colonial administration. After World War II, the first native political party, the *Mouvement Democratique de la Renovation Malgache* (MDRM), appeared. Under the Constitution of the Fourth French Republic in 1946, Madagascar became an overseas territory of France. But the imperial adjustments France was willing to make did not satisfy the Malagasy nationalists. Despite the MDRM's success in the 1946–1947 elections, a revolt exploded in 1947 in the Mananjary region on the coast where French land expropriations and forced labor had been especially exploitive. French troops brutally suppressed the rebellion. From 1947 to 1954 Madagascar experienced an iron-fisted administration along with a series of elections without the MDRM.

But the successful Vietnamese revolt against France in 1954 damaged forever the French Empire*. France moved quickly to increase self-government in her African colonies. A second native political party, the *Parti Social Democrate* (PSD), was founded by Philibert Tsiranana. In 1956, when the French government passed the *Loi Cadre** extending universal suffrage to the territories, Madagascar nationalism received another boost. On May 27, 1957, Tsiranana was elected vice president of Madagascar's first government council. During the 1958 visit of the premier of France, General Charles de Gaulle, Tsiranana solicited the nullification of the Law of Annexation of 1896 and the restoration of statehood to Madagascar. On September 28, 1958, a colony-wide referendum voted overwhelmingly for independence. On October 14, 1958, the PSD declared Madagascar an autonomous republic within the French Community*, with the new name of the Malagasy Republic. Tsiranana was elected president on May 1, 1959. The French parliament ratified the agreement on June 9, 1960. The proclamation of Madagascar's complete independence came on June 26, 1960. (Nigel Heseltine, *Madagascar*, 1971; Mutibwa Phares Mukasa, *The Malagasy and the Europeans: Madagascar's Foreign Relations, 1861–1895*, 1974.)

Said El Mansour Cherkaoui

MADEIRA. The Madeira Islands are an archipelago in the North Atlantic Ocean, 520 miles southwest of Portugal and 400 miles west of Morocco*. It consists of two inhabited islands, Madeira and Porto Santo, and two groups of uninhabited islets—the Desertas and the Selvagens. Their total land mass is 307 square miles. Although the Madeiras were probably reached by Genoese traders in the fourteenth century, the first recorded landfall came in 1418 when the Portuguese explorer João Goncalves Zarco was driven there by a storm while he was exploring the West African coast. The Portuguese navigator Tristao Vaz visited there in 1419. Prince Henry the Navigator claimed the islands for Portugal. They were uninhabited, and in 1420 Henry began colonizing them. Sugarcane from Sicily and grapes from Cyprus* created a plantation economy in the islands. Between 1580 and 1640 the Madeira Islands, along with all of Portugal, were under Spanish domination, but after Portuguese sovereignty was restored, the Madeira Islands became known as the Funchal District, one of Portugal's 22 political subdivisions. After the 1974 revolution in Portugal, the Madeiras sought greater political autonomy, and in 1976 they received their own Regional Assembly. (B. W. Diffie and G. D. Winius, *Foundations of the Portuguese Empire*, 1977; Francis M. Rogers, *Atlantic Islanders of the Azores and Madeira*, 1979.)

MADRAS. Madras is a major port city on the east coast of India*. The city had its beginnings in 1640 when Francis Day of the British East India Company* obtained from a local ruler the right to build a fort there. Completed in 1640 and named St. George, Madras prospered under the monopolistic direction of the company. In 1653 Madras gained recognition as an independent presidency of the company. The French captured Madras in 1746 but in the Treaty of Aix-la-Chapelle of 1748* it was restored to the British, in whose hands it remained until Indian independence. (Peter Kemp, *The Oxford Companion to Ships and the Sea*, 1976.)

MADRID CONFERENCE OF 1880. The Madrid Conference of 1880 was an attempt by the European colonial powers to extend their influence in North Africa. The conference was convened in Madrid from May 19 to July 3, 1880, in order to address complaints levied by the government of Morocco* alleging violations of the French-Moroccan Agreement of 1863. This treaty had established a system of *samsars* (brokers) who were employed by the European governments for the purpose of circumventing Moroccan laws against European purchases of land and other property. In effect, the French-Moroccan Agreement established *samsar* immunity from local law (the *samsars* were technically under the sole jurisdiction of their respective employer's legation) and exemption from taxation. By 1875, through approximately 2,000 *samsar* "brokers," European interests in Morocco had trebled. In 1876 the Moroccan government appealed to the European diplomats in Tangiers to help put an end to the corrupt practices. Conferences among the resident diplomats failed in both 1877 and 1879, whereupon the British minister, Sir John Drummond Hay, proposed an international conference for the following year. The Madrid Conference of 1880, however, which included delegations from Britain, Spain, Portugal, Belgium, France, and Germany, refused to consider any alteration in the *samsar* policy. The major provisions of the 1863 French-Moroccan Agreement were upheld and, in effect, European influence in Morocco and the rest of North Africa increased. In addition, the internationalization of the "Morocco question" allowed both Britain and Germany to exert increased influence in the region, largely at the expense of France. (J. C. Hurewitz, ed., *The Middle East and North Africa in World Politics*, Vol. I, 1975; Magali Morsy, *North Africa, 1800–1900: A Survey from the Nile to the Atlantic*, 1984.)

William G. Ratliff

MAGELLAN, FERDINAND (FERNAO DE MAGALHAES). Ferdinand Magellan was born in northern Portugal in 1480. He became a page to the Portuguese queen in 1492, and in 1505 he sailed to India* with Francisco de Almeida. In 1509 Magellan was present at the Portuguese defeat at Malacca*, but he returned with the Portuguese armada which reconquered it. Magellan went back to Portugal in 1513, but when he was charged with official corruption, he lost the support of King Manuel and went instead to Spain. In Spain he convinced King Charles I (Charles V*) that the Moluccas were within Spain's sphere of influence under the Treaty of Tordesillas of 1494. He also told Charles that the Moluccas* could be reached by sailing west across the Pacific rather than trying to make it past Portuguese patrols on the the Cape of Good Hope. Charles I provided him with five ships, and Magellan left Spain in September 1519. He went first to the Canary Islands* and then down the West African coast. From present-day Sierra Leone*, the expedition crossed the Atlantic to Rio de Janeiro. Magellan then began his search for the strait leading to the Pacific Ocean. On October 21, 1520, he entered what is today the Straits of Magellan and spent a month getting through it before reaching the Pacific Ocean.

Suffering from a dearth of water and provisions, as well as from scurvy, they headed northwest to the Marianas* and landed there in March 1521. Several weeks later Magellan made it to the Philippines*, where he was killed on

April 27, 1521, in a fight with local natives. The ships reached the Moluccas in December 1521 but left as soon as they heard that a Portuguese naval force was nearby. They sailed around the Cape of Good Hope and reached Spain on September 8, 1522, with one ship and seventeen men. In addition to being the first Europeans to sail around the globe, Magellan's voyage had established Spain's claim to Argentina, Chile, the Marianas, and the Philippines. (Samuel Eliot Morison, *The European Discovery of America: The Southern Voyages, A.D., 1492–1616*, 1974; Charles McKew Parr, *Ferdinand Magellan, Circumnavigator*, 1964.)

MAHAN, ALFRED THAYER. Alfred Thayer Mahan, an officer in the United States Navy, was born September 27, 1840, at the U.S. Military Academy at West Point, New York. His father, Colonel Dennis Hart Mahan, was an influential professor at West Point. Alfred grew up at West Point but to his father's dismay decided to pursue a naval career. The elder Mahan, to his credit, acquiesced when he realized he could not change his son's mind. Young Mahan entered the Naval Academy in September 1856 and graduated second in his class in June 1859. He served in a variety of commands. Mahan preferred shore duty where he had the time and facilities to pursue his interest in naval history. The most important assignment of his career was his appointment to teach at the new Naval War College in Newport, R.I., from 1886 to 1893.

Teaching at the War College was important, but the main contribution of his work there was the publication of his famous books on seapower. *The Influence of Seapower Upon History, 1660–1783* (1890), and its companion work, *The Influence of Seapower Upon the French Revolution and Empire, 1793–1812*, (1892), made his reputation as the foremost naval scholar of his time. Although not widely read at home, these books were studied thoroughly by naval officers in other countries, notably in Great Britain and Germany. His books analyzed in a comprehensive way the reasons for the rise of the British Navy to its commanding position among the world's navies, including geographic, political, and economic factors. His elucidation of the role of the merchant marine as a foundation for British naval dominance, together with his exposition of the role of trade and colonies both as a cause and a result of naval dominance, were distinctly original contributions which established a comprehensive concept of seapower as he defined it. Mahan's ideas on seapower were particularly influential in convincing German leaders of the importance of building a powerful navy and in providing the British Admiralty with the arguments it needed to persuade parliament to vote naval appropriations sufficient to allow the Royal Navy to maintain its superiority in the face of the German threat.

While Mahan's writings on seapower did not become widely popular in the United States, they influenced a small but powerful group of men, the most important of whom were Theodore Roosevelt and Henry Cabot Lodge. Roosevelt in particular became an advocate of seapower. He and Mahan maintained a close correspondence and friendship, and Roosevelt called upon him frequently to lend his expertise on many naval questions during Roosevelt's presidency.

Mahan reluctantly went back to sea after 1892, serving as commanding officer of the U.S.S. *Chicago* until 1895. On November 17, 1896, he was formally retired from the naval service, although he continued to serve in various missions for the government until his death. Perhaps the best-known of these missions was as an American delegate to the first Hague Disarmament Conference in 1899, where he took positions opposing the prohibition of the use of gas in warfare and the establishment of compulsory arbitration of international disputes. He continued to write and to publish articles and books on naval matters, his expertise being avidly sought on naval questions arising out of the Spanish-American War, the establishment of an American empire, the Russo-Japanese War, and the naval armaments race in the period prior to World War I. Yet he managed to continue historical research; his last published historical work, *The Major Operations of the Navies in the War of American Independence*, appeared in the autumn of 1913. Increasing ill-health forced him to curtail his writing commitments, and he died on December 1, 1914. (William E. Livezey, *Mahan on Sea Power*, rev. ed. 1980; Robert Seager, *Alfred Thayer Mahan: The Man and His Letters*, 1977.)

Ernest Andrade, Jr.

MAKASSAR. Makassar (also spelled Makasar, Mangkasar, and Macassar, modern name Ujung Pandang) is a port on the southwest coast of the irregularly shaped Indonesian island of Celebes* (Sulawesi), facing west toward the Makassar Strait and the Java Sea. It lacks a productive hinterland, as there is only a small plain between the coast and rugged mountains, and coral reefs make the harbor itself somewhat dangerous, but Makassar nonetheless occupies a very strategic location. From Makassar a navy can dominate the entire maritime world of eastern Indonesia*. The Makassarese people, who speak their own distinct language, live by fishing, farming and trade. They were influenced by Buddhism and Hinduism, but these Indic religions were grafted onto native animism, and then subordinated to Islam after 1605, when the King of the Makassarese Gowa state converted and took the title sultan.

Makassar was an expanding military and commercial power, frequently at war with its archrival, the Buginese state of Bone, when the sultan allowed the new Dutch East India Company* to build a small trading station in 1607. This led to trouble, because the Dutch were only interested in monopolizing the lucrative Moluccan spice trade. They took it poorly when the Makassarese allowed the English and the Danes to build "factories" in 1613 and 1618. To compel Makassarese acceptance of their hegemony, the Dutch waged a series of military campaigns. Peace treaties were signed in 1637, 1655, and 1660, but hostilities continued. Finally, in 1667 the Dutch naval commander Cornelius Speelman, with Buginese help, defeated Makassar and compelled Sultan Hasanuddin to sign the humiliating Treaty of Bongaya. Makassar promised not to trade with any of Holland's European rivals. The city-state also had to pay a massive indemnity and accept a Dutch governor. Deprived of an outlet for their skills, some Makassarese seamen turned to piracy while others hired on with the Dutch company itself. Makassar's importance eroded. The spice trade declined and the Dutch turned to growing coffee on Java*. The Makassarese kept right on fighting the Buginese, and even invaded Java in 1765. Nor did they hesitate to attack the British, who occupied Celebes during the Napoleonic Wars. The Netherlands Indies* government finally pacified Makassar in 1860.

The Dutch did not greatly change Makassar's economy. Some small plantations produced copra, resins, spices, coffee, and rubber, but there was not much level land. Makassar did export tropical hardwood, and also trafficked in Buginese slaves. When world commerce intruded on the Indonesian island world in the late nineteenth century, Makassar became an important distribution point for goods traded between eastern Indonesia and the rest of the world. Some Arabs, Chinese, and Europeans came to live in Makassar. Its population reached 40,000 by 1915, and is more than ten times that today.

Makassar's strategic location figured in naval battles between the Allies and the Japanese during World War II. When the war ended, and the Indonesians declared independence, the Dutch made Makassar the capital of their puppet state of East Indonesia. After the Dutch surrendered in 1949 the independent Makassarese unsuccessfully resisted incorporation into Indonesia. The Indonesians made Makassar the capital of South Celebes and renamed the city Ujung Pandang. Sultan Hasanuddin University was established in 1956. Some factories have been built, but few roads yet connect Makassar to the interior of Celebes. (M. C. Ricklefs, *A History of Modern Indonesia*, 1981.)

Ross Marlay

MALABAR COAST. The Malabar Coast is located in southwestern India* on the Arabian Sea. In the early 1650s the Dutch began to establish a commercial presence there, primarily to gain a foothold in the lucrative pepper traffic, which was then dominated by the Portuguese. In 1663 the Dutch captured Cochin from the Portuguese, and it became the headquarters of their Malabar Coast colony. During the eighteenth century, however, increasing British and French competition severely cut into Dutch trade there, and in 1795 the British seized the Dutch posts along the coast, bringing them under British rule in India. See INDIA.

MALACCA. Malacca (modern spelling, Melaka) is now a quiet provincial city on the west coast of Malaysia*, but once was the heart of a great sultanate and the object of successive imperial conquests by the Portuguese, Dutch, and British. It is the capital of a Malaysian state by the same name, but its prosperity has never rested on its hinterland. Malacca commands a vital strait, the best trade route between Asia and the west. Ships must pass through to avoid the sometimes perilous passage around Sumatra, but the Strait of Malacca has perils of its own, including sandbars and pirates. The city is located just north of the equator, and has a monsoon climate. Most Malaccans are Chinese, but there are also Malays, Indians, and Europeans.

Malacca's rise from fishing village to commercial entrepôt began about 1400 when a Sumatran named Parameswara set up his own kingdom there. It might have been extinguished quickly, but a deal seems to have been struck with the expansionist Ming Dynasty of China by which Parameswara suppressed local piracy and protected Chinese merchants. The Ming, in turn, protected Malacca from Siam* and Java*. This all coincided with an expansion of Asian trade. Malacca became the site where Asian goods were exchanged for those of Europe, Arabia, and India. Malay seamen brought cinnamon, pepper, and other spices. Chinese brought silks and porcelains. Indians brought cotton cloth. Arabs and Persians brought wool, gold, and silver from the West. They also brought Islam.

Sources differ on when the king of Malacca became a Muslim and began to call himself sultan, but it was probably in the 1540s. Hindu court rituals were retained for their impressive effect, but the Sultanate transmitted Islam to the rest of maritime Southeast Asia. Malacca entered its golden age. Literature and learning flourished along with trade. Malaccan military expansion encompassed the entire Malay peninsula, the Riau and Lingga islands, and parts of Sumatra. Malay became the market language for the whole region.

Malacca's radiant age proved brief. Its wealth attracted the first Portuguese to sail to the Far East. The Sultanate was already torn by internal dissension in 1509 when Diogo López de Siqueira arrived on the scene. He got into a fight with the sultan and a score of his men were taken hostage. They were not rescued until Affonso d'Albuquerque conquered Malacca for Portugal two years later, ending Malay rule for the next four and a half centuries. The Portuguese made Malacca their Asian headquarters, and St. Francis Xavier established a mission there, but the city slipped from its former preeminence. Merchants went elsewhere and British, Dutch, and Achehnese forces harassed the Portuguese, who in the end had to rest content with Macao* and Timor*, after the Dutch expelled them from Malacca in 1641. Dutch policy suppressed trade at Malacca in favor of Batavia, on Java. Malacca served as a strategic outpost protecting the Dutch East Indies*, but was otherwise unprofitable.

When Holland was overrun by France in the Napoleonic Wars, Great Britain moved to acquire Dutch overseas territory. The English had already established a port on Pinang*, at the northern end of the Malacca Strait, in 1786. They took Malacca itself in 1795, gave it back to the Dutch in 1818, only to take it back again in a treaty of 1824. The British employed steam gunboats to suppress piracy, and gradually consolidated their control over all of what is now Malaysia. They joined Malacca with Penang and Singapore* into a territory called the Straits Settlements*, administered from India until 1867 and as a crown colony later.

British Malacca exported tapioca, rubber, coconuts, and tin, brought from the interior over new roads and railways, but was otherwise put in the shade by the spectacular growth of nearby Singapore*. The muddy Malacca River silted up the harbor. Oceangoing vessels ceased calling. Only coastal craft enter Malacca now and the population is less than at the turn of the century. Tourists find romantic reminders of past glory in architectural gems that survive from imperial times: forts, civic buildings, merchant houses, temples and mosques. (Barbara Andaya, *A History of Malaysia*, 1982; Wang Gungwu, *Malaysia: A Survey*, 1964.)

Ross Marlay

MALAGASY REPUBLIC. See MADAGASCAR.

MALARIA. See QUININE.

MALAWI. See NYASALAND.

MALAYA. See MALAYSIA.

MALAYSIA. Malaysia is an independent nation of 127,581 square miles in Southeast Asia. The country consists of two major divisions: Peninsular Malaysia, which used to be known as West Malaysia, on the Asian mainland, and Sarawak* and Sabah, or East Malaysia, on the island of Borneo*. Ancient Malaysia was settled by immigrants from southern China, but Europeans did not get a foothold there until 1511, when the Portuguese conquered Malacca* and came to dominate the commercial traffic between India and China*. Portuguese Malacca fell to the Dutch in 1641.

The British Empire* established itself in Malaysia in 1786 when the British East India Company* secured a leasehold on the island of Penang*, which sits off the west coast of Peninsular Malaysia approximately 500 miles north of Singapore*. In 1800 the British East India Company negotiated another leasehold, this one on the mainland across from Pinang, which the British named the Province Wellesley. In 1819, led by Thomas Raffles, the British established a settlement in Singapore, which the British East India Company took over in 1824. That same year, to pay off a large debt to the British, the Dutch ceded Malacca to Great Britain. The British combined Penang, Province Wellesley, Singapore, and Malacca into one jurisdiction, the Straits Settlements*, in 1826. Until 1867, the Straits Settlements was part of British India, but it became a crown colony that year. The Straits Settlements became the foundation for British Malaya. In 1858 the British government assumed sovereignty over all property of the British East India Company, including the Straits Settlements.

In 1874 Britain negotiated a protectorate with Perak*, an independent sultanate on the western side of Peninsular Malaysia. A similar protectorate was negotiated with Selangor*, another sultanate on the southern border of Perak. Between 1874 and 1889 Great Britain negotiated a protectorate with the sultans of Negri Sembilan*, a federation of nine small states on the southern border of Selangor. The sultan of Pahang* signed such a treaty with the British in 1888. Pahang was an independent state bordering Negri Sembilan but on the eastern side of the peninsula. In an attempt to unify the region, Great Britain created a Federated Malay States* in 1895 out of Perak, Selangor, Negri Sembilan, and Pahang, complete with its own British governor and a central government.

The Bangkok Treaty of 1909 between Siam and Great Britain ceded to England four states of southern Siam: Kelantin*, Trengganu*, Perlis*, and Kedah*. The state of Johor*, located at the southern tip of the peninsula just north of Singapore, signed a protectorate treaty with Great Britain in 1914. Johor, Kedah, Kelantin, Trengganu, and Perlis became known as the Unfederated Malay States*.

During World War II Japanese troops invaded and occupied the Straits Settlements, the Federated Malay States, and the Unfederated Malay States, but when the war was over it had become clear that the British could not maintain the colony indefinitely. After the war, the government of the Straits Settlements was not re-established. In September 1945 Great Britain formed the Malaya Union out of the three administrative units, with the exception of Singapore, which became a separate crown colony in 1946. The Malaya Union became the Federation of Malaya in 1948. A bitter communist insurrection nearly destroyed the colony in the early 1950s, but the British and Malayans managed to suppress it. On August 31, 1957, the Federation of Malaya joined the British Commonwealth as an independent nation.

Five years later negotiations began to form the nation of Malaysia from a union of the Federation of Malaya, Singapore, and the British colonies on Borneo—Sarawak, British North Borneo*, and Brunei*. Brunei violently resisted the move, but on September 16, 1963, the Federation of Malaya, Singapore, Sarawak, and Sabah (North Borneo) formed the new nation of Malaysia. Two years later Singapore seceded from Malaysia and became an independent country. (Stanley Bedlington, *Malaysia and Singapore: The Building of New States*, 1978; Joseph Kennedy, *A History of Malaysia*, 1970; R. S. Milne and K. J. Ratnam, *Malaysia—New States in a New Nation*, 1974.)

MALDIVES. The Maldives is an archipelago of 1,201 small coral atolls stretching across 500 miles of the Indian Ocean on a north-south axis, south of Sri Lanka*. Their total land mass is only 120 square miles. Male is the main island and the most heavily populated of the archipelago. Although the Maldives were originally settled by Sinhalese and Dravidian migrants from southern India* and Ceylon*, they came under Muslim influence in the twelfth century. Portuguese sailors first landed in the Maldives in 1507, and beginning in 1558 they assumed political control of the islands, administering them from their colony of Goa* on the west coast of India. When the Dutch replaced the Portuguese as the dominant European power on Ceylon, they also established control over the Maldives in the 1650s, but for the most part the Dutch left internal affairs to the Maldivians.

Dutch control over the Maldives gave way to the British in 1796 when the

Dutch were expelled from Ceylon. Because of very limited natural resources and a tenuous water supply, the Maldives were important to Great Britain as a naval base but not as a full-fledged colony. Like the Dutch and Portuguese before them, the British left the Maldivians alone in terms of domestic affairs. To prevent France from establishing a base on the islands, Great Britain declared the Maldives a protectorate in 1887, leaving the ruling Islamic sultan in complete charge of internal affairs and Great Britain in control of defense and foreign policy.

During the 1930s and 1940s a movement toward constitutional republicanism developed in the Maldives, and it reached fruition in 1953 when the traditional sultanate was dissolved and a popularly elected president, Muhammad Amin Didi, assumed power. The experiment in democracy lasted only seven months before Muslim conservatives deposed him and restored the sultanate. Prime Minister Ibrahim Nasir came to dominate the colony.

In the late 1950s the differences between Maldivians on Male and those people on southern islands like Suvadiva, Addu, and Fua Mulaku erupted into a separatist movement led by Abdullah Afeef. Resentful of what he considered the power and relative prosperity of Male, Afeef established the United Suvadivan Republic in 1959. Great Britain refused to sanction the new country and Maldivian troops from Male crushed the rebellion. Six years later, on July 26, 1965, Britain granted independence to the Maldives. The new country elected not to become part of the British Commonwealth of Nations* and in 1968 became known as the Republic of the Maldives. Its population in 1988 was just under 165,000 people. (Urmila Phadnis and Ela Dutt Luithui, "The Maldives Enter World Politics," *Asian Affairs*, 8, January/February 1981, 166–79; Rinn S. Shinn, "Maldives," in Frederica M. Bunge, ed., *Indian Ocean. Five Island Countries*, 1982.)

MALI. Except for a scattering of romantics and adventurers in search of the legendary city of Timbukto, there was little European contact with the area of western Africa known today as the Republic of Mali until the second half of the nineteenth century. At that time, the French, who had established themselves in Senegal* and along the Upper Guinea Coast, became concerned about the rise and expansion of warlike Muslim "empires in the interior," perceiving them as a threat to French coastal possessions. One such indigenous state, the Tukulor empire, founded by El Hadj Umar Tall in the 1850s, covered at its zenith much of what is now central and western Mali and eastern Guinea. French military penetration of the western Sudan (the region of West Africa immediately south of the Sahara) began from Senegal around 1880. After numerous military campaigns, accompanied by diplomatic maneuvering, France created the territory of French Sudan in 1892. A year later, the French advance under the command of Colonel Louis Archinard, a brilliant but insubordinate officer who sometimes mounted campaigns without the approval of his superiors in the French government, brought the Tukulor empire to an end.

An even more serious challenge to the extension of French rule in Africa was posed by Samori Touré, a Malinke leader (imam), whose conquests embraced large parts of what would one day be southern Mali as well as the hinterlands of Guinea*, Ivory Coast*, and Ghana*. A soldier of audacity and genius, Samori held off the French for many years with his large, well-led and well-armed army. He was finally captured by the French in 1898 and exiled to Gabon* where he died two years later. While the French acknowledged the military prowess of Samori, calling him "the Bonaparte of the Sudan," they regarded him essentially as a bloodthirsty slave-raiding bandit. In more recent times, however, historians frequently have depicted Samori as one of the great African resistance leaders in the struggle against the encroachment of European imperialism.

From 1899 to 1904 the French Sudan was administratively merged with Senegal and parts of present-day Mauritania*, Niger*, and Burkina-Faso under the name Senegambie et Niger. In 1904 these districts were renamed the Haut-Senegal et Niger, a name which lasted until 1920. From 1920 to 1958 the area was again known as the French Sudan. In early 1957, as a result of France's *loi-cadre**, the territorial assembly obtained extensive powers over internal affairs and was permitted to form a cabinet with executive authority over matters within the assembly's competence. After the 1958 French constitutional referendum, Sudan became a member of the French Community and enjoyed complete internal autonomy as the Sudanese Republic (though still under general supervision of France). The following year, along with Senegal, the Sudanese Republic joined a federation known as the Mali Federation, taking its name from the Manding empire of Mali which flourished between the thirteenth and sixteenth centuries around the headwaters of the Niger River. The Mali Federation was given its independence from France on June 30, 1960, but broke apart on August 20, 1960, because of serious political differences between the two members. On September 22, 1960, the Sudanese Republic declared itself the independent Republic of Mali. (Michael Crowder, *Colonial West Africa: Collected Essays*, 1978.)

Eric C. Loew

MALTA. Malta is an independent nation consisting of three small islands—Malta, Gozo, and Comino—located in the Mediterranean Sea approximately 58 miles south of Sicily and 220 miles from Libya. Because of its strategic location, Malta has a history of involvement with larger empires, including the Phoenicians, Greeks, Carthaginians, Romans, and Arabs. The Normans conquered Malta in 1090 and brought the Roman Catholic Church to the island, and in 1193 Malta became a fiefdom of Sicily. As a reward for their loyalty in fighting the "infidel Turks," Charles V* of the Holy Roman Empire awarded Malta to the Knights of St. John of Jerusalem in 1530. On several occasions in the sixteenth century the Ottoman Turks laid siege to Malta but failed to dislodge the Knights from their fortifications. They ruled the island until the nineteenth century.

In 1798, as part of his campaign to conquer Egypt*, Napoleon invaded and seized Malta. He immediately declared French to be the official language and imposed a variety of other restrictions which the Maltese people found to be completely obnoxious. The Maltese fought a guerrilla war against the French and asked for British intervention. In 1799 British naval forces under the command of Horatio Nelson drove the French out of Malta. The Treaty of Amiens of 1802* returned Malta to the Knights of St. John. Afraid that the end of the Napoleonic Wars would return Malta to French control, the Maltese demanded the imposition of British sovereignty, and by the Treaty of Paris of 1814 Malta became a British crown colony.

Throughout the nineteenth century the Maltese gradually demanded more and more self-government, and the British responded to those requests. Between 1829 and 1836 the Maltese received freedoms of speech and the press, as well as an appointed council of government. R. Moore O'Ferrall became the first civil governor in 1847, and in 1849 the constitution of the executive council was changed to provide for ten appointed and eight elected members. During World War I the Maltese fought with the Allies against the Central Powers, and in 1921 Britain rewarded them by granting responsible government* on Malta. The constitution of 1921 provided for an elected senate and assembly. Great Britain revoked the constitution in 1936 because of increasing political intervention in Malta by Mussolini's Fascist Italy. A council of government of 30 people, with only 10 elected members, assumed power. Throughout World War II the Maltese suffered through daily attacks by German and Italian bombers.

During the 1950s Great Britain made steady progress toward independence for Malta, and on November 1, 1961, a new Maltese constitution gave the islands complete internal self-government, although the British still supervised the civil service, foreign policy, and defense matters. A political struggle ensued on Malta between the Maltese Labour Party, which wanted complete independence outside of the British Commonwealth of Nations*, and the Nationalist Party, which wanted independent status within the Commonwealth. The nationalists won the election held in 1962 and George Borg Oliver became the first prime minister. On September 21, 1964, Malta became a fully independent member of the Commonwealth. (Edith Dobie, *Malta's Road to Independence*, 1967.)

MANDATE SYSTEM. During World War I* the Allied powers defeated Germany, Turkey, and Austria-Hungary and seized control of the German and Ottoman colonies. Jan Smuts* of South Africa proposed and the victorious powers accepted the notion that the colonies should be regarded as temporary wards of the "advanced nations" until they were able, in the words of Article 22 of the League of Nations* Covenant, "to stand by themselves under the strenuous conditions of the modern world." It was a perfect compromise for the European empires which wanted to keep the colonies without offending the United States, an avowed opponent of old-fashioned imperialism.

The mandate system designated three classes of colonies. "A" mandates consisted of the Arab territories of the Middle East, formerly part of the Ottoman

Empire, which were regarded as being on the brink of independence. France received mandates over Syria* and Lebanon*, while Great Britain received mandates over Palestine*, Transjordan*, and Iraq*. The "B" mandates consisted of the former German colonies of Africa, except for South West Africa*, which became a "C" colony. They were deemed not ready for independence but worthy of protection from slavery and drug and liquor trafficking. They were also to be kept open for the free trade of all countries. France received a mandate over part of the Cameroons* and part of Togoland; Great Britain received the other part of the Cameroons and Togoland, and Tanganyika*; and Belgium received Ruanda and Urundi. Finally, the "C" mandates comprised South West Africa and the former German colonies in the Pacific, all of which were deemed unfit for independence. South Africa received a mandate over South West Africa; Japan received the Caroline*, Marshall*, and Mariana* (except Guam*) Islands; New Zealand received Western Samoa*; Australia received Papua New Guinea* and the island of Nauru*.

Although the mandate system spoke of independence in lofty language, the European empires were bent on maintaining their control. Iraq received her independence from Great Britain in 1932, but the other mandated colonies found themselves in a struggle for sovereignty and independence which did not end until the conclusion of World War II and establishment of the new idea of "trusteeship." (F. S. Northredge, *The League of Nations. Its Life and Times 1920–1946*, 1986.)

MANIFEST DESTINY. First coined in 1845 by John L. O'Sullivan, editor of *The United States Magazine and Democratic Review*, "Manifest Destiny" became a diplomatic and popular catchword in the late 1840s and 1850s to justify United States expansion across the North American continent. It referred to an idea held by many Americans that God intended the United States to reach from the Atlantic to the Pacific, and that Great Britain and Mexico should surrender their territorial possessions in North America to fulfill that destiny. "Manifest Destiny" played an important role in providing political support for the annexation of Texas in 1845, the acquisition of the Oregon Territory in 1846, and the Mexican War (1846–1848), in which the United States eventually seized much of the American Southwest. (Albert K. Weinberg, *Manifest Destiny*, 1935.)

MANILA. The city of Manila was founded by the Spanish in 1571 as the capital of their colony on Luzon* in the Philippines*. Soon it was the commercial center for a global trade in bullion and Asian goods, with the famous Manila Galleon* leaving Manila for Acapulco, Mexico. Gold and silver mined in Mexico and Peru would be shipped to Acapulco and then Manila to purchase Asian goods, which would then be returned to Spain via Manila and Acapulco. The trade declined in the seventeenth and eighteenth centuries when Dutch power in the East Indies increased. Great Britain captured Manila in 1762 during the Seven

Years' War but returned it to Spain in the Treaty of Paris of 1763*. In 1898, during the Spanish-American War*, a United States fleet captured Manila, and later in the year all of the Philippines were transferred to American sovereignty. Manila was part of that colonial system until the Philippines received independence in 1946. (Peter Kemp, *The Oxford Companion to Ships and the Sea*, 1976.)

MANILA GALLEON. Spain conquered most of the New World during her "great century" (1492–1588) but only took one colony in Asia, the Philippines*. For 250 years (1565–1815) all Spanish commerce and communication with its Far Eastern outpost was carried by the annual "Manila Galleon." Galleon trade was crucially important not only for Manila Spaniards, but for China and the whole Far East, Mexico, Peru, and Spain itself. Spaniards had found stupendous quantities of silver in Peru and Mexico. Some of that precious metal was taken across the Pacific in ships plying a long, perilous northern route, sometimes taking half a year to reach Manila. There the silver was exchanged for exotic, luxurious oriental goods prized in Europe. The vessel would depart Manila* on the eastbound journey to Acapulco, its cargo then carried across Mexico and loaded onto other ships bound for Europe. All other trade routes between Europe and Asia ran the other way, around India.

The galleon trade ruined Mexico and Peru, as their wealth was taken away, and they got nothing in return. For merchants in Spain, the galleons brought unwanted competition. The Manila galleon flooded China with Spanish silver. In fact, Spanish silver dollars became a medium of exchange across Asia, greatly stimulating regional trade. Manila was the entrepôt. Chinese junks brought porcelains and fine cloth, velvet, damask, satins, taffetas, and above all, silken goods, already finished as stockings, handkerchiefs, and priests' robes. Indian and Arab ships brought cotton from the Malabar coast* and carpets from Persia. Spices from the Moluccas*, ivory and sandalwood from the jungles of Southeast Asia, even slaves and gemstones were all shipped eastward, to Mexico and Spain, from Manila. On the return voyage, in addition to silver, Spaniards brought horses, cows, and a variety of New World plants that revolutionized farming in Asia, including tobacco, peanuts, corn, and tomatoes. The westbound galleon also brought governors and priests, and welcome letters that might be two years old before they were delivered.

The fabulous galleon trade benefited the Philippines little, if at all. Exports stagnated, since few Philippine products were in demand. On the other hand, imported Indian cotton, distributed through a growing network of provincial Chinese middlemen, ruined local cottage industries. The trade encouraged Spanish indolence since it was much easier to engage in trade and speculation while awaiting the galleon's arrival than to pioneer the interior forests. Manila society became so dependent upon the galleon that if one disappeared, the victim of shipwreck or piracy, fortunes were lost and economic depression descended on the city. Meanwhile, so many Chinese came to trade and live in Manila that

Spaniards and Filipinos, fearing a "yellow peril," sometimes massacred them in terrible pogroms. The galleon trade petered out in the eighteenth century, as the Spanish empire sank into decline. Dutch and English traders, with their free trade policies, eroded Manila's significance as an entrepôt. The last galleon left for Acapulco in 1815. (William L. Schurz, *The Manila Galleon*, 1959.)

Ross Marlay

MAO ZEDONG. Mao Zedong (Mao Tse-tung), born in 1893, was a giant of twenticth-century politics. It is sometimes said that he directly affected more people than anyone else in human history. Mao was the leader of the Chinese Revolution, the Chairman of the Communist Party of China*, and the seldom-questioned dictator of the People's Republic of China from the day he proclaimed its existence in 1949 until he died twenty-seven years later. Mao may be thought of as a military strategist, a political schemer, a Marxist theoretician of brilliant originality, a ruthless dictator, a Chinese patriot, a utopian dreamer, even an anarchist. In fact, he was all the above, and more. Mao was looked up to by Third World revolutionaries as a leader in the anti-imperialist movement. China itself was an empire, but one that had slipped into such humiliating straits by the mid-nineteenth century that "dogs and Chinese" were barred from a Shanghai park reserved for Europeans. China was a semi-colony, shamed all the more for having been at one time, in her own terms, the very center of civilization. When Mao was born, thinking Chinese were in despair. Some wanted to expel the barbarians and return to old ways; others wanted to abandon the past and westernize.

Mao's childhood in Hunan province as the son of a moderately well-off peasant was unremarkable except for the violent dislike the boy harbored for his tyrannical father, against whom he openly rebelled, in complete defiance of Confucian norms. He rebelled at school too, against a harsh teacher. When Mao was fifteen, he boarded at "higher primary school." Most of the other students were sons of landlords, better dressed and better mannered than Mao. His later classification of intellectuals as the "ninth stinking category" goes back to these years, but Mao himself was an intellectual, though one whose curiosity was wide-ranging and undisciplined. He read everything he could get his hands on, from ancient Chinese adventure tales to Darwin, Rousseau, and Montesquieu. He also insisted that thought was sterile if divorced from practice. He was a man of action. Above all, Mao believed in the invincible power of the human will. Men who thought correctly, and who refused to quit, could overcome all obstacles.

Japanese encroachments and demands on China during World War I* threw the country, and students in particular, into turmoil. Mao went to Peking in 1918, worked in a library, studied under the Marxist scholar Li Dazhao, and wrote patriotic tracts. Bolsheviks had seized power in Russia, and Lenin proclaimed the imminent death of imperialism, which was, he said, the highest stage of capitalism. Chinese students could now be modern and anti-western at the same time. Mao started a Marxist study group in 1920, and was present at the founding congress of the Chinese Communist Party (CCP) in Shanghai in 1921. He rose fast in the party and was elected to the CCP central committee in 1923.

For the next four years the CCP, on orders from Moscow, joined an artificial "united front" with the Kuomintang (KMT) of Sun Yat Sen and Chiang Kai-shek, and so operated legally in Canton*. Mao ran a "Peasant Movement Training Institute" in Canton, to train agitators to organize Chinese peasants—long scorned by orthodox Marxists as "rural idiots"—for revolution. One night in 1927 the KMT turned on the Communists and slaughtered all they could catch. The survivors escaped to the countryside, where Mao eventually organized a "Kiangsi Soviet," his first attempt to wed ancient Chinese principles of guerrilla warfare to modern communist egalitarianism. Chiang Kai-shek's forces surrounded and nearly annihilated the communists, but the reds broke out and started on the legendary Long March that took them thousands of miles west through the mountains, then northward across wild grasslands. They finally arrived at Yenan, in the barren treeless northwest, in 1937. For the next ten years Mao tested and refined his theories of politics, war, and human nature.

Mao's political insights, strategic decisions, and forceful personality made him the unchallenged leader of the CCP. Rivals were pushed aside, though never fully eliminated. Mao seized the initiative against the Japanese, organizing the north Chinese countryside, while Chiang's KMT forces stayed isolated in Chungking. The KMT grew ever more corrupt, while Mao's red army practiced "revolutionary morality." Worst of all, the KMT depended on landlords while the CCP bet its future on peasants. There were more of the latter. When the Japanese surrendered in 1945, the CCP and the KMT resumed their civil war, which ended in 1949 when defeated nationalist forces fled to Taiwan. Mao stood on the gate of the Forbidden City, in Peking, and proclaimed that "The Chinese people have stood up." He was no longer a guerrilla leader but the dictator of Communist China.

Mao knew that the struggle to remake China had just begun, and he threw the country into an unprecedented experiment in social engineering, an attempt to remake the human personality, to build a true communist society where greed would be gone and people would desire only to "serve the people." Much was accomplished, but at a heavy cost. During the first decade of the People's Republic, the old society was broken forever. Landlords were dispossessed or killed. Peasants were organized into cooperatives. Railroads, factories, schools, and clinics were built. America was fought to a standstill in Korea. Adults were taught to read. And everyone was propagandized night and day.

The Chinese now say that Mao began to go astray in the late 1950s. Perhaps power went to his head. Perhaps he had simply been right so often that he could no longer imagine being wrong. He wanted to leap ahead of the Soviet Union, to the final stage of communism, and thought that if people were sufficiently dedicated, material obstacles would not count. His mass campaign, the Great Leap Forward, turned into an economic disaster that brought famine, a rupture with the Russians, and the temporary political eclipse of Mao himself. Less utopian communists argued for retrenchment. Mao nursed his wounds, but struck back in 1966 with his Great Proletarian Cultural Revolution, one of the strangest episodes in the history of communism.

Mao, leader of the CCP, distrusted and scorned the party itself. He saw that communist bureaucrats were becoming a new class, and trusting only "the people," encouraged them to attack the party. Teenagers, in particular, heeded his call, and marched all over China brandishing a little red book of Mao's sayings. They terrorized their elders, paralyzed industry, shut down the school system, and were responsible for uncounted deaths. They were in the end betrayed by Mao, who banished them to the remote countryside to "learn from the peasants." From 1969 until his death in 1976 Mao may have been senile. Power struggles raged all around him. When he died, he was entombed in a crystal coffin at Tien An Men square. His wife was jailed. His policies were largely reversed by his successors. (Ross Terrill, *Mao: A Biography*, 1980; Dick Wilson, *Mao Tse-tung in the Scales of History*, 1977.)

Ross Marlay

MARANHÃO. The colony of Maranhão, which sat on the north coast of Brazil* just east of the Amazon estuary, was given to two donatárias in 1534, but no effective settlement began until the early 1600s. By that time Portugal was concerned about French colonization efforts in the Maranhão area. In 1621 Portugal created the "Estado do Maranhão" to govern Brazil's east-west coastal axis, and the new political unit began its effective existence in 1626. During the rest of the sixteenth century, the Portuguese crown granted a number of donatárias in Maranhão, including Cameta (1633–1754), Cuma (1633–1754), Caete (1634–1753), Cabo Norte (1637–1695), Ilha Grande de Joanes (1665–1754), and Xingu (1685). Each of these subsequent donatárias, however, eventually reverted to the crown and was reincorporated back into Maranhão. Maranhão lost its position as the seat of Portuguese government in 1737 when that post shifted to Belem in Grão-Pará.* To manage the area more efficiently the Estado of Maranhão was divided into four separate administrative units in 1775: Grão-Pará, São Jose do Rio Negro*, Piaui*, and Maranhão. Maranhão became a province in the empire of Brazil in 1822. (David P. Henige, *Colonial Governors from the Fifteenth Century to the Present*, 1970.)

MARGARITA. Margarita is a small island off the coast of Venezuela in the Caribbean Sea. Between 1525 and 1600 it was under the private control of the Villalobos family, which appointed its governors. The island reverted to the crown in 1600 and it was under the administrative authority, albeit with its own governor, of the Audiencia of Santo Domingo until 1739. Between 1739 and 1777 the Audiencia of New Granada supervised Margarita, and after 1777 it fell under the control of the captaincy-general of Venezuela. Effective royal control of Margarita ceased to exist after 1810 and the island eventually became part of Venezuela. See VENEZUELA.

MARIANAS. The Marianas are a series of volcanic islands located in the western Pacific ocean area of Micronesia*, approximately 1,500 miles east of the Philippines*. The major islands in the group are Guam*, the southernmost island, Saipan, Tinian, Rota, and Pagan. On a north-south axis, the islands stretch over 450 miles. Ferdinand Magellan* first discovered the Marianas in 1521, and for the next 375 years the islands remained Spanish territory. Colonists from Spain settled Guam in the early 1560s and other locations in the Marianas in 1668 and intermarried with the native people, known to the Spaniards as Chamorros.

The political status of the Marianas as a colony of Spain did not change until the Spanish-American War*. Spain's defeat at the hands of the United States in 1898 was a strategic disaster—the elimination of Spain as a Pacific power. As part of the Treaty of Paris* ending the war, Spain ceded the island of Guam to the United States. One year later, Spain sold the rest of the Mariana Islands to Germany for $4.5 million. When World War I* broke out, Japan exploited Germany's preoccupation in Europe and seized the Marianas, except for the American territory of Guam. At the Versailles Conference in 1919 ending World War I, Japan received what became a League of Nations* mandate over the northern Marianas Islands. Shortly after the bombing of Pearl Harbor in December 1941, Japan attacked and captured Guam from the United States, giving her complete control over the Marianas. American forces recaptured Guam and all the other Marianas in 1944.

When World War II ended, the United States received a United Nations trusteeship* over the scattered island groups of Micronesia, including the Marianas. In 1947 the area became known as the Trust Territory of the Pacific Islands*. The United States initially hoped to create a single commonwealth out of the entire Trust Territory, but ethnic differences between the various islanders made it impossible. In 1969 voters on Guam rejected an offer to be reunited politically with the northern Marianas, and all the other districts of the Trust Territory of the Pacific Islands, except the northern Marianas, rejected the notion of unification. United States officials then began negotiating with representatives of the northern Marianas. Those negotiations commenced in earnest after creation of the Northern Marianas Political Status Commission in 1973. With the overwhelming approval of native voters, the northern Marianas were separated from the rest of the Trust Territory of the Pacific Islands in 1976. In January 1978 the Commonwealth of the Northern Marianas Islands elected its own governor and legislature and became a self-governing entity in free association with the United States. (J. C. Beaglehole, *The Exploration of the Pacific*, 1968; Donald F. McHenry, *Micronesia: Trust Betrayal. Altruism vs Self-Interest in American Foreign Policy*, 1983; and Samuel McPhetres, ''Elections in the Northern Mariana Islands,'' *Political Science*, 35, July 1983, 103–16.)

MARQUESA ISLANDS. Part of French Polynesia*, the Marquesas consist of twelve islands in the South Pacific, about 750 miles northeast of Tahiti. The Spanish explorer Alvarao de Mendana first came across the Marquesas in 1595, and the next visit by a European was not until 1774 when Captain James Cook* of England arrived. Like so many other places in the Pacific, contact with Europeans led to rapid population decline in the Marquesas. Although Protestant missionaries from England arrived in the Marquesas in the 1790s, they made little headway. French Catholic missionaries were more successful when they arrived in the 1830s. The missionary success paved the way for French imperialism, and late in the 1830s and early in the 1840s, France established control over the Marquesas. The islands formally became part of the *Etablissements Francais de l'Oceanie* (EFO) in 1880, along with the Society, Tuamotu, Austral, and Gambier Islands. The capital of the EFO was at Pape'ete on Tahiti. After World War II France gradually extended more and more political power to the islands, along with French citizenship. An elected assembly meeting at Pape'ete governed local affairs throughout French Polynesia, and in 1977 French Polynesia gained the right to send representatives to the French parliament. (Robert Thomas, *The Marquesas Islands: Their Description and Early History*, 1978.)

MARSHALL ISLANDS. The Marshall Islands are an archipelago in the central Pacific Ocean between the Gilbert Islands to the southwest and Wake Island* to the north. There are 34 islands in two groups. Kwajalein is the largest island in the Ralik chain, while Majuro is the main island of the Ratak chain. Spanish explorers first reached the Marshall Islands in 1526 but they never developed their claim there. Germany established a presence in the Marshall Islands in 1874, and in 1885 Pope Leo XIII arbitrated a dispute between Germany and Spain, confirming Spanish sovereignty over the Marianas* and Caroline Islands* and German control over the Marshalls. But when World War I broke out, Japan occupied the Marshall Islands. Japan was confirmed in its possession of the Marshall Islands by the League of Nations* under the mandate system*.

During World War II the United States conquered the Marshall Islands, and after the war the United Nations* gave the United States a trusteeship* over them. In 1947 the Marshall Islands became part of the Trust Territory of the Pacific Islands*, along with a number of other Pacific island groups. The United States wanted the Trust Territory to evolve into a single independent nation, but ethnic differences and the vast distances made that impossible. In 1978 the people of the Marshall Islands voted in a referendum against a single nation-state for all of Micronesia, and on May 1, 1979, they declared self-government and established the Republic of the Marshall Islands. (Stanley De Smith, *Microstates and Micronesia: Problems of America's Pacific Islands and Other Minute Territories*, 1970.)

Joseph M. Rowe, Jr.

MARTINIQUE. Martinique is an island of approximately sixty square miles located in the southern Caribbean, between Dominica* on the north and St. Lucia* on the south. On his second voyage in 1493, Christopher Columbus* first sighted the island, but no European landed there until Columbus's fourth voyage in 1502. After exploring the island, the Spaniards decided it had little economic value, and they left it to its native Carib and Arawak inhabitants. In 1635 Pierre Belain d'Esnambuc took possession of Martinique for France, and because of the sugar plantations he established, the island became an economic jewel in the French Empire*. African slaves were imported to work the sugarcane fields, and the Caribs and Arawaks died out, victims of European diseases. In 1674 France formally assumed sovereignty over Martinique.

The social structure evolved with French-speaking whites at the top of the economic ladder and African slaves and laborers at the bottom. Throughout the seventeenth, eighteenth, and early nineteenth centuries, the sugar economy prospered, with Martinique sugar being shipped to France for refining before it was exported to the rest of Europe and to the United States. During the Seven Years' War, England seized Martinique, but the Treaty of Paris in 1763* restored the island to France. England took over the island again in 1794 during the Napoleonic Wars, but France regained Martinique at the Congress of Vienna of 1815*. When France abolished slavery in 1848, the economy of Martinique came on hard times and the colony declined in economic significance.

A local governor, appointed by France, administered Martinique beginning in 1674. In 1854 France gave the Martinique colonial council the authority to levy all taxes and approve local expenditures, and in 1860 France expanded the powers of the general council and required the island to become self-sufficient in the cost of government. In 1946 Martinique became an overseas department of France, with three seats in the national assembly and two in the senate. During the 1970s and 1980s an anti-French nationalism developed on Martinique, inspired by the economic hegemony of the white, French upper class, high unemployment rates, and Cuban agitation. France signed an agreement with Cuba in 1980, promising French economic assistance for the Cuban economy if Fidel Castro would stop trying to undermine the political stability of Martinique. Castro agreed and in the early 1980s some of the political insurgency disappeared. (Herbert Ingram Priestley, *France Overseas. A Study of Modern Imperialism*, 1966; W. Adolphe Roberts, *The French in the West Indies*, 1942.)

MARYLAND. Maryland lies at the center of the eastern seaboard of the United States and consists of three major physiographic regions: the Tidewater, or Atlantic Coastal Plain, the Piedmont Plateau, and the Appalachian Mountains. When European explorers entered the area in the fifteenth century, relatively peaceful Algonquian Indian tribes had established farms in the region and were being pressured by the Iroquois from the north for control of the land. John Cabot* may have explored the coast of Maryland as early as 1498. The Spanish and French took little interest in this region before the sixteenth century, but in 1524 the French government commissioned Giovanni da Verrazano*, an Italian navigator, to explore the Chesapeake Bay. Bartholomew Gilbert visited the coastline of Maryland in 1603 and in 1608 Captain John Smith came from

Virginia to explore the region and to publish his findings. By the seventeenth century Europeans were taking a greater interest in present-day Maryland.

In 1631 William Claiborne established a fur-trading post on Kent Island. One year later the King of England, Charles I, reluctantly granted a charter and proprietorship of the domain of Maryland lying between the Potomac River and the fortieth north parallel to George Calvert, First Lord Baltimore. With the death of Calvert on April 15, 1632, the proprietorship was transferred to his son Cecil. Maryland became the first enduring proprietorship in the New World and was established as a refuge for persecuted Roman Catholics in Protestant England. Colonization began on March 25, 1634, when two ships, the *Ark* and the *Dove*, transported 200 settlers to St. Clement's Island, on the lower Potomac. The first settlement was established at St. Mary's City. The early settlers, mainly British in origin and Catholic by faith, developed friendly relations with the Indians and established farms and trading posts.

The proprietor held absolute authority and ownership of the land in Maryland, and he encouraged settlement by awarding large grants of land to nobles. Maryland became feudal and proprietary in character, as yeoman farmers, indentured servants, and black slaves made up the majority of the population. The proprietor appointed the governor. By 1636 the settlers were allowed to elect a general assembly with law-making powers. The most notable piece of legislation coming forth from this assembly was the Act of Toleration in 1649, which granted religious freedom to Protestants and Catholics, but not to non-trinitarians. Internal rebellions began in Maryland in the 1630s and the colony soon became the scene of bitter political, economic, and religious strife. The proprietor lost control of the government on three occasions—1642, 1654 to 1658, and 1692 to 1715. Power was restored to the proprietorship in 1715, but the French and Indians War* caused further strain between the proprietor and the assembly, as well as defense disputes between the crown and the assembly. Proprietary control was retained, however, until the American Revolution*.

The 1700s witnessed continued strife in Maryland. Boundary disputes were resolved in 1732 when Maryland lost control of 3 million acres of land to Virginia* and Pennsylvania* and when the Mason and Dixon line was established in 1767. Inept proprietors failed to eliminate corruption and illegal taxation during the 1760s. Marylanders opposed Britain's attempt to impose taxes on the colony with the Stamp Act in 1765 and the legislature repudiated the law in November 1765. The Marylanders staged their own tea party in 1774 at Annapolis, when the *Peggy Stewart*, a ship filled with tea, was burned. In that same year Maryland held an independent convention, and in 1775 the Association of the Freeman of Maryland passed a resolution protesting British practices. Delegates drew up a state constitution which was adopted in November 1776. Statesmen from Maryland played a major role in the First and Second Continental Congresses and Marylanders were active participants in the war for independence. (M. P. Andrews, *History of Maryland*, 1979.)

Veula J. Rhodes

MASSACHUSETTS. Massachusetts was founded as an English colony on the coast of North America. Eventually it comprised 8,284 square miles of diverse land, hilly in the west, indented by the Connecticut River plateau in the center, and then low and sandy in the southeast, with a rocky coast and several important islands. The name comes from an Algonquian word meaning "near the great hill." Although the region was explored by Giovanni da Verrazano in 1524, no whites settled it until 1620 when the Pilgrims, fearing the dissolution of their religion and culture, beached at Plymouth*. The Pilgrims had been given a charter for land in Virginia*, but mistook Cape Cod for it, signed their famous "Mayflower Compact," and settled in for their first long winter at Plymouth.

Six years later the Dorchester Company settled Naumkeag (soon to be called Salem), but it wasn't until 1628 that large-scale immigration commenced. Puritans under John Endicott went first to Salem and from there to found Boston. Their old charter from the New England Company was superceded by that of the Massachusetts Bay Company. In 1630 the first large group followed them to Boston, under Governor John Winthrop. John Cotton's strong religious leadership quickly established a connection between church and state, although both were viewed as parts of the effort to create a New Jerusalem. This "City upon the hill" limited citizenship to members of the church until 1664, but most other rights were free and soon a prospering trade and agricultural community had been launched. Massachusetts's remarkable degree of religious and political homogeneity can be explained, in part at least, as a result of the strong measures carried out by the state against dissenters. Banishment was the sentence against Anne Hutchinson and Roger Williams, the heresies of each of whom threatened the cohesiveness of the colony.

While major dissent was prohibited, nonmembers increasingly gained civil rights. In 1632 freemen were allowed to take part in the direct election of the governor. Two years later they started voting for members of the general court, the popular assembly. Indian wars, especially the Pequot War of 1637 and King Philip's War* in 1675–1676, brought together the various colonies of New England, but it was a weak order, designed basically for defense purposes. A more serious effort at uniting the colonies was made by the Crown in 1684 with the revocation of Massachusetts's charter and the creation of the Dominion of New England*, which finally brought Massachusetts and Plymouth under one rule.

The Dominion, however, was short-lived and fell apart as soon as word (1689) arrived of England's Glorious Revolution. Although a new liberal charter was granted by the Stuarts in 1691, the interim period was a time of confusion. The concurrent Salem witch trials further eroded the traditional power bases of the local elite, the Puritan leaders. This left Massachusetts unsteady and open to the increased influence of a rising merchant elite.

Access to the colonial interior was limited, but its major ports did carry trade for a larger hinterland. This meant that Boston, and to some extent nearby Salem, would dominate the colony. Flourishing during a time of salutary neglect, Yankee

traders brought cloth, manufactured goods, and marine supplies around the Atlantic trade arena. As trade grew, however, the imperial government came to
realize that Massachusetts was not serving its mercantilist role adequately. A
succession of navigation acts, starting near the end of the century and increasingly
offensive with 1764's Sugar Act, 1765's Stamp Act, and the ill-conceived Coercive Acts of 1774, ignited a crisis of empire. By 1776 the breach was formally
complete. (Francis J. Bremer, *The Puritan Experiment*, 1976; John Demos, *A
Little Commonwealth*, 1970; Samuel Eliot Morison, *Builders of the Bay Colony*,
1930.)

Mark R. Shulman

MATABELELAND-MASHONALAND. See RHODESIA.

MATO GROSSO. By the eighteenth century, as settlement of the Brazilian
highlands took place, it became increasingly difficult to govern the new territories
from the coastal colony of São Paulo. The Portuguese government began creating
new administrative entities in the internal highlands, and Mato Grosso was one
of them. It received its first governor in 1751. Mato Grosso became a province
of the empire of Brazil* in 1822. See BRAZIL.

MAURITANIA. Mauritania is located in the western Saharan region of Africa,
with Morocco* (former Western Sahara) and Algeria* at its northern border,
Senegal* and Mali* at its southern and eastern borders, and the Atlantic Ocean
on the West. A proto-Berber people, the Bafour, and predecessors of the Toucouleur and Wolof tribes inhabited the region about one thousand years before
the Christian era. The Sanhadja confederation of Berber tribes dominated the
major caravan routes through Mauritania from the Mediterranean to Ghana* and
eastward to Timbuktu* until the tenth century, when the Ghana empire conquered
the Sanhadja. The Almoravids, Berbers from northern Mauritania, initiated an
Islamic holy war in 1040, and extended their conquests from Senegal northward
along the African coast and then into Spain. In the twelfth century the Sanhadja
dominated Mauritania again. The Mali empire controlled Mauritania during the
thirteenth century, but fell to the Songhai of Goa in the late fifteenth century.
At the end of the sixteenth century Moroccans defeated the Songhai in Mauritania.
By the end of the seventeenth century nomadic Arabic-speaking Maures (Moors)
who migrated to Mauritania from the north beginning in the eighth century,
dominated the entire region.

In 1448 the Portuguese established a trading post at Arguin Island on the
northern Atlantic coast of Africa. When the Portuguese and Spanish crowns
merged in 1580, the Spanish dominated slave and gold trade in the area. In 1638
they were replaced by the Dutch. The French drove out the Dutch in 1678 and
established a permanent base at Saint Louis at the border of the Senegalese and
Mauritanian coastlines. By 1763 the British had expelled France from the west

coast of Africa. However, after the Congress of Vienna of 1815*, France's sovereignty over the Mauritanian and Senegalese coasts was formalized.

Gum arabic was the valuable trade commodity coming from Mauritania and Senegal during the nineteenth century. The two areas were administered by the French government of Senegal. However, the Maures of Mauritania still claimed independent sovereignty. The Maures attacked Saint Louis in northern Senegal in 1855, but they were repulsed. In 1856 they were defeated in Mauritania as well by the French governor of Senegal, Louis Faidherbe. In the 1880s the French lost interest in Mauritania while pursuing the Malinke warrior, Samori Toure, in Guinea*, Sierra Leone*, and Ivory Coast*. The Maures resumed autonomy in Mauritania.

From 1899 to 1905 the French delegate-general of the territory of Mauritania, Xavier Coppolani, instituted a policy to separate Mauritania from Senegal. Coppolani, who was killed by Islamic assassins in 1905, is known as the "father of the French Colony of Mauritania," and to the Maures he is the "Pacific Conqueror" because of his policy of pacification of the inhabitants of Mauritania. By 1904 Coppolani had established French military posts across the middle of southern Mauritania, creating the Civil Territory of Mauritania. But the Adrar region of the north had yet to be subdued. With help from Morocco, the Maures in the north, led by Ma al Aynin, resisted French conquest until 1912.

In 1920 the French Colony of Mauritania was proclaimed. Divided into cercles—administrative districts based on traditional emirates—Mauritania was ruled by commandants. Under the control of commandants, local Maure emirs oversaw their areas and delegated authority to chiefs of factions and subfactions. The policy of assimilation sought to maintain the traditional social structures while modernizing Mauritania. With the fall of France to the Germans in 1940, the Vichy government ended assimilation and condoned racial discrimination and forced labor. In 1944, at the Brazzaville Conference, the French resolved to follow a course of colonial reform. The 1946 constitution of the Fourth French Republic established Mauritania as an overseas territory in the French Union*, instead of a colony. Forced labor was abolished and French citizenship was extended to inhabitants of French territories. Mauritania gained a general council to be elected by Europeans and Africans, as well as representation in the assembly of the French Union and the national assembly in Paris.

Extension of suffrage began in 1947 when those literate in French were entitled to vote. Heads of households were enfranchised in 1951, and by 1956 Mauritania enjoyed universal suffrage. Leading the call for independence, the Entente Mauritanienne (EM) was organized in 1946. The Union Progressiste Mauritanienne (UPM), which represented the traditional Maure ruling class, dominated the political scene in the early 1950s. In 1956, as a provision of Loi-Cadre, functions that had been carried out by a Paris-appointed colonial official were given to an executive council elected by and responsible to the territorial assembly. The ministers of the executive council, chosen from the dominant political party, then elected a vice president (the president remained the high commissioner), in effect if not in name designating a prime minister. In 1957 the UPM dominated the election to the territorial assembly. Mokhtar Ould Daddah filled the executive council's vice presidency. In 1958 the constitution of the Fifth Republic provided for a French Community*, replacing the French Union, and Mauritania became an autonomous republic within the community—the Islamic Republic of Mauritania. However, Mauritanian nationalists were not satisfied, and under the leadership of the UPM and Daddah, Mauritania declared its independence on November 28, 1960. (Alfred G. Gerteiny, *Mauritania*, 1967.)

Karen Sleezer

MAURITIUS. Mauritius is an island of 650 square miles in the Indian Ocean approximately 490 miles east of Madagascar. It also includes the island of Rodrigues, about 480 miles further east. The island was first explored by Arab sailors in the tenth century, and the Portuguese mapped its waters in the mid-sixteenth century. The Netherlands took control of Mauritius in 1598, but the first Dutch colonists did not arrive until 1638. They named the colony after Maurice of Nassau, the Stadtholder of Holland. The colony soon failed, as did another attempt in 1664. The Dutch completely abandoned Mauritius in 1710, leaving behind some runaway slaves and thousands of acres of sugarcane.

The French then filled the vacuum. France had seized Rodrigues and Reunion* in 1638, and in 1715 the French East India Company claimed jurisdiction over Mauritius. In 1722 the company financed a colony there, naming it the "Ile de France." Corporate control gave way in 1764 when Mauritius became a crown colony. Sugar plantations thrived and by 1800 more than 60,000 people lived on the island—80 percent of them slaves. Mauritius became a prosperous colony in the French Empire*.

By the beginning of the nineteenth century, French pirates and privateers operating out of Mauritius were harassing British ships in the Indian Ocean. The Napoleonic Wars gave England the excuse she needed and in 1810 a fleet with 10,000 soldiers sailed from India and conquered Mauritius. In the Treaty of Paris of 1814, France ceded the colony, along with the Seychelles* and Rodrigues islands, to England. Under English direction the sugar plantations boomed. When England abolished slavery in 1833, Mauritius lost its labor supply, but that need was filled by immigrant, contract laborers from India—nearly 450,000 of them by the late 1870s. They became the largest ethnic group in the colony, constituting 70 percent of the population. The descendants of African slaves totaled 25 percent, leaving the French-Mauritian contingent at only 5 percent.

In 1885 England expanded the appointed council of government to include several elected, wealthy French-Mauritian property owners. Soon after England permitted the establishment of elected municipal councils to govern the major cities. The Indian-Mauritian majority began demanding more control over local affairs and the right to vote. The franchise was gradually expanded to more and more Mauritians, and in 1926 the first Indian was elected to the council of government.

Politics on the island after the 1930s was a struggle between the French-dominated Social Democratic Party and the Indian-dominated Labor Party. The Labor Party wanted independence while the Social Democrats wanted to maintain the connection with Britain. Early in the 1960s the blacks and the Muslim Committee of Action endorsed independence, and a national referendum on August 7, 1967, did the same. Labor Party leader Seewoosagur Ramgoolam then requested independence and England agreed. Mauritius became independent on March 12, 1968, and joined the Commonwealth of Nations*. (Burton Benedict, *Mauritius: Problems of a Plural Society*, 1965; Adele Smith Simons, *Modern Mauritius: The Politics of Decolonization*, 1982.)

MAXIMILIAN. Archduke of Austria and emperor of Mexico, Ferdinand Maximilian Joseph was born in Vienna, Austria, on July 6, 1832. He was the second son of Archduke Franz Karl and Archduchess Sophia of Bavaria. The younger brother of Emperor Francis Joseph I, he served as governor general of the Lombardo-Venetian kingdom. Mexican conservatives in France seeking to regain their confiscated lands and to overturn the liberal government of Benito Juárez persuaded Louis Napoleon* III, emperor of France, to establish a monarchy in Mexico*. Napoleon, eager to further his own imperial ambitions, offered the Mexican throne to Maximilian. He accepted the offer in April 1864, on condition that the Mexican people vote in favor of the proposition. Marshall Bazaine, commander-in-chief of the occupying French army, duly obtained a favorable plebiscite.

Maximilian was not the man conservatives had envisioned; he possessed none of the qualities needed to govern an empire. He was weak, irresolute, and naive. The strongest element of his character was the pride he held for his Habsburg ancestry. It was this pride that had been played upon to bring him to Mexico, and it would be used to keep him there long after it was prudent to remain. His weakest point was his adored wife, the Belgian princess Carlotta. High-strung and passionate, she would eventually become insane while seeking support for her husband from Napoleon and Pope Pius IX. She would live the remainder of her days in Belgium, never regaining her sanity, until her death in 1927.

Crowned emperor on June 10, 1864, Maximilian soon displayed his liberal bent. Animated by a noble faith in democracy and liberalism, Maximilian viewed himself as one who would abolish injustice and help the oppressed. He upheld the liberal reforms of Juárez, which antagonized conservative land owners, and he angered the Roman Catholic hierarchy by not restoring their confiscated estates. It appeared to the conservatives that they might as well have come to terms with Juárez instead of importing an emperor. It soon became evident, however, that Maximilian would not be able to bring order out of the chaos in Mexico. His primary problem was the depleted Mexican treasury, which could not meet the obligations being placed on it by the French, who had seized the customs to finance the Mexican debt owed to France. Maximilian, meanwhile, spent his time drafting detailed schemes and regulations that were never implemented or if implemented, never obeyed. Maximilian's liberal plans were ultimately doomed when the American Civil War ended in 1865.

The American government, invoking the Monroe Doctrine, was determined that the French should leave Mexico. To this end, the Americans began covertly to aid the Mexicans. American pressure combined with French discontent at home over the Mexican venture and a new threat arising out of Prussia, convinced Napoleon to quit Mexico. The French forces withdrew in March 1867, and Juárez moved back into Mexico City. Napoleon put pressure on Maximilian to abdicate, but Carlotta counseled against it and traveled to France in a failed attempt to persuade Napoleon to support her husband. Finally, at Queretaro, Maximilian and his small force were betrayed and captured on May 15, 1867. A court martial tried the emperor and sentenced him to death. Although half the crowned heads of Europe petitioned Juárez to pardon Maximilian, he was adamant that foreign interventionists be taught a lesson. On June 19, 1867, the emperor of Mexico was executed by a firing squad on the Hill of Bells outside Queretaro. (Joan Haslip, *The Crown of Mexico: Maximilian and His Empress Carlotta*, 1971.)

Michael Dennis

MAYOTTE. Mayotte is one of the Comoro Islands*. The tribal ruler of Mayotte ceded the island to France in 1841, and in 1843 the first French settlers arrived. French interest in the region was fueled by a desire to gain a stronger foothold in the Indian Ocean and to offset the British presence there. France established protectorates over the other Comoro Islands—Grand Comoro, Anjuan, and Mohilla—in 1886, but in 1908 they all came under the administrative supervision of Mayotte. In 1914 all of the Comoro Islands became part of Madagascar. See COMORO ISLANDS.

MELAKA. See MALACCA.

MELANESIA. The term Melanesia is used by geographers, ethnologists, and historians to describe the islands of the western Pacific, south of the equator. Melanesia includes Indonesia*, Papua New Guinea*, the Solomon Islands*, the Bismarck Archipelago*, New Caledonia*, Vanuatu, and Fiji*. Some today consider the term a racist label invented by nineteenth-century academics who were preoccupied with the racial distinctions between people. The term ''Melanesia'' is derived from *mela*, meaning black, and *nesos*, meaning island. (Frederica M. Bunge and Melinda W. Cooke, *Oceania. A Regional Study*, 1984.)

MELILLA. Melilla is a Spanish city located on the Mediterranean coast of Morocco*, approximately 165 miles east of Tangier. The city has been a major port in North Africa for two thousand years, but it did not become Spanish territory until 1497. Five years after the expulsion of the Moors from Granada in 1492, Spanish troops crossed the Mediterranean and conquered Melilla. Ever since then the city has been a Spanish possession administered from the province of Malaga. Its population in the mid–1980s was approximately 82,000 people. When Morocco became independent in 1956 Melilla was one of the areas of the former colony of Spanish Morocco over which Spain retained sovereignty. (J. H. Parry, *The Spanish Seaborne Empire*, 1966.)

MENDAÑA DE NEIRA, ÁLVARO DE. Álvaro de Mendaña de Neira was born in Galicia in 1542. He left Spain for the New World in 1567. Later in the year, Mendaña sailed from Callao, Peru, through the Pacific Ocean, hoping to locate islands which, according to Incan legends, were laden with silver and gold. He also hoped to find the great southern continent often indicated on Renaissance maps. Mendaña crossed the Pacific and first sighted one island in the Ellice* group. In February 1568 the expedition reached Santa Isabel in the central Solomon Islands.* Mendaña remained in the Solomons for six months, exploring several islands in the group. In August Mendaña made preparations for the long and arduous journey to western America. After a three-month voyage afflicted with terrible hardships, the expedition reached lower California in December 1568, wintered there, and finally returned to Callao on September 11, 1569.

In April 1595 Mendaña left on another voyage of exploration. He reached a heavily populated island group in July which they named Las Marquesas de Mendoza in honor of the viceroy of Peru. Bloody battles occurred with the people of the Marquesa Islands*. The Spaniards survived the struggles but fled the region and established a settlement on an island that they named Santa Cruz (now Ndemi). But internal bickering, native hostility, food shortages, and epidemic disease doomed the colony at Santa Cruz. Mendana died from tropical fever on October 18, 1595. The starving survivors made their way to Manila in February 1596. (William A. Amherst and Basil Thomson, eds., *The Discovery of the Solomon Islands by Alvaro de Mendana in 1568*, 1901; John C. Beaglehole, *The Exploration of the Pacific*, 1966.)

MERCANTILISM. Mercantilism refers to a set of ideas and practices, associated with the period from 1500 to 1800, by which the national state sought to enhance its power through the use of certain economic policies. The term lacks precise meaning, and policies advocated in its name were not always consistent. Mercantilist writers and government officials believed that they had the right answers to various problems and acted accordingly. They were less concerned with developing a systematic economic philosophy than with creating policies that would yield national power and prosperity. Consequently, mercantilism is not a very cohesive theory. It manifested itself in different ways in various nations, but it was closely associated with the rise of capitalism in Europe and the acquisition of colonial empires. Moving away from medieval values, Europeans began to embrace capitalistic business as the path to wealth and power. Occasionally there were conflicts between businessmen and mercantilist officials.

On balance, however, mercantilism aided the capitalist by supporting him with the power of the government.

Although the ingredients of mercantilism were different in each country, there were certain core policies and concepts that were generally found in all major European nations. A fundamental principle of mercantilism was bullionism, which called for the acquisition and retention of as much gold and silver as possible as the key to national wealth. The example of Spain in the sixteenth century convinced observers of the importance of money. To other European nations it seemed that Spain had achieved greatness mainly because of the bullion she obtained from colonies.

Most of the other policies recommended by mercantilists were linked to bullionism. They called, for example, for the development of gold and silver mines domestically or in colonies. Laws were promulgated to either prohibit entirely, or greatly restrict, the export of bullion, the strategy being to keep the gold and silver that flowed into a nation. Some countries, of course, had no gold or silver mines. Under these circumstances, mercantilists advocated increasing exports and decreasing imports so as to gain funds from international trade. This approach became associated with the concept of balance of trade, which maintained that only through an excess of exports over imports could a nation increase its comparative wealth. To achieve a favorable balance of trade, mercantilists called for import and export duties, government promotion of industry, mining, and agriculture, the building of a large merchant marine, and colonial possessions.

The mercantilists recommended high tariffs on the importation of manufactured goods and the exportation of raw materials. On the other hand, they called for low tariffs on the importation of raw materials and promotion of the exportation of finished goods. Following this formula, raw materials would be available for domestic industries and foreign industrial products would be kept out. Home industries would occupy a monopolistic position in the domestic market while also being encouraged to export.

Colonies were important for a number of reasons. First, they provided an additional market for the mother country's manufactured goods; second, they served as sources of supply of raw materials; third, colonial trade would provide income for the merchant marine; fourth, the colonial population was a source of inexpensive labor; fifth, colonies provided locations for commercial and military bases; and, sixth, colonies increased a nation's prestige.

Portuguese mercantilism was highly developed and its main objective was to control the eastern spice trade, which was a royal monopoly. Under the Spanish mercantilist system, the colonies were dependent directly on the king. Spain tried, but not always successfully, to maintain a trading monopoly with her colonies. Dutch mercantilism was unique in that industry in Holland was unusually dependent on the export market. Consequently, the government was very active in supporting commerce, fighting a number of wars for economic reasons, and using its navy to obtain concessions for its merchants. English mercantilism can be illustrated by the following examples. A law passed in 1621 required colonial tobacco to be shipped to Great Britain before being sent to foreign ports. A 1624 law called for colonial tobacco to be transported only on English ships. (Shepard B. Clough and Charles W. Cole, *Economic History of Europe*, 1952.)

Roy E. Thoman

MÉRIDA-LA GRITA. In 1575 the Spanish crown created the province of Espiritu Santo de La Grita in what is today Venezuela and assigned a governor there. The province fell administratively under the authority of the Audiencia of New Granada. Because of population changes the province was dissolved in 1608 and La Grita was united into a single *corregimiento* with the settlement at Mérida, which was under the jurisdiction of the Audiencia of Santo Domingo. Spain then raised Mérida-La Grita to a province in 1625. Maracaibo was added to the province in 1676. To resolve a great deal of administrative confusion, Mérida was transferred to the authority of the Audiencia of New Granada in 1740, and the name of the entire colony was changed to Maracaibo in 1751. In 1777 Maracaibo became part of the Captaincy-General of Venezuela. Effective Spanish control over the region was over by 1810 and Maracaibo became part of Gran Colombia and then Venezuela. See COLOMBIA; VENEZUELA.

MEXICO. See NEW SPAIN.

MICRONESIA. The term Micronesia is used by geographers, ethnologists, and historians to describe the islands of the western Pacific, north of the equator. Composed of more than 2,000 volcanic islands and coral atolls, Micronesia includes the Caroline Islands*, Palau*, the Gilbert Islands*, the Marianas*, the Marshall Islands*, and Nauru*. (Frederica M. Bunge and Melinda W. Cooke, *Oceania. A Regional Study*, 1984.)

MIDDLE CONGO. See FRENCH CONGO.

MIDWAY. An unincorporated territory of the United States, Midway consists of two islands, Sand and Eastern, and the surrounding atoll. They are located in the central Pacific 1,150 miles northwest of Honolulu. The total area of Midway is about 2 square miles. Midway was discovered by the United States in 1859, and in 1867 Captain William Reynolds of the U.S.S. *Lackawanna* annexed it in the name of the United States. In 1903 a cable station was opened on the island, and in 1935 Midway became a stopping point for Pan American Airways. It was fortified by the United States in 1941. One of the great naval battles of history took place nearby in 1942 when a Japanese fleet was attacked and destroyed by United States aircraft. Currently, Midway is a naval installation administered by the United States Navy. (*Associated Press Almanac, 1973*, 1973; *The World Almanac and book of Facts, 1982*, 1982.)

Joseph M. Rowe, Jr.

MINAS GERAIS. An area rich in gold and diamonds, Minas Gerais was part of Sao Vicente* until 1710 when it was transferred to Sao Paulo* authority. The region attracted large numbers of settlers, and in 1720 Portugal created the captaincy of Sao Paulo e Minas do Ouro, an administrative combination of Sao Paulo and Minas Gerais. That arrangement proved too unwieldly, since the geography and distances between the two regions was too great, and in 1720 the two areas were separated. Minas Gerais became a province of the new empire of Brazil* in 1822. See BRAZIL.

MINDANAO. Mindanao is the second largest island of the Philippines*, more than 36,000 square miles in area. Its coastline is highly irregular, with long peninsulas and wide bays. The complex topography includes mountains, plateaus, lakes, swampy river basins, and some remaining virgin jungle in the interior where small tribes dwell in isolation from the outside world. Mindanao was long considered an island of opportunity, waiting to be developed, but intensive immigration has almost erased its frontier character.

All of Mindanao would be Islamic today had the Spaniards not intervened, just after expelling Muslims from Spain itself. They were not happy about traveling halfway around the globe only to run into more Muslims. Spain took Luzon* and the Visayas (central islands) and struggled ceaselessly against the "Moros" (Tausug, Samal, Maguindanao, Maranao, and other groups) but could never really defeat them. To check the spread of Islam, the Spaniards colonized the northern coast of Mindanao with Cebuano-speaking Filipino Christians.

Sovereignty over the Philippines went to the United States after the Spanish-American War* (1898). America forced the recalcitrant Muslims into the state, but only after a series of bloody battles that continued as late as 1912. American colonial authorities thought of Mindanao as a safety valve for the overpopulation and poverty that threatened social order in Luzon. Land could be cleared, and Filipinos encouraged to homestead. The independent government of the Republic of the Philippines has continued that policy. There is now a three-to-one Christian majority in Mindanao, but prejudice and hatred characterize relations between Christian and Muslim Filipinos.

Mindanao has considerable mineral deposits: coal, copper, chromite, iron ore, manganese, and tin. The economy, however, is presently more dependent on plantation agriculture. Huge tracts of land have been planted in pineapples and bananas. Illegal logging is out of control due to corruption and chaos in Philippine politics. A three-way war between the Philippine army, the communist New People's Army, and Moro separatists leaves the future of Mindanao very uncertain. (Alfred W. McCoy and Edilberto de Jesus, *Philippine Social History*, 1982; Frederick Wernstedt and J. E. Spencer, *The Philippine Island World*, 1967.)

Ross Marlay

MINORCA. Minorca is one of the Balearic Islands in the western Mediterranean. During the eighteenth century the British, Spanish, and French considered the island to be of great strategic importance in terms of controlling the sea lanes to North Africa and the Middle East, equally as important as Gibraltar*. In 1708 the British navy seized control of Minorca from Spain and appointed its own governor. In the Treaty of Utrecht* of 1713, Spain formally recognized the British claim. But at the outset of the Seven Years War* in 1756, France captured Minorca, only to return it to the British seven years later in the Treaty of Paris* ending the war.

By that time, however, the British had decided that Gibraltar was indeed strategically more significant, and in 1782 they returned Minorca to Spanish sovereignty. When the Napoleonic Wars erupted, however, the British wanted Minorca back, so they took it again from Spain in 1798. Four years later they returned the island permanently to Spain. (David P. Henige, *Colonial Governors from the Fifteenth Century to the Present*, 1970.)

MIQUELON. See ST. PIERRE AND MIQUELON.

MOLUCCAS. The Moluccas are the easternmost islands of Indonesia*, grouped together for administrative purposes into the province of Maluku. They once were known as the Spice Islands*—the goal of early European explorers who discovered many other lands and continents while searching for the source of the cloves, nutmeg, mace, cinnamon, and peppers that fetched such high prices in Europe. The Moluccas include the following islands and groups: Halmahera (the largest), Ternate, Tidore, Obi, Sula, Ceram and Buru, tiny Amboina, plus Wetar, Kai, Aru, the Banda Islands, and the Tanimbar group. In addition, there are hundreds of smaller islands scattered around the Banda Sea, Arafura Sea, Molucca Sea, and Timor Sea that are considered part of the Moluccas. These islands actually have little in common. Some are mountainous and some are swampy; some dry and some well-watered. Some are populated mainly by Malays, some by Melanesians. There are Muslims, Christians, and animists. The unifying factors are historical and political: They were fought over by the Portuguese, Spanish, Dutch, and English, and when the Dutch expelled their rivals spice production was organized along mercantilist lines. The Dutch monopoly yielded high profits for a while but was abandoned when Dutch policy shifted to free trade. The Moluccas became a remote backwater when economic development transformed Sumatra* and Java*. Today the Moluccas account for less than 2 percent of Indonesia's population. Separatist movements have challenged Indonesian sovereignty. Rebels tried to establish an independent "Republic of East Indonesia" in 1950, but now even Christian Amboina is resigned to being, in effect, a peripheral part of a Javanese empire called "Indonesia." (J. J. Van Klavern, *The Dutch Colonial System in the East Indies*, 1953.)

Ross Marlay

MOMBASA. Mombasa is an island city just off the east coast of Africa in what is today Kenya*. The Portuguese first took control of Mombasa in 1593 in an attempt to block Ottoman expansion down the east coast of Africa. At first

Portugal hoped it would become an important link in its chain of forts across the Indian Ocean—Mozambique, Portuguese India*, Ceylon*, and Malacca*. But Mombasa never assumed a role of much importance, and in 1698 it was seized by Omani Arabs. Portugal regained the colony in 1728 but then abandoned it permanently in 1729. (David P. Henige, *Colonial Governors from the Fifteenth Century to the Present*, 1970.)

MONROE DOCTRINE. The Monroe Doctrine, a fundamental statement of United States hemispheric policy, developed from deep concern about the rumored danger of Spanish-French intervention in Latin America and expansive Russian claims to the Pacific coast of North America. President James Monroe of the United States announced the policy in his annual address to Congress on December 2, 1823. He enunciated four basic principles: (1) the American continents, made up of independent nations, were no longer subject to future colonization by European nations; (2) the political systems of the European powers (monarchy) were different from that of America, where independence and republicanism were won at the cost of great bloodshed and treasure, and the United States would regard attempts to spread the European system to the western hemisphere as "dangerous to our peace and safety"; (3) the United States had never nor would ever interfere with colonies already established in this hemisphere; and (4) the United States had never involved itself in the wars of the European nations, "nor does it comport with our policy to do so." Although it was hardly noticed at the time, President Monroe's statement evolved to the status of national dogma by 1900. (Dexter Perkins, *The Monroe Doctrine, 1823–1826*, 1927; E. H. Tatum, Jr., *The United States and Europe, 1815–1823: A Study in the Background of the Monroe Doctrine*, 1936.)

Joseph M. Rowe, Jr.

MONTREAL. From their initial base in the town of Quebec*, French settlers (in the colony of New France) expanded out and established the settlement of Montreal in 1642. As such, it was a separate administrative entity, complete with its own governor, in New France* from 1642 until its capture by the English in 1760. Montreal became the center of the fur trade in New France. See NEW FRANCE.

MONTSERRAT. Montserrat is an island of 39 square miles, one of the Lesser Antilles* in the Caribbean. Europeans first sighted the island in 1493 during Christopher Columbus's second voyage to the New World, but for 150 years neither the Spanish nor the English saw much economic use in the island, particularly because of the ferocity of the native Carib Indians. In 1632 Thomas Warner brought a group of English and Irish settlers to Montserrat, and they were soon joined by other immigrants from the British North American colonies of Virginia* and Maryland*. They built a local economy based first on tobacco and eventually on cotton, indigo, and sugar. Beginning in 1664 African slaves were imported to work the land. The plantation system was the backbone of the economy until the nineteenth century, when the abolition of slavery in 1834 and steadily falling sugar prices impoverished the island.

Over the years Montserrat suffered at the hands of French adventurers and naval officials. France attacked and temporarily seized Montserrat in 1664, lost it in 1665, retook it in 1667, and in the Treaty of Breda in 1668 returned it to British sovereignty. During the War of the Spanish Succession, France attacked Montserrat again but lost control in the Treaty of Utrecht of 1713*. When France formed an alliance with the colonies during the American Revolution*, she again looked longingly on Montserrat, seizing the island in 1782. The Treaty of Paris* ending the revolution in 1783 restored Montserrat to English control, where she has remained ever since.

Beginning in 1871 Montserrat accepted membership in the Federal Colony of the Leeward Islands, an English colony which included the British Virgin Islands*, Dominica*, St. Kitts, Nevis*, and Anguilla*. That colony was dissolved in 1956, and Montserrat became a crown colony in its own right. Between 1958 and 1962, Montserrat was part of the West Indies Federation*. The people of Montserrat ratified their own constitution in 1960, which provided for a British-appointed governor and a locally elected legislature. In recent years a budding nationalist movement has emerged on Montserrat, led by the People's Liberation Movement (PLM). Since 1978 the PLM has controlled the colonial legislature, and although PLM leaders talk eventually of complete independence from Great Britain, they are reluctant to take that step until the local economy has diversified and achieved a measure of self-sustaining growth. (George R. Margetson, *England in the West Indies*, 1977; W. Adolphe Roberts, *The French in the West Indies*, 1942.)

MOROCCAN CRISIS OF 1911. The first years of the twentieth century were marked by a succession of crises between France and Germany over Morocco*, with the most serious one occurring in 1911. The Algeciras Conference of 1906* had acknowledged the predominant role of France in Morocco, in spite of German attempts at shared influence there. When a local rebellion had driven the sultan of Morocco, who was a protégé of France, out of his capital at Fez in 1911, French troops were sent to restore order. As Germany was determined to extract compensation for any French gain in the area, it declared that the French action nullified the Algeciras agreement. On July 1, a German gunboat, the *Panther*, was sent to Agadir as a demonstration of Germany's interest in the affair. German demands for French Congo* as compensation were at first rejected by France. But the French premier, Joseph Caillaux, was known to be friendly to Germany. On the other hand, the British government became alarmed at the private bargaining going on between France and Germany, which might have led to the cession of Agadir to Germany as a base on the Atlantic coast. In a speech delivered in July, British Premier Lloyd George stated that Great Britain was not indifferent to possible changes in the area. This constituted a warning to

France as much as to Germany. Tension built up throughout the month of August, leading to preparations for war in Great Britain, France, and Germany. In September there was a financial panic in Germany. However, in November, a new agreement was ultimately negotiated. Germany recognized France's right to establish a protectorate over Morocco in return for part of the French Congo with access to the sea, an area of about 100,000 square miles. War had been averted for the time being. Because the assumption of French power in Morocco appeared imminent, Italy resolved, with French and British assent, to seize Tripoli from the Ottoman Empire. (Edmund Burke III, *Prelude to Protectorate in Morocco*, 1976.)

Alain G. Marsot

MOROCCO. Morocco occupies a strategic location at the northwestern corner of Africa, separated from western Europe by the narrow straits of Gibraltar*— the columns of Hercules of antiquity. It therefore controls partly the passage from the Mediterranean into the Atlantic. Populated in the past by Berber peoples, just as the rest of North Africa, Morocco has been subjected to successive invasions and influences, from the Phoenicians and the Carthaginians to the Romans, the Vandals, the Visigoths, and the Byzantine Greeks. But the most significant invasion and influence was that of the Arabs in the seventh century A.D., who brought with them Arab civilization and Islam, plus a large immigration of Arabs. Direct Arab rule by the caliph from the Middle East did not last very long, and the four states of North Africa started to develop in an autonomous fashion, with the rise, from the eleventh to the thirteenth century of two large empires, that of the Almoravids (1042–1147) and that of the Almohads (1147–1269), who united all of the Maghrib and Islamic Spain. After them, separate kingdoms arose in Tunis, Tlemcen, and Fez. Ottoman rule came to North Africa in the middle of the sixteenth century, but Morocco was never occupied by the Ottoman Empire. It has had a ruling monarchy for twelve centuries with the present dynasty, the Alawis, in power from the seventeenth century. Part of the Alawis' legitimacy derives from the fact that they descend from the Prophet Muhammad.

Because of its location and its resources, Morocco became an area of interest to the European powers, notably France, in the first part of the nineteenth century. Having conquered Algeria* in 1830 and established a protectorate over Tunisia* in 1881, the French wanted to complete their control of the whole Maghrib. Neighboring Spain also had ambitions in Morocco. The Moroccan monarchy was in a state of stagnation, increasingly unable to control the mountain Berbers. Moroccan sultans fell into the familiar trap of borrowing money from European bankers, mostly French, in order to reassert internal control, buy weapons, and modernize the economy generally. By 1900 the country was so much in debt that the French took over the management of its finances. In 1904 the major European powers signed a secret agreement, recognizing France's and Spain's spheres of influence in Morocco, which was formalized in 1906 at the Algeciras

Conference. Anti-foreign agitation in Casablanca and Fez in 1912 led to French military intervention from Algeria and the signing of a Franco-Spanish treaty establishing a French protectorate over most of Morocco, and a Spanish protectorate over the country's northern and southern zones, while Tangier became an international city ruled by several European powers.

It took the French more than twenty years to pacify the country, where resistance was most active in the mountains, and they also intervened militarily to put down a rebellion in the Spanish zone of the Rif. Most of the organization of the protectorate was the work of the first resident-general, Marshall Lyautey*, who was intent on preserving Moroccan traditions and culture, while modernizing its political institutions and its economy. But the traditional elites were maintained, and the French worked with local chiefs, the *qaids*, with different administrative systems for the Berber-speaking regions in an effort at "divide and rule" which antagonized both Arab and Berber populations. The sultan remained a figurehead. Meanwhile, French settlers were given preferential treatment, economic incentives, and invited to buy land and develop vineyards and citrus groves. They also built modern cities alongside Moroccan cities.

The nationalist movement for independence started slowly, but acquired momentum in the late 1920s with economic difficulties and increased frustrations in the cities, notably on the part of western-educated young men. The first nationalist party, the Comite d'Action Marocaine, was formed in 1934 but dissolved by the French three years later. That nationalist movement received a further boost from World War II, with the foundation of the Istiqlal (Independence) party in 1943, which based its arguments for independence on the Atlantic Charter and the Allies' claim of their support for the self-determination of the colonized peoples after the end of the war. Originally based on urban elites, the Istiqlal provided the main leadership for the independence movement, became progressively a mass party, and benefited from the open support of the throne. The French continued to rely upon traditionalist elements in the countryside, notably the powerful rural *qaids*, and arrested most of the Istiglal leaders.

By then, the sultan, Muhammad ben Yusuf, had become involved in the independence movement, and the French decided to get rid of him and replace him with someone more to their liking. In 1953, in collusion with a powerful local chief, al Glawi, pasha of Marrakesh, they demanded the sultan's abdication. When he refused, the French deposed and deported to Madagascar Muhammad ben Yusuf and replaced him with an older and pliable relative, Ben Arafa. But this move had the opposite effect to what the French had hoped. It triggered massive nationalist agitation for independence and in favor of the deposed sultan, regarded as a martyr. It was also accompanied by violence against French settlers and the appearance of guerrilla fighters in the countryside. Already under pressure in Tunisia, and most of all in Algeria, the French government gave in. Muhammad ben Yusuf returned in triumph in November 1954 and reascended the throne. Negotiations leading to independence soon began. Independence was finally achieved in March 1956, with the end of the French and Spanish protectorates.

Tangier was reintegrated into Morocco in October of the same year, but retained its free port status for a few more years. Spain kept control of Ifni* in the south until 1969, and of the small enclaves of Ceuta* and Melilla* in the north, which it has retained to this day in spite of sporadic Moroccan claims. On the other hand, when Spain relinquished its rule over its colony of Western Sahara in 1976, Morocco annexed most of it, in spite of local opposition on the part of a nationalist guerrilla force, the Polisario Front, which has received some assistance from neighboring countries, such as Libya and Algeria. (Robin Bidwell, *Morocco Under Colonial Rule: French Administration of Tribal Areas, 1912–1956*, 1973; John P. Halstead, *Rebirth of a Nation: Origins and Rise of Moroccon Nationalism 1912–1944*, 1967.)

Alain G. Marsot

MOSKITO COAST. Beginning in the late seventeenth century, Great Britain developed a strategic and economic interest in the eastern coast of Central America. British companies maintained large-scale logging operations on the coast, and the British government forged an alliance with the Moskito Indians, who wanted to break the back of Spanish power there. In 1740 Great Britain appointed a superintendent to administer the logging settlements, but they dissolved that office in 1782 when their economic interests shifted to British Honduras (Belize*). In 1860 Great Britain ceded what had been the Moskito Coast territory to Nicaragua*. See BELIZE; NICARAGUA.

MOUNTBATTEN, LORD LOUIS. Born June 25, 1900, in Windsor, England, the First Earl Mountbatten of Burma was a British admiral and the last viceroy of India. Mountbatten was the son of Prince Louis of Battenburg and Princess Victoria, a granddaughter of Queen Victoria. In 1913 Louis Mountbatten entered the Royal Navy as a midshipman and saw service during several major engagements in World War I, including the battle of Jutland. Mountbatten became a lieutenant in 1920 and later served as personal aide-de-camp to his cousin, the Prince of Wales, the future King Edward VIII.

At the beginning of World War II, Mountbatten was a Royal Navy captain and personal aide-de-camp to King George VI. In 1939 he was given command of a destroyer flotilla. In the battle of Crete in May 1941, his own destroyer HMS *Kelly* was sunk. Mountbatten was then given command of the aircraft carrier *Illustrious* until he was appointed chief of combined naval operations in March 1942. In this capacity, Mountbatten was responsible for planning commando raids against German-held Channel ports. He became Supreme Allied Commander of the Southeast Asia Command in 1943. By 1944–1945, Mountbatten had skillfully organized the campaign that drove Japanese military forces from Burma. In 1946 he was made viscount, and in 1947 he was promoted to rear admiral and created earl.

Mountbatten was named viceroy of India in 1947 and was charged with carrying out the plans for independence of the subcontinent. The Mountbatten

Plan for independence, announced by the government of Great Britain on June 3, 1947, provided for the partition of India into two states—a Hindu state, Hindustan, and a Muslim state, Pakistan*. Both states received the rights of a dominion in the British Commonwealth. In the northwestern border province and in the Sylhet District of Assam, the question of which state to join was settled by referendum and in Sind, by vote of the local legislative assembly. In Punjab and Bengal the issue of demarcation was decided by vote of the legislative assemblies; deputies from Muslim-majority areas and deputies from Hindu-majority areas voted separately. Autonomous princes were given the right to choose either to join one of the two dominions or to retain their previous relations with Great Britain. After these measures were carried out, the constituent assembly of India was divided into the assemblies of Hindustan and Pakistan. On August 5, 1947, the partition was complete and both states became dominions. The Mountbatten Plan was confirmed by parliament and crown as the statute on the independence of India.

Mountbatten resigned as governor-general of India in 1948 and returned to navy duty. In 1950, he became lord commissioner of the Admiralty, fourth sea lord, and chief of supplies and transport. From 1952 to 1954 he served as NATO (North Atlantic Treaty Organization) commander in chief. From 1959 until his retirement in 1967 he was chief of the defense staff. Lord Louis Mountbatten was killed on August 28, 1979, by an Irish Republican Army terrorist bomb which destroyed his fishing boat off Mullaghmore, Ireland. (Judith M. Brown, *Modern India: The Origins of an Asian Democracy*, 1985; Philip Ziegler, *Mountbatten*, 1985.)

William G. Ratliff

MOZAMBIQUE. Mozambique, formerly known as Portuguese East Africa, is an independent country on the southeastern coast of Africa opposite the island of Madagascar*. It is bordered by the Indian Ocean on the east, the Republic of South Africa* and Swaziland* on the south, Zimbabwe on the west, Zambia* and Malawi on the northwest, and Tanzania* on the north. Early inhabitants of the area were Bantu farmers. Over the centuries Arabs came across the Indian Ocean and established trading posts along the coast. In 1498 the Portuguese navigator Vasco da Gama* explored this area and stopped at Arab trading stations along the coast. The Portuguese soon set up their own trading posts and ports of call along the sea route to the East Indies. The first Portuguese settlement was established in Sofala in the early 1500s. Other Portuguese settlements were soon established at Quelimane and Sena. Portuguese expeditions went into the interior and searched for gold, with disappointing results. By the middle of the seventeenth century Mozambique was an important slave-trade market.

The most significant effort by the Portuguese to colonize the interior involved the granting of vast *prazos* (estates), which began in the seventeenth century. These were to be controlled by white settlers—*prazeros*—who would also serve as the Portuguese administrators of their areas. Title to the land was held by

Portugal and was leased to the *prazeros* on a long-term basis. The Portuguese hope of a white enclave along the upper reaches of Zambezi River began to be diluted by miscegenation with the Africans. The mixed race people were referred to as "Mesticos." Beginning in 1677, laws were passed to reduce the size of the *prazos* which had become very large and powerful. Even though laws limiting *prazos* to 15 square kilometers were enacted, some families still managed to create very powerful estates through intermarriage. As time went on the *prazeros* became less dependent on Portugal, and ultimately many large estates refused to acknowledge any Portuguese authority. In the late seventeenth century, Portuguese efforts to penetrate into the interior received a setback when the *prazeros* were driven out of the gold-producing Zimbabwe highlands by the rise of the Changamire Empire.

During the eighteenth century Portugal persisted in the effort to exercise control over the *prazo* system in Mozambique, and in 1752 appointed a governor to preside over civil and military affairs in the colony. Before that time, Mozambique had been administered out of Goa*. Throughout the eighteenth century Portugal resisted the attempts of other European countries to open markets in Mozambique. The Dutch East India Company* opened a trading post in 1721 in Delagoa Bay. The British also became active in trading at Delagoa Bay. The French during the Napoleonic Wars attacked Portuguese coastal settlements.

In the early nineteenth century Portugal was still having a difficult time attracting colonists to Mozambique. There were few incentives, and most settlers who did come were political prisoners or convicts. In the 1820s the slave trade reached its zenith in Mozambique with the exportation of 15,000 Africans. The slave trade was banned by royal decree in 1836, but the export of slaves from Mozambique continued despite the ban. Reacting to British complaints based on reports of David Livingstone, Portugal again totally abolished slavery in all Portuguese possessions in 1878. Making this decree effective in Mozambique, however, required many more years. Because Portugal lacked the economic strength to pursue a vigorous policy of colonial expansion, the Portuguese presence in Mozambique was limited to the coastal areas and the Zambezi Valley until the late 1800s. At that time, Portugal joined the "scramble for Africa*," overcoming African resistance in the hinterlands and establishing the present borders of Mozambique in treaties with the other European powers.

In 1888 the *prazero* system was decisively ended with the defeat of the powerful de Cruz family. With the help of a rival *prazero*, Manuel Antonio de Sousa (Gouveia), Portuguese troops used heavy artillery, killing 6,000 people and taking the Massangano fortress of the de Cruz prazo. After this victory, only the Gouveia *prazo* retained any influence in Mozambique. Finding the *prazo* system unworkable, the Portuguese turned to the British system of chartered companies, granting them rights to develop the country. Until 1926 much of the governing of Mozambique was done through chartered companies. These companies forced the people to pay taxes and work the land. Forced labor on a road-building project in 1914, and conscription into the army during World War I, caused the Zambezi Revolts of 1917. Twenty thousand Portuguese troops were required to subdue the rebellion, but guerrilla activity continued until 1920. In the 1930s, the Portuguese government began to revise its colonial policy, becoming even less progressive than before. The colonial statute of 1930 reduced the powers of colonial authorities and gave Portugal more direct control over its colonial empire. By 1951 Mozambique had become an overseas province of Portugal.

After British and French colonies in Africa began to gain their independence, resistance to Portuguese colonialism grew. Nationalist movements emerged in Mozambique. The foremost of these was the Mozambique Liberation Front (FRELIMO) led by Eduardo C. Mondlane. An armed struggle began on September 25, 1964, and by 1968 FRELIMO claimed it controlled one-fifth of the country. Mondlane was assassinated in 1969 and was replaced by Samora Machel. The FRELIMO struggle continued into 1975, with Mozambique becoming independent on June 25, 1975. Machel was the first president. (Allen and Barbara Isaacman, *Mozambique: From Colonialism to Revolution*, 1983.)

Amanda Pollock

MUSCAT AND OMAN. See OMAN.

MUSLIM LEAGUE. European imperialism sometimes revived and at times created the nationalism that would eventually bring colonialism to its end. British rule in India* is a case in point. British introduction into India of a western system of education also brought about ideas of liberalism and constitutionalism. The Hindus of India—the majority—whose culture had been despised under Muslim rule at the time of the Mughals, availed themselves rapidly of the new opportunities presented by western education. In time, they would turn western ideas against their present rulers, leading to the creation of a nationalist movement, incarnated in the Indian National Congress Party, founded in 1885. At first, the Indian Muslims remained aloof. But the appeal to the Hindu past heritage as the basis of nationalist sentiment, an indispensable move for the sake of unity in a people divided by race, language, and the pervasive caste system, was bound to create fear and hostility within the sizable Muslim minority, which constituted more than a quarter of the total population. The result was the foundation, in 1906, of the Muslim League, to protect Muslim interests. The fledgling movement, supported by the British, aimed at safeguarding Muslim rights in the context of gains achieved by the Hindu nationalists, but it led to Hindu accusations of British use of the "divide and rule" approach for their own ends. In any case, the Muslims could not afford to take on two adversaries at the onset, and the British supported the League as a counterweight to the Congress. This was manifested in the 1905 temporary partition of Bengal into two provinces, one with a Muslim majority, and the creation of special constituencies for Muslims in the framework of the 1909 Morley-Minto reforms, accompanied by lower tax base requirements for voting participation for Muslims.

World War I saw a lull in nationalist agitation as India gave wholehearted support to Britain in the conflict. The period was also marked by a rapprochement between the Congress and the League and a tentative agreement on special representation for Muslims. At the end of the war the Muslims were disturbed by the dismemberment of the Ottoman Empire and the threat to the caliphate. Their agitation in the Khilafat movement was supported by Gandhi*, until the Turks themselves abolished the caliphate. But in the interwar period, separatist Muslim feelings grew, because of the failure to reach an agreement between the two nationalist movements to protect Muslim religious and economic rights. There was also a series of bitter communal disturbances. By then, the League benefited from the guidance of an able, astute, and thoroughly westernized leader—Mohammad Ali Jinnah*.

The idea of a separate Muslim nation, or nations, emerged in the 1930s, even though many Muslims and Hindus have a common racial origin, some having converted to Islam more or less recently. The concept of a separate nation was publicly endorsed by Jinnah, at the All India Muslim League meeting in Lahore on March 23, 1940. This came to be known as the Pakistan* Resolution. From then on, the two-nations theory became the foundation of the Muslim League's ideology, based as it was on the fear that Indian Muslims would lose their cultural and religious identity under Hindu domination. But what sort of state would Pakistan be? Would it be an Islamic state, based on traditional ideology, or would it be adapted to modern times? Most of the League's leaders were western-educated lawyers or landowners, using Islam as a rallying and unifying factor against the more numerous Hindu nationalists, much more than against the British imperialists. In fact, British civil servants found it easier to work with conservative Muslim politicians than with more progressive and demanding Congress party members. To be sure, there were Muslim politicians who were receptive to social democracy, economic planning, nationalization of key industries, land reform, and a better distribution of wealth. But in the final analysis, the Muslim League was not a political party in the traditional sense, but first and foremost a movement for national independence. The organization of the League influenced its ideology. It was marked by a centralization of power under the charismatic Jinnah, with most great landowners in the leadership, and a disproportionate number in the leadership of people from Punjab and Sind. Provincial rivalries were rampant, and after Jinnah's death, no collective leadership emerged and no machinery existed to settle intra-party disputes.

However, the League prospered during World War II, helped by the fact that most Congress leaders were in and out of jail for the duration. By 1944 the League's membership had reached two million. When the prospect of British departure from India became increasingly likely, the Congress and the League failed to reach an agreement for an interim government and a constitution. In June 1947 Britain announced it would grant full dominion status to two successor states, India and Pakistan, the latter made up of two wings separated by 3,000 miles of Indian territory. The birth of the new states was marked by communal rioting, massive losses of life, and the transfer of populations, ending in more than 5 million refugees. But the League's goal of Pakistan, an independent state for most of the Muslims of India, had been achieved.

After 1948 the Muslim League gradually disintegrated, following the death of Jinnah and the assassination of his most able lieutenant, Liaqat Ali Khan. Relations between India and Pakistan remained tense, mostly over the disputed territory of Kashmir (over which there was more trouble in 1989–1990), leading to armed conflicts in 1949, 1965–1966, and 1971, the latter marked by the break-up between the two wings of Pakistan and the birth of a new Muslim nation, Bangladesh. (C. H. Philips and M. D. Wainwright, eds., *The Partition of India*, 1971.)

Alain G. Marsot

N

NAGASAKI. Nagasaki is a city in the extreme southwest of Japan, on the island of Kyushu, with a current population of about half a million. It has one of the finest harbors in the country in a fjord-like inlet two and a half miles from the open sea and protected by offshore islands. Nagasaki's role in Japanese history is unique—the city was Japan's only "window on the West" for more than two centuries. From 1641 to 1854 the Tokugawa seclusion policy sought to protect Japan from European imperialism by drastically restricting, while not totally eliminating, diplomatic and commercial intercourse. Nagasaki was the sole point of entry for Western goods and ideas. Japanese ships were designed for sailing the inland sea, not the open ocean, so all long-range trade was in the hands of foreigners. Nagasaki's location made it a natural port of call for Chinese and European ships.

The Portugese arrived in 1571, followed by the Spaniards, English, and Dutch, all motivated by a different mix of strategic, commercial, and religious interests. The Iberians mostly wanted to save souls, and their alarming success led to their undoing. They were not cautious about meddling in Japanese politics. When Japanese authorities learned that the Catholic Church in Europe wielded vast political as well as religious power, they concluded that Christianity could subvert the traditional Confucian order regulating the state. The Spaniards were expelled in 1624 and the Portuguese in 1639. The English, finding little commercial gain, left of their own accord. That left the Protestant Dutch, who were so much more interested in trade than in proselytizing that they actually lent artillery to government forces slaughtering Japanese Christians on the Shimabara Peninsula in 1637. As many as 30,000 were killed and the survivors practiced their religion in secret for 250 years without benefit of church or clergy.

Suppression of Christianity was only one aspect of the extreme xenophobia that characterized Tokugawa policy. All Japanese were forbidden to travel abroad. Any who did, and returned, were killed. All foreigners except the Dutch were excluded, and they were confined to one tiny island, Dejima, connected to Nagasaki city by a guarded bridge. Only Japanese merchants and prostitutes could cross. The gates were shut at night. The dozen or so resident Dutch could walk no further than up and down the two streets of their small enclave. Unpromising as this situation seemed, Dejima became the place where "Rangaku" (Dutch learning) entered and eventually transformed Japan.

At first language problems hindered all but the most rudimentary commercial deals, as Dutch and Japanese struggled to understand each other using Portuguese. Later the Japanese compiled Dutch-Japanese dictionaries and supplied official interpreters, who translated lists of goods, medical books, astronomical tables, and treatises on military fortification and naval strategy. In 1720 the government lifted the ban on importing Dutch books. More cracks appeared in the Tokugawa seclusion policy, and Japanese scholars traveled to Nagasaki for what was now called "yogaku" (Western learning). Interest spread from science and technology to Western artistic techniques, and then to lively European philosophical and political debates. By the first half of the nineteenth century there were private Dutch academies in the major cities.

Nagasaki lost its monopoly on Western trade when Japan opened up to the west after Admiral Matthew Perry* visited, but prospered as a coaling station, and as the winter port for the Russian Asiatic fleet until 1903. Industrial growth, particularly shipbuilding, transformed Nagasaki, but bigger industrial centers such as Osaka and Yokohama eclipsed it economically. Nagasaki's history of involvement with the West reached an ironic and tragic denouement on August 9, 1945, when a single atomic bomb killed 100,000 people. (Grant Goodman, *The Dutch Impact on Japan, 1650–1853*, 1967; Donald Keene, *The Japanese Discovery of Europe, 1720–1830*, 1969.)

Ross Marlay

NAMIBIA. See SOUTH WEST AFRICA.

NAPOLEON, LOUIS. (Charles Louis Napoleon Bonaparte, Napoleon III). Born April 20, 1808, in Paris, the son of Hortense de Beauharnais (the stepdaughter of Napoleon I) and Napoleon's brother Louis Bonaparte, Louis Napoleon lived in exile after the downfall of Napoleon I in 1815. Following the death of the Duke of Reichstadt (Napoleon's son) in 1832, the Bonapartists declared Louis Napoleon the legitimate pretender to the French throne. Based on that support, in 1836 and in 1840 he tried to instigate military revolts and seize power in France. Napoleon was subsequently arrested and sentenced to life imprisonment.

After escaping to Britain in 1846, he returned to France during the 1848

Revolution. Drawing on the support of ecclesiastics and the association of his name with that of Napoleon I, plus his support for stability and order which appealed to the middle class, Louis Napoleon was elected president of the French Republic on December 10, 1848. Prevented from reelection by constitutional provision, on December 2, 1851, he carried out a successful coup d'état, which was ratified by a plebiscite a short time later. Following a second plebiscite, Louis Napoleon established the Second Empire on December 2, 1852, calling himself Napoleon III.

Politically, Napoleon III's rule was autocratic from 1853 to 1860. From 1860 until 1870, however, he introduced a number of liberal reforms, many of them under pressure from his political opponents. In foreign affairs, Napoleon III worked for good relations with Britain, strongly backed the Roman Catholic Church, and fomented a war with Russia (Crimean War, 1853–1856). In 1857, provoked by pressure from Catholic and commercial interests in France, Napoleon III's government moved to restore French influence in Southeast Asia. Following an unsuccessful naval assault at Da Nang, Vietnam*, a French fleet attacked further south and defeated the Vietnamese imperial forces. By 1883, France had assumed control over the entire region of Indochina*, including the protectorates of Tonkin*, Annam*, and Cochin-China*.

Napoleon III's other major colonial venture failed completely. In 1862, supported by Britain and Spain which, along with France, had seized the Mexican customshouse at Veracruz following the Mexican government's repudiation of its national debt in October 1861, France began the invasion of Mexico. In 1863 Napoleon III's troops captured Mexico City. Napoleon chose Archduke Maximilian* of Austria to assume the imperial throne of Mexico. Mexican liberals, however, still recognized Benito Juárez as president of the Republic of Mexico, and a war between Mexican nationalists and French occupation troops lasted until 1867. In May 1867 Emperor Maximilian was captured and executed. The failure of the Mexican imperial enterprise weakened Napoleon III's position in France and abroad. The collapse of the French government was hastened by the Franco-Prussian War (1870–1871). On September 2, 1870, Napoleon III was taken prisoner by Prussian troops in battle at Sedan. By September 4, 1870, a revolution had broken out in Paris and the emperor was removed from his throne. Following the conclusion of the Treaty of Frankfurt in 1871, Louis Napoleon was released from Prussian captivity and exiled to Great Britain. He died January 9, 1873 in Chislehurst, near London. (William E. Echard, *Napoleon III and the Concert of Europe*, 1983.)

William G. Ratliff

NASSER, GAMAL ABD al-. The eldest son of a village postal clerk, Gamal Abd al-Nasser was the first Egyptian to govern Egypt* for any period of time (1954–1970) since the Pharaohs. Nasser was trained in the Egyptian Military Academy at a time when Britain controlled Egypt, even though Egypt was theoretically an independent kingdom. A corrupt and subservient government caused nationalist sentiment to arise against the British, who controlled the Suez Canal* Zone, and against the king, who was supported on his throne by the British. The disastrous war with Israel in 1948 infuriated the army officers, especially Nasser, who had been besieged by the Israeli forces in Faluja. From then on he was determined to overthrow the king and oust the British from Egypt, and with a group of young officers he founded a secret society to that end. On July 23, 1952, the Free Officers, as they came to be known, carried out a bloodless coup d'état which sent King Farouk into exile and declared his infant son king, with a regency council. A year later Egypt was proclaimed a republic and Nasser became its second president.

Nasser's first major preoccupation was to negotiate a treaty to secure Britain's evacuation of the Canal Zone, which was successfully done. While Nasser had come to power with the aid of the United States, his independent stand soon alienated his former supporters. His opposition to regional defense pacts of the NATO and SEATO variety soon earned him the enmity of United States Secretary of State John Foster Dulles. Problems with Israel also loomed large, and since the west had placed a moratorium on the sale of arms to any Arab country, but continued to supply Israel, Nasser had no recourse but to arm himself from the eastern bloc, which he did in 1955. This caused Dulles to turn down financing the High Dam project in Egypt, reneging on an earlier promise, so that in retaliation, and as a means of financing the dam, Nasser nationalized the Suez Canal. British Foreign Secretary Anthony Eden saw this move as a premeditated Nasser plot to renege on the Suez Canal agreement. Angered by these events, Britain, France, and Israel attacked Egypt in 1956. The attack failed when the United States firmly ordered them to evacuate Egypt, and Nasser became a hero in the Arab world.

Internally Nasser nationalized foreign banks and resources in order to pay for the industrialization of Egypt. A program of import substitution was followed. Anything that was done in terms of reform was done with an eye to pleasing the poorer classes, and ended by alienating the bourgeoisie and the members of the ancient regime who found themselves dispossessed as landowners and industrialists. Nasser had to cope with the enmity of many Arab leaders, especially the monarchies, who saw him as a dangerous element inciting their populations to revolt. Egypt was soon enmeshed in a costly and useless war in the Yemen, and in constant verbal attacks with other Arab leaders, each of whom was jealous of his position within the Arab world and most of whom resented the public adulation given Nasser.

Another war broke out with Israel in 1967. Egypt and her allies were once again defeated and the Sinai occupied by the Israelis. For the next three years Nasser tried to carry out a war of attrition and he and the Arabs followed a policy of "no war no peace" which resulted in extensive Israeli raids into Egypt. The situation both internally and externally had degenerated, for the army leaders were accused of incompetence and blamed for the defeat, while the civilians demonstrated against the repressive form of government of the day. In 1970 King Hussein attacked the Palestinian refugee camps in Jordan*, causing a massive emigration of refugees. Worn out after arranging a new home for the refugees in Lebanon*, Nasser suddenly died in 1970. Though he had caused the Sinai to fall under Israeli occupation, Nasser had ousted the British from the Suez Canal and had given the Egyptians pride in self as leaders among the Third World. He had also been the first ruler to do something for the masses, who adulated him. (Joachem Joesten, *Nasser: The Rise to Power*, 1974; Mary Shivanandan, *Nasser: Modern Leader of Egypt*, 1973.)

Alain G. Marsot

NATAL. One of the four colonies which became part of the Union of South Africa* in 1910, Natal is surrounded by the Orange Free State* on the northwest, the Transvaal* on the north, Swaziland* and Mozambique* on the northeast, the Indian Ocean on the east, Transkei on the south, and Lesotho on the southwest. Vasco da Gama*, the Portuguese navigator, explored the coast of Natal in 1497 on his way to India, and in 1824 the British established a trading post at Port Natal, today known as Durban. Dutch (Boer) settlers from the Cape Colony* moved into Natal in 1836 and 1837 and controlled it until 1843, when Great Britain annexed it as a colony. The next year Britain attached Natal to the Cape Colony. In 1856 Natal became a separate colony again, and it earned a limited form of self-government in 1893. Natal annexed Zululand* in 1897. During the Boer War*, Boer soldiers controlled much of Natal from 1899 to 1900 until the British drove them out. Natal became a province of the Union of South Africa* in 1910. See UNION OF SOUTH AFRICA.

NAURU. Nauru is a volcanic atoll in the Pacific Ocean, located 25 miles south of the equator, east of the Gilbert Islands* and north of the Solomons*. Its indigenous population was Micronesian, with Gilbertese and Tuvaluan roots. John Fearne, the English explorer, was the first European to discover the island, when he landed there in 1798, and by the 1830s Nauru was an important depot for whalers working the Pacific. The island became more attractive to Europeans when they learned that its phosphate deposits were the purest in the world. In 1888 Germany landed troops on Nauru and annexed the island, incorporating it into the German colony of the Marshall Islands*. British and German mining interests received long-term concessions on Nauru and neighboring Ocean Island*.

Germany lost control of Nauru as a result of World War I. The League of Nations gave a mandate to govern Nauru jointly to Great Britain, Australia, and New Zealand, with a British phosphate commission controlling all mining profits on the island. Japan occupied Nauru during World War II, and after the war a United Nations trusteeship* again gave control of the island to Great Britain, Australia, and New Zealand. Late in the 1940s a burst of nationalism swept through Nauru as islanders demanded self-government and the profits from the phosphate mines. Gradually, new political and economic agreements were negotiated on both accounts under the leadership of such Nauruan nationalists as Timothy Detudamo and Hammer DeRoburt. On January 31, 1968, the Republic of Nauru was proclaimed an independent member of the British Commonwealth of Nations*. (Nancy Viviani, *Nauru: Phosphate and Political Progress*, 1970.)

NAVIGATION ACTS. The Navigation Acts were a series of laws passed by the English parliament in the seventeenth, eighteenth, and nineteenth centuries to implement the philosophy of mercantilism. The Navigation Acts of 1660 and 1663 established the basic regulations of mercantilism*. They prohibited all trade with the North American colonies except that carried in British-built ships manned by British crews. The acts required that sugar and tobacco be exported only to England or another colony. Most European goods shipped to the colonies had to pass through England first. Over the years new navigation acts tightened the regulations and expanded their authority. Rice, indigo, and naval stores were added to the restricted list, and in the 1690s England gradually increased the number of customs officials enforcing the regulations. To limit the colonial economy to the production of food, fiber, and natural resources, a series of eighteenth-century navigation acts restricted colonial manufacturing enterprises. The Woolens Act of 1699, the Hat Act of 1732, and the Iron Act of 1750 prohibited the colonial production of finished goods.

After the American Revolution*, parliament continued to pass legislation governing international commerce. Because American supplies were selling so well in the British West Indies, parliament passed the American Navigation Act of 1783 admitting only British-built ships to the West Indies* and imposing heavy tonnage duties on American ships at other British ports. The American Navigation Act of 1786 prevented fraudulent registration of American ships. The American Navigation Act of 1787 prohibited importation of American goods by way of foreign countries. The American Navigation Act of 1818 prohibited British ships sailing from an American port from landing in the West Indies or entering an American port if they had already been to the West Indies. In 1820 a new American Navigation Act directly restricted much trade between the United States and the British West Indies. The Navigation Acts gradually were repealed in the nineteenth century when the mercantilist philosophy gave way to the new panacea of free trade. (Bernard Bailyn, *The New England Merchants*, 1965; Harold Underwood Faulkner, *American Economic History*, 1960.)

NEGRI SEMBILAN. Negri Sembilan was a group of nine small sultanates located on the western side of the Malay Peninsula. Intense conflict characterized relations between the nine states, and between 1874 and 1889 the British signed treaties with each one, creating the colony of Negri Sembilan under one ruler and a British counselor. In 1895 Negri Sembilan became one of the four states in the Federated Malay States*. See MALAYSIA.

NEGRITUDE AND THE FRENCH COLONIAL IDEOLOGY. The concept of Negritude was elaborated between 1933 and 1935 by Caribbean and African students living in Paris: Senegal's L. S. Senghor, Martinique's A. Cesaire, and Guyana's L. Damas had formed a group of young black intellectuals. They published a journal, *L'Etudiant Noir* (1934–1939). On the one hand, they responded to the Marxist position of Martinique's writer E. Léro, publicized in *Légitime Défense* (1932); on the other, they reinterpreted the findings of the new school of theology (the French translation of L. Frobenius's *Kulturgeschichte Afrikas* came out in 1936). They significantly adopted the derogatory term "nègre" as a battle cry. As defined by L. S. Senghor (*Ce que l'homme noir apporte*, 1939, and *La negritude est un humanisme, L'Esthétique négro-africaine*, 1956), Negritude aims at defining the black soul in contrast to "white rationality" and rests on five major tenets: "personalism" (in politics), emotionalism (in psychology), orality (in aesthetics), symbolism (in philosophy), and communal solidarity.

J. P. Sartre gave considerable exposure to Negritude by prefacing Senghor's Anthology (*Orphée noir*, 1948). Yet, at the same time he pointed out its transitory relevance, likening it to an Hegelian antithesis to white and colonial discourse. As a point of fact Senghor's insistence on "affective" and "earthly" values to define black consciousness was too reminiscent of Heideggerian existentialism to have escaped Sartre's attention. Frantz Fanon, who for a while adhered to Negritude, saw in this cluster of concepts the main shortcoming of Senghor's reading of African culture: "The white man creates the black man" (*Peau noire et Masques blancs*, 1952). In fact, Negritude developed in parallel if not in opposition to Dahomey's K. T. Houénou's *Ligue Universelle de Défense de la Race Noire* (1924) and Lamine Senghor's *Comité de Défense de la Race Nègre* (1927), whose anti-imperialist and internationalist activities were abruptly curtailed by the Regnier-Rollin decrees of 1935. To a large extent Negritude may be seen as the African stream of French neo-humanism, which also fought against colonialism (L. S. Senghor, *Négritude et Humanisme*, 1954). After World War II Negritude gave its cultural backbone to most of the newly independent Francophone African states while, in correlation with Senghor's concept of "francite" (1966) and Mauritian writer E. Maunick's idea of "plural blood," it has now taken place in a utopian group of post-colonial French-speaking cultures. (Jean Chevrier, *Littérature nègre*, 1974.)

Philippe-Joseph Salazar

NEHRU, JAWAHARLAL. Jawaharlal Nehru was born on November 14, 1889, at Allahabad, India*. His father, Motilal Nehru, was a prosperous attorney. Although Nehru described his life as middle class, he was born into the aristocratic Brahmin caste. Until he was 15 Nehru was educated at home by tutors. The tutor who made the greatest impression on the young Nehru was an Irish theosophist, Ferdinand Brooks. In 1905 Nehru attended Harrow and then Trinity College, Cambridge, where he studied natural sciences. After Cambridge he studied law at Inner Temple and was called to the bar in 1912. Upon his return to India, Nehru worked in his father's law chambers, but he had little interest in practicing law. In 1916, at the age of 26, he married Kamala Kaul, seventeen, in an arranged marriage.

Nehru had an interest in politics and the future of Indian independence but he did not know how liberation could be achieved. Two events changed his life: the brutal killing of Indian protesters by the British army at Amritsar in 1919 and Mohandas Gandhi's first campaign of non-violent disobedience in 1921. Gandhi* attracted Nehru because he offered direct non-violent action against the British. In 1929 Nehru was elected president of the Indian National Congress and presided over the Lahore session, which proclaimed complete independence as India's goal, rather than accepting dominion status. In 1921 he went to jail for the first time when the Congress Party was outlawed by the British. The British government had become alarmed at the tone of his speeches, which attacked the British Raj and the Indian liberals and landed aristocracy whom he labeled the ''Indian lackey'' of the Raj. During the struggle for Indian independence Nehru would spend a total of nine years incarcerated. While in jail Nehru took the opportunity to write three important books: *Glimpses of World History, Towards Freedom*, and *The Discovery of India*.

He also studied the writings of Karl Marx, a man whose ideas he admired but with whom he disagreed over the methods of achieving a socialist state. As a result of his studies and experiences he inclined toward socialism as a more equitable economic system. His tour of Europe in 1926–1927 included a visit to the Soviet Union and attendance at the communist-sponsored Congress of Oppressed Nationalists in Brussels. Later, in 1938, after visiting Spain to observe the civil war, Nehru became increasingly alarmed at the spread of fascism and tilted further toward communism. What sympathy Nehru held for communism ended, however, with Stalin's 1939 pact with Adolf Hitler.

During the fight for Indian independence, Nehru worked closely with Gandhi. He disagreed with the Mahatma over the benefits of industrialization and the mixing of religion and politics. Unlike Gandhi, Nehru wanted India to become a secular state, and he saw industrialization as the key to economic prosperity. Although they had differences, Gandhi was instrumental in elevating Nehru to the leadership of the Congress Party in 1929. Gandhi hoped the responsibility would moderate Nehru's extremism. Nehru would hold the position of president four times until independence elevated him to the office of prime minister in 1946. Because of his reputation and the added prestige of being designated Gandhi's political heir, it was inevitable that he become the first leader of an independent India.

In 1935 the Government of India Act* provided for provincial autonomy in India. As a result of the elections, the Hindu-dominated Congress Party gained power in the majority of provinces. The Muslim League* led by Mohammad Ali Jinnah* was unhappy at the results and suggested a coalition of Congress Party and Muslim League governments in some provinces. The Congress Party's rejection of his proposal reinforced Jinnah's desire to create a separate Muslim state. Nehru agreed with the decision of his party and sought to weaken Muslim League support throughout India. When World War II broke out in September 1939, the viceroy, Lord Linlithgow, committed India to war without consulting the Congress Party. Nehru's views on the war differed from Gandhi's. Gandhi believed that India's support should be unconditional but non-violent. Nehru, on the other hand, believed that India should support Britain but only as a free nation. In 1940 Gandhi abandoned his original position and launched a civil-disobedience campaign in which Nehru participated and was arrested, spending less than a year in jail. In the spring of 1942 the British government renewed attempts to compromise with Indian opposition. The mission led by Sir Stafford Cripps failed, however, because Gandhi would accept nothing less than complete independence. Nehru, reluctant to hinder the war effort, nevertheless, joined with Gandhi in his opposition to Britain. On August 8, 1942, the Congress Party passed the Quit India Resolution, an ultimatum for Britain to quit India. Although Nehru realized that the resolution would be perceived by the British as a stab in the back from India, he hoped it would arouse Muslims to side with Congress and away from Jinnah. Britain attacked Gandhi for wanting to leave India without any form of constitutional government or effective administration. On August 9, 1942, all members of the Congress working committee were arrested, including Gandhi and Nehru. This was to be Nehru's last but longest imprisonment. He was released on June 15, 1945, but he found that Congress's discomfiture had strengthened Jinnah's Pakistan* movement.

By 1947 the question was no longer if India would become independent, but whether or not it would be split into one or more states. A final attempt that year by the Viceroy Lord Wavell to bring the Congress Party and the Muslim League together failed. The new Labour government in Britain, determined to be rid of India, replaced Wavell with Lord Louis Mountbatten*. During the interim government from September 2, 1946, to March 22, 1947, when Mountbatten became viceroy, Nehru established the basic framework for an independent India by establishing the form and principle of a constitutional secular state and launching his non-aligned foreign policy. Mountbatten presided over the creation of India and Pakistan as independent states on August 15, 1947. Although Gandhi refused to accept partition, Nehru pragmatically acceded and became the first prime minister of India, a position he held until his death on May 27, 1964. (Beatrice Pitney Lamb, *India: A World in Transition*, 1966; Bishwa Nath Pandey, *Nehru*, 1976.)

Michael Dennis

NEO-COLONIALISM. Neo-colonialism is primarily a Marxist term that has been employed, mainly by Soviet writers, to attack Western policies toward Third World countries in Asia, Africa, and Latin America. It is a comprehensive theory of what is alleged to be the current manifestation of capitalistic imperialism and, as a propagandist device, has enjoyed much success. Its recent prominence has been spawned by two factors: first, the Marxist insistence that bourgeois states resort to colonialism to defer national economic collapse and a subsequent proletarian revolution; and second, the undeniable historical fact that traditional colonialism has virtually disappeared from today's world. The apparent contradiction is resolved, according to Marxist ideologists, by pointing out that while the traditional colonial system has all but vanished, a new type of colonialism has arisen to replace it. Thus, according to this view, the peoples of Asia, Africa, and Latin America have achieved formal political independence and the termination of their colonial regimes, but they continue to suffer from foreign exploitation and interference in their internal affairs. The imperialists employ methods of exploitation which reflect contemporary international conditions, thereby creating modern colonialism, or neo-colonialism.

It is asserted that the aims and methods of imperialism have become substantially more complicated than they were under traditional colonialism. The new colonialism attempts to steer the evolution of radical social changes taking place in the Third World in directions that suit its objectives. Neo-colonialism therefore differs from historical colonialism in that its manifestations and methods are more varied and its content more complex. Viewed through the lenses of Marxism, the two types of colonialism yield essentially the same results.

Not surprisingly, Soviet writers regard the United States as the leading practitioner of neo-colonialism. Their analysis of the Vietnam* conflict is, of course, diametrically opposite to that given by those adhering to the doctrine of containment. Soviet historians contend that after the 1954 Geneva Conference on Indochina* brought down the curtain on French rule in South Vietnam, an imperialistic America proceeded to set up its neo-colonialist control over the country. Military aid agreements were forced on the "puppet" South Vietnamese regime, and American advisers began to occupy key positions in the nation's army and bureaucracy. Eventually this situation led to what the Soviets have labeled America's war of aggression in the region. A similar neo-colonial interpretation is given to America's alliance with the Chinese Nationalists. When Chiang Kai-shek's government was forced to retreat to Taiwan, Marxists view the subsequent American protective posture as tantamount to colonial occupation of the island. They assert that Taiwan was turned into an American military base for the purpose of promoting reactionary policies in that region of Asia. South Korea is also perceived as an important part of America's neo-colonial empire.

A major difference between traditional colonialism and neo-colonialism is that under the latter indigenous officials, rather than colonial administrators, make up the formal governments. Technical sovereignty is maintained but actual control is in the hands of the imperialists. The new empires are therefore classified as "invisible" empires.

According to their dialectical philosophy, Marxists believe that the eventual annihilation of capitalistic governments and imperialism is inevitable. Before the achievement of this utopia, however, Marxists expect the imperialists to engage in defensive battles and counteroffensives against the forces of socialism.

Concerning tactics, the methods of neo-colonialism are more subtle and sophisticated than those of traditional colonialism. The new approach emphasizes
economic measures and ideological domination. The old methods of outright
seizure of alien lands and maintenance of legal title are relatively unimportant
today. The ideology of neo-colonialism opposes the position taken by many
Western writers that the old, vanishing imperialism has been replaced by a system
of equality between the former metropolitan states and Third World countries.
In disputing this claim, Marxists charge that neo-colonialists have created a
military and political organization to squelch the progressive national-liberation
movement. This organization, according to Soviet writers, has a number of
elements, including multilateral and bilateral military alliances, and networks of
military bases around the world. (Y. Zhukov et al., *The Third World: Problems
and Prospects*, 1970.)

Roy E. Thoman

NEPAL. Nepal is an independent kingdom in Asia between India* and China*.
The Himalayan Mountains form its northern border. The ancient and early medieval history of Nepal is shrouded in myth, and it was not until 1324, when
Harisinha-deva, the rajah of Simraun, conquered Nepal that the kingdom's reliable history began. The modern kingdom of Nepal was established in 1769
when Prithwi Narayan Shah imposed some political order on the 46 small principalities and states which made up Nepal. Prithwi Narayan was the ruler of
Gurkha (Gorkha), a small state west of the main Nepalese center in the valley
of Kathmandu. He incorporated Kathmandu into his kingdom and the Gurkhas
became the dominant force in Nepal. The Hindu religion also spread through
Nepal during his tenure.

Modern Nepalese history has been characterized by problems inherent in her
geographic location between British India* and China. In 1790 the Gurkhas
invaded Tibet* and came into contact with the Chinese, who in return invaded
Nepal in 1791. At about the same time the Gurkhas had negotiated a commercial
treaty with the British in India, who sent a military force into Nepal to protect
their new trading partner from the Chinese. The British signed another commercial treaty with Nepal in 1801, but in 1814 Great Britain declared war on
Nepal to stop what they considered to be Gurkha encroachments on the frontier
with India. After two years of intense fighting, the Gurkhas signed a peace treaty
with Great Britain which forced them to withdraw behind their original border
with India and allow a British resident to be established at Kathmandu.

Border disputes continued to destabilize British-Nepalese relations until 1846
when Jung Bahadur came to the throne in Kathmandu. He visited Great Britain
in 1850 and from that point on the relationship between Nepal and Britain steadily
improved. Bahadur instituted a series of political reforms, and in 1857, when
the Indian Mutiny* erupted, he sent 12,000 Gurkha soldiers to assist the British
in quelling the rebellion. That set the pattern for Nepalese-British relations. Jung
Bahadur died in 1877 but his family dynasty ruled Nepal until 1951. During the

British-Tibet War of 1902, Gurkha troops fought side-by-side with the British, and in World War I Nepal sent 40 regiments of Gurkha soldiers to fight with the British forces against the Central Powers. Another 2,000 Gurkha troops fought with the British in the brief Afghan war in 1919. On December 21, 1923, Great Britain signed a new treaty of friendship with Nepal to replace the Treaty of Segowlie of 1815. One provision of the new treaty was a formal recognition by the British government of the complete independence of Nepal. (Leo E. Rose and John J. Scholz, *Nepal: Profile of a Himalayan Kingdom*, 1980; Sir Francis Ivan Simms Tuker, *Gorkha: The Story of the Gurkhas of Nepal*, 1957.)

NETHERLANDS ANTILLES. The Netherlands Antilles consist of five islands and the southern half of a sixth island, divided into two groups located in the southern Caribbean Sea. The three northern islands are Saba, St. Eustatius, and the southern part of St. Martin, while the southern group includes Aruba, Bonaire, and Curacao. On his second voyage to the New World in 1493, Christopher Columbus* discovered Saba, St. Eustatius, and St. Martin. Aruba, Bonaire, and Curacao were discovered by the Spanish explorer Alonso de Ojeda in 1499. Spanish colonists settled in Bonaire in 1501 and established a large cattle industry on Curacao after 1527. But because the islands contained no gold and only poor Indian tribes, Spain maintained only a marginal interest in them. Large numbers of Indians were transplanted to Hispaniola* as slaves in 1513, leaving only Aruba with a sizable Native American population. Spain exercised political jurisdiction over the islands between 1493 and 1634.

In the seventeenth century, as Spanish fortunes on the world stage declined and those of England and The Netherlands rose, Spain lost control of Aruba, Bonaire, Curacao, Saba, St. Martin, and St. Eustatius. The Dutch West Indies Company took control of Curacao in 1634 and began importing large numbers of slaves from West Africa. Curacao became a central depot in the Caribbean slave trade. England seized Curacao during the Napoleonic Wars, but the island was returned to the Dutch by the Treaty of Paris in 1815. Between 1636 and 1795 Bonaire was the property of the Dutch West India Company, and after seven years of British control between 1807 and 1814, it too was restored to the Dutch. French pirates settled on St. Martin in 1638, and when Spain withdrew from the island in 1648, France and The Netherlands divided it between them, with the Dutch taking the valuable southern half where large salt deposits existed. French and English settlers moved on to St. Eustatius in 1625, and remained there after the Dutch seized the island in 1632. Like Curacao, St. Eustatius became an important Caribbean link in the African slave trade. The Dutch seized Aruba in 1634 and prohibited settlement there, leaving the native Arawak Indians alone and the island as a military garrison in the Caribbean. The Dutch took control of Saba in 1632, but because of its rugged terrain, it attracted no European settlers except some pirates hiding from the Dutch and British navies.

The absolute control of the Dutch West India Company over the Netherlands Antilles lasted only a few years, when responsibility for the islands fell to different provinces. Amsterdam assumed supervisory control of Curacao, Aruba, and Bonaire in 1635. Company control over St. Martin, Saba, and St. Eustatius gave way to the supervision of Zeeland until 1773, when Rotterdam took over. In 1791, when the Dutch West India Company was dissolved, all six of the islands came under the direct control of the states general of The Netherlands. The new constitution approved in 1815 formalized that control.

In 1865 The Netherlands approved the Regeeringsreglement, or Fundamental Colonial Law, which provided a colonial council to the islands, and in 1922, when the constitution and the colonial law were revised, the islands formally changed from colonies to territories. The head of the government in Curacao was a governor, and in both Aruba and Bonaire a lieutenant-governor was the chief administrator. He was responsible to the governor in Curacao. A lieutenant-governor also presided over St. Martin, and he reported to the governor in Curacao. In Saba and St. Eustatius, colonial administrators report to the lieutenant-governor in St. Martin.

After World War II, the Netherlands Antilles moved closer to autonomy and independence. In 1954 the government of The Netherlands signed a document designating the Netherlands Antilles an autonomous part of the nation. The debate over independence was a controversial one in the islands; nationalists wanted it as soon as possible, but more conservative economic interests feared the loss of the economic lifeline to The Netherlands. Not until 1978 did all six of the islands agree to independence, and not until 1981 did The Netherlands agree to work for complete independence. A strong separatist movement had long existed in Aruba. Its ethnic mix, because of the survival of large numbers of its original Indian population, distinguished Aruba from the other islands, and its oil refineries, which processed Venezuelan petroleum, gave it a strong economic base. In 1986 Aruba formally ended its participation in the federation of the Netherlands Antilles, while retaining its traditional political affiliation with The Netherlands. (Cornelis C. Goslinga, *A Short History of the Netherlands Antilles and Surinam*, 1978; Philip Hanson Hiss, *Netherlands America. The Dutch Territories in the West*, 1943.)

NETHERLANDS BRAZIL. By the early 1600s the Dutch were making their moves to establish lucrative sugar plantations in the New World, particularly in the Caribbean islands and in Brazil*. On the mainland, of course, they faced the challenge of Portuguese occupation of Brazil, but beginning in 1624, with the occupation of Bahia*, the Dutch established themselves there. In 1630 Dutch settlements began to appear in the northeastern corner of Brazil, near the Guianas, and by 1640 they had seized control of several Portuguese captaincies there. Their official name for the colony was New Holland. The Dutch then shipped in large numbers of slaves from Angola* to supply the labor needs of their plantations. But the Portuguese retaliated in the late 1640s and by 1654 they had driven the Dutch from Brazil. See BRAZIL; SURINAM.

NETHERLANDS INDIA. Early in the seventeenth century, the Dutch established a foothold in India* primarily to be able to participate in the Asian textile
traffic. Beginning in 1608 the Dutch assigned a governor to administer the several
Dutch forts which had developed on the Coromandel Coast. By the 1670s,
however, the Dutch were beginning to feel pressure from the expanding British
presence in the area, and by the turn of the century their trade volume began a
long decline. In 1795 the British occupied the Dutch forts along the Coromandel
Coast and remained there until 1818. The Dutch gave in to the inevitable in
1825 when they ceded their interests on the Coromandel Coast to the British in
return for British concessions in Malacca* and Bencoolen*. (David P. Henige,
Colonial Governors from the Fifteenth Century to the Present, 1970.)

NETHERLANDS NEW GUINEA. See DUTCH NEW GUINEA.

NEVIS. Nevis is a small island in the Caribbean Leewards, consisting of 36
square miles of stiff clay soil studded with volcanic boulders from the almost
perfectly conical Nevis Peak, which at 3,232 feet dominates the island. On his
second voyage of 1493, Columbus* was the first European to visit Nevis, claiming it for Spain. In 1628 a small plantation was founded at Jamestown by Captain
Anthony Hilton, a failed English colonist of St. Christopher* who had procured
a patent from the Earl of Carlisle and support from the London merchant Thomas
Littleton. The next year a Spanish fleet retook Nevis, only to lose it again.
Jamestown was wiped out by a hurricane in 1680, and replaced by a new capital—
Charlestown. Exporting tobacco from the beginning, Nevis's economy was able
to withstand the French and Spanish wars of the seventeenth and eighteenth
centuries. Sensibly fearing overproduction, however, the English (and some
French) settlers also had planted sugar.

  With black slaves tending the cash crops, a luxurious white colonial society
developed in the eighteenth century. Nevis became famous for its mineral baths
which created a center for fashion among the wealthy of the West Indies*.
Alexander Hamilton was born on Nevis in 1755. After the Napoleonic Wars
Nevis enjoyed peace, although prosperity diminished with the end of slavery in
the British Empire in 1833. The nineteenth century saw the economy considerably
diminished so that the "Queen of the Caribbes" became a poor island which
could not support local government without the help of the British Empire.

  The road to decolonization was not especially bitter. In 1951 Nevis was
grouped with its neighbors to form the "Associated State" of St. Kitts-Nevis-
Anguilla, under a British governor. Indirect rule commenced for St. Kitts-Nevis,
but the Anguillans staged a bloodless coup in order to revert to direct British
colonial rule. This was formally accomplished in 1981. A governor-general
remains the representative of the crown but since September 18, 1983, the
Federation of St. Kitts-Nevis is fully self-governing, and the governor-general
must act in accord with the wishes of the prime minister whom he nominally

appoints. (Sir Alan Burns, *History of the British West Indies*, 1965; Arthur P. Newton, *Colonizing Activities of English Puritans*, 1914.)

Mark R. Shulman

NEW AMSTERDAM. See NEW NETHERLAND.

NEW ANDALUCIA. The region of New Andalucia included what is today eastern Venezuela*. Spaniards settled the area early in the 1520s and founded the town of New Córdoba, or Cúmana, in 1523. It was the first permanent Spanish settlement in South America. In 1569 officially created the province of New Andalucia with its own governor, and it was subject to the Audiencia of Santo Domingo until 1739. It then became part of the Viceroyalty of New Granada. In 1777 New Andalucia was placed under the authority of the new Captaincy-General of Venezuela, where it remained throughout the wars of independence. In 1821 New Andalucia became part of Gran Colombia and then of Venezuela. See VENEZUELA.

NEW BRITAIN. See BISMARCK ARCHIPELAGO.

NEW BRUNSWICK. New Brunswick is one of the maritime provinces of Canada*. It is bounded by Quebec* on the north, the Gulf of St. Lawrence and Nova Scotia* on the east, the Bay of Fundy on the south, and Maine on the south and east. The original inhabitants of New Brunswick were Micmac Indians, who were decimated by contact with European settlers. Jacques Cartier* in 1534 was probably the first European to sight the New Brunswick coast, and the French established the first European settlement in 1604 at the mouth of the St. Croix River. This colony was moved in 1605 across the Bay of Fundy to Port Royal, but the French established a small fur trade in the St. John River Valley early in the seventeenth century. For most of the first half of the seventeenth century the English and French disputed political control of the area which was called Acadia*. The Treaty of Utrecht of 1713* ceded Acadia to Great Britain, but the French denied that the cession included the present area of New Brunswick. After 1713 the British required an oath of loyalty from settlers in Acadia, but the policy was sporadically enforced and there were no penalties for non-compliance until 1755. Then, alarmed by French activity at Fort Beausejour on Chigneto Bay, the British deported several thousand Acadians who had settled in the St. John River Valley and along the Bay of Fundy.

Between the 1760s and 1784 the present New Brunswick was administered by the British as part of Nova Scotia. British settlement of the area began slowly in the 1760s, but after the American Revolution* approximately 14,000 Loyalists moved into the St. John and the St. Croix River valleys and established the town of St. John. The new arrivals felt that the distance to Halifax, Nova Scotia, was too far for effective government, and they petitioned for their own administration.

In 1784 the British government separated the area from Nova Scotia and named it New Brunswick.

The early nineteenth century brought prosperity to New Brunswick. Immigration, primarily from England, Scotland, and Ireland, pushed the population past 100,000 by the mid–1830s. Lumbering, shipbuilding, and fishing were the principal occupations. The former was largely responsible for the bloodless Aroostock War in 1839. Both the United States and Great Britain brought troops to the border, but the issues were resolved without fighting by the Webster-Ashburton Treaty* of 1842.

New Brunswick was slow to move toward responsible government*, which it achieved in 1848, and it was slow to see any value in confederation with other British colonies in North America. This view was reinforced by renewed prosperity in the 1850s and early 1860s, a result of the Reciprocity Treaty of 1854 with the United States and the American Civil War. This situation began to change in the mid–1860s with the non-renewal of the Reciprocity Treaty, and the active promotion of confederation by New Brunswick's British lieutenant governor, Arthur Gordon.

In 1864 representatives of the maritime colonies of British North America met in Charlottetown, Prince Edward Island*, to discuss the possibilities of a maritime union. At the urging of a Canadian delegation, the maritimers agreed to meet later in Quebec to discuss a larger confederation of the maritimes, Newfoundland*, Canada East, and Canada West. In 1865 the people of New Brunswick repudiated the government of Samuel L. Tilley, who favored the larger union. However in the following year, fear of Fenian raids from the United States, desire for railroads, and continued adroit political activity by the lieutenant governor brought a new election which returned Tilley to office. New Brunswick became a province of the Dominion of Canada under the terms of the British North America Act of 1867. (W. S. MacNutt, *New Brunswick: A History 1784–1867*, 1963 and *The Atlantic Provinces, 1712–1857*, 1965.)

Peter T. Sherrill

NEW CALEDONIA. The Territory of New Caledonia and Dependencies, an overseas territory of France, is in the South Pacific approximately 900 miles east of Australia. In addition to the main island of New Caledonia, also called Grand Terre, it includes the Loyalty Islands, which are parallel to Grand Terre and 60 miles to the east; the Isle of Pines, about 80 miles to the southeast; and the Chesterfield Islands, 240 miles west in the Coral Sea. The small Belep Islands are 30 miles northwest of Grand Terre. Unlike the rest of the Pacific islands, New Caledonia is neither volcanic nor coral in its origins. The islands are metamorphic and sedimentary in their formations and rich in nickel, chrome, cobalt, and iron.

Part of the Melanesian cultural area, New Caledonia was inhabited by more than 70,000 native people when the first Europeans arrived. Because the island was far south of the prevailing Portuguese, Spanish, and Dutch trade routes, it was not discovered until September 1774 when Captain James Cook* arrived. Because the island's steep cliffs reminded him of Scotland, Cook named it New Caledonia. In 1785 King Louis XVI of France commissioned Jean-Francois de Galaup to determine New Caledonia's economic significance, but the expedition was lost at sea. In 1791 France sent out a new expedition under Antoine de Bruni d'Entrevasteaux*, and from then until the early 1830s several French expeditions charted the islands.

European traders arrived in New Caledonia in 1841 to harvest its rich supplies of sandalwood for sale in China. Roman Catholic missionaries soon followed and in 1843 France established a colony there. The British drove them out in 1846, but in 1853 Napoleon III ordered Admiral Auguste Fevrier-Despointes to seize the island. After completing negotiations with native leaders, he formally annexed New Caledonia as a French colony. France annexed the Loyalty Islands in 1866.

Relations with the native people were based on hostility. Between 1866 and 1897 France transported more than 20,000 convicts to the colony and offered free land to immigrating farmers and ranchers. Native New Caledonians were herded into tiny reservations where they suffered and died. From its peak of 70,000 in 1774, the native population dropped to 60,000 in 1878, 42,000 in 1887, and 27,000 in 1921. Under tribal chief Atai, the natives rose up in violent rebellion in 1878–1879, but the French ruthlessly crushed it and relocated the entire native population. As the native population declined, France imported laborers from Vietnam, China, Japan, and the Philippines to work the cattle ranches, railroads, harbors, and gold, iron, cobalt, lead, zinc, silver, and copper mines. In the process, New Caledonia became an ethnically diverse society.

Politics in New Caledonia revolved around a struggle between a wealthy, conservative French minority wanting close ties with France, and a more liberal, poor Melanesian population seeking independence. In 1946 France abolished the requirement that all native New Caledonians live on the reservations and in 1951 extended voting rights to them. That year New Caledonia sent its first deputy to the French national assembly. In 1956 France discontinued New Caledonia's status as a colony and declared the island an overseas department. In the 1960s and 1970s conservatives on the island increased their political control and further secured New Caledonia's close ties to France. (K. R. Howe, *The Loyalty Islands: A History of Culture Contacts, 1840–1900*, 1977; Georges Kling, *En Nouvelle Caledonie*, 1981.)

NEW ENGLAND. Today the term ''New England'' is a regional geographic term describing the states of Connecticut*, Massachusetts*, New Hampshire*, Rhode Island*, Vermont, and Maine in the United States. Between 1610 and 1614 Sir Ferdinando Gorges, an English trader and former stockholder in the London Company, sponsored several exploring expeditions up the North Atlantic. The leader of one of the expeditions was John Smith, who had played such an important role in the founding of Jamestown*. Smith returned to England in

1614 with a map of the region. He described the area as ''New England.'' In November 1620, just one week before the Pilgrims reached Cape Cod, Gorges established the Council of New England to govern the region. The English colonies eventually established at Plymouth*, Boston, Providence, New Haven, Hartford, and New Hampshire were all part of this ''New England.'' Ever since then the term ''New England'' has been used by the settlers of the area as well as by geographers and cartographers. (J. T. Adams, *The Founding of New England*, 1921.)

NEWFOUNDLAND. Newfoundland is the newest and most easterly of Canada's ten provinces. It consists of the island of Newfoundland and of Labrador on the North American mainland to the northwest. The island of Newfoundland is also the most easterly part of North America, and hence it is the nearest part of North America to Europe. Even more than most areas, Newfoundland's history is inextricably linked to its geography. Newfoundland and Labrador were inhabited by various native cultures long before Europeans arrived. They were known as the Beothuk or ''Red Indians,'' a people who became extinct in the early nineteenth century. The first Europeans to visit Newfoundland were probably Norsemen in the tenth century.

Newfoundland was rediscovered in 1497 by John Cabot* who noted the extraordinary number of fish in the waters around the island. By the mid–1500s large numbers of English, French, Spanish, and Portuguese ships were fishing the area. In 1583 Sir Humphrey Gilbert* claimed Newfoundland for England, a claim not accepted by France. Much of Newfoundland's history in the seventeenth and early eighteenth centuries consists of repeated efforts at colonization by various English groups, and repeated efforts by English west country merchants, particularly from Dorset and Devon, to frustrate colonial development and protect their fishing grounds. Custom, later confirmed by the Western Charter of 1633, gave the fishermen an important advantage. The captain of the first British ship arriving in a Newfoundland harbor each spring had the right to act as the admiral and governor of the harbor for the season. This practice was continued by the Newfoundland Act of 1699, which served as a constitution for Newfoundland for over a century. This act specified the rights of the fishermen, but it ignored the colonists.

France was also interested in Newfoundland. In 1662 the French established a colony at Placentia. The Treaty of Utrecht of 1713* ceded Newfoundland to England, but Anglo-French conflict continued until the end of the Seven Years' War. The Treaty of Paris of 1763* confirmed French fishing rights on the north shore, and allowed France her only possessions in North America, the islands of St. Pierre and Miquelon* off Newfoundland's south coast. The power of the fishing admirals declined in Newfoundland after the appointment of Captain Henry Osborne as the first governor in 1729. Osborne and his successors gradually expanded the powers of the office, and conditions for the colonists slowly improved. In the late eighteenth century Newfoundland experienced serious tensions between the established English community and the newer Irish immigrants, whose Roman Catholic religion and geographic segregation brought them under suspicion. In the early 1800s an increase in the number of Irish settlers and Irish dissatisfaction with the existing political system led to a demand for representative government. This was granted in 1832 and responsible government was achieved in 1855. Representatives from Newfoundland participated in the Quebec Conference of 1864* to consider a union of British colonies in North America. Pro-confederation forces initially appeared to be in a majority. However, legislative inertia, notwithstanding prodding from the imperial government, and a sudden improvement in the economy allowed an anti-confederation movement to develop. In 1869 Newfoundland voters rejected confederation with Canada.

Fishing remained the mainstay of the Newfoundland economy in the late nineteenth century, but mining, logging, and pulp and paper production also became important industries. The Great Depression of 1929 struck Newfoundland hard as her markets almost totally collapsed. Greatly expanded public relief brought bankruptcy and forced the government in 1933 to ask Great Britain to reassume administration of Newfoundland as a colony. The resultant commission government lasted with considerable success through World War II. In 1948 Newfoundlanders were given an opportunity to determine their political future by choosing between a continuation of the commission government, confederation with Canada, or a return to responsible government. The first vote on June 3, 1948, resulted in a plurality for responsible government, but because a majority vote was necessary for a decision, a second referendum was held on July 22, 1948. In the second referendum confederation received 78,323 votes and responsible government 71,334. On March 31, 1949, Newfoundland became a province of the Dominion of Canada. (Frederick W. Rowe, *A History of Newfoundland and Labrador*, 1980.)

Peter T. Sherrill

NEW FRANCE. Other Europeans preceeded the explorers who established the French Empire* in the land now known as Canada*. The first, by modern consensus, was probably Leif Ericsson who discovered "Vinland" by accident around the year 1000. Portuguese and possibly other sailors discovered the rich Grand Banks fisheries. The earliest recorded voyage of discovery in the area was made by John Cabot*, a Venetian in the English service, who probably reached Cape Breton Island* in 1497 and claimed the land he found for King Henry VII. The earliest recorded French voyage to the New World occurred in 1524 when Giovanni Verrazano sailed from France with a commission from King Francis I to search for a northern passage to Asia as well as deposits of precious metals or stones. Verrazano reported back to the French that he had found no passage, but his detailed observations of the American coast gave later French explorers an unrivaled knowledge of the area. More importantly France used Verrazano's voyage as their "right of discovery" to claim all of North America.

The real French claim to a New World empire, however, occurred a decade later when Jacques Cartier* led an expedition across the Atlantic in 1534. Cartier's interest in the New World led him to ask Francis's permission for a new voyage to look for the northern passage to Asia. Cartier entered the Gulf of St. Lawrence, and coasted Newfoundland*, Prince Edward Island*, and New Brunswick*. There he raised a wooden cross bearing a shield with the royal fleurs-de-lis and the inscription "Vive le Roi de France." Cabot had probably claimed virtually the same area for England approximately forty years before. French settlement of the region began the next year when Cartier's second expedition constructed a small fort at the Indian village of Stadacona, present-day Quebec*, to protect them during the winter of 1535–1536. Cold and disease, especially scurvy, threatened to wipe out the group altogether, and Cartier had to abandon one of his ships because of his lack of sailors. Nevertheless, before he left in the spring of 1536, he raised another wooden cross and claimed this region for France.

The name New France was given to this area around 1541 when Francis granted Jean Francis de la Roque, Sieur de Roberval, a commission to establish colonies and forts, establish government, conduct war, and establish a feudal society in the area. Roberval's commission marked the beginning of a serious competition by the leading European powers for the interior of North America. It was Cartier, nevertheless, who established a new French fort at Cap Rouge, just upriver from Stadacona in the autumn of 1541. Rivalry between Roberval and Cartier, however, led the French to abandon this colonization effort.

In the following years French interest in the area was limited primarily to fishing fleets and occasional merchants who traded for beaver pelts along the coast. Samuel de Champlain* changed that focus in 1608 when he established his first trading post in present-day Quebec*, from which he began searching for the elusive northwest passage*. After 1613, however, he turned his attention increasingly to settlement and exploitation of the vast population of fur-bearing animals, especially beaver, in the region. Champlain established a network of company monopolies to control the fur trade and the French coureur de bois (literally "woods runners") probed deeper and deeper into the continent in search of untapped sources of furs. This quest led to an expansion of New France. In 1641 Catholic missionaries founded Montreal*. By 1663, New France consisted of Quebec, Montreal, and Three Rivers, while French Acadia* consisted of Port Royal and a string of small fishing settlements along the Annapolis Basin.

These settlements were enough, however, to attract the attention of England, France's chief rival for North America. English interest in New France dated back to Cabot's voyages, but English colonization had begun in earnest only after the establishment of the first successful colony at Jamestown* in 1607. In 1627 English interests in the north were revived with the founding of an English Canada Company, which in 1628 established a colony on the Annapolis Basin, blockaded Quebec, and successfully beat back a French attempt to relieve it. Champlain surrendered the colony in 1629, but the Treaty of St. Germain-en-Laye transferred both New France and Acadia back to France in 1632. In 1665 King Louis XIV assumed direct control of French overseas territories in an attempt to save them from being taken by other European powers.

His efforts and those of subsequent French officials ultimately proved futile. The French New World empire was lost in two stages. Border skirmishes between the two empires continued for decades, while on the high seas the English navy achieved a mastery which helped bring about the downfall of New France by effectively cutting the empire off from the mother country. In 1701 war broke out between England and France, the War of the Spanish Succession (or Queen Anne's War, as it was known to the British colonists), which ended in the Treaty of Utrecht in 1713*. The Treaty recognized the reality of a shifting balance of power revealed by the war: England received Acadia, Newfoundland, and Hudson Bay.

The two rivals renewed their struggle for North America in 1753 when French forces pushed southward from Lake Erie and established Fort Duquesne (present-day Pittsburgh). This expansion helped lead to the Seven Years' War (or the Great War for Empire) in 1756. British leader William Pitt* made conquest of New France and other French colonies a primary war effort in 1757 in order to weaken France sufficiently to defeat it in Europe. The British strategy began to bring rewards in the summer of 1758 as the Ohio area fell to British domination, thus separating New France from France's vast Louisiana colony to the southwest. In July Louisbourg* fell to British control, and in September 1759 a British army, cleverly transported to the Plains of Abraham against fantastic odds by James Wolfe, forced the surrender of Quebec. In September 1760 Montreal fell to the British.

Peace negotiations resulted in the Treaty of Paris of 1763* which further recognized the end of French North America. France transferred to Britain New France and all other French territory east of the Mississippi River except New Orleans. In order to repay its Spanish ally for losses suffered elsewhere in the war and to prevent Britain from claiming all of French North America, France also transferred the Louisiana colony, including New Orleans east of the Mississippi, to Spain. The French dream of a New World empire to rival or surpass that of England and Spain thus came to an end. (W. J. Eccles, *France in America*, 1972; Gerald S. Graham, *A Concise History of Canada*, 1968.)

Jerry Purvis Sanson

NEW GEORGIA. See SOLOMON ISLANDS.

NEW GUINEA. New Guinea is the second largest island in the world, and the last extensive area of truly primitive, stone-age human cultures. It lies 95 miles north of Australia*, across the Torres Strait. To the north is the Pacific Ocean; the Ceram, Banda, and Arafura seas are to the west; and the Coral, Solomon, and Bismarck seas are to the east. New Guinea was divided three ways: the Dutch claimed the western half, the Germans the northeastern quadrant, and the British the southeastern part, but borders were almost entirely theoretical. In reality the island was so vast, the jungle so impenetrable, and the tribesmen so dangerous that even in the twentieth century maps of New Guinea showed great blank spaces.

New Guinea is more than 300,000 square miles in area, (1,500 miles long and up to 500 miles wide.) It overlies tectonic plate margins and so has a complex geology dominated by high mountains and active volcanoes. The central spine of mountains (the Sneeuw, Victor Emanuel, Muller, and Owen Stanley ranges) includes peaks above 16,000 feet with permanent icecaps. To the north are more mountain ranges and long river valleys. The only extensive flat land on New Guinea is a swampy plain in the south crossed by the Fly and Digoel rivers. There is no transportation other than by footpath or by small airplanes able to land in jungle clearings. The Fly River is theoretically navigable for 580 miles upstream, but a dangerous tidal bore races upriver on the first three days of every new moon. The tropical climate has little seasonal variation. Temperature depends on elevation. Above 12,000 feet there are alpine grasslands. Perhaps because of continental drift, New Guinea's plant life is Southeast Asian, but its animals, including wallabies and tree kangaroos, are basically Australian.

The first Europeans to see the island were the Portuguese who gave New Guinea its name because the dark-skinned Melanesian natives reminded them of Africans. Iñigo Ortíz de Retes claimed the island for Spain in 1545, but the claim was not pursued, perhaps because of the sad fate that befell a Dutch expedition under Willem Janszoon in 1606. Nine crew members sent to fetch water were eaten by cannibals. A century and a half later the French explorer Louis de Bougainville* wrote in his journal, "People have long argued about the location of hell. Frankly, we have discovered it." There were practically no Europeans at all on New Guinea until the 1870s and the island exported only bird-of-paradise feathers.

The Negrito, Melanesian, and Papuan people who inhabit New Guinea intrigue anthropologists because they seem to offer a glimpse into mankind's past. Some tribes wear nothing but penis-gourds and bamboo slivers stuck through the nasal septum. Christian missionaries were appalled to find one tribe whose members used their own mothers' skulls for pillows. Seven hundred and fifty separate languages are spoken in the eastern half of New Guinea. Many tribes exist in a state of constant warfare with their neighbors. Those who farm grow yams, taro, cassava, and plants introduced from the New World such as sweet potatoes and tobacco.

Rival European claims to New Guinea were laid in the nineteenth century. Dutch suzerainty over the western half, inherited from the sultan of Tidore, was recognized in 1814, but control was purely nominal. Luigi D'Albertis's expedition (1875–1878) was the first to penetrate the interior. Germans began trading on the north coast in 1873. Englishmen discovered gold near Port Moresby in

1877 and the scramble was on, but it was driven more by fear that a rival power might take the island than by any serious prospect of commercial gain. Australia, a colony itself, demanded in 1883 that London annex New Guinea, but was turned down. The foreign office became less reticent the following year after Germany annexed northeast New Guinea and named it Kaiser Wilhelmsland. Great Britain proclaimed a protectorate over the southeast coast on November 6, 1884, raising the Union Jack and ceremoniously giving a local chief a walking stick with Queen Victoria's effigy on an inlaid silver coin. Britain and Germany agreed on a boundary in 1885—a perfectly straight line crossing mountains no European had laid eyes on.

British New Guinea (renamed the Territory of Papua) was lightly governed by paternalistic officials who suppressed head hunting but did little else. The native constabulary numbered less than 200. Health and education were left to missionaries. Commercial investment was not encouraged. No Europeans lived in German New Guinea when that territory was annexed in 1884, but the Neu-Guinea Kompagnie developed coffee and cacao plantations around Madang, using indentured labor. When World War I broke out, the Germans had to surrender to an Australian expeditionary force. German New Guinea was given to Australia as a League of Nations* mandate in 1921. An astounding discovery was made in the 1930s: previously unknown highland valleys containing an estimated one million natives who knew nothing of the world beyond their mountains.

In sum, New Guinea was hardly affected at all by imperialism. Japan occupied parts of the coast during World War II, but most islanders remained unaware there was a war. When it was over, the former German colony was united with Papua. All the land east of the 141st meridian was given self-government in 1973 and independence (with Australian aid and defense guarantees) in 1975. Papua New Guinea* exports copra, rubber, sugar, and timber. Deposits of chrome, copper, zinc, and silver have been found, but not extensively developed. Two very large gold deposits are known to exist, and high-grade oil was discovered in 1986. Dutch New Guinea, an area the size of Spain, has been made an Indonesian province against its will and named Irian Jaya. The Dutch had scarcely occupied it at all, but Indonesia claims to have inherited all former Dutch rights in the region, and the United Nations has agreed. Jakarta sent 15,000 troops. A Free Papua Movement fights for the independence of western New Guinea. (James Griffin, *Papua New Guinea: A Political History*, 1979; John Ryan, *The Hot Land*, 1969.)

Ross Marlay

NEW HAMPSHIRE. One of the original thirteen colonies of England in North America, New Hampshire lies along the North Atlantic coast between Massachusetts* and Maine. The English first explored the coast of New Hampshire in 1603, and Samuel de Champlain* arrived there two years later. Captain John Smith, one of the founders of the Virginia* colony, ventured up the New England coast in 1614. In 1623 John Mason, a wealthy London merchant with land grants from the council for New England, commissioned a small settlement in what today is Portsmouth, at the mouth of the Piscataqua River, and another one several miles up the river. In 1629 Mason used the name New Hampshire to describe an area extending from the mouth of the Merrimack River to the mouth of the Piscataqua and reaching 60 miles inland.

The Puritans settled Massachusetts Bay in 1629, and as the colony at Boston flourished, new settlements gradually reached north into New Hampshire. Puritan clergymen left Boston and initiated settlements in Exeter in 1638 and Hampton in 1639. In 1641 the various towns of New Hampshire voted to accept the administrative jurisdiction of Massachusetts, which they accepted until 1679, when New Hampshire was designated a separate royal colony. Boundary disputes with Massachusetts continued until 1741 when the crown fixed the boundary between the two colonies. The western boundary of the colony was in dispute with New York* until a 1764 royal decree set the boundary at the Connecticut River.

Settlement of the colony was slow until the mid-eighteenth century when more and more settlers began pushing up the Connecticut, Merrimack, and Picataqua river valleys. At the time of the American Revolution*, New Hampshire had a population approaching 90,000 people. Upset about what they considered British usurpation of their traditional rights, New Hampshire declared its independence on June 15, 1776, three weeks before the signing of the Declaration of Independence. In 1788 New Hampshire became the ninth state to ratify the United States Constitution. (Charles E. Clark, *The Eastern Frontier: The Settlement of New Hampshire, 1610–1763*, 1970; Jere R. Daniell, *Experiment in Republicanism: New Hampshire Politics and the American Revolution, 1741–1794*, 1970.)

NEW HAVEN. In 1638 Puritan settlers from Massachusetts* Bay headed south toward Long Island Sound and settled the region which became New Haven, Connecticut*. Since geography and economic commerce pushed New Haven into the orbit of New Netherlands* more than toward Massachusetts, Great Britain decided to give the colony its own governor in 1643. He was Theophilus Eaton. By that time there were other prosperous settlements developing in Connecticut, especially around Hartford, and in 1664 Great Britain allowed Connecticut to annex New Haven. See CONNECTICUT.

NEW HEBRIDES. The New Hebrides consist of approximately eighty islands and islets located between the Solomon Islands* to the north and New Caledonia* to the south in Melanesia*. The major islands and groups in the New Hebrides are the Torres Islands, the Banks Islands, Vanua Lava, and Espiritu Santo (the largest island). The New Hebrides are scattered across 560 miles at 15 degrees south latitude and total just over 5,000 square miles of territory. The Spanish explorer Pedro Fernández de Quiros was the first European to locate the New

Hebrides when he landed at Espiritu Santo in 1606. Quiros tried to establish a colony there, but it was abandoned after only three weeks because of the heat, illness among the crew, and intense opposition from natives. When Quiros left, the New Hebrides remained untouched by Europeans for the next 160 years. Louis Antoine de Bougainville*, the French explorer, mapped the Torres Islands, Banks Islands, and Vanua Lava in 1768, and in 1774 English Captain James Cook* explored the other islands and named them the New Hebrides.

Another fifty years passed before European imperialism reached the New Hebrides. In 1825 the English trader Peter Dillon inaugurated the sandalwood trade on Erromango, and by 1860 the trade dominated the economy of the islands. Australian planters also established a lucrative contract labor system using workers from the New Hebrides. Other planters from Fiji*, New Caledonia, and Samoa* soon joined the forced labor system, and by the 1880s more than half of the adult population was working abroad. Not until 1906 did the labor traffic end. Beginning in 1839, a series of European and Polynesian missionaries, sponsored by the London Missionary Society, the Anglicans, and the Presbyterians, arrived at the New Hebrides and converted most of the population to Protestantism.

European settlement of the New Hebrides began in the 1870s when prospective cotton planters arrived. When cotton proved to be marginal economically, they switched to raising coffee, cacao, bananas, and coconuts. At first the settlements were on Tanna and Efate in the south, but gradually they moved northward. Most of the European settlers were British until 1882, when French investors established the Caledonian Company of the New Hebrides. By 1900, of the 500 European settlers there, the French outnumbered the British by two to one.

Both England and France wanted to maintain their strategic interests in the New Hebrides, and in 1887 both countries agreed to allow their naval commanders in the region to jointly administer the islands. In 1906 England and France established the Anglo-French Condominium of the New Hebrides. It was a cumbersome arrangement, with both countries setting up separate administrative systems to serve their own nationals and a joint commission to deal with the native population. The Anglo-French Condominium of the New Hebrides was revised in 1922, but after that it served as the constitution of the islands until they achieved independence in 1980.

The native people of the New Hebrides had always resented European domination, and in the 1960s those feelings began to find political expression. Jimmy Stephens led a movement on Espiritu Santo calling for the return of all undeveloped land to natives, and in 1971 Walter Lini established the New Hebrides National Party, which began campaigning for independence. They succeeded in 1980 and Lini became prime minister of the new country of Vanuatu. On Espiritu Santo, French interests, allied with followers of Jimmy Stephens, tried to declare Espiritu Santo an independent nation, but Lini used Australian troops to crush the independence movement there. (W. P. Morrell, *Britain in the Pacific Islands*, 1960; Chris Plant, ed., *New Hebrides: The Road to Independence*, 1977.)

NEW HOLLAND. By 1600 the Dutch East India Company had planted deep roots in Java*, and throughout the seventeenth and eighteenth centuries the company expanded its influence throughout South Asia, expanding in Java, Borneo*, Celebes*, western New Guinea*, and Sumatra*. Dutch explorers gradually made their way along the northern coast of Australia and down the western coast, led by the voyages of Abel Tasman* in the 1640s. The Dutch East Company called Australia "New Holland," but the company made no effort to invest resources. Western Australia was unmatched anywhere in the world for geographic isolation and barren territory, and the northern coast did not appear to be much more promising. In 1826 Great Britain formerly claimed the area of Western Australia and the Dutch did not contest the claim. New Holland faded into history. (Kristof Glamann, *Dutch-Asiatic Trade, 1620–1740*, 1958; Russell Ward, *Australia*, 1965.)

NEW IRELAND. See BISMARCK ARCHIPELAGO.

NEW JERSEY. New Jersey is bounded on the north by New York*, the west by Pennsylvania*, the south by Delaware River Bay, and on the east by the Atlantic Ocean and the Hudson River. When European explorers entered the region in the sixteenth century, they found settlements of Lenni and Lenape Indians of the Algonquian group, whose numbers gradually declined due to migration and disease. The region has been claimed by the French, Dutch, and British on the basis of exploration. In 1524 Giovanni Verrazano, an Italian navigator commissioned by France, made contact with the New Jersey coast. In 1609 Henry Hudson*, in his ship *Half Moon*, sailed up the Hudson River and explored the region for the Dutch East India Company*. The Dutch claimed the area in 1618 and established Bergen as a trading post. By 1623 the province of New Netherland* was established and Fort Nassau was built. The Delaware River was further opened to exploration by Cornelius Jacobsen Mey, who was later followed by Cornelius Hendricksen. The Dutch claim to the Delaware River region was first challenged in 1638 by Swedish settlers. In 1655 the Dutch defeated the Swedes, and claimed the disputed territory. Dutch control, however, was shortlived. In 1664 James, Duke of York and brother of Charles II of England, was granted control of the Dutch holdings. James, in turn, granted the territory between the Hudson and Delaware rivers to John, Lord Berkeley, and Sir George Carteret. This grant was named in honor of Carteret, who had defended Jersey in the Channel Islands after the deposition of Charles I.

On February 10, 1665 the "Concessions and Agreements" were published in hopes of attracting settlers. They provided for a governor, a governor's council, and an assembly chosen by freemen and empowered to impose taxes. The Dutch reclaimed New Jersey in 1673, but one year later with the signing of the Treaty of Westminster, England reestablished control over the colony. In 1676 the Quintpartite Deed divided New Jersey into East Jersey (Carteret's portion) and West Jersey (Berkeley's portions). East Jersey was placed under the control of a proprietorship as a part of a real estate venture. A diverse group of settlers were attracted to the area. In March 1674 Lord Berkeley sold West Jersey to an English Quaker, John Fenwick, and by 1680 Quaker settlements were established there. East Jersey was sold to William Penn, a trustee of West Jersey, and his associates in 1682. In 1702 the proprietors relinquished their rights of authority to the British Crown, but retained their claim to the land. East and West Jersey were united to form the royal colony of New Jersey, sharing a governor with New York until 1738. Between 1745 and 1755 land disputes were frequent.

New Jersey was active during the American Revolution* as individual loyalties and sentiments resulted in bitter conflict within the colony. In 1774 a provincial congress convened in New Brunswick and selected delegates to attend the first Continental Congress at Philadelphia. In June 1776 royal authority was brought to an end with the removal of the governor. New Jersey signed the Declaration of Independence on July 2, 1776. (Thomas Budd, *New Jersey, Colonial Period*, 1966.)

Veula J. Rhodes

NEW MUNSTER. The term New Munster refers to a brief British colonial experiment in New Zealand*. In 1848 Great Britain divided New Zealand into two administrative units. New Munster included a portion of North Island, while New Ulster included the rest of North Island and all of South Island. The two provinces each had a lieutenant governor as chief executive officer, but five years later, in 1853, Great Britain dissolved both provinces. See NEW ZEALAND.

NEW NETHERLAND. In 1621 the Dutch West India Company was given a charter by the government of The Netherlands and the power to establish colonies in Africa and the Americas and "advance the peopling of those fruitful and unsettled parts." For the next three years the company sold stock and issued licenses to traders who traveled to the Hudson and Delaware River valleys and exchanged goods with the local Indian tribes. England had already established a colony at Jamestown* in the Chesapeake Bay area, and in the early 1620s more English colonists settled in the Plymouth area.

In March 1624 thirty Dutch families left Amsterdam and headed for the New World, where they set up three small colonies. One group settled on Nut Island, present-day Governors Island in New York harbor; a second went up the Hudson River and built Fort Orange in present-day Albany; and the third headed south and established Fort Nassau, or present-day Gloucester, New Jersey. In May 1626 another group of Dutch families, led by Peter Minuit, settled on the lower tip of Manhattan island. He became director of the colony. The Dutch colony became known as New Netherland, and the city on Manhattan as New Amsterdam. Because it was owned by the Dutch West India Company, the colony had no legislature. Assisted by an appointed council, the director-general had legislative, executive, and judicial powers. Although the arrangement seemed acceptable to the Dutch settlers in New Amsterdam, it became intolerable to the English colonists who had crossed Long Island Sound from Connecticut* and settled on the north shore of Long Island in the 1630s.

The discontent which the English settlers felt soon spread to the Dutch, at least in regard to the arbitrary nature of company government. The frequent hostilities between England and The Netherlands in the 1640s and 1650s only exacerbated the colony's difficulties. The colony was beset with economic problems, and by the 1650s also found itself increasingly isolated. The English colonies in New England* had grown large and prosperous, as had the English presence in the Caribbean. By 1650 there were 30,000 settlers in New England and only 1,700 in New Netherland, including its farming settlements on the Hudson River. By the early 1660s, with the English Civil War over and the English settlers on Long Island complaining more and more about Dutch rule, King Charles II decided to conquer New Netherland and eliminate the Dutch presence in North America. He granted all of New Netherland to his brother James, the Duke of York. In August 1664 an English fleet sailed into New Amsterdam, and with hardly a fight, the Dutch colony surrendered. New Netherland became New York, an English colony. (Michael Kammen, *Colonial New York*, 1975; E. L. Raesly, *Portrait of New Netherland*, 1945.)

NEW PLYMOUTH. See PLYMOUTH.

NEW SOUTH WALES. New South Wales, a state in the Commonwealth of Australia*, totals 309,433 square miles along the southeastern coast of the continent. In 1606 the Dutch explorer Willem Janszoon first reached the northeast coast of Australia, at the Cape York Peninsula. Although the Dutch continued their explorations along the northern coast of Australia throughout the 1600s and early 1700s, the eastern coast was not reached by Europeans until 1770 when the British seafarer James Cook* reached Botany Bay near present-day Sydney. He claimed the continent for Great Britain and named it New South Wales.

Settlement of New South Wales waited another eighteen years. Once the American Revolution had ended in 1783, British officials needed a place to send English subjects convicted of major crimes. Since the United States would not receive them, Great Britain began to view Australia as a possibility. An English colony there might also be able to raise flax for sails and rope to supply the British navy. On January 20, 1788, more than 1,000 convicts and their supervisors landed at Sydney in New South Wales. The first governor of the colony was Arthur Phillip. In 1823 parliament provided for a legislative council in New South Wales, appointed by the royal governor.

Over the years, until 1840, England continued to transport many convicted felons to New South Wales. Not surprisingly, it was a tumultuous colony. As late as 1840 the large majority of colonists were either convicts, ex-convicts, or the children of convicts and ex-convicts. The colony had no middle class. Its population in 1840 totaled approximately 56,000 people, of whom more than 50,000 were servants, laborers, and craftsmen. The end of transportation of convicts in 1840 soon led parliament to pass the New South Wales Act of 1842, which changed the New South Wales legislative council to a combined council-assembly with 24 elected seats and 12 appointed seats. The property requirement for voting was quite low.

New South Wales evolved into the oldest, most prosperous, and most populated colony in Australia. Settlers from New South Wales expanded out to Queensland, Western Australia, Victoria*, South Australia*, and Tasmania. The colony of New South Wales joined the other continental colonies on January 1, 1901, in forming the federated Commonwealth of Australia. (Manning Clark, *Short History of Australia*, 1963.)

NEW SPAIN. At the time of the Spanish conquest of what they came to call New Spain, the Aztec empire was dominant in the Valley of Mexico and the surrounding area. The Aztecs had arrived there only recently, in the fourteenth century, when they constructed their capital city—Tenochtitlán. Montezuma II came to the Aztec throne in 1502, by which time the Aztec empire had acquired a powerful military control in central Mexico. As late as the 1490s Aztec expansion had reached the Gulf of Mexico when Aztec warriors conquered Vera Cruz. The local tribes hated and resented Aztec power, and the Spaniards would be able to exploit those feelings when they arrived a few decades later.

Rumors of fabulous Indian riches on the mainland of the Gulf of Mexico had been filtering back to Cuba*, Hispaniola*, and Spain for years, and in 1519 Hernán Cortés* received a commission from Diego Velásquez, governor of Cuba, to make contact with the leader of the Aztec empire. With several hundred soldiers, Cortés landed on the Gulf coast and then marched inland toward the Valley of Mexico, making allies all the way out of Aztec-hating Indian tribes. By the time he reached Tenochtitlán, Cortés's army had swelled to several thousand people. Cortés took Montezuma prisoner and began to systematically plunder the gold of Tenochtitlán. The Aztecs rose up in rebellion in 1520 and expelled the Spaniards, but Cortés returned in 1521 and reconquered the Aztecs. Montezuma had died in the rebellion of 1520 and was succeeded by his son Cuauhtemoc.

From that base in the Valley of Mexico, the Spaniards conquered the rest of Mexico. In 1535 Francisco de Montejo attacked the Mayan civilization of the Yucatán, but only after ten years of bloody fighting did the region come under Spanish control. Francisco de Coronado* led an expedition into the northern borderlands which established Spanish claims to northern Mexico, Lower California, Upper California, and present-day Texas, New Mexico, Arizona, and Colorado. By the 1540s the Spaniards had for all intents and purposes completed their conquest of Mexico. Spain established an *audiencia** in Tenochtitlán in 1528, and in 1535 Spain created the viceroyalty of New Spain with the full array of crown offices there. Antonio de Mendoza was the first viceroy. The Roman

Catholic church established a bishopric in Mexico City in 1527 and the first bishop, Juan de Zumarraga, arrived the next year. As the rest of Central America came under Spanish control, the jurisdictional domain of New Spain increased. The viceroyalty of New Spain had jurisdiction over the *audiencias* of Mexico City (1528), Santo Domingo (1511), Panama* (1538), Guatemala* (1542), and New Galicia*, or Guadalajara (1548).

The early economy of New Spain, once the Indians had been robbed of their gold, revolved around mining, ranching, farming, and commerce. During the mid-sixteenth century rich silver mines were opened at Zacatecas, Guanajuato, and San Luis Potosí in Mexico, and Spanish treasure ships regularly carried the bullion back to Spain. In rural areas, large haciendas appeared. Spaniards in Mexico raised cattle for meat, tallow, and hides. They also raised sheep, horses, and a variety of grains. When New Spain expanded north into the borderlands in the seventeenth century, even larger cattle ranches appeared.

Although the formal era of conquest was over by the early 1540s, the Indians of New Spain found themselves in a demographic catastrophe. King Charles I*, responded to the complaints of Bartolomé de Las Casas*, by outlawing the *encomienda** in 1520, but Cortés disobeyed the orders and established the labor institution throughout New Spain, giving Spaniards control over Indian labor. The exploitation from the *encomienda*, combined with the devastating effect of European diseases, reduced the Indian population of New Spain from as many as 25 million people in 1520 to less than 1 million in 1605. Most Spanish men living in New Spain married Indian women, and in the process a large mestizo class emerged.

By the early eighteenth century Spanish society revolved around four groups. The *peninsulares*—people born in Spain—dominated the civil, religious, and military bureaucracies through crown appointments. The *criollos* were people of European descent who had been born in New Spain. They tended to dominate commercial and economic life. The mixed race *mestizos* constituted the large working class of artisans, small farmers, soldiers, and small businessmen. Finally, at the bottom of the social scale were the surviving Indians. At the end of the colonial period the population of New Spain exceeded seven million people.

By the end of the eighteenth century a growing restlessness had appeared among the people of New Spain. The local *criollo* elite resented the patronizing attitude and monopoly on appointed offices maintained by the *peninsulares*, as well as the commercial restrictions imposed by imperial regulations. *Mestizos* felt similar hostilities, as well as resentments over racism among *criollos* and *peninsulares*. Indians were upset over their poverty and the rampant racism toward them among all other social classes in New Spain. When France invaded and occupied Spain in 1808, this smoldering resentment burst into the independence movement. Father Miguel Hidalgo y Costilla launched the war for independence in 1810, and although he was captured and executed in 1811, he had set in motion a political movement which could not be stopped. Eventually, the social classes of New Spain united temporarily to cast off the *peninsulare* domination they had come to despise.

José María de Morelos emerged as the new independence leader, a position he maintained until his capture and execution in 1815. For the next five years the independence movement degenerated into a series of guerrilla actions, with Vicente Guerrero the most prominent nationalist. Finally, under the leadership of Agustín de Iturbide, Mexico declared independence in 1821. (Ruben V. Austin, *The Development of Economic Policy in Mexico with Special Reference to Economic Doctrines 1600–1958*, 1987; John F. Bannono, *The Spanish Borderlands Frontier 1513–1821*, 1974; Louis Hasbrouck, *Mexico from Cortes to Carranza*, 1976.)

NEW SWEDEN. The colony of New Sweden was located on the Delaware River in what is today the state of New Jersey in the United States. In 1638, under the sponsorship of the Swedish monarchy, it was established by rebellious Dutch settlers disaffected from the Dutch West India Company. Its first governor was Pieter Minuit who had formerly lived in the New Netherlands colony further north. The Swedes also established several other posts along the river. But in 1655 Governor Peter Stuyvesant of New Netherlands conquered New Sweden and all of the posts along the river and incorporated them into New Netherlands. (Adrian Coulter Leiby, *The Early Dutch and Swedish Settlements of New Jersey*, 1964.)

NEW ULSTER. See NEW MUNSTER.

NEW YORK. New York is bordered on the east by Vermont, Massachusetts*, and Connecticut*, the southeast by the Atlantic Ocean, the south by Pennsylvania* and New Jersey*, the west by Lake Erie and Ontario*, and the north by Quebec*. When European explorers came into the region, they found two groups of Indians: the Algonguins and the Iroquois. In 1570 the Iroquois League, or League of Five Nations, was formed and consisted of the Mohawk, Oneida, Onondaga, Cayuga, and Seneca tribes. It was later expanded in 1714 to include the Tuscaroras and served as a balance between the French and the British as they competed for control of the region. On his voyage to the New World in 1524, Giovanni de Verrazano, an Italian navigator sailing for the French, discovered New York harbor. The area was explored in 1603 and 1609 by Samuel de Champlain* and in 1609 by Henry Hudson*. In his ship *Half Moon*, Hudson sailed up the river which now bears his name and claimed the valley for the Dutch East India Company*. In 1614 and 1615 Dutch settlers established fur-trading posts at Fort Nassau and on Manhattan Island.

The Dutch West India Company, formed in 1621, was granted a charter and a monopoly on fur trading which lasted for twenty-four years. New Netherland* was founded, as trade and colonization increased, and by 1624 thirty Dutch families had established the first permanent settlement at Fort Orange in present-day

Albany. The next year brought more settlers into the area and by the end of the year the company had purchased Manhattan from the Indians and founded New Amsterdam. By 1629 the company adopted the system of patronage, which awarded large land grants to individual settlers. This system proved unsuccessful, however, because it was based on a tenant farm system rather than outright ownership. The Dutch maintained control over New Netherland until 1664.

In the seventeenth century the Dutch relinquished their monopoly on the fur trade and encouraged manufacturing as settlers were slow to enter the region because of increased Indian attacks. The colony was also plagued with mismanagement and neglect from the company. In 1650 the Dutch governor was forced to sign the Treaty of Hartford, which ceded Long Island and the territory west of the Connecticut River to England. On March 22, 1664, King Charles II of England granted his brother, the Duke of York, all the land from the west side of the Connecticut River to the east side of the Delaware Bay, including the whole of New Netherland. The Dutch governor relinquished all claims to the land in September 1664 and New Netherland became the English province of New York. In 1673 the Dutch briefly regained control of the colony when a Dutch fleet captured New York. The Treaty of Westminster was signed in 1674 and England again had control of New York. By 1683 the colonists had been granted a charter of liberties, which allowed them greater voice in the governance of New York. In 1688 James II consolidated New York, New Jersey, and the New England* colonies to form the Dominion of New England. With the abdication of James II in 1688, control of New York eventually went to William and Mary.

New York was a crucial region during the colonial wars between 1689 to 1763. England and France fought to control North American trade and territory. The defeat of France and the Treaty of Paris of 1763 freed New York from the threat of warfare waged by the French. The Treaty of Fort Stanwix was signed in 1768 ceding all Indian lands in New York to the colony. In the 1770s New York refused to comply with the Stamp Act and the Sugar Act, the Townshend Duties, and other British imposed taxes. This resistance led to the British government's repeal of most of the Townshend Duties in 1770. Protests continued throughout 1773, however, and in 1774 New York sent delegates to the First Continental Congress. Representing a moderate and loyalist view, the New York assembly at first refused to send delegates to the Second Continental Congress. A provincial convention was called in 1775 to select delegates to attend the Congress. This marked the beginning of revolution in New York. On July 9, 1776, representatives from New York signed the Declaration of Independence and a constitutional convention was appointed to frame a new state constitution. (D. M. Ellis, *A History of New York*, 1967.)

Veula J. Rhodes

NEW ZEALAND. In 1642 Abel Tasman*, an explorer working for the Dutch East India Company*, reached the western coast of South Island of New Zealand. Tasman named the land after his home in Holland—New Zealand. Because of a hostile reception from the native Maoris, Tasman did not land, simply recording the location of the island in his logs. Europeans did not return to New Zealand until 1769 when the British explorer James Cook* sighted and landed on South Island. Between 1773 and 1777 Cook returned to New Zealand three more times, sailing around North Island and South Island and mapping both coastlines. James Cook claimed the islands for Great Britain.

The first European settlements in New Zealand began in the early 1790s when British and American whalers started landing on the coast for resupply. Samuel Marsden brought Protestant missionaries to the Bay Islands off the coast of North Island in 1814. The missionaries established relatively good relations with the Maoris. In the 1830s Edward Gibbon Wakefield set his sights on the "systematic colonization" of New Zealand. Wakefield wanted the government to sell land to English settlers who would then move to the colony. In 1837 he formed the New Zealand Association to lobby for systematic colonization. In 1839 Wakefield established the New Zealand Company and sent an expedition. They landed at Port Nicholson, later known as Wellington, on North Island in January 1840. Shortly thereafter 500 Maori chiefs signed the Treaty of Waitangi, surrendering sovereignty over New Zealand to the British but retaining their property rights. Great Britain made New Zealand part of New South Wales* in 1840, but a year later New Zealand was separated from New South Wales and declared a separate crown colony.

In 1842 parliament passed the Waste Lands Act, providing for a price of 20 shillings an acre for all land in New Zealand and Australia*. The New Zealand Company established a settlement in Nelson on South Island in 1842 and contracted with religious groups for more settlers. In association with the Presbyterian Church of Scotland, the New Zealand Company settled Dunedin in 1848 on South Island and Canterbury on South Island in 1850, with the cooperation of the Church of England. In 1848, New Zealand was divided into New Munster*, which consisted of part of North Island, and New Ulster*, which included the rest of North Island and all of South Island. The division was discontinued in 1853. The New Zealand Constitution Act of 1852 granted provincial legislatures to each of the six major settlements in New Zealand (Auckland, New Plymouth, Wellington, Nelson, Canterbury, and Otago), as well as a federal legislature with control over taxing authority. By 1856 New Zealand enjoyed an elective parliament and a cabinet government. In 1862 New Zealand received complete control over Maori affairs and land sales. More change in the political structure took place in the 1870s. the British government withdrew its last troops from New Zealand in 1871 after the conclusion of the last Maori War, and in 1875 New Zealand abolished all the provincial councils in favor of a unitary political system.

Economic development in New Zealand was impeded by the intense, bitter wars between colonists and the Maoris, who felt their traditional land rights were being usurped by the ever increasing numbers of British colonists. But once those wars were over in the early 1870s, the New Zealand economy boomed, stimulated by the discovery of gold, huge increases in the number of sheep being raised on pastureland, and by the invention of refrigeration in 1882, which permitted large-scale exports of meat and dairy products.

During the 1890s New Zealand flirted with the idea of becoming part of the Australian Commonwealth, then in the planning stages; but because her ties to the mother country were among the strongest in the British Empire*, New Zealanders decided not to become part of Australia. By that time the country was known worldwide for its enactment of a comprehensive social welfare system for all of its citizens, as well as full civil rights for women. The British acquired the Cook Islands in 1888, and in 1901 Britain ceded the Cook Islands* and Niue* to New Zealand. Great Britain gave New Zealand full dominion status in 1907, but it was not until 1947 that New Zealand acted on its authority under the Statute of Westminister of 1931 and proclaimed itself fully autonomous. At that time New Zealand also acquired sovereignty over the Tokelau Islands. (John Cawte Beaglehole, *The Discovery of New Zealand*, 1961; John Bell Cunliffe, *The Welfare State in New Zealand*, 1959; Keith Sinclair, *A History of New Zealand*, 1960.)

NICARAGUA. Nicaragua, a province of the Captaincy General of Guatemala during the Spanish colonial period, received its name from the principal *cacique* Nicarao or Nicaragua whom the Spaniards first met. The province, bordered by the Atlantic and Pacific Oceans, contained two large lakes which determined its development and settlement patterns during this period. On September 12, 1502, Columbus made the first discovery of the region on his fourth voyage when forced to seek refuge in a cape named Gracias a Dios on the Atlantic side. On the Pacific side, it was Gil González Dávila who explored Costa Rican and Nicaraguan territory. He and Andrés Niño left Panama on January 21, 1522, to explore Central American territory. Niño continued the expedition along the Pacific coast as Gil González went inland. In Nicaragua, he came upon various Indian groups and was kindly received by them. He came upon the *cacique* Nicarao and his Indians. Many were baptized and he received a great deal of gold from them. The *cacique* Diriangen also talked to Gil González and promised to return. He returned at the head of three to four thousand armed Indians to attack the Spaniards. González retreated and arrived in Panama in June 1532 where he left for Santo Domingo to prepare another expedition.

In 1524, Pedrarias Dávila, governor of Castillo de Oro, arranged an expedition under Francisco Hernández de Córdoba to go to Nicaragua. On his arrival, Córdoba faced very little resistance from the Indians. He founded many towns, including Granada and León. Gil González landed in Honduras, went inland, and met Hernández's troops, under the command of Hernando de Soto. González won the ensuing battle, but he returned to Puerto Caballos when news of another expedition arrived. Meanwhile, Hernández attempted to free himself from Pedrarias who sent troops under Martín de Estete to arrest him. He was executed in Leon in 1526 when Pedrarias arrived. Pedrarias returned to Castilla de Oro, leaving Estete as governor in León, when Pedro de lo Ríos replaced him as governor. Diego López de Salcedo, governor of Honduras, declared Nicaragua under his jurisdiction and went to León in April 1527. Pedrarias convinced de los Rios to go to Nicaragua, but when he arrived Salcedo sent him away. Pedrarias received the title of Governor of Nicaragua in June 1527 but did not take his post until March 24, 1528. On his arrival he imprisoned Salcedo for seven months. Pedrarias's administration was noted for its cruelty to the Indians, as was that of his successor, Francisco de Casteneda, who took over upon Pedrarias's death in 1531.

The conquest of Peru depopulated the region, as did the flourishing Indian slave trade. Pedro de Alvarado founded Realejo on his journey to Peru. In February 1531, the Bishopric of Nicaragua was founded and Diego Alvarez Osorio named bishop in 1532. A new governor, Rodrigo de Contreras, was named and Casteneda left for Peru leaving Osorio in charge from January to November 1535. Under Contreras, Nueva Segovia was founded in a region with some mines. Also, in 1539, the San Juan river was explored by Alonso Calero and Diego Machuca de Zuazo.

In 1542, the New Laws put Nicaragua under the jurisdiction of the *Audiencia de los Confines* and did away with the governor's post, replacing it with that of *alcalde mayor*. Contreras was given a *judicio de residencia* because of his treatment of the Indians and other abuses. Nicaragua's third bishop, Antonio de Valdivieso, demanded enforcement of the royal orders for the protection of the Indians. This inflamed Contreras's sons, Hernando and Pedro, who assassinated the bishop in León on February 26, 1550. They continued their rebellion and went as far as Panama where they were stopped and managed to escape. Juan Gaitán, another rebel coming from Guatemala and Honduras, attacked León but was captured and executed. In 1566, the title of governor was reestablished. Explorations of the Atlantic side of the province continued.

At the end of the sixteenth century, León was the capital city although Granada was the richer of the two. The main economic activity was agricultural exports. Besides Spanish and Indian revolts, a major problem was pirate attacks, which began in 1572 and continued throughout the seventeenth century and into the eighteenth. English pirates joined forces with the Miskito Indians to sack and burn the province's principal centers. Matagalpa was attacked in 1644; Granada in 1665, 1670, and 1683; León and Realejo in 1685 and various other towns. Pirates commanded the mouth of the San Juan river impeding commercial traffic. The response to these attacks were forts and attempts to colonize and settle the Atlantic coast, known as Tologalpa, but there was little success. A major earthquake in 1663 destroyed León. In 1693, the inhabitants of Sebaco, tired of being recruited for the province's defense, rebelled. In 1699, William Pitt (not *the* William Pitt) established himself in Taguzgalpa.

The Miskitos continued their attacks at the beginning of the eighteenth century. In 1711, the New Segovia citizens tired of the constant attacks decided to leave. In 1724, Governor Antonio de Poveda organized a militia to attack the Miskitos and he was victorious. Under the next governor, Tomás Duque de Estrada, the León militia rebelled and Poveda returned in 1727. Ecclesiastics organized a rebellion but they were discovered. Poveda ordered the vicar general, Clemente Reyes Alvarez, to put an end to these meetings, which he did by firing the seminary's rector. A number of prominent people opposed to this decision and Alvarez asked for the governor's protection. They left Masaya for León but on July 7 unknown assailants assassinated the governor. In 1740, a militia company of *pardos* attempted to revolt when José Antonio Lacayo de Briones was named governor, but it was discovered and those responsible were executed. That same year the English and Miskitos attacked Jonotega, which they sacked. They also burned *haciendas* and took prisoners. In 1748, the English took San Juan del Norte but returned it after the Treaty of Aix-la-Chapelle.

A difference existed between the Atlantic and Pacific side of Nicaragua as the former was colonized by the English with the Miskitos as allies and the latter had the major Spanish populations. The English used their Atlantic bases to attack and harass the Spaniards and for contraband trade. The governors asked the Captain General, as well as the king, for protection, but it was always late in coming or never in sufficient amounts. In 1786, a treaty between Spain and England recognized Spain's rights to the Miskito territory. The Miskitos got closer to the Spaniards but still harassed the province. In 1786, Nicaragua was made an intendancy and the first intendant, Juan de Ayasa, toured the Atlantic coast trying to pacify the region.

The beginning of the nineteenth century saw disputes between public functionaries and more Miskito attacks. In 1811, León, Granada, Masaya, Rivas and other towns revolted. On December 13, 1811, León rebelled against the intendant José Salvador, who resigned to avoid bloodshed. The rebels demanded the establishment of a new government, reductions in the prices of some goods, and abolition of some taxes. These demands were agreed upon but the rebels continued their revolt until Bishop Nicolás García Jérez established a *junta gubernativa* on December 14, which recognized him as president and as intendant of the province. In Granada, a similar revolt occurred in December which deposed the peninsular employees of their offices replacing them with *criollos*. These former employees went to Masaya where they received help from the Captain General José Bustamante y Guerra, who sent troops under the command of Pedro Gutiérrez. In April 1812 the Granada rebels surrendered and were promised guarantees of which Bustamante did not approve. About two hundred rebels were condemned to different punishments, ranging from prison sentences to death.

When Guatemala declared independence on September 15, 1821, the province's last Spanish intendant, Miguel González Saravia, along with Bishop Jérez, issued in León the "*Acta de los Nublados*", which declared Nicaragua independent from Spain and Guatemala. Granada, under Crisanto Sacasa, declared independence in agreement with Guatemala on October 3. On October 11, León accepted independence on the terms presented by Agustín Iturbide and the Mexican empire. The issue would not be resolved until Guatemala declared in favor of Mexico in 1822. (Bernardo Portas, *Compendio de la Historia de Nicaragua*, 1927; Sofónias Salvatierra, *Contribuciones a la Historia de Centroamerica*, 2 vols, 1930.)

Carlos Pérez

NIGER. The history of Niger, located in the region of the central Sudan, began with the emergence of an agricultural and cattle-herding society of Libyan, Berber, and Negro groups in the area. The Hausa tribe was dominant in the south until the early sixteenth century, when the Songhai empire invaded from the west and established its dominance over the Hausa and Berber lands. Less than a century later the Songhai empire fell to the Moroccans, and the Bornu empire, centered around Lake Chad, expanded throughout eastern Niger. The Hausa were restored in the south. During the early nineteenth century Muslims from the Fulani sect, led by Uthman dan Fodio, confronted the Hausa and Bornu states in a holy war. At about the same time the Scottish explorer Mungo Park entered the area, trying to determine the course of the Niger River—a quest which ultimately cost him his life.

When French military expeditions began to push across Niger from the French colonies in west Africa, in order to secure the perimeters of France's other holdings in the Sahara and to access the lucrative trade around Lake Chad, the three states of Bornu, Hausa, and Fulani resisted French expansion with limited success. By 1900 the French had established military rule around Lake Chad, and one year later Niger was named as a district in the colonial administration of Upper Senegal* and Niger, which involved the southern region of Niger between the Niger River and Lake Chad. The northern desert regions had not yet experienced a permanent French presence. South Niger was important to the French as a line of communication linking west Africa with Chad* in the interior. In 1906 the French began to move northward and established posts at Agades and Bilma to prevent German encroachment into the area, which threatened to isolate Chad from French strongholds in the north. While expanding north, the French confronted, subjugated, and ultimately dislocated the Tuareg tribes.

During World War I a major uprising of Taureg warriors, supported by Germany, occurred at Zinder. Full-scale rebellion was averted by the French with British assistance from Nigeria* by 1922. The Taureg, as well as most of the indigenous population, lost nearly all of their property, freedoms, and political power. Niger was declared a separate French colony in 1922. The administration of Niger was in the hands of the governor-general in Dakar, Senegal. He received direction from Paris. Local government was the responsibility of commandants. At the beginning of World War II, the economy of Niger was too underdeveloped to be considered of any great importance. However, when France fell to Germany and the Vichy government was installed, Niger was bordered by two territories hostile to Vichy France: Free French, or Gaullist, Chad, which seceded from Vichy France in 1940, and British Nigeria. Niger became strategically important to the Vichy government, but the Gaullists were successful in seizing control of most of northern and western Africa, including Niger, in 1943.

In 1944, at the Brazzaville Conference, France adopted a change in colonial policy. Instead of extracting labor and resources and offering little economic assistance, the French initiated a system whereby economic development and political reforms could take place. In 1945 the new constitution of the Fourth French Republic conferred the right to vote upon colonial inhabitants. African colonies received representation in the French assembly. However, revisions were made to the constitution and most of its reforms before it was ratified in 1946. The 1946 constitution renamed the colonies overseas territories, and these, with the French Republic, constituted the French Union*. Africans in that Union were made French citizens.

Africans elected their own representatives in the national assembly or chamber of deputies, the council of the Republic, and the assembly of the French Union. They were allowed to participate and hold offices in local government as well. In addition, an economic policy of state-planning and state-expenditure was adopted, bringing about the Fund for Economic and Social Development. The financial strain of developing Niger consequently led French opinion to accept the notion of eventual Nigerian independence. Political parties began to emerge and maneuver in anticipation of independence.

With the ratification of the constitution of the Fifth French Republic and a favorable vote in the Niger territorial assembly in 1958, Niger became the Republic of Niger within the French Community*. Under the leadership of Hamani Diori, the *Ressemblement Democatique Africain* (RDA) was successful in eliminating opposition to independence by packing the territorial assembly with ''yes'' votes and outlawing opposition parties. On August 3, 1960, Niger proclaimed its independence from France. (Finn Fulgestad, *A History of Niger 1850–1960*, 1983.)

Karen Sleezer

NIGERIA. The Portuguese were the first Europeans to reach the Nigerian coast. By 1486 they had established a trading depot near Benin to carry out commerce in ivory, gold, and slaves. After 1650 the Dutch, French, and British trade competition undermined the Portuguese. In 1807 Great Britain passed legislation making the slave trade illegal, and in 1833 outlawed slavery throughout the British Empire*. Interest in the palm oil trade developed thereafter. Inland exploration from the northwest, led by the Scottish explorer Mungo Park, began in 1796. Park advanced European knowledge of the interior but failed to track the Niger River through to the coast. In 1830 the Lander brothers finally reached the Niger River delta from the interior. By the mid–1800s this penetration had led to significant trade links between the north and south along the Niger and Benue rivers.

The most important coastal organization, formed by Sir George Goldie in

1879, was the National African Company. Renamed the Royal Niger Company after receiving a charter from the British government in 1886, Goldie's group established wide governmental and commercial authority along the coast. Great Britain also established the Oil Rivers Protectorate in 1885. After further extension inland along the Niger River, it was renamed the Niger Coast Protectorate in 1893. At the same time the threat of German and French expansion from the north forced the consolidation of British inland territories. In 1900 the British government withdrew the Royal Niger Company's charter of 1866 and established the Protectorate of Northern Nigeria. Frederick Dealtry Lugard was appointed high commissioner and assumed full responsibility for Northern Nigeria. At the time Northern Nigeria was a vast territory with limited resources. Forced to rule the country through the agency of its African leaders, Lugard's policies gave rise to the method of "indirect rule," which became the model of British colonial administration in Africa.

Meanwhile the lucrative Niger Coast Protectorate had been amalgamated with other southern territories under the name of the Protectorate of Southern Nigeria in 1900. In 1906 the British government established the Colony and Protectorate of Southern Nigeria—including Lagos Colony—operating under the British Colonial Office. The Protectorate of Northern Nigeria and the Colony and Protectorate of Southern Nigeria existed separately from 1906 to 1914, though both were administered as a single unit under the British Colonial Office*. In 1914 the two entities were unified into the Colony and Protectorate of Nigeria with Lugard as governor-general.

Between World War I and World War II, regional animosities emerged between the north and the south and between the southwest and the southeast. Conflicting economic interests and religious differences contributed to these animosities, though most of the hostilities between the Yoruba, Ibo, and Hausa were based on ethnicity. Increasing pressures for self-government resulted in a series of constitutions between 1946 and October 1960. The constitution of 1954 firmly established the federal principle and substantially reduced the powers of the governor. After constitutional conferences in May and June 1953, both Western and Eastern regions formally became self-governing. The Northern region received the same status in 1957. Constitutional conferences in London in 1957 and 1958 prepared the final steps and set the final dates for the change from colonial self-government to independence.

The leading delegates at both conferences were Chief Obafemi Awolowo for the Action Group (Yoruba); Nnambi Azikiwe for the National Council of Nigeria and the Cameroons (Ibo); and Alkaji Ahmadu and Abubakar Tafawa Balewa for the Northern People's Congress (Hausa and Fulani). On October 1, 1960, Nigeria became the sixteenth African state to achieve independence. Balewa became the first prime minister and Azikiwe the governor-general. (Donald L. Wiedner, *A History of Africa South of the Sahara*, 1962.)

Eric C. Loew

NINE POWER TREATY. The Nine Power Treaty was the third of the major agreements to emerge from the Washington Conference* of 1921–1922. It was the product of United States concern over the growing Japanese presence in China. The signatories were the United States, Belgium, the British Empire, China, France, Italy, Japan, the Netherlands, and Portugal. All of them agreed to "respect the sovereignty, the independence, and the territorial and administrative integrity of China." They also promised not to take advantage of China's instability or to acquire undue influence in China. China promised to play fair with foreign economic interests which had invested there. The text of the treaty was a close copy of the United States's Open Door Note of 1900. Essentially this agreement meant that the United States had succeeded in making its own policy a multilateral arrangement for the first time since initially proposed in 1900. (J. Chalmers Vinson, *The Parchment Peace*, 1950.)

Joseph M. Rowe, Jr.

NIUE. Niue is a small coral atoll in the southern Pacific. Self-governing in free association with New Zealand*, Niue is part of the (British) Commonwealth of Nations. The island is located approximately 560 miles southeast of Samoa*. The indigenous people of Niue are Polynesian, and the first European contact came on June 24, 1774, when Captain James Cook* landed there. Blessed with a fierce pride, the people of Niue resisted the European presence—missionary and military—until the 1850s, by which time most of them had been converted to Christianity. The English initially called Niue "Savage Island." By the 1860s whalers were regularly landing on the island, as were slavers, who kidnapped Niueans to labor in the mines of other Pacific islands. King Fataaiki of Niue requested establishment of a British protectorate over the island in 1898, and in 1900, in order to prevent French expansion there, the British agreed. In 1901 the British included Niue as part of New Zealand. Self-government then evolved very slowly. A local council was established in 1904 to advise the British-appointed governor, and that form of administering the island prevailed until 1960, when an elected assembly was convened. On October 19, 1974, Great Britain extended independence to Niue, placing them in "free association" with New Zealand. The Niuean assembly was responsible for all internal affairs, while New Zealand conducted foreign affairs and provided defense. (Edwin M. Loeb, *History and Traditions of Niue*, 1926; Angus Ross, *New Zealand's Record in the Pacific Islands in the Twentieth Century*, 1969.)

NKRUMAH, KWAME. Kwame Nkrumah was born on September 21, 1909, in the village of Nkroful in Nzima in the Gold Coast colony. His father was a goldsmith. Nkrumah was educated at the Half Assini elementary schools, the Government Training School in Accra, and the Prince of Wales College in Achimota. A convert to Catholicism, he taught in a number of Catholic schools before enrolling at Lincoln University in Pennsylvania, where he received a degree in economics and sociology in 1939. In 1942 he was awarded a Bachelor of Theology from Lincoln and a master's degree in education from the University of Pennsylvania. Nkrumah remained in the United States until 1945, serving as a full-time instructor at Lincoln University. During this time Nkrumah organized the African Students' Association of America and Canada and published the *African Interpreter*.

In May 1945 Nkrumah left America and moved to London to study law and complete his thesis for a doctorate degree. A political activist, he joined the West African Students' Union and was a participant in planning the Fifth Pan-African Congress. From 1945 to 1947 he served as general secretary of the West African National Secretariat which supported African socialism and positive action without violence. Nkrumah edited *The New African* and used this magazine to stress his ideas of political freedom and economic advancement for the West Africa colonies. In 1947 he was invited to return to the Gold Coast* and serve as general secretary of the United Gold Coast Convention (UGCC). Seeking to hasten independence, Nkrumah organized this nationalist party in an effort to awaken the political conscience of his people. Boycotts and demonstrations were staged and Nkrumah and other leaders of UGCC were placed under arrest. Viewing education as a means by which to free the minds of the youth, Nkrumah created the Ghana National College and several national secondary schools and colleges. Nkrumah used the *Accra Evening News*, the *Morning Telegraph*, and the *Daily Mail* to promote the ideas of the movement. The Committee on Youth Organization (CYO), founded in 1948, issued the Ghana Youth Manifesto and met in 1949 to protest the dismissal of Nkrumah as general secretary of the United Gold Coast Convention. CYO was later converted into the Convention People's Party (CPP) and was dedicated to the promotion of immediate self-government through "non-violent positive action."

When the British administration commissioned the Coussey committee to propose a new constitution for the Gold Coast, Nkrumah convened the Ghana People's Representative Assembly to discuss strategies for resistance and to urge the people to action against the forces of imperialism in the country. On January 8, 1950, positive action went into effect as citizens took to the streets in non-violent strikes and demonstrations. The government reacted with censors, closings of all propaganda newspapers, and general curfews. Rioting and the death of two African policemen led to the arrest and imprisonment of Nkrumah and other party leaders. While serving a three-year sentence, Nkrumah was elected to the general assembly for Accra Central, receiving 22,780 of 23,122 possible votes. He was released from prison on February 12, 1951, as the leader of the majority party, holding the position of leader of government business. In 1952 Nkrumah was named prime minister for the Gold Coast.

In 1954 the Coussey constitution was overturned and a new one adopted. Nkrumah still faced opposition from the Ashanti and Northern Territory chiefs. Forming the National Liberation Movement, this group reverted to the use of violence as an attempt was made on Nkrumah's life on November 10, 1955. This violence delayed Britain's awarding of independence to the Gold Coast by more than a year. On March 6, 1957, Ghana* became an independent state as a part of the British Commonwealth*, and Nkrumah became prime minister. By 1960 Ghana emerged as a republic with centralized power in the hands of her new president, Nkrumah. He established himself as an absolute authority with power to veto legislation and power to dissolve parliament. He was the head of the army and controlled the civil service.

In 1961 Nkrumah attended the Belgrade Conference and made a trip to the Soviet Union. In his absence, the railway and harbor workers went on strike in protest against Nkrumah's economic policies. When Nkrumah returned home, he successfully suppressed the strike and expelled many of his earliest supporters. Opposition leaders were arrested along with the strikers and the politically powerful market women. Nkrumah's governing method became increasingly dictatorial as he declared that such controls were necessary for a new nation facing rapid economic and social reform. His policies soon precipitated violence in Accra* and other regions as bombings became commonplace.

Nkrumah had a lifelong ambition to develop African unity. He hoped to create a West Africa federation and in July 1961, the Union of African States, comprised of Ghana-Guinea-Mali, was chartered. On February 24, 1966, while on a peace mission in Beijing, Nkrumah was overthrown and replaced by a military government headed by General Joseph A. Ankrah. Forced into exile in nearby Guinea*, Nkrumah died in 1972. (Sophia R. Ames, *Nkrumah of Ghana*, 1961; Peter Jones, *Kwame Nkrumah and Africa*, 1965.)

Veula J. Rhodes

NORFOLK ISLAND. Norfolk Island is a 13-square mile land mass in the Pacific Ocean, approximately 800 miles northeast of Sydney, Australia. Captain James Cook* discovered the island in 1774, and between 1788 and 1855 it was a penal colony for Great Britain. In 1856, 200 people from Pitcairn Island relocated there, and Norfolk Island was placed under the political jurisdiction of New South Wales*, Australia. It became a formal territory of Australia in 1914. (Merval Hoare, *Norfolk Island: An Outline of Its History, 1774–1968*, 1969.)

NORTH BORNEO. See BRITISH NORTH BORNEO.

NORTH CAROLINA. In 1663 Charles II of England, in order to repay a political debt to several individuals who had helped restore him to the throne and to promote a mercantilist philosophy, made a huge proprietary grant of land in an area south of Virginia* in British North America. Settlers from Virginia had already settled there. At the same time, a number of prominent English planters from Barbados* were suffering from an economic depression and were interested in relocating their plantations. Charles II made the land grant to Sir John Colleton and several other prominent individuals who had politically supported the royal cause. The proprietors initially set out three counties: Albermarle, which included the Chowan River-Albermarle Sound area in the northeast; Clarendon, which was south of Albermarle and included Cape Fear Valley; and Craven, which is present-day South Carolina. The Clarendon settlement failed after only a few years.

The colony at Albermarle succeeded. It attracted settlers from Virginia because of the possibility of raising tobacco and cattle where land was cheap and abundant. But because of its isolated geography and lack of a good harbor, growth was slow. Eventually the proprietors decided that the South Carolina* settlement had more potential, and they invested most of their resources there. Most early settlers in Albermarle came from Virginia and Barbados, and they were primarily lower middle-class workers and farmers. Small farms became very common and the people exhibited a highly independent spirit, perhaps because their geographic isolation prevented much political interference. By 1700 there were only 3,000 people living there, and they were scattered from the Virginia line south to the Neuse River and up to fifty miles inland.

Beginning in 1691 the Albermarle colony became known as North Carolina with its own deputy governor, and in 1694 John Archdale, a proprietor and governor, established separate administrations for North Carolina and South Carolina. Edward Hyde became governor of North Carolina in 1712, when its independence from South Carolina was legally established. The colony continued to grow slowly in the eighteenth century, although immigration of poor settlers from Scotland and Northern Ireland helped create an even more independent minded population. In 1776 North Carolina joined with the other twelve mainland British North American colonies in declaring its independence from England. (V. W. Crane, *The Southern Frontier, 1670–1732*, 1928.)

NORTHERN AUSTRALIA. Settlement of the northern reaches of New South Wales* in Australia* began in 1824 when the communities of Fort Dundas (Melville Island) and Fort Wellington (Raffles Bay) were established. Both of those settlements were abandoned in 1829. In 1838 British settlers reached the inlet of Port Essington, which became the site of the first settlement in the area. In 1863, Great Britain created a new territorial government named Northern Australia, which was then transferred for administrative purposes to the colony of South Australia.* Northern Australia remained an administrative district of South Australia until 1910. At that point it became a territory of the new Commonwealth of Australia. See AUSTRALIA.

NORTHERN IRELAND. Northern Ireland, which remains today a much troubled part of the United Kingdom*, came into existence in 1920 when the Government of Ireland Act partitioned Ireland into two political entities, Northern Ireland and Southern Ireland, the latter becoming (in 1922) the Irish Free State. But the origins of Northern Ireland reach back into the early seventeenth century. Ever since the 1200s England had been attempting to take control of Ireland, but beginning in 1607 King James I began the "Plantation" experiment, inviting poor English Anglicans and Scots Presbyterians to relocate to Ireland, where he promised them long leases on the land they seized from native Irish peasants. During the rest of the seventeenth century, English and Scots immigrants used assassination, disenfranchisement, and relocation to push the native Irish off the land. Protestants became the dominant group—politically, economically, and socially—in the six northern counties of Ireland: Antrim, Down, Armagh, Tyrone, Londonderry, and Fermanagh. They also came to outnumber the native Irish Catholics by two to one. Gradually in the eighteenth and nineteenth centuries the northern counties became more and more integrated into the British industrial and commercial network.

During the nineteenth century drive for Irish Home Rule, most northern Protestants intensely opposed nationalism, demanding instead a continuation of the union with Great Britain, knowing that in an autonomous Ireland, they would be outnumbered by the Roman Catholic majority. When Home Rule for Ireland became inevitable after World War I, the Protestants, known as Unionists, became committed to the partition of Ireland. They were opposed to any settlement awarding sovereignty over all of Ireland to a nationalist, Roman Catholic government in Dublin. The Unionists enjoyed considerable support from English conservatives. In the Government of Ireland Act of 1920, parliament acceded to the Unionist's demands, establishing Northern Ireland, with 5,452 square miles and 1,256,000 people, as part of the United Kingdom. The law permitted Northern Ireland, upon a vote of its legislature, to join the Irish Free State, but the Unionist majority had no intention of letting that happen. For nationalists who had fought for a democratic, united Ireland, the partition was a bitter disappointment.

Widespread Catholic displeasure over the settlement, as well as fear of guerrilla raids by the nationalistic Irish Republican Army, inspired parliament to pass the Civil Authority Act (Special Powers Act) of 1922 permitting British authorities to arrest people who were members of ''suspicious organizations,'' search homes and businesses without warrants, and prohibit entry into Northern Ireland of ''undesirable people.'' Unionists controlled the Northern Ireland parliament. Lord Craigavon, who served as the prime minister of Northern Ireland between 1921 and 1940, was openly anti-Catholic and permitted widespread discrimination against the Roman Catholic minority in voting rights and access to government social benefits. His successors, J. M. Andrews (1940–1943) and Lord Brookborough (1943–1963), were just as anti-Catholic. Roman Catholics in Northern Ireland became an oppressed, impoverished minority.

During the late 1950s radicals in the outlawed Irish Republican Army began conducting a terrorist campaign, in Northern Ireland as well as in Great Britain, to unify Ireland under the Catholic majority. Not until 1962 did the Irish Republican Army renounce terrorism. By that time a civil rights movement was emerging among Roman Catholics in Northern Ireland. Led by Gerry Fitt and the Northern Ireland Civil Rights Association, they demanded an end to discrimination against Roman Catholics. By 1969 Bernadette Devlin had become an outspoken leader of the movement, but when rioting broke out in Londonderry over Catholic demands for equal opportunity, the British sent 3,000 troops to Northern Ireland to keep the peace. The disturbances of August, 1969 marked the beginning of the continuing turmoil known as the "troubles" in present-day Northern Ireland. Although Catholics at first welcomed the soldiers, they soon came to see them as the military arm of the Protestant majority. Increasingly the target of attacks by a revitalized Irish Republican Army (IRA), those 3,000 troops had become 11,500 by 1971. Violence and terrorism became more and more common, with Protestants and their paramilitary organizations like the B-Specials (officially disbanded in 1970) fighting for the preservation of a separate Northern Ireland and Roman Catholics and the Irish Republican Army demanding union. Hundreds of people have died in bombings and sniper attacks.

In March 1972, facing enormous pressure to do something about the violence, Great Britain dismissed the Northern Ireland parliament and assumed direct rule. The motivation behind direct rule was noble. As long as Protestants controlled the parliament of Northern Ireland, discrimination against Roman Catholics would never cease. By assuming direct rule, Great Britain hoped to end some of the oppression against Catholics; but since most Catholics wanted Northern Ireland to become a part of the Republic of Ireland, Great Britain could never really please them. In assuming direct rule, Great Britain also enraged the Protestant majority who wanted to continue their domination of the government and discriminatory treatment of Roman Catholics. In 1974 Great Britain returned to home rule by restoring the parliament of Northern Ireland but also requiring a sharing of government posts by Catholics and Protestants. The experiment lasted only five months when Protestant trade unionists protested the power-sharing arrangement and brought the Northern Ireland government to a standstill. Great Britain resumed direct rule later in 1974. Eight years later the British authorized creation of a provincial assembly, with guaranteed Catholic participation, as a transitional step toward the restoration of home rule for Northern Ireland. The Anglo-Irish Agreement of November 15, 1985, was another attempt to calm the political tensions in Northern Ireland. The agreement gave the Republic of Ireland an official but only advisory role in the affairs of Northern Ireland in exchange for formal recognition that Northern Ireland would not be reunified with Ireland unless a majority of its population wished to do so. Ireland also agreed to cooperate in fighting the Irish Republican Army. But because the agreement depends on mutual goodwill in a land where the animosity between Protestants and Catholics is unrivaled, it has had to date little effect on the violence. (Denis P. Barritt and Charles F. Carter, *The Northern Ireland Problem: A Study in Group Relations*, 1972; James Beckett, *The Making of Modern Ireland, 1603–1923*, 1966; John O'Beirne Ranelagh, *A Short History of Ireland*, 1983.)

NORTHERN RHODESIA. See ZAMBIA.

NORTH-WEST FRONTIER PROVINCE. For thousands of years the classic invasion route into India* from the Middle East and from the steppes of Asia had been through the northwest corridor, territory which is in Pakistan* today.

To stabilize that frontier, Great Britain established the North-West Frontier Province in 1901. The region became a governor's province in 1932, and in 1947, with the political division and independence of the subcontinent, the North-West Frontier Province became part of Pakistan.* See PAKISTAN.

NORTHWEST ORDINANCE. The Northwest Ordinance, passed by the United States Congress on July 13, 1787, was one of the most constructive solutions to the problem of colonialism ever devised. The Land Ordinance of 1785, which had provided for the orderly survey and sale of land in the United States Northwest, had opened that area to settlement. Thus, some provision had to be made for the governance of the territory. This brought to the forefront the old question of how to deal with colonial areas. Were they to be kept subordinate and underdeveloped? Or could some way be found to grant them equality? The answer was found in the Northwest Ordinance of 1787. This law set forth a policy which bridged the gap between wilderness and statehood by providing for progressively greater self-government until a state of complete equality was reached.

The ordinance virtually repeated the colonial experience in the United States. In the earliest stage of development, the territory would be governed by a governor, secretary, and three judges appointed by Congress. When the population reached a total of 5,000 free, male inhabitants of voting age, the first representative government would emerge with the election of a bicameral legislature. From the Northwest Territory, no more than five nor less than three states would be formed. When a population of 60,000 was achieved, the people of the territory could draft a constitution and request admission to statehood in the Union equal in all respects to the original states. During the territorial stage, all rights of citizenship were guaranteed. The ordinance barred slavery and involuntary servitude from the Northwest Territory, and encouraged "schools and the means of education." (William MacDonald, ed., *Select Documents Illustrative of the History of the United States, 1776–1861*, 1920.)

Joseph M. Rowe, Jr.

NORTHWEST PASSAGE. It was the quest for the fabled Northwest Passage which inspired most of the great voyages of exploration in the sixteenth and seventeenth centuries and gave birth to the modern age of European imperialism. For centuries Europe had imported Asian spices across the overland caravan routes in the Middle East, but in the late fifteenth century the expansion of the Ottoman Empire effectively closed them off. The need to find another way to Asia led to the Portuguese voyages of Bartholomew Dias * and Vasco da Gama* around the Cape of Good Hope to India* and the voyages of Christopher Columbus* and other Spaniards. By the early 1500s, especially after Pope Alexander VI had delineated the Portuguese and Spanish spheres of influence, the other European powers felt left out of the Asian trade. Spain controlled one route to Asia—across the Atlantic, through the Straits of Magellan, and across the Pacific—while the Portuguese controlled the other—south around the Cape of Good

Hope in Africa and east across the Indian Ocean. The Dutch and the English then spent centuries trying to find the Northwest Passage, some other way of getting to Asia besides the southern routes around the tips of South America or Africa. Such a route, of course, did not exist, but it was not until the seventeenth century decline of the Spanish and Portuguese empires, when the English and the Dutch navies were able to make their way to Asia by the traditional routes anyway, that the search for the Northwest Passage lost some of its urgency. (Peter Kemp, *The Oxford Companion to Ships and the Sea*, 1976.)

NORTH YEMEN. North Yemen, which eventually became the Yemen Arab Republic, occupied the southwestern corner of the Arabian Peninsula. From 1630 until the nineteenth century the coastal areas of North Yemen were controlled by the Ottoman Turks, while the Zaydi imams, an Islamic tribal group, ruled the interior. In 1840 the Zaydi imams accepted Ottoman sovereignty over the entire area, although periodic political instability in the large desert hinterland was common. Between 1872 and 1918 the Ottomans left a large troop contingent in North Yemen in hope of controlling the Arabian Sea and access to the Suez Canal*, but when World War I ended, the Ottomans withdrew as their empire disintegrated.

During World War I* British troops occupied Al-Hudaydah, and when the British withdrew in 1921 it fell under the control of the Idrisi imams, a rival to the Zaydi group. The Zaydis defeated the Idrisis in 1925, seized Al-Hudaydah, and invaded the Western Aden Protectorate, a British possession to the south. In 1934, with the Treaty of Ta'if, Great Britain and Saudi Arabia recognized the independence of North Yemen. In September 1962 General Abdullah al-Saleh overthrew the government of Yemen and declared the existence of the Yemen Arab Republic, an Islamic state in southwestern Arabia. In May 1990, North Yemen and South Yemen (Aden*) united to form a single nation—the Republic of Yemen. (Harold Ingrams, *The Yemen*, 1963; John E. Petersen, *Yemen. The Search for a Modern State*, 1982.)

NOSY BE. Nosy Be is a small island off the northwest coast of Madagascar*. France acquired the island in 1840 from its tribal ruler and established a naval station there. French settlement was extremely sparse throughout its colonial history. Although Nosy Be had its own governor from 1840 to 1895, it was under the administrative supervison of Reunion* from 1840 to 1843 and Mayotte* from 1843 to 1878, when it became a separate colony. Like Diego-Suárez, Nosy Be was incorporated into Madagascar in 1896. See MADAGASCAR.

NOVA COLÔNIA DO SACRAMENTO. In the later years of the seventeenth century, the Spanish and the Portuguese were busily competing for control of the Rio de la Plata estuary between Argentina* and Brazil.* In 1680 Portugal established the Nova Colônia do Sacramento on the north bank of the river directly across from the Spanish settlement at Buenos Aires*. Spaniards immediately seized the colony but returned it in 1683. They seized it again between 1705 and 1713 but then returned it under the terms of the Treaty of Utrecht*. In response to the Sacramento colony, Spain established a settlement at Montevideo in 1724, and the Portuguese responded by settling Santa Catarina* and Rio Grando do Sul*. The dispute was not resolved between the two powers until the Treaty of Madrid* of 1750 and the Treaty of San Ildefonso* of 1777, both of which confirmed Sacramento as Spanish territory. In return, Spain formally recognized Portuguese control of the Amazon interior. See BRAZIL; TREATY OF MADRID; TREATY OF SAN ILDEFONSO.

NOVA SCOTIA. Nova Scotia, including Cape Breton Island,* is one of the maritime provinces of Canada*. It is bounded by the Atlantic Ocean on the east and south, the Bay of Fundy on the west, and the Gulf of St. Lawrence on the north. The first Europeans to visit Nova Scotia were probably Norsemen in the eleventh century. In modern history John Cabot* made landfall in 1497 and claimed the area for England. Numerous explorers and fishermen visited the area between 1497 and the establishment of the first permanent settlement, Port Royal, by Samuel de Champlain* in 1605. In 1621 James I of England granted a charter for New Scotland (Nova Scotia) to Sir William Alexander. The Scots made several unsuccessful efforts at settlement, and for most of the seventeenth century control of the area alternated between England and France. This ceased in 1713, when Nova Scotia, excluding Cape Breton Island, was ceded to Great Britain under the terms of the Treaty of Utrecht*.

Between 1713 and 1749 the area was neglected. Neither Great Britain nor New England* attempted colonization, and British control was represented by a few troops, some New England merchants, and a fishery at Canso. The main body of inhabitants were the French-speaking Acadians, or "French Neutrals," a term derived from their argument that they be considered neutral in any Anglo-French conflict. The French fortress on Cape Breton Island—Louisbourg—encouraged the Acadians to maintain their French culture and ignore a sporadically demanded oath of allegiance to Great Britain. In 1745 an expedition sent by Governor William Shirley of Massachusetts* captured Louisbourg, but to Shirley's disgust he was forced to return it to the French under the terms of the Treaty of Aix-la-Chapelle*. The existence of Louisbourg, however, did spur the British to establish Halifax as a counterweight in 1749. Several thousand Protestant settlers came to the colony from Europe and New England, and in 1753 German Protestant immigrants founded Lunenburg.

French activity at Fort Beausejour alarmed the British governor of Nova Scotia in 1755, just prior to the outbreak of the Seven Years' War. Because many of the Acadians had not taken the oath of allegiance, approximately 6,000 were deported and their property seized in 1755. Many of these Acadians later returned only to find their lands distributed to new immigrants. In 1758 the influence of immigrants from England and New England, who were accustomed to self-government, and the influence of a New England lobby in London, resulted in the grant of a representative assembly to Nova Scotia. This was the first elected assembly to meet in what is now Canada. By 1775 Nova Scotia had over 17,000 inhabitants, more than half of whom were former New Englanders. The colonial origins of so many Nova Scotians ensured that the colony would take a neutral posture during the American Revolution*.

The Napoleonic Wars and the War of 1812 brought prosperity to Nova Scotia. Lumbering and shipbuilding developed and privateering also added to the colony's income. Cape Breton Island, which had been annexed to Nova Scotia and then separated, was reannexed permanently in 1820. By mid-century Nova Scotia's population was more than 250,000. Constant political struggle between Halifax and the townships sharpened the political skills of many Nova Scotians. In 1835 a former printer and journalist, Joseph Howe, successfully ran for office with a promise to bring responsible government to the colony. Howe and his reform supporters won the election of 1847, and in 1848 Nova Scotia became the first colony in the British Empire to achieve responsible government.*

In 1864 representatives of the maritime colonies of British North America met in Charlottetown, Prince Edward Island*, to discuss the possibility of a maritime union. At the urging of a Canadian delegation, the maritimers agreed to meet later in Quebec* to discuss a larger confederation of the maritimes, Newfoundland*, and Canada. Pro-confederation forces in Nova Scotia feared an expansionist United States on its border and argued that confederation would bring a stronger defense, new railroads, and new markets. Although Joseph Howe opposed it, the British parliament approved a bill to create a federal Dominion of Canada composed of Ontario,* Quebec, New Brunswick*, and Nova Scotia on July 1, 1867. (J. B. Brebner, *The Neutral Yankees of Nova Scotia*, 1937; W. S. McNutt, *The Atlantic Provinces, 1712–1757*, 1965; Kenneth G. Pryke, *Nova Scotia and Confederation*, 1979.)

Peter T. Sherrill

NYASALAND. Nyasaland was the British colonial name of what is now the independent country of Malawi, located in southeastern Africa, bordering Mozambique*, Zambia*, and Tanzania*. Although landlocked, two-thirds of its eastern border comprises Lake Nyasa (Lake Malawi). An African group of peoples called "Malawis" established themselves in the Shire valley and the lands west of it by 1500. They created a powerful empire a century later, based on control of long-distance trade through their territory. Two other peoples, the Ngoni and the Yao, invaded and settled in the area in the 1830s. The latter became heavily involved in the slave trade, which dominated long-distance commerce between the interior and the Indian Ocean coast, especially after 1830. The conflict and violence visited on the entire region by invasions and slave raiders was exacerbated by the increasing use of guns, especially after European armies converted to breech-loading rifles in 1866 and dumped thousands of older model guns on the market.

The remarkable Dr. David Livingstone arrived in Africa in the mid–1800s, and became determined to open up the interior of tropical Africa to Christianity and new types of commerce in order to end the horrors of the slave trade and to promote "civilization" in general. His efforts, both in Africa and in Britain, were instrumental in creating a wave of missionary efforts, several of which followed him to what later became Nyasaland. Two years after his death in 1873, Scottish missionaries established the first "Livingstonia" mission station on the shores of Lake Nyasa. It was moved the next year to the Shire highlands and named after the Scottish town where Livingstone was born; Blantyre is now Malawi's largest city.

The name Nyasaland technically applied only to the years 1907–1964. From 1889 to 1891 the area was part of a British protectorate proclaimed by Harry Johnston, the first British commissioner and consul-general in Nyasaland. In 1889–1890, Johnston and Cecil Rhodes carved out "Trans-Zambesia," which comprised the area of today's Malawi, Zimbabwe, and Zambia. In 1891 Trans-Zambesia, which had been claimed previously by Portugal, was split into three protectorates. The area near Lake Nyasa was given the name "British Central Africa Protectorate," which was changed in 1907 to "Nyasaland." In 1953, as part of British experiments in decolonization, Nyasaland became part of the Federation of Rhodesia and Nyasaland*, which geographically was an attempt to recreate Trans-Zambesia. Politically, it consisted of the British protectorates of Nyasaland and Northern Rhodesia, and the colony of Southern Rhodesia, which was "self-governed" by its European minority. The federation was dissolved in 1963, in large part due to fears by Nyasaland and Northern Rhodesia of domination by the minority white regime in Southern Rhodesia. Nyasaland became independent Malawi in 1964, led by the American-educated nationalist leader, Hastings Kamuzu Banda. (R. J. Macdonald, ed., *From Nyasaland to Malawi: Studies in Colonial History*, 1975; R. Rotberg, *Rise of Nationalism in Central Africa: The Making of Malawi and Zambia, 1873–1964*, 1965.)

Charles W. Hartwig

NYERERE, JULIUS. Julius Kambarage Nyerere was born in March 1922 at Butiama, Musoma District, Tanganyika*. The son of a Zanaki chief, he received his early education in village schools. When he was twelve, he was transferred to the government secondary school in Tabora. He completed his studies at Makerere College, Uganda*, in 1945, with an education degree. Having taught history and biology for four years in Catholic mission schools in Tanganyika, Nyerere received a scholarship to Scotland's Edinburgh University, where he earned a master's degree in 1952. He returned to Tanganyika to teach and, by this time, he had begun formulating his political ideology.

In 1953 Nyerere served as president of the nonpolitical Tanganyika African Association, but in 1954 he organized the Tanganyika African National Union (TANU) as a political party. He espoused increased militant agitation for independence. To devote his full energies to the cause, Nyerere resigned his teaching position. During the next two years he became the acknowledged spokesman for Tanganyika and began vigorously to petition the United Nations for a tentative date for Tanganyikan independence. (Tanganyika had become a UN trust territory in 1946.)

Nyerere was nominated by the British government in 1957 as a member of the legislative council, a position he resigned in protest against British imperialism. By 1958 TANU had gained the momentum to win national elections and Nyerere was appointed chief minister in 1960. Tanganyika was granted full independence on December 9, 1961, and Nyerere became the first prime minister. In early 1962 he resigned to devote full time to strengthening TANU and deciding the future of Tanganyika. In the 1962 presidential elections, he claimed 97 percent of the total votes and became the first president of the Tanganyikan Republic. On April 26, 1964, Tanganyika merged with the new Republic of Zanzibar*, becoming the United Republic of Tanganyika and Zanzibar, but shortly afterward changing the name to Tanzania*. Nyerere became the president of this unified state.

Believing that an independent political economy could not withstand the threat of an election, Nyerere established a one-party state in 1965. Two years later, as a moderate socialist president in one of the world's poorest countries, he nationalized banks, heavy industry, and large business firms. This he did while keeping an "open door" for outside investments in his country and calling for black and white cooperation in the peaceful development of Africa. He worked collaboratively with the National Development Corporation and joined the East Africa Community, a customs union with Uganda* and Kenya*. As Nyerere became more dictatorial in his administration, Tanzania was torn by internal and external strife. In the 1970s Nyerere had several of his closest associates placed on trial for treason and sentenced to life imprisonment. Though he professed to be an advocate of the Pan-African movement and the East Africa Community, Nyerere refused to attend or support an African summit which was held in Idi Amin's Uganda in 1975. His wisdom and motives are questioned in the role he played in overthrowing three of his neighboring states—the Comoros Islands*, the Seychelles*, and Uganda. In 1985 Nyere retired formally from his position as president, although he remained a powerful figure in Tanzanian politics. He did not resign as chairman of the ruling party, Chama Cha Mapinduzi, until the summer of 1990. (I. M. Kimambo and A. J. Temu, *A History of Tanzania*, 1970; W. E. Smith, *Julius Nyerere*, 1971.)

Veula J. Rhodes

O

OCEAN ISLAND. Ocean Island is part of the independent nation of Kiribati* in the west central Pacific. British sea captains visited Ocean Island early in the 1800s, and in 1900 Great Britain annexed the island, making it part of the new colony of the Gilbert and Ellice Isl Protectorate. The Tokelau Islands, Fanning Island, and Washington Island were added to the protectorate in 1917, when it officially became a British colony. The Phoenix islands were added in 1937.

OGASAWARA ISLANDS. The Ogasawara Islands are a series of small volcanic islands located in the Pacific Ocean approximately 600 miles southeast of Japan. The Spanish explorer Ruy López de Villalobos visited the Ogasawara Islands (also known as the Bonin Islands) in 1543. Although both the United States and Great Britain at one time or another during the nineteenth century laid claim to the islands, Japan successfully annexed them in 1876. During World War II*, the United States and Japan fought a bloody battle on Iwo Jima, which the Americans won. After the war the United States removed all of the surviving population from the Ogasawara Islands and administered them until 1968, when the islands were returned to Japan. (Mark Peattie, *Nan'Yo: the Rise and Fall of the Japanese in Micronesia, 1885–1945*, 1987.)

OMAN. Oman is an independent nation of 116,000 square miles located in the southeast extremity of the Arabian Peninsula. It is south of the Strait of Hormuz, southwest of the Gulf of Oman, west and north of the Arabian Sea, northeast of the Republic of Yemen, east of Saudi Arabia*, and southeast of the United Arab Emirates*. Oman has been an Islamic nation since the seventh century, but its Ibadhi denomination insisted on the election of the imam, a practice which has continued for 900 years. Although Oman's geographical location had been a commercial crossroads for centuries in the Middle East, the first contact with Europeans did not come until 1507 when the Portuguese overran Muscat, the Omani city located at the southeastern tip of the Arabian Peninsula. The Portuguese kept control of Muscat until 1649, when a combined Persian-Omani army dislodged them. Oman then entered upon its own period of imperial expansion, overrunning a number of Portuguese bases in East Africa. In 1798 the sultan of Muscat signed a treaty giving the British East India Company* exclusive trading rights, in return for an annual British stipend to sustain the sultanate. Britain then maintained an uneasy political balance between the imam of Oman and the sultan of Muscat, which was formalized by the Treaty of Seeb in 1920, which recognized the independence of the imamate of Oman.

The Treaty of Seeb was in force for nearly forty years. But the oil concession in the area had been awarded to the Petroleum Development Company, a British-managed corporation which maintained its own British-led army. In 1959 the Muscat and Oman Field Force overthrew the iman of Oman and the sultan of Muscat assumed control of the country of Muscat and Oman. In 1962 Great Britain declared Muscat and Oman an independent nation. Periodically since then the followers of the imam have tried to overthrow the government but to no avail. The sultan changed the name of the country from Muscat and Oman to Oman in 1971, and although other Middle Eastern nations accused Great Britain of maintaining its imperial status there, the government of Oman continued in the 1980s to nurture close relations with the English. (J. E. Peterson, *Oman in the Twentieth Century*, 1980; John Townsend, *Oman: The Making of a Modern State*, 1977.)

ONTARIO. Ontario is the most populous province of the Dominion of Canada*. It is bounded on the north by Hudson Bay, on the east by Quebec*, on the south by the Great Lakes, and on the west by Manitoba. Ontario became a province of the Dominion of Canada by the terms of the British North America Act of 1867, recently renamed the Constitution Act of 1867.

Peter T. Sherrill

OPEN DOOR POLICY. In 1898, as a result of the Spanish-American War*, the United States acquired the Philippines* from Spain in the Treaty of Paris*. One of the primary American objectives in acquiring the Philippines was to gain access to lucrative Asian markets for United States goods. The largest market by far was China. But just when the United States had acquired a foothold in Asia, the British, French, and Germans were busy expanding their spheres of influence in China. Afraid that the European powers would transform China into one or a series of colonies, effectively locking out the United States, Secretary of State John Hay issued what he called his "Open Door Notes"—proposals to the European powers that the territorial integrity of China be respected and that the country remain open to the commerce of all nations. The so-called "Open Door Policy" became a backbone of United States Far East policy in the twentieth century. (Marvin Kalb and Elie Abel, *Roots of Involvement: The U.S. in Asia, 1784–1971*, 1971.)

OPIUM WAR. See TREATY OF NANKING OF 1842.

ORÁN. Orán is a city on the coast of North Africa where fleeing Muslims took refuge after the Spanish crown reconquered Granada in 1492. Spanish forces then occupied the city in 1509 and stationed a governor there. Spain never tried to penetrate the interior. Forces of the Ottoman Turks seized the city in 1708 and held it until 1732, when Spain recaptured it. Spain finally abandoned Orán in 1792. During the years in which France colonized Algeria, Orán was under French control. (David P. Henige, *Colonial Governors from the Fifteenth Century to the Present*, 1970.)

ORANGE FREE STATE. The Orange Free State was one of the original four colonies making up the Union of South Africa*. It is separated from Transvaal* by the Vaal River and is bordered by Transvaal on the north, Natal* and Lesotho on the east and southeast, and by the province of the Cape of Good Hope on the south and southwest. Boer settlers from the Cape Colony* first made their way into the area between 1810 and 1820, but the mass migration of Boers did not take place until the 1830s. By that time they were tired of being under British rule in the Cape Colony. The British annexed the new territory in 1848 and named it the Orange River Sovereignty, but in 1854—in the Bloemfontein Convention—Britain returned it to the Boers. The colony, now independent, became known as the Orange Free State. The Orange Free State remained independent until 1900 when British troops invaded it during the Boer War*. They renamed it the Orange River Colony. At the conclusion of the Boer War in 1902, the people of the region reluctantly accepted British sovereignty. They received responsible government* in 1907. In 1910 the Orange River Colony joined the Union of South Africa as the province of the Orange Free State. See SOUTH AFRICA.

ORANGE RIVER COLONY. See ORANGE FREE STATE.

OREGON TREATY OF 1846. When the United States purchased the Louisiana Territory from France in 1803, the question of boundaries was left undetermined. After the War of 1812, the Convention of 1818 between the United States and Great Britain extended the northern boundary from the Lake of the Woods to the crest of the Rocky Mountains along the 49th parallel. Beyond that, the territory to the Pacific (Oregon country) was unresolved. Both nations agreed to joint occupation, an arrangement continued indefinitely in 1827. The Oregon country extended from the 42nd parallel, the northern limit of Mexican California, to 54 degrees 40 minutes latitude, the southern boundary of Russian America.* As United States interests in the region increased, demands for a resolution of the boundary question became stronger. In the election of 1844, "the re-occupation of Oregon" was one of the major planks of the Democratic Party in the United States. After his election to the presidency, James K. Polk pursued the issue aggressively, and the dispute was finally settled by the Oregon Treaty of June 15, 1846.

Article I extended the United States-Canadian boundary along the 49th parallel from the crest of the Rocky Mountains to the Straits of San Juan de Fuca, around the south of Vancouver Island, and to the Pacific Ocean. Article II granted to British subjects the right to navigate the Columbia River south of the 49th parallel. Article III guaranteed the property rights of British subjects south of the 49th parallel. And Article IV guaranteed the property rights of the Puget Sound Agricultural Company north of the Columbia River. The United States Senate ratified the treaty on June 15, 1846. (Henry S. Commager, ed., *Documents of American History*, 1948.)

Joseph M. Rowe, Jr.

ORISSA. Orissa is a region of India* located southwest of Bengal*. British forces occupied Orissa in 1803 and incorporated it administratively into Bengal. Between 1912 and 1936, Orissa was part of Bihar* in British India. It became a separate province with its own governor in 1936, and in 1947 Orissa became an individual state in an independent India*. See INDIA.

OUDH. The Kingdom of Oudh was located in the northern part of what is today India*. Great Britain annexed the Muslim state in 1856, claiming that its royal family was incompetent. Oudh was a separate province with its own chief commissioner until 1877 when it was incorporated into the United Provinces of Agra and Oudh*. See INDIA.

L'OUVERTURE, TOUSSAINT. Francois Dominique Toussaint L'Ouverture was born on May 20, 1743, on Breda Plantation at Haut du Cap in St. Domingue, French West Indies. Reputedly the grandson of an African chieftain and the son of a slave, he was taught to read, write, and use arithmetic; he also learned French, the Arada language, and the rudiments of Latin. He had a basic knowledge of the use of herbs, which proved useful while he was in charge of livestock as horsebreeder, tamer, and veterinarian. A convert to Catholicism, he was taught the tenets of the religion by the local priests. In 1777, when he was 34, Toussaint was granted *liberte de savanna* which allowed him many personal freedoms. He was assigned the position of coachman for the plantation manager and proved to be trustworthy and dependable. Later he oversaw the general operations of the plantation and Breda was soon recognized as the most prosperous estate on the island. When he was 40, Toussaint chose Suzanne Simon as his wife because she was a woman worthy of his talents and promise.

In 1791 as slave rebellions erupted in St. Domingue, Toussaint organized more than 150 slaves at Breda and joined the revolutionary forces of Jean

Francois. The initial revolt had been staged by the French government in an attempt to frighten landowners into total submission to French authority. But as the rebellions became more violent and the French government lost control, Toussaint quickly moved through the ranks to gain a leadership position. His military successes earned for him the name L'Ouverture, a term meaning "opening" and used by the French to describe Toussaint's success in breaking through enemy lines. In 1792 he demanded the French government improve the status of slaves in St. Domingue pending emancipation, to grant freedom to all rebel leaders, and to pay an indemnity. When these demands were rejected, fighting was renewed on the island. On May 15, 1793, Toussaint temporarily entered the service of the Spanish forces to fight the French in St. Domingue. In the following year he rejoined the French forces when the National Convention of France promised to extend freedom to all slaves in St. Domingue. For his role in the campaign against the Spanish and British forces, Toussaint was promoted to the rank of brigadier general. By 1796 Toussaint had been appointed lieutenant governor and major general as French officials were expelled from the island.

With the signing of a treaty in 1795, France and Spain made peace as Spain ceded control of Santo Domingo to France. The British control along the west coast included Port-au-Prince, Jeremie, L'Arcahaye, St. Marc, and Mole St. Nicolas, in addition to several cities and villages. Toussaint took a leadership role in driving the British forces from the island in 1798 with a brilliant attack against the British lines. An agreement for British evacuation of the island was issued, recognizing Toussaint as the king of St. Domingue. A commercial and military treaty was negotiated between Britain and St. Domingue and later extended to the United States in 1798–1800 as Toussaint was faced with opposition from Spain and the Haitian mulattoes. The French government refused to recognize the treaty negotiated by the commander in chief of the Haitian army.

By 1801 Haiti had its own constitution, its own laws, and its own army as Toussaint proclaimed himself governor-general for life of the entire island. As Toussaint worked to unify the island under his command, France, Britain, and the United States were working to restore peaceful relations on the island. In 1802 Napoleon sent a major force to Haiti to subdue the island and restore slavery. Through treachery and trickery, Toussaint was forced to retire and was later arrested and imprisoned at the Chauteau of Joux (Fort de Joux), where he died on April 7, 1803. (Stephen Alexis, *Black Liberator: The Life of Toussaint L'ouverture*, 1949.)

Veula J. Rhodes

P

PACIFIC ISLANDERS PROTECTION ACT OF 1872. See PACIFIC IS-
LANDERS PROTECTION ACT OF 1875.

PACIFIC ISLANDERS PROTECTION ACT OF 1875. Early in the 1800s
Protestant missionaries began settling in the Pacific islands. Most of them were
British. Along with the missionaries came a host of businessmen out of Australia*
and New Zealand* who did a brisk trade in sandalwood, tea, coconut oil, and
copra. By the 1860s the demand for labor on the commercial plantations of the
islands began to increase dramatically, and it was stimulated by the Civil War
in the United States, which led to the establishment of cotton plantations. Although Britain had outlawed slavery in 1833, the traffic in Pacific islander
indentured servitude virtually resurrected slavery. Kidnapping of Polynesian
islanders became quite common, and when the traders began disguising themselves as missionaries, a vigorous protest movement developed in Great Britain.
Demands for legislation outlawing indentured servitude gained momentum, especially after 1871 when natives murdered the English bishop of Melanesia*,
whom they confused with a slave trader.

In 1872 parliament passed the Pacific Islanders Protection Act, which prohibited British vessels from transporting indentured native labor. The traffic
continued, however, in French, Dutch, and American ships. To deal with the
traffic, parliament annexed the Fiji* Islands in 1874 and in 1875 passed a second
Pacific Islanders Protection Act. It established a British high commissioner in
New Zealand to enforce the legislation and prohibited British subjects from
participating in the slave traffic. The end of the American Civil War had reduced
somewhat the demand for native labor, but the trade continued in spite of the
legislation. (W. P. Morrell, *Britain in the Pacific Islands*, 1953; A. Grenfell

Price, *The Western Invasions of the Pacific and its Continents. A Study of Moving Frontiers and Changing Landscapes, 1513–1958,* 1963.)

PAHANG. Pahang was a large independent sultanate on the eastern side of the Malay Peninsula between Johor* and Trengganu*. In 1887 the sultan of Pahang negotiated a treaty with the Straits Settlements* and admitted a British consular agent. In 1888, despite a rebellion over British insistence on suppressing the slave trade, the sultan signed a formal protectorate with Great Britain. In 1895 Pahang became one of the Federated Malay States*. See MALAYSIA.

PAKISTAN. Pakistan, caught geographically between the Arabian Sea to the southwest, India* to the east, and Iran to the west, has been the scene of dynamic historical events for 2,000 years. In the late 900s Islamic expansion swept through the land that would become Pakistan and set the tone for Pakistani social and cultural development. But when the political power of the Mughal empire began to decline in the eighteenth century, Europeans moved into the vacuum and set up the great colonial empires which did not disappear until the nationalist rebellions of the twentieth century.

Located on the trade routes between Europe and the Far East, India was a ripe plum for European entrepreneurs and their political agents. They had been there ever since the Portuguese explorer Vasco da Gama* reached Calicut in 1498 and Affonso de Albuquerque conquered Goa* in 1510. The Portuguese proceeded to eliminate Arab political influence in the Indian Ocean. In the seventeenth century Dutch, British, and French trading companies—the Dutch East India Company*, the British East India Company* and the French East India Company—arrived and the real competition for control of the subcontinent began. By the early 1700s Portuguese power was waning and the French, Dutch, and British power was rising.

Local Indian rulers made political as well as commercial arrangements with the western intruders in return for military support, and in that way the Europeans eventually came to govern large areas of India. In the 1750s and 1760s the British East India Company became collector of revenue in Bengal*, Bihar*, and Orissa*, and gradually during the late eighteenth century and early nineteenth century it became the sovereign power over an increasingly large part of the subcontinent. Missionaries from England began pouring into India, and in the 1820s and 1830s they began building an English school system and making English the official language. It was not until the great Indian Mutiny of 1857* that the authority of the British East India Company was seriously challenged; and in 1858, as a result of the mutiny, parliament assumed direct responsibility for the government of India.

Muslim nationalism emerged in India after the Indian Mutiny. Sir Syed Ahmad Khan of Delhi led the movement. Insecure about their minority status in a Hindu-dominated India, the Muslims viewed the British Empire as a protection. Sir Syed urged his followers to take full advantage of British education, demonstrate loyalty toward British rule, avoid political activism, and work to develop Muslim self-respect. When the Hindus formed the Indian National Congress to represent all Indians, Sir Syed discouraged his followers from joining. Until Muslims could compete for political power with the Hindu majority, they had to support British rule. In 1906 Muslim nationalists established the Muslim League* to promote Muslim interests, as well as loyalty to British rule. They demanded that in all elections Muslims should be represented only by other Muslims, elected only by Muslim voters, and receive political representation in greater proportion than their numbers in the population justified. The Indian National Congress, naturally, opposed the Muslim League, but in the India Councils Act of 1909, the British recognized the Muslim demands for a separate communal electorate.

By the 1920s and 1930s, as nationalist aspirations swept through the subcontinent, Muslim demands began to find expression in the two-nation theory. Muslim philosopher Sir Muhammad Iqbal, convinced that a unitary government was unthinkable, began to campaign for a confederated India with a Muslim state incorporating the Punjab*, the North-West Frontier Province*, Sind, and Baluchistan*, a country "based on unity of language, race, history, religion, and identity of economic interests." Mohammad Ali Jinnah* became the leader of the Muslim League in 1934 and he adopted the two-nation theory as well. The Indian National Congress, led by Mohandas Gandhi*, opposed the idea, demanding instead one country, which clearly would be Hindu-dominated. At the Muslim League meeting in 1940, Jinnah demanded creation of two independent states for the Muslim majorities in the northwest and the northeast. The new nation would be named Pakistan, and would include the major Muslim homelands: Punjab, Afghan (meaning the North-West Frontier Province), Kashmir, Sind, Tukharistan, and Baluchistan. Jinnah rejected federation with Hindu India outright and said that no independence plan was acceptable to Muslims unless it provided for partition of the subcontinent.

During World War II* the debate continued. Jinnah and the Muslim League insisted on partition and Gandhi and the Congress demanded independence for one India. It was increasingly clear to both Hindu and Muslim nationalists that the days of the British Empire* were numbered. The war had drained British resources and the increasingly strident demands of subject peoples for independence made continuation of the colonial era impossible. By 1946 rioting and violence between Muslims and Hindus in India held out the prospect for a bloody, religious civil war. In February 1947 Lord Louis Mountbatten* was appointed viceroy of India and charged with preparing, within a year, for independence. To stop the rioting, Gandhi and the Congress agreed to partition. On July 14, 1947, the British parliament passed the India Independence Act, creating two independent countries on the subcontinent. Pakistan, which came into existence one month later, on August 15, 1947, was itself divided into two separate areas. West Pakistan consisted of Baluchistan, Sind, the North-West Frontier Province, and much of the Punjab. East Pakistan consisted of the area which is contemporary Bangladesh. (K. K. Aziz, *The Making of Pakistan*, 1967; Leonard Binder, *Religion and Politics in Pakistan*, 1963.)

PALAU. The Palau Islands group consists of six islands and dozens of uninhabited coral atolls and small volcanic islands at the far western edge of the Caroline Islands*, about 480 miles east of the Philippines*. The largest islands in the group are Kayangel, Babelthuap, Koror, Urukthapel, Eilmalk, Peleliu, and Angaur. Spanish explorers visited the Palau group in the mid-sixteenth century but made little effort to colonize the islands. In 1899 Spain sold the Caroline and Marshall Islands*, including the Palau Islands, to Germany for $4.5 million, but when World War I* broke out in 1914, Japan occupied all of them and then began to fortify the most strategic of the islands. The United States captured all of the Marshall and Caroline Islands during World War II. In 1947 Palau became one district in the newly created Trust Territory of the Pacific Islands*, a United Nations* trusteeship* granted to the United States.

In the 1960s the United States began negotiations to create a single nation in "free association" with America, but the people of Palau preferred to take a more independent route. The Trust Territory of the Pacific Islands was a vast, ethnically complex entity which eventually defied transformation into a single political unit. Along with the Marshall Islands, Palau called for independence, and instead of a single country, the Trust Territory of the Pacific Islands evolved into four political entities: the Commonwealth of the Northern Mariana Islands, the Republic of the Marshall Islands, the Federated States of Micronesia*, and the Republic of Palau. The people of Palau ratified their own constitution in 1979 and became an internally self-governing republic on January 1, 1981. (Homer Barnett, *Palau Society: A Study of Contemporary Native Life in the Palau Islands*, 1949; John Wesley Coulter, *The Pacific Dependencies of the United States*, 1957; Barrie MacDonald, "Current Developments in the Pacific: Self-Determination and Self-Government," *Journal of Pacific History*, 17, January 1982, 51–61.)

PALESTINE. The importance of Palestine lies essentially in its historical and religious significance to three of the world's major religions: Judaism, Christianity, and Islam. In those circumstances, it is not surprising that emotional motivations about this small territory have been intertwined with imperialism and nationalism. The idea of a Palestinian national entity is a new one. Before the Christian era the Biblical nation of Israel conquered a territory, previously inhabited by a number of peoples, which they believed had been granted to them by their God—Yahweh—in exclusivity, the Promised Land. This independent nation lasted for a brief period before it was subsequently conquered by neighboring empires, its people deported or enslaved until its final dispersion, the diaspora, under the Roman empire. Since that time and until 1948 there has never been an independent national entity in Palestine. After the fall of the Roman empire, Palestine became a province of the Byzantine empire until its conquest by the Arabs in the early days of the spread of Islam. After the Arabs came the Seljuk Turks. For a brief interlude during the Crusades, part of the area was the Christian Kingdom of Jerusalem, under the Crusaders whose religious zeal to save the Holy Land was accompanied by all sorts of imperialistic economic and social motivations.

The next imperial power was the Ottoman Turks, who remained in control until World War I*. During that time European nations such as France and Russia exercised some measure of protection over the holy places in Palestine, through the system of capitulations. But Arab nationalism encompassed the whole region known as the Fertile Crescent, and Palestinian aspirations were simply part of the movement for Arab nationalism. It was an external European movement, Zionism, which triggered the emergence of a distinct brand of Palestinian nationalism. When Zionist nationalism appeared in Europe at the end of the nineteenth century, Jews had a deep feeling of cultural identity and shared tribulations but not a distinct territory, since the Jews were scattered over many countries and even continents. Early Zionist leaders, who were essentially secular in their outlook, were quite prepared to settle for any territory they might get, be it in Uganda, Canada, or Argentina.

But they quickly realized that traditional Jewish communities would only follow them if they set as their territorial objective the land of Palestine, where an independent Jewish entity had existed more than 2,000 years ago. Eventual return there by the Jewish people, the cultural descendants of the biblical Israelites, was a powerful belief which had endured throughout the centuries. While a small number of Jews continuously lived in Palestine, most of the local population were Arabs, mostly Muslims, but with a sizable number of Christians. Those Palestinian Arabs had been there for centuries, descendants of those who came as a result of the seventh-century Arab conquest, as well as descendants of people who had lived there long before the Arab conquest. From the beginning of the twentieth century, Jewish emigration to Palestine occurred in successive waves, encouraged by the British imperialists for their own motives, notably in the Balfour Declaration* favoring the establishment of a Jewish homeland in Palestine, supposedly at the same time protecting the rights of the local Arabs.

But British and French imperialist behavior after the war showed they had little regard for the wartime promises of independence made to the Arabs. The Arab dream of unity was trampled and the territory parceled out between England and France in the mandate system*. To those Arab frustrations, resulting from the shattered dream of independence and unity, was now added the reality of European domination, and in the case of Palestine, a growing influx of culturally alien immigrants. Arab, and now Palestinian nationalism, was soon on a collision course with the British and Jews.

From the 1920s onward riots occurred frequently in Palestine and tension mounted between the Arab and Jewish communities, leading to numerous instances of armed conflict. The British attempted to mediate between the two peoples, proclaiming their desire to preserve Arab rights, while displaying a fundamental hostility to Arab nationalism and making sure the Arabs would not be adequately led and armed. The Jews, on the other hand, enjoyed substantial financial assistance from external sources, which allowed them to embark on a continuous policy of land acquisition, often from willing Arab absentee landlords. Jewish immigration increased massively as a result of Nazi persecution in Europe. During World War II*, many Jews volunteered to fight Germany on the Allied side, thereby receiving military training which would prove useful in the war for independence. Meanwhile the Arab Palestinians, who were sometimes receptive to German propaganda, remained disorganized and ill-prepared before the violent clash that was fast approaching.

At the end of the war the British faced an explosive situation in Palestine. Palestinian nationalists, buoyed by the success of neighboring Arab countries achieving independence, were aggravated by the steady arrival of new Jewish immigrants. The Jews, unified by the horror of the Holocaust and a common sense of purpose, were determined to extract their independence from a weakened colonizer. They had set up an official but underground army, the Hagganah, supplemented by several terrorist groups which targeted both the British and the Arabs. The British, economically and militarily weakened, faced tremendous pressure from world public opinion, and notably from the United States, to allow unrestricted Jewish immigration into Palestine, which they knew could only provoke further unrest among the Arab population. With opposition from all quarters, unable to placate either side, the British finally came to the conclusion that the only solution for them was to quit, advocating a partition which they left in the care of the newly formed United Nations*. That partition plan was rejected by the Arabs, who still constituted a large majority of the population, while the Jews hurried to proclaim an independent state of Israel on May 14, 1948.

As a result, several armies from the neighboring Arab countries attempted to invade the new state. But they were poorly armed, disorganized, and without a unified command, unlike the Israelis, who came out of the war with even more territory than they had been allocated by the United Nations. What followed has been a succession of wars—in 1956, 1967, 1973, and 1982—between Israel and several of the Arab states, all related, in theory, to the Palestinian Arabs who had been dispossessed and evicted from their ancestral lands. The 1948 war caused the displacement of several hundred thousand Palestinians who became refugees, while the 1967 war doubled the amount of territory under Israeli control and resulted in even more refugees or Palestinians chafing under Israeli control. It is a human tragedy that the Jewish diaspora could only end with the creation of a new diaspora, that of the Palestinians.

But what has also emerged, especially after 1967, is a distinct brand of Palestinian nationalism, supported by all the Arab states, sometimes for reasons of self-interest, and identified with a guerrilla movement, the Palestine Liberation Organization (PLO). The PLO has resorted to terrorist actions mostly to get noticed. Grudgingly, but with increasing success, the PLO has come to be seen, even by the United States at the end of 1988, as the representative for the legitimate demands of the Palestinians. This recent development was greatly helped, since the end of 1987, by the "intifada," the general insurrection against

Israeli military occupation. In spite of often ruthless repression, the Israeli army, supposed to be one of the three or four best and most effective armies in the world, has not been able to stamp out a rebellion which is using only stones as weapons. The logical outcome would seem to be an independent Palestinian state on most of the West Bank and Gaza. The other alternatives are equally unpalatable: (1) either the outright expulsion and/or massacre of the Palestinian Arabs in Israeli controlled territory; (2) a *de jure* as well as *de facto* state of apartheid, in which Israel would lose its vaunted democratic character; or (3) the integration of the occupied Arabs into a democratic Israel, in which, because of their higher birth rates, the Arabs would become the majority within a few decades. As a result of the last alternative, Israel would no longer be a Jewish state. By siding with Iraq in the Gulf War of 1991, however, the Palestinians lost a great deal of support around the world. (Michael J. Cohen, *Palestine and the Great Powers, 1945–1948*, 1982; Isaiah Friedman, *Germany, Turkey, and Zionism, 1897–1918*, 1977; Alvert M. Hyamson, *Palestine Under the Mandate, 1920–1948*, 1950.)

Alain G. Marsot

PALMYRA. Palmyra is a small island in the Central Pacific Ocean located about 1,000 miles southwest of Hawaii. The U.S.S. *Palmyra* discovered the island in 1802, and it was annexed by the Kingdom of Hawaii in 1862. Great Britain seized it in 1889. The United States did not annex Palmyra until 1912. Palmyra remained under the jurisdictional control of the territory of Hawaii until 1959 when Hawaii became a state. At that point the island fell under the administrative jurisdiction of the United States Department of the Interior. (*Webster's Geographical Dictionary*, 1986.)

PANAMA. Darién was the first Spanish settlement on the North American mainland. In 1509, Alonso de Ojeda received the territory known as New Andalucia, which stretched from modern day Panama's Gulf of Darién eastward. Ojeda attempted to lead an expedition there but he was gravely wounded and returned to Santo Domingo, leaving Francisco Pizarro, the future conqueror of Peru, in command. Ojeda died in 1510 in Santo Domingo, at which time Pizarro was replaced by Martín Francisco de Enciso. Enciso led an expedition to Darién and established the town of Santa María La Antigua de Darién, or simply, Darién. Enciso was not an able leader, and he relied heavily on the guidance of Vasco Núñez de Balboa. Balboa eventually accused Enciso of mismanagement, arrested him and sent him back to Spain. He then stabilized Darién. Balboa defeated the Indians of region, and obtained sizable amounts of gold and pearls. He established an agricultural economy for Darién, based on Indian labor, and the settlement thrived. Darién served as the base for Balboa's expedition to find the "Southern Sea." On September 29, 1513, Balboa was the first European to sight the Pacific Ocean, claiming all that it bordered for Spain. Back in Spain, Enciso filed formal complaints against Balboa and the Crown sent Pedro Arias de Ávila to relieve Balboa's command. In 1517, nonetheless, Pedrarias had Balboa convicted of treason and beheaded. Darién suffered under Ávila's administration. A rapacious and ruthless man, he showed little mercy toward the local natives, and disease, mistreatment and overwork decimated the local population. In 1519, he moved the Spanish population from the pesthole of Darién to the more healthful climate of Panama City. In 1524, Darién was abandoned. Panama City was destroyed by the English sailor Henry Morgan in 1671 and then reconstructed a few miles away. Located at the isthmus between the Atlantic and Pacific oceans, Panama benefited historically from the trans-world commerce, especially from Spanish commercial regulations which required all commerce to and from Peru to move through Panama. It prospered particularly as the point at which bullion shipments from Peru were sent to Spain. After 1740, however, the city's fortunes declined when Spain permitted the bullion galleons to sail around the Cape of Good Horn between Peru and Spain. Panama quickly became a backwater of the empire. With the re-creation of the Viceroyalty of New Granada in 1739, Panama came under its jurisdiction, and remained there until 1821 when it became part of Gran Colómbia. (Basil C. Hedrick and Anne K. Hedrick, *Historical Dictionary of Panama*, 1970; R. L. Woodward, Jr., *Central America: A Nation Divided*, 1983).

PANAMA CANAL ZONE. The Panama Canal Zone was an area granted "in perpetuity" to the United States by the Republic of Panama in the Hay-Bunau-Varilla Treaty* of 1903. The zone of territory was ten miles wide, or five miles on each side of the center line of the Panama Canal, beginning in the Caribbean Sea three miles from the low-water mark and extending through Panama into the Pacific Ocean to a distance of three miles from the low-water mark. The zone did not include the cities of Panama and Colon or the harbors adjacent to the cities. Other lands outside the zone were also granted, lands deemed necessary for the construction, maintenance, operation, and protection of the canal. In all the area granted totaled 552.8 square miles, of which 361.86 square miles were land.

In 1932 Harmodio Arias was elected president of Panama, and a dispute broke out between Panama and the United States in 1934 when he refused to accept the annual $250,000 payment from the United States. President Franklin D. Roosevelt had devalued the dollar in 1933, undermining the value of the payment in Arias's opinion. Negotiations took place to resolve the dispute along with other problems, and in 1936 the United States signed a treaty which was ratified in 1939. In the treaty the United States received the right to send troops to Panama to defend the Panama Canal but lost the right to interfere in Panamanian internal affairs.

In 1951 the United States Congress passed the Panama Canal Act which provided for a U.S.-appointed governor to preside over the Panama Canal Zone, with the Panama Canal Company, a U.S. government-owned corporation, operating a variety of commercial enterprises. That political arrangement lasted until 1977 when the United States Senate ratified a new treaty with Panama gradually turning over control of the Panama Canal to the Panamanians. Under the terms of that treaty the government of the Panama Canal Zone dissolved in 1979. American troops were still stationed there, however, and in 1990 they invaded Panama in order to overthrow the government of Manuel Noriega. (Michael J. Hogan, *The Panama Canal in American Politics. Domestic Advocacy and the Evolution of Policy*, 1986.)

Joseph M. Rowe, Jr.

PAPUA NEW GUINEA. The island of New Guinea is a large land mass in the western Pacific Ocean, located off the northern coast of Australia*. New Guinea is divided between Irian Jaya, the western half of the island which is part of Indonesia, and Papua New Guinea, the eastern half of the island. Papua includes Papua New Guinea, New Britain*, and the Bismarck Archipelago*, Bougainville in the Solomon Islands*, and the Louisiade Archipelago. Characterized by extraordinary ethnic diversity and geographic inaccessibility, New Guinea had episodic contact from European traders in the seventeenth and eighteenth centuries, but it was not until the 1790s that ships from the eastern colonies of Australia began passing by New Guinea regularly on their way to Asia. In the 1830s whalers began working the waters near New Guinea and set up a brisk trade with coastal tribes. The New Guineans quickly acquired a reputation for ferocity.

It was not until the 1870s that European missionaries established permanent settlements along the New Guinea coast, and they were soon followed by fishermen, pearl harvesters, copra traders, scientists, geographers, and gold prospectors. The imperial scramble of the late nineteenth century soon engulfed New Guinea, with Germany, the Netherlands, and Great Britain all establishing claims there. In the mid–1880s the three rivals agreed on a division. To the Dutch went all of west New Guinea to the 141st meridian; to Germany went the northeast region of New Guinea, the Bismarck Archipelago, and Bougainville; and to Great Britain went the southeast region of New Guinea and the Louisiade Archipelago.

German Papua had mixed success at best. The New Guinea Company tried to settle there in the 1880s and 1890s, but disease, lack of capital, and mismanagement doomed the colony to failure. The New Guinea Company relinquished control of the colony in 1899. More success was achieved, however, on Bougainville and the Bismarck Islands where Christian missionaries and large plantations established permanent settlements. From those settlements came the first small colonies on the mainland in the early 1900s. But when World War I broke out in 1914, German rule in New Guinea came to a swift end. Australian forces immediately seized all German possessions there, including German Papua, Bougainville, and the Bismarck Archipelago.

British Papua had become a reality in 1884 when England reluctantly declared a protectorate over the southeastern portion of New Guinea and the Louisiade Archipelago, but the British had few visions about the potential of the island and intended the Australians to administer the area. In 1906 the Papua Act changed British New Guinea into the territory of Papua, part of Australia. Although the Australians hoped to make the territory an economic success, and worked to treat the native New Guineans with fairness, the colony was an economic failure, achieving none of the prosperity or population growth the Dutch were experiencing in west New Guinea. When World War I ended, Australia also received a League of Nations* mandate over the former territories of German Papua, placing all of New Guinea east of the 141st meridian in Australian hands.

During World War II, Papua was a battleground between Japanese soldiers and American and British troops under the command of General Douglas MacArthur. The Japanese attempt to take Port Moresby and seize all of New Guinea failed when Japan lost the Battle of the Coral Sea in 1942. Although the interior of Papua was largely undisturbed during the war, the coastal areas, especially in the north, became part of MacArthur's promised march back to the Philippines*. Between 1942 and 1944 American, British, and Australian soldiers conquered Japanese forces and brought New Guinea completely back into Allied hands.

When World War II ended, Australia received eastern New Guinea as a United Nations trusteeship* and combined the Territory of Papua with the former German possessions into the Australian New Guinea Administrative Unit. Gradually the Australians moved New Guinea toward self-government. A legislative council was established in 1951 and a house of assembly with legislative powers in 1964. Michael Somare, a leading New Guinea nationalist, developed controlling power in the house of assembly in the early 1970s and began demanding complete self-government. Australia granted the Somare government complete control over internal affairs in 1972 and conceded complete independence in 1975 to the nation of Papua New Guinea. (Paul Hasluck, *A Time for Building: Australian Administration in Papua and New Guinea 1951–1963*, 1976.)

PARAGUAY. Paraguay is one of the more unfortunate nations of the world. Geographically, the country is landlocked and situated between two much larger neighbors, Argentina* and Brazil*. Through much of her history, Paraguay has been forced to defend herself from the ambitions of these two rivals. The terrain of Paraguay features extreme contrast. The eastern one-third of the country—that which is east of the Paraguay River—is a well-watered plateau with rich soil and a pleasant semitropical climate. To the west of the Paraguay is the Chaco, a low, poorly drained plain with extremely poor soil and a climate that features a few weeks of heavy rainfall followed by months of very hot, dry weather. Only a few of the hardiest souls live in the Chaco.

Paraguay has the most homogeneous population in Latin America. Nearly all of the 3,500,000 people are mestizos, the result of miscegenation between the

Spanish settlers and the Guarani natives. Paraguay is also the only truly bilingual nation in Latin America. The official language is Spanish, but most Paraguayans also speak Guarani. With little mineral wealth, the country is predominantly agricultural and poor. Industry, transportation, and commerce are controlled by foreigners, mostly Argentines and Brazilians, and much of the more productive land is owned by foreigners. Another misfortune of Paraguay, and probably the major cause of the retarded development, is that she has been governed by a succession of dictators whose rule makes Spanish colonial administration appear benevolent by comparison.

Spanish sovereignty was established in Paraguay in 1537 when Domingo Martinez de Ivala founded Asuncion, Spain soon made it the administrative center for the entire area east of the Andes. Asuncion lost favor with Madrid when the Spaniards realized that there was no wealth to be exploited, that it was not feasible to export Andean gold and silver across the Chaco to Atlantic ports, and that Buenos Aires was of greater strategic and economic importance. Buenos Aires left Asuncion's administrative control in 1620, and Paraguay was transferred in 1776 from the viceroyalty of Peru to the new viceroyalty of La Plata. The neglect and isolation perceived by the Paraguayans contributed to the introverted national personality that appeared later.

Colonialism in Paraguay was much less exploitative of Indians than in the other Spanish colonies, partly because there was less wealth and thus less need for labor and also because the Jesuits* established themselves as the protectors of the Indians. From 1588 until their expulsion from the New World in 1767, the Jesuits kept the Guarani in communal enclaves where the Indians were taught Christianity, modern farming methods, and the virtue of hard work. Spanish landowners, jealous of the wealth and power of the Jesuits and angry at being deprived of cheap labor, led the first Latin American revolt against Spanish authority. The *comuneros* overthrew the local governor in 1721, who was protecting the Jesuit missions, and defied the viceroy until they were finally defeated in 1735. The revolt was a major factor in Madrid's decision to evict the Jesuits. Without the paternal and authoritarian direction of the priests, the communities disintegrated rapidly, and the Indian population of Paraguay declined precipitously as the Indians fell prey to less paternalistic Spanish landowners and Portuguese slave raiders.

The intransigence exhibited in the Comunero Revolt appeared again after 1810 in Paraguay's fight for independence. When the Buenos Aires council in effect declared independence from Spain in 1810, they expected the Asuncion council to join them and to remain under the control of Buenos Aires. Long resentful of the power of Buenos Aires, the Paraguayans refused and successfully defeated an Argentine army sent to force compliance. The Asuncion council then deposed the Spanish governor and declared the independence of Paraguay in 1811. (George Pendle, *Paraguay: A Riverside Nation,* 1967; Harris Gaylord Warren, *Paraguay: An Informal History*, 1949.)

Bruce R. Drury

PARAÍBA. Late in the 1570s settlers from Pernambuco* in Brazil* began to settle the area of Paraíba. Paraíba became a captaincy in 1582, but until 1635 it was under the control of Pernambuco. That ended temporarily from 1635 to 1645 when the Dutch seized control of Paraíba. When the Dutch were expelled, Paraíba returned to the administrative supervision of Pernambuco. That lasted until 1799 when Paraíba became a separate, autonomous captaincy. In 1822 Paraíba became part of the empire of Brazil. See BRAZIL; NETHERLANDS BRAZIL.

PENNSYLVANIA. Pennsylvania covers 45,305 square miles stretching westward from the Delaware River to Lake Erie on its northwest frontier. The east is flat and low, while the west consists of level land on the Allegheny plateau. The Appalachians and the Great Valley break up the landscape. There were only about 15,000 Shawnee, Susquehanna, and Iroquois Indians scattered around the region when the Dutch explored the Delaware River in 1614. In 1643 Swedes settled near today's Chester, but a dozen years later New Amsterdam's Peter Stuyvesant brought New Sweden under Dutch authority, only to lose all his holdings to the Duke of York (later James II of England) in 1664. The crown ceded the lands to William Penn in 1681 in lieu of repaying debts which had been owed to Penn's father.

Penn's followers founded Philadelphia in 1682. The most liberal colony in North America—with widespread voting privileges, religious toleration, enlightened penal codes, and decent treatment of Indians—Pennsylvania grew quickly, with 30,000 European residents in 1700. Although in 1692 Penn's personal control was taken away and the province made a royal colony, most of his rights were restored by 1701. Penn then extended a great deal of power to Pennsylvania's unicameral legislature.

By 1776 there were 300,000 Pennsylvanians, and Philadelphia was the second largest city in the British Empire. But these demographic pressures had already brought strife to the young colony. In the 1750s traders and settlers in the west had forced the Indians to take a stand; they sided with the French in the French and Indian War*. Between 1754 and 1763, as part of a global struggle, the colonists successfully fought to secure land in the west. The conclusion of the French and Indian War meant that Pennsylvania had little to fear domestically. Strong local leadership emerged, most conspicuously under Benjamin Franklin. By 1775 Pennsylvania was ready to play the key role as birthplace of the revolution. The first Continental Congress, sitting in Philadelphia in April, appointed the Virginian veteran of the previous war, George Washington*, to command the troops of the Continental Army, then fighting the British near Boston. On July 2, 1776, the Second Continental Congress concluded that the "United Colonies are, and of Right ought to be Free and Independent States; that they are absolved from all allegiance to the British Crown," legally ending the colonial era in Pennsylvania. (Philip S. Klein and Ari Hoogenboom, *A History of Pennsylvania*, 1987.)

Mark R. Shulman

PEOPLE'S DEMOCRATIC REPUBLIC OF YEMEN. See ADEN.

PERAK. Perak was an independent sultanate on the western side of the Malay Peninsula between Selangor* and Pinang*. In 1874 the sultan of Perak signed a protectorate treaty with the British, and in 1895 Perak became one of the four Federated Malay States*. See MALAYSIA.

PERLIS. Perlis was once a sultanate in southern Siam*. In the Treaty of Bangkok, Siam ceded Perlis to Great Britain, and administratively Perlis became one of the Unfederated Malay States*. See MALAYSIA.

PERNAMBUCO. In 1534 the Portuguese granted a *donatário* in Pernambuco, which is located in northeastern Brazil*, and it soon evolved into the most important captaincy in sixteenth century Brazil. It was known at the time as New Lusitania. It was governed by the resident *donatários* until 1576, when it began to employ capitaes-mores appointed by the *donatário*. The Dutch took control of Pernambuco from 1637 to 1654, and it was the heart of the Netherlands empire in Brazil. When the Portuguese crown recovered Pernambuco in 1654, it took over administration of the region from the donatários. In 1716 the last of the donatários sold his rights in Pernambuco to the crown. Pernambuco had administrative supervision of Ceará* from 1656 to 1799, Paraíba* from 1582 to 1799, Rio Grande do Norte* from 1701 to 1808, and Alagôas* until 1817. Pernambuco became part of the empire of Brazil in 1822. (David P. Henige, *Colonial Governors from the Fifteenth Century to the Present*, 1970.)

PERRY, MATTHEW CALBRAITH. Matthew Perry was born on April 10, 1794, in Newport, Rhode Island. He joined the United States Navy in 1811 and in 1845 was one of the people who helped found the Naval Academy at Annapolis. During the 1840s Perry commanded several American vessels which were actively involved in trying to suppress the African slave trade, and during the Mexican War he fought in the Gulf of Mexico. He is best remembered for being the American naval commander who sailed into Tokyo Bay on July 8, 1853. Perry negotiated the Treaty of Kanagawa with Japan, effectively opening up Japan to Western commerce and missionary activity. The treaty protected American property and sailors in Japanese waters. His *Narrative of the Expedition of an American Squadron to the China Seas and Japan*, published in 1856, stimulated American interest in the Pacific and Far East. Matthew Perry died in 1858. (Joseph B. Icenhower, *Perry and the Open Door to Japan*, 1973.)

PERSIAN GULF. The interest of the British in the Persian Gulf originated in the sixteenth century and steadily increased as the importance of British India* grew in the imperial system of the eighteenth and nineteenth centuries, and as the demand for oil escalated in the twentieth century. When the Portuguese seized Hormuz* in 1515, England eventually realized its strategic significance. Great Britain steadily increased its presence in the commercial traffic of the Persian Gulf. In 1763 the British East India Company* established a residency at Bushir and several years later another one at Basar. Both of them were joined in 1822 and became the Persian Gulf residency. A chief political resident was the chief executive officer of the political unit, and he was subordinate to the governor of Bombay* until 1873 and to the viceroy of India until 1947 when India became independent. In 1946 the headquarters of the Persian Gulf residency was moved from Bushir to Bahrain*. From there the British also directed their other political agents in Bahrain, Kuwait*, Qatar*, and Oman* until those regions became independent. (David P. Henige, *Colonial Governors from the Fifteenth Century to the Present*, 1970.)

PERU. The first news of Peru reached Panama in 1522. Francisco Pizarro*, Diego de Almagro, and Hernando de Luque became associates for a Peruvian expedition in which they hoped to discover great riches and conquer new lands for Spain. In 1524 the expedition departed but quickly returned after running out of provisions. A second expedition left two years later and Bartolome Ruiz, a pilot, continued along the Pacific coast and "discovered" Peru when he sighted a raft with Indians who told him about the Incas and Cuzco. With this news, Pizarro continued while Almagro returned for provisions. Pizarro stayed on Gallo Island but Panama's governor learned about the privations which his men were undergoing and sent a rescue mission. Pizarro then moved with thirteen men to Gorgona Island. When provisions arrived he continued on to Tumbez before returning to Panama.

From there Pizarro traveled to Spain where he received a *capitulación* in 1529, which made him governor and captain-general. The crown provided funds and conferred titles on the men who had been with Pizarro on the islands as well as on his other associates. He went to his home town in Spain—Trujillo—to get his brothers Hernando, Gonzalo, Juan, and Martín. Pizarro then outfitted another expedition, leaving Diego de Almagro out of the planning. Almagro felt cheated but in 1531 Pizarro headed once again for Peru. They fought Indians at Puna Island, found that their original village at Tumbez had been destroyed, and then founded the first Spanish town—San Miguel.

When the Spaniards arrived a bitter feud was raging between the Indian rulers—Atahualpa of Quito and Huascar of Cuzco. Atahualpa's army was at Cajamarca. Pizarro arrived at Cajamarca on November 15, 1532, and soon captured Atahualpa. During the next several months Atahualpa tried to negotiate with the Spaniards for the conquest of Huascar, but on August 29, 1533, Pizarro had Atahualpa executed. Two months later Pizarro entered Cuzco. During the next several years the Spaniards completed the conquest of Peru and its Inca empire. In 1535 Pizarro founded the cities of Trujillo and Lima. But the Spaniards also suffered from internal dynastic struggles of their own. Diego de Almagro had arrived in Lima in 1533 and in June 1541 his followers assassinated Francisco Pizarro.

Gonzalo Pizarro emerged as the heir apparent but he revolted when the New Laws of 1542 were introduced to limit exploitation of the Indians. The first viceroy of Peru—Blasco Nunez Vela—attempted to enforce the New Laws but Gonzalo Pizarro and his followers would have none of it. A civil war raged for several years. Vela was killed in battle in 1546, but on April 9, 1548, Pedro de la Gasca pacified the country and executed Gonzalo Pizarro, ending the rebellion. Royal authority was quickly established under the leadership of a new viceroy— Antonio de Mendoza. He established the University of San Marcos in Lima in 1551 and after his death he was succeeded by Andrés Hurtado de Mendoza, who managed to secure an oath of allegiance from a powerful Inca leader, Sayri Tupac.

Under the reign of the fifth viceroy, Francisco de Toledo, from 1569 to 1581, a major reorganization took place which remained in place until the eighteenth century. Toledo developed laws to suit the viceroyalty's needs. He executed the last Inca, Tupac Amaru, in 1572. Toledo put the Indians into *reducciones* and in *mitas* for the booming silver mines, but allowed the *curacas*—Indian nobility—to govern local villages. To bring order to Peru's major export industry, Toledo developed a highly useful mining code. After Toledo left, the Spanish imperial system was firmly entrenched in Peru and remained untouched until 1781.

During the seventeenth and much of the eighteenth centuries Peru developed as one of the crown jewels of the Spanish empire*. The colonial population grew rapidly; the economy revolved around mining, textiles, and the commercial export of products from Chile, Bolivia, Paraguay, Ecuador, and Argentina; and Lima developed into a major urban and cultural center. But the prosperity bred certain resentments. *Criollos* (individuals of Spanish descent but born in Peru) and *mestizos* (individuals of European and Indian descent) resented the domineering paternalism of royal officials and grew increasingly restless. Indians, of course, hated the Spanish for the oppression and exploitation meted out to them. High taxes and exploitation led to the uprising of Tupac Amaru II* from 1780 to 1781. It not only involved the Indians but also *criollos* and *mestizos*. After Tupac Amaru's execution, revolts continued sporadically throughout the viceroyalty, but Spain strengthened the local militia, weakening the forces demanding independence.

By the mid-eighteenth century the viceroyalty of Peru had grown large and unwieldly. The viceroyalty of New Granada was permanently established in 1739 and the viceroyalty of Rio de la Plata went into operation in 1776. Spain introduced the intendancy system in 1784 and created the audiencia of Cuzco in 1787. These moves re-oriented trade away from Lima and economically weakened the colony while reducing its size. Lima's first newspaper, the *Mercurio Peruano*, began publishing in 1791.

The early years of the nineteenth century saw an increasing number of rebellions in Peru which eventually led to independence. Indians in Huanuco rebelled in 1811 but were crushed in 1813. In 1814 Mateo García Pumacahua, a former royalist who fought against Tupac Amaru II, rebelled and proclaimed himself president of the audiencia of Cuzco. Royalist forces captured him and defeated his supporters in 1815. José de San Martín* sent Argentinian troops into Chile to strike at Peruvian royalist forces in 1817, and he landed troops in Peru in 1819. The cabildo of Trujillo declared independence from Spain in 1820, as did a number of other towns north of Lima. The capital city, however, remained a royalist stronghold until San Martín invaded it on July 12, 1821. On July 28, 1821, San Martín proclaimed Peruvian independence. He organized Free Peru by issuing decrees and calling for free elections. But the royalist powers were stronger in Peru than in any other region of the Spanish empire. Simón Bolívar* entered Peru in 1822 after his victories in present-day Colombia and Venezuela in order to wipe out royalist power in Lima. Struggles for power divided the rebel forces for the next two years, giving the royalists some power again, but on December 9, 1824, Bolívar's forces defeated the royalists at the Battle of Ayacucho, consummating the Peruvian drive for independence. (Paul L. Doughty, *Peru: A Cultural History*, 1976; Clements R. Markham, *A History of Peru*, 1892.)

Carlos Pérez

PETERS, CARL. Carl Peters, the founder of German East Africa*, was born into a pastor's household in Neuhaus, Lower Saxony, on September 27, 1856. As a young history student at the University of Berlin, Peters enthusiastically endorsed the central theses of the philosopher Arthur Schopenhauer: an ingrained pessimism about life and the premier role of will. Colonial Africa ultimately provided Peters with the opportunity to assert his will through the dominance of East Africans and the forging of a new colony for the Second Reich.

Prior to going to Africa Peters spent two years in London (1881–1883). Here he developed an ambivalence toward his host country composed of equal parts of admiration and envy: admiration for the way England supported its citizenry from the proceeds of empire; envy that the English had outstripped the Germans in the colonial contest. A German colonial empire was essential, Peters reasoned, if the fatherland was to maintain a constant level of national commitment after Sedan.

Upon his return to Germany in 1883 Peters secured his Ph.D. from the University of Berlin. Instead of teaching, the young intellectual sought the fulfillment of his colonial dream in the Society for German Colonization, which he founded in March 1884 with two of his associates. Although greatly undercapitalized, the society provided Peters the vehicle to go to East Africa to do, as he said, "a great deed for the fatherland and to emblazon my name, once and for all, on German history.'' Peters concluded treaties of protection with chiefs in the territories of Usagara, Iseguha, Nguru, and Uhami. These gave the society sovereign rights and ownership over about 60,000 square miles of contemporary Tanzania*. Thus Peters, who cast himself as a German Robert Clive*, established the basis for his "German India"—to stretch, he said, from the Limpopo River in the south to the Nile sources in the north.

On February 27, 1885, Otto von Bismarck* granted an imperial charter to Peters's society which became the German East African Company in 1887. In the years 1885–1889 Peters participated in East Africa expeditions to secure territory beyond that obtained in the original treaties of 1884. His attempt to establish effective control over this enlarged empire led to an Arab revolt in 1888. The result was imperial military intervention to prevent the demise of German East Africa*. By 1890 Berlin decided that the island of Heligoland was more valuable than Peters's paper empire. Essentially it traded Uganda* and Witu to England for possession of Heligoland. Peters recorded his reaction to this treaty as a "fistblow" which nullified all gains achieved since 1885. The demise of Peters's company came in 1890 when the Reich assumed governance of the remaining portions of German East Africa.

In 1891 Berlin compensated Peters by appointing him imperial commissioner in German East Africa. The enactment of his philosophy that "the Negro is created by God for manual labor" led to brutalities against Africans which resulted in Peters's dismissal from imperial service in 1897. The frustrated imperialist returned to Africa to search for gold from 1899 to 1905. With the onset of the First World War, Peters returned to Germany where Emperor William II restored his titles and pension. Peters's controversial colonial career ended with his death in Bad Herzburg on September 10, 1918. (Hans-Ulrich Wehler, *Bismarck und der Imperialismus*, 1969.)

Arthur J. Knoll

PHILIPPINE-AMERICAN WAR. The Philippine-American War of 1899–1902, sometimes called the Phillippine Insurrection, was a bloody clash between the United States and Filipino guerrillas. Few Americans even knew where the Philippine Islands were when war was declared after the U.S.S. *Maine* sank in Havana on February 15, 1898. Spain still held title to the Philippines, and Germany seemed suspiciously interested, so United States Admiral George Dewey was sent to Manila Bay. He destroyed the entire Spanish fleet in a single battle on May 1. Spain's sovereignty was little more than a legal fiction, for the islands had risen in revolt. Dewey had brought along Emilio Aguinaldo, a revolutionary leader temporarily exiled to Hong Kong. Aguinaldo proclaimed an independent Philippine Republic (June 12, 1898) expecting that America, having defeated Spain, would withdraw. It was not to be. The Spanish governor of Manila surrendered to the Americans after a mock battle to preserve his honor. General Wesley Merritt then refused to let Aguinaldo's troops enter Manila*.

The Treaty of Paris of 1898*, ending the Spanish-American War, gave the United States title to the Philippines.

Conflict between American and Filipino soldiers was inevitable. Shooting started on the night of February 4, 1899, in Santa Mesa, a Manila suburb. For the next nine months American troops steadily pushed Aguinaldo's untrained, poorly equipped forces northward across the central Luzon* plain. At the end of November Aguinaldo escaped into the mountains and called on Filipinos to continue the struggle any way they could. The guerrilla phase of the war began. American soldiers could not distinguish enemy soldiers from civilians. The Filipino people were sullen and hostile. They came forward en masse to take the oath of allegiance to America but secretly supported the *insurrectos*, collecting contributions and supplies, recruiting men, and reporting American troop movements. Tactics were ruthless. Filipinos learned to wave a white flag, and then when the Americans approached, to open fire. American soldiers, for their part, were veterans of the plains Indian Wars, and brought to the battlefields of Luzon a low opinion of non-whites. They called Filipinos "gugus" and sometimes used water torture to extract information.

Public opinion in the United States was bitterly divided between imperialists and anti-imperialists. The former believed in America's mission to (in President McKinley's words) "uplift and Christianize" Filipinos, 85 percent of whom were Roman Catholic. Anti-imperialists denounced the whole venture as a betrayal of America's anti-colonial heritage. Military men in the field felt undermined by opponents of the war, and especially by reporters. It seemed that the best way to close the debate was to hand over control to a civilian government as soon as order could be established. William H. Taft was appointed head of the Philippine Commission over his own protest that he knew nothing about the Philippines. The Taft Commission exercised legislative power beginning in September 1900, and quickly co-opted influential Filipinos. Resistance continued even after Aguinaldo himself swore allegiance to America in April 1901. A particularly treacherous attack on American troops on Samar in 1901 sparked an orgy of destruction across that island. General Smith's orders included the words "I want no prisoners. I wish you to kill and burn. The more you kill and burn, the more it will please me." He was eventually court-martialed. The following year, in Batangas, the Americans had to declare a free-fire zone to starve out recalcitrant rebels.

Sporadic fighting broke out in remote parts of the islands for the next decade, but in spite of such an unpromising beginning, American rule proved very popular. Colonial policy emphasized public education, civic improvements, and rapid Filipinization of the civil service. The hatreds of wartime were soon forgotten. Only the most abbreviated and sanitized version of events was mentioned in textbooks. Today, most Filipinos are only vaguely aware of the bitter fighting at the turn of the century in which 4,200 American soldiers and hundreds of thousands of Filipinos died. (Joseph L. Schott, *The Ordeal of Samar*, 1964; Leon Wolff, *Little Brown Brother*, 1960.)

Ross Marlay

PHILIPPINES. The Philippines is an island nation in Southeast Asia, unique in its geography, history, and culture. It is the only Christian nation in Asia. Filipinos are highly educated but very poor. They had a long tutelage in democracy but have had to endure the worst misrule. The roots of the country's problems lie in its colonial history. Other Southeast Asian nations conceive their "true" identity to have emerged from precolonial kingdoms and empires. Filipinos like to joke that they spent "three hundred years in a convent, fifty years in Hollywood, and three years in a concentration camp," referring to Spanish, American, and Japanese imperialism. A more accurate metaphor compares the Filipino identity to layers of onionskin. The casual observer sees a superficial veneer of Americanization, but may overlook the Hispanic layer underneath, and not see the true Asian identity.

There was no "Philippines" before Spain created that political unit from an archipelago of dozens of islands, large and small, inhabited by local groups of Malays who spoke eighty-eight different languages. The islands lay too far east of the trade route between India and China to have been affected much by the waves of Hinduism, Buddhism, and Islam that washed over the rest of Southeast Asia. What Magellan found when he reached the Visayas (central islands) in 1521 were tropical islands where self-sufficient coastal Malays grew paddy rice and fished. The mountainous, forested interior regions were inhabited by different tribes, some quite primitive and some who maintained elaborate rice terraces. The reconquest of Spain for Christendom being fresh in their minds, the Spaniards were horrified to find that Islam was spreading in the islands.

Spain's motives for taking the islands were threefold: (1) There might be gold and silver, and there certainly were spice islands nearby; (2) Filipinos, mostly animists, seemed ripe for conversion; and (3) The archipelago had marvelous deepwater bays almost on the doorstep of China. Conquest was not too difficult, as local feuds made it easy to play one group against another. Filipinos were awed, too, by Catholic religious rituals and clerical garb. Starting with Miguel López de Legazpi's settlement at Manila (1571), Spanish control extended to all coastal areas of the islands, except Mindanao*. The islands, an ocean away even from Mexico, remained always the remotest part of Spain's empire. Religious orders (Augustinians, Dominicans, Jesuits*, and Franciscans) cleared vast estates, but most Spaniards preferred to wait in Manila for the annual arrival of the Manila Galleon*, which brought mail and goods from Acapulco. A stratified class society emerged as Spaniards conferred titles on tribal chiefs. In the villages, local priests, assisted by retainers of elite mestizo families, ran everything. Few Filipinos learned Spanish and few Spaniards other than priests mastered Philippine languages. The authorities were completely uninterested in teaching anyone to read or write. Insular society persisted in this sleepy pattern for two centuries until an upswing in global trade changed everything.

When the last galleon came from Acapulco in 1815, Manila was thrown back on its own resources. Filipinos now were encouraged to plant export crops: indigo, sugar, rice, hemp, and tobacco. Spain gave up trying to exclude English and American merchants, and the transforming effects of world commerce were felt everywhere. Regional economies depended on a single crop: sugar in central Luzon and Negros, tobacco in the Ilocano-speaking coastal regions of northern Luzon, and hemp in Bicol. Chinese immigrants went to live in provincial towns, where they bought and sold plantation crops, loaned money, and ran retail stores. The social structure grew more rigid as landowners found new sources of wealth. Rapid population growth provided plenty of cheap labor.

Free trade in goods eventually brought free circulation of ideas. The mestizo elite found Spanish arrogance increasingly difficult to endure. Wealthy families sent their children to be educated in Manila or Spain. Anger focused on the Spanish monopoly of church posts. Three Filipino priests—Fathers Burgos, Gómez, and Zamora—were executed in Cavite in 1872, becoming the first martyrs to Philippine independence. A sense of national identity grew where none had existed before. Spaniards called the natives "indios" and islanders defined themselves by language group: Tagalog, Cebuano, Ilocano, etc. Only in the 1890s did nationalists begin to call themselves "Filipinos."

Revolution was already in the air in 1892 when the brilliant novelist Jose Rizal* was sent into internal exile in Mindanao. He was executed in 1896, though quite innocent of revolutionary agitation. Fighting broke out that year. The Philippne Revolution (1896–98) was Asia's first struggle for a modern republic, but it petered out when General Emilio Aguinaldo signed the Pact of Biak-na-Bato in 1897, accepting exile in Hong Kong and a generous sum of money. He was brought back by American Admiral George Dewey in 1898, and immediately resumed his revolutionary war against Spain. Aguinaldo believed that after the Americans quickly disposed of Spain's fleet (May 1, 1898) and took Manila in June, they would simply withdraw. He was badly mistaken. Instead, the United States bought the islands from Spain for $20,000,000. The only problem was that American forces actually controlled only Manila itself. Shooting broke out on February 4, 1899, and the Philippine-American War* was on. It was shockingly vicious on both sides, but ended with a complete American victory.

The Americans established civilian rule as quickly as possible. They were pleasantly surprised to find that Filipino notables, once convinced of the impossibility of revolutionary victory, flocked to their side. Filipinos enthusiastically joined what Americans liked to call their "great experiment" in creating "a showcase for democracy in Asia." American imperialism had one unique and important feature: From the beginning, Americans planned to leave when their Filipino subjects were "ready" for independence. Schools had to be built in every barrio, for education was the foundation of democracy. Roads were improved. Boards of health were set up to improve public sanitation. Commerce was encouraged. A democratic constitution was written and elections held. Americans retained control only over defense, foreign relations, and the treasury after the Philippine Commonwealth was proclaimed in 1935. Filipinos were promised independence in ten years. Only one serious flaw marred this otherwise progressive paternalism—the rich were getting much richer. The land-owning class was very pro-American, and economic leveling was hardly part of America's ideology, so the situation was allowed to grow worse.

Japanese planes bombed the Philippines on Pearl Harbor Day. An invasion force landed at Lingayen Gulf and pushed rapidly southward. Manila was declared an open city and American forces retreated to the Bataan peninsula, where they held out until April 1942. Most Filipinos remained loyal to America throughout the occupation. Japanese sneered at the Filipinos for allegedly trying to imitate the whites, and exhorted them to assume a true Asian identity. But Japanese actions belied all their talk of pan-Asian friendship. General Douglas MacArthur was practically deified by Filipinos when he returned, as promised. The Philippines became independent on July 4, 1946. (Renato Constantino, *A History of the Philippines*, 1975; Alfred W. McCoy and Edilberto de Jesus, *Philippine Social History*, 1982; John L. Phelan, *The Hispanization of the Philippines*, 1967; David J. Steinberg, *The Philippines: A Singular and Plural Place*, 1982.)

Ross Marlay

PIAUÍ. In 1682 settlers moving out of Bahia* settled in Piauí in northeastern Brazil*. The region was transferred from Bahia to Maranhão* in 1715, and in 1759 Piauí was raised to a separate captaincy, although that individual still reported to the chief executive officer of Maranhão. Paiuí was separated out as a province in its own right in 1811, and in 1822 it became part of the empire of Brazil. See BRAZIL.

PIGS. Among the biological transplants the Europeans brought to the New World, pigs were among the most important. Unlike cattle, which consume plants indigestible to humans, pigs need concentrated carbohydrates and protein, but they convert one-fifth of what they eat into food for human consumption, compared to only 5 percent for cattle. In the early years of the New World colonies, where carbohydrates and protein were plentiful in the environment and human consumers few, pigs became ideal food for settlers. Although they do not do well in extremely cold climates or intense heat, they found enough shade and moisture in the Americas and Australia to thrive. Also, pigs are omnivorous—able to eat a wide variety of products—so they were very adaptable to different habitats. Columbus brought pigs in 1493 and Spaniards regularly left pigs behind in an area so that future explorers would have plentiful supplies of meat. Pigs multiplied so rapidly that within a few years they would be in abundant supply. This was called "seeding" of remote areas. Pigs multiplied by the tens of millions, often reverting to a wild state, and for the first generations of colonists, pork was the main source of protein. (Alfred W. Crosby, Jr., *Ecological Imperialism. The Biological Expansion of Europe, 900–1900*, 1986.)

PINANG. Pinang is a small island off the western coast of Malaysia*, approx-imately 500 miles north of Singapore. Interested in gaining a foothold in the Straits of Malacca in order to protect their commercial ships plying between China and India, the British East India Company* negotiated a lease in 1786 with the sultan of Kedah* for control of Pinang. Pinang become part of the Straits Settlements* in 1829, along with Singapore, Malacca, and Province Wellesley. See MALAYSIA.

PIRACY. Some historians have called pirates the "shock troops of European imperialism." There was, of course, often a very fine line between a legitimate merchant trader and a pirate. Along the African coast in the 1560s, legitimate Portuguese businessmen often forced African tribes at gunpoint to do business. The transition from forcing others to do business and piracy was often quite easy. Francis Drake*, John Hawkins*, and other sixteenth century English sea-dogs did not start out as pirates. They were armed, commercial smugglers who forced local officials to cooperate. By attacking and plundering Spanish treasure ships returning from the New World to Spain, the pirates indirectly enhanced British and Dutch attempts to increase their influence and control in the Carib-bean. English pirates like Drake actually worked closely with the English navy in defeating the Spanish Armada*.

The centers of European piracy were in the Caribbean Sea around the hundreds of islands of the West Indies* and along the coast of East Africa and Mada-gascar*. The pirates in the Caribbean spent most of their time trying to seize Spanish treasure fleets or attacking Spanish ports-of-call. Silver and gold taken from New Spain*, Bolivia*, and Peru* were all transported through Panama before shipment to Spain, and the Manila Galleon* from the Philippines* de-livered its goods to Acapulco for transshipment to Spain. The Caribbean was the perfect place to harass Spanish shipping. The coastline of East Africa and Madagascar provided similar opportunities for pirates attacking Portuguese and Dutch ships crisscrossing the Indian Ocean bearing spices and rare goods from China, India, and the Dutch East Indies*.

The seventeenth century was the great age of European piracy. The Spanish, Dutch, French, and English were all vying for control of the islands of the Caribbean, and political stability was limited at best. Various islands changed hands frequently. St. Eustatius of the Netherlands Antilles*, for example, changed hands ten times between 1664 and 1674. Pirates took advantage of the vacuum in political authority. The pirates were ruthless, raiding various settle-ments, especially Spanish ports, attacking ships, and serving as mercenaries in the intercolonial wars. The height of piracy occurred between 1640 and 1690. The most prominent pirate centers were in the French-held island of Tortuga off the coast of Hispaniola* and Port Royal in Jamaica*. The pirates on Tortuga led by Jean-David Nau—eventually gave France its entré to seize sovereignty over the western part of Hispaniola and establish St. Domingue*, or Haiti*. From his headquarters at Port Royal, Jamaica, the pirate Henry Morgan attacked

Spanish settlements and ocean traffic throughout the Caribbean. Like his sixteenth-century predecessors Francis Drake and John Hawkins, Henry Morgan was knighted by a grateful England. Eventually he became lieutenant governor of Jamaica. English pirates established the foothold on Central America which gave rise to British Honduras*.

By the eighteenth century, however, European piracy went into a long period of decline. Spain and Portugal had fallen on hard times and the volume of valuable goods being taken back to the Iberian peninsula had declined. Political control stabilized somewhat in the West Indies, depriving the pirates of many opportunities. Also, the British navy had become the largest and most powerful in the world. By the 1740s the British had established naval squadrons on Jamaica and Antigua*, eliminating whatever freedom of movement the pirates still enjoyed. Admirals replaced buccaneers as the most powerful individuals in the Caribbean and piracy lost much of the significance it had enjoyed in the sixteenth and seventeenth centuries. (Elisabeth Wallace, *The British Caribbean*, 1977).

PITCAIRN ISLANDS. The Pitcairn Islands are located east of French Polynesia* in the South Pacific*. They consist of four islands: Pitcairn, Henderson, Ducie, and Oeno. British sailors first discovered the Pitcairn Islands in 1767, and although there is archaeological evidence of ancient inhabitants, they were uninhabited at the time of the British landing. English cartographers, however, misplaced the islands on Pacific maps, and it was not until 1789 that eight mutinous crew members of the H.M.S. *Bounty*, led by Fletcher Christian and accompanied by nineteen Polynesians, settled on Pitcairn Island hoping to escape the reach of British law. They went undiscovered for years. The British navy again "found" Pitcairn Island in 1808, and it was annexed by the British government in 1838. By 1850 approximately 200 people of mixed English and Polynesian descent were living on Pitcairn Island. Henderson, Ducie, and Oeno were uninhabited. The Pitcairn Islanders relocated to Norfolk Island* in 1856, but some of them later returned. The four islands remain British dependent territories. (Peter Clark, *Hell and Paradise: The Norfolk-Bounty-Pitcairn Saga*, 1987.)

PITT, WILLIAM. Born May 28, 1759, William Pitt served twice as prime minister of Great Britain. He was the son of William Pitt, the first earl of Chatham (called The Elder), and Hester Grenville, sister of Prime Minister George Grenville. Like most boys born to aristocratic families during the eighteenth century, Pitt was educated at home by a private tutor. At age twenty-one, he entered the practice of law and soon after secured a seat in parliament. During the ministry of Lord Shelbourne, Pitt entered the cabinet as chancellor of the exchequer in July 1782. He made a name for himself as a political reformer, championing the cause of electoral reform. While Pitt proposed no radical change in the franchise, he argued for "honest government" and more equitable representation in parliament. Pitt's reformist measures were defeated, yet his dynamic personality and tireless leadership of the reform faction in the house of commons catapulted him to the political vanguard in parliament. In December 1783, King George III* asked Pitt to form a government in the wake of the failure of the Charles James Fox-Lord North coalition cabinet.

During Pitt's first ministry the government was beset by political divisiveness, but Prime Minister Pitt received the full support of the king. Pitt's domestic policies centered largely on erasing the considerable national debt incurred by the American Revolution*. By imposing new taxes, reducing fraud and waste in government, simplifying customs duties, and shrewdly investing government revenues, Pitt wiped out the deficit. His foreign policy was based upon a series of alliances with Prussia and Holland, the purpose of which was to cripple French influence and expansionist tendencies in Europe. While Pitt counseled neutrality during the early stages of the French Revolution, the French declaration of war on February 1, 1793, prompted the Prime Minister to defend forcefully the commercial and colonial interests of Great Britain. Pitt refused consistently, however, to push for the restoration of the French monarchy.

In imperial affairs, Pitt introduced in 1784 an India bill in which he set up a government agency, the board of control, to supervise the British East India Company's activities in the subcontinent. Pitt further enhanced the powers of the British government in India by greatly expanding the authority of the governor-general. Regarding Canada, Pitt presided over the passage of the Constitutional Act of 1791 which divided the province of Quebec* into a predominantly English province of Upper Canada and a French Province of Lower Canada. As early as 1792 Pitt argued for the ultimate union of Ireland and Britain, going so far as to propose Catholic emancipation and civil rights for Catholics and dissenting clergy. Parliamentary and royal opposition to the Prime Minister's plan forced Pitt to resign on February 3, 1801. Pitt's second ministry from 1804–1806 was much less successful than his first, due largely to his own ill health and the utter failure of the Third Coalition to defeat Napoleon Bonaparte. Upon the Allied defeats at Ulm and Austerlitz, Pitt's health declined further, and he died in London on January 23, 1806. (John Ehrman, *The Younger Pitt*, 1969; Derek Jarret, *Pitt the Younger*, 1974.)

William G. Ratliff

PIZARRO, FRANCISCO. Francisco Pizarro, the conquerer of the Incas, was born around 1470 in Trujillo, Extremadura, a region of Spain which produced dozens of explorers and conquistadores in the sixteenth century. Pizarro was the illegitimate son of an officer in the Spanish army. In 1502 Pizarro traveled with Nicolás de Ovando's expedition to Hispaniola*. He went to the Gulf of Uraba with Alonso de Ojeda in 1509 and rose to become second in command. Pizarro was with Vasco Núñez de Balboa* in 1513 when Spain claimed the Pacific Ocean. He turned on Balboa in 1516 and arrested him on the orders of Pedro Arias de Ávila. In the province of Darién, Pizarro rose to a position of respect and power.

During 1520 rumors of rich tribes to the south filtered up to Darién and Pizarro joined forces with Diego de Almagro. Between 1524 and 1526 they explored the Pacific coast of Colombia* and returned to the area of present-day Ecuador* in 1528 to discover the Inca outpost on the Gulf of Guayaquil. Pizarro returned to Spain in 1530 to try to raise money for another expedition south, and in 1531, equipped with the requisite money and titles, Pizarro returned to Peru and conquered Atahualpa, the Inca emperor, at Cajamarca. He conquered Cuzco in 1533 and founded Lima in 1535. Pizarro and his brother Gonzalo squeezed Diego de Almagro out of his share of the Incan gold and conquest. Diego de Almagro received a commission to what is today Chile*, but after two years of unsuccessful searching for other rich Indian tribes, he returned to Peru in 1537, captured Cuzco, and imprisoned the Pizarro brothers. A full-scale civil war erupted between those supporting Almagro and those supporting Pizarro. Pizarro had Almagro executed in 1538, but Almagro's supporters assassinated Francisco Pizarro in 1541. (James Lockhart, *The Men of Cajamarca: A Social and Biographical Study of the First Conquerers of Peru*, 1972.)

PLAISANCE. France established Plaisance on southern Newfoundland* in 1640 to support their fishing expeditions to the Grand Banks. A few settlers and a governor—Thalour du Perron—arrived in 1662. The colony was a French possession until 1713, when the Treaty of Utrecht* ceded it to Great Britain. See NEWFOUNDLAND.

PLYMOUTH. In the late sixteenth century one of the most powerful religious movements in Europe was the spread of Calvinist ideas. The English Calvinists became known as "Puritans" because of their desire to cleanse the Anglican Church of its "Catholic corruptions," and one group of Puritan dissenters was known as Separatists because of their conviction that they had to reject totally the Anglican communion. To separate completely from Anglican society, they relocated to Holland in 1608, living for more than a decade in Leyden. But by 1620 they were ready to move again, primarily to protect their children from assimilation into Dutch society. With financing from a joint stock company, 101 Separatists headed for America on the *Mayflower* in 1620. They landed on Cape Cod in Massachusetts* on November 21, 1620. Before heading ashore they signed the Mayflower Compact agreeing to establish a government of their own. After a month the colony relocated from what is today Provincetown on the tip of Cape Cod to a mainland settlement, which they named Plymouth. For several years they eked out a meager existence fishing and farming. Eventually they built a stronger colony based on lumber and furs. But only ten years after the Separatist settlement at Plymouth, a much larger body of Puritans settled the Massachusetts Bay colony at Boston. For the next sixty years Plymouth retained its independence, even though the expansion of Massachusetts Bay gradually surrounded them. In 1691 Massachusetts Bay annexed the Plymouth colony. (J. A. Goodwin, *The Pilgrim Republic*, 1921.)

POLYNESIA. The term "Polynesia" commonly refers to a large section of Oceania, particularly the central and southeast regions of the Pacific Ocean. The most well-known islands in the Polynesia group are Samoa*, Hawaii*, Easter Island*, and the Marquesa Islands* and Society Islands.

POMEROON. Pomeroon was a tiny Dutch colony in western Guiana settled by Dutch fugitives fleeing the Portuguese attacks on Dutch settlements in Brazil in the 1650s. The colony was periodically devastated by British, French, and Karib Indian attacks and remained highly dependent upon the Dutch colony of Essequibo*. In 1689 the colony ceased to exist as a bureaucratic political entity, becoming part of the Essequibo settlement. See BRITISH GUIANA.

PONCE DE LEÓN, JUAN. Juan Ponce de León was born around 1460 to a noble family in Santervas de Campos in Valladolid Province, Spain. He served as a page in the royal court and in 1493 sailed with Christopher Columbus* on his second voyage to the New World. Ponce de León returned to Puerto Rico* in 1508 and served with the troops who crushed the Indian rebellion on Hispaniola*. Between 1509 and 1511 Ponce de León served as governor of Puerto Rico, where he heard repeated tales of a Caribbean island endowed with a "fountain of youth." With a royal commission to discover the island, Ponce de Leon set sail in 1512 and landed on the Florida coast. He explored the western coast of Florida, sailed around the peninsula, explored as far north as present-day Tampa, and then returned to Cuba* and Puerto Rico. Juan Ponce de León spent the next several years exploring the Bahamas* before returning to Florida in 1521, where he was wounded by an Indian arrow. He died shortly thereafter. (Murga V. Sanz, *Juan Ponce de León*, 1982.)

POPAYÁN. The region known as Popayán was located in southwestern Colombia and was settled by people moving out of Peru. Its first governor arrived in 1536. Popayán fell under the authority of the audiencias of Peru (1536–1549), New Granada (1549–1563), and Quito (1563–1717). When the Audiencia of Quito was suppressed in 1717, Popayán came under the Viceroyalty of New Granada. Spanish authority was eliminated in Popayán by 1820 and the region became part of Gran Colómbia after the wars of independence. See COLOMBIA.

PORTUGUESE EAST AFRICA. See MOZAMBIQUE.

PORTUGUESE EMPIRE. Portugal, the first of the western European countries to embark on imperial expansion, launched a new era in human history in 1415 when she crossed the Mediterranean and conquered Ceuta* on the North African coast. Motivated by an intense economic desire to find a new route to secure Asian spices and discover fabled, wealthy kingdoms laden with gold, as well as a powerful crusading zeal to convert "infidels" to Christianity, Portugal began looking toward Africa early in the 1400s. The fact that Portugal was a united kingdom throughout the fifteenth century—free of the dynastic struggles afflicting Spain, Italy, and England, or the Hundred Years War affecting France—made overseas expansion easier to begin. Portuguese voyages of discovery down the coast of Africa began in 1433 and continued throughout the century, culminating when Bartolomeu Dias* rounded the Cape of Good Hope in 1487–1488 and Vasco da Gama* reached India* in 1498. To the west, Pedro Álvares Cabral* discovered Brazil* in 1500. The Treaty of Tordesillas* in 1494 divided the newly discovered lands of the world between Spain and Portugal, drawing a line from north to south through the South American continent and giving Portugal lands east of the line and Spain lands to the west.

Those voyages of discovery initiated the first stage of Portuguese imperialism—the sixteenth century triumphs on the African coast, the Indian Ocean, and Asia. From bases in the Cape Verde* Islands, Portugal began exploiting the Upper Guinea region, and from São Tome and Principe* they projected into the Gulf of Guinea. Portuguese settlements at Luanda and Benguela led to the penetration of what became Portuguese West Africa, or Angola*. Angola became the bastion of Portuguese power in Africa, and Angolan slaves built the Portuguese colony of Brazil on the other side of the Atlantic.

On the east coast of Africa, Portugal had planted isolated settlements along the coast of what is today Mozambique* and developed large, landed estates in the Zambezi river valley. The entire region eventually evolved into Portuguese East Africa. With those beginnings in the early sixteenth century, Portugal became involved in the gold, ivory, and slave trade which had long been part of Indian Ocean commercial markets. From the Portuguese trading settlements at Goa* and Gujerat on the west coast of India, cotton cloth and a variety of spices were sent to east Africa in exchange for gold, ivory, and slaves. A Portuguese naval base at Hormuz*, captured in 1515, helped secure another of the traditional spice routes to Europe. The capture of Malacca* in 1511 gave Portugal control of the spice traffic in the South China Sea, and the establishment of Portuguese posts at Macao* in China and Nagasaki* in Japan provided access to East Asian markets. By the middle of the sixteenth century, the Portuguese empire stretched from the coast of China in the east to the coast of Brazil in the west.

But the Portuguese empire peaked in the sixteenth century and then entered a long period of decline. The population of Portugal stagnated at 1,200,000, and as its economy also faltered in the late sixteenth and early seventeenth centuries, it became increasingly difficult for the Portuguese to maintain control over such a vast empire. Between 1580 and 1640, just when Dutch and English fortunes were on the rise, Portugal was an appendage to Spain, losing her sovereignty for sixty years. She regained that sovereignty and the wealth of the Brazilian trade helped her maintain it, but in 1821 Brazil declared independence, a fact which Portugal recognized in 1825. It was the beginning of the end of the Portuguese empire.

Portugal was left only with her outposts in Africa and Asia. The Asian settlements were not capable of being exploited. England's power in India prevented Portugal from doing anything with Goa and Gujerat, while Dutch expansion on Timor* and throughout the Dutch East Indies* confined Portugal there. Nor were the British or the French willing to let Portugal expand her interests in China beyond the small settlement at Macao. Only Africa held out any possibilities for a "new Brazil." West Africa, however, was not conducive to much expansion. British and French interests effectively confined Portuguese Guinea to the coast. So Portugal invested her energies in Portuguese West Africa and Portuguese East Africa. For a time in the nineteenth century Portugal managed to export slaves from both areas, but the anti-slavery movement in Europe doomed the trade, which Portugal finally conceded in 1888. In the twentieth century Portugal developed metals, textiles, machinery, paper, and chemical industries in Africa, but she had neither the resources nor the will to maintain the empire once the nationalistic rebellions erupted in the 1950s and 1960s. In 1961 India seized the last Portuguese outposts along the western coast of the sub-continent.

Internal Portuguese politics finished off the rest of the empire in the 1970s. A new government seized power in Portugal in 1974 and let it be known that it was interested in a peaceful settlement of the colonial problem. In 1975 Angola achieved independence, as did Mozambique, destroying the old colonial order of Portuguese West Africa and Portuguese East Africa. The Portuguese empire was all but dead, and Macao was slated to be returned to China in 1999; and by the late 1980s Portugal was the poorest country in Western Europe. (C. R. Boxer, *Four Centuries of Portuguese Expansion, 1415–1825*, 1961; Gervase Clarence-Smith, *The Third Portuguese Empire 1825–1975. A Study in Economic Imperialism*, 1985.)

PORTUGUESE GUINEA. Portuguese Guinea (now Guinea-Bissau) was a Portuguese colony on the western coast of Africa bordered to the north by Senegal*, and to the east and south by French Guinea*. Exploration of the area by the Portuguese began in the mid-fifteenth century. During the sixteenth and seventeenth centuries, European slave trade in the region was centered around the city of Bissau (São Jose de Bissao) on the central coastline of Portuguese Guinea. The Portuguese, and their colonial henchmen, the Cape Verde* Islanders, dominated the Bissau slave trade. Of the imperial powers in the area—Portugal, England, and France—only Portugal was wholeheartedly in favor of permanent occupation of its claims on the Guinea coastline. But limited military resources prevented Portugal from expanding its interests further than the area around its trading posts. Due to the politics of the slave trade, relations with the Africans in the area were touchy, and the European coastal settlements were frequently attacked. Only a small portion of the western coastline had been ceded to the colonial powers by the Africans at the beginning of the nineteenth century.

Portugal formally abolished slavery in the nineteenth century but still sought to control Portuguese Guinea as an overseas province. At this time, the British, from their stronghold on the Gambia River, began to assert claims to the coastal regions tenuously held by the Portuguese. These claims were dismissed in 1870 by United States President Ulysses S. Grant, who had been called upon to act as arbitrator in the dispute. In 1885 quarrels with France concerning the lands around the Casamance River were settled by the Berlin West Africa Conference*, and Portugal's holdings in the area were reduced to the size of present-day Guinea-Bissau.

Portuguese Guinea was declared a Portuguese dependency in 1879, with its capital at Bolama just south of Bissau on the central coast. The interior regions of Portuguese Guinea were not occupied until the second decade of the twentieth century, due to tenacious African resistance to Portuguese rule by the Papel, Balante, and Mandinga tribes. Portuguese military campaigns conducted by Captain Teixeira Pinto and Lieutenant Abdul Indjai, a deserter from the Senegalese army, and a force of less than five hundred soldiers, subdued Portuguese Guinea by 1917.

In 1951 Portuguese Guinea was declared an overseas province of Portugal. Independence movements began in 1956 when the African Party for the Independence of Guinea and Cape Verde (PAIGC) was organized, predominantly by Cape Verdean Africans, with Amilcar Cabral as its secretary-general. Work strikes and public riots ensued, culminating in the bloody 1959 dockworkers strike in Bissau. In 1959 Cabral declared a war for independence. Guerrilla warfare against the Portuguese army in the colony was well underway by 1963. In January 1973 Cabral, who favored a union of Cape Verde and Portuguese Guinea, was assassinated, reportedly by a PAIGC member. Aristides Pereira took control of the movement and proclaimed the independence of the Republic of Guinea-Bissau in September of the same year. By November the new republic was welcomed into the United Nations as an independent state. However, the civil war continued until April 1974, when Portuguese General Antonio de Spinola, who favored a peaceful settlement of the war, seized control of the Portuguese government. In August 1974 an agreement on Guinea-Bissau's independence was signed. Guinea-Bissau would become independent of Portugal by September. Portuguese troops would withdraw from the country by the end of October and a referendum concerning Guinea-Bissau's relationship with the Cape Verde Islands would be held. In September 1974 a Marxist government led by President Luis de Almeida Cabral was established in Guinea-Bissau. The Cape Verde issue was resolved when Cape Verde attained a separate independence from Portugal in 1975, with Aristides Pereira as president. (Michael Crowder, *West Africa Under Colonial Rule*, 1968; J. M. Gray, *A History of the Gambia*, 1966).

Karen Sleezer

PORTUGUESE INDIA. The Portuguese, because of the voyages of Bartholomeu Dias* and Vasco da Gama,* were the first Europeans to be able to exploit the trade of India.* In 1510 they seized Goa* on the western coast of India and, several hundred miles to the north, they took Diu* in 1535 and Damao* in 1538.

Together those three colonies constituted Portuguese India. The Portuguese crown placed a governor-general or viceroy at Goa, and he exercised political authority for all of Portuguese India as well as for Mozambique,* Mombasa,* Ceylon,* Timor, and Macao* at various times. Portugal retained Goa, Diu, and Damao until 1961 when India forcibly occupied them. See DAMAN; DIU; GOA.

PORTUGUESE TIMOR. Already in the thirteenth and fourteenth centuries, Japanese and Chinese were interested in Timor's sandalwood for its reputed medicinal properties. The Portuguese arrived in the 1520s, followed by the Dutch a century later. In the fierce struggle among European powers, generally for hegemony over the natural riches of the East Indies, the indigenous Timorese rulers (*liurai* or *rajas*) of some fifty small pre-colonial principalities (called *suku* or *fukun*) offered little resistance. In 1653 the Dutch overran the small Portuguese trading settlement at Kupang, building a fortress there and driving the Portuguese toward the northeastern part of the island. Boundary lines between the Portuguese and Dutch spheres of influence remained undefined, allowing *liurai* and *rajas* periodically to assert their authority. The British ruled over Timor and other Dutch East Indies* possessions from 1811 to 1816, but after the Napoleonic Wars, Portuguese and Dutch control was restored. It was not until 1859 that the boundary between East (Portuguese) and West (Dutch) Timor was determined by treaty. The treaty demarcation was further refined by another pact in 1893. But this agreement did not come into force until 1914, in part because of wrangling or resistance among *suku* territories. The town of Okusse and a surrounding enclave, though in the western part of the island, also remained under Portuguese control.

Considered a distant colonial backwater, and largely administered from the much more lucrative Portuguese possession of Macao*, East Timor's development stagnated, remaining mired in feudal land tenure traditions. Beyond the East Timorese capital of Dili, little was known of Timorese life. In much of the interior, the *liurai*, though often bitterly divided, held sway. In Dili a small Portuguese mestizo elite, some with ties to leading families in Portugal itself, held power, along with a small garrison and civil service. In 1889 a Portuguese embargo on the import of firearms ignited a protracted rebellion among power conscious *liurai*. The last resistance was not fully crushed until 1912. In 1896 East Timor was given the status of a separate province, free from Macao's influence. Though Portugal officially was neutral during World War II, the Japanese occupied much of the coastal section of East Timor. Local inhabitants suffered severely as a result of ruthless Japanese security measures and food shortages.

The successful revolution of the Indonesians against the Dutch (1945–49), and the assumption by Indonesia* of control over West Timor, slowly activated nationalist sentiment in East Timor. In 1959 a group of Indonesians briefly stirred up a revolt in the Vieqeque area, but the Salazar government in Lisbon, determined to maintain its power, quickly quelled the uprising. Though the new

Indonesian government of President Sukarno confirmed existing East Timorese boundary treaties with Portugal, an underground "Unirepublic (i.e., united) Timor" movement arose in 1961. It possibly was inspired by dissident, anti-Sukarno Indonesian nationalists in West Timor and came as the culmination of another chain of brief, violent, anti-colonial eruptions in the Viqueque area. The "Unirepublic Timor" movement appears to have been a seedbed for East Timorese independence circles a decade later.

Sparked by growing nationalist and Marxist unrest in the 1960s within Portugal's African colonies, and by the increasing political restiveness in Portugal itself caused by the tottering Portuguese economy in the waning years of the dictatorship of Antonio de Salazar, East Timorese nationalists became more vocal. The death of Salazar in 1970 led to ever more persistent demands for democratic reforms and complete decolonization in Portugal itself. A focal point for such reforms also was a radical "Young Turk" officers' movement in the Portuguese armed forces, some of whose members had connections in East Timor. On April 25, 1974, they staged a successful coup in Lisbon, and by November 1974 a number of the new Portuguese "Armed Forces Movement's" representatives also had arrived in East Timor, presumably to assist the East Timorese in preparing for self-determination. Local officials were replaced if they refused to cooperate.

Having had no experience in self-government, the East Timorese uncertainly began moving toward one of three emerging political parties. The first, the UDT (*Uniao Democratica Timorense*), favored a gradual evolution toward independence, while retaining close economic and cultural ties with Lisbon. Segments of the urban mestizo elite, some senior civil servants, and prominent *liurais* supported the UDT. The second party, *Fretilin (Frente Revolucionaria do Timor Leste Independente)*, with a following primarily among the lower strata urban mestizo population, a handful of professionals and junior civil servants, and especially among leading local military elements, favored complete independence, advocated "anti-colonialism" and "non-alignment" in foreign affairs, and "new forms of democracy and social justice." To the post-Sukarno government of President Suharto in Indonesia, having come to power in the wake of an abortive communist coup attempt on September 30, 1965, Fretilin's rhetoric, its connections with leading leftists in Lisbon's military and government, and its seemingly rising popular appeal in East Timor increasingly spelled a security danger. East Indonesia, where resistance against the Jakarta government still was in progress in Western New Guinea, and on Seran, in the Moluccas, already was a source of strategic concern to Suharto.

The third, and initially the smallest, of the three East Timorese political groups, Apodeti (*Associacao Popular Democratica de Timor*), was committed to union with Indonesia. From their bases in Indonesian Western Timor, Indonesia's watchful military early on were active in covertly supplying Apodeti—including weapons during its armed clashes with Fretilin bands. Apodeti's main support came from *liurai* along the western border, Muslim East Timorese, and some of the wealthier, conservative anti-Fretilin landowning mestizo families and Roman Catholic clergy. The deepening political quarrel between UDT and Fretilin, often spilling over into violence, vitiated emergence of a popular independence movement in East Timor.

Meanwhile, during a strident Indonesia media campaign that East Timor was a danger right on Indonesia's doorstep, Jakarta officials kept affirming that Portugal, though in effect all but powerless in East Timorese affairs, remained the sovereign power in East Timor. But on November 28, 1975, amid the widening political chaos, Fretilin leaders in Dili lowered the Portuguese flag and proclaimed a "Democratic Republic of East Timor" (DRET). DRET's President, Xavier do Amaral, pronounced the new state to be "anti-colonialist and anti-imperialist." Two days later a rival *Movimiento Anti-Communista*, inspired by Apodeti and also with UDT following, announced that East Timor had been "integrated" with the Indonesian Republic.

DRET quickly was recognized by the newly independent states of Angola* and Mozambique*, both former Portuguese colonies and both with Fretilin-type leaderships. The Indonesians, however, prepared to annex the territory. Within hours after the Indonesian parliament, on December 6, 1975, unanimously adopted a resolution calling on the Suharto government "to restore peace and order" in East Timor, 2,000 Indonesian commandos, assisted by some UDT and Apodeti bands, stormed ashore at Dili. Within two days they had occupied not only the city, but also most of the territory. Fretilin units retreated to the hilly interior to continue their resistance.

Ignoring UN Security Council resolutions passed on December 22, 1975, and again on April 22, 1976, to withdraw its forces and afford East Timorese the opportunity to exercise freely the right to self-determination, Indonesia staged a series of semi-plebiscitary and carefully supervised mass "consultation" meetings in major East Timorese population centers. These gatherings reportedly unanimously voiced approval of incorporation of East Timor into Indonesian territory. A "People's Representative Council" of an Indonesian-supervised "provisional government" forwarded the plebiscitary results to Jakarta, where the Indonesian parliament on August 14, 1976, ratified Law no. 6/1976, which formally made East Timor (*Timor Timur*) into Indonesia's twenty-seventh *propinsi* (province).

In the years since then, Indonesia successfully has staved off various diplomatic attempts at the United Nations and at conferences of the Non-Aligned Nations, as well as sharp criticism by international human rights groups of alleged abuses by Indonesian "pacification" forces of East Timorese, particularly Fretilin guerrillas and their sympathizers. None of the major or surrounding powers has been willing to risk their relationship with Indonesia by pressing the question of the legitimacy of Indonesia's seizure of East Timor, or persistent reports of human rights abuses. As the territory remains closed to all but a very limited number of foreign visitors, conditions in East Timor have been difficult to verify. Indonesia claims to have initiated some $8 million in development projects in the area, but reportedly about 500 Fretilin guerrillas still remain active in the interior. Also, periodic attempts by the Portuguese government to reopen the issue of East Timor have led nowhere. As recently as December 1, 1988, Indonesian Foreign Minister Ali Alatas dismissed Portugal's inquiries about human rights problems in East Timor. (Jill Jolliffe, *East Timor. Nationalism and Colonialism*, 1978; Torben Retboll, ed., *East Timor: The Struggle Continues*, 1984; Justus M. van der Kroef, "East Timor: The Problem and the Human Rights Polemic", *Asian Thought and Society*, 7, November 1982, 240–263.)

Justus M. van der Kroef

PORTUGUESE WEST AFRICA. See ANGOLA.

PRINCE EDWARD ISLAND. The first recorded European sighting of Prince Edward Island (today one of the maritime provinces of Canada) occurred in 1534 when Jacques Cartier*, sailing for France, explored the Gulf of St. Lawrence. The island was largely neglected by the French—who named it Ile St. Jean— until after the Treaty of Utrecht of 1713* and the loss of Acadia* to the British. French efforts to colonize Ile St. Jean started in the 1720s. Over the next several decades the colony, which was administratively attached to Ile Royale (Cape Breton Island*), developed slowly and precariously, the small population of settlers having to confront the danger of forest fires, plagues of crop-destroying field mice, and the constant threat of attack by the British. In 1758, during the French and Indian War*, a British military force took over the island and expelled most of the French inhabitants in an episode reminiscent of the removal of the Acadians from Nova Scotia* just a few years before.

The British officially gained possession of Ile St. Jean, which they called the Island of St. John, by the Treaty of Paris of 1763*. It was administered as part of Nova Scotia until 1769. In that year it was separated from Nova Scotia and was given its own colonial government. The first elected assembly of the Island of St. John met in July 1774 at Charlottetown. In 1779 the assembly voted to change the name of the colony to Prince Edward Island in honor of the Duke of Kent, the fourth son of King George III* (and father of Queen Victoria).

The most persistent political controversy in the history of the province prior to Confederation was the "eternal land question." In 1767 most of the land on the island—which had been surveyed and divided into 67 townships of 20,000 acres each—was granted in large lots to favored absentee proprietors by the British government. In return for these grants, the landlords were obligated to develop their estates, encourage settlement, and pay annual quitrents to the crown to finance the governing of the colony. Since most of the proprietors were perpetually delinquent in paying their quitrents and held their unimproved lands for purposes of speculation, thus driving up rents and purchase prices for those who wanted farms, a long, bitter, and sometimes violent struggle soon began between landlords and tenants. The land question hindered the development of the colony and impeded its growth. Demands for distraint and escheat proceedings to end the curse of absentee proprietorship were not supported by the British government, which assiduously defended the sanctity of property rights instead. Consequently, the land question was not finally resolved until Prince Edward Island joined the Canadian confederation.

Despite the embroilments of the land question, the colony progressed toward the achievement of responsible government (i.e., internal self-government) in the mid-nineteenth century. Among the leaders in the struggle for responsible government in Prince Edward Island were Edward Whelan, a journalist-politician who learned his craft and his politics as an apprentice in the printing office of Joseph Howe, the tribune of Nova Scotia, and George Coles, a brewer and distiller who, in 1851, became the premier of the first responsible government in Prince Edward Island.

In September 1864 a conference was held in Charlottetown to discuss the possibility of a union of the maritime provinces. A proposal for a wider union, promoted by visiting delegates from the Province of Canada, led to expanded discussions at Quebec (October 1864) and, ultimately, to the creation of the Dominion of Canada on July 1, 1867. Initially Prince Edward Island remained outside the new federation, largely because of local pride and patriotism. After six years, however, the province, burdened by a massive railway construction debt, was persuaded to reconsider by promises of financial assistance and other inducements. On July 1, 1873, Prince Edward Island became the seventh province to enter the Confederation of Canada. (J. M. Bumsted, *Land, Settlement, and Politics on Eighteenth-Century Prince Edward Island*, 1987; W. Ross Livingston, *Responsible Government in Prince Edward Island*, 1931.)

Robert Shadle

PRINCIPE. See SAO TOME AND PRINCIPE.

PROVIDENCE. The island of Providence is located in the Caribbean Sea approximately 100 miles off the coast of Nicaragua*. In 1630 merchants from the Providence Company, an English concern, placed settlers on Providence Island. Strategically located on the sea lanes to the Isthmus of Panama*, Providence was taken by the Spanish in 1641 and renamed Santa Catalina Island. England took it back in 1665, but only for a year, after which it became Spanish territory again. See NICARAGUA.

PROVINCE OF CANADA. See CANADA.

PUERTO RICO. Historians trace the ancestry of early Indian tribes of Puerto Rico to the first wave of Asiatic nomads that inhabited the Western Hemisphere. One of the early groups were the Ciboney (Siboney) from whom the Arawaks descended. At the time of European contact the Tainos of the Arawak branch inhabited Puerto Rico. They were a peaceful, agricultural people who raised corn, manioc, and cotton. Christopher Columbus* was the first European to contact the island of Puerto Rico. On his second voyage on November 19, 1493, he claimed the island for Spain. At the time it was called Broiquen (Borinquen). However, Columbus renamed it San Juan Bautista (St. John the Baptist). The Spanish did not attempt rigid colonization during the first fifteen years of occupation. The island was named San Juan, the main city was named Puerto Rico ("Rich Port"), and the Indians were left to their own devices.

This period of indifference ended in 1508 with the arrival of Juan Ponce de León*. As a member of Columbus' maiden crew, he was rewarded with the governorship of Puerto Rico. He initially settled at Caparra, changed the name to Ciudad de Puerto Rico (1511), and began mining for gold. Gold was not to be of major importance on this island except for its decimating effect on the Indian population. Dark, water-filled, poorly ventilated mines were not conducive to good health and many Indians died. The real "gold" of the area was found upon the introduction of the sugarcane plant from Hispaniola* between 1511 and 1515. African slaves arrived in 1518 to work the fields. Other crops of economic value during the latter 1500s were cotton, ginger, cacao, and indigo. By the seventeenth century tobacco was becoming important and within another century had become a cash crop. After the introduction of sugarcane, the coastal Indian population declined, mostly due to forced labor and such European diseases as measles and smallpox. Those Indians that survived intermarried with the Europeans, thus diluting the Taino strain.

After 1521 the island became known as Puerto Rico and the main city, San Juan. Shortly thereafter the strategic location of Puerto Rico came to the notice of other European powers. For a 200-year period ending in 1797, it underwent numerous attacks by the Dutch and the English. San Juan became a heavily fortified, walled city that withstood most attempted takeovers. The English succeeded in 1598 but were eventually doomed by a tropical disease outbreak.

The nineteenth century was marred mainly by outbreaks against Spanish rule. None equaled a major revolution but Spain did acknowledge the actions and gave Puerto Rico the status of a province in 1869. Following quickly was the peaceful abolition of slavery. By the time of the appearance of the United States in 1898, Puerto Rico and Spain had gained a remarkable compatibility as to the governing of the island. Shortly before United States intervention, Spain had extended limited autonomy to Puerto Rico.

At the end of the Spanish-American War* in 1898, Puerto Rico was ceded to the United States. The United States quickly granted a return to the civil government. The Foraker Act of 1900 provided Puerto Rico duty-free trade with the United States and exemption from payments to the federal treasury, and the Jones Act of 1917 granted American citizenship to the Puerto Ricans. "Operation Bootstrap," a post-World War II economic development program instituted by the government under the direction of Luís Marin, changed Puerto Rico from an agrarian to an industrial economy. At the present time Puerto Rico is officially a commonwealth of the United States, neither a territory nor a state. Some Puerto Rican nationalists want independence, but more conservative leaders feel that independence would be an economic disaster. Independence is ever present in some minds and may be a reality before the twentieth century concludes. (Robert Carr, *Puerto Rico*, 1984; Antonio López, *The Puerto Ricans: Their History, Culture, and Society*, 1980.)

Catherine G. Harbour

PUNJAB. The Punjab is a region in western India* which, historically, was the homeland of the Sikhs. British India annexed the eastern Punjab in 1846 after prevailing in the First Sikh War, and in 1849 annexed western Punjab as well. British India directed Punjab affairs through an appointed Board of Administration until 1856 when Punjab received its own chief commissioner. A lieutenant governor arrived in 1859 when Delhi* was placed under the Punjab administration. Delhi was separated out as a province in 1912 and Punjab became a governor's province in 1921. When the Indian subcontinent received its independence in 1947, the Punjab was divided between India and Pakistan. See INDIA; PAKISTAN.

Q

QATAR. Qatar is an independent nation of 4,416 square miles located on the Arabian Peninsula. The peninsula projects north into the Persian Gulf and has been occupied for thousands of years. By the eighteenth century the Khalifah family of what is today Bahrain* claimed sovereignty over the region, much to the dismay of the al-Thani family, which already dwelled there. Great Britain, interested in protecting the sea lanes to India, intervened in the dispute and all parties signed the Perpetual Maritime Truce of 1868, in which the Khalifahs surrendered their claim to Qatar in return for an annual tribute payment. The Ottoman Empire seized Qatar in 1872 and maintained its control until World War I when the Turks withdrew from the Arabian Peninsula and the British replaced them as the paramount influence. Qatar became independent in 1916, although a treaty that year with Great Britain gave England virtual control over Qatarian foreign policy.

In 1940 high-quality oil was discovered in Qatar, but World War II prevented its development until 1949. British influence in Qatar was still powerful, but Great Britain's declining resouces guaranteed a decline. In 1968 the British announced their intention to withdraw troops from the Arabian Peninsula in 1971, ending the special political relationship she had maintained with Qatar and several other local states. That withdrawal took place, and on September 3, 1971, the fully independent nation of Qatar came into being. (John B. Kelly, *Britain and the Persian Gulf, 1795–1880*, 1968; David Long, *The Persian Gulf*, 1976; Rosemarie Said Zahlan, *The Creation of Qatar*, 1979.)

QUEBEC. Quebec is the largest province in the Dominion of Canada*. It is bounded on the north by the Northwest Territories, on the east by Labrador and the Gulf of St. Lawrence, on the south by New England* and New York*, and on the west by the province of Ontario*. Quebec's total area is 636,400 square miles. Over 80 percent of the population is Francophone, and the French language, tradition, culture, and institutions set Quebec apart from the rest of Canada. The original inhabitants of Quebec were Algonkian, Huron, Montaignais, and Cree Indians and small numbers of Inuit in the far north. In July 1534 Jacques Cartier* landed on the Gaspe Peninsula, raised a thirty-foot cross, and took possession of the land for France. After an unsuccessful effort at colonization in the 1540s, France's interest in the new territory waned until the seventeenth century. Not until 1608 did Samuel de Champlain* establish the first permanent settlement at the site of modern Quebec City.

The growth of the new colony was painfully slow. Agriculture, which would support more population, meant a decline in fur trapping, which was the economic mainstay of the colony. This confict was unresolved through the seventeenth century. By mid-century small posts at Trois Rivieres and Montreal were established, but a series of wars with the Iroquois Indians interrupted the fur trade and almost brought an end to the French settlements. In 1663 Louis XIV and his great minister, Jean Baptiste Colbert, removed the settlements from private hands and made them a royal province, New France*. A new intendent, Jean Talon, vigorously promoted a mixed mercantile economy, and the arrival of a regiment of French troops significantly improved the Indian problem. The population was boosted by the arrival of several hundred *filles du roi*, peasant girls of good character, primarily from Normandy, who were married to settlers as soon as they arrived in the colony. New France began a period of slow and steady growth, but the colony reflected the authoritarianism of the mother country.

Through the first half of the eighteenth century the economic health and the expansion of New France were inseparable from the fur trade. As trapping played out in the St. Lawrence Valley, French explorers and fur traders moved into the Ohio River Valley, down the Mississippi River, north and west of the Great Lakes, and north to Hudson's Bay. Farm sites multiplied along the banks of the St. Lawrence River, but compared to the English settlements to the south, New France remained underpopulated. Clashes between the English and the French were frequent and the conflict reached a climax in the Seven Years' War, 1756–1763. On September 15, 1759, the fate of New France was sealed by the British victory at the Battle of Quebec.

By the terms of the Treaty of Paris of 1763* Great Britain acquired New France. They renamed the entire colony Quebec, the same name as the city, and assumed responsibility for governing 60,000 Roman Catholic Francophones. In a remarkable display of tolerance and in an effort to win their cooperation, the British allowed the French to retain their language, religion, and part of their legal system, but an authoritarian system of government was also retained. This policy proved troublesome when large numbers of Anglophones moved into the colony after the American Revolution*. To satisfy the new settlers, who demanded a more representative form of government, Great Britain divided Quebec into two provinces, Upper Canada (Ontario) and Lower Canada (Quebec), by the Constitutional Act of 1791. This act retained French language rights, Roman Catholic religious rights, and French civil law in Lower Canada, but it added an elected assembly for each province.

Initially Lower Canada was controlled by a conservative group of Anglophone merchants, senior Catholic clergy, and wealthy seigneurs or large land owners, the "Chateau Clique." Gradually this group was opposed by a young reform movement led by Louis Joseph Papineau, the first of a long line of Quebec proponents of French Canadian nationalism. In 1837 a series of petty skirmishes was quickly crushed, but an alarmed Great Britain was determined to investigate the cause of the violence in Lower Canada and a similar episode in Upper Canada. The British government sent an extraordinary politician, John George Lampton, Earl of Durham, who, after a brief visit, composed the Durham Report, one of the most crucial documents in the history of the British Empire. Durham recommended the reunion of Lower Canada and Upper Canada in order to swamp the French in an English legislature with English laws and the English language. However, he also recommended that the colony be granted responsible government. The Union Act of 1840 merged the two provinces, but it did not grant responsible government. Between 1840 and 1848 the newly merged and renamed Canada East (Lower Canada) and Canada West (Upper Canada) won responsible government by demonstrating that government without it was unmanageable. One British governor frankly admitted that whether or not it was approved by the mother country, responsible government virtually existed. The election of a Liberal government in Great Britain brought new instructions for the governor general in Canada, which conceded the issue, and the acceptance by the governor general of the Rebellion Losses Bill in 1849 confirmed the existence of responsible government.

The reunion of the two assemblies did not eliminate the French culture in Canada East as Durham had hoped. Rather, there was continued development of a distinct French Canadian identity. Responsible government did not solve many old political problems, and the equality of the two areas in the new legislature created new problems which gradually brought the government to a standstill. Twenty years after the passage of the Union Act a combination of factors, including the political stalemate and the American Civil War, made it clear that a confederation of all the British colonies in British North America offered the greatest hope for the future.

A remarkable coalition of Canadian politicians, including George Brown, John A. Macdonald, and Macdonald's ally from Canada East, George Etienne Cartier, fathered the Canadian Confederation. It was not easy to persuade any of the colonies to accept federation under a strong central government, and Cartier found it especially difficult to convince his suspicious Francophone colleagues in Canada East that their interests would be best served by the creation of a larger political entity in which they would be a minority. He argued that if a united Canada were not created, the United States would eventually absorb the separate British North American colonies, and the French culture would not survive in a greater United States of America. Moreover, the proposed confederation included specific protection for traditional French rights in Canada East. Even with these assurances, the representatives from Canada East voted in favor of confederation by the narrow vote of 27 to 22, and the general population of Canada East was not given the opportunity to vote at all. By the terms of the British North America Act of 1867 (Constitution Act of 1867) Canada East became the province of Quebec in the Dominion of Canada. (W. J. Eccles, *Canada Under Louis XIV, 1663–1701*, 1964; Fernand Ouellet, *Lower Canada, 1791–1840*, 1980; Marcel Trudel, *The Beginnings of New France, 1524–1663*, 1973.)

Peter T. Sherrill

QUEBEC CONFERENCE OF 1864. The Quebec Conference of 1864 was, in effect, Canada's constitutional convention. On October 10, 1864, 33 delegates from Canada*, New Brunswick*, Nova Scotia*, Prince Edward Island*, and Newfoundland* met in Quebec City to discuss the feasibility of a political union of British North America. The conference continued with reasonable smoothness until October 27 when, with the main work of the conference complete, the delegates dispersed to attend public receptions in Montreal, Ottawa, and Toronto. The Seventy-Two Resolutions adopted by the Quebec Conference provided the core of the subsequent British North America Act of 1867, which confirmed the federal union of Canada and served as the constitution of the Dominion of Canada. Among other provisions, the Seventy-Two Resolutions provided that the Queen rule the Dominion through the governor general assisted by the federal cabinet, which he appoints. The real executive power of the Dominion, however, lay in the prime minister, who is the majority leader in the legislature and selects his own cabinet colleagues. The Quebec Conference delegates provided that the legislature be elected for five years, with the legislative body holding the authority to dissolve the government and call new elections at any time. To ensure a united Canada, the Quebec Conference decided to require that the federal government provide for the building of a transcontinental railway. Provision was also made for incorporating the western territories into the Dominion. Overall, the conference delegates created a strong federal system for Canada at the expense of local, or provincial, authority. (James M. S. Careless, *Canada: A Story of Challenge*, 1974; Bruce Willard Hodgins, *Canadian History Since Confederation*, 1972.)

William G. Ratliff

QUININE. European exploitation of the African interior was delayed until the nineteenth century for a variety of reasons, but among the most important of them was the effect of malaria. As early as 1485 a Portuguese expedition on the Congo River was devastated in only a few days by malaria, and for the next 350 years Europeans communicated with interior tribes primarily through coastal tribes. Each time a European expedition headed inland, malaria destroyed most members of the party. Dysentery, typhoid, and yellow fever took their toll as well, but malaria was the real killer.

The cure for malaria came to Europe by way of the New World. In the 1600s Jesuit missionaries in Brazil and Peru began grinding up and chewing chinchona bark as a medicinal treatment for malaria, and in 1820 two French chemists, Pierre Peletier and Joseph Caventou, extracted the alkaloid of quinine from chinchona bark. By 1830 quinine was being manufactured on a large scale, and by the 1840s Europeans in Africa were keeping quinine pills by their bedstands. The death rate from malaria dropped dramatically. Use of quinine was common by the 1860s. In the wake of its discovery came explorers, soldiers, traders, settlers, and missionaries. Quinine also came into common use among Europeans in Asia. The British in India and the Dutch in Java began commercially planting the chinchona trees, creating a reliable supply of the bark by the 1880s and 1890s. The discovery of quinine was a major force in the expansion of the European empires into Africa. (Daniel R. Headrick, *The Tools of Empire. Technology and European Imperialism in the Nineteenth Century, 1981.*)

R

RAILROAD. During the nineteenth century the most powerful technological agent of European imperialism was the railroad. Until the invention of the railroad, the imperial powers depended on water transportation—ocean travel and river navigation—to explore new territories and ship goods to and from their colonies. Railroad construction provided economic infrastructures which permitted political unification in areas where geography militated against it. By linking Vancouver, British Columbia, with Montreal, Quebec, and Toronto, for example, the Canadian Pacific Railroad played a major role in making the Canadian confederation a reality. Railroad construction provided similar benefits in Latin America, the Indian subcontinent, Africa, and Australia. Without the railroad, European domination of the colonial world would have been confined to coastal enclaves or settlements near major navigable river systems. (Donald R. Headrick, *The Tools of Empire: Technology and Imperialism in the Nineteenth Century*, 1981.)

RAS AL-KHAIMAH. See UNITED ARAB EMIRATES.

RECIPROCITY TREATY OF 1854. Also known as the Elgin-Marcy Treaty, the Reciprocity Treaty of 1854 initiated the period of reciprocal trade between the United States and the Canadian colonies of British North America. The agreement was concluded following a brief period in the early 1850s when colonial sentiment in Canada* favored closer relations with the United States. Dissatisfaction with a change in British commercial policy, specifically the repeal of the corn laws and the resulting loss of Canada's preferred status in British markets, produced a movement for peaceful separation from the British Empire* and possible annexation to the United States. Any potential union between the

Canadian colonies and the United States was opposed by Britain. The British government therefore suggested closer trade relations with the United States as a means of assuring Canada's economic health without the danger of future American annexation of the colonies.

A trade agreement, the Reciprocity Treaty, was negotiated by Secretary of State William L. Marcy and the Earl of Elgin and Kincardine, governor general of Britain's North American Provinces, and signed on June 5, 1854. The agreement provided the free entry from Canada and the Maritime Provinces to the United States of a long list of enumerated products including raw and semifinished commodities, agricultural produce, timber, mineral ores, and fish. The United States received the same concession from Canada. The treaty admitted American fishermen to the inshore fisheries of the British provinces from which they had been excluded under the treaty of 1818. Similar privileges were granted Canadian fishermen on the eastern coast of the United States north of the 36th parallel of latitude. The treaty opened the St. Lawrence river and its canals to navigation by American citizens and, in return, allowed British subjects unrestricted navigation on Lake Michigan.

The Reciprocity Treaty was to remain in effect for ten years, after which either signatory could terminate it by giving one year's notice. The agreement proved beneficial to both the United States and the Canadian colonies, but the United States terminated it in 1865. The central reason for canceling the treaty was Washington's anger at alleged Canadian pro-Confederacy sentiments during the American Civil War. In addition, by 1865 United States economic policy had become increasingly dominated by the protectionist Republican party. (Gerald M. Craig, *The United States and Canada*, 1968; David R. Deener, *Canada-United States Treaty Relations*, 1963; C. C. Tansill, *The Canadian Reciprocity Treaty of 1854*, 1922.)

William G. Ratliff

REPUBLIC OF EASTERN INDONESIA. See BORNEO.

REPUBLIC OF THE MARSHALL ISLANDS. See MARSHALL ISLANDS.

RESPONSIBLE GOVERNMENT. By the early nineteenth century responsible government was understood in Britain as meaning that the advisors of the crown were responsible to the elected house of commons. In the 1830s reformers in the British North American colonies demanded that the same principle should be applied there. Lord Durham in his 1839 report advocated a limited form of responsible government for the colonies, but the British government was reluctant to concede the principle. After 1841 a working system of responsible government was established in the United Province of Canada* and the governors of New Brunswick* and Nova Scotia* sought to find advisors acceptable to the assembly, but the British government refused to endorse the principle of responsible government until 1847 when the colonial secretary, the 3rd Earl Grey, instructed the governors of the larger British North American colonies that they must choose as members of their executive council those who could command the support of a majority in the assembly.

By 1848 responsible government was clearly established in Nova Scotia and the United Province of Canada and within a few years extended to the other North American colonies. Inevitably the demand for responsible government was heard in the other colonies of settlement, and the colonial office* came to see the measure as a panacea for alleviating colonial discontent. Although there continued to be clashes over the extent to which the principle could be applied without destroying the unity of the Empire, it provided a method by which Britain could gradually reduce its overseas commitments and devolve authority while retaining a residual control over its colonies. Initially the British government denied that responsible government could be applied to its colonies in Africa and Asia, but in the twentieth century it was compelled to extend the principle throughout the Empire. (Phillip A. Buckner, *The Transition to Responsible Government: British Policy in British North America, 1815–1850*, 1985.)

Philip A. Buckner

REUNION. One of the Mascarene Islands, Reunion is located in the Indian Ocean, about 110 miles southwest of Mauritius and 400 miles southeast of Madagascar*. It was first discovered by the Portuguese navigator Pedro de Mascarenhas in 1506, but it was not formally colonized until 1643 when France took control of the island. Settlers began arriving in 1662. They quickly established coffee and spice plantations and African slaves to work the land. The French named the colony Bourbon. Later in the seventeenth century France introduced sugarcane to the colony and a new plantation economy emerged. In 1793, after the French Revolution, the destruction of the French monarchy, and the rise of Napoleon, Bourbon was renamed "La Reunion," or Reunion. Between 1810 and 1814, during the Napoleonic Wars, England took control of Reunion, but French sovereignty was restored with the peace treaty in 1815. The British had no permanent interest in Reunion because it lacked a harbor.

France abolished slavery in 1848 and Reunion planters began importing contract laborers from East Africa, India, and Indochina, giving the island its polyglot ethnic character. In 1946 Reunion was designated an overseas department of France with representation in the national assembly. By the 1980s, an independence movement had appeared, although it had little momentum. The Anti-Colonial Front for the Self-Determination of Reunion campaigned for independence, but they were opposed by the Association for the French Department of Reunion. Most people in Reunion realized that because of their weak economy, they were heavily dependent on France for survival. (Frederica M. Bunge, *Indian Ocean. Five Island Countries*, 1982.)

RHODES, CECIL. Cecil John Rhodes was born on July 5, 1853, at Bishop Stortford in Hertfordshire, England, where he lived until leaving for South Africa* in 1870. His father became vicar of Bishop Stortford in 1849 and remained in that position for the rest of his life. The vicar's second wife bore him nine sons and two daughters. Although the family was not poor, young Cecil did not enjoy the benefits of either wealth or membership in the aristocracy. He began his work at Oriel College, Oxford, in 1873; he would return to college from time to time from South Africa and was finally awarded his B.A. pass degree in 1881.

In 1870 Cecil traveled to South Africa to join his brother Herbert in a farming venture in Natal*. Before long, however, he was drawn to the diamond fields of Kimberley. Here, Rhodes began the business maneuvers that eventually led to his amassment of an incredible fortune. By the end of 1876, the colonial office* had removed all impediments to the acquisition and consolidation of prospector claims. From this time the partnership formed by Rhodes and Charles Rudd began systematically buying up claims in the De Beers mine. In 1880 most of the claims were bought out, and the partnership was floated as the De Beers Mining Company with a capital of £200,000. Rhodes later pushed for monopolistic control of the diamond industry. De Beers Consolidated Mines was registered on March 13, 1888, as the result of a dramatic amalgamation of claims; in 1891 virtual monopoly was attained with the acquisition of other mines. He now controlled all South African diamonds, or 90 percent of the entire world's production. In 1890 the Diamond Syndicate was established to fix prices and control the supply of diamonds; from that time on prices were stabilized.

Rhodes was given an opportunity to become involved in Cape Colony* politics in 1880, when the Cape annexed Griqualand* West. He was elected to parliament from Barkly West, which was heavily populated by Dutch farmers. To the north of Kimberley lay Bechuanaland*, a vast region composed mainly of the Kalahari Desert. On its eastern flank, however, was a zone of fairly good land with water which ran along the borders of the Orange Free State* and the Transvaal*. Called the "missionaries road," this area was critical to Rhodes' plans for gaining control over possible gold-bearing regions to the north populated by the Ndebele and Shona tribes. It was the only practical route to construct a railway from Kimberley into the highlands of what would later be named Rhodesia*. Rhodes achieved a political victory when the British agreed to split the Bechuanaland Protectorate. The land south of the Molopo River, which included the Dutch-settled Stellaland and Goshen areas, was established as the crown colony of British Bechuanaland. The Boer farmers, supported by Rhodes, were confirmed in their land titles and thus suffered no economic disadvantages. British Bechuanaland was later absorbed by Cape Colony. The route north could therefore be exploited by Rhodes without fearing that it would be blocked by the westward expansion of either the Orange Free State or the Transvaal.

After important gold discoveries were made on the Rand, Rhodes moved to acquire major claims in this region of the Transvaal throughout 1886 and 1887. In the latter year he formed Gold Fields of South Africa, which he later transformed into Consolidated Gold Fields of South Africa. In future years the vast wealth generated from his gold operations would be twice that derived from his diamond interests. The 1880s saw a revival of the "chartered company," which was a type of private company organized and authorized by the crown to rule colonial lands. In 1888, for example, the Conservative prime minister Lord Salisbury had chartered the Imperial British East Africa Company to secure British interests in Kenya and Uganda. His government was also quite interested in reserving the Ndebele country, Mashonaland, and the Zambezi valley as regions for British colonization. An energetic chartered company could resolve the issue without troubling the treasury or the taxpayers. Rhodes was now ready for such an undertaking. In forming the Gold Fields company, he had obtained powers to use its finances for the type of administrative expenses a chartered company would incur.

By this time Rhodes' economic and political power was such that he had great influence on imperial officials in South Africa. Sir Hercules Robinson, the high commissioner, had become a personal friend and fully supported Rhodes' solutions to the region's problems. In 1889 Robinson became a significant shareholder in several companies linked to the charter; he also became a member of the board of directors of De Beers. As a preliminary step to obtaining a charter, Rhodes sent Charles Rudd to conduct negotiations with King Lobengula, the Ndebele ruler of much of the territory in question. In a signed document, known as the Rudd concession, it was agreed that the king would receive guns, ammunition, and money in exchange for granting exclusive mining rights. There were certain other provisions written in a clever way that were later claimed to provide a basis for the acquisition of extensive territorial rights. In fact, no rights of sovereignty had been conceded.

The colonial and foreign offices encouraged Rhodes to extend the scope of his operations far beyond his original proposal, suggesting, for example, that he include the Nyasaland* region. A royal charter of October 29, 1889, created the British South Africa Company and granted it the right to colonize a vast area of south-central Africa. British officials simply ignored the fact that the charter application had lacked any legitimate claim to Ndebele territory. Thus, Rhodes was given the task of building an empire without effective governmental constraints concerning his methods. His power to exercise a free hand in ruling the lands to the north was facilitated in May 1890 when he became the Cape prime minister, a post he held until 1896. In the early years there was no railway into the company's territory and pioneers found the 1,600-mile trek from Kimberley to Fort Salisbury grueling. Rhodes felt that the best way to solve the problem would be to control a port on the east coast of Africa. Beira, in Portuguese Mozambique, located only 370 miles from Fort Salisbury, was an ideal prospect. He was not deterred from taking action by the fact that Britain had recognized Portugal's claim to the Mozambique* coastline since 1817. He thus demonstrated incredible boldness by instructing Leander Jameson to invade the Portuguese colony and seize the port. In the end, after some complicated maneuvers, the city remained in Portugal's possession. However, in the Anglo-Portuguese convention of June 11, 1891, the British achieved the economic objective by obtaining permission from Lisbon for the British South Africa Company to build a railway from Mashonaland to Beira.

There had been tensions and incidents involving white settlers and Ndebele which resulted in a short war. On November 4, 1893, troops entered Lobengula's capital of Bulawayo after the king had burned the town and fled; shortly thereafter Lobengula died. In an order-in-council of July 18, 1894, the British government proclaimed that all of the king's lands were to be treated as conquered territory and handed over to the British South Africa Company. Rhodes, ruler of a gigantic private empire, was now at the pinnacle of his career. The company owned the land and was the sovereign. Rhodes was its managing director and exercised its power of attorney. As a symbol of his personal power he adopted Lobengula's sons and brought them to live in his house in the Cape, where they worked as gardeners. In 1897 the name of the territory was officially proclaimed to be "Rhodesia."

Toward the end of 1894 serious disagreements were developing between Rhodes and Paul Kruger's regime in the Transvaal. Rhodes began thinking in terms of overthrowing Kruger's government by force, setting in motion a pattern of developments which climaxed in the disastrous Jameson Raid*. The attack ended in failure. Transvaal's General Piet Cronje defeated the invaders on January 1, 1896, and captured Jameson the following day. The raid ended Rhodes' friendship and political alliance with Jan Hofmeyr and he lost all support from the Afrikaner Bond; his political strength in the Cape had collapsed. Rhodes' great wealth benefited the men who had been captured. Fines for minor prisoners were set at £2,000 each; the ringleaders were fined £25,000 each. In all, the Jameson Raid and its aftermath cost Rhodes approximately £400,000.

The Boer War* began in October 1899. Rhodes went to Kimberley to assist in the defense of the city, which was subjected to a four-month siege. While there he used De Beers' resources to construct a fort on the edge of the city and formed a cavalry group composed of 800 De Beers workers. Cecil Rhodes died on March 26, 1902. His will provided that the greater part of his fortune would fund Rhodes Scholarships. The recipients were to be drawn from the British self-governing colonies, the United States, and Germany, and would attend Oxford University. (John Flint, *Cecil Rhodes*, 1974.)

Roy E. Thoman

RHODESIA. A landlocked country in south-central Africa, Rhodesia (now Zimbabwe) was the home of prehistoric cultures at least 100,000 years ago. The ancestors of the San people (also known as Bushmen, Twa, Sarwa) were probably the original inhabitants of Rhodesia. Invading Bantu-speakers began to enter the country early in the first millenium A.D. By the fifteenth century the Shonan Munhumutapa state had been established in the northern part of Rhodesia and present-day Mozambique*, dominating the trade routes to the Muslim ports of the east coast and the inland sources of gold. In the sixteenth century Portuguese forces occupied the Muslim trade centers and attempted to reach and control the gold area in the hinterland. The Portuguese made little headway in subduing the interior during this earlier period; however, repeated forays did serve to weaken the Munhumutapa empire. During the seventeenth century breakaway Shona states secured their autonomy and, in the early 1690s, the Changamire armies under Dombo invaded the vulnerable Munhumutapa territories and while at it routed most of the Portuguese from the region. Historiographical evidence of the eighteenth century Changamire empire is not abundant. Succession disputes and droughts had disabled the central authority, and by the 1830s the non-Shona Ndebele (Matabele) people began to invade the country. In 1866 Tohwechipi, the reigning Changamire king, was captured, and throughout the rest of the century, the newly established Ndebele/Matabele kingdom dominated the country's politics and commerce under the rule of Mzilikazi Khumalo (c. 1790–1868) and his successors.

In 1888 Cecil Rhodes*, seeking to forestall both the Portuguese and the Boers, obtained exclusive mining rights to Matabeleland (the area occupied by the Ndebele people) from Lobengula, king of the Ndebele. In 1889 Rhodes was able to secure a British Royal Charter for his newly formed British South Africa Company (BSAC). In 1890 the BSAC sent a group of 200 settlers protected by 500 Company police into the country, where they established the town of Salisbury (now Harare) on the Mashonaland plateau. The vast territory which the company brought under its rule, including Mashonaland and Matabeleland, was formally named Rhodesia in 1895 and was granted representative government (a legislative council for the European settlers) in 1898.

British settlement and economic development continued under the BSAC during the next 25 years. However, bitter African resentment over land and cattle seizures and forced labor abuses peaked during King Lobengula's futile Ndebele Revolt in 1896. By 1923 the BSAC, due to costs and disputes with the settlers, was forced to surrender its responsibility for Rhodesia to the British government. Although Britain retained imperial control over African affairs in Southern Rhodesia, the new crown colony was granted internal self-government (responsible government), and from 1923 until the 1960s, the settler-dominated local government, under alternating ruling parties, enacted discriminatory laws to safeguard the interests of the white minority in many important areas. Following the abrogation of the BSAC charter, Northern Rhodesia (present-day Zambia*) became a separate British protectorate.

In 1953 Southern Rhodesia joined with Northern Rhodesia and Nyasaland* (present-day Malawi) in forming the Central African Federation (Federation of Rhodesia and Nyasaland*) in an effort to pool resources and secure markets. Although the Federation generated economic benefits—mostly for Southern Rhodesia—it proved to be an unworkable arrangement, with the African populations of Northern Rhodesia and Nyasaland becoming increasingly dissatisfied. Following the secession of Nyasaland and Northern Rhodesia in 1962, the Central African Federation was officially dissolved in 1963. Nyasaland and Northern Rhodesia were granted independence in 1964 and became the black-ruled states

RIFLE

of Zambia and Malawi. The British government refused to accede to similar demands for independence from Southern Rhodesia's white-controlled dominion without amendments to the colony's constitution, including a guarantee of African majority rule. Rhodesia's prime minister, Ian Smith, in an effort to retain the settler government's dominant position, issued a Unilateral Declaration of Independence (UDI) on November 11, 1965. World criticism and sanctions were immediate. The British government considered the declaration illegal and unconstitutional, but stopped short of using force. Nevertheless, regional and international political pressure mounted, various African nationalist movements emerged, and African guerrilla activities escalated into a full-blown civil war. Rifts between African political and military leaders, as well as active hostility among separate guerrilla forces, hindered the formation of a unified liberation movement until October 1976, when Robert Mugabe's ZANU (Zimbabwe African National Union), based in Mozambique, and Joshua Nkomo's ZAPU (Zimbabwe African Political Union), operating from Zambia, formed the Patriotic Front.

On March 3, 1978, Smith acknowledged his government's conditional acceptance of majority rule by signing an "internal settlement" agreement in Salisbury with Bishop Abel Tendekali Muzorewa, Reverend Ndabaningi Sithole, and Chief Jeremiah Chirau. Following the elections of April 1979, Bishop Muzorewa, whose party won a majority, became the first black prime minister of the country (renamed Zimbabwe-Rhodesia). The Patriotic Front dismissed it as a sham, and the guerrilla conflict continued. Meanwhile British initiatives led to the Lancaster House negotiations in England between September and December 1979. As a result, agreement was reached on a new, democratic constitution and on the transition to independence. Sanctions were lifted, a ceasefire was implemented, and Rhodesia, for the time being, reverted to the status of a British colony. Elections were held in February 1980. Robert Mugabe's ZANU won a majority; and Mugabe became the first prime minister of the independent nation of Zimbabwe (formally granted by the British government on April 18, 1980). (Collin Stonemen, *Zimbabwe's Inheritance*, 1981.)

                                                                                      Eric C. Loew

RIFLE. Nineteenth-century developments in rifle technology gave Europeans an overwhelming advantage in firepower which allowed them to defeat far larger armies in Africa and Asia. In the first half of the nineteenth century, the invention of percussion caps, rifling, oblong bullets, and paper cartridges brought the muzzle-loading rifle to its technological peak. Its range, accuracy, and all-weather capabilities greatly improved. But in the second half of the nineteenth century it was the invention of the breechloading technique which provided for rapid fire capability. Instead of having to reload each bullet through a laborious process, the breechloader allowed an infantry soldier to shoot several rounds a minute.The breechloading rifle gave the smaller European armies in Africa and Asia a tremendous advantage over native soldiers armed only with spears, bows and arrows, and old muskets. The brass cartridges and smokeless explosives held up better against the hazards of long-distance shipment and tropical climates. They also weighed less. (Daniel R. Headrick, *The Tools of Empire. Technology and European Imperialism in the Nineteenth Century*, 1981.)

RIO DE JANEIRO. In 1555 France established a small colony at the site of present day Rio de Janeiro in Brazil*, and they called the settlement Antarctic France. Portuguese forces overran the settlement in 1560, and Portuguese colonists began arriving in 1563. Rio de Janeiro became a captaincy in 1565, subject to the administrative supervision of Bahia.* Huge discoveries of gold and diamonds in the interior of southern Brazil in the seventeenth century gradually made Rio de Janeiro a more significant trading center. In the process, Bahia declined in significance. In 1763, that reality was confirmed when the seat of the Brazilian viceroyalty was transferred from Bahia to Rio de Janeiro. When the Estado of Maranhão* was suppressed in 1775, all of Brazil was under the administrative supervision of Rio de Janeiro. See BRAZIL.

RÍO DE LA PLATA. Sebastián Cabot first explored the Río de la Plata in 1526, and nine years later the first Spanish settlers arrived. The city of Buenos Aires was established in 1536 but it was abandoned in 1537 because the city of Asunción in what is today Paraguay seemed more viable, primarily because it was more accessible to the prosperous colonies in Bolivia and Peru. The first Spanish governor of the province of Río de la Plata was Pedro de Mendoza. The province was subject to the Audiencia of Charcas. In 1618, to make the colonial government more efficient and to end the constant political struggles between its two primary regions, the province of Río de la Plata was divided into two new provinces—Asunción and Buenos Aires. See ARGENTINA; PARAGUAY.

RIO DE ORO. See SPANISH SAHARA.

RIO GRANDE DO NORTE. The area of Rio Grande do Norte in Brazil* was declared a donataria by the Portuguese crown in 1534, but settlement of the region was hampered by geography and climate. The area reverted to the crown at the end of the sixteenth century, but in 1597 settlers began making their way there from Pernambuco.* Except for the years of Dutch rule between 1633 and 1654, Rio Grande do Norte was governed by a *capitae-more* until 1701 and then by a governor until Rio Grande do Norte became a province of the empire of Brazil in 1822. See BRAZIL.

RIO GRANDE DO SUL. The region of Rio Grande do Sul in Brazil* was settled by ranchers and gauchos early in the 1700s. Portugal believed the settlements there were critically important to link up the area south of Sao Paulo* with the Nova Colônia do Sacramento* on the Rio de la Plata estuary. Military commandants governed the region from 1737 to 1761, when a governor was installed. Rio Grande do Sul was elevated to a separate captaincy-general in 1807 after being under the supervision of Rio de Janeiro* from its inception. For much of its colonial history, Rio Grande do Sul was known as Rio Grande do Sao Pedro. It became part of Brazil in 1822. See BRAZIL.

RIZAL, JOSÉ. Born on June 19, 1861, José Rizal is considered the Philippines'* national hero. His short life was filled with accomplishment: He is variously described as a linguist, doctor, patriot, freethinker, novelist, ethnographer, poet, and zoologist. There is no doubt that the man was a genius, the foremost Asian exemplar of enlightened thought. Rizal's novels stimulated the growth of Filipino nationalism, and his martyr's death symbolized the injustice and cruelty of Spanish rule in the islands. Rizal was of the privileged *mestizo* class, which in Philippine colonial society occupied a niche above all darker-skinned natives but below pure-blooded Spaniards. The *mestizos*, of mixed Chinese-Malay ancestry, were usually wealthy and socially prominent. Rizal's father ran a sugar plantation in Calamba, Laguna Province, on land he leased from Dominican friars. His mother was highly educated. They sent Jose to the best schools: The Ateneo and the University of Santo Tomas in Manila, and later to the University of Madrid.

Upper class *Indios* and *mestizos* (few yet called themselves "Filipinos") chafed under Spanish rule and particularly resented the monopoly of high clerical appointments enjoyed by Spaniards. Insular society was outraged by the execution of three Filipino priests in 1872. It was a formative event: Rizal's novels are merciless in their sarcastic depiction of abuses by Spanish friars.

Rizal arrived in Spain in 1882 and became a leader of Filipino students there. He traveled to England, France, and Germany, making the acquaintance of prominent European intellectuals. While studying medicine in Heidelberg (1886), he finished his famous novel *Noli me Tangere* (lit. "Touch Me Not" but sometimes translated as "the Social Cancer" or "The Lost Eden"). The book was an immediate sensation in the Philippines, despite condemnation by friars who told people they would fall into mortal sin by reading it. Rizal returned to his homeland in 1887, but was followed by government agents and soon left again for Europe. In 1890 he annotated a new edition of an old history book, Antonio Morga's *Sucesos de las Islas Filipinas*, which argued that Filipinos had a national history predating Spanish conquest. In 1891 Rizal finished a second novel, *El Filibusterismo*, sometimes translated as "The Reign of Greed" and sometimes as "The Subversive." He also contributed to a crusading journal, *La Solidaridad*, published in Spain, where the authorities were considerably more liberal than in Manila. In all this, Rizal never asked for more than justice and political equality. He called for Philippine representation in the Spanish parliament, not independence. He shunned violent revolution but warned that it might come if Spain ignored the warning signs.

Rizal returned to Manila in 1892, and in July that year founded an innocuous group, La Liga Filipina, to publicize his reformist agenda. The Spaniards panicked, arrested Rizal, and sent him to internal exile at Dapitan, a backwater town on the coast of Mindanao*. He stayed there for four years, practicing medicine, teaching school, and collecting specimens of local plants and animals. During those years, the Philippine nationalist movement gathered strength without him, and swerved increasingly toward violent revolution. Rizal wanted no part of it and volunteered to serve as a surgeon with Spanish forces in Cuba. The Spaniards at first agreed, but then stupidly arrested him. José Rizal faced the firing squad in Manila on December 30, 1896. (John Schumacher, *The Propaganda Movement, 1880–1895*, 1973.)

Ross Marlay

RODRIGUES. See MAURITIUS.

ROTUMA. Rotuma is an island of approximately 17 square miles located in western Polynesia, 300 miles south of Fiji*. British explorers discovered the island in 1791, and in the early nineteenth century a series of whalers, labor recruiters, and missionaries landed on the island. England annexed Rotuma in 1881 and administered it as part of its colony in Fiji. When Fiji became an independent dominion within the British Commonwealth in 1970, Rotuma was part of the new nation. (William Eason, *A Short History of Rotuma*, 1951.)

RUANDA-URUNDI. See RWANDI-BURUNDI.

RWANDA-BURUNDI. Rwanda and Burundi (formerly Ruanda-Urundi) are two separate nations located just south of the equator in east-central Africa. They were first inhabited by the Twa, a Pygmy group of hunters and gatherers, but between the seventh and tenth centuries Bantu-speaking Hutu people moved into the area. By the fourteenth or fifteenth century the Tutsi arrived in the area and gradually established a number of small independent chiefdoms. Around 1500 the first state was formed near Kigali (the capital of Rwanda today) by a few of those chieftaincies under the leadership of Ruganzu I Bwimba. The Tutsi then began a process of expansion which lasted into the nineteenth century. In both Burundi and Rwanda, the Tutsi became the political leaders of a feudal landlord system in which the majority of the Hutu were subjugated and performed all the manual labor.

The first Europeans in the region were John Hanning Speke and Richard Burton, who traveled to Lake Tanganyika in 1858 in search of the headwaters of the Nile. In the early 1870s the region was also explored by Henry Morton Stanley and David Livingstone. German explorers reached the area in the 1890s, and Count Von Gotzen discovered Lake Kiva in 1894. Roman Catholic missionaries of the Order of White Fathers soon followed these explorations. Colonial control came about after the Berlin West Africa Conference of 1884–1885*. The German sphere in East Africa was expanded to include Rwanda and Burundi. In 1896 a military post was established in Usumbura, which became the administrative center for both kingdoms until the Germans appointed separate residents for Burundi (1906) and Rwanda (1907). The Germans utilized the existing system of royal government in both territories because of the limited size of the German presence. This arrangement was advantageous to the monarchs as they were able to use the Germans to strengthen their own positions. The Germans carried out punitive expeditions against the Hutu chiefs in Rwanda.

Since both Rwanda and Burundi lacked the economic potential of nearby British and Belgian colonies where gold, diamonds, and copper were mined, the German resident, Richard Kandt, decided in 1913 to promote the production of coffee as a much-needed cash crop. The plan was carried out and money was introduced into the economy for the first time. This had the far-reaching effect of enabling the Hutu to look on money rather than cattle as wealth. In the past the Tutsi, having established that the ownership of cattle was wealth, had traded cattle for the land of the Hutu. As a result, the Tutsi had gained control over the Hutu by controlling the grazing land. Tutsi domination was further weakened when the Germans instituted the head tax in 1914. This caused the Hutu to look upon the Germans as their lords rather than the Tutsi.

The German administration in Rwanda and Burundi had visions of creating a great German empire in Central Africa. However, they had so few people in Rwanda or Burundi at the begining of World War I* that their dream of empire was shortlived. The two territories, now designated Belgian East Africa, were taken over by Belgium in 1916 without a major battle. Belgium's postwar plans for Rwanda and Burundi (then known as Ruanda and Urundi) involved a three-way trade with Great Britain and Portugal in which Belgium would swap the Central African territories for the southern bank of the lower Congo River adjacent to its Congo* Colony. These negotiations failed, and Belgium administered Rwanda and Burundi under a League of Nations* mandate of August 1923. The mandate called for the Belgian government to promote peace, order, good administration, and social progress. Belgium was also enjoined to protect the population from fraud, arms traffic, and alcohol.

Belgium used the existing political structure as had the Germans. Rwanda and Burundi each had a separate resident-administrator and chieftains and subchieftains. During all of the Belgian administration, the leader of Burundi was Mwambutsa IV. The ruling class in Rwanda came from the so-called favored race, the Tutsi. In Burundi, those who held power were members of the favored families (Ganwa). The early government policy for education concentrated on the sons of the Ganwa and lesser Tutsi chiefs in Burundi, and on the sons of the ruling Tutsi families in Rwanda. The Belgium mandate ended in 1946 when the United Nations* made Rwanda and Burundi a trust territory under Belgian administration. Belgium attempted to help Rwanda and Burundi become economically self-sufficient. Since neither country had natural resources to exploit, the Belgian effort concentrated on developing agriculture and expanding cultivation of coffee as a cash crop.

The United Nations' instructions to the Belgian trusteeship* were more specific than were those of the League of Nations, with the major difference being the emphasis upon the development of a more representative type government. United Nations inspection teams visited Rwanda and Burundi every three years starting in 1948. They determined insufficient progress was being made in accordance with the agreement. As a result, Belgium proposed significant reforms, including the launching of a 10-year development plan in 1952. In Rwanda the growth of democratic institutions was resisted by the Tutsi, who saw them as a threat to Tutsi rule. A Hutu revolt began in 1959. As a result Tutsi power was overthrown, and many Tutsi either were killed or fled to neighboring countries. The Hutu had the support of the Belgium authorities and the Roman Catholic Church during this period, and by October 1960 the Hutu-dominated party PAR-MEHUTU set up a republican form of government. A republic was established in January 1961. Although this new government was recognized by the Belgian administration, the United Nations declared it had been established by irregular and unlawful means. Under United Nations supervision, a referendum was held in September 1961, on retaining the old monarchy. The outcome was an overwhelming 4 to 1 vote to abolish the monarchy. Rwanda became an independent country in July 1962 under the leadership of Gregoire Kayibanda. The exiled Tutsi attempted an abortive invasion of Rwanda in December of 1963. Government reprisals led to the deaths of an estimated 12,000 Tutsi. This massacre caused many more Tutsi to flee to Burundi, Uganda, Tanzania, and the Congo (Zaire).

As independence approached in Burundi, the government became a constitutional monarchy under King Mwambutsa IV, a Tutsi. Burundi gained its independence on July 1, 1962. Although the Tutsi were in the minority, they had well-established government control in the 64-seat National Assembly. This was accomplished through the formation of a coalition with some Hutu leaders. That arrangment continued until 1965, when a Hutu-backed coup deposed Mwambutsa but failed to gain control of the country. In July 1966 Mwambutsa was succeeded by his heir, Mwami Ntare V, who, after a reign of 89 days, was overthrown in a military coup by Prime Minister Michel Micombero. Burundi was proclaimed a republic in November 1966. With the Tutsi controlling the government and the army, the persecution of the Hutu continues in Burundi, just as persecution of the Tutsi by the Hutu continues in Rwanda. (A. E. Afigbo, *The Making of Modern Africa*, 1971; J. D. Fage, *A History of Africa*, 1978.)

Amanda Pollock

RUPERT'S LAND. See HUDSON'S BAY COMPANY.

RUSSIAN AMERICA. See ALASKA.

S

SAAVEDRA CERON, ALVARO DE. Alvaro Saavedra de Cerón, a Spanish navigator and explorer, was the first European to sail across the Pacific from North America to the East Indies. Hernando Cortés* had received orders from Charles V* to find the *Trinidad*, one of the ships of Ferdinand Magellan*. Alvaro de Saavedra Cerón, a relative of Cortés, led the expedition. On October 31, 1527, they sailed from Zihuatanejo on the western coast of New Spain. Late in December they sailed past Guam* and reached the Philippines* in February 1528. Saavedra then proceeded to the Moluccas* and in March 1528 reached the island of Tidore. Saavedra sailed along the coast of New Guinea, discovering islands in the Marshall* and Caroline* groups as well as the Admiralty Islands* off the northern coast of eastern New Guinea. He died at sea during a second expedition in 1529. (Ione Struessy Wright, "The First American Voyage Across the Pacific, 1527–1528: The Voyage of Alvaro de Saavedra Cerón," *Geographical Review* 24, 1939: 472–82; Ione Struessy Wright, *Voyages of Alvaro de Saavedra Ceron, 1527–1529*, 1951.)

SABA. See NETHERLANDS ANTILLES.

SABAH. See BRITISH NORTH BORNEO.

ST. BARTHELEMY. St. Barthelemy is an irregularly shaped rocky island of nearly 30 square miles located 12 miles southwest of St. Martin in the Leeward Islands of the West Indies*. France first occupied the island in 1648. In 1784 France ceded St. Barts, as it is called, to Sweden but then bought it back in 1877. St. Barthelemy has remained within the French Community as part of the overseas department of Guadeloupe*. Sugar production dominates the economy. See GUADELOUPE.

Mark R. Shulman

ST. CHRISTOPHER. St. Christopher (St. Kitts) is a small island in the Caribbean Leewards, consisting of 65 miles of rugged mountainous terrain dominated by Mount Misery (3,792 feet). The capital is Basseterre. Although Columbus* was the first European to sight St. Christopher, no effort was made to settle it until English Puritans, under Sir Thomas Warner, made their first landing in 1623. The next year some French colonists followed. The Puritans welcomed the Catholic settlement as assistance against Carib Indian resistance. Both groups of Europeans planted tobacco from the start. As the Carib natives died away, they were replaced with African slaves. They grew the tobacco and later cotton, and they are the majority of the population today.

The economy suffered under the succession of Anglo-French wars in the late seventeenth and eighteenth centuries. Although France took the island in 1682, it was ceded formally to Britain in 1713. The Treaty of Paris of 1783* permanently secured St. Kitts for the British. Within fifty years, however, slavery was abolished in the British Empire, and St. Kitts started its economic decline as it could no longer successfully compete with American cotton and Cuban and Brazilian sugar, staples still grown by slaves.

Devolution from the Empire started relatively early, as 1951 saw creation of the state (with dominion-like status) of St. Christopher-Nevis-Anguilla. In 1967 the state assumed the status of association with the United Kingdom, although Anguilla* withdrew from the state in 1981. In 1983 St. Christopher-Nevis became a fully self-governing nation within the British Commonwealth. The new sovereign and democratic federal state is headed by a governor-general who is appointed by the British Crown. The governor-general, in turn, appoints the prime minister who has the best chance of holding a majority in the house of assembly. (Sir Alan Burns, *History of the British West Indies*, 1965; Arthur P. Newton, *Colonizing Activities of English Puritans*, 1914.)

Mark R. Shulman

ST. CROIX. Leading the United States Virgin Islands* in area, population, agriculture, and industrial production, St. Croix lies 65 miles southeast of Puerto Rico*. Carib warriors clashed with Columbus'* landing party at Salt River Bay in 1493, and Europeans did not settle the island until 1625. In the space of two decades, the English managed to gain control of St. Croix's polyglot community, thus precipitating Spain's surprise attack from Puerto Rico that wiped out the colony in 1650.

A short time afterward, Philippe de Lonvilliers de Poincy left French St. Kitts with a force that succeeded in capturing St. Croix's Spanish garrison. Three years later he donated the island to the Knights of Malta, a Catholic religious order. France acquired it in 1674 from the French West India Company, which had ruled since the Knights had disposed of their Caribbean enclave nine years earlier. The Crown found St. Croix difficult to defend and unprofitable, and its 1,200 colonists were evacuated to St. Domingue in 1696. When English pirates and settlers encroached upon the abandoned possession, the French sold the island to the Danish West India Company in 1733. At the time, 150 Englishmen and their 456 slaves lived on St. Croix. While few Danes came as planters, British, Dutch, Jewish, French, and German migrants were attracted by the company's liberal land policy, so that by 1748, all of the island's level areas were under cultivation and the capital of the Danish West Indies was shifted there from St. Thomas*. St. Croix became a royal colony in 1754, ushering in a period of prosperity based upon sugar cultivation.

Denmark's harsh slave code led to severe reprisals against blacks suspected of plotting insurrections. Nevertheless, due to a mixture of motives, the Scandinavian nation's 1792 Royal Ordinance was the first in Europe to outlaw traffic in human chattel, effective January 1, 1803. It was not until 1847, however, that Copenhagen abolished the institution of slavery. St. Croix's slaves refused to accept an apprenticeship program that would delay their full emancipation for twelve years. In July 1848, Moses "Buddoe" Gottlieb marched on Fredericksted at the head of a crowd demanding immediate freedom. Governor Peter von Scholten, influenced by his free-mulatto mistress, Anne Heegaard, bowed to these wishes by issuing the Proclamation of Emancipation, subsequently confirmed by a royal decree on September 22, 1848.

Falling sugar prices, poor agriculture practices, and a large number of absentee estate owners were several of the many factors responsible for St. Croix's economic doldrums in the 1830s. After emancipation, Crucian planters forced freedmen to work on their estates for minimal wages under the Labor Act of 1849. Deteriorating socioeconomic conditions resulted in serious unrest in 1878 and 1916. Denmark's colonies, increasingly expensive and restive, now constituted a burden rather than a source of wealth. The United States, primarily for strategic reasons, purchased the Danish Virgin Islands in 1917. St. Croix continued to sink into a deep depression that prompted Washington in the 1930s to create the Virgin Islands Company (VICO) in order to pull the island out of its misery. World War II brought a large air base, jobs on St. Thomas, higher wages, and an influx of Puerto Rican workers. An industrial incentives plan during the 1960s drew manufacturers, notably Harvey Alumina and Hess Oil. These companies offered only limited employment to native Virgin Islanders. Compared to St. Thomas, few tourists visited St. Croix.

Social tensions ran high in the 1970s. Alien service workers and prejudiced mainland whites clashed with locals. Many young males rebelled by adopting Rastafarian hairstyles and music while rejecting the cult's peaceful ways by committing violent acts against visitors. On September 6, 1972, seven whites and one black were gunned down at Fountain Valley Golf Course. Other white slayings followed. Racial unrest was still evident in the 1980s, along with environmental, industrial, and drug-related woes. Hurricane Hugo in 1989 devastated large sections of the island and led to widespread looting. (William W. Boyer, *America's Virgin Islands: A History of Human Rights & Wrongs*, 1983; Florence Lewisohn, *St. Croix Under Seven Flags*, 1970.)

Frank Marotti

ST. DOMINGUE. See HAITI.

ST. HELENA. The island of St. Helena is located in the Atlantic some 1,200 miles from the southwest coast of Africa. St. Helena was discovered by João de Nova Castella, a Portuguese navigator, on May 21, 1502. Captain John Cavendish, in 1588, was the first Englishman to visit St. Helena. By the early seventeenth century both the English and the Dutch had begun to call at the nearby Cape of Good Hope for victuals and repair. In 1652 the Dutch took formal control of the Cape and began to organize settlements there. The British East India Company*, excluded from the Cape, began to search for an alternative stopover for its India-bound ships. In 1659 a small British force under the leadership of John Dutton seized and garrisoned St. Helena. The Dutch captured the island in 1673, but within the year St. Helena was retaken by the British. A charter to occupy and govern St. Helena was issued by King Charles II to the East India Company in December 1673.

The island was brought briefly under the authority of the Crown when it served as Napoleon Bonaparte's place of exile from 1815 until his death in 1821. After Napoleon died, the East India Company resumed control of St. Helena until the island was placed under the direct rule of the British Crown by an act of parliament in 1833.

Following completion of the Suez Canal* and the opening of the red Sea route in 1869, St. Helena lost its significance as a port of call and coaling station on the way to India. During the second Boer War* (1899–1902) thousands of Boer prisoners were shipped to St. Helena by the British government. St. Helena also served as a place of exile for Chief Dinuzulu (1889–1897) and for the ex-Sultan of Zanzibar, Khalid Bin Barghash (1916–1921).

In an effort to reform and enlarge the British Continental Army to meet the growing threat of European military rivals, parliament passed the Territorial and Reserve Forces Act in 1907. This measure reduced the occupying soldiery of various Pacific and non-Continental outposts, including the abolition of the garrison at St. Helena. In 1922 the island of Ascension* and, in 1938, the islands of Tristan da Cunha*, Nightingale, Inaccessible, and Gough became dependencies of St. Helena.

The United Nations Committee on Decolonization has called for measures to transfer power to elected officials of the islands, as well as independence. The St. Helena Labor Party advocates such a position. The St. Helena Progressive Party supports close economic ties with the United Kingdom. At present the government of St. Helena and its dependencies Tristan da Cunha and Ascension form a crown colony administered by Britain through a governor assisted since

January 1967 by an executive council and an elected legislative council. (Tony Cross, *St. Helena with Chapters on Ascension and Tristan da Cunha*, 1981.)

Eric C. Loew

ST. JOHN. In November 1493 Christopher Columbus* sighted St. John, located three miles east of St. Thomas* in what is today the United States Virgin Islands*. The Danes claimed it as early as 1684, but they did not settle there until 1717. From this date the island has been linked administratively to St. Thomas. Between 1717 and 1733, St. John rapidly developed sugar estates based upon slave labor. By the latter year 208 whites held 1,087 slaves, most of them of African descent, on 109 plantations.

One of the most famous slave revolts in West Indian history took place on St. John in 1733. A drought, two hurricanes, and an insect plague preceded the revolt. When Governor Philip Gardelin (1733–1736) enacted an especially harsh slave code, the uprising began. The island's white population perished and its main fort was captured. From the bush, the rebels waged a guerrilla war that St. Thomian and English troops could not quell. French forces eventually crushed the rebels. Though only about 146 of St. John's slaves actively participated in the fighting, they managed to control the colony for six months. Those captured by the French endured public torture before being executed on St. Thomas.

The number of St. Johnians declined from 2,555 in 1841 to 746 in 1950. The abolition of slavery in 1848 meant the end of the plantation economy. Approximately 85 percent of the land reverted to forest or scrub. In 1939, under United States rule, plans were formulated to preserve St. John's natural beauty. The United States had purchased the island from Denmark in 1917. World War II postponed these proposals, but after the war millionaire Laurance Rockefeller bought half of the island. He proceeded to create an exclusive resort at Caneel Bay. The wealthy philanthropist then decided to donate his holdings for the establishment of a national park. Two-thirds of St. John now lies within the borders of the Virgin Islands National Park, which came into existence in 1956.

Rockefeller's philanthropy managed to stir periodic local controversy. In 1958 the Caneel Bay resort faced charges of racial discrimination. Also, St. Johnians feared that the scion would dominate community development in the remaining private areas of the island. Virgin Islanders learned in 1962 that Rockefeller and the United States Congress were considering increasing the park's size. The land was to be acquired by eminent domain. At the last minute, the territorial government thwarted the scheme. Today, 3,000 people permanently dwell on St. John. Tourism in the major economic activity. The local government center is Cruz Bay, and the one at-large senator in the legislature of the Virgin Islands must be a St. Johnian. (William W. Boyer, *America's Virgin Islands: A History of Human Rights and Wrongs*, 1983; Gordon K. Lewis, *The Virgin Islands: A Caribbean Lilliput*, 1972.)

Frank Marotti

ST. KITTS. See ST. CHRISTOPHER.

ST. LUCIA. St. Lucia is a small island of 240 square miles in the Lesser Antilles of the Caribbean, lying between Martinique* and St. Vincent*. Columbus* discovered St. Lucia on his third voyage in 1502, but the native Carib inhabitants were fierce people and European colonization was delayed until the seventeenth century. England made an attempt at settling the island in 1605 and again in 1638, but the Caribs put up a violent defense and the settlements collapsed. From their colony at Martinique, the French posted a successful settlement on St. Lucia in 1650 and formalized a peace treaty with the Caribs a decade later. England seized St. Lucia in 1664 but surrendered it back to France in the Treaty of Breda in 1677. For the rest of the seventeenth century the colony at St. Lucia remained in French hands.

In the eighteenth century sugar and cotton plantations, worked by African slaves, thrived on St. Lucia, and both England and France lusted after the colony. The colonial wars of the eighteenth century left St. Lucia in a most confusing position, gravitating back and forth between French and British sovereignty. England captured the island in 1762 during the Seven Years' War, but then returned it to France in the Treaty of Paris of 1763*. During the American Revolution*, England took control of St. Lucia, but again restored it to France, this time in the Treaty of Versailles of 1783*. During the Napoleonic Wars, the island switched back and forth, depending upon which navy had invaded, but the Treaty of Paris of 1814 awarded St. Lucia to the British, and the island soon became a crown colony. By that time the French influence ran deep in the island's 16,000 inhabitants, most of whom were French-speaking, Roman Catholic blacks.

St. Lucia remained a crown colony until 1838, when it became administratively a part of Barbados*. That ended in 1885. A new constitution in 1924 created an elected legislative council, and another constitution in 1936 required a St. Lucian majority on that body. Between 1958 and 1962 St. Lucia was part of the West Indies Federation*, but when the Federation dissolved in 1962, the island reverted to its former position as an autonomous crown colony. Led by Allan Lousy, the St. Lucia Labour Party campaigned vigorously for independence along socialist lines; independence and formal membership in the British Commonwealth of Nations* was achieved on February 22, 1979. (Sir Alan Burns, *A History of the British West Indies*, 1965.)

ST. MARIE OF MADAGASCAR. St. Marie of Madagascar is a small island located off the northeastern coast of Madagascar*. Its Malagasy tribal leader ceded the island to France in 1750, but settlement did not begin until 1819 when its first governor, Jean-Louis-Joseph Carayon, arrived. Between 1840 and 1843, St. Marie was an administrative unit of Reunion*, and from 1843 to 1853 it was part of Mayotte*. France gave St. Marie separate colonial status between 1853 and 1877, but in 1878 it was returned to Reunion. Like Nosy Be and

Diego-Suárez, St. Marie was incorporated into the colony of Madagascar in 1896. See MADAGASCAR.

ST. MARTIN. See NETHERLANDS ANTILLES.

ST. PIERRE AND MIQUELON. St. Pierre and Miquelon, along with Langdale, are small islands located in the North Atlantic Ocean, about 15 miles off the southern coast of Newfoundland. French settlers, soon followed by hundreds of Basques, settled on the islands in 1604, and they have remained under French sovereignty ever since. Even at the end of the French and Indian War, the Treaty of Paris of 1763* left St. Pierre and Miquelon in French hands as the last vestiges of the once great French Empire* in the New World. They were used primarily by French fishermen working the Grand Banks off Newfoundland. (Herbert Ingram Priestley, *France Overseas. A Study of Modern Imperialism*, 1938.)

ST. THOMAS. St. Thomas, the site of Charlotte Amalie, the territorial capital of the United States Virgin Islands*, lies 40 miles east of Puerto Rico. Christopher Columbus* discovered the island in 1493. European occupation began in the early seventeenth century, but no permanent settlement existed until 1672, when George Iverson arrived from Denmark with 189 indentured servants and convicts. English, French, German, Jewish, and Dutch colonists bolstered the Danish population. Soon, Dutchmen outnumbered all other nationalities.

The Danish West India Company ruled St. Thomas, whose fine harbor, strategically located near the Anegada Passage, an important shipping route, was its most valuable asset. Since Denmark tended to remain neutral during European wars, Dutch traders based on the island could continue to operate in periods of international conflict. The colony also provided a haven for buccaneers, especially under Governor Adolph Esmit (1682–1684). A flourishing commerce in African bondsmen developed after the Danes permitted the Elector of Brandenburg to establish a slave warehouse in 1685. Most of the human cargo was exported to other West Indian destinations, but the Brandenburg presence stimulated sugar cultivation. By 1733 blacks were seven times as numerous as whites.

In 1717 the Danes annexed nearby St. John* and turned it into a sugar colony. Sixteen years later, however, a serious slave revolt rocked that island, paralyzing its young economy. Denmark compensated by purchasing St. Croix*, 40 miles to the south, from the French. The 1733 acquisition proved to be a cane-producing bonanza. Indeed, St. Croix became the islands' seat of government within two decades. St. Thomas' importance as a commercial entrepot grew in the same period, though its agricultural output diminished. Illicit trade with British North America prospered when Copenhagen designated St. Thomas as a free port in 1764.

The English seized the Virgin Islands during the Napoleanic Wars in 1801–1802 and in 1807–1815. After the restoration of peace, Charlotte Amalie's future appeared bright. Two banks, a coaling station, and the headquarters of the Royal

Mail Steam Packet Company all were established there between 1837 and 1842. Nevertheless, the long-term consequence of the rise of steamships was a gradual economic downturn. St. Thomas' slaves were emancipated in 1848, subsequent to a black uprising on St. Croix. Still, the Danes transferred their Caribbean capital back to Charlotte Amalie in 1871. The United States came very close to acquiring St. Thomas in 1867 and 1902. Attempts by Denmark early in the twentieth century to revive St. Thomas' fortunes failed. The effects of World War I worsened the island's economy. Finally, on March 31, 1917, the Danish West Indies were handed over to the United States, which had purchased them several weeks earlier. United States naval rule (1917–1931) produced material benefits, but racial incidents perpetrated by the Marines aroused local resentment. Labor unrest occurred, notably in 1920.

St. Thomas' situation improved when Congress granted United States citizenship to Virgin Islanders in 1927. The number of vessels visiting Charlotte Amalie climbed between 1931 and 1935. Tourism, which also expanded during this time, received government support by the construction of Bluebeard's Castle Hotel. Those residents who could read and write English won the right to vote by the Organic Act of 1936. Furthermore, a Marine Corps air station and a submarine base were built. The wartime activities of the 1940's boosted employment opportunities to the extent that labor was imported from nearby European possessions.

The end of World War II spelled hard times for St. Thomas, but by the mid–1950s, a tourist boom had begun to soften the impact of a drop in defense-related jobs. Tourism ballooned in 1961, when Havana, Cuba*, was declared off-limits to Americans. During that year 4,000 ships called at Charlotte Amalie, a number not seen since the early nineteenth century. Between 1960 and 1970, a five-fold increase in visitors took place.

Local political control also expanded during these decades. The Organic Act of 1954 established a unicameral legislature and nine government executive departments. Virgin Islanders first elected their governor in 1968. Since 1973 residents have sent a non-voting delegate to the United States House of Representatives. The tourist influx brought problems along with a higher standard of living. Tensions between St. Thomians and both mainland whites and "alien" service workers was one area of conflict. Crime, water shortages, juvenile delinquency, official corruption, environmental concerns, land alienation, a troubled school system, power outages, and traffic jams plagued the island in the 1970s and early 1980s. Hurricane Hugo, which swept through the Virgin Islands in September 1989, devastated many of the islands and led to widespread looting, requiring the stationing of National Guard troops there. (William W. Boyer, *America's Virgin Islands: A History of Human Rights and Wrongs*, 1983; Darwin D. Creque, *The U.S. Virgins and the Eastern Caribbean*, 1968.)

Frank Marotti

ST. VINCENT AND THE GRENADINES. Today St. Vincent and the northern Grenadine Islands are an independent nation in the Caribbean. St. Vincent is twenty miles southwest of St. Lucia* and 100 miles west of Barbados*. The largest of the northern Grenadines are Union Island, Bequia, Canouan, Mustique, and Mayreau. St. Vincent was inhabited by the fierce Carib Indians when Columbus* discovered the island in 1498, but Spain generally disregarded the area. Shipwrecked African slaves reached St. Vincent in 1673 and married into the Carib society, and a series of French, Dutch, and English settlements followed. French control was established early in the eighteenth century, but England captured the island in 1762, during the Seven Years' War, and the Treaty of Paris of 1763* turned the island over to the British.

Like other areas of the British Caribbean, the St. Vincent economy was damaged by the abolition of slavery in 1834, limiting the availability of cheap labor for the sugar plantations. St. Vincent and the Grenadines remained a British colony, dependent economically on the mother country, until the late 1950s, when the move for regional autonomy gained momentum. St. Vincent joined the West Indies Federation* in 1958 and remained there until 1962 when the Federation dissolved. In 1969 Great Britain changed St. Vincent's status from that of a colony to a state in association with the United Kingdom, and full independence was granted to St. Vincent and the Grenadines on October 27, 1979. (Sir Alan Burns, *A History of the British West Indies*, 1965.)

SAMOA. The Samoan Islands, once called the Navigators Islands, are located in the south Pacific Ocean, about 2,250 miles southeast of Hawaii and 1,750 miles northeast of New Zealand. The islands east of longitude 171 degrees W. form the territory of American Samoa*, while those east of that line constitute Western Samoa*. See AMERICAN SAMOA and WESTERN SAMOA.

SAN MARTÍN, JOSÉ DE. José de San Martín was born on February 25, 1778, in Yapeyu, Viceroyalty of La Plata. His mother was Gregoria Matorras and his father was Juan de San Martín, a professional soldier and administrator of Yapeyu. The family returned to Spain in 1784, where San Martín was educated at the Seminario de Nobles from 1785 until 1789, when he began his military career as a cadet in the Murica infantry regiment. From 1808 until 1811 he served as an officer against the forces of Napoleon. Having attained the rank of lieutenant colonel in 1808, he was offered the command of the Sagunto Dragoons following the Battle of Albuera. Instead of accepting, he requested assignment to Lima, Viceroyalty of Peru. He proceeded to Peru* via London, where he met other disaffected Spanish-Americans and was recruited by James Duffy, 4th Earl of Fife, to fight against the Seville Junta (Ferdinand VII was imprisoned by Napoleon). San Martín claimed that he chose to fight for his native land in revolt against the Junta. He was probably motivated by his belief in constitutional liberalism, and he identified with the creole revolutionaries with whom he had earlier become associated in Cádiz. Furthermore, as a creole serving in the Spanish army, he undoubtedly experienced prejudice from Peninsular Spaniards.

Upon his arrival in Buenos Aires in March 1812, he was given the task of organizing a corps of mounted grenadiers to be used against the Spanish royalists in Peru who were threatening the government in Argentina. In September 1812 San Martín reinforced his ties with Argentina when he married María de los Remedios Escalada, the daughter of an upper-class Argentine family. On February 3, 1813, San Martín fought his first engagement, defeating a royalist force at San Lorenzo. Before replacing General Manuel Belgrano at Tucumán, San Martín had already come to the conclusion that the Rio de la Plata provinces would never be secure until the royalist stronghold in Peru had been crushed. To accomplish this task he trained the army around Tucuman so it could sustain a holding operation. Then, on the pretense of ill health, he got himself appointed governor-intendent of Cuyo in western Argentina. The capital city, Mendoza, was the key to routes through the Andes mountains. His plan was to travel west from Argentina to Chile* and from there by sea to the Peruvian coast. The design and execution of his plan were carried out with meticulous care, and San Martín would not move until he was fully equipped, including his bugles. A setback occurred in October 1814 when the Chilean patriot regime collapsed. However, San Martín's army benefited from the influx of Chileans, including Bernardo O'Higgins. In January 1817 San Martín set out on his expedition to Chile. Initially he was able to elude the Spanish by misleading them as to the trail he would take. From January 18 until February 8, 1817, he fought his way across the Andes, concentrating his forces at the enemy's weakest point. He took the main part of his army through passes that reached altitudes of 10,000 to 12,000 feet. On February 12, 1817, San Martín surprised and defeated the royalist army at Casas de Chacabuco and occupied Santiago.

Turning the governorship over to O'Higgins, San Martín took a year to clear the country of the remaining royalist troops, defeating them on April 5, 1818, at the Battle of Maipú. While the government in Buenos Aires was embroiled in domestic quarrels, San Martín proceeded without its assistance with the next phase of his plan. With a newly created Chilean fleet under the command of Admiral Thomas Cochrane, San Martín sailed from Valparaiso, landing south of the port of Callao by September 1820. San Martín, not prepared to attack the superiorly defended Lima, waited a year until royalist support deteriorated and they withdrew to the mountains. On July 28, 1821, San Martín entered the city unopposed and declared the independence of Peru, accepting the title Protector of Peru from a grateful populace.

In the newly liberated areas, he began to enact a series of liberal reforms, including the gradual emancipation of black slaves and the abolition of Indian forced labor. He was criticized, however, for not pursuing the royalists, who remained numerous and well entrenched in the Peruvian Andes. There was also mistrust of San Martín's monarchist views. Earlier, at the Congress of Tucumán in 1816, he had supported a scheme to establish a limited monarchy under a prince of the Inca royal family. Prior to his 1821 victory in Peru, San Martín had negotiated with Spain to create an autonomous monarchy in which one of the princes of the Spanish royal family would rule over an independent Peru. Although nothing came of these schemes, San Martín believed that a liberal constitutional monarchy was the best hope for stability in the new nations. San Martín thus faced growing resentment and distrust among Peruvians when he left Peru to meet with Simón Bolívar*.

The two great revolutionary leaders met in Guayaquil in July 1822. Although the content of the meeting was secret, San Martín presumably sought support for his monarchist plans in Peru. He also hoped to secure Guayaquil as a port for Peru. San Martín's request for troops hinged on the type of government that would be established in Peru. Bolívar stood firmly in favor of a republic and would not entertain San Martín's plans for creating a constitutional monarchy. Historians debate the substance of the meeting, but it was clear that although they disagreed over the type of government, both men remained committed to independence and felt the need to continue the revolution. Whether he decided before or after his meeting to resign is unclear, but upon his return to Lima on September 20, San Martín resigned as Protector of Peru and departed. In February 1824 he sailed for Europe, where he lived most of his life in France. He returned to South America in 1828 hoping to aid in the political consolidation of the new nations, but nothing came of his efforts, and he returned to France in 1829. San Martín died in Boulogne-sur-Mer, France, on August 17, 1850. (Richard Rojas, *San Martín, Knight of the Andes*, 1945.)

Michael Dennis

SAN REMO AGREEMENT OF 1920. British foreign policy interests centered increasingly on the Middle East in the years immediately following World War I*. Of particular interest to the British government was the retention of Mesopotamia in the form of a British-dominated Arab state in order to prevent the incursion of any other great power into the Persian Gulf area, thus creating a possible future threat to India. An international meeting was convened at San Remo, on the Italian Riviera, to decide the future of the former territories and other possessions of the defeated Ottoman Empire. The conference, held from April 19 to April 26, 1920, was attended by Prime Minister David Lloyd-George of Britain, French Prime Minister Alexandre Millerand, and Prime Minister Francesco Nitti representing Italy. An American representative was present only as an observer, and the representatives of Greece and Belgium took part only when the specific interests of their respective countries were discussed.

The conference considered several questions: a peace treaty with Turkey and the assignment of League of Nations* mandates in the Arab countries; Germany's fulfillment of the military articles of the Versailles Peace Treaty of 1919; and the position of the Allies toward Soviet Russia. The San Remo agreement, signed by the delegates on April 26, 1920, awarded Great Britain the mandates in Palestine* and Iraq*, including Mosul, and awarded France the mandates in

Syria* and Lebanon*. Great Britain guaranteed France 25 percent of the oil production from Mosul, and France promised to ensure the delivery of oil to the Mediterranean. The draft peace agreement with Turkey approved at the conference was the basis for the Treaty of Sevres of 1920*. The conference also demanded that Germany meet the military reduction and reparation stipulations of the Versailles Treaty. On the Russian question, the conference adopted a resolution in favor of restoring trade with the Soviet Russian government. (Max Beloff, *Imperial Sunset*, Vol. I, 1970; W. N. Medlicott, *British Foreign Policy Since Versailles, 1919–1963*, 1968; F. S. Northedge, *The Troubled Giant: Britain Among the Great Powers, 1916–1939*, 1966.)

William G. Ratliff

SANTA MARTA-RIO HACHA. Spanish conquistadores founded the settlement of Santa Marta in northern Colombia* in 1525, with Rodrigo de Bastidas as the first governor. Santa Marta then became the base of operations for the conquest expeditions into New Granada and was an important export point for Peruvian bullion headed for Spain. After 1600 the colony was referred to as Santa Marta-Rio Hacha. When the wars for independence accelerated, Santa Marta-Rio Hacha long remained under Spanish control and was the seat of the viceroy of New Granada after 1810. In 1821, however, when Spanish authority evaporated, Santa Marta-Rio Hacha became part of Gran Colombia and then later of the republic of Colombia. See COLOMBIA.

SÃO JORGE DA MINA. Convinced that substantial gold deposits existed on the Gold Coast* of West Africa, Portugal established a post there in 1482, naming the settlement São Jorge de Mina. It proved to be a misguided investment, at least in terms of mining possibilities. São Jorge da Mina declined in significance, especially in the seventeenth century when French and Dutch competition began undermining the limited markets which did exist there. The Dutch seized São Jorge da Mina in 1637 and the Portuguese then lost their foothold completely on the Gold Coast. See GOLD COAST.

SÃO JOSÉ DO RIO NEGRO. Until the Treaty of Madrid* of 1750, both Spain* and Portugal* had extensive claims to the same territory in the Amazon River Valley. The treaty settled some of those claims, but the boundaries were imprecise and both countries set out to firm up their claims. In 1757, Portugal created a new colony—São José do Rio Negro—and placed its capital at Manaus, Brazil*. The colony received its first governor in 1758 but remained subordinate to Grão-Pará* until 1822. When the new empire of Brazil was established in 1822, the colony was discontinued, the only colonial province not to be retained. See BRAZIL.

SÃO PAULO. São Vicente* was a captaincy of Brazil*, with its capital city at Santos. But as the southern coastal areas of Brazil developed rapidly in the late seventeenth and early eighteenth centuries, São Paulo assumed greater importance. The capital of São Vicente was moved to São Paulo in 1681. In 1710 a number of older donatárias—including São Vicente, Santo Amaro, and Itanhaêm—reverted to the Portuguese crown and together with a huge section of interior highlands of Brazil became the new province of São Paulo e Minas do Ouro. Subsequent gold and diamond discoveries in the highlands created a rush of population settlement and resulted in the establishment of the new interior provinces of Minas Gerais*, Goiás*, and Mato Grosso*. São Paulo became part of the empire of Brazil in 1822. See BRAZIL.

SÃO TOMÉ AND PRÍNCIPE. São Tomé and Príncipe are two small islands of 333 square miles and 39 square miles respectively, located in the Gulf of Guinea approximately 225 miles off the west coast of Gabon*. Portuguese navigators first reached the islands in 1471 as part of Prince Henry's exploring crusade down the west coast of Africa. In 1485 the Portuguese crown awarded a *donatario* (a proprietary concession) over São Tomé to João da Paiva. Over the years the islands were settled by a variety of people. More than 2,000 Jewish children were relocated there in 1493 during the great anti-Semitic pogroms in Spain* and Portugal*. Portugal also regularly deported criminals to São Tomé and Príncipe. Finally, African slaves were imported to work the sugar plantations, which became very profitable early in the 1500s. The Portuguese crown formally assumed sovereignty over São Tomé in 1522 and Príncipe in 1573. The population of São Tomé and Príncipe became a racially mixed group over the years.

São Tomé and Príncipe remained Portuguese colonies until 1975. In the nineteenth century coffee and cocoa production had displaced sugar as the colony's principal products, but natives of the islands began to feel exploited by the Portuguese. Periodic eruptions of labor violence between plantation laborers and Portuguese soldiers protecting the interests of Portuguese landlords occurred throughout the nineteenth and twentieth centuries. In 1953 one episode left more than 1,000 workers dead. The Committee for the Liberation of São Tomé and Príncipe was organized by native nationalists in 1960 but had to function in exile in Gabon because of Portuguese opposition. Later renamed the Movement for the Liberation of São Tomé and Príncipe (MLSTP), the group gained Portuguese recognition in 1974. By that time the last vestiges of the once proud Portuguese empire were disintegrating. Portugal granted São Tomé and Príncipe independence as a single nation on July 12, 1975, and Manuel Pinto da Costa, head of the MLSTP, became president. (David Abshire and Michael A. Samuels, eds., *Portuguese Africa: A Handbook*, 1969; Francisco Teneiro, *A Ilha de São Tomé*, 1961.)

SÃO VICENTE AND ITANHAÊM. The first Portuguese settlement in Brazil* began in São Vicente in 1532, and the *donatária* of São Vicente also held the neighboring *donatárias* of Santo Amaro, Santana, and Itamaraca. Itanham, for the most part a *donátaria* on paper only, was always closely linked with São Vicente, usually with the same *capitae-more* administering it. The Sao Vicente *donátarias* were sold back to the Portuguese crown in 1710 and they were all integrated into the province of Sao Paulo* e Minas do Ouro. The *donátaria* of Itanhaêm was purchased by the Portuguese crown in 1755 and integrated into São Paulo. See BRAZIL.

SARAWAK. Sarawak, with more than 50,000 square miles of jungle and swamp on the northwest coast of Borneo*, is the largest state in Malaysia*. It borders Indonesian Kalimantan, the independent sultanate of Brunei, and the other East Malaysian state, Sabah, and has a long coastline on the South China Sea. There is no reliable census but the population of Sarawak is thought to be about 30% Iban, 30% Chinese, 20% Malay, with the remainder divided between small numbers of Europeans in the towns and primitive tribes in the interior. Sarawak is underdeveloped by modern standards. There is only one short highway and no railway. The capital and main port, Kuching, lies twenty miles from the sea on the Sarawak River. The only way to reach the interior is by river boat or airplane. Much of the territory has not yet been thoroughly prospected, but there are known coalfields and deposits of bauxite and gold. An oil refinery at Miri, near the border with Brunei*, is almost played out, but offshore wells are being drilled. The true wealth of Sarawak lies in its equatorial rain forest. Parts of the territory receive 200 inches of rain per year.

The history of Sarawak is particularly interesting because of the unique role played by the "white rajas"—the Brooke family that ruled Sarawak for a century. James Brooke moved into practically virgin territory when he arrived off the coast of Borneo in 1839. The young adventurer, filled with imperial dreams, had used his inheritance to buy a 142-ton schooner. Sarawak was under the nominal "control" of the sultan of Brunei, but in fact local tribes had nearly complete autonomy. Brooke helped the sultan of Brunei suppress a rebellion, and in return was named raja (governor) of Sarawak, which was understood then to include only a small area around the mouth of the Sarawak River. Brooke and his successors enlarged their realm by successive treaties of 1861, 1882, 1885, 1890 and 1905. Each time the Brookes paid the sultan an annual pension greater than he had been getting from local chiefs. The result was that Sarawak grew huge while Brunei declined to insignificant size.

To put James Brooke's rule in its best light, he suppressed piracy along the coast and extinguished head-hunting among the interior tribes. He established a stable government, with Malay and Iban advisers. When Brooke offered Sarawak to Great Britain but was refused (1843), he ruled as a traditional Bornean potentate, administering personal justice and remaining personally accessible to "his" people. Brooke was always controversial at home, and although knighted in 1848, he had to endure parliamentary inquiries into his unorthodox personal imperialism. Brooke encouraged Chinese to come to Sarawak until an 1857 incident in which he escaped with his life from a nighttime raid by Chinese rebels only by diving into the river, hiding behind a barge, and swimming to the other shore. He returned to England six years later, leaving Sarawak to his nephew, Charles Johnson, who took the surname Brooke and was crowned the second white raja upon Sir James' death in 1868. Sarawak had already been recognized as an independent state by the United States and Great Britain.

Sir Charles Brooke (knighted 1888) ruled Sarawak for half a century, continuing his uncle's paternalism. He worried that the Iban language, which he spoke, and customs, which he respected, might be destroyed by modernity. The Brookes did not allow large-scale plantation agriculture but did permit Chinese immigrants to engage in commerce and grow some cash crops, including pepper, sago flour, and rubber. Sir Charles' domestic policy of benign neglect contrasted with his aggressive expansion of Sarawak's boundaries in all directions. He negotiated a treaty with Great Britain in 1888 by which the Crown assumed responsibility for Sarawak's defense but left internal matters up to Brooke. He permitted Anglican and Catholic missionary schools, and in 1902 established state primary schools for Malays and Chinese.

As Charles Brooke advanced in years he turned day-to-day government over to his son, Charles Vyner Brooke, who reigned as the third Raja Brooke from 1917 to 1946. His heart seemed not to be in it, but he conscientiously tried to prepare Sarawak for independence. His plan to proclaim a constitution was aborted by the Japanese occupation (1941–1945) and after the war he simply gave Sarawak to Great Britain and went into retirement. The three Brookes' legacy to modern Sarawak is mixed. By allowing only the most measured intrusions of modernity they spared Sarawakians the terrible social disruption common to other parts of Asia. On the other hand, most people in Sarawak are uneducated and poorly prepared to deal with the problem of how to earn a livelihood after the jungle is cut down, which may not be long, given present logging practices.

Sarawak gained a written constitution in 1956. It united with Malaya and Sabah to create Malaysia in 1963. Loss of separate Sarawakian identity was not universally popular. There was some political turmoil until 1970, revolving around questions of land use and communal rights. Sarawak today is still thinly populated and resource-rich, a frontier zone for Malaysia. (Robert Milne, *Malaysia: New State in a New Nation*, 1974; Robert Pringle, *Rajahs and Rebels: The Ibans of Sarawak Under Brooke Rule, 1841–1941*, 1970.)

Ross Marlay

SAUDI ARABIA. Saudi Arabia, the largest country on the Arabian Peninsula, has been home for nomadic Semitic tribes for thousands of years. Except for the cities of Mecca and Medina, which are spiritual centers for Muslims, Saudi Arabia had little geographical significance until the nineteenth century. The Saud family conquered Mecca and the surrounding area of Hejaz early in the 1800s, forcing out the Ottoman rulers, but Egyptian soldiers, fighting on behalf of the Ottomans, retook the area in 1819. The Turks withdrew in 1840 and bitter civil wars raged throughout Arabia, with the Saud family fleeing to Kuwait*.

But in 1901 Ibn Saud came out of Kuwait with his own army and conquered

Riyadh. By 1911 he had brought much of the peninsula under his control. The British, interested in political stability along the Red Sea and the commercial routes to India, signed a treaty of protection with Ibn Saud in 1915, gaining the authority to direct Saudi Arabian foreign relations in return for an annual subsidy paid to the Saud family. Between 1915 and 1925 Ibn Saud pacified other areas not yet under control, entering Jiddah in triumph on December 23, 1925. On May 27, 1927, the the British recognized Saudi Arabia as a sovereign, independent nation, nullifying the 1915 agreement. All of the major regions were integrated into the Kingdom of Saudi Arabia on September 22, 1932. (Willard Beling, *King Faisal and the Modernization of Saudi Arabia*, 1980; Richard H. Sanger, *The Arabian Peninsula*, 1954.)

SELANGOR. Selangor was an independent sultanate located between Perak* and Negri Sembilan* on the Malay Peninsula. In 1874 the sultan of Selangor signed a protectorate treaty with Great Britain, and in 1895 Selangor became one of the Federated Malay States*. See MALAYSIA.

SENEGAL. Precolonial Senegal can be described as the area around the valley of the Senegal River inhabited by the Wolof, Seres, and Toucouleur peoples who migrated to the region from the northeastern Sahara between the tenth and fifteenth centuries. Before the great Mali empire occupied most of Senegal in the thirteenth century, the Tekrur empire was the predominant state in the area. Later three Wolof states rose to control Senegal: Djolof, dominant in the fourteenth century, and Kayor and Boal, powerful during the sixteenth and seventeenth centuries.

The Portuguese arrived at Cape Verde* off the coast of Senegal in 1455, and soon began to explore the mainland. Senegal and Gambia* became major suppliers of slaves to Europe during the sixteenth and seventeenth centuries. By this time the Dutch, French, and English had entered the region and a militant revival of Islam throughout the Western Sahara had begun. The French obtained control of most of the Senegal coast when they established a fort at Saint Louis in 1659 and took Gorree from the Dutch in 1677. Meanwhile the British established themselves to the south along the Gambia River. Although rivals for the slave trade and gold, neither France nor England were strong enough to monopolize the region entirely or to expand into the Senegalese interior, which remained under the control of Africans.

Beginning in 1776 Muslim Tukolors in the northwest established a theocratic oligarchy throughout the region. The Islamic jihad, led by Muslim warrior al Haj Umar Tall, challenged the French in the 1850s. In defeating Umar, the French, under the command of Louis Faidherbe, extended their influence up the Senegal River to Bakel. Umar's successor, Ma Ba, reunited most of Senegal, including Djolof and Kayor, against the French intrusion. But after building several more forts throughout the interior of Senegal, the French were finally able to vanquish the Islamic resistance with their victory over the Wolof in 1886.

French rule in Senegal was more democratic than in other French colonies. Africans born in the major cities of Dakar, Gorree, Rufisque, and Saint Louis were granted French citizenship. They could vote and hold elected offices. The urban Senegalese had their own territorial assembly, municipal councils, and a representative who sat in the French chamber of deputies in Paris. In 1895 French West Africa—which included French Sudan*, Mauritania*, French Guinea*, Ivory Coast*, Niger*, Senegal, and Dahomey*—was created and its capital was in Dakar. Rural Senegelese were made subjects of the French imperialists and did not enjoy the privilege of participating in electoral politics. Instead, the rural population was ruled autocratically by French commandants. In 1914 the election of Blaise Diagne, a colonial customs official who favored France's assimilation policy, to the French parliament marked the beginning of black African leadership in Senegal. By 1920 black Africans held most local elective offices, and the territorial assembly was expanded to include chiefs from rural Senegal. Peanuts became the major cash crop of Senegal and established the colony as the wealthiest in West Africa. However, the colonial subjects in rural Senegal benefited very little from the peanut industry. Other food crops were underdeveloped. Farmers went into debt, and regions of Senegal that could not produce peanuts were neglected. The Great Depression of the 1930s devastated rural Senegal as peanut prices fell.

In 1936 the socialist-led Popular Front government was established in France, and new laws restricting forced labor in the colonies and granting the Africans the right to organize trade unions were passed. Reform in the colonies was brought to a halt during World War II*. The next step towards Senegalese independence did not come until 1946 when four reforms were adopted: abolition of forced labor, elimination of the distinction between citizen and subject status, extension of suffrage and representation in assemblies, and the creation of the Economic and Social Development Investment Fund. In 1948 Senegal's deputy to the French parliament, Leopold Sedar Senghor, disappointed with the administration's policy of assimilation and its failure to accept African tradition, founded the *Bloc Democratique Senegalese* (BDS), with most of its support coming from the rural Senegalese peasantry. During the 1950s Senghor and the BDS began to dominate African politics in Senegal. However, the French capitalists still controlled the peanut-based economy.

As a result of the French *Loi-Cadre** of 1956, the territorial assemblies of Senegal and other colonies were given broadened powers, and universal suffrage was established in 1957. Charles de Gaulle, who appreciated that time was running short for colonialism, came to power in France in 1958 as a consequence of the failure of previous French governments to resolve the Algerian dilemma. In a referendum on the new French constitution that same year, De Gaulle allowed French colonies around the world to choose their future course—with or without France. Senegal and most of the French African territories rejected immediate independence (Guinea* was the exception) and accepted the status of autonomous republics within the French Community*. In April 1959 Senegal joined with

Sudan* to form the Federation of Mali. On June 20, 1960, the Mali Federation, at its request, was granted complete sovereignty within the French Community. Eight weeks later political disagreements between Senegal and the Sudanese Republic caused the Federation to break apart. On August 20, 1960, Senegal became an independent republic; Leopold Senghor became the first president of Senegal. (Michael Crowder, *Colonial West Africa*, 1978; Sheldon Gellar, *Senegal: A Nation Between Islam and the West*, 1982.)

Karen Sleezer

SENEGAMBIA. Senegambia was the first British crown colony in Africa. In 1758 the British occupied the French colony of Senegal*, and gave administrative authority over the region to the Royal African Company until 1765. That year Great Britain incorporated the area, along with its forts on the Gambia River, into the colony of Senegambia. The first governor—Charles O'Hara—arrived in 1765. French forces retook Senegal in 1778, and the Treaty of Paris* of 1783 confirmed Britain's control only over the Gambia River forts. The last British governor had already left the region in 1779. (David P. Henige, *Colonial Governors from the Fifteenth Century to the Present*, 1970.)

SEPOY MUTINY OF 1857. Possibly the most written-about event in Indian history is the uprising of 1857. Interpretations of the upheaval reflect a wide diversity of opinion: was it a military mutiny or national revolt? Was it a Russian plot, a Muslim conspiracy, or a Brahmanical protest movement? Or was the war of 1857 the result of a social revolution, reacting to capitalism (the last gasp of the ancient regime)? According to early Marxist analyses, 1857 was a "national war of liberation." Regardless of the interpretation, the events of 1857, especially the much-publicized massacres of English women and children, generated a deep, irrational fear among the British in India* and left a legacy of racism which conditioned British attitudes toward India and its people well into the twentieth century.

There is no single explanation for the rebellion. The upheavals reflect cumulative tensions which had built up during nearly a century of interaction between western influences and Indian society. This tension unfolded during a period of British political consolidation in the first half of the nineteenth century. India was also subjected to an ideological onslaught between 1800 and 1850 which had profound effects on relations between the British Raj and Indian society. Finally, urbanization and modernization played key roles in precipitating the violence.

Following a series of frontier wars in the first part of the nineteenth century, the British eventually gained control of roughly two-thirds of the Indian subcontinent. The significance of the territorial conquests lay in the fact that additional funds were required to police and administer the new areas. The British East India Company* effected several plans to raise revenue, including seizure of land from Indian princes under the "doctrine of lapse," centered around

British insistence that only "natural" heirs could inherit land or it reverted to the company. This action, and the elimination of long-standing privy purses to a number of princes, led to disaffection among this segment of the elite.

India was also subjected to three important western ideologies carried to India. Evangelicalism made its way to India in the early nineteenth century as the company policy of limiting missionary activity slowly eroded. The evangelical impulse spurred an active intrusion in socio-religious spheres, particularly of Hindus, where a spate of legislative acts directed at Hindu social practices (e.g., suttee, thugee, etc.) upset many orthodox Hindus. Utilitarian ideals were carried to India by individuals like Thomas Babington Macaulay and William Bentinck, who felt that English law, language, and education were best suited for Indians. Finally, the steady gains of free trade, laissez-faire liberalism in England had a marked effect on the monopoly of the East India Company. With each charter renewal (1813, 1833, 1853), the company lost more of its monopoly of Indian and Chinese trade, and new traders to India had less empathy or understanding of Indian affairs, which often led to tensions.

India was also subjected to an array of modernizing efforts in the first part of the nineteenth century. The penny post came to India, and an extensive program of railways and telegraph building provided India with a modern communication and transportation infrastructure. Moreover, large areas of northwest India were brought under cultivation with construction of government public works. These innovations, however, cost money, and efforts to raise revenue contributed, in part, to the upheavals of 1857 by angry landlords and peasants. Finally, British military reforms contributed to the war of 1857. The General Services Enlistment Act required Indian soldiers to serve overseas, while the introduction of the breechloading Enfield rifle*, which required greased cartridges, precipitated much anxiety by both Muslims and Hindus fearful of pollution by either pork or cow fat respectively.

The bloody uprising of the British East India Company's sepoys at Meerut, in the North-West Provinces on Sunday, May 10, 1857, came as a complete surprise to the British. Most British officers were blind to the unrest created, in part, by the rapid imposition of direct British control over two-thirds of India. Even at the time of the outbreak, British officers were boasting among themselves about the loyalty of their troops. The Sepoy Mutiny was the most serious threat to British authority yet encountered, but it cannot be considered a general nationalistic uprising. Most of the trouble was confined to the Punjab, the Ganges valley, and central India. As a consequence of the uprising, the British government would take permanent control of India in 1858 and assert rights over India far greater than those the company had exercised prior to 1858. The bloody mutiny at the garrison in Meerut in May 1857 caught the British completely off guard. Once the mutineers murdered every European they could lay their hands on, they marched to Delhi and placed themselves under the leadership of the impotent and bewildered Moghul Emperor Bahadur Shah. Throughout May and June the mutiny spread through the Ganges valley. By June Cawnpore had

surrendered to Nana Sahib, and Lucknow, the only British-held outpost in Oudh,*
was besieged. On July 17, 1857, it was discovered by British troops that 200
British men, women, and children had been murdered at Cawnpore, and venge-
ance was exacted on the Indian population. Suspected mutineers were usually
tied to cannon and executed. In six months the mutiny had been broken, and
within the next year British power was restored. Remarkably, the majority of
Indians displayed no ill will toward the British, and even protected endangered
civilians. Most of the Indian princes also remained aloof from the rebellion. It
is therefore difficult to view the uprising as a nationalist event.

In England public opinion tended to place the blame on the East India Company. On February 12, 1858, a new India Bill was proposed before parliament,
out of which came the Government of India Act of 1858*. This act turned control
of India over to the British government. The Crown gradually asserted much
greater control over India than the company had claimed. The British government
not only controlled India's foreign policy but also asserted the right to direct
internal affairs as well. By guaranteeing their thrones, the British secured the
loyalty of the princes even though the British policy of paramountcy, or overlordship, stripped Indian royalty of any real power. (C. E. Carrington, *The British
Overseas: Exploits of a Nation of Shopkeepers*, 1968; A. T. Embree, *1857 in
India: Mutiny or War of Independence*, 1963; T. R. Metcalf, *The Aftermath of
Revolt in 1857*, 1964.)

Arnold P. Kaminsky

SERGIPE D'EL REI. In 1590 settlers from Bahia* in Brazil* began moving
to northeastern Brazil and settling the area of Sergipe. Except for the period of
Dutch occupation between 1633 and 1648, Sergipe d'el Rei was governed by a
capitae-more who reported to Bahia. Sergipe d'el Rei was raised to a separate
province in 1821—the last new province in colonial Brazil—and in 1822 it
became a province of the new empire of Brazil. See BRAZIL.

SEVEN YEARS' WAR. See TREATY OF PARIS OF 1763.

SEYCHELLES. The Seychelles are a group of one hundred islands located
northeast of Madagascar in the Indian Ocean. The major islands in the group
are Mahe, Praslin, Silhouette, and La Digue. Portuguese sailors first sighted the
islands in the 1490s, but the first Europeans to land there were English traders
from the British East India Company* in 1609. Except for pirates hiding out
there, the islands were uninhabited. Afraid the British might take permanent
control, the French sent an exploring party there in 1742 under the command
of Lazare Picault. France made formal claim to the islands in 1756, and French
settlers colonized it in 1770. They soon brought in West African slaves to work
their plantations, and by 1800 there were 2,000 people living in the Seychelles.

The Seychelles remained under French control until the Napoleonic Wars
altered their status. When France surrendered, the Treaty of Paris in 1814 shifted

the Seychelles from French to English jurisdiction. Gradually the English introduced a degree of self-government. In 1872 a board of civil commissioners, appointed by parliament but composed of natives, gained jurisdiction over a variety of internal affairs, and in 1888 England established an appointed legislature and executive council. The Seychelles became a crown colony in 1903.

In the 1960s the movement to gain independence became more and more vocal. The left-wing Seychelles People's United Party, as well as the more moderate Seychelles Democratic Party, demanded independence. England approved a new constitution in 1970, complete with greater control over internal government, universal suffrage, and an elected legislature. Elections that year gave power to the Seychelles Democratic Party, whose leader, James R. Mancham, headed the government. On June 29, 1976, England granted the Seychelles its independence. (J. T. Bradley, *The History of the Seychelles*, 1940; Guy Lionnet, *The Seychelles*, 1972.)

SHARJAH. See UNITED ARAB EMIRATES.

SHEEP. Although slower to adapt to the environs of the New World and Australia than horses and cattle, sheep were nevertheless one of the most important biological entities in European imperialism. Sheep ranching was a key industry in fifteenth-century Spain, and in 1493 Columbus* brought sheep with him to the New World. Sheep did not do well in the Caribbean or in the wet lowlands of Brazil nor, like pigs and horses, did they do well on their own in the wild. But in Mexico and Peru, the sheep industry provided meat and wool to the colonial economy. Beginning in 1535 Antonio de Mendoza, the viceroy of New Spain*, imported high quality sheep, and by 1580 there were more than 200,000 head there. Sheep ranching also did well in the Peruvian highlands, northern Chile, and northern Argentina. And when the British reached Australia and New Zealand in the late eighteenth and early nineteenth centuries, sheep production boomed, becoming central to the colonial economy. In the presence of the sheep, native animals like the llama and alpaca declined rapidly in population and economic significance. (Alfred W. Crosby, Jr., *The Columbian Exchange. Biological and Cultural Consequences of 1492*, 1972.)

SIAM. Traditional name for modern Thailand. The name "Siam" was changed to "Thailand," meaning "land of the free," in a burst of nationalism in 1939. It was changed back to "Siam" from 1945 to 1949. The country has officially been named the Kingdom of Thailand since 1949.

Ross Marlay

SIERRA LEONE. Sierra Leone is located on the coastal "bulge" of West Africa, bordered by Liberia* and Guinea*. With the exception of the mountainous peninsula that marks the mouth of the Rokel River, the site of Freetown, Sierra Leone's coastal areas consist of a fairly narrow band of swamplands, which give way to plains, which in turn rise to an eastern region of plateaus. The latter are occasionally broken by hill and mountain areas, including Loma Mansa, West Africa's highest point, at 6,390 feet. The climate is tropical, with a single rainy season occurring between May and November—average rainfall is about 100 inches a year, although up to 200 inches per year may fall on the coast. The current population of around 4 million is divided into some eighteen different ethnic groups, the largest of which are the Mende and the Temne, who each comprise around 30 percent of the total population. The important Creoles, discussed below, make up no more than 2 percent of the country's people.

Sierra Leone got its name from the Portuguese, who began to explore the western coast of Africa in the mid-fifteenth century, in their bid to reach India and who thought that the abruptly appearing mountains of the peninsula cited above looked like lions—hence it was called "Serra Lyoa," or Lion Mountain. This name evolved into "Sierra Leone," and eventually was applied to the surrounding areas as well. The Portuguese and other Europeans established a few trading posts to exchange goods with the small African kingdoms in the coastal areas, such as the several "factories" (run by a representative or "factor") established by British and French trading companies in the mid–1600s. The commodity desired by the traders soon became people, however, as the Atlantic slave trade began. Sierra Leone was to supply slaves for 300 years.

Prior to the American Revolution, a number of blacks had been brought as slaves to England from the Western Hemisphere. A test case arranged by English abolitionist Granville Sharp in 1772 led to a decision by Lord Chief Justice Mansfield that Africans could not be held in slavery on English soil, which led to the creation of a group of people in England known as the "Black Poor," who were no longer slaves but were generally unemployed. Sharp organized a colonization effort which received British government support, and which resulted in the arrival of around 400 Black Poor and a few Europeans on the Sierra Leone Peninsula in 1787, with the objective of founding a self-governing colony. Sharp supplied a democratic constitution for the new colony, which he named the "Province of Freedom." With the help of the British naval escort, arrangements were made with the local chief to allow the settlers to use much of the peninsula, in return for goods worth 59 pounds sterling. A treaty the following year with the king of the regional Temne state led to the "sale" of the area to the settlers, although it is rather unlikely that the Africans really understood what the settlers had in mind with their request for a permanent "purchase" of land. Disease, lack of experience in agriculture, and conflict with the African tribes in the area led to the demise of Sharp's experiment in 1789 when the settlement at Granville Town was destroyed by an angry local chief.

In 1791 the settlement was reestablished with about 50 survivors of the original 411 settlers, although this time the funds and directions came from a trading company, the Sierra Leone Company. The company, which included Sharp and abolitionist spokesman William Wilberforce among its directors, attempted to combine business and philanthropy. In 1792, after rebuilding Granville Town and renaming it "Freetown," the struggling settlers were joined by about 1,000 "Nova Scotians." These newcomers were former American slaves who had joined the Loyalist cause during the American Revolution (spurred by the promise of freedom), and who had been evacuated to Canada at the end of the conflict. Tired of broken promises of land from the British in Canada, the black Loyalists sent an ex-British army sergeant and escaped slave named Thomas Peters to England as their spokesman. He contacted the Sierra Leone Company, and was offered the chance to send his people "back" to Africa. These hardy new settlers saved the colony, although the settlement faced many other problems, such as conflict with the local Temne kingdom, and the unanticipated attack and subsequent sack of Freetown by a French naval squadron in 1794. The town was once more rebuilt, and in 1800 the struggling colony was again rescued by newcomers, in the form of 550 additional black settlers, called "Maroons," who came from Jamaica. The Maroons were a well-organized community of escaped slaves who had managed to maintain their independence in the mountains of Jamaica* for 130 years after the British took the island over from the Spanish. One group surrendered in 1796, and ended up in Sierra Leone four years later, when they arrived just in time to save the company representatives from a revolt by the Nova Scotians. Although distinctions between the three groups of settlers were initially significant, they eventually blurred, and the "Creole" segment of the population of Sierra Leone evolved. This group of people were culturally very distinct from the native African inhabitants of the area.

The Sierra Leone Company kept losing money, and handed its settlement over to the British government in 1807, effective the following year when it became a crown colony. The British parliament also outlawed the slave trade in 1807, and sent a naval unit to West Africa, headquartered in Freetown, to enforce the law and intercept slave ships. When captured, these ships were taken to Freetown. The cargo of newly freed slaves was then released in the colony, where they became known as "recaptives." The ships were sold at auctions, which attracted buyers and generally enhanced the prominent position of the colony in British West Africa* during the mid-nineteenth century. By the time the anti-slavery patrol ended in 1870, over 70,000 recaptives had been released in Freetown. Although many died of disease or injuries suffered in their enslavement, and a few managed to return to their original homelands, most remained in Sierra Leone, and the more successful eventually became part of the Creole culture.

During the last half of the nineteenth century the Creoles attained a very prominent position in many parts of West Africa, thanks in part to their stress on education, and the reputation of the area as the "white man's graveyard," which discouraged European colonial administrators and settlers alike. When the Anglican Church, for example, removed its foreign clergy in 1861, the priesthood became completely Creole. The Anglicans had a major role in establishing educational institutions for the African population, such as Fourah Bay College, which was founded in 1814, and was the sole source of African university training in the continent until 1918. In addition, Creoles sat on executive councils and supreme courts of Gambia*, Nigeria*, and the Gold Coast*. One was even elected president of neighboring Liberia*—Charles D. B. King.

Contacts between the colony on the coast and the interior gradually increased through the nineteenth century, thanks to the efforts of traders and missionaries alike. Their pressures on the British colonial government to expand the colony's territory inland were met initially with official reluctance to add to the cost of administration. This attitude eventually changed, owing to concerns about French efforts to expand French West Africa* in the area, and a British protectorate was established over the interior areas in 1896. An attempt to resist the colonization move erupted two years later among the Temne and Mende, but was crushed in six months. This was the last serious challenge to British rule, and the colony and protectorate remained intact until the rise of African nationalism led to the transition to independence in the post-World War II era. The discovery and exploitation of major diamond and iron ore resources, starting in the 1930s, helped the colonial service toward its objective of making Sierra Leone a self-sustaining colony. In 1961 Sir Milton Margai, leader of the Mende-based Sierra Leone People's Party (SLPP), became independent Sierra Leone's first prime minister. The country became a republic, headed by a president, in 1971. (J. R. Cartwright, *Politics in Sierra Leone, 1947–67*, 1970; C. F. Fyfe, *A History of Sierra Leone*, 1962.)

Charles W. Hartwig

SIMLA CONFERENCE OF 1945. In the last year of World War II, British policy in India focused largely on the impending move for Indian independence. After conciliation talks between Mohandas Gandhi* and Muslim leader Mohammad Jinnah* failed, the British government assumed the task of bringing together the disparate religious factions in India. The immediate problem was appointment of Indian ministers to the cabinet of viceroy and governor-general Field Marshal Viscount Archibald Wavell. Following a visit to London for consultation with the British cabinet on June 14, 1945, Wavell proposed that all Indian cabinet portfolios, except for that of minister of war, should be transferred to Indian hands. The cabinet positions opened to Indians included the ministries of home and finance, and external affairs. The Wavell plan also allowed for the appointment of fully accredited diplomatic representatives abroad, and was intended to promote India's position as an independent international actor. In selecting his council, Wavell promised to secure a balanced representation of the main Indian communities, including equal proportions of Muslims and Hindus. The governor-general's executive would thus be made representative of organized Indian political opinion. If these proposals were agreed to by the Indian political leaders, ministerial government, suspended since the war, would be resumed on a coalition basis in the provinces.

On his return to India, Wavell called a round table conference of 21 representatives of the Indian political parties at Simla to discuss his plan. The Simla

Conference delegates, meeting on June 25, 1945, were expected to submit lists of names from which the viceroy would choose his ministers. After protracted discussions, however, the conference dissolved when Jinnah, head of the Muslim League*, refused to submit a list of nominees without a guarantee that all the Muslim members would come from his organization. This was a condition unacceptable to the rest of the conferees. The Hindu delegates especially feared Muslim League domination of the cabinet. The failure of the Simla Conference to reach an accomodation on representation helped postpone eventual transferral of governmental authority from Great Britain to India. (M. E. Chamberlain, *Britain and India: The Interaction of Two Peoples*, 1974; Stanley Wolpert, *A New History of India*, 1977.)

William G. Ratliff

SIMONSTOWN AGREEMENT OF 1921. A strategic anchorage on the eastern side of the Cape Peninsula, thirty miles south of Cape Town, Simonstown was occupied by the British navy in June 1795 when British forces invaded the Cape region. As the main naval base in southern Africa, vital to the protection of trans-Cape of Good Hope trade routes, Simonstown retained its importance even after the opening of the Suez Canal* in 1869. British naval and land forces maintained defense of the port until the end of World War I. In 1921 the British government, mindful of Commonwealth defense policy and intent on reducing military expenditures, signed an agreement with South Africa* regarding control over the strategic base. In the Simonstown Agreement of 1921, Britain gave up control of the Simonstown naval installations in return for a South African guarantee to defend it with land and air forces and to make it available to the British navy in case of hostilities with a third power. The agreement was in force even if South Africa was not engaged as a belligerent. In addition, South Africa agreed to buy British-made naval vessels. The agreement was abandoned in 1924 when the British Labour government refused to sell weapons of war to South Africa, based upon the latter nation's racial policies. From 1921 to 1924 the Simonstown Agreement both signaled increased Commonwealth cooperation and evidenced the desire for greater autonomy among the constituent elements of the British Empire*. (David Austin, *Britain and South Africa*, 1966; Monica Wilson and Leonard Thompson, eds., *The Oxford History of South Africa*, 2 Vols., 1971.)

William G. Ratliff

SIND. Sind is an area in southwestern India* which British India annexed in 1843. A commissioner operating under the supervision of the governor of Bombay* served as chief executive officer. In 1936 the British raised Sind to the status of a separate governor's province. It became part of newly independent India in 1947. See INDIA.

SINGAPORE. Singapore is an island, a city, and a country. It is best thought of as a Chinese city-state incongruously located in the middle of the Malay world. Singapore island is about 27 miles long by 14 miles wide, and is dominated by one big city where most of the country's 2.5 million people live. This tiny, densely populated sovereign state has no resource except a granite quarry, yet is prosperous beyond the dreams of other Southeast Asian countries. Singapore's modernity and wealth stem from the booming colonial economy that grew up under British imperial rule. It had one cardinal virtue: its location at the southern end of the Strait of Malacca, halfway between India and China. It dominated the sea lanes between Asia and the West.

The island may have been settled early, for the old *Malay Chronicles* mention a "Temasek" (Sea Town). The area was controlled, in succession, by the Sumatran Srivijayan empire, the Javanese Majapahit empire, the Malay Malacca sultanate, the Portuguese, and the Dutch. But when Sir Stamford Raffles landed on the swampy island in 1819, only about 200 Malays lived there. Temasek had been renamed "Singapura" (Sanskrit for "Lion City") though no one knows why, since lions are not native to the area. Raffles saw that Singapore could be the foundation on which would rest British maritime domination of all Asia. It would be the most vital link in a chain of ports and bases stretching from Aden to Tientsin.

Raffles wangled a dubious treaty from one claimant to the island and immediately set about building a port city that would function on the basis of completely free trade. Batavia* and Malacca* had for centuries thrived as entrepots in which spices, silks, and other exotic Asian products had been exchanged for goods from India and Europe, but Singapore's spectacular growth put them in the shade. In 1826 the British created the Straits Settlements*, administratively uniting Singapore with Malacca and Penang. Despite its muggy climate, Singapore became the administrative capital for the Straits, and eventually for Malaya and North Borneo.

Raffles encouraged immigration and merchants came to Singapore from all across Asia. The city had neighborhoods for Malays, Javanese, Indians, and Chinese. Sumatrans, Thais, Vietnamese, Buginese, and Achehnese visited too. Europeans, Indians, and Arabs brought their own goods, languages, and religions. Englishmen remained the unchallenged political masters, but Singapore gradually acquired a Chinese character. Men from South China came as merchants, dockworkers, and pepper farmers. If they prospered, they sent home for wives. Chinese coolies built the wharves, bridges, and the railroads that opened the Malayan interior to world capitalism. Chinese laborers dug vast tin mines in Malaya, and cleared jungle for rubber plantations. Speaking different dialects, the Chinese did not form a cohesive social group, but governed themselves through "secret societies" impenetrable to outsiders.

The city's growth slowed after Hong Kong* was founded in 1842, but the opening of the Suez Canal* (1869) stimulated rapid economic development throughout Southeast Asia. Half the world's tin was smelted in Singapore. Rubber was processed there. Banks and trading houses arose. Singapore became the financial and commercial capital of Southeast Asia. The Chinese (75 percent of the population) eschewed politics to concentrate wholly on earning a living. Singapore never had any nationalist or independence movement; politically aware Chinese looked instead to their homeland, and beginning in the 1920s, chose sides between the Communists and the Kuomintang.

When Japan industrialized and built a navy, Britain, fearing for its Asian empire, fortified Singapore. Twenty percent of the colony's revenue went for military defense, but in 1942 Japanese troops invaded down the Malayan peninsula on bicycles. Singapore was vulnerable to assault across the half-mile Strait of Johore and fell on February 15, after a six-day seige. The Japanese planned to make Singapore a key part of their Greater East Asia Co-Prosperity Sphere, but they treated Singaporean Chinese brutally. Singapore welcomed the British back in August 1945. For the next twenty years, developments in Singapore were dictated by the more volatile politics of Malaya.

Malaya was a political hodge-podge of sultanates on which the British imposed limited political unity in the form of a ''Malayan Union'' (1946) that became the ''Federation of Malaya'' (1948). Malays did not agitate strongly for independence, but the British were engaged throughout the 1950s in suppressing a communist insurgency in Malaya confined to the Chinese community there. A gradual transition to separate nationhood was planned for Singapore. Elections in 1955 brought the People's Action Party, purged of radicals, to power. When Malaysia* was created in 1963, Singapore was part of it, but that marriage foundered on racial incompatibility. Malaysia expelled Singapore in 1965. The colonial city became a sovereign republic and a member of the United Nations*.

Independent Singapore continued its tradition of political apathy and single-minded concentration on building fortunes. An austere, honest strongman, Lee Kuan Yew completely dominated the government, which favored free market capitalism alongside generous subsidies for housing and education. Banks, insurance companies, and oil companies made their regional headquarters in Singapore. The government has encouraged manufacturing and electronics. Oil refining is the largest industry. The port of Singapore is still one of the world's busiest. (Stanley Bedlington, *Malaysia and Singapore*, 1978; P. P. Lee, *Chinese Society in Nineteenth-Century Singapore*, 1978.)

Ross Marlay

SINO-JAPANESE WAR OF 1894–1895. After the Meiji Restoration of 1868 Japan emerged from two centuries of feudal isolation anxious to assert herself on the world stage. At the same time China* was acutely vulnerable to foreign exploitation because of massive economic problems and political instability. Following the example of the ''neoimperialist'' Western powers, Japan sought to extend her influence into Korea where China could make only the feeblest attempt to buttress her ancient but by then virtually defunct hegemonial position. The upshot was the Sino-Japanese War of 1894–1895 in which the military and naval forces of China were destroyed. By the Peace Treaty of Shimonoseki on April 17, 1895, China recognized the independence of Korea and surrendered Formosa*, the Pesacadores Islands, and the Liaotung Peninsula to Japan. Amid mounting Western speculation about the new "Yellow Peril," European diplomatic pressure led Japan to abandon her claim to Liaotung.

The interventionist powers then proceeded to exact from China some rich rewards. The French secured extensive commercial and territorial concessions in the southern-most provinces of China on June 20, 1895. Russia took another step in her emerging rivalry with Japan and toward the disastrous armed confrontation of 1904–1905 by concluding with Peking the defensive alliance of June 1896 in return for the right to construct and operate the Chinese Eastern Railway in Manchuria. Also winning new railroad concessions and various other rights in southwestern China were the British, even though they had refused to intervene against Japan over the Treaty of Shimonoseki and thereby took a first step toward the rapprochement that culminated in the Anglo-Japanese Alliance of 1902*.

The German incursion was a milestone only in the limited sense that Berlin demonstrated to the other powers a new diplomatic device; namely, the "lease" agreement, which set a precedent for similar arrangements to be extorted from Peking—by Russia in the southern part of Liaotung Peninsula (March 27, 1898), by France in Kwangchowan Bay and vicinity (April 10, 1898), and by Great Britain in Kowloon (June 9, 1898) and Weihaiwei (July 1, 1898). China had agreed to "lease" Kiaochow* to Germany on March 6, 1898. By these and other agreements Paris, St. Petersburg, Berlin, and London gained further railroad concessions and consolidated their control over their spheres of influence in China. (William Langer, *The Diplomacy of Imperialism, 1890–1902*, 1956.)

Bascom Barry Hayes

SLAVERY. The fortunes of slavery and the fortunes of European imperialism were inextricably linked throughout the sixteenth, seventeenth, eighteenth, and nineteenth centuries. Beginning in the sixteenth century, Portuguese slavers seized Africans and carried them off to Europe, but by the seventeenth century those slaves were headed for the huge Portuguese plantations in Brazil* and the Cape Verde* Islands. The Portuguese monopoly of the Atlantic slave trade gave way to the British monopoly of the Royal African Company, which supplied slaves to the cotton plantations of the American South and the sugar plantations of Danish, Dutch, French, Spanish, and British colonies in the West Indies*. By the time of its abolition in the mid-nineteenth century, the Atlantic slave trade had taken approximately 20 million Africans from their homes in West Africa. Access to slaves was a major source of competition among the European imperial powers.

The Atlantic slave trade was a corrupt business, particularly in its cruel treatment of the slaves. In the late eighteenth century, Quakers in Great Britain and the United States began to call for the abolition of slavery, but powerful economic interests prevented most attempts to outlaw the institution. But the American Revolution* and the French Revolution, with their rhetoric of equality and individual rights, gave the abolition movement a boost. In 1776 Pennsylvania* abolished slavery and several Northern states in the United States soon followed suit.

But it was the slave trade which first fell victim to the ideology of freedom. The death rate among slaves being carried across the Atlantic—the dreaded "Middle Passage"—approached 40 percent, and humanitarian cries for an end to the slave trade, if not slavery itself, became more and more intense. In 1792 Denmark outlawed the slave trade in its colonies in the Virgin Islands*, with the prohibition to go into effect in 1802. The United States and Great Britain outlawed the slave trade in 1807, and Great Britain then assumed the lead in securing the cooperation of the other European powers. Sweden prohibited the slave trade in 1813. At the Congress of Vienna in 1814, the participants stated in principle that the slave trade should be abolished. The Dutch abolished the slave trade that same year. France abolished the traffic in 1818. Spain outlawed the slave trade in 1820 when Great Britain offered her £400,000 in compensation. In return for £300,000 compensation, the Portuguese agreed to cease participating in the slave trade by 1830, and in 1836 Portugal issued a decree prohibiting the export of slaves from any of its possessions. Although an illegal traffic in slaves continued for several decades, it was largely suppressed by the 1860s.

The movement to abolish slavery itself encountered even more opposition. Planters realized that they could probably still survive the elimination of the Atlantic slave trade through the natural reproduction of the existing slave population, but the abolition of slavery altogether posed a real threat to their economic well-being. Nevertheless, the antislavery movement acquired a political momentum in the early 1800s which proved to be unstoppable. Once again, Great Britain led the way, although most Northern states in the United States had already abolished slavery by 1830. In 1833 Great Britain outlawed slavery, providing £20 million sterling to compensate the planters. France did the same in 1848. Portugal began a gradual, twenty-year emancipation process in 1858, and the Dutch launched a similar abolition scheme in 1863. In the United States, the Civil War resulted in the Emancipation Proclamation of 1863 and the outright end of slavery with the Thirteenth Amendment to the Constitution in 1865. Spain lost most of its New World empire in the revolutions of the early 1800s, but in 1886 Spain outlawed slavery in Cuba. Brazil finally eliminated slavery in 1888. Slavery, however, was still a powerful institution in Africa. At the Berlin West Africa Conference of 1884–1885* the European powers pledged to suppress African slavery. They renewed that pledge at the Brussels Conference of 1889–1890*. Gradually during the next fifty years the Europeans fulfilled that pledge. By the 1920s slavery, although certainly not other forms of forced servitude, was largely under control in Africa. (Philip Curtin, *The Atlantic Slave Trade*, 1969; Suzanne Miers and Richard Roberts, eds., *The End of Slavery in Africa*, 1988.)

SMALLPOX. Of all the diseases the Europeans brought with them to the New World, smallpox was the most devastating to the native populations. Because it spread from one victim to another by breath, smallpox was one of the world's most communicable diseases. It was especially deadly among children. Smallpox spread into the Americas in 1519 when it appeared in the West Indies, destroying nearly half of the Arawak population on Hispaniola and Puerto Rico. One of Cortes' soldiers carried it to Mexico. Smallpox reached Peru even before Francisco Pizarro, killing thousands of Incas. Because the disease has an incubation period of fourteen days, it is possible for a healthy person to flee a smallpox-ridden area for safety and carry the disease to another region. For the next 400 years smallpox reduced native populations to sickness and death, paving the way for the triumph of imperial institutions. The English brought the disease to New England in the 1630s, and by the 1640s it had raced through New England, upstate New York, and the Great Lakes region, reducing the population of Amerindians there by half. By the end of the eighteenth century it had spread throughout much of North America. The story was the same throughout the pampas of Argentina and in Brazil. Within a year of the arrival of the English in Australia in 1788, Aborigines were dying of the disease. The pandemic killed fully one third of all Aborigines. It was one of the Europeans' most powerful weapons in establishing their power over colonial peoples. (Alfred W. Crosby, Jr., *Ecological Imperialism. The Biological Expansion of Europe, 900–1900*, 1986.)

SMUTS, JAN CHRISTIAN. Jan Christian Smuts was born on May 24, 1870, in Riebeek West, South Africa*. He attended college at the Victoria College in Stellenbosch and at the University of the Cape of Good Hope. Early in his life Smuts acquired the political loyalties of the Afrikaaner Bond. In 1891 he went to Christ's College, Cambridge University, to study law. Blessed with a keenly analytical mind and excellent work habits, Smuts distinguished himself as one of the best law students in England. Smuts returned to South Africa in 1895 and began practicing law. Politically he supported the imperial aspirations of Cecil Rhodes*. But after the Jameson Raid*, Smuts became an ardent advocate of Afrikaaner nationalism. In 1897 he settled in Johannesburg, where he worked diligently for the independence of the Transvaal* Republic. After service as a prosecuter in Johannesburg, Smuts joined Afrikaaner military forces when the Boer War * erupted. He gained fame in 1901 when he assembled and led a Boer army into the Cape Colony* against British forces.

After the Boer War, Smuts settled in Pretoria to practice law. He stayed out of politics until 1905 when the British tried to Anglicize the schools and import Chinese workers into the colony. Early in 1906 Smuts went to England to campaign for independence for the Transvaal and the Orange River Colony, and he had some success in representing the Afrikaaner position. In 1907 Smuts became colonial secretary in the Transvaal government of Louis Botha*. From that position Smuts worked for the union of the four British colonies in South

Africa. He drafted a constitution for the union government and in that sense became the father of the Union of South Africa. During World War I, Smuts led British forces fighting in German Southwest Africa*, and in 1916 he represented South Africa at the Imperial War Conference in London. At the conference Smuts first proposed a "British Commonwealth"* of free and equal nation states. In 1917 Smuts became a member of the British government's war cabinet. From that position Smuts wrote the plan which evolved into the League of Nations* after the war.

Smuts returned to South Africa in 1919 and after Botha's sudden death he became prime minister. At the Imperial Conference of 1921*, Smuts wrote the memorandum which later became the foundation of the Balfour Declaration and the Statute of Westminster* creating the British Commonwealth. In 1924, after losing reelection, Smuts returned to private life. He spent the next decade in scientific and philosophic pursuits, but in 1933 Smuts reentered the government as minister of justice and deputy prime minister. He became prime minister in 1939 one week after Great Britain declared war on Germany. He became a field marshall in the British army in 1941. Smuts saw South Africa through the war, but in 1948 he was not reelected. Jan Smuts died on September 11, 1950. (W. K. Hancock, *Smuts. Volume I. The Sanguine Years 1870–1919*, 1962, and *Volume 2. The Fields of Force 1919–1950*, 1968.)

SOLOMON ISLANDS. The Solomon Islands form an archipelago in the southwest Pacific Ocean, east of New Guinea*. Eight large islands and island groups arranged in two parallel chains make up the region: islands in the western-most chain include Vella Lavella, Kolombangara, New Georgia*, Guadalcanal, and San Cristobal, while Bougainville, Choiseul, Santa Isabel (Ysabel), and Malaita are to be found in the eastern chain. Economic activity in the Solomons had historically been based upon agriculture, copra and coconuts being the most important crops, but cacao, rubber, timber, rice, bananas, taro, sweet potatoes, and pineapples have also been cultivated.

Melanesians from the Malayo-Asian area arrived in the Solomon Islands in canoes sometime between 2000 and 1000 B.C. Settlers from this racial group colonized the various islands; they formed numerous tribes speaking about 60 different languages, and still comprise a majority of the population of the region. Spaniards were the first Europeans to reach the Solomon Islands. Alvaro de Mendaña de Neyra, in search of the source of King Solomon's wealth, landed at Santa Isabel on February 7, 1568, with 70 soldiers, 4 Franciscan friars, and a number of slaves. He was unable to establish peaceful relations with the natives, and the following August his expedition returned to Peru*. Twenty-seven years later, in 1595, Mendaña returned to the "Islas de Salomon," as he named them, in four ships carrying over 300 colonists. Unable to locate Santa Isabel, this group attempted to settle in the Santa Cruz Island group, which is far to the southeast of the rest of the Solomons and inhabited by a particularly fierce tribe of Melanesians. This fact, combined with disease and general dissatisfaction, led to the abandonment of the project less than two months after its beginning. Pedro de Quiros, who had served in Mendaña's second voyage as chief pilot, reached Taumako in the eastern Solomons in April 1606. He was vainly searching for the legendary Terra Incognita, and eventually made landfall in the New Hebrides*. After his colony there failed, Quiros returned to Peru and brought to an end Spanish interest in the Solomon Islands.

The Solomons were rediscovered by the Europeans late in the following century. An Englishman, Captain Philip Carteret, repaired his leaky vessel in the Santa Cruz Islands sometime in early 1767, but sailed on without making any attempts either to colonize or explore the group. Later that year Louis de Bougainville* discovered, mapped, and named the western Solomons, including Bouganville, Buka, and Choiseul. Several French and English explorers followed Carteret and Bougainville to the Solomons over the next thirty years, but because of the hostility of the natives, no settlements were planted. Throughout the first quarter of the nineteenth century, however, whalers and traders regularly landed in the Solomon Islands, and by 1840, trading schooners from Sydney had established profitable commercial relations with some of the more peaceful islanders. Catholic missionaries arrived at Santa Isabel in 1845 led by Bishop Jean-Baptiste Epalle. Epalle, a man of strong personality and drive, had been hand-picked for the job of converting the Solomon Islanders, who by now had a well-earned reputation for ferocity. The widespread consternation among Catholic officials, therefore, was understandable when Epalle was murdered just two weeks after his arrival in the region. The killing of three more missionaries over the course of the next three years persuaded the Catholic authorities in 1852 to abandon the endeavor.

In 1850, shortly before Catholic missionary attempts came to an end, the Australasian Board of Missions was formed to bring Christianity to all of Melanesia* under the guidance of the Anglican Bishop of New Zealand. The Solomons were first visited in 1851, but little was accomplished on the mission. The Anglican missionaries returned under the leadership of John Patteson in 1856, gathering native boys from the islands of Rennell, San Cristobal, Guadalcanal, Malaita, and the Santa Cruz group. The young natives were taken to New Zealand, educated in Anglican doctrine, and later returned to the Solomons to spread the Christian message among their own people. This policy was immensely successful, but the practice of "blackbirding" eroded the natives' trust in the whites, resulting in the murder of John Patteson in 1871.

The cessation of transporting convicts from Europe to Australia had induced in the region a severe labor shortage. In the 1860s some Europeans began kidnapping islanders (blackbirding) and carrying them off to serve as slaves on the sugar plantations of Queensland and Fiji. Malaita was particularly hard hit by the blackbirders. Patteson's murder in 1871 underscored the seriousness of the problem and strong measures were instituted to halt the practice. Five naval vessels were added to the Australian squadron of the Royal Navy in 1872, and in the same year the Pacific Islanders Protection Act* was passed to curtail the illegal labor recruitment by the blackbirders. The demand for labor was stronger than the Royal Navy, however, and blackbirding continued without respite for 30 years.

In the 1870s Anglican missionaries began a systematic study of Melanesian culture in the Solomons. They compiled dictionaries, grammars, and translations of the Bible, which helped foster the spread of literacy in the islands. Yet the hostility of the natives, manifested in the occasional murder of Europeans, led the British government to reconsider its interest in the Solomons. No real profits had to date resulted from British possession of the islands, but Germany's entrance into the race for Pacific colonies in the 1880s raised the value of the Solomons, especially for use as naval bases and coaling stations. The German New Guinea Company claimed the northern Solomons in 1885, leading to the issue in 1886 of a joint declaration defining the two powers' respective areas of interest in the region. Great Britain was thereby committed to continue her administration of the troublesome Melanesians, especially after the Germans in 1900 transferred to Great Britain control of the islands they had received fifteen years earlier.

A British protectorate over the Solomons was proclaimed in 1893 in an attempt to establish more firmly the rule of Anglo-Saxon law and order. C. M. Woodford was appointed the first resident commissioner of the Solomons, with the task of maintaining law and eradicating headhunting. The goals set for Woodford's small force, which consisted of six policemen for the entire protectorate, were unachievable; constant tribal warfare and violence disrupted the Solomons, although, to Woodford's credit, it was much less widespread than it had been before he accepted his post.

When global war erupted in 1914, the Solomons were largely unaffected: shipping dropped off some, and after the war, Germany's few remaining possessions in the Solomons became part of the Australian mandate of New Guinea. The natives, however, were far from content with European rule. As late as 1927 islanders on Malaita were still attacking British administrators. Fifteen Europeans were killed in that incident, and after the administration of justice, 31 islanders were executed. An official investigation into the affair was conducted; a number of social and governmental reforms were recommended and eventually enacted in the late 1940s.

The Solomon Islands witnessed some of the most savage battles of World War II*. Japanese forces overran Tulagi on May 3, 1942, and by July had conquered all the major islands. In August the United States launched an amphibious assault on Japanese-held Guadalcanal and Tulagi; after a bloody struggle (24,000 Japanese were killed in action) which lasted until February 1943, the Americans took control of Guadalcanal. It was not until 1945, however, that Bougainville was finally recaptured from the Japanese. During the war an independence movement known as "Marching Rule" had arisen on Malaita. It advocated agricultural improvement, concentration of population into large villages, and non-cooperation with the British government and mission societies.

The Marching Rule movement culminated in the establishment of the Council of Malaita in 1952.

A new constitution approved by the British government in 1970 provided the Solomon Islands protectorate with a governing council and limited local representation. Five years later the protectorate was granted internal self-government, which was intended to smooth the transition from protectorate to independent nation. This status was granted to the Solomon Islands by the British Crown in 1978. (Frederica M. Bunge and Melinda W. Cooke, *Oceania: A Regional Study*, 1985; Janet Kent, *The Solomon Islands*, 1972.)

Jay O. Boehm

SOMALIA. Located at the crossroads of Asia and Africa, at the meeting of the Red Sea and the Indian Ocean, the Somali region has had great strategic significance for centuries. Inhabiting approximately 400,000 square miles of savannah grassland in the Horn of Africa are between five and six million ethnic Somalis. Because of the legacy of European imperialism and African politics, they are divided into four separate political entities. About 3.5 million Somalis live in the Somali Republic, while another 2 million are in the Ogaden region of Ethiopia. Approximately 250,000 live in the northern provinces of Kenya, while the rest are in the Djibouti. The Somali Republic is bordered by the Indian Ocean and the Gulf of Aden to the east, by Kenya to the southwest, by Ethiopia to the northwest, and by Djibouti to the north. The Ethiopian empire of Aksum ruled the area from the second to the seventh centuries, when Arab tribes assumed control. The Somali people began migrating into the region in the thirteenth century. By then Arab rule had degenerated into small sultanates and independent states, many of them governed by Somali chiefs. The Somalis were a pastoral, nomadic people whose livelihood revolved around cattle, sheep, and camels.

The first Europeans to take a real interest in Somalia were the British. Seeking a place to harbor their ships on the way to India, the British East India Company* negotiated treaties with the sultan of Tajura and the governor of Zeila in 1840. They had previously taken possesion of Aden* in 1839. For a while the British were content to let the Egyptians, over whom they exercised strong influence, extend their authority down the Somali coast, but when Egypt withdrew her troops in 1884, the British were faced with a dilemma. They were worried about the Suez route to the east, wary of French and German intentions in east Africa, and desperate to keep control of the headwaters of the Nile River, which they considered essential to Egyptian prosperity. Between 1884 and 1886 Great Britain concluded treaties with a variety of Somali chiefs and occupied Zeila, Berbera, and Bulhar. The British sphere of influence extended along the Gulf of Aden some 400 miles from Djibouti in the west to Bandar Ziyada, 180 miles west of Cape Guardafui (Ras Asir), and 80 to 220 miles inland from the coast. The region became known as British Somaliland.

French Somaliland was at the entrance to the Red Sea. It extended from Ras Dumeira on the straits of Bab-el-Mandeb, just north of Perim Island, to Ras

Gurmarle, just south of the Gulf of Tajura. French interest in the area originated in the Second Empire when France acquired Ambabo and Obock in 1862. It took formal possession of Obock in 1883. A series of treaties with various Somali chiefs gave France complete control of the Gulf of Tajura between 1883 and 1887. In February 1888 the French signed an agreement with Great Britain outlining the boundaries between British Somaliland and French Somaliland.

Italian Somaliland extended on the coast from Bandar Ziyada east to Cape Guardafui and then south to Dick's Head (Ras Chiambone). Italian Somaliland was bordered on the north and east by the Indian Ocean, on the south by the British colony of Kenya, and on the west by Ethiopia and British Somaliland. In the 1880s Italy negotiated a series of agreements with local Somali chiefs securing the coast east of British Somaliland. In 1892 the sultan of Zanzibar* gave Italy a fifty-year lease on the Benadir ports. Thirteen years later, in 1905, the sultan of Zanzibar surrendered sovereignty over the ports to Italy in return for a cash payment. An 1894 agreement with the British established the boundaries between British Somaliland and Italian Somaliland and declared the Ogaden off-limits to British expansion. The Anglo-Italian Agreement of 1925 then ceded part of Jubaland to Italy, which the Italians merged into Italian Somaliland, while the British retained the interior of shrublands which later became known as the Northern Frontier District of Kenya.

Finally, Ethiopia carved out a sphere of influence in Somalia. In 1889 Menelik II acceded to the Ethiopian throne, and with considerable assistance from Italy, he proceeded to conquer the rich Oromo province of Jimma in 1886 and Harar in 1887, establishing the Ogaden region as Ethiopian Somaliland.

So by 1900 the Somali region, which ironically was one of the few relatively homogenous regions of Africa, was divided up among the British, French, Italians, and Ethiopians. Because the European empires really did not extend deeply into the Somali interior or disrupt the essentially nomadic, pastoral lifestyle of the Somali people, Somalian nationalism was not directed against them. It was the Ethiopians who first inspired Somali ire. Menelik II, in order to recoup financial losses from the wars and famines of the 1890s, began to seize and sell livestock indiscriminately in the Ogaden. The European armies, living on the coast, survived off supplies shipped from home, but the Ethiopians lived off the land in the Ogaden, imposing a terrible burden on Somali herdsmen. Between 1890 and 1907 Menelik II seized nearly one million head of livestock from Ogaden herdsmen. The first pan-Somali resistance movement, known as the Dervish rebellion, was directed at the Ethiopians.

The Somalian rebellion began in 1895 under the leadership of Sayyid Muhammad Abdille Hasan, who raised an army of 6,000 warriors and began attacking Ethiopian forces from his base in the Dulbahante country. Eventually, the British and Italians joined forces with the Ethiopians in their battle against Hasan, whom they dubbed the "Mad Mullah," but who was, in fact, the first great Somali anti-colonialist resistance leader. The war went on until 1920, when the British brought in air strikes against Hasan's forces and broke the rebellion. Hasan died in December 1920. The Europeans then set about the task of consolidating their colonial administrations.

In 1935 the Italians, bent on expanding their African empire, conquered Ethiopia and formally brought the Ogaden into Italian Somaliland. Italian Somaliland, Eritrea, and Ethiopia became known together as Italian East Africa*. But in January 1941, during World War II, British forces from South Africa, Kenya, Uganda, Nigeria, Gold Coast, Southern Rhodesia, and Northern Rhodesia captured Italian Somaliland. With the exception of French Somaliland, the whole Somali region was under British control by 1942. But by that time the winds of nationalism were blowing across Africa. Worried about a repartitioning after the war, Somali intellectuals and nationalists formed the Somali Youth League in 1943 and began demanding complete unification of the Somali region and independence.

But it was not to be. Emperor Haile Salassie of Ethiopia successfully lobbied for a return of the Ogaden, and between 1948 and 1954 the British gradually returned the region to Ethiopian sovereignty. British Somaliland continued to function as it had before the war, and the Northern Frontier District remained a part of Kenya. French Somaliland continued as it had before the war; and in 1950 Italy was given a United Nations trusteeship* over Italian Somaliland. Throughout the 1950s a variety of Somali nationalist groups—led by the Somali Youth League, the United National Front, and the Somali National League— campaigned for reunification and independence. In 1949 the United Nations had ordered that Italian Somaliland be given its independence in 1960, and the British decided to work toward the same goal for British Somaliland. Ethnic rivalries between the Issa and the Afar in French Somaliland stalled independence in that area, even though the Issa wanted reunification with their Somali kin in British and Italian Somaliland. In 1960 Italian Somaliland and British Somaliland became independent, and a month later they united into the Somali Republic. French Somaliland did not become independent until 1977 when it was renamed Djibouti. Ethnic Somalis in the Ogaden of Ethiopia and the Northern Frontier District of Kenya are still agitating for reunification. (David D. Laitin and Said S. Samatar, *Somalia. Nation in Search of a State*, 1987.)

SOMALI REPUBLIC. See SOMALIA.

SOUTH AFRICA. The origins of the Republic of South Africa are traced to an expedition of three ships dispatched by the Dutch East India Company* that led to the founding of a colony on Table Bay at the Cape of Good Hope in 1652. Dutch ships involved in trading in Asia used the port to obtain fresh water and food. It was also a strategic location that provided protection for ships. The British occupied the colony from 1795 to 1803, and, again, in 1806. Great Britain gained sovereignty over the Cape Colony* through a treaty with the Netherlands in 1814. The British government encouraged immigration, and approximately 5,000 Englishmen came to Cape Colony in the 1820s. It was only after the discovery of diamonds and gold in the 1860s, however, that Europeans came to South Africa in significant numbers. The Boers (South Africans of Dutch origin) disliked British policies, which they regarded as excessively liberal. The British had, for example, abolished slavery in 1834, and English missionaries often took a protective approach toward the Bantu. In an attempt to place themselves beyond the reach of British jurisdiction, many Boers joined the Great Trek of 1836–1854. These *Voortrekkers*, or pioneers, established the Orange Free State* and the South African Republic (Transvaal). Great Britain annexed the Transvaal in 1877. In the aftermath of a rebellion that erupted in 1880, Britain agreed to reestablish internal self-government in 1881. Under the terms of the Convention of 1884, Britain permitted the Transvaal to carry on its own foreign relations, subject to London's right to review treaties.

The discovery of diamonds and gold around 1870 in the two Boer republics resulted in a great number of *uitlanders*, or foreigners, coming to these territories. Tensions and conflicts involving such issues as the right of the uitlanders to obtain citizenship and to participate in voting, as well as bitter feelings resulting from Jameson's Raid*, finally resulted in the Boer War* (1899–1902). As a result of her victory, Britain annexed the two republics.

Attainment of self-government in South Africa proceeded in a piecemeal way. In Cape Colony responsible government was extended in 1872. Natal*, annexed by Britain in 1843, and made a part of the Cape Colony, became a separate colony in 1856; it was granted self-government in 1893. The Orange Free State and the Transvaal were given self-government in 1907. When the Union was created in 1910, the component colonies gave up the right of self-government. The new political unit, however, had a popularly elected parliament and a ministry responsible to it. In Cape Colony, coloreds were given the right to vote for white members of the Union parliament; elsewhere, nonwhites did not have the franchise. Both Dutch and English were made official languages of the Union.

When Great Britain declared war on Germany in August 1914 the prevailing legal opinion was that South Africa had automatically assumed the status of a belligerent. South Africa was part of the British Empire*; when Great Britain entered the war, so did all segments of the Empire. South African military forces made a significant contribution to the war effort by conquering the neighboring German colony of South West Africa*. James Barry Hertzog, leader of the National party, waged a campaign for South African independence during the war. He was encouraged in his quest by statements made by President Woodrow Wilson of the United States and British Prime Minister Lloyd George concerning self-determination and the rights of small nations. Hertzog headed a delegation of nine to Great Britain and the Paris Peace Conference to demand complete, sovereign independence for his country. In his formal reply, the British prime minister pointed out that the Hertzog delegation seemed to want to go back to a Balkanized South Africa, as indicated by their apparent request for sovereignty for the Transvaal and the Orange Free State. This, he stated, was no longer

permissible. Lloyd George further stated, in wording that seemed self-contra-
dictory, that South Africa was one of the dominions of the British Confederation
and could determine its own national destiny in the fullest sense. He also said
that South Africa took part in imperial conferences on a basis of absolute equality.
Hertzog understood the statement to imply that the Union possessed the right of
self-determination in the fullest sense, including the controversial right of secession.

When the Hertzog delegation returned to Cape Town they asked Prime Minister
Jan Christian Smuts if he concurred with Lloyd George's position that South
Africa possessed the right of self-determination to the fullest extent. Smuts gave
a negative answer, apparently holding the view that the dominions possessed all
sovereign prerogatives except the right to secede. In a speech he had delivered
in May 1917, Smuts had stated that the Empire was not a state, but a system
of nations. He referred to the dominions as ''almost independent states,'' and
seemed to prefer a common foreign policy for the entire British Empire.

Hertzog, now prime minister, attended the Imperial Conference of 1926*
determined to resolve the confusion concerning the international legal status of
South Africa. He wanted to secure a declaration of equality of Commonwealth
members. Resulting from the conference was the Balfour Declaration*, which
asserted that the dominions were autonomous communities within the British
Empire, equal in status, and in no way subordinate one to another in any aspect
of their domestic or external affairs. Prime Minister Hertzog was satisfied and
felt that the conference had been both a Nationalist and personal victory. By the
1931 Statute of Westminster, the British parliament gave its approval to the
principle of equality stated in the Balfour Declaration.

In accordance with formal recognition of South Africa's sovereign independence, Hertzog created a department of external affairs in 1927, which he decided
to head. In 1929 diplomats were exchanged with the Netherlands, the United
States, and Italy. The governor-general's status was altered in 1927; in 1937,
for the first time, a South African citizen was appointed governor-general. A
national flag was adopted in 1927. The right to appeal to the privy council was
abolished by the Nationalist government in 1950.

There were a series of developments in 1960 and 1961 that led to a break
with the Commonwealth. In February 1960 British Prime Minister Harold Macmillan made his ''wind of change'' speech to the South African parliament. In
March racial tensions culminated in the tragic loss of lives at Sharpeville; in
April there was an attempt to assassinate Prime Minister Hendrik Verwoerd. In
a referendum, held on October 5, 1960, a majority of the voters favored changing
the nation into a republic, and the government set May 31, 1961, as the date
for the inauguration of the Republic of South Africa. Notwithstanding, the government petitioned for continued membership in the Commonwealth, and the
application was taken up by the Prime Ministers' Conference which met in
London during March 8–17, 1961. Several prime ministers strongly criticized
South Africa's racial policies and maintained that an unqualified approval of the

request would be viewed as an endorsement of apartheid. Due to tensions and disagreements, South Africa withdrew from the Commonwealth in March 1961. (Amry Vandenbosch, *South Africa and the World: The Foreign Policy of Apartheid*, 1970.)

Roy E. Thoman

SOUTH AFRICA HIGH COMMISSION. The South Africa High Commission was the charge (or responsibility) of the governor of the Cape Colony* and later, after the formation of the Union of South Africa,* the governor-general of the Union of South Africa. That individual, as high commissioner, headed the South Africa High Commission, which served as the chief executive body directing the affairs of the protectorates of Basutoland,* Bechuanaland,* and Swaziland.* Each of those protectorates had its own resident commissioner who answered to the South Africa High Commission. In 1931 the office of the governor-general and the high commissioner were separated, and the high commissioner was given responsibility for the protectorates. When it became obvious that Basutoland, Behuanaland, and Swaziland were headed for independence, Great Britain dissolved the South Africa High Commission in 1964. See BASUTOLAND; BECHUANALAND; SOUTH AFRICA; SWAZILAND.

SOUTH AFRICAN REPUBLIC. See SOUTH AFRICA.

SOUTH ARABIAN FEDERATION. During the nineteenth century Great Britain began to establish a variety of political relationships with the emirates, shiekdoms, and sultinates in the Arabian Peninsula, eventually combining them loosely into the Western Protectorate and the Eastern Protectorate, which were administered by the government of Aden* until 1959. Several of those principalities formed the Federation of Arab Emirates of the South in 1959, and the British assigned a High Commissioner to administer it. The name of the coalition was changed to the Federation of South Arabia in 1962, and by 1963 most of the other principalities had joined. Aden also joined the federation in 1963 and ceased to be a crown colony. The Federation of South Arabia became independent in 1967 as the Republic of South Yemen. See SOUTH YEMEN.

SOUTH AUSTRALIA. South Australia is one of the six confederated states of Australia*. Unlike the others, however, it was not settled initially as a penal colony. Its capital city—Adelaide—was constructed on a large coastal plain of fertile soil, and its original settlers tended to be more middle-class than working class. The leading figure in the early settlement of South Australia was Edward Wakefield. Following his lead, parliament passed the South Australia Act in 1834 establishing the colony, and two years later colonists began arriving in Adelaide. By 1840 South Australia had more than 15,000 people, and by 1860 the colony had become the breadbasket of Australia, producing more wheat than the rest of the continent combined. On January 1, 1901, South Australia joined

Tasmania, New South Wales, Victoria, Western Australia, and Queensland in forming the commonwealth of Australia. (Douglas Pike, *Paradise of Dissent*, 1957.)

SOUTH CAROLINA. South Carolina, located on the southeastern coast of the present-day United States, was inhabited by 25 to 30 tribal groups who spoke either the Iroquoian, Siouan, or Muskhogean dialects. In 1521 a Spanish expedition captained by Pedro de Queros and Francisco Gordillo landed at the mouth of the Winyah River searching for Indian slaves to be used in the West Indies. A Spanish colony began there in 1526, but a slave rebellion destroyed it. The result, though, was a stimulating report of good land and harbor that encouraged further Spanish interest. Other European explorers like Giovanni da Verrazano and Hernando de Soto* reached present-day South Carolina as well.

French Huguenots established a colony there in 1562 under the leadership of Jean Ribaut, who explored the Atlantic coast from St. Augustine northward, trying to locate a suitable place that did not infringe on Spanish soil. His colony settled on present-day Parris Island. He built a fort, named the area Charlesfort, left a number of men to set up a town, and returned to France to seek more colonists and funds. But they did not farm, hunt, fish, or establish any form of government. After the goodwill of local Indians was depleted, mutiny broke out and the survivors constructed a vessel and abandoned the colony. Ribault tried unsuccessfully to get French then English aid for his colony. Eventually the Spanish, led by Hernando de Manrique de Rojas, destroyed the remains. In 1566 Pedro Menéñdez de Aviles built a fort, San Felipe, close to Ribault's Charlesfort. An interior expeditionary force, led by Juan Pardo, succeeded in leaving minor garrisons along de Soto's former route. Unfortunately, they were cruel to the Indians and created a lasting bitterness toward the Spanish there.

England succeeded where the Spanish and French failed. In 1629 King Charles I of England granted to Sir Robert Heath all lands between the 31st and 36th north latitudes and extending to the Pacific Ocean. Though Heath did not get to settle it, he did name it Carolina after Charles I. Problems in England kept colonization attempts at a standstill until Charles II granted a new charter on March 24, 1663. The new titleholders, called lord proprietors of Carolina, were eight titled men. By 1670 they had established a permanent colony with a land-tenure plan and a governing body. South Carolina proved to be England's southernmost outpost in the North American continent. During the next seven-year period Charles Town, the English name for the colony, was settled, abandoned, and resettled by New Englanders, Barbadians, and finally Englishmen. New Englanders wrote disparaging accounts of the area; immigrants from Barbados, hoping to establish sugar plantations, put their hope in a pamphlet, "A Relation of a Discovery," by Captain William Hilton. The pamphlet made South Carolina sound like every settler's paradise. By May 1670, 148 settlers, mainly English immigrants, reached Albemarle Point. Within ten years the Barbadians had relocated to present-day Charleston. Two other groups arrived in the next twenty years—a large group of Barbadians, who openly conducted the Indian slave trade and were concerned only with profit, and the French Huguenots, who were highly skilled, hard-working, and intelligent. The Barbadians caused constant conflicts which divided South Carolina for many decades, while the Huguenots helped create a firm base in colonial America.

During the latter days of the seventeenth century, Henry Woodward, a Barbadian planter, introduced the growing of rice to the colony, creating a cash crop that was to help South Carolina gain importance throughout the New World. It also brought an increase in the number of African slaves. The early eighteenth century was marked with political conflicts and monetary problems. The colonists felt that the lord proprietors were too engrossed in profit and not concerned enough about defense. Problems peaked in 1719 when the colonists elected their own governor and declared themselves free of the lord proprietors. By 1729 parliament had reacted and made them a royal colony with North Carolina. Three years later South Carolina became a separate colony. The census of that year (1732) estimated a population of 30,000 inhabitants, including African slaves.

By this time South Carolina had fair-sized settlements at Beaufort, Georgetown, and as far inland as thirty miles. In 1735 there were nine more towns toward the interior. As the colony became more populated, Indian trade, a former source of funds, took second and then third place to the production of rice and indigo. By 1750 the royal colony had gained a sense of economic prosperity, had settlements in the back country beyond what was referred to as the fall-line (the point where rapids hindered river navigation), and was divided culturally as well as geographically into Low Country and Up Country.

The division created societies that were independent of each other. This cultural independence was aided by the arrival of various immigrants—Germans, Swiss, and Welsh Baptists in the 1730s, and the Scots-Irish in the 1750s. The Up Country settlers were small farmers who had to make do with vigilante laws, which developed by 1769 into a court system. They had been denied representation by the planter-dominated Charleston government. This led to intense disputes over representation and eventually a relocation of the capital to Columbia, an inland settlement.

The years between 1770 and 1776 were marked with prosperity and an increase in trade. The problem of the northern colonies did not hinder South Carolinians to any great extent. The colony had a good working relationship with the Crown so it did not participate in the early tax and trade infractions. However, it did send delegates to the Continental Congresses in 1774 and 1775, and in 1776, along with the other twelve British North American colonies, South Carolina declared its independence from Great Britain. (Verner W. Crane, *The Southern Frontier, 1670–1732*, 1959; Anne Riggs Osborne, *The South Carolina Story*, 1988.)

Catherine G. Harbour

SOUTHERN RHODESIA. See RHODESIA.

SOUTH GEORGIA. South Georgia is a large island of nearly 1,600 square miles in the South Atlantic Ocean, approximately 800 miles east of the Falkland Islands*. It is a British dependency administered as part of the Falkland Islands. See FALKLAND ISLANDS.

SOUTH RIVIERA. See FRENCH GUINEA.

SOUTH WEST AFRICA. South West Africa (independent Namibia is located north of the Orange River on the Atlantic coast of southern Africa. Until March 21, 1990, it was under the control of South Africa*, which gained authority over the former German protectorate following World War I. The coastal area was first reached by Portuguese sailors in 1486. They were followed by other Europeans, but these explorers were hindered in the penetration of the interior by the harsh and inhospitable expanse of the Namib Desert. By the early 1880s German missionaries, traders, and soldiers had come to the Namibian coast, and in 1885 Germany declared South West Africa a protectorate. There was periodic resistance from native groups. In 1904 the Herrero and other African tribes of the region began a bloody revolt that was put down by the Germans in 1907 with the loss of over 60,000 African lives.

During World War I troops from the Union of South Africa campaigned against the Germans and took control of South West Africa. The South Africans hoped to formally annex South West Africa following the war, but international pressures prevented that from happening. Instead, in 1919, South Africa was granted the right to administer the territory under a League of Nations* mandate. Because supervision by the League of Nations through the Permanent Mandates Commission was not stringent, South West Africa was governed virtually as a fifth province of the Union of South Africa, which moved to exploit the agricultural and mining potential of the territory. By the early 1920s nearly 10,000 South Africans had settled in the country as farmers, entrepreneurs, and public servants. The Germans who remained in South West Africa were treated generously and, in 1924, were offered South African citizenship. For the most part, they accustomed themselves to the new order. The African majority—including Nama and Herrero pastoralists and Ovambo migrant laborers—had little choice. In the years between the wars there was no serious challenge to the authority of South Africa. During World War II, however, evidence of the spread of pro-Nazi sympathies among the German population forced the Union government, as an ally of Great Britain, to take stern action. Well over a 1,000 people of German extraction were interned and numerous pro-Nazi organizations were proscribed.

After World War II the United Nations assumed the authority of the League of Nations, which formally went out of existence in 1946. When the General Assembly recommended that South West Africa be placed under a United Nations trusteeship, South Africa refused to accept the legal authority of the United

Nations over South West Africa and rejected the trusteeship system, which would have required movement of South West Africa toward self-government. In 1949 the new National Party government of South Africa, led by Dr. Daniel Malan, sought to incorporate South West Africa into the Union through the passage of the South West Africa Affairs Amendment Act, which allowed South West Africa whites to elect six representatives to the South African parliament. The United Nations General Assembly, denying the legitimacy of the incorporation, passed several more resolutions in the 1950s stating that South Africa had an obligation to place South West Africa under United Nations trusteeship, but these were ignored as well.

In 1966 the United Nations declared that since South Africa had failed to pursue the best interests of South West Africa, it had forfeited the right to govern the territory. The United Nations then voted to place South West Africa under the control of an 11-member council which would administer the territory until independence was established. South Africa still refused to relinquish control. In 1971 the International Court of Justice at the Hague (after handing down somewhat ambiguous rulings in 1962 and 1966) declared South Africa's presence in the territory illegal and ordered South Africa to end its occupation. The South Africans, regarding the International Court as a biased tool of the United Nations, rejected this decision and remained in South West Africa.

Meanwhile, in the 1960s, South West Africa blacks formed an anti-colonial liberation movement known as the South West African People's Organization (SWAPO), which drew its support largely, though not exclusively, from the Ovambo people in the northern part of the country. They began to refer to South West Africa as Namibia and sought independence and black majority rule in contrast to the apartheid policies of South Africa. Failing to shake South African control through political means, SWAPO resorted increasingly in the 1970s to guerrilla actions against South African military forces and non-SWAPO blacks, whose opposition to SWAPO was based chiefly on ethnic grounds—fear of Ovambo domination. The South African Defence Force countered by massing troop strength along the borders with the "frontline" states of Zambia* (in the geographical anomaly known as the Caprivi Strip) and Angola* where, after the collapse of Portuguese colonial power in 1974, SWAPO had established its principal guerrilla bases and training camps.

In 1977 South Africa, concerned with the diplomatic as well as the economic costs of a protracted Namibian conflict, proposed to grant independence to South West Africa under a plan that would give local political control to a multi-ethnic, though white-dominated, party—the Democratic Turnhalle Alliance (DTA). Elections in 1978 (sponsored by South Africa and boycotted by SWAPO) resulted in an overwhelming victory for the DTA, but the United Nations, strongly opposed to any plan which did not grant Namibian blacks full political freedom, refused to recognize elections that had been held without United Nations participation. Finally, under pressure from the United States and Canada, South Africa agreed to reformulate its plan in accordance with United Nations guidelines and to hold a new election in South West Africa under UN supervision.

Predictably, negotiations to implement the United Nations guidelines—as stated in UN Security Council Resolution 435 of 1978—proved difficult and dragged on for years, often being overshadowed by a military conflict that involved SWAPO raids in Namibia and South African incursions into Angola. In 1981, due to the Cuban presence in Angola, the South African government, with the support of the newly elected Reagan administration in Washington, began to link the withdrawal of Cuban forces from Angola to the implementation of the United Nations Namibian independence plan. For a number of years, progress toward a settlement stalled on the issue of "linkage," but in the late 1980s, vigorous United States diplomatic efforts moved negotiations forward and resulted in a Namibian peace accord. On December 22, 1988, South Africa, Cuba, and Angola signed an agreement at the United Nations setting in motion a Namibian independence process that called for elections in the territory on November 1, 1989, and promised the achievement of Namibian independence by April 1990. A second pact between Cuba and Angola established a timetable under which an estimated 50,000 Cuban troops would be withdrawn from Angola by July 1, 1991. South West Africa became the Republic of Namibia on March 21, 1990, and former SWAPO guerrilla leader Sam Nujoma was sworn in as Namibia's first president. (Graham Leach, *South Africa*, 1986; *Southwest Africa*, 1963.)

Joseph L. Michaud

SOUTH YEMEN. See ADEN.

SPANISH-AMERICAN WAR. The war between the United States and Spain in 1898 arose out of several developments going back before the beginning of the decade. One was the increasing trade of the United States and subsequent American investment abroad. American businessmen had sunk money into Cuban tobacco and sugar production and in various industrial and commercial enterprises. The development which eventually exerted the major influence leading to war was the outbreak of a rebellion in Cuba* against Spanish rule. This uprising began in 1895 and soon took the form of guerrilla war and widespread destruction of economic and transportation resources, including plantations and other businesses owned by foreigners.

American concern over the situation in Cuba was aroused partly by the destruction of American-owned businesses, but mainly by the public perception of inhumanity exhibited by the Spanish authorities in their conduct of the anti-guerrilla operations. Under the Spanish commander, General Valeriano Weyler, much of the rural population in guerrilla-infested areas was relocated to refugee camps where living conditions and sanitation facilities caused great suffering and death. The giant American newspaper chains like Pulitzer's and Hearst's saw the events in Cuba as an opportunity to increase circulation, and they did not hesitate to embellish or even to invent stories which would attract a wide readership. By early 1898 public pressure upon the administration of William McKinley to do something to help end the bloodshed led to American efforts to get the Spanish government to agree to a ceasefire and to grant internal self-government to the Cubans. This American interference was widely resented both in Spain and by pro-Spanish people in Cuba.

The impetus to war, already started by American fervor on behalf of the Cubans, became irreversible on the evening of February 15, 1898, when the American battleship *Maine*, stationed at Havana to provide a means of evacuating Americans if necessary, was racked by a huge explosion and sank in the harbor with the loss of 260 of her crew. The United States held Spain responsible, although the cause of the explosion has never been firmly established. The cry "Remember the *Maine*" made it impossible to resist the clamor for war to free the Cubans, and after more than two weeks of debate and a formal recognition of Cuba's independence, Congress declared war on April 25.

The U.S. navy was ready for war. On May 1, Commodore George Dewey took the Asiatic squadron past the Corregidor fortifications into Manila Bay and destroyed the Spanish fleet in the Philippines*, while at about the same time naval vessels in the Atlantic blockaded Cuban ports. The Army meanwhile began a haphazard and inefficient expansion. Americans had no clear strategy except the implied objective of driving the Spaniards out of Cuba. The discovery of the main Spanish fleet in the harbor of Santiago in southeastern Cuba in the latter part of May greatly relieved those who had feared enemy naval bombardment of East Coast ports.

The Cuban campaign began on June 22, 1898, when an American army of 17,000 troops under General William R. Shafter landed at Daiquiri, about 15 miles east of Santiago. In the face of strong opposition from a small Spanish force, the ill-organized and poorly equipped American army spent a week driving the Spaniards back to Santiago. Partly because of lack of coordination and unclear expectations, the Americans got no real help from the Cuban rebels around Santiago, although the guerrillas elsewhere in the island kept the Spanish forces, numbering over 100,000 troops, from concentrating against the Americans.

The culminating stage of the campaign in Cuba came on July 1 when the American army, now assembled before Santiago but increasingly demoralized by supply difficulties and illness, launched assaults against the Spanish fortified positions at El Caney and San Juan Hill. The imagination of Americans was captured by the spectacle of ragged lines of blue-clad American troops under the leadership of Generals Henry W. Lawton, Jacob F. Kent, and Joseph Wheeler, assisted by the irrepressible Colonel Theodore Roosevelt, moving bravely against the heavy fire of the entrenched Spanish defenders. The capture of those positions placed the Spaniards in a difficult position. Unaware of the desperate plight of the American besiegers, now running short of ammunition and supplies and with yellow fever beginning to appear among the troops, the Spanish commander in Santiago decided to give up after prolonged negotiations with General Shafter. On July 17 the Spanish garrison of nearly 24,000 men surrendered.

The capture of Santiago was something of an anticlimax. The post had been chosen for attack because of the presence of a Spanish fleet in the harbor, but by the time Santiago was given up, the fleet was no longer there. On July 3 Admiral Pascual Cervera brought his fleet out in a daring but hopeless attempt to break free of the American naval blockade. In the ensuing running battle westward along the coast the four Spanish cruisers and their two escorting torpedo boats were all either sunk or driven ashore in flames. The American ships suffered no serious damage and only a few casualties.

By the time Santiago was captured the Spanish government was ready to negotiate a peace treaty. The war had been a disaster for Spain. Besides the loss of Santiago, the Spaniards had lost two fleets. In addition an American expedition had taken Puerto Rico*, the only other Spanish possession in the New World, while it was obviously only a matter of time before Manila* and the Philippines fell. On August 12, 1898, the French ambassador in Washington signed a ceasefire agreement on behalf of the Spanish government, preceding by one day the fall of Manila and the surrender of Spanish forces in the Philippines.

At the peace conference held in Paris from September to December 1898, the Spaniards agreed that Cuba would become independent and that Guam* and Puerto Rico, which had been taken by the Americans, would be annexed by the United States. They opposed American retention of the Philippines, however, because Manila had not been captured until the day after the ceasefire. They accepted $20 million in lieu of a restoration of the Philippines, which the Americans would not permit, and a treaty was signed on December 10. After intense debate about the consequences of establishing an overseas empire, the Senate approved the treaty on February 6, 1899, shortly after the outbreak of an insurrection by Filipino rebels against the American occupation.

The most important result of the war was that it gave the United States an overseas empire, largely in the Pacific. In addition to the Spanish conquests, the annexation of Hawaii* was a direct consequence of the war. The acquisition of empire brought the United States directly into the cross currents of international rivalries in the Far East, increased greatly the propensity for interference in the Caribbean, and forced the nation to deal with the many problems of colonial policy. (Frank Freidel, *The Splendid Little War*, 1958; David F. Frost, *The War with Spain in 1898*, 1981; H. Wayne Morgan, *America's Road to Empire: The War with Spain and Overseas Expansion*, 1965.)

Ernest Andrade, Jr.

SPANISH ARMADA. In 1588 Philip II of Spain sent a fleet of 130 ships commanded by the Duke of Medina Sidonia—and commonly known as the Armada—to facilitate the invasion of England by Spanish troops in the Netherlands. The enterprise was part of an undeclared war between Spain and England that began in 1585 and lasted until 1604, overlapping with their involvement in hostilities in the Netherlands and France. Traditionally the attempted invasion has been regarded as the result of commercial and/or religious rivalry, and the defeat of the Armada has been seen as a decisive victory for well-prepared English naval forces, whose superiority to those of Spain was clearly proven. But the overall picture of the causes, course, and consequences of the Armada campaign is more complex. Neither Philip nor Elizabeth I* of England really wanted a war, and while competition for wealth and Catholic/Protestant antagonism were important factors making conflict unavoidable, so also were internal pressures in Spain and England and the exceedingly complicated international situation in the 1580s. In addition, the English—though they had long anticipated a Spanish invasion—were caught by surprise upon the Armada's arrival at the end of July 1588. Finally, the failure of Philip's scheme was less significant for the subsequent history of the war than other circumstances.

Philip had a dynastic claim of a sort to the English throne because of his marriage to Elizabeth's sister, Mary I, from 1554 to 1558. As the leading Catholic ruler in Europe, he was also the focus of hopes to return the English to the Roman church. Prior to the 1580s, however, he showed relatively little interest in plans for a Catholic crusade directed against the British Isles—his orders to the Duke of Alba for an invasion of England at the time of the Ridolfi plot in 1571 were altogether half-hearted, and he gave no support to papal invasions of Ireland in 1579 and 1580. By the beginning of the 1580s Philip's attitude began to change. In 1580 he inherited the Portuguese throne, but Elizabeth gave sanctuary to the pretender Dom Antonio and in 1581–1582 abetted his unsuccessful attack on the Azores. She also showed no sign of ceasing her support for anti-Spanish, Calvinist rebels intent on overthrowing Philip's rule in the Netherlands, and after the assassination of their leader William of Orange in 1584, she formally took them under her protection. Sir Francis Drake's* circumnavigation of the world in 1577–1580 increased Spain's concern about the safety of its empire, and these fears were borne out in 1585—after Philip seized English ships in Iberian ports—by Drake's raids on Baiona and Vigo and Caribbean shipping and by English attacks on Spain's Newfoundland fishing fleet.

Philip was also worried by English overtures to Fez-Morocco and the Ottoman Empire in 1584–1585, particularly given the tension caused in Spain by the "New Christians" (converted Muslims, or moriscos). In France the death of the Duke of Anjou in 1584 left the Huguenot Henri (Bourbon) of Navarre as heir to Henri III, which—along with Dutch overtures to the latter in 1585—raised the spectre of an Anglo-French-Dutch alliance against Spain. Finally, Philip's rapprochement with the powerful Catholic Guise family in France made him more amenable to English Catholic schemes to put Mary, the Queen of Scots (whose Guise blood had troubled Philip), on England's throne.

Already in 1583 the Marquís of Santa Cruz had suggested an attack on England, which Philip rejected as impractical, but by late 1585 he had changed his mind and was negotiating with Pope Sixtus V for financial aid and the right to name a successor to Mary if she replaced Elizabeth. In March 1586 Santa Cruz proposed sending an invasion force of 55,000 men from Spain, which would require a fleet of over 500 ships, while in June the Duke of Parma suggested transporting 30,000 men across the English Channel from the Netherlands, for which secrecy was essential. Philip began assembling ships and men in various ports and urgently desired the invasion to occur in 1587, but repeated delays prevented this, and word of his plans leaked out, giving the English the chance to prepare a defense. Further impetus was given Philip's enterprise by the execution of Mary, Queen of Scots, in February (for complicity in the Bagington Plot of 1586) and Drake's raid on Cadiz in April, though these were not the causes of the invasion.

The Armada sailed from Lisbon on May 30, but bad weather forced it to put in at La Coruma on June 19 for supplies and repairs, and it did not depart until July 22. By the 18th the English concluded that the invasion was off, and their fleet sailed from Plymouth to attack Spanish ports, but was driven back by adverse winds. Thus the appearance of the Armada off the Lizard on July 29 surprised the English, but the bulk of their fleet was still at Plymouth under Lord Admiral Charles Howard (Earl of Nottingham) and Drake and hastily put out to sea, getting the wind advantage on July 31. Superior tactics, greater maneuverability, and the longer range and more rapid fire of their guns gave the English the advantage in skirmishes off Portsmouth, Plymouth, and the Isle of Wight on July 31 and August 2 and 4. But the turning point was Medina Sidonia's halt off Calais on August 6 necessitated by poor communications with Parma—blame for this belongs to Philip. The English sent fire-ships among the Spanish on the 7th, and thereafter did considerable damage to the Armada before a "Protestant wind" blew it northward. The English broke off pursuit on August 12, and the Armada had to sail home around Scotland and Ireland, where many men and ships were lost.

The Armada's defeat was not decisive with regard to the war. Drake's expedition against Portugal in 1589 failed, and Philip attempted invasions again in 1596 and 1597, though these were foiled by storms. But the victory of 1588 convinced English Protestants that God was on their side and made loyalists of many English Catholics who could not countenance foreign invasion. It shattered the image of Spanish invincibility and over the long run made peace with the English a compelling alternative in Spanish foreign policy and made empire more attractive and attainable for England. (Simon Adams, *The Armada Campaign of 1588*, 1988; M. J. Rodriguez-Salgado, et al., *Armada*, 1988.)

William B. Robison

SPANISH EMPIRE. Although the Kingdom of Castile reached the Canary Islands* in 1402, the real beginnings of the Spanish Empire did not come until 1492, when Ferdinand* and Isabella* expelled the Moors from Spain after a 700 year occupation and Christopher Columbus* reached the New World. Intent on finding a new water route to the Indies, the Spanish monarchs sponsored three more voyages by Columbus and dozens of other expeditions of exploration and conquest during the next half century. In the 1490s and early 1500s Spaniards conquered the Greater Antilles—Cuba*, Puerto Rico*, and Hispaniola*—and reduced the native Arawak population to extinction. Ferdinand Magellan* began his voyage around the world in 1519 and in the process established the Spanish presence in the Pacific Ocean, which eventually evolved into colonial establishments in the Caroline Islands*, the Marshall Islands*, the Marianas*, and the Philippines*. That same year Hernán Cortéz* moved into the Valley of Mexico* and conquered the Aztecs. The Spanish conquest of Central America took place between the 1520s and the 1530s, and in the 1530s Francisco Pizarro* conquered the Inca empire. From those bases in New Spain* and Peru*, the Spanish empire expanded north into what is today Florida and the American Southwest; south and southeast into Chile*, Bolivia*, Paraguay*, Argentina*, and Uruguay*; and north into Ecuador*, Colombia*, and Venezuela*.

From its very inception, the Spanish empire was a political enterprise governed directly from the mother country. The imperial apparatus was heavy handed, with power resting in the hands of *Peninsulares*—political appointees born in Spain who spent several years in the colonies as a means of moving up through the ranks of the civil service, the military, and the church. Spain discouraged the development of indigenous political institutions and tried to exercise all power, but nationalistic movements developed in the late eighteenth century in South America and the Caribbean and late in the nineteenth century in the Philippines. By that time the Spanish economy entered its long period of decline which eventually left Spain one of the poorest countries in Europe. Spain took thousands of tons of gold and silver out of Mexico and South America, but the riches bought pleasure for the Spanish nobility and royal family, not an infrastructure or economic development for the country as a whole. The Spanish population actually declined from eight million to six million people in the late sixteenth and seventeenth centuries. With a declining population and a stagnant economy, Spain could not sustain the empire she had been building since 1492.

During the Napoleonic Wars of the early nineteenth century, Spain was cut off from her New World colonies, and in the process the nationalists received a new sense of independence. Between 1810 and 1830 revolutions erupted throughout Latin America, and in the process Spain lost control of its colonies. When the political dust settled, Spain retained only Cuba, Puerto Rico, and her Pacific and African colonies. But they too were doomed. Cuban nationalists fought sporadically against Spanish rule until the 1890s, when full-scale revolution broke out. The revolution merged with the Spanish-American War* in 1898. Spain suffered a humiliating defeat at the hands of the United States, and in the subsequent treaty, the United States assumed a protectorate over Cuba, seized Guam and Puerto Rico, and purchased the Philippines from Spain. The next year Spain sold the remaining Marianas and Marshall Islands to Germany.

By the twentieth century the Spanish empire had been reduced to a few African possessions. In 1778 Portugal ceded what became Spanish Equatorial Guinea* to Spain. To counter British naval activity on the coast of Africa, Spain established a trading post on the Rio de Oro Bay, and that post evolved into the colony of Spanish Sahara*. Spanish Sahara, Spanish Equatorial Guinea, and the two small zones of Morocco known as Spanish Morocco*, along with Ceuta*, Melilla*, and Ifni*, constituted the Spanish empire in Africa. During the period of revolutionary nationalism which swept throughout Africa in the 1950s, 1960s, and 1970s, Spain lost those colonies as well, except for Ceuta and Melilla. Both parts of Spanish Morocco were ceded to Morocco* in 1956 and 1958; Ifni went to Morocco in 1969, and Spanish Sahara was divided up between Mauritania and Morocco in 1976. The Spanish empire, which had once reached around the world, existed no more. (J. H. Parry, *The Spanish Seaborne Empire*, 1966.)

SPANISH EQUATORIAL GUINEA. Spanish Equatorial Guinea, now the Republic of Equatorial Guinea, consists of a small enclave on the west coast of equatorial Africa called Rio Muni, plus the islands of Bioko (formerly Fernando Po), Annobon, and Corisco, as well as some other very small islands. The island of Bioko was discovered around 1469 by Portuguese explorer Fernando Po. The Portuguese controlled the commercial activities of the island and the mainland between the Niger and Ogooue Rivers (Río Muni) until 1778 when the Portuguese ceded their interests to the Spanish. Until 1900 the area was explored only along the coast. The French also made formal claims to the bulk of the mainland coast, and the English settled former slaves on Fernando Po in the nineteenth century.

With the Treaty of Paris in 1900 the mainland was conceded to Spain and a colonial administration was organized by 1904. The Spanish left the mainland interior unexplored until the 1920s. By 1926–1927 intermittent resistance from the region's dominant ethnic group, the Fang, was defeated. Under colonial rule the Spanish permitted Fernando Po's indigenous Bubi to assimilate into Spanish commerce and culture. However, the populations of the mainland were allowed to make little economic progress.

After World War II African nationalist movements began to influence the people of Spanish Guinea. An underground nationalist movement was organized in Spanish Guinea in 1954. The colonial regime responded quickly. Nationalist leaders Enrique Nvo and Acacio Mane were assassinated, but the movement persisted. In 1958 the colony, formerly governed by an admiral, was named a Spanish province—the Spanish Equatorial Region. Africans were allowed to participate in the political administration, and all Africans in the province became citizens of Spain. By 1960 three African representatives were sent to the Spanish Cortes, or parliament. Even though the Spanish Equatorial Region was ruled by an appointed governor-general, who had military and civilian powers, elections for selected village, municipal, and provincial councils were held. In 1963 limited autonomy was granted, and the province was renamed Equatorial Guinea. A joint legislature and a cabinet of eight African councillors was established, and a president was elected by the legislature. The governor-general was replaced by a high commissioner, who was supposed to leave considerable initiative in formulating laws to the legislature.

Nationalist movements were recognized legally as political parties. The National Union Movement of Equatorial Guinea (MUNGE), the National Liberation Movement of Equatorial Guinea (MONALIGE), and the Popular Idea of Equatorial Guinea (IPGE), all in Río Muni, favored independence for the islands and the mainland as one political entity. The Bubi Union and the Fernandino Democratic Union preferred a separate independence for the island of Fernando Po or a loose federation. MUNGE, headed by Bonifacio Ondo Edu, emerged as the principal party of the provincial government.

Under increasing pressure from the United Nations, the Spanish made plans for Equatorial Guinea's independence by 1968. At the constitutional convention the five political parties disagreed over the arrangement between the mainland and the islands as well as the extent of future ties with Spain. Francisco Macias Nguema, a Fang, led the protest against the draft constitution, but with its ratification Macias Nguema ran for president on a constitutional platform favoring a union of the islands and the mainland and close ties to Spain. Once elected, Macias Nguema chose former presidential candidate Edmundo Bosio Dioco as vice president and suspended many of the provisions of the compromise constitution. The Republic of Equatorial Guinea was established on October 12, 1968. He then implemented a reign of terror which did not end until the coup d'etat of 1979 and his execution. (Robin Cohen, ed., *African Islands and Enclaves*, 1983).

Karen Sleezer

SPANISH MOROCCO. The Spanish presence in Morocco* was the first and among the last ventures of Spain in overseas imperialism. Five years after the expulsion of the Moors from Granada, Spain crossed the Mediterranean and seized Melilla*, a city on the coast of what is today northeastern Morocco. Spain then annexed Ceuta*, a city on the Mediterranean coast about 165 miles east of Tangier, in 1668, winning it from Portugal in the Treaty of Lisbon. Although Spain did not press into the interior from those coastal possessions, she had nevertheless established a foothold in northern Morocco.

The foothold in southern Morocco took much longer to establish. From bases in the Canary Islands*, Spain established a few trading posts along the West African coast in the sixteenth century, but she was soon diverted by wealthier prospects in the New World. Spain did not return to West Africa until the nineteenth century. Throughout the eighteenth and early nineteenth centuries, European sailors were periodically shipwrecked along the coast and sold into slavery, so European countries began negotiating treaties with local potentates. In 1860 Spain won from the rulers of Morocco a 579-square-mile colony at Ifni*, a town on the Atlantic coast approximately 200 miles southwest of Marrakech. Donald MacKenzie of Scotland negotiated the rights to establish a commercial trading post at Cape Juby in 1879 and Spain, concerned about possible British penetration of the area, placed trading posts at Dakhla on Rio de Oro Bay and at La Guera. Madrid officially declared these areas Spanish protectorates in December 1884. Still, Spain made no attempt to extend and consolidate her holdings beyond those coastal enclaves.

By the early twentieth century Germany was expressing interest in Morocco, inspiring Spain, France, and Great Britain to conspire to keep the North African coast in French and Spanish hands. In 1904 they signed a secret agreement recognizing France's and Spain's spheres of influence in Morocco, and the Algeciras Conference of 1906* formalized those claims. Anti-foreign political insurgency in Casablanca and Fez in 1912 led to French military intervention from Algeria and the signing of a Franco-Spanish treaty establishing the French protectorate over most of Morocco, as well as a Spanish protectorate, known as Spanish Morocco, over the country's northern and southern zones. Tangier became an international city.

Spanish Morocco consisted of two zones. The northern zone, known as the Spanish Protectorate in Morocco or the Northern Zone of the Protectorate, stretched from just south of Larache on the Atlantic Coast of Morocco east to the Moulouya River and then north to the Mediterranean. The southern zone, separated from the northern zone by more than 500 miles, was known as Cape Juby, Southern Morocco, the Southern Protectorate of Spanish Morocco, Tarfaya, or the Tekna Zone. Covering more than 8,500 square miles, the Southern Zone included land between the northern boundary of Spanish Sahara at the latitude of 27 degrees 40 minutes north to the Qued Draa, and reaching 150 miles into the African interior. In 1934 Ifni and the Northern Zone of Spanish Morocco* were united administratively with Spanish Sahara, and in 1946 the Southern Zone of Spanish Morocco was included, creating the new colonial entity of Western Sahara.

But by that time the seeds of nationalist rebellion had already been sown. During the 1920s Spain and France found themselves in the middle of a bloody civil war in Morocco and the Northern Zone against the Rif rebels, a group of anti-foreign Berber tribesmen led by Abd-el-Krim. Beginning in 1921 Krim's guerrilla troops repeatedly defeated Spanish troops from bases in the rugged Rif Mountains, which extend along the Moroccan coast from Ceuta to the Algerian border. Only after years of bitter fighting did combined Spanish-French forces crush the rebellion. During the Spanish Civil War in the 1930s, local Moroccan nationalists like Al-Quazzani and Abdelhaleq Torres began pressing their demands for independence from Spain. When Moroccan and Algerian nationalists fought successfully for independence from France in the 1950s, the continuing colonial status of Spanish Morocco was doomed. When Morocco became independent from France in 1956, Spain ceded the Northern Zone of Spanish Morocco to the new country. Two years later, in April 1958, Spain signed the Agreement of Cintra, handing over the Southern Zone of Spanish Morocco to Morocco. Finally, in 1969, Spain ceded Ifni to Morocco. All that remained of Spanish Morocco were the two tiny enclaves at Ceuta and Melilla. (Richard M. Brace, *Morocco. Algeria. Tunisia*, 1964.)

SPANISH SAHARA. Portugal and Spain first explored the Saharan coastline opposite the Canary Islands* in the fourteenth and fifteenth centuries. The Spanish fort Santa Cruz de Mar Pequena served as a trading post and a slaveholding base until it was sacked by local tribes in 1524. The Portuguese were evicted in turn from their fort at Agadir in 1541, though they retained control of the island of Arguin until 1638, when it was seized by the Dutch. Meanwhile, imperial ambitions in the Americas diverted the Spaniards, who were not to return to the Sahara coast until the end of the nineteenth century.

Between the late eighteenth century and the 1860s, western sailors trading at the nearby Canary and Madeira* Islands often became shipwrecked along the dangerous Saharan coast and were sold by their captors to nomadic traders. As a consequence, western interests negotiated a number of peace and trading treaties with local potentates during the second half of the nineteenth century. In 1879 Donald MacKenzie of Scotland signed a trading agreement with Mohammed Ben Beyrouk. As a result, the British North-West Africa Company near Cape Juby became the first successful European commercial operation on the Saharan coast in 350 years, competing with the southern trading activities of the sultan of Morocco. When the business of the BNWA Company began to decline in the early 1890s, MacKenzie's trading station was sold to Morocco* (March 13, 1895).

Meanwhile the Spanish government, fearing that the British might establish a presence on the African coast opposite the Canary Islands, established trading posts at Dakhla on the Rio de Oro Bay (later the settlement of Villa Cisneros) and at La Guere. The Madrid government officially declared these enclaves to be protectorates in December 1884. On April 6, 1887, a Spanish decree consolidated the protectorate to include the whole coastal region from Cape Juby to Cape Blanco. This new territory was under the administration of a sub-governor in Villa Cisneros who was responsible to the captain-general of the Canaries. The borders of the protectorate were subsequently extended and more clearly delineated by three Franco-Spanish conventions in 1900, 1904, and 1912. Despite these extensions, the Spanish presence remained confined, in practice, to the tiny enclaves of Villa Cisneros, Tarfaya, and La Guere on the Bay of Levrier. No attempts were made to occupy the interior until 1934, although in principle the area, by then known as Rio de Oro, extended 150 miles inland.

During the 1930s, under the prodding of France, Spain sought to strengthen its control over Spanish possessions in the Western Sahara region. The Spanish, unlike the French who were aggressively trying to pacify their part of the region, had established a reasonably amicable relationship with the nomads operating along the nearby trans-Saharan trading routes. Spanish negligence, however, enabled anti-French resistance forces to establish sanctuaries from which they could stage *ghazzis*, or raids, against French positions in the neighboring territories. Following the French call for more control, Spanish occupation stretched inland to include the Saguia el-Hamra region in the north and the small enclave of Ifni*, nominally claimed by Spain since 1860 but not really occupied until the 1930s. In 1934 the Spanish Sahara region and Ifni were unified administratively with the Northern Zone of the Spanish protectorate in Morocco. Ultimate responsibility for the Spanish Sahara rested with the Spanish high commissioner of Spanish Morocco. This arrangement was called "Spanish Western Sahara," or more simply, "Spanish Sahara." As a response to growing Moroccan nationalism, the Southern Zone of Spanish Morocco was attached to the Spanish Sahara in 1946. This new overseas entity was dubbed Spanish West Africa, or AOE (Africa Occidental Espanola), with its own governor-general in Ifni and with a sub-governor in Western Sahara.

Spanish West Africa was dissolved in January 1958 when the Army of Liberation, a radical partisan movement which had played a role in gaining Moroccan independence from France in 1956, launched a guerrilla campaign against the Spanish in Ifni and Western Sahara. The Spanish government had no intention of quitting either Ifni or Western Sahara and turned both into Spanish provinces. As a Spanish "providence," Western Sahara was ruled by its own governor-general with a very wide range of powers, but he was responsible in military matters to the captain-general of the Canary Islands and in administrative matters to the president of Spain.

The threat from the Army of Liberation was largely removed following a joint Spanish-French counterinsurgency operation in February 1958. In April 1958 the Spanish government agreed to hand over the Southern Zone of Spanish Morocco to Morocco in the Agreement of Cintra. The protectorate over the Northern Zone of Spanish Morocco had come to an end with Moroccan independence in 1956. A detente between Spain and the Kingdom of Morocco followed and was further strengthened when Ifni was finally ceded to Morocco in 1969.

In 1974 Spain announced its intention of withdrawing from the Spanish Sahara province (by then, generally referred to as Western Sahara). King Hassan II of Morocco and Mokhtar Ould Daddah of Mauritania* reiterated their claims to the area, and in September 1974 Spain agreed to partition Western Sahara between them despite an advisory opinion from the International Court of Justice (October 16, 1975) rejecting the claims. In November 1975 Hassan, in an effort to force the integration of Western Sahara into Morocco, sent 350,000 unarmed Moroccans across the Western Sahara border (The Green March) and persuaded Spain to yield. On November 14, 1975, the Spanish government withdrew; and on February 26, 1976, the country was formally partitioned. Morocco received the largest and most valuable area, including the richest phosphate deposits in the world; Mauritania got the rest—mostly useless desert. (In 1979 Mauritania relinquished its claims in Western Sahara, leaving Morocco to annex the entire territory.)

The partition, however, was opposed by the Polisario Front, an indigenous nationalist group of Western Sahara Saharawi, formed in 1973. From the spring of 1975 the Polisario Front received substantial Algerian aid, and on February

27, 1976, declared the formation of the Saharan Arab Democratic Republic (SADR). By the 1980s the Polisario guerrilla army had swelled to 20,000 men, well-equipped and trained by Algeria and Libya. Battles frequently raged between the SADR guerrillas and the Moroccan army. By 1989 neither camp could claim outright victory and neither seemed ready to compromise. The status of Western Sahara has yet to be resolved. (John Mercer, *Spanish Sahara*, 1975.)

Eric C. Loew

SPICE ISLANDS. The romantic, mysterious ''Spice Islands'' are the Moluccas* of eastern Indonesia. They are not a geographical unit, for they actually consist of several separate island groups and contain a mixture of human races and cultures. The larger Spice Islands are Halmahera, Ceram, Buru, and the Tanimbar group, although some of the smaller islands such as Ternate,* Tidore, and Ambon were historically more significant. The Spice Islands are situated between Mindanao* on the north, Australia on the south, Celebes* on the west, and New Guinea* on the east. They straddle the equator.

Spices were highly prized in Europe, not for their taste but for their ability to preserve meat. Before the age of discovery, spices reached Europe via Javanese seamen, Malay traders, Arab merchants, and Venetian distributors. With all these middlemen, the price was exorbitant in western Europe. No European actually knew where the fabled Spice Islands were, only that they were very distant. They acted as a magnet, drawing first Portuguese and Spanish explorers, then Dutch and English merchants. Christopher Columbus* and John Cabot* both failed to reach the Spice Islands, but the Portuguese concluded an alliance with the sultan of Ternate in 1512 and built a fort there ten years later. Later in the sixteenth century Portuguese power in Asia waned and that of England and Holland waxed. Sir Francis Drake* brought a cargo of spices back to England in 1580. In 1602 the Dutch East India Company* was formed to organize procurement of spices and their shipment to northern Europe.

For the entire first half of the seventeenth century the Dutch had to fight Spaniards, Englishmen, and Indonesian natives for control of the spice trade. They evicted the Spanish from Ternate in 1608, and massacred a score of Englishmen and Javanese at Amboina (Ambon) in 1623. From 1650 to 1656 they fought to suppress a native rebellion. The Dutch monopoly yielded profits of up to 1,000 percent, but regulating the trade was hard. Foreign privateers had to be chased away, and ''bootleg'' spice plants uprooted. Overproduction was a constant danger. More than once the Dutch destroyed planted fields to reduce the supply and drive up the price. They tried assigning clove production exclusively to Amboina, Ternate, and Tidore; mace and nutmeg to Amboina and the Banda Islands. Black pepper was more widely cultivated. Dutch interest shifted when changing European tastes created a new, more lucrative market for Javanese coffee. Batavia* became the capital of the Netherlands East Indies, and Dutchmen referred to the former Spice Islands as the ''great east.'' Indonesians today think of them as part of the "Outer Islands." (Anthony Reid, *Southeast Asia in the Age of Commerce, 1450—1680*, 1988.)

                                                                                      Ross Marlay

SRI LANKA. Sri Lanka was formerly known as Ceylon. It is a large, teardrop-shaped island off the southeast coast of India*, about 270 miles long and 140 miles wide. There is one mountainous region in the center; rivers radiate outward in all directions to the coast. A wide coastal plain in the north is dry, but most of the rest of the island catches two monsoons a year and is lushly tropical. The climate and soils favor plantation crops: coffee, tea, cinnamon, cacao, coconuts and rubber. There are few minerals, but some iron ore. Gemstones are found. Sri Lanka's location, so close to India and directly on the maritime trade route between Europe and China, brought foreigners to the island from earliest times. The first known inhabitants were the primitive Veddas, few of whom survive. The Sinhalese, an Aryan people from north India, came by boat in the fifth century B.C. They dominate the political life of Sri Lanka today. Dark-skinned Tamils from southern India came in the first millenium of the Christian era. They are called Sri Lankan Tamils, to distinguish them from Indian Tamils, more recent immigrants brought by the British in the nineteenth century as coolie workers for the plantations.

A high civilization arose very early on Ceylon. The Sinhalese adopted Buddhism in the third century B.C. and built magnificent temple cities dominating the northern plain from Anuradhapura and Polonnaruwa. Irrigation generated a rice surplus. Monuments, reservoirs, and canals showed superior mathematical and engineering skills. Religious literature flourished. Great stupas housed venerated relics of the Buddha. Sri Lanka became a homeland for Buddhists after that religion was extinguished in India by Hindu reaction.

Because Sri Lanka is only 40 miles from the coast of India, Sinhalese kings became embroiled in south Indian wars. Tamils invaded in the thirteenth century, and the Sinhalese retreated to impregnable mountains in the south, from where they were able to dominate most of the island until Europeans came. A ship rounding the southern tip of India and heading for the far east will run into Sri Lanka. Arab traders came in the eighth century and today about 4 percent of the population is Muslim. Portuguese ships first appeared in 1505. The Sinhalese foolishly allowed them to build a fort in 1518. Soon they were taking sides in local wars, and got control of the whole island except the central highlands and part of the east coast. The Portuguese levied excessive taxes and tried to enforce a monopoly on the valuable export trade in cinnamon and elephants. They encouraged missionary work. Augustinians, Dominicans, Jesuits*, and Franciscans met with some success in converting elite Sinhalese to Roman Catholicism. In the process, some learned to speak Portuguese, too. But fiercely independent Sri Lankan kings, who were invulnerable in the mountains around Kandya, waited only for a chance to evict the foreigners. They could not do so without sea power, the dominant technology of the age, and so allied themselves with the Dutch, who were taking away Portuguese colonies all across Asia.

The Sinhalese soon found that the Dutch were less interested in their welfare than in usurping the Portuguese export monopolies. A three-way struggle developed. By 1658 the Portuguese were beaten and the Dutch controlled the coast and all the lowlands. Their regime was hardly better than that of the Iberians. They promoted Calvinism, with far less success than Portuguese Catholic missionaries had met, but did better at developing cinnamon production. The Kandyan kingdoms remained free, but isolated, during the whole Dutch period, which lasted until the Napoleonic Wars. In 1796 the Netherlands fell under French control, so British troops were sent from India to take the island they called Ceylon. The Dutch put up only a half-hearted resistance, and British control was formalized by the Treaty of Amiens of 1802*. The last independent Sinhalese kingdoms in the mountains were absorbed in 1818.

English rule was more progressive than that of earlier European imperialists. They abolished slavery and applied a unitary administrative and judicial system to the whole island. Monopolies were abandoned in favor of free trade. Immediately, commercial agriculture began to transform the island. Coffee plantations spread over the hills. Roads and railways were built. The harbor at Colombo* was deepened. Indentured laborers (Hindu Tamils) were brought from India. Ceylonese coffee plants succumbed to disease in the 1870s, but planters quickly substituted tea, for which the climate was perfect. Jungle was cleared for rubber and coconut plantations. English expatriates controlled banking and insurance houses, but an indigenous capitalist class arose, eventually to lead a peaceful independence movement.

The first stirrings of modern Sri Lankan nationalism were religiously inspired: Buddhists chafed under perceived British slights. But as a secular independence movement gained ground in India, the same occurred in Sri Lanka. The Ceylon National Congress was founded in 1919. Sri Lankan Tamils, fearing Sinhalese domination if the British should leave, organized to protect their own communal rights. The 1931 Donoughmore Commission made Ceylon the first colony in Asia to be granted universal suffrage. A second commission, in 1944, drafted a constitution that in modified form became the governing document of independent Ceylon on February 4, 1948.

Ceylon (renamed Sri Lanka in 1972) is an anomaly among third world countries. It has remained a democratic welfare state, although divided by terrible racial hatred. It is rated one of the poorest countries in the world according to standard economic criteria, yet boasts excellent health care and very good schools. Sri Lanka is regarded as a virtual paradise by western tourists, but the economy is still based on plantation exports and therefore remains at the mercy of an unpredictable global market. (K. M. DeSilva, *A History of Sri Lanka*, 1981; and K. M. DeSilva (ed.), *Sri Lanka: A Survey*, 1977.)

Ross Marlay

STATUTE OF WESTMINSTER. The Statute of Westminster was the legislative instrument which formally established the British Commonwealth of Nations*. Passed by the British parliament on December 11, 1931, it specifically defined the powers of Canada's parliament and those of the other dominions. The Imperial Conference of 1926* had declared the United Kingdom and its dominions as "autonomous communities . . . equal in status, in no way subordinate to one another," and the Statute of Westminster gave legal substance to that declaration. It specifically declared the parliaments of Canada*, Australia*, New Zealand*, the Union of South Africa*, the Irish Free State*, and Newfoundland* independent of United Kingdom legislative control. They could nullify British laws if they so chose, and the United Kingdom had no power to pass laws for them without their consent. See BRITISH COMMONWEALTH OF NATIONS.

STEAMBOAT. The steamboat gave Europeans the power to travel upriver and penetrate the interiors of Asia and Africa. First invented in the United States early in the 1800s, the steamboat was used sparingly in Europe because of the well-developed road system. But Europeans found the steamboat perfect for upriver navigation. It had taken the Portuguese more than 300 years to subdue the Amazon interior, and one of the reasons was their vulnerability to Indian attack while rowing upstream. But in the nineteenth century the Europeans developed the armed, shallow-draft steamboat, called a gunboat, to open up the two continents to colonization. In the 1820s the British East India Company* went into Burma* with gunboats, and gunboats played a key role in the British victory in the Opium Wars of the 1840s. The British, Dutch, French, and Portuguese used gunboats in their Third World conquests of the 1800s and 1900s. (Daniel R. Headrick, *The Tools of Empire. Technology and European Imperialism in the Nineteenth Century*, 1981.)

STRAITS SETTLEMENTS. In 1826 Great Britain created a single administrative unit out of the British protectorates of Singapore*, Malacca, Pinang, and Province Wellesley. At the time the Straits Settlement was under the sovereignty of the British East India Company.* The British East India Company ceded the Straits Settlements to the crown in 1858, and in 1867 the Straits Settlements became a crown colony. The Straits Settlements became part of the Malayan Union in 1945. See MALAYSIA.

STRONG, JOSIAH. A nationally prominent Congregational minister, Josiah Strong made a significant contribution to both the imperialistic impulse and social gospel movement. Born in Napierville, Illinois, on January 19, 1847, and educated at Western Reserve College, B.A., 1869, and Lane Seminary, 1869–1871, he held a succession of pastorates and religious posts, mostly in the Midwest: minister, Cheyenne, Wyoming, 1871–73; instructor and chaplain,

Western Reserve College, 1873–76; minister, Sandusky, Ohio, 1876–81; regional secretary, Congregation Congregational Home Missionary Society, 1881–84; minister, Cincinnati, Ohio, 1884–86; secretary, New York City, American Evangelical Alliance, 1886–98; and president, New York City, American Institute for Social Service, 1898–1916.

His first book, *Our Country: Its Possible Future and Its Present Crisis* (1885), struck a responsive chord among American imperialists and ensured the minister's prominence. He attributed American greatness to its Anglo-Saxon heritage of democracy and Christianity and boldly asserted that it was the nation's destiny to expand. "If I do not read amiss," wrote the parson, "this powerful race [Anglo-Saxon] will move down upon Mexico, down upon Central and South America, out upon the islands of the sea, over upon Africa and beyond." Similar arguments were put forth in *The New Era; or the Coming Kingdom* (1893), in which Strong declared that American expansionism was "like a ring of Saturn— a girdle of light—around the globe," and *Expansion Under New World Conditions* (1900). While many American ministers had reservations about the conquests of the Spanish-American War, Strong was not among them. By wedding the idea of Anglo-Saxon superiority to that of Christian responsibility to the "less fortunate," the minister easily justified the conflict with Spain and bestowed divine approval upon American imperialism. He believed God was preparing Anglo-Saxon America to impose its democratic and religous institutions upon inferior races.

It seems somewhat incongruous that such an avowed racist should also have been a leading social gospel minister, but such was the case. Indeed, the very writings in which Strong rationalized American imperialism and spoke condescendingly of "weaker races" often voiced concern for the plight of the poor and encouraged a practical application of the gospel. He was especially important in focusing the attention of the churches on the urban environment, particularly industrial centers characterized by monopolistic wealth and alienated working people. To Strong, the Kingdom of Jesus was of this world as well as the next, and so he challenged the churches to concern themselves with social conditions adversely affecting human welfare.

Strong not only publicized social problems, but also actively worked toward their resolution. He collected statistical data, carefully analyzed urban conditions, and strove for interdenominational cooperation. Convinced that righting the wrongs of modern industrial society required the unified resources of the churches, he attempted from 1886 to 1898 to use the Evangelical Alliance as a vehicle for interdenominational activity. Unsatisfied with the Alliance, he established the League (changed to Institute in 1902) for Social Service in 1898, over which he presided until his death in New York on April 28, 1916. In the meantime, he joined enthusiastically in the formation of the Federal Council of Churches in 1908. Strong, along with Walter Rauschenbusch, another major figure of the social gospel movement, deserves considerable credit for making the churches aware of the social dimensions of Christianity. Josiah Strong died in 1916. (Josiah Strong, *Religious Movements of Social Betterment*, 1900; *The Challenge of the City*, 1907; and *My Religion in Every Day Life*, 1910).

John W. Storey

SUDAN. See ANGLO-EGYPTIAN SUDAN.

SUEZ CANAL. The brainchild of Ferdinand de Lesseps, the Suez Canal, which connects the Mediterranean and the Red Sea, was opened in 1869. The Canal, dug with the blood and sweat of Egyptian peasants, 20,000 of whom died during construction, was the creation of a French company, which at first was boycotted by the British because of their interest in railways. Later Benjamin Disraeli bought shares in the Canal when the British realized that 90 percent of shipping going through the Canal was British. It became the major communication line between Britain and its Asian empire, especially India, and resulted in an occupation of Egypt in 1882, ostensibly to help the ruler put down a nationalist insurrection. The Canal was eventually evacuated by British forces in 1954 and nationalized the following year by Gamal Abd al-Nasser.

Of great importance to British supply routes during the two world wars, the Canal was an international waterway that cut sailing times between Europe and Asia and was credited with being one of the reasons for the scramble for Africa in terms of colonies on the part of England and France. With the demise of the British Empire in Asia, especially in India, it became necessary for the British government to cut down expenses overseas and consider an evacuation of the Canal. Today the Canal is important as a waterway bringing oil from the Gulf regions to the western world, even though passage through it was interrupted twice, a first time briefly, in 1956, and a second time for eight years (1967–1975), following the Six Days War. (Patrick B. Kinross, *Between Two Seas, the Creation of the Suez Canal*, 1969).

Alain G. Marsot

SUKARNO. Born on June 6, 1901, Sukarno was a great nationalist leader and brilliant spellbinder who led "his" Indonesian people to independence and then down the road of ever more bizarre domestic and foreign policies. Sukarno's father was a Javanese Muslim, his mother a Balinese Hindu. His childhood was suffused with magical themes; indeed, for Javanese his very name resonates with folk tales of a long-ago mythic prince. Sukarno's upbringing instilled in him the idea on which he based his entire life and thought, that he could synthesize opposites. Sukarno attended elementary and secondary school in Surabaya, boarding at the home of the famous intellectual Tjokroaminoto, leader of Indonesia's first modern political movement, Sarekat Islam. In that stimulating environment, he listened to debates about religion, nationalism, democracy, and communism. There is no doubt that Sukarno was highly intelligent, for he is said to have mastered four Indonesian languages, four European languages, plus

Arabic and Japanese. He read European political philosophy, too, and his pursuit of a civil engineering degree at the Bandung Technical Institute (1921–1925) was inappropriate to his talents.

Sukarno founded a Bandung Study Club in 1926, and the Indonesian Nationalist Party the next year. Sarekat Islam had dissipated, and the fledgling communist party had gone underground. The way was open for an eclectic nationalism with no goal more specific than throwing out the Dutch. He was inspired by the Non-Cooperation Movement in India, but not by its pacifism. Sukarno discovered that he had charisma. His voice swayed crowds, his radiant style riveted their attention. He propounded a doctrine he called "Marhaenism," which was simply Indonesian populism. He revived ancient Javanese prophecies and interpreted them to mean an imminent end to Dutch imperialism. Sukarno was arrested, but turned his own trial into a defense of Indonesian nationalism. When he was released from jail in 1931, crowds again flocked to hear him speak, so the Dutch arrested him again and kept him safely tucked away in remote places until the Japanese set him free in 1942.

Sukarno admired the Japanese and worked closely with them, managing to enhance his nationalist credentials in the process. Collaboration was not shameful in the eyes of Indonesians, so hated were the Dutch. Sukarno's voice was heard on the radio preaching nationalism and pan-Asianism. The Japanese sponsored Indonesian youth groups, a civil administration, and a militia—all of which became core institutions in the Republic of Indonesia after the war. After initially wavering, Sukarno proclaimed Indonesian independence on August 17, 1945. Allied troops did not land until six weeks later.

The Dutch wanted to reconstitute their Netherlands East Indies empire, but Asian nationalism was an irresistable force in the changed postwar political climate. Four years of bitter fighting ended with complete victory for the nationalist side in December 1949. Sukarno was made president of the United States of Indonesia, but parliamentary democracy was not for him. His syncretic philosophy of *Pantjasila* (Five Principles: nationalism, internationalism, democracy, social welfare, and belief in God) was too vague to offer concrete guidance. The next five years were boring and frustrating. Politicians bickered. The public grew disillusioned. Sukarno sought relief by convening a conference of Asian and African leaders in Bandung, where his flamboyant speeches attracted the international attention he increasingly seemed to need.

Sukarno proclaimed in 1957 that henceforth Indonesians should solve their differences by the old Javanese village institution of *gotong-royong*, or self-help. Consensus would emerge. Hidden in this seemingly innocuous formulation was Sukarno's fascist belief that he embodied the general will of the Indonesian nation. It was all downhill from there. In 1959 he abandoned what he contemptuously called "50% plus one democracy" for a "new" system called Guided Democracy. He suspended parliament in 1960 and named himself president for life in 1963.

The economy began to slide. Inflation reduced the value of the rupiah from ten to the dollar to 12,000 to the dollar. Sukarno's solution was to go on the radio and tell Indonesians to draw a line through the last two zeroes on their paper currency. He diverted attention by staging a confrontation with the Malaysian Federation, the formation of which he said was an imperialist plot. He convinced the United Nations to expel the Dutch from New Guinea. He denounced both the United States and the Soviet Union, saying he represented the Nefos (New Emerging Forces) of the world. Acronyms became the discourse of politics. His progressive megalomania expressed itself in monuments that still disfigure Jakarta today. He began to spend more time with his newest wife, the beautiful Japanese barmaid Ratna Sari Dewi. Finally, in 1965, it all came undone.

Sukarno believed he had a magical ability to make contradictions disappear, but actually they were growing, especially the political contradiction between left (the Partai Kommunis Indonesia) and right (the Army). On the night of September 30, 1965, six generals were murdered and their bodies thrown down a well. Whoever the conspirators were, they missed an officer named Suharto. Under his leadership the army killed all communists they could find. A reign of terror spread through Java and Bali. No one knows how many people died; perhaps about 500,000. Sukarno went into involuntary retirement and died on July 21, 1970. (John D. Legge, *Sukarno: A Political Biography*, 1972.)

Ross Marlay

SUMATRA. Sumatra is the thousand-mile-long westernmost island of Indonesia. It is three times the size of Java and thirty times that of Holland, its former colonial ruler. Sumatra is separated from the Malayan peninsula by the Strait of Malacca, and from Java by the Sunda Strait. The Indian Ocean lies to the south, but most of the coastline is protected from the full force of its winds and waves by a line of offshore islands. The Sumatran mountains follow one great tectonic arc that actually begins in Burma and continues eastward through the rest of Indonesia. Sumatra has many active volcanoes; the famous Krakatoa lies just off the island's southeast coast. West of the mountains the land falls off steeply to the sea, but to their east lies a wide, low, swampy alluvial plain stretching to the mangrove swamps that border the Malacca strait. Silty rivers are constantly rearranging the coastline so all east coast ports, including the notable towns of Djambi and Palembang, are actually many miles upriver. The equator runs right through the middle of Sumatra, dividing it neatly in half, so temperature depends on altitude rather than season. There is plenty of rain to support a dense jungle with wild animals, including the orangutan, gibbon, elephant, tiger, rhinoceros, and crocodile.

Had the Dutch not imposed political unity, Sumatra might today consist of four or five separate countries, for its people belong to distinct ethnic groups, each with its own proud history. The strongly Islamic Achehnese have little in common with the Christian and animist Bataks, or even with the Minangkabau, who adopted some Islamic beliefs while retaining their ancient Hindu-Buddhist culture. There are Malays along the east coast, Javanese in the south, and small tribes in the remote mountains. Until the late nineteenth century, most Sumatrans not engaged in trade or piracy were subsistence farmers and fishermen.

Sumatra's strategic position at the midpoint of the trade route between east (China, the Spice Islands) and west (India, Arabia, and Europe) attracted foreigners. Sumatra traded with India from the dawn of the Christian era, and with China from at least the fifth century. An early state called Malayu had its capital at Djambi in the east. It was soon absorbed by the great Buddhist Srivijayan empire centered on Palembang. Srivijaya waxed powerful around 700 A.D. by controlling trade through the Strait of Malacca. Srivijaya dominated much of what is now Malaya, placed a king on the throne in Cambodia, and made its influence felt as far away as Ceylon* and Formosa*. Palembang became a center of Buddhist scholarship, but left no great stone monuments like those in Java and Cambodia. Srivijaya's fortunes waned when the collapse of the Chinese T'ang dynasty depressed commerce. It was attacked by Cholas from India, and then disintegrated into separate sultanates after Islam spread to Sumatra in the 1200s.

Acheh, an especially aggressive sultanate on the northern tip of Sumatra, seized control of the straits and grew confident enough to fight the Portuguese and Dutch. The Dutch first allied themselves with Acheh against the Portuguese, but then turned on Acheh, using a tactic they repeated over and over again for the next 300 years: divide and conquer. They persuaded a number of sultans to sell pepper only to the Dutch East Indies Company (VOC) in return for a guarantee of protection against Acheh. One by one, Sumatran towns fell under nominal Dutch suzerainty: Djambi in 1615; Palembang in 1616; Padang in 1662; Indrapura in 1664. The British established their own pepper station at Bencoolen* on the southwest coast in 1685.

The Dutch concentrated their efforts on Java in the eighteenth century, but in the late nineteenth century, influenced by ideas of free trade and fearful of other European imperialists, they imposed direct rule on Sumatra. The Treaty of London (1824) designated all Sumatra a Dutch sphere in return for Dutch recognition of British Singapore. Whenever local chiefs or sultans faced domestic rebellion, the Dutch sent troops. First, they supported Minangkabau chiefs who were locked in civil war with zealous Islamic reformers. Skirmishes in the 1820s and major campaigns in the 1830s culminated in a Dutch victory in 1837. The Dutch quickly downgraded the chiefs and imposed compulsory coffee planting. Rebellions in Palembang triggered repeated military expeditions. An insurrection in Djambi kept the Dutch busy from 1858 until 1904. Battles were fought on the Nias Islands in 1847, 1855, and 1863. The Batak War lasted from 1872 to 1895. The upper Hari River area was subdued in a five-year campaign, 1890–1895. The Acheh War was the most bitter of all. It dragged on from 1873 until 1903. The Dutch tried everything. They bombarded Kutaraja, cut off trade, sent 10,000 native troops recruited from other islands, burned villages, and drove the Islamic guerrillas into the mountains. The war finally sputtered out due to Achehnese exhaustion. The Netherlands Indies treasury was nearly drained.

Asian trade and commerce accelerated dramatically after the Suez Canal opened in 1869. Tobacco planting around Medan began in the 1860s and quickly escalated into something Sumatra (and Southeast Asia) had not known before: huge plantations where imported Chinese and Javanese coolie laborers cleared forests for commercial export agriculture. Englishmen and Americans joined Dutchmen in constructing almost autonomous societies in an area known as the Oostkust, or East Coast Residency. Planters diversified into coffee, ramie fiber, copra, palm oil, tea in the highlands, and the most valuable crop of all, rubber. Demand for rubber grew in the twentieth century, with the western automobile industry. Three unconnected railroads were built to bring out coal, timber, and plantation crops. In all this the planters were aided by an 1880 law, the "Coolie Ordinance for Oostkust Residency" which allowed overseers to impose penalties for idleness. Dutch policy shifted after 1900. New laws protected workers from abuse, but compulsory labor in Medan was not abandoned until 1928.

Oil was discovered in Sumatra in the 1890s. Soon Royal Dutch Shell and Standard Oil of California were drilling and building pipelines in the Palembang-Djambi area. Sumatra's resources became so vital to the industrial powers that Japan believed she could not live without them. Sumatran oil and rubber seemed essential to war planners in Tokyo. Sumatrans endured Japanese brutality from 1942 to 1945 and joined Sukarno's fight for independence from 1946 to 1949, but have not always liked being part of independent Indonesia. A 1958 rebellion, aided by the CIA, was the strongest, but not the sole, recent expression of Sumatran separatism. Since the island continues to provide most of Indonesia's foreign exchange, but receives few benefits from Jakarta, future rebellions are not unlikely. (David Steinberg, *et al.*, *In Search of Southeast Asia*, 1971.)

Ross Marlay

SURAT. In 1612 the British East India Company established its first factory in India*—at Surat on the west coast of the subcontinent. For the next fifty-six years Surat was the headquarters of British operations in India, until Bombay* assumed that role in 1668. Until 1687, however, the presidency remained in Surat. After that, the governor of Bombay served as Surat's president. Beginning in 1687, Surat was governed out of Bombay until 1947 when India won its independence. See INDIA.

SURINAM. See DUTCH GUIANA.

SWAN RIVER COLONY. The Swan River drains the barren lands of Western Australia into the Indian Ocean near present-day Perth. For years after the settlement of Sydney, Australia, Britain showed no interest in Western Australia because of its isolation and the Dutch claim that the area was "New Holland." But the Dutch had neither the resources nor the inclination to develop New Holland and it remained uninhabited by Europeans. In 1826, frightened by news of French expansion on the islands of the Indian Ocean, Great Britain laid claim to Western Australia. On December 25, 1826, the British established the colony of Albany when 44 soldiers and convicts settled at King George's Sound. At the same time, some British investors began looking on Western Australia as a place to raise sheep and supply wool to England's booming textile mills. Government officials thought the scheme a worthy one, especially if they could settle some of England's unemployed workers in the distant land. In 1828 the government granted Thomas Peel 250,000 acres of land in Western Australia in return for his agreement to invest 80,000 pounds in the venture and settle 400 free laborers there. On June 18, 1829, James Stirling, the first governor, reached the Swan River Colony.

The Swan River Colony grew slowly and economic life was marginal at best. Geographically isolated on the Indian Ocean, without any roads, railroads, or telegraphs to the rest of Australia, Swan River found it almost impossible to attract settlers. By 1841 there were only 2,760 Europeans living in an area of more than one million square miles, and by 1850 that number had reached only 7,186. Between 1850 and 1868 the British government sent 10,000 convicts to work the land in Swan River, but even then the colony struggled along.

It was not until the 1890s, when gold was discovered there, that the Swan River Colony, now known as Western Australia, experienced substantial population growth. Tens of thousands of miners rushed into the territory, boosting its population and integrating it culturally and economically with the eastern regions of Australia. At the time there was considerable nationalist sentiment in eastern Australia and the federation movement was gaining momentum. The discovery of gold made Western Australia an important entity for the first time to easterners; and they appealed to Western Australia to join Queensland, Victoria, South Australia, and New South Wales in creating a new, continental nation. In Western Australia, politicians agreed to the federation if the easterners would construct a transcontinental railroad connecting Perth with the east coast. The easterners agreed and on January 1, 1901, the new Commonwealth of Australia was created, including Western Australia. The railroad to Perth was completed in 1917. (F. K. Crowley, *Australia's Western Third*, 1960.)

SWAZILAND. Swaziland is a landlocked country in southern Africa bounded on the north, west, and south by the Republic of South Africa, and on the east by South Africa* and Mozambique*. The Swazi sprang from the Nguni group of the Bantu-speaking peoples, who moved into southeastern Africa from the north in the sixteenth century. The Dlamini—one of the clans of the Nguni-Bantu—migrated from lands west of Delagoa Bay around the year 1750, conquering and absorbing numerous other clans and tribes, and settling eventually in what is today Swaziland, under the leadership of Sobhuza I (c. 1780–1839). In the early nineteenth century, the Dlamini kingdom faced a constant military threat from the powerful Zulu nation to the south. Mswati (a.k.a. Mswazi), Sobhuza's son and successor, appealed to the British in Natal for help against the Zulu in the 1850s and was given assurances of British protection. Thus the name of the Swazi tribe is taken from that of Mswati, who delivered his people from the danger of Zulu domination.

The dread of Zulu power led the Swazi to deal with the Boer Voortrekkers who, by the 1850s, had moved into areas of the Transvaal* adjacent to Swaziland. Seeking alliances against the Zulu and other enemies, the Swazi ceded land to the Boers in order to create a buffer zone between themselves and Zululand, beginning a period of European encroachment on Swaziland which would continue for several decades. In the 1870s and 1880s, Boer settlers and unscrupulous European entrepreneurs flocked into the country to acquire land and valuable concessions of every kind; and the discovery of gold in 1882 only exacerbated the situation. Swazi independence had been guaranteed in Anglo-Boer treaties in 1881 and 1884, but the excessive granting of concessions to Europeans by Mbandzeni, a young and inexperienced Swazi ruler (c. 1857–1889), had created such confusing conditions that the British and Transvaal governments in 1890 agreed to set up a provisional government in Swaziland to represent the interests of the Swazi, British, and Boers. This arrangement soon proved unworkable, and in 1894 a further Anglo-Boer convention placed Swaziland under the administration of the South African Republic (Transvaal).

After the Anglo-Boer War of 1899–1902, Britain somewhat reluctantly assumed the burden of administration in Swaziland. In 1906, Swaziland was officially declared a British protectorate and was placed under the authority of the British High Commissioner for South Africa, who was represented in the territory by a Resident Commissioner.

Sobhuza II (1899–1982), who became king in 1921, launched a costly legal battle to recover the lands that had been signed away to concession-hunters by previous Swazi rulers. In 1926, the Judicial Committee of the Privy Council, the highest court of appeal in the British Empire, ruled against Sobhuza, leaving at least half of Swaziland in the possession of European landholders. In 1941 the British recognized the Paramount chief (Sobhuza) as the supreme African authority in the Swaziland and granted him the power to issue legally enforceable laws applicable to the Africans in the territory.

The most serious threat to the existence of Swaziland in the first half of the twentieth century was the provision in the South Africa Act (1909) for the incorporation of the High Commission territories—i.e., Swaziland, Basutoland, and Bechuanaland—into the Union of South Africa. Several attempts were made by South Africa in the 1920s and 1930s to absorb Swaziland into the Union; however, Great Britain's insistence over the years that such incorporation must be contingent upon the agreement of Swaziland kept South Africa from ingesting its small, landlocked neighbor.

In the early 1960s an independence movement began to take shape in Swaziland. In 1960 the first Swazi political party, the Swaziland Progressive Party, was formed; and in 1964 a party called the Imbokodvo National Movement was established with the backing of King Sobhuza II. Imbokadvo began to advocate immediate independence. Swaziland was granted internal self-government in

1967. Elections for the House of Assembly were held in that year, and the Imbokodvo Party won a resounding victory. An independence conference met at Marlborough House in London in February, 1968; and Swaziland regained its independence and became a member of the Commonwealth of Nations on September 6, 1968.

As an independent nation, Swaziland functioned in the beginning under a Parliamentary system, with Prince Makhosini Dlamini serving as Prime Minister and Sobhuza II reigning as a constitutional monarch. In 1973, Sobhuza suspended the constitution and placed the government of Swaziland under royal control. (Potholm, Christian P. *Swaziland: The Dynamics of Political Modernization*, 1972; Grotpeter, John J. *Historical Dictionary of Swaziland*, 1975; Stevens, Richard P. Lesotho, *Botswana and Swaziland*, 1967.)

Joseph L. Michaud

SYKES-PICOT AGREEMENT OF 1916. The Sykes-Picot Agreement of 1916 was concluded between Great Britain and France and concerned the division of the Middle Eastern, primarily Arab, territories of the Ottoman Empire. Negotiated and prepared by the British diplomat Sir Mark Sykes and the French diplomat Georges Picot, the accord was coordinated with the government of Tsarist Russia in March 1916 and concluded in London in the form of an exchange of notes between May 9 and May 16. The Sykes-Picot Agreement provided for Anglo-French domination of most of the Middle East. The specific arrangements included Russian control over the Ottoman provinces of Erzurum, Trebizond, Van and Bitlis. Great Britain would acquire hegemony over southern Mesopotamia, including Baghdad, plus the Mediterranean port towns of Haifa and Acre. France was to be given control of Lebanon and the greater part of Syria. The Sykes-Picot Agreement also promised that between the French and British spheres of influence there should be created a confederation of independent Arab states or a single independent Arab state, with economic and political control divided between France and Britain. Palestine, containing the holy city of Jerusalem and other religious sites, was to be placed under an international administration.

The Sykes-Picot agreement was concluded in secret and most of the treaty's arrangements were inherently contradictory to solemn promises made in 1915 to the Hashemite Arabs, notably Hussein Ibn Ali, the most influential anti-Turkish Arab leader. While both Britain and France were contemplating the division of the former Turkish provinces, Britain was negotiating for Arab aid against Turkey and promising eventual independence for the Arab states, to be guaranteed by Britain, France, Russia, and Italy. The terms of this independence were the subject of secret correspondence (not revealed until 1939) between the British high commissioner in Cairo, Sir Henry McMahon, and Hussein. In his letters to Hussein, McMahon specifically excluded Syria and the "Holy Places" from the future independent Arab states, but the high commissioner made no specific reference to Palestine.

With Russia's exit from the Allied war effort, the Sykes-Picot plan for Russian hegemony in Armenian Anatolia was canceled. In April 1917, Italy, having joined the Allied Powers in 1916, was promised southern and southwestern Anatolia by the Agreement of Saint-Jean-de-Maurienne. When made public by the Bolshevik Revolutionary government in 1917, the Sykes-Picot terms infuriated the Arabs, who were certain that their efforts on behalf of the Allies in the war against Turkey were to be rewarded with Arab independence. The Sykes-Picot Agreement never came into force, but Arab resentment continued despite territorial revisions made in favor of the Arabs in the subsequent Conference of San Remo in April 1920. (Ronald Sanders, *The High Walls of Jerusalem: A History of the Balfour Declaration and the Birth of the British Mandate for Palestine*, 1983; Ann Williams, *Britain and France in the Middle East and North Africa, 1914–1967*, 1968.)

William G. Ratliff

SYRIA. The geographic area known today as Syria was the center of a much larger entity and of an advanced Semitic civilization and empire which, around 2500 B.C., spread from Turkey to the Red Sea and from the Mediterranean to Mesopotamia. Dating from that time, the capital city of Damascus has been one of the oldest continuously inhabited cities in the world. Located at the crossroads of three continents, Syria has been on the path of many invasions and has been occupied throughout the centuries by peoples such as the Canaanites, Phoenicians, Aramaeans, Assyrians, Babylonians, Persians, Greeks, Romans, and Byzantines. With the spread of Islam, it came early under Muslim rule in 636, four years after the death of the Prophet Mohammed. From 661 to 750, Damascus was the capital of the Islamic empire under the caliphs of the Ummayyad dynasty. Then, the center of gravity of the empire moved to Baghdad with the advent of the Abbasid Caliphate, and Syria lost its autonomy until the present century. Briefly affected by the Crusaders from western Europe, Syria became a province of the Mameluke empire in the thirteenth century. In 1400 Damascus was nearly entirely destroyed by the Mongol conqueror Tamerlane, but was soon rebuilt. In 1516, together with Egypt, Syria fell under Ottoman rule, which lasted for the next 400 years. Ottoman rule was interrupted for eight years (1833–41) as a result of conquest by Mohammed Ali of Egypt, whose son Ibrahim governed Syria well, with reforms in the areas of education and taxation, which ushered the beginning of the modern age, as well as that of Arab nationalism, as some Arab historians claim.

In the countries of the Fertile Crescent, until World War I, Western educators revitalized Arab intellectualism. They were mostly Catholic missionaries from France and Presbyterian missionaries from America. They set up schools and printing presses, spreading among the young, Muslims and Christians alike, ideas of human rights and a renewed perception of their common Arab cultural heritage, leading to nationalism and a desire for independence. In that part of the Middle East, nationalism was directed at the Ottomans in the guise of secret societies, aiming at independence for Syria, including Lebanon. This was exacerbated by repression and programs of Turkification implemented by the Young Turks in Istanbul. During World War I the British and the French persuaded Arab nationalists in the Levant to revolt against the Ottomans, with vague promises of independence such as in the Sharif Hussein-MacMahon correspondence, accompanied by secret deals between the Allies, proposing to share between themselves the spoils of the Ottoman Empire. One such secret deal was the Sykes-Picot Agreement in 1916*.

At the end of the war Syria as well as the rest of the Fertile Crescent found itself in a confused situation, characterized by deceptions and contradictions, exacerbated by the Fourteen Points of United States President Woodrow Wilson, which acknowledged the right of dependent peoples to self-determination. As a result, Amir Faisal, of the powerful Hashemite family, who had ousted the Ottomans from Syria with British help, was proclaimed king of an independent Arab kingdom centered in Damascus in 1920. But his new independence was soon frustrated by Western imperialism. The Allies' secret agreements governing the fate of the spoils of the Ottoman Empire had promised Syria to the French. The French sent an ultimatum to Faisal, which was rejected. Then they defeated Syrian forces at the battle of Maysalu and occupied Damascus; Faisal went into exile, later to be compensated by being made king of Iraq by the British authorities. Against the expressed rejection of the Syrian population, the League of Nations granted France a mandate over Syria and Lebanon.

The French fragmented their Middle Eastern mandate, attempting to play religious and ethnic groups against each other. But bitter resistance to their rule persisted from 1920 to 1946, marked by revolts and uprisings, notably in the Jebel Druze, and on two occasions the French bombed Damascus. At the time of the Popular Front in France, the Socialist government signed a treaty with Syria, providing for a Syrian provisional government and constitutional assembly. But that treaty was not ratified in Paris. With World War II, and after the fall of France, Syria was controlled by Vichy France until British and Free French forces occupied it in 1941. While the Gaullist authorities went through the moves of appointing a Syrian president and holding elections in the country, they intended to maintain there a preponderant political and cultural influence, as well as a military presence. Under British, American, and Russian pressure, the French agreed in principle to withdraw their troops. But when Syria manifested its independence, declaring war on Germany in February 1945 and becoming a charter member of the UN, the French tried to reassert their presence and again shelled Damascus in May 1945. At that point, Winston Churchill issued an ultimatum to Charles De Gaulle, who even considered a direct confrontation with England. But the last French forces ultimately left Syria in April 1946, when the Syrian republican government, formed in the last years of the mandate, finally took over control of an independent Syria. (Ann Williams, *Britain and France in the Middle East and North Africa, 1914–1967*, 1968.)

Alain G. Marsot

T

TAHITI. See FRENCH POLYNESIA.

TANGANYIKA. Tanganyika comprised territory of approximately 360,000 sparsely populated square miles in central east Africa. Its history was closely tied in with that of its off-shore neighbor Zanzibar*, with which it formed the nation of Tanzania* in 1964. For Tanganyika, the colonial era opened in the early nineteenth century when Arab traders pushed into the interior in search of slaves and ivory. The routes to Lake Tanganyika became well-worn from the passage of such black and white ivory from Ujiji, through Tabora, and on to Zanzibar. These places became important Arab trading centers, although their formal rule was limited to ejecting local chieftains who interrupted the trade.

European missionaries were the first whites to show an interest in the interior, discovering Mt. Kilimanjaro in the 1840s. The great explorers soon followed, with Richard Burton and John H. Speke traveling to Lake Tanganyika in 1857–1858. Speke went on to Lake Victoria. In 1860 Speke set out again, this time with J. A. Grant to find the source of the Nile in Lake Victoria. Dr. David Livingstone set out in 1866 for Lake Nyasa, hoping to open the interior to trade more legitimate and Christian than that of the slave traffic. Livingstone was followed by the journalist-explorer Henry M. Stanley who presumably found him at Ujiji in 1872.

The age of great explorers was rapidly followed by the age of empire. Karl Peters, a German acting with the approval of Otto Von Bismarck, claimed land in the interior, mostly by striking deals with local chieftains. The Anglo-German Agreement of 1886 acknowledged Peter's efforts, ceding to Germany what became Tanganyika, while Britain took Kenya*. The sultan of Zanzibar retained some rights to a ten-mile strip along the entire coast. An Arab rebellion along the Tanganyikan coast two years later gave the European powers the excuse to crush any indigenous power, which German troops and the British navy promptly did. During the 1890s the Germans consolidated their rule, taking the sultan's littoral strip, and then integrating Tanganyika to the international commodities market with the introduction of sisal hemp production. A new railway system permitted the interior to produce coffee, rubber, and cotton for the international market.

But Tanganyika balked at joining this system. The struggle for labor brought great oppression and resentment. The Maji Maji rebellion exploded in 1905 and was not put down until 1907. So great was the outburst that the repression was successful only when all remnants of resistance were obliterated. The Germans crushed traditional societies throughout the land, leaving only famine and extreme discord. With all dissent crushed the Germans could afford to experiment in a more liberal colonialism, starting in 1907. During World War I, the British occupied Tanganyika, and were given a formal League of Nations mandate over the territory with the peace. Sir Donald Cameron, the British governor (1925–31), tried to make the country strong enough to play a viable role in providing raw materials for the international market.

The Great Depression and World War II wreaked havoc on these efforts, closing down much of the trade upon which the country was growing dependent. With the close of the war, Britain made grand plans to "develop" the Tanganyikan economy. The Colonial Development and Welfare Act of 1940 sought to provide imperial financing for long-term colonial development, and by 1949 £35,870,000 had been spent on a ground nuts scheme which failed miserably. The scheme had been designed with little attention paid to the needs of the Tanganyikan economy to develop more than another weak cash crop. All it served to do was to assuage the British conscience as the Empire started to pull out of east Africa. Tanganyika was an intensely poor country, and Britain no longer had any strategic or economic use for it. The Tanganyika African National Union (TANU) was given power within the government in the 1950s, and by 1959 the nation was prepared for elections. An African majority was elected to the government in 1960, under the leadership of the charismatic Julius Nyerere*. He formed the first independent government of the country as prime minister in December 1961. A year later Nyerere was elected the first president of the Republic of Tanganyika. In 1964 Tanganyika entered into a national union with its neighbor Zanzibar, with Nyerere as president. (Martin Bailey, *Union of Tanganyika and Zanzibar: A Study in Political Integration*, 1986; John Iliffe, *A Modern History of Tanganyika*, 1979.)

Mark R. Shulman

TANGIER. Tangier is a city on the northwest tip of Africa right at the entrance to the Strait of Gibraltar,* and as such has held strategic significance for Spain, France, Great Britain, and Portugal. Portugal first conquered Tangier in 1471, but in 1661 it was transferred to Great Britain as part of Catarina of Braganca's dowry when she married Charles II of England. The British kept Tangier only until 1684, when they decided it was not worth keeping, especially in view of the intense military pressure from Morocco.* Great Britain abandoned Tangier in 1684 and Morocco seized it. (David P. Henige, *Colonial Governors from the Fifteenth Century to the Present*, 1970.)

TANZANIA. The United Republic of Tanganyika and Zanzibar was proclaimed on April 27, 1964, with the merger of Tanganyika* and Zanzibar*, which had achieved independence from Great Britain in 1961 and 1963 respectively. On October 29, 1964, the union was renamed Tanzania. At the time of the merger, Tanzania had a population of just over ten million people. The country is located on the eastern coast of Africa, along the Indian Ocean, south of Kenya and Uganda. See TANGANYIKA and ZANZIBAR.

TASMAN, ABEL JANSZOON. Abel Janszoon Tasman was born in Gronigen, The Netherlands, in 1603 and went to work for the Dutch East India Company* in 1633. In 1642 Governor Anthony van Dieman assigned Tasman to make an exploratory voyage from the Dutch East Indies* south along the edge of New Holland* in search of rich new land for Dutch conquest. He sailed from Java* to Mauritius* and from there south of Australia to Tasmania, which he named Van Dieman's Land*. Tasman sailed on to the east and reached New Zealand*. His voyage continued into 1643 when he reached the islands in the Tonga* and Fiji* group. The ship went on to the New Hebrides* and returned to Batavia* on June 15, 1643. Tasman later completed several other voyages for the Dutch East India Company before his death in 1659. (Anthony Sharp, *The Voyages of Abel Janszoon Tasman*, 1968.)

TASMANIA. See VAN DIEMAN'S LAND.

TAYOWAN. The term Tayowan was used by the Dutch to refer to their colony on the island of Formosa*. See FORMOSA.

THAILAND. Thailand is the modern name for the kingdom formerly known as Siam. The country is mountainous in the north and west, where it borders Laos* and Burma*. Northeastern Thailand, bordering Cambodia*, is mostly a dry plateau. The south is a long, narrow peninsula stretching down to Malaysia*. The most densely populated area, and the political heart of the country, is the central plain around the Chao Phraya river valley, where rice is grown on flat, easily irrigated land, and where a network of estuaries and canals enables Thais to get around easily by boat. Thailand is not without natural resources but lacks the natural bounty that attracted Europeans to other Asian countries.

Thailand is the only country in Southeast Asia to have escaped colonization, so Thais entered the modern world free from the defensive nationalism common to their neighbors. Their openness and self-confidence in dealing with foreigners contrasts sharply with the truculent isolationism of Burmese, the xenophobia of Cambodians, and the fierce self-reliance of Vietnamese. Thai kings recognized Western strength and yielded to European demands, even to the extent of surrendering outlying satrapies. They thereby preserved their independence.

Another difference between Thailand and most other Southeast Asian countries is in the homogeneity of its population. The usual dichotomy between hill tribes and lowlanders is here blurred because the Thais themselves came from the mountains of Chinese Yunnan. Thailand is 95 percent Buddhist. The only unassimilated minority is a small Muslim population near the border with Malaysia. Siamese culture was profoundly influenced by the Hinduized people the Thais overran in their southward march from the wilds of Yunnan. Thai architecture, cosmology, and writing are all Indian in inspiration. Theravada Buddhism, so central to the daily lives of Thais, also originated in India. Hindu-Buddhist notions of statecraft and kingship encouraged passivity on the throne—the king's role was to perform rituals to keep kingdom and cosmos in balance—but here the Thais broke with Indic tradition. Thai kings, especially in the modern period, have been activists who not only reigned, but governed.

Early European contact with Thailand made little impact. Some Portuguese adventurers visited Ayudhya in the 1500s, and in the next century Dutchmen came seeking a trade monopoly. The English wanted to trade too, and the French to proselytize, but in 1688 the Thais expelled all Europeans to concentrate on their more immediate enemies, the Burmese, who invaded in 1764 but were driven back. Burmese fortunes declined when they became embroiled in wars with the British, and the Siamese may well have noted Burmese helplessness against modern arms. It was Thailand's great good fortune that in 1851, just when the British invaded lower Burma and shortly before the French embarked on their conquest of Indochina*, a 47-year-old monk named Mongkut was crowned king. Mongkut was energetic and far-seeing. He mastered many modern Asian languages, as well as the ancient Sanskrit and Pali scripts of India, then Latin and English. He had no fear of Westerners, but saw the dire threat they posed. Rather than resisting, he bent with the wind.

Mongkut invited foreign missionaries to teach him Western science and decreed changes in Thai customs he deemed backward. He reformed the bureaucracy and popularized the monarchy. He granted Westerners free trade and diplomatic relations and signed humiliating treaties with the British, French, and Americans. He even ceded Siamese suzerainty over western Cambodia to France. But Mongkut would not surrender Thai sovereignty nor would he be provoked into a military response that might give the British or the French a pretext to intervene. Mongkut died in 1868, and was followed on the throne by another progressive ruler, the young Chulalongkorn. After a five-year regency, during which he traveled around Southeast Asia seeing British and Dutch colonies firsthand, Chulalongkorn ruled until 1910. He continued his father's twin policies of modernization at home and accomodation abroad. He founded public schools, created a modern army, and updated Thai laws. Foreign affairs posed a knotty problem. The British were clearly the strongest power in Asia. To appease them, Chulalongkorn actually allowed them to regulate Thai finances. But the French threatened too, and when they trained guns on his palace in 1893, Chulalongkorn gave them Laos. Finally, to the immense relief of all Thais, the Anglo-French Treaty of 1896 established Siam as a buffer zone between French Indochina and British Burma*.

Thailand was economically but not socially transformed by the great increase in Asian trade and commerce that accompanied the age of imperialism. The international trade in rice multiplied many times over. Thai farmers expanded production, but royal decrees supported smallholders and discouraged landlordism. Chinese middlemen, who elsewhere in Asia formed a class apart, were assimilated into Thai society by intermarriage. Chulalongkorn traveled to Europe twice and lived to see Westerners accept Thailand as a sovereign equal. He created a modern state and thereby undermined the foundation of monarchy. A 1912 revolt by young army officers was suppressed, but it was a precursor of the 1932 revolution that ended absolute monarchy.

Thailand has been governed by a confusing succession of military leaders since then. The coup d'etat has become a way of life at the top, while ordinary people go about their business undisturbed. The king remains an important, respected symbol of national unity. Intermittent attempts at democratic, civilian rule have foundered. All Thai governments since 1932 have sought to modernize the nation, while tailoring foreign policy to the prevailing winds. (Charles Keyes, *Thailand, Buddhist Kingdom as Modern Nation-State*, 1987; Walter F. Vella, *The Impact of the West on Government in Thailand*, 1955; David Wyatt, *Thailand: A Short History*, 1984.)

Ross Marlay

TIBET. Tibet is today an autonomous region of the People's Republic of China*. An overwhelmingly Buddhist country, Tibet is bordered on the south by Burma*, India*, Bhutan*, and Nepal*, and on the west by India. Huge mountain systems surround and isolate Tibet. China acquired sovereignty over Tibet in the seventeenth century. But by the end of the nineteenth century, preoccupied with their own internal problems from European imperialism, the Chinese were unable to assert much authority over the mountain kingdom. In 1790 Gurkhas from Nepal, enjoying British support, invaded Tibet. Chinese troops drove the Gurkhas out of Tibet in 1792 and then sealed off the whole country to foreign, especially British, influences.

Protestant and Roman Catholic missionaries from France and Great Britain made it into Tibet periodically in the 1800s, but the Chinese expelled them each time. British India, on a number of occasions, tried to make sustained diplomatic contact with Tibet, but each time the Tibetans and the Chinese refused to negotiate. In 1904, worried about possible Russian expansion into the area, the British sent an armed diplomatic mission into Tibet. The Tibetans and the Chinese were unable to expel the British and signed a treaty with them in 1904. Two years later an Anglo-Chinese Convention recognized Chinese sovereignty over Tibet. Britain withdrew her troops in return for a huge indemnity, and both Russia and Great Britain agreed not to establish a sphere of influence there. But when the Chinese Revolution broke out in 1911, the Tibetans managed to drive the Chinese out of their country. At the Simla conference of 1914 China agreed to Tibetan autonomy, but in 1917 China disavowed the agreement and tried but failed to retake Tibet. British-Tibetan relations improved, but the Tibetan problem with China continued. In 1950, one year after the Communist triumph in China, Chinese troops invaded Tibet and have been in control ever since. (A. T. Grunfeld, *The Making of Modern Tibet*, 1987; Alastair Lamb, *British and Tibet*, 1986.)

TIMBUKTU. Timbuktu is a city in central Mali* near the great bend of the Niger River. Its location, about nine miles from the Niger and on major caravan routes crossing the Sahara, established it as an important trading and cultural center by the fourteenth century. In 1324 a great caravan of the Mali emperor, Mansa Musa, arrived in Cairo after crossing the desert from West Africa on a pilgrimage to Mecca. It carried with it such great wealth, presumably the treasure of Timbuktu, that word of it reached Europe. In 1353 an Arab traveler, Ibn Battuta, brought back even more tales of vast riches from Mali and Timbuktu. Leo Africanus, a Spanish Moor, visited Timbuktu in 1510. He later published a book in which he told of the city's great wealth. Thus the legend of Timbuktu as a far-away "El Dorado," inaccessible to most and possessing wealth beyond the wildest dreams, was born. This legend, which was to live and grow for centuries, spawned many European expeditions, few of which achieved their quest. Unfortunately, by the time any Europeans set foot in the city, it had already passed its pinnacle as part of the Songhai Empire of the fifteenth and sixteenth centuries.

The first European said to have entered Timbuktu was Paul Imbert, a French sailor who was taken there as an Arab captive around 1670. Imbert died in captivity, but rumors of him reached Europe and increased the aura of mystery about Timbuctu. A shipwrecked American sailor named Benjamin Rose also may have been a visitor to the fabled city. In 1810–1811 Rose supposedly was taken to Timbuktu as a captive but was able to return to civilization and tell his story. However, his description of Timbuktu was in sharp contrast to a city of wealth and splendor, and his story was not believed by many, then or since.

A few European explorers did unquestionably reach Timbuktu in the early nineteenth century. One of these, Major Alexander Gordon Laing, a British officer, encountered unbelievable hardships on his journey. He entered Timbuktu on August 13, 1826, after crossing the mid-Sahara from Tripoli and traveling a distance of 2,650 miles in thirteen months. He survived a bout with an unknown plague which killed many around him, and left him ill for many weeks. By some miracle, he lived through an attack by fearsome Tuareg warriors who shot him and inflicted eighteen saber wounds on his person, three of which fractured his skull. Regretfully, Gordon Laing did not live to enjoy wealth and fame that surely would have been his had he returned to England. He was killed on the return journey. His journals, thought to have been left in Timbuktu for safe keeping, were never found.

Rene-Auguste Caillie, a Frenchman, had learned Arabic by trading with the Moors. He entered Timbuktu in 1828 disguised as an Arab and traveling with a desert caravan. For his exploit of reaching Timbuktu and living to tell about it, he received 10,000 francs, a pension, and admission into the Legion of Honor. Caillie wrote of Timbuktu: "The idea I had formed of the city's greatness and wealth hardly correspond to what I saw, a cluster of dirt houses, surrounded by arid plains of yellow-white sand." Heinrich Barth, a German scholar acting as an emissary of the British government, reached Timbuktu in 1853. He returned not only with an accurate description of Timbuktu but also with a history of the Sonhgai people and much other scholarly and scientific information.

After Barth only one other European (Dr. Oskar Lenz, in 1880) successfully traversed the desert to Timbuktu before the French under Major Joseph Joffre captured the town in 1894. By then Timbuktu was in rapid decline. It was no longer a center for Muslim academic studies or a flourishing crossroads of trade. Nevertheless, the name of Timbuktu—which drew into the interior of Africa those all-too-often doomed explorers who were the vanguard of European imperialism—remains a symbol of far-off, exotic, and mysterious places. (Brian Gardner, *The Quest for Timbuctoo*, 1968.)

Amanda Pollock

TIMOR. See PORTUGUESE TIMOR.

TOBAGO. Reputedly discovered by Christopher Columbus* in 1498, Tobago lies off the coast of South America, eighteen miles northeast of Trinidad*. Some authorities claim that Daniel Defoe used the island as the setting for his novel, *Robinson Crusoe* (1719). Until the early 1600s, when many Caribs started migrating to nearby St. Vincent*, Tobago was the stronghold of fierce cannibals. Caribs still held its northern and central portions in 1650. Europeans valued Tobago's excellent harbors, as well as its timber, fresh water, and strategic location along Spanish shipping routes. In fact, during the seventeenth and eighteenth centuries, the island changed hands more than any other Caribbean territory.

A Dutch colony, New Walcherin, operated intermittently from 1628 to 1678. Spanish-Indian forces from Trinidad wiped it out in 1637. In 1640 England's Charles I "gave" it to his godson, the Duke of Courland. Courlanders, present-day Latvians, arrived in 1654, followed closely by the Dutch, who drove them away in 1659. The triumphant Zeelanders developed a sugar enterprise and entrepot, which by 1665 employed 1,500 settlers and 7,000 slaves. The British captured New Walcherin during the Second and Third Dutch Wars but were forced to relinquish it by the treaties of Breda (1667) and Westminster (1672).

France continued to battle the Netherlands after Britain's withdrawal from the struggle, and, as a consequence of the Treaty of Nijmegan, wrested the island from its owners in 1678.

France's victory did little to halt European arguments over Tobago. Thus, the Treaty of Aix-la-Chapelle (1684) declared the island neutral. Violations of this neutrality resulted in a similar proclamation in 1748. During the Seven Years' War (1756–1763), Britain was awarded Tobago under the terms of the Treaty of Paris*, only to lose it in 1783, after being defeated in the American Revolution*. Ten years later, while engaged in armed conflict with France, Britain recovered the West Indian bone of contention. Nevertheless, the Treaty of Amiens of 1802* restored Tobago to France, which again lost it to Britain in the Napoleonic Wars. This time, the British held Tobago for good, their possession being confirmed in 1814 by the Treaty of Paris and in 1815 by the Congress of Vienna*.

After the English acquisition of 1763, commercial agriculture was strongly encouraged. Tobago prospered due to burgeoning exports of sugar, rum, cotton, and indigo. Scarborough became the capital in 1769. A plantation economy also brought slave uprisings, two of which took place in 1770–1771. The French occupation of 1783–1793 put an end to this period of expansion. After the British returned, Tobago's growth resumed until sputtering in the first half of the new century. By 1886 Tobago exported only a tenth of what it had in 1839. Soil exhaustion was a contributory factor to this decline. After the emancipation of the slaves, 1834–1838, freedmen deserted the estates in order to farm small plots. A devastating hurricane in 1847 left planters with neither capital nor labor. *Metayage*, a sharecropping system, became increasingly popular. It proved satisfactory until 1884, when the London firm upon which most of Tobago's estate owners depended for credit collapsed. Cacao and coconuts began replacing sugar and cotton as the chief cash crops in the latter years of the nineteenth century.

Great Britain granted Tobago a legislature chosen by a very restricted electorate. After social unrest culminated in the 1876 Belmanna riots, local elites, threatened by the discontented masses, relinquished their representative institution. Tobago became a crown colony under the direct control of an autocratic royal governor on June 6, 1876. Economic catastrophe in 1884 led to political ties to Trinidad in 1889. As conditions worsened, the impoverished island became its wealthier neighbor's ward in 1899. Tobago was neglected for the next fifty years, until the People's National Party rose to power in the wake of three decades of gradual constitutional reforms. Although Tobagonians failed to support the Trinidad-based party in the elections of 1956, Eric Williams' government committed itself to the development of the island's infrastructure. From 1958–1962, Tobago, with Trinidad, was part of the West Indies Federation*. On August 31, 1962, it won independence under the banner of the united nation of Trinidad and Tobago. (David L. Niddrie, *Tobago*, 1980; C. R. Ottley, *The Story of Tobago: Robinson Crusoe's Island in the Caribbean*, 1973.)

Frank Marotti

TOGO. The first Europeans to see the Togolese coast were Portuguese explorers during the fifteenth and sixteenth centuries. Their principle interest was in items such as pepper, gum, wax, ivory, and gold. By the seventeenth century the slave trade had become the principle European pursuit in the region. During the nineteenth century present-day Togo was an area of contention among a number of colonial powers including France, Great Britain, and Germany. (Previously, the Danes were active in the area but they withdrew following the sale of the port town of Keto to Britain in 1850.) As the search for slaves escalated, Petit Popo (also known as Anecho), a small slave-port, came to be established with various European nationalities.

On July 4, 1884, Gustav Nachtigal, the German imperial commissioner, signed a protectorate agreement with Chief Mlapa III over a short stretch of the Togoland coast. The Germans gradually pushed inland from the coast, encountering resistance from the indigenous population, but extending their control over the hinterland and building an infrastructure of roads, railroads, schools, and legal and administrative institutions. In their slow penetration to the north, however, the Germans failed to attain one of their primary goals—a foothold on the Niger River. Meanwhile, British and French commercial domination along the present-day coast of Benin (Dahomey*) and Ghana* curbed further German growth to the east and west. Between 1887 and 1889 Germany, France, and Great Britain set the boundaries of Togo.

In August 1914, during the onset of World War I, Togoland was invaded by joint French and British forces and fell after a brief German resistance. Soon after the war, in a provisional agreement, the French assumed control of the entire coast region, and the British exerted control over the interior. In 1922 the two occupying powers were given League of Nations* mandates over the re-partitioned territories. Following World War II, both the United Kingdom and France placed their administrative spheres under the United Nations Trusteeship Council. By that time, the Ewe (who constitute an ethnic majority of the area), were under three different administrations: the Gold Coast, British Togoland, and French Togoland. The ''Ewe Problem'' proceeded to preoccupy the Trusteeship Council for nine years during the 1940s and 1950s. British and French reluctance to grant Ewe demands of autonomy, as well as deep divisions among the various Ewe tribes, delayed any resolution. However, on May 9, 1956, a plebiscite held in British Togoland under United Nations supervision decided in favor of the integration of that area with the neighboring Gold Coast, which, on March 6, 1957, became the independent state of Ghana.

Independence for French Togoland was advanced when, on October 28, 1956, 72 percent of the registered voters, in their own referendum, chose to terminate the French trusteeship and become an autonomous republic within the French Union*. The United Nations refused to end the trusteeship status of the territory at that time because, although the new Republic of Togo had internal autonomy, France retained control of defense, foreign affairs, and currency. In April 1958 new elections were held under UN supervision. The Committee of Togoland

Union (pledged to secure complete independence) won control of the Togo assembly. The Committee's leader, Sylvanus Olympio, subsequently became premier. On October 13, 1958, France announced that full independence would be granted. On April 27, 1960, the Republic of Togo became a sovereign nation, with Olympio as president. (Donald L. Wieder, *A History of Africa South of the Sahara*, 1962.)

Eric C. Loew

TOGOLAND. See TOGO.

TOKELAU ISLANDS. Also known as the Union Islands, the Tokelau Islands are three coral atolls in the South Pacific, nearly three hundred miles north of Western Samoa* and 2,400 miles southwest of Hawaii*. The English landed in the Tokelau Islands early in the 1790s, and by the 1820s whalers were making regular stops there. The indigenous population was Polynesian in origin, and in the mid–1840s Samoan missionaries, sponsored by French Catholics, converted most of the islanders to Christianity. Late in the 1850s the London Missionary Society sent Samoan Protestants to proselyte in the Tokelau Islands. Great Britain established a formal protectorate over Tokelau in 1889 and in 1916 made the islands part of the Gilbert and Ellice Islands Colony. New Zealand* assumed jurisdiction over Tokelau in 1925, and in 1948 the Tokelau Islands Act formally made the islands part of New Zealand. (Federica M. Bunge and Melinda W. Cooke, *Oceania: A Regional Study*, 1984.)

TONKIN. Tonkin (Tongking or Tonking) was a French protectorate in the northern part of Vietnam*. It comprised the Red River valley and delta, and the surrounding mountains and plateaus. Tonkin was bounded on the north by China, on the east by the Gulf of Tonkin (part of the South China Sea), on the south by the French protectorate of Annam*, and on the west by the French protectorate of Laos*. As far as the native Vietnamese were concerned, the mountainous frontiers were dangerous regions inhabited by "savage" tribes. The heart of Tonkin was the Hanoi-Haiphong area. Tonkin was the cradle of Vietnamese culture. As long ago as the time of Christ, Vietnamese of the Red River valley were conscious of the cultural and racial distinctions between themselves and the Chinese. Proximity to China made Vietnamese jealous of their national independence—even though Tonkin was incorporated into China for 900 years. They freed themselves from China temporarily in the tenth century. Thereafter all foreign occupations of Tonkin—Mongol, Chinese, French, Japanese, French again—were relatively brief and unsuccessful. In the long run of Vietnamese history, the 70-odd years of French control of Tonkin were but a moment. Tonkinese society, however, was irremediably altered.

The French were first attracted to Tonkin because they thought the Red River might be a convenient route into Chinese Yunnan through the back door. It was not to be, as the river proved unnavigable through all its upper course, but French military probes in 1873 were followed by an all-out attack ten years later. Legal sovereignty passed to France after the Emperor of Annam, under duress, agreed to protectorate status for Tonkin (1885) and China renounced her traditional claim to suzerainty. But Tonkinese guerrilla resistance continued into the 1890s, and flared again before World War I, during the Great Depression, under the Japanese occupation, and after World War II.

Densely settled Tonkin was not an economic asset like the southern rice-basket of Cochin-China*. There were some profits to be made in rubber and hemp plantations, as well as in gold, tin, and coal-mining, but Tonkin's value to France was primarily strategic: Occupation of Tonkin denied rival European powers a foothold on the doorstep to South China. Tonkin suffered extensive bombing, but no invasion during the years of American fighting in Vietnam (1961–73). Hanoi is today the capital of the Socialist Republic of Vietnam. (Chester A. Bain, *Vietnam: The Roots of Conflict*, 1967; John F. Cady, *The Roots of French Imperialism in Eastern Asia*, 1967.)

Ross Marlay

TORTUGA. Tortuga is a small island, approximately 32 miles long by 5 miles wide, located off the northern coast of Haiti*, 8 miles from Port-de-Paix. Today part of Haiti, Tortuga was once Spanish property, but in the early 1600s, as Spanish fortunes began to decline, French pirates began using the island as a base for attacking Spanish shipping in the Caribbean. During the mid–1600s those French pirates played a key role in the French conquest of western Hispaniola and the founding of Haiti. See HAITI.

TRANQUEBAR. To exploit economic opportunities in Asia, Danish merchants established the Danish East India Company in 1611 and in 1620 purchased Tranquebar from the Rajah of Tanjore. Tranquebar was located near the French outpost of Pondicherry* on the Coromandel coast of southeast India*. The company later established outposts at Dennemarksnagore in 1698, Frederiksnagore in 1755, and the Nicobar Islands in 1756. During the Napoleonic Wars, Great Britain occupied the outposts between 1806 and 1815, returning them to Denmark only with the conclusion of the peace. But it was clear to the Danes that they would not be able to defend her possessions. In 1845 she sold the coastal outposts to Great Britain and abandoned the post on the Nicobar Islands. Denmark ceded the islands to Great Britain in 1869. That concluded the Danish presence in Asia. (David P. Henige, *Colonial Governors from the Fifteenth Century to the Present*, 1970.)

TRANSJORDAN. Transjordan was the former name of present-day Jordan, an independent nation of 34,820 square miles located south of Syria, west of Iraq and Saudi Arabia, north of Saudi Arabia and the Gulf of Aqaba, and east of Israel. From the sixteenth century until the end of World War I, Transjordan was part of the Ottoman Empire, but the demise of the Ottomans liberated the former colonies. When World War I erupted in 1914, nationalist sentiments in Transjordan appeared immediately. With the blessing of Great Britain, Hussein ibn Ali, the sharif of Mecca, led the Arab revolt against the Ottoman Turks. Hussein's forces joined with British troops in conquering Palestine* in 1917 and 1918. In 1920 the Allied nations awarded Great Britain a mandate over Palestine, and that mandate by 1921 included Transjordan. The next year Britain separated Transjordan from the Palestine mandate and placed Abdullah ibn Hussein, a son of Sharif Hussein, in charge of the government.

As emir of Transjordan, Abdullah Hussein spent the next five years fighting against Bedouin tribal guerrillas who were financed by ibn Saud, sultan of Nejd. The Saudi Arabs believed southern Transjordan was part of their kingdom. British forces assisted Abdullah in resisting the Saudi attacks until 1927, when ibn Saud recognized the southern border of Transjordan. In 1928 the British established an elected legislative council in Transjordan to advise Abdullah.

During World War II, Transjordan provided troops to the British army in its successful effort to depose a pro-Nazi government in Iraq. Although Abdullah hoped to create a united Transjordan, Syria, and Palestine under his own control, the plan never really got off the ground. On March 22, 1946, by the terms of the Treaty of London, Great Britain ended the mandate and granted independence to Transjordan. Abdullah became the first king of Transjordan. Two years later, when Great Britain ended the mandate over Palestine, Transjordan joined in the war against the new state of Israel, occupying the West Bank of the Jordan River, which previously had been part of Palestine and was populated by ethnic Palestinians. In 1949 Abdullah dropped the name Transjordan and called his country the Kingdom of Jordan. One year later Jordan's national assembly formally annexed the West Bank, which has remained an area of conflict and contention in the Middle East down to the present day. (Uriel Ldann, *Studies in the History of Transjordan*, 1984; Mary C. Wilson, *King Abdullah, Britain, and the Making of Jordan*, 1988.)

TRANSVAAL. The Province of Transvaal was one of the four colonies making up the Union of South Africa*. Boer settlers who had left the Cape Colony* in the 1830s to get away from British influence founded the state of the Transvaal, or the South African Republic, in 1848. Great Britain recognized the South African Republic in 1852. Bitter factionalism among the Boers, as well as constant fighting between the Boers and African tribes in the 1860s and 1870s, nearly destroyed the Transvaal. Hoping to restore political stability to the area, the British annexed the Transvaal in 1877. The Boers revolted against British rule in 1880 and one year later Great Britain, after defeat at Majuba Hill, agreed to the autonomy of the Transvaal, even though the British retained suzerainty. When gold was discovered in the Transvaal in 1886, thousands of English prospectors poured into the area, quickly outnumbering the original Boer settlers. The Boers refused to extend civil rights to the newcomers (*uitlanders*), who began appealing to Great Britain for intervention. In 1899 the Boers revolted against British sovereignty, precipitating the Boer War*, which England won. The British governed the Transvaal directly until 1907, when it was given its own system of responsible government. In 1910 the Transvaal joined the Cape Colony, Natal*, and the Orange Free State* in forming the Union of South Africa. See UNION OF SOUTH AFRICA.

Robert Shadle

TREATY OF AIX-LA-CHAPELLE OF 1748. The weakness of the Austrian empire in 1740, exacerbated by the lack of a male heir to the Emperor Charles VI, led to renewed territorial conflict among the European powers. Despite the Pragmatic Sanction having been signed by the major European states, thus guaranteeing Maria Theresa's succession to all the Habsburg domains, Prussian King Frederick II seized the Austrian province of Silesia in 1740. This exercise ignited a general conflict, the War of the Austrian Succession, with Bavaria, Spain, and France also interested in annexing Austrian territory. France joined Spain and Prussia against Great Britain and Austria, with Maria Theresa forced to cede Silesia to Frederick of Prussia. Until 1748 the struggle continued in Bohemia and in the Austrian Netherlands where Maria Theresa suffered further setbacks. Austria ultimately was forced to negotiate by the threat of diminished subsidies from Britain. The Treaty of Aix-la-Chapelle, signed October 18, 1748, resulted in little territory changing hands in Europe. In the European colonies, however, the treaty was marked by the mutual restitution of conquests, including the fortress of Louisbourg* on Cape Breton Island, to France, and British reacquisition of Madras in India*. The treaty settled little of the economic rivalry between Britain and France in the New World, Africa, and India, thus setting the stage for further colonial conflict. The war itself signaled the emergence of Prussia-Brandenburg as one of the two German powers, with the Habsburgs seriously weakened by the Prussian gain of Silesia. (Edward Crankshaw, *Maria Theresa*, 1970; Robert A. Kann, *A History of the Habsburg Empire, 1526–1918*, 1974.)

William G. Ratliff

TREATY OF ALCAZOVAS OF 1479. This treaty ended the War of the Succession (1474–1479) between Castile and Portugal in which Afonso V, the king of Portugal, supported the claim of Juana, a niece of Isabella of Castile*, to the throne of Castile in opposition to Isabella and her husband Ferdinand*. The war merged with a long-standing Portuguese-Castilian rivalry over the Canary Islands*. Castile claimed the Canaries on the basis of a papal grant made in 1344. Early in the fifteenth century Norman pioneers established settlements on the islands of Lanzarote, Ferro, and Fuerteventura, in spite of determined opposition from the indigenous inhabitants of the Canaries, the warlike Guanches. Meanwhile, starting in 1419, the Portuguese began exploring the west coast of Africa and established a profitable trade there. They also settled the Madeira* Islands in the 1420s and the Azores* and Cape Verde* Islands beginning in the early 1460s. As a result they came to fear Castilian attacks on their trade routes from the settlements on the Canaries and wanted the islands for themselves as a base. They established their own settlements on the Canaries and encouraged the Guanches to attack the Castilians.

Savage piratical warfare broke out between the Castilian and Portuguese settlers in the Canary Islands during the 1460s, becoming part of the War of the Succession in 1474. Although the Portuguese and their allies were defeated on land, they had achieved considerable success at sea by 1479. The Treaty of Alcazovas, which ended the conflict, was the first treaty between European nations to deal with conflicts concerning overseas possessions. While the treaty established the legitimacy of Isabella's claim to the throne of Castile, it also favored the further expansion of the Portuguese empire*. Portugal abandoned all claims to the Canary Islands in favor of Castile. In return Castile (soon to be united with Aragon in 1481 as Spain) recognized Portugal's monopoly of the African trade and its possession of the Azores, Madeira, and Cape Verde Islands and all lands south of the Canaries. The treaty was confirmed by Pope Sixtus IV in 1481 by the bull *Aeterni Regis*. Later John II of Portugal (1481–1495) would use this treaty to lay claim to Columbus's discoveries of 1492. The resulting confrontation between Spain and Portugal would lead to the Treaty of Tordesillas of 1494* and its division of the Atlantic world between the two countries. (Bailey W. Diffie and George D. Winius, *Foundations of the Portuguese Empire 1415–1580*, 1977.)

Ronald Fritze

TREATY OF AMIENS OF 1802. Despite the formation of the Second Coalition (1798) against France, the Allies were unable to mount concerted action against Napoleon. Great Britain lost control of the Mediterranean, and Napoleon was able to withdraw safely from Egypt*. Only with the accession of Tsar Alexander in 1801 and the increased cooperation between Britain and Russia was peace made possible in Europe. In addition, by early 1802 Napoleon, now first consul of France, needed a respite to consolidate his victories over Austria. Thus Britain, France, Spain, and the Batavian Republic (Netherlands) entered into peace negotiations at the cathedral town of Amiens, France. After lengthy negotiations, an agreement was signed on March 27, 1802. The treaty declared that there should henceforth be peace, friendship, and "good intelligence" between the contracting parties. Article 2 concerned exchange of prisoners. Articles 3 and 4 stipulated that the possessions and colonies which had been taken by the British forces be restored to France, Spain, and the Batavian Republic. Great Britain retained, however, control over Trinidad* (Spanish) and Ceylon* (Dutch). The Cape of Good Hope was returned to the Dutch in full sovereignty. The territories and possessions of Portugal were to be preserved as they existed before the outbreak of hostilities in 1798, except that France was granted possession of part of Portuguese Guinea*. The territory, possessions, and rights of the Ottoman Empire were guaranteed. The Republic of the Seven Isles (Greek Ionia) was recognized. And the island of Malta* was restored by Britain to the Order of Saint John of Jerusalem.

The treaty was most notable for the provisions forcing Britain to restore Egypt (evacuated by the French) to the Ottoman Empire and the restoration of Malta, an island of considerable strategic value in the Mediterranean, to the Knights of Malta. The resulting peace, which lasted only fourteen months, was inevitably shortlived due to the unresolved rivalry in Europe, the continued aggression of Napoleon, and the economic warfare between Britain and France engendered by Napoleon's Continental System. (R. B. Mowat, *The Diplomacy of Napoleon* 1971; R. B. Mowat, *International Relations*, 1966.)

William G. Ratliff

TREATY OF ASIENTO OF 1713. After her defeat in the War of the Spanish Succession (1702–1713), Spain ceded to Great Britain the monopoly of supplying African slaves to the West Indies*. The contract to deliver slaves was known as an *asiento*. Although the treaty limited the number of slaves to 4,000 per year for thirty years, British slavers far exceeded those restrictions. Spain grew more and more upset over British violations of the treaty limits, precipitating, in part, the War of Jenkin's Ear between Great Britain and Spain in 1739. The Treaty of Asiento was not renewed in 1743. (Peter Kemp, *The Oxford Companion to Ships and the Sea*, 1976.)

TREATY OF GHENT OF 1814. The Treaty of Ghent ended the War of 1812 between the United States and Great Britain. The two belligerents agreed to meet in Ghent, in present-day Belgium, to discuss the peace. The meeting convened on July 11, 1814, but quickly broke down because of incompatible instructions. The United States insisted on provisions dealing with maritime rights and impressment; the British wanted territorial concessions in the Northeast and Northwest. Relative to territorial matters, the United States rejected anything but a *status quo ante bellum* settlement; the British wanted an *uti possidetis* settlement. However, as news of British failures in America reached Ghent, the British delegation received permission to abandon that demand and accept a *status quo* settlement. With that obstacle removed, both sides gave up their original objectives and accepted a treaty which simply ended the war, restoring all territories taken during the war and returning all captured ships and prisoners of war. Both nations also pledged to cooperate in suppressing the African slave trade. (William Macdonald, ed., *Select Documents Illustrative of the History of the United States*, 1920.)

Joseph M. Rowe, Jr.

TREATY OF GUADALUPE-HIDALGO OF 1848. The Treaty of Guadalupe-Hidalgo ended the United States-Mexican War of 1846–1848. Nicholas P. Trist signed the treaty for the United States on Feruary 2, 1848, with the government of Manuel de la Pena y Pena, a moderate who had replaced General Antonio Lopez de Santa Anna as president of Mexico after the fall of Mexico City. In

the treaty, Trist achieved for the United States the basic objectives set forth in
the original instructions from Secretary of State James Buchanan. The critical
Article V of the treaty set forth the new boundaries between the United States
and Mexico: the Rio Grande boundary for Texas from the Gulf of Mexico to El
Paso, then westward to the Pacific, giving the United States possession of New
Mexico and Upper California. The treaty recognized the right of Mexican residents in the acquired territories either to remain or remove themselves to Mexico
without loss of their property or assets, and it guaranteed civil rights to Mexican
residents in the acquired territories and their right to citizenship in due course.
The United States agreed to pay $15 million for the territories. Other articles of
the treaty dealt with the return of prisoners of war, navigation rights on the Gila
and Colorado rivers, and resolution of debt claims against both countries. After
intense debate, and more than a little concern from Northerners about the question
of slavery in the newly acquired territories, the United States Senate approved
the treaty on May 30, 1848. (William Macdonald, ed., *Select Documents Illustrative of the History of the United States*, 1920.)

Joseph M. Rowe, Jr.

TREATY OF LAUSANNE OF 1923. The onerous terms of the Treaty of
Sèvres* (August 10, 1920), which included the loss of much of the former
Ottoman Empire's territory to the Western Powers (including the British and
French mandates in the Middle East), led to the overthrow of the sultan's government and the rise to power of the Turkish Nationalists led by Mustafa Kemal.
Kemal and the Nationalist Assembly in Ankara rejected the terms of the Treaty
of Sèvres. In March 1921, Kemal concluded a treaty with Bolshevik Russia
which settled Turkey's eastern frontier without reference to the Allied claims
and rejected the validity of any treaty imposed on Turkey following World War
I*. In the same year a reorganized Turkish army crushed Armenia, whose sovereignty had been guaranteed by the Treaty of Sèvres. Kemal's growing strength
prevented the Allies from attempting to enforce the Treaty of Sèvres by force,
especially after the United States declined to join an Allied military expedition.
In June 1921 Italy evacuated all its troops from Asia Minor. Hostilities between
Turkish and French troops ended with the conclusion of the Treaty of Ankara
on October 20, 1921. The treaty also created a new frontier between the French
mandate in Syria and Turkey which erased the former boundary established by
the Treaty of Sèvres. France also recognized Kemal's government and the Grand
National Assembly in Ankara.

By August 1922 Kemal had decisively defeated the Greek army in Asia Minor.
By the Armistice of Mudanya between Turkey, Italy, France, and Britain on
October 11, 1922, Kemal succeeded in regaining eastern Thrace and the city of
Adrianople from Greece and reestablished Turkish sovereignty over Istanbul
(Constantinople) and the Straits (Dardanelles and Bosporus). Following a series
of conferences at Lausanne (November 21, 1922–February 4, 1923, and April
23–July 24, 1923), a final settlement of the territorial disposition of the former

Ottoman Empire was concluded. The Treaty of Lausanne between the Allied Powers and the Turkish Republic recognized the 1923 Turkish boundaries. Turkey made no claim to its former Arab provinces and recognized British possession of Cyprus* and Italian possession of the Dodecanese islands. The Allies dropped their demands of autonomy for Turkish Kurdistan and Turkish cession of territory to Armenia. In addition, the allies relinquished all claims to spheres of influence in Turkey, and imposed no controls over Turkey's finances or armed forces. The Straits were declared open to all shipping. In a separate agreement, Greece and Turkey agreed to a compulsory mutual transfer of national minorities. (W. N. Medlicott, *British Foreign Policy Since Versailles, 1919–1963*, 1968; F. S. Northedge, *The Troubled Giant: Britain Among the Great Powers, 1916–1939*, 1966.)

William G. Ratliff

TREATY OF MADRID OF 1750. The Treaty of Madrid of 1750 between Portugal and Spain consolidated Portuguese claims in Brazil*. During the colonial period Brazil expanded beyond the line established by the Treaty of Tordesillas of 1494* to include the slopes of the Andes, north to the Amazon, and south to the Rio de la Plata. Portuguese expansion inevitably led to clashes with Spanish colonial interests in South America. It was Portuguese activity on the northern and southern extremities of Brazil, especially in the upper Parana region and Paraguay to the goldfields of Mato Grosso and up the Amazon, that spurred negotiations with Spain. The Spanish-Portuguese territorial negotiations culminated in the Treaty of Madrid, signed January 3, 1750.

The Treaty of Madrid superceded all previous treaties from the Treaty of Tordesillas to the Treaty of Utrecht of 1713*. The Treaty attempted to delimit the frontiers of Spanish and Portuguese possessions in America, Africa, and Asia on the basis of logical geographic features and actual occupation. The Treaty of Madrid was a diplomatic triumph for Portugal and King Joao V, for it officially recognized the contested Portuguese possession of almost half of South America. A secondary result of the Treaty was the expulsion of the Jesuits* from Portuguese territory. As the Jesuits had been the principal protectors of the numerous Indian tribes in Brazil, their removal allowed for widespread colonial exploitation of Indian lands. (Leslie Bethell, ed., *The Cambridge History of Latin America*, Vol. I, 1984; C. H. Haring, *The Spanish Empire in America*, 1947.)

William G. Ratliff

TREATY OF METHUEN OF 1703. Portugal's foreign affairs were complicated in the early eighteenth century by the War of the Spanish Succession. During the war, Portugal first sided with France, but under pressure from England, which dispatched a naval squadron to Portugal in the spring of 1702, it joined the anti-French coalition on May 16, 1703. The same day, Britain and Portugal signed the Lisbon Treaty, which proclaimed a perpetual alliance between

the two countries. A second Anglo-Portuguese agreement, the Treaty of Me-
thuen, was signed on December 27, 1703. This treaty, also known as the Methuen
Commercial Treaty, was named after Lord John Methuen, the British envoy in
Lisbon. Under the terms of the agreement, Great Britain was permitted to export
wool cloth to Portugal (the Portuguese government had banned the import of
English woolens in 1677) and Portugal received the right to export its wines to
Britain on favorable terms. The political consequences of the treaty, while not
explicitly mentioned, were of considerable value to both participants. The Methuen Treaty proved to be the anchor for the continuation of the Anglo-Portuguese
alliance which guaranteed the integrity of Portugal and Brazil*. While the agreement failed to fulfill the commercial aspirations of British merchants, especially
their goal of securing eventual direct trade with Brazil, British traders were given
free access to indirect trade with the Portuguese colonies. In addition, the Methuen Treaty had the indirect result of securing for Britain the crucial western
flank for the defense and maintenance of Gibraltar*, the key to Great Britain's
emergence as a Mediterranean power. (A. D. Francis, *The Methuens and Portugal, 1691–1708*, 1966; G. D. Ramsay, *English Overseas Trade During the
Centuries of Emergence*, 1957.)

William G. Ratliff

TREATY OF MÜNSTER (WESTPHALIA) OF 1648. The agreement that
ended the Thirty Years War of 1618–1648 in Europe, the Treaty of Westphalia
consisted of two peace treaties concluded on October 24, 1648, after lengthy
negotiations that began in the spring of 1645 in the Westphalian cities of Münster
and Osnabruck. The Treaty of Osnabruck was negotiated largely between the
Holy Roman Empire and its allies and Sweden and its allies. The Treaty of
Münster concerned the Holy Roman Empire and France. The Treaty of Westphalia dealt with territorial changes, religious relations, and political arrangements throughout Europe. According to the treaty, Sweden received from the
Holy Roman Empire, in addition to a large cash indemnity, Rugen Island, all
of West Pomerania and part of East Pomerania with the city of Stettin, the city
of Wismar, the secularized arch-bishopric of Bremen, and the bishopric of Ver-
den. Sweden thus gained not only several of the major ports on the Baltic but
also, with the town of Bremen, an important North Sea port.

By the Treaty of Münster, France received the former Habsburg possessions
in Alsace and her sovereignty over the Lorraine bishoprics of Metz, Toul, and
Verdun was confirmed. France and Sweden, as the victorious powers, were
declared the chief guarantors of the fulfillment of the provisions of the Treaty
of Westphalia. The allies of the victorious powers—the German principalities
of Brandenburg, Mecklenburg-Schwerin, and Brunswick-Luneburg—enlarged
their territories at the expense of bishoprics and monasteries; the Duke of Bavaria
was confirmed in his possession of the Upper Palatinate and in his title of Elector.
The treaty recognized the German princes' complete independence from the Holy
Roman Emperor in conducting domestic and foreign policy, provided that the

external alliances were not directed against the interests of the Empire. In matters of religion the Treaty of Westphalia gave to the Calvinists in Germany equal rights with the Catholics and Lutherans and legalized the secularization of church lands carried out before 1624.

The Treaty of Westphalia, which consolidated the victory of the anti-Habsburg coalition in the war, was of considerable international significance. The attempt to create a Catholic world empire under the aegis of the Spanish and Austrian Habsburgs and their plans for suppressing the Reformation movement in Europe and subjugating the United Netherlands failed. Both Switzerland and the Netherlands obtained international recognition of their sovereignty. France ensured herself of a dominant position in Western Europe for a century. The treaty, however, did not completely break the power of the Habsburgs. Although in decline since the early seventeenth century, Spain used the Fronde rebellion (1648–1653) in France to prolong her struggle with the French until 1659. The Treaty perpetuated German division and political weakness into the nineteenth century, thus maintaining Austria as the dominant power in Central Europe. (Samuel R. Gardiner, *The Thirty Years War, 1618–1648*, 1972; S. H. Steinberg, *The Thirty Years War and the Conflict for European Hegemony, 1600–1660*, 1966.)

William G. Ratliff

TREATY OF NANKING OF 1842. The Treaty of Nanking ended the Opium War of 1840–1842. The Anglo-Chinese Opium War was an aggressive war waged by Britain against China* in order to place China in a position of economic and political dependency. In June 1840, under the pretext of the destruction of large supplies of opium by the Chinese commissioner, Britain launched an attack on China in the area of Kuangchou. The contraband trade of opium was widely practiced by British merchants in Asia and the opium trade with China constituted a considerable proportion of the exports for British India*. Armed conflict between British and Chinese naval forces continued from 1840 to 1842. By the summer of 1842, British military forces had seized Hong Kong* and the cities of Tinghai, Ningpo, Hsiamen, Shanghai, and Chenchiang. In August 1842 British forces approached the vicinity of Nanking and the Chinese government surrendered. On August 29, 1842, the first of the "unequal treaties," the Treaty of Nanking, was signed by both governments.

Under the terms of the agreement, China paid the British government an indemnity, ceded the territory of Hong Kong, and agreed to establish a favorable tariff for British imports. In addition, British merchants, who had been allowed to trade only at the South China port of Canton*, were allowed to conduct commerce at five "treaty ports," including Canton and Shanghai. The Treaty of Nanking was followed the next year by the British Supplementary Treaty of the Bogue, signed October 3, 1843, which, *inter alia*, granted British citizens in China an exemption from Chinese legal jurisdiction and which included a most-favored-nation clause granting Britain all trade privileges that China might extend to any other nation. In subsequent years China was forced to conclude other humiliating agreements (''unequal treaties'') with foreign powers granting similar rights. (Jack Beeching, *The Chinese Opium Wars*, 1973; Michael Greenberg, *British Trade and the Opening of China, 1800–1842*, 1979.)

William G. Ratliff

TREATY OF PARIS OF 1763. With the end of the War of the Austrian Succession, Austro-Prussian rivalry over possession of the province of Silesia continued apace. Maria Theresa of Austria, determined to win back her lost territory, entered into secret agreements with Russia, the ultimate purpose of which was the crippling of Prussia-Brandenburg. As British policy in the 1750s continued to be focused on maintaining the balance of power in Europe, London backed Prussia as a counter to French interests in northern Europe. Thus, the Anglo-Prussian Treaty of Westminster (1756) laid the groundwork for British military support of Prussia in any conflict with France or Austria.

The Anglo-French rivalry of the 1750s also included the struggle for overseas empire, especially in North America and India. In North America, Britain feared most the possibility of French expansion into the valuable Ohio and Mississippi valleys. By 1754 an undeclared war already existed between the two powers in North America. The smoldering conflict on the frontier of America, however, was quickly fanned into conflagration in Europe. In 1756 France agreed to support her old rival, the House of Habsburg, in its claim to Silesia, the restoration of which was to be the condition of the cession to France of the southern Netherlands. On August 26, 1756, Frederick II of Prussia, aware of the Austro-Russian plan for the dismemberment of Prussia-Brandenburg, attacked Austria, thus opening the Seven Years' War pitting Britain and Prussia against France and Austria.

The war in Europe quickly found the French, although defeated in western Prussia, successful in subsidizing the Austro-Russian armies which inflicted a near-decisive defeat on Frederick in the east. Prussia was on the brink of collapse, despite massive British war subsidies, until 1762 when Tsarina Elizabeth of Russia died, bringing to the throne Tsar Peter III, Frederick of Prussia's most devoted admirer. Peter immediately made peace with Prussia, thus forcing Austria in 1763 to accept the *status quo ante bellum*, most significantly Prussia's retention of Silesia.

In the West, France was forced into peace negotiations with Britain following serious defeats in Europe and North America, most particularly in September 1759 when the French army in Canada was defeated at Quebec* City by the British army under General James Wolfe. Under the terms of the Treaty of Paris, signed February 10, 1763 (and which included both Spain and Portugal as signatories), France was forced to cede many of its colonial possessions to Great Britain. In North America, France lost Canada, Cape Breton Island*, and all territory east of the Mississippi, excluding New Orleans. In the West Indies*, the islands of Dominica*, St. Vincent*, Grenada*, and Tobago* were ceded to

Great Britain. The island of Minorca, which had been captured by the French in 1756, was returned to Great Britain. In return for ceding Florida to Britain, Spain received western Louisiana and cash compensation from France. French troops were ordered to evacuate the territory of Hanover, and French and Spanish troops were to leave Portugal. Ultimately, France received from Britain several footholds in India*, at Pondicherry* and Chandernagore. The sugar islands of Guadeloupe* and Martinique* were restored to the French.

The Seven Years' War and the Treaty of Paris were leading causes for both the American and French Revolutions. France, though still possessing sources of colonial income, was no longer a great colonial power. The Spanish empire* remained largely intact, but the British were still determined to penetrate its markets. On the Indian subcontinent, Britain increased its colonial holdings, and the British East India Company* continued to press against the weakening indigenous governments and to impose its own authority. (Walter L. Dorn, *Competition for Empire, 1740–1763* 1940; Z. E. Rashed, *The Peace of Paris, 1763*, 1951.)

William G. Ratliff

TREATY OF PARIS OF 1783. After the British defeat at the Battle of Yorktown in 1781, the ministry of Lord Frederick North resigned. The succeeding ministries under Rockingham and Shelburne, pursuant to an act of parliament, initiated peace negotiations with the United States to end the American Revolution*. The extended negotiations resulted in the signing of preliminary terms of peace on November 30, 1782, leading to a cessation of hostilities on January 20, 1783. But the task of reaching peace terms with the other nations involved in the war proved to be more difficult. France was an ally of the United States in the war, and Spain was an ally of France. Although France was eager to end the war, Spain was somewhat intractable, having failed to achieve her major objective—the recovery of Gibraltar*. Not until September 3, 1783, was the definitive treaty of peace signed at Paris and Versailles.

The Treaty of Paris, which pertained to the American Revolution, secured a generous peace settlement for the new nation. The treaty acknowledged the independence of the United States; set the boundary between the United States and Canada*, a western boundary along the Mississippi River, and the southern boundary with Florida; granted fishing rights to Americans off Newfoundland*; provided for settlement of prewar debts; made vague references to guaranteeing the property of loyalists and to making compensation for loyalists' property seized; required the British to evacuate American territory "with all convenient speed"; provided for the return of prisoners; and guaranteed mutual rights of navigation on the Mississippi River. The American portion of the treaty was signed at Paris because the British representative refused to go to Versailles to sign the treaty.

The treaty ending the European phase of the war was signed on September 3 at Versailles. Thus, its proper title was the Treaty of Versailles. In it England retained possession of Gibraltar but returned to Spain the Floridas in America and Minorca in the Mediterranean. French gains were minimal. England agreed to remove restrictions which had been placed on the French port of Dunkirk and made minor concessions to the French in the West Indies* and Africa. Conclusively, the only nation to benefit from the wars of the American Revolution was the United States. For good reason many American diplomatic historians consider the treaty the greatest triumph in the history of American diplomacy. (Richard B. Morris, *The Peacemakers*, 1965.)

Joseph M. Rowe, Jr.

TREATY OF PARIS OF 1898. The Treaty of Paris formally ended the Spanish-American War* of 1898. As early as July 1898 Spain had sought French mediation to determine what terms of peace the United States would demand to end the war. As a result of this effort, the two nations signed a protocol on August 12 which provided for a peace treaty to be negotiated at Paris. Hostilities ended under the stipulation that Spain give up Cuba* and cede to the United States the island of Puerto Rico* and also Guam* in the Marianas*. In addition, the United States was to occupy and hold Manila* in the Philippines* until its disposition was determined at the peace conference.

Between August 12 and October 1, 1898, when the peace conference convened in Paris, United States policy toward the Philippines changed. In mid-September President William McKinley seemed determined to have only Luzon*. But by October 26, the President insisted that the United States have all of the Philippines. Although his explanations for this policy varied from time to time, the decision was clearly based on the commercial advantage that possession of the Philippines would give the United States in the Far East. Spain strongly protested against the injustice of this policy, but was left with no choice but to accede to United States demands.

The final treaty, signed on December 10, 1898, contained the following provisions: Spain would give up Cuba, and the United States would occupy the island; Spain would cede to the United States the islands of Puerto Rico in the West Indies and Guam in the Marianas; Spain would cede the Philippine Islands to the United States in return for a payment of $20 million. During the debate over the treaty in the United States Senate, anti-imperialists protested the implications of a new American empire*, but ratification was approved on February 6, 1899, by a close vote of 57 to 27. The effect of the war and the Treaty of Paris was to diminish Spain's overseas empire and initiate the era of United States imperialism. (Henry Steel Commager, *Documents of American History*, 1948; Julius W. Pratt, *A History of United States Foreign Policy*, 1955.)

Joseph M. Rowe, Jr.

TREATY OF SAN ILDEFONSO OF 1777. The Treaty of San Ildefonso of 1777 was the last in a series of eighteenth-century agreements between Spain and Portugal affecting the colonial boundaries of South America. Territorial disputes between Portugal and Spain remained unresolved during the period following the Treaty of Madrid of 1750* which, among other results, gave recognition to Portuguese control over most of present-day Brazil*. In 1761 the Treaty of El Pardo between Spain and Portugal nullified most of the Portuguese gains inherent in the Treaty of Madrid, thus reopening negotiations over the territorial boundaries between Brazil and Spanish Latin America. The Treaty of San Ildefonso, signed October 1, 1777, was less favorable to Portugal since her only advantage was to retain her sovereignty over a small disputed area in the Rio Grande de Sao Pedro and the island of Santa Catarina.* Spain gained former Portuguese territory in the Seven Missions region between the Uruguay and Ibicui rivers and Colonia do Sacramento* on the Rio de la Plata. The Treaty of San Ildefonso was followed by further attempts at fixing the colonial frontiers in South America, both north and south, culminating in the Treaty of Badajoz of 1801, in which the Portuguese losses under the Treaty of San Ildefonso were confirmed. (Leslie Bethell, ed., *The Cambridge History of Latin America*, Vol. I, 1984; C. H. Haring, *The Spanish Empire in America*, 1947.)

William G. Ratliff

TREATY OF SAN STEFANO OF 1878. From the end of the Crimean War through the early 1870s, Turkey attempted to enact a number of political, economic, and social reforms intended to modernize the tottering Ottoman Empire. The leaders of the national minorities within the empire, however, remained intensely hostile to any ameliorations which might weaken their already established positions. In 1875 revolts erupted in the provinces of Bosnia and Herzegovina which quickly spread to Bulgaria. Sultan Abdul Hamid reacted to these rebellions with immediate military force and canceled any further plans for the reform of the empire. With the revolt of the Ottoman Empire's Slavic territories, Russia, as the "protector" of the Slavic peoples, entered into hostilities with Turkey on April 24, 1877. By early 1878, Russia was able to threaten Constantinople, thus gaining the leverage with which to dictate a peace agreement to Turkey.

The Treaty of San Stefano, which brought an end to the Russo-Turkish War of 1877–1878, was signed on March 3, 1878, at San Stefano, near Constantinople. According to the terms of the treaty—which greatly enhanced the political position of Russia in the Balkans—Montenegro, Serbia, and Romania were granted full independence. Bosnia-Herzegovina was made a dependency of the Ottoman Empire. Bulgaria was made a dependency of the Ottoman Empire, but was also given the right to elect its own prince. Russia was given the authority to place troops in Bulgaria for two years. Russia also received most of the territories, including southern Bessarabia, which it had lost to Turkey following the settlement of the Crimean War (Treaty of Paris, 1856). The sultan in Constantinople pledged to pay Russia an indemnity of 310 million rubles.

The Treaty of San Stefano was opposed by the Western Powers, especially Great Britain and Austria-Hungary, which feared the extension of Russian influence into the Balkans. At the Congress of Berlin of 1878* it was supplanted by a multilateral agreement much less favorable to Russia and Bulgaria. The Congress of Berlin greatly reduced the extent of the Slavic territorial gains, largely to the advantage of Slavic nationalism in the Balkans for the succeeding decades. (Matthew S. Anderson, *The Eastern Question, 1774–1923: A Study in International Relations*, 1966; Richard Millman, *Britain and the Eastern Question, 1875–1878*, 1979.)

William G. Ratliff

TREATY OF SÈVRES OF 1920. With the conclusion of World War I the Allied powers planned to partition Turkey. At Versailles, the Allies intended that the subject national groups were to be stripped from the Ottoman Empire, with Turkey proper to be placed under the influence of the Western democracies. The Ottoman Empire's Middle Eastern territories were disposed of during protracted negotiations resulting from the Sykes-Picot Treaty of 1916*. The mandate system* was devised to attempt to reconcile Arab and Zionist claims for national development. France claimed the mandate for Syria* and Great Britain was named the mandate power in Palestine* and Mesopotamia. A United States mandate for Armenia was refused by Congress in 1920. Any conclusive settlement of the disposal of the former Ottoman territories, however, was prevented by Italian and Greek claims in Asia Minor. In April 1919 the government of Italy landed troops at Adalia, on the southern coast of Asia Minor. In the following month Greece sent troops to occupy Smyrna. With the subsequent Allied occupation of Constantinople in May 1920, the Turkish government was in no position to resist Allied territorial claims. By the Treaty of Sèvres, signed on August 10, 1920, eastern Thrace and most of the Aegean islands were ceded to Greece. The Dardanelles and Bosporus were left under Turkish control, but the waterway was declared neutral and open to all merchant ships in both peace and war, guaranteed by a League of Nations* commission. Smyrna and western Anatolia were to be administered by Greece for five years, with the region's ultimate fate left to a plebiscite. Armenia was granted independence, and Kurdistan was permitted autonomy. The sultan of Turkey recognized both the French and British mandates. (Richard D. Robinson, *The First Turkish Republic*, 1963; Albert F. Vali, *Bridge Across the Bosporus: The Foreign Policy of Turkey*, 1971.

William G. Ratliff

TREATY OF TORDESILLAS OF 1494. When Columbus* returned from his first voyage to America, he landed at Lisbon on March 4, 1493. At that point the Portuguese King John II, on hearing of his new discoveries, laid claim to them on the basis of the Treaty of Alcazovas*. His purpose was to safeguard Portugal's investment of time and treasure into the African trade and the sea-route to India* confirmed by Bartolomeu Dias'* discovery of the Cape of Good Hope in 1487. He even went so far as to begin gathering a fleet to prevent further westward expeditions from Spain.

Unfortunately for John II, Ferdinand* and Isabella* of Spain refused to be intimidated by his bellicose posturing. Instead, they launched their own diplomatic offensive by securing papal recognition of their discoveries by Pope Alexander VI, a fellow Spaniard. The Pope quickly responded to their request by issuing the bull *Inter Caetera* on May 3, 1493. It granted Spain the right to all discoveries made or to be made in the west while recognizing previous concessions made to Portugal in Africa and the East. Two further bulls, *Eximiae Devotionis* and *Inter Caetera*, were officially dated May 3 and 4, 1493, respectively. Other evidence indicates, however, that these documents were actually formulated in June and July and then backdated. They basically repeated the first *Inter Caetera* except that the second *Inter Caetera* contained the famous provision for a line of demarcation lying 100 leagues west of the Azores* and Cape Verde* Islands.

The papal line of demarcation appears to have arisen out of on-going Portuguese-Spanish negotiations and, while it was not what John II had hoped for, he found it acceptable in principle. Ferdinand and Isabella, however, became even more greedy and on September 26 the bull *Dudum Siquidem* appeared at their behest. This momentous document rescinded all papal grants to Portugal concerning Africa and freed Spain from its obligations under the Treaty of Alcazovas. It even forbade anyone from sailing the eastern seas without the permission of Ferdinand and Isabella. In effect, the papacy had given to Spain the trading monopoly that Portugal had spent decades developing.

King John II chose to ignore the latest papal grant to his rivals and by the beginning of 1494 the Spanish monarchs had come to realize that their diplomatic triumph could only be sustained at the risk of implacable Portuguese resistance. Realistic negotiations occurred in the spring of 1494. Employing superior diplomats and well-cultivated friends in the Castilian court, the Portuguese managed to negotiate a treaty that was quite favorable to their interests. It was then signed on June 7, 1494, at Tordesillas on the Spanish frontier with Portugal.

The Treaty of Tordesillas actually consisted of two separate treaties. One treaty provided for the famous line of demarcation. It placed the line 370 leagues west of the Cape Verde Islands, which was at least 600 miles further west than the earlier papal line of demarcation. All lands west of the line were to be Spanish territory while all lands east of the line were to be Portuguese territory. Spanish ships were allowed to sail through Portuguese waters by the most direct route to reach their own territories. In the second treaty, the Spanish monarchs agreed to refrain from sending any ships south of Cape Bojador in West Africa for the next three years.

An exact interpretation of the Treaty of Tordesillas is impossible. Its provisions were vague because the fluctuating and inaccurate geographical knowledge of the time. Furthermore, Spain and Portugal never even sent out the agreed demarcation commission to fix the location of the line which then remained under dispute. Whether the line of demarcation went merely from pole to pole or completely encircled the globe was another matter of disagreement. Most modern scholars feel that the original intention was simply to divide the Atlantic Ocean from pole to pole. Only later when Spain saw a strong possibility that the Molucca Islands might be located in their half of the world, did they argue that the undetermined line of demarcation extended all around the world. Portugal countered by getting Pope Leo X to issue the bull *Praecelsae Devotionis* on November 3, 1514, which placed no limits on its expansion in the East. Ownership of the Moluccas* was later settled by the Treaty of Zaragosa of 1529*.

After the expeditions of Vasco da Gama* and Pedro Cabral* reached India, King Manuel sought and received papal confirmation of Portugal's rights in the Treaty of Tordesillas in the bull *Ea Quae* on January 24, 1506. As a result of the treaty relative peace was maintained between Portugal and Spain since their spheres of influence were realistically defined. Their resources could be directed toward exploration and development of the discoveries rather than war. In fact, the treaty even provided Portugal with the unexpected bonus of New World territory when Brazil* was discovered in 1500. Its details, however, remained under dispute until 1777 when both countries simply agreed to drop the matter. The other European powers, meanwhile, did not consider themselves bound by the treaty and soon began poaching on the Portuguese and Spanish discoveries. Francis I of France spoke for them all when he quipped "I should very much like to see the passage in Adam's will that divides the New World between my brothers, the Emperor Charles V and the King of Portugal." (Frances Gardiner Davenport, ed., *European Treaties Bearing on the History of the United States and its Dependencies*, 4 vols., 1917 rpt. 1967; Charles Edward Nowell, "The Treaty of Tordesillas and the Diplomatic Background of American History," in *Greater America: Essays in Honor of Herbert Eugene Bolton*, 1945.)

Ronald Fritze

TREATY OF UTRECHT OF 1713. The Treaty of Utrecht is the name for a series of peace treaties that, along with the Treaty of Rastatt of 1714, ended the War of the Spanish Succession. The basis of the war was the increasing entropy of the Spanish empire* by the end of the seventeenth century. By 1700 a number of treaties had already attempted to divide the Spanish empire, largely through the recognition of the claims of the Austrian Habsburgs. The death of the heirless Spanish king, Charles II, led to a general European conflict after he ceded the whole of the Spanish empire to the Duke of Anjou, the grandson of the king of France, Louis XIV. With Austria, Britain, and the Netherlands against France, the first years of the war saw the French armies suffering major defeats by the Duke of Marlborough at the battle of Blenheim, and later at the battles of Ramillies and Oudenarde. The stiffening of French resistance by 1709 at the battle of Malplaquet, combined with British reluctance to carry on the war, led to the opening of peace talks in 1711. Treaties were signed in Utrecht on April 11, 1713, between France and Great Britain, the Dutch Republic of the United Provinces, and on February 6, 1715, between Spain and Portugal.

The treaties recognized the right of Philip V (formerly the Duke of Anjou) as king of Spain and to the Spanish colonial possessions on the condition that he and his successors renounce all rights to the French crown. Great Britain gained from Spain the fortress of Gibraltar* and the important coastal town of Mahon. From France, Britain received a number of possessions in North America, most notably the Hudson's Bay Company's territory, Newfoundland*, and Acadia*. Britain also acquired special trading rights with the Spanish colonies in the Americas, especially the right of *asiento*, trading privileges which included the right to introduce African slaves in Spanish America. The Kingdom of Savoy gained Sicily, Montserrat, and part of the duchy of Milan from Spain. Prussia received part of upper Gelderland and several other territories, and France agreed to recognize the royal title of Frederick I as king of Prussia. The treaties marked the definite end of French aggrandizement under the Old Regime and signaled the end of Spain as a significant power in European politics. The Treaty of Utrecht was an important step toward establishing the commercial and colonial supremacy of Great Britain for the succeeding two centuries. (Henry A. F. Kamen, *The War of Succession in Spain, 1700–1715*, 1969, James Leitch Wright, *Anglo-Spanish Rivalry in North America*, 1971.)

William G. Ratliff

TREATY OF VERSAILLES OF 1783. See TREATY OF PARIS OF 1783.

TREATY OF VERSAILLES OF 1919. See WORLD WAR I.

TREATY OF ZARAGOSA (OR SARAGOSSA) OF 1529. The Treaty of Tordesillas of 1494* had settled the immediate rivalry between Portugal and Spain over the Asian spice trade that resulted from Columbus's discovery of America. Magellan's voyage of 1519–22 reopened that conflict by proving that a southwestern route to the Spice Islands* existed. A conference between the two powers was held at Badajoz-Elvas during April and May of 1524 to determine ownership of the Moluccas*. It broke up without reaching a decision. As a result, Emperor Charles V* sent a second expedition of seven ships under the command of Garcia de Loaysa to the Moluccas by the new southwestern route in order to strengthen his claim. Only one ship survived the Pacific passage to join the survivors of Magellan's ship *Trinidad* on Tidore Island. A third expedition of three ships was dispatched from Mexico in 1527. Once again only one ship survived the passage and like the *Trinidad* of Magellan, it proved unable to find the right sailing route to make a return trip across the Pacific.

Meanwhile, as early as 1526, Charles V was coming to the conclusion that he needed Portugal as an ally in Europe more than he needed to control the distant Spice Islands. In that year he married the Portuguese Infanta and even began negotiating a treaty that would have given up any Spanish claims to the Moluccas. It was not until April 22, 1529, however, that a satisfactory treaty was finally negotiated at Zaragosa. The Treaty of Zaragosa is a vague agreement, probably because Charles V wished to avoid offending his own Cortes of Castile, which opposed any renunciation of Spanish claims to the Moluccas. Instead, in the Treaty of Zaragosa, Charles V pawned his claim to the Moluccas in exchange for

350,000 ducats. When the ownership of the islands was finally decided between Spain and Portugal, he was to return the money if the decision went in favor of Portugal. Meanwhile Portugal promised to build no new fortifications on the islands, and a line of demarcation was set up 297½ leagues east of the Mollucas to keep the contending Spanish and Portuguese apart. Final ownership of the Moluccas was never decided. Portugal kept its shaky control over the turbulent islands until the Dutch drove them out at the beginning of the seventeenth century while Charles V kept his money. The Spanish also chose to ignore the treaty's line of demarcation in their settlement of the Philippines* later in the sixteenth century. (Frances Gardiner Davenport, ed., *European Treaties Bearing on the History of the United States and its Dependencies*, 4 vols., 1917 rpt. 1967; Donald Lach, *Asia in the Making of Europe, Vol. 1: The Century of Discovery*, 1965.)

Ronald Fritze

TRENGGANU. Trengganu was a sultanate located along the Malay Peninsula on the South China Sea in Siam*. In the Treaty of Bangkok of 1909, Siam ceded Trengganu to the British, who made it one of the Unfederated Malay States. See MALAYSIA.

TRINIDAD. A large population of 20,000–30,000 Arawaks inhabited Trinidad when Christopher Columbus* discovered it on July 31, 1498. Spain valued the island, which lies seven miles off Venezuela's coast, as a base for expeditions in search of El Dorado, and as a source of slaves for nearby pearl fisheries. The Arawaks stubbornly blocked colonization efforts, but a sixteenth century "demographic disaster" eroded their numbers, thus permitting a permanent Spanish settlement in 1592. By 1797, 1,082 Amerindians survived. For most of the Spanish period, Trinidad remained an isolated, undeveloped outpost exporting small quantities of tobacco, cacao, vanilla, timber, and turtles. Only two towns, Port-of-Spain and St. Joseph, were founded. Indian attacks harassed settlers. Smuggling thrived, since few Spanish ships called. Despite trading and raiding by the Dutch, French, and English, Spain prevented rival footholds. In 1777 less than 3,500 people lived on the island, 6 percent of whom were slaves.

During Governor Jose Maria Chacon's administration, 1783–1797, Spanish Trinidad's prosperity peaked. Imperial reforms led to liberalized commercial and immigration policies. Madrid granted land to Catholic foreigners who migrated to the island with their bondsmen. French refugees, fleeing revolutionary upheaval or British rule, flocked in from other Caribbean isles. Between 1777 and 1797 the colony's population climbed to nearly 18,000. For the first time in its history, slaves preponderated. Sugar became the top export. Trinidad's racially mixed citizenry further diversified. Those of French background accounted for 60 percent of its non-slave inhabitants. A significant British segment also existed. Moreover, most freeman were classified as "colored."

England captured the island while at war with Spain and France in 1797. Five years later Madrid formally ceded it by the Treaty of Amiens*. The Treaty of

Paris confirmed British sovereignty on May 30, 1814. Britain ruled Trinidad directly, through a royal governor, as a crown colony, rather than creating a local assembly. London refused to provide a predominantly non-Anglo populace with a legislature. Furthermore, the slave trade had been abolished in 1807 and slavery itself was under attack. Humanitarians feared that if they granted Trinidadian planters political power, the institution would become entrenched in yet another West Indian possession.

While crown colony rule did enable Britain to enact model slavery legislation in Trinidad, it also caused considerable uproar. Popular discontent with the governmental system, brewing since 1850, culminated in serious 1903 disturbances. After World War I, veterans of the West Indies Regiment, led by Arthur A. Cipriani, agitated for social, political, and economic improvements. The governor's absolute power was not curbed until 1925, when a tiny electorate voted for a limited number of his legislative council. In the same period other developments shaped Trinidad's destiny. As a consequence of the emancipation of the slaves in 1838, London sought to ameliorate a shortage of agricultural workers by importing labor from India*. Some 150,000 East Indians arrived between 1838 and 1917. They now comprise 40 percent of the island's population. Great Britain detached Trinidad from the Windward Islands in 1842 and linked nearby Tobago* to it in 1889. Ten years later, Tobago became Trinidad's ward. Both islands would win independence as a united country. Oil in commercially viable quantities was discovered in 1910. By 1938 oil amounted to 70 percent of the colony's exports.

Trinidad gradually obtained a government responsible to its citizens between 1925 and 1956. Rising nationalism, coupled with economic depression, resulted in a vigorous trade-union movement and a proliferation of political parties. Grave labor unrest in the dominant oil and sugar industries erupted in 1935 and 1937. Uriah Butler figured prominently in these protests. A rash of similar outbreaks throughout the British West Indies prompted an inquiry that brought about increased financial assistance and democratization. World War II revived the economy and gave origin to the steel band, a national musical institution. On the other hand, an American military base at Chaguaramas would embitter Trinidad-United States relations after the war. Universal adult suffrage was extended to Trinidad in 1946. Constitutional advances in 1950 and 1956 ushered in ministerial government. The renowned scholar, Dr. Eric Williams, founder of the People's National Movement, the island's first lasting political party, became the colony's chief minister after a victorious 1956 campaign.

From 1958 until 1962, Trinidad belonged to the West Indies Federation*, headquartered in Port-of-Spain. When Jamaica seceded in 1961, Trinidad followed suit. The United Kingdom dissolved the Federation in May 1962. On August 31 Trinidad and Tobago achieved fully independent nationhood under Williams' leadership. (Selwyn D. Ryan, *Race and Nationalism in Trinidad and Tobago: A Study of Decolonization in a Multiracial Society*, 1972; Eric Williams, *History of the People of Trinidad and Tobago*, 1962.)

Frank Marotti

TRIPOLITANIA. Tripolitania is the northwestern region of Libya*. Tripoli is its major city. Italy attacked and seized the region from the Ottoman Turks in 1911, and in 1919 Tripolitania was separated from Cyrenaica* and administered as a separate colony. The Italians rejoined Tripolitania with Cyrenaica in 1934, forming the single colony of Libya. See LIBYA.

TRISTAN DA CUNHA. Tristan da Cunha is a system of four islands—Tristan da Cunha, Inaccessible, Nightingale, and Gough—totaling 80 square miles and located 1,500 miles southeast of St. Helena* in the South Atlantic. Only Tristan da Cunha is inhabited, and its 1985 population was less than 325 people. The islands were first discovered in 1506 by the Portuguese navigator Tristao Da Cunha. Because of their strategic isolation and the fact that they were uninhabited, the islands were of little interest to Europeans. When Napoleon was exiled to St. Helena between 1815 and 1821, British troops were stationed on Tristan da Cunha, and in 1816 England formally annexed the islands. No formal political arrangements were made for the government of Tristan da Cunha until 1938, when the islands became a dependency of the colony of St. Helena. In 1950 St. Helena appointed an administrator for Tristan da Cunha, and in 1952 residents elected the first island council. See ST. HELENA.

TRUSTEESHIP. The term trusteeship, as defined in international law, refers to an international system administered by the United Nations* following World War II under which states, as trustees, assumed an obligation to administer trust territories in such a manner that the latter would progress toward self-government or independence. The United Nations trusteeship system was patterned after, and was successor to, the mandate system* of the League of Nations*. Established by chapters 12 and 13 of the United Nations Charter, the system was designed to apply to territories transferred from the mandates system, territories which were detached from the enemy states as a result of World War II, and other territories preparing for independence.

The Trusteeship Council of the United Nations was created in 1945 to act on behalf of the United Nations with regard to the territories administered as part of the international trusteeship system. The primary responsibility of the Trusteeship Council was to see that the states entrusted with territories promote the political, economic, and social advancement of the inhabitants of the trust territories, and oversee their progressive development toward self-government and independence. The Trusteeship Council consisted of three categories of United Nations members—those members administering trust territories, Security Council members not administering trust territories, and additional members (for a three-year term) elected by the General Assembly.

By 1960 all territories under the original United Nations trusteeship administration had either achieved independence or were moving toward political independence. Therefore, on December 14, 1960, the United Nations General Assembly adopted the Declaration on Granting Independence to Colonial Countries and Peoples, which effectively abolished the trusteeship system. (Ramendra N. Chowdhuri, *International Mandates and Trusteeship Systems: A Comparative Study*, 1955.)

William G. Ratliff

TRUST TERRITORY OF THE PACIFIC ISLANDS. The Trust Territory of the Pacific Islands was a United States territory consisting of more than 2,200 islands and atolls scattered across more than four million square miles in the western Pacific Ocean. The three major island groups in the Trust Territory of the Pacific Islands were the Marianas Islands*, the Marshall Islands*, and the Caroline Islands*. Although the Marianas and Marshalls were relatively compact and they constituted distinct geographic areas, the larger Caroline Island archipelago was logically composed of five separate groups: the Palau*, Yap, Truk, Ponape, and Kosrae systems.

Spain established its claim to the Marianas and Caroline Islands during the sixteenth century but did little to consolidate its power there. Germany established its presence in the Marshall Islands in 1874, and in 1885 Pope Leo XIII arbitrated a dispute between Germany and Spain, confirming Spanish sovereignty over the Marianas and Carolines and German control over the Marshalls. After losing the Spanish-American War* of 1898, Spain ceded Guam*, the southernmost of the Marianas, to the United States, and in 1899, for $4.5 million, Spain sold her claims to the other Marianas and the Carolines to Germany.

German power in Micronesia* was shortlived. When World War I broke out, Japan occupied many of the German islands in the Pacific. After the war Japan received a League of Nations mandate over the former German territories, which she then fortified. In 1941, shortly after the bombing of Pearl Harbor, Japan captured Guam. Between 1942 and 1945 United States armed forces launched a successful counteroffensive against the Japanese islands, conquering them in an east to west campaign. When World War II ended, the United States was in complete control of the Marianas, Marshalls, and Carolines, and in 1947 the United Nations gave the United States a trusteeship over the islands. The political unit was known as the Trust Territory of the Pacific Islands.

Between 1947 and 1951 all of the islands were administered by the United States Navy. The Marshalls and Carolines were turned over to the Department of the Interior in 1951, and the Marianas, in 1962. The capital of the territory was located on Saipan after 1962; and in 1965 the congress of Micronesia assumed legislative authority over the Trust Territory of the Pacific Islands. In the late 1960s negotiations and constitutional deliberations were begun to secure independence for the Trust Territory along with a relationship of "free association" with the United States. Both the United States and the United Nations wanted the Trust Territory to evolve into a single independent nation, but ethnic differences and the vast distances between the islands made that impossible. Some regions wanted to remain close to the United States, while others wanted independence.

In 1972 the United States began to negotiate separately with the Marianas Islands. Guam had been a United States territory independent of the Trust Territory of the Pacific Islands, but the other Marianas islanders argued against independence from the United States and in favor of a close association. In 1975 Marianas islanders overwhelmingly approved a proposal to create the Commonwealth of the Northern Marianas Islands*, and Congress approved the decision in 1976, staging a gradual separation of the northern Marianas from the Trust Territory of the Pacific Islands, a move which became complete in 1984.

The people of Palau and the Marshalls then began to express misgivings about long-term association with the economically disadvantaged Caroline Islands. In 1978 Palau and the Marshalls voted against creation of a single, federated Micronesian republic. On May 1, 1979, the Marshall islanders declared self-government and established the Republic of the Marshall Islands. On May 10, 1979, the districts of Yap, Truk, Ponape, and Kosrae established the Federated States of Micronesia. The people of Palau created the Republic of Palau on January 1, 1981. All three of the former states of the Trust Territory of the Pacific Islands voted in 1983 to maintain a "free association" with the United States, a political arrangement in which they exercised full control over internal and foreign affairs but considered themselves part of the larger United States strategic and military presence in the Pacific. The United States agreed to provide economic assistance and military protection for the area well into the next century. (John Wesley Coulter, *The Pacific Dependencies of the United States*, 1957; Stanley De Smith, *Microstates and Micronesia: Problems of America's Pacific Islands and Other Minute Territories*, 1970; C. J. Lynch, "Three Pacific Island Constitutions: A Comparison," *Parliamentarian*, 61 (July 1980), 133–41.)

TSHOMBE, MOISE. Born in 1919 to a wealthy and prominent businessman in the Belgian Congo, Moise Tshombe was educated by American Methodist missionaries, married into tribal royalty, and worked in his father's business prior to entering public life. Tshombe was relatively incompetent as a businessman and his abilities as a politician were limited to currying the favor of European, particularly Belgian, economic and military interests. Tshombe's rise to prominence began in November 1958 when a number of tribal and ethnic associations formed the *Confederation des Associations du Kananga* (Conakat). Conakat soon accepted the political agenda of the resident European community as Tshombe became the organization's leader. Through extensive contact with the Europeans, Tshombe had learned that intense "anti-communism" (meaning opposition to anyone who challenged white economic interests or the dominant positions of whites in the local community) and the enhancement of white economic interests produced powerful friends and supporters.

Western nations and the white community, concerned about impending independence from Belgian colonial rule, generally believed the Congo* should remain a unified country. However, Belgian and European residents were more concerned with protecting their economic investments, particularly the giant holding company *Union Miniere du Haut Katanga*. Because Katanga was rich in natural resources, producing approximately 50 percent of the Congo's revenues, it represented the heart of Europeans' Congo investments. These investments supposedly were threatened by "radical nationalists" such as Joseph Kasavubu and Patrice Lumumba*, the soon to be president and prime minister respectively of the Republic of the Congo.

Tshombe and Katangan separatism were seen as a way of protecting these economic interests. This explains the apparent ambivalence of Belgium, the United States, and other European nations toward Katangan secession. The apparent objective was to see the establishment of a relatively loose Congolese federation in which Katanga maintained substantial political autonomy and Tshombe's political position was preserved. Consequently, Belgium, while formally supporting a unified Congo, sent army units into Katanga at Tshombe's request after he declared independence on July 11, 1960, provided him with both military equipment and advisors after international political pressure forced the withdrawal of Belgian troops, and encouraged Tshombe in recruiting a mercenary army which included former members of the French Algerian OAS (*Organisation de l'Armee Secrete*) and white South Africans.

Ensuing efforts by Prime Minister Lumumba to end the secession resulted in his being dismissed by President Kasavubu, imprisoned by Colonel Joseph Mobutu, and delivered to Katangan troops for assassination in January 1961. A series of United Nations military operations against Tshombe ensued. Tshombe was briefly imprisoned for "high treason" in April 1961 but continued to lead secession efforts until January 1963. Shortly thereafter Tshombe went into voluntary exile in Europe and planned a return to power. However, it was a peasant revolt rather than Tshombe's mercenary army which enabled his return. In June 1964 he was asked to become prime minister and quell the rebellion. He promptly turned operation of the country over to white mercenaries and European interests. With active assistance from Belgium and the United States, the peasant revolt was brutally suppressed.

At this point, Tshombe's ambition outstripped his abilities. He openly challenged President Kasavubu, who dismissed Tshombe on October 13, 1965, just as he had previously dismissed Lumumba. Tshombe fought back, but on November 25, 1965, General Mobutu led a coup, establishing himself in power with the support of the United States. Tshombe returned to European exile where he plotted a return to power. After two failed uprisings he was kidnapped and taken to Algeria where he died, reportedly of a stroke, on June 29, 1969. (Ian Colvin, *The Rise and Fall of Moise Tshombe: A Biography*, 1968.)

Samuel Freeman

TUCUMÁN. Late in the 1540s settlers from Peru began moving into the area of Tucumán in what is today northern Argentina. Spain erected a province there in 1550 with Juan Núñez del Prado serving as the first governor. For the next century, Tucumán was the jewel of Argentina, the most densely populated and prosperous colony in the region. By 1650, however, Buenos Aires* was rapidly eclipsing her. Tucumán was under the jurisdiction of the Audiencia of Charcas until 1776, when the Viceroyalty of Rio de la Plata was created. Tucumán ceased to exist as an administrative unit in 1783 when the Spanish crown imposed the intendencia system. Tucumán was divided into two intendencias: Córdoba and Salta. See ARGENTINA.

TUNISIA. Smallest of the three states of the Maghreb (North Africa), Tunisia shares with the other two a population made up of Berber tribes, to which were added Arab elements from the seventh century onward. The Arabs brought with them their civilization and their religion. Islam and the blending of those ethnic groups resulted in a fairly homogeneous society. Before the Arabs, Tunisia had been subjected to various invasions and influences, of which the most notable were the Phoenicians, who founded the city and empire of Carthage, ultimately defeated and destroyed by the Romans. Later there were Vandals and Byzantine Greeks. With the Arabs, Tunisia became a center of Islamic culture and in 1574, after a Turkish invasion, it was integrated into the Ottoman Empire, to which it paid formal allegiance. But the local regime became increasingly autonomous, while the Ottoman Empire had entered into a period of progressive decline at a time of Western expansion.

The last quarter of the nineteenth century saw the spread of European colonization to all corners of the globe, notably Asia and Africa. In the latter's case, the 1880s was marked by the famous "scramble for Africa," when most of the continent was divided up between several European nations. France, which had conquered Algeria in 1830, ultimately aspired to control the whole of the Maghreb. In Tunisia's case, the French faced some competition from the recently unified and geographically closer nation of Italy. There were already a sizable number of Italian settlers in Tunisia. Bismarck* shrewdly encouraged France to annex Tunisia, in order to deflect French interest and energy away from her lost provinces of Alsace-Lorraine, and keep her busy with colonial ventures. This had the added advantage—from Bismarck's point of view—of creating a lasting divisions between the French and the Italians, whose Tunisian ambitions were thereby frustrated. It also led a resentful Italy to join Germany and Austria-Hungary in forming the Triple Alliance the following year in 1882.

So France won out, and in 1881 a French army invaded and occupied Tunisia, using as a pretext the protection of their investments in Algeria, and claiming along the familiar pattern that the bey's government was broke and could not pay back its debts to French businessmen. The French also claimed that they had acted to protect the interests of the Europeans who had settled there because of lucrative possibilities. With the signing of the Bardo treaty in the same year (1881), Tunisia became a French protectorate.

French settlers continued to move in and the country's economy became increasingly geared toward France's export needs, while the protectorate system was gradually transformed into a system of direct French rule. Progressively, a

Tunisian French-educated elite developed. Through the normal process, and in the wake of the disquiet agitating the colonial world after World War I, a Tunisian nationalist movement took shape in the 1920s under the name of "Destour," which means "Constitution." It had been helped by native trade unions, which were allowed by the French, and which became the organized mass basis for the movement. At this stage, Tunisian nationalists under the leadership of Habib Bourguiba formed a splinter group, which called itself "Neo-Destour." Their goal was total independence.

The Neo-Destour succeeded in mobilizing the whole nation in the struggle for independence, masses as well as the educated elite. There were strikes, demonstrations, and violence. Bourguiba, the "Supreme Fighter," was repeatedly jailed by the French. World War II temporarily halted the nationalistic movement. Tunisia, which had been delivered to the Germans by Vichy France in 1942, became the final battleground in North Africa between the Allies and the Axis Powers. In 1943 the remainder of Rommel's Afrika Corps, close to 300,000 men, surrendered in Tunisia.

The nationalist struggle for independence was resumed after World War II, climaxing with massive demonstrations in 1952. In July 1954 the French promised internal autonomy, and the French premier, Pierre Mendes-France, started direct negotiations with Bourguiba, which led to an agreement in 1955 on the country's progress toward independence. By then, the French were involved in the repression of a difficult rebellion in Algeria*. For them, Algeria was more important because of economic reasons and the presence of a sizable number of European settlers, and they were more willing to grant independence to Morocco* and Tunisia in order to concentrate on Algeria. In any case, the European minority constituted only 6 percent of Tunisia's population. Tunisia became independent on March 20, 1956. French economic interests were protected and Tunisia joined a customs union with France. In 1958 the French withdrew all their troops from the country, except those in the leased naval base at Bizerta. In the same year Tunisia became a member of the Arab League. A constitution was proclaimed on June 1, 1959, and Bourguiba became President for Life. (Dwight L. Ling, *Tunisia: From Protectorate to Republic*, 1984; Norma Salem, *Habib Bourguiba, Islam and the Creation of Tunisia*, 1984.)

Alain G. Marsot

TUPAC AMARU II. Tupac Amaru II was christened Jose Gabriel Condorcanqui in 1742. Born into the Peruvian nobility, he was fifth in descent from Tupac Amaru I, an earlier insurrectionist who was executed by the Spaniards in 1571. Tupac received an excellent education at the College of Nobles in Cuzco where he proved to be an outstanding student. At the age of twenty he succeeded his father as cacique, or chief, of Tinta (Tuita), an outlying province of the Cuzco region. The Spaniards acknowledged his Inca descent with the title Marqués de Oropesa. Holding positions of power and prestige, he established a regular association with Spanish priests and officials. He earned his livelihood as a transport agent in the Andes, as the demand for gold, silver, maté, and salt was great.

Under the Spanish regime in Peru*, the native Indians were at the bottom of the social ladder. They became legal minors or wards of the Spanish crown. Their religion was suppressed and their culture was violated. Tupac Amaru was outraged as he watched the reestablishment of the *repartimiento* and *mita* in 1777. Tupac watched the Spaniards force Indians to work Spanish-owned farms, serve on construction projects, and labor in the silver mines. Tupac attempted to bring about reform through peaceful means. He first presented a petition to the attorney-general in Lima asking that the Indians be exempted from paying the unfair labor taxes and performing servile labor. His request was denied. The attorney-general claimed Tupac lacked evidence to substantiate the exploitation of the Indians. In another petition, Tupac included all inhabitants of the Tinta province. That, too, went unheeded. Failing to get support for his measures, Tupac returned to Tinta in late 1778.

In early 1779 peasant unrest had become apparent in the Cuzco region. Taking this unrest as a sign of support, Tupac began to plan his strategy and to organize the rebellious forces. On November 4, 1780, Tupac captured the local corregidor, Don Antonio Arriaga, a brutal tyrant, who had committed outrages against the Indians. Tupac demanded the abolition of unfair taxes and the replacement of the Spanish-appointed corregidores with Indian governors. When these demands also went unheeded, Arriaga was tried and later brutally executed by being forced to drink molten gold in the public square of Tungasuca on November 10, 1780.

By the end of 1780 Tupac Amaru II was the self-proclaimed liberator of the people. This he did for personal and perhaps ideological reasons. Sharing power with the Indian, Thomas Catari, Tupac initiated a nativist movement which was to last until 1783. Initial support for this movement came from the Indians, mestizos, and Creoles. With the promise of rebirth for those who fell in battle against the Spaniards, Tupac garnered an estimated force of two hundred thousand men. Tupac's movement thus acquired a millenarian tone. He used his forces to wage a bloody war against the Spanish governors in hopes of driving them out of Peru. Thousands of lives were claimed as Tupac's forces, although not as well-armed or as well-trained as the Spanish army, fought courageously. Violence swept into Upper Peru and Ecuador*, leaving vast amounts of private property violated. The insurrection, now being led by the Indians, was taking on a racial quality. All mestizos and Spaniards were considered enemies, and the rebellious forces held more than 600 Spanish soldiers at Sangarara. All but twenty-eight of these Spanish captives were either burned or massacred, acts of terrorism which alienated many earlier followers as they withdrew their support from the movement.

In 1781 by orders of Inspector General Jose del Valla, Tupac Amaru, his family, his captains, and thousands of his followers were captured, tortured, and savagely executed. Tupac's tongue was cut out, and he was drawn and quartered with the use of four horses. Finally he was decapitated, and the Spanish government ordered that his body parts be placed in leather bags on mule-back and be carried to all the towns where Tupac had incited rebellion. (Jean Descola, *Daily Life in Colonial Peru*, 1968; Marion Lansing, *Liberators and Heroes of South America*, 1940.)

Veula J. Rhodes

TURKS AND CAICOS ISLANDS. The Turks and Caicos Islands is a British colony in the West Indies*, lying between the southern end of the Bahamas* and north of Hispaniola*. There are eight islands in the Turks group, but only Grand Turk and Salt Cay are inhabited, and six islands in the Caicos group— South Caicos, East Caicos, Grand Caicos, North Caicos, Providenciales, and West Caicos. Juan Ponce de Leon* discovered the islands in 1512 during his quest for the legendary fountain of youth, but Spain showed little permanent interest in them. In 1678 English settlers from Bermuda* began visiting the Turks to acquire supplies of salt, but permanent settlement of the Caicos did not begin until 1781 when Loyalists fled the colonies at the end of the American Revolution. For more than a century the Turks and Caicos had a separate political existence, until the Bahama Islands annexed them in 1799. That arrangement lasted only until 1848, when Great Britain granted the Turks and Caicos their own colonial charter, although they shared a governor with Jamaica.

The colony came on hard times after the abolition of slavery in 1838. The sugar plantations declined in value, abandoned by the English planters unable to secure the labor needed to work the fields. The Turks and Caicos' financial problems were so severe that in 1873 they were annexed by Jamaica*. They remained part of Jamaica until the Jamaican independence movement gained momentum late in the 1950s. The Turks and Caicos separated from Jamaica in 1959 and became a crown colony in 1962. Three years later they associated themselves politically with the Bahama Islands, but when the Bahamas became independent in 1973, the Turks and Caicos again returned to their former status as a crown colony. Although the Turks and Caicos experienced a nationalist movement of their own, it was not powerful enough to secure the legislative majority required before Great Britain would give them independence. (Sir Alan Burns, *History of the West Indies*, 1965.)

U

UBANGI-SHARI. See CENTRAL AFRICAN REPUBLIC.

UGANDA. Uganda, a former British protectorate which Winston Churchill once called "the Pearl of Africa," is a heavily populated country located in East Africa. Black Africans comprise well over 98 percent of the people of Uganda and are divided into more than twenty discrete ethnic groups, nearly all of which have their own language. Since there is no indigenous language that is understood by all Ugandans, English serves as the official language of the country—one of the many legacies of British colonial rule. Europeans became interested in the region in the early 1860s. The British explorers J. H. Speke and J. A. Grant traversed the western shore of Lake Victoria in 1862, searching for the source of the Nile, and they were the first Europeans to enter the Kingdom of Buganda, the name of which they incorrectly rendered as "Uganda." Another English explorer, Sir Samuel Baker, reaching Uganda from the north, discovered Lake Albert in 1864. In the 1870s Baker and General Charles Gordon, serving successively as governor of the Egyptian Sudan and seeking to suppress the Arab slave trade, attempted—without permanent success—to expand the dominion of Egypt into what is today the northern part of Uganda. The journalist-explorer H. M. Stanley visited the Kingdom of Buganda in 1875 and conveyed to the outside world the need for Christian missionaries in the country. As a result, missionaries from both the Protestant and the Catholic religions were sent to the area—Anglicans from the Church Missionary Society of Great Britain arriving in 1877, followed in 1879 by French priests of the Roman Catholic White Fathers of Algeria. All too soon, disputes began to arise between the Christian sects. At the same time Arab ivory and slave traders, active in the region since the 1850s, strove to gain converts for Islam and intrigued against the Christians.

Initially the Christian missionaries were welcomed by the kabaka (king) of Buganda, Mutesa I, in the hope that they would help counter the threat of Egyptian encroachment from the north. However, Mutesa I died in 1884 and was succeeded by his son, Mwanga, then only about eighteen, but already suspicious, hostile, and cruelly dissolute. Mwanga feared the influence of the missionaries over his people and encouraged the persecution and slaughter of Christians in Buganda. These atrocities culminated in the murder of the Anglican bishop, James Hannington, in 1885 (speared to death and mutilated) and in the wholesale martyrdom of 32 young Roman Catholic and Anglican converts in 1886 (rolled up in reed mats and burned alive in one great execution pyre). Mwanga also turned against the Muslims, suspecting danger from that quarter. The Bugandan adherents of Christianity and Islam then united and, in 1888, succeeded in driving Mwanga from his kingdom. The Muslims soon afterward attacked the Buganda Christians and seized control of the country. Finally the Christian factions and Mwanga came to terms, joined forces to defeat the Muslims, and in 1890 restored the kabaka to power.

In 1888 the Imperial British East Africa Company received a royal charter and authorization to administer the British sphere of influence in East Africa. After the Anglo-German Agreement of 1890 officially demarked the boundaries of the British sphere, including what is now Uganda and Kenya*, and the German sphere, which was later called Tanganyika*, the IBEA Company sent Capt. Frederick Lugard to Uganda to establish a company (and British) presence. From the beginning Lugard's objectives were more political than commercial. In December 1890 he concluded a treaty with Mwanga, placing the Kingdom of Buganda under IBEA protection. Later, in 1892, Lugard, with the aid of Sudanese troops and the only Maxim gun in the country, intervened in a civil war between the Ba-Fransa (Roman Catholic) and Ba-Ingleza (Protestant) factions, enabling the Ba-Ingleza to gain the upper hand. When in that same year the IBEA Company was brought to the verge of bankruptcy (its representatives seemed to do more fighting than trading), it was Lugard who traveled to London to persuade the British government not to abandon Uganda and the headwaters of the Nile. In 1894 the Kingdom of Buganda was declared a British protectorate; and in 1896 the protectorate was enlarged to include the neighboring Kingdom of Bunyoro and other areas encompassing most of what is present-day Uganda.

In 1897 Mwanga attempted an uprising against the British but was unsuccessful. He was captured and exiled by the British to the Seychelles* in 1898, dying there in 1903. His infant son, Daudi Chwa, was installed as kabaka, and the British special commissioner, Sir Harry Johnston, concluded the Uganda Agreement of 1900, in which the kabakaship and the lukiido (council of chiefs) were formally recognized by the British government. The dominant tribe of the region, known as Ganda, or Baganda, was granted a great deal of political autonomy under British supervision in exchange for its allegiance. The agreement also provided for freehold land tenure and allocated these land tracts (called mailo) to both the individual Ganda leaders and the hierarchy of appointed chiefs who made up the bulk of the Bugandan administration. The British used their appointive powers to assert control over the Buganda government. Elsewhere in the region British rule was extended through a system of expatriate officers and Bugandan agents. The agreement solidified the privileged position of the Bagandan people in Uganda. Subsequently, treaties establishing "indirect rule" were concluded with the other kingdoms in the region—Toro in 1900, Ankole in 1901, and finally, Bunyoro in 1933.

British policy in Uganda did not encourage settlement of Europeans, but instead supported the cultivation of cash crops which would benefit the British Empire*, and Uganda as well. By focusing on cotton and, later, coffee crops, the policy directly affected the development of the infrastructure of the region through the building of improved roads, railroads, and public services. This modernization was dramatically accelerated in the post–World War II economy when higher prices resulted in greater prosperity for the country.

Political development occured primarily along tribal lines until a sense of nationalism began to emerge in the 1950s due to British efforts to establish a unitary state in Uganda. Governor Sir Andrew Cohen was charged with carrying out this policy and was met with extreme opposition from the Non-Ganda Nationalist movement, which feared the domination of Buganda. A crisis soon emerged between Cohen and Kabaka Mutesaa II over the demands of the Bagandan people for a separate independent state. The kabaka was exiled to Britain in 1953 for refusing to order his chiefs to follow British policy. He was restored in 1955 in another attempt to secure Bugandan participation in a united Uganda. The role of Buganda within a united Uganda continued to be a stumbling block until 1961. At a constitutional conference held in London in October 1961, it was decided that Buganda would be given a federal relationship with the government of a united Uganda. Thus Bugandans would enjoy limited autonomy within their kingdom and yet play a role in the national government of Uganda. It was also decided at the London conference that Uganda would become officially independent of Great Britain on October 9, 1962. (Jan Jorgenson, *Uganda: A Modern History*, 1981).

Joseph L. Michaud

ULSTER. See NORTHERN IRELAND.

UMM AL-QAIMAIN. See UNITED ARAB EMIRATES.

UNFEDERATED MALAY STATES. The Unfederated Malay States was an administrative unit created by the British in 1914 to make bureaucratic supervision of the Malay Peninsula simpler. The Unfederated Malay States included Johor*, Kelantin*, Perlis*, Trengganu*, and Kedah*. In 1945 the Unfederated Malay States became part of the Malayan Union. See MALAYSIA.

UNION OF SOUTH AFRICA. See SOUTH AFRICA.

UNITED ARAB EMIRATES. The United Arab Emirates is an independent nation of approximately 30,000 square miles located along the Persian Gulf in the eastern Arabian Peninsula. It is composed of seven states, each of them formerly an independent kingdom: Abu Dhabi, Dubai, Sharjah, Ras al-Khaimah, Al-Fujayrah, Umm al-Qaiwain, and Ajman. The United Arab Emirates are bordered on the north by the Persian Gulf and Qatar*, on the east by Oman, and on the south and west by Saudi Arabia*. The Portuguese first set up a base in Ras al-Khaimah in the late 1500s to harrass the Persian Empire, and they maintained a presence in what is today the northern Arab Emirates—Ras al-Khaimah, Umm al-Qaiwain, and Sharjah—until the late 1600s. In 1820 and 1835 Great Britain signed a series of treaties with the Persian Gulf states, and for the next 150 years the British maintained a military presence there. In an 1853 treaty the sheiks of the various Arab kingdoms agreed to allow Great Britain to mediate their disputes, and in 1892 the British agreed to protect the area from external aggression. By that time the Persian Gulf was becoming increasingly important to the British as a strategic site to protect their Asian interests.

But in 1968 the British announced their intention to withdraw troops from the region, forcing the Persian Gulf nations to make new political and military arrangements of their own. The region had assumed great importance to Great Britain, however, because of the huge oil reserves there. Great Britain then supervised negotiations to create a political federation of Bahrain*, Qatar, Ras al-Khaimah, Abu Dhabi, Dubai, Sharjah, Umm al-Qaiwain, Al-Fujaryah, and Ajman. But the talks broke down. Bahrain, Qatar, and Ras al-Khaimah decided to become independent. On December 2, 1971, the other six states formed the United Arab Emirates, a sovereign nation. Ras al-Khaimah joined the federation one year later. (Muhammad Morsy Abdullah, *The United Arab Emirates: A Modern History*, 1978; Ali M. Khalifa, *The United Arab Emirates: Unity in Fragmentation*, 1979.)

UNITED ARAB REPUBLIC. The concept of pan-Arabism, or a union of Arab states, had been a pious wish for many Arabs from the end of the nineteenth century. It was only with the advent of a charismatic leader like Gamal Abd al-Nasser* that it seemed on its way to becoming a political reality. The push toward such a union of Arab states came from Syria*, where some moderate politicians, led by Shukri al-Quwatli, fearing a communist take-over of the government, and strongly supported by Baath party elements, induced Nasser to create a union between the two countries in 1958. Coming as it did on the heels of the Tripartite aggression against Egypt* in 1956, which resulted in turning Nasser into a hero who had resisted a major attempt to topple him, the United Arab Republic was pieced together hurriedly and presented more problems than it was to solve. Syrian political parties were dissolved, as those of Egypt had been, resulting in a Baath Party grievance against Nasser and the resignation of all Baathist ministers. Nationalization decrees did not sit well with a commercial center such as Syria, and the choice of a tough-minded dictator to rule over Syria ended by exacerbating Syrian feelings against what they called the "Egyptian occupation." Expecting to be treated as equals, the Syrians found the Egyptians treating them as a very junior partner. In 1961 a military coup ousted the Egyptians from Syria and disbanded the United Arab Republic. Although Yemen had become a member of the United Arab Republic, Egypt and Syria were the two effective partners, so that after the Syrian defection the union was ended. Nasser continued to use the name until it was finally changed to the Arab Republic of Egypt under Sadat. (R. Hrair Dekmejian, *Egypt Under Nasir: A Study in Political Dynamics*, 1971.)

Alain G. Marsot

UNITED NATIONS. Created in 1945, the United Nations is an international organization whose principal function is to maintain international peace and security. The United Nations's activities and structure were developed during World War II* by the Allied Powers. The most important stages in the creation of the United Nations were the Moscow Conference of Foreign Ministers of the Soviet Union, United States of America, and Great Britain in 1943; the Dumbarton Oaks Conference in 1944; the Yalta Conference in 1945; and the San Francisco Conference in 1945. At the San Francisco Conference on June 26, 1945, representatives of 50 nations signed the United Nations Charter. The Charter came into force on October 24, 1945, after the Soviet Union, the United States, Great Britain, France, China, and most of the other signatories had ratified it.

The United Nations Charter included such principles of international cooperation as the sovereign equality of all United Nations members, the settlement of international disputes by peaceful means, the renunciation in international relations of the threat or use of force in any way inconsistent with the aims of the United Nations, and nonintervention by the United Nations in matters that essentially fall under the domestic jurisdiction of a sovereign state. The Charter established the basic structure of the United Nations. Among the most important bodies are the General Assembly, the Security Council, the Economic and Social Council, the Trusteeship Council, the International Court of Justice, and the Secretariat. The General Assembly has the right to discuss any question within the scope of the Charter or affecting the powers and functions of any United Nations organ and to make recommendations where they do not conflict with the special powers of the Security Council. The Security Council bears the main responsibility for maintaining international peace and security, and all United Nations members may bring their disputes to the forum of the Security Council for mediation.

Since its inception, the United Nations has focused attention on the movement for independence among colonial territories of the European powers. The United Nations Charter provisions on non-self-governing territories are delineated in Article XI, which contains the Declaration Regarding Non-Self-Governing Territories. Under the terms of this declaration, member states administering such territories were to recognize that the interests of the inhabitants of these territories were paramount and undertake to promote to the utmost their well-being. More specifically, they agreed to assure the peoples of these territories political, economic, social, and educational advancement, just treatment, and protection against abuse. They also undertook to promote self-government for these peoples, take account of their political aspirations, and assist them in the progressive development of free political institutions.

In addition to the declaration, which is applicable to all non-self-governing territories, Articles XII and XIII of the Charter provided for an International Trusteeship System to be applied to all territories brought under it by the administering states. It was intended that all territories formerly under League of Nations* mandate should be placed under trusteeship* unless they had acquired full independence. The Charter specifically committed the United Nations to the economic, social, and political development of these former mandate territories instead of limiting its responsibilities to the prevention of abuses. Furthermore, in order to more effectively supervise the trusteeship system, the Charter placed overall control in the General Assembly. The Trusteeship Council, an arm of the General Assembly, was given extensive powers of inquiry and report. Among the former mandate territories placed under United Nations trusteeship since World War II—including the two Togolands, the two Cameroons, Somaliland, Tanganyika*, Ruanda-Urundi, Nauru*, New Guinea*, and Western Samoa*— all have achieved independence. By 1975 virtually all the non-self-governing territories not under trusteeship, including all the major colonial possessions in the former British, French, Belgian, and German colonial empires, had been granted full independence. (Clark M. Eichelberger, *United Nations: The First Twenty-Five Years*, 1970; D. K. Fieldhouse, *The Colonial Empires*, 1966; Ruth B. Russell, *A History of the United Nations Charter*, 1958.)

William G. Ratliff

UPPER CANADA. See CANADA.

UPPER VOLTA. The Upper Volta region of west Africa first attracted European attention in the late nineteenth century when various colonial powers sought to increase their influence north and east of their coastal colonies. The German explorer Gottlob Krausse first visited the region in 1886. He was followed two years later by a French officer, Louis Binger, who failed to persuade the local tribes to accept the protection of France. In 1896 French Lt. Paul Voulet was sent with army troops to subjugate the area before the English could bring it under their control. He was successful. The capitol of Ouagadougou fell and the local people, known as Mossi, accepted French occupation as a form of protection from their hostile neighbors. In 1898 an Anglo-French agreement set the boundries between the Upper Volta region and Britain's Gold Coast territory.

Between 1904 and 1919 the Upper Volta region was administered as part of

the Upper Senegal-Niger territory. In 1919 the French created the colony of
Upper Volta in the landlocked area that is now Burkina Faso. In 1932, for
economic reasons stemming from the worldwide depression, the colony was
abolished and divided among French Sudan, Niger*, and the Ivory Coast*.
Nevertheless, the area continued to develop, and by 1934 a railroad connected
the city of Babo-Dioulasso with the Ivory Coast port of Abidjan. Soon thousands
of Mossi were migrating annually to work in the cotton fields of the Ivory and
Gold Coast regions.

In 1947 France re-created the Upper Volta region as a separate colony, with
its pre–1932 boundaries intact, to satisfy Mossi desires for a separate territory
and to reduce the influence of the RDA (*Rassemblement Democratique Africain*),
a radical intercolonial party that espoused independence. The RDA had failed
to heavily influence the Mossi but it had gained prominence among the smaller
tribes of the area such as the Bobo, Lobi, and Fulani—all of whom hated the
Mossi. In 1948 France curtailed the activities of the RDA and in its place a
number of small regional independence movements took shape. By the mid–
1950s the regional groups were uniting around national issues. The RDA soon
re-emerged as the dominant political party. Led first by Quezzin Coulibaly and
then by Maurice Yameogo, the independence movement slowly gained strength.
During this period the national railroad was also extended to the capitol city of
Ouagadougou, creating a tremendous boom in the exports of various cash crops
such as cotton, livestock, and peanuts.

From 1947 to 1958 Upper Volta enjoyed the rights and privileges of an official
overseas territory of France. Elected representatives were sent to both a national
assembly and the parliament of France. In 1956 the *Loi Cadre* established a
predominantly African territorial executive whose primary responsibility was the
domestic policy of the colony. Two years later the people of Upper Volta voted
to make the colony an autonomous state within the French Community* and
also approved the constitution of the Fifth Republic. By this time the traditional
chiefs had lost influence and power in governmental affairs. Most of the authority
now rested with a young French-educated elite, who were slowly modernizing
the country in political matters. Upper Volta became independent on August 5,
1960, with Maurice Yameogo as president. After a series of relatively short-
lived governments Upper Volta was re-named Burkina Faso, or Land of the
Honest People, in 1984. (Daniel M. Mcfarland, *Historical Dictionary of Upper
Volta*, 1978.)

Joseph L. Michaud

URDANETA, ANDRÉS DE. Born in 1508, Andrés de Urdaneta was a Spanish
mathematician, cartographer, navigator, and Augustinian priest who accompanied the Spanish expedition to the Moluccas* in 1525 and remained in the
Far East until 1536. He then returned to Spain, sailing around the Cape of Good
Hope, and prepared a detailed account of his travels. He had the honor of being
received in audience by the emperor Charles V* in Valladolid. Urdaneta left for

New Spain* in the fleet of the governor of Guatemala* in October 1538. They arrived in the New World in April 1539, after which time Urdaneta served in various important administrative capacities under the viceroy, Antonio de Mendoza. Urdaneta turned his attention to religious matters in the spring of 1552, entering upon a novitiate in the Augustinian order. He took his solemn vows in March 1553 in Mexico City. Because of his eminence as a cosmographer, he had an unexpected opportunity for further travel when Philip II commanded him to serve as a guide for a new Spanish voyage to the Pacific. Miguel López de Legazpi* was named commander of this enterprise.

Legazpi's expedition consisted of two three-masted galleons, two pinnaces, and a small frigate attached to the flagship. Esteban de Rodríguez served as chief pilot. This expedition left from the port of La Navidad on 21 November 1564. While at sea the *San Lucas* parted from Legazpi's fleet, reached Mindanao*, and returned to New Spain, arriving in August 1565. Meanwhile the rest of the fleet reached the Philippines* in February 1565, and in late April the Spaniards anchored off the island of Cebu. Legazpi was able to establish a colony on Cebu after overcoming the initial hostility of the islanders. This colony remained the principal base for Spanish operations in the area until 1571, the date of the founding of Manila*. On June 1, 1565, Legazpi sent his flagship, *San Pedro*, back to New Spain. Urdaneta finally succeeded in returning to the western coast of North America, making the first landfall off the California coast near the present site of Santa Barbara; and on October 8th the voyage terminated at Acapulco. Urdaneta had succeeded in discovering the route from the Far East to New Spain that approximated the passage used by the Manila galleons* for many years. He then journeyed to Spain, reported the story of his voyage to Philip II, and returned to New Spain. He died in Mexico City in June 1568 at the age of sixty. (Mariano Cuevas, *Monje y arion; la vida y los tiempos de Fray Andrés de Urdaneta*, 1943; Mairin Mitchell, *Friar Andrew de Urdaneta*, 1964; Henry R. Wagner, ''Urdaneta and the Return Route from the Philippine Islands,'' *Pacific Historical Review* 13, no. 3, 1944, 313–16.)

URUGUAY. Uruguay is distinctive on a number of counts. Its populace of just over three million people is the most homogeneous in Latin America, has the highest literacy rate, and is among the most prosperous. Uruguay created the first welfare state in Latin America and, in the first half of the twentieth century, was considered to be the most democratic nation of the region. Unlike most Latin American nations, Uruguay has no physical extremes. There are no mountains, deserts, or jungles. The topography is rolling plains and the climate is temperate.

The Banda Oriental (Eastern Bank) de la Plata was claimed by Sebastián Cabot for Spain in 1527. Because there were no riches to be exploited, the Banda Oriental was generally neglected except as an occasional battleground between the imperial forces of the Spanish and Portuguese. The Spanish did not consolidate control over Uruguay until 1777, when the Portuguese signed their outpost of Colonia over to Spain. The interior of the region had been settled sparsely by gauchos from the Argentine side of the La Plata, who crossed the river to round up the wild cattle which roamed the Uruguayan plains.

Banda Oriental was under the administrative control of the Spanish viceroy of La Plata centered in Buenos Aires. When the *criollos* of Buenos Aires deposed the viceroy in 1810, the Uruguayans were expected to be part of an independent Argentina, but the governor of Montevideo refused to recognize the authority of the Buenos Aires junta. José Gervasio Artigas, a Uruguayan gaucho, then led a rural revolt against the governor. The effort was joined by forces from Buenos Aires, and the Spanish commander in Montevideo finally surrendered in 1814. Artigas, however, refused to accept Argentine domination and forced the Argentines to withdraw in 1815, only to be confronted by Portuguese troops from Brazil* the next year. Artigas's guerrillas were defeated in 1820, and Uruguay became a province of Brazil. Artigas, the architect of Uruguayan nationalism, fled to Paraguay, where he lived in exile until his death in 1850.

Uruguayan nationalists, with Argentine help, went to war against the Brazilians in 1825. After a three-year struggle, the British, whose lucrative trade was obstructed by the conflict, persuaded the Brazilians and the Argentines to sign a treaty guaranteeing the security of the independent Republica Oriental del Uruguay. The British saw an independent Uruguay as a useful buffer between the two giants of South America. (Martin Alisky, *Uruguay: A Contemporary Survey*, 1969; Martin Weinstein, *Uruguay: The Politics of Failure*, 1975.)

Bruce R. Drury

V

VAN DIEMEN'S LAND. Today known as Tasmania, Van Diemen's Land is a 26,215 square-mile island state of Australia* located south of Victoria, across the Bass Strait. It was first discovered by a Dutch explorer, Abel J. Tasman*, who was exploring the southern and eastern coasts of Australia under the direction of Anthony van Diemen, the governor-general of the Dutch East Indies*. Tasman discovered the island in 1642 and named it after Governor Van Diemen. At the time of the discovery the native population of the island totaled only a few thousand people, probably because the soil is low in fertility. Founded as a British penal colony, Van Diemen's Land received its first prisoners in 1803. Other British colonists began arriving soon after, and almost immediately the native population began to decline because of disease and brutal treatment. The colonists relocated the native population to a reservation on Flinders Island, where the last native Tasmanian died in 1876.

Van Diemen's Land was formally administered as part of the colony of New South Wales* from 1803 to 1825, when it became a separate colony. In 1856 Van Diemen's Land, which had been renamed Tasmania in 1853, became a self-governing colony. When the Commonwealth of Australia was formed in 1901, Tasmania was one of its original states. (Lloyd Robson, *A History of Van Diemen's Land from Earliest Times to 1855*. Vol. I, 1983; *Lloyd Robson, A Short History of Tasmania*, 1986.)

VENEZUELA. In 1498, on his third voyage to the New World, Christopher Columbus* sailed into the Gulf of Paria and then along the coast of the Orinoco Delta of what is today Venezuela. One year later, Alonso de Ojeda and Amerigo Vespucci made a more extensive exploration of the coastal region. During the next two decades several other Spanish and Portuguese explorers reached the area, but settlement was slow to occur. In 1528, hoping to realize immediate financial gains from its New World discoveries, the Spanish crown under Charles I leased Venezuela to the House of Welser, a prominent German banking group headquartered in Augsburg. Along with the lease went the right to establish cities and develop mineral properties and an *asiento* to import African slaves. The Welsers brought in several thousand slaves from West Africa in 1528 and in 1536. The first blacks they brought were primarily Yoruba, Ibo, and Fon tribes people. Father Bartolomé de las Casas* promoted the program because he felt that such a plan would give the crown control over the trade and guarantee that the slaves were distributed only to individuals willing to give them a Christian education. In 1546, the Spanish crown refused to renew the lease, and the program was officially terminated in 1556.

Settlement in the area then occurred piecemeal over the next decades. The island of Margarita*off the coast of Venezuela had been given to the Villalobos family as a private domain in 1525. They established a small settlement there, but it reverted to crown control in 1600. Caracas*, the capital city of Venezuela, was established in 1567 as Santiago de León de Caracas. Its founder was Diego de Losada. The city of Maracaibo was founded in 1569. The Spanish crown erected the province of Espiritu Santo de La Grita in 1575, and in 1576 Caracas became the colonial capital. Another Spanish settlement developed in Merida. For the most part, Venezuela was an economic backwater in the sixteenth and seventeenth centuries, its economy revolving around subsistence agriculture, small-scale mining, and stock raising.

But it began to assume commercial importance in the early 1700s with the export of gold, silver, cacao, tobacco, hides, and indigo to Spain from the region. By the early 1700s the Dutch had established a near monopoly on the cacao trade coming out of northern South America, and the Spanish crown resented the losses of revenue. King Philip V authorized creation of the Caracas Company in 1728 to stimulate commerce and trade between Spain and what is today Venezuela. Also known as the Guipuzcoa Company because Basque investors in Guipuzcoa Province financed the venture, the Caracas Company first sent a fleet to the New World in 1730. The company was an immediate success, crushing Dutch trade and pirates in the lower Caribbean and exporting Venezuelan gold, silver, hides, tobacco, indigo, and cacao to Spain. The crown granted the Caracas Company a monopoly in 1742 over the Venezuelan trade, a move which alienated *criollo* traders in Caracas. They revolted violently against the company in 1749, prompting the crown to relocate the company's board of directors to Spain in 1751. The revolt was led by Juan Francisco de León. After two years of rebellion which even drove the Spanish governor from the capital, royal troops restored order. The revolt, however, did influence company policy. In 1752 the Caracas Company invited and received substantial *criollo* investment and in 1759 allowed small cacao merchants to use company warehousing and shipping space to export their product. Under the economic operations of the Caracas Company, Venezuela came into its own economically and became an important political and economic center in the Spanish empire.

From the beginning of the colonial period until 1717, the region of contemporary Venezuela was under the administrative authority of the Audiencia of Santo Domingo*. From 1717 to 1723, Venezuela came under the authority of the Audienca of Santa Fe (de Bogotá). When the Viceroyalty of New Granada was suppressed, Venezuela returned to the jurisdiction of the Audiencia of Santo Domingo, where she remained until 1739. For the next three years, Venezuela was back under the authority of the Audienca of Santa Fe (de Bogotá). From 1742 until 1786, Venezuela went back to Santo Domingo jurisdiction. In 1786, however, with her population growing and economy expanding, Venezuela deserved her own audiencia. That year, Charles III established the Audiencia of Caracas, and it was installed on July 19, 1787. The Audiencia of Caracas functioned until the end of the colonial period.

The *criollo* revolt against the monopoly of the Caracas Company was a precursor to the subsequent Venezuelan independence movement. Local, Venezuelan-born elites resented the social, political, and economic power of the Spanish-born government and church officials, and in 1797 Manual Gual and José María España led a brief, poorly planned revolt. Spain easily crushed it but the winds of revolutionary sentiment were blowing in Venezuela. In 1806 Francisco Miranda sailed from New York with a small expedition to liberate Venezuela from Spanish control, but he too was unsuccessful. But after the Napoleonic invasion of Spain and the deposition of the Spanish monarchy, the independence movement became irreversible in Venezuela. In April 1810 rebel leaders deposed the captain-general of Caracas, and on July 5, 1811, a revolutionary *junta* was created which formally declared Venezuelan separation from Spain and drew up a constitution. Fighting continued for the next ten years until Simón Bolívar's forces finally eliminated royalist power. Venezuela was part of Gran Colómbia before finally becoming an independent nation in 1830. (Roland D. Hussey, *The Caracas Company, 1728–1784: A Study in the History of Spanish Monopolistic Trade*, 1934; John V. Lombardi, *Venezuela, The Search for Order, the Dream of Progress*, 1982; Guillermo Moron, *A History of Venezuela*, 1963.)

Said El Mansour Cherkaoui

VICEROYALTY OF NEW CASTILE. The Viceroyalty of New Castile, later renamed the Viceroyalty of Peru, was the administrative unit responsible for governing all of Spanish South America, including the colonial settlement at Panama. But unlike the Viceroyalty of New Spain, which had reasonable communication links with its colonies, the Viceroyalty of New Castile was unable to effectively administer its colonial settlements, particularly those at great distances from Lima. To relieve the problem, Spain created the Viceroyalty of New Granada in 1717, dissolved it a few years later, and then reconstituted it in 1739. The Viceroyalty of New Granada assumed responsibility for the colonial settlements in Panama*, Colombia*, Venezuela*, and much of Ecuador*. In 1776 Spain created another viceroyalty—the Viceroyalty of the Rio de la Plata—to assume direction of the colonial settlements in Argentina*, Chile*, Uruguay*, Paraguay*, and most of Bolivia. (Charles Gibson, *Spain in America*, 1966.)

VICEROYALTY OF NEW SPAIN. By 1535 Spanish settlements had appeared throughout Mexico*, Central America, and the Caribbean—particularly in the Greater Antilles*—and Spain needed to impose some administrative rationality over her growing empire. In 1535 Spain established the Viceroyalty of New Spain, with its headquarters in Mexico City. The viceroyalty was the primary administrative unit of government in the Spanish empire*, and the *audiencias* of New Galicia, Mexico, Guatemala*, and Santo Domingo were within its jurisdiction. Throughout the colonial period, the Viceroyalty of New Spain governed all of Spanish America north of Panama*. (Charles Gibson, *Spain in America*, 1966.)

VICTORIA. By the 1830s, as the English textile mills boomed and enormously increased the demand for wool, Australian settlers began squatting on range land south of New South Wales* just as other settlers from Van Dieman's Land* made similar moves crossing the Tasmanian sea to raise sheep*. They settled the area of Melbourne in 1835. The explorer Thomas Mitchell crossed the Murray River and named the lands south of it "Australia Felix." By the early 1840s settlers directly from Scotland and England were colonizing the area south of the Murray River. Late in the decade the area's population exceeded that of South Australia*. In 1850 parliament passed the Australia Colonies Government Act, which among other items provided for the creation of new, separate colony of Victoria out of southern New South Wales. Local self-government was established in 1853 and responsible government in 1855. On January 1, 1901, Victoria became a state in the new Commonwealth of Australia*. (Manning Clark, *Short History of Australia*, 1963; S. M. Roberts, *Squatting in Australian History*, 1935.)

VIETNAM. Vietnam is a small, resource-poor nation located in Indochina, and throughout history it has been a focus of great-power rivalry. The Vietnamese fought tenaciously and successfully for national independence against the Chinese, Mongols, French, Japanese, and Americans. Vietnamese history offers a convincing demonstration of the efficacy of "people's war" against foreign occupation. Vietnam already possessed a distinct national culture when first conquered by the Chinese Han Dynasty in 111 B.C. The Trung sisters' rebellion (39 A.D. to 43 A.D.) may be seen as an embryonic version of Vietnam's many later "wars of national liberation," except that it failed, while later wars succeeded. Vietnam was governed as a frontier province of China* for more than a thousand years. Sinicization was inevitable. Vietnam absorbed all three strands of Chinese religion (Confucianism, Daoism, and Mahayana Buddhism), grafting them to native Southeast Asian animism. Vietnamese scholars rose through the highly developed Chinese bureaucracy, learning to read and write Chinese and absorbing Chinese political philosophy. When the Vietnamese won independence in the tenth century, they set up a miniature version of the Chinese empire, but with distinctive Vietnamese characteristics. The Vietnamese language and national identity endured despite the long centuries of incorporation into China.

A major theme of Vietnamese history, even to the present day, has been their slow, steady, seemingly inexorable southward march. Vietnamese culture spread out of its original home in the Red River delta and flowed south at the expense of the Cham empire, which ceased to exist in 1695, and the Cambodian empire, which declined as Vietnam expanded. The price for this expansion was that transportation and communication became tenuous along the coastline. It proved impossible to maintain central control. Even before Europeans interfered, Vietnam had split into rival halves. A Nguyen family dynasty ruled southern Vietnam from Hue, while the Trinh dynasty in Hanoi ruled the north.

At first European contact with Vietnam produced little effect, but the French missionary Alexandre de Rhodes did succeed in baptizing thousands of adults in 1624. As elsewhere in East Asia, Christianity seemed to threaten the Confucian foundations of the state. Vietnamese converts were persecuted and missionaries were executed. Catholic orders in Paris agitated for French military action. By the middle of the nineteenth century, conditions were ripe for French annexation of Vietnam. There was no French master plan. A punitive expedition (1857) against the port of Tourane (Da Nang) was turned back. The French went south, instead, where Vietnamese control was weaker, and annexed three provinces around what became Saigon. Emperor Tu Duc was forced to recognize the initial French penetration in 1862, and events quickly led to the loss of all Vietnam, and Cambodia* and Laos* as well. The French took Cambodia in 1863, attacked Hanoi in 1873, and consolidated their rule over all Vietnam in 1885. The Indochina Union* was created in 1887. Laos was added as the fifth and final part of French Indochina in 1893. Imperialism rested rather lightly on Cambodia and Laos; nationalist movements there never grew strong enough to oust the French. Vietnam was another story altogether.

Frenchmen could not foresee the impact of their policies, which appeared to them progressive. A new (romanized) writing system, for example, replaced cumbersome Chinese characters with a phonetic alphabet and brought literacy within reach of the masses. A new class of intellectuals was thereby cut off from Vietnamese classics—but could read Voltaire, Rousseau, and Marx. Likewise, draining the delta land south of Saigon seemed progressive but created conditions that undermined French control. Large commercial plantations employed armies of seasonal male laborers. Vietnamese had known only small farms and compact, coherent villages. Villagers had produced whatever they needed. Their very identities were bound up with their families and villages, where ancestors' bones hallowed the ground. By contrast, social cohesion was completely lacking on the sugar, rice, banana, coffee, and rubber plantations. Rural proletarians, far from home, at the mercy of harsh overseers and subject to unpredictable layoffs if world market prices fell, were ripe indeed for revolutionary agitators. Labor on construction projects was worse yet. Twenty-five thousand Vietnamese died building a useless French railroad up a river valley into Yunnan. Peasants who remained in their traditional villages suffered from French policies, too. France was determined that Vietnam should pay for its own colonial administration, and to that end imposed ruinous taxes. Revenue from the salt monopoly went up 5,000 percent. Vietnamese emperors had taxed, too, but relented in hard times. The French kept better records; they updated surveys and censuses. Taxes were now collected in cash, not in rice, as before. Villagers were enmeshed in a cash economy they could neither understand nor control.

Vietnamese resentment eventually expressed itself in various revolutionary movements. The French allowed no democratic opposition, and drove Vietnamese patriots underground, where they found brilliant leadership and coherent organization in the Indochinese Communist Party, founded and led by Ho Chi Minh*. The Japanese occupied all Indochina* during World War II*, with the acquiescence of French *colons* who answered to the pro-fascist Vichy regime in Paris. They so disrupted the colonial order that the French were never able to reassert control after 1945. A long war to win Vietnamese independence ended with a complete Vietnamese victory over the French in 1954.

Legally, imperialism in Vietnam ended with the signing of the 1954 Geneva Accords that established two temporary regroupment zones north and south of the 17th parallel. Two sovereign states emerged to claim legitimate rule over independent Vietnam: The communist Democratic Republic of Vietnam, with its capital at Hanoi, and the non-communist Republic of Vietnam, ruled from Saigon. In political terms, however, as defined by the victorious North Vietnamese, imperialism persisted. Vietnam was still occupied by a destructive foreign presence whose expulsion would perfect Vietnamese independence. Americans had simply stepped into the shoes of the departed French. Because this simple idea carried such popular force, the American-backed government in Saigon could never establish political legitimacy with Vietnamese villagers. Saigon was politically defeated long before the matter was settled militarily in 1975. (Joseph Buttinger, *Vietnam: A Political History*, 1968; Stanley Karnow, *Vietnam: A History*, 1983; David Marr, *Vietnamese Anticolonialism, 1885–1925*, 1971.)

Ross Marlay

VIRGINIA. Virginia was originally inhabited by a number of Indian tribes. Spanish sailors were the first Europeans to visit the area, which Spain claimed as part of Florida, in either 1560 or 1561. An unsuccessful attempt in 1566 by Pedro Menendez to settle along the Chesapeake Bay was followed by the establishment of a Jesuit mission in September 1570, probably on the York River, among the Occaneechi tribe. Six months later the Indians attacked the Spanish missionaries, sparing only an altar boy who eventually made it back to Florida. Further missionary efforts in Ajacan, as the Spanish called the Chesapeake region, were seen as too dangerous and were suspended.

Walter Raleigh in 1584 received a grant to establish a colony in the New World and dispatched Philip Amandas and Arthur Barlowe to undertake the task. They landed at Roanoke Island and returned to England with a bag of pearls, a few Indians, and some fanciful tales about the region, which Raleigh named "Virginia" (to both honor and flatter Queen Elizabeth I). Two privately financed efforts in 1585 and 1587 to establish a permanent settlement failed, the colonists having experienced difficulties with bad weather, hostile Indian tribes, and inadequate supplies. Although unsuccessful, Raleigh's attempts at colonization aroused English interest in the region, which led to the London Company's expedition in 1607.

James I, Elizabeth's successor, had granted a charter to the London Company authorizing it to send to Virginia colonists who would search for Raleigh's lost colony at Roanoke Island, seek the mythical northwest passage to the Pacific Ocean, convert the Indians to Christianity, guard against Spanish encroachment, and prospect for gold and other treasure. In May 1607 the settlers arrived from England and moored on a peninsula in the James River, where they established a stockaded village they named Jamestown*. The site was badly chosen, for it was located in a malarial swamp with inadequate fresh water supplies and little tillable soil. For the next two years, the Jamestown settlement was subjected to incompetent leadership, internal dissension, disease, hunger, thirst, and the constant threat of Indian attack. Conditions reached their nadir during the winter of 1609–1610, which the colonists called "the starving time." The colony was rescued by the fortuitous arrival of Thomas West, Lord De La Warr, who brought fresh supplies and new colonists. Under De La Warr's competent yet stern leadership, Virginia began to flourish, especially after John Rolfe successfully introduced West Indian tobacco seeds in 1612, thereby providing the Virginians with a valuable cash crop they could export.

In 1619 it appeared that the colony of Virginia was well established: all free colonists had been granted land, a representative legislative body (the House of Burgesses) was formed, and the London Company, for the first time, judged it safe enough to allow women to emigrate. Dutch traders that year brought to Virginia the first African slaves, a source of labor upon which Virginian planters grew increasingly dependent. Although profitable, tobacco production in Virginia had not produced for the London investors the immense returns they had hoped. In 1624, consequently, the London Company declared bankruptcy. The corporate charter was revoked and Virginia was placed under direct royal administration, giving the Crown great control over the colony's economy.

When Charles I was executed during the English Civil War, Virginia recognized without hesitation the future Charles II as the lawful monarch. Many loyalists and aristocratic refugees fled to the colony, eventually reaching positions of leadership and economic importance. Throughout the second half of the seventeenth century, the drift toward an aristocratic and hierarchical culture was encouraged and strengthened by the social and economic ramifications of the growing tobacco industry. As the plantation owners relied more heavily on slave labor, it became more important for them to regularize the status of African slaves as property. This process, begun in the 1670s, culminated in 1705 with the issue of a slave code in which African slaves were defined by the House of Burgesses as real estate. By 1730 the labor-intensive tobacco industry dominated Virginia. Over 40 percent of the population was black, and fear of a violent slave insurrection resulted in a rigid slave code.

At the turn of the eighteenth century Virginia was the largest and most important of Great Britain's North American colonies. As the population grew, it also expanded westward. English settlers eventually came into conflict with French trappers in the Ohio Valley; skirmishes and border raids erupted into full-scale war during the French and Indian War (1754–1763). Under the terms of the Treaty of Paris of 1763*, France ceded all her territorial claims in North America to Great Britain. Land-hungry colonists, especially those from Virginia, the colony with the best claim to the disputed western lands, were enraged by the Proclamation of 1763, which closed to the American colonists the fertile lands of the Ohio Valley and allowed a standing army at colonial expense. The disappointment of would-be settlers and land speculators over the decision by George III* to close the frontier came during a time of growing dissatisfaction with royal administration. Virginians served with distinction throughout the subsequent and successful War for American Independence. (Warren M. Billings, John E. Selby, and Thad W. Tate, *Colonial Virginia: A History*, 1986.)

Catherine A. Boehm

VIRGIN ISLANDS. The Virgin Islands, composed of a group of seven islands and approximately ninety cays and islets, were originally inhabited by the Siboney (Ciboney) Indians. A later branch of the Arawaks, the Caribs, lived there upon arrival of the Europeans. The Caribs were the scourge of the other Caribbean tribes for they were extremely hostile, aggressive, and independent. Christopher Columbus* became the first European to visit the Virgin Islands when he landed on the islet of Ayay (which he renamed Santa Cruz) on November 14, 1493. The Spanish opted not to colonize either this or the other islands because they were more interested in the Greater Antilles. Therefore, other European nations, mainly the English and the Dutch, settled Santa Cruz (St. Croix). The Dutch established present-day Christiansted, and the English settled near Fredricksted, both in 1625. The Dutch settlement was joined by French Protestant refugees from St. Christopher's. The Dutch abandoned Christiansted in 1645 after Indians killed the governor.

In 1650 the Spanish became alarmed at the English presence and drove them from Santa Cruz. Still not opting to colonize, the Spanish left the island open to the French colonial efforts of the governor of St. Christopher's. The name was changed to its present-day name of St. Croix and planters arrived. Prosperity did not follow because of restrictive trade laws, but smuggling, piracy, and illegal trading were successful. In 1653 the Knights of Malta took control of St. Croix and brought in bonded labor. From 1665 to 1674 the French West India

Company was in charge of St. Croix. It replaced bonded labor with African labor and the growing of tobacco with that of sugar.

In 1666 Denmark attempted to settle St. Thomas*, but poor weather, tropical illness, and English privateers brought it to an end. In 1668 Christiann V, King of Denmark, entered a treaty of alliance with the English and chartered the Danish West India Company, thus beginning successful colonization of the island. In 1672 Fort Christian was built in an effort to increase military authority on the island. The population of St. Thomas consisted of imported workers, artisans, soldiers, and convicts. However, 80 percent of those sent died and more convicted felons replaced them, creating a period of lawlessness which ended only with the arrival of new European immigrants, the majority of whom were Dutch. The main city became Tap Huis, later changed to Charlotte Amalie in honor of Christiaan V's consort, and the main language became Dutch.

St. John* remained uninhabited by Europeans until 1717 when the Danes, who had asserted sovereignty as early as 1684, overcame English hostility and colonized it. Like St. Thomas and St. Croix, St. John's economy was based on plantations with slave labor. In 1733 a slave revolt on St. John caused the Danes to eye St. Croix as an alternative colony. Denmark purchased St. Croix from France in 1753 and set up a colony immediately, made up of English settlers and slaves. The agreement had an addendum that stated France had final say on who could purchase the island from Denmark. This colonization period was marked with continual harassment from the Spanish who wanted Denmark out of the Caribbean. Due to intervention by the king of France because of Denmark's continued neutrality in European conflicts, the security of her Caribbean holdings was ensured.

The slave trade brought notoriety as St. Croix became known as the world's largest slave market. This ended with the Danish prohibition of slave trade in 1803. The abolition of slavery occurred in 1848 following a slave rebellion. Government of the islands was in the hands of a governor and council, composed of whites appointed by the Danish king. Several colonial laws were instituted to keep the blacks in their "place." The Colonial Law of 1863 divided the islands into two groups—St. Croix in one and St. Thomas and St. John in the other. This law, with its bill of rights and strict voting franchise, remained the norm until 1936. The Danes were never interested in maintaining the islands for any purpose other than profit. Therefore they instituted no reforms or programs to aid the populace socially or economically.

The United States expressed an interest in St. Croix, St. Thomas, and St. John in the 1860s but did not follow through and acquire them until fifty years later. The strategic location of the group became apparent upon completion of the Panama Canal. The United States felt it had to control the islands in order to maintain its control over the canal. When World War I broke out, the United States also began to worry about the possibility of Germany buying the islands. On March 3, 1917, the United States purchased the islands. The founding of any type of government or economic programs was delayed until after World

War I. The years between and immediately following the World Wars saw little economic growth in the three islands. However, a resurgence occurred with the advent of tourism. Today the islands' main economy is tourism, and the governmental policies, both economically and socially, are directed to enhancing it. Beginning in 1970 the governor was elected. Two years earlier the first black governor came to office, thus soothing tensions that had erupted occasionally since the days of slave labor. In 1972 the Virgin Islands were given a no-vote delegate to the United States House of Representatives. Today the territory looks toward independence.

The islands to the east of the American Virgin Islands were included by Spain when she claimed the New World as her own dominion. As with the western Virgin Islands, Spain claimed them in name only, never establishing colonies. The Dutch placed a small settlement on Tortola in 1648, but in 1666 Tortola, Virgin Gorda, and Anegada were settled by English planters. The Dutch were driven from Tortola in 1672. The islands were not as suited for agriculture as those to the west. However, England continued to maintain control of the group mainly due to the Anegada Passage—one of the main entrances into the Caribbean Sea. Control of it ensured the British access to the area. The Spanish names for the islands—Tortola, Virgin Gorda, and Anegada—remained. The Dutch tried unsuccessfully to found a colony on Jost Van Dyke during the same time period they were attempting settlement of the western Virgin Islands. Only their name for the island survived.

The economy of these islands was based mostly on piracy, smuggling, and slave trading. It was lucrative, though illegal. No colonization of any importance was undertaken and the islands' population was composed mainly of descendants of plantation slaves. Government until 1871 was undertaken by the British colonial office. For the next eighty-five years, they belonged to the colonial Leeward Islands Confederation. However, they did not join the West Indies Federation* (1958–1962) in order to maintain their close ties with the American Virgin Islands. By 1980 the British Virgin Islands were internally self-governing with a governor and executive and legislative council. (Darwin D. Creque, *The U.S. Virgin Islands and the Eastern Caribbean*, 1968; James E. Moore, *Everybody's Virgin Islands*, 1979.)

Catherine G. Harbour

W

WAKE ISLAND. An atoll of about 2.5 square miles located in the Central Pacific between Hawaii* and Guam*, Wake consists of three islets: Wake, Wilkes, and Peale. It was discovered around 1567 by Spanish explorers and then visited by the British in 1796. Wake was acquired by the second United States expedition to the Philippines* on July 4, 1898. The United States formally took possession of the island on January 17, 1899. Although small in area, Wake became an important commercial air base on the way to Asia in 1935 and a military base later in the decade. On December 7, 1941, Japanese forces attacked the island, which fell on December 23 after a heroic defense by a small Marine garrison. Wake was bombed heavily during World War II and was surrendered by the Japanese in September 1945. Since World War II Wake has continued to be an important commercial and military base. In 1962 administrative responsibility for Wake was vested in the United States Deparmtnet of the Interior, but in 1972 that function was turned over to the United States Air Force. (*Associated Press Almanac, 1973*, 1973; *The World Book Almanac and Book of Facts, 1982*, 1982.)

Joseph M. Rowe, Jr.

WALLIS. See WALLIS AND FUTUNA.

WALLIS AND FUTUNA. Wallis and Futuna is an overseas department of France. Closely associated with Futuna is the island of Alofi, just about one mile away. Wallis and Futuna are located at the far western edge of Polynesia*, about 110 miles from each other. Western Samoa* is to the east, Tonga to the southeast, Fiji* to the south and west, and Tuvalu to the north and west. Futuna and Wallis are both volcanic islands. Samuel Wallis, the British navigator, was the first

European to sight Wallis when he arrived there in 1767. Father Pierre Bataillon, a French Catholic missionary, arrived on Wallis in 1837 to try to convert the local population, which was composed of descendants of Samoans and Tongans who had arrived there centuries earlier. Bataillon converted most of the local chiefs to Catholicism and in 1842 France established a protectorate over Wallis.

Dutch navigators Jacob Lemaire and Willem Cornelius van Schouten first reached Futuna in 1616. Father Pierre Chanel, a French Catholic priest, arrived there in 1837 but he was killed by native islanders in 1841. Futuna became a French protectorate in 1888, and in 1909 France began to administer them from the same budget. By that time nearly everyone on the islands was Roman Catholic. Wallis was made a colony of France in 1913, and in 1959, after a referendum on the islands, Wallis and Futuna became a single overseas territory of France, with one deputy in the French national assembly and one member of the French senate. (Virginia Thompson and Richard Adloff, *The French Pacific Islands: French Polynesia and New Caledonia*, 1971.)

WALVIS BAY. Situated on the Atlantic coast in southwestern Africa, the district of Walvis Bay (434 square miles) is controlled and administered by the Republic of South Africa, although geographically it is separated from that country by the vast arid expanse of Namibia*. Its name is derived from the large number of whales observed in the bay by Portuguese explorers. The Dutch called the bay Walvisch Bay, and the British subsequently changed the name to Walvis Bay. The Portuguese explorer Bartolomeu Dias* discovered Walvis Bay in 1487. During the eighteenth and nineteenth centuries, Walvis Bay was used as a port for whaling ships operating in the south Atlantic. A German mission station was established nearby in 1845. The British annexed a fifteen-mile circle around the bay in 1878; and the area was placed under the jurisdiction of Britain's Cape Colony* in 1884—the same year that a German protectorate was formally established over South West Africa.

After South Africa defeated German forces in South West Africa in 1915, Walvis Bay developed into the region's principal port. It was administered as part of South West Africa from 1922 until 1977 when it once again was made a part of the distant Cape Province. With the advent of Namibian independence in 1990s, Walvis Bay has become the center of controversy. The government of South Africa maintains that Walvis Bay should not be included in any settlement of the Namibian question since the enclave was never part of the 1920 League of Nations* mandate for South West Africa. Needless to say, those on the other side of the argument insist that Walvis Bay should belong to independent Namibia. In 1990, when Namibia gained independence, Walvis Bay remained part of South Africa. (Lynn Berat, *Walvis Bay. Decolonization and International Law*, 1990; J. J. Wilkins and G. J. Fox, *The History of the Port and Settlement of Walvis Bay*, 1978.)

Joseph L. Michaud

WAR OF THE SPANISH SUCCESSION. See TREATY OF UTRECHT OF 1713.

WAR OF AMERICAN INDEPENDENCE. In July 1776 delegates from the thirteen British North American colonies, assembled as the Second Continental Congress, declared their independence from Great Britain. A bloody war ensued which lasted until 1783. At first the odds seemed stacked against the rebellious colonists. They faced the most formidable military and naval power on earth, and they had few resources of their own. At the same time, they were wracked by severe political divisions between the various colonies. But eventually they prevailed. The colonies produced a remarkable leader—George Washington*— who inspired the colonists and provided them with steady military and political leadership. After the Battle of Saratoga in 1778, when the colonists inflicted a substantial military defeat on the British, France established an alliance with the Americans, providing them with financial, naval, and military support. The colonists fought an extended guerrilla war against the British, retaining the tactical initiative and waiting for political support for the war to erode in England. Gradually it did. After the American victory at the Battle of Yorktown in 1781, the British lost the will to continue, and in 1783 they extended independence to the thirteen former colonies and ceded to the United States of America all of the land between the Appalachian mountains and the Mississippi River. (John Alden, *The American Revolution, 1776–1783*, 1957.)

WASHINGTON, GEORGE. Known to Americans as the "Father of His Country," George Washington was born in Westmoreland County, Virginia, on February 22, 1732. A surveyor and land developer by profession, Washington was an officer in the colonial forces during the French and Indian War*, when Britain and France fought for control of the Upper Mississippi Valley. In 1759 Washington was elected to the House of Burgesses, the colonial legislature in Virginia*, and from that position he became a leading figure in the American movement for independence from Great Britain in the 1760s and 1770s. Washington was a delegate to the First and Second Continental Congresses and in 1775 he was selected to command the Continental Army. During the war he led the colonial forces to a victory over the more powerful British army, primarily through judicious tactical decisions on when and where to fight. When Great Britain acknowledged American independence in 1783, Washington retired to private life at his family estate in Mount Vernon.

In 1787 Washington came out of retirement to preside over the convention which wrote the United States Constitution. He was unanimously elected the first president of the United States and assumed office in 1789. Washington served two terms as president, and both administrations were characterized by a judicious foreign policy which emphasized neutrality and isolationism and fiscal policies designed to restore the government's fiscal reputation. Washington declined to serve a third term and returned to private life in 1797. He died on December 14, 1799. (James Thomas Flexner, *George Washington*, 1965–1972.)

WASHINGTON CONFERENCE OF 1921–1922. To deal with the question of the naval arms race after World War I*, the United States convened the Washington Conference in late 1921 and early 1922. In addition to limiting naval arms, the conferees wanted to deal with problems in the Pacific inspired by Japan's occupation of the German concession of Shantung in China. The United States feared for the future of the Open Door policy. Another problem for the United States was the possibility of the renewal of the Anglo-Japanese alliance. The results of the conference were considered a great victory for Secretary of State Charles Evans Hughes and United States diplomacy. Three major treaties were agreed to: The Five Power Pact*, which accepted the principle of naval arms limitation and maintenance of the status quo in the Pacific; the Four Power Treaty*, which pledged the signatories to respect each other's possessions in the Pacific and resolve any differences through negotiations; and the Nine Power Treaty*, which essentially gave multilateral acceptance to the Open Door policy. (Dexter Perkins, *Charles Evans Hughes and American Democratic Statesmanship*, 1953.)

Joseph M. Rowe, Jr.

WEBSTER-ASHBURTON TREATY. The Webster-Ashburton Treaty of 1842 settled a longstanding dispute over the United States-Canadian boundary on the Northeast. Article II of the Treaty of Paris of 1783* originally set the boundary in the Northeast, but it was much too vague, leading to a number of disputes. In 1838–1839 the conflict between the province of New Brunswick* and the state of Maine over the boundary came to a head with the outbreak of a small border war. The mediation of General Winfield Scott averted a broadening of the war, and the United States and Great Britain agreed to negotiate a settlement. Alexander Baring, 1st Baron Ashburton, was sent from England as special envoy to conclude an agreement with Daniel Webster, United States secretary of state. Webster and Ashburton were personal and business acquaintances and the negotiations were conducted amicably. The treaty was signed on August 9, 1842.

Articles I and II set forth in minute detail those geographical points which delineated the boundary. As a result, about 7,000 of the 12,000 square miles of territory in dispute were awarded to the United States. Maine and Massachusetts* were awarded $150,000 each to settle their claims in the issue, the money to be paid by the United States government. The other articles in the treaty guaranteed mutual rights of navigation on border waterways, validated property rights and claims, provided for extradition of criminals, and committed the two nations once again to cooperate in the suppression of the African slave trade. The United States Senate ratified the treaty on August 20, 1842. (William Macdonald, *Select*

Documents Illustrative of the History of the United States, 1920; Thomas G. Paterson, et al., *American Foreign Policy*, 1983.)

Joseph M. Rowe, Jr.

WEIHAIWEI. During the scramble for China* which occurred during the 1890s, the European powers were intent on securing a logistical foothold there in order to increase their commercial opportunities. On July 1, 1898, Great Britain leased from China the port of Weihaiwei in Shantung Province. A commissioner was assigned to direct government affairs there in 1901, and Great Britain maintained its presence there until 1930, when Weihaiwei was returned to China. (David P. Henige, *Colonial Governors from the Fifteenth Century to the Present*, 1970.)

WESTERN AUSTRALIA. See SWAN RIVER COLONY.

WESTERN SAMOA. Western Samoa, consisting of the major islands of Savai'i, Upolu, Manono, and Apolima, is located in the southwest Pacific Ocean. Its population of 60,000 people is primarily of Polynesian extraction. The Dutch explorer Jacob Roggeveen became the first European to reach Samoa when he landed there in 1722, and after him a variety of European navigators had encounters, often bloody ones, with Samoans throughout the eighteenth and early nineteenth centuries. The first systematic contact between Europeans and Samoans came in 1830 when Protestant missionaries from the London Missionary Society began arriving on the islands trying to convert people to Christianity. European imperial interest in the Samoan Islands grew in the late nineteenth century when Asian markets became increasingly important. For the United States, Samoa seemed a perfect Pacific port, a way-station, between Asia and California. But the Germans and the British were interested as well. In 1879 the three nations signed an agreement to stop interfering in Samoan politics because it was destabilizing the islands, but the agreement did little to change the fact that the three powers were trying to secure protectorate agreements from local chiefs.

Tensions mounted throughout the 1880s and in March 1889 German, American, and British warships gathered in Apia harbor in Samoa. They were ready to attack one another to prevent a rival from gaining a foothold in the islands. However, a devastating hurricane nearly destroyed the fleets, averting a war; and in 1889 the three countries signed an agreement creating a tripartite commission to jointly run the islands. The arrangement was cumbersome and unworkable. In 1900 Great Britain agreed to abandon her claims to Samoa in return for German and American recognition of her claim to the Tonga Islands. The United States received the eastern Samoan Islands, which became known as American Samoa*, while the Germans received the western Samoan islands.

German rule lasted just fourteen years. When World War I erupted in 1914, a military force from New Zealand* attacked and conquered the western Samoan islands. When the war ended the League of Nations* awarded New Zealand a mandate over western Samoa. But many Samoans found the New Zealanders to be racist and corrupt. A nationalist movement, led by O. F. Nelson and known as the *Mau*, began demanding respect and equal treatment in the 1920s; however, they did not promote either democracy or independence, both of which might undermine the traditional local political and social power of Samoan chiefs. The *Mau* remained powerful until 1936 when it began to decline. When World War II ended, western Samoa became a New Zealand trust territory under a United Nations grant. Throughout the 1950s New Zealand extended more and more local governing authority to Samoans, and in 1960 the Samoans wrote their own constitution. They became the independent nation of Western Samoa on January 1, 1962. (J. W. Davidson, *Sanoa Mo Samoa: The Emergence of the Independent State of Western Samoa*, 1967.)

WEST FLORIDA. From the first explorations of Juan Ponce de Leon* in the early sixteenth century, Florida and the Gulf Coast came under Spanish control. Great Britain briefly controlled the region between 1763 and 1783. Eventually Spain divided the area into East Florida* and West Florida. West Florida extended from the Mississippi River east to the Perdido River. When President Thomas Jefferson completed the Louisiana Purchase* from France in 1803, he concluded that the territory included what Spain considered West Florida. Spain disagreed, and the two countries disputed the area for the next seven years. American expansionists led a revolt in 1810 and captured the Spanish fort of Baton Rouge on the east side of the Mississippi River, proclaiming on September 26, 1810, the Republic of West Florida. On October 27, 1810, President James Madison declared that the United States owned West Florida from the Mississippi River to the Perdido River. On May 14, 1812, the former Spanish territory of West Florida was incorporated into the Mississippi Territory. Spain protested but there was little she could do. The war for independence had begun in Mexico and she was preoccupied there. When the War of 1812 erupted, the United States then completed its military occupation of West Florida. General James Wilkinson captured the Spanish fort at what is today Mobile, Alabama, on April 15, 1813. West Florida had become American territory. (Robert F. Fabel, *The Economy of West Florida, 1763–1783*, 1988; Gloria Jahoda, *Florida: A History*, 1984.)

WEST INDIES. Also known as the Antilles*, the West Indies are a series of islands stretching in a 1,000 mile arc from the Yucatan Peninsula toward Florida and then south to the coast of Venezuela. With a land area of approximately 91,000 square miles, the archipelago separates the Gulf of Mexico and the Caribbean from the Atlantic Ocean. When Columbus* first entered the West Indies in 1492, the islands were inhabited by Arawak and Carib Indians. Spaniards exploited native labor on the island plantations, and by 1600, on most of the islands, the Indians were extinct. They died of disease, starvation, and forced labor. Spain replaced the labor losses by importing West African slaves in the seventeenth century. Spain established strongholds on Cuba*, Puerto Rico*, Hispaniola*, and Jamaica*, but early in the 1600s English settlers began populating several other islands in the West Indies. The French made similar inroads between 1635 and 1650, as did the Dutch between 1630 and 1648. The English conquered Jamaica in 1655, and the French seized control of the western half of Hispaniola (Haiti) in 1697. Eventually all the West Indies came under the control of the major European powers. The West Indies were governed by the following arrangements:

Spanish West Indies

Cuba	Margarita Island
Dominican Republic	Coche
Nueva Esparta	Cubagua
Puerto Rico	

French West Indies

Haiti	Petite Terre
Guadeloupe	La Desirade
Basse-Terre	St. Barthelemy
Grand-Terre	St. Martin (northern)
Marie Galante	Martinique
Les Saintes	

British West Indies

Bahamas	Trinidad
Barbados	Tobago
Cayman Islands	Turks Islands
Jamaica	Caicos Islands
LEEWARD ISLANDS	WINDWARD ISLANDS
Antigua	Dominica
Barbuda	Grenada
Redonda	Carriacou
St. Kitts	Nevis
Montserrat	So. Grenadines
Tortola (Virgin Is.)	No. Grenadines
Anegada (Virgin Is.)	St. Vincent
Virgin Gorda (Virgin Is.)	St. Lucia
Jost Van Dyke (Virgin Is.)	

Netherlands Antilles

Curacao   LEEWARD ISLANDS

Aruba   St. Martin (southern)

Bonaire   St. Eustatius

                                                       Saba

Danish Antilles

VIRGIN ISLANDS   Navassa Island

   St. Thomas

   St. John

   St. Croix

   Culebra Island

   Vieques Island

(J. O. Cutteridge, *Geography of the West Indies*, 1956; J. H. Parry and P. M. Sherlock, *Short History of the West Indies*, 1956.)

WEST INDIES FEDERATION. The West Indies Federation (1958–1962) was comprised of ten British colonies and their dependencies. Antigua*, Barbados*, Dominica*, Grenada*, Jamaica*, Montserrat*, St. Kitts*-Nevis*-Anguilla*, St. Lucia*, St. Vincent*, Trinidad*-Tobago*, Barbuda*, the Cayman Islands*, the Grenadines, Redonda, and the Turks and Caicos Islands* all were members. Jamaica and Trinidad-Tobago, however, held 83 percent of its land, 77 percent of its population, and 75 percent of its wealth. Lord Patrick Hailes, the governor-general, represented the Queen. Sir Grantley Adams of Barbados served as prime minister.

Since the seventeenth century Great Britain had sought to impose various forms of closer association upon its Caribbean possessions. In general, these efforts were resisted. For the most part, England's West Indian territories inherited a spirit of rivalry rather than cooperation. During the heyday of sugar, they had competed for markets and had communicated more with London than with one another. A combination of factors resulted in a West Indian desire to unite under one government. The dismal socioeconomic conditions of the 1930s fostered nationalism in the region as labor unions and the political parties that they spawned strove to wrest power from local elites. Furthermore, intellectuals and politicians came to believe that federation was the only viable way for a string of small, insulated island communities to gain independence from their British colonial masters.

This drive for a federal union peaked in the immediate post-World War II period, when questions concerning the future of colonies loomed large in the minds of world leaders. At the Montego Bay Conference (1947), enthusiasm for a West Indian federation reached its high-water mark. British officials and delegates from their Caribbean possessions discussed plans for a unified political entity. During the next eleven years civil servants and statesmen tediously hammered out the specifics of federation. On February 23, 1956, representatives from the British West Indies agreed to join together in a common government. Several months later, on August 2, parliament assented by passing the British Caribbean Act. The Federation of the West Indies came into being on January 3, 1958. Princess Margaret opened the federal parliament's inaugural session in Port-of-Spain, Trinidad, on April 22, 1958.

Unfortunately, by this date much of the fervor for federation had dissipated. Between 1947 and 1958 the two dominant units, Jamaica and Trinidad, made significant economic and political advances. For these islands, federation no longer offered the quickest path to independence. In fact, Jamaica had attained more autonomy than had the federation as a whole. Therefore, it advocated a weakening of the central government so that it would be free to follow a "Jamaican" road to prosperity. Actually, the West Indies Federation lacked even the power to tax its constituent units. Also, the United Kingdom managed its foreign relations, defense, and various internal matters. The federal government mainly occupied itself with the financing of the University College of the West Indies, the distribution of colonial grants, and the maintenance of the West Indies Regiment. A constitutional provision which forbade the holding of local and national offices simultaneously further hampered the government. Most of the prestigious local leadership, notably Norman Manley of Jamaica and Eric Williams of Trinidad, chose to retain their insular posts rather than stand for federal elections. Yet, considering its limitations, the federation did score "respectable though modest" successes. In fact, Britain pledged to relinquish all of its controls by granting full independence under a new constitution by May 31, 1962.

The union first unraveled in Jamaica, which contained over half of the federation's area and citizenry. Opposition leader Alexander Bustamante charged that the central government's economic policies were stifling the island's developing industrial sector. Bustamante claimed that Jamaicans were being forced to endure sacrifices for the benefit of smaller, poorer neighbors. Norman Manley, who headed the ruling party, made a questionable decision to settle the matter by referendum. On September 19, 1961, a majority of Jamaicans casting ballots chose secession. Manley accepted the outcome. As a result, Jamaica sought independence outside the federal framework. Trinidad reacted by following suit. Consequently, on May 23, 1962, Great Britain formally dissolved the West Indies Federation.

A major cause of the federation's downfall was the failure of its officeholders to cultivate a spirit of compromise. Instead of concentrating on common goals, the foci of discussions frequently centered upon inter-unit conflicts. Often the atmosphere surrounding these discussions was one of intense personal acrimony. Such confrontational patterns were more appropriate for dealing with the colonial office than with West Indian colleagues. Antigua-Barbuda-Redonda (1981), Barbados (1966), Dominica (1978), Grenada (1974), Jamaica (1962), St. Kitts-

Nevis (1983), St. Lucia (1979), St. Vincent and the Grenadines (1979) and Trinidad-Tobago (1962) achieved independence separately. Anguilla, the Cayman Islands, Monserrat, and the Turks and Caicos Islands remain British possessions. (Sir John Mordecai, *The West Indies: The Federal Negotiations*, 1968; Elisabeth Wallace, *The British Caribbean: From the Decline of Colonialism to the End of Federation*, 1977.)

Frank Marotti

WEST TIMOR. See PORTUGUESE TIMOR.

WHITE MAN'S BURDEN. The title of a famous poem by English Nobel Laureate Rudyard Kipling*, the term "White Man's Burden" became an early twentieth-century euphemism for English and American imperialism. In their arrogant sense of cultural and racial superiority, English and American imperialists argued that the Anglo-Saxon world had a moral responsibility to share its values and institutions—Protestant Christianity, democracy, and capitalism—with all the people of the world. Such an idea became an important rationale for imperialism. See KIPLING, RUDYARD.

WINDWARD ISLANDS. The Windward Islands was a British colony which existed from 1885 to 1960. Great Britain organized it with St. Lucia*, St. Vincent*, Tobago*, Grenada*, and the Grenadines as constituent parts. Until then those islands had been under the authority of Barbados.* Like the Leeward Islands government, the Windward Islands government was dissolved in 1960. (David P. Henige, *Colonial Governors from the Fifteenth Century to the Present*, 1970.)

WORLD WAR I. World War I had a dramatic impact on the European colonial empires. In the short term, most observers in Great Britain, France, and the United States assumed that the war had made the empires stronger and confirmed the benevolence of imperialism. Great Britain and France both recruited colonial troops in their struggle with Germany and the Austro-Hungarian Empire. Although there were outbreaks of nationalistic violence in many colonies, the more striking development was the British and French success in recruiting troops and suppressing debates about independence in most areas.

For the German empire, of course, World War I was an unmitigated disaster. Germany's most important possessions were in Africa: German Southwest Africa*, Togo*, Cameroon*, and German East Africa*. In the Pacific Germany controlled northeastern New Guinea*, western Samoa*, the Bismarck Achipelago*, the Marshall Islands*, the Caroline Islands*, the Marianas* (except Guam*), and Kiaochow* on the Shantung Peninsula. Expecting the war to be shortlived and to end in victory, Germany left her colonies to fend for themselves. They did so with varying degrees of success. Most of the Pacific colonies fell to the British and Australians in 1914. Kiaochow fell the same year to the

Japanese, as did Togo to the British. In 1915, after a hard-fought engagement, South Africa conquered Southwest Africa. In 1916 a joint British-French expedition gained control of Cameroon. And German East Africa held out against forces from Britain, South Africa, India, Belgium, and Portugal until after the 1918 armistice.

World War I also marked the final demise of the Ottoman Empire. Turkey sided with Germany and Austria-Hungary in World War I, and against Russia, France, and Great Britain, and when the Allies emerged victorious, Turkey witnessed the loss of her former colonies, the region of the Middle East now represented by the countries of Israel, Jordan*, Iraq*, Syria*, and Lebanon*.

The Treaty of Versailles* of 1919 represented the zenith of the European colonial empires. The treaty created the League of Nations* and the mandate system*, awarding former German and Ottoman colonies to the victors under individual mandates, austensibly until the former German colonies were ready for independence but in essence preserving the paternalistic order in which the imperial powers exercised virtual total control over colonial life. Great Britain received most of German East Africa, part of Togo and Cameroon, and the island of Nauru* in the Pacific. France acquired three-fourths of Togo and most of Cameroon. Belgium got Ruanda and Urundi in the northwestern section of German East Africa. New Zealand was given Germany's territory in Samoa*. South Africa picked up German Southwest Africa. Portugal received the district of Kionga, formerly part of German East Africa. Japan won Germany's holdings on the Shantung Peninsula as well as Germany's Pacific islands north of the Equator—the Carolines, the Marianas, and the Marshalls. Mandates also resolved the future of the Ottoman colonies. Great Britain received mandates over Palestine*, Transjordan*, and Iraq, while France received mandates over Syria and Lebanon.

But in the long run, World War I was the beginning of the end for the remaining European empires. When the war was over, nationalistic leaders around the world began demanding independence as a reward for their loyal support of Great Britain and France in the war against Germany. But far more important in contributing to the demise of the imperial systems was the economic decline of Europe which came in the wake of World War I. The war ravaged European economic resources; indeed, when the war was over the United States had become the premier economic power in the world and Japan seemed poised for dominance in Asia and the Pacific. Great Britain, France, and The Netherlands would be hard-pressed to protect their political and economic investments in such scattered parts of the world. Although most of the decolonization would not occur until after World War II*, it was World War I which set decolonization in motion. Finally, the mandate system created by the League of Nations tacitly acknowledged that independence was the ultimate goal for the colonies. In 1932 Great Britain extended independence to Iraq, the first of the mandates to become free. Other European colonies would soon demand similar treatment. (R. F. Holland, *European Decolonization 1918–1981*, 1985; F. S. Northredge, *The League of*

Nations. Its Life and Times 1920–1946, 1986; Woodruff D. Smith, *The German Colonial Empire*, 1978.)

Randy Roberts

WORLD WAR II. World War II was enormously significant in leading to the demise of the European empires. The war was so costly, in terms of money and personnel, that the British, French, and Dutch emerged from World War II without the assets to maintain their colonial empires, especially in the face of growing nationalist sentiments. When Germany invaded and conquered France and The Netherlands in 1940, cutting them off from their Asian and African empires, the beginning of the end was in sight. And even though Germany did not conquer Great Britain, the war was so intense that the British colonies, especially those in Asia, could not be defended from Japanese attack. Japan moved into Indochina* in 1940 and 1941 and conquered Singapore*, the Dutch East Indies*, and the Philippines* in 1942. When World War II ended, the momentum for independence was unstoppable. The United States awarded independence to the Philippines in 1946. That same year the Fourth French Republic allowed most of her African colonies to become internally self-governing members of the French Union*. Although France hoped to hold on to her Indochina empire, Ho Chi Minh* and the Vietminh had other ideas, and after eight years of bloody combat, France lost Vietnam*, Cambodia*, and Laos*. The Fifth French Republic in the late 1950s allowed most of her African colonies to become fully independent members of the French Community*, an option most of them exercised. Another bloody war in Algeria* ended in independence as well. The British soon lost India* and Pakistan* to independence in 1947 and began to prepare their other Asian and African colonies for independence in the 1950s. The major European empires really did not survive World War II. (T. O. Lloyd, *The British Empire 1558–1983*, 1984.)

Y

YEMEN ARAB REPUBLIC. See NORTH YEMEN.

YUCATÁN. The Yucután Peninsula comprises the Mexican states of Yucatán, Campeche, and Quintana Roo. This final state is not an exotic Maya word but is instead named after a military hero. The vast area of the peninsula is flat with low rolling hills in the Puuc region of the north-central part of the peninsula. Until recently few roads led to Yucatán, although currently a modest paved highway system circles the peninsula. Current population, while not exact, runs about 2,000,000 people, largely Maya Indians. In 1517 Francisco Fernández de Córdoba was the first European to reach Yucatán, and settlement and conquest began a decade later. Even today, close ties with the central government of Mexico leave something to be desired, the region often being at odds with the central government of Mexico. Its people speak with a decided accent, different from the rest of Mexico, and many of them still speak a Maya dialect. Yucatán was part of the Audiencia of Mexico City from 1527 to 1543, and then it was shifted to the Audiencia of Los Confines. In 1549 it was transferred back to Mexico City, and only one year later it became part of the Audiencia of Guatemala. That lasted until 1560 when it became part of the Audiencia of Mexico City again. The governor's office of Yucatán was elevated to that of a captain-general in 1617. In 1789, when Charles III's Bourbon reforms brought the intendencia system to New Spain, the Yucatán was organized as the intendencia of Mérida. It retained that status until 1821 when the area became part of the republic of Mexico. See NEW SPAIN.

YUKON TERRITORY. The Yukon Territory is a possession of the Dominion of Canada*. The territory covers an area of 207,076 square miles in the northwest corner of Canada. It is bounded by Alaska on the west, British Columbia on the south, the Northwest Territories on the east, and the Beaufort Sea on the north. The total population of the Yukon Territory is less than 25,000. The first European to reach the territory was Sir John Franklin, the British explorer, who traveled along the Arctic coast in 1825. Hudson's Bay Company* fur traders pushing west from the Mackenzie River system established permanent contact in the 1840s. Robert Campbell established Fort Selkirk at the junction of the Pelly and Yukon Rivers in 1844. The establishment of Fort Selkirk and several other posts weakened the Russian fur trade by drawing Indians away from the coastal trade and to the interior posts.

Late in the nineteenth century gold prospectors pushed north from British Columbia into the Yukon Territory. On August 17, 1896, George Carmack and two Indian companions discovered gold on a small tributary of the Yukon River, what was to become Bonanza Creek. This discovery triggered the world's greatest gold rush. Between 1897 and 1899 an estimated 100,000 people poured into the Yukon, primarily through Skagway, Alaska, and the upper Yukon River. In a few months Dawson, which had been a tiny outpost at the junction of the Yukon and Klondike Rivers, became the largest Canadian city west of Winnipeg. In 1898 by act of the Canadian parliament the Yukon was separated from the Northwest Territories and was made a territory in its own right. Dawson, "the Paris of the North," became the first capital, and the Royal Canadian Mounted Police maintained law and order in the new territory.

By the first decade of the twentieth century the glory days of the gold rush were over. Large gold companies replaced individual prospectors, and the population of the territory declined almost as rapidly as it had risen. Dawson gave way as an economic center to Whitehorse, which was connected to Skagway by a railroad, but overall the economy faltered. The Yukon economy remained at a low level until World War II when the United States asked Canada for permission to build an all-weather military supply route to U.S. forces in Alaska. Notwithstanding exceptionally difficult terrain the Alaska Highway was officially dedicated in November 1942, after only nine months of continuous work. The highway runs essentially northwest for 1,520 miles from Dawson Creek, British Columbia, through Whitehorse in the Yukon Territory to Fairbanks, Alaska. The Arctic coast of the Yukon Territory is now linked to the Alaska Highway by the Dempster Highway, which was opened in 1979. (Melody Webb, *The Last Frontier*, 1985).

Peter T. Sherrill

Z

ZAIRE. See BELGIAN CONGO.

ZAMBIA. Zambia is a landlocked independent state in southeastern Africa, slightly larger than Texas. Its nearly 7 million inhabitants, almost 45 percent of whom live in urban areas, speak eight different languages, although English is the official language. Since most of the country comprises a level plateau at an elevation of around 4,000 feet, the climate is relatively temperate. Zambia was a British protectorate known as Northern Rhodesia for forty years until its independence in 1964. The British era began in 1889, when Cecil Rhodes'* British South African Company was chartered by the British government to attempt colonization efforts north of South Africa*, as part of Rhodes' vision of a "Cape to Cairo" corridor of British rule along all of eastern Africa. Often aided by British and French missionaries in the area, some of whom were worried about Portuguese and German expansion, Rhodes' agents were able to extract a series of "treaties" with African rulers. This led to the proclamation by Rhodes and Harry Johnston, the first British commissioner and consul-general in Nyasaland, of an area they called "Trans-Zambesia." This British sphere of influence comprised what today is Zambia, Zimbabwe, and Malawi. By 1891, after competing British and Portuguese territorial claims had been settled and African objections silenced, the British South African Company administered the area, now known as "Northern Rhodesia." The company ran into financial difficulty, and handed Northern Rhodesia over to the British government in 1924, when it became an official protectorate. The discovery of large copper deposits in the late 1920s brought a rush of European immigrants. Within a decade the copper industry was established, creating the "copperbelts," located along the border of the Belgian Congo*.

In 1953 the British established the Federation of Rhodesia and Nyasaland*, which comprised the protectorates of Northern Rhodesia and Nyasaland*, plus the colony of Southern Rhodesia, which was governed internally by its minority white population. Since the emerging African nationalist movements had no interest in links with the regime in Southern Rhodesia, the federation was dissolved in 1963. Northern Rhodesia and Nyasaland became independent the next year as Zambia and Malawi, respectively. Southern Rhodesia's white minority regime declared its independence from Britain in 1965, which led to United Nations economic sanctions being imposed on the illegal government in December 1966. Zambia cut its economic ties to Southern Rhodesia, although this cost the country dearly. Sharp drops during the 1970s in the price of copper, Zambia's main export, added to the country's economic woes. President Kenneth David Kaunda, Zambia's first and (to 1991) only president, faced increasing unrest during the 1980s, as economic problems became more severe. Zambia has continued to play a major role in the "frontline states" struggle against South African apartheid, while also endeavoring to promote economic cooperation among the other countries of Southern Africa. (A. D. Roberts, *A History of Zambia*, 1976; Robert Rotberg, *Rise of Nationalism in Central Africa: The Making of Malawi and Zambia, 1873–1964*, 1965.)

Charles W. Hartwig

ZANZIBAR. Zanzibar is an island off the east coast of Africa whose history was closely tied to that of its littoral neighbor—Tanganyika*—throughout much of the modern colonial era. In the early sixteenth century the people of Zanzibar allied themselves with the Portuguese. In 1571 the "king" of the island offered it to the Portuguese, who instead established a trading factory and an Augustinian mission. The first English ship visited the island two decades later. The rise of Islam brought the expulsion of the Europeans, as Zanzibar, along with the islands of Mafia Pemba, came under the control of Oman*. The local *hakim* (governors) ruled the island without much interference from the sultan, until Seyyid Sa'id of Muscat settled there in 1832 to escape domestic troubles in Oman and to extend his influence on the Zanzibari coast. On Sa'id's death, his dominions were split between two sons, Seyyid Majid taking Zanzibar and the east African coast. In 1870 Majid's successor Bargash ibn Said found himself with an African empire increasingly under British control.

Sir John Kirk, Britain's consular representative from 1866 to 1887, used the suppression of the slave trade to bring Zanzibar under British control, while shutting out the other European powers. By the end of the 1870s, however, trade between Zanzibar and the international economy was carried mostly by American ships, carrying to Europe and the United States the native cloves as well as the spices and fine cloths which Arab traders had brought from the rest of their Indian Ocean trading world. When Commodore Robert E. Shufeldt (USN) visited Zanzibar in 1879, he recommended that the United States strengthen its diplomatic and naval presence to secure increased trade, but the nation turned its back on this fruitful coast of Africa. As the American merchant presence declined, the British were able to re-establish control over most of the trade.

Kirk's efforts to secure trade for the British closed out all but the most persistent Germans. His brand of imperialism was flavored by the unique control he exercised over the sultan. Kirk did all he could to help the British enjoy free trade and to keep out that of others. For instance, he did very little to help Henry M. Stanley on his expeditions into the interior, fearing that increased American trade or power might result. By the end of Seyyid Bargash's reign (1888), Kirk found reason to take the coastal holdings from the sultan, dividing the lands between Germany (Tanganyika) and Britain (Kenya). The ensuing scramble for Africa has been ascribed to this division of East Africa and the headlands of the Nile which it controlled.

Whatever the cause for the scramble, by 1890 the European rivalries were so intense that Britain felt forced to proclaim a formal protectorate over Zanzibar. A revolution over succession to the nearly impotent sultanate in 1896 caused the British to shell the city of Zanzibar, and the island was finally and completely subdued. The installation of Hamoud ibn Mohammed as sultan with a British first minister ensured the end of political resistance. The final abolition of slavery in 1897 ensured the end of economic autonomy, as Zanzibar was left with only one crop, cloves, and only one buyer, Britain.

Mostly, Britain assumed that the political status of Zanzibar would never change, that as a colony it would thrive and always play a useful role within the British Empire*. But by 1960 that empire was no longer serviceable. Between 1960 and 1963 Britain found herself dismantling what had become something of a progressive East African empire since World War II. In this scramble, Zanzibar was stripped of its final holdings on the mainland—the Islam-oriented Mombasa. But some of the old imperial truisms were correct, and Zanzibar was unstable alone. Zanzibar received internal self-government in June 1963 and complete independence in December 1963, but a communist revolution overthrew the sultan one year later. In April 1964 the People's Republic of Zanzibar joined in a union with the Republic of Tanganyika to form the United Republic of Tanzania*, under the Tanganyikan president Julius Nyerere* and Zanzibari vice-president, Sheikh Abeid Amani Karume. With President Nyerere's first five-year economic plan the colonial era in east Africa can said to be closed. (Norman R. Bennett, *A History of the Arab States of Zanzibar*, 1978; Abdul Sheriff, *Slaves, Spices, and Ivory in Zanzibar*, 1987.)

Mark R. Shulman

ZIMBABWE. See RHODESIA.

ZULULAND. Zululand is a district in South Africa* located in the northeastern Province of Natal*. It encompasses 10,362 square miles and is mainly inhabited by the Zulu people. The Zulu are descendants of the Nguni Bantu people. The name Zulu was originally applied to a small tribe living near the Mfolozi River.

This tribe was one of many among the Nguni Bantu people. Each of the Nguni tribes numbered from 2,000 to 10,000 under its own independent chief. By 1775 these tribes were settled across the southeastern region of Africa. As the population of each tribe grew, a segment would frequently break off to form a new tribe under a kinsman of the old chief. Sometimes this breaking away was peaceful and sometimes it was not. There was no real attempt to unite the tribes until the early 1800s. At that time Shaka (Chaka), a Zulu chieftain, began to conquer and bring other tribes under his control, forging a powerful Zulu nation.

In 1824 the first British trading company, The Farewell Company, was established in Port Natal. The British made contact with Shaka, and as a matter of political expediency assisted him in some raiding expeditions. Shaka in return deeded Port Natal to the British. Shaka's brother Dingane assassinated him in 1828 and took over as leader of the Zulu nation. The first missionary, Captain Allan Gardiner with the Church Missionary Society of England, arrived in 1835 and was followed by a Reverend Francis Owen. Six American missionaries arrived in Zululand the next year. Boer settlers, descendants of the original Dutch colonists of the Cape Colony*, arrived in 1837.

The Zulus were now faced with an invasion of white settlers wanting land. Even though the Zulus vastly outnumbered the Boers and British in Natal, they were very inferior in weapons and equipment. Dingane, being particularly fearful of the Boers, invited Pieter Retief and seventy of his men to a meeting and celebration in February, 1838. After Retief and his men were lulled into a false sense of security, Dingane and his followers killed them. Dingane then sent warriors after the Boer families who were camped in wagons along nearby mountain streams. In these attacks, 41 men, 56 women, 185 children and 250 Hottentot servants died. Dingane had hoped to force the Boers out of the land of the Zulu. However, Boer retaliation spelled the beginning of the end for the Zulu nation.

Late in 1838 Andries Pretorius led a force of 464 Boers including their servants across the Buffalo River in search of the Zulu. They camped at the Ncome River on a steep high bank that formed a point. Pretorius felt that this was an excellent position to defend. Scouting reports indicated that the main force of Zulus were in the vicinity so he formed his 64 wagons into a laager. Each tongue was lashed to the next wagon, and the wheels were covered with rawhide to form a shield. Upon arising the morning of December 16, 1838, the Boers were astonished to find what appeared to be the entire Zulu nation watching their campsite. In reality there were about 12,000 Zulu warriors. As the Zulu tried to cross the river, they were slaughtered by the Boer gun fire. The rush was so intense many Zulus were trampled by their own warriors. The final outcome of the battle was approximately 3,000 Zulu killed with only four Boers wounded, including Pretorius. The Ncome River was from this time called the Blood River. Dingane was soon overthrown by his half brother Panda (Mpande). Panda ruled for thirty two years over the independent Zulu nation.

Their defeat at Blood River had forced the Zulus into an area north of the

Tugela River. The Zulus began to steadily lose land to white settlers. Panda ceded territory beyond the Blood River to the Boers in 1854, and this became the Utrecht District. However, the Zulus in Zululand remained relatively free of European influence from 1838 to 1879. In January 1879 the British, fearing the impressive military force of the Zulu, issued an ultimatum to Cetewayo, who was then the Zulu king, demanding the abolishment of his army. Cetewayo ignored this demand, and in January 1879 a British force under Lord Chelmsford invaded Zululand and set up a base camp at Isandhlwana. Chelmsford took a large number of men with him on a reconnaissance mission, leaving the camp too thinly defended. When the Zulu attacked the base camp, the British were unable to form the defensive square. Another major problem was the inability of the quartermasters to open the ammunition boxes fast enough. The Zulu wiped out the base camp with just a few Europeans escaping. Chelmsford finally got his revenge at Ulundi (July 4, 1879), where he was able to form a huge square and decimate the Zulu forces with rifle, rocket, and artillery fire. The royal residence was burned before Chelmsford withdrew his troops. This defeat convinced the Zulu of the futility of further resistance to British military might.

Chelmsford's successor, Sir Garnet Wolseley, became supreme civil and military commander in Natal, Transvaal*, and adjacent territories. He had arrived just before the defeat of the Zulus at Ulandi and was in charge of the settlement made with them. Cetewayo was exiled and Zululand was divided into thirteen chiefdoms. Wolseley's intention was to destroy the power of the House of Shaka with little regard to the desires of the Zulu people. Wolseley based his choice of the kings who would serve over these chiefdoms not on their leadership ability but on their subservience to the Crown. There was considerable unrest among the Zulu people toward these chosen leaders and fighting broke out among the various chiefdoms.

Dinizulu, who was Cetewayo's eldest son and the head of one of the chiefdoms, sought help from the Boers living in Utrecht and Vryheid against Usibepu, a rival chief. In exchange for their assistance, the Boers took considerable land and created the New Republic. The New Republic was recognized by a Natal court but with considerably less land. Within a year this republic became a part of the Transvaal as the District of Vryheid.

The fighting between chiefdoms caused the British in 1887 to declare what was left of Zululand a protectorate and to banish Dinizulu to St. Helena*. In 1897 Zululand was made a part of Natal. In 1902 the Delimitation Commission created reserves exclusively for the use of the Zulu, and opened the balance of Zululand to private business. In 1906 an outbreak of Zulu violence in Natal, following the imposition of a poll tax by the colonial government, served to accelerate the movement toward closer union of the four colonies of South Africa. Natal became a province of the Union of South Africa* on May 31, 1910. (Donald Morris, *The Washing of the Spears*, 1965.)

Amanda Pollock

APPENDIX A: LANGUAGES OF THE FORMER EUROPEAN COLONIES AND/OR SPHERES OF INFLUENCE

Judith E. Olson

COUNTRY	OFFICIAL LANGUAGE(S)	OTHER MAJOR LANGUAGES
Afghanistan	Pashto, Dari (Afghan (Persian)	Baluchi, Kazakh, Kirghiz, Turkoman, Uigur, Uzbek
Algeria	Arabic	French, Kabayle, Tuareg (Tamashek)
Angola	Portuguese	Cicokwe, Kikongo, Kimbundu, Umbundu, Ovambo
Antigua and Barbuda	English	English Creole
Antilles	Creole French	
Argentina	Spanish	English, German, Guarani, Italian, Portuguese, Quechua, Tehuelche
Australia	English	
Azores	Spanish	
Bahamas	English	Creole, French
Bahrain	Arabic	English
Bangladesh	Bengali	Burmese, English, Urdu
Barbados	English	
Belize	English	Creole, Garifuna, German, Mayan, Spanish, Yucatec

COUNTRY	OFFICIAL LANGUAGE(S)	OTHER MAJOR LANGUAGES
Benin	French	Bariba, Ewe-Fon, Fulani, Kabre, Tem (Kotokole), Yoruba
Bhutan	Dzongkha (Tibetan dialect)	Bumthangka, Sarchopkha, Tibetan
Bolivia	Spanish	Aymara, Quechua
Botswana	English	Setswana, Sisuthu
Brazil	Portuguese	English, French, German, Italian, Japanese, Spanish
Brunei	Malay	English, Chinese dialects: Hokkien, Hakka, Cantonese, Mandarin
Burkina (Upper Volta)	French	Dyula, Gourounsi, Kasem, More, Samo, Songhai, Soninke
Burma	Burmese	Akha, Kachin, Lisu, Lolo, Manipuri (Meithei), Mon, Pwo, Sgaw, Shan
Burundi	French, Kirundi	kinyaRuanda-kiRundi
Cambodia	Cambodian	Vietnamese, French
Cameroon	English, French	Duala, Fang-Bulu, Fulani, Hausa
Canada	English, French	Chinese, Dutch, German, Inuit, Italian, Portuguese, Ukrainian, Yiddish
Cape Verde Islands	Portuguese	Crioulo
Central African Republic	French	Banda, Sango, Zande
Chad	French	Arabic, Kanuri, Sara, Sengo
Chile	Spanish	Araucanian, German
Colombia	Spanish	Goajiro
Comoro Islands	Arabic	French, Malagasy, Shaafi Islam, Swahili
Congo	French	Banda, Kikongo, Lingala, Kiteke
Costa Rica	Spanish	English
Cuba	Spanish	
Cyprus	Greek, Turkish	
Djibouti	Arabic, French	Afar, Somali
Dominica	English	French Creole
Dominican Republic	Spanish	Creole, English
Ecuador	Spanish	Quechua
Egypt	Arabic	Beja, English, French, Nubian

COUNTRY	OFFICIAL LANGUAGE(S)	OTHER MAJOR LANGUAGES
El Salvador	Spanish	Nahuatl
Equatorial Guinea	Spanish	English Creole, Fang-Bulu
Ethiopia	Amharic	Afar, Beja, English, Nuer, Oromo, Sidamo, Somali, Tigray, Tigrinya, Welamo
Fiji	English	Fijian, Hindi, Hindustani
Formosa	Mandarin	Hokkien, Hakka, Japanese, Malay-Polynesian dialect
French West Indies	French	French Creole
Gabon	French	Fang-Bulu
Gambia	English	Mandinka, Wolof
Ghana	English	Akan, Anyi-Baule, Dagomba, Ewe-Fon, Fanti, Ga, Kasem, Tem (Kotokole), Twi
Grenada	English	
Guam	English	Chamorro, Spanish
Guatemala	Spanish	Cakchikel, Carib, Chol, Mam, Pocoman, Quekchi, Quiche, Yucatec
Guinea	French	Bassari, Cohiagui, Dan, Fulani, Guerze, Kisse, Kpelle, Loma, Malinke, Madelkan, Mano, Susu, Toma
Guinea-Bissau	Portuguese	Balante, Crioulo
Guyana	English	Chinese, Hindi, Portuguese, English Creole
Haiti	French, Haitian	Creole French, English, Spanish Creole
Honduras	Spanish	English, Miskito, Paya, Xicaque, Zambo
India	Hindi	Assamese, Awadhi (Eastern Hindi), Bengali, Bhojpuri, Boro (Kachari), English, Garo, Gondi, Gujerati, Ho, Kannada, Kashmiri, Khasi, Kurukh, Lahnda (Western Punjabi), Magadhi, Maithili, Malayalam, Manipuri (Meithei), Marathi, Nepali, Oriya, Punjabi, Rajasthani, Sanskrit, Santali, Sindhi, Tamil, Telugu, Tibetan, Tulu

COUNTRY	OFFICIAL LANGUAGE(S)	OTHER MAJOR LANGUAGES
Indonesia	Bahasa Indonesia (Malay)	Achinese, Balinese, Karo Batak, Simalungun Batak, Toba Batak, Belu, Buginese, Gorontalo, Javanese, Madurese, Makassarese, Menangkabao, Ngadju, Sangir, Sasak, Sudanese
Iran	Farsi	Azerbaijani, Baluchi, Kurdish, Persian-Tajiki, Turkoman
Iraq	Arabic	Arabic dialects: Mandaean, Persian, Syriac, Turkic; Kurdish
Ireland	English	Gaelic
Israel	Arabic, Hebrew	Circassian, English, Yiddish
Ivory Coast	French	Agni, Anyi-Baule, Baule, Bete, Dan, Kru-Bassa, Malinke-Bambura-Dioula, Mandekan, Senari
Jamaica	English	English Creole
Jordan	Arabic	Circassian, English
Kampuchea	Khmer	Chinese, French, Vietnamese
Kenya	Swahili	Achooli-Luo, English, Gujarati, ikiGusii, Kikamba, Kikikuyu, Kipsigis, Luluhya, Masai, Nandi, Oromo, Punjabi, Somali, Teso
Kiribati	English	Gilbertese (I-Kiribati)
Kuwait	Arabic	English
Laos	Lao	Lolo dialects, Miao, Mon-Khmer dialects, Thai-Lao, Vietnamese, Yao
Lesotho	English, Lesotho	
Liberia	English	Bassa, Dan, Kissi, Kpelle, Loma, Mano, Vai
Libya	Arabic	Berber, English, Italian
Madagascar	French, Malagasy	
Malawi	English, Chichewa	Chilomwe, Chinyanja, Chitumbuka, Chiyao, iMakua
Malaysia	Bahasa Malaysia (Malay)	Arabic, Chinese dialects: Cantonese, Hokkien, Hakka, Mandarin; Dusun, English, Hindustani, Javanese, Jawi, Kadazan, Punjabi, Rumi, Tamil
Maldive Islands	Maldivian (Divehi)	English

COUNTRY	OFFICIAL LANGUAGE(S)	OTHER MAJOR LANGUAGES
Mali	French	Bambara, Fulani, Mandekan, Songhai, Soninke, Suppire, Tuareg (Tamashek)
Malta	English, Maltese	
Mauritania	Arabic (Hassaniyah), French	Peular, Soninke, Tukulor, Wolof
Mauritius	English	Bhojpuri, Chinese, Creole French, Hindi
Mexico	Spanish	Maya, Mazatec, Miztec, Nahuatl, Otomi, Papago, Tarascan, Totonac, Tzeltal, Tzotzil, Yucatec, Zapotec
Monaco	French	Monegasque
Morocco	Arabic (classical)	Berber dialects: Tamazirt, Tashelhit, Zenatiya; French, Maghribi Arabic, Rif, Shilha, Spanish
Montserrat	English	English Creole
Mozambique	Portuguese	Chichopi, Chimakonde, iMakua, Chinyanja, Chishona, Chiyao, Shitonga, Swahili
Namibia	Afrikaans, English, German	Herero, Ovambo
Nauru	Nauruan	English
Nepal	Nepali	Bhojpuri, English, Maithili, Newari, Tibetan
Netherlands Antilles	Dutch	Papiamento
New Zealand	English	Maori
Nicaragua	Spanish	English
Niger	French	Djerma, Fulani, Hausa, Kanuri, Songhai, Tuareg (Tamashek)
Nigeria	English	Bini (Edo) Efik, Fulani, Hausa, Igala, Igbo, Western Ijaw, Ishan, Kanuri, Nupe, Tiv, Urhobo, Yoruba
Oman	Arabic	English, Farsi, Urdu
Pakistan	Urdu	Baluchi, Gujerati, Hindi, Kashmiri, Lahnda (Western Punjabi), Pashto, Punjabi, Sindhi
Panama	Spanish	English
Papua New Guinea	English	Enga, Motu, Pidgin

COUNTRY	OFFICIAL LANGUAGE(S)	OTHER MAJOR LANGUAGES
Paraguay	Guarani, Spanish	
Peru	Spanish, Quechua	Aymara, Huayhuash
Philippines	English, Philipino	Bicol, Cebuano, Ibanag, Ilocano, Pampanga, Panay-Hiligaynon, Pangasinan, Spanish, Sulu, Tagalog, Visayan
Puerto Rico	Spanish	English
Qatar	Arabic	English, Farsi
Rwanda	French, Cinyarwanda	kinyaRuanda-kiRundi
St. Christopher and Nevis	English	English Creole
St. Lucia	English	French Creole
St. Vincent and the Grenadines	English	English Creole
Sao Tome and Principe	Portuguese (Creole dialect)	
Saudi Arabia	Arabic	English
Senegal	French	Crioulo, Fulani, Mandekan, Serer, Soninke, Wolof
Seychelles	English, French	Creole, Gujerati, Tamil
Sierra Leone	English	Kisse, Krio, Mende, Susu, Temne, Vai
Singapore	English, Malay, Mandarin, Tamil	
Somalia	Somali	Arabic, Italian, English
South Africa	Afrikaans, English	Gujerati, Pedi, Sesotho, Sisuthu, Swazi, Tsonga, Tswana, Venda, Xhosa, Zulu
Sri Lanka	Sinhala	Tamil
Sudan	Arabic	Achooli-Luo, Bari, Beja, Dinka, English, Lugbara, Nubian, Nuer, Zande
Surinam	Dutch	Javanese, Sranang-Tongo (Takki-Takki); Hindi, Chinese, Amerindic, and African languages and dialects
Swaziland	English, Siswati	
Syria	Arabic	Aramaic, Armenian, Circassian, Kurdish
Tahiti	French	Tahitian

COUNTRY	OFFICIAL LANGUAGE(S)	OTHER MAJOR LANGUAGES
Tanzania	Kiunguja	Arabic, Chigogo, Chimakonde, Chitumbuka, Chiyao, Ekihene, English, iMakua, Kinyamwezi-kiSukuma, KinyaRuanda-kiRundi, Masai, Swahili
Thailand	Thai	Albanian, Amoy, Cambodian, Chinese, English, Indonesian-Malay, Lisu, Mon, Sgaw, Shan, Vietnamese
Tibet	Tibetan	
Togo	French	Ewe-Fon, Hausa, Kabre, pidgin English, Tem (Kotokole)
Tonga	Tongan	English
Trinidad and Tobago	English	Hindi, Urdu, Tamil, Telegu, English Creole
Tunisia	Arabic	Berber, French
Turks and Caicos Islands	English	
Tuvalu	English, Tuvaluan	Gilbertese
Uganda	English	Achooli-Luo, Luganda, Lugbara, Luluhya, Kinande, OrunyororunyNkoleruHaya, kinyaRuanda-kiRundi, Teso
United Arab Emirates	Arabic	English, Farsi
United States	English	Chinese, French, German, Italian, Polish, Spanish, Ukrainian, Yiddish
Uruguay	Spanish	Portuguese
Vanuatu	English, French	Melanesian, Pidgin English (Bislama, Bichelama)
Venezuela	Spanish	Goajiro
Vietnam	Vietnamese	Cambodian, French, Miao, Tho, Yao
Yemen, Arab Republic of	Arabic (Yemeni dialect)	
Yemen, People's Democratic Republic of	Arabic	English, Mahri
Zaire	French	Cicokwe, Ekihauu, iciBemba, Kinande, kinyaRuanda-kiRundi, Kiteke, Lingala, Lomongo, Lugbara, Sango-Ngbandi, Swahili, Zande

COUNTRY	OFFICIAL LANGUAGE(S)	OTHER MAJOR LANGUAGES
Zambia	English	Bemba, Cicokwe, Chiluba, Chitumbuka, Ila, Lozi, Luvale, Nyanja, Tonga
Zimbabwe	English	Chikaranga, Chirowzi, Chishona, Chivenda, Chizezuru, CiIla-ciTonga, Ngoni, Shitongax

APPENDIX B: A CHRONOLOGY OF THE EUROPEAN EMPIRES

1402
Castile claims the Canary Islands

1415
Portugal conquers Ceuta from the Arabs

1420
Portugal colonizes Madeira

1433
Gilianes sails southward from Portugal along the West Coast of Africa, rounding Cape Bojador for the first time

1456
Alvise da Cadamosto discovers Cape Verde Islands

1462
Portugal establishes settlement on the Cape Verde Islands
Spain takes Gibraltar

1470
Portuguese explorers reach modern-day Gabon

1479
Treaty of Alcazovas

1482
Diogo Cão of Portugal discovers mouth of Congo River and explores part of the coast of West Africa (1482–1486)
Portuguese build Elmina Castle in Ghana

1488
Bartolomeu Dias of Portugal explores Algoa and Mossel bays in South Africa, observing and naming Cape of Storms, later renamed Cape of Good Hope

1492
Christopher Columbus discovers America

1494

Treaty of Tordesillas

1497

John Cabot of Italy makes two voyages (1497–1498) under the English flag. He discovers Cape Breton Island, Nova Scotia, and explores parts of Greenland, Labrador, Baffin Island, and Newfoundland

Vasco da Gama of Portugal begins his voyage (1497–1499) in which he sails around the Cape of Good Hope and across the Indian Ocean to India

Amerigo Vespucci of Italy begins his voyage (1497–1498) in which he sails through Caribbean, around Gulf of Mexico, and along coast of Florida

Spain takes Melilla

1499

Alonso de Ojeda of Spain begins his voyage (1499–1500) in which he explores the northern coast of South America

1500

Vicente Yañez Pinzón of Spain touches the coast of Brazil not far from Pernambuco, and discovers the Amazon River

Pedro Alvares Cabral of Portugal touches the coast of Brazil and rounds the Cape of Good Hope

1501

Gaspar de Corte-Real of Portugal explores the northeastern coasts of Canada and New-foundland

Spain colonizes Bonaire

1505

Portugal discovers the Comoros Islands

1507

German geographer Waldseemuller publishes the accounts of Amerigo Vespucci's voyages and suggests that the New World be named America

1508

Sebastian Cabot of Italy begins voyage to Labrador (1508–1509) while searching for the Northwest Passage, possibly sailing as far as Hudson Bay

1510

Diego Velásquez commissioned to conquer and settle Cuba

1511

Portugal establishes trading post on Malacca

1513

Juan Ponce de Leon of Spain discovers and names Florida

Vasco Núñez de Balboa of Spain traverses Panama and discovers the Pacific Ocean

1514

Diego Velásquez completes the conquest of Cuba

1518

Portugal builds fort at Ceylon

1519

Ferdinand Magellan leaves for voyage (1519–1521) in which he explores the estuary of Rio de la Plata, sails southward, proceeding through strait which bears his name, and traverses the Pacific Ocean to Philippine Islands, where he is killed by natives. He was the first man to have sailed westward around the globe to a longitude he had previously reached on an eastward voyage

Juan Sebastian del Cano of Spain, a commander in Magellan's expedition, commands the expedition of *Victoria* after Magellan's death and returns to Spain by way of Moluccas and the Cape of Good Hope. He was the first to circumnavigate the globe

Hernando Cortés of Spain begins his voyage (1519–1536) in which he explores the east coasts of Mexico and Yucatán, conquers Mexico, and discovers Lower California

1521

Magellan lands on Guam and the Marianas and claims them for Spain

1523

Francisco Pizarro of Spain begins his voyage (1523–1535), exploring west coast of South America and conquering Peru

1524

Giovanni da Verrazano of Italy explores the east coast of North America northward to Newfoundland, discovering New York and Narragansett bays

1525

Rodrigo de Bastidas establishes Santa Marta, the first European settlement in Colombia

1526

Portuguese land in Papua

Loaysa sights Marshall Islands

1527

Alvar Núñez Cabeza de Vaca of Spain begins his voyage (1527–1542) in which he explores the south coast of North America and heads an expedition to the Rio de la Plata region—1,000 miles across South Brazil to Asunción, Paraguay

1529

Treaty of Zaragosa

1532

Portugal establishes first permanent settlements in Brazil

1533

Inca Atahullpa executed by Pizarro

Spaniards conquer Cuzco, the Inca capital, in Peru

Last Indian resistance crushed in Cuba

1534

Jacques Cartier of France begins his voyages (1534–1536) in which he explores the west coast of Newfoundland and Gulf of Saint Lawrence, sailing up the St. Lawrence River until sighting Montreal

1535

Diu is ceded to Portugal

1538

City of La Plata (Sucre) founded in Bolivia

1539

Hernando de Soto of Spain begins his voyage (1539–1542) in which he explores the southeastern United States

1540

Francisco Vasquez de Coronado of Spain begins his voyage (1540–1542) in which he traces the Colorado River northward, discovers the Grand Canyon, and explores southern California, New Mexico, north Texas, Oklahoma, and east Kansas

Pedro de Valdivia of Spain begins his voyage (1540–1552) in which he explores Chile.

Francisco de Orellana of Spain begins his expedition (1540–1541) in which he discovers the Amazon River, tracing it from its headwaters in the Andes to its outlet in the Atlantic Ocean.

1541

Pedro de Valdivia establishes first permanent European settlement in Chile

1542

Juan Rodríguez Cabrillo and Bartolome Ferrelo of Portugal begin their voyage (1542–1543) in which they explore the west coast of Mexico and land at Point Loma, California

1557

Portugal establishes trading post on Macao

1559

Portugal annexes Daman

1565

Spain takes part of Marianas

1567

Mendana sights Solomon Islands

Mendana sights Nui, Tuvalu

1570

Portuguese establish trading post at Nagasaki

1574

Portugal establishes colony in Angola

1576

Sir Martin Frobisher of England begins voyage (1576–1578) in which he discovers Frobisher Bay and Hudson Strait

1577

Sir Francis Drake of England begins his voyage (1577–1580) in which he completes the second circumnavigation of the globe in the *Golden Hind*

1580

The crowns of Spain and Portugal unite under Philip II

1581

Prince William I of Orange, Stadtholder of Holland, Zeeland, and Utrecht, and the States-General of the Seven Provinces, renounce their allegiance to Philip II of Spain.

1583

Spanish colony established at Buenos Aires.

1584

William I is assassinated.

1585

John Davis of England begins his voyage (1585–1593) in which he skirts the east coast of Greenland southward to Cape Farewell, turns northward and sails along the west coast of Greenland to Baffin Bay

1588

The English and the Dutch defeat the Spanish Armada

1590

Expansion of Dutch seaborne trade to the Mediterranean, West Africa, and Indonesia begins (1590–1600)

1592

John Davis discovers Falkland Islands

1594

Willem Barents of the Netherlands begins his voyage (1594–1597) in which he discovers Novaya Zemlya, Barents Sea, and Barents Island

1595

Mendaña lands on Santa Cruz, Solomon Islands

Mendaña visits Marquesas, sights the northern Cook Islands

Sir Walter Raleigh of England explores Guiana, the coasts of Trinidad, and Orinoco River

Pedro Fernandes de Queiros of Portugal begins his expedition (1595–1606) in which he discovers New Hebrides in 1606.

1596

Sebastian Vizcaino of Spain begins his voyage (1596–1603) in which he explores the west coast of Mexico between Acapulco and Lower California and sails up San Diego and Monterey bays.

1597

Dutch establish trading post on Bali

1598

Dutch seize Mauritius

1600

English East India Company is founded

First Dutch ship reaches Japan.

Unification of Japan under the *de facto* rule of the Tokugawa Shogunate after the battle of Sekigahara (1600–1863)

1602

Dutch East India Company is founded

1603

Samuel de Champlain of France begins his expedition (1603–1613) in which he traces course of St. Lawrence River northward to Lachine Rapids above Montreal, explores the east coast of North America southward from Nova Scotia to Vineyard Haven, and founds and names Quebec

Dutch establish trading post on Borneo

1604

French settlement begins at Cayenne in what becomes French Guiana

1605

Dutch capture Amboina and drive the Portuguese from the Moluccas

1606

Quiros visits New Hebrides

Quiros sights Gilbert Islands

Dutch fleet blockades the Tagus.

Spanish expedition from the Philippines recaptures part of the Moluccas.

Unsuccessful Dutch attacks on Mozambique and Malacca

1607

English colony at Jamestown, Virginia, established

Dutch establish trading post in Makassar

1608

England established colony on Grenada

1609

Henry Hudson of England begins his voyage (1609–1610) in which he discovers the
   Hudson River, Hudson Strait, and Hudson Bay

Inauguration of the Ten Year Truce between Holland and Spain

Dutch factory at Hirado in Japan

Sir George Somers of England lands on Bermuda

1610

Dutch settlements founded in Guiana and Amazon region (1610–1612)

1612

Dutch found Fort Mouree on the Guinea Coast

1614

Dutch fur traders active on the Hudson River

1615

Jakob Le Maire and Willem Cornelis Schouten of the Netherlands begin their expedition
   (1615–1617) in which they round the southern tip of Tierra del Fuego, pass through
   Le Maire Strait, observe and name Cape Horn, and reach Moluccas.

1616

Schouten and Le Maire visit Futuna and Tonga

William Baffin of England rediscovers and explores Baffin Bay

1618

Islamization of Macassar

1619

Anglo-Dutch rivalry in East Indies temporarily changes into an alliance (1619–1623)

Dutch establish commercial port at Batavia on Java

1620

English colony at Plymouth, Massachusetts, established

1621

Twelve Years Truce expires

Dutch West India Company is established

Dutch East India Company conquers the Banda Islands

1623

English settlement at Portsmouth, New Hampshire, established

Amboina "Massacre"

1624–1625
Dutch take and lose Bahia
Dutch repulsed at Puerto Rico and Elmina
Great Britain settles St. Christopher (St. Kitts)

1625
Dutch establish the colony of New Netherland

1626
First French settlement placed on Madagascar
France establishes fort at St. Louis, Senegal

1629
Mataram unsuccessfully besieges Batavia
English colony of Massachusetts Bay established
Treaty of St. Germain-en-Laye
English colonists establish a settlement on Barbados

1630
Dutch begin the conquest of Pernambuco, Northeastern Brazil

1632
English settlers colonize Montserrat
Dutch West India Company seizes St. Eustatius and Saba

1634
English Catholics establish the colony of Maryland
Dutch West India Company seizes Curacao and Aruba

1635
Massachusetts Bay colonists establish the Connecticut colony
France establishes colony on Guadeloupe
France claims Martinique

1636
Massachusetts Bay colonists establish the Rhode Island colony

1637
John Maurice completes conquest of Pernambuco
Van Diemen makes an alliance with Raja Sinha of Kandy against the Portuguese in
    Ceylon

1638
Dutch capture Elmina in Guinea and begin conquest of coastal Ceylon
British sailors establish a settlement in what becomes British Honduras
Swedish settlement established in Delaware

1640
Dutch defeat a Portuguese Armada off Pernambuco

1641
Dutch capture Malacca, the Maranhão, and Luanda from the Portuguese
Ten Year Truce between Dutch and Portuguese ends at The Hague
Dutch are the only Europeans allowed in Japan (until 1853)

1642
Abel Janszoon Tasman of the Netherlands begins his voyage (1642–1644) in which he
    discovers New Zealand and Tonga and Fiji islands, Gulf of Carpentaria, and Tasmania

1643

Tasman visits Fiji

France annexes Reunion

1644

Rebellion in northeastern Brazil follows John Maurice's departure from Pernambuco

1648

Spain recognizes Dutch independence by the Treaty of Munster

Portuguese recapture Luanda and Benguela

Treaty of Westphalia

1650

English Navigation Act which discriminates against Dutch seaborne trade is passed

1651

Great Britain takes St. Helena

1652

First Anglo-Dutch War begins (1652–1654)

Van Riebeeck founds the Dutch settlement at Cape Town

Portuguese expel the Dutch from northeastern Brazil

Arnold de Vlaming completes conquest of the Amboina group (1650–1656)

1654

First Anglo-Dutch War ends in a decisive Dutch defeat in the North Sea and regional
    Dutch victories in the East Indies and the Mediterranean

1655

The Dutch seize control of the Swedish settlement in Delaware

1658

Dutch complete the conquest of coastal Ceylon

1661

Dutch make peace with Portugal and complete conquest of Malabar from the Portuguese

Manchus capture Formosa from the Dutch

Spaniards evacuate the Moluccas

First Dutch attack on Macassar occurs

1663

English colony of the Carolinas established

1664

English take some Dutch forts on the Gold Coast and the North American colony of New
    Netherland in time of peace, renaming it New York

English acquire the Dutch and Swedish settlements of New Jersey

English capture the Dutch settlement in Delaware

French West India Company establishes foothold in western Hispaniola

1665

Second Anglo-Dutch war begins

Portugal establishes military presence in Cabinda

1667

Second Anglo-Dutch war ends in the Dutch raid on the Medway and the Treaty of Breda

Final subjugation of Macassar by Speelman and Aru Palakka

1668

Jesuit missionaries arrive in Guam and Marianas

Spain recognizes independence of Portugal

Triple alliance between Dutch Republic, England, and Sweden

Portugal cedes Ceuta to Spain

1670

Guamanian revolt against Jesuits

Spain cedes Cayman Islands to Great Britain

1672

Spanish-Chamorros War begins (1672–1700)

Third Anglo-Dutch War begins

Denmark settles St. Thomas

1673

Jacques Marquette and Louis Joliet of France travel down Wisconsin and Mississippi
    rivers to the mouth of the Arkansas River and trace the Illinois River back to Lake
    Michigan

1674

Revolt of Trunajaya inaugurates the decline of Mataram which recognizes Dutch suz-
    erainty by Treaty of 1677

Treaty of Westminster

1675

King Philip's War in North America

1678

Treaty of Nymegen

1680

New Hampshire becomes a separate British colony

1682

Robert Cavelier, Sieur de la Salle, of France traces the Mississippi River to its mouth in
    the Gulf of Mexico

Dutch begin subjugation of Bantam (1682–1684)

English colony of Pennsylvania is launched

1689

War of the League off Augsburg begins (1689–1697)

1695

Northern Marianas peoples moved to Guam

1697

Treaty of Ryswijk

Coffee tree introduced into Java from Arabia

1702

War of the Spanish Succession begins (1702–1713)

Civil war in Mataram and first Javanese War of Succession (1702–1713)

East Jersey and West Jersey unite to form New Jersey

1703

English settlement of Delaware acquires self-government from Pennsylvania

1704
Great Britain takes Gibraltar from Spain

1710
Spanish exploration of Carolines

1713
Treaty of Utrecht
France cedes Acadia, Nova Scotia, and Cape Breton Island to Great Britain

1715
France seizes Mauritius

1717
First Revolt of the Vegueros in Cuba
Denmark annexes St. John

1722
Roggeveen sights Samoa and Easter Islands

1725
Vitus Bering of Denmark begins his expedition (1725–1741) in which he discovers the
  Bering Sea and the Bering Strait

1733
English colony of Georgia established
France sells St. Croix to the Danish West India Company

1740
Massacre of Chinese at Batavia followed by extension of fighting into the interior of Java
  and a new war in Mataram, ending with further cession of territory by the Susuhunan
  (1740–1743)

1742
Pierre Gaultier de Varennes, Sieur de La Verendrye, of France, explores Manitoba, North
  Dakota, South Dakota, western Minnesota, and possibly a portion of Montana

1745
British colonial troops conquer Louisbourg

1747
Dutch Republic becomes involved in the War of the Austrian Succession (1747–1748)
French invade territory of Dutch Republic

1748
Treaty of Aix-la-Chapelle

1749
Third Javanese Succession War begins

1750
Treaty of Madrid

1755
Battle of Monongahela (Braddock's defeat).

1756
Seven Years' War begins (1756–1763)

Dutch profit as neutrals in Seven Years' War but suffer from considerable English interference with their seaborne trade (1756–1763)

France seizes Seychelles Islands

1759
Dutch expedition to restore their position in Bengal miscarries completely and is annihilated by the English

1761
Treaty of El Pardo

1762
English capture and occupy Havana, Cuba

1763
Treaty of Paris ends the Seven Years' War. Quebec, Canada, is ceded by the French to the English

1765
England formally annexes Falkland Islands

1766
English Parliament passes the Declaratory Act

1767
Carteret claims New Guinea for Britain, sights Solomon Islands

Wallis visits Marshall Islands

Wallis visits Tahiti and Wallis Islands

Jesuits expelled from Spanish America

1768
Captain James Cook of England begins his exploration (1768–1779) and charting of the coast of New Zealand. He finishes the charting of the world's major water bodies by 1778 and disproves the long-standing theory that a large, habitable land remained undiscovered in the Southern Hemisphere

1769
Cook arrives in Tahiti

1773
East India Tea Act

1774
Cook visits New Caledonia, New Hebrides

Great Britain passes the Intolerable Acts

1776
Thirteen British North American colonies declare their independence as the United States of America

1777
Treaty of San Ildefonso

1778
Captain James Cook sights Hawaii

1780
Uprising of Tupac Amaru II
Revolt of the *comuneros* in New Granada
Fourth Anglo-Dutch War begins and causes catastrophic effects on Dutch seaborne trade
    and colonial power
1783
Antelope wrecks on Palau, crew makes way to Philippines
Treaty of Paris ends the American Revolution. Great Britain cedes land east of Mississippi
    West to the United States
Great Britain receives control over Dominica
1784
Fourth Anglo-Dutch War ends
New Brunswick becomes a separate British colony
1786
British East India Company acquires Pinang
1788
Captain Marshall explores islands and names them
New South Wales settled
Great Britain establishes settlement at Sierra Leone
1790
Bounty crew reaches Pitcairn Island
1791
English Parliament passes Corn Law
Dutch West India Company dissolved
Slave revolt begins in Santo Domingo
1795
First English occupation of the Cape of Good Hope
1796
British place a settlement on Ceylon
1797
English missionaries arrive in Tahiti, Tonga, and Marquesas
1798
British East India Company secured exclusive trade rights in Oman
1799
Dutch East India Company formally dissolves, and its debts and possessions are taken
    over by the Batavian Republic
Irish Act
1800
Sandalwood trade begins in Fiji
British East India Company establishes Province Wellesley in Malaysia
1801
Treaty of Badajoz
1802
Bernardo O'Higgins returns to Chile
Treaty of Amiens

1803
United States buys the Louisiana Purchase from France

1804
Haiti becomes independent

1806
Miranda's expedition to Venezuela
First English invasion of Buenos Aires

1807
Bolivar returns from Europe to Venezuela
Second English invasion of Buenos Aires
Sierra Leone placed under control of British crown.

1808
Charles IV abdicates
Ferdinand VII imprisoned by Napoleon

1810
Junta established in Caracas (Venezuela); Spanish authority defied
De facto independence of La Plata
Paraguayans reject Buenos Aires leadership
New Granada (Colombia) declares independence
Grito de Dolores—Hidalgo initiates revolution in Mexico
Junta formed in Chile

1811
Paraguay declares independence
Venezuela declares independence

1812
Jose Antonio Aponte leads slave revolt in Cuba
Spanish-galleon Pacific trade via Guam ceases
Cortes in Spain proclaims liberal constitution
Bolivar returns from exile to Cartagena

1813
Bolivar invades Venezuela from New Granada
Bolivar declared Liberator of Venezuela
United States seizes West Florida from Spain

1814
Ferdinand VII returns to Spanish throne
Ferdinand VII abolishes Constitution of 1812
Battle of Rancagua (Chile)
Congress of Vienna convenes
Great Britain gains the Cape Colony
France cedes Mauritius to Great Britain
Protestant missionaries establish a mission in New Zealand
Dutch claim western New Guinea
Treaty of Ghent

1815
English Parliament passes Corn Law

1816
United Provinces of the Rio de la Plata declares independence from Spain
1817
San Martin and O'Higgins cross Andes into Chile
Battle of Chacabuco (Chile)
1818
Chile formally declares independence
Battle of Maipu (Chile)
1819
Republic of Gran Colombia declared
Battle of Boyaca (Venezuela)
United States purchases East Florida from Spain
Great Britain establishes colony at Singapore
1820
American whalers begin visiting Micronesia
ABCFM missionaries in Hawaii; Bellinghausen surveys Tuamotus
1821
Protestant missionaries in Cook Islands
Plan of Iguala established
Second Battle of Carabobo (Venezuela)
Independence of Mexico achieved
Guatemala declares independence
1822
Protestant missionaries in Tonga
Battle of Bombona (Ecuador)
Battle of Pichincha (Ecuador)
Iturbide crowned Agustin I, Emperor of Mexico
Ecuador proclaims its incorporation into Gran Colombia
Brazil declares its independence from Portugal
Moresby Treaty
American Colonization Society establishes colony in what is today Liberia
1823
Ferdinand VII restores absolute despotism in Spain
Central American Federation secedes from Mexico
First Anglo-Burmese War begins
1824
Kotzbue surveys Marshall Islands
Duperrey surveys Caroline Islands
Battle of Junin (Peru)
Battle of Ayacucho (Peru)
British merchants establish post in Natal
Dutch take Sumatra
Battle of Ayacucho secures the independence of Peru
1825
Sandalwood found in New Hebrides
Administration of Guam shifts to Philippines under Spanish rule

Dutch annex western New Guinea (Irian Jaya)
Bolivia (Alto Peru) declares independence

1826
First Anglo-Burmese War ends
Britain establishes colony of Western Australia
Britain establishes the Straits Settlement

1828
Uruguay achieves independence
Treaty of Turkmanchai

1830
Tahitian Protestant missionaries land in Fiji
Protestant missionaries arrive in Samoa
Venezuela, Colombia, and Ecuador separate
France seizes Algiers

1832
Ecuador annexes the Galapagos Islands

1834
French Catholic missionaries in Mangareva

1835
LMS Protestant missionaries arrive in Fiji

1836
Catholic missionaries arrive in Tahiti, are expelled
Texas declares independence from Mexico

1837
Spanish crown ends Cuban representation in the Cortes

1838
Nicaragua, Costa Rica, and Honduras secede from Central American Federation

1839
First Afghan War begins
LMS missionaries to New Hebrides
U.S. commercial treaty with Samoa
Guatemala and El Salvador form separate republics
Great Britain takes Aden

1840
French Catholic missionaries arrive in New Caledonia
Britain establishes a crown colony in New Zealand
Canadian Union Act

1842
Webster-Ashburton Treaty
France annexes Marquesas; protectorate over Tahiti and dependencies
First Afghan War ends
Treaty of Nanking declares Hong Kong a British colony

1843
British sea captain Paulet seizes Hawaii, but cession revoked
Gambia becomes a separate British colony

1844
Catholic missionaries arrive in Fiji
Dominican Republic declares its independence

1845
Unsuccessful Catholic mission to Solomon Islands
United States annexes Texas
Hamerton Treaty

1846
United States acquires Oregon Territory from England

1847
First recruitment of laborers from New Hebrides to New South Wales
Jarnac Convention
Republic of Liberia claimed
Great Britain takes control of Labuan

1848
Anglican missionaries in New Hebrides
Treaty of Guadelupe-Hidalgo ends the war between the United States and Mexico. United States acquires California, Nevada, Utah, Colorado, Arizona, and New Mexico

1852
Second Anglo-Burmese War begins
U.S. Protestant missionaries in Carolines

1853
Second Anglo-Burmese War ends
France seizes New Caledonia
United States completes the Gadsden Purchase with Mexico
Matthew Perry visits Japan

1854
Orange River colony becomes the Orange Free State
Reciprocity Treaty

1855
United States establishes consulate in Guam

1857
U.S. missionaries in Gilberts and Marshalls
Sepoy Mutiny

1858
France establishes colony of Cochin China
Government of India Act

1860
Anglo French Treaty
Morocco cedes Ifni to Spain

1862
Great Britain formally acquires what becomes the colony of British Honduras from Spain

1863
France establishes protectorate in Cambodia

1864
France annexes the Loyalty Islands
French convicts sent to New Caledonia

1865
First Chinese laborers arrive in Hawaii

1867
United States acquires Alaska from Russia
United States occupies Midway Islands
English Parliament passes the British North America Act

1868
Beginning of the Ten Years War in Cuba
Perpetual Maritime Truce

1869
Germany acquires land in Carolines
Suez Canal opens

1870
Gold rush begins in New Caledonia
LMS missionaries in Tuvalu

1872
United States signs treaty with Samoa
French Catholic missionaries arrive in Hawaii
Pacific Islanders Protection Act

1873
Prince Edward Island joins the Confederation of Canada

1874
Britain annexes Fiji

1875
Britain establishes protectorate over Perak

1876
United States-Hawai'i reciprocal trade treaty; first LMS missionaries in Papua

1877
Great Britain annexes the Transvaal

1878
New Caledonian uprising against the French
Germany acquires coaling station in Marshalls
First Japanese laborers arrive in Hawai'i
Pact of Zanjon ends Ten Years War in Cuba
Second Afghan War begins
Great Britain leases Cyprus from Turkey
Treaty of San Stefano

1879
Britain establishes naval station in Samoa
"Little War" begins in Cuba
Portuguese Guinea formally declared a Portuguese dependency

1880

France annexes Tahiti and dependencies

Madrid Conference

Second Afghan War ends

1881

France establishes protectorate over Tunisia

British North Borneo Company takes control of Sabah

1882

France controls New Hebrides

British army occupies Cairo

France takes Tonkin

1883

France establishes formal control over Annam

1884

Britain establishes a protectorate over southeast New Guinea

Germany annexes northeast New Guinea, the Bismarck Archipelago, and the northern
    Solomon Islands

Germany annexes the Admiralty Islands

Berlin West Africa Conference convenes

Germany establishes the colony of German Southwest Africa

London Convention

Germany establishes protectorate over Togoland

Germany establishes claim to Cameroon

French troops occupy Dahomey

1885

Spanish protectorates established over Cape Juby, Rio de Oro, and La Gyera

Dispute between Spain and Germany over Carolines, with Spain gaining control

General Gordon killed at Khartoum

Third Anglo-Burmese War

Colony of French Congo established

British establish protectorate over Bechuanaland

1886

Germany takes Marshalls, Spain takes Carolines

Slavery abolished in Cuba

Anglo-German Treaty

Burma becomes part of British India

France acquires Congo-Gabon

France establishes protectorate over most of the Comoros Islands

1887

Caroline islanders revolt

Wallis Islands become French protectorate

Colonial Conference of 1887

1888

Anglo-French joint naval commission for New Hebrides

Brunei becomes a British protectorate

Great Britain establishes protectorate over the Southern Cook Islands

Chile annexes Easter Island
Germany annexes Nauru

1889

Gold fields open in New Guinea; British protectorate over New Guinea
Hurricane in Samoa; Britain, United States, Germany hold Berlin conference and divide
    Samoa into three units
Anglo-German Treaty
Brussels Conference convenes
Berlin Act
Treaty of Uccialli
Great Britain establishes protectorate over Tokelau Islands

1890

Italy annexes Eritrea
Heligoland-Zanzibar Treaty
Great Britain establishes protectorate over Zanzibar

1891

Anglo-Portuguese Treaty

1892

Britain declares protectorate over Gilbert and Ellice Islands
India Councils Act

1893

Britain declares protectorate over the southwestern Solomon Islands
Siam cedes Laos to France

1894

Great Britain establishes protectorate over Uganda
Sino-Japanese War begins

1895

Cuban war of independence begins
Federated Malay States formed
French West Africa formed
Japan takes control of Formosa in Treaty of Shimonoseki
Jameson Raid
Great Britain forms the East Africa Protectorate

1896

Treaty of Addis Ababa
France conquers Upper Volta

1897

Colonial Conference of 1897
Natal annexes Zululand

1898

Germany establishes base at Kiaochow
Spanish-American War
United States seizes Guam, Philippines, Puerto Rico, and Wake Island from Spain
United States annexes Hawaii
United States establishes protectorate over Cuba

Fashoda Incident

1899

Anglo-Egyptian Agreement on the Sudan

Spain sells Marshalls, Carolines, and Northern Marianas to Germany

Tripartite Convention

Samoa divided into American Samoa and German Samoa

Boer War begins

Hague Conference

United States formally annexes Wake Island

1900

Ocean Island annexed by Great Britain

Boxer Rebellion in China

Great Britain establishes protectorate over Niue and Tonga

1901

Commonwealth of Australia comes into existence

New Zealand annexes Cook Islands

1902

The Republic of Cuba proclaimed

Anglo-Japanese Alliance

Boer War ends

Colonial Conference of 1902

French-Siamese Treaty

1903

United States acquires Panama Canal Zone

1904

Anglo-French Entente

Herero Uprising

Russo-Japanese War

1905

Papua Act establishes Australian control over British New Guinea

1906

Anglo-French condominium in New Hebrides

Tripartite Treaty guarantees Ethiopian independence

1907

Treaty of Punakha

Imperial Conference

British Central Africa Protectorate becomes Nyasaland

1908

Western Samoan revolt, men deported to Mariana Islands

Anglo-French Convention

Congo Free State becomes the Belgian Congo

1909

Treaty of Bangkok

1910

Union of South Africa created

1911
Italy conquers Libya from the Ottoman Turks
Imperial Conference
Anglo-Portuguese Convention

1912
Franco-Spanish Treaty on Morocco; Spanish Morocco established

1914
World War I begins, Australia gains German New Guinea and Nauru
Japan gains German colonies: Marianas, Marshalls, Carolines
New Zealand seizes Western Samoa
Great Britain declares protectorate over Egypt

1915
Great Britain annexes Gilbert and Ellice Islands Colony

1916
United States purchases Virgin Islands from Denmark
British-Hedjaz Agreement
Sykes-Picot Agreement
Qatar becomes independent

1917
Advisory council of Guamanians established
Great Britain issues the Balfour Declaration

1918
Anglo-French Convention

1919
Allied Powers seize and distribute among themselves the former German and Ottoman
     colonies under the League of Nations mandate system
Government of India Act
Tripolitania becomes a separate Italian colony
Upper Volta becomes a formal French colony

1920
League of Nations gives Australia mandate over German New Guinea
League of Nations mandate given to colonial powers for control of Pacific islands
Government of Ireland Act
East Africa Protectorate becomes the Kenya Colony
Northern Ireland created
Chad becomes a separate French colony
French Equatorial Africa created
Treaty of San Remo
Treaty of Sevres

1921
Denmark formally claims sovereignty over Greenland
Imperial Conference
Treaty of Ankara
Simonstown Agreement

1922
English Parliament passes Empire Settlement Act

1923
Imperial Conference
Rwanda and Burundi become Belgian mandates
Treaty of Lausanne

1924
Union of Free Church of Tonga and Wesleyan church

1926
Imperial Conference

1927
Canary Islands become formal provinces of Spain

1930
Gandhi launches the protest against the salt tax in India

1931
Guam gains an elected Congress
Statute of Westminster

1932
Japan annexes Micronesian states
British mandate over Iraq ends
Imperial Economic Conference

1933
Newfoundland reverts to status of British colony

1934
United States Congress passes the Tydings-McDuffie Act providing for independence of
    the Philippine Islands in 1945
Treaty of Sana
Treaty of Ta'if

1935
Japan withdraws from League of Nations, establishes military in Micronesia
Italy invades Ethiopia
United States settles the Equatorial Islands
Government of India Act

1936
Anglo-Egyptian Treaty

1940
World War II begins in Europe. Gaullists take over French territories
Japan invades Indochina

1941
Guam occupied by the Japanese
Japan bombs Pearl Harbor, United States declares war
Lebanon proclaims independence

1942
United States establishes bases on Funafuti

1944
Brazzaville Conference

1945

New Guinea becomes Australian trust territory
U.S. awarded trust territories in Micronesia
World War II ends
France returns to Indochina
Indonesia declares independence
Great Britain forms the Malaya Union
Simla Conference

1946

Philippine Islands receive independence
New Caledonia becomes French overseas department; anti-colonial movements in Solomons
Bikini Atoll nuclear tests
French Guiana becomes French overseas department
Guadeloupe becomes French overseas department
Syria becomes fully independent
Transjordan becomes independent

1947

South Pacific Commission established
Eniwetok Atoll nuclear tests
Trust Territory of the Pacific Islands established
Comoros Islands become a separate colony of France
India Independence Act—India becomes independent
Pakistan becomes independent

1948

Burma becomes independent
Israel established
Ceylon becomes independent

1949

Merger of Papua and New Guinea
Republic of Ireland declared
Newfoundland becomes part of Canada

1950

Organic Act of Guam

1951

Libya becomes independent

1953

Central African Federation formed

1954

Vietminh defeat the French at the Battle of Dien Bien Phu
Geneva Accords divide Vietnam at the 17th parallel, creating the Democratic Republic of Vietnam (North Vietnam) and the Republic of Vietnam (South Vietnam). Laos and Cambodia gain independence from France

1956

Tunisia becomes independent
Morocco declares independence

Cabinda becomes part of Angola
Spain cedes Northern Zone of Spanish Morocco to Morocco

1957
Malaya becomes a self-governing dominion
Ghana becomes independent

1958
French West Africa dissolved
French Equatorial Africa dissolved
Agreement of Cintra
Spain cedes Southern Zone of Spanish Morocco to Morocco
West Indies Federation formed
United Arab Republic formed

1959
Hawaii becomes U.S. 50th state; Wallis and Futuna become French territories
Singapore becomes independent

1960
Legislative and executive councils in Solomons
Guam gains first appointed Guamanian governor
Western Samoan constitution
Central African Republic declares independence
Belgian Congo becomes the Independent Congo Republic (Zaire)
Cameroon declares independence
Dahomey declares independence
Cyprus declares independence
People's Republic of Congo established
Gabon declares independence
Madagascar declares independence
Mali declares independence
Chad declares independence
Niger declares independence
Republic of Togo proclaimed
Somali Republic established
Senegal becomes independent
Upper Volta becomes independent

1961
India takes Daman from Portugal
India takes Goa from Portugal
Kuwait declares independence
Tanganyika becomes independent
Sierra Leone becomes independent
United Arab Republic dissolved

1962
Mariana Islands under U.S. Department of the Interior
Western Samoa becomes independent
Rwanda becomes independent
Burundi becomes independent

Trinidad and Tobago becomes independent
West Indian Federation dissolved

1963
Singapore joins Federation of Malaysia
Central African Federation dissolved
Aden joins the Federation of South Arabia
Zanzibar becomes independent
Kenya becomes independent

1964
Malawi becomes independent
Zambia becomes independent
Tanganyika and Zanzibar join to form Tanzania

1965
Congress of Micronesia held
Cook Islands gain internal self-government
Gambia becomes independent
British Indian Ocean Territory formed
Maldives becomes independent
Southern Rhodesia issues Unilateral Declaration of Independence
Singapore leaves Malaysia

1966
Botswana becomes independent
British Guyana becomes the independent nation of Guyana
Lesotho becomes independent
Barbados becomes independent

1968
Nauru becomes independent
Mauritius declares independence
Swaziland becomes independent
Republic of Equatorial Guinea proclaimed

1970
Fiji becomes independent
Tonga becomes independent

1971
Bahrain becomes a member of the United Nations
British troops withdraw from the Arabian Peninsula

1973
Commonwealth of the Bahamas becomes independent

1974
Niue gains self-government
Grenada becomes independent
Portuguese Guinea becomes independent

1975
Papua New Guinea becomes independent
Plebiscite establishes Commonwealth of the Northern Mariana Islands

Gilbert and Ellice Islands separated; Ellice Islands become Tuvalu
North Vietnam conquers South Vietnam and creates the Socialist Republic of Vietnam
Angola becomes independent
Cape Verde Islands declare independence
Federal Islamic Republic of Comoros declared
Sao Tome and Principe becomes independent

1976
Western Samoa joins United Nations
Spanish Morocco partitioned
Seychelles becomes independent

1977
Djibouti declares independence

1978
Solomon Islands declare independence
Tuvalu becomes independent
Dominica becomes independent

1979
St. Vincent and Grenadines becomes independent
Federated States of Micronesia formed
St. Lucia becomes independent
Kiribati becomes independent

1980
New Hebrides becomes independent state of Vanuatu
Zimbabwe becomes independent
Palau becomes internally self-governing

1981
U.S. trusteeship of the Pacific Islands ends
Antigua and Barbuda become independent
Belize becomes independent

1982
Falkland Islands War

1983
St. Christopher-Nevis (St. Kitts–Nevis) declares independence

1984
Brunei becomes independent

1985
Commonwealth of the Northern Marianas Islands established

1990
Namibia becomes independent

APPENDIX C: OCEAN ISLAND GROUPS OF THE WORLD

J. Larry Murdock

Entries are arranged by island group, subdivided by subgroups, with individual islands in alphabetical order. The islands are listed in a word-by-word alphabetical order. Cross references were made for (1) all island groups that seemed to be plural; (2) former names of island groups; and (3) a few common or political names. Geographic names were used when possible. Current, or former, political names or designations for current island groups were avoided where possible.

Actaeon Group
  See Tuamotu Islands

Admiralties
  See Admiralty Islands

Admiralty Islands
  See Bismarck Archipelago

Aegadean Islands
  See Egadi Islands

Aegean Islands
  Astipalaia
  Bozcaada
  Chalke
  Corfu
  Crete
  Cyclades
  Dodecanese
  Euboea
  Embros
  Kalymnos
  Karpathos
  Kasos
  Kastellorizo
  Khalki
  Kos
  Leips
  Lemnos
  Leros
  Lesbos
  Lipsos
  Nisiros
  Patmos
  Rhodes
  Samos
  Samothrace
  Simi (Syme)
  Sporades
  Tilos
  Thasos

Aeolian Islands
  See Lipari Islands

Agalega Islands
  See Mascarene Islands

Aland Islands (Ahvenanmaa)
Aland
Eckerd
Lemland
Lumparland
Vardo

Alcester Islands
See Woodlark Islands

Aldabra Islands
See Seychelles

Aleutian Islands
Andreanof Islands
  Adak
  Amlia
  Atka
  Kanaga
  Tanaga
Fox Islands
  Akutan
  Umnak
  Unalaska
  Unimak
Near Islands
  Agattu
  Attu
Rat Islands
  Amchitka
  Kiska
  Semisopochnoi

Alexander Archipelago
Admiralty
Baranof
Chicagof
Kuiu
Kupreanof
Mitkof
Prince of Wales
Revillagigedo
Wrangell (Ostrov Vrangelya)

Alexander Island

American Samoa
See Samoa, Eastern

Amindivi Islands
See Laccadive Islands

Amirantes
See Seychelles

Anagai Islands
See Caroline Islands

Anchorite Islands
See Sea Islands, Bismarck Archipelago

Andaman Islands
Baratang
Little Andaman
Middle Andaman
North Andaman
Ritchie's Archipelago
Rutland
South Andaman

Andreanof Islands
See Aleutian Islands

Anjou Islands
See New Siberian Islands

Anou Islands
See Duke of Gloucester, Tuamotu Islands

Ant Islands
See Caroline Islands

Antilles
See West Indies

Antipodes Islands
See New Zealand

Aran Islands
See Ireland, British Isles

Archipelago de las Perlas
See Pearl Islands

Arctic Archipelago
See Canadian Arctic Archipelago

Arnavon Group
See Solomon Islands

Aroe Islands
See Malay Archipelago

Ascension Island

Ashmore Islands

Auckland Islands
See New Zealand

Aurora Islands
See Tuamotu Islands

Austral Islands (Tubuai Islands)
Hull (Maria Islands or Sands)
Marotiri (Bass Rock)

Raivavae (Vavitao or High)
Rapa Islands
  Bass
  Rapa
Rimatara
Rurutu
Tubuai

Azores
Corvo
Faial
Fayal
Flores
Graciosa
Pico
San Miguel
Santa Maria
Sao Jorge
Sao Miguel
Terceira

Babuyan Islands
See Philippine Islands

Bahama Islands
See West Indies

Baker Island

Balearic Islands
Cabrera
Ibiza (Ibitza)
Formentera
Majorca
Minorca

Balintang Islands
See Philippine Islands

Balleny Islands
Sturge
Young

Banaba
See Ocean Island (Banaba)

Banda Islands
Bandalontar
Bandanaira
Gunung Api

Banks Island [Australia]

Banks Island [B.C. Canada]

Banks Island
See Canadian Arctic Archipelago

Banks Islands
See New Hebrides

Batan Islands
See Philippine Islands

Belep Islands
See New Caledonia

Bermuda Islands (Somers Islands)
Boaz
Bermuda (Great Bermuda or Long Is-
    land)
Coney
Damel
Ireland
Ireland Island North
Ireland Island South
Nonsuch
St. David
St. George
Somerset

Berry Islands
See West Indies

Bismarck Archipelago
Admiralty Islands
  Baluan
  Fedarb Islands
    Chokua
    Lolau
    Olan
    Sisiva
    Uh
  Johnson Islands
  Los Negros
  Los Reyes
  Lou
  Manus
  Mbuke Islands
    Jambon
    Mbuke
    Vogali
  Mok
  Pak
  Pam Islands
  Pam Ling
  Purdy Islands
    Bat
    Mole

Mouse
Rat
Rambutyo
St. Andrew Group
Tong
Towi
Ulunau
Albert Reef
Aris (Boisa)
Aua
Bagabag
Circular Reef
Crown
Hermit Islands
  Jalun
  Luf
  Marion
Kairiru
Kaniet Islands
  Tatak
Karkar
Lavongai (New Hanover)
Long
Manam
Manu
Mushu
New Britain
New Ireland
  Djaul
  Duke of York Islands
  Feni Islands
    Ambitle
    Babase
    Balum
  Lihir Group
    Lihir (Gerrit Denys)
    Mahur
    Malie
    Masahet
  Mait
  Niguria Group
    Nugarba (Goodman)
    Sable
  St. Matthias
    Eloaue
    Emananus
    Emirau (Storm)
    Mussau

Tench
Tabar Islands
  Simberi
  Tabar
  Tatau
Tanga Group
  Boang
  Lif
  Malendok
  Nekin
  Tefa
Tingwon Islands
  Beligila
  Tingwon
Tsoi Islands
  Kawulikiau
  Mirimbang
  Tsoi Boto
  Tsoi Buga
  Tsoi Guka
Ninigo Islands
  Ahu
  Awin
  Awin Atoll
  Heina Atoll
  Liot Atoll
  Longan
  Mal
  Maletin
  Meman
  Ninigo Atoll
  Pelleluhu Atoll
  Sama Atoll
  Sumasuma Atoll
Ottilien Reef
Ritter
Sakar
Schouten Group
  Kadovar (Blosseville)
  Koil
  Viai
  Wogeo
Sea Islands
Sherbourne Shoal
Siassi Group
Sydney Shoal
Tendanye
Tolokiwa Group

Umboi
Valif
Victoria Reef
Vitu Islands
  Garove
  Mundua
  Narage
  Undaga
  Unea
  Vambu
Whirlwind Reef
Wuvulu

Blasket Islands
See British Isles

Bonin Islands (Ogasawara Islands)
Chichi-shima Retto
  Ani Shima (Buckland)
  Chichi Shima (Peel)
  Ototo Shima (Stapleton)
Hahashima Retto
  Haha Shima
  Kazan Retto (Iwo Retto or Volcano
    Islands)
    Iwo Jima (Naka Iow or Sulphur)
    Kita Iwo
    Minami Iowo
Marcus Island (Minami Tori Shima)
Mukoshima Retto
  Harino Shima
  Kitano Shima
  Muko Shima
  Nakano Shima
  Nakodo Shima
  Sasago Shima
  Yome Shima

Borneo
See Malay Archipelago

Bounty Islands
See New Zealand

British Isles
Achilli
Aran Islands
Channel Islands (Norman Islands)
  Alderney
  Guernsey
  Herm

Jersey
Jethou
Lithou
Sark
Great Britain [main island]
Hebrides (Western Islands)
  Inner
    Coll
    Colonsay
    Eigg
    Iona
    Islay
    Jura
    Lismore
    Mull
    Oronsay
    Raassay
    Rum
    Scarba
    Skye
    Staffa
    Tiree
    Ulva
  Outer
    Barra
    Benbecula
    Flannan Islands
    Harris
    Lewis
    North Uist
    St. Kilda
    South Uist
Ireland
  Achilli
  Aran Islands
  Blasket Islands
    Great Blasket
    Tearaght
Isle of Anglesey
Isle of Man
Isle of Wight
Orkney Islands (# 90)
  Hoy
  Mainland (Pomona)
  Rousay
  Sanday
  South Ronaldsay
  Stronsay

Westray
Scilly Islands
  Bryher
  St. Agnes
  St. Martin's
  St. Mary's
  Tresco
Shetland Islands

Bressay
  Fair Isle
  Fetlar
  Foula
  Mainland
  Noss
  Papa Stour
  Trondra
  Unst
  Whalsey

British Leeward Islands
  See West Indies

British Solomon Islands
  See Solomon Islands

British Virgin Islands
  See Virgin Islands, West Indies

British Windward Islands
  See West Indies

Bubiyan

Caicos Islands
  See West Indies

Calvados Chain
  See Louisiade Archipelago

Canadian Arctic Archipelago (Arctic Archipelago)
  Baffin
  Banks
  Bylot
  Prince of Wales
  Queen Elizabeth Islands
    Ellesmere
    Parry Islands
      Bathurst
      Cornwallis
      Devon
      Melville
      Prince Patrick

Sverdrup Islands
  Amund Ringnes
  Axel Heibeerg
  Ellef Ringes
Resolution
Somerset

Canary Islands
  Alegranza
  Fuerteventura
  Gomera
  Graciosa
  Grand Canary
  Hierro
  Isla de Lobos
  Lanzarote
  La Palma
  Tenerife

Cape Verde Islands
  Deserted
    Branco
    Razo
    Santa Luzia
    Secos
  Leeward Group
    Brava
    Fogo
    Maio
    Sao Tiago
  Sal Rei
  Windward Group
    Boa Vista
    Sal
    Santa Luzia
    Santo Antao
    Sao Nicolau
    Sao Vicente

Caroline Islands (Carolines)
  Palau Group
    Angaur
    Arakabesan
    Auluptagel
    Aurapushekaru
    Babelthuap
    Banna
    Eilmalk (Amototi)
    Helen Reef
    Kayangel Islands

Kayangel
Koror (Korror)
Malakal
Merir (Warren Hastings Island)
Negargol
Peleliu
Pulo Anna
Sonsorol
Tobi (Lord North Island)
Urukthapel
Uruktapi
Ponape Area
  Ant Islands
  Kapingamarangi Islands
    Hare
    Nunakitsu
  Kusaie Islands
    Lele
  Mokil Atoll
    Mokil
    Urak
  Ngatik Atoll
    Ngatik
  Nukuoro Islands
  Oroluk Lagoon
    Baxotrista (Rock)
    Orlouk
  Pakin Atoll
  Pingelap Atoll
    Pingelap
  Senyavin Islands (Seniavin)
    Ponape
Truk Area
  East Fayu Island
  Hall Islands
    Murilo
      Murilo
      Numurus
      Ruo
    Nomwin (Namolipiafan)
      Elin
      Fananu
      Setoaneris
  Kuop Islands
  Losap Atoll
    Laol
    Losap
    Pis

Nama
Namoluk Atoll
  Amas
  Namoluk
  Toinom
Namonuito Islands (Onon Islands)
  Magur
  Pisaras
  Ulul
Nomoi Islands (Mortlock Islands)
  Etal
    Etal
  Lukunor
    Lukunor
    Oneop
    Sopunur
  Nukuor
  Satawan
    Kutu
    Satawan
    Ta
Pulap Islands (Tamatam)
  Fanadik
  Pulap
  Tamatam
Pulusuk (Shukku)
Puluwat Islands
  Alet
  Puluwat
Truk Atoll (Hologu or Hogoleu Islands)
  Dublon
  Eiol
  Eot
  Eten
  Fala-Beguets
  Falo
  Fanan
  Fefan
  Mesegon
  Moen
  Onamue
  Param
  Salat
  Tarik
  Tol
  Tsis
  Udot

Uijec
Ulalu
Uman
Yap Area
  East Fayu (Rukute)
  Eauripik Atoll (Yorupikku)
    Eauripik
    Oao
  Elato Atoll (Erato)
    Falipi
    Kari
    Oletel
  Fais Atoll (Fuhaesu or Tromelin)
  Faraulep Atoll (Furaarappu)
  Gaferut (Gurimesu or Grimes)
  Ifalik Atoll (Furukku)
    Ella
    Flalap
    Ifalik
  Lamotrek Islands (Namochikku)
    Falaite
    Lamotrek
    Pugue
  Mereyon (Woleai or Ulie)
  Ngulu Atoll (Kurru)
  Nomwin (Namolipiafane)
  Olimarao Atoll
    Falifi
    Olimarao
  Onomarai (Olimarao)
  Pikelot (Pigerotto)
  Satawal (Sasaon or Tucker)
  Sorol Islands (Sororu or Philip)
    Sorol
  Toas Atoll
    Toas
    Ulor
  Ulithi Atoll (Mackenzie Islands)
    (or Urushi)
    Asor
    Falalop
    Fassarai
    Lossau
    Mogamog
  West Fayu Islet (Fuiyao)
  Yap Group
    Gagil
    Map

    Rumung
    Yap
  Woleai Islets (Anagai Islands)
    Mariaon
    Raur
    Woleai

Carolines
  See Caroline Islands

Carteret Islands
  See Kilinailau Islands, Solomons

Cartier Islands

Catherine Archipelago
  See Aleutian Islands

Cayman Islands
  See West Indies

Ceylon (Sri Lanka)
  Delft

Chagos Archipelago (Oil Islands)
  Diego Garcia
  Peros Banhos
  Salomon Islands
  Six Islands
  Three Brothers

Chain Islands
  See Tuamotu Islands

Channel Islands
  See British Isles
  See Santa Barbara Islands

Chatham Islands
  See New Zealand

Chesterfield Islands
  See New Caledonia

Christmas Island [Indian Ocean]

Christmas Island (Kiritimati) [Pacific Ocean]
  See Line Islands

Clipperton Island

Cocos Island

Cocos Islands (Keeling Islands)
  Direction
  Home
  West

Coiba Island

Coloane Island

Colon Archipelago
See Galapagos Islands

Commander Islands
See Komandorski Islands

Comoro Islands [Archipelago]
Anjouan
Grand Comore
Mayotte
Moheli

Con Son Island

Conflict Group
See Louisiade Archipelago

Cook Islands
Northern Group
Danger Islands
Pukapuka
Manihiki
Nassau
Palmerston
Palmerston Atoll
Penrhyn
Rakahanga
Savorov (Suvarov)
Tongareva (Penrhyn)
Southern Group
Aitutaki
Atiu
Manihiki
Manuae
Mauke
Mitiaro
Rarotonga
Takutea
Te Au o Tu

Coral Sea Islands

Corsica

Cosmoledo Group
See Seychelles

Cousin Islands
See Seychelles

Crete

Crozet Islands
East
Hog
Penguin
Possession
Twelve Apostles

Cyprus

Dampier Archipelago
Delambre
Dolphin
Enderby
Lewis
Rosemary

Danger Islands
See Cook Islands

Dangerous Islands
See Tuamotu Archipelago

Deboyne Islands
See Louisiade Archipelago

De Long Islands
See New Siberian Islands

D'Entrecasteaux Islands
Fergusson
Dobu
Kawea
Nabwageta
Neumara
Oiaobe
Sanaroa
Uama
Urasi
Wamea
Watota
Wawiwa
Yabwaia
Goodenough
Normanby
Pwasiai (Vaseai)
Ubuia
Ventenat Islands

Desolation Islands
See Kerguelen Islands
See Tierra del Fuego

Diomede Islands
  Big Diomede
  Fairway Rock
  Little Diomede
  Ratmanov

Disappointment Islands
  See Tuamotu Islands

Dodecanese
  See Aegean Islands

Duchateau Islands
  See Louisiade Archipelago

Duff Islands
  See Taumako Islands, Solomon Islands

Duke of Gloucester Group
  See Tuamotu Islands

Duke of York Island (Atafu)
  See Tokelau Islands

Duke of York Islands
  See Bismarck Archipelago

Dutch Antilles
  See West Indies

Dutch East Indies
  See Malay Archipelago

Dutch West Indies
  See West Indies

East Indies
  See Malay Archipelago

Easter Island (Isla de Pascua)

Egadi Islands
  See Sicily

Ellice Islands (Lagoon Islands)
  Funafuti
  Nanumanga
  Nanumea
  Niulakita
  Niutao
  Nui
  Nukufetau
  Nukufalae
  Vitupu

Engineer Group
  See Louisiade Archipelago

Equatorial Islands
  See Line Islands

Exploring Islands
  See Fiji Islands

Faeroe Islands (Faroe Islands)
  Ostero
  Steymoy
  Stromo
  Sudero

Falkland Islands (Islas Malvinas)
  East Falkland
  Jason
  Pebble
  Weddell
  West Falkland

Farne Islands (The Staples)
  Farne
  Longstone
  St. Aidan
  St. Cuthbert

Faroe Islands
  See Faeroe Islands

Farquhar Islands
  See Seychelles

Fedarb Islands
  See Bismarck Archipelago

Feni Islands
  See Bismarck Archipelago

Fiji Islands
  Bau
  Beqa
  Cicia
  Kadavu
  Kanacia
  Kandavu
  Lakeba
  Lau Group
    Exploring Islands
      Avea
      Kanathea
      Munia
      Namalata
      Nataiumba
      Nggilanggila
      Thikobia i Lau
      Thikombia i Lau
      Vanua Mbalavu
      Vatu Vara

Wailagilala
Yathata
Kaimbu
Katafanga
Kimbombo Islets
Lakemba Group
  Aiwa
  Bacon
  Komondriki
  Koroni
  Lakemba
  Lau
  Naiau
  Navtutu i Loma
  Navutu Ira
  Olorua
  Oneata
  Ongea Levu
  Ongeadriki
  Ono i Lau
  Thithia
  Tuvana i Tholo
  Tuvanaira
  Tuvutha
  Uangava
  Vanua Masi
  Vanua Vatu
  Vatoa
  Vuata Vatoa
  Yangasa Levu
Laucala
Mango
Matuku
Moala
Naitamba
Nayau
Ono Group
  Ndavura
  Ndoi
  Ono Levu
Southern Islands
  Fulanga
  Kambara
  Komo
  Marambo
  Mothe
  Namuka i Lau
  Olorua

Ongea Levu
Tavunasithi
Vuanggava
Totoya
Yangasa Islands
  Navutuiloma
  Navutuira
Lomai Viti Group
  Batiki
  Gua
  Koro
  Makogai
  Makongai
  Mbatiki
  Moturiki
  Nairai
  Ngau
  Ovalau
  Wakaya
Mago
Makagai
Mbenga
Quamia
Taveuni (Somo Somo)
  Nggamea
Vanua Balavu
Vanua Levu
  Bekana
  Kavewa
  Kia
  Kioa
  Lambu
  Lauthala
  Mali
  Mathuata
  Motualevu
  Namukalau
  Nandogo
  Ndrua
  Ngamea
  Ngelelevu
  Nukuira
  Nukumbalate
  Nukumbasanga
  Nukunuku
  Rambe (Rambi or Rabi)
  Talailau Nangano
  Tavea

Thikombia
Thombia
Thukini
Tutu
Vatuka
Vendrala
Yandua (Yadua)
Yangganga
Yanutha
Yavu
Vatu Lele
Viti Levu
  Malolo
  Mamanutha Group
    Mana
    Tavua
    Tokoriki
    Vomo
    Yanuya
  Manggewa
  Mataivai
  Mbengga
Viwa
Yasawa Group
  Kowata
  Lailai
  Matathawa Levu
  Nanuya
  Nanuya Levu
  Nathula
  Naviti
  Tavewa
  Viwa Islands
  Waya Lailai
  Yangasa Levu
  Yanggeta
  Yasawa
  Yasawa i Lau
  Yuvutha

Flannan Islands
  See British Isles

Florida Keys
  Big Pine Key
  Boca Chico Key
  Cudjoe Key
  Elliott Key
  Grassy Key

Key Biscayne
Key Largo
Key West
Long Key
Lower Matecumbe Key
Old Rhodes Key
Pigeon Key
Plantation Key
Ramrod Key
Saddlebunch Key
Sands Key
Sugarloaf Key
Summerland Key
Torch Keys
Upper Matecumbe Key
Vaca Key
Virginia Key
West Summerland Key

Formosa (Taiwan)
  Lan Yu
  Liu-Ch'iu Yu
  Lu Tao
  Pescadores (P'Eng-Hu Ch'un-Tao)

Fox Islands
  See Aleutian Islands

French Antilles
  See West Indies

French West Indies
  See West Indies

Friendly Islands
  See Tonga Islands

Frisian Islands
  East Frisian Islands
    Baltrum
    Borkum
    Juist
    Langeoog
    Langenoog
    Neuwerk
    Norderney
    Scharhorn
    Spikeroog
    Wangerooge
  North Frisian Islands
    Amrum
    Fohr

Fano
  Helgoland
  Mando
  Nordstrand
  Pellworm
  Romo
  Sylt
  Trischen
  West Friesian Islands
    Ameland
    Boschplaat
    Rottum
    Schiermonnikoog
    Terschelling
    Texel
    Vlieland

Fur Seal Islands
  See Pribilof Islands

Furneaux Islands
  Cape Barren
  Clarke
  Flinders

Futuna Islands (Hoorn Islands)
  Alofi
  Futuna

Galapagos Islands (Archipelago de Colon or Tortoise Islands)
  Blindloe
  Charles
  Culpepper
  Espanola (Hood)
  Fernandina (Narborough)
  Floreana (Santa Maria or Charles)
  Genovesa (Tower)
  Hood
  Isabela (Albemarle)
  Marchena (Bindloe)
  Pinta (Abingdon)
  Pinzon (Duncan)
  Rabida (Jervis)
  Roca Redondo
  San Cristobal (Chatham)
  San Salvador (Santiago or James)
  Santa Cruz (Chaves or Indefatigable)
  Santa Fe (Barrington)
  Tower

Tortuga (Brattle)
Wenman

Gambier Islands
  Akamaru
  Aukena
  Fangataufa
  Makaroa
  Mangareva
  Maria
  Marutea
  Minerva Reef
  Morane
  Portland Reef
  Taravai
  Tema Tangi
  Temoe (Timoe)
  Tureia
  Vanavana

Gardner Islands
  See Tabar Islands, Bismarck Archipelago

Gijuabeana Islands
  See Solomon Islands

Gilbert Islands
  Abaiang
  Abemama
  Aranuka
  Butaritari
  Kingsmill Group
    Arorae
    Beru
    Nonouti
    Onotoa
    Tabiteuea
    Tamana
  Kuria
  Little Makin (Makin Meang)
  Maiana
  Makin
  Marakei
  Nikunan (Nukunau)
  Tarawa

Great Barrier Islands
  See New Zealand

Greater Antilles
  See West Indies

Greater Sunda Islands
See Malay Archipelago

Green Islands
See Solomon Islands

Greenland
Disko

Grenadine Islands
See West Indies

Guam
See Mariana Islands

Ha'apai Group
See Tonga Islands

Habomai Islands
See Kuril Islands

Hall Islands
See Caroline Islands

Hawaiian Islands (Sandwich Islands)
Johnston Atoll
    Johnston
    Sand
Leeward Islands
    French Frigate Shoal
    Gardner
    Gardner Pinnacle
    Hermes Reef
    Ocean (Kure)
    Laysan
    Lisianski
    Midway Islands
        Eastern
        Sand
    Necker
    Nihoa
    Pearl Reef
Windward Islands
    Hawaii
    Kahoolawe
    Kauai
    Kaula
    Lanai
    Maui
    Molokai
    Molokini
    Niihau
    Oahu

Heard Island [Indian Ocean]

Hebrides
See British Isles

Herald Islands
See Kermadec Islands

Hermit Islands
See Bismarck Archipelago

Hervey Islands
See Cook Islands

Hetau Islands
See Solomon Islands

Hogoleu Islands
See Truk Atoll, Caroline Islands

Hong Kong
Dangan Dao
Hong Kong
Jiapeng Liedao
Kat O Chau
Lan Tao
Leung Shuen Wan Chau (High)
Neilingding Dao
Po Toi Is
Pok Liu Chau
Sanmen Liedao
Shek Kwu Chau
Soko Islands
Tap Mun Chau
Wailingding Dao

Hoorn Islands
See Futuna Islands

Howland Island

Hunters Islands
Hunter (Barren)
Robbins
Three Hummock

Huon Islands
See New Caledonia

Hyeres Islands
Ile du Levant
Porquerolles
Port Cros

Iceland
Grimsey
Surtsey
Vestmannaeyjar

Île de France
    See Mauritius, Mascarene Islands

Inaccessible Islands
    See South Orkney Islands

Indonesia
    See Malay Archipelago

Ionian Islands
    Cephalonia
    Cerigo
    Corfu
    Cythera
    Ithaca
    Kefallinia
    Kerkira
    Kithira
    Leukas
    Paxos
    Zakinthos
    Zante

Ireland
    See British Isles

Japan
    Awaji
    Hokkaido
    Honshu
    Kyushu
    Sado
    Shikoku
    Tsushima

Johnson Islands
    See Bismarck Archipelago

Johnston Atoll
    See Hawaiian Islands

Jomard Islands
    See Louisiade Archipelago

Juan Fernandez Islands
    Mas Afuera
    Mas a Tierra
    Santa Clara (Goat)

Kaniet Islands
    See Bismarck Archipelago

Kapingamarangi Islands
    See Caroline Islands

Kayangel Islands
    See Caroline Islands

Keeling Islands
    See Cocos Islands

Keila Islands
    See Solomon Islands

Kerguelen Islands (Desolation Islands)
    Kerguelen

Kerkenna Islands
    Chergui
    Rharbi

Kermadec Islands
    Cheeseman
    Curtis
    Herald Islands
      Meyer
    L'Esperance Rock
    Macauley
    Raoul (Sunday)

Kilinailau Islands
    See Solomon Islands

King George Islands
    See Tuamotu Islands

Kingman Reef
    See Line Islands

Kingsmill Group
    See Gilbert Islands

Komandorski Islands (Commander Islands)
    Bering (Beringa)
    Medny

Knox Islands
    See Marshall Islands

Kotu Group
    See Tonga Islands

Kuop Islands
    See Caroline Islands

Kuril Islands (Kurile)
    Habomai Islands
      Shibotsu
      Shuishio
    Iturup (Etorofu)
    Kunashir
    Onekotan
    Paramushir
    Shiashkhotan

Shikotan-to
Shimushir
Shumshu
Urup

Kusaie Islands
See Caroline Islands

**Laccadive Islands, Amindivi Islands, &
Minicoy**
Amindivi Islands
  Amini
  Kadmat (Cardamum)
  Karvaratti
  Kiltan
Laccadive Islands
  Agatti
  Androth
  Bingaram
  Cheriyam
  Chetlat
  Kalpeni
  Kalpeni
  Kalputhi
  Kavaratti
  North
  Peremul Par
  Pitti
  South
  Suhelipar
Minicoy

Ladrone Islands
See Mariana Islands

Lagoon Islands
See Ellice Islands

Lakemba Group
See Fiji Islands

Lamotreck Islands
See Caroline Islands

Lau Group
See Fiji Islands

Lesser Antilles
See West Indies

Lesser Sunda Islands
See Malay Archipelago

Lieutenant Islands
See Solomon Islands

Lihir Group
See Bismarck Archipelago

Line Islands (Equatorial Islands)
Caroline
Christmas (Kiritimati)
Fanning
Flint
Jarvis
Kingman Reef
Malden
Palmyra
Starbuck
Vostock
Washington

Lipari Islands
See Sicily

Lofoten Islands
Austvagoy
Flakstadoy
Rostoya
Moskenes
Vaeroya
Vestvagoy

Lomai Viti Group
See Fiji Islands

Loochoo Islands
See Ryukyu Islands

**Lord Howe Island [S.W. Pacific
Ocean]**

Lord Howe Island
See Santa Cruz, Solomon Islands

Lord Howe Islands
See Ontong Java, Solomon Islands

Louisiade Archipelago
Calvados Chain
  Abaga Gaheia
  Bagaman
  Hemenahei
  Jomard Islands
  Montemont Group
  Moturina
  Nimoa
  Panasia
  Panatinani
  Panawina

Utian
Conflict Group
  Auriroa
  Bunora
  Irai
  Lunn
  Muniara
  Panasesa
  Sarupai
Deboyne Islands
  Horuga Rara
  Nivani
  Panaeti
  Panapompom
  Panauya
  Wana
Engineer Group
  Anagusa (Bentley)
  Berriberrije
  Kuriva (Watts)
  Naranarawai (Sketton)
  Nari (Mudge)
Misima
  Managun
Renard Islands
  Kimuta
  Nivabeno
  Oreia
Rogeia-Moresby Group
  Moresby
    Haines
    Katai
    Katokatoa
  Rogeia
    Doini
  Sariba
    Samarai
  Sideia
Rossel
Tagula Reef
  Duchateau Islands
    Kukuluba
    Pana Boboi Ana
    Pana Rura Wana
  Yeina (Piron)
Torlesse Islands
  Bonabonakai (Pana Nui)

Bonabonawan
Tinolan

Low Archipelago
  See Tuamotu Archipelago

Loyalty Islands
  See New Caledonia

Luchu Islands
  See Ryukyu Islands

Lusancay Islands
  See Trobriand Islands

Lyakhov Islands
  See New Siberian Islands

McDonald Islands [Indian Ocean]

Mackenzie Islands
  See Caroline Islands

Madagascar
  Nossi Be Islands
  Sainte Mare Islands

Madeira Islands
  Desertas
  Madeira
  Porto Santo
  Selvagens

Malay Archipelago
  Northeast Chain
    Aroe Islands
      Dobo
      Tanabesar
    Borneo
    Celebes
    Kei
    Moluccas (Spice Islands)
      Amboina (Ambon)
      Abu Islands
      Aru
      Babar Islands
      Bachan (Batjan)
      Banda Islands
      Buru
      Ceram
      Halmahera
      Kai Islands
      Kisar
      Leti
      Makian

Morotai
Obi Islands
Sula Islands
Tanimbar Islands
Ternate
Tidore
Wetar
Natuna
New Guinea
South Natuna
Southwest Chain
Banka
Billiton
Java
Lesser Sunda Islands
　Alor
　Bali
　Flores
　Leti
　Lomblem
　Lombok
　Madura
　Riau Archipelago
　Roti
　Solor
　Sumba
　Sumbawa
　Timor
Mentawai Islands
Sumatra
Tanimbar Archipelago
Tenimber
Wetter

Malaysia
See Malay Archipelago

Maldive Islands (Maldives)
Addu Atoll
　Abuhera
　Fadu
　Gan
　Haratera
　Hitaddu
　Maradu
　Midu
　Wilingill
Aliff
Ari Atoll

Baa
Daalu
Faafu
Fadiffolu Atoll
Felidu Atoll
Gaafu Aliff
Faafu Daalu
Haa Alifu
Haa Daalu
Haddummati Atoll
Horsburgh Atoll
Ihavandiffulu Atoll
Kaafu
Kolumadulu Atoll
Laamu
Laviyana
Makunudu Atoll
Male Atoll
　Hulule
　Male
　Wilingili
Meemu
Miladummadulu Atoll
Mulaku Atoll
Naviyani
Noonu
North Malosmadulu Atoll
North Nilandu Atoll
Raa
Sheenu
Shaviyani
South Male Atoll
South Malosmadulu Atoll
South Nilandu Atoll
Suvadiva Atoll
Tiladummati Atoll
Thaa
Waavu

Maldives
See Maldive Islands

Malpelo Island

Malta
See Maltese Islands

Maltese Islands
Comino
Gozo
Malta

Maluku
See Moluccas

Malulu Islands
See Solomon Islands

Mamanutha Group
See Fiji Islands

Mangareva Islands
See Gambier Islands

Manu'a Islands
See Samoa Islands

Maramasike Islands
See Solomon Islands

Maria Islands
See Hull, Austral Islands
See Windward Islands, West Indies

Mariana Islands (Ladrone Islands)
Northern
Agrihan
Alamagan
Anatahan
Asuncion
Farallon de Pajaros (Uracas)
Guguan
Maug Islands
East Island
North Island
West Island
Pagan
Sariguan (Sarigan)
Southern
Agiguan
Farallon de Medinilla
Guam
Cabras Island
Cocos Island
Managaha
Rota
Saipan
Maniagassa Island
Tinian
Naftan Rock

Marianas
See Mariana Islands

Marquesas Islands
Cotar (Coral)
Eiao

Fatu Hiva
Fatuuku
Hiva Oa
Hatutu (Chanal)
Mohotani (Motane)
Motu Iti (Hergest Rock)
Nuku Hiva
Tahuata
Ua Huka
Ua Pu (Uapou, Marchand or Adams)

Marshall Bennet Islands
See Woodlark Islands

Marshall Islands
Ralik Chain
Ailinginae
Mogiri
Ailinglapalap (Elmore or Odia)
Ailinglapalap
Bigatyeland Islands
Jeh
Wotja
Bikini Atoll (Escholti)
Bikini
Eninman
Enirikku
Enyu
Ebon Atoll (Boston Island)
Ebon Island
Eniwetok Atoll (Brown)
Engebi
Eniwetok
Parry
Jabwot Island
Jaluit
Ai Islands
Elizabeth Islands
Enybor
Imrodj Islands
Jabor Islands
Jaluit
Kabbenbock Islands
Kili Island
Kwajalein (Menschikov)
Ebadon
Kwajalein
Namur
Roi

Lae Atoll
  Lae Island
  Lotj
  Ribong
Lib Island
Namorik Atoll
  Matamat Island
  Namorik Island
Namu Atoll (Mosquillo)
  Kaginen
  Lauen
  Namu
Rongelap Atoll
  Arubaru
  Enigan
  Enlaidokku
  Enybarar
  Rongelap
Rongerik
  Enyvertok
  Rongerik
Ujae (Katherine)
  Ebbetyu
  Enylamieg
  Ujae
Ujelang (Areficos or Providence)
  Ujelang
Wotho (Schane)
  Kabben
  Medyeron
  Wotho
Ratak Chain
  Ailuk Atoll
    Ailuk Island
    Kapeniur
  Arno Atoll
    Enirikku Island
    Ine Island
    Tagelib Island
    Terranova
  Aur Atoll (Ibbetson)
    Aur Island
    Bigen Island
    Tabal Island
  Bikar Atoll (Dawson)
    Bikar
  Erikub Atoll
    Enego Island

  Erikub Island
  Log Island
  Jemo Island
  Likiep Atoll
    Kapenor Island
    Likiep Island
    Roto Island
  Knox Islands
  Majuro Atoll (Arrowsmith)
    Calalin Island
    Ejit Island
    Djarrit Island
    Majuro Island
  Maloelap Atoll
    Airik Island
    Bogen Island
    Kaven Island
    Taroa Island
  Mejit Island
  Mili Atoll
    Alu
    Burrh Island
    Enajet Island
    Jobenor Island
    Lukunor Island
    Mili Island
    Tokowa
  Pokaakku Atoll (Taongi)
    Sibylla Island
  Taka Atoll (Suvorov Island)
    Taka
  Wotje Atoll (Romanzov)
    Goat Island
    Ormed Island
    Wotje Island

Mascarene Islands
  Agalega Islands
  Cargados Carajos Shoals
  Mauritius (Ile de France)
  Reunion (Bourbon or Bonaparte)
  Rodriguez

Matthew Islands
  See New Hebrides

Maug Islands
  See Mariana Islands

Mbuke Islands
  See Bismarck Archipelago

Mentawai Islands
  See Malay Archipelago

Mergui Archipelago
  Bentinck
  Daung
  Domel
  Elphinstone
  Kadan
  Kanmaw Kyun
  King
  Kisseraing
  Lanbi
  Letsokaw
  Mali
  Ross
  St. Mathew's
  Saganthit
  Sellore
  Sullivan Islands
  Thayawthadangyi

Midway Islands
  See Hawaiian Islands

Minicoy Islands
  See Laccadive Islands

Misore Islands
  See Schouten Islands

Moluccas
  See Malay Archipelago

Montemont Group
  See Louisiade Archipelago

Morlock Islands
  See Tauu, Solomon Islands

Mortlock Islands
  See Nomoi Islands, Caroline Islands

Mulatas Islands (San Blas Islands)

Murua
  See Woodlark Islands

Namonuito Islands
  See Caroline Islands

Nansei Islands
  See Ryukyu Islands

Natuna Besar Islands
  See Malay Archipelago

Nauru (Pleasant Island)

Navigators Islands
  See Samoa Islands

Near Islands
  See Aleutian Islands

Netherlands Antilles
  See West Indies

Netherlands East Indies
  See Malay Archipelago

Netherlands Indies
  See Malay Archipelago

Netherlands West Indies
  See West Indies

New Caledonia
  Baaba
  Balabio
  Balade Reefs
  Belep Islands
    Art
    Pott
  Bogota Reefs
  Chesterfield Islands
    Avon
    Bampton
    Longue
    Sandy
  Colnett Reefs
  Cook Reefs
  D'Entrecasteaux Reefs
  Huon Islands
    Fabre
    Le Leizour
    Suprise
  Isle of Pines
    Koutomo (Lesser of the Pines)
  Loyalty Islands
    Astrolabe Reefs
    Beautemps-Beaupre
    Leliogat
    Lifou (Lifu)
    Mare
    Ndoundoure
    Ouvea (Uvea)
    Pleiades
    Tika
    Uo
    Uvea

Nani
Neba
New Caledonia
Nou
Quen
Pam
Poudiou
Pouma Reefs
Seine Reefs
Toupeti
Walpole
Yande

New Georgia Group
See Solomon Islands

New Guinea
See Malay Archipelago

New Hebrides
Ambrym (Ambrim)
Aneityum (Aneytum)
Aniwa
Aoba
Banks Islands
  Gaua (Santa Maria)
  Mera Lava (Star Peak)
  Merig
  Mota (Sugarloaf)
  Mota Lava (Motlav or Saddle)
  Rowa
  Saddle
  Ureparapara
  Vanua Lava
  Vatganai
Efate (Sandwich)
  Nguna
  Pele
Epi
Erromango (Eromanga or Erromanga)
Espiritu Santo (Santo)
  Aore
  Dolphin
  Elephant
  Malo
  Tangoa
  Venui
Futuna
Hunter Islands
Lopevi

Maewo
Maskelyne Islands
Malekula (Makakula)
  Hambi
  Uri
  Uripiv
Matthew Islands
Omba
Paama
Pauma
Pentecost
Raga
Shepherd Islands
  Buninga
  Efate
    Emau
    Leleppa
    Mau
    Moso
    Nguna
    Pele
  Emae
  Ewose
  Falea
  Iwose
  Laika
  Mai
  Makura
  Mataso
  Tevala
  Tongariki
  Tongoa
Tanna (Tana)
Torres Islands
  Hiu
  Loh
  Metoma
  Tegua
  Toga
Wot (Monument Rock)

New Siberian Islands
Anjou Islands
Belkovski
De Long Islands
Faddei
Figurin
Kotelny

Lyakhov Islands
New Siberian
Novaya Sibir
Zheleznyakol

New Zealand
  Antipodes Islands
  Auckland Islands
  Bounty Islands
  Chatham Islands
    Chatham
    Pit
    The Sisters
    Star Keys
    Great Barrier Islands
    North
    Snares Islands
    South
    Stewart
    Three Kings Islands

Nggela Group
  See Solomon Islands

Nicobar Islands
  Car Nicobar
  Chowra
  Great Nicobar
  Katchall
  Lamorta
  Little Nicobar
  Nancowry
  Teressa

Nieue
  See Niue

Niguria Group
  See Bismarck Archipelago

Ninigo Islands
  See Bismarck Archipelago

Niue (Savage Island or Selyagens)

Nomoi Islands
  See Caroline Islands

Nomuka Group
  See Tonga Islands

Norfolk Island

Norman Islands
  See British Isles

Nossi Be Islands
  See Madagascar

Novaya Zemlya

Nukuoro Islands
  See Caroline Islands

Ocean Island (Banaba)

Ocean Island (Kure)
  See Hawaiian Islands

Ogasawara Islands
  See Bonin Islands

Oil Islands
  See Chagos Archipelago

Okinawa Islands
  See Ryukyu Islands

Olu Malau Group
  See Solomon Islands

Ono Group
  See Fiji Islands

Onon Islands
  See Namonuito Islands, Caroline Islands

Orkney Islands
  See British Isles

Otu Tolu Group
  See Tonga Islands

Palau Group
  See Caroline Islands

Palmyra Island
  See Line Islands

Pam Islands
  See Bismarck Archipelago

Pangutaran Group
  See Philippine Islands

Pantelleria (Cosyra or Cossyra)

Parry Islands
  See Canadian Arctic Archipelago

Paumotu Archipelago
  See Tuamotu Archipelago

Pearl Cays (Pearl Islands) [Caribbean]

Pearl Islands (Archipelago de las Perlas) [off Panama]
  Gonzalez
  Pedro

Saboga
San Jose
San Miguel

Pemba Island

Peter Island

Philippine Islands
Babuyan Islands
  Babuyan
  Calayan
  Camiguin
  Dalupiri
  Fuga
Balintang Islands
Batan Islands
Bohol
Camiguin
Catanduanes
Cebu
Leyte
Luzon
Marinduque
Masbate
Mindanao
Mindoro
Negros
Palawan
Panay
Romblon
Samar
Sulu Archipelago
  Jolo (Sulu)
    Cabucan
    Capual
    Pata
  Pangutaran Group
    North Ubian
    Panducan
    Usada
  Samales Group
    Balanguingui
    Simisa
    Tongquil
  Sibutu
  Tapul Group
    Cabingaan
    Lapac
    Lugus

    Siasi
    Taluc
    Tapul
  Tawitawi Group
    Bilatan
    Bongao
    Kinapusan
    Sanga Sanga
    Simunul
    South Ubian
    Tandubas
    Tawi Tawi
    Tumindao
Visayan Islands

Phoenix Islands
Birnie
Canton
Enderbury
Gardner
Hull
McKean
Phoenix
Sydney

Pitcairn Island(s)
Ducie
Henderson (Elizabeth)
Oeno
Pitcairn

Pleasant Island
See Nauru

Ponape Area
See Caroline Islands

Portuguese Timor
See Malay Archipelago

Pribilof Islands (Fur Seal Islands)
Otter
St. George
St. Paul
Walrus

Prince Edward Island [Canada]

Prince Edward Island [Indian Ocean]
Marion
Prince Edward

Pulap Islands
See Caroline Islands

Puluwat Islands
  See Caroline Islands

Purdy Islands
  See Bismarck Archipelago

Queen Charlotte Islands
  Graham
  Kunghit
  Louise
  Lyell
  Moresby

Queen Elizabeth Islands
  See Canadian Arctic Archipelago

Ralik Chain
  See Marshall Islands

Rapa Islands
  See Austral Islands

Rat Islands
  See Aleutian Islands

Ratak Chain
  See Marshall Islands

Reef Islands
  See Solomon Islands

Renard Islands
  See Louisiade Archipelago

Revillagigedo Island
  See Alexander Archipelago

Revillagigedo Islands (Revilla Gigedo Islands)
  Clarion (Santa Rosa)
  Roca de la Pasion
  Roca Partida
  San Benedicto
  Socorro

Rogeia-Moresby Group
  See Louisiade Archipelago

Roosevelt Island

Ross Island

Rotuma
  Hatana
  Hofliua
  Uea

Russell Islands
  See Solomon Islands

Ryukyu Islands (Luchu, Loochoo, or Nansei Islands)
  Amami-Gunto
    Amami-o-shima
    Kikai-shima
    Okinoerabu-shima
    Tikara-gunto
    Tokuno-shima
    Yoron-jima
  Okinawa Islands
    Daito-shima
    Ie-jima
    Iheya-shoto
    Kerama-retto
    Kume-shima
    Okinawa
  Sakishima Islands
    Ishigaki-shima
    Miyako-jima
    Sebkaku-gunto
    Tarami-jima

Sable Island

St. Andrew Group
  See Bismarck Archipelago

St. George's Island
  See San Jorge (Solomon Islands)

St. Helena [Atlantic]

St. Helena Islands
  See Sea Islands

St. Paul Island [Canada]

St. Paul Island [Indian Ocean]

St. Paul Island
  See Pribilof Islands

St. Paul Rocks
  See St. Peter and St. Paul Rocks

St. Peter and St. Paul Rocks [Atlantic]

Sainte Marie Islands
  See Madagascar

Sakhalin Island (Saghalien or Saghalin)

Sakishima Islands
  See Ryukyu Islands

Sala y Gomez

Salomon Islands
  See Chagos Archipelago

Samales Group
  See Sulu Archipelago, Philippine Islands

Samoa Islands (Navigators Islands)
  Eastern (American)
    Aunu'u
    Manu'a Islands
      Ofu
      Olosega
      Ta'u
    Rose Atoll
    Swains Island
    Tutuila
  Western
    Apolima
    Manono
    Savai'i
    Upolu
      Fanuatapu
      Namua
      Nuulua (Nuula)
      Nuusafee
      Nuutele

San Ambrosio

San Blas Islands
  See Mulatas Islands

San Felix

Sandwich Islands
  See Hawaiian Islands

Santa Barbara Group
  See Santa Barbara Islands

Santa Barbara Islands (Channel Islands)
  Santa Barbara Group
    Anacapa
    Santa Cruz
    Santa Miguel
    Santa Rosa
  Santa Catalina Group
    San Clemente
    San Nicholas
    Santa Barbara
    Santa Catalina

Santa Catalina Group
  See Santa Barbara Islands

Santa Cruz Islands
  See Solomon Islands

Santanilla Islands
  See Swain Islands

Sao Tome (St. Thomas)
  Principe

Sardinia
  Asinara
  Caprera
  Maddalena
  San Pietro
  St. Antioco

Savage Island
  See Niue

Schouten Group
  See Bismarck Archipelago

Schouten Islands (Misore Islands)
  Biak
  Numfoor
  Sup'ori

Scilly Islands
  See British Isles

Scott Island

Sea Islands [off South Carolina]
  Amelia
  Cumberland
  Daufuskie
  Edisto
  Folly
  Hilton Head
  Hunting
  Isle of Palms
  James
  Jekyll
  Johns
  Kiawah
  Ladies
  Morris
  Ossabaw
  Parris
  Port Royal
  Sapelo
  Sea
  Skidaway
  St. Catherines
  St. Helena Islands
  St. Simons
  Tybee

Wadamalaw
Wilmington

Sea Islands
See Bismarck Archipelago

Selvagens
See Niue

Senyavin Islands
See Ponape Area, Caroline Islands

Seychelles
African Banks
Aldabra Islands
Alphonse Atoll
Amirantes
Aride
Assumption
Astove
Bancs Providences
Bijoutier
Bird (Sea Cow)
Cerf
Coetivy
Conception
Cosmoledo Group
Cousin Islands
Cousine
Curieuse
D'Arros
Denis
Desnoeufs
Farquhar Islands
Felecite
Frigate
Grande Soeur
Ile au Cerf
Ile aux Fous
Ile aux Recifs
Ile aux Vaches
La Digue
L'Ilot
Mahe
Marie Anne
Mamelle
North
Petite Soeur
Plate
Poivre Atoll
Praslin

Providence Island
Providence Reef
Recif
Remne
Sainte Ann
St. Francois Atoll
St. Joseph's Atoll
St. Pierre
Silhouette
The Sisters
Therese

Shag Island

Shepherd Islands
See New Hebrides

Shetland Islands
See British Isles

Shortland Islands
See Solomon Islands

Siassi Group
See Bismarck Archipelago

Sicily
Egadi Islands
Favignana
Levanzo
Marettimo (Marittimo)
Lipari Islands (Eolian)
Alicudi
Basiluzzo
Filicudi
Lipari
Panarea
Salina
Stromboli
Vulcano
Pantelleria
Ustica

Six Islands
See Chagos Archipelago

Snares Islands
See New Zealand

Society Islands
Leeward Group
Bora-Bora
Fenua Ura (Scilly)
Huahine

Maupiti
Mopihaa (Lord Howe Island)
Motu One (Bellingshausen)
Raiatea
Tahaa
Tubai (Motu-iti)
Windward Group
Mehetia
Moorea
Tahiti
Tapuaemanu (Maiao)
Tetiaroa

Solomon Islands
Antua (Cherry)
Arundel
Bellona
Bougainville
Katitj
Madehas
Toiokh
Buka
Hetau Islands
Malulu Islands
Cherry
Choiseul
Dillimore
Rob Roy
Vagina
Duff Group
Tammmumako
Fatutaka
Florida (Gela)
Ganongga
Gatukai
Gizo
Green Islands
Nissan
Guadalcanal
Beagle
Komachu
Malapa
Kilinailau Islands
Irinalan
Piuli
Yeharnu
Yovo
Kolombangara

Malaita (Mala)
Maramsike Islands
Mitre
Ndai
New Georgia Group
Arundel
Ganongga
Gatukai
Gizo
Kolombangara
New Georgia
Rendova
Simbo
Tulagi
Vangunu
Vella Lavella
Wanawana
Nggela Group
Florida (Nggela)
Olevuga
Vatilau
Nissan
Nukumanu
Ontong Java (Lord Howe Islands)
Keila Islands
Luangiua
Ramos
Reef Islands
Fenualoa
Lomlom
Matema
Nalogo
Nufiloli
Nukapu
Nupani
Pileni
Rendova
Rennell (Mangana)
Russell Islands
Banika
Buraku
Pavuvu
San Cristobal (Makira)
Bio
Olu Malau Group
Aliiti
Malaulalo
Malaupaina

Santa Ana
Ugi
Yanuta Islands
Santa Cruz
  Anuda
  Fataka
  Lord Howe
  Ntendi (Ndeni, Santa Cruz)
  Tevai
  Tinakula
  Tucopia
  Utupua
  Vanikoro
Savo
Shortland Islands
  Fauro
  Shortland
Sikiana (Stewart Islands)
  Barena
  Faore
  Manduiloto
  Matu Avi
Taumako Group
  Obelisk
  Taumako
  Treasurers
Tauu
  Nugurigia
  Taku
Tetipari
Tikopia
Treasury Islands
  Mono
  Stirling
Ulawa
Vangunu
Vella Lavella
Ysabel (Bogotu)
  Anker
  Arnavon Group
    Kernikapa
    Sikapo
  Barora Fa (Barola)
  Barora Ite
  Bero
  Captain
  Gagi
  Gijuabeana Islands

  Papatura Fa
  Papatura Ite
  Langton
  Lieutentant Islands
  Nidero
  San Jorge (St. Georges)

Somers Islands
  See Bermuda Islands

Sorol Islands
  See Caroline Islands

South Orkney Islands
  Coronation
  Inaccessible Islands
  Laurie
  Powell
  Signy

South Sandwich Islands

South Shetland Islands
  Clarence
  Deception
  Elephant
  Greenwich
  King George
  Livingston
  Low (Jameson)
  Nelson
  Robert
  Smith (James)
  Snow

Spice Islands
  See Moluccas, Malay Archipelago

Spitsbergen
  Barents
  Bear
  Edge
  Hopen
  Kong Karlsland
  Kvitoya
  North East Land
  Prince Charles Foreland
  West Spitsbergen

Sprately Islands (Storm)

Sri Lanka
  See Ceylon

The Staples
  See Farne Islands

Stewart Islands
  See Solomon Islands

Sullivan Islands
  See Mergui Archipelago

Sulu Archipelago
  See Philippine Islands

Summer Islands
  See Bermudas

Sunda Islands
  See Malay Archipelago

Sverdrup Islands
  See Canadian Arctic Archipelago

Swain Islands (Santanilla Islands)

Swallow Islands
  See Reef Islands, Solomon Islands

Tabar Islands
  See Bismarck Archipelago

Taipa Islands

Taiwan
  See Formosa

Tanga Group
  See Bismarck Archipelago

Tanimbar Archipelago
  See Malay Archipelago

Tanimbar Islands
  See Moluccas, Malay Archipelago

Tapul Group
  See Sulu Archipelago, Philippine Islands

Tasmania

Taumako Group
  See Solomon Islands

Tawitawi Group
  See Sulu Archipelago, Philippine Islands

Three Brothers
  See Chagos Archipelago

Three Kings Islands
  See New Zealand

Thurston Island

Tierra del Fuego
  Clarence
  Dawson
  Desolation Islands

  Diego Ramirez
  Horn
  Hoste
  Isla de los Estados
  Navarino
  Santa Ines
  Staten
  Tierra del Fuego
  Wollaston

Tingwon Islands
  See Bismarck Archipelago

Tokelau Islands (Union Islands)
  Atafu (Duke of York)
  Fakaofo
  Nukunonu (Nkunono)

Tolokiwa Group
  See Bismarck Archipelago

Tonga Islands (Friendly Islands)
  Ha'apai (Hahaapai) Group
    Foa
    Fotuha'a
    Ha'ano
    Kao
    Kotu Group
      Fonoaika
      Ha'afeva
      Kotu
      Lekaleka
      O'ua
      Putuputua
      Tokulu
      Tungua
    Lifuka
    Lofanga
    Mo'unga'one
    Niniva
    Nomuka Group
      Fonoifua
      Mango
      Nomuka
      Tonumea
    Ofolanga
    Otu Tolu Group
      Fetokopunga
      Telekivava'u
    Tofua
    Uiha

Uoleva
Niuafo'ou
Northern Islands
 Fotuha'a
 Niuatoputapu (Bu)
 Tafahi
Tongatapu Group
 Ata
 Eua
 Fonuafo'ou (Falcon)
 Hunga Ha'apai
 Hunga Tonga
 Toku
 Tongatapu
Vava'u Group
 Ava
 Euakafa
 Faioa
 Fofoa
 Hunga
 Kapa
 Kenutu
 Koloa
 Late
 Manfana
 Maninita
 Niuatobutabu (Niuatoputapu)
 Niuafoo (Niuafoou)
 Nuapapu
 Ofu
 Okoa
 Olo'ua
 Ota
 Ovaka
 Pangaimotu
 Tafahi
 Taula
 Taunga
 Umuna
 Uta Vaua'u
 Utungake
 Vaka'eitu
 Vavau

Tongatapu Group
 See Tonga Islands

Torlesse Islands
 See Louisiade Archipelago

Torres Islands
 See New Hebrides

Torres Strait Islands
 Badu
 Banks
 Boigu
 Coconut
 Darnley
 Dauan
 Deliverance
 Dungeness
 Friday
 Goode
 Hammond
 Horn
 Jervis
 Long
 Mabuiag
 Mer
 Moa
 Mulgrave (Badu)
 Murray
 Prince of Wales
 Saibai
 Stephens
 Tuesday
 Thursday
 Turnagain
 Wednesday
 Yam
 Yorke

Tortoise Islands
 See Galapagos Islands

Treasury Islands
 See Solomon Islands

Tristan da Cunha Islands
 Gough
 Inaccessible
 Nightingale
 Tristan da Cunha

Trobriand Islands
 Boimagi
 Bompapau
 Kadai
 Kaileuna
 Kiriwina

Kitava
Lusancay Islands
Muua
Muwo
Tuma
Vakuta

Truk Area
See Caroline Islands

Tsoi Islands
See Bismarck Archipelago

Tuamotu Islands or Archipelago
(Dangerous Islands)
Actaeon Group
  Matureivavao
  Tenararo
  Tenarunga
  Vahanga
Ahe (Peacock)
Ahunui
Akiaki
Amanu
Anaa (Chain Islands)
Angatau (Fangatau)
Anuanuraro
Apataki (Hagemeister)
Aratika
Arutua (Rurik)
Disappointment Islands
  Napuka
  Teppoto
Duke of Gloucester Group
  Anuanurunga
  Nukutipipi
Faaite
Fakarava (Wittgenstein)
Fangahina (Fakahina or Enterprise)
Fangataufa
Hao
Haraiki
Hereheretue (San Pablo)
Hikueru
Katiu
Kauehi (Vincennes)
Kaukura
King George Islands
  Takapoto
  Takaroa

Makatea (Aurora Islands)
Makemo
Manihi (Waterland)
Manuhangi
Maria (Morenhout)
Marokau
Marutea (Furneaux)
Matahiva
Morane (Cadmus)
Motu Tunga (Adventure)
Murruoa
Nengonengo
Niau (Greig)
Nihiru
Nukutavake
Paraoa
Pinaki
Pukapuka (Honuake)
Pukarua
Raevski Group
  Hiti
  Teppoto
  Tuanaka
Rangiroa
Raraka
Raroia (Barclay de Tolly)
Ravahere
Reao
Reitoru
Rekareka
South Marutea
Taenga (Holt)
Tahanea
Takume
Talaro (King)
Tatakoto
Tauere
Tekokoto
Tematangi
Tikehau
Tikei
Toau (Elizabeth)
Tureia (Papakena)
Vahitahi
Vairaatea
  Pukararo
  Pukarunga
Vanavana

Tubuai Islands
  See Austral Islands
Turks Islands
  See West Indies
Tuvalu
  See Ellice Islands
Uap
  See Yap
Union Islands
  See Tokelau Islands
U.S. Trust Territory of the Pacific Islands
  See Mariana Islands
Vancouver Island
Vanuatu
  See New Hebrides
Vava Islands
  See Torres Islands, New Hebrides
Vavu'u Group
  See Tonga Islands
Ventenat Islands
  See D'Entrecasteaux Islands
Vesteralen Islands
  Andoy
  Hadseloy
  Hinnoy
  Langoy
Virgin Islands
  See West Indies
Visayan Islands
  See Philippine Islands
Vitu Islands
  See Bismarck Archipelago
Viwa Islands
  See Fiji Islands
Volcano Islands
  See Bonin Islands
Wake Atoll
  Peale Island
  Wake Island
  Wilkes Island
Wallis Islands (Uvea)
  Akimao
  Faiao

Fougalei
Lonaniva
Nukuafo
Nukufetao
Nukuloa
Nukulufala
Nukufutu
Nukutea
Nukuteatea
Tukuaviki
Uvea
West Indies (Antilles)
  Bahama Islands (Bahamas)
    Acklins
    Andros
    Anguilla Cays
    Berry Islands
    Biminis
    Caicos Islands
      East Caicos
      Grand Caicos
      North Caicos
      Providenciales
      South Caicos
      West Caicos
    Cat Island
    Cat Cay
    Conception
    Crooked
    Eleuthera
    Grand Bahama
    Great Abaco
    Great Exuma
    Great Inagua
    Harbor
    Little Abaco
    Little Exuma
    Little Inagua
    Little Ragged
    Long Cay
    Long Island
    Mariguana
    Mayaguana
    New Providence
    Nurse
    Ragged
    Rum Cay

St. George's Cay
San Salvador (Watlings)
Turks Islands
  Grand Turk
  Salt Cay
Walker Cay
Cayman Islands
  Cayman Brac
  Grand Cayman
  Little Cayman
Greater Antilles
  Cuba
    Cayo Coco
    Cayo Romano
    Isla de la Juventuo
    Isle of Pines
    Jardines de la Reina
  Hispaniola
    Grande Cayemite
    La Gonave
    Isle a Vache
    Isla Beata
    Isla Saona
    Island of la Jortue
    Navassa
    Tortuga
  Jamaica
  Puerto Rico
    Culebra
    Vieques
Lesser Antilles (Caribbees)
  Aruba (Oruba)
  Barbados
  Bonaire
  Curacao
  Leeward Islands
    Anguilla
    Antigua
    Barbuda
    Dominica
    Guadeloupe
      Basse-Terre
      Desirade
      Grande-Terre
      Marie Galante
      Petite-Terre
      St. Barthelemy
      St. Martin [N. part]

      Les Saintes
    Montserrat
    Nevis
    Redonda
    Saba
    St. Christopher
    St. Eustatius
    St. Kitts
    St. Martin [S. pt]
    Sombrero
    Virgin Islands
      British
        Anegada
        Dead Man's Chest
        Fallen Jerusalem
        Guana
        Jost Van Dyke
        Norman
        Peter
        Salt
        Tortola
        Virgin Gorda
      United States
        St. Croix
        St. John
        St. Thomas
Margarita
Tobago
Trinidad
Windward Islands
  Grenada
    Calivigy
    Green
    Sandy
  Grenadine Islands (Grenadines)
    Bequia
    Caille
    Canovan
    Carriacou
    Diamond
    Frigate
    Large Island
    Little Martinique
    Little Sainte Vincent
    Mayreau
    Mustique
    Ronde
    Saline

Les Tantes
Union
Martinque
St. Lucia
Maria Islands
St. Vincent

Western Islands
See Hebrides, British Isles

Western Samoa
See Samoa, Western

Whitsunday Island

Woleai Islets
See Caroline Islands

Woodlark Islands
Alcester Islands
Egum Group

Laughlan Group
Madau
Marshall Bennet Islands
Nusam
Woodlark (Murua)

Yangasa Islands
See Fiji Islands

Yanuta Islands
See Solomon Islands

Yap Area
See Caroline Islands

Yap Group
See Caroline Islands

Yasawa Group
See Fiji Islands

SOURCES

The Columbia Lippincott Gazetteer of the World. ed. by Leon E. Seltzer. New York: Columbia University Press, 1952.

Countries of the World and Their Leaders: Yearbook 1984. v. 1–2. Detroit: Gale Research Co., 1984.

Gellhorn, Eleanor Cowles. *McKay's Guide to Bermuda, the Bahamas and the Caribbean*. New York: David McKay Co., 1955.

Great Britain. Naval Intelligence Division. *Pacific Islands*. v. 2, *Eastern Pacific*, v. 3, *Western Pacific (Tonga to the Solomon Islands)*, v. 4, *Western Pacific (New Guinea and Islands Northward)*. (Geographic Handbook Series B.P. 519B restricted) London: Naval Intelligence Division, 1944.

Huxley, Anthony, ed. *Standard Encyclopedia of the World's Oceans and Islands*. New York: G. P. Putnam's Sons, 1962.

Kennedy, Thomas F. *A Descriptive Atlas of the Pacific Islands*. New York: Praeger, 1968.

National Geographic Atlas of the World. enlarged 2d ed., ed. by Melville Bell Grosvenor. Washington, D.C.: National Geographic Society, 1966.

The New Columbia Encyclopedia. 4th ed., ed. by William H. Harris and Judith S. Levey. New York: Columbia University Press, 1975.

Platt, Raye, John K. Wright, John C. Weaver, and Johnson E. Fairchild. *The European Possessions in the Caribbean Area: A Compilation of Facts Concerning Their Population, Physical Geography, Resources, Industries, Trade, Government, and Strategic Importance*. (Map of Hispanic American Publication, no. 4) New York: American Geographical Society, 1941.

Robson, Robert W., comp. *The Pacific Islands Handbook: 1944*. North American ed. New York: Macmillan Co., 1945.

U.S. Central Intelligence Agency. *The World Factbook, 1988*. Washington, D.C.: Central Intelligence Agency, 1988.

U.S. Department of Defense. Department of the Army. *Area Handbook for Oceania,* by
  John W. Henderson and others. (DA Pam 550–94) Washington, D.C.: Government
  Printing Office, 1971.
U.S. Department of Defense. Department of the Army. *Indian Ocean: Five Island Coun-
  tries.* ed. by Frederica M. Bunge. 2d ed. (DA Pam 550–154) Washington, D.C.:
  Government Printing Office, 1983.
U.S. Department of Defense. Department of the Army. *Oceania: A Regional Study.* ed.
  by Frederica M. Bunge and Melinda W. Cooke. 2d ed. (DA Pam 550–94) Wash-
  ington, D.C.: Government Printing Office, 1984.
Webster's New Geographical Dictionary. Springfield, MA: G & C Merriam Co., 1977.

INDEX

Main entries appear in **bold** type.